Gender
Stereotypes and Roles
Third Edition

Gender
Stereotypes and Roles
Third Edition

Susan A. Basow

Lafayette College

 Brooks/Cole Publishing Company
Pacific Grove, California

ITP™ The trademark ITP is used under license.

A CLAIREMONT BOOK

Brooks/Cole Publishing Company
A Division of Wadsworth, Inc.

Printed in the United States of America
10   9   8   7   6   5   4

Library of Congress Cataloging-in-Publication Data
Basow, Susan A.
    Gender: stereotypes and roles / Susan A. Basow. — 3rd ed.
      p.   cm.
    Rev. ed. of: Gender stereotypes, c1986.
    Includes bibliographical references and index.
    ISBN 0-534-12120-9
    1. Sex role. 2. Stereotype (Psychology) I. Basow, Susan A.,
[date]– Gender stereotypes. II. Title.
    HQ1075.B36   1992
305.3—dc20   91-38410
                                                        CIP

Sponsoring Editor: *Claire Verduin*
Editorial Associate: *Gay C. Bond*
Production Editor: *Penelope Sky*
Manuscript Editor: *Lorraine Anderson*
Permissions Editor: *Mary Kay Hancharick*
Interior Design: *Katherine Minerva*
Art Coordinator and Cover Design: *Cloyce C. Wall*
Interior Illustration: *Roger Knox*
Typesetting: *ExecuStaff*
Printing and Binding: *Malloy Lithographing, Inc.*

To Jade:
For the joy you've brought me.

Preface

Gender: Stereotypes and Roles is intended for students on the introductory level, and the comprehensive references and recognition of complexities make it an excellent resource for advanced students and faculty. It can be used in psychology and sociology courses on women, men, gender, sex roles, and sex differences, and in women's and men's studies programs. Individual sections can supplement broader psychology, sociology, or interdisciplinary courses that include units on sex roles, sex differences, human sexuality, or male–female relations. The book can also be used with traditional social psychology texts.

Development I began to write the first edition, *Sex-Role Stereotypes: Traditions and Alternatives* (1980) because there were no adequate teaching materials, and I wanted to put all the existing material together coherently. Research on sex differences was starting to increase, but in the absence of theory and without social–historical context. As a full-time clinical psychologist, I was very aware of the damaging effects of sex-role stereotypes on individuals and their relationships. I was convinced that there were few basic sex differences, and that androgynous development made the best sense.

When the second edition, *Gender Stereotypes: Traditions and Alternatives* was published (1986), research was booming. The change of title from "sex" to "gender" reflected the shift in the field from a biological and psychological perspective to an increasingly sociocultural one. I became more sensitive to interdisciplinary work in women's studies and to issues of race, class, and sexual preference, and added new topics accordingly.

This third edition also reflects the changes both in the field and in my personal development. I have gone considerably beyond gender stereotypes, focusing on the nature of gender itself: its meanings, its social construction, its influence on our lives. Research on gender has matured. Major projects have developed in nearly every discipline, transforming the knowledge base in fields as diverse as biology, history, political science, and sociology. There is new interest in theory and in inclusivity. Although research is still based disproportionately on White heterosexual college students, more information is available than ever before on people in more representational groups. Gender as a status variable is widely recognized. Although the field has grown increasingly complex, as has my thinking, I've tried to convey the major points in broad strokes, neither oversimplifying complexities nor exaggerating them.

My major theme is that there is little physical or psychological evidence to justify gender stereotypes as reflecting clear distinctions between the sexes. Most of the differences that do exist are the result of gender roles, not the cause. Gender is constructed by every socializing agent and force in society: parents, teachers, the media, religion, and so on. The power differential is an essential component of gender construction in Western culture. That is, the sexes aren't viewed simply as different from each other, but as superior or inferior, dominant or subordinate. The effects of gender stereotypes and roles are pervasive, intense, and generally damaging to *all* individuals, to their relationships, and to society as a whole. To break free is a difficult yet beneficial process that requires a complete transformation of society.

This remains a viewpoint book. My perspective is feminist; I never lose sight of how gender encodes inequality. By claiming this bias at the outset, I can help the reader evaluate the material I present.

Organization   The structure of the book is the same as in previous editions. Part 1 begins with a discussion of the nature and meaning of gender, gender roles, and gender stereotypes. In Part 2 we examine research on gender similarities and differences, with respect to physical, cognitive, personality, social, and sexual functioning. In Part 3 we explore how gender stereotypes and roles developed, both historically and from one generation to the next. In Part 4 we delve into the effects of stereotypes and roles on individuals, relationships, and society. Finally, in Part 5 we explore alternatives to traditional gender stereotypes and roles, and consider ways to achieve them.

The actual content of the book is more new than old: there are more than 2000 new references, and many sections are completely reorganized. Overall, I have paid more attention to families, both traditional and non-traditional, and to issues of race, ethnicity, class, and sexual orientation. Theoretical debates are discussed in greater detail, as are social and structural perspectives. I have included frequent summaries, and highlighted important concepts. The focus is on gender roles, rather than on stereotypes.

Research issues are discussed in Chapter 1, "Gender Stereotypes and Roles," which also includes issues of sexual stratification. Chapter 2, "Comparisons of Physical and Cognitive Functioning," includes research on hormonal effects, and contains a new section on "women's ways of knowing." Chapter 3, "Comparisons of Personality and Social Behavior," includes a discussion of achievement behavior, as well as theory. Chapter 4, "Comparisons of Sexual Behavior," includes same-gender behaviors and sociocultural factors. Chapter 5, "Historical Perspectives," focuses on the development of gender stratification in societies, with additional attention to theories. Chapter 6, "Socialization Theories and Agents," pays attention to feminist psychodynamic theories, the lifespan perspective, and the influence of fathers and peers. Chapter 7, "Social Forces," is completely updated, especially the media section. Chapter 8, "Consequences for the Individual," has a section on the relevance of body image to the sense of self, a discussion of depression, and generous attention to physical health. Chapter 9, "Consequences for Friendships and Love Relationships," includes a discussion of marital satisfaction; Chapter 10, "Consequences for Family Relationships," contains analyses of both mothering and fathering, and includes such diverse types of families as those headed by single parents and married couples, and gay and lesbian households. Chapter 11, "Consequences for the Labor Force," considers structural barriers and theories of inequality. Chapter 12, "Structural Power and Abuses of Power," includes political attitudes and voting patterns, and violence against women. Chapter 13, "Beyond Stereotypes and Roles," is partly theoretical, and looks at current debates between liberal and cultural feminists, and at the men's movement.

Acknowledgments   Many people helped me bring this edition into being. My thanks go to particular students who helped during the past three years: Laura Brader, Christy Chandler, Michelle Noll, Heather Stoddard, Ligia Zamora, and Malena Zamora. Lorraine Merli, my secretary, was invaluable in assisting me in the final stages: her grace under pressure kept me from going off the deep end time and time again. The Feminist Research Group of the Lehigh Valley assisted with their helpful comments, as did the following reviewers: Joan M. Fayer, The University of Puerto Rico; Nancy Kenney, University of Washington; Edward LaFontaine, Keuka College; Susan E. Marshall, University of Texas at Austin; Bonnie Tyler, University of Maryland; and Joseph Ventimigla, Memphis State University. I continue to appreciate working with the Brooks/Cole staff, including publisher Claire Verduin, who bore with me through numerous delays; senior production editor Penelope Sky, who effectively shepherded the book through to publication; and, most especially, copyeditor par excellence Lorraine Anderson, who treated the manuscript with the love and care one expects only of the author.

Most of all, I thank my family, particularly my mother, Faye Basow, and my daughter, Jade B. Miller; and my friends, especially Stacey Schlau and Jay K. Miller. They put up with my neglect while I devoted most of my time and energy to this book. Without their support (especially Jay's), I couldn't have done it. I hope the product justifies the sacrifices.

Susan A. Basow

Contents

**Part 4
Consequences of
Gender Stereotypes
and Roles   171**

Chapter 10
Consequences for
Family Relationships   230

Chapter 11
Consequences for
the Labor Force   259

Gender
Stereotypes and Roles
Third Edition

Part 1
Introduction

Masculinity. Femininity. These words engender clear pictures of two opposite sets of behavior and personal attributes. To some degree, we all know what these characteristics are. In fact, one of the most impressive aspects of these images is the extent to which we Americans share them. Men should be strong, rational, aggressive; women should be weak, emotional, submissive. And yet, to what extent do these images fit the majority of real people? That is, do men and women really conform to these images, or are these images stereotypes?

If men and women do not conform to the stereotypes, how did such stereotypes and distinct gender roles come into being? Once established, how are the stereotypes and roles maintained and transmitted? Once transmitted, how do these stereotypes and roles affect women and men in our society? Once affected by the stereotypes and roles, how does one break free, and toward what does one change? This book is dedicated to answering these questions. We will begin by defining our terms.

Chapter 1
Gender Stereotypes and Roles

This book will examine gender—the meanings we assign to the terms *female* and *male*—as well as gender stereotypes. It will argue that gender is socially constructed, not biologically given. Each culture creates its own meanings for the terms *female* and *male*. These meanings involve a series of expectations regarding how each gender should behave (that is, gender roles). When exaggerated, these expectations become gender stereotypes. In this book, we will examine all these aspects of gender—their bases, transmittal, and consequences. It will be argued that rigid gender roles and stereotypes are based on few actual sex differences, but rather on a differential power relationship between men and women. Furthermore, rigid gender roles and stereotypes seriously limit individual functioning and have a negative effect on relationships as well as on society.

▲ Definitions

What's the difference between sex and gender? Although frequently used interchangeably, the two terms actually differ in important ways. *Sex* is a biological term; people are termed either male or female depending on their sex organs and genes. In contrast, *gender* is a psychological and cultural term, referring to one's subjective feelings of maleness or femaleness (*gender identity*). *Gender* may also refer to society's evaluation of behavior as masculine or feminine (*gender role*). The degree to which a person identifies with societal definitions of masculinity or femininity is referred to as *gender role identity* or *sex typing*. It is possible, indeed common, for women and men to vary in their adoption of sex-typed characteristics.

The importance of distinguishing between the terms *sex* and *gender* rests on the importance of distinguishing between biological aspects and social aspects of being either male or female. All too frequently, people assume that apparent behavioral and personality differences between males and females are due to *sex* differences—that is, that the differences are biologically based. As we shall see in this book, to the extent that behavioral and personality differences between males and females exist, most are due to social factors—socialization practices, social rewards, status variables, and observer expectations, to name a few. As Rhoda Unger (1989b) summarizes, "In the new psychology of sex and gender, maleness and femaleness are viewed largely as social constructs that are confirmed by sex-characteristic

A boy and his father were involved in a serious automobile accident. The father was killed instantly; the son was severely injured. An ambulance rushed him to the nearest hospital, and a prominent surgeon was summoned to perform an immediate operation. Upon entering the operating room, however, the surgeon exclaimed, "I can't operate on this boy. He's my son." Question: how can this be?

If this apocryphal story is unfamiliar to you, and you came up with an answer involving a stepfather, an adopted father, reincarnation, a mistake, or such, you are part of the majority of Americans who think of surgery as a male occupation. The answer to the riddle is simple: the surgeon is the boy's mother. The fact that most people do not guess the answer demonstrates the pervasiveness and strength of certain gender stereotypes—in this case, occupational ones.

styles of self-presentation and the differential distribution of females and males into different social roles and statuses and maintained by intra-psychic needs for self-consistency and the need to behave in a socially desirable manner" (p. 17). Thus, gender is constructed by people, not by biology, and this construction is shaped by historical, cultural, and psychological processes. For example, in the United States, dentistry is viewed as a male profession; and, indeed, most dentists today are men. In Sweden and the Soviet Union, however, most dentists are women, and the profession is viewed as a female one. Clearly, then, the skills involved in dentistry are not inherently male- or female-related but are only labeled as such by a society.

Given the socially constructed nature of gender, why do so many people believe in *sex* differences? Deaux and Kite (1987) suggest that the answer lies in a shared "gender belief system," which refers to "a set of beliefs and opinions about males and females and about the purported qualities of masculinity and femininity" (p. 97). Such a belief system shapes the way we perceive and evaluate others. Two fundamental aspects of a gender belief system are the culture's stereotypes of women and men and the roles assigned to women and men.

Consider the following example. If you were giving a toy to a girl, would you give her a doll? A catcher's mitt? A coloring book? A chemistry set? Which of these toys would you give to a boy? Such choices tap our basic assumptions about boys and girls, males and females. Although for a particular child your choice may not reflect the typical assumptions we make about female and male interests, how about your response for an unknown boy or girl? If that distinction makes a difference, you have come face to face with the meaning of the term *stereotype*. Stereotypes are strongly held overgeneralizations about people in some designated social category. Such beliefs tend to be universally shared within a given society and are learned as part of the process of growing up in that society. Not only may stereotypes not be true for the group as a whole because they are over-simplifications (most boys may not want a chemistry set), but they also are unlikely to be true for any specific member of the group (Johnny Doe, in particular, may not want a chemistry set). Even when a generalization is valid (that is, it does describe group averages), we still cannot predict an individual's behavior or characteristics. For example, if we know that men are taller than women, we still don't necessarily know that John Doe is taller

than Jane Doe. Stereotypes, because they are more oversimplified and more rigidly held than such generalizations, have even less predictive value.

When we speak of *gender* or *sex role stereotypes*, we are speaking of those "structured sets of beliefs about the personal attributes of women and men" (Ashmore & Del Boca, 1979, p. 222). These beliefs are *normative* in the sense that they imply that gender-linked characteristics not only exist but also are desirable. Gender stereotypes exist both on the cultural level (for example, as reflected in the media) and on a personal level (for example, our implicit personality theory regarding the attributes linked with being female or male) (Ashmore, Del Boca, & Wohlers, 1986). We acquire gender stereotypes as we acquire information about the world and our roles in it.

Children in every culture need to learn their roles and the behaviors that go with them. They need to learn what a child, a student, a brother or sister, son or daughter, man or woman should do. With gender roles, as with other roles, the expectations are not always clear, nor does everyone adopt them to the same degree. For example, the male role in many working-class families involves being physically aggressive and settling disagreements by a show of physical strength; in many middle- and upper-class homes, the expectation for men is to be verbally and intellectually aggressive and to settle disagreements through the use of reasoning powers. Yet there are many working-class men who disdain physical violence and many upper-class men who use it. The former group, particularly, are likely to be accused of not being masculine enough. Such charges reveal the operation of specific role expectations.

Because roles are learned, the possibility always exists that they can be unlearned and the definitions of the roles themselves redefined. Even stereotypes can be modified. Indeed, some modification of gender stereotypes appears to be occurring. The possibility of such changes is important to bear in mind as we examine the specific gender stereotypes in more depth.

▲ Gender Stereotypes

A number of aspects of gender stereotypes need examining—their content, their implications, their bases, and their effects. We will begin with the content of gender stereotypes.

What Are the Gender Stereotypes?

List as many descriptors as you can for the terms *masculine* and *feminine*. If you're like most people, a number of descriptors come readily to mind. See if they match the ones listed in Table 1.1.

For most people, masculinity is associated with competency, instrumentality, and activity; femininity is associated with warmth, expressiveness, and nurturance. Studies conducted during the late 1960s and early 1970s with nearly 1000 males and females (I. Broverman, Vogel, Broverman, Clarkson, & Rosenkrantz, 1972; Rosenkrantz, Vogel, Bee, Broverman, & Broverman, 1968) demonstrated a broad consensus regarding the existence of different personality traits in men as compared with women. This consensus was found regardless of the age, sex, religion, educational level, or marital status of the respondents. More than 75% of those asked agreed that 41 traits clearly differentiated females and males. Table 1.1 lists these traits in the two categories suggested by statistical analysis: 29 male-valued items (competency cluster) and 12 female-valued items (warmth-expressiveness cluster). Similar clusters have been found by more recent researchers as well (for example, P. A. Smith & Midlarsky, 1985; Spence & Sawin, 1985). Although a research design that involves questions about how males differ from females may exaggerate sex differences, requests for open-ended descriptions of males and females show the same distinctive clusters of traits (Cicone & Ruble, 1978; Kite & Deaux, 1987). In general, using Bakan's (1966) terminology, women most often are characterized as communal (that is, selfless and other-oriented); men most often are characterized as agentic (that is, assertive and achievement-oriented).

Children as young as 7 years make these distinctions (Davis, Williams, & Best, 1982; Hensley & Borges, 1981), and even cross-cultural research finds considerable generality in those characteristics seen as differentially associated with women and men (Ward, 1985; Zammuner, 1987). For example, in all 25 of the countries sampled by J. E. Williams and Best (1990), men were associated with such descriptors as "adventurous" and "forceful," whereas women were associated with such descriptors as "sentimental" and "submissive."

Variations in Gender Stereotypes

Despite general agreement on a number of sex-stereotypic traits, variations in gender stereotypes do occur (Lii & Wong, 1982; J. E. Williams & Best, 1990). The specific traits listed in Table 1.1 appear to be based on people's image of a prototypic male and female. In the United States, the prototype basically is White,* middle-class, heterosexual, and Christian. For groups that differ from the prototype, different stereotypic traits exist. For example, the stereotypes of African-American males and females are more similar to each other in terms of expressiveness and competence than are the stereotypes of Anglo-American males and females (Millham & Smith, 1981; P. A. Smith & Midlarsky, 1985). Compared with White women, Black women are viewed as less passive, dependent, status conscious, emotional, and concerned about their appearance (Landrine, 1985; Romer & Cherry, 1980). Compared with White men, Black men are viewed as more emotionally expressive and less competitive, independent, and status conscious.

Less research has been done on gender stereotypes of other racial or ethnic groups, but cultural images of women suggest other variations do exist. Hispanic women tend to be viewed as more "feminine" than White women in terms of submissiveness and dependence (Vazquez-Nuttall, Romero-Garcia, & De Leon, 1987). A similar stereotype holds for Asian women, but with the addition of exotic sexuality (Chow, 1985). Native-American women typically are stereotyped as faceless "squaws"— drudges without any personality (Witt, 1981). And Jewish women are stereotyped as either pushy, vain "princesses" or overprotective, manipulative "Jewish mothers" (S. W. Schneider, 1986).

Besides racial differences in gender stereotypes, there are social class differences, sexual orientation differences, and age differences (Cazenave, 1984; Del Boca & Ashmore, 1980; Kite & Deaux, 1987; Landrine, 1985). For example, working-class women are stereotyped as more hostile, confused, inconsiderate, and irresponsible than middle-class women; male homosexuals are stereotyped as possessing feminine traits while lesbians are stereotyped as possessing masculine traits.

What these variations in gender stereotypes suggest is that gender is not the only variable by which people are stereotyped. Each one of us is situated in sociological space at the intersection of numerous categories—for example, gender, race or ethnicity, class, sexual orientation, and able-bodiedness. These social categories interact with

---

* The racial descriptors "White" and "Black" are capitalized to indicate the terms refer to designated social categories and not to physical characteristics.

Table 1.1 Stereotypic sex role descriptors (responses from 74 college men and 80 college women, 1972)

Competency Cluster: Masculine Pole Is More Desirable

Feminine	Masculine
Not at all aggressive	Very aggressive
Not at all independent	Very independent
Very emotional	Not at all emotional
Does not hide emotions at all	Almost always hides emotions
Very subjective	Very objective
Very easily influenced	Not at all easily influenced
Very submissive	Very dominant
Dislikes math and science very much	Likes math and science very much
Very excitable in a minor crisis	Not at all excitable in a minor crisis
Very passive	Very active
Not at all competitive	Very competitive
Very illogical	Very logical
Very home-oriented	Very worldly
Not at all skilled in business	Very skilled in business
Very sneaky	Very direct
Does not know the way of the world	Knows the way of the world
Feelings easily hurt	Feelings not easily hurt
Not at all adventurous	Very adventurous
Has difficulty making decisions	Can make decisions easily
Cries very easily	Never cries
Almost never acts as a leader	Almost always acts as a leader
Not at all self-confident	Very self-confident
Very uncomfortable about being aggressive	Not at all uncomfortable about being aggressive
Not at all ambitious	Very ambitious
Unable to separate feelings from ideas	Easily able to separate feelings from ideas
Very dependent	Not at all dependent
Very conceited about appearance	Never conceited about appearance
Thinks women are always superior to men	Thinks men are always superior to women
Does not talk freely about sex with men	Talks freely about sex with men

Warmth-Expressiveness Cluster: Feminine Pole Is More Desirable

Feminine	Masculine
Doesn't use harsh language at all	Uses very harsh language
Very talkative	Not at all talkative
Very tactful	Very blunt
Very gentle	Very rough
Very aware of feelings of others	Not at all aware of feelings of others
Very religious	Not at all religious
Very interested in own appearance	Not at all interested in own appearance
Very neat in habits	Very sloppy in habits
Very quiet	Very loud
Very strong need for security	Very little need for security
Enjoys art and literature	Does not enjoy art and literature at all
Easily expresses tender feelings	Does not express tender feelings at all easily

From "Sex Role Stereotypes: A Current Appraisal," by I. Broverman, S. R. Vogel, D. M. Broverman, F. E. Clarkson, and P. S. Rosenkrantz, *Journal of Social Issues*, 1972, *28*(2), 59–78. Copyright 1972 by the Society for the Psychological Study of Social Issues. Reprinted by permission of the author and publisher.

each other in complex ways. A woman who is White, working-class, lesbian, and differently abled will be viewed very differently from a Black, middle-class, heterosexual, able-bodied woman. Thus, women and men do not form two homogeneous groups but rather represent striking diversity within each gender. Most people, including social scientists, have tended to ignore this diversity and have used

White middle-class heterosexuals as the norm. It behooves us, however, to recognize this limitation in much of the research presented in this book.

Stereotypes are not fixed but respond, albeit slowly, to cultural changes. Since the 1970s, distinct subtypes of both female and male stereotypes have appeared (Ashmore, Del Boca, & Wohlers, 1986; Deaux & Kite, 1987; Deaux, Winton, Crowley, & Lewis, 1985; Six & Eckes, 1991). For women, there are at least three distinct stereotypes: the housewife (the traditional woman), the professional woman (independent, ambitious, self-confident), and the Playboy bunny (sex object). Although the subtypes are perceived as differing on many traits, behaviors, and occupations, they still share commonalities. For example, all three subtypes are expected to be concerned with having and caring for children.

Subtypes of the male stereotype are less clear, partly because less research has been done on this topic, partly because the image of "man" seems less differentiated than the image of "woman," and partly because women and men may hold slightly different subtypes (see also Hort, Fagot, & Leinbach, 1990). The traditional man stereotype has been found to be comprised of three main factors: status (the need to achieve success and others' respect), toughness (strength and self-reliance), and antifemininity (avoidance of stereotypically feminine activities) (E. H. Thompson & Pleck, 1987). In addition, the traditional man is seen by men as sexually proficient. Women, however, distinguish a sexual man subtype—the stud or Don Juan. For many people, a liberated man stereotype also exists that incorporates such stereotypically feminine traits as gentleness and sensitivity (Ehrenreich, 1984; Keen & Zur, 1989; Kimmel, 1987a; Pleck, 1981b). Some writers in the emerging field of men's studies argue for use of the term *masculinities* rather than *masculinity* to acknowledge the pluralism in definitions based on race, class, sexual orientation, and so on (for example, Brod, 1987). Still, when most people think of a typical man or woman, they apparently have the traditional (White) middle-class stereotype in mind.

Although most research on gender stereotypes has focused on personality traits, Deaux and Lewis (1984) and others (J. Archer, 1989; P. A. Smith & Midlarsky, 1985; Spence & Sawin, 1985) have shown that gender stereotypes exist in at least three other areas as well. Not only can one talk about masculine and feminine traits (such as independence and gentleness, respectively), but one can also talk about masculine and feminine roles (such as head of household and caretaker of children, respectively), masculine and feminine occupations (such as truck driver and telephone operator, respectively), and masculine and feminine physical characteristics (such as broad shoulders and grace, respectively). The four components, although related, can operate relatively independently. A graceful individual can be male or female, independent or gentle, a head of household or a caretaker of children, and a truck driver or a telephone operator. Of all the domains (personality, role behaviors, occupations, and physical appearance), the most important in terms of eliciting an individual's gender belief system is the physical (Deaux & Lewis, 1984; Freeman, 1987). For example, if the only information people are given about a man is that he has a slight build, people are likely to predict that he has stereotypically feminine traits, is employed in a feminine occupation, and possibly is homosexual. Such far-reaching predictions would be much less likely if all we knew about the man was that he was gentle. Given the fact that the first thing we notice or know about a person is her or his physical appearance, it's clear that gender stereotypes can get activated very quickly.

Although gender stereotypes appear to have considerable generality and to be quite strong and stable, some indication exists that people's attitudes about socially desirable traits for men and women may be changing. For example, T. L. Ruble (1983) found that although college students believed that the typical female and male differed on nearly 53 traits, these students also believed that it was desirable for males and females to differ on only 12 traits (such as aggressiveness and neatness). Women appear to perceive fewer characteristics as desirable for one sex only than do men (Canter & Meyerowitz, 1984; M. Lewin & Tragos, 1987). Thus, men appear to view gender stereotypes as more appropriate than do women, a finding that will reappear repeatedly in different contexts throughout this book.

The evidence that gender stereotypes exist is strong. What are their implications?

Implications of Gender Stereotypes
A number of issues regarding gender stereotypes merit further consideration: their social desirability, the opposition they imply between the two sexes, and their all-or-none categorizing.

Social desirability   The general social desirability of masculine and feminine traits is related to gender stereotypes. Traditionally, stereotypically masculine traits have been viewed more positively and as more socially desirable than stereotypically feminine traits (I. Broverman et al., 1972; Rosenkrantz et al., 1968). Masculine traits are viewed as showing more strength and activity than feminine traits (Ashmore et al., 1986; J. E. Williams & Best, 1990), and the qualities of strength and activity have been highly valued by Western cultures. Traditionally, the only exceptions to this pattern have been the few feminine traits that relate to sensitivity to the needs of others. These few traits have been rated more highly than any masculine ones (S. L. Bem, 1974).

More recently (since 1980), increased value has been attached to certain stereotypically feminine traits, especially by women (Eagly & Mladinic, 1989; P. A. Smith & Midlarsky, 1985; P. D. Werner & LaRussa, 1985). This increased valuation probably has stemmed from a deliberate attempt by many feminists and nonfeminists alike to counteract the "masculinization of values" that occurred as a product of the women's movement during the 1970s. As will be discussed in Chapter 13, the women's movement during the 1970s seemed to emphasize women moving into traditionally male roles (for example, the executive suite) and adopting traditionally male traits (for example, assertiveness and dominance). The other side of social change—men moving into traditionally female roles and adopting traditionally female traits—was relatively neglected. Consequently, during the 1980s we saw the rise of attempts to valorize the feminine traits involved with being relational (communal)—in moral reasoning (Gilligan, 1982), in cognitive processes (Belenky, Clinchy, Goldberger, & Tarule, 1986), and in personality in general (Chodorow, 1978; J. B. Miller, 1976, 1984). The irony of this attempt is that arguing for the value of stereotypically feminine traits strengthens the stereotypes themselves. The identification of these traits with women rather than as valuable but "human" ones perpetuates the myth that these traits are indeed sex-linked (see M. Crawford, 1988, and Hare-Mustin & Marecek, 1988, for an interesting discussion of the debate between maximizing and minimizing claims of gender differences).

Today, although a number of stereotypically feminine traits are viewed more positively than stereotypically masculine traits, especially by women, a number of stereotypically feminine traits are still viewed extremely negatively, such as being submissive, emotional, easily influenced, sneaky, and unambitious. Of course, a number of stereotypically masculine traits (such as restricted emotionality, aggressiveness) are viewed negatively as well, at least by women. Thus, the value attached to stereotypic gender traits appears to be changing, at least for women. Still, masculine traits are culturally supported more than feminine traits and are associated with power and control. In contrast, feminine traits are associated with powerlessness and being controlled. The effects of such differential valuations on self-image and attitudes toward women will be examined in Part 4.

The "opposite" sex   The traits listed in Table 1.1 reveal another common finding related to gender stereotypes: the characteristic traits for men and women are commonly viewed as being opposite each other. Thus, whereas males are thought of as dominant and objective, females are thought of as submissive and subjective. This all-or-none distinction may have been a function of the questionnaire used by the Broverman group (Brannon, 1978). The items were presented as two endpoints on a line, and each respondent was asked to check where on the line the typical male or female could be placed. Thus, a female could only be rated as either submissive or dominant, not as more or less submissive, or more or less dominant. Even when responses are free form, however, nearly identical lists and distinctions emerge; for example, males are strong, females weak; females are emotional, males are unemotional. Furthermore, as many researchers (Deaux & Lewis, 1984; Foushee, Helmreich, & Spence, 1979) have found, most people think that masculinity and femininity are negatively related— that is, that being low on masculine traits implies being high on feminine traits.

If sex-typed traits were opposites, we would expect a strong inverse relationship between how a person scores on stereotypically masculine traits and how she or he scores on stereotypically feminine traits; that is, being high on one dimension (for example, dominance) would mean being low on the other dimension (for example, nurturance). However, research that has correlated individual scores on the masculinity and femininity scales has found little relationship between the two (S. L. Bem, 1974; Marsh, Antill, & Cunningham, 1989; Spence & Helmreich, 1978). How high someone scores on masculinity is unrelated to how high he or she scores on femininity. Thus, the bipolar model of masculinity and femininity, which postulates that instrumentality and expressivity fall at opposite ends of a single dimension, is not completely correct. However, a few aspects of the gender stereotypes may be bipolar. In particular, ratings of the terms *masculine* and *feminine* do seem to be negatively correlated; that is, people who rate themselves high on one tend to rate themselves low on the other (Marsh et al., 1989). In sum, three factors appear to be involved in determining masculinity or femininity: two factors, characterized as active-instrumental and expressive-nurturant, that are independent, and one factor that is bipolar.

All-or-none categorizing   The all-or-none categorizing of gender traits is misleading. People just are not so simple that they either possess all of a trait or none of it. This is even more true when trait dispositions for groups of people are examined. Part a of Figure 1.1 illustrates what such an all-or-none distribution of the trait "strength" would look like: all males would be strong, all females weak. The fact is, most psychological and physical traits are distributed according to the pattern shown in Part b of Figure 1.1, with most people possessing an average amount of that trait and fewer people having either very much or very little of that trait. Almost all the traits listed in Table 1.1 conform to this pattern.

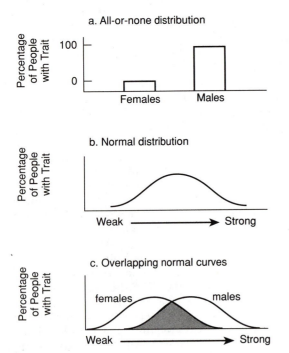

Figure 1.1 Three types of distributions for the trait "strength."

To the extent that females and males may differ in the average amount of the trait they possess (which needs to be determined empirically), the distribution can be characterized by *overlapping normal curves*, as shown in Part c of Figure 1.1. Thus, although most men are stronger than most women, the shaded area indicates that some men are weaker than some women and vice versa. The amount of overlap of the curves generally is considerable. Another attribute related to overlapping normal curves is that differences within one group are usually greater than the differences between the two groups. Thus, more variation in strength occurs within a group of men than between the average male and the average female. Most of the stereotypic traits in Table 1.1 fit this pattern. For example, although males on the average may be more aggressive than females on the average, greater differences may be found among males than between males and females. Indeed, recent investigations of college students' conceptions of typical men and women reveal much overlap in the descriptions (De Lisi & Soundranayagam, 1990).

This concept of overlapping normal curves is critically important in understanding gender stereotypes because it undermines the basis of most discriminatory regulations and laws. Although most men are stronger than most women, denying women access to jobs requiring strength simply on the basis of sex is unjustified, because some women are stronger than some men (see shaded area in Part C of Figure 1.1). Thus, if most of the stereotypic traits are actually distributed in normal curves along a continuum (that is, people may be more or less dominant, more or less submissive) rather than distributed in an all-or-none fashion—dominant or submissive—then setting up two opposite and distinct lists of traits for females and males is entirely inappropriate and misleading.

Not only is it inaccurate to view traits as all or none; it may also be inaccurate to view gender stereotypes in terms of personality traits. As noted earlier, recent research on gender stereotypes suggests that most people think of the terms *masculinity* and *femininity* as related to biological sex (male, female), sex-appropriate physical characteristics (muscular, petite), and appearance descriptors (handsome, pretty) more than to personality traits (dominant, submissive). Thus, most of the scales used to measure sex typing (that is, people's conformity to gender stereotypes) may be inadequate.

Furthermore, strong debate exists over whether personality can be viewed in trait terms altogether. Despite their popularity, trait theories of personality have little empirical validity (see, for example, Chaplin & Goldberg, 1985). People are simply not as consistent in their behavior across a variety of situations as one might like to believe. Mischel (1968) concludes that cross-situational consistencies rarely produce correlations greater than +.30; that is, a person does not usually exhibit the same trait to the same degree in every situation. Rather, human behavior is a function of both the person and the situation. The situation, in many cases, accounts for more than 90% of the variability in a person's behavior. For example, one's behavior during a church service or at a red light is almost entirely a function of the situation. As another example, how assertively a person acts depends not only on the person but on the situation itself. This can be readily verified from one's own experience. An individual can be very assertive in one situation (for example, in a class or group meeting) and markedly unassertive in another (for example, with a close friend).

Of course, some people may be more consistent than others in their behaviors in general and with respect to specific behaviors in particular (D. Bem & Allen, 1974). That is, some people may generally be more predictable than others across a wide range of situations. For example, people who strongly identify with a sex role are more predictable because they more often act according to sex role expectations than people who don't identify with such a role (S. L. Bem, 1975b, 1985). And some people are more consistent than others with respect to a particular behavior (for example, "You can always count on Mary to be assertive"). On the whole, however, the trait approach to personality needs to be modified. Specific people interact with specific situations and produce specific behaviors; generalized traits rarely apply.

With reference to gender stereotypes, then, it can be concluded that (1) people cannot be viewed simply as collections of consistent traits, because situations also are important; (2) males and females specifically cannot be viewed as having unique traits that are opposite each other; and (3) whatever attributes are thought of as distinctly masculine or feminine are also possessed by at least some members of the other sex.

Bases of Gender Stereotypes
If women and men are not accurately described solely as collections of feminine or masculine traits,

respectively, and, in fact, if the application of trait terms to personality is generally not appropriate, on what are the stereotypes based? Two basic theories exist regarding the origin of gender stereotypes: the "kernel of truth" theory and social-role theory. The *"kernel of truth" theory* rests on the assumption that gender stereotypes have some empirical validity—that is, there are real differences in behavior between the sexes that the stereotypes just exaggerate. This approach suggests that the differences exist first and that the stereotypes simply reflect them. In this case, what have been called stereotypes would be simple generalizations. Carol Martin (1987) examined this question and found that most of the gender stereotypic traits were indeed oversimplifications and exaggerations of minor group differences. Polling 139 college students regarding which of 32 gender-typed traits they viewed as typical of male college students and which as typical of female college students, Martin found significant differences on all of them, in the expected direction. For example, a very large sex difference was expected for the trait "loves children." (This trait was viewed as much more characteristic of women than of men.) However, when these same students were asked to rate these 32 traits as either descriptive or not descriptive of themselves, male and female students differed on only 5: male students were more likely than female students to see themselves as egotistical and cynical; female students were more likely than male students to see themselves as aware of others' feelings, whiney, and fussy. Although these 5 differences were as predicted, the major finding was of gender similarity on the 27 other sex-typed traits, including "loves children." Thus, although a few gender differences might exist with respect to personality traits, people expect many more. Unger and Siiter (1975) found similar exaggerations made by college students with respect to values. Gender stereotypes, thus, may not be based on statistically significant differences between the sexes, but, at best, are exaggerations of a grain of truth. Most of the research on differences in behavior and traits that we will review in the next part of the book shows the same pattern of greater gender similarity than gender difference. Yet people continue to exaggerate the number and magnitude of differences between the sexes.

The *social-role theory* of gender stereotypes (Eagly, 1987b; Eagly & Steffen, 1984) maintains that the stereotypes arise from the different social roles typically held by women and men. Males are likely to play with guns, know how to change a flat tire, mow the lawn well, and be employed when they are adults. Females are likely to bake well, change diapers, play with baby dolls, and be homemakers as well as employed when they are adults. Eagly and Steffen (1984, 1986b) argue that it is *because* men and women typically do different things that people make assumptions about men's and women's innate traits and abilities. These researchers found that people's beliefs that females possess more communal (concerned with others) and fewer agentic (masterful) qualities than men are a result of perceiving women as homemakers and men as full-time employees. When women are specifically described as full-time employees, they are perceived as more similar to men in terms of communal and agentic qualities (low communal, high agentic). When men are described as full-time homemakers, they are perceived as more similar to (traditional) women (high communal, low agentic). Other research confirms that when men and women are in identical roles, they are perceived as similar (L. A. Jackson & Sullivan, 1990). Therefore, it is the division of labor and tasks between women and men that accounts for the content of gender stereotypes. Even when both women and men are employed, they tend to be employed in different types of jobs (Chapter 11 will explore this process in more detail). Traditionally female jobs (for example, elementary school teacher, social worker) require mainly communal qualities, whereas traditionally male jobs (for example, manual laborer, executive) require mainly agentic qualities (see also C. Hoffman & Hurst, 1990; Yount, 1986). (The division of labor by gender will be discussed further in Chapter 5.)

Figure 1.2 summarizes the social-role theory of gender stereotypes and gender differences in social behavior. The division of labor between the sexes gives rise to different expectations regarding women and men (gender stereotypes); that is, women are expected to behave more communally (because of their domestic role) while men are expected to behave more agentically (because of their occupational role). Because men and women are doing different things, they develop different skills and beliefs; for example, because women do more child care, they may develop more proficiency in that role, while men, who are more likely to be full-time employees, may develop more proficiency in that role. These differences in sex-typed skills (and their accompanying beliefs) combined with gender stereotypes may lead to observable gender

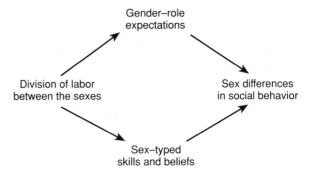

Figure 1.2 The social-role theory of sex differences in social behavior. From *Sex Differences in Social Behavior: A Social-Role Interpretation*, by A. H. Eagly, p. 32. Copyright © 1987 by Lawrence Erlbaum Associates. Reprinted by permission.

differences in social behavior in the stereotypic direction; for example, women may more often engage in nurturant behaviors whereas men may more often engage in task-oriented behaviors.

The social-role theory of gender stereotypes is provocative because of the circular nature of the process. As we will see in Part 3, boys and girls are encouraged in many ways to learn gender-stereotypic roles and behaviors. Once they have learned these roles and behaviors, college men and women report greater ability, enjoyment, and performance of gender-stereotypic behaviors than of nonstereotypic behaviors (Canter & Meyerowitz, 1984). Further strengthening the stereotypes is the tendency for people to overestimate the frequency with which gender-stereotypic behaviors occur (Hepburn, 1985). Culminating the process is the fact that once stereotypic roles are acquired, people may look at the differences in behavior and conclude that they are a product of different innate traits or abilities, rather than a product of learning. Thus the stereotypes themselves become strengthened.

The social-role theory is compatible with *social stratification theories*, which suggest that gender roles are actually status roles; that is, that the male role is the socially dominant one while the female role is the socially subordinate one. The stereotypic behaviors, traits, and jobs that are viewed as *gender*-linked are actually *status*-linked. For example, a person (female or male) assigned to play a dominant position will be more authoritative and more agentic than someone (female or male) assigned to a subordinate position. Similarly, a person (female or male) assigned to a subordinate position will display more passivity and communal traits than someone assigned to a dominant position. This theoretical approach is supported by the fact that the main dimension differentiating masculine traits from feminine traits is "potency" (Ashmore et al., 1986). Indeed, some writers argue that the male sex role doesn't even exist since it is purely a power-based role (for example, Carrigan, Connell, & Lee, 1987). This approach also allows us to tie together a number of disparate findings regarding social behaviors that will be described in Chapter 3. Of note here is the value of this approach in understanding other status differences, such as between Whites and Blacks, with Whites relative to Blacks being viewed as more agentic and less communal (Romer & Cherry, 1980). This approach also explains why national stereotypes are based on the stereotypes of men in that nation (Eagly & Kite, 1987). Because men hold the higher status, their behavior is more visible and valued by observers, who then equate men's qualities and behaviors with that of their country.

In sum, the social-role theory, which suggests that gender roles create gender stereotypes, is fairly persuasive, especially when combined with social stratification theory. Social-role theory differs from the "kernel of truth" theory only with respect to the causal factor—do existing small sex differences create the stereotypes, or do assigned gender roles create the stereotypes and gender differences in behavior? The next three chapters will examine whether stereotypic sex differences indeed are supported by research. Although some differences exist and may have a physiological basis, the bulk of the research suggests that gender differences, to the extent they exist, are a *function* of gender roles rather than their cause (for example, Epstein, 1988).

Effects of Gender Stereotyping
What are the consequences of the gender stereotypes themselves? Although a more thorough examination of the consequences will be presented in Part 4, it will be helpful to review some of the general effects of stereotypes at this point.

As we have just seen, rather than reflecting real behavioral differences, it is more likely that belief in the stereotypes may give rise to some behavioral differences. If the stereotypes function as part of sex role expectations, then people will learn them and be influenced by them. Even though sex-typed distinctions between the sexes may not fit individuals, stereotypes themselves have power as standards to which to conform, against which to rebel, or with which to evaluate others.

One way stereotypes operate is by serving as *perceptual filters* through which we see individuals. We're actually more likely to notice and remember stereotype-consistent behaviors than other behaviors (Bodenhausen, 1988; Stangor, 1988). If we see a White man acting assertively, we're more likely to remember that incident than if we see the same behavior in an Asian woman. When it comes to promotion time, who might be seen as the better candidate for a leadership position? This perceptual filter function of stereotypes also explains why stereotypes are so resistant to change. If we observe someone conforming to the stereotype (for example, a woman being helpless about changing a tire), we notice and remember it ("Isn't that just like a woman!"). Consequently, the stereotype (in this case, of helplessness) is strengthened. If, however, we observe someone not conforming to the stereotype (for example, we see a woman competently changing a tire), we either don't notice or remember it, or we view it as an exception to the "rule." ("Oh, *she's* just different. Most women can't take care of their cars.") The strength of the stereotype itself is undiminished. The self-perpetuating nature of stereotypes is further enhanced by the finding that even if we only *imagine* that an individual conforms to stereotypes, we remember the imagining as an actual confirmation (Slusher & Anderson, 1987).

Another way stereotypes operate is by setting up a *self-fulfilling prophecy*. If females are viewed as having more negative characteristics than males, some females may view themselves this way and may, in fact, develop those very characteristics. For example, if females are expected to be less rational than males, some may view themselves that way and not participate in problem-solving activities or take advanced math courses, since such behaviors are not gender-appropriate. As a result, some females may indeed develop fewer problem-solving abilities than some males who have had those experiences, thereby fulfilling the stereotype. Such beliefs can powerfully influence behavior in either a negative way, if the expectations are negative, or a positive way, if the expectations are positive (M. Snyder, Tanke, & Berscheid, 1977).

An example of the critical role of other people's expectancies in determining our own behavior was demonstrated by Skrypnek and Snyder (1982). In a laboratory study, males were led to believe that they were paired with either another male or a female in a task requiring a division of labor. Males selected more gender-stereotypic activities for themselves and for their partner when the partner was thought to be female than when the partner was thought to be male. More important, the female partner later chose more stereotypically feminine tasks when her partner believed that she was female, even though she wasn't informed directly of his expectations. Thus, other people's expectations become fulfilled.

As this study suggests, another way gender stereotypes affect us is through *impression management.* All of us, at some level, want to be socially acceptable, at least to some people. To the extent that we desire such approval, we may engage in impression-management strategies in order to obtain it. That is, we will try to present ourselves (our image) in a way that we think is acceptable to another person. Zanna and Pack (1975) found that female Princeton undergraduates when meeting a man they viewed as a desirable partner would present themselves as extremely conventional women when the ideology of the man was conventional and as more liberated women when his ideology was nontraditional. When the man was viewed as undesirable, his views did not have much impact on the images presented by the women.

In a similar study by von Baeyer, Sherk, and Zanna (1981), 53 female undergraduates acted as job applicants and were interviewed by a male confederate who supposedly held either traditional or nontraditional views of women. The women who saw the traditional interviewer presented themselves in a more traditional way (they wore makeup and clothing accessories, talked to and gazed at the interviewer less, and gave more traditional answers to a question concerning marriage and children) than the women who saw the nontraditional interviewer. These changes were unrelated to the women's own degree of sex typing. Thus, one way the gender stereotypes function is to define expected gender behavior and thereby shape people's self-presentations. This is as true for men as it is for women. As the stereotypes change, so might gender behaviors. Such changes, however, may simply define new images rather than reflect a general reduction in impression management. To the extent that individuals, male or female, are stereotyped, realization of their full human potential in all its complexity is impeded.

Stereotypic expectations can be overcome by specific information about an individual (Berndt & Heller, 1986; Deaux & Lewis, 1984; Locksley, Borgida, Brekke, & Hepburn, 1980). In this sense, stereotypic beliefs appear to operate as intuitive estimates of the probabilities of traits in social

groups. If we know nothing else about a person except that she's female, we're likely to guess that she's expressive, nurturant, dependent, and so on. But when we learn more about her, we will use the specific information instead of gender stereotypes to make predictions.

Although it is encouraging that once someone gets to know us, he or she will stop using stereotypes to predict our behavior, this doesn't mean that stereotypes stop affecting judgments. For example, boys who engage in feminine activities are viewed as less popular than are other boys (Berndt & Heller, 1986). Women who act in a feminine (modest, family-oriented) manner during an interview are viewed as better suited for traditionally feminine jobs (such as preschool teacher) than for traditionally masculine ones (such as high school principal) (Towson, Zanna, & MacDonald, 1989). Furthermore, although both men and women would like to get away from gender-stereotypical behavior, both men and women (but especially women) tend to experience the other sex as demanding conformity (L. R. Davidson, 1981).

In sum, gender stereotypes, which are based on few real sex differences, are powerful forces of social control. People can either conform to them and be socially acceptable but restricted, or they can rebel and face the consequences of being socially unacceptable.

How much *do* people conform to gender stereotypes? Research on sex typing and androgyny can give us some idea, at least with respect to personality traits.

▲ Sex Typing and Androgyny

Research in the mid-1970s on the degree to which individuals were sex-typed (that is, conformed to gender stereotypes) led to a redefinition of the older concept of androgyny. Since the two sets of personality traits viewed as stereotypically masculine (active-instrumental traits) and stereotypically feminine (nurturant-expressive traits) were statistically independent (that is, the way an individual scored on one set of traits was unrelated to the way she or he scored on the other set of traits), terms were needed to describe individuals who were high on both sets of traits and others who were low on both. Sandra Bem (1974, 1975b, 1976) and others (for example, Spence & Helmreich, 1978) used the term *androgynous* to describe those individuals who scored high on both active-instrumental traits (such as assertiveness, self-reliance, and independence) and nurturant-expressive traits (such as understanding, compassion, and affection). These people were different from masculine-sex-typed individuals (high on instrumental-active traits, low on nurturant-expressive traits), feminine-sex-typed individuals (high on nurturant-expressive traits, low on instrumental-active traits), and *undifferentiated* individuals (those who scored low on both sets of traits) (Spence, Helmreich, & Stapp, 1974). Figure 1.3 presents this fourfold classification. One virtue of this fourfold typology is that it separates biological sex from psychological sex typing. Any person can be masculine-sex-typed, feminine-sex-typed, androgynous, or undifferentiated.

Being androgynous does not mean being neuter or imply anything about one's sexual orientation. Rather, it describes the degree of flexibility a person has regarding gender-stereotypic behaviors. The complex characteristics of androgynous individuals can be evidenced, depending on the situation, all in a single act or only in a number of different acts. Thus, a person may be an empathic listener when a friend has a problem, an assertive leader propelling a group to action, and an assertive and sensitive boss when an employee needs to be fired. The implications of androgyny for various behaviors will be explored throughout the book.

The percentage of people who could be classified as androgynous varies as a function of many factors: the specific population studied, the measuring instrument and the scoring procedure used, and even the year in which a study is done. For example,

	Masculinity: Low	Masculinity: High
Femininity: Low	Undifferentiated 18% females 27% males	Masculine 12% females 42% males
Femininity: High	Feminine 39% females 12% males	Androgynous 30% females 20% males

Figure 1.3 Fourfold classification of sex typing. Numbers are percentages of college students who typically fall into each cell. From S. L. Bem, 1981a.

males seem to have increased their level of androgyny during the 1970s compared to the 1960s, whereas females showed higher levels of androgyny in the 1960s (Heilbrun & Schwartz, 1982). One should note that there are no absolute cutoff points for the categories of androgynous and sex-typed individuals. Rather, the cutoffs typically are based on the median scores of a particular sample. The vast majority of studies have been conducted on college populations. In general, about 40% of all college students describe themselves as possessing traits viewed as more characteristic of their sex than of the other (that is, traditionally sex-typed). (See Figure 1.3.) About one-fourth of college populations are classified as androgynous (somewhat more females than males). Another 20% are characterized as undifferentiated (that is, low in both sets of traits). Finally, about 10% describe themselves as possessing traits viewed as more characteristic of the other sex than of their own (that is, cross-sex-typed). Thus, more than half of all college students are *not* traditionally sex-typed, although more males than females possess instrumental traits (masculine-sex-typed and androgynous) and more females than males possess expressive traits (feminine-sex-typed and androgynous).

Among other populations, degree of sex typing is unclear. As will be discussed in Chapter 6, there is evidence of increasing androgyny as people reach middle age. Racial differences in sex typing may also exist. One study of young adult women, most of whom had completed high school, found that the Black women had higher instrumentality scores than the White women (Binion, 1990). In terms of sex typing, more Black women (37%) than White women (16%) fell in the androgynous category, whereas more White women (38%) than Black women (28%) fell in the undifferentiated category. Again, we must be careful not to generalize from young, primarily White, well-educated individuals to the entire population.

More recently, Sandra Bem (1981b, 1985, 1987) has reconceptualized androgyny and sex typing to refer to cognitive schemata rather than personality types. Sex-typed individuals seem to be more aware than non-sex-typed individuals (both the androgynous and the undifferentiated) of gender and such gender-related issues as the number of men and women in a room, whether the topic discussed is masculine or feminine, and whether an occupation is gender-appropriate or not (Frable, 1989; Frable & Bem, 1985; J. B. Miller, 1984; C. J. Mills, 1983). Thus, sex typing may refer to the process of construing reality in terms of gender. Non-sex-typed individuals seem less ready to impose a gender-based classification system on reality. (Gender schema theory will be discussed further in Chapter 6.)

The concept of androgyny, when first articulated, was hailed by some as a signpost leading the way toward gender equality and deplored by others as signifying the end of sex differentiation and thus the end of the world. Neither extreme view now seems justified. As we will see in succeeding chapters, the concepts of sex typing and androgyny do have some utility in helping us understand how and why some males and females differ on some behaviors. For example, more behavioral differences exist between feminine-sex-typed and masculine-sex-typed people than between women and men as social groups, because most men and women are *not* traditionally sex-typed. This finding explains why there are so few strong gender differences in behavior at the same time that it suggests why we *think* there are (because we *expect* most men to be masculine-sex-typed and most women to be feminine-sex-typed). These concepts also emphasize the importance of looking for factors other than biology to account for gender differences.

For all its value, the concept of androgyny still has its limitations. Theoretically, androgyny may be a self-defeating concept in the sense that it depends on the existence of two separate sets of traits—masculine and feminine. Thus, it may serve to perpetuate the gender stereotypes themselves. One solution to this problem is to refer to masculine and feminine traits by their qualities—instrumental-agentic and expressive-nurturant—rather than by their stereotyped labels (Spence, 1983; Spence & Helmreich, 1980). Another solution is to go beyond the concept of androgyny altogether and speak in terms of sex role transcendence (Rebecca, Hefner, & Olenshansky, 1976). This issue will be discussed further in the last chapter.

A related problem is whether these two sets of traits adequately distinguish what is feminine from what is masculine (J. Archer, 1989; Deaux & Kite, 1987; Locksley & Colten, 1979). As we've already noted, gender refers to more than simply personality traits and indeed, to more personality traits than can be summarized by the terms *instrumental* and *expressive*. Gender and sex typing are multidimensional constructs, and bidimensional measures, such as the Bem Sex-Role Inventory (S. L. Bem, 1974, 1981a) or the Personal Attributes Questionnaire (Spence & Helmreich, 1978; Spence, Helmreich, & Stapp, 1974) are not sufficient. They tell us something but not everything we need to know about gender.

Another issue (discussed further in Chapter 8) is whether androgyny is actually a unique type (an interaction between instrumental and expressive traits) or just the sum of its parts—that is, a linear combination of instrumental and expressive traits. Research suggests that androgyny does not have unique predictive power (J. A. Hall & Taylor, 1985; Lubinski, Tellegen, & Butcher, 1983). For example, with respect to self-esteem, creativity, and psychological adjustment, it is high scores on the instrumental-agentic trait scale that are beneficial (true of both masculine-sex-typed individuals and androgynous individuals), not high scores on both scales (Harrington & Andersen, 1981; Whitley, 1984, 1988a). Thus, the androgynous "ideal" may turn out to be a traditionally masculine one (Morawski, 1987). We need to understand why that is, and explanations in terms of personality traits alone will not help us.

Finally, a host of empirical problems have been raised with respect to measuring androgyny and sex typing. Different scales do not all seem to measure the same thing (A. C. Baldwin, Critelli, Stevens, & Russell, 1986; F. R. Wilson & Cook, 1984). Different scoring methods yield different results (for example, Handal & Salit, 1985). Sex-typing scales seem to measure more than two different factors (for example, Marsh et al., 1989; Pedhazur & Tetenbaum, 1979). Different researchers use different definitions of androgyny (for example, Heilbrun & Mulqueen, 1987). Sex-typing categories do not always predict stereotypic attitudes and beliefs (for example, J. Archer, 1989; Beauvais & Spence, 1987; Binion, 1990). And sex-typing categories do not always predict behavior (Lubinski et al., 1983; Myers & Gonda, 1982).

Many of these problems stem from inadequate understanding of the nature of androgyny and overly general use of the term (Morawski, 1987; Sedney, 1989). On the whole, however, if we view androgyny as a limited but valid construct whose parameters are still being explored, we will have a useful tool with which to understand some of the research on gender. We should not expect sex typing and androgyny, however, to be the only explanatory tools we will need. The concepts of power or status and the importance of situational determinants still play pivotal roles in any exploration of gender, since gender is not primarily a psychological variable but a socially constructed one. Psychologists have a tendency to overlook the latter variables, whereas sociologists have a tendency to overlook the former ones. Since gender is right at the intersection of the two fields, we need to keep as broad a perspective as possible.

▲ Tying It All Together: A Multidimensional View

What is the connection among gender roles, gender stereotypes, sex typing, and sex-typed attitudes? Although we frequently assume that individuals who hold sex-typed attitudes (for example, who believe in gender stereotypes and in traditional roles) will themselves be strongly sex-typed and in traditional roles, this assumption is not always borne out. For example, Phyllis Schlafly, one of the strongest voices in the fight to defeat the ERA during the late 1970s and an advocate of traditional roles for women and men, is herself a lawyer and a nationally renowned public speaker (nontraditional roles for a woman). The relationship among attitudes, personality traits, and behaviors is complex in the area of gender as well as in other areas of social psychology (J. Archer, 1989; Deaux & Kite, 1987; Del Boca, Ashmore, & McManus, 1986). Although under some circumstances, traditionally sex-typed individuals are more likely than others to accept and use traditional gender ideology and to engage in gender-stereotypic behaviors (see, for example, Frable, 1989), under other circumstances sex typing seems unrelated to attitudes and behaviors (Beauvais & Spence, 1987; V. J. Edwards & Spence, 1987). Gender is a multidimensional construct and the relationships among the dimensions are just beginning to be explored.

Janet Spence (1985) has proposed replacing the more limiting concept of sex typing (that is, conformity to stereotypical personality traits) with the more multidimensional concept of gender identity (a phenomenological sense of one's own femaleness or maleness). One can have a strong gender identity as a male and still evidence expressive personality traits and behaviors and an egalitarian attitude toward gender roles. Spence's theory of gender identity suggests that age affects the relationships among sex-typed traits, behaviors, and beliefs. When children first develop their sense of themselves as male or female (by age 3), they tend to adopt gender-stereotyped behaviors and beliefs. As they get older, however, and their gender identity becomes more firmly established, other factors (such as parental models and peer expectations) start shaping their behaviors and beliefs. We must remain sensitive to the complexity of human behavior.

Moreover, what seems very clear is that gender must always be viewed within a social context (Ashmore et al., 1986; Deaux & Major, 1987; Del Boca et al., 1986; Eagly, 1987b; Epstein, 1988). Gender-related behaviors are influenced by the gender belief systems of the individual, the gender belief systems of others, and by a host of situational cues (such as the role the individual is in and the reinforcement for engaging in the behavior). Furthermore, a person's gender belief system is influenced by her or his gender-linked social role (Figure 1.2), other social roles, and socialization experiences. As we examine the findings of research on gender, we will need to keep this multidimensional and interactive model in mind. First, however, we need to examine how research in this area is conducted.

▲ Research on Gender

How much of human behavior is a direct product of biological factors, how much a product of cultural factors, and how, much a function of situational forces interacting with biological predispositions? This is the question that research on gender attempts to answer. Before you read about the findings of such research, which are often quite complex and at times inconsistent, it is important to get a general idea of the ways in which psychologists and other social scientists ask and answer questions about behavior.

Research Methods

In psychological research, scientists make hypotheses about how people will behave in certain situations. These hypotheses, or guesses, generally are based on theories about why behavior occurs. The actual testing or verification of these hypotheses can be done in a variety of ways, each with its own advantages and disadvantages. The four most common research methods are case history, survey, naturalistic observation, and experiment.

In the *case history* method, one or a few individuals are studied in depth. For example, Freud based his entire theory of human behavior on intensive examination of a few patients and himself. The advantages of this method are that a great deal of information can be collected in a short time and in a relatively natural setting. However, because so few people are examined, the information obtained may not be generalizable to others. Therefore, this method's value is to help in developing hypotheses and theories, not in definitively testing them.

The *survey* uses a standardized questionnaire or interview to obtain information from a large sample of people. The advantage of this method is that a great deal of information from many people can be gathered in response to the same questions. For example, questions relating to menstrual discomfort and emotional changes can be given to a large number of people in a relatively short amount of time. However, people also may respond in ways to make themselves look good (responding in a way to seem socially desirable), or to please the experimenter (responding to what is expected of them, called *demand characteristics*). People also may not remember their behavior. Therefore, this method's value is in getting rough estimates of people's attitudes or in obtaining preliminary information to guide later research.

Naturalistic observation involves studying people's reactions to naturally occurring events in natural settings. For example, a researcher may put video cameras in nursery schools and observe how teachers react to male and female children. The advantages of this method are that it allows firsthand observation rather than retrospective reporting; people are more likely to respond naturally because demand characteristics are not obvious; and natural environments are most likely to elicit behavior as it usually occurs. However, naturalistic observations may be difficult to analyze precisely because responses are wholistic and not easily broken down into discrete components; results are difficult to verify because natural events seldom reoccur in exactly the same way, and such observations cannot establish cause-and-effect relationships. Just noting that two events co-occur does not mean that one causes the other. For example, finding that the amount of attention each student gets from the teacher is positively correlated with the child's performance on problem-solving activities does not mean that teacher attention causes improved problem solving. Good problem solvers may elicit more attention from teachers. Or both factors could be related to a third unmeasured one, such as the child's level of intelligence. In general, naturalistic observations are valuable in providing important information that then can be tested in experiments.

The *experiment* generally is the sine qua non of scientific methodology. In an experiment, a researcher directly manipulates one variable, called the *independent variable*, while measuring its effects on some other variable, called the *dependent variable*. In doing so, the researcher also must control for all other factors that might possibly influence the results. For example, a researcher may be interested in the effects of training on visual-spatial performance. Subjects are randomly assigned to either the experimental group, which receives the specific training, or to a control group, which performs some unrelated activity for the same amount of time. The two groups then are tested and the results are statistically analyzed to determine how likely it is that the group difference is due to chance. The generally accepted standard is that if the difference between the two groups has less than a 5% likelihood of being due to chance, the findings are termed *statistically significant*. The experimental hypothesis then is supported, and the *null hypothesis* (that there is no difference between the two groups) is rejected. Rigid controls must occur in an experiment. Subject selection must be unbiased and assignment to groups random. Subjects' expectations also must be controlled to avoid demand characteristics. This may mean some withholding of information. For example, subjects may not know that their training is intended to improve their performance or that the experimenter expects males to do better. Experimenter bias also needs to be controlled—for example, by the tester not knowing which group has received specific training, or by the trainer not knowing the hypotheses. The advantages of experiments are that ideally they can establish cause-and-effect relationships, they are repeatable by anyone who replicates the conditions, and they can be used to analyze the variables precisely. However, experiments also have disadvantages: subjects know that they are being studied, and too much control may make the situation very artificial regarding both the independent and dependent variables. An experiment conducted outside the laboratory (field experiment) may solve some of these problems but is not always practical.

Thus, no one method is perfect. A finding supported by more than one method is more persuasive than one obtained by just one method. For example, case studies of couples in marital counseling may reveal that husbands seem to have more difficulty than wives communicating their feelings to their spouse. Husbands also seem to have more difficulty picking up and understanding emotional messages from their spouse than do wives. Naturalistic observations of couples waiting to talk to their child's teacher at parent-teacher conferences may confirm this observation. Surveys that ask husbands and wives how often they tell their spouse how they feel, how well they feel understood by their spouse, and so on may provide some ideas about how common a problem this may be. Laboratory studies may reveal more information about the dynamics of the whole communication process. For example, it may be that husbands have the most difficulty understanding nonverbal forms of expression; or that certain feelings are the most difficult to communicate; or that it is mainly unsatisfactory marriages that show this communication problem. Thus, all methods have something to offer, and our understanding of people can be furthered when different approaches point to the same conclusion.

Now let us look at some of the research problems that are particularly important in research on gender.

Research Problems

In many of the studies reported in this book, certain research problems occur that serve to place limits on the reported results. Although research problems are liable to occur in any research area, the areas of sex comparisons and gender-related behaviors are particularly vulnerable to such problems, because these areas are very personal and, in many ways, political. It is thus necessary to highlight some of the possible problems, so that you can keep them in mind in reviewing the research presented in this book. By necessity, the discussion will be brief. The interested reader is encouraged to consult Denmark, Russo, Frieze, and Sechzer (1988), M. Eichler (1988), or Wallston and Grady (1985) for further discussion of research problems and how to correct them.

Problems can occur in one or more areas of any research project: the basic assumptions of the researchers, choice of subjects, experimental design and methodology, and interpretation of the results. We will look at each in turn.

Basic assumptions   All experimenters bring certain assumptions to bear on their research, mainly because as human beings we cannot help but be influenced by our personal experiences and the sociohistorical contexts in which we live. Perhaps the most basic problem in examining the research on gender is the underlying assumption that *sex differences exist* and that *these differences are important* (see Hare-Mustin & Marecek, 1990, and Rhode, 1990, for theoretical explorations of this assumption). As A. Kaplan and Bean (1976) point out, because researchers study areas already thought to reflect male-female differences, such as hormonal cyclicity, the data reflecting these differences may be exaggerated. For example, much

research has been done on the effect of female hormone cyclicity on moods; very little has been done on the effect of male hormones. The implication is that hormones play a larger role in female behavior than they do in male behavior. Similarly, Petersen (1983) observed that as research reveals fewer sex differences in cognitive abilities than previously had been thought, more and more research is done on the few remaining areas that do suggest a gender difference. Thus, we get an exaggerated picture of a male-female dichotomy and a limited understanding of the full range of human potential.

This emphasis on sex differences, as opposed to similarities, is further perpetuated by the policy of most journals to publish only statistically significant findings. The null hypothesis, meaning that there is no difference between groups, can never be proved. The strongest statement that can be made is that the null hypothesis cannot be rejected. Therefore, findings reflecting no difference usually do not get reported in the literature. Additionally, because journals have limited space, they have to reject a high percentage of submitted articles, and they naturally tend to accept those with positive findings. The number of studies testing for sex differences that were published in mainstream psychology journals increased during the 1970s, then decreased during the 1980s (Lykes & Stewart, 1986; Signorella, Vegega, & Mitchell, 1981). Whether this change is because the heyday of "sex difference" research has passed, or because fewer sex differences are found, or because editors of mainstream journals no longer find such research valuable or politically correct, is unclear. A debate has arisen recently regarding whether *every* study that uses people should test for sex differences (Baumeister, 1988; Eagly, 1987a, 1990; McHugh, Koeske, & Frieze, 1986). Doing so would give a more representative picture of how infrequently men and women differ, but it would also increase chance findings of difference.

Journals generally select articles on the basis of importance of the research topic. Although published research on topics related to gender has increased tremendously during the last 20 years, it is found mostly in feminist journals and books (M. Fine & Gordon, 1989; Lott, 1985; Lykes & Stewart, 1986). In mainstream psychology journals, the percentage of articles relating to gender still is small (10–17% in 1986) and only slowly increasing. In addition, most of this research is on gender differences or sex-typing differences, so the differences again are highlighted. And the emphasis is on individual factors rather than structural ones when behavior is explained or changed. Thus, basic assumptions and theories operating in psychology are difficult to challenge and revise.

Another basic assumption in research on gender is that *sex differences can be attributed to either nature* (that is, biology—the essentialist position) *or nurture* (that is, the environment—the constructivist position). Even calling this topical area *"sex differences"* suggests that the underlying reason for any differences found is likely to be biological (related to sex) rather than cultural (related to gender). As many writers have noted, it is nearly impossible to separate the influences of biology and environment in humans because socialization begins at birth, and humans have such a tremendous capacity for learning. As we shall see in Chapter 2, even gender identity is formed through a complex interaction of biological, psychological, and sociocultural factors. All these factors need to be taken into account when examining human behavior. The upsurge of interest in sociobiological theories since 1975 demonstrates that belief in pure biological determinism still has appeal (see Bleier, 1984, and Fausto-Sterling, 1985, for critiques). An interactionist perspective is needed, and we must determine the way this interaction operates for various behavior patterns in various contexts.

The third basic assumption influencing research is that *what males do is the norm*; what females do, if it is different from what males do, is deviant. Thus McClelland and colleagues (1953) based an entire theory of achievement motivation primarily on male subjects. The fact that this theory does not fit females as well as males should have made the validity and generalizability of the theory suspect but did not. Similarly, Kohlberg (1969) based a theory of moral development almost entirely on male subjects; females have been shown not to conform to his theory as well (Gilligan, 1982). Indeed, Grady (1981) reports that males appear as subjects in research nearly twice as often as do females. The important point here is that theories based solely or primarily on males have been generalized to all people even though the theories may not fit 51% of the human race. When women's behaviors and thoughts are included, the theories themselves frequently must be revised drastically. Such work already has begun.

Hare-Mustin and Marecek (1988) have analyzed the degree to which researchers have defined gender in terms of difference. They have noted two tendencies: the exaggeration of difference,

which they call *alpha bias* (such as viewing men as instrumental, women as expressive); and the minimization of difference, which they call *beta bias* (such as ignoring women's greater child-care responsibilities in research on workplace productivity). Both biases support the existing gender hierarchy by making what is male normative and by focusing on individuals rather than on the power differential embedded within the organization of society (see also M. Fine & Gordon, 1989; A. S. Kahn & Yoder, 1989). This postmodern perspective is a result of two developments: the recognition on the part of social science researchers that science itself is socially constructed (K. J. Gergen, 1985; Harding, 1987; Unger, 1989a) and the application of postmodern theories, such as deconstruction, to psychology (Flax, 1987; Hare-Mustin & Marecek, 1988).

The assumptions that we have just reviewed all fit in with a positivist empiricist model of research in psychology, one that restricts analysis to a few clearly observable units of behavior. Such a model shapes research questions, findings, and interpretations. Yet this model ignores the inevitable effects of social constructs, such as status and power, on the research process itself. Mary Gergen (1988) and others (for example, M. Fine & Gordon, 1989; Unger, 1983, 1989a; Wittig, 1989) suggest a more reflexive model of research, which requires an understanding of the reciprocal and interactive relationship that exists between the person and reality, and therefore between the experimenter and the "subject." The researcher, together with the persons being researched, exists within a specific cultural and historical setting. Such settings affect the entire research enterprise. For example, the assumption that men are the sexual aggressors and women are sexually passive has affected scientific research on the process of conception (E. Martin, 1991). The egg traditionally has been depicted as passively awaiting "penetration" by active sperm (like Sleeping Beauty), whereas recent biological research finally has acknowledged that both the egg and the sperm play active roles in conception.

New methods are being developed that recognize the interdependence of researchers and participants and that avoid decontextualizing the two. This new framework (entitled "transformative" by M. Crawford & Marecek, 1989) is clearly distinct from three others: the focus on exceptional women, the focus on women as problem or anomaly, and the current focus on the psychology of gender (that is, the social construction of male and female). For interesting examples of new feminist research approaches, see Hollway (1989), Kitzinger (1987), and Warren (1988).

Choice of subjects Research problems arise in choosing whom to study. Some researchers have used animals, because human experimentation in the biological area presents serious ethical and practical problems. The choice of which animals to study, however, is often a product of the experimenter's assumptions and biases. Donna Haraway (1989) forcefully demonstrates how the study of primates has reflected gender politics. For example, rhesus monkeys, who show different behaviors by sex, are studied more frequently than gibbons, who do not show such differences; yet gibbons are evolutionarily closer to humans than rhesus monkeys (Rosenberg, 1973). The generalizability of findings from animals is also questionable, because humans are unique in their development of the neocortex and in the plasticity of their behavior. Human behavior is extremely modifiable by experience. Although there may be similarities in behavior between humans and animals, the antecedents of behaviors may be quite different. It is curious, in this regard, to note the overwhelming number of studies on aggression that have used nonprimates, particularly rats and mice, and have generalized their findings to humans. (See Bleier, 1979, for an excellent discussion of this topic.)

Subjects may be selected to fit preexisting assumptions. For example, in examining the effect of menopause on women, one study simply excluded from the sample all women who worked outside the home, apparently on the grounds that such women were deviant (Van Hecke, Van Keep, & Kellerhals, 1975). Similarly, studies of attachment in infants nearly always look at mothers rather than fathers, on the assumption that infant-mother attachment is more important. Another example of bias in subject selection is the fact that 90% of all research on aggression has used male subjects, whereas females have been involved in only half the studies (McKenna & Kessler, 1977). As noted previously, males more often are used to represent all human beings, despite the frequent importance of gender as regards the topic studied. Indeed, significant self-selection may occur in some studies. Signorella and Vegega (1984) have found that women are most interested in signing up for experiments on "feminine" topics, such as revealing feelings and moods, whereas men are most interested in signing up for experiments on "masculine" topics, such as power and competition. Results

from such studies may be biased and thus limited in generalizability.

Studying people with some abnormality or who need some form of treatment also is problematic, because by definition, these are individuals whose development differs from normal. Women who consult doctors for menstrual problems, for example, are a select group and cannot be assumed to represent women in general. People with inconsistent sex characteristics may be treated differently by their parents from other children, and research may be designed to specifically highlight their differences (for example, Stoller, 1968). Such problems limit the generalizability of findings.

Most research has used White, North American, middle-class, presumedly heterosexual subjects, which severely limits the generalizability of findings. For example, "women" have been found to be less assertive than "men," but this finding is not necessarily true for Black women and Black men (K. A. Adams, 1983; Reid, 1984). Who then is meant by the terms *women* and *men*? Elizabeth Spelman (1988) and others argue that we must become aware of our (usually hidden) assumptions about who represents the norm. As pointed out previously, each of us is embedded in a complex social matrix with respect to gender, race or ethnicity, class, sexual preference, able-bodiedness, and so on. Not only must researchers learn to stop privileging White, middle-class, heterosexual, Christian norms, but they must also actively seek out other groups to study (for example, Cannon, Higginbotham, & Leung, 1988; Scarr, 1988). The relative impossibility of speaking for all women or all men when the differences within each sex or gender group are enormous must constantly be borne in mind.

Some behaviors seem to be situation- or age-specific. Yet the vast majority of social psychological studies published in the mid-1980s were conducted on college students, especially within an experimental laboratory (Lykes & Stewart, 1986; Sears, 1986). We are left with a great deal of information about a select group of young men and women in atypical situations and very little information about the majority of men and women in natural situations. We therefore are likely to have an incomplete view regarding the great complexity of human behavior as it occurs outside the laboratory. Even the gender of the researcher/experimenter has been shown to be a very influential contextual variable, yet it is rarely even reported (Basow & Howe, 1987; Rumenik, Capasso, & Hendrick, 1977). Also not frequently reported is age of subject in topical areas where age may be influential. For example, menstrual problems appear to be age-related (Golub & Harrington, 1981). Clearly, such variables are important to control and need to be borne in mind when generalizations are made from research findings.

A major problem in many studies is the lack of an adequate control group. For example, female behavior during the menstrual cycle has been extensively studied but rarely compared to male behavior during a similar length of time. When men and women are compared (for example, on mood and behavioral variability over a four-week period), no differences are found (Dan, 1976; McFarlane, Martin, & Williams, 1988; J. S. Stein & Yaworsky, 1983). Thus, studies that focus on mood changes only in women distort the nature of the findings.

Design As we have seen, feminist critiques of psychological research have emphasized the importance of getting outside the experimental laboratory and exploring issues of gender in more naturalistic contexts with a more diverse population than predominantly White middle-class college students. This is important because different methodologies will lead to different types of results. We now know that quantitatively oriented experimental research tends to minimize findings of gender differences (beta bias), whereas qualitatively oriented clinical research tends to maximize findings of gender differences (alpha bias) (M. Crawford, 1988). The point is not to determine which finding is "correct" but to understand how gender operates within different contexts. The increased use of different methodologies is apparent in feminist journals but, unfortunately, not in mainstream ones (M. Fine & Gordon, 1989; Lykes & Stewart, 1986). Thus the transformative potential of feminist methodology in the social sciences is not being realized (M. Crawford & Marecek, 1989).

Other problems afflict research design: lack of precise objective definitions of the behavior studied, selective perception of raters, and shifting anchor points. This last problem refers to the fact that we often evaluate male and female behavior differently. For example, what is seen as active for a boy may be different from what is seen as active for a girl. The use of different definitions of a behavior as a function of the sex of the ratee also may be a function of the sex of the rater. For example, men and women may use different definitions of "active behavior." Imprecise measures of behavior may also limit a study's findings. Besides the premenstrual syndrome

having various definitions, actual physiological measures of cycle phase have varied enormously from study to study, some relying on self-reports, others relying on varying physiological measurements taken at varying intervals (Parlee, 1973).

Using an appropriate baseline, or standard, when measuring gender differences is imperative but not frequently found. For example, with respect to the menstrual cycle, it may be as accurate to posit a follicular phase (midcycle) syndrome of positive traits and behaviors as to posit a premenstrual syndrome of negative traits and behaviors (McFarlane et al., 1988; Parlee, 1973). Yet we hear far more of the latter than the former.

Three research designs used in studying sex differences should be examined particularly carefully since each has serious limitations:

1. *Correlation studies* do not demonstrate causation, although they are frequently interpreted that way by unsophisticated readers and, at times, by researchers themselves. Thus, a correlation between anxiety and the premenstrual phase has led many to assume that hormones determine mood in females, although such a relation may be caused by a third variable such as expectation of amount of flow (Paige, 1971). The causation also may occur in the opposite direction. For example, anxiety can bring on menstruation (see Parlee, 1973).

2. *Retrospective questionnaires* suffer from reliance on an individual's memory. For example, complaints of mood impairment during or before menstruation typically are found when mood is assessed retrospectively, but not when mood is assessed daily (for example, McFarlane et al., 1988). Questionnaires also may selectively lead the respondent to provide certain information—for example, by asking only about negative mood changes as a function of menstrual phase.

3. *Self-reports or observations* are affected by people's need to respond in a socially desirable way. As an example, men may be reluctant to admit mood changes because such changes contradict societal gender stereotypes. These methods also have a problem with selective perception or selective reporting by the respondent. For example, only negative mood changes may be observed in or admitted by women because that is the cultural and/or the reporter's expectation (McFarland, Ross, & DeCourville, 1989; D. N. Ruble, 1977).

An important problem in all psychological research, especially in this area, is the effect on the results of the experimenter's beliefs. Robert

Rosenthal (1966; Rosenthal & Jacobson, 1968) has ingeniously demonstrated that in unconscious, nonverbal ways, experimenters can influence the outcome of an experiment to conform to the experimental hypotheses. Thus, in studies in which the experimenter expects to find moods varying with menstrual phase, she or he may indeed find them (Moos et al., 1969). Because most researchers have been male, they unconsciously may have misperceived certain situations with humans and animals to put males in the better light. For example, Harry Harlow's (1962, 1965) research with monkeys has contributed a great deal to our understanding of attachment behavior. But reading some of Harlow's observations of the behavior of monkeys sometimes resembles viewing a soap opera with females "scheming" and acting "helpless" and males acting "intelligently" and "strongly." (See also Hrdy, 1986.) This brings us to the question of interpretation.

Interpretation Statistical reporting and analysis are often a function of an experimenter's hypotheses and biases. To illustrate, although Dalton (1969) found that 27% of her female subjects got poorer grades before menstruation than at ovulation, she ignored the 56% who had no changes and the 17% who actually improved.

Another reporting problem arises in reviews such as that by Maccoby and Jacklin (1974). Although the reviewed studies varied greatly in quality, the results were simply tabulated without giving greater emphasis to the better research. Therefore, a finding of a high percentage of studies reporting no difference in an area may be due to there being no difference, or it may be due to a large number of inadequate experiments. More use of the statistical technique of *meta-analysis* is needed in order to truly integrate the findings in this area. This technique is a quantitative way of reviewing the research on a specific topic. It provides us with two estimates: one of effect size and one of degree of variability. Because a gender difference can be significant in the statistical sense yet still unimportant in a practical sense, such estimates can provide much needed information. With increasing use of this technique in recent years, many of the findings cited in Maccoby and Jacklin have been qualified greatly (see Eagly, 1987b; Hyde, 1990). Meta-analyses are not a panacea, however: they can include studies that may be inadequate on grounds previously mentioned, and they still must be interpreted. Still, the technique of meta-analysis has brought more objectivity and organization to a field nearly overwhelmed by individual studies. Results of meta-analyses will be reported wherever available in succeeding chapters.

Interpretation of scientific facts has sometimes determined the facts themselves. Recent feminist examinations of the history of science reveal numerous illustrations of gender, race, and class prejudices (Bleier, 1988; Hubbard, 1990; Katz, 1988; Russett, 1989; Sayers, 1987). For example, Shields (1975) found that when the frontal lobes of the brain were regarded as the main area of intellectual functioning, research studies found men had larger frontal lobes, relative to the parietal lobes, than women. When parietal lobes were regarded as more important, the findings themselves changed. Men now were found to have relatively larger parietal lobes, relative to their frontal lobes, than women. Today, there is no firm evidence of sex differences in brain structures or proportions, so interest has turned to sex differences in brain organization, following a predictable pattern. When men were thought to be less lateralized than women, that was thought to be the superior organization. When men were thought to have more brain lateralization than women, then *that* was thought to be the superior organization. As we will see in Chapter 2, the research on sex differences in brain lateralization is so confounded with methodological and interpretational problems that we cannot draw any meaningful conclusions at this point.

▲ Summary

We have seen that the terms *sex* and *gender* are distinct, the former referring to biological aspects of being female or male, the latter referring to sociocultural aspects of being female or male. Strongly entrenched stereotypes exist regarding what constitutes being female or male, with the former being associated with expressive-communal traits and the latter with agentic-instrumental traits. Although these gender stereotypes are complex in structure and vary somewhat by race or ethnicity, class, sexual orientation, and so on, gender stereotypes function very powerfully to shape our expectations of others and our own behavior. Furthermore, people differ in the degree to which they possess traits stereotyped as gender-appropriate. In fact, most people do *not* possess only those traits that are considered gender-appropriate.

In examining the studies on female and male behaviors and characteristics, one must be aware of the many research problems that can invalidate the results. Science is constructed by people, and people are never value-free or impervious to social forces. As Sue Rosser (1988) notes, until our society is neutral with respect to gender, class, race, and sexual preference, it is impossible to assume that science will be. Therefore, it is incumbent upon all researchers to understand how the social context influences the research process. With this caution in mind, we will examine the current findings.

▲   Recommended Reading

Ashmore, R. D., Del Boca, F. K., & Wohlers, A. J. (1986). Gender stereotypes. In R. D. Ashmore and F. K. Del Boca (Eds.), *The social psychology of female-male relations: A critical analysis of central concepts* (pp. 69–119). New York: Academic Press. An excellent summary of research on gender stereotypes with guidelines for future research and theory on this topic.

Deaux, K., & Kite, M. E. (1987). Thinking about gender. In B. B. Hess & M. M. Ferree (Eds.), *Analyzing gender: A handbook of social science research* (pp. 92–117). Newbury Park, CA: Sage. A brief review of the study of gender in psychology plus the development of the concept of "gender belief systems."

Eichler, M. (1988). *Nonsexist research methods: A practical guide.* Boston: Allen & Unwin. Written by a sociologist, this book presents a good overview of how to avoid doing sexist research.

Hare-Mustin, R., & Marecek, J. (1988). The meaning of difference: Gender theory, postmodernism, and psychology. *American Psychologist, 43,* 455–464. An interesting article discussing the tendency to either exaggerate or minimize sex differences in research on gender, using a deconstructionist approach.

Hyde, J. S. (1990). Meta-analysis and the psychology of gender differences. *Signs: Journal of Women in Culture and Society, 16,* 55–73. A review article explaining meta-analysis and its advantages when examining gender differences.

Sedney, M. A. (1989). Conceptual and methodological sources of controversies about androgyny. In R. Unger (Ed.), *Representations: Social constructions of gender* (pp. 126–144). Amityville, NY: Baywood. Excellent review of the status of the concept of androgyny with suggestions for resolving the conflicts.

Part 2
Current Findings from Female-Male Comparisons

*A*n infant girl is in the babbling stage of development. An observer laughingly remarks, "A typical female. You can't keep them from talking."

After hearing that his son was sent home from school for being disruptive in class and fighting with other boys, a father remarks, with a smile, "Well, boys will be boys."

In both these incidents, certain assumptions are made regarding emotional and behavioral differences between females and males. Boys are assumed to be more active, unruly, and aggressive; girls are assumed to be more emotional, talkative, and passive. Our very use of the term *opposite sex* assumes that females and males are diametrically different from each other not only in their sexual characteristics but in their behaviors as well. To understand these stereotypic expectations, it is important to know what differences between the sexes actually do exist. Are any of the stereotypic differences listed in Chapter 1 based on fact? If so, which ones are factually based and to what degree? This part will attempt to answer these questions by examining the current findings related to male and female characteristics in four major areas: physical, cognitive, social, and sexual.

Chapter 2

Comparisons of Physical and Cognitive Functioning

The examination of the differences and similarities between the sexes in the areas of physical and cognitive functioning requires a clear understanding of some complicated physiological phenomena. How sex is determined needs to be understood, as do the specific areas in which sex differences have been found or suggested: anatomy, physiological processes, brain organization, physical vulnerability, and motor performance. Because some people cite biology as the ultimate justification for stereotypes such as "boys will be boys" or "girls are just naturally more verbal than boys," it is necessary for us to understand just what is biologically given and how biology and the environment may interact. Then we can examine whether and how these factors affect cognitive functioning.

▲ How Sex and Gender Are Determined

As we saw in Chapter 1, *sex* is a biological term whereas *gender* is a psychological and cultural term. Figure 2.1 indicates a *sex* difference. It is quite possible to be genetically of one sex with a gender identity of the other. Such may be the case of people born with ambiguous reproductive structures (anatomical *hermaphrodites*) or with other unusual physical conditions. A mismatch between sex and gender identity also occurs in *transsexuals*, who often report feeling "trapped in the wrong body" (Kessler & McKenna, 1978; Money, 1988). Furthermore, as we saw in Chapter 1, it is common for women and men to vary in their adoption of sex-typed personality traits. A man could be stereotypically sex-typed, cross-sex-typed, androgynous, or undifferentiated and still be a heterosexual male.

The distinction between sex and gender, explored in the research of John Money and others (see Ehrhardt, 1985; Money, 1986; Money & Ehrhardt, 1972) is important precisely because it points out that one's behavior—indeed, one's basic identity as a female or male—is not directly determined by one's genes or hormones; that is, by one's biological sex. Through the study of sexually anomalous individuals (people born with ambiguous sex organs or with organs that do not correspond to their genetic sex), it becomes clear that "sex of assignment and rearing" is "better than any other variable as a prognosticator of the gender role and orientation" of individuals (Money, 1986, p. 171). That is, a person's gender identity, for the most part, conforms to the sex according to which the parents rear that person, regardless of the person's genes or hormones or sexual equipment. As we've seen, gender can be viewed as a social construction, independent of objective criteria. It is mainly on the basis of people's differential reactions to the labels "male" and "female" that we construct gender.

How gender can be viewed as a social construct will be clearer after examining the variables that determine one's biological sex. For most people, sex is determined simply and obviously by the external genitalia. Other criteria are internal genitalia, hormones, and chromosomes. Although these indexes are usually in concordance, in some cases they are not. It is these unusual cases, these sexual anomalies, that shed light on the process of sexual differentiation.

The Role of Chromosomes
Usually, two X chromosomes produce a female, and an X and a Y chromosome produce a male. This

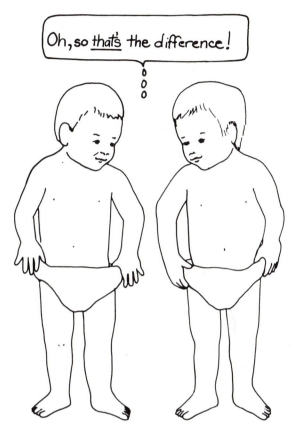

Figure 2.1 The basic sex difference.

initial sex determination occurs at the moment of conception and remains the only difference between male and female fetuses until the seventh week after conception. At this time, a single gene on the Y chromosome (the "testes determining factor") initiates the differentiation of internal reproductive organs (Angier, 1990). Generally, if this gene is present, the gonads (sex glands) of the fetus will develop into testes; if this gene is not present, the gonads will develop into ovaries. Thus, the fetus is basically bipotential, capable of developing with male or female organs. Indeed, in one sense, the basic course of development is female in that female sex organs will develop unless a Y chromosome is present. Thus, the fundamental form is female. To form a male, something must be added: in the first fetal stages, a specific gene on the Y chromosome; in the next stage of fetal development, the hormone androgen.

Besides the normal genetic patterns of XY for males and XX for females, anomalies occasionally occur in which individuals are produced with just one X chromosome (XO), three Xs (XXX), an extra Y (XYY or XXY), or other variations. Again, the presence or absence of the Y chromosome determines the development of the sex organs. A person with either an XYY or an XXY chromosome pattern will develop testes, and an XO or an XXX person will develop ovaries.

Endocrinological research suggests that the X chromosome is molecularly more information-packed than the Y chromosome (S. Gordon, 1983). It is not clear what this means except that males, who typically have just one X chromosome, are more susceptible to any recessive X-linked disorder they might have inherited, such as color blindness and hemophilia. Females, having two X chromosomes, are usually protected by the second X chromosome from developing such recessive disorders. Of course, if both X chromosomes carry such an ailment, the female will also manifest the disorder. In other cases, however, the female will merely be a carrier of the disorder. This genetic process has been thought to account partially for males' greater physical vulnerability. The exact influence of genes on behavior is quite controversial and will be examined further as we go along in this and the next two chapters.

The Role of Hormones

Prenatally, hormones have been found to be extremely important in the sexual differentiation of a fetus. After the first seven weeks of embryonic development, the internal reproductive organs (testes or ovaries) develop in response to either the presence or absence of the testes determining factor on the Y chromosome. Once these organs develop, hormone production begins, and further differentiation of the fetus occurs. Figure 2.2 shows the ensuing sexual differentiation.

During the third prenatal month, if the hormone dihydrotestosterone (one of the androgens) is produced, male external organs (urethral tube, scrotum, and penis) and male ducts (seminal vesicles, vas deferens, and ejaculatory ducts) will develop, and female ducts will regress. If dihydrotestosterone is not produced, female sex organs (labia minora, labia majora, and clitoris) and female ducts (uterus, fallopian tubes, and upper vagina) will develop, and male ducts will regress. Once again, unless something is added—in this case, the hormone dihydrotestosterone—female structures will develop. The critical period for this

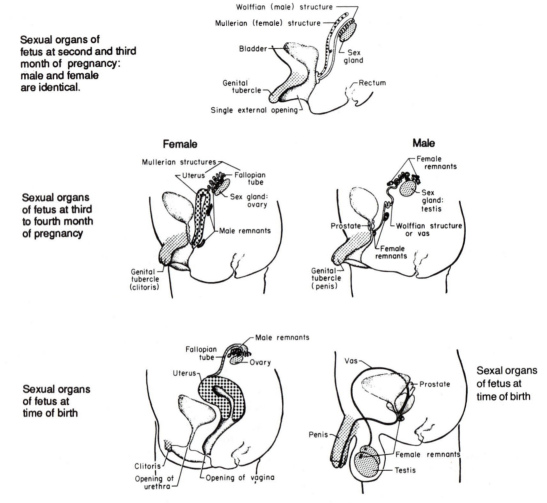

Sexual organs of fetus at second and third month of pregnancy: male and female are identical.

Sexual organs of fetus at third to fourth month of pregnancy

Female

Male

Sexual organs of fetus at time of birth

Sexal organs of fetus at time of birth

Figure 2.2 Sexual differentiation in the human fetus. Note the early parallelism of sex organs. Adapted from *Man and Woman, Boy and Girl,* by J. Money and A. A. Ehrhardt, p. 42. Copyright 1972 by The Johns Hopkins University Press. Reprinted by permission.

development occurs between the second and third prenatal months.

If hormone production or hormone sensitivity is impaired, or hormones are externally administered to the mother during this critical period, an infant with sexual anomalies may develop (Hines, 1982; Money, 1986; Money & Ehrhardt, 1972). Thus, if a genetically female fetus is exposed to androgens, structural development will proceed along male lines—that is, male external sex organs will develop. This occurs in the *adrenogenital syndrome,* caused by excessive fetal androgen production signaled by an abnormally functioning adrenocortical gland,

and in *progestin-induced hermaphroditism.* This latter disorder arises in some cases in which the mother is given the synthetic hormone progestin early in pregnancy to avert the danger of a miscarriage. Conversely, if a genetically male fetus is deprived of the androgens either through an inherited androgen insensitivity or through a metabolic error, a female system will be produced. From these cases it is clear that genes only predispose, not guarantee, the development of the corresponding reproductive structures.

During the critical period for the differentiation of the external sex organs, another major differentiating development occurs, at least in animals, in response to the presence or absence of testosterone (S. Gordon, 1983; Money, 1986; Money & Ehrhardt, 1972). This differentiation is in the brain in the area called the hypothalamus. This region is located at the base of the brain and controls the release of hormones at puberty by the attached pituitary gland. When testosterone is present during this prenatal period, the pituitary will function at puberty to cause a regular production of androgens and sperm. The presence of testosterone causes the pituitary gland to function at puberty with low levels of continuous hormone release. When testosterone is absent during the prenatal period, the pituitary will function at puberty to cause high levels of cyclical hormonal activity, resulting in ovulation and menstruation. These differences in pattern of hormone production do not appear until the full functioning of the pituitary gland at puberty, yet the patterns seem to be set during the second to third month of gestation. Again, hormonal errors during this critical period of gestation will affect pituitary functioning at puberty unless corrective hormones are administered after birth. It must be emphasized, however, that most of the evidence for brain differentiation is based on work with animals. Such differentiation in humans is somewhat more speculative.

According to the preceding information, after eight weeks male and female fetuses can be differentiated by hormone production. After birth, however, and until the child is about 8 years old, hormone production is negligible. Hormones, therefore, do not differentiate the sexes during this period. At puberty there is an increased production of all sex hormones in both sexes. Males generally have a greater increase in gonadal androgen production than do females, and the production of androgens becomes fairly regular and continuous. Females generally have a greater increase in ovarian estrogen and progesterone production at this time than do males, and this production becomes cyclic (the menstrual cycle). Hormones at this time result in the development of the secondary sex characteristics, such as facial and ancillary hair, enlarged genitals, and deeper voice in males, and development of breasts and menstruation in females.

It is important to note that these hormone differences are not absolute. Both sexes have all the hormones, are receptive to all the hormones, and, as is the case with most other human attributes, individuals differ greatly in the relative amounts and proportion of the sex hormones they possess. An overlapping normal curve distribution for all

hormones demonstrates that some genetic females may have more androgen than some genetic males, at least some of the time. Distinctions between the sexes based on hormone production are proportional, not absolute (S. Gordon, 1983; Money & Ehrhardt, 1972).

The effect of prenatal hormones on later behavior is a subject of great debate. As will be seen later in this chapter, prenatal hormone levels have been linked to the development of certain cognitive abilities (T. Adler, 1989a). A hypothesis put forward by Norman Geschwind (Geschwind & Behan, 1982; Geschwind & Galaburda, 1985) is that prenatal testosterone levels affect the development of certain cortical regions, especially the organization of language functions. Excess testosterone or unusual sensitivity to testosterone during fetal life may consequently affect a variety of later behaviors including left-handedness, dyslexia, immune system disorders, and mathematical genius, all apparently found more often in males. Such a hypothesis, although intriguing, remains speculative and controversial (Bleier, 1986, 1988; Kolata, 1983). We will discuss some of this research later in the section on brain organization.

Prenatal hormones have also been linked to the development of either a hetereosexual, bisexual, or homosexual orientation, at least in some individuals (Ehrhardt et al., 1985; Money, 1988; Sanders & Ross-Field, 1987), although there is considerable controversy over this hypothesis as well (T. Adler, 1990b). Even here, it seems clear that sexual orientation is not completely determined by prenatal hormones but rather is strongly dependent on postnatal socialization experiences.

Hormones are currently thought to have two types of effects: a sensitizing effect, whereby prenatal hormones sensitize the organism to respond to later hormones in certain ways; and an activating effect, whereby hormones produced at and after puberty activate or interact with the sensitized brain to produce different behaviors (Jacklin, 1989). Because males are exposed to more prenatal hormones than females, they appear to be more sensitive to the effects of pubertal hormones than females (Susman, Nottelmann, Inoff-Germain, Dorn, & Chrousos, 1987). Prenatal hormones, by affecting certain areas of the brain, also may influence the ease with which certain behaviors (such as nurturant behaviors and rough-and-tumble play) are acquired. In all cases, the behaviors themselves are still markedly affected by environmental factors (DeBold & Luria, 1983; Ehrhardt,

1985; Money, 1986; Reinisch, Rosenblum, & Sanders, 1987). Because hormones, as well as genes, can never be fully separated from environmental and socio-cultural factors, at least in humans, we can never know the "pure" effects of hormones or genes.

Genitalia and Gender

The external sex organs are the primary means by which sex is determined at birth. Males have an external penis and a scrotum; females, a clitoris and a vagina. Until the second to third month of pregnancy, however, the external genitalia, as well as the internal reproductive organs and tracts, are in an undifferentiated state (see Figure 2.2). Differentiation begins during the second to third month as a result of the presence or absence of the Y chromosome, which determines the internal organ development. Differentiation then proceeds during the third month as a function of the presence or absence of the hormone testosterone, which determines the external organ development. At each stage, development can go either way—toward the male form or toward the female form. That is, development is *bipotential*.

This bipotentiality continues at birth. With the doctor's pronouncement, based on external genitalia, that the infant is a boy or a girl, two different patterns of infant-adult interactions begin. These differentiating behaviors can be observed in the giving of blue or pink blankets, in the naming and handling of the infant, and in verbalizations to the infant. Again, it is the sexually anomalous individual who sheds light on the development of gender identity. Studies of hermaphrodites, pseudo-hermaphrodites (those born with external genitalia of the other sex), and children who have suffered surgical accidents that have affected their genitals (for example, damage to the penis during circumcision) vividly demonstrate that the single most important variable in the development of gender identity is the sex of assignment—that is, the sex one's parents raise one to be (Money, 1986). This influence can override other influences of genes, hormones, and external organs and demonstrates very fundamentally how plastic and malleable is human behavior.

A striking example of the bipotentiality of the human infant is the case of identical twin boys, one of whom had his penis severely injured by an electrical needle during circumcision (Money & Ehrhardt, 1972). Rather than attempt reconstructive surgery, which would have been complicated and time consuming and would have had a low probability of success, the doctors recommended that the boy be given an artifical vagina, which was a simpler operation, and be raised as a girl. The parents agreed, and follow-up studies at ages 5 to 6 showed the two children to be clearly differentiated in terms of activities, toy preferences, and mannerisms as a result of different child-rearing practices. In fact, these children were more clearly differentiable than are most girls and boys. However, genetic and prenatal hormonal effects on behavior cannot be dismissed: a report from the girl's psychiatrist in 1982 describes a very gender-confused adolescent (Diamond, 1982). There may be many nonbiological reasons for such confusion, not the least of which may be knowledge of what happened to her after birth, but it behooves us to be properly open-minded until research findings are more conclusive.

As for other stages of development, there appears to be a critical period for the postnatal development of gender identity—up to 18 months or the time the child acquires language (Money, 1986). This identity becomes consolidated by age 3 or 4, depending on the consistency of child-rearing experiences. Any attempt to change sex assignment after a child has acquired language is usually unsuccessful and may lead to later emotional problems. It is interesting, in this regard, that transsexuals do not seem to have formed a gender identity of their biological sex at this stage. Whether this deficit is due to parental up-bringing, to rigid societal gender stereotypes, or possibly to a prenatally determined predisposition is unclear at this time (Finney, Brandsma, Tondoro, & Lemaistre, 1975; Money, 1986; J. G. Raymond, 1979).

Having detailed the differentiation of sex in a fetus and in an infant and having examined some problems that may arise, it remains to be emphasized that for the vast majority of infants all physiological sex characteristics are in agreement. That is, most babies with female external genitalia also have female internal genitalia, have an XX chromosome pattern, and will produce a preponderance of female sex hormones at puberty. Of these indicators, the external genitalia are the most important because they determine the sex of assignment. It is the sex of assignment that has been found critical in determining an individual's gender identity.

Implications

The research in this area has two major implications. The first is that research that searches for simple biological reasons for gender stereotypes and gender roles is misdirected. Given the enormous plasticity of human behavior and the fact that biological and environmental factors never can be fully separated in humans, the question of whether any particular behavior or trait is caused by nature or nurture is unanswerable. Indeed, the nature/nurture question is moot in the area of gender development as well as in virtually all aspects of human functioning. What is in question is the relative weights of the experiential and physiological influences. Money's studies (1986, 1987, 1988; Money & Ehrhardt, 1972) demonstrate that postnatal experiential factors can override prenatal, physiological ones in the majority of cases. Although Money's research has been criticized as biased and methodologically flawed, his conclusion regarding the overriding influence of sociocultural factors has been supported (L. Rogers & Walsh, 1982).

The second implication is that human beings are bipotential in their psychosexual identity and behavior at each stage of development. Which path (male or female) is followed at each stage depends on both the internal and external environment. A fetus can develop male or female gonads, depending on its chromosomes; male or female external genitalia and possibly brain (hypothalamic) differentiation, depending on its hormones; and a male or female gender identity, depending on sex of assignment. There is a critical period for each stage of development to occur, after which the male or female path is relatively fixed. The sex of the infant usually is fixed by birth; its gender, by 18 months. After this time, people ordinarily do not change their image of themselves as male or female, although what traits and behaviors are implied by those terms may change. What is important to note is that even on a biological level, many sex differences are differences in degree, not kind (Freimuth & Hornstein, 1982). On a behavioral level, this is even more the case.

▲   Physical Functioning

Some physical differences do exist between the sexes, although their implication for behavior is unclear and many differences are culturally determined. First let us examine the findings. We will look specifically at anatomy, physiological processes, brain organization, physical vulnerability, and activity levels. Remember: there is a tremendous amount of overlap in virtually all human traits and characteristics.

Anatomy

Clearly, the most basic difference between the sexes at birth lies in their external genitalia. These organs usually determine the sex of assignment, and some writers, especially Freud, think they determine the personality structure of the child as well ("anatomy is destiny"; see Chapter 5). Although the possibility of getting pregnant, as opposed to impregnating, probably has meaningful consequences for one's personality, these consequences surely will vary with the individual, the family, the culture, and other external forces to such a degree that a simple deterministic explanation is untenable.

The sexes also typically differ in size and weight at birth, males generally being slightly larger, although these differences are minimal until age 13 or 14. Indeed, because female puberty begins two years earlier than male puberty on the average, for two years girls generally surpass boys in height and weight (Monagan, 1983). Males have a narrower pelvic outlet, broader shoulders, more cardiovascular power, and tend to have a smaller body-fat-to-muscle ratio than females at all ages (McDonald, 1984; Percival & Quinkert, 1987; Wardle, Gloss, & Gloss, 1987). These differences all increase significantly during and after puberty and contribute to males generally having more strength, more ease in running and overarm throwing, less flexibility, and poorer ability to float and withstand cold. These are average differences, of course, and may also be a function of athletic training.

Training and experience have been found to eliminate sex differences in many physical and athletic endeavors. E. G. Hall and Lee (1984) found that after one or more years in a coeducational physical education program, prepubescent girls and boys performed at similar levels on most physical fitness test items. Improvement by girls over the years was significant, and by the last year of testing, girls actually performed better than same-age boys from the previous two years. Similarly, the army found in 1977 that when 825 women were given regular basic training and compared to men, there was little difference in relative performance ("Arms," 1977). Another example of the effect of training is the fact that between 1970 and 1982, women's best performance in the marathon run improved by a little over 20% whereas the men's record improved by .1%. In the 1983 Boston Marathon, Joan Benoit's women's world-record time would have beaten the 1961 male winner in the race.

These relative differences in size and strength may have accounted for certain sex-role distinctions in the past or resulted from such distinctions, such as the assignment of males to certain forms of hunting that required strength. However, they certainly have little importance in our modern technological society. Most work that formerly required brute strength is now performed with the aid of equipment, levers, and push buttons.

Physiological Processes

Generally, females mature faster than males. This difference can be observed as early as the seventh week of embryonic life and continues through puberty. Girls also tend to have a slightly lower metabolic rate and consume fewer calories than do boys. After puberty, boys tend to have greater respiratory volume and higher systolic blood pressure than do girls. It currently is debatable as to which sex is capable of more physical endurance, males with their better ability to use oxygen or females with their extra fat, more efficient heat regulatory system, and higher amounts of estrogen that may increase blood circulation (McDonald, 1984; Wardle et al., 1987).

Small sex differences in sensation may exist, with some variation in women as a function of their estrogen level (M. A. Baker, 1987). Females seem somewhat more sensitive than males to taste, smell, touch, and high tones; males tend to have slightly better visual acuity. The better performance of females in odor identification has been found across a variety of cultural groups and thus probably is not due to cultural factors per se (Doty, Applebaum, Zusho, & Settle, 1985). The effects of these slight differences on behavior have yet to be determined, especially since there is considerable overlap between the sexes.

One major process in which the sexes do differ is in hormone functioning and production after puberty. Differences occur in actual hormone levels, in the pattern of secretion, in the sensitivity to particular hormones, and in the sources of hormone production (gonads or adrenals). Males tend to have continuous androgen secretion; females have cyclical hormonal fluctuations of estrogen and progesterone as part of the menstrual cycle. The different patterns of hormone production represent reproductive fertility for the adolescent and result in the development of secondary sex characteristics (for example, facial hair in males, breast development in females). However, it is important to remember that females also produce androgens; and males, estrogens. Thus it is incorrect to refer to androgen as the male hormone and estrogen as the female hormone. We will take a closer look at the menstrual cycle and the effects of the androgens.

Menstrual cycle   The menstrual cycle has been the focus of much research and controversy. Consequently, we will describe it in some detail. The beginning of the cycle, which averages 28 days but which may range from 15 to 45 days, is usually set at the day menstruation begins. From that time, estrogen production increases to a high point around the 12th day. During this first part of the cycle, the lining of the uterus thickens to prepare it to receive the fertilized egg. On the basis of a 28-day cycle, an egg is released from an ovary around the 14th day and travels down a fallopian tube to the uterus. During its transit, if the egg encounters a sperm, it will most likely become fertilized. The fertilized egg will then become embedded in the thickened lining of the uterus. If fertilization does not occur, estrogen production decreases, and production of progesterone increases. Both hormones drop precipitously a few days before actual menstruation (the shedding of the uterine lining) begins. A new cycle then starts. Figure 2.3 charts the hormonal changes for one average 28-day cycle, although it should be emphasized that such an "average" cycle occurs in no more than 16% of the female population (Ryan, 1975).

These hormonal changes that occur during the menstrual cycle may be related to some physical changes, but there are large individual differences in this area. Most common are reports of fluid retention and slight weight gain premenstrually and increased basal temperature and smell acuity around ovulation (Dan, 1979; McFarland et al., 1989). Diane Ruble (1977) has found, however, that even physical-symptom reports can be heavily affected by psychosocial factors. She found that by misleading college women as to their actual cycle phase, she could obtain reports of severe physical symptoms, such as water retention and pain, if the subjects believed they were premenstrual, even though they were not really in that phase. Thus, learned associations or beliefs can lead a woman to exaggerate or overstate a feeling. Such results must temper any conclusions based on self-report data regarding the magnitude of menstrual-related changes as well as the physiological bases of such changes.

Much attention has been paid to the psychological changes, especially of mood, thought to be associated with the menstrual cycle. These supposed changes, including anxiety, irritability, unrest, and depression, were called the premenstrual syndrome (or PMS) by

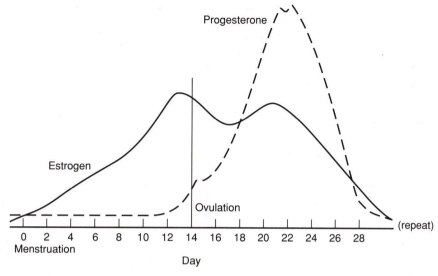

Figure 2.3 Hormone levels during a 28-day menstrual cycle.

Dr. Katharina Dalton in 1948. PMS has received much recent attention because of its use as a legal defense for murder in England and because of its inclusion in an appendix in the *Diagnostic and Statistical Manual of Mental Disorders* (DSM-III-R) (American Psychiatric Association, 1987; Sommer, 1984). Its inclusion in DSM-III-R (under the label "Late Luteal Phase Dysphoric Disorder") was protested by many researchers, practitioners, and activists on both scientific and political grounds.

On scientific grounds, the evidence for such a syndrome is weak, especially since research on this topic has suffered from serious deficiencies in definition, measurement, design, and interpretation (Hopson & Rosenfeld, 1984; Parlee, 1973, 1982b). Some premenstrual symptoms have been found in 20 to 90% of all women, depending on the definitions and the methodology used (T. Adler, 1990a). For example, when women in two studies were asked to recall their moods at different points in the menstrual cycle, most reported negative mood changes premenstrually. However, when these same women's daily mood ratings were examined, no increase in negative moods was found during the premenstrual phase (McFarland et al., 1989; McFarlane et al., 1988; see also Golub & Harrington, 1981). Thus it is the *belief* that one should experience negative moods premenstrually that seems most powerful in the reporting of those moods. And the belief in a premenstrual syndrome of negative moods is quite prevalent in the United States and other Western countries (Clarke & Ruble, 1978;

Koeske & Koeske, 1975; McFarland et al., 1989). Moods do vary, of course, quite frequently. But when negative moods occur and a woman is premenstrual, both she and others are likely to notice and attribute her mood to her cycle phase; when those moods occur at other times of the month, no menstrual attribution is made. Thus, we see how stereotypes can distort memory and affect behavior. Moreover, positive moods, which are not thought to vary as a function of the menstrual cycle, are almost never attributed to it. Yet some women say they feel better premenstrually (Alagna & Hamilton, 1986; Parlee, 1982a), others during the ovulation phase of the cycle (McFarlane et al., 1988).

More to the point, the variability of moods in females has not been found significantly different from the variability of moods in males, especially when the males are matched for lifestyles and ratings of moods are made daily (Alagna & Hamilton, 1986; Dan, 1976; McFarlane et al., 1988). People's moods change more over the course of a week (lows on Mondays, highs on Saturdays) than over the course of a menstrual cycle. Overall, environmental events, expectations, and social variables have been found to account for more of the variance in mood than does cycle point (see also P. R. Good & Smith, 1980; Paige, 1971).

A small percentage of women do seem to experience dramatic negative mood changes premenstrually that are related to hormonal level. Since the definition of PMS, even the one given in *DSM-III-R*, is vague, the estimate of how many women actually suffer from it has varied from 5 to 20% (T. Adler, 1990a). Furthermore, most women who suffer from PMS suffer from other psychological disorders as well, especially depression, so it is hard to pinpoint the exact cause of the premenstrual changes, if indeed they are separate. For these and other reasons, the causative factors in PMS have proven elusive (T. Adler, 1990a, 1990c). However, most researchers in the field think the cause is biological—somehow related to the sex hormones (estrogen and progesterone) or the hypothalamus. Much work remains to be done.

Since so little is known with respect to PMS, it seems premature to include it among the psychiatric disorders, even on a trial basis. Politically, the inclusion of PMS as a psychiatric disorder is undesirable since it reinforces the stereotype that women, as a group, are mentally disordered, at least at "certain times of the month." Furthermore, even if a small percentage of women experience marked and disruptive mood changes linked to their menstrual cycle, if the causes are biological, then the disorder should be considered a physical and not a psychiatric one.

Besides moods, the menstrual cycle also has been thought to affect behavior. The bulk of the research suggests, however, that the menstrual cycle is not an important source of gender differences in performance tests (Asso, 1987), especially when men are included as a control group. When only women are studied, some variation in performance across the menstrual cycle occasionally is found. Doreen Kimura and associates (Hampson & Kimura, 1988; Kimura, 1989a, 1989b) have linked these changes to variations in estrogen level. When estrogen levels are low (at the beginning of the menstrual cycle and just before menstruation begins), women may perform better on tasks involving spatial relationships; when estrogen levels are high (after ovulation, with estrogren replacement therapy), women may perform better on tasks involving verbal skills and muscular coordination.

The effect of the menstrual cycle on women's sexual desires and activity is also complicated by expectations, but only heterosexual women have been investigated. It has been found that heterosexual women's sexual desires appear to peak at midcycle for all but two groups of women: those taking oral contraceptives, suggesting a hormonal link, and those using the rhythm method of birth control, suggesting a psychological factor (D. B. Adams, Gold, & Burt, 1978; Morris, Udry, Khan-Dawood, & Dawood, 1987).

Androgens   The interest in the hormonal cycle and its correlates in females has obscured the fact that cycles are a part of all living things, and that both males and females have similar hormonal endowment and a pattern of cyclical secretion of different hormones (Asso, 1987). This neglect of males is evidence of how societal stereotypes (males are "unemotional" and "rock-steady") may affect the questions researchers ask. Because males have no external indication of cycles like menstruation, such questions have been easy to ignore. As noted earlier, in those few studies that have examined men's moods, evidence of variability is notable and similar to their female peers (Alagna & Hamilton, 1986; Dan, 1976; McFarlane et al., 1988). In fact, recent research suggests that the link between hormones, moods, and behavior may be even stronger in males than in females (Susman, Nottelmann, et al., 1987). However, research relating men's moods and behaviors to their hormonal levels is much less common than research on the menstrual cycle (Doering, Brodie, Kramer, Becker, & Hamburg, 1974; Petersen, 1979). For example, we know that testosterone level is influenced by circadian rhythmns and rises in the morning, but we don't know what effect such levels have on men's moods or cognitive performance.

More recently, testosterone level has been linked to certain personality traits in adolescents and college students (Baucom, Besch, & Callahan, 1985; Udry & Talbert, 1988). For example, a high testosterone level in both males and females is correlated with such traits as dominance, cynicism, and extraversion. It is not clear, however, what the causal sequence is. Prenatal hormones may directly lead to the development of certain personality traits or they may sensitize the individual to prefer certain activities, which in turn encourage the development of certain traits. Additionally, prenatal hormones may be linked to pubertal hormone levels, which may produce personality traits. Of some interest is the finding that although testosterone concentration is higher in adolescent males than in females, females respond more to each unit of testosterone than do males. Thus, the net effect is that testosterone level should not increase sex differences in personality at puberty (Udry & Talbert, 1988).

Androgens have been linked with both anger and aggression in males and females, but the relationships are complex (Goleman, 1990a; Inoff-Germain et al., 1988; Susman, Inoff-Germain, et al., 1987; Treadwell, 1987). Even with animals, the relationship between testosterone level (for example) and aggression is not clearly linear, since, in some cases, aggressive behavior may cause a rise in testosterone level (R. M. Rose, Gordon, & Bernstein, 1972). In general, however, high levels of androgen seem related to a greater predisposition to physically aggress, and males tend to have higher levels than females. (Aggression will be discussed in more depth in Chapter 3.)

Androgens also have been associated with increased libido, or sexual desire, and increased erotic reactivity in both females and males (Money & Ehrhardt, 1972; Morris et al., 1987; Udry, Talbert, & Morris, 1986), although this is not a consistent finding even in animals (Rosenberg, 1973). To the extent that males, on the average, have larger amounts of androgen than females, some may argue that the male sex drive is greater. However, as will be discussed in Chapter 4, human sexuality is so much a function of learning and of social forces that a simple, biologically deterministic approach would be completely inappropriate.

In sum, hormones have complicated effects on humans, and hormonal activity constantly interacts with social and psychological factors. Individual differences in moods and behavior are the norm, and this is true for males as well as females—even for such hormonally influenced events as menstruation, pregnancy, postparturition, and menopause (Fausto-Sterling, 1985).

Brain Organization

Since 1974, research has accumulated suggesting that men's brains are organized differently from women's for certain tasks and activities (see Treadwell, 1987, for a summary). Thus, a certain degree of sexual dimorphism appears to exist in the human brain, as it does in the brains of other animals. It had previously been suggested that each side of the brain was specialized and functioned differently. Language and language-related skills were thought of as being contained in the left hemisphere; nonverbal and spatial skills, in the right hemisphere. More recent research suggests that although this may be true for most right-handed men, it does not seem true for left-handed individuals or for many women (Bryden, 1979, 1986; Hines, 1982; McGlone, 1980).

On the average, the degree of *hemispheric specialization* may be different in females and males (Geschwind & Galaburda, 1985; Kimura, 1987). For right-handed individuals, more males than females tend to have their verbal abilities primarily in their left hemisphere, and their spatial abilities primarily in their right hemisphere. For more females than males, however, performance of verbal and spatial tasks seems to involve both hemispheres. This may explain why women, compared to men, suffer less often from speech disorders or aphasia after left-hemisphere damage. This does not mean that females are less lateralized than are males, as some researchers have concluded. In fact, Kimura (1987) suggests that certain language skills are *more* focalized in the left hemisphere (only in the anterior portion) for women than for men. In contrast, other language skills are *less* focalized in the left hemisphere (in the posterior regions) for women than for men. Differences appear, then, in the distribution of left- and right-hemispheric receptive processes, not in their magnitude. For example, whereas 90% of right-handed males show a right-side advantage (showing left-hemispheric activity) for verbal materials, only 80% of right-handed females show right-side advantage (Bryden, 1983).

As a result of such asymmetries, some females may have greater flexibility between hemispheres (Jorgenson, Davis, Opella, & Angerstein, 1979; Witelson, 1976). For example, such asymmetry may make it easier for women than for men to put a verbal label (left-hemispheric function) on an emotion (right-hemispheric function). This hypothesis is partly supported by the finding that part of the corpus callosum (the part of the brain that connects the two hemispheres) is larger in women than in men (De Lacoste-Utamsing & Holloway, 1982; Goleman, 1989). Although this finding has been hard to replicate (Bleier, 1988), if confirmed, it might explain some cognitive sex differences. For example, Hines (reported in Goleman, 1989) has linked the part of the corpus callosum that is larger in women than in men to three different measures of verbal fluency.

These differences in brain organization, to the extent that they exist, may be genetic, or, more likely, are influenced by different prenatal sex hormones (Hines, 1982; Hines & Shipley, 1984; Kimura, 1987). As we saw earlier, Geschwind speculates that high levels of fetal testosterone delay the development of the left hemisphere, making males more likely to be left-handed and better in visual-spatial skills than females (Geschwind & Behan, 1982; Geschwind & Galaburda, 1985). Such differences in genes and/or hormones themselves may reflect a long historical adaptation to sociocultural mandates. However, it is not known whether sex differences in laterality are present at birth or develop over time. There is some evidence support-ing both possibilities (Hahn, 1987; Treadwell, 1987; Turkewitz & Ross-Kossak, 1984). The corpus callosum, noted earlier as possibly mediating females' greater use of both hemispheres on certain verbal tasks, is relatively nonfunctioning at birth. This brain struc-ture matures gradually over the first five to ten years of life, thereby making it extremely sensitive to experiential factors (Trevarthen, 1974).

Therefore, it is possible that some sex differences in brain functioning *result from* differential socialization practices (Petersen, 1982). Even if such differences are somehow inherent from birth, dif-ferential treatment may still drastically affect the development of each sex. In particular, socializa-tion appears to influence the type of cognitive strategies each sex develops. These strategies may then interact with cerebral organization to cause different patterns of behavior (Bryden, 1979; Star, 1979). Thus, we must use a biosocial interactionist model to understand any sex differences in physiology (Ehrhardt, 1985; Kenrick, 1987).

The finding of small sex differences in brain organization is still tentative and may prove a result of methodological problems (see Hahn, 1987). Furthermore, the implications of the findings are unclear. Differences in brain organization may contribute to gender differences in verbal, mathe-matical, and visual-spatial skills, which are dis-cussed later in this chapter, and to sex differences in discerning emotions, discussed in Chapter 3. However, it should be kept in mind that all such differences are average differences, not absolute ones, and, as the percentages in Bryden's (1983) research reveal, focusing on differences obscures the basic similarities between the sexes. In fact, there is more variability in brain organization patterns from person to person than between men and women (Hahn, 1987; Kimura, 1985). Because of the relatively small intersex variation in cognitive function and the lack of an adequate theory to explain such a small variation, Alper (1985) argues that focus-ing on sex differences in brain asymmetry cannot lead to significant scientific progress in understanding either sex differences or brain functioning.

Physical Vulnerability

Another physical area that has been thought to differentiate the sexes is physical vulnerability, especially in terms of *mortality* (death rate) and *morbidity* (illness rate). At every stage of life, males, particularly Black males, are more vulnerable than are females to disease, physical disorders, and death (Gibbs, 1988; Stillion, 1985). The life span of females is nearly universally longer than that of males. In the United States in 1989, the average female life span for Whites was 79.1 years and for others, 75.7; the average male life span for Whites was 72.6 and for others, 67.5 (U.S. Department of Health and Human Services, 1990a). In 1900, the average life span for women and men was 48.3 and 46.3 years, respectively. Although life expectancy rates improved for both sexes during the 1980s, they improved more for males than for females (Schmid, 1990). The main reason for this greater improve-ment in men's life expectancy is the change in disease patterns, discussed later. For example, women's rate of death from cancer increased dur-ing the 1980s while men's declined.

Still, males tend to die earlier than do females, especially in industrialized countries. Although the X and Y sperm appear to be produced in equal numbers, between 108 and 140 males are conceived for every 100 females. At birth, the ratio of males to females is reduced to between 103 and 106 to 100. Thus, between conception and birth, more males than females die. Four times as many males as females are miscarried or stillborn and 29% more males than females die soon after birth (U. S. Department of Health and Human Services, 1990b). In the first year of life in the United States, more male than female babies die: 35% more for Whites, 22% more for Blacks. After age 34, females begin to outnumber males in the United States (Schmid, 1990), and the differences increase with age: after age 65, there are about 150 women to 100 men. These ratios fluctuate as a function of societal changes. (See Guttentag & Secord, 1983, for an interesting discussion of this point.)

Cultural factors affect longevity. Although indus-trialized countries generally contain more women than men (106 females to every 100 males), in Asia and the Pacific there are only 95 females for every 100 males (United Nations, 1991). The major reasons for this discrepancy are the poorer nutrition and health care girls receive relative to boys in these countries, combined with high rates of violence against females, as demonstrated in female infan-ticide and dowry deaths.

Males are more vulnerable than females to a wide range of physical handicaps that are genetically linked. As was previously discussed, because males have one X chromosome, if that chromosome carries genes related to any one of a possible 62 specific recessive disorders, ranging from hemophilia to color blindness, males will manifest it. Females, with a second X chromosome to balance out the abnormal one, do not develop the disorder. Males are also more susceptible to degenerative and infectious diseases and to death from them. Males also show a greater incidence than females of a wide range of developmental problems, ranging from enuresis to stuttering to mental retardation (Geschwind & Galaburda, 1985).

In examining the major causes of death in 1972, James Harrison (1978) found that for four of the five major causes—the four being diseases of the heart, malignant neoplasms, accidents, and influenza and pneumonia—the death rate for males exceeded the death rate for females. Only in deaths from cerebrovascular diseases (such as strokes, the third most frequent cause) did the rate of female deaths exceed that of males. The 1988 data presented in Table 2.1 show a similar pattern. Of the five major causes of death, males have higher rates in three: malignant neoplasms, accidents, and chronic obstructive pulmonary diseases (bronchitis, emphysema asthma). Women still die more than men from cerebrovascular diseases, and the sexes now are fairly equal in deaths from heart disease. The highest male-to-female death ratios occur for human immunodeficiency virus infection (AIDS, eight times more males than females), suicide (nearly four times more males), homicide (three times more males), and accidents and chronic liver diseases (about twice as many males), mainly preventable causes. In contrast, two of the four diseases women die more of relate to aging—cerebrovascular diseases (strokes) and atherosclerosis.

This greater physical vulnerability of males goes against one of our most basic stereotypes—that of the strong male and the vulnerable female. Perhaps the stereotype needs to be restricted to muscular strength, although muscular strength is distributed normally in the population, indicating that some females are stronger than some males. Perhaps the stereotype refers to the greater strength surviving males must have over their less fortunate brothers. Or perhaps the stereotype of strength is a cognitive defense against this very vulnerability.

It is important to examine possible explanations for this difference in physical vulnerability. There are two main ones: women have a biological advantage, and women have a more healthful lifestyle. In terms of biology, because the basic fetus is female and something—chromosome and gonadal hormones—must be added to make the fetus male, more can go wrong with the developing male embryo (Money & Ehrhardt, 1972; Reinisch, Gandelman, & Spiegel, 1979). Other evidence suggests that female hormones may be protective. Risk of heart disease, for example, increases in females as estrogen decreases (Rodin & Ickovics, 1990). It may be that ability to withstand infection is transmitted via the X chromosome or that females' lower metabolic rate contributes to their superior capacity for survival (Hatton, 1977; McCoy, 1977).

Another possible explanation for superior female survival is that males may be more active, more subject to stress, and therefore more likely to have accidents, to be exposed to germs, to die of stress-related diseases, and to be victims of war. We shall

Table 2.1 Major causes of death (1988 data)

	Percentage of All Deaths	*Ratio of Males to Females*
Diseases of the heart	35.3	1.01
Malignant neoplasms	22.4	1.14
Cerebrovascular diseases	6.9	.66
Accidents and adverse effects	4.5	2.10
Chronic obstructive pulmonary diseases	3.8	1.44
Pneumonia and influenza	3.6	.90
Diabetes mellitus	1.9	.72
Suicide	1.4	3.80
Chronic liver disease and cirrhosis	1.2	1.87
Kidney diseases and renal failure	1.0	.94
Atherosclerosis	1.0	.60
Homicide and legal intervention	1.0	3.14
Septicemia	1.0	.77
Certain causes in infancy	.8	1.33
Human immunodeficiency virus infection	.8	8.27

From U.S. Department of Health and Human Services, 1990b.

see in the next section that the research on exploratory behavior does not support the explanation that boys are more active than girls simply because of biology. Nonetheless, it is true that male children are usually allowed more freedom of movement than females and are often encouraged to take risks and be more aggressive, thereby increasing their vulnerability to accidents and illnesses.

As these findings suggest, lifestyle factors play an important role in physical vulnerability (Rodin & Ickovics, 1990; Strickland, 1988). Harrison (1978) and others (Jourard, 1971; M. Perry, 1982) go further and assert that the male gender role is dangerous to men's physical health. The emphasis on conformity to the male role and on achievement may give rise to anxiety about failing. This anxiety may lead to the development of certain compensatory behaviors that are health hazards. Examples include taking risks, exhibitions of violence, smoking, and excessive consumption of alcohol. Other aspects of the male role encourage the development of aggressive, competitive behaviors, also known as Type A, or coronary-prone behaviors. Research has shown that Type A personality traits are significantly correlated with measures of instrumental (stereotypically masculine) traits (for example, Grimm & Yarnold, 1985). Additional stress may occur because males are expected not to show their emotions and therefore must suppress most feelings. All of these patterns would lead to the higher male-to-female ratios found in Table 2.1. In fact, Waldron (1976) estimated that three-quarters of the difference in life expectancy between males and females in 1975 (eight years) could be attributed to behaviors related to gender roles. One-third to one-half of the difference was due to smoking alone. Today, that difference has decreased, at least for Whites, mainly as a result of women's increased smoking.

Black males are particularly vulnerable to a host of physical disorders and death. Both Black males and females are more likely than White children to grow up in poverty, with its attendant stresses and poor access to health care and adequate nutrition. Both also suffer the added stress of inequality and discrimination. Black males' death rate is skyrocketing to such an extent that they have been called "an endangered species" (Gibbs, 1988). Among Blacks, males have higher rates of infant mortality, low birth weight, sickle cell anemia, elevated blood pressure levels, nonfatal and fatal accidents and injuries, and sexually transmitted diseases. They are more likely to die before the age of 20 than any other race-sex group. Between the

ages of 15 and 24, the major causes of death among all youth are accidents, homicide, and suicide. However, among Black males, homicide is the leading cause of death. A young Black male has a 1 in 21 chance of being murdered before he reaches the age of 25. The greater physical vulnerability of Black male youths has been attributed to various high-risk behaviors that exacerbate their poor health, such as substance use and abuse, involvement with gangs, use of guns, smoking cigarettes, and poor health care.

Thus, we see an example of the negative effects of our socialization practices on males. Indeed, as females begin to experience many of the same stresses and behaviors as males, like smoking, their susceptibility to stress-related diseases also increases (Rodin & Ickovics, 1990; Waldron, 1976). As an example, male smoking has been on the decline since the early 1950s, but female smoking has actually increased since then. Starting in 1976, slightly more girls than boys have been smokers (19% of female high school seniors smoke daily, compared to 18% of their male peers; Reinhard, 1991). Since lung cancer takes about 35 years to develop, we're just now seeing a marked jump in lung cancer rates for women. Women's deaths from lung cancer (the most common type of cancer death in women since 1985) increased by more than one-third between 1980 and 1987, whereas for men, the rate of increase during those same years was less than 5% ("Lung Cancer," 1990). Consequently, we're seeing a decrease in the male-to-female death ratio from malignant neoplasms and bronchitis, emphysema, and asthma. (Further discussion of gender and health will occur in Chapter 8.)

Some of the differences in physical vulnerability probably reflect aspects of Western society, yet not all do; across a variety of cultures with different stresses, males still seem to die earlier and have a greater incidence of chromosomal abnormalities than do females (H. E. Fitzgerald, 1977). It seems likely that a biological predisposition interacts with social factors in unclear ways to make males more physically vulnerable.

Motor Behavior

Motor behavior can be examined in terms of both general activity level and performance on specific motor tasks. Boys tend to score higher than girls on both sets of measures.

Gender differences in *activity level* appear to increase with age from infancy through middle adolescence, with boys nearly always receiving higher average ratings than do girls on measures of motor activity, physical exertion, and rough-and-tumble play (Eaton & Enns, 1986; Ehrhardt, 1985; Maccoby & Jacklin, 1974; Tauber, 1979). This is true of other primates as well. This finding does not mean that girls are passive; rather, girls seem to be active in different activities—for example, playing house and hopscotch—thus making a quantitative distinction difficult (H. E. Fitzgerald, 1977).

Eaton and Enns's (1986) meta-analysis found the average difference between boys' and girls' ratings was about one-half a standard deviation ($d = .49$), a moderately sized difference. This means that of those children scoring above average on an activity-level rating, 62% probably will be boys, 38% girls. These differences were most pronounced in situations that maximized individual differences—familiar, nonthreatening, unrestricted social situations—and were strongest after puberty, weakest during infancy. Studies investigating the amount of activity shown by male and female infants have produced inconsistent results, largely because of methodological problems (Maccoby & Jacklin, 1974; McCoy, 1977). Generally, female and male infants evidence equal amounts of total activity; but males show more large body movements, and females show more refined and limited movements. The magnitude of the difference is such that approximately 57% of male infants would be rated above average in motor activity compared to 43% of female infants (Linn & Hyde, 1989). Male infants also tend to be more fretful and wakeful than females, a finding not completely explained by the fact that males have more birth problems and may suffer from the effects of circumcision (Barfield, 1976; Maccoby & Jacklin, 1974; Phillips, King, & DuBois, 1978). This difference in fretfulness has implications for parent-infant interactions because an infant's irritability may lead to decreased parental contact (M. Lewis & Weinraub, 1979; Segal & Yahraes, 1978).

Although gender differences in activity level increase with age, the absolute level of activity appears to decrease. Thus, physical maturation appears to be associated with activity level. Since girls mature faster than boys, girls' somewhat lesser activity level during infancy and childhood may be due to their faster maturation. A study by Eaton and Yu (1989) with 5- to 8-year-olds suggests that maturation does affect activity level, but only for males. One implication of this finding is that girls' activity levels must be determined by something else, possibly socialization factors.

Gender differences in childhood activity levels also may be due in part to prenatal androgen levels, as suggested by the increased display of tomboy behavior (more physical activity) in females who experienced prenatal androgen produced either internally, as in the adrenogenital syndrome, or externally, as when the mother is given drugs to avoid a miscarriage (Ehrhardt, 1985; Money & Ehrhardt, 1972). Similarly, some evidence exists that high doses of progesterone prenatally may reduce "masculine" play behavior in both boys and girls (Meyer-Bahlburg, Feldman, Cohen, & Ehrhardt, 1988). However, socialization factors cannot be ruled out since masculinization of the genitals of androgenized girls also occurs in some of these cases. Thus, it is possible that the parents of these children may have expected more such behaviors in these girls, thereby subtly reinforcing them. In support of this interpretation is Hines's (1982) conclusion from a review of the literature that when research involved individuals who were exposed to unusual hormones prenatally but who were born without physical abnormalities, many studies failed to find evidence of masculinized play comparable to that reported for androgenized girls. Additionally, because most females engage in tomboy behaviors (estimates range from 51% to 78%, according to Hyde, Rosenberg, & Behrman, 1977), the use of this index to define a masculine activity pattern is highly questionable. Indeed, some recent writers have taken issue with the definitions Money and his colleagues used to determine masculine play styles (for example, girls not wearing dresses), as well as these researchers' methods of data collection and use of control groups (Hines, 1982; L. Rogers & Walsh, 1982). In conclusion, the role of prenatal androgen in activity level and style still is unclear, but the evidence points strongly to the more important role of socialization (Ehrhardt, 1985).

With respect to *motor performance*, boys again generally excel, but the size of the gender difference ranges from small (for balance, $d = .09$) to large (for throwing velocity, $d = 2.18$), with most tasks falling in the moderate range (J. R. Thomas & French, 1985). Both biological and socialization forces seem to be operative, depending upon the specific motor task. For example, gender differences with regard to both throwing speed and throwing distance are among the largest to be found, averaging two standard deviations. This size difference means that nearly everyone who scores above average on these tasks will be a boy. Since this difference is found as early as age 3, it is likely to be at least partly biologically based (fat/muscle ratio, arm measurements). However, since the difference increases substantially during childhood, whatever biological differences exist probably are augmented by practice differences. Boys are more likely to receive training and experience in throwing than are girls. For some motor tasks—dash, grip strength, long jump, shuttle run, sit-ups, vertical jump—gender differences increase sharply after puberty, suggesting that increases in boys' size and strength probably are responsible. Before puberty, however, differential experience probably is more important. For still other motor tasks—agility, balance, eye-motor coordination, flexibility, and reaction time—differential treatment and practice probably account for most of the gender differences.

In sum, boys generally score higher than girls when motor behavior is measured. Most of these differences appear to be due to an interaction between biological and environmental factors.

Discussion

The physical underpinnings of gender stereotypes are complex. We have seen that even sex differentiation is not simple. It occurs in stages, first influenced by chromosomes, then by hormones prenatally, then by genitalia and socialization postnatally. At each stage, the developing fetus is bipotential; that is, it can develop along either female or male lines. Furthermore, differences between the sexes even on a physical level are usually differences in degree, not in kind. The most critical factor in gender identity (one's concept of oneself as a male or a female) is culture, which can override the biological factors, as demonstrated in cases of sexual anomalies. We need not argue about nature or nurture. It is logical that an interaction occurs, with nature possibly predisposing, and nurture either reinforcing or contradicting that predisposition. Most of the research evidence is consistent with this interactionist position.

This interaction is true in the areas of physical functioning as well. Although, on the average, males tend to be bigger and stronger than females, nutrition and athletic training can decrease the gap. In physiological processes, females tend to mature faster at all age levels and are slightly more sensitive to touch and smell than males, and they have cyclical hormonal fluctuations after puberty. The consequences of these differences are dependent on socialization and societal expectations, as depicted clearly in the research on menstrual cycle. Particular mental functions may be organized differently

in some male brains than in some female brains. Males tend to be more physically vulnerable to disease, death, and physical disorders than females, although these differences also can be affected by the environment. Differences in activity levels and motor performance exist, but these, too, depend on an interaction between biological and environmental factors.

People tend to accept three myths when thinking about biological factors. *Myth 1:* Biological factors are primary; that is, if they co-occur with a behavior, they must be the *cause* of the behavior. *Fact:* Behavior also can change biological factors. For example, we know different types of experiences can affect neural connections. Thus, the relationship between biology and behavior is bidirectional. *Myth 2:* Biology is fixed; therefore if something has a biological basis it cannot be changed. *Fact:* Human behavior is enormously flexible, predominantly affected by cultural factors, not biological ones. *Myth 3:* Biology is natural; therefore, it indicates what *should* be. *Fact:* "Shoulds" are imposed by humans, not by biology. The shifting trends in research on gender differences clearly bear this out. It probably is not coincidental that research on the possible biological bases of gender differences has skyrocketed at a time when the behavioral and role differences between women and men are decreasing.

In summary, the only "basic irreducible element of sex differences which no culture can eradicate, at least not on a large scale, are that women can menstruate, gestate, and lactate, and men cannot" (Money & Ehrhardt, 1972, p. 14). For their part, men can impregnate, and women cannot. The explanation for nearly all other human behaviors is "not in our genes" (see Lewontin, Rose, & Kamin, 1984). A similar picture of the importance of social factors, perhaps in interaction with biological ones, occurs with respect to cognitive functioning.

▲   Cognitive Abilities

Many gender stereotypes about thinking and reasoning abilities exist, such as that boys are more analytical than girls, and girls are better at simple repetitive tasks. Despite the popularity of such stereotypes, however, research has found few clear-cut gender differences in cognitive abilities. What is striking in reviewing research in this area is how much attention has been paid to the very few and very small gender differences in cognitive functioning that are sometimes found, especially those differences in which males, as a group, appear to show an advantage.

An unavoidable problem with research in this area is the fact that cognitive ability cannot be measured directly but only indirectly through performance. And performance is affected by many factors other than innate ability, such as mood, motivation, expectations, and social factors. For example, Golden and Cherry (1982) found that average-ability 11th- and 12th-grade girls performed better on verbal and math tests when they thought their results would not be made public than when they thought their results would be publicized. In contrast, boys and high-ability girls showed no difference in performance across conditions. Thus, even when performance differences do appear between males and females, the cause of the difference is not always clear.

It will be instructive to review research on the performance of females and males in the following cognitive areas: intellectual aptitude, memory, verbal abilities, quantitative abilities, visual-spatial abilities, cognitive styles, and creativity. As we will see, only three differences appear fairly consistently: girls have a slight edge in verbal skills, while boys have an edge in quantitative abilities and in visual-spatial skills. Even these differences are small, however, and may not show up until after age 8. Unfortunately, the literature abounds with studies of the differences, not the similarities, so that a reader gets the impression that these differences are large and very important.

Intellectual Aptitude

Are boys smarter than girls? According to research, the answer is no. There are no known differences between males and females in overall intelligence after age 6, an unsurprising finding, because IQ tests were specifically designed to eliminate sex differences (Maccoby & Jacklin, 1974); that is, test items were selected that specifically did not show differential responding by males and females, because it was assumed there were no sex differences in intelligence.

It is true, however, that there are more male than female retardates. A number of possible explanations for this have been offered, most centering around the greater vulnerability of males in general to a host of developmental problems. Although IQ has not been found related to the X chromosome (Wittig, 1979) or to prenatal hormones (Hines, 1982) in general, there does seem to be a particular type of mental retardation called the "fragile X syndrome"

(Maugh, 1991; Vandenburg, 1987). Because males inherit only one X chromosome, they are more vulnerable to this disorder.

Intellectual performance may vary as a function of sex-role conformity. Eleanor Maccoby (1966) found that nonconformity to gender stereotypes was positively related to IQ scores. Thus, the more assertive and active the female, the greater her intellectual abilities and interests; the less active and aggressive the male, the less developed his physique and the greater his intellectual abilities and interests. Here is a possible example of how conformity to gender stereotypes may limit one's capabilities. Although intelligence is partially inherited, socialization does play a large role in the actual development of intellectual abilities. For example, mothers who strongly believe in gender stereotypes tend to have daughters with lower IQ scores as toddlers than do other mothers, mainly because sex-stereotypic mothers play less actively with their daughters (Brooks-Gunn, 1986).

Overall, then, there are no basic gender differences in intelligence.

Memory

Neither sex has a better memory than the other, although there is some evidence that information-processing strategies may differ for males and females (N. S. Anderson, 1987; Maccoby & Jacklin, 1974). Gender differences in memory tasks also may appear in situations where there are gender differences in familiarity or interest. For example, some suggestion exists that girls have better social memory than boys—that is, girls are better at remembering people's names and/or faces. Although there has been some support for this hypothesis among adults (for example, Borges & Vaughn, 1977; Hamilton, 1983), gender differences in social memory have not been found consistently among preschoolers (Etaugh & Whittler, 1982). Such a pattern of results suggests that socialization factors probably account for whatever difference in social memory exists, rather than any biological differences in memory capacity or efficiency.

Supporting this hypothesis that socialized interest patterns may affect memory is the finding that gender-related words and information may be recalled differently by men and women, especially as a function of the individual's degree of sex typing or sexism. Children through adults seem to recall sex-stereotyped people and activities better than nonstereotyped people and activities, and this memory preference is most marked for students with strong gender stereotypes (Hepburn, 1985; Liben & Signorella, 1980; Stangor, 1988). Males also seem more likely to remember information about other males and about "masculine" activities and words than they do information about females and "feminine" activities and words (Brown, Larsen, Rankin, & Ballard, 1980; Halpern, 1985). The reciprocal pattern is found for females—that is, females are more accurate in recalling female-related information than male-related information. This pattern of results is consistent with self-schema theory (Markus, Crane, Bernstein, & Siladi, 1982), that people remember best information that is congruent with the way they define themselves.

Sandra Bem's gender schema theory (described in Chapter 1) suggests that it is only sex-typed individuals who remember gender-related information better than non-gender-related information. That is, those individuals with a strong gender schema (sex-typed individuals) use that schema to process incoming information. Bem's hypothesis has received inconsistent support. Bem (1981b, 1985) and some others (for example, G. D. Levy, 1989a) have found that individuals who are strongly sex-typed do indeed recall gender-related information more quickly and cluster gender-related information more than do non-sex-typed individuals. However, a number of other studies have failed to find this effect (Deaux, Kite, & Lewis, 1985; Edwards & Spence, 1987; Payne, Connor, & Colletti, 1987).

In summary, there are no overall differences in memory abilities between males and females, although gender may affect the type of information best remembered.

Verbal Abilities
Females frequently perform better than males in a variety of verbal tasks (Feingold, 1988; Hyde & Linn, 1988; Maccoby & Jacklin, 1974). However, the size of the gender difference is so small, especially in recent years, that some researchers view the differences as negligible. For example, in Hyde and Linn's recent (1988) meta-analysis of 165 studies, average gender differences in verbal abilities were the size of only one-tenth of one standard deviation $d = .11$). What this means is that of people scoring above average on verbal ability tests, 53% are probably girls and women, 48% are boys and men. Another way of looking at the findings is that 99% of a person's score on verbal tests is determined by factors other than a person's sex (Hyde, 1981). The practical implications of such small gender differences are virtually nil.

Although no particular type of verbal ability shows very strong gender differences, Hyde and Linn (1988) found that the female edge appears greatest in measures of speech production, anagrams, and general or mixed abilities. On tests of vocabulary and reading comprehension, the differences are close to zero. On one type of test, verbal analogies, males showed a slight edge. Girls have been found to acquire language earlier than boys, as measured by acquisition of phonemes, amount of vocalization in infancy, age of use of first word, vocabulary size, articulation, comprehensibility, and fluency (Maccoby & Jacklin, 1974). Tests of spelling and grammar also generally show a female edge (Feingold, 1988). Furthermore, more boys than girls suffer from speech difficulties (such as stuttering, three to four times more common in males) and reading problems (such as dyslexia, five to ten times more common in males) (Geschwind & Galaburda, 1985; Halpern, 1989).

The finding of fewer gender differences in studies published since 1973 than in those published earlier suggests that whatever small gap existed between females and males in verbal abilities is shrinking (Hyde & Linn, 1988). Whether this shrinkage is because gender differences really have narrowed or because more studies reporting no differences have gotten published isn't clear. Since Feingold (1988), in reviewing performance on the Differential Aptitude Test (DAT) given to national samples in grades 8–12 between the years 1947 and 1980, also found a decrease in gender differences over time, it may be that the gender performance gap indeed has narrowed.

This decreasing female edge in tests of verbal abilities has been particularly apparent in performance on the verbal portion of the Scholastic Aptitude Test (SAT), a test taken by college-bound high school juniors and seniors. Before 1972, females scored somewhat higher than males; since 1972, males have scored somewhat higher than females, although this difference is very small ($d = .01–.08$) (Feingold, 1988; Hyde & Linn, 1988). (In 1989–90, the average SAT verbal score for women was 419; for men, 429; Dodge, 1990.) These findings may be due to the more heterogeneous (in terms of ability) population of females taking the SATs; that is, the males who take the SATs are more highly selected than the females. Studies by the Educational Testing Service (reported by Landers, 1989) support this hypothesis. In the case of SATs, however, even small differences can be meaningful since a number of scholarships are based on SAT scores. This will be discussed further in the section on quantitative abilities.

Although recent research suggests that gender differences in verbal abilities are so small as to be nonexistent, other researchers argue that this pattern partially may be an artifact of the increasing dropout rate of more poorly performing male students (Halpern, 1989). Thus, comparisons made during high school are between girls of wide-ranging abilities and better-performing boys. Gender differences thus would be underestimated. Therefore, it is worthwhile to examine reasons for this small female advantage in verbal abilities. We will briefly review biological and social reasons, which probably interact.

Biological explanations As was noted earlier in this chapter, a small gender difference may exist in patterns of brain organization, probably as a result of prenatal hormones. Most language functions appear localized in the left hemisphere, especially for right-handed males. For females, some language functions appear more localized, some less localized than in males. For example, Kimura (1985, 1987) found that the site responsible for speech production is more localized in women's than in men's brains, whereas the site responsible for defining words (vocabulary) is less localized in women's than in men's brains. On other verbal tasks, there is no gender difference in location.

The left hemisphere may develop earlier in females than in males, giving females a lead in childhood language skills (Kimura, 1985; J. Levy & Reid, 1978). Owing to this earlier lead, girls may use language more in processing their environment. Boys develop language abilities later than other cognitive abilities; because boys' shift to linguistic skills occurs later, more language-related disorders may arise, as has been found. Language-related disorders have also been related to excessive levels of prenatal testosterone, which cause anomalous patterns of cerebral dominance to develop (Geschwind & Galaburda, 1985). Because it is mainly male fetuses who are exposed to testosterone in utero, males suffer from more language-related disorders than females.

This line of research is suggestive but certainly not conclusive at this time. The precise relationship between degree of hemispheric specialization and performance of a particular skill is still an open question, especially since there is such tremendous overlap between the sexes in terms of both brain lateralization and verbal abilities. Furthermore, it is not known whether sex differences in laterality

are present at birth or develop over time. Prenatal hormonal factors, which have been implicated in brain lateralization patterns, have not been found predictive of verbal ability (Hines & Shipley, 1984). Even if sex differences in brain organization were in some way inherent, social factors could still be important in the development of particular abilities.

More recently, Kimura (1989a, 1989b) has suggested that estrogen level in women affects their verbal skills. Women at the midpoint of their menstrual cycle (when estrogen levels are high) compared to premenstrually (when estrogen levels are low) perform better at speeded articulation (saying tongue-twisters) and verbal fluency (saying as many words as possible that begin with a particular letter) tasks. Although the media made a big fuss over this research (see Benderly, 1989), the implications of these findings are unclear since these tasks have little real-life relevance, the differences were small, and no comparisons were made with men.

Social explanations The environment can affect the development of gender differences in children in a number of ways, particularly through differential treatment and differential expectations. The finding of diminishing gender differences in verbal skills over the last 20 years suggests social factors may be responsible for such differences.

Evidence of differential parental treatment according to the sex of the child has been substantial although not unquestioned (Bee, Mitchell, Barnard, Eyres, & Hammond, 1984; Maccoby & Jacklin, 1974). Males appear to be handled more often and more vigorously than females during the first six months of life, whereas females are more frequently vocalized to, especially by mothers. More frequent parental vocalizations to daughters may lead to increased vocalization on the part of female infants. Conversely, these differences in parental treatment may result from female infants' more frequent vocalizations. Evidence for both positions is available, and it is highly likely that these factors interact to strengthen each other from the earliest days of the child's life.

Females in a number of countries are expected to do better than males in reading and other verbal skills. For example, a recent study of youngsters in the United States, Taiwan, and Japan found that mothers rated girls as better than boys in reading, despite there being no gender difference in performance tests (Lummis & Stevenson, 1990). In the United States, socioverbal and artistic skills are seen as "feminine" beginning in the second grade

(Hill, Hobbs, & Verble, 1974; Nash, 1979). In cultures where reading is considered to be male-appropriate (for example, England and Germany), males' reading and vocabulary performance is generally the same as or superior to that of females (Finn, 1980; D. D. Johnson, 1973–74).

Teachers' expectations regarding what subject matters are more appropriate to each sex also may be important, as well as their own modeling of academic interests. The International Association for the Evaluation of Educational Achievement recently reported from a five-year examination of writing samples of over 40,000 students from 14 nations on five continents that girls write better than boys because girls get more encouragement to develop those skills ("Study: Girls Encouraged," 1989). Some studies report that males perform better when tested and/or taught by males, particularly when verbal materials are presented, and females perform better when tested and/or taught by females (S. C. Nash, 1979; Shinedling & Pedersen, 1970).

In sum, research on verbal abilities indicates very small gender differences in the direction of some females performing better than some males on some tasks. These differences are extremely small and are likely to be due to differences in the socialization process interacting, perhaps, with differences in brain organization.

Quantitative Abilities

Tremendous interest has been shown in the last few years in the area of gender differences in mathematical ability. Recent evidence from meta-analytic studies based on literally millions of subjects indicates that gender differences in math ability are extremely small and are a function of the age group examined, the selectivity of the sample, and the type of mathematical ability tested (Feingold, 1988; Hengkietisak & Cleary, 1989; Hyde, Fennema, & Lamon, 1990).

The overall effect size for general populations is close to zero ($d = -.05$; negative value meaning female superiority). Very few gender differences are found in mathematical achievement before high school. Those found slightly favor females on computation subtests ($d = -.14$). Starting in high school and continuing through college, males perform somewhat better on problem-solving subtests ($d = .29–.32$). There are no gender differences in understanding mathematical concepts at any age. Girls in most cases still get better math grades in school (Kimball, 1989). Furthermore, gender differences in math performance have decreased in studies since 1973 (from $d = .31$ for studies published before 1974 to $d = .14$ for studies published since). Also of note is the finding that the slight male edge overall is restricted to White populations in the United States, Canada, and Australia. Among Blacks and Hispanics, gender differences are near zero (Hyde, Fennema, & Lamon, 1990). Figure 2.4 shows two normal distributions that are apart by the size of the average gender difference found over all groups (general and selected) in all types of mathematical performance ($d = .15$). The overlap between the two groups is considerable.

What exactly does the small male edge in problem-solving ability during and after high school mean? It means that for everyone taking such a test in high school, about 57% of those scoring above

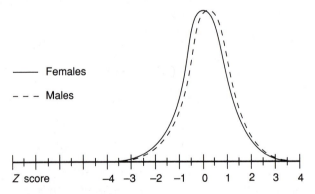

Figure 2.4 The average gender difference in mathematics performance, averaging over all samples. From "Gender Differences in Mathematics Performance: A Meta-analysis," by J. S. Hyde, E. Fennema, and S. J. Lamon, *Psychological Bulletin*, 1990, *107*, 139–155. Copyright 1990 by the American Psychological Association. Reprinted by permission.

average will be male and 43% will be female. The size of this difference does not seem impressive, yet the public has been bombarded with reports of "large" and "sizable" gender differences in math ability (Benbow & Stanley, 1980, 1983).

Why the big fuss if there are so few gender differences and the ones that exist are small and selective? One reason is that the area in which gender differences typically are found, that of problem solving, is a very important area for both future academic and career endeavors. Even with a small edge for males in this area, many females will be screened out of careers not only in math but also in science, engineering, and computers (Hyde, Fennema, & Lamon, 1990; Sells, 1980).

Another reason gender differences in math have aroused so much attention is that when only selective samples are examined—for example, college students and precocious youth—the male edge in problem solving is greater ($d = .33–.54$). These are the differences reflected in males' consistent edge in the math portion of the Scholastic Aptitude Test (SAT) and research on mathematically gifted youth. And these are the differences that make the news each year when SAT scores are released to the media.

SAT performance is, of course, important since it is one of the filters for college admission and for many college scholarships. In 1989–90, the average score on the math portion for males taking the test was 499, for females 455 (Dodge, 1990). The male edge on these tests has occurred every year, although the magnitude of the difference has varied and is smaller among African Americans and Asian Americans than among Whites ($d = .42$ in 1983; K. J. Cooper, 1989; Feingold, 1988). The gender difference in SAT math performance is best explained by the greater heterogeneity of female test-takers (more males drop out of high school, leaving a more selective sample of males in high school and applying to college) and the greater likelihood of male test-takers' having had advanced math courses (Feingold, 1988; Hyde, Fennema, & Lamon, 1990). When these two factors are controlled for, gender differences in SAT math scores generally disappear. In addition, the context of the questions used on the SATs has been found to favor males (more questions relating to sports and science, fewer to interpersonal relationships and sewing) (P. Rosser, 1989).

Overall, then, the SAT may not be the best reflector of mathematical *ability*. It certainly seems to underpredict math performance by females during their first year of college (P. Rosser, 1989). For all

these reasons, both the SAT itself and the National Merit Scholarship program have been accused of sex bias. Because the National Merit Scholarship program awards scholarships based on Preliminary SAT scores, more than 60% of the scholarships have gone to males. In 1989, New York State was prohibited from using the SAT as the sole basis for their awards because it was found to be sex discriminatory (Landers, 1989). In 1990, with the formula for awarding the New York Regents Scholarship changed to include high school grades, girls for the first time won a majority of the scholarships, 51.3% (Verhovek, 1990).

The research on mathematically gifted youth by Camille Benbow and Julian Stanley (1980, 1983; Benbow, 1988) also has led to an emphasis on gender differences in quantitative ability. Since 1972, these Johns Hopkins University researchers have tested more than 50,000 7th and 8th graders, seeking those who scored in at least the top 2–5% on standardized math and verbal achievement tests. These select students then were given the SAT math and verbal subtests, more usually taken by 11th and 12th graders. Benbow and Stanley found that more than twice as many boys as girls had math scores greater than 500 on the SAT (highest possible score is 800) and score differences were the greatest between highest-scoring boys and girls. For example, among students who scored greater than or equal to 700, boys outnumbered girls 13 to 1. Even among high school students taking the SAT during its regular administration, males are greatly overrepresented among the highest scorers (84% of those scoring 750 or more are male; 96% of those scoring 800) (Dorans & Livingston, 1987). These percentages make sense when we realize we are examining individuals at the upper extreme of the distribution in Figure 2.4. This needs to be kept in mind since group differences using the entire sample were almost nonexistent (Rossi, 1983). The use of the SAT as a pure measure of aptitude has been questioned as well because these tests also involve knowledge of particular techniques (L. H. Fox, 1981; Tobias, 1982).

But perhaps more controversial than Benbow and Stanley's findings have been the reasons invoked to explain their findings and those of others showing male superiority in quantitative performance. These explanations again fall generally into two groups: those that primarily emphasize biological factors, and those that primarily emphasize social factors.

Biological explanations Although Benbow and Stanley (1980) suggested that male superiority in mathematics was probably due to both biological and social factors, the media picked up mainly on the former; for example, in *Time* magazine, males were described as "naturally abler than females" ("Gender Factor," 1980). Yet no strong evidence for genetic influence on gender differences in mathematics has been found (Petersen, 1983; Sherman & Fennema, 1978). Even the pattern of results belies a genetic factor, since consistent female inferiority among the mathematically talented was not found (Tobias, 1982).

An alternative hypothesis that involves prenatal hormones to explain math genius has been put forward by Geschwind (Geschwind & Behan, 1982; Geshwind & Galaburda, 1985; Kolata, 1983). As described earlier, Geschwind proposes that brain anatomy can be altered during fetal life due to excess testosterone or unusual sensitivity to testosterone. The right hemisphere of the brain then will become dominant for language-related abilities as well as for mathematical and spatial abilities. The result is either mathematical genius or learning disorders, depending on whether some delicate balance is obtained. Further implications of such prenatal hormone activity are that such people should be more likely to be left-handed (right hemispheric dominance) and more prone to immune system disorders (which have been found linked to testosterone production and sensitivity). As already noted, males do seem more likely than females to be math geniuses and to suffer from learning disorders. They also are more likely than females to be left-handed and to have immune system disorders, such as allergies and asthma. When Benbow and Stanley contacted those students who scored above 700 on the SAT math test, they found that 20% were left-handed, twice the percentage expected in the general population, and 60% had immune system disorders, five times the incidence in the general population. In contrast, when average scorers were examined, the incidence of left-handedness and of immune system disorders was the same as in the general population. These findings, although still tentative, provide a possible mechanism that may underlie math genius in some cases. For most individuals, however, such a mechanism would not be operating, and we need to look at other factors that might explain why some males score higher than some females.

Social explanations Researchers in this area generally agree that most of the difference in math performance between males and females can be explained by environmental factors. Even biological factors can be modified by a child's surroundings. Among the most powerful social influences are the attitudes of fellow students plus parents and teachers toward mathematics performance, as well as actual differences in mathematics-related behaviors.

The most common and reliable finding in this area is that females tend to take fewer math courses than males as soon as such courses become optional, usually in high school (Kimball, 1989). A study of those taking the SATs in 1988 showed that whereas 68% of male test-takers took four years of math, only 59% of female test-takers did (Mitgang, 1988). On the average, college-bound females take about one-half year less mathematics and about one year less physical sciences than do their male peers (National Science Foundation, 1986). As noted earlier, when number of math courses taken is controlled for, gender differences in math achievement usually are eliminated, especially on the SATs. It thus is encouraging to note that the gender difference in participation in math courses appears to be decreasing (Chipman, Brush, & Wilson, 1985).

Why do girls tend to take fewer math courses than boys? A number of factors seem important, most of them attitudinal. Compared to boys, girls have less confidence in their own math ability, see math as less valuable than English, and have less interest in math and science as careers (Eccles, 1989; Hyde, Fennema, Ryan, Frost, & Hopp, 1990; Kimball, 1989). Girls also tend to attribute their success in math to effort rather than ability. Therefore, the fact that they get better math grades than boys does not make girls feel more confident. Bright girls in particular (when compared to less bright girls and bright boys) appear to suffer from achievement fears and confusions that would lead them to be less motivated toward mathematics than toward verbal tasks (Dweck, 1986). These attitudinal differences emerge during junior high school (seventh grade) at the same time that math becomes viewed as a male domain. Indeed, the belief that math is a male domain is related significantly to girls' lower self-confidence in learning math and their poorer math performance during these years (J. Sherman, 1978, 1982a, 1982b). Negative attitudes toward math increase during high school, for girls more so than for boys (American Association of University Women, 1991).

Although differences in course taking did not account for the gender differences in mathematical achievement among the gifted seventh and eighth graders in Benbow and Stanley's research, these students may have had different math-related experiences outside of school. For example, L. H. Fox and Cohn (1980) found that more boys than girls in the Johns Hopkins program reported that they had systematically studied mathematics and science textbooks with a parent or teacher before entering the talent search. Other reports also suggest that parents of mathematically gifted children are more likely to work with and encourage their sons than their daughters (L. H. Fox, 1981; Tobias, 1982). Such encouragement appears critical for later math and science achievement, especially for girls. Follow-up studies of more than 1200 mathematically talented youth found that the best predictors of later math and science achievement were schooling variables (such as number of semesters of math and science, and number of math and science exams) and family variables (such as encouragement from parents to pursue career and educational goals) (Benbow & Arjmand, 1990). Such environmental variables were better predictors of later achievement than attitudinal variables or even absolute level of ability, especially for girls.

Girls receive less encouragement than boys with respect to math from parents, teachers, and peers. Parents tend to view their daughters as having less ability in math than their sons, despite there being no gender difference in math performance (Yee & Eccles, 1988). This is true in Taiwan and Japan, as well as in the United States (Lummis & Stevenson, 1990). Parents consequently have lower expectations for girls than boys, which is particularly unfortunate since parental expectations are strong predictors of a child's math attitudes and achievement (Eccles, 1989; J. Sherman, 1983). Males, starting in junior high and extending into adulthood, are particularly likely to view math as a male domain ($d = .90$; Hyde, Fennema, Ryan, Frost, & Hopp, 1990). This may translate into subtle (or not-so-subtle) pressure on girls from their male peers not to achieve (see also L. H. Fox, 1981; Webb, 1984). Many teachers, especially men, also view math as a male domain and convey this attitude both directly and indirectly—for example, by giving males and females different kinds of feedback (Eccles, 1989; J. Sherman, 1982a). One study (Hallinan & Sorensen, 1987) found that teachers were more likely to assign boys who scored high on a math achievement test to a high-ability math group than they were to assign high-ranking girls to such a group. Not only may girls receive less encouragement for math achievement than boys, but girls also seem more responsive to the kinds of

evaluative feedback they receive than boys (T. Roberts, 1991). The result may be girls' increasing disinterest in math.

Some aspects of girls' typical socialization experiences also may disadvantage them on problem-solving and standardized tests during and after high school. In particular, boys' greater risk-taking tendencies and autonomous approach to learning math may make them more likely to guess on tests and to apply rules learned in the classroom to new situations. Girls' greater tendency toward caution and toward "playing by the rules" appears to cause them to leave more questions unanswered on tests and to answer word problems more slowly (Kimball, 1989; Linn & Hyde, 1989; Linn & Petersen, 1985; P. Rosser, 1989).

In sum, boys and girls show many similarities with respect to quantitative abilities, although beginning in high school, boys demonstrate an edge in problem-solving tasks and are overrepresented among those with the greatest mathematical ability. Except for SAT math performance, gender differences have been diminishing. Although math genius may have a biological foundation, social factors provide the most convincing explanations for math achievement for most individuals. Overall, the fact that females take fewer math courses, have lower confidence in their mathematical ability, have less interest in math and science, and receive less encouragment than their male peers explains females' slightly poorer performance on standardized math tests. Girls need extra support and encouragement to feel as confident as their male peers and to take the same types of courses (Eccles, 1989; L. H. Fox, 1981).

Visual-Spatial Abilities

Look at Figure 2.5. If finding the simple figure in the complex figure is relatively easy for you, you likely have good visual-spatial ability. This ability

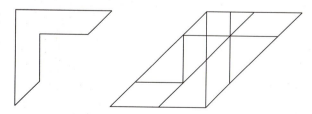

Figure 2.5 The embedded figure test. Find the simple shape (on left) in the complex shape (on right).

refers to the visual perception of objects or figures in space and the way they are related to each other. Such perception usually requires some mental transformation of the object, as in disembedding a visual figure from its context (the embedded figure test—Figure 2.5) or aligning a figure independent of its field (the rod-and-frame test—Figure 2.6) (Witkin, Dyk, Faterson, Goodenough, & Karp, 1962).

In all the research done on gender differences, one of the two most consistent findings has been a male advantage in visual-spatial ability after age 8 (Linn & Petersen, 1985; Maccoby & Jacklin, 1974). (The other consistent gender difference occurs in aggressive behaviors, discussed in the next chapter.) This male superiority in visual-spatial ability after age 8 is one gender difference that appears across social classes in most cultures and is maintained through old age, although the magnitude of the difference has been decreasing since 1974 (Becker & Hedges, 1984). Overall, gender accounts for less than 5% of the variability of scores on visual-spatial tests (Hyde, 1981).

The size of the gender difference in visual-spatial ability varies from small to relatively large depending upon the specific visual-spatial task examined. Of the three subtypes of visual-spatial ability— spatial visualization, spatial perception, and mental rotation—only the latter subtype shows strong gender differences. *Spatial visualization* tasks, such as the embedded figure test (Figure 2.5) and the Spatial Relations subtest of the Differential Aptitude Test, require analytic ability for completion,

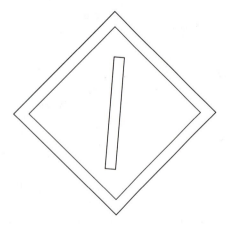

Figure 2.6 The rod-and-frame test, used to measure field dependence/independence. The center rod must be aligned to the true vertical despite the tilt of the frame.

and do not demonstrate significant gender differences, especially recently (Feingold, 1988; Hyde, 1981; Linn & Petersen, 1985). Studies since 1974 have found $d = .13$, down from .30 in studies before 1974. In fact, the more recent the publication, the smaller the size of d found (Rosenthal & Rubin, 1982).

Spatial perception, a second subtype of visual-spatial ability, involves measures of horizontality/verticality, as in the rod-and-frame test (Figure 2.6), where the subject must adjust a luminous rod inside a luminous frame to the true vertical. Both the frame and the rod are tilted, and, since the room is darkened, the subject has few cues with which to align the rod. Those who are accurate in their judgment of the true vertical are termed *field independent*; those who are inaccurate are termed *field dependent* (theoretically, they are assumed to be influenced by the frame or "field"). Some spatial perception tests, such as the rod-and-frame test, rely heavily on kinesthetic cues for solution, whereas other tests requiring judgments of horizontality rely on spatial knowledge. Supporting the importance of spatial experience in these tasks are the age trends found. Gender differences in this ability increase after age 18 ($d = .64$); smaller differences are found with students aged 7 to 17 ($d = .37$) (Linn & Petersen, 1985). When differential experience and knowledge are controlled for, gender differences are reduced or reversed (De Lisi & McGillicuddy-De Lisi, 1988: Liben & Golbeck, 1986).

The third subtype of visual-spatial ability involves *mental rotation* of pictures and shows the strongest gender difference in favor of males, although the strength of the difference varies with the test used (Linn & Petersen, 1985; Wattenawaha & Clements, 1982). Typically, a two- or three-dimensional figure is presented and questions are asked that require the observer to picture the figure from a different perspective. (Imagine how Figure 2.5 would look upside down.) On tests like these (for example, the space subtest of the Primary Mental Abilities test), $d = .26$ starting at age 10 (Linn & Petersen, 1985). These differences remain throughout the life span (Willis & Schaie, 1988). However, on tasks such as the Shepard-Metzler mental rotations test, which measures speed of response to different amounts of figure rotation, the gender difference is $d = .94$, close to one full standard deviation, starting at age 13. Such a large effect means that among those scoring above average, 74% will be male, 26% female. Thus the largest gender difference in cognitive ability yet found occurs on a mental rotation task requiring rapid analog processing. Such gender differences may reflect differential strategy usage, differential rate of rotation, or differential caution. Training has been found to reduce or eliminate gender differences on these tasks (Lohman, 1988; Willis & Schaie, 1988).

Thus, some males appear to have an advantage over some females on tasks that require rapid mental rotation of objects and, after age 18, on tasks requiring recognition of verticality and horizontality. The implications of these findings are unclear because these specific abilities are not required for many tasks. Although map reading and finding one's way in an environment may appear to tap such abilities, the relationship is a modest one and gender differences on these tasks generally are non-significant (J. L. Pearson & Ferguson, 1989; J. L. Pearson & Ialongo, 1986). Visual-spatial ability may be involved in some aspects of engineering and architecture, although social factors play a larger role in achievement in those fields. For example, women were only 2% of all engineers in the United States in 1978, although the size of even the largest gender difference in visual-spatial ability would suggest that women should comprise at least 25%.

Visual-spatial ability sometimes has been linked to performance in math and science, but such correlations probably reflect different contributing factors (Connor & Serbin, 1985; Linn & Hyde, 1989; Linn & Petersen, 1986). For example, Sherman (1983) found that girls' visual-spatial skill (measured by spatial visualization) in the eighth and ninth grades predicted their continuation of math for four more years. However, such skills were not predictive of males' continuing with math. Nor did such skills account for gender differences in math performance. Nor, as we just saw, is spatial visualization the type of visual-spatial skill that shows strong gender differences. The main way visual-spatial ability may be linked to math and science is through use of problem-solving strategies. As discussed later, males and females may develop and use different strategies as a result of different types of experiences. Differences in such strategies then may affect performance in all three areas.

Because this skill, or set of skills, appears to be the one area where the most gender differences are found, much attention has been paid to the reasons for such differences. Interestingly, there has been more interest in biological than social processes affecting gender differences in this area and little emphasis on the fact that the differences themselves frequently are small and do not occur on all tasks measuring this ability. (See Caplan, MacPherson, & Tobin, 1985, 1986, for a critique of these approaches.)

Biological explanations A number of biological factors have been examined in the search for explanations of the gender differences in visual-spatial ability—genetic, hormonal, and brain lateralization factors. The research still is inconclusive, and none of it rules out the likelihood of interactions with social factors.

Substantial research into genetic influences on visual-spatial ability has been conducted, but the research findings have been inconsistent (Linn & Petersen, 1986, Vandenberg & Kuse, 1979). Although there is some inferential evidence that genetic control over these abilities may be recessive and carried on the X chromosome, the research frequently has been flawed with regard to statistical techniques, age corrections, and types of tasks used. At this point, then, the X-linked hypothesis is still a tentative one.

Hormone levels appear related to some forms of spatial ability but not in predictable ways. High estrogen levels may be associated with poorer visual-spatial performance than low estrogen levels, whereas moderate androgen levels appear related to better visual-spatial performance than either high or low androgen levels (Hood, Draper, Crockett, & Petersen, 1987; Kimura, 1989b). However, effects of these hormones are not always found and do not occur across all visual-spatial tasks. Furthermore, gender differences in visual-spatial ability appear as early as age 8, before pubertal hormonal changes make the sexes hormonally distinct; therefore, it seems unlikely that hormone levels by themselves can account for such gender differences.

Yet, the fact that gender differences in visual-spatial ability appear to increase at adolescence suggests pubertal hormones may be involved, perhaps in indirect ways. Such hormones may affect brain organization or interact with a brain already presensitized by prenatal hormones. As we have seen, male fetuses typically are exposed to higher androgen levels prenatally than are female fetuses. Research trying to link prenatal hormone level to later cognitive abilities is just beginning and the preliminary results suggest that the relationships are quite complex (T. Adler, 1989a; Hier & Crowley, 1982; Hines & Shipley, 1984; Jacklin, 1989). In some cases, girls exposed prenatally to unusually high levels of androgen evidence better visual-spatial skills than other girls, whereas boys exposed prenatally to unusually low levels of androgen evidence poorer visual-spatial skills than other boys. These findings may be mediated by preference for different types of toys. (The effects of toy usage on visual-spatial ability will be discussed in the next section.)

Prenatal hormones also may have an effect on visual-spatial ability through their organizing effect on the brain. Females appear to use both hemispheres more than males on a variety of tasks. Spatial ability, primarily located in the right hemisphere and generally nonlinguistic in nature, may require use of the right hemisphere without the left, which may be more difficult for some females than some males. Estrogen levels, higher in postpubertal females than males, seems to facilitate activation of the left hemisphere more than the right, perhaps accounting for women's lesser visual-spatial skills (Kimura, 1989b). Yet the relationship between brain organization and visual-spatial skills is not simple or direct (Bryden, 1986; Geschwind & Galaburda, 1985; Hines & Shipley, 1984; Newcombe, Dubas, & Baenninger, 1989). For example, greater use of the right hemisphere does not always lead to better visual-spatial performance. Furthermore, differences in brain organization patterns can *result* from differential socialization experiences and/or use of different cognitive strategies. Thus, even if evidence that males and females differ in brain organization becomes better established, we still will not know whether this difference is due to prenatal hormonal factors or postnatal environmental ones.

The fact that girls typically reach puberty before boys also may account for some gender differences in visual-spatial ability. Deborah Waber (1976, 1977) suggested that, regardless of gender, later-maturing children scored better than early-maturing children on spatial-ability tasks, perhaps because early maturity is associated with predominant use of the left hemisphere of the brain. Although intriguing, the relationship between maturity and visual-spatial ability is much more complex than originally hypothesized and may be most salient among extremely late or extremely early maturers (Bryden & Vrbancic, 1988; Linn & Petersen, 1985; Newcombe & Dubas, 1987; Newcombe et al., 1989; Waber, Mann, Merola, & Moylan, 1985). Furthermore, psychosocial variables still appear more powerful. For example, Newcombe and Bandura (1983) found that although spatial ability in 11-year-olds was significantly related to timing of puberty, it was more related to psychological variables, such as instrumental personality traits and math/science interests.

Thus, the research on biological factors, although suggestive, clearly presents only part of the picture with respect to causes of visual-spatial ability.

Social explanations   Of all the social factors studied, the most evidence has accumulated regarding the positive effects of experience and practice on visual-spatial skills for both females and males (Baenninger & Newcombe, 1989; Connor & Serbin, 1985; De Lisi & McGillicuddy-De Lisi, 1988; Kalichman, 1988; Lohman, 1988; Signorella, Jamison, & Krupa, 1989). For both sexes, participation in spatial activities positively correlates with high scores on tests of spatial ability, and both sexes benefit from specific training in visual-spatial skills. Thus, the general group gender difference found in visual-spatial ability is likely to be due to the differential experience the two sexes have in using this ability.

Why do boys have more experience with tasks requiring visual-spatial skills than girls? The primary reason appears to be that toys and activities that are considered masculine, such as using hand tools and building models, utilize such skills. Differential experience with such toys and activities begins by preschool and is strongly correlated with later visual-spatial ability (Serbin & Connor, 1979; Serbin, Zelkowitz, Doyle, Gold, & Wheaton, 1990; Tracy, 1987). Boys' greater access to and play with such toys may reflect the gender typing of the toys, or they may reflect the greater interest such toys hold for boys than for girls. It is possible that prenatal hormones may make play with such toys more satisfying for boys than girls. This suggestion is supported by the finding that girls exposed to androgens prenatally appear to prefer to play with stereotypic boys' toys over stereotypic girls' toys (reported in T. Adler, 1989a). The gender-typing explanation also has support from the finding that masculine-sex-typed individuals are most likely to favor "masculine" toys and activities and also are likely to have the best spatial performance (Newcombe & Bandura, 1983; Signorella & Jamison, 1986; Signorella et al., 1989).

The fact that the largest gender differences on a visual-spatial task appear on timed mental rotation tasks suggests that gender differences in visual-spatial ability may be less a function of actual ability than of speed of response. As discussed earlier with respect to performance on the SATs, females appear more cautious when confronted with novel tasks than males, which tends to slow females down (see also Gallagher, 1989). In cultures where female autonomy is encouraged—for example, among the Canadian Eskimos—no gender difference in visual-spatial ability has been found (Berry, 1966; MacArthur, 1967). This lack of gender differences among the Eskimos also may be due to both sexes' using the same problem-solving strategies. Visual strategies appear more effective than verbal ones on certain visual-spatial tasks (Kearins, 1981), and such strategies appear to be more common among males than females. Such findings may explain why training programs are so effective in improving visual-spatial performance.

In sum, males as a group tend to perform better than females as a group on visual-spatial tasks, especially those involving fast mental rotation of images and field independence. These differences can best be explained by differential experience with tasks involving visual-spatial ability, perhaps interacting with hormonally induced differences in brain organization. The implication of such specific differences in ability for life tasks and activities remains unclear, especially since training appears to eliminate the differences altogether.

Cognitive Styles
Are males better learners than females or more likely to use analytical reasoning? The answer to both questions is no. However, there may be gender differences in cognitive style or preferences for certain styles. In this section, we will examine research that relates to learning facility, analytic ability, field dependence, cognitive styles, and problem-solving strategies. This research then will be connected to a topic of increasing importance, computer literacy.

There are no overall gender differences in *learning ability*, based on reviews of over 2000 studies (Maccoby & Jacklin, 1974). Both boys and girls are equally capable with respect to concept mastery, reasoning ability, and learning repetitive tasks. Women tend to be faster in processing certain types of information (McGuinness & Pribram, 1978), perhaps because they do better than males in perceptual speed and accuracy tests (Antill & Cunningham, 1982). On mechanical reasoning tests, males generally perform better than females, probably as a function of experience and sex typing.

In research focusing directly on *analytic ability*, few gender differences have been found. There are no differences in analytic ability when verbal or auditory materials are employed, nor when spatial ability is controlled (Petersen & Wittig, 1979). Even with materials tapping the subtype of visual-spatial ability that requires some type of analytic strategy for solution (spacial visualization), such as the embedded figure test (Figure 2.5), males have only a slight edge (Linn & Petersen, 1985). Early research

(D. M. Broverman, Klaiber, Kobayaski, & Vogel, 1968) that suggested that females perform better on simple, overlearned perceptual-motor tasks that involve little thinking, whereas males perform better on tasks requiring inhibition or perceptual restructuring—a "higher" cognitive process—has been discredited (Maccoby & Jacklin, 1974).

Historically, analytic ability was conflated with *field independence*. As we saw in the previous section, field independence involves responding to a stimulus without being distracted by its context, such as required by the rod-and-frame test (Figure 2.6). Such a task actually taps a subtype of visual-spatial ability labeled horizontality/verticality. Males typically perform better than females on such tasks, especially after age 18. From research done in the 1940s and 1950s, Witkin and colleagues (1962) characterized males as field independent and females as field dependent. Field dependence/independence was viewed not just in terms of visual-spatial ability but as a cognitive style, a personality trait, a way of being in the world (Witkin & Goodenough, 1981). The terms themselves suggest a pejorative view of female performance, which might also be described as demonstrating field "relatedness," "sensitivity," or "adaptation" (Haaken, 1988). In any case, the size of the gender difference is not large enough to label males one way and females another.

But there is other suggestive evidence that males and females may differ in *cognitive style*. Recently, controversy has erupted over whether women have particular "ways of knowing." Belenky and colleagues (1986) reported from their interviews with 135 women that a woman assumes one of five major epistemological positions: silence, in which she feels she has nothing to say; received knowledge, in which she learns by listening to others; subjective knowledge, in which she values her own personal experiences and feelings above all else; procedural knowledge, in which she uses (in either a connected or alienated way) objective procedures for learning and communicating; and constructed knowledge, in which she integrates objective and subjective ways of knowing. Although men weren't studied, the authors imply that unlike men, women learn best or at least prefer constructed knowing and a connected type of procedural knowing. In a way, this hypothesis fits in with Witkin's view that women are more influenced by and "connected" to the "field." Such stylistic preferences may be why women are less interested in fields emphasizing purely objective procedural styles, such as math, science, and technology, and prefer fields in which they can feel connected to people and use their subjective experiences, such as in the arts, humanities, and social services. Although the work of Belenky et al. has generated much public interest, its scientific basis is weak (see M. Crawford, 1988). Thus, at this point, although there may be different ways of knowing, it's not clear that there are particular *gendered* ways of knowing.

However, some evidence exists that males and females tend to use different *problem-solving strategies*. Boys tend to use visual cues and spatial strategies more often and more effectively than girls (M. J. Allen & Hogeland, 1978; Linn & Petersen, 1986). As discussed previously, these differences partially may account for the somewhat better and faster performance by males on mathematical problems and certain visual-spatial tasks. Boys also may use autonomous learning strategies more than girls, which facilitates performance in novel situations (Kimball, 1989). In contrast, females may be more affected by the context of a problem than males (Fagley & Miller, 1990). All these differences in problem-solving style appear to be based on experience. Boys generally receive more practice in, and reinforcement for, problem-solving behavior from parents and teachers than do girls, making boys more familiar with such activities and more proficient at them. Fortunately, gender differences in problem solving may be decreasing, probably because of increasing equality in the ways girls and boys are treated (Berger & Gold, 1979).

No gender difference has been found with respect to *cognitive complexity* (preference for complex rather than simple information-processing demands) (Tanaka, Panter, & Winborne, 1988). However, females compared to males have been found to *persist* longer in cognitive tasks—that is, females appear to try to maximize the utility of limited amounts of information (Tanaka et al., 1988). Such a tendency may relate to previously mentioned hypotheses of women's greater field "dependence" and preference for connected knowing. These tendencies, to the extent that they actually exist, have been linked to women's subordinate status in our culture. For survival purposes, it is more important for the individual in a subordinate role to pay attention to all environmental cues than it is for the individual in the more powerful role. However, more research is needed to substantiate these hypotheses.

A question of increasing interest, given that gender differences with respect to cognitive styles

may exist, is how such styles might affect use of computers. Research on computer programming suggests that males and females may differ in programming styles (Turkle, 1984; Turkle & Papert, 1990). Males appear more likely than females to prefer a formal and abstract approach, which heavily emphasizes logic and control; females appear to prefer a more personal and concrete approach, which emphasizes intuition and creativity. If the more formal style of programming is the one that's rewarded, females may feel more discouraged than do males with respect to programming. Females and males also appear to differ in their general orientation toward computers, with females more likely than males to use computers just for a particular purpose and males more likely than females to use computers for fun, to amuse themselves (as seen in any video arcade) (Vernon-Gerstenfeld, 1989). Whether such stylistic differences discourage girls from using computers or whether other social factors are involved, it is clear that girls' interest in computers decreases with age. One study (L. S. Gray, 1983) found that among first graders, girls were as interested as boys in learning to program computers. By the sixth grade, however, boys interested in computers outnumbered girls two to one, and by the ninth grade, more than four-fifths of the interested students were males.

Boys are not only more interested in computers but also increasingly use computers with respect to programming, video games, home usage, computer courses, and computer camps (Kiesler, Sproull, & Eccles, 1985; Lips & Temple, 1988; Miura, 1987; L. J. Nelson & Cooper, 1990). For example, in 1983, boys outnumbered girls in computer camps five to one. Furthermore, boys know more than girls about computers and are more confident of their ability with them. Thus, by college, males have vastly more experience with computers than females. Yet, males have no greater aptitude for computers than females. Why, then, do females use computers less and express less interest? Cultural factors, such as the sex typing of computer software and use context, combined with social expectations appear to play critical roles.

Most computer games and educational programming involve such "masculine" themes as sports, war, and violence. Such themes are less likely to appeal to girls. Evidence exists that both boys and girls become anxious when forced to use other-sex-oriented software in a public setting, like the computer center (J. Cooper, Hall, & Huff, 1990). Since most software is male-oriented, it is not surprising that girls stay away. Computers also generally are associated with math and technology, often introduced into schools and used in math programs (Griffiths, 1988; Kiesler et al., 1985). To the extent that girls prefer other subjects and activities to math and science, they also will prefer other subjects and activities to computing. The reasons for these preferences may be based on preferences for more connected knowing styles over more separate knowing styles, as just noted, and/or to the masculine sex typing of the fields themselves.

Parents too tend to view computers as a male domain since boys are more likely than girls to have a computer at home (L. J. Nelson & Cooper, 1990). Since having a computer at home is related to computer usage, and computer usage is related to feeling competent with computers, these factors alone can explain gender differences in perceived competence. When computer experience is held constant or when it is required for a course, female and male college students express similar attitudes toward computers and similar aptitudes (Arch & Cummins, 1989; Ogletree & Williams, 1990). Thus, it is important for females to receive specific encouragement to use computers. Otherwise, girls tend to shy away, a trend that has serious implications for future career opportunities and the future of our technological society (R. Perry & Greber, 1990).

In sum, no gender differences exist in analytic or computer abilities, although males and females may use or prefer different cognitive strategies or styles. Preliminary hypotheses suggest that an autonomous cognitive style (perhaps preferred by males) may facilitate performance on mathematical problem-solving tasks, whereas a more connected cognitive style (perhaps preferred by females) may facilitate performance on interpersonal tasks. Cognitive styles are a product of experience and, as is clear in the case of computers, boys and girls tend to have different experiences.

Creativity

Another area in which cognitive differences have been thought to exist is creativity. A problem here is with the definition and tasks used to measure the construct. When creativity is measured by the number of responses produced to a stimulus (for example, "List all the possible uses of a paper clip") or by the uniqueness of the responses, females are superior, especially if verbal materials are used (Kershner & Ledger, 1985; Maccoby & Jacklin, 1974). When creativity is measured by career accomplishments, however, males excel, because most awards and recognition go to males.

The relationship between sex typing and creativity is unclear. There is some evidence that androgynous individuals show more creativity than sex-typed individuals, perhaps because such individuals are gender-aschematic (Harrington & Andersen, 1981; Lott, 1978). Sex-typed individuals may be more cognitively bounded by their gender schema than androgynous individuals. Creative individuals tend to rate themselves high on instrumental traits, but this relationship appears clearer for males than for females. For whatever reason, there is not much current research on this topic.

▲   Summary

Males and females show a pattern of both similarities and differences with respect to physical and cognitive functioning. Given the strong expectation that gender differences are large and widespread, the research findings reveal more similarities than differences, especially in the cognitive area. In the physical area, the sexes differ most clearly on those aspects related to male and female reproductive roles: anatomy and hormone production. In other physical areas, gender differences are greatest with respect to life expectancy and motor behavior, both a function of biological and social factors.

In the cognitive area, gender differences are nil in overall intelligence, memory, analytic ability, computer ability, and creativity (unless measured verbally). Females have a small edge in verbal abilities, males a small edge in mathematical problem-solving abilities after age 11 (although there are far more male than female math geniuses), and males have a moderate-size edge in visual-spatial ability after age 8, especially when mental rotations are involved. Gender differences in cognitive strategies may exist in certain situations.

A variety of physical and environmental explanations have been suggested to account for the three cognitive differences that have been found. Prenatal hormones may affect the organization of the brain, which indirectly may be related to cognitive performance, but this research still is speculative at this time and would account for only some of the gender differences found—mainly mathematical genius and strong visual-spatial ability. Environmental explanations emphasizing differential expectations and differential experiences have good support. Boys are expected to excel in math and visual-spatial ability and boys receive more encouragement and experience than girls in activities related to the development of these skills. Girls are expected to excel in verbal abilities and receive more encouragement and experience in these areas.

Some sort of interactional hypothesis seems warranted. It seems likely that some biological predisposition, possibly due to prenatal hormones, interacts with the environment to determine whether the ability itself will be actualized. The environment can either reinforce or discourage such actualization, depending on the behavior's gender-appropriateness in that society. The fact that most gender differences are not apparent in early childhood and emerge before puberty undercuts a purely physiological explanation. Expectations of performance shape a child's behavior, and these expectations vary along gender lines.

An important question to keep in mind as we continue to look at reported gender differences involves the implications of such differences. Because individual differences are so broad and because adult achievement and performance involve so much more than pure ability, no clear-cut predictions on the basis of sex are possible. The similarities between the sexes are as notable as, if not more notable than, the differences.

▲ Recommended Reading

Benbow, C. P. (1988). Sex differences in mathematical reasoning ability in intellectually talented preadolescents: Their nature, effects, and possible causes. *Behavioral and Brain Sciences, 119,* 169–232. A summary of the controversial research on precocious math achievers, followed by commentaries from over 40 other prominent researchers in the field.

Benderly, B. L. (1987). *The myth of two minds: What gender means and doesn't mean.* New York: Doubleday. A clearly written review of assumed sex differences, showing how cultural biases have affected research on gender.

Kimura, D. (1989, November). How sex hormones boost or cut intellectual ability. *Psychology Today,* pp. 62–66. A good overview of recent research on the effects of sex differences on cognitive tasks. The article by Beryl Lieff Benderly that follows in the same issue of *Psychology Today* explores how such research gets misrepresented by the media.

Linn, M. C., & Petersen, A. C. (1986). A meta-analysis of gender differences in spatial ability: Implications for mathematics and science achievement. In J. S. Hyde & M. C. Linn (Eds.), *The psychology of gender: Advances through meta-analysis* (pp. 67–101). Baltimore: Johns Hopkins University Press. An important article showing the power of meta-analysis to further our understanding of cognitive gender differences.

Chapter 3

Comparisons of Personality and Social Behavior

Generally, when we talk about masculinity and femininity, we are talking about certain personality and social characteristics. Females are seen as emotional, submissive, talkative, aware of others' feelings, and so forth; males are seen as possessing opposite traits. Figure 3.1 exemplifies one part of the stereotype.

In examining the factual bases for stereotypes in the areas of personality and social behavior, a number of difficulties arise. Although research problems can and do plague all areas of gender research, there are particular problems we need to be aware of in reviewing research on personality and social behavior. First, we need to remember that situational factors interact with individual factors in determining behavior. Thus, it is inaccurate to speak of social traits, such as assertiveness,

existing solely within the individual. A person in isolation is not assertive.

A second problem arises when social behavior must be operationally defined—that is, described in terms of objective measurement. Although cognitive differences, such as verbal ability, can be measured by a variety of paper-and-pencil tests (for example, spelling, reading comprehension), it is much more difficult operationally to define and measure concepts like dependence, which can refer to clinging behaviors, social responsiveness, number of friends, and so forth. If researchers use different definitions of the same concept, the results are difficult to compare.

A variety of person-related problems must also be considered. Many social behaviors and the way they are measured change as a function of age. Thus, it is important to take the age of the participants into account in comparing studies and in drawing conclusions. For example, research done with college students, generally aged 18 to 22, may not accurately generalize to all adults. Similarly, findings from research based on male participants may not accurately be generalized to females, as many researchers have done (for example, Kohlberg, 1969). A related problem occurs when research on White participants is generalized to people of different racial and ethnic backgrounds. Especially in the area of social behavior, different ethnic and racial groups may demonstrate different patterns (for example, K. A. Adams, 1980, 1983).

It is important to recognize the tremendous range of individual differences in the area of personality and social behavior. Such differences overshadow any gender-based ones. Thus, clear-cut differences between males and females are difficult to find and of little use in predicting an individual's performance.

The behaviors discussed in this chapter can be grouped into four major areas: personality and temperament, communication patterns, prosocial behaviors (those that facilitate interpersonal relationships), and power-related behaviors. Although much overlap occurs among these four areas, the prosocial and power distinction parallels those made by personality theorists (for example, Buss & Finn, 1987) as well as the stereotypic view of women as being more interpersonal and of men as being more agentic or active. We will come across a number of common themes: the importance of gender as opposed to sex, the importance of person-situation interactions, and the importance of race of subject.

Figure 3.1 Illustrative sex "difference" in personality? (Copyright 1973 by Bülbül. Reprinted by permission.)

▲   Personality and Temperament

The term *personality* refers to the distinctive character of an individual, which includes traits, behaviors, emotions, and thoughts, whereas *temperament* refers to emotional mood or disposition only. Both areas have been assumed to show gender differences. Most personality theorists, however, emphasize individual, rather than sex-specific, differences. Psychodynamic theorists, starting with Freud, are exceptions. For our purposes, a brief look at personality development as related to sex typing will prove instructive.

Personality Development

When one talks about personality development, the distinction between stereotypic gender differences and true gender differences often is difficult to determine. As noted in Chapter 1, people generally are in a great deal of agreement as to what constitutes the gender stereotypes, and these stereotypes are learned by ages 3 to 5. However, children do not necessarily behave accordingly. In particular, girls show much less behavioral sex typing than boys (Maccoby & Jacklin, 1974; Stericker &

Kurdek, 1982; Urberg, 1982). Between ages 3 and 11, it is very unusual for boys to prefer activities or toys ascribed to girls, but it is quite common for girls to choose "boys'" toys and activities. In fact, between ages 6 and 9, most girls prefer "male" activities, perhaps because such activities are more interesting or more fun.

In contrast to behavioral sex typing, sex-typed personality traits are slower to develop in boys than in girls, perhaps because the traits associated with masculinity are relatively more adult and perhaps unnatural than the traits associated with femininity (S. W. Davis, Williams, & Best, 1982; Stericker & Kurdek, 1982). For example, the independent, assertive, and unemotional parts of the male stereotype are difficult for most children and, perhaps, for most adults to acquire. With puberty come increased societal pressures to conform to gender expectations. From grades 6 to 12, increasing consistency between self-description and sex-role expectations is found (Donelson, 1977; Feather, 1984). These gender differences conform to the two sets of stereotypes discussed in Chapter 1, variously labeled as expressive and instrumental (Parsons & Bales,

1955) or communal and agentic (Bakan, 1966). After grade 7, females tend to rate themselves significantly higher than males on expressive-nurturant traits; males tend to rate themselves significantly higher than females on instrumental-active traits, differences that have been quite stable despite societal changes over the last 30 years (R. O. Baldwin, 1984; Galambos, Almeida, & Petersen, 1990). These results hold true for Blacks as well as Whites, at least among college students (R. O. Baldwin, 1987). Nonetheless, recent research does suggest that gender differences with respect to instrumental-active traits are decreasing (Gill, Stockard, Johnson, & Williams, 1987; Snell, 1989). Remaining are gender differences in the expressive-relational dimension.

With gender stereotypes being as pervasive as they are, it is not surprising that most people see themselves as behaving in gender-appropriate ways. Whether they actually behave this way is a different matter. This question will be the focus of the rest of the chapter. Even when behavioral differences are found, they are as or more likely to be due to situational factors, differential learning opportunities, or societal rewards as to differences in personality.

The question of the causal sequence between personality and behavior is an important one. Given the pervasive pattern of women rating themselves higher than men on expressive-communal qualities and men rating themselves higher than women on instrumental-agentic qualities, it is easy to view these traits as being innate, or at least basic to women and men. It therefore seems to follow that gender differences in personality *cause* gender differences in behavior. However, as discussed in Chapter 1 (see Figure 1.2), it is just as likely that gender differences in behavior *cause* gender differences in personality. That is, it is because of the particular roles each sex plays and thereby the distinctive situations each sex encounters that different traits develop (Deaux & Major, 1987; Eagly, 1987b; Epstein, 1988). For example, individuals who spend a large amount of time caring for others, especially young children, will be encouraged to develop nurturant and expressive traits. Individuals who spend a large amount of time in a competitive hierarchical employment situation will be encouraged to develop agentic and assertive traits. In cross-cultural research, Whiting and Edwards (1988) found just that: an individual who spends enough time with infants will become a nurturer. In most but not all cultures, it is females who spend much time with infants.

Not only do females in North America take care of young children more than do males, but during adolescence, girls and boys spend much of their spare time doing different things as well (Timmer, Eccles, & O'Brien, 1985). Adolescent girls spend much more time than their male peers doing household work and grooming activities, while adolescent boys spend much more time than their female peers engaged in sports. These different activities, conforming as they do to gender stereotypes, may encourage different traits and behaviors to develop. For example, participation in sports may facilitate competitive traits more than does housework.

This view of roles and experiences as affecting personality also fits in with certain developmental findings. Although most research concentrates on children and college students, personality development continues throughout the life span. When personality development is defined in terms of ego development (increasingly complex perceptions of the self and others; Loevinger, 1976), gender differences increase from childhood to early adolescence (around age 13), remain moderately large during adolescence, then decline among college students to essentially no difference among the post-college-aged (Cohn, 1991). The direction of the difference favors females, who consistently score about one stage higher than males in maturity as they go from impulsiveness, to self-protection, to social conformity, to self-awareness, to conscientiousness, and finally to individuality and autonomy (few reach this last stage). The different social experiences of children and adolescents noted earlier seem the most likely explanation for these developmental patterns.

A number of studies report that people tend to become more androgynous (that is, combine both expressive and agentic competencies) as they mature from late adolescence to middle adulthood (Gutmann, 1987; Jung, 1956; Levinson, 1978; V. Mitchell & Helson, 1990). Men appear to become more acceptant of communal-expressive characteristics with age, while women appear to become more agentic and confident. The process, however, may not be linear. Women college graduates appear to become more feminine-sex-typed during their 20s as they prepare for or engage in parenting (Helson & Moane, 1987). However, these same women become more androgynous between their late 20s and mid-40s as their child-rearing days recede. Thus, it is important to speak cautiously of generalized gender differences in personality across the life span.

Despite strong evidence that gender differences in personality are a function of gender differences in social expectations, experiences, and roles, and are most apparent starting at adolescence, many believe gender differences in personality are either biological or arise from early childhood experiences. The biological evidence is tentative and stems from recent research with twins and adolescents. One study found genetics accounted for 20% to 48% of the observed individual differences in instrumental-active and nurturant-expressive traits in a sample of twins aged 8 to 14 (J. E. Mitchell, Baker, & Jacklin, 1989). The remaining 52% to 80% of the variance was due to environmental influences specific to each individual. Replication of these findings, especially with twins at different ages and who were reared apart, is needed. Another study attempted to link sex-typed traits with hormonal changes at puberty (Udry & Talbert, 1988). Although some sex-linked personality traits were found to be correlated with testosterone level (traits such as dominance, outgoingness, sensitivity, and understanding), gender differences in testosterone level did not explain gender differences in personality since girls are much more sensitive than boys to this hormone. Furthermore, other research that has attempted to link pubertal timing with increased sex typing of personality traits has found little support (Galambos et al., 1990). Thus, biological explanations of gender difference in personality are still speculative at this time.

Nonetheless, a number of personality theorists, mainly psychodynamic ones, do posit basic gender differences in personality. Freud suggested that anatomical differences combined with psychosexual dynamics lead girls and boys to develop different personality traits by age 5 or 6 (this theory will be discussed in more depth in Chapters 4 and 6). Because Freud thought that the penis was the intrinsically superior sex organ, he stated that boys' recognition that they had one, and that girls did not, led boys to feel superior and to develop active-autonomous traits at the resolution of the phallic stage of psychosexual development. At the same time, according to Freud, both boys and girls develop their gender identity after identifying with the same-sex parent. In this view, girls must identify with someone who has an inferior sex organ, and therefore girls develop feelings of inferiority and traits of vanity, passivity, and dependence; feelings and traits that are "normal" and "natural." This aspect of Freud's theory has very little empirical support, as we will see in other chapters. Nonetheless, it figures prominently in cultural theories of gender differences.

More recently, feminist psychodynamic theories (for example, Chodorow, 1978, 1990; J. B. Miller, 1976, 1984) have posited basic gender differences in personality due to the fact that it is mainly women who raise children. According to these theories, girls develop their sense of self, which starts to emerge during the first year of life, in the context of a relationship with a similar other. In contrast, boys experience a disjunction between their first "object" of attachment and their own developing sense of self. Consequently, boys develop an identity characterized by independence and autonomous strivings and a rejection of the feminine, whereas girls develop an identity characterized by interpersonal involvement and empathy. Direct empirical tests of these theories are sorely lacking, but their implications with respect to gender differences in behaviors and attitudes are far-reaching. We will evaluate these theories further as we examine specific personal and social behaviors.

Temperament

With regard to temperament, females have often been thought to be more passive than males. However, the term *passivity* can mean a variety of different things: submissiveness, lack of sexual interest, dependence, inactivity, and so on. From the research on the possible components of passivity, it is clear that little support exists for the assumption that females are uniformly more passive than males.

Among researchers, *temperament* generally refers to basic emotional dispositions. Studies of infants show few consistent gender differences in the area of emotionality, but male infants do appear to be more irritable, emotionally labile, less attentive, and less socially responsive than female infants (Haviland & Malatesta, 1982; Maccoby & Jacklin, 1974; D. Phillips et al., 1978). The situations that occasion emotional outbursts are different for boys and for girls from age 3 to 5. Boys react most to frustration situations, conflicts with adults, and fear-inducing situations; girls respond most to conflicts with other children. Girls also decrease their total emotional responsiveness at a faster rate than boys.

Among adolescents, boys and girls experience the same intensity of emotions but differ with respect to the types of emotions they feel most strongly and most frequently and the context in which these emotions occur. In one study (Stapley & Haviland, 1989), 5th graders through 11th graders rated 3 (out of 12) emotions as most salient—joy, interest, and anger. Girls reported somewhat greater salience than boys of negative emotions, especially sadness, shyness, shame, guilt, and self-hostility. On the other hand, contempt was more salient for boys than girls. Boys and girls also differed with respect to emotional contexts. Girls found affiliation events to be associated with the strongest emotions; boys found activities and achievement events to be associated with the strongest emotions. Thus, it's not that girls experience more intense emotions than boys, but that the types of and contexts giving rise to emotions differ by gender.

Perhaps because females report more sadness than males, females also report crying significantly more frequently and intensely than males, and in a wider variety of situations (Lombardo, Cretser, Lombardo, & Mathis, 1983). However, both males and females agree on the kinds of situations in which crying is most likely to occur. Why females may in fact be sadder than males will be discussed in Chapter 8, when the effects of gender roles on mental health, and in particular depression, are examined.

A small tendency has been found for girls to be more timid than boys in early childhood (Jacklin, Maccoby, & Doering, 1983). Girls also consistently report more fears than boys and are rated as more fearful by others (W. K. Silverman & Nelles, 1987). However, observational studies do not show females, in childhood and adolescence, actually to evidence more timid behaviors than males of that age (L. R. Brody, 1984; Maccoby & Jacklin, 1974). This apparent gender difference in fearfulness may be a function of sex typing, since reported fears correlate significantly with femininity scores (L. R. Brody, Hay, & Vandewater, 1990; Krasnoff, 1981). The difference in fearfulness also may be a function of gender expectations. Girls, especially those high in "feminine" traits, may be more likely to admit to fear or anxieties because such admissions are more socially acceptable from, and more expected of, them.

In this regard, Birnbaum and colleagues (Birnbaum & Croll, 1984; Birnbaum, Nosanchuk, & Croll, 1980) found that preschoolers had marked stereotypes about sex differences in emotionality. Females were more associated with fear, sadness, and happiness, and males were more associated with anger. Similar stereotypes were held by parents and were reflected in television programming. Parents, in practice, accepted anger in boys more than in girls and accepted fear in girls more than in boys. Thus, girls actually may show more fear than boys because fear is more socially acceptable for girls than boys. These stereotypes may also lead more females than males to report fearfulness. The equation of fear with femininity also may explain why males often engage in risk-taking activities to prove that they are not fearful; that is, not feminine.

Thus, in terms of emotionality, male infants appear somewhat more emotionally expressive than female infants, but these differences disappear and then reverse themselves during grade school and adolescence, especially for the specific emotions of fear and sadness. With respect to anger and hostility, however, girls increasingly inhibit displaying and even recognizing such emotions. A curious aspect of research in this area is defining emotionality solely as fear or as the number of emotional upsets. Emotions, of course, cover a wide range of feelings, including hostility. Yet, although more males than females display and report hostile feelings, males are rarely described as "emotional," as illustrated in Figure 3.1. We need to recognize that the term *emotion* is itself socially constructed (Shields, 1987).

The developmental pattern just noted suggests that socialization practices may actively work to encourage boys to minimize or mask their emotional expressiveness. For example, Buck (1977) found that boys between ages 4 and 6 increasingly inhibited and masked their overt reactions to emotion-producing situations (in this case, slides depicting emotion-laden scenes). Girls, however, continued to respond relatively freely to such situations. Such differences, becoming more extreme during adolescence, clearly conform to gender stereotypes of females as being emotional. This developmental pattern suggests that gender differences in emotional expressiveness may be more a consequence of gender socialization and social roles than a basis for them. Research on socialization practices supports this conclusion (Balswick, 1988; L. R. Brody, 1985; Fivush, 1989).

In sum, it is not accurate to say that females are more emotional than males. Much depends on the definition of emotionality used, the age group studied, the social context, and the specific emotions examined. Females do appear to be more emotionally expressive than males with respect to most emotions except anger. This gender difference in emotional expressivity is related to gender differences in communication patterns, to which we now turn.

▲ Communication Patterns

The stereotype of female emotionality may be related to the greater frequency with which females display or communicate their emotions. The area of communication is an extremely important one in the study of gender, since most of our information and knowledge of others comes through their verbal or nonverbal cues. In ground-breaking work, Nancy Henley (1977; Mayo & Henley, 1981) found gender differences in communication patterns to be pervasive in both verbal and nonverbal behaviors.

Verbal Communication
Overall, males tend to dominate verbally and females tend to listen. Contradicting the "talkative female" stereotype, Henley and others (for example, Aries, 1987; Lakoff, 1975) have found that males talk more and for longer periods of time than females. Males interrupt other speakers more, control the topic of conversations more, make more jokes, speak less in standard English (that is, they use slang more), and more often use a familiar form of address (first name, "honey") when talking to a female than would a female talking to a male. Females talk at a much higher pitch, allow themselves to be interrupted more, listen more, and disclose more personal information to others. Women more than men use tag questions ("It's hot, isn't it?"), qualifiers ("maybe," "I guess"), and compound requests ("Won't you close the window?" rather than "Close the window"). These three speech style differences are assumed to indicate a lack of assertiveness and more politeness on the part of females. Indeed, women are expected to be polite in their speech, regardless of the gender of the person addressed or the content of the speech (Kemper, 1984). In contrast, males are expected to modify their speech as a function of the gender-appropriateness of the content and the gender of the addressee. For example, it is rarely all right for women to use profanity, but men can use it as long as they don't use it with women. The use of profanity by males appears to demonstrate a degree of social power that women do not have (Selnow, 1985).

These gendered linguistic patterns appear early in life and increase in frequency with age. Even among preschoolers, males tend to talk more, initiate more topics, and use more attention-getting speech devices than their female peers (Austin, Salehi, & Leffler, 1987; Cook, Fritz, McCornack, & Visperas, 1985). In contrast, young girls' speech uses more conversation facilitators and reinforcers than boys' speech. Research on parental directives to young children suggests that children learn these different linguistic styles from their parents (Bellinger & Gleason, 1982). For example, fathers appear to issue more direct commands than mothers ("Put the screw in"), and mothers appear to issue more indirect requests than fathers ("Can you put the screw in?"). Cross-cultural research confirms that gender differences in language use, although fairly universal, are socially constructed (Philips, Steele, & Tanz, 1987).

Differences in content of conversation are not clear because males and females often engage in different activities and occupations. Content differences also are unclear because content of conversation appears to depend not only on the gender of the speaker but also on the gender of the listener (Haas, 1981; J. A. Hall & Braunwald, 1981). Among White middle-class children, boys talk more about sports to both boys and girls, and girls talk to girls more about school, identity, and wishing and needing. When girls talk to boys, they are more verbally compliant and they laugh more. When boys talk to girls, they use more direct requests. College women talk more frequently about a third person than do college men, but there is no gender difference in the frequency of derogatory remarks about that person (Levin & Arluke, 1985). In general, males more often are talked about by both sexes, perhaps a reflection of their greater importance or interest.

With respect to self-disclosure of intimate information, such as personality and bodily matters, women are more self-disclosing than men (Balswick, 1988; Derlega, Durham, Gockel, & Sholis, 1981; C. T. Hill & Stull, 1987). However, when personal topics are considered neutral, such as tactfulness, or masculine, such as aggressiveness, no gender difference regularly appears. With respect to feelings, men are less expressive of positive emotions than negative ones (Saurer & Eisler, 1990).

Why are men less likely than women to disclose positive feelings and personal information about themselves? The answer seems to be that such behaviors are seen as feminine, revealing emotionality and vulnerability (E. T. Lewis & McCarthy, 1988). As such, they may be considered socially unacceptable for males. Indeed, it is only the men who are experiencing gender role stress or who are low in expressive-nurturant traits (masculine and undifferentiated males) who limit their disclosure of positive emotions and personal information (Lavine & Lombardo, 1984; Narus & Fischer, 1982; Saurer & Eisler, 1990). Androgynous people of both sexes appear to be flexible with regard to self-disclosure, responding more to their partner's level of disclosure and to the nature of the topic than their sex-typed peers (Sollie & Fischer, 1985).

Certain aspects of the masculine gender role, such as restrictive emotionality and inhibited affection, clearly work against intimate self-disclosure (Snell, Miller, Belk, Garcia-Falconi, & Hernandez-Sanchez, 1989). The association of intimate self-disclosure with femininity suggests that the social costs and rewards of such behavior will differ for males and females. This was demonstrated in a study by Derlega and Chaikin (1976), who found that self-disclosing college men were perceived by college students of both sexes as significantly more psychologically maladjusted than non-self-disclosing men. For women, however, the reverse was true; that is, the non-self-disclosing women were seen as significantly more maladjusted.

Overall, the type of verbal communication typical of men (verbal dominance, direct statements, limited intimate self-disclosure) reflects men's greater social dominance and their concern with power and competition. Men use talk to negotiate and maintain their higher status. Reciprocally, the type of verbal communication typical of women (listening, qualifying, politeness, personal self-disclosure) reflects women's relative subordination and greater interpersonal involvement. Women use talk to signal support and to maintain relationships. The outcome of these different styles and goals may be problems in male-female communication (Tannen, 1990). Social perception research confirms the effects of these different communication styles: the "feminine" linguistic style is perceived by others of both sexes as higher in social warmth but lower in competence and assertiveness than the "non-feminine" linguistic style (Mulac, Incontro, & James, 1985; Quina, Wingard, & Bates, 1987). Given the social functions different linguistic styles support, it is not surprising that people who deviate from these gender expectations would be socially denigrated. For example, men who use the "female" linguistic style are perceived by others of both sexes as homosexual; women who use the "male" style are perceived as uppity (Rasmussen & Moely, 1986).

Nonverbal Communication

In studies of nonverbal behavior, the observed gender differences are of even greater importance than in the verbal behaviors just noted, since the impact of nonverbal communication is so much stronger and so much more subtle than verbal communication (Henley & Thorne, 1977). Generally, females are more restricted in their demeanor and personal space, have more frequent eye contact during conversations (but avoid eye contact otherwise), smile more when it is unrelated to happiness, touch less in impersonal settings but are touched more,

and are more sensitive to nonverbal cues than males (J. A. Hall, 1984, 1987; Henley, 1977; Mayo & Henley, 1981). The size of the gender differences in this area is medium to large. Few of these differences appear among children, however, and many of these general findings must be qualified by situational, cultural, and sex-typing factors.

For example, the finding related to females' skill at decoding nonverbal cues is complex. Although above-average ability in decoding is found in 61% of females and 39% of males ($d = .43$), research suggests that this superiority is present mainly when the nonverbal message appears to be intentional and overt, such as in facial expressions, rather than more covert or unintended, such as in body position (Blanck, Rosenthal, Snodgrass, DePaulo, & Zuckerman, 1981; Rosenthal & DePaulo, 1979). The interpretation of this pattern has been in terms of "politeness"; that is, females learn to refrain from effectively decoding the less controllable cues of the sender. The finding that this pattern increases with age from the year 9 to 21 suggests that this phenomenon results from social learning; that is, girls may be trained through modeling and rewards to develop this decoding pattern.

As was found with verbal behaviors, males are less expressive nonverbally than are females, a gender difference that appears regularly among adults but inconsistently among children (Buck, 1977; J. A. Hall, 1984; Haviland & Malatesta, 1982; Yarczower & Daruns, 1982). Facial expressiveness is one of the largest gender differences found ($d = 1.01$), with above-average expressiveness characteristic of 75% of females and only 25% of males. The age pattern suggests that learning this skill is part of learning one's gender role, a hypothesis supported by finding a stronger relationship between encoding skill and sex typing than between encoding skill and sex (M. Zuckerman, DeFrank, Spiegel, & Larrance, 1982). Accuracy of encoding intentional nonverbal cues is positively correlated with expressive ("feminine") traits, and negatively correlated with instrumental ("masculine") traits.

The importance of sex typing with respect to nonverbal behavior is clearly illustrated by a study conducted by LaFrance and Carmen (1980; LaFrance, 1982). Androgynous and sex-typed male and female undergraduates were observed in same-sex pairs in either a situation requiring instrumental qualities (debating an abstract issue) or expressive qualities (sharing feelings about starting college). Some nonverbal behaviors were coded as feminine (for example, smiling, gazing) and some were coded as masculine (for example, interrupting, vocalizing while pausing "uh . . . ," "mmm . . ."). Both types of nonverbal behaviors were present in androgynous individuals, whereas sex-typed students were more restricted to sex-consonant behaviors, regardless of the topic. Similar results (that non-sex-typed individuals were less sex-typed behaviorally) have been found with respect to how people move their bodies (Frable, 1987). It is interesting that "feminine" language styles have been found to contribute to a communicator's credibility, perhaps because listeners interpret sharing feelings, smiling, and gazing as linked to personal openness. In contrast, "masculine" language styles appear to contribute to the perception of the communicator as extroverted, perhaps because frequent and constant vocalizations are interpreted as a desire to affect the listener (Berryman-Fink & Wilcox, 1983). Thus it may be an advantage to use different speech modes in a flexible fashion, as androgynous individuals seem to do.

One must keep situational cues in mind when discussing all social behaviors, especially nonverbal ones. For example, the gender of the person to whom one talks may be as important as or more important than the gender of the person communicating (M. Davis & Weitz, 1982; J. A. Hall & Braunwald, 1981). Such factors also are important in research on personal space (Berman & Smith, 1984; Hayduk, 1983), smiling (J. A. Hall & Halberstadt, 1986), and touching (Berman & Smith, 1984; Major, Schmidlin, & Williams, 1990; Stier & Hall, 1984).

Another important variable is culture. Females tend to sit closer than males during conversations, but the actual distance varies as a function of cultural background and the language being spoken (N. M. Sussman & Rosenfeld, 1982). The pattern of gender differences in nonverbal behavior just described may be more characteristic of Whites than Blacks. For example, Black women appear to smile and lean less than Black men, look at one another less often than White female pairs, and move together in synchrony more often than both White female and Black male pairs (Halberstadt & Saitta, 1987; A. Smith, 1983). Hispanic females appear less likely than Anglo females to show nonverbal behaviors indicative of leadership (for example, physical touch and intrusiveness) (Moore & Porter, 1988).

Still, the general pattern of research suggests that females nonverbally display more submission and warmth and males display more dominance and high-status cues (Frieze & Ramsey, 1976).

Explanations

Physiological factors and gender-related traits have been suggested to explain gender differences in communication patterns. The main physiological explanation rests on research in hemispheric processing of the brain (see Chapter 2). The right hemisphere appears to be dominant in mediating the perception of emotional material; the left hemisphere, in forming verbal codes for emotion (Saxby & Bryden, 1985). The female advantage in discerning the emotions of others may be due to women's somewhat greater use of both hemispheres. This gender difference, which is quite small, may reflect innate differences in brain structure, or it could come from early conditioning. The age patterns suggest the latter. Because males generally are discouraged from acknowledging their emotions verbally as part of their sex role, fewer males than females may build the necessary hemispheric connections.

Male and female infants may present different patterns of emotional reactivity and different forms of signaling behaviors very early in life (L. R. Brody, 1985; Haviland & Malatesta, 1982; Trotter, 1983). Parents, particularly mothers, may view these behaviors differently as a function of infant gender, with girls' expressions viewed more positively, boys' more negatively. Furthermore, high maternal expressiveness may overstimulate highly reactive infant males. Perhaps as a consequence of these factors, mothers appear to be more restrictive in the range of emotions they express toward and encourage in their sons, as opposed to their daughters. The result would be girls' enhanced understanding of emotional expression.

Although physiological and learning factors may be important in understanding communication behavior, the most persuasive explanations focus on the role and status differences between males and females. The status explanation (first suggested by Hacker, 1951) rests on the assumption that males and females hold different statuses and have differential access to power in our culture. Differences in communication behaviors, then, reflect differences in status and power, and are not specific to gender.

Henley (1977; Mayo & Henley, 1981) has compared gender differences in verbal and nonverbal behavior to differences based on other status dimensions, summarized in Table 3.1. In this scheme, females' politeness, smiling, emotional expressiveness, smaller personal space, less frequent touching and talking, and greater frequency of being interrupted all reflect their subordinate status. Females' greater sensitivity to nonverbal

Table 3.1 Gestures of power and privilege (examples of some nonverbal behaviors with usage differing for status equals and nonequals, and for women and men)

	Between Status Equals		Between Status Nonequals		Between Men and Women	
	Intimate	*Nonintimate*	*Used by Superior*	*Used by Subordinate*	*Used by Men*	*Used by Women*
1. Address	Familiar	Polite	Familiar	Polite	Familiar	Polite
2. Demeanor	Informal	Circumspect	Informal	Circumspect	Informal	Circumspect
3. Posture	Relaxed	Tense (less relaxed)	Relaxed	Tense	Relaxed	Tense
4. Personal space	Closeness	Distance	Closeness (option)	Distance	Closeness	Distance
5. Time	Long	Short	Long (option)	Short	Long	Short
6. Touching	Touch	Don't touch	Touch (option)	Don't touch	Touch	Don't touch
7. Eye contact	Establish	Avoid	Stare, ignore	Avert eyes, watch	Stare, ignore	Avert eyes, watch
8. Facial expression	Smile?	Don't smile?	Don't smile	Smile	Don't smile	Smile
9. Emotional expression	Show	Hide	Hide	Show	Hide	Show
10. Self-disclosure	Disclose	Don't disclose	Don't disclose	Disclose	Don't disclose	Disclose

From *Body Politics: Power, Sex, and Nonverbal Communication,* by N. M. Henley, p. 181. Copyright 1977 by Prentice-Hall, Inc. Reprinted by permission.

cues may reflect a survival mechanism. Because a female's well-being is likely to depend on her "superior's" moods or desires, it is to her advantage to learn to read them well, especially because these "superiors" try to hide them. Henley's analysis has received some but not unequivocal support (C. E. Brown, Dovidio, & Ellyson, 1990; Halberstadt & Saitta, 1987; Porter & Geis, 1982; Snodgrass, 1985; Stier & Hall, 1984). Henley's conclusions apply mainly to adults and are situation-specific. For example, although men tend to display more visual dominance behavior than women, when women are viewed as knowledgeable or expert with respect to a particular task, their visual dominance behavior increases (C. E. Brown et al., 1990; Dovidio, Ellyson, Keating, Heltman, & Brown, 1988).

Gender differences in communication also may reflect gender differences in social roles (Eagly, 1987b). Although gender roles may incorporate a status differential, they involve much more. As described in Chapter 1, the female role emphasizes affiliation aspects whereas the male role emphasizes agentic ones. Thus, gender differences in communication patterns may reflect gender differences in warmth and affiliation (J. A. Hall, 1987; Major et al., 1990).

One problem with the status analysis is that it implies that higher status behaviors are "better" than lower status behaviors. However, an argument can be made that the communication pattern more typical of women has many positive aspects. Because females (or feminine- and androgynous-sex-typed individuals) generally use more self-disclosure, display greater eye contact and smiling behavior, have smaller personal space, and exhibit greater listening and attending skills than males, they generally facilitate close personal interactions. Rosenthal, Hall, DiMatteo, Rogers, and Archer (1979) have determined that people who are more skillful at decoding nonverbal cues are more effective in their interpersonal relationships. Because more women have this skill and use it politely, their proficiency in interpersonal situations is strengthened. Males (or masculine-sex-typed individuals), who have greater domination of conversations, space, and touching, and have minimal self-disclosure, generally impede close personal interactions but facilitate interpersonal control. These differences in spheres of influence (personal interactions versus power interactions) again reflect gender differences in social roles.

In sum, females communicate feelings verbally and nonverbally more than males. In contrast, males communicate dominance and power more than females. These communication patterns seem to serve the different roles assigned women and men—interpersonal and agentic, respectively. Communication styles appear to be learned and are related to both sex-typed characteristics and social status.

▲ Prosocial Behaviors

As noted earlier, females generally are assumed to be more concerned with relationship-centered interactions than males, who are assumed to be more concerned with power-centered interactions. The research evidence supports this assumption to some extent. From a wide variety of different research studies, females appear to be more concerned with and expert in interpersonal relationships than males. However, it is important to examine the specific behaviors included in this category: affiliation, empathy, nurturance, altruism, and morality. As we will see, not all of these behaviors show clear-cut gender differences.

Affiliation
When interest in and concern about other people are assessed after childhood, females tend to show a greater interest in affiliation and more positive feelings about social interactions than males (Maccoby & Jacklin, 1974; Pollak & Gilligan, 1982; Swap & Rubin, 1983; Veroff, Depner, Kulka, & Douvan, 1980). For example, when adolescents were asked to rank a number of concerns in the order of the importance they felt each had for them personally, both sexes ranked identity and sexuality as the top two items. For the third item, however, a gender difference appeared. Girls ranked interpersonal relationships as the third most important concern to them, whereas boys ranked autonomy third (Strommen, 1977). Indeed, interpersonal concerns appear to be a core aspect of a young woman's identity, whereas beliefs and ideology appear more important for males. Girls appear to inhabit a world where connections between people figure prominently (Bilsker, Schiedel, & Marcia, 1988; Gilligan, Lyons, & Hamner, 1990; Gilligan, Ward, & Taylor, 1988). Not only are relationships more important to females than males, but adolescent girls also have been found to outperform boys at resolving interpersonal problem situations (Murphy & Ross, 1987). Thus, there does seem to be a gender difference

here, corresponding to gender expectations, although it does not show up until adolescence. During childhood, few gender differences have been found.

Females' greater interest in relationships may be due to a possibly fundamental gender difference in personality, as discussed previously; to differential social reinforcement for affiliative interests and behaviors; or to the effect of the social roles in which females and males are placed. Related to the role explanation is the explanation based on differential status. High interpersonal orientation may develop as an adaptation to "a chronic position of relative powerlessness" (Swap & Rubin, 1983). Because low-power people are more likely to be affected by the actions of other people than are high-power people, it is to the advantage of low-power people to pay close attention to others. All these explanations have some support and it is likely that they all contribute to this gender difference.

Interestingly, this greater interest in affiliation on the part of females has led many to assume that females are more dependent on males for love and fulfillment than males are on females (for example, Dowling, 1981). Men, on the average, actually fall in love more quickly and easily, become more upset at the end of a relationship, are more likely to remarry, and generally are in worse emotional and physical shape when unmarried than women (see, for example, Gove, 1973, 1979). Thus, simple generalizations about females needing others are unwarranted. (Relationships will be discussed in more detail in Chapter 9.)

As these findings suggest, dependency, which is most commonly associated with females, is not actually more characteristic of them. Much depends on the definition used. When dependency is defined as seeking the presence of others or as resistance to physical separation, no consistent gender difference for this trait emerges during the childhood years (Maccoby & Jacklin, 1974; Wasserman & Lewis, 1985). When dependency is defined as willingness to seek and receive help, females, especially feminine-sex-typed ones, show the most consistent help-seeking behaviors (Nadler, Maler, & Friedman, 1984). When dependency is defined by number of friends or susceptibility to their influence, boys appear more dependent during childhood and adolescence (Lott, 1978; Maccoby & Jacklin, 1974; Strommen, 1977).

The importance of consistent research definitions cannot be sufficiently stressed. In a cross-cultural study of 3- to 11-year-old American (from Mexico and the United States), Asian (from the Phillipines and Okinawa), Indian, and African (from Kenya) children (Whiting & Edwards, 1973), younger girls (ages 3 to 6) were found to be more dependent than boys only when dependency was defined as seeking help and physical contact. Older boys (ages 7 to 11) were more dependent when dependency was defined as seeking attention. Across six cultures, sex differences were found to be a reflection of style and of task assignment (more away-from-home chores for males, more domestic chores for females) rather than a reflection of innate sex differences.

In sum, females, by the time they reach adolescence, evidence more interest in interpersonal relationships than males. Whether such interest makes females more dependent on others is a matter of subjective evaluation. Certainly, research using various operational definitions of dependency reveals no consistent gender pattern. It is important to recognize that this term is often used pejoratively, especially in the United States, which values autonomy and independence (for example, the lone cowboy is a cultural hero). However, women's affiliative interests might also be viewed as interdependence, a mutual connectedness vital for the establishment of relationships.

Empathy

One component of empathy is the degree of sensitivity to others' thoughts and feelings. Females and feminine-sex-typed individuals, as was previously discussed, tend to be better than males and masculine-sex-typed individuals at interpreting nonverbal cues, perhaps because they have greater eye contact or because they take more of an interest in people. When other forms of empathy are examined, however, as in responding to people with problems or in describing the feelings or plans of characters in a story or picture, no consistent gender differences emerge (Brehm, Powell, & Coke, 1984; Eisenberg & Lennon, 1983; Maccoby & Jacklin, 1974). Rather, people tend to be more accurate about people of the same sex and about situations with which they are familiar.

When self-report measures are used, females express more concern and sympathy toward other people than males. However, when behavior is observed unobtrusively, fewer gender differences are found (Eisenberg & Lennon, 1983). Perhaps females express more concern because of gender-related expectations. Supporting this hypothesis is the finding that sex typing affects empathy scores. People with high femininity scores (androgynous or feminine-sex-typed people) appear more empathic

than those scoring low on this scale (S. Bem, Martyna, & Watson, 1976; Jose, 1989; Jose & McCarthy, 1988). Because more females than males score high on this scale, females may appear more empathic than males. However, there is no support for the hypothesis that self-report differences in empathy are due to an innate mechanism or predisposition.

Another factor affecting interpersonal sensitivity is the status of the participants. People in subordinate roles tend to be more sensitive to the feelings of another person than do people in leadership roles (Snodgrass, 1985). To the extent that women are more likely to be in a subordinate role than men, a gender difference in interpersonal sensitivity is likely to be found that in actuality is a status difference. Status differences may be related to cultural differences. Patricia Hill Collins (1989) argues that an ethic of caring, which involves empathy, is a critical component of African-American culture, yet race is rarely investigated in research on empathy.

In sum, females and feminine-sex-typed individuals report more interest in the feelings and concerns of others than males and masculine-sex-typed individuals, but actual behavior shows few differences. If women tend to be more empathic than men, are they better at jobs requiring empathy, such as direct-care medicine? A controversy exists over the answer to this question (Klass, 1988; S. C. Martin, Arnold, & Parker, 1988), but the key variable probably is sex typing, not biological sex. Empathy appears strongly linked to possession of expressive-nurturant traits.

Nurturance

Females traditionally have been thought to possess exclusively the capability of nurturing others—that is, facilitating the development of others. This belief is an outgrowth of the fact that only women can bear and nurse children. Because only women can bear and nurse them, it might follow that women must "naturally" be more qualified to take care of them and, by extension, take care of others. The problem with this assumption is twofold. First, there is no evidence at all of a maternal instinct. Second, there is no evidence that females are consistently more nurturant than males. In responses to infants and other vulnerable creatures, males and females have been found capable of equally nurturant behavior (Berman, 1980; Melson & Fogel, 1988). Males and females do differ, however, in their self-report of their reactions to infants, and indeed in their behavioral reactions when observed or when assigned the caretaking role (Berman, 1980;

Blakemore, 1990; S. C. Nash & Feldman, 1981). These differences, which appear to increase with age and are more marked during adolescence, seem primarily a response to gender expectations, because there is no gender difference in physiological responding to infants and children nor in behavior when the individuals are not directly observed or evaluated.

The important variables related to nurturant behaviors seem to be (1) contact with a newborn during a critical period after birth (Bronfenbrenner, 1977), (2) previous experience (females are usually given more preliminary practice with such behaviors—for example, playing with dolls, baby-sitting), (3) gender expectations (A. S. Rossi, 1985), and (4) sex typing (high nurturant-expressive trait scores are associated with more nurturant behavior; S. Bem et al., 1976). An interesting finding with respect to sex typing is that when nurturant behavior necessitates active initiation of a response, feminine-sex-typed college women were less nurturant than androgynous women and androgynous men. Thus, because feminine women are behaviorally constricted in instrumental functioning, they are less able to be nurturant when the situation also requires assertion.

Although there is no such thing as a maternal instinct, some indication exists that it is easier to trigger the nurturant response to infants in women than in men. This may be a function of prenatal hormonal history (Ehrhardt, 1985; Hines, 1982). Specifically, exposure to androgens seems to inhibit such behavior. Although most studies have been done with animals, some studies of adrenogenital females show them to be less interested in rehearsing parental behaviors, such as baby-sitting and playing with dolls, during childhood. This, of course, may be a function of competing athletic interests and/or socialization and not a consequence of prenatal hormone exposure. These girls do eventually marry and have children; so again, the hormonal effect seems, at most, to make nurturant behaviors easier to learn. Hormones in the mother during the birth process also might make nurturant behaviors easier to acquire (Talan, 1986). However, hormones clearly do not make maternal behaviors inevitable, as evidenced by numerous cases of maternal child abuse and infanticide in the general population. Nor do hormones prevent males from learning nurturing behaviors.

The fact that women are more likely to be in nurturant roles in our society (mothers, nurses, social workers, and so forth) is more a consequence of gender stereotypes than a direct reflection of any fundamental sex difference in nurturing ability. As Whiting and Edwards (1973, 1988) found in their cross-cultural study, differences in nurturance do not show up until ages 7 to 11, and then they are a clear function of differential socialization pressures. In those cultures where girls do not engage in infant care as well as in cultures where boys do care for infants, fewer sex differences in behavior are found. For example, in Fiji, both sexes are involved in infant care, and no difference in sex typing between males and females is found (Basow, 1984a).

In sum, females are not naturally more nurturant than males. When experience and sex typing are similar, behavioral differences between males and females are negligible. However, females are expected to be more nurturant than males and are more likely to be in nurturant roles.

Altruism
Because females are expected to be more concerned about others, one might also expect them to be more altruistic—that is, to live and to act for the good of others, as in helping someone in distress. Indeed, girls do score significantly higher than boys on measures tapping their reputation for altruistic behaviors (Shigetomi, Hartmann, & Gelfand, 1981; Zarbatany, Hartmann, Gelfand, & Vinciguerra, 1985). In the yearly survey of college freshmen conducted by the American Council of Education, the only attitude question that consistently differentiates males and females is the question regarding how important it is to help others who are in difficulty. In 1990, 71% of first-year college women rated this objective as "essential" or "very important" in contrast to 51% of the men (A. W. Astin, 1991). Furthermore, this objective ranked third for women (behind raising a family and being very well-off financially) and fifth for men (behind being very well-off financially, raising a family, becoming an authority in own field, and obtaining recognition from colleagues). However, when actual helping behavior is assessed, no consistent sex differences appear (Maccoby & Jacklin, 1974; Piliavin & Unger, 1985). Where differences are found, it more often is in the direction of greater male than female helpfulness. The meta-analytic review by Eagly and Crowley (1986) revealed a moderate effect size of .34, or about one-third of a standard deviation in the direction of more helping by men than by women. This means that in a particular helping situation, of those scoring above average on helpfulness, about 58% will be male, 41% female. The

magnitude of the effect size has been decreasing as a function of the year of publication.

Many methodological, situational, and attitudinal factors account for the gender differences in helping behaviors. In Eagly and Crowley's (1986) meta-analytic study, a combination of such variables accounted for nearly 70% of the variability in the findings. Among the important variables are (1) the nature of the response required (men are more likely than women to help if some initiative on the part of the respondent is required); (2) the nature of the task (females are more likely than males to perceive a situation as dangerous and are less likely to respond to such situations; males are more reluctant than females to engage in activity inappropriate to their sex role), (3) the gender of the person requiring help (other-sex helping is more likely for men than same-sex helping; for women, gender of the person needing help appears less salient), (4) the presence of witnesses (males are more likely to help if witnesses are available), and (5) helper sex typing, although the evidence here is inconsistent and may depend upon the other variables (N. Eisenberg et al., 1988; Senneker & Hendrick, 1983; Siem & Spence, 1986; Tice & Baumeister, 1985). Many of these results fit in with the norms for men to be more chivalrous, assertive, and heroic. All these variables point to the importance of social factors in determining helping behavior.

In sum, although women are viewed as more helpful than men and seem to care more about helping, behavioral research suggests men may be more helpful than women, at least in public situations with strangers. What these studies do not generally assess is helping in the context of a relationship. It is in such settings that helping by women is most likely to occur.

Morality

Since the 1960s, moral development has been conceptualized as a series of stages that children pass through. These stages relate to a child's level of cognitive development. As Lawrence Kohlberg (1969) describes the six stages grouped into three levels, children move from a level of *preconventional morality* (concern with obedience and punishment as well as instrumental considerations) to a level of *conventional morality* (concern with social acceptance and following authority), and then perhaps to a level of *postconventional morality* (concern with individual rights and with individual principles). Although not everyone achieves the highest of the six stages, the sequence was seen as invariant. Early

research using Kohlberg's framework typically found that males tended to score around stage 4 (concern with authority) whereas females tended to score around stage 3 (concern with feelings and social opinions). These findings supported the belief, based on Freudian theory, that females were less developed morally than males, although Kohlberg's focus was on cognitive development, while Freud emphasized emotional development.

This theory of moral development had fundamental flaws, not the least of which was that it was based entirely upon the study of male participants responding to male protagonists in a story. Using Kohlberg's original stories but varying the sex of the protagonist, Bussey and Maughan (1982) found that males reasoned differently as a function of the protagonist's sex: they scored at stage 3 when the character was female, but at stage 4 when the character was male. Females did not change their reasoning as a function of the sex of the protagonist. Although these results have not been replicated consistently (for example, Donenberg & Hoffman, 1988), they suggest that a new way of viewing moral reasoning is needed.

Carol Gilligan (1982; Gilligan et al., 1988, 1990), in attempting to correct the male bias in Kohlberg's research by talking with women and girls, discovered that many females conceptualize morality very differently and that Kohlberg's stages do not capture the ways some females think about moral problems. When people talk about a personal moral dilemma, males seem more concerned than females with the "right" thing to do, whereas females seem more concerned than males with the "responsible thing to do." Females are much more concerned than males with the social context and with the feelings of others than with abstract principles of justice when thinking about real personal dilemmas. These two orientations toward moral reasoning, *rights* and *care*, are exemplified in Figure 3.2. Gilligan relates these differences to females' greater interpersonal orientation and connections to others, stemming from a greater early childhood connection to mother.

Strong debate is taking place about many aspects of Gilligan's theory. One criticism is that males typically do *not* score higher than females in moral reasoning using Kohlberg's criteria (Thoma, 1986; L. J. Walker, 1984, 1989). Education is a much better predictor of moral reasoning than gender. Second, even using Gilligan's framework of two different moral orientations, justice and care, gender differences in use of these orientations are not always found (Ford & Lowery, 1986; W. J. Friedman, Robinson, &

Figure 3.2   Gender differences in moral reasoning: "rights" versus "care"? (copyright 1989)
Reprinted with special permission of North America Syndicate, Inc.

Friedman, 1987; Garrod, Beal, & Shin, 1990). Even when gender differences are found in the predicted direction, they tend to be small (Brabeck & Weisgerber, 1988; Donenberg & Hoffman, 1988; Mills, Pedersen, & Grusec, 1989).

In general, both care and justice concerns can be found in the moral reasoning of most males and females. Still, Gilligan's point that a care orientation may be somewhat more present in the lives of females than males does have some support. When studies look at those people who use only one orientation, the primary users of an exclusive care orientation tend to be female (Gilligan & Attanucci, 1988). In addition, considerations of care appear to be more consistent for women than men, whereas considerations of justice appear to be more consistent for men than women (Ford & Lowery, 1986). Other research suggests that the care orientation may be more important than justice in women's reasoning in real-life moral dilemmas, perhaps because women are more likely than men to have or focus on moral dilemmas involving interpersonal relationships and such dilemmas are more likely to elicit a care orientation (Brabeck & Weisgerber, 1988; Mills et al., 1989; L. J. Walker, de Vries, & Trevethan, 1987; L. J. Walker, 1989). Certainly, women are *expected* to care more than men, and this may affect self-reports in research.

It is important to note that most research on moral reasoning uses White participants. Yet theorists who have studied African-American thought have suggested that Black men and women use similar patterns of moral reasoning, and both emphasize a care orientation (P. H. Collins, 1989; Stack, 1974). The few studies that have used racially diverse groups have found some differences among subsamples

(for example, Gilligan & Attanucci, 1988). Certainly, more research is needed on this topic.

Somewhat related to the division between justice and care orientations in moral reasoning is the division between *equity* and *equality* orientations in situations where rewards must be distributed. A norm of equity involves allocating rewards according to inputs, whereas a norm of equality involves allocating rewards equally regardless of inputs. As with the research on moral reasoning, gender differences in distributive justice situations are very confusing. Most research suggests that in same-sex situations, men tend to distribute rewards equitably whereas women tend to distribute rewards equally. In cross-sex situations, however, gender differences are negligible (L. A. Jackson, 1987; Reis & Jackson, 1981). What appears critical is the expectations for appropriate behavior in a particular setting, the status of the individual, and a variety of personality factors, including sex typing and personal orientation (A. Kahn & Gaeddert, 1985; Major & Adams, 1984; Stake, 1985). Gender by itself is not the best predictor of what orientation an individual will use, although men do seem to have a greater sense of personal entitlement than women, especially in an occupational setting (Major, 1987; Major, Bylsma, & Cozzarelli, 1989). The implications of these findings in the workplace will be discussed in Chapter 11.

Even if males and females do differ in the way they reason about moral dilemmas, determining which approach is more "moral" is clearly a subjective evaluation. Gilligan's point is not that all men use one and only one orientation and all women the other, but that two paths to morality exist and that both are needed in this world. We need to use principles of both care and justice in resolving the moral issues of our times. A new theory of morality that incorporates the experiences of both men and women, people of different ethnic groups and identities, and thinking about both real and hypothetical moral problems needs to be developed. We have a long way to go on this quest. (See Tronto, 1987, for some ideas about a theory of care.) Focusing on gender differences or similarities in this area may blind us to the larger issue.

Discussion

In the prosocial areas, women seem more concerned than men about relationships and about the feelings and ideas of others. In many situations, women are more empathic and more nurturant than men, although men appear more likely to help someone else, at least when that person's a stranger. However, gender differences are small and inconsistent and are overshadowed by situational and sex-typing factors. Of note is the fact that more gender differences are found with regard to self-reports and people's expectations of others than with respect to actual behavior. It seems likely that differential gender stereotypes and roles shape these results. A similar pattern is found with respect to power-related behaviors, although here the differences give men the edge.

▲   Power-Related Behaviors

In the area of power-centered interactions, males generally are thought to be more proficient than females. Such interactions encompass the behaviors of aggression, assertion, dominance, competition, achievement, and nonconformity versus compliance.

Aggressiveness

The most commonly and strongly held assumption about gender differences concerns males' greater aggressiveness. Although this assumption has been substantiated repeatedly across many situations and cultures, the size of the difference actually is only moderate. In a meta-analysis of 143 studies investigating gender differences in aggression in both child and adult populations, Hyde (1986) found that the size of the difference was about one-half a standard deviation in scores ($d = .50$). That is, above-average amounts of aggression were found in 63% of males and 38% of females. Yet gender accounted for only 5% of the variation in scores. As with gender differences in spatial ability, it is easy to overestimate the importance of the difference by exaggerating the frequent findings of a difference.

Although males consistently are found to be more aggressive in nearly all studies regardless of the design or definition used, a number of methodological factors affect the magnitude of the gender difference (Eagly & Steffen, 1986a; Hyde, 1986). Age of subject is one important factor. The largest gender differences are found among young children, especially preschoolers. Type of aggression studied is another important factor: the largest gender differences are found for fantasy and physical aggression in contrast to verbal or psychological aggression. Research design also affects the magnitude of the findings, with gender differences largest in naturalistic studies (where the aggression is relatively spontaneous) rather than in experimental ones. Furthermore, gender differences are larger when aggression is directly observed or reported by peers than when it is reported by self or adult others. Interestingly, generational trends exist as well, with larger differences found in studies before 1973 than after 1978.

It is important to differentiate behavioral aggression from both the ability to aggress and the propensity to aggress. Although males seem to have a greater readiness to respond in aggressive ways, they still must learn the behavior and choose to display it. As Albert Bandura (1973) has demonstrated, girls learn aggressive behavior to about the same degree as boys but are more inhibited in performing that behavior. When the social situation allows it, however, girls exhibit the same amount of aggression as boys.

A meta-analysis of 63 studies of adult aggression demonstrated that the best predictor of the gender difference in aggression was participants' belief about the consequences of aggression (Eagly & Steffen, 1986a). People who believed that aggression might prove dangerous to themselves or who thought they would feel guilt or anxiety about hurting someone else were less likely to display aggressive behaviors. Women held both of these beliefs significantly more than men. More than one-third of the variation in the magnitude of the gender difference in aggressive behaviors among adults was explained by these two beliefs. Similar differences in beliefs about the consequences of aggression have been found among children (Boldizar, Perry, & Perry, 1989; D. G. Perry, Perry, & Weiss, 1989). Other important variables affecting the display of aggression in both males and females are sex of victim and observer, empathy, amount of provocation, attitude toward women, and sex typing of the situation (Frodi, Macaulay, & Thome, 1977; D. Richardson,

Vinsel, & Taylor, 1980; H. L. Thompson & Richardson, 1983; Towson & Zanna, 1982).

From these findings we see that the largest gender differences in aggression occur during childhood when physical aggression is observed in a naturalistic setting. As children get older, attitudinal and situational factors appear to play a greater role in modifying the display of aggression. However, even among adults, men tend to be more physically aggressive than women. How do we explain these modest but consistent findings? Most explanations for this gender difference center either on physiological or social factors, although it is probably more accurate to say that these factors interact.

Physiological explanations Physiological explanations have centered primarily on the role of the androgens—the hormone testosterone and the prehormone adrenostenedione (Goleman, 1990b; Hopson, 1987; Susman, Inoff-Germain, et al., 1987). Male fetuses during the third prenatal month normally produce androgens, which set the brain for a fairly regular production of hormones at puberty. Prenatal androgen level also may affect behavior after birth, even before pubertal hormones kick in. There is some evidence, particularly from studies on animals, that high testosterone levels may be related to high aggressiveness (Olweus, 1986; Susman, Inoff-Germain, et al., 1987; Treadwell, 1987). For example, rhesus monkeys raised with cloth and wire "mothers" exhibit sex differences in aggressive play, which must be due to physiological and not social factors (Harlow, 1965). It's important to note, however, that males are not always more aggressive than females among nonhuman primates (Dixson, 1980).

In humans, the relationship between testosterone level and aggressive behavior is more equivocal. First, many studies do not find a significant correlation between the two variables and even in animals, such a relationship is not always found (Doering et al., 1974; Fausto-Sterling, 1985). Second, the relationship between the two variables is bidirectional. High levels of testosterone may increase aggressiveness, but aggressiveness also may increase testosterone levels (R. M. Rose, Gordon, & Bernstein, 1972). Third, studies of genetic females exposed to prenatal androgens (those with the adrenogenital syndrome) have found higher levels of rough-and-tumble play and self-assertion, but not always aggression (Hines, 1982; Money & Ehrhardt, 1972). Fourth, levels of testosterone vary widely among males and can be enhanced or reduced by environmental

factors, such as stress and weight training, and by socioeconomic status (Dabbs & Morris, 1990; Treadwell, 1987). Fifth, whereas hormones may affect the aggressive behavior of males, they may not have the same effect on females, or their effect on females may be more mediated by environmental factors (Inoff-Germain et al., 1988; Susman, Inoff-Germain, et al., 1987). Not surprisingly, aggressive behavior, like other human social behaviors, cannot be explained primarily by hormonal factors.

The most parsimonious explanation of these findings is that prenatal exposure to androgens may predispose an individual to behave aggressively. Such a predisposition may increase sensitivity to certain stimuli, like rough contact, or may make certain patterns of reactions, such as large muscle movements, more rewarding and thus more likely to occur (Hamburg & Lunde, 1966). This predisposition may arise through the effect of androgens on the amygdala, a structure in the limbic system of the brain that appears to affect aggressive behavior. Pubertal hormones may predispose individuals toward aggression due to heightened tension or irritability (Susman, Nottelmann, et al., 1987). For any predisposition to be actualized, however, various social influences are needed.

Social explanations The importance of social factors in the expression of aggression can be seen clearly in the previously cited research on the innumerable situational and methodological factors that affect aggressive behavior. Regardless of any physiological predisposition, society plays the determining role in the development of aggressive behavior, a point dramatically illustrated by the classic cross-cultural studies of Margaret Mead (1935). Rather than males always being more aggressive than females, she found one New Guinean tribe where both sexes were aggressive as adults (Mundugumor); one where both sexes were nonaggressive (Arapesh); and one, where females were aggressive and males passive (Tchambuli). In more modern Western cultures as well, norms regarding aggressiveness by males vary (J. H. Block, 1973). Compared to England and Scandinavia, the United States particularly encourages aggression in males. Parents seem more tolerant of certain forms of aggression in their sons than in their daughters (for example, physically defending oneself in a fight with a same-sex peer), although they generally discourage other forms (such as picking fights with someone younger or weaker or, for boys, with girls). Peers, too, appear to reinforce boys more than girls for their aggressive behavior, even at the toddler stage (Fagot & Hagan, 1985). The male role in the United States incorporates expectations of both aggressiveness and chivalry (Eagly, 1987b), a complexity that may account for the moderate effect size found for gender in aggregated research on aggressive behavior. Many stereotypically male activities, such as team sports and military service, deliberately encourage aggressive behavior. Thus, differential gender roles may give rise to gender differences in aggressive behavior.

Many parents have the experience, similar to that of the mother in Figure 3.3, of consciously discouraging aggressive behavior in their sons, only to have such behavior appear anyway; in this situation, the first explanation considered may be biological. However, parents may encourage aggressive behavior inadvertently simply by paying a great deal of attention to such behavior. Furthermore, other socialization forces, such as the media, may exert even more influence on children than parents. As will be discussed in Chapter 7, television in particular is filled with images of males acting aggressively. Such images dramatically affect the behavior of many viewers (see, for example, Slife & Rychlak, 1982).

Thus, even a behavior with a possible physiological basis, such as aggression, can be augmented or diminished by cultural norms. Other evidence indicates that this environmental and biological interaction is true with animals as well. Aggressive behavior is influenced by rearing, previous encounters, situational factors, and amount of fighting experience (Bleier, 1979).

In sum, males may have a greater predisposition to act aggressively than females, but aggressive behavior is determined primarily by social norms, situational factors, attitudes, and previous learning history. The value of males' greater predisposition to act aggressively is questionable, since in industrialized societies, physical aggressiveness does not necessarily help one survive or achieve high status. Rather, physical aggression may be maladaptive for the individual as well as for society if it leads to violence and crime. These societal effects of aggression will be discussed in Chapter 12.

Assertiveness

Although the terms *assertiveness* and *aggressiveness* are frequently confused, they refer to different verbal and nonverbal behaviors. Whereas *aggressiveness* refers to behaviors that infringe upon the rights of others, *assertiveness* refers to the ability to speak up for oneself while continuing to respect the rights of the other person. Assertiveness can also be differentiated from passivity, which in this regard refers to allowing others to infringe upon one's own rights (Alberti & Emmons, 1978; Phelps

Figure 3.3 The roots of aggression are complex. DOONESBURY Copyright 1987 G. B. Trudeau. Reprinted with permission. All rights reserved.

& Austin, 1975). Research on gender differences in assertiveness is problematical for both method-ological and conceptual reasons (see Gervasio & Crawford, 1989, for an excellent critique). Labora-tory simulations of assertiveness generally lack ecological validity; that is, they tend to ignore how assertiveness might fit into a real-life interpersonal encounter between people who have not only a gender but also an ethnic background, a class, and a particular age. Such research also tends to assume that assertiveness, which embodies a focus on the self as opposed to the other, is always better than nonassertiveness. This assumption can be seen as male-biased, since it tends to value autonomy over interpersonal connection.

In research studies, females generally are assumed to be deficient in assertiveness (Gervasio & Crawford, 1989). We previously noted that women let men dominate conversations, allow themselves to be interrupted, and are less likely to initiate actions. Whether these behaviors show an *inability* to speak up for oneself, or a *choice* not to speak up so as to facilitate the ongoing social interaction or to avoid negative repercussions, has not been examined. Fur-thermore, the generalization about women lacking assertiveness may not apply to African Americans. Black females have been found to have little diffi-culty asserting themselves with Whites or Blacks, males or females (K. A. Adams, 1980).

Gender stereotypes have associated femininity with passivity and masculinity with assertiveness. Such stereotypes have been found to influence judgments of assertiveness (L. K. Wilson & Gallois, 1985). In general, assertive behavior is less posi-tively evaluated when engaged in by a female than the identical behavior when engaged in by a male (Connor, Serbin, & Ender, 1978; Gervasio & Crawford, 1989). Thus, women who act assertively may be seen as violating sex role norms and may experience social disapproval for assertive behaviors. No wonder some women might hesitate to engage in such behaviors! In fact, men appear to respond less positively to a woman when she speaks assertively than when she speaks tentatively, although women listeners respond more to the assertive style (Carli, 1989b). The ethnic identity of the participants also may affect how assertiveness is perceived (Garrison & Jenkins, 1986).

Given the association between assertiveness and gender stereotypes, it is not surprising that sex typing has been found related to assertiveness as well. Androgynous individuals, both female and male, appear to be the most effective in situations involving both positive (commendatory) assertions and negative (refusal) assertions (S. L. Bem, 1975a; Darden, 1983; J. A. Kelly, O'Brian, & Hosford, 1981). The least assertive individuals are the undifferen-tiated, low on both expressive and instrumental traits.

Situational factors are quite important with regard to assertive behavior, as they are to most social behaviors. Some people may find it easier to be assertive with friends than with strangers; some may find it easier to be assertive with same-sex rather than other-sex individuals. Some research suggests that only in mixed-sex groups, especially ones that are structured, can one observe lower female than male assertiveness (Kimble, Yoshikawa, & Zehr, 1981). In such groups, a female may be reluc-tant to be assertive due to expected social rejection for her behavior and/or due to her lower social status. And there are different types of assertions. In some contexts, such as expressing negative feel-ings to a close friend of the other sex, assertion by females is viewed as more appropriate than asser-tion by males (Linehan & Seifert, 1983).

Assertiveness is an important topic to research. While many of the positive aspects of power, such as standing up for one's rights, displaying leader-ship, and so forth, have been associated with the trait of aggressiveness, they are really assertive behaviors. Because aggression may be biologically based, some people have assumed that males more naturally are leaders. This is totally unwarranted, since most leadership behaviors involve asser-tiveness, and assertiveness is definitely learned and has been successfully taught (Alberti & Emmons, 1978). Indeed, some have argued that males more than females need to be trained in assertiveness in order to modify their more typical aggressive social behaviors (Smye & Wine, 1980).

Dominance

The image of males as the more dominant sex is strongly held in our culture. Think of the standard picture of our prehistoric ancestors—a caveman dragging a cavewoman about by the hair. (No evidence of such behavior in prehistoric groups has been found; this image is a 20th-century projection of male dominance onto our ancestors.) *Dominance* refers to a relationship in which one member of a group has control and influence over the behavior of others (Frieze & Ramsey, 1976). As noted in the discussion of communication patterns, males clearly dominate conversations and physical space. Males also dominate when behaviors are related to physical toughness and force, as in children's play groups. However, even here a considerable amount of overlap exists between the behavior of the sexes (Maccoby & Jacklin, 1974, 1987). These early differences in dominance may be related to differences in aggression, which, in turn, may be related to androgen production. However, Money and Ehrhardt (1972) found in their study of adreno-genital females that although these girls did compete more in the dominance hierarchy of boys than did other girls, they did not compete for the top positions, a suggestion that social factors may also be operating. In addition, other researchers have found that aggression does not automatically lead to dominance even in animals, although the two may be correlated (Fausto-Sterling, 1985; R. M. Rose, Holaday, & Bernstein, 1971).

One problem with research in this area has been the lack of specificity of the definition of dominance. Defining dominance as control and influence over others is not sufficient. Control and influence over others can be for selfish ends, such as self-enhancement, a kind of dominance called agentic or egoistic (for example, persuading one person to perform another person's menial tasks). Cross-culturally, boys tend to be more egoistically dominant than girls (Whiting & Edwards, 1988). In contrast, control and influence over others can also be for the furthering of group goals or group harmony, a kind of dominance called communal or prosocial (for example, settling disputes among group members) (D. M. Buss, 1981; Whiting & Edwards, 1973). These two types of dominance might also be labeled "power-over" in contrast to "power-with" or "power-to." Male undergraduates have been found to judge agentic dominance as more desirable than communal dominance, but to engage in both types of dominant behaviors (D. M. Buss, 1981). In contrast, female undergraduates rate communal dominance as more desirable than agentic dominance, and they express dominance primarily in group-oriented communal ways. Cross-culturally, prosocial dominance in children has been found related to caring for siblings (Whiting & Edwards, 1988). Such care in the United States is assigned primarily to girls. Unfortunately, most research designs study mainly agentic dominance; thus, research results typically find males to be more dominant. Communal dominance, in which females may excel, has been understudied.

Leadership The distinction between agentic and communal dominance parallels the distinction between task-oriented and socioemotional leadership in human groups. These distinctions relate to the gender stereotypes of males as more agentic, females as more nurturant-expressive. Such social norms should affect the kinds of dominance-related behaviors people engage in and the degree of social support they receive for engaging in such behaviors, especially in mixed-sex groups. Indeed, meta-analyses of research on what types of leaders emerge in newly created mixed-sex groups typically find that men tend to assume leadership and be viewed as leaders because they tend to specialize in task-oriented behaviors (Eagly & Johnson, 1990; Eagly & Karau, 1991). Women, who tend to be more attentive than men to the socioemotional functioning of the group, are less likely to be recognized as leaders. Interestingly, once a group has functioned for a while, women have more chance of being recognized as leaders.

Thus, the results indicate that in laboratory studies, men seem primarily interested in the task functions of a group, whereas women tend to be interested in both task and socioemotional functions. These gender differences are small and seem clearly role-related. These differences generally do not appear when people who actually hold a leadership position in an organization are examined, probably because the selection criteria and the organization role itself overshadow the effects of gender role. One interesting gender difference that remains and is fairly strong regardless of the setting is women's preference for a democratic as opposed to an autocratic leadership style. Perhaps men are more likely to be perceived as leaders than women because an autocratic style is perceived as more "dominant" and "leaderlike" than a democratic style. (Leadership in the workplace will be discussed in Chapter 11.)

The distinction between dominance or leadership in same-sex as opposed to mixed-sex groups is an important one. All-female groups appear to function very differently from all-male and mixed-sex groups (Maccoby & Jacklin, 1987; Paikoff & Savin-Williams, 1983). Whereas all-male and mixed-sex groups tend to develop a relatively linear dominance hierarchy, with a strong leader and clear ranking of subordinate positions (a "pecking order"), all-female groups tend to be less structured and less linear. Leadership may be rotated or fall to two people rather than one. Dominance, as traditionally defined, appears to be less salient. All-female groups also tend to be more cohesive than all-male groups, at least among late adolescents. Thus, our traditional ideas about dominance are based on a male norm and do not adequately reflect female behavior, at least when only females are studied. The fact that leadership in mixed-sex groups tends to conform to the male model probably reflects both the nature of agentic dominance and the fact that what males do is seen as the norm. Evidence that females may not feel as comfortable in mixed groups as they do in all-female groups can be found as early as age 3. Eleanor Maccoby and Carolyn Jacklin (1987) found that it is girls who initiate gender segregation in childhood play groups, possibly because they find play with boys to be a negative experience.

Status is a major factor in social dominance. As we have seen, gender functions as a diffuse status characteristic, with males holding higher status. Thus, by virtue of their gender, men tend to be accepted as leaders whereas women are likely to encounter resistance, especially from men, if they try to exercise leadership in a mixed-gender group (Bartol & Martin, 1986; Kanter, 1977; Lockheed & Hall, 1976). Not only is the higher status person usually viewed as leader, but also the lower status person usually attends to the interpersonal group functions, paralleling the findings with respect to gender.

Other situational and personal variables also appear to interact with gender in shaping social dominance. The ethnic identity of the participants is one factor that may interact with gender. For example, Black females consistently appear more dominant than White females regardless of the race of their partner, whereas Black males appear dominant only with partners of their own race (K. A. Adams, 1980). In contrast, Hispanic elementary school females are least likely to be perceived as leaders by their peers (H. A. Moore & Porter, 1988). The gender-appropriateness of the task is another important factor. For example, women are more likely to be viewed as leaders on a "feminine" task, men on a "masculine" task (Eagly & Johnson, 1990; Wentworth & Anderson, 1984). However, men also are more likely to be viewed as leaders on a "neutral" task, supporting the view of gender as a diffuse status characteristic. A third important factor is the sex typing of the group members. There is evidence that in groups that have functioned together for a while, sex typing may overshadow gender in determining whether an individual will be perceived as a leader (Goktepe & Schneier, 1989). In particular, masculine-sex-typed people emerge as leaders significantly more frequently than those from other sex-typing groups.

As should now be evident, becoming a leader depends upon being seen as a leader. One group of researchers (N. Porter & Geis, 1982; N. Porter, Geis, & Jennings, 1983) found that women simply were unlikely to be seen as leaders in mixed-sex groups despite the presence of customary leadership cues, such as sitting at the head of the table. This was true regardless of the observer's sex, sex typing, or feminist ideology. Such perceptions, then, appear to be cultural stereotypes that operate on a nonconscious level. Even when a woman and a man engage in similar group behaviors, observers are more likely to view the man as the leader than the woman (Butler & Geis, 1990; N. Porter, Geis, Cooper, & Newman, 1985). Even equally participating group members are likely to view only the men as leaders, unless they've been exposed to a number of women in positions of authority (Geis, Boston, & Hoffman, 1985).

Gender stereotypes suggest that in terms of personality traits, women should be less dominant and have less need for power than men. Although no evidence supports this stereotypic idea (Winter, 1988), how power and dominance are displayed seems very much a function of gender roles, expectations, and experiences. For example, when college students who differ in the dominance trait are paired, the high-dominant individual tends to assume leadership the vast majority of the time, except when the high-dominant individual is a female paired with a male. In such pairings, the male usually assumes leadership, despite his lower dominance score (Fleischer & Chertkoff, 1986; Megargee, 1969; Nyquist & Spence, 1986). Again, the findings suggest the importance of a gender-role-and-status interpretation of gender differences.

Intimate relationships   In intimate relationships, men traditionally have been able to dominate women physically and economically. However, power in intimate relationships is also a function of emotional commitment and investment. The person with less invested tends to have more power. Whether gender differences exist in this area is unclear. Where gender differences do appear is with respect to the types of power strategies used to get one's way (Cowan, Drinkard, & MacGavin, 1984; Falbo, 1982; Falbo & Peplau, 1980; Howard, Blumstein, & Schwartz, 1983). Among heterosexual couples, men are more likely than women to report using bilateral and direct strategies, such as bargaining and reasoning, whereas women are more likely to use unilateral and indirect strategies, such as evasion and negative affect (like crying). These apparent gender differences in influence strategies actually are linked to a variety of other factors that frequently covary with gender. For example, use of bilateral, direct strategies is linked with possession of instrumental personality traits and having more power within the relationship, whereas use of unilateral, indirect strategies is linked to being low in instrumental traits, being more dependent within the relationship, and having a male partner. When these variables are unconfounded—for example, among homosexual couples and among friends who generally are equal in power—women and men do not use different power strategies. Again, we must recognize how gender's link to differential status and thus differential power may affect social behaviors. Furthermore, when asked to rank strategies they would prefer to use, men and women exhibit a similar pattern (J. W. White & Roufail, 1989). Both would start by using rational strategies, such as "stating my desire" and "using reason." The fact that women may wind up using more unilateral and indirect strategies in intimate relationships may be because direct and bilateral strategies may be less successful for them than such strategies are for men. That is, men may be able to get their way simply by stating their wishes, but in order for women to get their way, they may need to resort to crying or pouting.

Overall, males generally are perceived as and act more dominant in mixed-sex groups. In fact, dominance appears to be a more salient interpersonal dimension for males than for females. Undoubtedly, the importance of dominance in males' lives is linked, at least in part, to the importance of dominance in the expectations of the male gender role. Females, for whom interpersonal interests are more expected and encouraged, do not seem as interested as males in setting up hierarchical relationships. Nonetheless, actual behavioral differences are small and are determined by a host of situational and personal factors, especially status and sex typing. Although males and females may have somewhat different leadership styles and strategies, no one style is clearly superior for all purposes.

Competitiveness

According to gender stereotypes, males are generally more competitive than females. Research studies examining this question typically do find males to score higher than females on measures of competitive orientation. That is, males compared to females appear to be more concerned with winning, especially if money is concerned, and in surpassing an opponent. Females appear more concerned than males with interpersonal aspects of the situation, such as minimizing losses (Deaux, 1976; D. L. Gill, 1986).

Socialization and situational factors appear important in explaining these differences. Among young children, gender differences in competitiveness are not found consistently (Lott, 1978; E. E. Maccoby & Jacklin, 1974). There may be a developmental pattern, with competition most marked in cross-sex situations among young girls and boys (aged 4 to 5) (Moely, Skarin, & Weil, 1979). As children get older (by ages 7 to 9), boys show a general tendency to compete regardless of partner sex and instructional set, whereas girls appear to retain their response selectivity. Participation in competitive activities, such as playing competitive sports, is directly linked to high scores on a test of competitive orientation among high school and college students (D. L. Gill, 1986). Since males are more likely than females to have such experiences, differential experiences may account for males' greater competitive orientation. Hormonal factors cannot be ruled out, although the relationship between hormones and behavior is complex and bidirectional. For example, testosterone levels increase in male university tennis players before a match and after winning (Booth, Shelley, Mazur, Tharp, & Kittok, 1989).

Since competitiveness is more expected of males than females, competitive females may worry about social approval. Indeed, research has found that women's performance but not men's is particularly affected by peer approval or disapproval of competition (Alagna, 1982). During college, males seem to maintain a generalized competitive approach, whereas females appear to reduce their competitiveness if their partner is a male peer (Bunker, Forcey, Wilderom, & Elgie, 1984). Supporting the importance of gender stereotypes is the finding that masculine-sex-typed and androgynous individuals have better performance and greater perceived success under competitive conditions than feminine-sex-typed and undifferentiated individuals (Alagna, 1982; Coutts, 1987). Androgynous and masculine-sex-typed college women also feel more comfortable competing in a mixed-sex group than feminine-sex-typed women. Other variables affecting competitive performance are the nature of the task, group composition, significance of the behavior, training, and race and racial ideology of participants (Deaux, 1976; A. D. Jackson, 1982; Lockheed & Hall, 1976; E. E. Maccoby & Jacklin, 1974).

In sum, after early childhood, males (and masculine-sex-typed individuals) seem to have a more competitive orientation than females (and feminine-sex-typed individuals), at least when competition emphasizes winning over an opponent.

Achievement

As with competition, men have been thought to be more motivated to achieve than women. History books amply demonstrate that women have not been considered major contributors to Western civilization beyond their reproductive role. Although the reasons for this fact may lie in the biases of historians themselves, in institutionalized sexism, in the lack of effective means of birth control, and in other social forces, many people have focused on individual factors within women, particularly their low motivation to achieve or their fear of success. After more than 20 years of intense research on this topic, it now is clear that the sexes do not differ in their motivation to achieve or in their motive to avoid success (A. S. Kahn & Yoder, 1989; Paludi, 1984; Tresemer, 1977; Veroff, Depner, Kulka, & Douvan, 1980). However, gender does affect achievement behavior in a couple of ways: in how achievement is defined and in the appropriateness of achievement.

Definition issues Part of the confusion about gender differences in achievement motivation and behavior has been due to using men as the norm, and then trying to understand why women don't act like men. In David McClelland and associates' (1953) original work, only male participants were used. The researchers found that male achievement behavior was a direct function of motive to achieve (measured by projective tests), expectancy of the consequences of success, and the value attached to such consequences. However, when women were tested, their achievement behavior did not follow the same pattern (Atkinson & Feather, 1966); that is, their achievement behavior was not a direct function of the same variables. As a result of the failure of many women to conform to the proposed theoretical model of achievement behavior, they simply were neglected from study for many years (an example of the sexist nature of science).

In the late 1960s, Matina Horner (1968, 1972) posited that in order to understand women's achievement behavior, a new variable needed to be considered—a motive to avoid success. This fear of success was evident in the stories women told about a successful woman. When writing a story about "Anne," who found herself at the top of her medical school class after first-term finals, about 65% of women college students told stories indicating denial of success, unhappiness about it, or negative consequences that followed it. For example, fear of success would be scored for responses such as the following: "A mistake has been made. Anne is not really at the top of the class" and "Anne is ugly, studies all the time, and will never get married." Only 10% of male college students writing a story about "John" in the identical context told stories indicating fear of success. Not only did more females than males demonstrate this motive to avoid success using a projective technique, but Horner also found this fear to predict behavior in competitive achievement situations. Females high in fear-of-success imagery performed better in noncompetitive situations than females low in such imagery. Males in general performed better in competitive situations. From these findings, Horner concluded that fear of success was a stable personality trait and was caused by the negative consequences expected to follow success.

Although initially attractive as an explanatory construct, especially since it appeared to blame women for not achieving, fear of success as a gendered variable did not stand up to further research. We now know that both females and males will avoid success if they expect negative consequences to follow (Bremer & Wittig, 1980; Cherry & Deaux, 1978; Janda, O'Grady, & Capps, 1978). Such behavior is reasonable and reflects situational factors, not personality traits. One of the key variables related to whether people expect negative consequences to follow success is whether the success occurs in an area considered gender-appropriate. In the original Horner study, success was in a traditionally male domain—medical school. When success is in a traditionally female domain, such as nursing school, the opposite results have been found (T. G Alper, 1974). That is, more males show fear of success. Furthermore, such fear does not always reduce achievement attempts on the part of females (J. Condry & Dyer, 1976; Paludi, 1984). Fear of success may lead to performance decrements only for highly achievement-motivated women in situations viewed as male-appropriate (Piedmont, 1988).

A more substantive issue with respect to achievement motivation is how it's defined. Traditional definitions of achievement have emphasized mastery and competitiveness, especially in such public domains as school, sports, and occupations. Yet achievement also can take other forms and occur in other domains, such as in personal or interpersonal areas. Although women and men don't differ with respect to which domain they pick when asked to describe an experience of success or failure, women seem more sensitive than men to the different characteristics of the different achievement domains (Travis, McKenzie, Wiley, & Kahn, 1988). Furthermore, women seem to define success more in terms of intrinsic criteria (for example, how they feel about it), while men seem to define success more in terms of extrinsic criteria (for example, how others evaluate it) (Gaeddert, 1985).

Achievement motivation is more than mastery and competitiveness, too. Using a questionnaire they developed to measure four independent factors of achievement motivation, Spence and Helmreich (1978, 1983) found that although males generally scored higher than females in competitiveness (enjoyment of interpersonal competition) and mastery (preference for challenging tasks), females generally scored higher in work orientation (desire to work hard). There was no gender difference on the fourth factor, personal unconcern (lack of concern over others' reactions to one's success), confirming the finding that "fear of success" is not a gendered construct. Interestingly, the pattern of motives or values most conducive to actual achievement, as measured by grades, salaries, and so on, is high mastery and work orientation and low competitiveness, at least in the United States. Thus, males' generally high competitiveness scores may not facilitate actual achievement.

How achievement fits in with people's life plans also may vary for women and men. Whereas achievement behavior for men typically follows a straightforward career track (Levinson, 1978), achievement behavior, and the importance of it, for many women may vary as a function of family life stage (Baruch, Barnett, & Rivers, 1983; Krogh, 1985; Paludi & Fankell-Hauser, 1986). For example, younger women and women with young children may be more concerned with relationships than with competitive achievement, but when children leave home, career achievement goals may become more important.

Gender-appropriateness As implied by the preceding discussion of definitions of achievement motivation and behavior, certain types of achievement are culturally associated with males, such as career and athletic achievement. Other types of achievement, such as nurturing interpersonal relationships, not usually even defined as achievement,

are associated with females. Women are expected to achieve less than men, especially in terms of money and career success, and when they don't, they frequently are viewed negatively (Janman, 1989; Monahan, Kuhn, & Shaver, 1974; Pfost & Fiore, 1990). Children learn these associations as part of their socialization, as we will see in Chapters 6 and 7. Because of these different social norms for males and females, both sexes may learn to channel their achievement motivation into socially sanctioned (gender-appropriate) domains and to perceive the other domain as somewhat threatening. Research using projective techniques does indeed find that competitive achievement situations appear more threatening to women than to men, whereas affiliative or intimate situations appear more threatening to men than to women (Helgeson & Sharpsteen, 1987; Pollak & Gilligan, 1982, 1983). In addition, considerable evidence exists that the sexes differ in how much value they attach to different achievement options, such as achieving in math (Eccles, 1985, 1987b). These different values and perceptions affect their achievement choices.

From these findings, it can be predicted that the more gender-stereotyped an individual, the more his or her achievement behavior will be affected by situational factors. Indeed, women with traditional female attitudes have been found to score lower on achievement-motivation measures than women with nontraditional orientations (Canter, 1979; Gralewski & Rodgon, 1980). Instrumental ("masculine") personality traits, but not expressive ("feminine") ones, are associated with high achievement motivation, low fear of success, high career achievement, and few achievement conflicts (Cano, Solomon, & Holmes, 1984; Orlofsky & Stake, 1981; Sadd, Miller, & Zeitz, 1979; Spence & Helmreich, 1978). Thus, "masculine" qualities seem most closely connected to achievement behaviors and motivations.

Although achievement research has often focused on the question of why women don't behave like men, we need to examine men's achievement behavior as well. The male sex role is primarily defined by success and status gained through working and achieving (Brannon, 1976; Cicone & Ruble, 1978; O'Neil, 1982). All that counts is the material rewards of achieving—money, possessions, power, and "winning" in sexual and athletic areas. In contrast to many women, many men achieve more for the social rewards of achieving than for the personal rewards of mastery. Success for many men means only economic success (Goldberg & Shiflett, 1981). This emphasis on achieving may prevent the development of other human abilities—sensitivity to others, nurturance, emotional expressiveness, and formation of relationships. The very nature of the male role, both traditional and modern, may be dysfunctional because it contains inherent role strain between role demands and more fundamental personal needs (Pleck, 1976b). In addition, in a competitive society like America, only a few can win or come out on top in terms of success or status. Even when success is obtained, it usually lasts for only a limited time, because there is always either something else to achieve or someone else who achieves more. Consequently, many males spend their lives competing endlessly with little possibility of reaching their goal. Furthermore, because masculinity is so tied to working and achievement, when unemployment occurs, some men also may experience a damaging loss of self-esteem. Research confirms that an unsuccessful man is downgraded much more than an unsuccessful woman (Fogel & Paludi, 1984). All these pressures may give rise to frustration, aggression, and/or stress-related ailments, among other consequences.

Racial and class issues   Not only is school and career achievement expected more of males than females, it's also expected more of Whites than Blacks and Hispanics, and more of upper- and middle-class individuals than working-class individuals. Minority and working-class children may need special encouragement to channel their achievement needs into school and career areas. Evidence exists that Black females may be steered toward social goals and away from achievement goals ("Study of Black Females," 1985). Fear of success among Black female college and graduate students or among talented Black female high school students is about the same as or lower than it is in their White female counterparts, perhaps because the Black women in these programs already have overcome achievement obstacles (Fleming, 1978, 1982; George, 1986; Mednick & Puryear, 1975). However, Black women who do have high fear of success appear to channel their achievement into more gender-appropriate professions than Black women low in fear of success. Research on Black men is scarcer, with some suggestion of greater fear of success for them than for either Black women or White men. This finding, if confirmed, may relate to the strong racial stereotypes of Black men as unreliable and unproductive. Therefore, they may see any success as role-inappropriate. Even middle-class Black men may

have conflicts over achievement (Cazenave, 1984; Cordes, 1985). Such conflicts may lead to a lack of striving. Indeed, fewer and fewer Black men are going to college (Collison, 1987; "Fewer," 1989). Whereas in 1976, Black males were 4.3% of all college students, in 1986, they were only 3.5%. Although the percentage of Black females in college has dropped as well, it has not dropped as much and Black women still outnumber Black men in college. As is the case among Whites, traditional sex role training is associated with higher achievement motivation in Black boys, but lower achievement motivation in Black girls (Carr & Mednick, 1988).

It is important to remember that for Blacks, as for White females, whatever internal factors may affect their achievement are secondary to external factors—racism, sexism, lack of economic and personal support, lack of role models, and so on.

In sum, achievement behavior for women and men is a function of both achievement motivation and gender expectations. Because of gender labeling of achievement domains, each sex may avoid achieving in gender-inappropriate areas. Traditionally, women have been discouraged from achieving in male-defined areas, such as sports and medicine, whereas men have been discouraged from achieving in female-defined areas, like nursing and interpersonal relationships. Some change seems to be occurring, at least with respect to high-ability women and high-prestige occupations. For example, about one-third of all law and medical school students were women in 1990.

Noncompliance and Nonconformity
Gender stereotypes hold that females are more easily persuaded and more conforming than males. Results from meta-analyses tend to support these assumptions, although the differences are small and show tremendous variability ($d = .11–.28$) (Becker, 1986; H. M. Cooper, 1979; Eagly & Carli, 1981). That is, of those people who conform more than average, from 52% to 57% will be female, 43% to 48% will be male. Findings of a gender difference in influenceability depend on the nature of the task itself, on the presence of others, on the gender of the researcher, on the sex typing of the individual, and on the race and status of the participants.

Since conformity is viewed as part of the female gender role and independence-nonconformity as part of the male gender role, gender differences should be most apparent when social evaluation occurs. Research supports this prediction. In group-pressure conformity situations and in laboratory studies where participants are observed, males appear to be much more resistant to influence than females (Becker, 1986; Eagly & Chrvala, 1986; Eagly, Wood, & Fishbaugh, 1981). However, when participants are not observed, or when no group pressure exists, females are no more likely to conform in their opinions than males. The change appears more at the level of behavioral expression than at the level of a genuine change of opinion. These results support a gender role analysis of this behavior.

A gender role analysis not only predicts more conformity by females than males, it also predicts most conformity by females *to* males and least by males to females. Observations of children's play groups support the prediction that boys, by age 3 or 4, tend to resist being influenced by girls (Maccoby & Jacklin, 1987). The result is that girls prefer to play with other girls, whom they can influence and be influenced by. This prediction also is supported by the findings in Eagly and Carli's (1981) meta-analysis. They found that gender differences in the direction of greater persuasibility and conformity among females was present mainly in studies authored by men, who were 79% of the authors of such studies. Female researchers generally found no gender difference. Thus, the findings of greater conformity by female participants in the literature may be due to their conforming to what they perceive to be the expectations of male experimenters.

The source of the influence attempt is important in another way. During childhood, girls comply more than boys with directives from parents and teachers; however, boys comply more than girls with peer pressure (Maccoby & Jacklin, 1974, 1987; Serbin et al., 1990). It is possible that girls may be more socialized for adult approval than boys. In any case, females receive more requests from adults than do boys, making the cause-and-effect sequence here very unclear.

Gender roles may affect the type of influence strategy an individual uses to persuade another to change his or her mind. College students tend to adopt a prosocial influence style (with more agreement) when dealing with women and a more task-oriented influence style (with more disagreements) when dealing with men (Carli, 1989a). Since the task-oriented influence style is less effective than the prosocial one, females are most likely to conform and males least likely to conform, especially to the influence attempts of men. Gender of the influencer needs to be studied more in persuasion research.

Knowledge or skill is an important variable in conformity studies. When a task is familiar or gender-appropriate, both sexes typically show independence; when it is unfamiliar or gender-inappropriate, both sexes are more likely to conform (Feldman-Summers, Montano, Kasprzyk, & Wagner, 1980; Karabenick, 1983; Morelock, 1980). Since by virtue of their gender role, men are considered more knowledgeable about "masculine" topics than women, female conformity is especially apparent in such situations (Eagly & Carli, 1981). Other evidence suggests that the gender relevance of a topic triggers different response styles in both males and females (Maslach, Santee, & Wade, 1987).

Women's greater conformity in the presence of others also may reflect their relatively lower status. Lower status individuals tend to conform more than higher status individuals, especially in the presence of others (Eagly, 1987b; Eagly & Chrvala, 1986; Eagly & Wood, 1982, 1985). Also needing more recognition is the important interaction between race and sex in research design. As noted in the previous section, Black females appear less easily influenced and more assertive than either their Black male or White female peers (K. A. Adams, 1980, 1983).

In line with a gender role socialization analysis is the finding that sex typing is an important factor in conformity research. In general, high "femininity" scores are correlated with greater conformity, whereas high "masculinity" scores are correlated with more frequent dissent (S. L. Bem, 1975b; Brehony & Geller, 1981; Maslach et al., 1987). Thus, feminine-sex-typed individuals tend to be the most conforming, especially when the social norm is strong in group-pressure situations.

Overall, although males show a slight tendency to be less conforming and less influenced by others than females, these results are apparent mainly when behavior is observed by others, the situation is a group-conformity one, and the individuals studied are traditionally sex-typed. The best explanation of these patterns is a combination of gender role and status analyses.

Discussion

We can conclude from research on power-related behaviors that males compared to females tend to be somewhat more aggressive, dominant, competitive, and nonconforming. Gender differences in assertiveness are less clear. However, the gender differences that exist are small and are overshadowed by situational and sex-typing factors.

▲ Summary

In this chapter, we have reviewed a wide range of social behaviors, from communication patterns to prosocial behaviors to power-related behaviors. A number of gender differences have been found in the direction predicted by gender roles and stereotypes. Males tend to be somewhat more agentic—more aggressive, dominating (both behaviorally and communicatively), competitive, and nonconforming. Females tend to be somewhat more communal—more expressive, smiling, friendly, empathic, nurturant, and agreeable. These results parallel the findings with respect to personality traits. The size of these gender differences ranges from small (noncompliance) to large (facial expressiveness), but most are in the small-to-moderate range (decoding skill, aggression, helping strangers). The amount of overlap between the sexes is greater than the differences between them in all areas surveyed.

In many areas, gender differences are unclear (for example, in fearfulness, moral reasoning, altruism, and assertiveness). Furthermore, many of the differences that appear in the literature seem to be differences in quality, not quantity. That is, males and females may have different styles of behavior (for example, moral reasoning, achieving, and dominance patterns) that may not be adequately measured by research designs defining terms in a male-biased way.

When gender differences are found, they nearly always depend upon certain situational and personal variables. In particular, status and sex-typing factors account for most of the findings of gender differences. That is, behavior that is typical of men is even more typical of high-status and masculine-sex-typed individuals. Behavior that is typical of women is even more typical of low-status and feminine-sex-typed individuals. The power of situational factors to increase or decrease gender differences in social behaviors is most impressive. Rather than asking *whether* males and females differ on a certain behavior, we need to ask under what circumstances males and females differ and under what circumstances they do not.

Explanations for gender differences in social behavior that rely on physiological or personality differences do not adequately explain the person-situation interactions generally found. Although some evidence exists that a predisposition toward aggressiveness may be related to prenatal androgen levels, aggressive behaviors must be learned and enacted by each individual within a social context.

Similarly, prenatal androgen exposure may inhibit nurturing behavior in adults, but this behavior is more clearly a function of learning than of hormonal predisposition. Personality theorists who posit that females are more connected to people while males are more separated also have difficulty accounting for the fact that people's behaviors change with situational factors, such as whether the person is being observed by another.

The best explanations of the gender patterns found are social-role theory and status theory (Eagly, 1987b). As we have seen, the gender differences that are found parallel gender stereotypes and role expectancies. The situations in which gender differences are greatest are ones in which role cues are most salient—for example, in a mixed-sex situation where behavior is observed by others. People who are most concerned about gender-appropriate behavior—sex-typed individuals—also show the most behavioral differences. Furthermore, since gender functions as a diffuse status characteristic and many of the roles women and men hold outside a laboratory setting differ in status in predictable ways, role theory can also incorporate status theory in predicting gender differences. For example, high-status jobs, such as manager and doctor, are most likely to be held by men; low-status jobs, such as secretary and nurse, are most likely to be held by women. Compliance by women to men in such situations would be predicted by both gender role and status analyses. Because men and women are socialized into different social roles (men into the higher status employment role, women into the domestic and lower status employment roles), men may develop more agentic qualities, women more communal ones.

Social-role theory and status theory explain the general pattern of social behaviors exhibited by women and men. However, these theories do not completely account for the kind of situational specificity frequently observed. To account for this specificity, a complex interactive model is needed, such as proposed by Deaux and Major (1987). Their model takes into account both the actor's and the observer's gender schema and gender beliefs, situational cues (including the gender of the people involved and the sex typing of the task), and the actor's concerns with self-presentation or self-verification. These factors affect the actor's interpretation of the situation and her or his behavior. The actor's behavior, in turn, affects both the actor's and the observer's gender belief systems. This interactive model predicts that gender differences in behavior will be maximized in situations where individuals who are strongly sex-typed (gender-schematic) interact with an individual with a strong belief in gender differences in a situation with strong cues about gender-appropriate behavior. In such a situation, the participants' gender schemas will be maximally activated. If the perceiver acts in such a way as to make clear his or her gender-related expectations to the target, the target will have to decide how important it is to make a good impression on the perceiver and thereby conform to the expectancy. Status cues might affect the interpretation made, since a person in a lower status position (for example, an employee) might want to fulfill the expectancies of a higher status person (an employer). Once a gender-congruent behavior occurs, the gender belief system of the perceiver is strengthened and the self-system of the target verified. Much of the research reviewed in this chapter that has found gender differences conforms to this model.

Overall, gender differences in social behaviors are found when personal and situational variables maximize the salience and importance of gender role conformity. Biological predispositions, which may be involved in aggressive and nurturant behaviors, play only a minor role. Gender differences in personality, to the extent they exist, actually may be a *result* of gender roles rather than an explanation of gender differences in social behavior.

▲   Recommended Reading

Balswick, J. (1988). *The inexpressive male*. Lexington, MA: Lexington Books. A thoughtful examination of one aspect of the male role. Research results and their implications plus an integrated theoretical framework are presented.

Deaux, K., & Major, B. (1987). Putting gender into context: An interactive model of gender-related behavior. *Psychological Bulletin*, *94*, 369–389. Presentation of a complex but convincing model integrating personal and situational factors to explain how gender affects social behaviors.

Eagly, A. H. (1987). *Sex differences in social behavior: A social-role interpretation*. Hillsdale, NJ: Erlbaum. A clearly presented argument for the importance of gender roles in shaping various social behaviors, supported by a number of meta-analytic studies. Eagly argues that sex differences in social behavior are not trivial and have meaningful implications in real-life situations.

Gilligan, C., Ward, J. V., & Taylor, J. M. (Eds.). (1988). *Mapping the moral domain*. Cambridge, MA: Harvard University Press. A collection of articles and studies, many by Gilligan and her students and co-workers, elaborating upon a new model of moral functioning.

Chapter 4

Comparisons of Sexual Behavior

Perhaps no area in the study of sex differences and similarities is more clouded by misconceptions than the area of sexual behavior. Part of this confusion is due to the very private nature of sexual experiences in our culture. Although a person's social behavior is observed by many people, an individual's sexual behavior is viewed by very few others—perhaps by only one other person in the course of a lifetime. This clearly limits factually based generalizations.

In the United States especially, there has been a taboo against talking about sexual feelings and behavior, particularly for females. This limits the information a researcher can obtain. When a researcher does obtain information from self-reports, it is difficult to know its accuracy. For example, a follow-up survey of teenagers two years after an initial interview found that male and Black adolescents were less likely to have been honest about their sexual experiences during the first interview than female and White adolescents (Newcomer & Udry, 1988). Yet survey data sometimes are all we have, and Kinsey's surveys in the 1950s (Kinsey, Pomeroy, & Martin, 1948; Kinsey, Pomeroy, Martin, & Gebhard, 1953), Hite's surveys of female and male sexuality (1976, 1981), and Pietropinto and Simenauer's survey of male sexuality (1977) have added tremendously to our knowledge of sexual functioning. Results of such research, however, must be used cautiously.

A major problem in sex research has been researcher bias. Because people have so many preconceived notions about sexual behavior, it is not surprising that these assumptions manifest themselves in the research questions asked. For example, women's reactions to visual stimuli have rarely been studied, since a pervasive myth has it that women do not get turned on by erotica. Similarly, some researchers generalize about human sexuality from animal data despite the fact that nonhuman female primates have no hymen, no orgasm, no menopause, and no voluntary birth control. In addition, nonhuman primate sexuality is determined by the female estrus cycle. The extent to which such researcher biases can influence our attitudes and beliefs is clearly demonstrated in the case of Freud, who postulated the vaginal orgasm as an index of a woman's psychological maturity. Despite the fact that there is no such thing as a vaginal orgasm (scientists now agree that all female orgasms result from clitoral stimulation), Freud was believed for 50 years and is still believed today by many people.

Heterosexism (the belief that heterosexuality is the only acceptable sexual orientation, backed by institutions such as the law to ensure its predominance) is so strong that most sex research has assumed respondents' heterosexuality. Yet we know that sexual attraction between same-sex partners is common and that by age 45, between one-fifth and one-third of all men and one-sixth of all women have had at least one same-gender sexual experience, mostly during adolescence (A. Bell & Weinberg, 1978; Fay, Turner, Klassen, & Gagnon, 1989; Hunt, 1974; Kinsey et al., 1948, 1953; "Sex on Campus," 1982). Since homosexuality and heterosexuality are points on a continuum of sexual orientation with many points in between, and since nonexclusive heterosexuality is so stigmatized, it is difficult to obtain precise figures for the numbers of men and women who are gay or bisexual during adulthood. Our best estimate is that from 3 to 10% of both men and women are primarily or exclusively gay, with more who are bisexual (another 10 to 25%). More males than females appear to be exclusively gay. If we want to understand sexual behavior, we need to consider all human beings, not just those who fit the majority pattern. Indeed, we need to broaden our definition of sexual behavior. Most people, including most researchers, define sexuality as penile penetration of the vagina (or vaginal engulfment of the penis). Obviously, this definition excludes many sexual behaviors (for example, kissing, fondling, oral stimulation) and is based on an exclusively heterosexual model. A more inclusive view of sexuality is needed.

Another research problem is in the use of volunteers. As Abraham Maslow (in Seaman, 1972) demonstrated, people who willingly participate in sex research without financial compensation are usually freer in their sex lives than most people and are less inhibited and more self-actualizing. Consequently, surveys may be using biased samples. Masters and Johnson, in their laboratory research (1966, 1979), paid participants and carefully screened them for psychological abnormalities, so such bias in their studies is reduced. One might argue, however, that people who would allow their sexual behavior to be studied in a laboratory still constitute an unrepresentative sample.

Gender of the researcher is also an important variable. Male anthropologists often get data only on the male sex life in other cultures, either because of their own bias or because females will not talk with them about sexual matters. Israel and Eliasson (1971) found an effect of interviewer bias that resulted in each sex giving more traditional answers to same-sex interviewers. This bias certainly would affect survey responses.

Once results are obtained, the data often are interpreted according to prevailing assumptions. Although a striking amount of similarity exists between male and female sexual responses, only the differences have been stressed. Thus, for example, based on the findings that more males than females engage in masturbation, it has been concluded that females are uninterested in sex for its own sake. Yet the same studies also show that more than half of all females do masturbate and achieve orgasm, contradicting the woman-as-asexual image.

Keeping these research problems in mind, we will review the current findings regarding sexual behavior—the physiology of sexual response; sexual interest, attitudes, and activity; and sexual fantasies and responses to erotic stimuli. Because sexual behavior is so complex and hard to break into its component parts, the explanations put forth for individual aspects of sexual behavior have a great deal of overlap. Consequently, we will examine these explanations as a group after we first examine the findings.

▲ The Physiology of Sexual Response

In Masters and Johnson's revolutionary work (1966), the authors shattered the myth of sex differences in sexual responding. In their laboratory study of 382 women and 312 men, they discerned four phases of human sexual response, each of which is virtually identical in males and females. These phases are summarized in Table 4.1.

The four phases are as follows:

1. The *excitement phase* is characterized by sexual stimulation producing vasocongestion (filling of the blood vessels). This vasocongestion results in lubrication and clitoral erection in females in 5 to 15 seconds and penile erection in males in 3 to 8 seconds. This response occurs for any kind of effective sexual stimulation, physical or mental.

2. The *plateau phase* results in sexual tension increasing if effective sexual stimulation continues. Both sexes experience generalized skeletal muscle tension, rapid breathing, fast heart rate, and, in some, a body flush. In females, the clitoris retracts while remaining extremely sensitive to traction on the clitoral hood, the vaginal passageway constricts, and the inner two-thirds of the vagina balloons out. In the male, the glans of the penis increases in diameter and the testes are pulled up into the scrotum.

3. In the *orgasmic phase*, a sequence of rhythmic muscular contractions occurs about every .8 seconds, markedly reducing the vasocongestion built up by stimulation. Breathing increases to at least three times the normal rate, blood pressure increases by one-third, and heart rate more than doubles. In males, semen is ejaculated. In females, muscular contractions continue longer, and many females can have a further orgasm immediately with continued stimulation. This repeated orgasm is very rare in males.

4. The *resolution phase* completes the cycle, with muscular tension subsiding and the body gradually returning to its preexcitement state. The speed with which this occurs is related to the speed with which excitement occurred—the more slowly the excitement builds up, the more slowly it recedes. If

Table 4.1 Four phases of human sexual response in males and females

Male	Female
Excitement Phase	
Erection of penis	Vaginal lubrication
Nipple erection	Nipple erection
Partial elevation of testes	Lengthening and distention of vagina
Plateau Phase	
Fast heart rate (100–175 beats per minute)	Fast heart rate (100–175 beats per minute)
Rapid breathing	Rapid breathing
Elevated blood pressure	Elevated blood pressure
Sex flush (25% incidence)	Sex flush (75% incidence)
Glandular emission of lubricating mucus from penis	Glandular emission of lubricating mucus into vagina
Sometimes deepened color change in head of penis (glans)	Vivid color change in labia minora
Increased circumference in ridge at the penile glans	Decrease in size of vaginal opening
Full elevation of testes	Elevation of uterus
	Retraction of clitoris
Orgasmic Phase	
Rapid breathing	Rapid breathing
Fast heart rate (110–180 beats per minute)	Fast heart rate (110–180 beats per minute)
Increased blood pressure elevation	Increased blood pressure elevation
Rhythmic penile contractions, beginning at .8-second intervals	Rhythmic vaginal contractions, beginning at .8-second intervals
Resolution Phase	
Return to normal breathing, heart rate, and blood pressure	Return to normal breathing, heart rate, and blood pressure
Loss of vasocongestive size increase in penis, scrotum, testes	Loss of vasocongestive size increase in vagina, labia majora, and labia minora
Rapid disappearance of sex flush	Rapid disappearance of sex flush
Perspiring reaction (33% incidence)	Perspiring reaction (33% incidence)
Refractory period—temporary loss of stimulative susceptibility	No refractory period—capable of repeated orgasm if stimulated

Data from Masters and Johnson, 1966.

orgasm does not occur, the resolution phase is prolonged, giving rise to a tense, uncomfortable feeling. This is true for both males and females. Males experience a refractory period in which they are temporarily unresponsive to sexual stimulation; females experience no refractory period.

These reactions occur in the same sequence regardless of the type of stimulation (manual, oral, genital) or the source of stimulation (fantasy, masturbation, same-sex partner, other-sex partner). However, many people's sexual responses do not fit neatly into these phases (Zilbergeld, 1978). Furthermore, intensity and duration of sexual responses vary. Women generally have more intense and quicker orgasms from manual clitoral stimulation, especially from their own stimulation, than from heterosexual intercourse. In fact, as Kinsey and colleagues (1953) found, during masturbation, a woman takes the same length of time to reach an orgasm as does a man—from two to four minutes. The fact that it usually takes a woman longer to achieve orgasm during intercourse is most often a function of poor coital technique and of poor communication between partners regarding what is most stimulating.

Masters and Johnson's research and that of others proved a variety of ideas about sexuality to be false. They found the following facts:

1. Women have sexual responses similar to men except that women are capable of multiple orgasms.

This finding is contrary to the belief that women are less sexual than men or that they are even asexual.

2. Women arouse and reach orgasm as quickly as men when stimulation is appropriate, contrary to the belief that women are inherently slower to respond than men.

3. Women, as well as men, may respond with physical discomfort to not reaching an orgasm, contrary to the belief that an orgasm doesn't matter for a woman.

4. Women can achieve full sexual satisfaction without genital intercourse, contrary to the belief that a woman's sexual enjoyment depends on a man. Vaginal penetration may stimulate the Grafenberg spot, which is located within the anterior wall of the vagina. This "G spot" appears to be erotically sensitive in some women (J. Perry & Whipple, 1981). With vaginal penetration, orgasm may be more diffuse (felt less specifically over wider areas of the body) than without it (Hite, 1976). This can be either more or less pleasurable for a woman, depending on individual preference.

5. Women have only one kind of orgasm, based in the clitoris, although contractions are felt in the vagina. This is contrary to Freud's distinction between a vaginal and a clitoral orgasm, the former, according to Freud, being more "mature." However, some researchers have suggested that stimulation of the Grafenberg spot leads to a different type of orgasm than does pure clitoral stimulation (J. Perry & Whipple, 1981). At this point, such a suggestion still is unproven.

6. The subjective experience of orgasm is essentially the same for females and males. This was confirmed in an experimental study in which people closely concerned with sexual behavior (for example, psychologists, obstetricians/gynecologists, medical students) were unable to distinguish the sex of a person from that person's written description of his or her orgasm (Proctor, Wagner, & Butler, 1974). Further gender similarities in the experience of orgasm are evidenced by the findings that some women may ejaculate through their urethras upon orgasm (Belzer, 1981; J. Perry & Whipple, 1981).

These findings have altered traditional thinking about female sexuality, but changes in awareness have come slowly. Shere Hite (1976) found that ten years after Masters and Johnson's research was published, many women still believed the traditional view of their sexuality, even though they knew that they did not conform to it. She found that most women have more intense, quicker orgasms

with masturbation than with intercourse but that they feel they should not do so. Lesbians and bisexual women also appear to have stronger and more numerous orgasms than heterosexual women in their sexual interactions, possibly because women are on the average more attuned than men to women's bodies (Bressler & Lavender, 1986). As Hite notes, there is no great mystery about why a woman has an orgasm. The key is adequate stimulation, and, for most females, this is simply not supplied by intercourse, since clitoral stimulation, if it occurs, is usually indirect.

Sexual dysfunction may occur in any stage, but gender differences are most commonly expected in the stage of sexual desire or excitement (H. S. Kaplan, 1979). A close examination of this phase is needed.

▲ Sexual Interest, Attitudes, and Activity

One misconception resistant to refutation is that men have a stronger sex drive than women. It is important to differentiate among sexual desire, sexual interest, and sexual experience. Although males compared to females generally have more sexual experiences (summing all types of experiences together) (Griffitt & Hatfield, 1985) and more permissive attitudes toward heterosexual activity (S. S. Hendrick, Hendrick, Slapion-Foote, & Foote, 1985), it does not necessarily follow that males have stronger sex drives. Bernard Zilbergeld (1978) points out that male sexuality tends to be focused solely on penile penetration, whereas female sexuality tends to include more variety in terms of enjoyable body parts and types of stimulation. If definitions of sexual desire are restricted to desire for genital intercourse, women's sexual desires may go unrecorded.

Genital intercourse appears to follow a clear and well-understood script (Geer & Broussard, 1990). Women and men agree on the typical sequence of sexual behaviors leading to coitus, starting with kissing, moving to caressing, manual stimulation, oral stimulation, and then penetration. Where the sexes differ is in their degree of arousal to each of the 14 behaviors in the script. The arousal level of male undergraduate subjects followed the script sequence very closely, building linearly with each of the steps. However, the arousal level of female undergraduate subjects was not significantly correlated with the sequence. The behaviors that females found most arousing had to do with the male stimulating the female, whereas males found most behaviors arousing, especially penetration. Thus, it appears that men and women react to the same sexual behaviors differently, possibly leading to miscommunication and misunderstanding. Furthermore, since it appears that male arousal may determine the sequence of sexual acts, females in heterosexual unions may not be as satisfied as males. Understandably, then, women's interest in sexual intercourse might be less than men's.

In fact, considerable evidence exists that women are less interested than men in sexual intercourse (Hite, 1976; Zilbergeld, 1978). For example, in a study of the recreational preferences of more than 500 middle-class couples, the wives were more likely to prefer reading a book to sexual and affectional activity (37% preferred the former; 26%, the latter). Husbands, on the other hand, preferred sexual and affectional activities over attending athletic events and reading books (45%, 41%, 33%, respectively) (Mancini & Orthner, 1978). The fact that women's lower interest in sexual activities may be a result of inadequate stimulation and not of a personal or female-related defect is usually neither known nor acknowledged. A woman's vulnerability to pregnancy also may affect her interest in intercourse.

Sexual Attitudes

One problem with assessing sexual desires is that self-reports of sexual feelings strongly reflect sexual attitudes. Major changes in the area of attitudes toward sexual activity have been observed over the last 40 years. From the 1950s to the early 1980s, U.S. society became more sexually permissive, especially of premarital sexual intercourse (D'Emilio & Freedman, 1988; Fink, 1983). However, since the early 1980s, sexual attitudes have become somewhat more conservative, probably due to an increase in sexually transmitted diseases (especially herpes and AIDS), increased societal conservatism, and a reaction against the sexual liberalism of the previous two decades (Gerrard, 1987; "How College Women," 1987; "The Revolution," 1984).

Liberal attitudes toward sexual activity may have reached their peak during the early 1980s, especially for individuals aged 18 to 29 and for those with some college education. Males and females began to hold more similar attitudes regarding sexual activity, at least in the context of a committed relationshp. For example, a Louis Harris and Associates poll taken in 1983 (Fink, 1983) found that 79% of men and 70% of women aged 18 to 29 thought it was all right for regularly dating couples to have sex. Among men and women aged 50 to 64, only 55% of the men and

40% of the women thought such behavior was all right. With respect to casual sex, however, gender differences in attitudes have remained marked. For example, the annual national survey of college freshmen in 1990 found that nearly twice as many men as women (66% to 38%) thought it was all right for people who like each other to have sex if they have known each other for a very short time (A. W. Astin, 1991). In fact, gender differences with respect to approval of sexual intercourse without love are among the strongest found, with an effect size (d value) of 1.34 (J. L. Carroll, Volk, & Hyde, 1985).

With respect to attitudes toward homosexuality, however, men are much more conservative than women. The 1990 survey of college freshman found that more than half of the men (56%) thought it was important to have laws prohibiting homosexual relationships. Only one-third (34%) of their female peers felt similarly. This gender difference, which existed even before the AIDS scare, is probably a result of the greater *homophobia* (fear and hatred of homosexuals and homosexuality) among men than women (Herek, 1987; Morin & Garfinkle, 1978) and the probability that both sexes interpret the word *homosexual* to refer to men only.

Sexual Activity

Not only did sexual attitudes in general become more permissive and the sexual double standard decline somewhat between the 1950s and the 1980s, but sexual behavior followed a similar pattern, with some retrenchment in the 1990s. Before the 1960s, less than 10% of White females and 40% of Black females had intercourse by age 16, compared to one-third to two-thirds of male teenagers (Brooks-Gunn & Furstenberg, 1989). Twenty years later, the gap between Black and White females had narrowed, as had the gap between females and males. Blacks still begin sexual activity earlier than Whites. By age 18, nearly all Black males, three-fourths of non-Black males, 60% of Black females, and more than 50% of White females have had sexual intercourse at least once (Brooks-Gunn & Furstenberg, 1989; Sonenstein, 1990, as cited in T. Adler, 1990d). Among college-age people, a similar increase in sexual experience over previous generations has occurred (Hopkins, 1977; Sacks, 1990). In fact, the incidence of premarital intercourse for college females has shown a greater increase than for males (from about 25% of all college females in the mid-1960s to about 80% in the mid- 1980s), probably because males already were close to ceiling level in terms of sexual activity. Yet, despite increasingly similar numbers of nonvirgins among males and females by age 18, men still tend to have more frequent intercourse and more sexual partners. For example, in a survey of single men and women, aged 18 to 44, more than half (56%) of the men had had sex with more than one partner in the past year, compared to one-third (38%) of the women ("Rubber Sales," 1988).

As noted previously, sex typically is defined as genital intercourse. Other forms of sexual behavior have rarely been examined. However, subjective reports of female sexuality make it clear that for women, kissing, touching, and holding count as sex and may be more sexually satisfying than intercourse (Denny, Field, & Quadagno, 1984; Laws & Schwartz, 1977). Females also may find oral sex more satisfying than intercourse. At least it avoids the risk of pregnancy. A study of oral sex among adolescents revealed that receiving oral-genital stimulation was more common than intercourse for females, although for males, intercourse was more common than either receiving or giving oral-genital stimulation (Newcomer & Udry, 1985). For both males and females, the incidence of both giving and receiving oral sex is much higher than Kinsey and colleagues found in the 1940s and 1950s. Masturbation too seems to be on the increase among females, although it is still more common in males (Abramson & Mosher, 1979; Hunt, 1974; Mosher & Abramson, 1977). Virtually all men and more than two-thirds of all women have masturbated. The fact that some women never masturbate is important in light of the findings that masturbation is strongly related to the ability to have coital orgasms (Kinsey et al., 1953).

These findings suggest that the younger generation of women may be more sexually active than previous generations, especially when sex is defined as genital intercourse. Virginity is no longer a necessity for marriage for young women; therefore, fewer feel compelled to retain it or to say they have retained it. Whether lesbian and bisexual women have increased their sexual behavior is difficult to determine. What is known about the sexual experiences of lesbians, gay men, and bisexuals is that males tend to have more sex with more partners and in the context of more short-term relationships than do females (A. Bell & Weinberg, 1978; Kinsey et al., 1948, 1953; N. Meredith, 1984; Peplau, 1981). Gay men also tend to act on their sexual feelings earlier than lesbians (Riddle & Morin, 1977), just as heterosexual males act earlier than heterosexual females.

Surveys of lesbian, gay male, and heterosexual relationships generally find that men in gay relationships have the most sexual interactions, followed by people in heterosexual relationships, with women in lesbian relationships having the fewest sexual interactions (Blumstein & Schwartz, 1983). Whether these differences, which follow gender lines, are due to gender differences in sexual desire, social conditioning, or gender-based norms and expectancies is hard to determine. Among married couples in the late 1970s, sexual activity became more frequent and more satisfying for both partners than it had been in previous generations (Blumstein & Schwartz, 1983; D'Emilio & Freedman, 1988). Both men and women expect a "good" sex life, and most couples seem relatively satisfied with what they have.

Sexual behavior showed marked changes during the 1980s, probably as a result of the AIDS scare, sex education, increasingly conservative values, and/or changing gender roles. Casual sex among gay men significantly declined and the use of condoms increased (Landers, 1990). Similar results have been found among heterosexual males. For example, the 1988 survey of teenage boys found that although more males were sexually active than a decade earlier, boys were having sex less often, with fewer girls, and at a later age (Sonenstein, 1990, as cited in T. Adler, 1990d). Furthermore, over half of the boys were now using condoms when they had intercourse. College students, too, had sex slightly less often in the late 1980s than they did in the late 1970s, and they had increased their use of effective contraception (Gerrard, 1987; "How College Women," 1987).

Despite the preceding findings—the convergence between males and females with respect to desire for sexual activity, at least in a love relationship—the belief persists that men have stronger sex drives than women (Byrne, 1977; A. E. Gross, 1978; Peplau, Rubin, & Hill, 1977). Because the male sex drive is believed to be stronger than the female drive, sex is perceived by both females and males as being more important and enjoyable for men than for women. This belief is particularly evident in married and dating couples.

Males usually do seem to take the lead in heterosexual activities, both in initiating sexual contact and in controlling the sexual interaction itself (Blumstein & Schwartz, 1983; Grauerholz & Serpe, 1985; Masters & Johnson, 1979). Women appear to exert more negative control; that is, they may resist or encourage sexual advances but may not initiate them. This double standard regarding sexual initiative still remains strong, although attitudes about its acceptability may be changing.

The Meaning Attached to Sex

Regardless of similarities or differences between the sexes in sexual interest and sexual activity, an important difference does seem to exist between males and females in the meaning attached to sex (Foa et al., 1987; Hatfield, Sprecher, Pillemer, Greenberger, & Wexler, 1988; S. S. Hendrick et al., 1985; Hite, 1976, 1981; Whitley, 1988b). Indeed, gender differences in this area may turn out to be the strongest of all gender differences. J. L. Carroll and colleagues (1985) estimate that gender accounts for 31% of the variability in attitudes toward casual premarital sex, a percentage much higher than the variability accounted for by gender in aggressive behaviors and in visual-spatial skills (around 6%).

The gender difference in the meaning of sex can be summarized as follows: females generally connect sex with feelings of affection and closeness; males often see sex as an achievement, an adventure, a demonstration of control and power, or a purely physical release. This is true before, during, and outside marriage and for same-gender relationships as well as female-male ones (Blumstein & Schwartz, 1983; A. Lawson, 1988). Women generally have fewer partners than men and their first experience is usually with someone with whom they are romantically involved. They also are more likely to use sex to get love, rather than to use love to get sex. For women, the chief pleasures of sex and intercourse appear to be the shared feelings, the emotional warmth, and the feeling of being wanted and needed, not the physical sensations per se. Men, on the other hand, are more likely to isolate sex from other aspects of relationships and to focus on the arousal aspects of sexual activity.

Gender differences in the meaning of sex should not be overstated, however. Most men, like most women, prefer having love and sex together, and most men, like most women, rank love far ahead of sex in terms of overall importance for their life satisfaction (Chassler, 1988; Pietropinto & Simenauer, 1977). In fact, with age, love and intimacy replace physical pleasure as the main motivator of sex for most men (Sprague & Quadagno, 1989). In contrast, physical pleasure becomes more important to women during middle-age than it was earlier. However, despite similar preferences, more men than women tend to differentiate between love and sex (Foa et al., 1987). These differences are most marked between gay men and lesbians, and least marked among married heterosexuals. Among teenagers, love is low on the list of reasons for having sex (peer pressure ranks first), but it is even lower for boys than for girls (6% of boys gave love as the reason compared to 11% of the girls) ("Teen Sex," 1989).

These gender differences in the meaning of sex may lead to differences in faking experiences. In the 1970s, faking orgasm was common among 50 to 70% of heterosexual women (L. B. Rubin, 1990; "Sex on Campus," 1982). In the 1980s, the percentage was down to about 30%. Some men also fake orgasm when they engage in sexual intercourse without really wanting to (L. Levine & Barbach, 1984). However, the reasons for faking appear to be different for women and men. Whereas women may fake orgasm to enhance their partner's ego, men appear to fake orgasm to maintain the myth of an omnipresent male sexual interest. Both heterosexual men and heterosexual women seem to be preoccupied with attaining orgasm, especially when contrasted with lesbians and gay men (Masters & Johnson, 1979).

These differences in the meaning of sex may be related to women's somewhat greater tendency to see all behaviors in the context of relationships, as discussed in the last chapter (Gilligan et al., 1990). Or women may emphasize intimacy because intercourse often is not satisfying for females or is less satisfying than is masturbation. Gender differences in the meaning of sex also may be a function of the different socialization experiences for males and for females in our society. As A. E. Gross (1978) and others have noted, sex is commonly viewed as a major proving ground of a male's masculinity. Quantity, more than quality, is stressed, with many negative consequences as a result.

Some of the negative consequences manifest themselves in sexual dysfunction. For males, problems with impotence or premature ejaculation often arise from pressure to perform and from an exclusive goal orientation, both being parts of the male role. As Masters and Johnson (1974) note, this very pressure can be self-defeating. In females, sexual dysfunction often takes the form of inability to have an orgasm. In the past, such women were termed frigid. Now they are called preorgasmic, because it is understood that with proper stimulation, any female can have an orgasm. Instruction on self-stimulation has been markedly effective in this regard. Modern sex therapists treat sexual problems more as learning and communication problems than as a reflection of physiological problems, although the latter sometimes occur. These physiological problems, too, usually can be successfully treated.

▲ Sexual Fantasies and Responses to Erotic Stimuli

Another strong belief in our society is that males are sexually aroused, especially by visual stimuli and by their own fantasies, more frequently and more easily than females. If one were only to look at which sex is the primary consumer of sex stimuli and pornography, such a conclusion seems reasonable. Women do appear to be less interested than men in sexual material. However, controlled research studies paint a more complex picture: erotic material and sexual fantasies arouse women as much as they do men, but the content of the material and fantasies may be different.

Erotica

Research on reactions to erotic stimuli generally has used only male subjects or has used materials with explicit sexual content aimed almost exclusively at heterosexual males. Hence, accurate data on female responsiveness have been minimal. Furthermore, when questioned, females generally report less sexual arousal than males to explicit sexual material (Griffitt, 1987). However, when actual physiological responses to a range of erotic and erotic-romantic stimuli (stories, pictures, films) are measured in well-controlled studies, women have been found to respond with levels of arousal equal to that of men (W. R. Fisher & Byrne, 1978; Heiman, 1975; Masters & Johnson, 1966; G. Schmidt, 1975). In one study (G. Schmidt & Sigusch, 1973), from 80% to 91% of the men were aroused, while 70% to 83% of the women were aroused, with considerable intragroup differences in responding.

Why should women report less sexual arousal than men to sexual stimuli when they are physiologically responding equally to men? As Heiman (1975) documented, women sometimes do not know when they are physiologically aroused, or else they feel reluctant to report this arousal. This reluctance may be due to conditioning and also to the fact that female sexual arousal (vaginal lubrication) is much less noticeable to the woman herself than is male arousal (erection) to the man. The conditioning explanation is supported by the finding that it is mainly women who feel guilty about sex who tend to report low sexual arousal while viewing an erotic videotape (Morokoff, 1985). Such self-reports contradict the objective finding that such women also tend to show *greater* physiological arousal during erotic videotapes than women low in sex guilt. Guilt may make women inhibit their conscious sexual arousal to erotic material, yet this inhibition actually may make such women more arousable.

The stimuli that arouse men and women differ, but not always in stereotyped ways. For example, females do not respond more to romantic stories than to erotic ones. Rather, both sexes respond most to explicit sex stories, women sometimes responding more than men (W. R. Fisher & Byrne, 1978; Heiman, 1975). Males, however, are much more likely than females to get aroused by stimuli depicting sexual aggression and violence, the content of most pornography (Malamuth & Donnerstein, 1984). Heterosexual women and gay men are most aroused by male erotic stimuli, heterosexual men and lesbians are most aroused by female erotic stimuli (Griffitt, 1987).

Although males and females are equally capable of being aroused by pertinent types of erotica, there is no question that males seem more interested in, are more positive about, and have more experience with such materials (W. R. Fisher & Byrne, 1978; Griffitt, 1987). In fact, most such materials, with their objectification and sexualization of the female body, are aimed at heterosexual males. Indeed, the female body has been sexually objectified in most visual stimuli, from pornography to shoe advertisements. (See Figure 4.1 for an example of the sexual objectification of the female body.) The multibillion-dollar pornography industry, in particular, aims its products almost exclusively at males, both heterosexual and homosexual. (The stores that sell this material disguise this fact by calling themselves *adult* bookstores, when they are *adult male* bookstores. The targeted clientele becomes clear, however, as soon as one steps in the door.) Whether female disinterest in erotica is due to inappropriate stimuli, sexual conditioning, greater sex guilt, or social conformity is unclear. We know, however, that the typical sequence of erotic stories about genital intercourse are more in line with male arousal needs than female needs (Geer & Broussard, 1990). Thus, females may be less interested in erotica because most sexual materials are not optimally arousing to them.

A disturbing implication of males' greater experience with erotic material is the finding that exposure to such material can have adverse effects on men's judgments of women (Kenrick, Gutierres, & Goldberg, 1989). Men, but not women, who were exposed to nude photographs taken from *Playboy*, *Penthouse*, and *Playgirl* later rated their mate and an unknown female as less sexually attractive than did a control group who saw pictures of abstract

Figure 4.1 Men have more experience with erotica because of the pervasive use of the female form in advertising products unrelated to the female form. (Courtesy of Sanders Bootmakers.)

art. When erotic stimuli are combined with violence against and degradation of women, as is the usual case with pornography, the negative effects of such materials are even more far-reaching. The effects include greater predisposition to act in sexually aggressive ways and more callous attitudes toward women and sexual violence. These effects of pornography will be discussed in Chapter 12.

Fantasies
In regard to erotic fantasies, it appears that both sexes are able to arouse themselves through fantasy (Heiman, 1975), and the majority of both sexes do arouse themselves in this way (Kinsey et al., 1948, 1953; Knafo & Jaffe, 1984). However, males may fantasize more frequently than females about sex. For example, a survey of college students found that

36% of the males said they had such fantasies every day in contrast to 17% of the women (Sacks, 1990). Another one-third of each sex admitted to fantasizing a few times a week, so the majority of both sexes fantasize frequently. The kinds of fantasies created by men and women may differ as well, depending upon sexual orientation. For example, most gay men and lesbians have same-gender fantasies, most heterosexuals, female-male fantasies (Masters & Johnson, 1979). Women are more likely than men to fantasize about submitting to another, romance, and seduction, whereas men are more likely than women to fantasize about sexual dominance and virility, and sex with strangers (Griffitt, 1987; Knafo & Jaffe, 1984). These fantasies relate to gender differences in the meaning of sex.

▲   Explanations for Sexual Behavior

To review the chapter thus far, females and males have similar sexual responses on a physiological level. In practice, however, and irrespective of sexual orientation, males compared to females begin sexual activity earlier, have more sexual experiences, are more interested in sexual materials, and are more likely to consider sex apart from love. Since the 1970s, the differences between males and females in sexual behaviors have decreased, mainly as a result of females' adopting traditionally male patterns of sexual activity. Still, some gender differences remain that somewhat support the stereotypic image of males as more sexually oriented than females, although not the image of females as asexual. We will now turn to some explanations for these gender patterns.

Because sex is necessary for the reproduction of the species and because it involves many physiological responses, some researchers lean toward a physiological explanation of sexual behavior. Others stress psychosocial and/or sociocultural factors. As will be demonstrated, all these factors interact. The strongest factors, however, seem to be the sociocultural ones.

Physiological Factors
"Men are just naturally more interested in sex than women." "Men's urges are stronger, you know." These comments reflect the belief that physiological factors underlie differences in sexual behavior. Explanations invoking physiological processes center on hormones, anatomy, and evolutionary development.

Hormones   Sexual interest, or libido, for both males and females has been related both prenatally and postnatally to the androgens, especially testosterone (Barfield, 1976; Money & Ehrhardt, 1972). Androgen secretion appears to lower the threshold of arousal and to increase the energy with which sexual activity is pursued in both humans and animals. Decreases in testosterone level with age are related to decreases in sexual interest (Bancroft, 1987). The increase in androgen production at puberty is primarily responsible for the increase in sexual interest at that time. However, the effect of testosterone level on sexual activities in boys is much stronger and more direct than the effect of testosterone level on girls' sexual activities, suggesting the importance of social factors in modulating or enhancing hormonal influences (Susman, Nottelmann, et al., 1987; Udry & Talbert, 1988; Udry et al., 1986). In our society, such behaviors are encouraged in males but not in females. Perhaps that is why hormonal effects on sexual behavior appear more direct and predictable in males than in females. Even in animals, social factors and past experience play a more important role in determining sexual behavior than do hormones (Barfield, 1976; R. D. Nadler, 1987). In humans, behavior is more variable and freer from direct hormonal control than is the case with other animals. Consequently, the effect of experience is even greater. Therefore, although generally higher androgen levels in males than females may tend to lower males' arousal threshold, social factors could either encourage or discourage related sexual behavior. It should also be recalled that although males typically have higher androgen levels than females after puberty, females are more reactive to androgens than males, thus equalizing some of the androgens' effects on behavior.

Few studies have directly examined women's sexual desires, especially as a function of hormonal factors. This negligence is probably due to viewing sex as natural for males, but less so for females. The few studies that have dealt with the timing of female desires have yielded contradictory results. Although some women appear to have a peak of sexual desire at a specific phase of their menstrual cycle, the precise phase varies from one woman to another, partly as a function of the form of birth control used (D. B. Adams et al., 1978; A. R. Gold & Adams, 1981; Money & Ehrhardt, 1972). Postmenopausal women typically report a reduction in sexual desire that corresponds to declining estrogen levels, but their orgasmic response is not affected and psychological-social factors may play the more important role (Leiblum, 1990). In general, testosterone levels appear to play a more important role than ovarian hormones in modulating a woman's sexual arousability (N. McCoy, Cutler, & Davidson, 1985; Morris et al., 1987; Svare & Kinsley, 1987). An examination of lesbians might throw more light on the question of whether women have predictable peaks of sexual desire that are related to hormone levels and not to reproductive desires or fears (see E. Cole & Rothblum, 1991).

Males and females seem to have different peaks of sexual activity. For males, the highest point of sexual activity occurs around the age of 18; for women, around the age of 30 (Griffitt & Hatfield, 1985). Here, too, hormonal explanations are unsatisfactory. Rather, such peaks reflect gender differences in sexual experience. In particular, women have most of their sexual experiences within marriage. For males, marital status is uncorrelated with sexual activity.

Although postnatal hormones may affect the amount of sexual energy present, they do not affect the choice of sex partner nor do they distinguish between heterosexuals and homosexuals (H. F. L. Meyer-Bahlburg, 1984; Money, 1987, 1988). Prenatal hormones, however, may predispose certain individuals toward homosexuality, bisexuality, or heterosexuality. The evidence here is quite complex and controversial (Ellis & Ames, 1987; Hines, 1982; LeVay, 1991; Money, 1987, 1988; G. Sanders & Ross-Field, 1987). Such a predisposition can occur in a number of ways; for example, it may be due to direct genetic-hormonal factors, drug-induced factors, maternal stress during pregnancy, or immunity factors. Prenatal hormones may affect brain structures and brain organization, which in turn are involved in sexual behavior. The crucial time for determining a sexual orientation predisposition may be between the middle of the second month of gestation and the middle of the fifth month. Evidence of the universality of homosexuality, both culturally and historically, as well as the experimental production of same-sex mating behaviors in other animal species, supports the possibility of some physiological basis of homosexual behavior in humans. However, a predisposition must be facilitated by postnatal experiences in order to become manifest. For example, although women who were exposed to a synthetic estrogen (DES) prenatally were more likely to be bisexual or lesbian than a matched control group, about 75% still were exclusively or nearly exclusively heterosexual (Ehrhardt et al., 1985). Sexual orientation requires both nature and nurture and appears relatively fixed by ages 5 to 8. It still is possible for sexual orientation to be completely determined postnatally for some people. Given the evidence, it is foolish and scientifically inaccurate to label one sexual orientation as more natural than another. Similarly, it is scientifically unacceptable to think that one can change one's sexual orientation at will. Although one might be able to change one's sexual behaviors, one's orientation (what sex stimuli one finds most sexually arousing) appears fixed well before puberty.

Anatomy   The fact that males and females have different sex organs has been held by some to account for gender differences in sexual behavior. By this reasoning, the greater visibility and accessibility of the penis (as opposed to the clitoris) and the use of the penis in urination may orient a boy to handling it and discovering its pleasurable qualities. This may account for males' greater likelihood of masturbation. At puberty, a male's attention is further focused on his genitals by the increased frequency of erections and by the start of seminal emissions. Female genitals, on the other hand, are easier to ignore, often remaining unlabeled (referred to only as "down there"), and their signs of arousal are subtler. As Heiman (1975) found, some women misread their physiological arousal. This may occur because females have relatively less experience than males in producing and identifying such states since they tend to masturbate less than males. Furthermore, since masturbation is clitoral, it would be difficult to imagine vaginal intercourse as pleasurable. Puberty for females is marked by menstruation, which has reproductive, rather than sexual, significance and which often is surrounded by fear or mystery. Thus, anatomical differences may lead to differences in attention paid to genitalia. This differential attention may be further socialized into two different scripts (behavioral blueprints) concerning sexual behavior for males and females (Simon & Gagnon, 1987; Laws & Schwartz, 1977).

Freud (1905/1964c, 1924/1964a, 1925/1964b) spelled out the "anatomy is destiny" approach quite comprehensively and is most closely identified with it. In brief, he posited that a child's gender development is based on unconscious reactions to anatomical differences. When a little boy (aged 3 to 6) discovers that a female does not have a penis, he becomes afraid of losing his. This castration anxiety forces him to repress his desire for his mother and to identify with his father. By identifying with the father, the little boy's fear of punishment for his incestuous desire is reduced because he believes that the father would not punish someone so much like him. This male form of resolution of the Oedipus complex leads to the development of a strong superego (through fear of punishment) and a strong male gender identification.

A little girl, however, on discovering she does not have a penis, envies a male and feels inferior. She rejects her mother because the mother also is "inferior" and looks to her father for a replacement penis. The resolution of her "Oedipus" complex (called the Electra complex by neo-Freudians) occurs when she accepts the impossibility of her wish for a penis and compensates for it by desiring a child. This penis envy on the part of females has enormous consequences for their personality development, according to Freud. He concluded that first, females have weaker superegos than males, because their Electra complex is resolved by envy, not fear. Second, he concluded that females feel inferior to males and consequently develop a personality characterized by masochism, passivity, and narcissism. Third, he believed that females give up their clitoral focus in masturbation and begin to prepare for adult gratification via vaginal stimulation.

Freud's theory has been criticized on a variety of grounds. What concerns us here are the criticisms of penis envy and its consequences. As was noted previously, there is no evidence that females are more passive or masochistic than males, or that they have inferior superegos. In addition, the vaginal versus clitoral orgasm differentiation is incorrect. All orgasms are clitorally based regardless of stimulation. Also, no evidence exists that little girls believe they are anatomically inferior to boys or that they blame their mothers for lack of a penis, and so on. Freud's theory reflects a strong male bias: he regards sexuality itself as male, he bases his theory on a patriarchal society, and he assumes that everyone recognizes a penis as inherently superior (see Millet, 1970, for an interesting critique). If young girls do envy boys, they more likely are envying males' higher status and greater power rather than the male anatomical appendage (Horney, 1922/1973). In support of this status interpretation, Nathan (1981) found in her cross-cultural analysis of dream reports that the occurrence of penis envy in a dream was a function of the status of women in that culture. Where the status of women was low, dream reports showed penis envy; where the status of women was higher, dream reports showed less penis envy. Furthermore, an equally persuasive argument can be made for male womb envy. This envy is theoretically manifested in the way males develop rituals and develop a greater achievement orientation and need for dominance as compensation for their inability to conceive (see Bettelheim, 1962; Chesler, 1978). Thus, although anatomy may influence an individual's sexual development, Freud's "destiny" edict is greatly overstated and very male biased. Indeed, Horney (1922/1973) suggests that Freud's ideas regarding female thoughts and feelings are really projections of Freud's own feelings and thoughts about girls.

Possessing a womb and being pregnable (able to be made pregnant) probably have some consequence in a girl's sexual development. Similarly, having a penis and not being pregnable probably have some consequence in a male's sexual development. However, culture determines the way these biological facts affect an individual's sexual feelings and behaviors, as we will soon see.

Evolution   Before leaving physiological explanations, the explanation based on evolutionary development merits consideration. The most well developed of these theories is the sociobiological one, whose major proponent with regard to human sexual behavior is Donald Symons. Symons (1979, 1987) has argued that differences in sexual conduct between women and men relate to different reproductive strategies in the sexes. These different strategies ultimately are dependent on the differences between sperm and egg cells. Because men produce a large number of sperm, their reproductive strategy is to have many sexual partners and transient relationships. Women, because they have a small supply of eggs and must carry a child for at least nine months, require stable relations with a good provider. Symons uses this theory to explain men's greater number of sexual partners, greater interest in casual sex, and greater arousability by visual stimuli. Symons argues that in same-gender sexual behaviors we see the true nature of male and female sexuality—multiple involvements for males, committed relationships for females.

Symons's arguments, albeit provocative, involve much speculation and ignore contradictory evidence that currently is available (for example, the research on responses to erotic stimuli, the occurrence of multiple sex partners among many female primates). He neglects any evolutionary explanation of what may be the major gender difference in human sexual behavior: a female's

capacity for multiple orgasms, which is completely unconnected to reproduction. Symons also bases his entire explanation on sexual conduct in the United States, despite the fact that sexual behavior varies widely in different cultures. Therefore, although his explanation has a certain simplistic appeal, it does not appear to be well substantiated (Benderly, 1987; Hrdy, 1986). (See Bleier, 1984, and Lewontin et al., 1984, for critiques of sociobiology.) The male-female dichotomy in sexual behavior can be explained better by social factors than by genes. A model that takes into account the complexity of both factors in human sexual behavior is just beginning to be developed (see Kenrick & Trost, 1987).

A different type of evolutionary theory has been proffered by Mary Jane Sherfey (1974), who argues that women have a biologically based inordinate sex drive. As evidence, she cites women's potential for multiple orgasms, and she includes the fact that the more orgasms a woman achieves, the more she can achieve. This sexual capacity may have evolved because the more erotic primates bred more and therefore reproduced more than the less erotic primates. In humans, however, women's inordinate sex drive had to be suppressed if family life and agricultural economies were to develop, since the female sex drive interfered with maternal responsibility and the establishment of property rights and kinship laws, all elements vital to patriarchal civilization. Thus, Sherfey describes how men had to suppress female sexuality to establish family life and maintain their own position of power and the power of patriarchy.

Sherfey's theory presents many problems. In the first place, no conclusive evidence has been found that female hypersexuality ever existed, even in tribal hunting societies (Tavris & Offir, 1977). Also, her theory cannot account for societal differences. As we shall see, female sexuality is not universally suppressed. In addition, the theory itself reflects a curious patriarchal bias in which men are viewed as coming to the rescue of society and in which women are viewed, in terms of their sexuality, as being unable to control themselves. Thus, although provocative, Sherfey's theory remains in the realm of speculation. It does highlight, however, the greater, often unused, potential that females have for sexual enjoyment.

In sum, physiological factors do not clearly explain male and female sexual behavior, although males' higher androgen levels and greater handling of their genitals may contribute somewhat to gender differences in desire and behavior. Psychosocial and sociocultural factors also need to be examined.

Psychosocial Factors

Four major psychosocial factors in the development of sexual behavior are parental influence, peer influence, personality variables, and sexual scripting.

Parental influence   The viewpoint that parent-child relationships are important in determining a child's eventual sexual behavior is an outgrowth of Freud's theory of personality development and the particular importance of the phallic stage (ages 3 to 5). It is during this stage that the resolution of the Electra and Oedipus complexes occurs. Successful resolution means an active sexuality for males and a passive sexuality for females. "Deviant" sexual behavior, including homosexuality, is seen as a result of some problem with resolving this stage. There is little support for this aspect of Freud's theory. For example, research on both lesbians and gay males does not consistently find a particular family constellation or particularly deviant or traumatic childhood experiences (A. P. Bell, Weinberg, & Hammersmith, 1981; Money, 1988; Pleck, 1981b).

One major influence on later sexual behavior is sexual rehearsal play during late infancy and childhood (Money, 1988). Children who are prevented from such play by excessive punishment or prohibition, who are isolated from playmates, or who are victims of sexual abuse may have their adult sexual behaviors negatively affected. Gender differences in terms of prohibitions and isolation from playmates are unclear, but evidence exists that girls are much more likely to be victims of sexual abuse than boys (approximately one-third of girls compared to less than 10% of boys have been victims of sexual abuse before the age of 18; Finkelhor, 1984; D. E. H. Russell, 1986). Evidence is growing that childhood sexual abuse may cause sexual problems later on, mainly by desensitizing the individual to her or his body. This may result in either restricted or excessive sexual behaviors.

Sexual rehearsal play during childhood and late infancy also may influence sexual orientation (Money, 1988). Although same-sex sexual rehearsal play during childhood does not necessarily lead to a same-sex or bisexual orientation in adulthood, cultures in which girl-boy sexual rehearsal play is permitted or encouraged during childhood tend to have a low incidence of adult homosexuality. Such early experiences may be a form of social learning and conditioning.

Parents appear to communicate about sex differently to their daughters versus their sons (Brooks-Gunn & Furstenberg, 1989; DeLamater, 1987). For example, parents are much more likely to talk to daughters than sons about both the reproductive significance and the morality of sex. These differences will be discussed in more detail later, in the context of sexual scripts. However, exactly how much influence parents have on their child's sexual behavior is unclear. Of far greater influence are peers.

Peer influence   Peers appear to influence the timing and frequency of sexual activity. A 1986 Planned Parenthood survey of teenagers found that the leading reason both girls and boys have sex in the teen years is peer pressure ("Teen Sex," 1989). For girls, pressure from peers far outweighs other reasons. One-third (34%) of girls gave peer pressure as the leading reason for having sex, followed by pressure from boys (17%), "everyone is doing it" (14%), curiosity (14%), love (11%), and sexual gratification (5%). For boys, one-fourth (26%) gave peer pressure as the leading reason, but this was followed by curiosity (16%), "everyone is doing it" (10%), sexual gratification (10%), and love (6%).

Other research supports the findings that peer pressure or modeling is probably the single most important reason, next to hormonal readiness, influencing teenagers' sexual activities, especially with respect to heterosexual intercourse (E. A. Smith, Udry, & Morris, 1985; Wilcox & Udry, 1986). Teenagers also may gravitate toward peer groups whose sexual behaviors are consistent with their own (Newcomb, Huba, & Bentler, 1986). Males, especially, appear pushed to have sex. For example, in a 1987 study of college students, 40% of the men and 28% of the women said they had felt peer pressure to be sexually active ("How College Women," 1987). However, these percentages were down from 1980, when 52% of the men and 45% of the women had felt such pressure.

Personality variables   As discussed in the last chapter, psychodynamic theory views males and females as developing different personalities. Recent feminist formulations of psychodynamic theory, especially the self-in-relation theory (Jordan, 1987; J. B. Miller, 1984; Surrey, 1985), suggest that women's sexuality mirrors their personality development. Because women's personality develops in the context of relationships, women's sexual self also is embedded in a relationship. On the other hand, men's sexuality, like their personality, develops as disconnected from relationships. Thus, women tend to emphasize and prefer sex in the context of an intimate relationship, and casual sex is less appealing to them than it is to men. Furthermore, because females expect sex to be mutually enhancing (as they expect most relationships to be), they become disappointed when their expectations are not met. Thus, girls may learn to split off their sexual self from the rest of their personality and stop trying to find pleasure in it. Rather, girls start to focus on what they can give to a partner. Although provocative and in line with some of the findings regarding gender differences in the meaning of sex, this theory remains speculative.

Freud's psychoanalytic theory asserted that traditional femininity, meaning passivity, was associated with female sexual satisfaction. This assertion has not been supported by research; that is, no significant relationship between femininity and sexual satisfaction has been found (C. S. Kirkpatrick, 1980). Rather, such "masculine" characteristics as assertiveness and self-confidence seem important for both male and female sexual fulfillment (Oakley, 1972; L. J. Snow & Parsons, 1983). For females, in particular, positive attitudes toward non-gender-stereotypic roles and behaviors are associated with sexual satisfaction.

Not only is sexual satisfaction linked to instrumental (stereotypically masculine) personality traits for females, but most sexual behaviors also are linked to such traits in both sexes. For example, instrumental personality traits in both female and male college students are associated with greater sexual experience, more sexual partners, earlier age of first intercourse, more permissive attitudes toward sex, and a more game-playing attitude toward love (W. C. Bailey, Hendrick, & Hendrick, 1987; Leary & Snell, 1988). Masculine-sex-typed females, in particular, are more sexually active and experienced than other females. Expressive (stereotypically feminine) personality traits are correlated with positive attitudes toward sex as an expression of love and negative attitudes toward casual sex.

Sex-typed characteristics are believed to be associated with sexual orientation. Most people believe that lesbians and gay men are sexually inverted—that is, that they are sex-typed in the direction opposite their biological sex. In other words, most people think male homosexuals must be feminine-sex-typed (and feminine-sex-typed males must be gay), and female homosexuals must be masculine-sex-typed (and masculine-sex-typed females must be lesbian) (Kite & Deaux, 1987; Storms, 1980; Storms, Stivers, Lambers, & Hill,

1981). Research supporting the implicit inversion theory, however, is weak. Although lesbians and gay men do appear to be less traditionally sex-typed than heterosexuals, lesbians and gay men are more likely to be androgynous than cross-sex-typed (Kurdek, 1987; Spence & Helmreich, 1978). Gay men still view themselves as more masculine than feminine, while lesbians still view themselves as more feminine than masculine. Yet, despite limited empirical support, people still believe in the sexual inversion theory. Because lesbians and gay men are stigmatized in the United States, all but feminine-sex-typed heterosexual women and masculine-sex-typed heterosexual men tend to be stigmatized as well. Such stigmatization is a powerful factor in producing gender conformity.

Although sex typing has some influence on sexual behavior and attitudes, gender actually is a stronger and more consistent predictor (Allgeier, 1981; Whitley, 1988b). The power of gender as a predictor is due to the different sexual scripts of women and men in our culture. Sexual scripts appear to override individual personality characteristics with respect to sexual behaviors and attitudes.

Sexual scripts   In our society, as in most societies, females and males have different sexual scripts (Simon & Gagnon, 1987; Laws & Schwartz, 1977; Zilbergeld, 1978). Sexual scripts refer to cultural blueprints for both engaging in and evaluating sexual behaviors. These cultural blueprints are internalized through the socialization experience and are evident in the context of interpersonal interactions.

In the United States, parents expect the adolescent son, but not the daughter, to have overt sexual activity. They therefore are more restrictive of the daughter's behavior, which retards her sexual experimentation. Consequently, adolescent rebellion in girls usually consists of sexual "offenses," whereas adolescent rebellion in boys usually does not involve sex. In fact, the labeling of adolescent female sexual activity as deviant or as an offense is itself an example of the sexual double standard. Such behavior in adolescent males is expected and often encouraged. With increasing sexual experience, males show an increasing conformity to gender role norms but females show an increasing nonconformity (Whitley, 1988b). Thus, sexual interest and activity is "written into" the male sexual script, but not the female one.

Because females can become pregnant, their socialization typically emphasizes this consequence of sexual activity. Females usually learn about sex as connected to reproduction, family life, and emotional ties. Indeed, sex is basically defined as genital intercourse. Females are thereby trained to think about "catching" a mate, using sex as a bait if necessary. Since genital intercourse is so closely tied to reproduction and marriage, it may be difficult for some females to connect such an activity to personal pleasure. The connection between sex and pleasure may be further limited for females by their limited sexual exploration of their own bodies. Thus, some females mature without having had any sexual gratification. Furthermore, even if girls have masturbated to orgasm, their clitoral stimulation may seem unconnected to vaginal penetration. It therefore may be difficult for them to connect heterosexual sex activity with pleasure. Female sexuality is never spoken of as valuable or worthwhile in and of itself, but only as a means to an end. Many females learn to use their sexuality in this way and become quite manipulative. One-fourth of the women answering a 1972 survey in *Psychology Today* magazine reported using sex to bind a person into a relationship (Tavris, 1973.) Thus, the sexual script for females values sexuality mainly in terms of a committed relationship, not as a pleasurable experience in and of itself. Consequently, heterosexual females are more likely than males to engage in sex in the context of an intimate relationship. Lesbians too are more likely than gay men to connect sex with love (N. Meredith, 1984; Peplau, 1981).

The devaluation of female sexuality is also evident in our double standard of shamefulness. Female genitals are either unlabeled or derogatorily labeled (for example, "down there," "cunt"). Indeed, few girls learn correct anatomical names for female genitalia. Gartrell and Mosbacher (1984) found that whereas the correct names for male genitalia were learned by 40% of boys and 29% of girls, the correct names for female genitalia were learned by only 18% of boys and 6% of girls. Girls are encouraged to conceal their "privates" with clothes, leg positions, and deodorant. It is therefore not surprising that some women never touch their genitals or learn to masturbate. When girls learn about sexual anatomy, they learn that boys have a penis and girls have a vagina. But the vagina is not homologous to the penis, nor is it the female sexual organ. The clitoris is. That most girls are not taught this fact further distances them from connecting sexuality with pleasure (H. G. Lerner, 1988).

Boys, however, are taught to view sex as a way of proving their masculinity. This emphasis reflects the pressure on males to consistently achieve in all areas of their lives (Fasteau, 1974; A. E. Gross, 1978;

O'Neil, 1981b; Zilbergeld, 1978). In the sexual area, this may result in males' trying to "score"—that is, have many sexual experiences with many partners and, for the "modern" male, bring their partners to many orgasms. Numbers matter, not the quality of the experience. Such an impersonal orientation toward sex was strikingly evident before the AIDS epidemic among many gay men, whose promiscuous behaviors greatly resembled the fantasized sexual life of many heterosexual men (N. Meredith, 1984).

This exclusive goal orientation may be a result of early male masturbatory experiences in which the focus is solely on producing an orgasm. As a result of this achievement focus, females are often viewed solely in their sexual roles (for example, "a piece of ass"), and sex itself is viewed as a conquest rather than as a form of communication. (See Figure 4.2.) Surveys of college men have found that from 20% to 50% admit to saying things they didn't mean to obtain sex from a woman against her will (Greendlinger & Byrne, 1987; Koss & Oros, 1982; Lisak & Roth, 1988). Such manipulative strategies are most often used by men who accept traditional gender roles and who believe men should be sexually dominant (Muehlenhard & Falcon, 1990). Many more men apparently misinterpret or ignore women's degree of sexual willingness. About 70% of all college women report having had a man misinterpret the degree of sexual intimacy they desired (Abbey, 1987; Koss & Oros, 1982). Some men apparently go even further than deception to obtain sex. As will be discussed in Chapter 12, about 35 to 60% of college men admit that they might rape a woman under some circumstances (Briere & Malamuth, 1983; Malamuth, 1981) and 1 in 12 male college students actually have (Warshaw, 1988). It is estimated that by midlife, nearly half of all women will have been a victim of an attempted or actual rape (Riger & Gordon, 1981).

Males are also expected to take the lead and be in control, in sexual areas particularly. This control sometimes may be a burden. In one study (J. E. Carlson, 1976), nearly half of the husbands felt that the responsibility for sexual initiation should be equal between husband and wife. Among college students, about 80% of the men rejected the idea that a man should always initiate sex (J. L. Carroll et al., 1985; Sacks, 1990). Interestingly, more women than men think men should be the initiators, perhaps because initiation violates their sexual script or because they sense men's ambivalence about losing control (Komarovsky, 1976; Safilios-Rothschild, 1977). Male attitudes toward sexually

Figure 4.2 A cartoonist's view of male and female communication about sex. (Copyright 1973 by Bülbül. Reprinted by permission.)

assertive women are related to their attitudes toward women in general; men who hold traditional views of women hold unfavorable views of sexually assertive women (Quante, 1981). Among college women, only those who are aware of sexual inequality and who have relatively liberal attitudes toward masturbation, instructing one's sexual partner, and so on, are likely to feel comfortable initiating sexual activity (Grauerholz & Serpe, 1985). The double standard of sexual behavior still exists in some form. Yet equalizing who initiates sexual activity may be critical in establishing gender equality. Warren Farrell (1982) argues that when men take all the risk of sexual rejection, defensive and protective attitudes commonly develop, such as depersonalizing the woman, de-emotionalizing sex, and developing anger and resentment toward all women.

The consequences of the male sexual role are many. The unstated permission to masturbate may limit male sexuality to the genitals and make sex entirely goal-oriented, thus limiting the pleasure of a sexual experience. The pressure to appear in charge may also make men hesitate to reveal ignorance or uncertainty, thereby inhibiting open communication

between partners about sexual interactions (A. E. Gross, 1978; Masters & Johnson, 1970, 1979; Zilbergeld, 1978). The constant pressure to achieve may lead to impotence (erectile dysfunction), since anxiety is inconsistent with sexual arousal. Yet if sexual difficulties occur, a man is more likely to be censured by other men for his "inadequacies" than a woman with similar difficulties is to be censured by other women (Polyson, 1978). Women do not show this same negative attitude toward sexually troubled men, although men may not be aware of, or believe, that. Thus, open communication with one's partner may be restricted. In recent years, the number of articles on impotence has increased dramatically, perhaps reflecting the increased pressure on men to be sexually ready at all times with all partners (Tiefer, 1987). A "real" man never says no.

If we consider the two different cultural scripts for males and females, we can better understand why more males than females express interest and participate in sexual activities. They must be more interested if they are "real" men. Sex for many is another area of achievement or of power, unconnected to feelings of intimacy. Similarly, we can understand why some women never learn to enjoy their own sexuality. They haven't had the experience, and, besides, they shouldn't enjoy it if they are "good girls." Sex is all right only in the context of a relationship, only as a means to an end. In this respect, R. G. Evans (1984) has found that college females have much greater sex guilt than college males, and these differences are most marked for sex-typed students. Furthermore, college women with a high degree of sex guilt tend to use contraception less frequently than college women low in sex guilt (Gerrard, 1982, 1987). For such women, use of contraception may suggest that they thought about engaging in a sexual activity ahead of time and were not just "swept away" by emotions or a dominating other. Thus, acceptance of the cultural sanction against enjoyable and premeditated sex for women actually may lead to unplanned pregnancies. Furthermore, women with traditional beliefs about sex and sexual scripts are most likely to engage in token resistance to sex (saying no when they mean yes) (Muehlenhard & Hollabaugh, 1988; Muehlenhard & McCoy, 1991). This token resistance, engaged in by about one-third of college women, not only reinforces the different sexual scripts for women and men, but also may lead to sexual victimization if men learn not to take a woman's "no" seriously.

These sexual expectations, or cultural scripts, combine with both a societal preoccupation with sex and a social taboo against talking about sex, especially for females. The results are serious misunderstandings, dishonesty ("scoring," "faking it"), and a lack of full sexual enjoyment for both sexes, particularly for females. Hence, we find that more women can achieve orgasm through masturbation or lesbian sexual activity than through genital intercourse.

Liberating men from their stereotype as sex agents and liberating women from their stereotype as sex objects will result in a sexuality based on authentic concern for the persons involved, whether it be part of play, affection, or love. This form of sexuality will undoubtedly be deeper and more rewarding for those concerned than the manipulative form of sexuality we now often have.

Overall, psychosocial factors are more powerful than physiological factors in accounting for gender patterns in sexual behavior. Although peers, parents, and sex-typed personality traits influence sexual behavior, the best explanation of gender patterns involves understanding the different sexual scripts for males and females. To understand the origin of these scripts, a sociocultural context is needed.

Sociocultural Factors

Understanding the different sexual scripts for males and females in the United States means understanding how sexuality is socially constructed rather than biologically given. Sexuality, its meanings, contexts, and values, varies historically as well as cross-culturally. We will look at some of the cultural variations before examining the social construction of sexuality and the particular power of patriarchy to shape sexual relations.

Cross-cultural studies   Nowhere can the social bases of our sexual behavior be more clearly seen than in comparisons with other cultures. When different cultures have different forms of sexual behavior, it is apparent that these behaviors cannot have a primarily physiological basis. In observing such behaviors in a wide range of cultures, enormous variability has been found.

Cultures vary on a number of factors related to sexual behavior:

1. The amount of sexual play permitted between children varies. For example, the Trobriand Islanders (Malinowski, 1932) and the Yolngu in Australia (Money & Ehrhardt, 1972) encourage such play; in the United States it is strongly discouraged.

2. The permissibility of intercourse before marriage varies. It is strongly encouraged in Mangaia, Polynesia (Marshall, 1971), and by Pilaga Indians in Argentina (Money & Ehrhardt, 1972), but is strongly discouraged in the Batak culture of northern Sumatra (Money & Ehrhardt, 1972) and in the United States.

3. The latitude of sexual activity after marriage varies widely, from strict monogamy among the Batak, to serial monogamy in the United States, to extramarital relations in Mangaia.

4. The importance attached to sexual activity itself ranges from highly important, as in the Truk Islands (Malinowski, 1932) and among Mangaians, to very unimportant and secondary, as among the Arapesh of New Guinea (Mead, 1935).

5. The extent to which sexual desire is seen as dangerous varies from the Manus (Malinowski, 1932), who encourage restraint, to the Balinese, who view the sex drive as very weak (Malinowski, 1932).

6. Attitudes toward same-gender sexual behavior differ from acceptance by American Mohave Indians (Devereux, 1937) to encouragement of

sequential bisexuality in Melanesia (Money, 1987) to nearly total rejection in the United States and Nicaragua.

7. The expectation of gender differences in sexual behavior ranges from no expectation of a difference, as in Southwest Pacific societies like Mangaia (Marshall, 1971), to an expectation that the female sex drive is stronger, as among the Trobriand Islanders and the Kwoma and Mataco (Malinowski, 1932), to an expectation that the male sex drive is stronger, as in Latin America.

In those societies where the sexes are seen as equal in sexual potential (for example, in Mangaia), the sexes do not have sexual peaks at different ages, sex is not linked necessarily to love for women, and orgasmic dysfunctions and premature ejaculation are rare. Thus, the cultural relativity of our sexual sex-role standards and their consequences are readily apparent.

Social construction   A study of the history of sexuality makes it very clear that human beings construct the meaning of sexuality in the context of specific historical, economic, and political events (see D'Emilio & Freedman, 1988, and Foucault, 1978, for enlightening reading on this topic). Indeed, there is not *one* meaning of sex at all, even during one historical period in one culture, but multiple meanings, as a function of an individual's gender, race, class, and sexual orientation.

As D'Emilio and Freedman (1988) illustrate, during the colonial period in the United States, church, state, and community functioned in concert to channel sexuality toward marital reproductive ends. Women and men shared responsibility for sexual regulation. The emergent middle class in the 19th century came to separate sexuality and reproduction. Sexual relations, as well as marriages, became associated with emotional intimacy, and women became primarily responsible for maintaining moral standards. Sexual "purity," however, was reserved for White middle-class women. Working-class, immigrant, and African-American women were viewed as strongly sexual, indeed as "loose" and "depraved." This projection of White middle-class male fantasies served to rationalize the oppression of these groups, especially the repeated rapes of Black women by White men.

The sexual reform movement in the early 20th century in Europe emphasized the positive and healthy nature of sexual activity. But this more permissive attitude toward sex actually was focused on male pleasure and came at a time of increasing economic and social progress for women (Jeffreys, 1986). Women who refrained from sex with men, often in order to retain some form of economic or personal independence, or who campaigned against sexual violence and abuse of women, were negatively characterized as "anti-sex, " "frigid," or "dried-up spinsters." The norm developed that "healthy" and "normal" women were interested in sex with men, especially in being submissive to and sexually dominated by men. Therefore, if a woman was uninterested in sex with men in the way that men liked, or if she preferred the company of women, something was wrong with her (she was "repressed," a "prude," or "sexually inverted").

During the 20th century in the United States and other Western cultures, sexuality has been further separated from reproduction. This separation has been related to the increasing power of psychology, the medical profession, and the media. Personal pleasure has become the primary goal of sexual relations and sexuality has become increasingly commercialized. Regulation of sexual relations has been appropriated by the state and often has come in conflict with messages from other social forces, such as the media and the church. Sexual relations have begun to be viewed as part of an individual's identity. For example, although people always have engaged in same-gender sexual behaviors, it was not until the 20th century that people self-identified (or were identified by others) as gay men, lesbians, or bisexuals. (For more details on the social construction of sexual identity, see D. F. Greenberg, 1988, and Kitzinger, 1987). The much-discussed sexual revolution of the 1960s following the discovery of the birth control pill was actually a continuation of the "revolution" that occurred during the early part of the century in England. The women's liberation and gay rights movements of the late 1960s and early 1970s further highlighted the political nature of sexuality.

The sexual liberalism that has prevailed during the last 30 years has started to wane. There are increasing restrictions on sexual behavior (for example, on contraceptive availability and abortions); a backlash against same-gender sexual behavior (due in large part to the AIDS epidemic); stronger promotion of chastity, restraint, and sex within marriage by church and state; and continuing attempts to control the reproductive processes of minority women. Romance may be back, sexual "scoring" may be out (L. B. Rubin, 1990). As we have seen, since the mid-1980s some decrease in the rate of sexual intercourse outside of marriage and some change in sexual ideology has occurred.

An analysis of sex education courses and materials in the 1980s reveals an emphasis on victimization and the absence of any notion of female desire, pleasure, or sexual entitlement (M. Fine, 1988). This missing "discourse of desire" coupled with an emphasis on how males will try to take sexual advantage of females, possibly leading to pregnancy or disease, constructs female sexuality as object—something that is acted upon by another. The notion of females as subjects—that is, agents who can act on their own sexual feelings—is rarely discussed. Ironically, the victimization message actually may interfere with the development of sexual responsibility in adolescents, especially low-income females. Unfortunately, conservative forces, currently dominant in most school districts, are against most sex education programs but are particularly uncomfortable with any discussion of female desires.

Patriarchy We live in a patriarchy, in which men hold economic and material power. This fact holds several direct consequences for sexual behavior.

One major consequence of patriarchy, as Millet (1970) points out, may be that for females to obtain economic and material security, they must barter their sexual availability either through marriage or prostitution. Thus, females may use sex as a means to an end, subordinating their own desires to those of the male, distorting their self-image and personality in the process. Men may end up distrusting women and being afraid of getting "hooked." Hite (1976) found that women were very reluctant to create their own orgasms either through masturbation or by requesting certain behaviors from their partner, for several reasons: habit, fear of losing their man's "love," and, especially, fear of economic recrimination. In most states, a married woman is required by law to have sexual intercourse with her husband; she need not enjoy it, and many do not enjoy it. If a woman is financially and emotionally dependent on a man, she is not in a good position to demand equality in bed.

Another consequence of patriarchy is men's control of women's biological functioning. Laws and institutions regulating contraception, pregnancy, and childbirth are made and run by men. Thus, many women are prevented from controlling their own bodies. Their sexuality remains tied to their reproductive functioning, whereas men's sexuality is not tied to reproduction. This may limit more

than a woman's sexuality—such dependence limits career and educational plans as well. Between the late 1960s and early 1980s, the women's movement was increasingly successful in challenging this aspect of patriarchy. Since the early 1980s, however, conservative forces have gained considerable political power. They have been able to impose their traditional views about gender roles and sexuality on the entire nation, particularly with respect to limiting the availability of both abortions and contraceptive information. As is clear to both sides, controlling women's reproductive functions is crucial to controlling women.

Patriarchy restricts sexual behavior in both women and men by making heterosexuality "compulsory" (A. Rich, 1980). The possibility of individuals finding emotional and sexual satisfaction with same-sex partners in egalitarian relationships is threatening to a system that relies on dominance of women by men. Consequently, gay men and lesbians are viewed as deviant and are heavily stigmatized. Lesbians, in particular, are viewed as a threat to male dominance, since they don't need men for sexual pleasure and therefore can be independent of male standards of appearance and behavior. Indeed, all women who are outside the control of men—lesbians, spinsters, sex resisters, nuns, and widows—are socially stigmatized in our culture (R. Weitz, 1989). Homophobia can be viewed as one of the major ways patriarchy and sexism are maintained (see Pharr, 1988). As long as people fear the stigma of being labeled homosexual, they will conform to traditional gender roles. (The dynamics of homophobia will be discussed further in Chapter 9.)

Patriarchy affects sexual relations by eroticizing dominance and submission and labeling that configuration "sexuality" (Dworkin, 1987; MacKinnon, 1987a). Even sexual relations between same-gender partners are viewed in the context of dominance and submission (*butch* and *femme*), despite evidence that many same-sex couples ascribe to a norm of equality (Peplau, 1981). Women's subordination, in particular, has been eroticized (Jeffreys, 1990) and is the main content of pornography and sexual fantasies. In addition, the patriarchal assumption that women's major role is to serve the needs of others, particularly the needs of men and of children, affects women's sense of sexual entitlement. In the various sexual "revolutions" of the 20th century, although both women and men were supposed to be sexually active and permissive, the emphasis was still on male-defined and male-dominated sexuality. Women were expected to live out men's sexual fantasies and to satisfy men's sexual needs without any thoughts about their own needs or any expectation of reciprocity.

Indeed, sexuality as currently constructed is male-centered—that is, *phallocentric.* As we have seen, sex typically is defined solely in terms of genital intercourse and male orgasm. Female satisfaction occurs in *fore*play or in *after*play, if it occurs at all, but it is not the main point of sexual activity (Rotkin, 1976). Many people still believe in vaginal orgasms because such orgasms require a penis; a clitoral orgasm does not have that requirement. Other evidence of phallocentrism can be seen in the following facts: (1) a female generally is considered to be a virgin as long as she has not had genital intercourse; (2) the clitoris usually is defined as a miniature penis rather than the penis being defined as an enlarged clitoris, though the latter definition is phylogenetically more accurate (see Chapter 2); (3) premature ejaculation is sometimes viewed as the cause of female "frigidity," although the penis does not provide the best mode for producing female orgasms; (4) what is sexual is what gives a man an erection, whether that be dominance, violence, or love.

The effects of phallocentricity are far-reaching for females and for males. Females often give up expecting sexual satisfaction and use sexual contacts to secure affection and security rather than for sexual pleasure. Or they feel guilty about their desires and think they are abnormal, immature, and so on. Men, on the other hand, are under increased pressure to identify themselves with their penis, and some see in it the answer to all problems. (See Figure 4.3 for one example.) Thus, any sexual difficulty for either the male or the female partner reflects on the male's masculinity, on his psychological effectiveness, and on his personal identity (Polyson, 1978; Zilbergeld, 1978). In addition, as females increase the substitute demands of love and commitment, males become more confused, guilty, and alienated. This further reduces compatibility (Masters & Johnson, 1974; Rotkin, 1976).

Discussion

We need to take a new look at sexuality, but this is difficult to do because sexuality is both so personal and so political, and it is hard to examine it directly. Recent writings by feminists (see Leidholdt & Raymond, 1990; Snitow, Stansell, & Thompson,

Figure 4.3 An often proposed solution to female unhappiness. (Copyright 1973 by Bülbül. Reprinted by permission.)

1983; Vance, 1984) have begun such an examination and have revealed tremendous diversity of opinions and approaches. At the very minimum, the clitoris needs to be recognized as equal with the penis as a center of human sexuality. Females need to be recognized as having separate sexual centers for gratification (clitoris) and for reproduction (vagina). Whereas reproduction requires intercourse, gratification does not, although intercourse may well provide secondary pleasures. Equality must be eroticized rather than dominance or submission. A liberation from constricting sex roles is needed as well as a change in the patriarchal system. As Masters and Johnson (1974) note, "The most effective sex is not something a man does to or for a woman but something a man and woman do together as equals" (p. 84).

▲ Summary

Overall, an examination of sexual behavior reveals both gender similarities and gender differences. The similarities reside in the nature of male and female sexual responses. The sexes have similar arousal patterns, except that females are capable of multiple orgasms, and most males are not. Both sexes have sexual fantasies and become aroused by erotic material, although most material is aimed solely at heterosexual males. Females have become increasingly similar to males in their rates of sexual activity, although males still are somewhat more sexually active. Where the sexes differ most is in the meaning assigned to sex and in degree of interest in sexual activities. In general, males express greater interest than females in sex and sexual materials. Males seem to receive more pleasure than females from sexual intercourse. Males are more likely than females to separate sex from the quality of a relationship; females are more likely than males to tie sex to love and affection.

Physiological factors do not adequately account for the differences between males and females in sexual behavior, although they may provide the basis for different socialization experiences. What is clear is that males and females have very different sexual scripts, and these scripts are socialized into each individual's fundamental view of herself or himself. Thus, sexuality is, to a large degree, socially constructed. Cross-cultural and historical evidence reveals the sociocultural basis of our current sexual scripts. Patriarchal culture, in particular, has shaped not only sexual scripts but our very definition of sexuality as well. What would sexuality be like in a nonpatriarchal culture? We have no idea. But we need to be careful about ascribing to biology or to evolution that which is culturally determined. For example, women may be less interested than men in sex not because women are less sexual or because they are by nature more monogamous. Rather, women may be less interested because they are supposed to be, or because sexual experiences with men are unsatisfying. We have a long way to go before we fully understand human sexual behavior.

▲ Recommended Reading

D'Emilio, J., & Freedman, E. B. (1988). *Intimate matters: A history of sexuality in America*. New York: Harper & Row. A fascinating examination of the changing social construction of sexuality in different historical periods as a function of race, class, and sexual orientation.

Geer, J. H., & O'Donohue, W. T. (Eds.). (1987). *Theories of human sexuality*. New York: Plenum. A broad range of articles, each viewing human sexual behavior in a different way, from the theological to the feminist-political.

Leidholdt, D., & Raymond, J. G. (Eds.). (1990). *The sexual liberals and the attack on feminism*. New York: Pergamon. A powerful collection of articles critiquing the assumptions underlying sexual liberalism.

Money, J. (1988). *Gay, straight, and in-between: The sexology of erotic orientation*. New York: Oxford University Press. A compilation of Money's years of research on the origins and nature of sexual orientation.

Rich, A. (1980). Compulsory heterosexuality and lesbian existence. *Signs, 5,* 631–660. A challenging and influential article delineating the political nature of the lesbian lifestyle, and female sexuality in general.

Zilbergeld, B. (1978). *Male sexuality: A guide to sexual fulfillment*. Boston: Little, Brown. A sensitive and humorous examination of male sexuality, and how sexual and sex role myths interfere with sexual fulfillment.

▲▲▲▲▲▲▲▲▲▲▲▲▲▲▲▲▲▲▲

Part 2 Summary

After reviewing the current findings related to gender differences and similarities, certain general conclusions can be stated. The Summary of Gender Comparisons summarizes the information in the physical, cognitive, personality, social, and sexual areas.

Summary of gender comparisons

Physical

Anatomy: Females have a uterus, ovaries, a clitoris, and a vagina. Males have testes, a penis, and a scrotum. Males tend to be bigger and more muscular.

Processes: Females mature faster and have slower metabolism. Females are more sensitive than males to taste, smell, touch, and high tones; males have better visual acuity. Hormone production is cyclic in females after puberty (ovulation and menstruation); it is mostly continuous in males. Hormones affect males as well as females.

Brain organization: Males tend to be more hemispherically specialized for verbal and spatial abilities. Differences are small and variable.

Vulnerability: Males are more vulnerable to disease, physical disorders, and early death.

Activity level: Boys tend to be more physically active during childhood, if activity is defined as large muscle movements.

Cognitive

Intellectual aptitude: No difference.

Memory: No difference.

Verbal skills: Essentially no difference, although girls show a slight edge on some tasks.

Quantitative skills: No difference before high school; males show an edge in problem-solving tasks and in the incidence of math genius.

Visual-spatial abilities: Males perform somewhat better, especially if tasks involve rapid mental rotation of images.

Cognitive styles: No difference in analytic or computer abilities. Possible difference in style preference, with males preferring an autonomous and females a connected style.

Creativity: Unclear. Females sometimes have an edge.

Personality and Temperament

Personality: Girls describe themselves as more people-oriented, males as more instrumental and power-oriented.

Temperament: Unclear. Females may be more timid.

Communication Patterns

Verbal: Males dominate conversations; females listen, qualify, and self-disclose more. Situational and sex-typing factors are important.

Nonverbal: Males dominate after childhood; females are more expressive and more sensitive to nonverbal cues. Situational, cultural, and sex-typing factors are important.

Prosocial Behaviors

Affiliation: Females show greater interest by adolescence.

Empathy: Unclear. Females express more interest in others' feelings. Situational and sex-typing factors important.

Nurturance: Unclear. Females more likely to be in nurturant roles.

Altruism: Unclear. Females express more concern, but males are more likely to help strangers. Situational factors important.

Morality: Unclear. Females may be more concerned about the feelings of others.

Power-Related Behaviors

Aggressiveness: Males tend to be more physically aggressive.

Assertiveness: Unclear. Situational and sex-typing factors important.

Dominance: Dominance appears more important to males. Definitional, sex-typing, and situational factors important.

Competitiveness: Males tend to be more competitive. Situational and sex-typing factors important.

Achievement: No difference in motivation. Definitional, sex-typing, and situational factors important.

Noncompliance-nonconformity: Males tend to be less compliant and conforming. Situational factors important.

Sexual Behaviors

Physical response: No difference; females are capable of multiple orgasms.

Interest, attitudes, and experience: Males express more interest and have more experiences. Males are more likely than females to separate love and sex.

Response to erotica: No difference. Males are more interested.

Fantasies: Slightly more frequent in males.

As the summary list indicates, aside from the physical area, few clear-cut differences between males and females have been found. Males, compared to females, tend to be more physically vulnerable, physically active, aggressive, power-oriented, and sexually active. Males have a slight edge in visual-spatial and quantitative skills after childhood, and they tend to dominate verbal and nonverbal communications. Females, compared to males, tend to mature faster and to be more people-oriented, more prosocial, and more emotionally expressive. Females have cyclic hormonal production after puberty and are capable of multiple orgasms. They may have a slight edge on some verbal tasks.

Far more numerous than the areas of gender difference are the areas in which no overall differences have been found or where differences are unclear because of the importance of situational factors. These areas include intelligence, memory, cognitive styles, creativity, temperament, empathy, nurturance, altruism, morality, assertiveness, achievement, and sexual responsiveness.

To give a clearer sense of how much the sexes differ, the magnitudes of the average gender differences are graphed in Figure S.1. Not all topics covered in Chapters 2 to 4 are included because d values were not always available. (Recall that d value is the size of the difference between male and female performance expressed in terms of a standard deviation.) Gender differences can be divided into small, moderate, and large effects. Most of the small gender differences (d value equal to or less than .20, one-fifth of a standard deviation) are cognitive ones: overall verbal ability, SAT verbal scores, overall math ability, problem solving, computation skills, and spatial visualization. Small gender differences are also found in balance, social smiling (child), and noncompliance. Of small to moderate size ($.20 < d < .40$) are gender differences in spatial perception (before age 18), helping others, democratic leadership style, aggression (by adults), and approval of intercourse in serious relationships. Of moderate size (around one-half of a standard deviation, $.40 < d < .60$) are gender differences in activity level, grammar, SAT math scores, decoding skill, body expressiveness, and aggression (all ages). Of moderate to large size ($.60 < d < .80$) are gender differences in dash, spatial perception (after age 18), mental rotations, social smiling (adult), gaze, and speech errors. Large gender differences (over .80) are found for only a few comparisons: height, throwing distance, facial expressiveness, and approval of sexual intercourse without love.

From these comparisons, it's obvious that the gender differences we are examining are mostly of small to moderate size—large enough to be noticed but not large enough to provide a basis for statements (such as "all men are more aggressive than all women") or job applicant choice. As Eagly (1987b) notes, the meaning of the size of any particular gender difference is a function of the value attached to it. For example, if people value quantitative skills, then the slight edge males may have in these skills may seem very important. If people don't value facial expressiveness, then even the large advantage females have in this area will be viewed as unimportant.

Furthermore, situational and individual variability in most of these behaviors is enormous. The numbers in Figure S.1 represent only the average findings. As was made clear in discussing specific behaviors, gender differences can be either magnified or minimized by situational factors, such as whether the person is observed by others or whether the research is conducted in the laboratory or in a natural setting. Individual factors, such as age, class, beliefs, and sex-typing category, also affect results. In general, masculine- and feminine-sex-typed individuals show stereotypical gender differences to a greater degree than androgynous or undifferentiated males and females. Another factor affecting results is the date of the research. Cognitive gender differences, in particular, have become smaller over time, probably due to changes in early childhood socialization and expectations.

In looking at explanations of the differences, social factors (roles, status, expectations, and learning history) seem to be the most powerful influences on gender differences, although biological predispositions may play a role in some cases (for example, aggression and nurturance). Even in these cases, however, nature and nurture interact, with environmental-social factors usually overpowering biological factors, shaping the behavior to conform to cultural expectations. We are all born with different physical, intellectual, and emotional potential, but these differences are not distributed by gender. The potentials that become actualized depend on the environment and the roles in which we are raised. And social factors and roles do differ on the basis of gender. Indeed, gender differences are maximized in situations in which gender roles are made salient, such as among strangers who are being observed, the traditional research

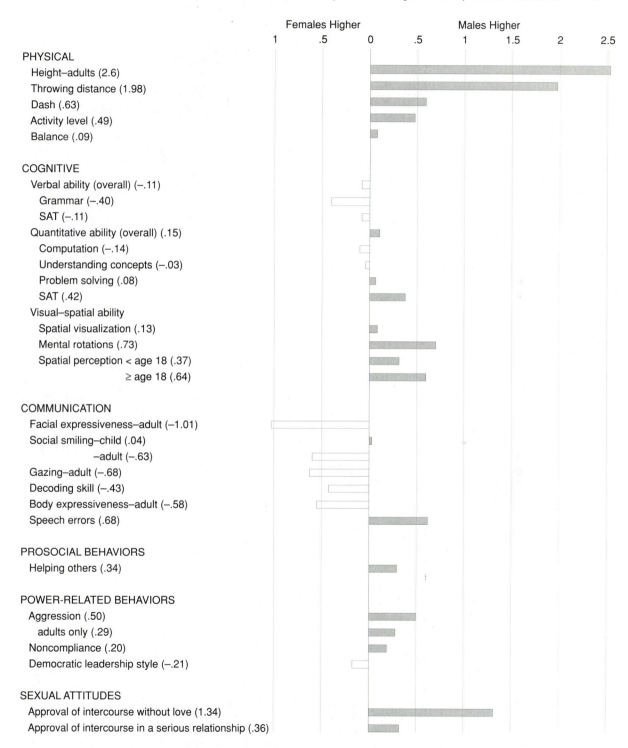

Figure S.1 Effect sizes of gender differences. Numbers are the difference between means expressed in terms of the standard deviation.

design. Gender also serves as a stimulus cue for others; that is, people perceive and react to an individual depending upon that person's biological sex.

The question remains as to why the gender stereotypes discussed in Chapter 1 remain and are so strongly believed when gender differences, to the extent that they exist, are relatively small and highly variable. To understand the tenacity of stereotypes, one needs to understand the nature of the stereotypes themselves. Once believed, stereotypes become confirmed and strengthened whenever someone behaves in the expected way. For example, whenever a female expresses fearfulness, an observer may remark, "That's just like a woman." The observer's belief in the stereotype then becomes stronger. On the other hand, when someone acts in a way contrary to the observer's expectation, instead of weakening the stereotype, the behavior in question is more likely to go unnoticed or to be classified as an exception. Thus, if a female does not act fearful, an observer might simply brush off the observation as unusual ("Oh, she's different"), if an observation is made at all. The stereotype itself remains inviolate and protected from refutation. Thus, we have the case where active athletic behavior on the part of girls is called atypical ("tomboyish") even though the majority of girls behave that way.

Another reason for the strength and persistence of stereotypes is that men and women tend to hold different roles, both in the home and in the workplace. The roles inhabited by women tend to be low-status and to involve nurturant-communal behaviors (mother, homemaker, nurse). Conversely, the roles inhabited by men tend to be high-status and to involve agentic-instrumental behaviors (paid employee, boss, political leader). Thus, in real life, women generally engage in more prosocial behaviors than men, and men generally engage in more power-related behaviors than women, but this apparent *sex* difference actually is a *role* difference. To the general observer, however, these different behaviors seem to confirm the stereotypes. The same is true with regard to sexual scripts and sexual behaviors. That is, males and females are given different scripts to follow, but when they follow the scripts, their behaviors are viewed as reflecting innate differences.

To challenge stereotypes, we need to get to the individual before he or she learns them; that is, we need to change the content of our gender socialization. In particular, we need to change the assignment of males and females to different social roles. In the next part, we will review how gender socialization occurs and how very difficult instituting such changes would be.

Part 3
Origins of Gender Stereotypes and Roles

As was shown in Part 2, few basic differences between the sexes aside from the purely physical have been found. Given that few differences are inherent, how do gender stereotypes and roles get transmitted to members of a society? The following three chapters are devoted to answering this question.

Before examining the transmission of gender stereotypes and roles from one generation to another, we might first ask how the gender roles began. Did a division of traits, behaviors, and activities always exist between the sexes? If so, on what was the division based, since there are so few innate differences between the sexes and since the gender stereotypes themselves differ to some degree cross-culturally?

Does such division necessarily imply differing statuses? To answer these questions, anthropological evidence is needed as well as an evolutionary and historical perspective. These will be covered in Chapter 5.

Given an evolutionary and historical background, we then can examine how children develop their gender roles and how they learn the gender stereotypes appropriate to their culture. *Socialization* is the process by which the values and mores of a society are inculcated. Four different theories of how gender socialization occurs, together with evidence regarding specific socializing agents, are reviewed in Chapter 6. Various socializing forces are discussed in Chapter 7.

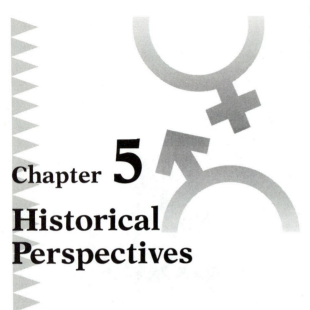

Chapter 5
Historical Perspectives

A survey of a broad cross-section of cultures over the course of human history reveals that gender stratification (male dominance) and a division of labor between the sexes are nearly universal. The precise division of labor, however, varies from one society to another, as does the rigidity with which such divisions are held. In most cultures, males primarily are responsible for hunting, fishing, and warfare, and females for gathering foods, cooking, and child care. Yet this division is not true for all cultures. For other activities, such as preparing soil and tending and harvesting crops, the cultural variations are considerable (Sanday, 1981a; Seager & Olson, 1986).

Like the division of labor between the sexes and male dominance, the presence of gender stereotypes is nearly universal. In a study of more than 30 countries, J. E. Williams and Best (1990) found that

nearly everywhere, males are characterized as adventurous, forceful, and independent, and females are characterized as sentimental, submissive, and superstitious. In all countries studied, the characteristics associated with males were stronger and more active than the characteristics associated with females.

Although Williams and Best studied gender stereotypes and not behavior, other cross-cultural research suggests that similar pancultural differences exist between women and men in actual behavior and in subjective world view. For example, a frequent finding is that males more often see the world in more instrumental and agentic ways and act in more aggressive, dominant, independent, and achievement-oriented ways than females. Females more often see the world in expressive and communal ways and act more nurturantly, responsibly, obediently, and expressively than males (Ember, 1981; R. L. Munroe & Munroe, 1980; Stockard & Dougherty, 1983; M. R. Welch & Page, 1981). The most compelling evidence suggests that such differences in behavior and world view are the result of the division of labor between the sexes. People who spend time with infants will become nurturing; people who are breadwinners will become agentic (Eagly, 1987b; Whiting & Edwards, 1988; Yount, 1986). Furthermore, a gender-based division of labor gives rise to gender stereotypes, particularly with respect to personality traits (C. Hoffman & Hurst, 1990).

In this chapter, we will examine briefly the gender-based labor division patterns in various societies and review the explanations proposed to account for the patterns. How these patterns relate to the status of females and males within a society is another important issue that will be discussed. Much controversy surrounds all research in this area, with many conflicting theories and interpretations of findings. Although this chapter will not do justice to the breadth of research relating to the origins of gender roles, it will summarize some of the major approaches. The interested reader should examine sources referred to in the chapter for further information.

▲ Patterns of Labor Division and Male Dominance

In nearly all cultures, women and men perform different tasks. The exact division of tasks depends on three factors: the particular subsistence base of a society, the supply of and demand for labor, and the compatibility of the needed tasks with child rearing. This last factor accounts for the fact that women's contributions to the subsistence activities of their society vary more than men's. Across all cultures, however, women contribute at least half the world's output of food (Seager & Olson, 1986). Furthermore, domestic labor (household maintenance, child care, food preparation) is virtually always women's work. As the 1980 United Nations report on the status of women found, "women constitute half the world's population, perform nearly two-thirds of its work hours, receive one-tenth of the world's income, and own less than one-hundredth of the world's property."

In this section, we will examine the various patterns of labor division by sex as a function of the technoeconomic base of the society. There are four major bases: foraging, horticulture, agriculture (wet and dry), and industry. Societies based on foraging and on horticulture are characteristic of almost all of the last 3 to 4 million years of human history, and in most of these societies, women were the primary producers.

▲   Foraging Societies

In foraging (also known as hunting and gathering) societies, which are the original form of social grouping, most food (60 to 80%) comes from gathering activities, which are performed predominantly by women (see Nielsen, 1990). The most common pattern is some division of labor between the sexes where game is available at a distance and vegetables are available nearby, as among the !Kung Bushmen of Africa. Men hunt and provide protein for the group; women gather roots and berries, thereby contributing most of the food supply. However, both sexes may work together to hunt and gather where game is close; this is the case, for example, with the Mbuti pygmies of the African Congo. Where hunting is the only food source, men provide all the food. This pattern, which is found, for example, among the Eskimos, is quite rare (Friedl, 1975). Except in the latter case, women generally are full economic partners in foraging societies. Although males still retain some degree of dominance in other areas, relations between the sexes tend to be warm, cooperative, and relatively egalitarian, and women tend to be unrepressed sexually (Blumberg, 1977; J. Chafetz, 1984; Etienne & Leacock, 1980). This type of society apparently

characterized all human groups for several million years—98% of all human history (Blumberg, 1979; G. Collins, 1979).

Most foraging societies have been nonterritorial and have been focused around the activities of both men and women, not solely around men as has sometimes been claimed (Bleier, 1979; Gough, 1975; Leibowitz, 1983). For example, in the !Kung society, groups of siblings and their offspring of both sexes band together, share food with all members of the group, and migrate to a new setting when any conflict arises (R. B. Lee, 1972). In such a society, women enjoy relatively high status, relative autonomy, and some ability to influence group decisions (G. B. Kolata, 1974). Fathers also tend to have a great deal of contact with children, including infants (G. Collins, 1979). Although there frequently is a gender-based division of labor, foraging societies have very little social stratification of any kind (Nielsen, 1990). That is, status differences are minimal.

Horticultural Societies

Societies in which food is cultivated by hoe emerged in the Middle East by 12,000 B.C. and are primarily found today in sub-Saharan Africa, the hills of southern Asia, the Amazon River basin in South America, and the islands of the Pacific. Here, women's contribution to subsistence is a direct function of the amount of warfare in that society and of certain natural environmental conditions (J. K. Brown, 1976; Sanday, 1973, 1981a). In general, because hoe cultivation is compatible with child care, women tend to make the predominant contribution. Indeed, it is now thought, though not widely acknowledged, that women rather than men probably invented agriculture (Bleier, 1979). In Africa, 75% of the cultivation is in the hands of women (Sciolino, 1985). Because neither sex automatically controls food, there is considerable flexibility in sex roles and some equality between the sexes on certain life options. For example, in the South Pacific nation of Fiji, male and female Melanesians are strikingly similar in instrumental and expressive characteristics (Basow, 1984a). Neither sex is sex typed according to U.S. standards, and both sexes can be described either as androgynous or undifferentiated. Both sexes also tend to have similar attitudes toward women's roles in society, although these attitudes appear to be relatively traditional (Basow, 1984b).

Women's status in horticultural groups varies tremendously, depending on the presence of three social practices—polygyny (one man with multiple wives), bridewealth (payment of a price by a man for a wife), and menstrual taboos (Nielsen, 1990). Although these practices sometimes can be viewed as supporting women's autonomy, they most often are present in male-dominated societies. Thus, although there is some equality, many horticultural societies appear somewhat male-dominated. However, status can also be based on principles other than gender (Ortner, 1981).

Agrarian Societies

When a group begins to lay claim to land and increase its food supplies through plow cultivation and the domestication of animals, certain social changes occur as well. Because land becomes property to be owned, defended, passed on, and bartered, inheritance factors, such as legitimacy of offspring, become very important. Thus, with the rise of agrarian societies about 5000 years ago in the valleys of the Tigris-Euphrates, Nile, and Indus rivers, *patriarchy* (societal organization based on the supremacy of the father in the family and the reckoning of descent and inheritance in the male line) and men's control of women's sexuality became firmly established. Women were not to engage in any sexual activity with men other than their husbands in order to ensure the "legitimacy" of their children. Consequently, women's behaviors and lives became more restricted. An extreme example of this restrictiveness is the practice of genital mutilation of young girls in certain African countries, such as the Sudan.

Thus, with the development of private property, male dominance became institutionalized. Many writers, particularly those holding to traditional Marxism, view the development of private property as the beginning of all inequalities, sexism as well as classism, racism, heterosexism, and so on (for example, Engels, 1884/1972; Meillassoux, 1981). For other writers, sexism has itself been viewed as the prototype of all other inequalities (Firestone, 1970; G. Lerner, 1986). In this latter viewpoint, male dominance precedes the development of private property; it was men's appropriation of women's reproductive capacities and their labor that led to male dominance, spurred by the development of alliances among men in intertribal conflicts.

In the overwhelming majority of agrarian societies, men tend to dominate the division of labor, and exploitation of women's reproductive processes is much more common than in foraging societies (Blumberg, 1979; Nielsen, 1990). The division of labor seems to be based on the fact that plow

cultivation is more efficient and also requires greater physical strength. In addition, because the activities required for plow cultivation range far from home and require full-time labor, they are generally not compatible with child care. The !Kung offer a case in point (G. B. Kolata, 1974). Although foragers for over 11,000 years, more and more of the !Kung have begun to live in agrarian villages since the 1960s. In 1974, fewer than 5% were still nomadic hunter-gatherers. Their society has changed dramatically as a result. Women have less mobility and contribute less to the food supply. Children now play in single-sex and -age groups as opposed to all playing together. Such segregated play encourages segregated roles. Aggression has increased because of such segregation, less supervision by adults, and less ability to leave the area. Fertility has also increased because of earlier age of menarche as a result of changing diet. All these factors have led to a marked decline in women's status.

In cultures that use wet irrigation—for example, for the cultivation of rice, as in Southeast Asia and Indonesia—more labor is required in a smaller area. There, women (at least those of the working class) contribute a great deal to the economy in the paddies and the marketplace. Consequently, their status is higher than that of their sisters in dry agrarian regions, such as in northern India and the Middle East. In these societies, there is a surplus of labor and women's economic importance is minimal. This, too, is reflected in their status (Blumberg, 1977, 1989). Indeed, in such societies, women are excluded almost completely from public life (for example, the Muslim practice of *purdah*).

In sum, the status of women in agrarian societies is low because of patriarchy, institutionalized male dominance, and the division of labor. Interestingly, every one of today's industrialized societies sprang from an agrarian base (Blumberg, 1979). Furthermore, most of the people in today's world live in industrializing agrarian societies—that is, traditionally agrarian societies undergoing industrialization.

Industrial Societies

The Industrial Revolution, begun about 1800 in England and northwest Europe, transformed basically agrarian societies but did little to improve the status of women. In fact, the position of women declined as men took over tasks formerly done by women and transferred these tasks from the home to the factory (Boserup, 1970). Men then assumed dominance of the public sphere with women relegated to the private sphere, which now decreased in societal importance as the means of production moved outside the home.

It's important to note, however, that from another perspective, the work women did (and still do) in the home was (and still is) vitally important both to the family and to society. Indeed, women around the world work more hours than men and have less leisure time (Seager & Olson, 1986; United Nations, 1991). Even in countries where the labor force is nearly half female, domestic responsibilities are unlikely to be shared. It is women who have a double day, who spend about eight hours in paid employment plus nearly four hours on household tasks, including family care. Employed men spend only a little more than an hour a day in domestic activities. Despite its value and importance, however, domestic work is never considered a part of a country's gross national product unless it is done for a wage. Nor is the work women do on their own land for their family's subsistence taken into account. This invisibility of much of women's work is a source of contention for many feminist economists and geographers (for example, Seager & Olson, 1986; Waring, 1989). It is estimated that only about two-thirds of women's work gets counted in official statistics. Furthermore, "development" projects in Third World countries, which have focused predominantly on moving men into the paid labor force, have led to a decrease in women's status (Tiano, 1987; Tinker, 1990).

Because factory work is not compatible with continuous child care, women were not encouraged to do such work except when their labor was needed and/or when they needed the money. Thus, it was mostly poor women who worked for pay and then mainly in low-status sweatshop activities. Women were viewed as a cheap and often nonessential labor pool. They were still viewed this way after World War II in the late 1940s and 1950s when service sector and low-level information-processing jobs boomed. In the early 1960s in the United States, the combination of these new jobs and a period of inflation pushed large numbers of White married women into the labor force (M. Harris, 1981). However, because these jobs were just as dead-end and low-level as the previous ones at the turn of the century, they did not improve women's status. Furthermore, women were not seen as competing with men, because the jobs women moved into were those that had long been dominated by women rather than men. Today, although women constitute from 40 to 50% of the labor force in industrialized societies, they still are not viewed as an integral or permanent part of the labor force (Blumberg, in press; Seager & Olson, 1986; United Nations, 1991).

This pattern of viewing women as cheap temporary labor when a society begins industrializing is strikingly evident in many Third World countries today (Fuentes & Ehrenreich, 1983; Lim, 1990; Nash & Fernandez-Kelly, 1983). Many manufacturing industries, especially textiles and electronics, have transferred production to export-processing zones in the Third World. These industries have shown an overwhelming preference for female workers, who are viewed as a cheap, abundant, and politically docile labor force.

In the transition from a subsistence to a market economy in the United States, which accelerated with the Industrial Revolution, specialized roles for men and women arose. For middle- and upper-class White women, the new role created by the Industrial Revolution during the mid-19th century in the United States was that of "true womanhood" (D'Emilio & Freedman, 1988; Welter, 1966). As more men became involved in an increasingly materialistic society, the traditional values of piety and purity became viewed as the province of women almost exclusively. In addition to the values of piety and purity, the cult of true womanhood involved the values of submissiveness and domesticity. Although rarely lived up to in their most extreme forms, these values served to constrain women's lives and to foster feelings of guilt and confusion in women. Working-class women and Black women, who continued their participation in the labor force, were stigmatized as less "pure" and therefore less "womanly."

Whereas the cult of true womanhood existed mainly until the latter part of the 19th century, the new role for men, that of the "good provider," lasted much longer. Bernard (1981) dates the good-provider role in the United States from the 1830s to the late 1970s, when more than half of all married women were in the labor force. This role created a heavy burden on men to achieve in the work force to support their families. This role also increased women's dependence on men and transformed marriage itself. Because men were supposed to be the main providers, employed women could be and were paid less. Consequently, even employed working-class women were made economically dependent on their husbands. Working-class men, who often did not feel they were good providers, may have felt pressured to exert their dominance by other means, such as through violence. Single women, of course, struggled to get by, often dependent upon other members of their family of origin.

Although birth control and modern child care and educational practices free a mother from having to structure her life solely around childbearing and child-rearing activities, such traditional activities still often are used to bar women from equal employment opportunity and equal pay. To some extent, industrialized society's low view of women's productivity and status may be a carryover from its agrarian heritage. Attitudes have not yet caught up with current realities.

Discussion

In sum, a review of gender roles and status over time reveals a decrease in women's status relative to men. From a position of relative equality in foraging groups, women started becoming subordinate to men in horticultural societies, and became very subordinate in agrarian and industrialized societies. From this perspective, the gains in women's status during the late 20th century in industrialized countries have been slight and have not led to a noticeable decrease in overall male dominance, which has become embedded in every institution of the culture. This historical review also highlights the fact that although societies have ranged from relative equality to total male dominance, no known society has been characterized by female dominance (J. Chafetz, 1984). There is speculation that societies that worshiped the Great Goddess or the Great Mother in prehistoric times may have been ones in which women held high status, but the evidence is open to a variety of interpretations (for example, Gimbutas, 1990; G. Lerner, 1986; Miles, 1988). Interestingly, even theories that suggest that matriarchal societies might once have existed posit relationships between men and women of relative equality, not of female dominance and male subordination. This is why the scenario imagined in Figure 5.1 seems highly unlikely.

▲ Explanations for Labor Division and Male Dominance

Why are men almost always the hunters and warriors and women the gatherers and domestics? Why is a division of labor associated with male dominance? The nearly universal division of labor by sex and male dominance have, at various times, been attributed to physical, psychological, and functional factors.

Physical Factors

The physically based explanations argue that because men are "naturally" bigger, stronger, and more aggressive, and women are "incapacitated" by childbearing, men are assigned the more strenuous, dangerous, and important societal activities. Marvin Harris (1977b) has gone so far as to say that a woman's most "essential characteristic" is her ability to make eggs, and this ability lays the groundwork for all differences between women and men in all societies for all times. This is part of the sociobiological viewpoint discussed in the previous chapter, which essentially holds that fundamental human behavioral similarities are based on genetic blueprints because they have some evolutionary significance.

The size difference between males and females that exists among almost all primates may play some role in the division of labor and the status of the sexes. Sarah Hrdy (1981) argues that large males were evolutionarily functional because males must

Figure 5.1 What a reversal of gender stratification might mean for the division of labor. (B.C. by permission of Johnny Hart and Creators Syndicate, Inc.)

be able to compete with each other for mates, but large females were not functional, because they would have less food to spare for babies. The result was male physical dominance, which, she argues, has led to the subjugation of women in patriarchy, where laws were made and enforced by men to secure paternity.

Males' greater predisposition toward aggressiveness, which appears to be biologically based, also may lead to a division of labor and male dominance (S. Goldberg, 1974). Because males are more prone to being aggressive, they are more suited to hunting and to warfare. These activities, traditionally seen as pivotal in the evolution of society, would account for men's higher status. Although the association of men with hunting and warfare may have some relationship to gender stratification, attributing these role assignments solely to men's aggressiveness is far too simplistic. Furthermore, the "man-the-hunter" theory of evolution has been soundly refuted by evidence that "woman-the-gatherer" was of at least equal if not greater importance in the evolution of human society (Dahlberg, 1981). For example, the first tools were probably created by women to dig tubers and carry food and babies.

Another physically based explanation relates to how the brain is organized. As was noted in Part 2, females appear to have a slight edge in verbal skills and a somewhat larger advantage in the ability to read nonverbal cues. These characteristics seem well suited to the traditional mother's role and may be based on the somewhat greater hemispheric flexibility of the female's brain. Males, in contrast, appear to have superior visual-spatial skills—traits that are appropriate to roaming in search of food and that may be based on more specific localization of function in male brains. Division of labor, then, may have followed from genetic blueprints. However, this explanation is based on much speculation and the gender differences involved are not strong and are highly variable. Furthermore, our understanding of brain organization and localization of functions is very limited at this time, and any difference may be a result of different experiences rather than different genes or hormones.

There is one biological difference that might account for the gender division of labor, although not necessarily male dominance. The fact that only women bear and nurse children does have significance for what women can do in societies where life expectancy is short, no efficient birth control methods are available, and the family is entirely responsible for the socialization of its young. In most primitive societies and in India until 1920, the average age at death was 20. Until about 1800, the average age at death in most countries was only 35 (Youssef & Hartley, 1979). In such societies, women spend most of their lives either pregnant or breast-feeding. Thus, women's activities must be compatible with simultaneous child care. This will be commented on further in the subsequent section on functional factors. Yet suggesting that the natural reproductive differences between the sexes may have led to some division of labor is not sufficient to explain why men became dominant. A more complicated explanation is needed, involving functional, ideological, economic, and structural factors (A. Ferguson, 1989; Firestone, 1970; Ortner, 1974).

The difficulties with purely physical explanations are numerous (Bleier, 1979; Leibowitz, 1979, 1983; J. Mitchell, 1971): (1) Physical differences between the sexes do not exist until puberty, and they vary considerably. In fact, such differences are often a function of different activities rather than a cause of them. (2) Motherhood does not require giving up work, not even in the paid labor force. (3) Women's activities require a great deal of physical strength and energy (for example, carrying water or lifting a 30-pound child). (4) Women generally do contribute substantially to a society's economic base. (5) In some societies, parenthood restricts male activities. For example, in some extreme cases, fathers—not mothers—are expected to have labor pains and a long recovery period after birth (Paige & Paige, 1973). (6) Male dominance and aggression are not universal, even among primates, and are not necessarily associated with better breeding opportunities. As Juliet Mitchell (1971) argues, it is not physical coercion or physical weakness that has led to the subjugation of women but rather social coercion interacting with the division of labor based on biological capacity.

Psychological Factors

Many theorists (Freud, Chodorow, Gilligan, J. B. Miller) have argued that there are fundamental psychological differences between the sexes based on anatomical and/or reproductive differences that underlie the division of labor. These theories were reviewed in Chapter 3. The most current arguments suggest that girls develop a personality embedded in interpersonal relationships and subjectivity whereas boys develop a personality based on autonomy and objectivity. Thus, females might be viewed as the best rearers of infants; males might be viewed as best suited for impersonal activities.

These psychological differences are assumed to result from nearly universal socialization experiences—that is, the fact that children are brought up by women. In this sense, presumed personality differences might be both the cause and the result of the division of labor.

Viewing psychological factors as the explanation of the division of labor and of male dominance is extremely controversial. Although certain gender stereotypes appear in a wide variety of cultures, as do certain sex-linked behaviors, most researchers conclude that there is no evidence of basic psychological differences between females and males. Mead (1935) and other cross-cultural researchers have noted that the sexes are quite variable on a number of different traits—jealousy, dependency, artistic interests, aggressiveness, and so on. Specific cultures may encourage the development of different traits in females and males, but these differences then are culturally, not biologically, derived. Indeed, it seems most likely that girls and boys are socialized into their work roles by the encouragement of different traits, skills, and interests. For example, males may be encouraged to develop agentic traits to facilitate their assumption of work-related roles, whereas girls may be encouraged to develop communal traits to facilitate their assumption of nurturing roles. Thus, the division of labor itself may shape the psychology of females and males, rather than psychological differences determining the division of labor.

The relationship between the division of labor and personality factors is complex. As we have seen in previous chapters, different gender roles (both occupational and domestic) may themselves produce differences in traits and behaviors, rather than the reverse (Eagly, 1987b). Interesting in this regard is the finding that people tend to attribute a gender-based division of labor to intrinsic personality differences, regardless of which sex is in a particular category (C. Hoffman & Hurst, 1990). For example, the vast majority of surgeons in the United States are male, a fact typically explained by the decisiveness and stamina required for the job. But in the People's Republic of China, the vast majority of surgeons are female, a fact typically explained by the fine motor movements and dedication to detail required. What's at issue here is not which sex gets assigned the job, but the rationalization of job assignment by attributions regarding the sexes' presumed basic personality differences.

Functional Factors

Functional explanations of the division of labor between the sexes stress the practicality of such divisions for a society. Claude Lévi-Strauss (1956) suggests that by having men and women responsible for different tasks in a society, mutual dependency between the sexes is established. This dependency serves to strengthen marriage and family ties. Thus, the division of labor exaggerates differences between the sexes and leads to marriages based on exchange. For example, a woman from Tribe A is "given" in marriage to a man in Tribe B, thus solidifying alliances between the two tribes. Although interesting, this theory does not fully account for the specific division of tasks by sex nor why it is women who are exchanged rather than men (J. K. Brown, 1976; Nielsen, 1990). Gerda Lerner (1986) extends Lévi-Strauss's theory by positing that women were exchanged rather than men because men became responsible for making political coalitions between groups as an outgrowth of their role in warfare. Women were "valuable" because of their ability to reproduce.

Another functional explanation involves women's childbearing capacity (Blumberg, 1979; Friedl, 1975; Leibowitz, 1983). Since women do bear and nurse children, it is more functional to have them perform tasks that are compatible with such activities in societies where no alternative exists. Because hunting, fishing, and warfare occur irregularly, last for unpredictable lengths of time, and require long-distance travel, these activities are not very compatible with childbearing and early child care; however, if hunting activities occur near home, women can and do participate in hunting, without detriment to their child-care activities (M. J. Goodman, Griffin, Estioko-Griffin, & Grove, 1985). Carrying young children around for a long distance is cumbersome, and leaving them home to be cared for by others is unfeasible when the children are still nursing, although in many societies, wet nursing (nursing by other women) is customary.

In addition, it would be impractical to train everyone to become hunters. Game is an uncertain commodity. Therefore, some members of society must be responsible for a more reliable food supply, such as berries and roots. Since foraging activities, hunting small game, and cultivating the land are perfectly compatible with childbearing and early child care, women became primarily responsible for these food-producing activities. Men, in turn, were assigned other tasks, perhaps by default or because of their expendability (Meillassoux, 1981; Sanday, 1981a). That is, because women's investment in the reproduction of the species is more extensive than men's (nine months of gestation plus a year or more of lactation, versus minutes), women's lives are more valuable to a society. Dangerous activities (such as warfare), then, should be done by men.

Thus, the most persuasive explanation of the division of labor involves an interaction of functional distinctions between the sexes and the economic bases of specific cultures. Tasks are divided according to the compatibility of tasks with child care, the subsistence base of the society, and the labor supply and demand. This still occurs today (M. Harris, 1981; Wojcicka-Sharff, 1981).

As is evident from this previous discussion, different scholars have variously seen gender stratification as a cause, a concomitant, or a consequence of the division of labor. Hence, a closer examination of this complex variable is warranted.

▲ Male Dominance and Its Relation to Labor Division

Men's having a higher status than women in terms of power and prestige is a nearly universal occurrence in the world today. Even in modern societies in which women hold what we, in the United States, would consider high-status jobs, their actual status is low. For example, most doctors in Russia are women, but practicing medicine is considered a low-status job there.

Although some controversy exists regarding the universality of male dominance, most writers agree that the status differential between the sexes seems to have existed in varying degrees since prehistoric times (J. Chafetz, 1984; G. Lerner, 1986; Ortner & Whitehead, 1981). Does this status differential arise from the division of labor between the sexes, does the differential give rise to the division of labor, or is some more complex interplay of causes and effects at work here? We'll look at theories of this relationship that posit a culture/nature, public/private split, and theories based on warfare and economics.

The Culture/Nature, Public/Private Split
Sherry Ortner (1974; Ortner & Whitehead, 1981) suggests one way male dominance may be related to the division of labor. She believes that cultures tend to put a higher value on things they can control than on things they cannot control. Thus, all activities that are regulated by humans (for example, hunting) are viewed by a culture as more valuable than all activities regulated by nature (for example, childbirth). Because women, by virtue of their reproductive functions, appear more controlled by nature than by their culture, their work and their status as people become devalued. Men, who do not seem as subject to natural forces as do women, are considered to be more in control of themselves. Therefore, they and their activities become more highly valued in a culture.

Ortner's thesis, although controversial (see MacCormack & Strathern, 1981), has been extended by other anthropologists. After examining more than 150 tribal societies, Sanday (1981a) concludes that male dominance is not universal but most likely occurs in societies severely stressed by migration, food shortages, or colonialism. In such circumstances, public and private life become split, and public life, that part separate from child rearing and family activities, becomes synonymous with the male collective. Etienne and Leacock (1980) put forth a similar view—that much of the male dominance found today in many societies is actually a result of the hierarchical relationships brought by the agents of colonialism (for example, priests, bureaucrats, and military personnel).

From these theories, it seems that functional factors may lead to a status differential, which in turn may play a role in assigning tasks within a society. The strongest evidence, however, is that gender stratification is a direct outgrowth of the division of labor, although such an outgrowth may be mediated by other factors. Many theories have been formulated to explain how a division of labor could lead to male dominance. We will explore the two main types: those based on warfare and those based on economics.

Warfare Theories
Gerda Lerner (1986) traces the beginning of male dominance to a time of economic scarcity and intense intertribal warfare among horticultural groups. Because males were the warriors, they formed coalitions with other men and used women as objects of exchange to facilitate intergroup alliances (kinship ties). Thus, women were the first property. Indeed, women from conquered groups were the first slaves. Male military power became

converted into generalized male dominance as groups became more land-based (agricultural societies) and men held sway in the public sphere. Although Lerner views women as equal partners in the development of the division of labor in the beginning (based on the incompatibility of warfare and child care), she posits that their later cooperation with male dominance was ensured through physical force, economic dependency on men, indoctrination, educational deprivation, and dividing women against themselves, especially through the development of class privileges and through the good girl–bad girl dichotomy (the "good girl" is attached to one man, while the "bad girl" is not attached to one man). Men further developed an ideology of male dominance, ensconced in Hebrew monotheism, in which an all-powerful male God usurps even women's procreative activities.

The fact that men were the warriors also figures prominently in Marvin Harris's (1977a) theory of gender stratification (see also Gilmore, 1990). He proposes that male supremacy has existed since prehistoric times as a way to counter the threat of overpopulation and the depletion of resources that such overpopulation would bring. Warfare is one means of controlling overpopulation as well as resources. Because during prehistory, muscle-powered weapons (clubs, bows, and arrows) were relied upon and because of the greater average strength and height of the human male, men were everywhere the principal, if not exclusive, combatants. To prepare to risk one's life in battle took years of mental and physical training via competitive sports and physical ordeals. Since a female's life cycle after puberty was constantly interrupted by pregnancy and breast-feeding, males were the logical sex to undergo such training.

The consequences of male responsibility for warfare were enormous. To get males to risk their lives and their comfort, a powerful system of rewards and punishments was needed. Sex was the reward; ostracism, the punishment. "If wives and concubines were to be the chief inducement for men to become masculine, women had to be trained from birth not for combat but for acquiescence to male demands" (Harris, 1977a, p. 117). Patriarchy, patrilocality (place of residence determined by males), exchange of women, polygyny, aggressiveness in males, passivity in females, and male chauvinism and supremacy all follow from assigning responsibility for warfare solely to males. Men's monopoly on weapons in prehistoric (as well as in current) times also led to the appropriation and

subordination of other people and their products (see Mies, 1988). This predatory mode of appropriation was (and is) the quickest way of accumulating goods and wealth without work. Consequently, domination/subordination became the paradigm not only of male-female relationships but of all other exploitative relationships as well.

The division of labor in other areas of society followed the initial division for combat. Women were assigned all the remaining tasks. Because maleness was associated with power and prestige through warfare, whatever men did was considered of high status. Because females were trained to be subordinate, whatever they did was considered of low status. This relationship between male status and female status continues into the present. Touhey (1974) found that the status of an occupation declined when respondents (female and male) thought more females than males would enter that occupation in the future. When more males than females were predicted as entering an occupation, the status of the occupation increased. Although replications of Touhey's study have not found the same results (for example, Suchner, 1979), the bias still appears to exist when actual increases in proportions of women in various occupations occur.

Because Harris sees the threat of overpopulation and the assignment of warfare exclusively to males as the cause of male supremacy, he foresees the development of safe contraceptives and the integration of women into the military as the way to end this domination by males. Not everyone shares his optimism or his thesis (Gailey, 1987). In the first place, as previously noted, not all societies were focused around warfare or hunting, nor were all societies patrilocal. Second, warriors do not necessarily have dominant positions in their societies. Third, some birth control (mainly infanticide and extended nursing) did exist in some foraging societies. Fourth, although Harris argues that male dominance was advantageous for the continued development of society, it seems more advantageous for males than females (Nielsen, 1990). On the whole, however, Harris's thesis is provocative and supported by findings in Israel. In that country, once the army stopped using women in combat, women's status in the military and in society regressed ("Israeli Women," 1982).

In both Lerner's and Harris's theories, the fact that men were the warriors led directly or indirectly to male dominance. An important part of both theories is the development of an *ideology* of male dominance and female subordination in order to socialize each generation into their roles. The ideology that maintains and justifies patriarchy is composed of four main beliefs (Iglitzin & Ross, 1986): (1) that women are apolitical, and therefore men should make laws and govern; (2) that the division of labor between the sexes is based on innate factors and therefore can't and shouldn't be changed; (3) that women's central identity is as wives and mothers, so that while men have a separate identity, women are viewed only in terms of their family relationships; and (4) that women are childlike and therefore need men for support and protection. All four assumptions are baseless, yet they survive to varying degrees in different cultures. In this way patriarchy is perpetuated and maintained, as we will see in more detail in the next two chapters.

Economic Theories

Economic theories see women's status in a culture as a function of their economic power, up to a point. Economic power refers less to the amount women contribute to the economic base of their society than to the degree to which women control both the means of production (land, tools) and the distribution of resources.

As noted earlier, female contributions tend to be greater in horticultural societies than in other societies. Their status in horticultural societies also tends to be higher than in other societies. In agrarian societies, in which women's contributions are low, their status also is low. Yet this relationship is not perfectly linear. Even when women contribute greatly to a society, their status still tends to be lower than men's. For example, in 1985, African women made up 60 to 80% of the agricultural labor force, yet their status vis-à-vis men remained low ("African Women," 1985).

One of the two key factors in determining status levels is who controls the distribution of resources (Blumberg, 1984; J. Chafetz, 1984; Collier & Rosaldo, 1981; Sanday, 1981a). Blumberg (1979), in examining 61 preindustrial societies, found that participation in production, by itself, was not directly related to control of certain life options, such as freedom to initiate and end a marriage. The strongest influence on female equality was women's relative degree of economic control over the group's productive resources and surpluses. For example, Iroquois women have an unusually high status in their society. They contribute about 50% of the food supply for their society (basically vegetables, fish, and game). But in other societies in which women contribute more, as in the Tikopia and the Azande

societies, their status remains low (Sanday, 1974) What differentiates the Iroquois from these other groups is that in the past, the Iroquois women also controlled the distribution of food because their men were frequently away hunting or at war for years at a time (J. K. Brown, 1970). Being in charge of food distribution was a form of power, and Iroquois women used this power in political areas as well. In societies where women do not have control of food distribution, even though they contribute 60% to 70% of the food supply, their status is low. In most societies, it is usually game that gets distributed among tribal members. Because men are in charge of hunting, they are generally in charge of food distribution. The vegetables and berries gathered by women are usually directed more toward family, rather than tribal, consumption (Friedl, 1975). Hence, women generally have less power and status than men.

In industrializing and industrialized countries, even when both husband and wife are in the paid labor force, men still control the distribution of resources (see Dwyer & Bruce, 1988). Men typically earn more than women, for one thing. For another, women's income goes primarily toward household needs, especially children's, while men spend their income in a variety of ways, including their own personal leisure activities, such as drinking with friends. Thus, men not only have more money than women, they also have more discretionary power over where and how it is spent.

Connected with the distribution of resources is the question of who is in charge of the relatively more vital and rarer resources. Since protein can be considered more vital and rarer than vegetables, and since meat is protein, men's contributions from hunting may have been more highly valued than women's contributions from gathering. Thus, we can see another way in which men may have accrued more power and status.

The second important factor in women's status in a society is who owns the means of production. As traditional Marxist theory has argued, with the development of private property came a class system. Those with the highest status and most power were those who owned the land and tools. As we have seen, the owners were mainly men, although not all men. Feminist revisions of this traditional approach have argued that women were subjugated even more than working-class men because of their role in reproduction (Eisenstein, 1979; Flax, 1981; Hearn, 1987; Mies, Bennholdt-Thomsen, & von Werlhof, 1988; O'Brien, 1981;

Vogel, 1984). Women were reduced to "factors of production" in the recreation of the human labor supply. Men "appropriated" women and their children and built institutions to support female chastity and monogamy. Custom and ideology then developed that promoted the idea of female inferiority and supported a still shaky sense of male power. This ideology thus reinforced the dominance of all men over women, at least over those in the same and lower classes.

A number of researchers have found that the economic power of women in society is further enhanced by their being strategically indispensable and by kinship arrangements that take females into account (Blumberg, 1979, 1984; Leibowitz, 1983; Mendonsa, 1981; Sanday, 1981a). Strategic indispensability arises when there is no reserve labor pool, such as slaves or homemakers; when specific expertise is needed; and when work is autonomous, as in the case of marketing handcrafted items in Africa. Strategic indispensability also occurs when there are fewer women than men in a society over a period of time (Guttentag & Secord, 1983; Secord, 1983). In societies where inheritance passes through the mother's side of the family or where the family residence is with the wife's family, women also tend to have considerable economic power. Economic power can be translated into political power and into some immunity to physical force. Thus, for full sexual equality, women must have economic power.

Not only did men develop control over the means of reproduction as well as production, but reproduction also removed middle-class women from the arena of production—which occurred outside the home—in agricultural and industrialized societies. This later developed into an emphasis on the socialization—in the home—of children by their mother. Such an emphasis on maternal child care serves to decrease women's influence in their community, since a mother's social network is relatively restricted even when she still contributes to the food supply (for example, the Mekranoti of Central Brazil, D. Werner, 1984). To achieve equality, women must not only participate equally in the production process, but they must also gain control of the reproductive process as well as transform societal norms regarding socialization and private property. As we have seen, in societies without private property (foraging societies), gender stratification was (and is) relatively absent. However, in socialist countries today, male dominance still exists, although women may fare better than do their sisters in capitalist countries, at least in such areas

as pay equity (Kruks, Rapp, & Young, 1989). Since the collapse of communism in Eastern Europe in the early 1990s, women's status has decreased (Bohlen, 1990). (Socialist feminism will be discussed further in Chapter 13.)

One of the main reasons male dominance still exists in socialist and communist countries is that although women participate relatively equally in the work force, they still have almost complete responsibility for domestic work and child care. Indeed, degree of responsibility for child-care activities may be the key to the status of women in a culture, more important than the degree of their labor force participation. Scott Coltrane (1988), in his examination of 90 nonindustrial societies, found that the greater was men's participation in child care (even just their presence), the higher was women's public status (participation in community decision making and positions of authority). This effect held true even when other indicators of male dominance, such as patrilineal and patrilocal social structures, frequency of warfare, and societal complexity, were taken into account. It may be that when males are raised with frequent exposure to their fathers, their need to dominate and exclude women is reduced, as Chodorow's personality theory suggests. (This theory will be discussed in more detail in the next chapter.)

In modern societies, the same pattern of economic power seems to exist as has been described for more primitive cultures. Even though women constitute nearly half the labor force in most industrialized countries, their status remains lower than men's (Seager & Olson, 1986). This may be because the goods and services produced by women (for example, social services and clerical work) are not valued as highly as those produced by men (for example, manufacturing and managerial work). Gender inequality may decrease only if women move into male-dominated professions with higher prestige. Furthermore, because men are assigned the role of breadwinner, they usually are in charge of the distribution of their earnings. Even if the wife works outside the home, men's generally higher salaries mean the men still are in control. The battle for equal pay for equal work has important ramifications for the balance of power in a family, as both opponents and supporters of the equal-pay position are well aware. Indeed, as a number of writers have recently argued (Blumberg, 1989; J. S. Chafetz, 1989), changing the "internal economy of the household" is pivotal to changing women's roles in society at large, although control over resources on a societal level is more likely to lead to power in the family than the reverse.

In sum, males' higher status can be viewed as both a cause and a consequence of the division of labor between the sexes. No one theory can account for male dominance. Indeed, most current theories are multicausal, taking into account a variety of economic and functional factors. Whatever the initial justification for male dominance, little is functional about it in today's world, at least for women. The ideology and institutions that maintain it, however, live on.

▲   Summary

The difference in status between the sexes, so visible in our society, seems to be a carryover from the division of labor in societies that preceded ours. This division of labor was initially necessary because of women's childbearing activities and was shaped by environmental conditions. Thus, the precise chores allocated to women were determined by the activities' compatibility with child care, with the supply and demand of labor, and with the subsistence base of the society. In hunting and gathering societies, men were the hunters; women, the gatherers. Men had slightly higher status because their activities were more dangerous and more vital for their tribes' survival and because their activities gave them more power in the distribution of food. But women and their economic contribution were very important. In horticultural societies, females generally contributed a great deal, but males were the warriors. This division of labor led to some gender stratification as a gender-based ideology developed and as women were viewed as objects of exchange between tribes. In agrarian societies, with the development of private property, women's economic contribution dropped dramatically, as did their status. The ideology of male superiority and female inferiority became embedded in cultural institutions. In industrialized societies like our own, the division of labor and the lower status of women have continued despite the fact that such divisions and status levels no longer are justified culturally. Today, everywhere in the world, women have a lower status than men. As Seager and Olson (1986) document, "In the world of women there are few 'developed' nations" (p. 8).

Thus, although childbearing is an unchangeable sex difference, the implications of this biological fact are different today in the United States from previous times in other societies. With the advent of reliable birth control, women no longer need to become pregnant frequently and unpredictably. Most women now use some form of birth control, plan on having fewer children, and are having them at a later age than in the past. Because of smaller family sizes and longer life expectancies, motherhood, if entered at all, occupies a much smaller proportion of an American woman's life than it used to. In highly industrialized countries, less than one-seventh of a woman's average lifetime is spent bearing children. In addition, because many child-care responsibilities previously borne by the family alone are now borne by society, such as by schools and day-care centers, no justification for a division of labor based completely on sex exists any longer.

One implication of our brief survey of labor division and status is that although productive labor does not automatically lead to equality, it does lead to economic power, at least in the form of control of a paycheck. This economic power, in turn, is the strongest determinant of a woman's freedom and status. Economic power is not, however, the only determinant. Political and military power are of even greater importance in determining the status of members of a society. Women's presence in these areas is just beginning (see Chapter 12).

▲   Recommended Reading

Gilmore, D. D. (1990). *Manhood in the making: Cultural concepts of masculinity.* New Haven: Yale University Press. An anthropological account of how culture constructs definitions of manliness, depending upon the roles assigned to men.

Lerner, G. (1986). *The creation of patriarchy.* New York: Oxford University Press. A grand theory of the origin of male dominance, spanning almost 2600 years of history. Male dominance of women is viewed as the model for oppression of other groups.

Nielsen, J. M. (1990). *Sex and gender in society: Perspective on stratification* (2nd ed.). Prospect Heights, IL: Waveland. An excellent review of gender stratification patterns and theories. Up to date and easy to read.

Sanday, P. R. (1981). *Female power and male dominance: On the origins of sexual inequality.* Cambridge, England: Cambridge University Press. An attempt to link cultural ideas about sex roles to the shifting ecological environments in which "sex-role plans" are created. In Sanday's view, there is no universal pattern of male dominance in tribal societies.

Seager, J., & Olson, A. (1986). *Women in the world: An international atlas.* New York: Simon & Schuster. Fascinating collection of data on the status of women worldwide, presented in colored maps and charts.

Chapter 6

Socialization Theories and Agents

In Part 2, a strong case was made for the overriding importance of socialization as opposed to biological factors in determining an individual's sex-typed behaviors. In Chapter 5, gender stereotypes and roles were found to be rooted in the division of labor based on economic conditions present in a society and on functional differences between the sexes. Although such a division based on biological sex is no longer either practical or necessary, the traditional pattern is embedded within the structure of society and gets transmitted to each succeeding generation as part of its socialization. Because socialization is such an important factor, it is productive to examine more closely how the socialization process occurs, who the socializing agents are, and what other forces operate.

In this chapter, four psychological theories of gender identity development—psychodynamic, social

learning, cognitive-developmental, and gender schema—will be reviewed and evaluated. As with other research in this area, the evidence is complex and contradictory, partly because of methodological problems and partly because of the complexity of human development itself. In general, some combination of the four theories is needed to account for the complex interaction among biological factors, the learning environment, and the level of cognitive development of the child. Reviews of research on the major socializing agents, which include parents, teachers, and peers, will follow, along with a summary of their influence. Chapter 7 will focus on the influence of other socializing forces in American society.

▲   Theories

The three traditional theories of gender development are psychodynamic theory, social learning theory, and cognitive-developmental theory. More recently, gender schema theory has been formulated. Each theory emphasizes different aspects of development and makes different predictions as to the sequence of development. These models mainly focus on early childhood; in particular, how children by age 7 develop a sense of gender—their own and that of others. But gender socialization continues throughout the life span. Therefore, we will conclude this section with a life-span perspective.

Psychodynamic Theories

Psychodynamic theories emphasize how early childhood experiences with the primary caretaker shape a child's personality. Such experiences affect the deep psychic structures of the mind (the unconscious) and therefore are relatively permanent. Why are females more communal, males more agentic? All psychodynamic theories emphasize identification with the same-sex parent, but different theories emphasize slightly different developmental dynamics. All, however, describe gender identity as a core part of one's personality.

Traditional psychodynamic theory, Freud's psychoanalytic theory, stresses the importance of biological (including anatomical) factors and parental identification. As was discussed in Chapters 3 and 4, this theory proposes that through the resolution at ages 5 to 6 of the Oedipus and Electra conflicts brought on by the recognition that only boys have penises, children become motivated to identify with the same-sex parent. Each child is thought to have incestuous desires that cause guilt and anxiety. Each views the same-sex parent as either responsible for the absence of a penis, in the case of girls, or able to remove the penis, in the case of boys. Identifying with the "aggressor" is thus a way to allay this anxiety. The fear of penis removal is considered stronger for males than is penis envy for females, because girls have already "lost" the coveted penis. Consequently, males' gender identity is viewed as stronger than females' gender identity. For Freud, same-sex identification is critical for healthy adjustment and for the development of masculine and feminine personalities. He viewed the sequence of development as innate and biologically based, proceeding from an awareness of the anatomical sex difference to identification with same-sex parent and eventually to adoption of sex-typed behaviors.

Little empirical support exists for these assertions, although L. H. Silverman and Fisher (1981) argue that the effects of the Oedipus complex on adult males can be discerned through careful laboratory testing. In previous chapters, we reviewed evidence of the nonuniversality of Freudian personality concepts, stages, and interpretation. In addition, contrary to psychoanalytic predictions that females should have a weaker identification with their same-sex parent than do boys, D. B. Lynn (1979) cites research that shows the reverse to be true. More females than males do seem to prefer other-sex activities (see, for example, Connor & Serbin, 1978), but interpretations other than "penis envy" are more likely. Some females may prefer male-related activities because of males' generally higher status and greater power. Or they may prefer such activities because of the intrinsic qualities of the activities themselves. For example, engaging in sports or playing with an Erector Set simply may be more fun than playing with dolls.

The prediction that identification with the same-sex parent is critical for mental health also has not been verified (Pleck, 1981b; J. H. Williams, 1973), nor has the importance of having appropriately sex-typed parents. Spence and Helmreich (1978) found that the healthiest homes (those in which children are able to function effectively and achieve a sense of worth) are homes in which both parents are perceived as androgynous; followed closely by homes in which only one parent is perceived as androgynous.

Part of Erikson's (1963, 1970) extension of Freudian theory emphasizes how the shape of one's genitals affects one's sense of space. This conclusion, resulting in the description of males as more outer-space oriented and females as more inner-space oriented, was based on one poorly controlled study of 11- to 13-year-olds (Erikson, 1964). These children were asked to build a scene out of a selection of toys. Erikson observed that boys tended to build towers, while girls tended to build enclosures. However, no controls were exerted on previous experience or on the types of toys chosen. More recent attempts at replication reveal that no difference in constructions emerges when children use the same toys (Budd, Clance, & Simerly, 1985; Karpoe & Olney, 1983). Children of both sexes make "feminine" constructions with "girl" toys such as dolls, and "masculine" constructions with "boy" toys such as trucks.

Current feminist psychodynamic thinkers (for example, Chodorow, 1978, 1990; J. B. Miller, 1976, 1984) break with Freud on the anatomy-is-destiny part of his theory but concur that psychodynamic principles are the prime shapers of an individual's gender identity. In particular, these theorists posit that being brought up primarily by a mother or other female figure causes boys and girls to develop different cognitive orientations and personalities. Girls, who continue a personal identification with the female socializer, develop a more personal and embedded style of being (a self-in-relation), whereas boys, who must shift to an abstract identification with a more distant and diffuse male figure, develop a more abstract and impersonal style of being (a more autonomous self). Boys also must reject their personal identification with the mother, which leads to rejecting everything connected with her—that is, everything female and feminine. But the mother's power during the pre-Oedipal phase is still strong. Therefore, in order to separate from her, boys are motivated to reverse that power by subordinating females, both personally and culturally. By the end of the Oedipal phase (age 5 or 6), this reversal is complete; male dominance and female subordination become part of male gender identity and the model of relationships between the sexes. Girls, who maintain an identity with the mother (see Figure 6.1, three generations of daughters), continue developing a self-in-relation unless thwarted by not having such a self validated by others. Since the father represents separation for the girl child as well as the boy, separation/connection becomes a gender issue for both sexes (Benjamin, 1988).

The evidence supporting feminist psychodynamic theories is mixed. For example, college women who grow up without a mother or mother substitute during their first few years do appear to have a lower sense of social connectedness than other young

Figure 6.1 Daughters tend to develop a self-in-relation.

women (Tolman, Diekmann, & McCartney, 1989). In cultures where fathers participate in child care, women's public status is higher, suggesting that boys brought up with fathers present may have less need than other boys to reject and dominate females (Coltrane, 1988). Certainly the agentic/expressive, impersonal/personal, objective/subjective distinctions between males and females characterize the gender stereotypes. With respect to personality traits, however, although some evidence of gender-linked differences in agentic and communal traits and behaviors (as discussed in Chapter 3) exists, a great deal of individual variability in these traits is not accounted for by the theory. In particular, the importance of situational factors and social roles in eliciting certain types of traits or behaviors is completely absent from psychodynamic theory. Furthermore, the tremendous influence on behavior of people and forces besides the mother is relatively ignored here, as it is in all psychodynamic theorizing (see H. G. Lerner, 1988; M. B. Lykes, 1985). Although there is some support for the idea that it may be more difficult for boys to form their gender identity than it is for girls, explanations other than a psychodynamic one can account for this. For example, there may be fewer male figures for a boy to model. Similarly, although mothers do seem to encourage separation in their sons more than in their daughters, such maternal behavior could be a cause rather than a response to the child's behavior (Aries & Olver, 1985).

The critical age for gender identity development varies in these different formulations. Feminist psychodynamic theory emphasizes the importance of the first two years of life (the pre-Oedipal phase) in the formation of gender identity. Traditional psychoanalytic theory emphasizes the Oedipal phase, ages 3 to 6. For Erikson, although gendered behavior is evident during childhood, adolescence is the key time for identity development, for answering the question, "Who am I?" In his life-span perspective, the sexes diverge during adolescence: boys generally establish a strong autonomous identity before establishing an intimate relationship, whereas girls frequently establish an intimate relationship first and may never establish a strong autonomous identity. Erikson's emphasis on autonomy, based on studying the life experience of men, has led to viewing women's emphasis on intimacy as unhealthy or immature. J. B. Miller (1984) argues the reverse: that women's emphasis on intimacy is a natural extension of self-in-relation development; men's avoidance of intimacy and emphasis on autonomy show a disjunctive development of self. Although their interpretations differ, both theorists posit gender differences in the timing and meaning attached to intimate relationships. As discussed in Chapter 3, there is evidence that the sexes differ in the importance placed on interpersonal relationships during adolescence. Evidence also exists that the attainment of ego identity during adolescence is related to the establishment and stability of later intimate relationships in different ways for women and men (S. Kahn, Zimmerman, Csikszentmihalyi, & Getzels, 1985). In particular, men with a strong adolescent identity are most likely to establish an intimate relationship; this doesn't hold for women. Yet the meaning and cause of such differences are open to various interpretations.

In summary, psychodynamic theories do not completely account for the development of an individual's gender identity, although the fact of being cared for by a woman during the first few years of life, as nearly all children are, may affect a child's developing sense of self. It is this emphasis on the self, and the fact that gender is an integral component of it, that is one of the major contributions of the psychodynamic theories. This view explains why challenging gender norms and ideology should be so threatening—because such challenges affect our basic and unconscious sense of our self. Since we view the world entirely through the subjective lens of the self, all challenges to traditional gender concepts are challenges to one's core self.

Social Learning Theory
One theory that contrasts strongly with the psychodynamic approach is social learning theory. Instead of viewing gender identity as an unconscious, in part biologically based development, social learning theory views gender identity as a product of various forms of learning. This theory, put forth by Mischel (1966), Bandura and Walters (1963), D. B. Lynn (1969), and others, emphasizes the importance of the environment in a child's gender development. The child learns his or her role directly through differential treatment, rewards, and punishments, and indirectly through observational learning and modeling.

From a social learning perspective, girls become more communal and boys more agentic because each sex is reinforced for different behaviors and either punished or not rewarded when they engage in behaviors seen as inappropriate. Furthermore, because powerful, nurturant, and similar models are most likely to be imitated (Bandura, 1969), children tend to model their same-sex parent (the one most similar to themselves), thus learning gender-appropriate behavior through observation. Unlike psychodynamic theories, however, social learning theory does not view communal and agentic behaviors as fixed or a core part of one's personality. Rather, these behaviors are learned the same way all behaviors are learned—through environmental factors. Thus, such behaviors can be modulated or even eliminated by changes in such factors.

According to social learning theory, differential treatment of girls and boys—from handling to clothes to toys—begins at birth. There is much evidence (to be reviewed in the next section) that this is true. Because different behaviors get reinforced in and modeled by males and females, children develop an awareness of gender-linked behaviors very early. Their own behavior becomes shaped to accord with one of the gender roles. Gender-linked behaviors have been observed by the end of the first year of life and are present in most children by age 2 or 3 (M. Lewis, 1987). Same-sex modeling also begins early and apparently precedes and gives rise to the formation of a stable gender identity—in other words, "I do girl things; I must be a girl."

D. B. Lynn (1959, 1969), in an expansion of this theory, posits that since the father is frequently absent from the home and since masculine-sex-typed activities are not directly observable by the child, boys have a more difficult time than girls in establishing their gender identity. They are forced to develop a more abstract identification with the male role, while girls identify directly with their mothers, who are observable. This early abstraction may account for gender differences in cognitive style and in males' greater attachment to a culturally defined masculine role. Although cognitive style differences have not been found consistently and can be explained better by differences in experience (see Chapter 2), there is some support for Lynn's hypothesis that boys may have a more difficult time forming their identity. For example, father-son similarity is less strong than mother-daughter similarity (D. B. Lynn, 1979). Boys also seem to be more rigidly and more consistently sex-typed than girls, suggesting a lack of flexibility and latitude in their interests and behaviors (Downs & Langlois, 1988; A. C. Huston, 1985). For example, whereas girls attend to both female and male models, boys tend to ignore or reject female models and attend to and imitate mainly same-sex ones (Bussey & Bandura, 1984; Bussey & Perry, 1982; Connor & Serbin, 1978; Raskin & Israel, 1981).

Since social learning theory emphasizes reinforcement history, stereotyped behaviors and knowledge should increase with experience and age. Some evidence exists that such is the case, up to a point. The number of sex-typed traits an individual possesses appears to increase with age through adolescence, especially for males (Galambos, Almeida, & Petersen, 1990; Silvern, 1977). A trend toward same-sex modeling increases from nursery school through high school and adulthood, especially for boys (Bussey & Bandura, 1984; Connor & Serbin, 1978). As reviewed in earlier chapters, gender differences in many behaviors appear more marked during adolescence than during childhood, suggesting the effect of differential experiences. Furthermore, knowledge about gender stereotypes increases with age from age 2 to college (Del Boca & Ashmore, 1980; C. L. Martin, Wood, & Little, 1990; J. E. Williams & Best, 1990). However, the relationship between age and degree of gender stereotyping is not linear; rather, it appears to be curvilinear, with most stereotyping occurring between ages 5 and 8 (Kohlberg & Ullian, 1974; Plumb & Cowan, 1984; Urberg, 1982), with less thereafter, especially for girls. For example, with regard to occupational gender stereotypes, sex-typed attributions are minimal during preschool, increase until first or second grade, and then decrease after fourth grade (Garrett, Ein, & Tremaine, 1977; O'Keefe & Hyde, 1983; Tremaine, Schau, & Busch, 1982). Thus, research on age patterns does not fully support social learning theory.

Developmental patterns do not present the only problem for social learning theory; there are other problems as well. First, like all learning theories, social learning theory views the child as relatively passive in the learning process. Yet the child, even an infant, brings her or his own qualities to any situation. For example, if female infants begin vocalizing earlier than males, parents may respond with more vocalizations to females. This parental response further reinforces the infants' vocalizations, and a sex difference in language development may ensue. Thus, an interaction model may be more applicable in many cases than a straightforward environmental model (see also M. Lewis, 1987).

Second, research on direct reinforcement has been equivocal. Clearly, it would be impossible for parents consistently and deliberately to reward and punish each behavior according to its gender appropriateness. Maccoby and Jacklin (1974), reviewing a large body of research, concluded that, at least in parental self-reports and in laboratory observations, there is surprisingly little differentiation in parent behavior according to the sex of the child. The one exception to this finding is that boys are subject to more intense socialization pressures than girls. Some differences in parent behavior do emerge outside laboratory settings, but not enough differences occur to account for the clear differences in gender expectations that boys and girls have.

Third, the importance of imitation of the same-sex parent in the acquisition of sex role behavior is unclear. Although identification can account for the acquisition of more behavior than can differential treatment, the evidence again is only partially supportive. Maccoby and Jacklin (1974) found that children do not always select same-sex models, that they do not necessarily resemble the same-sex parent, and that the sex-typed behavior, such as it is, is not a direct copy of adult behavior but tends to be more stereotyped and exaggerated.

The criticism regarding the extent of imitation by a child has been addressed by a more cognitive reformulation of social learning theory (D. G. Perry & Bussey, 1979). According to this reformulation, children learn gender-appropriate behaviors by observing differences in the frequencies with which female and male models, as groups, perform various behaviors in given situations. Children are more likely to imitate a model if that model usually displays sex-appropriate behavior than if that model usually does not display such behavior. Furthermore, boys appear to be more affected than girls by the gender appropriateness of the model's behavior (Eisenstock, 1984; Raskin & Israel, 1981). Hence, a child may imitate a same-sex parent or other model, but only if the parent or model is seen as representative of other members of his or her sex. Perry and Bussey's modification of social learning theory assumes a significant amount of abstracting ability on the part of children, as in noticing that the sexes differ in their frequency of performing some behaviors. It is important to note that research supporting this theory used 8- to 11-year-old children. Factors other than imitation must be involved in earlier sex differences, since a child's cognitive capacities need to be fairly well developed for the imitation process described by this theory to occur.

Social learning theory does offer an explanation of how modeling and reinforcement may interact, with the former process being involved in the acquisition of behavior and the latter determining the performance of the behavior. For example, Bandura (1965) found that boys were more likely than girls to act aggressively after viewing an aggressive model. When incentives for behaving aggressively were introduced, however, the gender difference disappeared. This study demonstrates that both sexes can learn aggressive responses, but girls are less likely to perform them because of their reinforcement history. Similarly, Perry and Bussey (1979) found that 8- and 9-year-old children were unaffected by the sex of a model in recalling a model's behavior, even though the sex of the model was an important variable with regard to whether the children actually imitated a behavior.

Thus, cognitive factors appear important in the development of gender identity, in addition to reinforcement history and modeling. A theory that can fully explain gender development must be able to take into account the changing cognitive abilities of young children. Cognitive-developmental theory provides one way of acknowledging these factors.

Cognitive-Developmental Theory
Cognitive-developmental theory, put forth by Kohlberg (1966; Kohlberg & Ullian, 1974), emphasizes the active role of the child in acquiring sex role behaviors. As Piaget has delineated, children go through various discrete stages in their cognitive

development. They first perceive the world in relation to their sensorimotor abilities, such as crawling and sucking. Then they learn how to categorize the world. Later they become capable of performing concrete operations on that world, as in taking both the height and width of an object into account when estimating its size. Finally, they become capable of abstract reasoning, but not usually until after age 8. A child's reality, then, is qualitatively different from an adult's.

Based on Piaget's theory of stages of cognitive development, Kohlberg argues that the way children learn their sex role is a function of their level of understanding of the world. Before about ages 4 to 7, children do not have an understanding of physical constancy. For example, they don't understand that water poured from a narrow glass to a wide glass is still the same amount of water. Therefore, before about age 5, they cannot have a firm gender identity. After that age, however, the permanence of gender is grasped, and this self-categorization (one's label of self as girl or boy) becomes an organizing focus of future behaviors. Children begin valuing same-sex behaviors and attitudes and begin devaluing other-sex ones. They then seek out models and situations in accordance with this categorization in order to remain self-consistent; that is, after establishing what they are (female or male), children look around to find out what people with that label do. Reversing the sequence proposed by social learning theory, cognitive-developmental theory posits that it is at this point, when gender identity is already established, that a child may identify with the same-sex parent. This identification is not important to cognitive-developmental theorists, however. A child can acquire information about appropriate sex role behaviors from many sources—adults, peers, stories, TV, and so forth. Kohlberg's theory posits that the establishment of gender identity guides the perception of gender stereotypes and the consequent development of gender attributes.

Because their cognitive development is still tied to concrete operations, children aged 6 to 7 often have very simplistic and exaggerated pictures of the two sex roles and have sharp gender stereotypes. It is only with further cognitive development that these stereotyped conceptions can become modified to incorporate exceptions and personal preferences. Thus, a cognitive-developmental theorist would explain the finding that fifth graders hold fewer occupational stereotypes than first and third graders by suggesting that the older children are at a cognitively more sophisticated level of classification competency than the younger children. They are able to use multiple classification schemes and do not need to rely on extreme either/or categories.

The cognitive-developmental explanation of gender identity development has considerable, although not complete, support. There is evidence for a rapid and early increase in the accuracy of gender differentiation and labeling from age 2 to 5, as well as evidence for important cognitive development changes relating to the recognition of gender constancy during the years from 2 to 8 (Coker, 1984; Etaugh & Duits, 1990; Leahy & Shirk, 1984; Stangor & Ruble, 1987). For example, prior to achieving gender constancy (say, at age 4), children might say that a pictured girl would be a boy if she wore "boy's" clothing or had a "boy's" haircut. After constancy is achieved, however, the girl would still be considered a girl no matter how she looked or what she wore.

Some of the strongest support for Kohlberg's theory comes from studies that find that children, boys more so than girls, do value their own sex more highly (Bussey & Perry, 1982; R. H. Munroe, Shimmin, & Munroe, 1984; Tremaine et al., 1982; Urberg, 1982). This preference facilitates the modeling process and the acquisition of gender-appropriate behavior. For example, McArthur and Eisen (1976) found that more than 90% of nursery school children preferred same-sex characters in a story. When asked why they had this preference, the children usually indicated some form of identification with that character (for example, "because I'm a girl [boy]"). Since children view same-sex characters as more similar and more likable, it is not surprising that they imitate them.

One controversial aspect of cognitive-developmental theory is the age at which gender identity is established. As we have just noted, gender constancy, and therefore gender identity, is not cognitively possible before age 5 or 6. Yet a significant amount of sex typing does seem to occur before this age. As early as age 2 or 3, children prefer gender-appropriate toys in comparison to other-sex toys, are knowledgeable about sex role behavior, and play more with same-sex than other-sex playmates (M. Lewis, 1987; E. E. Maccoby & Jacklin, 1987). Other evidence of early attainment of gender identity is Money and Ehrhardt's (1972) finding that changing a child's assigned sex up to age 2 is relatively easy, but after age 4 it is usually unsuccessful.

One way of accommodating these findings is to conclude, as do M. Lewis (1987) and others (C. L. Martin et al., 1990; Slaby & Frey, 1975), that gender identity exists at a variety of levels, at least some aspects of which are evident by age 2 or 3. With language, which develops rapidly between 18 and 24 months, children learn which sex they are and some of its cultural associations (like clothes and toys). This ability to label gender, which appears to be fairly reliable after 29 months (Etaugh, Grinnell, & Etaugh, 1989; Leinbach & Fagot, 1986), is followed by an awareness that gender remains the same over time (stability). This awareness of stability is then followed by an awareness that gender remains fixed across a wide range of situations and behaviors (constancy). This constancy, critical for the attainment of complete gender identity, occurs around age 5 or 6. As gender constancy increases, children spend more total time attending to models and therefore become more sex-typed. Sex-typed preferences do increase after age 6 and seem related to acquisition of gender stability, at least in part (Emmerich, Goldman, Kirsh, & Sharabany, 1977; C. L. Martin & Little, 1990; O'Keefe & Hyde, 1983). Of interest is the fact that although gender constancy judgments do not always follow a linear progression with age, explanations for these judgments do. For example, in response to the question "Is Paul a boy or a girl if he cooks?" the progression is from no explanation in early childhood (age 3) to use of societal norm information ("Paul is still a boy even if he cooks because my Dad cooks") around age 5 to constancy explanations ("It doesn't matter what Paul does; he's always a boy") after age 7 (Wehren & De Lisi, 1983). This orderly age progression in the attainment of gender stages has been supported by cross-cultural research as well (De Lisi & Gallagher, 1991; R. H. Munroe et al., 1984). All these findings support a cognitive-developmental perspective.

Another problem with cognitive-developmental theory is that Kohlberg used only male examples and interviews to support his theory (S. Weitz, 1977). Thus, the theory can explain why boys should see a physical size difference between men and women and learn to value it and, by extension, other males. But how do females learn to value the female role? Ullian (1984) suggests that for both boys and girls before age 6, sex role concepts are viewed as rooted in physical characteristics. For boys, this means that being a man involves strength and dominance. For girls, being a woman involves nurturance as well as physical vulnerability.

Furthermore, young girls see themselves as similar to adult women in that both groups are relatively small and powerless and potential mothers. Therefore, girls develop interests, skills, and values that correspond to this emerging female identity.

There are other problems with Kohlberg's theory. For example, methodological variations have found gender constancy in children as young as age 3 (S. L. Bem, 1989; C. L. Martin & Halverson, 1983), a finding not explainable by cognitive-developmental theory since children this age are at a preoperational stage of cognitive development. Furthermore, Kohlberg's specific prediction that the acquisition of gender constancy leads a child to become more sex-typed afterward and more likely to prefer same-sex activities and objects has not always been confirmed (Downs & Langlois, 1988; G. D. Levy & Carter, 1989; Marcus & Overton, 1978). Indeed, Urberg (1982) found gender conservation to be associated with decreased sex typing, perhaps because the children were more secure in their gender identity. Although this finding does not support Kohlberg's theory, it does recognize the importance of a child's level of cognitive development in the development of gender identity and gender stereotypes.

One way of resolving these conflicting findings is to posit that early acquisition of sex-typed behaviors is due to differential reinforcement and observational learning, as social learning theory predicts, whereas later sex typing, after gender constancy has been acquired, may be due to same-sex modeling, as cognitive developmental theory predicts. In this regard, it is possible that sex role preference and adoption are not the same as gender identity. For example, a girl can prefer male activities and toys and adopt male behavior, like wearing pants and playing ball, and still have a female identification, as in drawing herself as a female. This, in fact, seems to be true more often for girls than for boys (Downs, 1983; E. E. Maccoby & Jacklin, 1974). Thus, males are generally considered to be more strongly sex-typed at an earlier age than girls. Cognitive-developmental theory, although not ruling out learning principles, subordinates them to inborn cognitive processes.

For cognitive-developmental theorists, then, the answer to the question of why girls are more communal and boys are more agentic is a function of the age of the child. Preschool children do not show differences in these qualities, because they haven't yet established a complete gender identity. They do have gender labels, however, and once they realize those labels are stable and constant (after age 7), they are motivated to engage in gender-appropriate activities and develop gender-appropriate qualities, such as either communality or agency.

Gender Schema Theory
Some coordination of the three theories discussed thus far seems required to account for the complexity of gender development. Such a coordinated explanation would include an active role for children in developing concepts of masculinity and femininity and in organizing their world consistent with their level of cognitive development. In this process, differential treatment by primary socializing agents and observation of different models all add to the information the child gathers about appropriate gender behaviors. Interacting with this input are the affectional bonds formed with one or both parents and any biological predispositions the child may have.

A number of integrative theories of sex role development have been proposed (Cahill, 1983; Constantinople, 1979; Spence, 1985). A particularly promising one is Sandra Bem's (1981b, 1983, 1985) gender schema theory. Gender schema theory contains features of both social learning and cognitive-developmental theories, as well as acknowledging the importance of cultural factors. In this theory, sex typing derives in large part from gender-schematic processing, a readiness on the part of the child to encode and to organize information according to the culture's definition of the gender roles. By observing the distinctions made between males and females in their culture, children learn not only the specific content of the gender roles but also that gender and gender distinctions are important. This acquired gender schema is a cognitive structure that serves to organize and guide an individual's perception. Sex typing then results, in part, from the assimilation of the self-concept into the gender schema. For example, a child may observe that boys generally are described as "strong," "big," or "brave," whereas girls more often may be described as "good," "nice," and "cute." What this child learns is that the sexes not only differ but that certain attributes are more relevant for one sex than the other as well. By matching one's behaviors and attributes against the developing gender schema, one learns to evaluate one's adequacy as a person. In this way, cultural stereotypes can become self-fulfilling prophecies.

People differ in the degree to which they use gender schema in processing the world. Those who perceive the world, including themselves, in gender-specific terms are considered gender-schematic or sex-typed; those who do not process information primarily on the basis of gender are considered non-gender-schematic, such as androgynous individuals. This theory is noteworthy in its emphasis on the acquired nature of gender schema. If cultures did not make such broad distinctions between the sexes so that nearly everything is divided into masculine and feminine (for example, toys, speech, walking styles, personality traits, clothes, even colors and food: "Real men don't eat quiche"), then children would not develop or use such strong gender schemas. As discussed in Chapter 5, cultures do vary in the degree to which gender distinctions are made, although nearly all cultures make distinctions that go beyond the biological.

Bem's theory has received considerable although not complete empirical support (Bem, 1985; Bigler & Liben, 1990; Frable, 1987, 1989; Frable & Bem, 1985; Liben & Signorella, 1987; C. J. Mills, 1983; Spence, 1991). For example, sex-typed individuals sometimes show more clustering of gender-relevant items in a free recall memory test than do non-sex-typed individuals, suggesting that sex-typed individuals do organize and process information in terms of gender schema. Sex-typed individuals appear more likely than non-sex-typed individuals to organize other people into feminine and masculine categories. They pay more attention to the sex of a job applicant and then are more likely to devalue the interview performance of a woman. They even are more likely to confuse members of the other sex with each other, suggesting that for sex-typed individuals, members of the other sex are categorized mainly by their sex. Sex-typed individuals also are more likely than others to have a traditional sex-role ideology and to accept gender rules designating culturally appropriate behavior for women and men.

Gender schema theory is consistent with the cognitive-developmental assumption that children's cognitive processes change over time, and therefore their gender schema changes as well (Berndt & Heller, 1986; G. D. Levy, 1989a; C. L. Martin & Halverson, 1987). However, gender schema is viewed as more predictive than stage of gender constancy with respect to children's gender-stereotypic knowledge (G. D. Levy & Carter, 1989). For example, children as young as age 3 demonstrate gender constancy if they view gender as based in genitalia differences (S. L. Bem, 1989). Preschool children typically have a primitive schema, focused mainly on gender labeling of people. Children who apply gender labels to others early (prior to 28 months) are more sex-typed in their own toy choices than children who do not yet label people and things reliably, suggesting that early labelers already have a gender schema (Fagot & Leinbach, 1989). Whether a child uses gender labels early is predicted by how salient gender is in her or his family; for example, by how much attention his or her parents have paid to gender-appropriate play. As children get older (ages 4 to 8), their gender schema gets more complex: gender is viewed as related to specific behaviors and traits, but in a fairly rigid and categorical way. Children who were aware of gender labels early remain more aware of gender stereotypes, again suggesting that these children have a more developed gender schema. As we have seen, children are notably stereotypic at this age. For example, "If she is a girl, she must do only feminine things." Between age 8 and adulthood, the gender schema becomes more dimensional, incorporating a network of associations with respect to gender. For example, "She is a girl, but I can only tell how feminine she is by seeing what she does." At this point, gender schema can be measured by possession of predominantly gender-stereotypic personality traits. For sex-typed individuals, stereotypic masculine and feminine traits are negatively correlated, indicating a gender schema with a bipolar construct for masculinity/femininity. For non-sex-typed individuals, gender stereotypic traits are independent, indicating the absence of a strong gender schema (R. J. Larsen & Seidman, 1986; B. H. Schmitt & Millard, 1988).

Gender schema theory has been criticized as needing to take situational variables more into account (C. J. Mills & Tyrrell, 1983). For example, not all situations apparently elicit gender-schematic processing. Related to this critique is the view that gender identity is too multidimensional to be tapped by a single scale of personality traits (Spence, 1985). And indeed, not all research using a sex-typing scale has found evidence of gender-schematic processing (Beauvais & Spence, 1987; Deaux, Kite, & Lewis, 1985; V. J. Edwards & Spence, 1987; T. J. Payne, Connor, & Colletti, 1987). A third criticism suggests that one need not posit a separate gender schema to explain sex typing (Crane & Markus, 1982; Markus, Crane, Bernstein, & Siladi, 1982; C. T. Miller, 1984; Spence & Helmreich, 1981). Rather, a general self-schema of which gender is just one part may be sufficient to account for sex typing. Yet, these criticisms have not negated the major point of the theory—that is, that people do process the world in terms of schemata and that sex-typed

individuals are particularly likely to use a gender schema as their primary way of organizing their world and self-concept.

As to the question of why females are more communal and males more agentic, gender schema theory would respond that since our culture has made these traits part of the gender stereotypes, children learn to code these qualities as either female or male. As a child's gender schema develops, the child judges her or his own behavior as either gender-appropriate or inappropriate. This self-evaluation process motivates the child to conform to the gender norms of the culture. Only children who are gender-aschematic or who do not code communal and agentic traits as gender-related will avoid the self-fulfilling prophecy of these particular gender stereotypes.

Discussion

All four theories of gender identity emphasize early childhood, and each touches upon an important aspect of gender identity development. The psychodynamic theories emphasize the core nature of gender, while social learning theory describes how various environmental contingencies (rewards, punishments, models) shape gendered behavior. Both cognitive-developmental and gender schema theory emphasize the importance of an active, thinking organism in mediating the influence of family and culture. Gender-related information is filtered through a child's developing cognitive structures. Such structures shape how the message is perceived and influence both behaviors and attitudes.

Table 6.1 contrasts gender schema theory with psychoanalytic, social learning, and cognitive-developmental theory. The precursors of gender identity differ for each theory: for gender schema theory, the emphasis is on development of a gender schema; for cognitive-developmental theory, the emphasis is on awareness of sex categories; for social learning theory, the emphasis is on development of sex-typed behaviors; and for psychoanalytic theory, the emphasis is on identification with the same-sex parent.

All four theories have value, but integration is needed. Gender schema theory attempts some integration by incorporating cultural, child-rearing, and cognitive factors into one psychological theory. But a truly integrative theory must also have a life-span perspective. There is considerable evidence that gender identity continues to develop into adulthood (J. H. Block, 1984; Eccles, 1987a; Sinnott, 1986; Ullian, 1976). Figure 6.2 presents one model (based on P. A. Katz, 1986) of such development that takes

Table 6.1 Theoretical models of gender identity development: sequence of events

Psychoanalytic

Awareness of anatomical differences	Identification with same-sex parent	Gender identity	Sex-typed behaviors

Social Learning

Exposure to sex-typed behaviors	Imitation of same-sex models	Sex-typed behaviors	Gender identity

Cognitive-Developmental

Awareness of sex categories	Gender identity	Identification with same-sex model	Sex-typed behaviors

Gender Schema

Awareness of sex categories	Gender schema	Gender identity	Sex-typed behaviors

into account social and environmental factors as well.

Gender development begins with the initial labeling of a newborn as male or female, followed by differential treatment of the infant. With the acquisition of language, the child begins to self-label as to gender and to seek out gender-appropriate toys, activities, and so on. Following the recognition that gender is immutable (age 5 or 6) comes increased gender-role conformity and some anticipation of adult roles (for example, in the United States, girls start spending more time than boys in household tasks and with young children). Girls generally have more flexibility in their role than boys.

Adolescence is a time of many changes—biological, psychological, cognitive, and social (Eccles, 1987a; Gilligan et al., 1988, 1990; McNeill & Petersen, 1985). With puberty comes the sexual component of gender roles, with its attendant focus on sexual attraction and attractiveness. Although a heterosexual interest is considered normative, sexual orientation does not determine one's gender identity, which already is firmly established. As discussed in Chapter 4, lesbians retain a female gender identity and gay men a male gender identity, despite stereotypes to the contrary. Adolescents, who are capable of logic and hypothesis testing, also must cope with conflicting aspects of self, which at first may mean a return to rigidity of gender conceptions. Later, they may recognize that some aspects of gender roles are fairly arbitrary. Middle and late adolescence is a time of striving to develop

a secure personal gender identity in a social context, which may be extremely difficult in a society in which gender roles appear to be in flux. Labor force options also need to be considered. Girls appear to go through an intense struggle to reconcile their childhood sense of self, embedded in relationships and caring, with the adult (male) world expectations of autonomy and "objectivity."

With adulthood, those individuals who marry and/or have children add another component to their gender identity, that of wife/husband or mother/father. Socialization of future generations with respect to gender roles then ensues. Occupational roles also affect one's gender identity. As we have seen in previous chapters, the assumption of different social roles (breadwinner or homemaker; boss or secretary; and so on) encourages people to develop different traits and behaviors (Eagly's social-role theory). Thus, life experience itself socializes men and women with respect to gender. And it does not seem to stop. For example, middle age may be a time for both women and men to modify their gender roles more toward androgyny. The major gender task of males and females during childhood, adolescence, and young adulthood may be the preparation for and the socialization of a new generation. Once this major task is accomplished, strict gender roles may become less important and both sexes may allow other qualities and interests to emerge (J. H. Block, 1984; Costos, 1990; Helson & Moane, 1987; Sinnott, 1986, 1987).

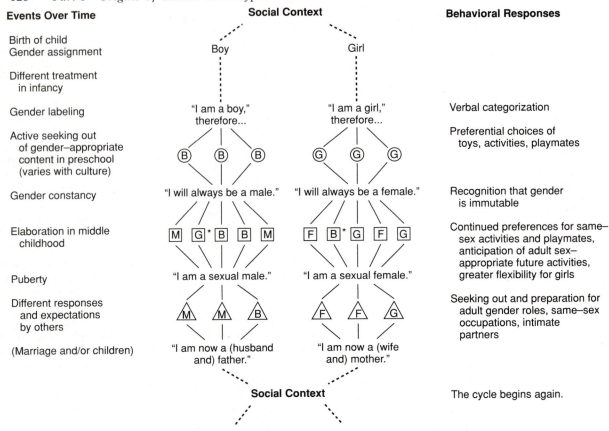

Key: B = boy; G = girl; F = adult female (actual and expected); M = adult male (actual and expected).
* No one is completely stereotyped; there are always some cross-gender interests.

Figure 6.2 An integrative model of gender identity development over the life span. Adapted from "Gender Identity: Development and Consequences," by P. A. Katz, p. 52. In R. D. Ashmore and F. K. Del Boca (Eds.), *The Social Psychology of Female–Male Relations: A Critical Analysis of Central Concepts*, pp. 21–67. Copyright © 1986 by Academic Press. Reprinted by permission.

Although young children initially may adopt gender-stereotyped behaviors and beliefs to match their sense of gender identity (the cognitive and schema theories), once gender identity is firmly established, other factors (for example, other people's opinions) may affect behavior more (Spence's 1985 gender identity theory). Therefore, self-descriptions of stereotyped personality traits may not be very predictive of behavior or attitudes. Evidence in support of this position is growing (Edwards & Spence, 1987; Signorella et al., 1989). Furthermore, people also socialize themselves by the choices they make and the company they keep (Jacklin, 1989). All-male and all-female peer groups may socialize group members in very different ways, as we will see in the later section on peers.

In sum, gender identity is a multidimensional and evolving construct, with different components and meanings at different life stages.

From our review of socialization theories, it is clear that both people and social forces, including social institutions, affect the development of sex typing and gender stereotypes. Although people and social forces operate together, for convenience we will discuss them separately, keeping their integration in mind.

▲   Socializing Agents

Clearly, because of the prolonged interaction, the differences in power, and the intense bonds between parents and children, parents serve as the initial and major socializing agents in our society. The term *parents* here refers to a child's legal guardians or to anyone who has major caretaking responsibilities, such as a grandparent or a regular babysitter. Little research has been done with these latter groups, although similar socialization procedures probably operate. Similarly, the influence of siblings has been markedly neglected, although some research has been done on this topic recently.

A child also receives input from people outside the home. Once school begins, teachers and peers become increasingly important. These agents will be examined following a discussion of the role parents and other kin play in the socialization of children.

Parents

To understand how families socialize children into their gender roles, it is important to begin by looking at parental beliefs about and treatment of daughters and sons. How these parental beliefs and behaviors actually affect the child's own developing beliefs, behaviors, and personality then will be examined.

First, however, there are various methodological problems to consider. One serious problem is the frequent use of self-reports of both parents and children. When people describe behaviors related to sex roles, it is often difficult to separate out socially desirable responses from an individual's true preferences or behavior. Thus, studies that find few parental differences in admitted treatment of sons and daughters (see E. E. Maccoby & Jacklin, 1974) may reflect more a parental ideal than actual parental practices. In addition, much parental behavior may occur beyond the parents' level of awareness or even intention and is thus difficult to measure.

Similarly, laboratory studies of parent-child interactions may not reflect what actually goes on in the home. Bronfenbrenner (1977) concluded from surveying a number of studies that interactions in the laboratory are substantially and systematically different from those in the home. Laboratory settings tend to increase anxiety and decrease behaviors showing social competence. This effect may be even more pronounced on working-class families, for whom the laboratory setting is especially likely to be anxiety-arousing. For example, parents may be so anxious about doing the "right" thing or being "good" subjects that they may refrain from punishing their child in the laboratory,

although they do so at home. Thus, generalizations from laboratory observations may be quite limited. Even home observations may be flawed. Fagot (1985) found that parents interacted with their child very differently during the first couple of hours of observation compared with later observations.

These and other research problems should be kept in mind as the research related to socializing agents is presented.

Parents' beliefs and stereotypes Parents socialize their children into appropriate gender roles in multiple ways, some overt, most subtle. Of importance are the parents' own gender role attitudes, the way they treat and react to their sons and daughters, and the behavior they model.

As we saw in Chapter 1, beliefs about sex differences are strongly held and nearly universal. Parents, of course, are among those holding such beliefs. Even before a child is born, stereotyped beliefs affect parents' preference for, and the value they attach to, a male or female child. Nearly everywhere in the world, most couples prefer male children to female children and base this preference on assumed sex differences (Steinbacher & Holmes, 1987; Williamson, 1976). In countries like India, where daughters are viewed negatively and represent a financial burden (a dowry must be paid for a daughter to be married) and where sons are a sign of status and represent income and financial support in old age, preference for sons is especially marked. Indeed, with the advent of amniocentesis and chorionic villa sampling, methods that can detect the sex of the fetus around the third or fourth month of gestation, a disproportionate number of female fetuses have been aborted (Kishwar, 1987). People who prefer sons are most willing to use sex selection technology (Steinbacher & Gilroy, 1990). Thus, even before the birth of a child, parental expectations of sons and daughters are different. Parents' differential preferences cannot help but be reflected in the way male and female children are treated by their parents.

Once a child is born, these gender-stereotyped beliefs and attitudes are activated by the pronouncement "It's a boy!" or "It's a girl!" In fact, these probably are the first three words a new parent will hear. Such gender labeling affects parental perceptions of their newborn, as J. Z. Rubin, Provenzano, and Luria (1974) found. These researchers interviewed 30 first-time parents within 24 hours after their child's birth and found that a significant amount of sex typing already had begun.

Girls were seen as softer, finer, and littler; boys as firmer, stronger, and more alert. These differences were posited even though hospital data indicated that the infants did not differ on any health or physical measure. Fathers made even more stereotyped ratings of their newborn than mothers, a finding that has received confirmation in other studies (Barry, 1980; J. H. Block, 1973; D. B. Lynn, 1979). Perhaps because a father's contact with a newborn is generally less than a mother's or maybe because males generally are concerned more about sex roles than females, fathers fill in their lack of knowledge with more stereotyped expectations.

Other research confirms the effect of gender labeling on adults' perceptions of infants, although the effects may be subtle (Delk, Madden, Livingston, & Ryan, 1986; M. Stern & Karraker, 1989). Figure 6.3 illustrates not only how gendered assumptions can affect perceptions of an infant, but also how important such labeling is to most people. When an otherwise unidentifiable infant is labeled a male, observers perceive what that infant does as masculine; when that same infant is labeled a female, observers perceive what that infant does as feminine. Interestingly, men perceive more sex differences than women, a finding parallel that found for fathers and mothers. The biggest effect of gender labeling is with respect to toy choices: infants, once labeled, typically are given only gender-appropriate toys.

Research on middle-class parents has found that most parents expect their sons to be more agentic (aggressive, noisy, rough, and so on) than their daughters, and their daughters to be more emotional than their sons (Antill, 1987). Cognitively, as we saw in Chapter 2, parents expect their sons to be better than their daughters at math and science (Eccles, 1989). These assumed gender differences were viewed as primarily or exclusively due to socialization factors by half the parents in one study, but one-third saw the influences of biology and socialization as equal, and 20% emphasized biological factors (Antill, 1987). Cross-sex activities by a child were viewed more negatively for sons than daughters, probably because such activities are seen as more connected to homosexuality for boys than for girls. In general, mothers compared to fathers tend to hold more egalitarian values, believe in fewer gender differences, and emphasize socialization rather than biological causes.

Parents' treatment of children   In studying how parents actually treat their children, a somewhat confusing picture emerges. Parents generally report that they treat their sons and daughters similarly (Antill, 1987; E. E. Maccoby & Jacklin, 1974). A recent meta-analysis of 172 studies found no significant systematic differences in parents' general treatment of daughters and sons (Lytton & Romney, 1991). Logically, however, parental beliefs and values should affect parental behavior toward their child, although the effects might be subtle and indirect. This seems to be the case (McGillicuddy-De Lisi, 1985). The strongest evidence of differential parental treatment appears in reactions to the child's behavior, toy selection, and household chore assignment.

If boys are viewed as stronger, they may be handled more roughly than girls, and girls may be protected more. There is some evidence that this does occur (Condry, Condry, & Pogatshnik, 1983;

Figure 6.3 How gender labeling shapes adult perceptions of infants. (CATHY Copyright 1986 Cathy Guisewite. Reprinted with permission of Universal Press Syndicate.)

Culp, Cook, & Housley, 1983; Frisch, 1977). For example, a crying infant is responded to more quickly by young women if it is thought to be a girl rather than a boy. Parents also tend to vocalize more to female than to male infants (Cherry & Lewis, 1976; Wasserman & Lewis, 1985) but to verbally stimulate their toddler sons more in ways facilitative of cognitive development, such as through teaching and questioning (N. Weitzman, Birns, & Friend, 1985). Although infant behaviors certainly can interact with parent behaviors (see, for example, Moss, 1967), the sexes start off remarkably similar in behavior. However, differential treatment by parents and others very quickly can lead to differential development. For example, Fagot and colleagues (Fagot, Hagan, Leinbach, & Kronsberg, 1985) found that caretakers of 1-year-old children attended more to boys' assertive behaviors than girls' and more to girls' communication attempts than to boys'. At the beginning, the infants did not differ in these behaviors, but about ten months later, differences emerged: the boys had become more assertive, the girls had increased their talk to the adults. Thus, differential reactions by caretakers to girls and boys appear to shape the development of different behaviors.

In terms of activities and toys, parental behavior is fairly stereotypic. Girls and boys are given different toys, different clothes, and different environments. A study of the rooms of 120 boys and girls 2 years of age and younger revealed that girls were provided with more dolls, fictional characters, children's furniture, manipulative toys, and the color pink; boys were provided with more sports equipment, tools, vehicles of all sizes, and the colors blue, red, and white (Pomerleau, Bolduc, Malcuit, & Cossette, 1990). Parents discourage their children, especially their sons, from engaging in other-sex activities or playing with other-sex toys (Antill, 1987; Fagot, 1978). In fact, encouragement of sex-typed activities was the only significant gender difference to emerge in a recent meta-analytic study ($d = .43$; Lytton & Romney, 1991). This encouragement of sex-typed activities is particularly true for fathers and may take somewhat subtle forms. That is, cross-sex play may not be explicitly prohibited or discouraged, but parents tend to show more positive reactions to play and toys viewed as gender-appropriate (Caldera, Huston, & O'Brien, 1989). Social learning theory would predict that differential reinforcement of behaviors should lead to differential frequency of the child engaging in those behaviors. Such seems to be the case. Children do

spend more time playing with gender-appropriate toys than gender-inappropriate toys. Interestingly, different toys elicit different types of parent-child interactions: play with "feminine" toys elicits closer physical proximity and more verbal interactions; play with "masculine" toys elicits low proximity and low levels of questions and teachings (Caldera et al., 1989). Thus, boys and girls may develop different patterns of interpersonal interaction as a function of play with different toys.

Boys and girls also tend to do different things and are assigned different chores as early as age 5 or 6 (Burns & Homel, 1989; Goodnow, 1988; McHale, Bartko, Crouter, & Perry-Jenkins, 1990; Timmer et al., 1985). Boys are more likely than girls to be assigned maintenance chores (for example, painting things, mowing lawns), whereas girls are more likely to be assigned domestic tasks (cooking, laundry, shopping). These gender differences in assigned chores increase from childhood through adolescence. Since domestic chores are daily ones whereas maintenance chores are sporadic, girls end up spending more time in chores than boys. These gender patterns are affected by social class, ethnic background, maternal employment, and size and gender makeup of family. For example, lower socioeconomic status families tend to make more gender-linked assignments than higher class families. When the mother is employed, both sons and daughters tend to perform domestic tasks. What is learned through this gender division of chores? Besides the content of the chores themselves (girls learn how to do domestic work better than boys; boys learn how to do maintenance work better than girls), children also learn to link certain types of work with gender, a linkage that may extend to later occupational choice. In addition, children may develop different personal qualities. Domestic work, associated with caring for others, may facilitate the development of nurturance and prosocial behaviors. Maintenance work, associated with caring for things, may facilitate different cognitive skills or strategies. The fact that girls spend more time doing chores than boys also may convey a message about male privilege.

As suggested by the research on chore assignment, race and class are important variables when discussing gender socialization. Working-class families tend to differentiate between the sexes more sharply than middle-class families in some respects, but not in others (Brooks-Gunn, 1986; Canter & Ageton, 1984; Cazenave, 1984; A. C. Huston, 1983). For example, higher socioeconomic level families are more likely to provide stereotypically male toys (associated with better visual-spatial and problem-solving skills; Serbin et al., 1990) to children of both sexes than lower socio-economic level families. Among Blacks, gender stereotypes are less strong and both sons and daughters are socialized toward independence, employment, and child care (Bardewell, Cochran, & Walker, 1986; Hale-Benson, 1986; Malson, 1983; E. J. Smith, 1982; Wallace, 1979). Indeed, Blacks seem to use a different female stereotype—that of the "strong Black woman"—in their training. However, Black girls still receive a very strong motherhood orientation, whereas Black boys receive much more training in street smarts, athletic prowess, and sexual competence. Gender socialization beliefs and practices in other ethnic groups have received little study. Since most of the research on gender socialization has focused on middle-class Whites, the generalizability of such findings may be limited.

Do mothers and fathers treat children differently? We already have reviewed evidence demonstrating that fathers tend to hold more stereotypic attitudes toward the sexes than mothers. Fathers also tend to enforce gender norms more than mothers, especially with respect to their sons. In particular, fathers are much more restrictive than mothers with respect to cross-sex play in their sons. Although most research on parental socialization practices uses mothers only, and indeed mothers do spend more time with children than do fathers even when both parents work outside the home, fathers have been found to be important socializing agents as well (Baruch & Barnett, 1981; B. E. Carlson, 1984; M. E. Lamb, 1981b, 1986).

Typically, fathers spend most of their time with young children playing with them, whereas mothers spend most of their time taking care of them (M. E. Lamb, 1981a, 1981b; MacDonald & Parke, 1986; Parke, 1981; Stevenson, Leavitt, Thompson, & Roach, 1988). The type of play in which fathers typically engage tends to be more physical and more emotionally arousing than the type of play in which mothers typically engage. In contrast, mothers' play tends to be more centered on toys and more didactic than fathers' play. These differences are especially evident with boys and seem to be reciprocated. That is, boys in particular seem to prefer the more physical and active play style typical of fathers (H. Ross & Taylor, 1989). Because mothers are more involved in child-care activities, mothers become more, and fathers become less, sensitive to the individual needs of their children after the newborn period (M. E. Lamb, 1986). Furthermore, compared to mothers, fathers also give more evaluative responses—that is, more approval and disapproval (Fagot & Leinbach, 1987). Thus, fathers seem to be the more playful, the less sensitive, and the more critical parent. In addition, each parent is inclined to encourage the interests and characteristics typical of her or his own sex (Antill, 1987). Overall, each parent tends to complement the other.

Despite these general patterns of treatment as a function of parent sex, the bulk of the research suggests that parent sex interacts with child sex. Each parent may be more involved with and attached to a child of the same sex than a child of the other sex, especially fathers (Dickie, 1987; Fagot & Leinbach, 1987; S. P. Morgan, Lyle, & Condran, 1988). Yet parents tend to be more permissive with a child of the other sex and more restrictive with a child of the same sex. That is, mothers tend to be more permissive with sons and more restrictive with daughters, whereas fathers tend to be more permissive with daughters and more restrictive with sons. These cross-sex effects have been found to be stronger than the sex of either the child or the parent alone in influencing parent-child interactions. That is, all sons are not treated one way and all daughters another, nor do all mothers treat children one way and all fathers another. Rather, each parent treats sons and daughters in specific and different ways.

In general, fathers tend to be more favorable toward and permissive with girls in regard to aggressive, dependent, and achievement behaviors than they are with boys. For mothers, the opposite is true—they tend to be more favorable toward, and permissive with, boys than with girls (Bronstein, 1984a; Gurwitz & Dodge, 1975; E. E. Maccoby & Jacklin, 1974). Parents even cuddle other-sex newborns more than same-sex ones (J. Z. Rubin et al., 1974). With respect to cognitive development, however, parents tend to challenge and encourage their child of the other sex more than their child of the same sex (McGillicuddy-De Lisi, 1988; N. Weitzman et al., 1985). Because mothers are often the only parent studied, these results may account for the predominant findings in the literature that boys receive more praise, are subject to stricter socialization, and are held more at birth than girls. In the home, with father present, these effects may be counterbalanced. However, because most fathers do not spend the same amount of time with their children as mothers, and because many children grow up in female-headed households without any paternal presence, girls appear to grow up receiving less positive treatment and more restrictiveness than boys, in general.

The reasons for this cross-sex effect are unclear, but it may result from a variety of sources. It may be a reaction to the other-sex child as a member of the other sex, or it may be a reaction to the same-sex child as a rival. Behavior by a same-sex child may also be a reminder of the parents' own negative impulses, which they then punish. In any case, such effects certainly need to be taken into account in drawing conclusions about parental behavior. It would be inappropriate to conclude, however, that the relationship between a parent and same-sex child is less important than that between a parent and other-sex child. For example, in divorce cases, children living with the same-sex parent appear better adjusted than children living with the other-sex parent (Hetherington, Stanley-Hagan, & Anderson, 1989). Overall, the relationship a child has with each parent appears important, but in different ways for boys and girls.

What parents model   Besides differential treatment, parents also model different behaviors. The most basic difference modeled by mothers and fathers is with respect to child care. Nearly all children are cared for primarily by a woman, signaling that child care and nurturance in general may be "women's work." Even if both parents are employed outside the home, mothers spend more time and energy than fathers in child-care and domestic activities. Fathers appear more involved than mothers with play activities, with maintenance chores, and with the labor force in general and higher status occupations in particular (Bronstein, 1984a; Burns & Homel, 1989; J. D. G. Goldman & Goldman, 1983).

As we saw earlier in this chapter, the importance of parents as models is discussed by all the theories of gender socialization, but is particularly stressed by psychodynamic and social learning theories. Children learn about the roles of women and men from observing their mothers and fathers. To the extent that their parents are traditionally stereotyped or engage in traditional behaviors, children should acquire a traditional view of gender roles. The research on this topic is contradictory, as we have seen in reviewing these theories. We need to take a closer look at what effect parental sex typing, behaviors, and beliefs actually have on a child's own sex typing, behaviors, and attitudes.

Parental effects on children's gender development   We have seen that most parents, especially fathers, believe that significant differences exist between males and females. We also have seen that parents treat their sons and daughters differently and themselves model different behaviors. What effect does all this have on children's gender-related views and behaviors?

Research on parental beliefs and values about gender suggest that although these factors affect children's sex-typed behaviors and attitudes, the connection is often indirect. For example, in couples with egalitarian gender role beliefs, fathers are more likely to share housework and child-care responsibilities (Pleck, 1983). Increased visibility of, and interaction with, fathers may lead to more egalitarian views in children. Furthermore, the relationship between parental beliefs and children's behaviors may vary depending upon the particular belief or even the particular parent (McGillicuddy-De Lisi, 1985). In general, the more specific the parental beliefs, the more clear the effect. For example, mothers who believe that boys have more talent for math than girls tend to have daughters who have little confidence in their own math abilities irrespective of the grades they receive in math (Eccles, 1989; Eccles & Jacobs, 1986). This low confidence leads girls to take fewer advanced math courses than boys, as discussed in Chapter 2. Overall, parents with traditional beliefs and values tend to actively discourage cross-sex and encourage same-sex characteristics and interests in their children. Parents with egalitarian gender beliefs and values tend to encourage cross-sex, and are neutral to same-sex, characteristics and interests in their children (Antill, 1987). Children whose parents hold strongly egalitarian beliefs and whose lifestyle reflects those beliefs tend to have greater knowledge of non-sex-typed objects and occupations than do other children (Weisner & Wilson-Mitchell, 1990).

Fathers' attitudes, in particular, may be related to their children's gender role development. Fathers with traditional attitudes toward women (and traditional roles in the home) tend to have children who begin labeling by gender early (before 28 months) (Fagot & Leinbach, 1989). Mothers' attitudes toward women are not related to their child's early gender labeling. Traditional gender attitudes in fathers have also been found to be significantly associated with traditional gender attitudes in their sons (Emihovich, Gaier, & Cronin, 1984).

Specific parent behaviors have been found linked to a child's gender role development. Both mothers and fathers who are reactive to their 18-month-old child's sex-typed play tend to have children who begin labeling by gender early (before 28 months) (Fagot & Leinbach, 1989). Early labelers show more sex typing in their own toy choices by 28 months, which appears to continue at least through age 4. Thus, parental reactions to a child's sex-typed play at a very young age seem to steer that child toward developing a gender schema and toward increased sex typing. Children who start to label by gender somewhat later still develop sex-typed preferences, but their preference seems less based on knowledge of gender stereotypes than does the behavior of early labelers. These results support gender schema theory. The relationship between parental behaviors and a child's development of sex-typed knowledge, behaviors, and identity is complex and appears to vary as a function of the realm examined and as a function of the child's sex (A. C. Huston, 1983; L. A. Jackson, Ialongo, & Stollak, 1986; J. A. Kelly & Worell, 1976; Levy, 1989b; M. Lewis, 1987; Orlofsky, 1979). For example, among college students, parental warmth and involvement are critical factors in determining males' sex typing, whereas cognitive encouragement and consistent discipline are most important for females' sex typing. Overall, each parent plays an important part in the sex role development of a child, with the influence of each parent varying as a function of the child's gender.

Fathers' behaviors, like their attitudes, seem particularly important in shaping their children's sex typing. Fathers are the primary role models of young boys, but only when the fathers are nurturant and the father-child relationship has been affectionate (Biller, 1981b; Radin, 1981). Sons seem more likely to exhibit the socially desirable characteristics of their fathers than of their mothers, whereas daughters seem likely to exhibit desirable characteristics of either parent regardless of their gender appropriateness (Spence & Helmreich, 1978). For daughters, then, both maternal and paternal behaviors are important. Sons and daughters of involved, nurturant fathers tend to have increased cognitive development and less stereotyped gender beliefs (Biller, 1981b; M. E. Lamb, 1986; W. H. McBroom, 1981; Pruett, 1987; Radin, 1981). Although the paternal relationship is important to children, children growing up in father-absent homes are not necessarily less well adjusted or less secure in their own sex typing than children growing up in father-present homes, when socioeconomic and stress factors are held constant

(Biller, 1981a, 1981b; M. E. Lamb, 1981b, 1986). One reason father-absent homes may not be deleterious compared to father-present homes is that most fathers, even when present in the home, tend not to be very involved with their children.

As suggested by the research on a father's nurturant behaviors, a parent's sex-typed personality may influence a child's sex typing. Results show, however, that parental sex typing is less important than parental behaviors or the parental relationship itself in determining a child's sex typing. This is particularly true for males. With few exceptions, the literature has failed to support the hypothesis that "masculine" fathers will have "masculine" sons or that boys raised in homes without fathers will be less "masculine" (Biller, 1981a, 1981b; L. A. Jackson et al., 1986; M. E. Lamb, 1981b, 1986). Parental sex typing may affect children indirectly, through specific parent behaviors. For example, fathers who score high on expressive-nurturant traits (that is, fathers who are androgynous or feminine-sex-typed) tend to be more involved with their children than fathers low on these traits (Palkovitz, 1984; G. Russell, 1978). Families in which one or both parents are androgynous appear to be highest in parental warmth and supportiveness and in encouraging achievement and a sense of self-worth in the children; "undifferentiated" couples appear to be the lowest (Spence & Helmreich, 1978). In general, androgynous children tend to have parents who are androgynous, loving, and egalitarian (see Sedney, 1987).

Overall, boys and girls are treated differently by their parents, both directly (in terms of specific toys and chores) and indirectly (in terms of parental reactions and parental modeling). Fathers, in particular, seem influential in making gender distinctions, and cross-sex effects (cross-sex permissiveness, same-sex restrictiveness) are common.

The general picture is one of boys being more intensely socialized than girls. Boys receive both more praise and more punishments than girls, and more pressure against engaging in gender-inappropriate behavior. Sons compared to daughters also receive more encouragement for independent explorations starting in early childhood, and more pressure for achievement in school and athletics. Girls' socialization involves more reinforcement for staying close and conforming to adult expectations (Aries & Olver, 1985; Fagot & Leinbach, 1987). In general, boys receive more attention. This is true in other cultures as well (M. R. Welch & Page, 1981). Although role pressures on girls intensify after puberty, these pressures are focused fairly narrowly upon being sexually attractive and finding a mate, even if doing so means limiting educational and career aspirations and talents (Gilligan et al., 1988; P. Katz, 1979).

Why this differential pressure exists is not clear. As Maccoby and Jacklin (1974) suggest, perhaps males' greater strength and aggressiveness make their adequate early socialization much more important. Or perhaps males simply are more valued, and, therefore, more attention is paid to them. This is supported by findings regarding parental sex preferences and other research that shows that sex is a status variable, with males having the higher status (Feinman, 1981, 1984). Another reason for differential pressure involves the greater demands of the masculine sex role. To get a child to accept the masculine role, as in suppressing his feelings, socialization must be intense. It may be that the masculine role is more unnatural, requiring young boys to separate from the intimate relationships that have sustained them from birth, and therefore more pressure must be exerted on males to conform. Females can continue to develop a self-in-relation. Or perhaps establishing a male identity is harder to do because of absence of male models. Therefore, socialization must be more intense to compensate. It also is possible that males' behaviors demand more attention, but this explanation overlooks the lack of major gender differences in infancy and early childhood.

The explanations with the most support involve the differential value placed on the male gender role and the greater demands attached to it, although it is undoubtedly true that children of each sex may bring different qualities to a parent-child interaction. The rigidity of the male gender role can be seen in the four basic themes of masculinity (David & Brannon, 1976; Pleck, 1981b): (1) rejecting all "feminine" behaviors and traits; (2) being strong, competent, and independent; (3) acquiring success and status; and (4) demonstrating aggressiveness and daring. Regardless of which explanation for differential pressures is accepted, such differential pressures have important consequences. We've already examined some of the consequences in the literature on cognitive, personality, social, and sexual behavior differences (Part 2). Other consequences will be discussed in Part 4.

Other Kin

Parents, of course, are not the only socializing agents in a family. Grandparents, aunts and uncles,

cousins, and siblings also are important, especially among low-income Blacks, where children frequently are cared for by members of the extended family (Stack, 1974). Among all cultural groups, the maternal grandmother plays a particularly strong socializing role, since children usually see her most frequently and feel closest to her (Bengtson & Robertson, 1985; Eisenberg, 1988).

Siblings also play an important part in the sex role development of a child, both directly, through their behavior with the child, and indirectly, through their effect on the parents (Barry, 1980; Bronfenbrenner, 1977; Cicirelli, 1982; Stoneman, Brody, & MacKinnon, 1986; Tauber, 1979). Both age and gender of siblings are important. For example, young children tend to play with an older sibling. If the older sibling is of the same sex, play activities tend to be gender stereotyped; if the older sibling is of the other sex, cross-sex play is common. In families where children are all one sex, household chores tend to be less stereotypically assigned than in families in which children of both sexes reside. Human behavior functions as part of a whole system, each part of which undoubtedly influences every other part. Thus, we must be aware of complex interactions among family members with respect to gender socialization.

Teachers

Whatever influence parents and other household members may have on a child's development, once school begins, other people share the responsibility for socialization. Teachers, in particular, are important.

From the time a child starts school, which for some children occurs as early as age 3, teachers provide additional messages regarding sex role development through provision of activities, reinforcement, modeling, and subtler forms of communication. In most cases, these messages reinforce those received at home, strengthening the sex typing. Even when teacher messages contradict parental messages, their influence is enormous and sometimes is greater than parental influence, especially if the messages are supported by other socializing forces.

From nursery school through college, teachers pay more attention to males than to females, and males tend to dominate the classroom environment. Compared to girls, boys are more likely to receive teacher attention, to call out in class, to demand help or attention from the teacher, to be seen as a model student, or to be praised by teachers (Epperson, 1988;

Sadker & Sadker, 1986). Girls receive reinforcement mainly for being quiet and compliant. For example, in an observational study of 15 nursery school teachers by Serbin and colleagues (Serbin, O'Leary, Kent, & Tonick, 1973), the teachers responded three times more often to boys who were disruptive than to girls. They also responded more to girls who clung or stayed nearby than to boys who exhibited similar behaviors. Teachers also actually taught boys more than girls. Boys were given more individualized instruction, thereby making them more capable of fending for themselves and more capable in problem solving. In general, boys were given more attention for their behavior, whether such behavior was appropriate or not. Other research with preschool teachers confirms these findings of greater attention paid to boys, especially for engaging in tasks appropriate to academic behaviors, and more compliance socialization for girls (Fagot, 1984; Fagot et al., 1985; Gold, Crombie, & Noble, 1987).

A similar pattern is found during elementary and middle school (Dweck, Davidson, Nelson, & Enna, 1978; Irvine, 1986; Wilkinson & Marrett, 1985). For example, researchers who observed more than 100 fourth-, sixth-, and eighth-grade classes over a three-year period found that boys consistently and clearly dominated classroom interactions at all grade levels, in all communities, and in all subject areas (Sadker & Sadker, 1985, 1986). Teachers tended to call on boys more often than girls and to encourage boys more. For example, if a girl gave an incorrect answer, the teacher was likely to move on to another student, whereas if a boy gave an incorrect answer, the teacher was likely to help him discover the correct answer and then praise him. Even when a girl gave a correct answer, she was more likely to receive a simple acceptance ("OK") than praise ("Excellent"). Thus, boys tended to receive a more specific and intense educational interaction. Furthermore, when a boy called out in class without first raising his hand, the teacher probably would accept his answer. However, when a girl called out in class, she was likely to receive a reprimand. These teacher behaviors sent the message that girls should keep quiet and be passive learners, whereas boys should be academically assertive and active.

Many variables interact with gender in the classroom, with race and age being particularly salient (Irvine, 1986; Wilkinson & Marrett, 1985). White female students exhibit more compliant, passive behaviors throughout elementary school and receive the least teacher feedback. Black female students start out with more active and interacting behaviors, but by third or fourth grade, they receive feedback similar to their White female peers; that is, they receive little teacher feedback, especially academic feedback, and few public response opportunities. Black girls from kindergarten through third grade tend to receive praise from teachers primarily for nurturing behaviors ("Study of Black Females," 1985). The consequences of this pattern of teacher behaviors for both White and Black girls may be quite serious. Girls learn to give up on academic work after a failure more quickly than boys. This learned helplessness by girls may stay with them throughout their school years. Black males also don't seem to fare very well in the classroom. Although some research finds that Black males receive more attention than White females (Irvine, 1986), other research finds that Black males, when compared with females of both races and with White males, receive the most unfavorable teacher treatment, such as the fewest response opportunities (Grant, 1985; Taylor, 1979). Black males also receive the most teacher recommendations for special education programs (McIntyre & Pernell, 1985). These findings might help account for the lower academic motivation and the greater dropout rate of Black students, especially males, compared with Whites. Although Black males may indeed demonstrate different classroom behaviors than other race-gender groups, even when behavior is controlled for by using written descriptions, teachers still predict lower success for Black males, especially if they are described as noncompliant (S. I. Ross & Jackson, 1991). Teacher behaviors and attitudes play a major role in student achievement, since the best predictor of school success for seventh- and eighth-graders has been found to be teacher's judgment (Farkas, Grobe, Sheehan, & Shuan, 1990). Teacher's judgment remains powerful even when cognitive performance variables (coursework mastery and basic skills) are controlled. Asian students are perceived as having the best work habits; Black students, especially Black males, the worst.

The greater attention and encouragement given to White boys have been found related to problem-solving ability and may explain boys' greater mathematical skills (Eccles, 1989; L. H. Fox, 1981). The lack of accurate and continuous feedback for girls may interfere with girls' realistic appraisal of their abilities. It may also interfere with the development of self-confidence and achievement motivation. The indirect reinforcement of aggressiveness in boys also may explain the higher incidence of behavior and learning problems in school-age boys than in girls, since such behaviors interfere with learning.

College teachers also tend to pay more attention to male than female students (R. M. Hall & Sandler, 1982; Krupnick, 1985; Sadker & Sadker, 1986). Compared to male students, female students are called on less frequently, receive less encouragement for speaking, and are interrupted, ignored, and devalued more often. As the Association of American Colleges' Project on the Status and Education of Women concluded, the classroom climate is a "chilly" one for female students. These college classroom encounters, which reinforce previous ones, may contribute to the drop in self-esteem college women in coed schools seem to experience (A. W. Astin, 1977; also see Chapter 8). Interestingly, women college professors (about 25% of college professors) tend to encourage a participatory classroom environment and to be less biased against female students (Brophy, 1985; M. Crawford & MacLeod, 1990; Krupnick, 1985; Statham, Richardson, & Cook, 1991). In such classrooms, women students participate more equally with their male peers. Female faculty members also serve as role models for female students (Basow & Howe, 1980; Erkut & Mokros, 1983; L. A. Gilbert, Gallessich, & Evans, 1983).

Unlike in colleges, teacher gender does not seem to be a particularly strong variable in elementary or secondary school classrooms, perhaps because teaching in these grades is so heavily female-dominated (Brophy, 1985; A. C. Huston, 1983; Sadker & Sadker, 1986). Both male and female teachers tend to have traditional sex role beliefs and to respond differently to male and female students. Male preschool teachers in one study gave more positive comments to, and were more physical with, both boys and girls than were female teachers (Fagot, 1981a). As is true with parents, male teachers tend to believe in the gender stereotypes even more strongly than female teachers (Fagot, 1981b). This is particularly unfortunate since male teachers may be more salient sources of information about sex role behaviors for very young children than female teachers (Koblinsky & Sugawara, 1984). Just the presence of a teacher in a particular area of the room has been shown to affect the likelihood of a preschool child playing with toys in that area (Serbin, Connor, & Citron, 1981). If preschool teachers are mostly female and stay in feminine-typed areas (for example, the kitchen), each sex may have little encouragement to play with other-sex-typed toys.

The differences in teacher behavior toward males and females at all grade levels parallel those found in parents. Boys receive more attention, more praise, and more punishment than girls. These findings are especially striking because teachers do not seem to be aware that they treat boys and girls differently, even when faced with direct evidence. For example, in the Sadkers' (1985) elementary school study, the researchers asked teachers and administrators to view a film made of a classroom discussion. In response to a question as to which sex was talking more, the teachers overwhelmingly said the girls were. In fact, the boys in the film outtalked the girls at a ratio of three to one. Without awareness, changing differential teaching practices is impossible.

Peers

Age-mates also serve as strong socializing agents. They become increasingly important during the school years. In many cases, peer pressure is stronger and more effective than parental or other adult pressure, particularly during adolescence. Even during preschool years, however, peers influence the sex role behaviors of their friends.

From preschool through adolescence, children who engage in traditional forms of sex role behavior are more socially acceptable to their peers than those who do not adopt traditional behaviors (Fagot, 1977, 1978, 1984; Hartup, 1983; C. L. Martin, 1989). This may be particularly true for boys, and it serves as another example of their more intense socialization and more rigid sex role. For example, preschool boys who preferred feminine-sex-typed toys received less positive feedback and were more likely to play alone than were other boys in their class (Fagot, 1984). The intense peer pressure toward gender conformity may be one reason why there is so little cross-sex-typing in elementary school children, even though the categories of "tomboy" and "sissy" exist (Hemmer & Kleiber, 1981; Stericker & Kurdek, 1982). Rather than denoting cross-sex-typing or androgyny, these labels seem to be used pejoratively by young children for peers who are regarded as socially difficult and antisocial. Given the more rigid sex role for males and the greater importance attached to the male sex role, it is not surprising that the term *sissy* is far more pejorative than the term *tomboy*. Being a "sissy" also may be seen more negatively than being a "tomboy" because such boys are viewed as more likely than such girls to reject their gender role and become homosexual (Antill, 1987; C. L. Martin, 1990).

Three behaviors, in particular, seem affected by peer responses—aggressiveness, assertiveness, and passivity. Connor and associates (1978) found that 9- to 14-year-old girls expect less disapproval from their peers for passive behavior and more disapproval for aggressive behavior than do their male classmates. Such expectations are indeed justified. Assertiveness is also regarded as more desirable for males than for females. Such gender stereotypes may influence the way children respond to other children and may influence their willingness to use other children as models.

Sex segregation begins in preschool years and intensifies once a child enters school. Both sexes prefer same-sex groups, a process observed in both Western and non-Western societies and even among some nonhuman primates (D. B. Carter, 1987; Feiring & Lewis, 1987; Whiting & Edwards, 1988). This sex-segregation process was studied longitudinally by Maccoby and Jacklin (1987; E. E. Maccoby, 1990) with children from birth to age 6. They found that girls seem to initiate such segregation around 3 years of age, but both sexes maintain it thereafter. In exploring various reasons why such segregation occurs, Maccoby and Jacklin concluded that the most likely explanation is that girls find playing with boys to be a negative experience. Whereas girls tend to enjoy mutual play and use conflict mitigation strategies, boys tend to play more roughly, use physical assertion to resolve conflicts, and ignore girls' attempts at influence. The result is that boys tend to dominate and bully girls in mixed-sex groups, and girls consequently try to avoid such situations.

In classrooms as well, girls get few rewards from interacting with boys. Whereas girls tend to offer help to both boys and girls, boys rarely help girls, leading to an imbalance in reciprocity (Lockheed, 1985). Teachers tend to support sex segregation by separating children by sex ("All the boys line up on the left, girls on the right"), encouraging competition between the sexes ("Let's have the girls against the boys"), and not promoting cross-sex interactions. Interestingly, status and power differentials between girls and boys are less apparent among Blacks than they are among White children, perhaps due to Blacks' less rigid sex stereotyping or the socialization of Black girls to be more assertive (Grant, 1985).

Although sex segregation seems to arise from differences in dominance relations between boys and girls rather than from any innate personality or temperament differences, the recognition of dominance differences by sex rests upon knowledge of gender labels (E. E. Maccoby & Jacklin, 1987).

In societies where men's higher status is obvious and differential treatment of male and female children pronounced, boys' struggle to disassociate themselves from females is particularly strong (Whiting & Edwards, 1988). Sex segregation continues throughout childhood and adolescence because it is both reinforcing and socially reinforced, especially as children approach puberty and wish to avoid romantic or sexually toned relationships.

The result of sex segregation is that boys and girls tend to grow up in different peer environments, different subcultures (E. E. Maccoby & Jacklin, 1987). The subculture boys inhabit, compared to that of girls, is characterized by larger groups, less proximity to adults, more public play, more fighting and physical contact, more dominance attempts, and the establishment of a hierarchical "pecking order." The subculture girls inhabit, compared to that of boys, is characterized by smaller, more intimate groups (twosomes or threesomes), closer proximity and connections to adults, a strong convention of turn-taking, and more mutuality in play and conversations. Such patterns have been found among both Blacks and Whites (D. L. Coates, 1987). These different peer groups continue to socialize members, further enhancing both real and perceived gender differences. With limited cross-sex interactions, stereotypes have an opportunity to flourish unchecked by disconfirming experiences. Young people also become more restricted in the range of behaviors and styles to which they are exposed and with which they can experiment. As Whiting and Edwards (1988) found in their cross-cultural research, we are shaped by the company we keep.

Peers seem to be particularly important to boys. From an early age through adolescence, boys spend more time with peers relative to adults than do girls. For example, in one study of 3-year-olds, 41% of the boys' contacts were with peers relative to adults whereas only 29% of the girls' contacts were with peers (Feiring & Lewis, 1987). This greater attention to peers than adults by boys compared with girls has been found in the first-grade classroom as well (Grant, 1985). Whereas girls spend more time interacting with teachers than with peers, boys spend more time interacting with peers than with teachers. Black boys show the greatest differential; that is, they spend the vast majority of their time interacting with peers instead of teachers. Furthermore, although the peer networks of White girls encourage being attentive to teachers, the networks of other children, especially Black boys, discourage such attention. Other research supports the critical role male peer groups play for African-American males (D. L. Coates, 1987; Rashid, 1989). Whereas African-American adolescent girls say they feel close to family members and to both male and female peers, Black males feel close mainly to male peers.

This turning to peers by boys rather than to adults may be due to the fact that most of the adults and teachers with whom young boys interact are female. Peers exert tremendous pressure on males of all ages to resist female influence (E. E. Maccoby & Jacklin, 1987). As Hartley (1959) suggests, a peer group may be more important to a male than to a female because he has to look to them for information about the male role, since adult males are less available than adult females. A Black male, more likely to be raised in a female-headed single-parent family than a White male, may be particularly dependent upon male peers. However, because his peers have no better source of information than he, the information a male child obtains is likely to be distorted and oversimplified. Males' conceptualizations of appropriate behavior therefore are often extremely rigid and stereotyped. In contrast, girls grow up surrounded by female models. Girls thus have a conception of the female role more grounded in direct observation and therefore don't need female peers as much to bolster their identity. Furthermore, as we have seen, girls are reinforced for staying around female adults, whereas boys are reinforced for their "autonomous" behaviors. Another reason girls may stay around adults is that adults appear to reduce boys' attempts to dominate girls in a competitive situation (Powlishta & Maccoby, 1990).

Male bonding, as it emerges during late childhood and early adolescence, plays a very important role in male lives. Such bonding serves to reinforce a male's identity as male, meaning separate from female. Such bonding also gives rise to and reinforces a sense of male dominance over females. This dominance usually is achieved by degrading all that is female (as in "girls have cooties") and later by developing exploitative attitudes toward women as sex objects. Males often feel great pressure to prove their masculinity throughout their lives, but especially during late childhood and adolescence, through athletic skill, physical strength, acts of daring, and sexual conquests (Raphael, 1988; Stockard & Johnson, 1979). (See Figure 6.4.) Even though males after puberty are expected to have sexual relationships with females, males still are expected to put "the guys" first in their priorities. In contrast, girls' proof of their femininity, which doesn't arise until adolescence, rests primarily on finding a mate. Peer status for girls then becomes contingent on their popularity with boys (J. S. Chafetz, 1978; S. Weitz, 1977). Adolescents with traditional gender attitudes appear to be more influenced by peers than adolescents with more nontraditional attitudes, supporting the important role of peers in gender socialization (Canter & Ageton, 1984).

In sum, peers play an important role in socializing children and adolescents into gender-appropriate behaviors and attitudes. Furthermore, the role peers play appears to be more influential for males than for females. (We will discuss friendships more thoroughly in Chapter 9.) Although little studied compared to other socializing forces, sex-typed peer preferences may be particularly powerful in encouraging sex typing in children. Such preferences certainly precede and are stronger than gender differences in personality traits and social behaviors (A. C. Huston, 1985).

Figure 6.4 Peers play a strong role in eliciting and reinforcing males' gender-stereotypic behaviors. (HAGAR reprinted with special permission of King Features Syndicate, Inc.)

▲ Summary

The theory that best explains gender socialization is an integrated one: it takes into account primary maternal caretaking during the first years of life (psychodynamic theory), differential treatment and modeling of gender-linked behaviors (social learning theory), developmental changes in cognitive abilities and structures (cognitive-developmental and gender schema theory), the strength of cultural messages regarding gender (gender schema theory), and differential social roles by gender (social-role theory). Both directly and indirectly, children are steered toward different modes of behavior through a developing gender schema. Boys are steered toward the agentic—achievement, competition, independence—and girls toward the communal—nurturance, sociability, dependence.

Children are strongly affected by socializing agents—parents, other kin, teachers, and peers—and generally learn the gender stereotypes early and well. Parents believe boys and girls are different and tend to treat them accordingly, especially with respect to toys and chores. Each parent also tends to model different behaviors, as do other kin. Teachers too believe in gender stereotypes and tend to show differential treatment of the girls and boys in their classes. Peers further reinforce the gender stereotypes in each other both directly, through differential approval for gender-linked behaviors, and indirectly, through sex segregation. The result is that by school age, children know what girls and boys "should" and "shouldn't" do and tend to behave accordingly, boys more so than girls. Boys tend to receive the more intense socialization pressures and consequently behave in more stereotyped ways than girls. One future implication of this differential socialization pressure is that androgyny may be more difficult for males, since they are more committed to the masculine stereotype.

Although the effects of socializing agents are enormous, socializing agents alone cannot account for the entire socializing process. Children formulate their conceptions of sex roles from a wide range of social forces acting on a more impersonal level, such as the media, the educational system, and religion. We now turn to an examination of these forces.

▲ Recommended Reading

Bem, S. L. (1983). Gender schema theory and its implications for child development: Raising gender-aschematic children in a gender-schematic society. *Signs, 8,* 598–616. An excellent description of gender schema theory for nonpsychologists with an instructive section on child-rearing implications.

Chodorow, N. J. (1990). *Feminism and psychoanalytic theory.* New Haven: Yale University Press. The most recent thinking of an important theorist whose work has had a tremendous impact on feminist researchers in a number of areas.

Huston, A. C. (1983). Sex-typing. In P. H. Mussen & E. M. Hetherington (Eds.), *Handbook of child psychology, Vol. 4: Socialization, personality, and social development* (4th ed.) (pp. 387–468). New York: Wiley. An excellent and detailed review of the literature to 1983.

Lamb, M. E. (Ed.). (1981). *The role of the father in child development* (2nd ed.). New York: Wiley. An excellent collection of articles by the most prominent researchers in the area of paternal effects on children.

Chapter 7
Socializing Forces

A 6-year-old child is overheard by her mother explaining to a friend that only boys can be doctors and only girls can be nurses. The mother remarks "But, Sally, you know I'm a doctor." Sally replies "You're no doctor; you're my mother."

This story illustrates not only the simplistic categories children use to understand their world but also the fact that children acquire information about the world from sources outside the home. This chapter examines the sex role messages the child's world contains.

That social contexts are crucial in understanding human behavior has been amply demonstrated by social psychologists. Under certain nonthreatening, innocuous conditions, people can be made nearly to kill other humans, while under other conditions they cannot be made to do so (Milgram's obedience experiments, 1965). People appear to react to their state of physiological arousal, induced by adrenalin, with either euphoria or anger depending upon their expectations and the behavior of another person (Schacter & Singer, 1962). Students can sometimes get better grades if their teachers expect them to be intelligent (Rosenthal & Jacobson, 1968). Given these findings, Naomi Weisstein concluded that "a study of human behavior requires a study of the social contexts in which people move, the expectations as to how they will behave, and the authority that tells them who they are and what they are supposed to do" (Weisstein, 1969, p. 58).

The influence of social contexts need not be direct or, in fact, deliberate. As Sandra and Daryl Bem (1970) suggest, the training of women and men to know their place is a function of a pervasive but nonconscious ideology. The sheer pervasiveness of such an ideology determines a child's developing gender schema and consequently how sex-typed she or he will become. As we argued in Chapter 1, gender is socially constructed. An examination of the social context in which a child develops is thus important to fully understand how gender stereotypes and gender expectations develop and are maintained. As we will see in this chapter, messages about gender and gender-appropriate behavior can be found everywhere—in our language, play activities, school, religion, and, of course, the media. Of all social forces, language is perhaps the most subtle.

▲ Language

From the moment a child begins to understand the spoken word, she or he also begins to receive messages about the way society views the sexes. Language plays a major role in defining and maintaining male power over women. Sexism in the English language takes three major forms: ignoring, stereotyping, and deprecating females (Henley, 1989; Lakoff, 1975, 1990; Thorne, Kramarae, & Henley, 1983).

Ignoring

The most striking way of ignoring females is by using the masculine gender to refer to human beings in general—for example, "chair*man*," "best *man* for the job," "*man*kind," "the working *man*," "everyone should do *his* best." This use of the male term to refer to all humans makes maleness the norm and femaleness the exception. That people do, in fact, perceive the masculine "generic" to refer predominantly to males has been demonstrated conclusively by numerous researchers (Fisk, 1985; Gastil, 1990; Hamilton, 1991; MacKay, 1980; Switzer, 1990). For example, when students from first grade through college were asked to make up a story about the average student in a school, only 12% who had read the pronoun *he* in the instructions told a story about a female. When the pronoun encountered was *they*, only 18% told a story about a female, but when the pronoun was *he or she*, 42% of the stories were about females (Hyde, 1984). Clearly, then, the use of male pronouns is not sex-neutral. Furthermore, most children in elementary school don't even know that *he* is supposed to include females. Children who are exposed to a constant flow of information about "him" appear to conclude that the typical person is male. Thus, use of the generic *he* allows many people to ignore the female half of the population. Even the seemingly neutral pronoun *they* may connote mainly males, as do other apparently gender-neutral terms like *he/she, person,* and *adult* (Gastil, 1990; Hamilton, 1991; Wise & Rafferty, 1982). These results are particularly true for male listeners, who appear to have difficulty understanding any generic term as pertaining equally to females.

Henley (1989) summarizes research that shows that use of the generic *he* can affect a reader's comprehension, memory, and career perceptions. For example, when a job description used only male pronouns, elementary and college students rated females as least able to do that job (Hyde, 1984; Shepelak, Ogden, & Tobin-Bennett, 1984). As this example suggests, the sex that most directly suffers from the use of male language is females. Although females are a little less likely than males to perceive the generic *he* as solely male (Hamilton, 1988; Henley, 1989; Switzer, 1990), most still do. Thus, use of the generic *he* is not just an arbitrary custom, but a continuing statement about the societal roles of women and men.

Stereotyping

Language also defines women by labeling what is considered to be the exception to the rule ("*lady* doctor," "*career* girl"), thereby reinforcing gender stereotypes. The message appears to be that the typical adult person and the typical worker is male—in other words, that being female is atypical. This implication that women are atypical is likely to be encoded into a child's developing gender schema. There may be important consequences for a child's self-esteem and self-confidence, as we will see in the next chapter, as well as for her or his career aspirations.

When women are described by their appearance while men are not, the implied message is that appearance is more important for women than for men, and that appearance may be the cause of a woman's circumstance. For example, when a newspaper reports, "Blonde found murdered," the reader knows that the corpse is a female (men rarely are referred to solely by their hair color) and gets the impression that her hair color had something to do with her death (If "blondes have more fun," are they also more likely to get murdered?). When a statement reads, "A doctor and his pert assistant," the reader has no question that the assistant is female. Why? Because a male rarely is described by his appearance, especially by the adjective *pert*.

Females are defined by the group with which they are linked. For example, the frequent grouping of "women and children" suggests a similar dependent status. Women are referred to as possessions, as in "pioneers moved West, taking their wives and children with them." Females also are defined by the order in which they are usually referred to—"he and she," "boys and girls"—that is, in second place. Women are predominantly referred to by relationships—"Jane Doe, *wife* of John Doe and *daughter* of Mr. and Mrs. Joseph Smith." When women marry, they traditionally lose their name (identity) and take on that of their spouse; thereafter, they are "Mrs. John Doe." Until recently, marriage ceremonies pronounced a couple "man and *wife*." He maintains his personhood; she becomes a role. Even the convention of referring to women as "Miss" or "Mrs." indicates that marital status is important for women in ways it is not for men. Indeed, women who use "Miss" or "Mrs." are perceived as lower in instrumental traits, like competence and leadership, but stronger in expressive traits and more likable than an identically described woman who uses "Ms." (Dion & Cota, 1991; Dion & Schuller, 1990).

Deprecating

A third sexist aspect of language is its use to deprecate women. One way to do this is by trivializing them ("poet*ess*," *girl* for *woman*). Another way to deprecate women is to sexualize them. For example, *dame* and *madam* have double meanings, while their male counterparts, *lord* and *sir*, do not. A third means of deprecation is to insult women. One researcher found 220 terms for a sexually promiscuous female, compared to 22 terms for a sexually promiscuous male (Stanley, 1977). Women belonging to an ethnic minority are especially likely to have sexually derogatory epithets applied to them

(I. L. Allen, 1984). These women appear to be doubly stigmatized, on the basis of both their sex and their race. A fourth form of deprecation is depersonalization ("chick," "piece of ass," "cunt," "broad").

Even the American Sign Language system used by most deaf people in this country mirrors gender stereotypes. For example, references to men and masculine pronouns are signed around the top portion of the head. This part of the body is also the reference point for signs depicting intelligence and decision making. References to women and feminine pronouns, however, are signed in the lower part of the face, the part of the body associated with signs for the emotions and feelings (Jolly & O'Kelly, 1980).

Changing Language

As noted in Chapter 3, the sexes also use language differently. Females typically use more polite and tentative speech modes; males typically use more direct and dominant speech modes. Thus, children are exposed to very distinct gender messages as they learn their language. Children learn that males are the norm and are dominant and that females are less important and less interesting. These messages are reinforced by other aspects of socialization. To begin to change these stereotypes, our language and our use of it must change. Publishers now issue guidelines for eliminating sexism in writing (Scott, Foresman & Co. was among the first in 1972). For example, use *he or she* instead of *he*; recast pronouns into the plural (*their* instead of *his*); neuterize occupational terms (*police officer* instead of *policeman*). (See C. Miller & Swift, 1988, for how-to tips on nonsexist writing.)

Changes in our use of language clearly can be made. Witness the change of the word *Negro* to *Black* (and now to *African American*) and the acceptance of *Ms.* by most businesses and organizations. Anything that makes people more aware of sexist language may become an impetus for language change (Adamsky, 1981). It may be hard to change, it may be awkward until a new habit develops, and it may be superficial compared to needed economic and social changes. But it is important. As Blaubergs (1978) notes, "Although language may be only one of the reflections of societal practices, nevertheless it is a reflection, and as such provides continuing inspiration for sexism" (pp. 246–247).

Social and linguistic changes are interactive, each promoting change in the other. For example, R. L. Munroe and Munroe (1969), in their study of ten cultures, found a significant relationship between structural sex bias in a culture, such as marital residence and inheritance regulations, and the proportion of male to female gender nouns in use. To develop a more egalitarian society, a more egalitarian language is needed. A particularly dramatic example of how threatening language change can be for those invested in traditional patriarchal roles occurred in a courtroom in Pittsburgh in 1988. A male judge insisted upon calling a female attorney trying a case before him by her husband's name (with "Mrs." before it) even though she had not changed her name when she married and preferred the title "Ms." Her co-counsel, who supported her position, was sentenced for contempt of court.

A positive sign of change can be seen in the 1982 edition of *Roget's Thesaurus*, a book of synonyms and antonyms first published in the 1850s. That edition eliminated sexist words—for example, changing *mankind* to *humankind*. Also in that year, the American Psychological Association mandated nonsexist language use in its journals and conference presentations. Although much change has occurred since the 1970s, it probably will take another generation for the changes to be fully incorporated into the language. Furthermore, unless the new language regulations actually are enforced, institutional compliance tends to be minimal (Markowitz, 1984).

▲ Play

Language is only one vehicle by which gender roles and stereotypes are taught. As soon as children start to play, they receive another lesson. Picture a group of children playing with trucks. Picture another group playing with dolls. What is the sex composition of these groups? Now picture a high school athlete who has just received a school letter for excellence in basketball. Does a boy or does a girl come to mind? From toys to sports, play activities help socialize children into their gender roles.

Toys

In the last chapter, we saw that girls and boys are given different toys starting at birth, and that children develop gender-appropriate toy preferences very early, some as young as 18 months (Caldera et al., 1989). Boys play with vehicles, construction toys (like blocks), balls, and guns; girls, with dolls, household goods, and stuffed animals. In general, girls' toys do not make many cognitive demands or prepare girls for any occupational future except the role of motherhood. Girls' toys generally elicit closer interactions with another person and more verbal behaviors. Boys' toys, on the other hand, tend to be more varied, expensive, aggressive, and creative (for example, scientific kits). These toys also tend to involve more physical activity and less interpersonal contact (Caldera et al., 1989; C. Lawson, 1989). Differential experiences with toys thus may develop different abilities, such as verbal and nurturance abilities for girls and visual-spatial and manual abilities for boys (C. L. Miller, 1987). These toys also may convey important occupational messages. One message is that careers are not important for girls but are important for boys. Another message is that child care is not important for boys but is important for girls.

A child's toy preferences, because of their stability and predictability, frequently have been used as an indicator of her or his degree of sex typing. Boys appear to develop sex-typed interests in toys at an earlier age than girls, and seem more reluctant to play with toys viewed as gender-inappropriate (C. C. Robinson & Morris, 1986). In general, choice of sex-typed toys among preschoolers is associated with other forms of sex-typed social behavior (see, for example, Cameron, Eisenberg, & Tryon, 1985). Whether toy choice encourages or just reflects children's other sex-typed behaviors is unclear.

Language probably plays a mediating role with respect to toy preferences: children are more likely to play with and be interested in toys that are labeled as gender-appropriate rather than gender-inappropriate regardless of the properties of the toy itself (Bradbard & Endsley, 1983; Cobb, Stevens-Long, & Goldstein, 1982; Downs, 1983). This is more true for boys than for girls. As we saw in the last chapter, gender labeling generally precedes sex-typed toy preferences. And gender labeling of toys by parents, other children, advertisers, and especially salespeople is very strong (L. A. Schwartz & Markham, 1985; Ungar, 1982). Advertisers rarely show a sex-typed toy being played with by a child of the nonstereotypic sex. Nintendo, the best-selling toy in 1989, is directed almost entirely at boys, and involves games of aggression and violence (C. Lawson, 1989). As we saw in Chapter 3, early experience with video games may lead to differential use of computers later on. As Figure 7.1 suggests, it is very hard for adults to find and buy toys that are not gender-labeled.

Sports

The play activities in which boys and girls engage also differ. Girls spend more time in individual activities that require little competition and have few rules—for example, jumping rope, playing house (Lott, 1978; E. E. Maccoby & Jacklin, 1974). Sports considered appropriate for females, such as skating, swimming, and horseback riding, also have few rules and usually involve no competition. The emphasis is on quality of performance, not on winning. Boys, on the other hand, are more likely to play in situations that involve sociability and coordinated action. They also are strongly encouraged to play in highly organized, complex, competitive team sports such as baseball, football, and basketball. Through such team sports, boys learn how to set goals and work with others to achieve those goals. They learn a degree of emotional detachment necessary in choosing players for a team. Boys come to understand and respect rules, and they learn to be persistent. They also learn the importance of winning and come to view it as a personal or team achievement. Failure can be spread among team members, keeping the individual ego protected (Hennig & Jardim, 1977).

It will surprise no one to read that males spend more time in sports activities than females, starting in preschool and continuing into adulthood (Timmer et al., 1985). Boys also spend more time than girls playing in general since, as we saw in the last chapter, girls are more involved than boys in domestic chores. Differences in sports participation increase with age through college. In 1982, about 37% of high school and 30% of college athletes were female ("How Title IX," 1984; Women's Sports Foundation, 1989).

Sports participation has many immediate and long-term consequences. The Women's Sports Foundation (1989) analyzed data from a six-year longitudinal study of a stratified national probability sample of more than 14,000 high school sophomores in 1980 from both public and private schools. They found that students who participated in athletic teams during high school were more popular and more involved in extracurricular and community activities. Four years after high school, more former athletes than nonathletes were actively involved in teams or sports clubs. The beneficial effects of sports participation held true for males and females of all racial groups (Blacks, Hispanics, and Whites). Minority athletes of both sexes also scored higher in achievement tests than their nonathlete cohorts, although their school grades and drop-out rates were not much different. In terms of continued education after high school, athletic participation was most helpful for Whites and Hispanic females.

Figure 7.1 The challenge of finding nonsexist toys. (CATHY Copyright 1987 Cathy Guisewite. Reprinted with permission of Universal Press Syndicate.)

Athletic participation may help Hispanic females expand their role expectations, which have traditionally emphasized domestic and maternal duties. Sports participation appears to add to the advantages already enjoyed by White students (higher socioeconomic class, better-educated parents, lack of impediments due to racism) after high school.

Other research confirms that although sports participation may have beneficial effects for Blacks, and is one way Black males from lower-class backgrounds may achieve status, such participation does not translate into upward mobility either in the educational sphere or in the labor force (H. Edwards, 1988; Messner, 1989).

Although the Women's Sports Foundation's study did not find that athletic participation made much difference in the types of jobs held by those who entered the labor force after high school, other research suggests that there indeed may be a link between athletic participation and future occupational performance. As sociologist David Riesman comments, "The road to the boardroom leads through the locker room" ("Comes the Revolution," 1978, p. 59). Hennig and Jardim (1977), in their book on women in management, attribute male dominance of business to early sports experience. Males transfer to the business world in an effective way what they learned from team sports—competition, emotional detachment, teamwork, and ego protection from failure. Females, however, usually have not learned these things. They are not used to delegating responsibility, tolerating people who do not perform well, or focusing on winning. Hennig and Jardim found that women who have "made it" in the business world have one thing in common— they were raised free from gender stereotypes. Other research (M. B. Nelson, 1991; Rohrbaugh, 1979) has found that female participation in sports enhances females' general sense of confidence and well-being.

Sports and sport terms play another important role in future occupational performance. Many terms used for business and political processes are based on sports—for example, *one-on-one, blitz, strike out*. People unfamiliar with the jargon, as are many women, are often at a loss to understand the messages being communicated. This lack of understanding further increases their difficulty in operating in traditionally masculine fields (Fasteau, 1974). In addition, many social activities and conversations revolve around sports, such as the business golf game and Monday night football. People who are not interested in, or are not familiar with, such activities, such as many women, often are left out.

Sports participation is a major form of male socialization, as Figure 7.2 suggests. (See Messner & Sabo, 1990, for an interesting analysis.) The traditional definition of masculinity (physical strength, courage, adventurousness, dominance) has increasingly been challenged by changes in the family and the workplace during the last century. Men's greater physical strength is less important in an industrial culture than it was in an agricultural one; men's sense of courage and adventure has less place in a nation no longer expanding geographically or globally; and men's dominance in the home and the workplace is challenged by women's increasing participation in the labor force. As these traditional bases of male identity have eroded, organized sport has become increasingly important as a source of gender identity validation for males (Dubbert, 1979). Indeed, sports and the military may be the "last bastions" of male power and identity (Raphael, 1988; Tolson, 1977). Some writers have argued that "sport is a crucial arena in which masculine hegemony is constructed and reconstructed" (Bryson, 1987, p. 349). Sport associates males and maleness with valued skills and sanctions the use of aggression, force, and violence.

The intimate association between athletics and masculinity is especially obvious in the resistance expressed by males when females try to join their games. Some writers even argue that such resistance to coed sports is necessary for boys to form an adequate male gender identity (for example, Monagan, 1983). The uproar over admitting qualified

Figure 7.2 The "character" that sports build. (CALVIN AND HOBBES Copyright 1990 Universal Press Syndicate. Reprinted with permission. All rights reserved.)

girls to Little League baseball teams in 1974 led to the development of Little League softball teams. Girls are encouraged to play softball and leave baseball to the boys (J. Y. Miller, 1989). Most do. In 1989, of the 2 million children participating in Little League activities, 200,000 girls played softball and 6000 played baseball. The attitude that baseball should be for boys reflects the belief that all-male sports are critical for boys to become men; therefore, female competition is masculinity-destroying. To get beaten by a girl has been viewed as a major humiliation for boys because girls are thought to be inferior. A study of ten different Little League baseball teams for three seasons revealed that the sport encourages male dominance over women through devaluation of the feminine and an ideology of male superiority (G. A. Fine, 1987b). Little Leagues also encourage dominance contests with other males through verbal sparring, homophobia, and racism. No wonder females are not welcome. Interestingly, the few sports that have resisted female "intrusion"—football and ice hockey—are seen as the most masculine and have become increasingly popular.

One indication of the relationship between sports participation and traditional sex roles is the finding that male varsity athletes in college have more traditional attitudes toward women's roles and more negative attitudes toward nontraditional sex role behaviors than do male nonathletes (Hirt, Hoffman, & Sedlacek, 1983; Houseworth, Peplow, & Thirer, 1989). Another indication of the relationship between sports participation and masculinity for males is the finding that male athletes tend to be more traditionally sex-typed than male nonathletes and female athletes, even when the female athletes play the same sport (Myers & Lips, 1978; Wrisberg, Draper, & Everett, 1988). Given the association among "masculine" sports, aggression, and male dominance over women, it should not be surprising that male athletes in such sports are disproportionately involved in cases of rape (Eskinazi, 1990; Neimark, 1991).

Although sports participation has many positive consequences, as we have noted, an overemphasis on sports can have many negative ones. Males who are not interested or talented in sports are strongly stigmatized (Fasteau, 1974; Pleck, 1976a; Stein & Hoffman, 1978). Such males may experience role strain and feelings of failure and inferiority for not living up to male sex role expectations. Picture a clumsy boy who gets ridiculed for dropping the ball. One of the worst insults that could be aimed at him

would be "You play like a girl!" If sports participation and success are the sole bases of one's identity, when such participation ends (due to injury or simply aging), a crisis of identity may occur (Messner, 1987). Even during participation, negative consequences appear. Intense competitiveness may limit personality growth, instill feelings of inadequacy, inhibit close relationships, and lead to violence (Fasteau, 1974; Miedzian, 1991; Ogilvie & Tutko, 1971; Pleck, 1976a). Excessive competitiveness may even impair performance (Reis & Jelsma, 1978; Spence & Helmreich, 1978). Furthermore, the emphasis on, and preoccupation with, high-level performance and winning may cause an athlete to play while in great pain or when injured (Hyland, 1978; Stein & Hoffman, 1978). The male role, however, does not allow the male either to acknowledge or to give expression to such pressures and pain. This puts great strain on the athlete and may cause lasting physical problems.

Because athletics and the male sex role are so closely related, many women have hesitated to become involved in sports for fear of becoming, or being labeled, masculine or lesbian (Bennett, Whitaker, Smith, & Sablove, 1987; Matteo, 1986, 1988). Lesbian-baiting is a classic social control mechanism to keep women in "their place." Although some female athletes are lesbian, so are some female nonathletes. Furthermore, contrary to cultural stereotypes, most lesbians are not "masculine." Recent research suggests that the stigma attached to female participation in sports has diminished somewhat, especially with respect to individual sports such as swimming, tennis, and track (Basow & Spinner, 1984; Desertrain & Weiss, 1988; Hoferek & Hanick, 1985; Rao & Overman, 1984). The Women's Sports Foundation (1989) study of high school athletes found that female athletes were more popular than female nonathletes; this was especially the case for female minority athletes. Although the stereotype of female athletes is that they are masculine, research does not completely bear this out. Female athletes generally do have more active-instrumental personality traits (higher masculinity scores) than nonathletes, but female athletes are no lower than nonathletes in expressive-nurturant traits (femininity scores) (Butcher, 1989; Marsh & Jackson, 1986; Wrisberg et al., 1988). Thus, the female athlete usually is androgynous. Feminine-sex-typed females tend to avoid masculine-rated sports; if they do participate in these sports, such females have less commitment to their sport than other females (Matteo, 1986, 1988).

The findings that the female athlete is less traditionally sex-typed than the female nonathlete, combined with the finding of masculine sex typing among male athletes, may explain why male and female athletes tend to have different attitudes toward sports (Myers & Lips, 1978). Male athletes typically score higher than female athletes on all questions dealing with the importance of competition, whereas females typically score higher than males on all questions dealing with the importance of social interactions (Croxton, Chiacchia, & Wagner, 1984; Reis & Jelsma, 1978). These responses parallel, and perhaps reflect, the stereotypic gender difference in interest areas and social orientations discussed in Chapter 3. However, no significant differences typically are found in males' and females' enjoyment of the sport or in their desire to perform well.

Female participation in sports is aided by encouragement from significant others (especially male peers during adolescence), the provision of financial and physical support (equipment expenses, scholarships, transportation, practice facilities), and the visibility of female role models, such as Florence Griffith Joyner and Martina Navratilova (Ames, 1984; B. A. Brown, Frankel, & Fennell, 1989; Women's Sports Foundation, 1988; U.S. Commission on Civil Rights, 1980). Although the sports situation for girls is improving, it still has a way to go.

Since 1972, when the Title IX regulation of the Education Amendments Act of 1972 was passed by Congress, female participation in sports has increased dramatically. Implemented in 1975, Title IX prohibits schools and colleges receiving federal funds from discriminating on the basis of sex in any educational program or activity. Before 1972, 300,000 high school girls participated in varsity athletics; in 1985–86, 1.8 million played, an increase of 600% (S. Messing, 1987). In colleges too, the number of women participating in varsity sports jumped from 16,000 prior to 1972, to 150,000 in 1985–86, a nearly tenfold increase. Expenditures on female athletes also have increased and some of the grossest inequities in budget allocations to male and female athletic activities have been reduced. For example, before Title IX, no colleges or universities offered athletic scholarships to women; now over 15,000 scholarships are offered ("How Title IX," 1984). In 1972–73, the average budget for women's athletics at Division I colleges and universities was $7,000; in 1985–86, it was $640,000 (Oberlander, 1989).

Although the situation for female athletes has improved, they still are getting less than their fair share of the pie. For example, in Division I in 1985–86, expenditures for women's athletic programs were less than one-seventh those for men's (Oberlander, 1989)—$4.6 million. Furthermore, many of the gains made in educational equity since Title IX was passed have been halted. During the Reagan administration, enforcement of Title IX regulations was lax, and the 1984 Supreme Court decision *Grove City College v. Bell* led many colleges to think that Title IX provisions did not apply to their athletic programs. Although the passage in 1988 of the Civil Rights Restoration Act restored to full strength the laws governing sex equity in education, most sports programs remain out of compliance. The future does not look promising with respect to complete sex equity, since football takes up a big chunk of personnel and economic resources, and football remains all male. Ironically, as women's participation in sports has increased on the high school and college levels, the number of women coaches has declined, due to increasing numbers of male applicants and the increasing presence of male athletic directors (Potera & Kort, 1986). Thus, although females have made tremendous gains in sports participation and support, they remain relatively disadvantaged. A similar situation exists with respect to professional sports (Engeler, 1989; Seidman, 1979).

In summary, although sports participation appears important in the development of many positive skills, and although female participation in sports is increasing, the sports world remains male-dominated. Indeed, sports participation still provides the basis for many males' gender identity and serves as a training ground for male dominance. Until the association between sports and masculinity is broken, male children will continue to be socialized into their gender role through sports and female children will be discouraged from equal participation. Recently, some proposals for a feminist transformation of sport have been proferred (for example, Bennett et al., 1987; Birrell & Richter, 1987; Theberge, 1987). We need to separate sport from the male sex role so that both sexes can receive the benefits of athletic participation and avoid its costs.

During childhood and adolescence, sports participation usually occurs within a school context. It is to a closer examination of that context that we now turn.

▲ School

As we have just seen, sport in schools reflects male dominance in terms of numbers, finances, and social support. Other aspects of the school environment also convey gender messages. In countries where school attendance is voluntary, boys are more likely to be sent to school than girls (United Nations, 1991). Not surprisingly then, females comprise 63% of the world's illiterates. As noted in the last chapter, teachers are a major source of gender socialization. In this section, we will examine the role played by instructional materials, curricula, counseling, school organization, and the general school atmosphere in the gender socialization of children. These factors come together to form a hidden curriculum on gender roles. This curriculum conveys the message, often without the conscious awareness of either the students or the teachers, that there are strong stereotypic gender differences. One way to discern this hidden curriculum is suggested by the Project on the Status and Education of Women, a division of the Association of American Colleges (R. M. Hall & Sandler, 1982, 1984). This project has published pamphlets that can help students, educators, and administrators assess whether their school is "chilly" toward women.

Raphaela Best (1983) observed an elementary school for four years and concluded that there actually are three curricula of sex role learning—the academic curriculum, with its sexist materials and sex typing of academic skills; the behavioral curriculum, with different roles and activities for girls and boys; and the sexual curriculum, with explorations of sexuality guided by different ideologies (for example, flirting for girls and "getting it" for boys). The title of her book, *We've All Got Scars*, conveys her sense that elementary school experiences negatively affect both girls and boys.

Instructional Materials
Students spend the vast majority of their learning time in school with instructional materials—textbooks, worksheets, tests, audiovisual media, and computer software. Computer usage and software were discussed in Chapter 2. Here we will focus mainly on textbooks. The absence of women in textbooks increases through grade school into high school and college.

At the elementary school level, children are exposed to marked gender stereotypes in their readers. Quantitatively, males outnumber females in elementary school books, although the situation has improved since 1972, when Women on Words and Images conducted their classic study "Dick and Jane as Victims." Their examination of 2760 stories revealed that males outnumbered females approximately three to one,

with even more male dominance in the category of biographies. A replication of the study, conducted in 1989 on 1883 stories in use in schools, found that the ratio of male to female characters was more equal, except in the sex of animal characters (still about 75% male) and in illustrations (two-thirds male) (Purcell & Stewart, 1990). However, significant differences still appear in how the sexes are portrayed. In the 1972 study, males predominated in situations with active mastery themes (cleverness, bravery, adventure, and earning money), and females predominated in situations with "second-sex" themes (passivity, victimization, and goal constriction). For example, Jane watches as John fixes a toy. In the 1989 study, although girls are presented fairly similarly to boys in many ways, females still typically need rescue more often than males, are shown as less adventurous than males, and are depicted in fewer occupations than males. Other differences in portrayals of the sexes have been found. Using Gilligan's (1982) distinction between a care and a justice orientation (see Chapter 3), female characters in children's stories have been found to demonstrate a care morality and a connected self, while male characters tend to demonstrate a justice morality and a separate self (Tetenbaum & Pearson, 1989). The greater visibility of males in children's readers plus their more active presentation alongside the greater invisibility of females, especially in occupations, and their less active and more caring presentation, may model gender differences in behavior and moral reasoning.

Some evidence has been found that children's stories do influence behavior. McArthur and Eisen (1976) report that nursery school boys persisted longer on a task (a measure of achievement motivation) after hearing a story depicting achievement behavior by a male character than after a story depicting the same behavior by a female character. The trend was in the opposite direction for girls. This change occurred after hearing just one story. Given that more central characters in children's books are male and that females, when depicted, are less often shown in achieving roles, it is not surprising that women have been underrepresented in achieving roles in our society. Similarly, Ashton (1983) found that preschool children exposed to a stereotypic picture book subsequently chose a sex-stereotypic toy more often than a nonstereotypic one, whereas those who were exposed to a nonstereotypic picture book more often selected a nonstereotypic toy.

Clearly, children can be affected by what they read. In this sense it is somewhat encouraging that a number of nonsexist preschool picture books have been published since the late 1960s, although they are not always as nonsexist as they purport to be. For example, compared to more conventional book characters, females in nonsexist books are more independent and males are less aggressive (Davis, 1984). However, females still are more nurturant and emotional, and less physically active than males.

In textbooks for specific subjects, gender stereotypes abound. L. J. Weitzman and Rizzo (1974) found that women are rarely mentioned as important historical figures, as government leaders, or as great scientists. This stereotyping is most extreme in science textbooks, in which only 6% of the pictures include adult women. Even when a scientist like Marie Curie, who won two Nobel Prizes, is presented, her achievements are likely to be minimized. (One text describes Madame Curie as a "helpmate" of her husband.) Even in college, women are strikingly absent from both textbooks and the curriculum (Banner, 1977; Ferree & Hall, 1990). The absence of women in textbooks can encourage readers to view the field depicted, particularly science, as a prototypic masculine endeavor. This may discourage females from entering the particular fields being studied, thereby perpetuating the stereotypes portrayed.

Schau and Scott (1984) examined more than 40 studies involving the effects of sex-typed and sex-neutral instructional materials. They concluded that most materials still are sexist and that they seriously affect the sex role attitudes of students from elementary school through college. One way these materials affect students' attitudes is through the use of male generic language. As noted earlier in this chapter, use of such language results in gender associations that predominantly are male. In contrast, use of gender-specific language referring to both females and males seems to lead to the most gender-balanced associations. A second way instructional materials affect students' sex role attitudes is through the portrayal of the sexes in stereotypical roles. Such exposure appears to increase sex-typed attitudes, especially among young children. In contrast, exposure to sex-equitable materials and to same-sex characters in nontraditional roles results in less sex-typed attitudes among students of all ages. This kind of attitude change increases with increased exposure to nonsexist materials. Other important findings of Schau and Scott were that exposure to sex-equitable materials does not decrease student interest in the

materials, nor does it adversely affect either males' or females' comprehension of the material.

Clearly, textbooks need to be rewritten with the elimination of sexism in mind. California was one of the first states to take systematic action in this regard, passing a code in 1977 requiring a balancing of traditional and nontraditional activities for each sex in textbooks used in state schools. Because California purchases huge quantities of books, the state's code has had some impact in all states. Change is slow, however, since replacing texts is expensive. Even recent books incorporate stereotypes, although not to as great a degree as before. However, many supplementary materials are now available to teachers to help them promote sex equity in the classroom (see, for example, S. S. Klein, 1985).

In addition to textbooks, test materials frequently reflect gender bias. Saario, Jacklin, and Tittle (1973) found frequent stereotypic portrayals in the content of test questions. For example, women were typically homemakers; men, responsible workers. Sex bias also occurred in the language used in the tests. Analysis showed more frequent use of male pronouns and referents than female pronouns and referents, since male characters predominated. As with the findings on textbooks, stereotypic portrayals in achievement tests, particularly in the mathematics sections, intensify as grade level rises. As was discussed in Chapter 2, there is some evidence that such a male bias in tests can depress the scores of many females, thereby giving an inaccurate picture of their abilities and negatively affecting their future with respect to college admission and scholarships.

Curricula

Who takes home economics? Who takes shop classes? Either formally or informally, the different curricula and activities prescribed for each sex are powerful conveyors of gender messages. Beginning in kindergarten, activities usually are segregated by sex. Boys and girls play different games, form different lines, carry out different classroom tasks, and learn different things.

Although Title IX prohibits "tracking" students by gender, many school systems, parents, and peers still exert informal pressure to keep tracking going. Males and females still tend to take different courses, especially in the vocational area (National Center for Education Statistics, 1984; U.S. Department of Health, Education, and Welfare, 1979). Girls are overrepresented in consumer and homemaking, home economics, health, and office occupations courses. In contrast, boys are overrepresented in agricultural, technical, trade, and industrial programs. This tracking system keeps students from learning many skills needed in their home as well as in their occupational lives. For example, girls don't learn how to make home repairs, and boys don't learn cooking and domestic skills. The consequences of this tracking are particularly pernicious, since such tracking prepares females for only a few jobs, which have low status and low salaries.

The Education Amendments of 1976 to the Vocational Education Act of 1963 went into effect in October 1977. They are helping to change some of the inequities just discussed. The law requires educational institutions to initiate programs to overcome sex discrimination and sex stereotyping in vocational education programs and to make all courses accessible to everyone. When given the opportunity and the encouragement, females do move into male-dominated, higher paying fields. The frequency of males moving into female-dominated, lower paying fields is much lower.

Males and females on the academic (college preparatory) track in high school also take different courses. As discussed in Chapter 2, females take fewer math and science courses than males. This differential course-taking has been shown to be responsible for the poorer performance of females on the math portion of the SAT. Even more significantly, such differential course-taking shuts out many females from careers in science and technology. As we have seen, social forces (parents', peers', and teachers' attitudes about females and math) contribute greatly to this differential course-taking.

Since the women's studies movement began in the late 1960s, traditional courses of study have been shown to suffer from and reflect a male bias. For example, history books traditionally have divided the past into periods based on men's lives—wars, political regimes, and so on—and have completely neglected women's lives and experiences. This neglect can be seen, for example, in discussions of the Renaissance. This period is usually viewed as a great step forward in terms of humanistic inquiry and values, yet it represented a step backward in the status of women (Kelly-Gadol, 1977). If half the population regressed, how can the time period legitimately be viewed as a rebirth for all? People involved in the women's studies movement have challenged traditional scholarship, made

new discoveries, revised academic fields, and rewritten textbooks (Aiken, Anderson, Dinnerstein, Lensink, & MacCorquodale, 1988; E. C. DuBois, Kelly, Kennedy, Korsmeyer, & Robinson, 1985; McIntosh, 1989). Yet changing the curriculum is slow, because it involves the revision of nearly all the academic disciplines and typically meets with strong resistance. Similar resistance has met attempts to make the curriculum more sensitive to other issues of cultural diversity (McMillen, 1989; National Association of Scholars, 1989; see also Chapter 13).

How-to manuals for help in implementing such curriculum change projects are available (for example, Schmitz, 1985). The kinds of changes that would decrease gender stereotyping have been of great concern. Guttentag and Bray (1975, 1977) set up a 6-week curriculum designed to make kindergartners and fifth- and ninth-graders more flexible in their assumptions about the sexes in occupational, familial, and socioemotional roles. These researchers designed curricula with the different developmental concerns and cognitive levels of the three grades in mind. Students read stories, saw films, acted out plays, and worked on special projects to accomplish the study's goals. Teachers were trained to use the materials and to treat boys and girls equally. The results were mixed. Attitude change was found to be a function of grade level, student sex, teacher attitude, background variables, and the particular stereotypes highlighted. Kindergartners decreased their occupational stereotypes but not the socioemotional ones. Girls were more willing than boys to accept the nonstereotyped ideas. Ninth-grade girls showed the greatest decrease in stereotyped attitudes; ninth-grade boys showed the greatest increase in stereotyped attitudes. The key factor seemed to be the degree to which the teacher implemented the curriculum effectively. With an enthusiastic teacher, even ninth-grade boys changed to nonstereotyped views in many areas.

This study, as well as many others (for example, Best, 1983), illustrates the complexity of the school environment as well as the potential for change. Changing the curriculum can be effective when implemented early and when the new curriculum coincides with the teacher's attitudes. Modeling, however, may be more important than specific lessons in the acquisition and maintenance of gender stereotypes. For example, decreases in stereotypic knowledge and preferences by young children were greatest when a nonsexist curriculum was presented by a same-sex teacher (Koblinsky & Sugawara, 1984). Male teachers may be particularly effective in this regard, perhaps because males tend to be both more sex-stereotyped and more privileged.

Counseling

Although many students never see a guidance counselor during secondary school for advice (V. E. Lee & Ekstrom, 1987), those who do frequently are exposed to gender-biased counseling. Sex bias on the part of counselors is not surprising, since it is so prevalent in society at large. It is most apparent with respect to vocational and career counseling.

Few counselors receive training on the special needs of girls and women (Farmer & Sidney, 1985; Minor, 1989). Thus, counselors often consider only the male career path (continuous employment, in many cases preceded by advanced education) when advising, ignoring the fact that for most females, education and employment may be interrupted due to family responsibilities. If counselors recognize the discontinuities in the work life of many women, they may stereotype all women and discourage them from pursuing advanced careers or high-commitment (and high-paying) jobs. They may use cultural stereotypes to steer boys and girls into gender-linked job tracks. Indeed, as we have seen with respect to the curriculum, females and males often do take different courses, which prepare them for different jobs. Females, in particular, are over-represented in low-paying service jobs, as we will discuss in Chapter 11.

A greater number of females than males graduate from high school with higher grades. Yet, until the 1980s, fewer females than males went on to college. Such figures suggest that a sex bias was operating in career counseling (Harway, 1980; Harway & Astin, 1977). Starting in 1986, women made up half of all the students in higher education in the United States, Canada, Finland, and France ("Women Account," 1986). In 1993, they are expected to be 53% of all undergraduates in the United States (U. S. Department of Education, 1988a). Many of these women are returning students.

Numerical equity in total enrollment disguises continued inequities. For example, a ten-year study of high school valedictorians found that two-thirds of the women had begun to lower their career aspirations by their sophomore year of college, although they got better grades than the men ("Where Have All," 1989). Males and females still take different courses, with males overrepresented

in engineering and applied science, and females overrepresented in education and the humanities. These different majors lead to different job opportunities, with the highest paying ones going to men. Bias in financial aid awards also may contribute to fewer women in higher education. A study during the 1981–82 academic year by the National Commission of Student Financial Assistance found that while women college students tend to need more student aid than their male counterparts, they typically do not get it (Project on the Status and Education of Women, 1984). As we saw in the section on sports, males are more likely than females to receive athletic scholarships.

As the education level increases, the proportion of women decreases. In 1988, 52% of all B.A.'s and 51% of all M.A.'s were awarded to women, but only 36% of the Ph.D.'s and 35% of the professional degrees were awarded that year to women (U. S. Department of Education, 1988a). Again we see gender differences in field of study. Whereas 55% of the doctorates in education and 45% of the doctorates in arts and humanities went to women, only 6.5% of those in engineering, 14% of those in computer science, and 17% of those in mathematics and the physical sciences did (National Research Council, 1989). The percentage of women earning doctorates in any field, especially in science and technology, is up somewhat from what it was in the 1970s, but this is partly because the number of men earning doctorates is down. Between 1977 and 1985, women's doctorates increased by one-third, whereas men's decreased by 14% (McMillen, 1986). Whether choice of career and pursuit of advanced education are influenced by faculty advising isn't clear, but there is some evidence that faculty advisors tend to be insensitive to the special concerns of female undergraduates (Lacher, 1978). In the valedictorian study mentioned earlier, interaction with involved faculty members increased the likelihood of the women's continuing on to a doctoral degree ("Where Have All," 1989). Substantial evidence exists that for women to pursue careers in math, science, and technology, they must take the appropriate courses in high school. As we have seen, girls tend not to do so, for many reasons, but adequate advising and support would help correct the imbalance.

Black women in particular may suffer from both racial and sex bias in the area of vocational counseling (E. J. Smith, 1982). Although more Black females than Black males go on to college, their educational and occupational aspirations are lower than those of Black males. Black women's choices of careers are markedly gender-stereotyped, particularly if they went to a predominantly White liberal arts high school as opposed to a more integrated vocational high school (Chester, 1983). Fewer Blacks now are enrolled in college and graduate school than in the 1970s, unlike the situation for Hispanics and Asians (Heller, 1986). How much of this decreased participation in higher education is due to guidance counselors is hard to ascertain, but they certainly play a role (M. Fine, 1987).

Several pieces of federal legislation during the 1970s attempted to eliminate discrimination in vocational and career education (Title IX of 1972, the Women's Educational Equity Act of 1974, the Vocational Educational Act of 1976, and the Career Incentive Act of 1977). These acts have helped promote programs aimed at reducing occupational stereotypes (Farmer & Sidney, 1985). They also have eliminated some of the grossest inequities. For example, until the 1970s, different tests, scores, and interpretations for boys and girls were used in counseling and testing for aptitudes and interests. In particular, the Strong Vocational Interest Blank had separate male and female versions (printed on blue and pink forms, respectively) with different occupations for each sex. The revised Strong Interest Inventory removes some of the sex bias but still uses single-sex criterion groups for some occupations, such as language teacher (female) and photographer (male).

In sum, guidance counseling on both the high school and college level tends to convey and support gender stereotypes.

Organization

From the very organization of the school itself, students receive messages regarding gender-appropriate behaviors and career opportunities. What they observe are men in positions of authority—coordinators, principals, superintendents, college professors—and women in positions of subservience—teachers and aides.

The percentage of male teachers generally rises with grade level, as does their status, and the percentage of female administrators decreases. As Table 7.1 shows, women teachers predominate in elementary school and junior high school, reach some parity with men in senior high school, and are a minority in colleges and universities. In contrast, the vast majority of principals are men, ranging from 82% in elementary school to 98% in senior high school. At the college and university level, 90% of the presidents were men in 1987 ("12-Year

Table 7.1 Percentage of women teachers and prinicipals/presidents

	Teachers	*Principals/Presidents*
Elementary (public)	86.2	18
Junior high (public)	61.4	3
Senior high (public)	47.0	2
College (all categories)	27.4	10

Data from *Academe*, 1990; Metha, 1983; U.S. Department of Commerce, 1989b.

Growth," 1988). The number of women presidents doubled between 1975 and 1984, but since then, the pace has slowed, at least among White women. Other senior administrative positions are similarly male-dominated, with college campuses averaging only one senior woman administrator apiece ("Women Gaining," 1985).

Within colleges and universities, as rank increases, the percentage of women decreases. In 1989–90, women were 40% of assistant professors, 26% of associate professors, but only 13% of full professors (*Academe*, 1990). For all the talk about Affirmative Action, the percentage of women on college faculties has increased only slightly, from 22.5% in 1974–75 to 27.4% in 1989–90 (*Academe*, 1990; National Center for Education Statistics, 1983). Women faculty are more likely to teach in community and undergraduate institutions than in doctoral-level research institutions. Blacks are even more strongly underrepresented in faculty positions, constituting only 4% of all faculty (T. D. Snyder, 1987). Given that small percentage, however, Black women constitute nearly half of the Black faculty, whereas White women are only 26% of the White faculty.

Not only are women and men found in different positions in the schools, they also are found teaching different subjects. In high schools, women predominantly teach English, foreign languages, humanities, and business education, whereas men predominantly teach math, science, and vocational education. In colleges and universities as well, females are underrepresented in the sciences and engineering, as suggested by the gender differences in area of doctoral study noted earlier. This disproportionate representation models for students the gender stereotypes.

How does this differential representation of women and men by field and status in the schools affect students? First, the organization of the school mirrors gender stereotypes. The message that males are dominant and females subordinate, which students receive from other sources, is reinforced in the school system. Second, since teachers serve as role models for many of their students, the underrepresentation of women teachers in certain fields, and in higher education in general, serves to perpetuate gender discrepancies in career aspirations. In fact, female college teachers may be particularly important role models for female students in their choice of careers and in their productivity (Basow & Howe, 1980; L. A. Gilbert & Evans, 1985; Goldstein, 1979). The same appears to be true for Black faculty and Black students (Fleming, 1984). Therefore, the predominance of White male faculty, especially in the higher ranks, may do little to encourage change in the gender status quo. A third effect of the differential representation of women and men in teaching roles is the creation of different school atmospheres for female and male students. We next turn to a closer examination of this aspect of gender socialization.

Atmosphere

The number of women and men teachers and administrators in a school contributes to the total school atmosphere. And the school atmosphere is another way in which gender messages get communicated.

Elementary school classrooms primarily are the province of female teachers. Some writers argue that the predominance of women, plus the emphasis on obedience and conformity instead of on more active learning, makes the early school environment a feminine one (Fagot, 1981a; Sugg, 1978). This feminine atmosphere has been blamed for the many school difficulties that boys have, especially in the early years, since such an atmosphere goes counter to the socialization boys receive elsewhere (Best, 1983). As was discussed in the last chapter, boys construct their gender identity, at least in part, by avoiding anything female or feminine. As students leave elementary school and move into junior high, high school, and college, the student role and the male gender role become more congruent because of the clearer linkage between academic achievement and future success. It is then that male academic performance substantially improves and becomes positively linked to male self-image (American Association of University Women, 1991; L. R. Roberts, Sarigiani, Petersen, & Newman, 1990). The picture for females is nearly the reverse. In elementary school, the female gender role and the student role are congruent. Both roles require obeying adults and being orderly. Females, therefore, do

well in elementary school—better than boys. As school achievement becomes more competitive and linked to future career achievements, however, the two roles for females become increasingly incongruent. Females' academic performance consequently declines, and the relationship between academic performance and self-image becomes more variable.

There is some support for the idea that at the preschool level, more girls than boys may feel comfortable in school. The kinds of activities girls prefer (for example, doll play and art activities) appear to receive the most positive teacher reinforcement (Fagot, 1981a). These female-preferred behaviors are more closely associated with school performance than those behaviors preferred by boys (for example, block and sandbox play). However, scholastic performance in later school years is better predicted by play with traditionally masculine activities than by play with traditionally feminine activities. Thus, the early school years may indeed emphasize "feminine" styles of play and behavior, although the benefits for girls are short-lived. Girls' better elementary school grades seem partly due to their greater social responsiveness to and compliance with teachers (Serbin et al., 1990). Both sexes need to be encouraged to play with and experience a wide variety of toys and activities in the early school years, and both sexes need to develop social responsiveness. During junior high school (sixth through eighth grade), there is evidence that students with more "feminine" gender identities (who see themselves as soft, girlish, smooth, weak, and emotional) receive higher grades than students who have more "masculine" gender identities (who see themselves as more hard, boyish, rough, strong, not emotional), regardless of student sex, race, grade, or sex of teacher (Burke, 1989). Thus, being studious may fit better with the female than the male gender role.

Although elementary school does seem more compatible with the female than the male gender role, it would not be accurate to conclude that elementary schools are feminine and that they "feminize" boys. First, the writers who equate femininity with passivity and masculinity with activity tacitly accept stereotyped definitions of sex-role behavior. Second, there is much evidence, reviewed before, that boys actually receive more teacher approval, attention, and direct instruction than girls. Third, girls continue to achieve better grades than boys from kindergarten through college, even though male teachers increasingly predominate and the school atmosphere becomes more "masculine." Fourth, as indicated by the preceding point and as discussed in the last chapter, teacher gender in the elementary grades makes very little difference in terms of teacher behaviors or student responsivity. Finally, it is more likely that boys' poorer achievement in grade school reflects the intense and often contradictory pressures on boys at that time. To be aggressive, independent, and athletic may be viewed as more important for a boy during grade school than achievement. Boys also are more likely than girls to enter school with information-processing difficulties and disturbing aggressive behaviors (Anastas & Reinharz, 1984). These two gender differences may make school a more difficult place for boys than girls.

In the classroom, teachers convey the message that boys are more important than girls. As described in the previous chapter, teachers treat students differently as a function of student gender and race. The classroom environment is most supportive of and attentive to the needs of White males. White females are relatively ignored. Black students, especially Black males, receive the least support. Because Black males are at such high risk for school failures, dead-end jobs, unemployment, violence, and crime, there has been a recent movement to create separate elementary schools or classes for Black males (Freiberg, 1991b). The hope is that in such classes, Black males will increase their self-respect, their racial and cultural pride, and hence their school achievement and aspirations. It is too soon to tell how effective such experiments will be, but the results of single-sex schools for females suggest that minority groups disadvantaged in heterogeneous settings may indeed do much better in settings that are all theirs (V. E. Lee & Marks, 1990; see following). Although Black males may need extra support, it is important to recognize that Black females have similar needs, which remain neglected.

At the college level, the male-dominated atmosphere of nearly all schools except women's colleges is marked and is reflected in student behavior. As we have seen, male students tend to be taken more seriously than female students, and they tend to dominate classroom discussions. Traditional pedagogical styles also appear to benefit males more than females (S. L. Gabriel & Smithson, 1990; Tannen, 1991). Male students also tend to dominate in extracurricular activities. At traditionally male-dominated colleges, especially those that went coed in the 1970s, women are urged to achieve at the same time as they are pressured to conform socially to the male-dominant style. Such pressures may be responsible for the lower self-esteem experienced by female college students at coed schools compared to their male peers, despite females' better grades. Female college students at coed schools also have lower career aspirations than male students with similar grades and aptitudes.

The campus climate outside the classroom appears to preserve, rather than reduce, gender-stereotypic differences between women and men (Collison, 1990; R. M. Hall & Sandler, 1984). College women often are made to feel like interlopers or "guests" on campuses where the social life, health services, athletic opportunities, and so on are focused predominantly around male needs and male interests. Peer harassment of women on campus is endemic and often seen as "normal" (Fitzgerald, Shullman, et al., 1988; Hughes & Sandler, 1988; Malovich & Stake, 1990; Paludi, 1990). Between one out of two or three college women have been sexually harassed, compared to one out of nine to twelve college men. Some of the unwanted sexual attention comes from male faculty members (Dziech & Weiner, 1984; Fitzgerald, Weitzman, Gold, & Ormerod, 1988). Thus, the atmosphere of a college campus is quite different for women than for men: men are the norm, women are marginal.

Black women have additional problems at predominantly White institutions. They suffer from the pressures of both racism and sexism (Fleming, 1983; Guy-Sheftall & Bell-Scott, 1989b; E. J. Smith, 1982). For example, not only are Black women a significant minority on campus, but they have few role models, must learn a curriculum that has little relevance to their lives, and face social isolation and sometimes overt harassment as well. Such women tend to be particularly self-reliant and assertive. In predominantly Black colleges, the sex role norms encourage social passivity on the part of Black women, although their self-esteem may be higher than White women's. Other minority women suffer similar marginalization during college (Ethier & Deaux, 1990; Nieves-Squires, 1991; C. S. Pearson, Shavlik, & Touchton, 1989).

In comparison to women at coed institutions, who experience sex role pressure with its attendant diminution of women's self-esteem and career aspirations, women at single-sex colleges fare very well. Compared to graduates of coed schools, alumnae of women's colleges are more likely to pursue doctoral degrees and to have high career accomplishments (J. K. Rice & Hemmings, 1988; Tidball, 1989; "Where Have All," 1989). At those colleges, female role models abound because women represent the majority of college presidents (71%) and of tenured faculty (51%). Women students do not have to deal with men students dominating classroom discussions and extracurricular leadership positions. They more easily can learn to develop their own potential. Although the number of women's colleges has decreased since the 1960s (there now are about 100) due to demographics and the increased number of women students interested in coed schools, interest in such schools is still strong among a segment of high school graduates (about 2%), and that percentage seems to be relatively stable (Wartik, 1986). Research on single-sex Catholic high schools finds similar positive effects for females (V. E. Lee & Bryk, 1986; V. E. Lee & Marks, 1990). In particular, girls at single-sex high schools compared to their coed peers are more academically inclined and, by their senior year, superior in reading, writing, and science. These girls also have less traditional views of gender roles than their coed peers. In contrast, boys in single-sex schools show no comparable advantage over their coed peers, suggesting that single-sex schools are beneficial mainly to females. Thus, the atmosphere of coed schools seems to disadvantage female students.

School, then, serves as a powerful socializing force, especially with regard to gender development. The message is that (White) males are most important. As Bernard (1989) notes, females in the educational system, especially higher education, are exposed to a "curriculum of inferiority." No wonder the achievement and aspiration gap between female and male students increases with grade level, and female self-esteem decreases. Steps need to be taken to correct gender inequities in the educational system. Although materials and ideas abound to facilitate educating the majority of students (White males are a minority), many educators do not take achieving gender equity seriously (Sadker, Sadker, & Steindam, 1989).

Children also learn about gender roles through religious education.

▲   Religion

To the extent that a child has any religious instruction, he or she receives further training in the gender stereotypes. Virtually all major religions of the world, including the Judeo-Christian religions dominant in America, place strong emphasis on the two sexes' acting in ways consistent with traditional patriarchal society (M. Daly, 1974; G. Lerner, 1986).

In the Old Testament, God clearly is perceived as a dominating male ("Lord" and "King") who has taken over women's procreative powers. He creates first a male human and then a female "helpmate" to be subservient to the male. The Adam and Eve story can be viewed as a rationalization of patriarchy. Because of Eve's gullibility and treachery, she brings about the downfall of Adam and of succeeding generations. Consequently, she is condemned to suffer childbirth, to work hard, and to be a faithful and submissive wife. However, in another version of Genesis, God creates a man (Adam) and a woman (Lilith) simultaneously and "in His own image," thus conveying both the equality of the sexes and the androgyny of God. This version was deemphasized over the 400 years (from the tenth century B.C. to the fifth century B.C) it took to write the Book of Genesis (G. Lerner, 1986), which paralleled the entrenchment of patriarchy. Completely left out in the final version was the tale of Adam and Lilith. Because Adam would not accord Lilith equal treatment, she went into exile, emerging in later mythology as the snake who tempts Eve (A. Cantor, 1983). Such a version of the Creation gives a picture of the status of the sexes that is very different from the one currently promulgated.

As Gerda Lerner (1986) describes it, Hebrew monotheism attacked and supplanted fertility cults in which females and their bodies were revered and female goddesses worshiped. In the Book of Genesis, women's connection to the divine becomes completely restricted to their function as mothers. Men in general, and the patriarchs in particular, become the primary religious figures, and men's power over women is meant to replicate God's power over men. Female sexuality other than for procreative purposes becomes associated with sin and death. In the New Testament, a double image of woman as Madonna (Virgin Mary) or whore (Mary Magdalene) is conveyed with all its double messages about female sexuality.

Feminists have been challenging the traditional interpretation of Scripture since at least the early 1800s. In 1895, Elizabeth Cady Stanton wrote *The Women's Bible*. More recently, feminists have expanded their critique not only to document and trace male ideological bias, but also to discover an alternative history and tradition that supports the inclusion and personhood of women (Fiorenza, 1985; Heschel, 1983; Plaskow & Christ, 1989; Ruether, 1987). An alternative feminist spirituality movement also has blossomed in which ancient goddesses have been rediscovered or reinvented and the female nature of the divine celebrated (Eisler, 1987; Starhawk, 1982; M. Stone, 1976).

In the religious hierarchies, power and prestige have been reserved exclusively for males. Until recently, only males could be priests, ministers, rabbis. The Catholic church still does not have female clergy, and men dominate the 19 top positions in U. S. dioceses (Catholics for a Free Choice, 1988). Although Roman Catholic women now are participating in the Mass as lectors and in the distribution of the Eucharist, and many within the church are urging female priesthood (Koenenn, 1987), Pope John Paul II's letter "On the Dignity of Women" in 1988 made clear that such equality will not happen in the near future. The Pope's letter, while asserting that women are equal to men and not subordinate or especially sinful, still views the sexes as fundamentally different and thus "destined" to play different roles. For women, maternal qualities are primary. In contrast to women in the Catholic church, women in various Protestant and Jewish sects have made considerable headway. The 1970s and 1980s witnessed a number of firsts—the first female cleric was ordained in 1970, the first female rabbi in 1972, the first female Episcopal priest in 1976, and the first female Episcopal bishop in 1988. In 1986, women were 8% of the nation's clergy, double the percentage of ten years previously (A. L. Goldman, 1990). During the same year, women comprised more than half the degree candidates at Harvard Divinity School (Koenenn, 1987). Women's presence in other religious seminaries continues to increase. However, their position still is controversial, and many female clerics have difficulty obtaining anything but low-level positions. This is especially the case for Black women ministers (A. L. Goldman, 1990).

Religious devoutness in general has been found to strongly predict stereotypical gender role attitudes (Herzog & Bachman, 1982; M. Y. Morgan, 1987). That is, those who are most devout also hold the most stereotyped attitudes toward gender roles. Religions do differ somewhat in their promotion of stereotypic attitudes. The degree to which different religions afford women equality is related to both occupational choice and attitudes toward women held by college students (Rhodes, 1983). In a study of a nationwide sample of college students in 1973, those students who identified themselves as Seventh Day Adventists, Mormons, or Baptists, particularly if they were White, showed the greatest gender differences in occupational choices and disapproval of careers for married women. Those students who identified themselves as Quakers, Unitarians, or of no religious preference showed the fewest gender differences in those two areas. Thus, religious training may affect gender-related attitudes and training, even if it is not, as John Wilson (1978) states, "the single most important shaper of sex roles" (p. 264).

Another recent change in male-dominated religious messages has been the rewriting of hymns, creeds, and prayers to remove sexist words. In 1983, *An Inclusive Language Lectionary* was released by the National Council of Churches. This book marked the first formal effort to revise Bible passages in order to eliminate patriarchal terminology and exclusively male metaphors for God. In substituting *humanity* for *mankind*, *community* for *fellowship*, *Creator* for *Father*, *Father and Mother* for *God*, and so on, the new guidelines should go a long way toward reducing the predominance of male imagery in religion. Many churches are trying to find ways to be less sexist, racist, and militaristic in hymnals as well (Lavelle & Ramunni, 1986). But since Judeo-Christian religions originated in a male-dominated and masculine-oriented culture, it is hard to eliminate all male and masculine references and still be historically correct ("Bishops Publish," 1987; "New Edition," 1977). Religions, as they currently exist, still reflect that male dominance, and not all religious personnel want that dominance to change.

Thus, children exposed to religious education receive further training in male dominance through the content, language, and form of their religion.

▲ Media

Of all the sources of gender stereotypes, the media are the most pervasive and, some would say, the most powerful. Television, films, print media, music, art—all communicate messages about sex roles that are far from subtle. Females and males are presented, for the most part, in stereotyped ways, usually with deviations from the stereotypes depicted negatively. Because the media both reflect and shape society, they are extremely influential, especially for young children who cannot clearly differentiate fantasy from reality. The last ten years have seen some improvement in the images of women presented in the media. However, the overall picture still is far from balanced.

Television

It has been estimated that children spend one-third of their lives at home and/or sleeping, one-third at school, and one-third in front of a TV set. Almost all households in the United States (98%) own at least one television set (Nielsen Media Research, 1989). TV viewing averages more than 7 hours a day in the average TV household. Half of the 12-year-olds in the country watch this amount or more, although the average child watches from 3 to 4 hours a day (Gerbner & Gross, 1976; Nielsen Media Research, 1989). By the time a child is 16, she or he has spent more time in front of a TV set than in a classroom. Black children and adolescents spend significantly more time watching TV than their White peers (J. Brown, Childers, Bauman, & Koch, 1990; Tangney & Feshbach, 1988). A similar differential is found between children from blue-collar families and those from the middle class. Consequently, whatever effects TV viewing has should be particularly strong for such children.

Regardless of what the viewer is watching—children's shows, daytime TV, prime-time TV, newscasts, music television, or commercials—stereotypic gender messages abound. This is not surprising, especially given the fact that over 95% of television writers, producers, and executives are male (Lichter, Lichter, & Rothman, 1986). Most of the research on television has focused on commercial TV rather than cable, with the exception of music television. However, cable stations are drawing more viewers every year, especially from among the middle class. The average TV household now receives nearly 28 stations (*American Demographics*, February 1990, p. 4). Although programs on these channels may not be significantly less gender-stereotypic than those on commercial TV—indeed, viewers say cable offers more sex, violence, and profanity (*Television Digest*, April 3, 1989, p. 3)—viewers can better avoid commercials. As we will see, such avoidance can reduce one's exposure to sexism.

Children's shows   The world that children see on TV is sex-typed and White-male-oriented. Children's TV, for example, has been found to depict more than twice as many male as female roles. The behaviors of the female and male characters are strikingly different, as are the consequences of these behaviors (N. S. Feldman & Brown, 1984; Sternglanz & Serbin, 1974). Male characters are more likely than female characters to be aggressive, constructive, direct, and helpful, and to be rewarded for their actions. Females are more likely to be shown as deferent and as being punished for displaying a high level of activity. Females also use indirect manipulative strategies to get their way (for example, acting

helpless or seductive). In general, female behavior has no environmental consequence. This pattern parallels the practices of socializing agents: males get more attention and reinforcement; females are usually ignored and are expected to be passive and sedate.

Beginning with the fall 1991 season, all Saturday morning programs began to feature dominant male characters with females playing peripheral roles, if any (B. Carter, 1991). This was a deliberate marketing decision by television executives based on the finding that girls will watch shows with male or female lead characters, but boys will only watch shows with male leads. Since commercial TV is driven by advertisers, and since boys are 53% of the Saturday morning television audience, programmers are concerned mainly about pleasing boys. And boys don't want to be seen liking the shows girls like. As we have seen repeatedly, young boys' gender identity is more rigid and more based on what they are not (female or feminine) than is girls'. Boys prefer animated, high-action programs (often involving violence) and so such programs predominate on children's TV (for example, "G. I. Joe") (V. M. Watson, 1990).

Even in educational programs like "Sesame Street," gender stereotypes can occur. The Muppets, the major characters on "Sesame Street," all have male names or voices or both. These puppets not only are the mainstays of the show but also are prominent in books, toys, and other commercial articles. Their influence on children is strong. In one study, children aged 4 to 6 would not play with non-sex-typed toys that had been labeled by two Muppets as appropriate only for the other sex (Cobb et al., 1982). This behavior change occurred after only five minutes of TV exposure.

Daytime TV   In daytime soap operas, viewed primarily by women, characters also are presented in traditional and stereotypic ways, although the subject matter has become more contemporary in recent years (M. G. Cantor & Pingree, 1983). Women on such shows as "All My Children" and "General Hospital" more often are depicted as nurturant, hopeless, and displaying avoidance behaviors than men on these shows. Men more than women are depicted as directive and problem solving, although at least one study suggests that neither sex demonstrates competent coping strategies on such shows (Hodges, Brandt, & Kline, 1981). The complex narrative structure of the shows allows for the creation of multiple meanings (R. C. Allen, 1985). This fact may account for the appeal of soap operas to women of all age groups and social classes as well as to an increasing number of men. These shows may particularly appeal to women because the ongoing nature of the stories and characters is typical of real life, and thus fits in with women's more interpersonal orientation. Soap operas appear to satisfy viewers' needs for a sense of connection, a sense of community, despite the fact that such a community is not real (Modleski, 1982).

In daytime talk shows, sensationalism and exploitation abound. As Rapping (1989) notes, such shows as Oprah Winfrey's take some of the contributions of feminism—consciousness raising, personal sympathetic questioning—and use them to exploit the feelings of both the guests and the studio audience. Whether any real light is shed on such personal and troubling issues as "women who love too much" is questionable.

Prime-time TV   Sexism on prime-time TV has been amply documented since the late 1960s, although it has been reduced somewhat in the last ten years (Lichter et al., 1986; Signorielli, 1989; Steenland, 1988; Steenland & Whittemore, 1987; U.S. Commission on Civil Rights, 1979). White men consistently outnumber women three to one as leading characters of shows. In exciting adventure shows, White men outnumber women more than four to one. Men are more likely than women to be depicted as wage earners, and men appear in a greater variety of jobs than women. Since 1979, increasing numbers of female characters on TV have had jobs, but their representation has been less than realistic. Not only are more women on TV now shown as employed (75%) than is the case in real life (56%), but most of these women have professional careers (for example, lawyers or managers), whereas most real women work in low-paying, low-status jobs. (Roseanne Barr's popular show is an exception to this trend.) Although professional women on TV (such as Claire Huxtable and Murphy Brown) can serve as positive role models for young girls, the lack of realism may cause viewers to underestimate the extent of gender inequities in the labor force (see Chapter 11). Furthermore, most shows with female professionals still focus on family issues rather than on work ones. Despite such changes in depictions of females, they still are more often identified by their relationships to males—as girlfriend, wife, mother—than males are identified by their relationships to females. In fact, both women and men on TV tend to interact with men much more frequently than they interact with women (Lott, 1989). Furthermore,

men on TV tend to distance themselves physically (through head or body movement) from women characters on TV. This distancing behavior may convey a subtle negative message to viewers about men's attitudes toward women. In general, most females on prime-time television are young, attractive, sexy, and ornamental (D. M. Davis, 1990). Figure 7.3 illustrates some of the typical female roles on TV.

Although the number of male and female characters on TV conveys an important message to viewers, even more powerful are the qualities such

I am a psychotic/mute/Indian/Chicana who is restored to normalcy and neatness by a young, attractive, white, middle class doctor from the east. (Lots of flashbacks showing me whipped, raped, and force-fed)

I am the sister/daughter of an unjustly imprisoned man or else the witness to a mafia crime. I am also the client of a blind freelance insurance investigator. I scream often and inopportunely. I always fall and twist my ankle when the investigator and I are fleeing the bad guys.

I am a black/white cop. I have a short snappy name. I am tough but feminine. I like to follow my own instincts about a case. This frequently gets me into trouble; I am inevitably rescued by my male, fellow officers, who are devoted to me . . . I never rescue them.

I am the woman behind the man. I spend a lot of time keeping dinner warm for my crusading policeman/coroner, lover/husband. Sometimes I nag about being left alone so much. Sometimes I am kidnapped by mafia thugs. This makes a welcome break in my routine.

Figure 7.3 Memorable television role models. (Copyright © 1979 by Nicole Hollander. From the book *I'm in Training to Be Tall and Blonde.* Reprinted with special permission from St. Martin's Press, Inc., New York, NY.)

characters portray. The previously cited studies have shown that female characters on TV are more concerned than males with sex and marriage; looks count more than brains for females; and female characters are more likely than males to show helpless and incompetent behaviors. For example, even in a show where a woman is a major character, she often must be rescued from a difficult situation by a male. Females are much more likely than males to be depicted in a negative light (for example, as a bimbo, dope addict, or prostitute), especially on adventure shows. Men, although depicted somewhat negatively in situation comedies, are more than twice as likely as women to be shown as competent (independent, skilled, leaderlike, self-confident). Men on TV also are more likely than women to be older, serious, and to hold prestigious jobs. Since 1986, men, such as David Addison in "Moonlighting" and Sam Malone in "Cheers," have gotten tougher and more hard-boiled (Boyer, 1986).

Given the fact that Black youth watch commercial television twice as often as White youth, it is particularly unfortunate that they see so few Black characters. Blacks and members of other minority racial or ethnic groups are a minority of TV characters, although there's been some improvement in the last few years with shows like "The Cosby Show" and "227" (H. Gray, 1986; Lichter, Lichter, Rothman, & Amundson, 1987; Stroman, 1989). The Black characters that are presented tend to be presented fairly positively—in professional roles, belonging to the middle or upper classes, in two-parent families, and demonstrating competent behaviors. However, Black male youths are portrayed less frequently than both Black female youths and Black men and women. When they are presented, they tend to be depicted as happy-go-lucky and lacking in ambition. These portrayals do not help young Black viewers, who tend to be poor and working-class, to prepare for the realities of adulthood. Members of other minority groups, especially Hispanics and Asians, are markedly absent. When Hispanic males are present, they are more likely than White and Black males to commit crimes (Lichter et al., 1987). When non-Black minority females are present, they are more likely to be crime victims. For example, if a character is a non-White, foreign-born, elderly woman, her life expectancy on a show is about 20 seconds (John Murray, as cited in V. M. Watson, 1990).

As noted earlier, new shows in prime time have tended to be less gender-stereotyped than older shows, perhaps because strong female characters appeal especially to women between ages 25 and 54 with annual incomes of more than $30,000 (P. Kerr, 1984). Such viewers are highly desirable to advertisers. Between 1979 and 1988, women on prime-time television became more racially diverse, older, more likely to be working, and less likely to be in nuclear families (Steenland, 1988). However, progress has not been steady. During the 1980s, programming tended to focus on the affluent rather than the majority of the population. Furthermore, since fall 1987, there has been a surprising resurgence of male prominence, pretty female sidekicks, female homemakers, and single (as opposed to married) working women. Almost 20% of the new shows in 1987–88 had no female characters at all (for example, "Jake and the Fatman"). A few of the new shows (for example, "My Two Dads") featured men raising and nurturing children on their own. Although nurturing men are good role models, their portrayal is very unrealistic. Most single parents are female, and very few fathers raise their children alone. Still, any programs that counter negative gender stereotypes (such as "L. A. Law" and "The Golden Girls") are to be welcomed.

Newscasts   Most Americans (65%) use TV as a primary source of news (*Television Digest*, April 3, 1989, p. 3). What they see are a lot of White men, although the percentage of female network news correspondents has increased somewhat from 1977, when 79% of the newscasters were White males, 10% White females, 8% non-White males, and 3% non-White females (U.S. Commission on Civil Rights, 1977, 1979). In 1989, women constituted 16% of the nightly network newscasters, although they filed only 10% of the nightly news stories ("Study Reports Sex Bias," 1989). Minorities still are seriously underrepresented, with less than 1% of the news stories filed by minority women (Lipsyte, 1989). Furthermore, the percentage of women in management positions in TV news still is small. For example, women were only 14% of all news directors in 1986, although this was an improvement over 1972, when less than 1% of the news directors were women ("Women Taking Charge," 1987).

As these statistics indicate, gender equality in TV newscasts is still far from being realized, despite the finding that most Americans would prefer to see a man and a woman anchoring the network news ("Progress Slow," 1985). Not only are women less visible than men as newscasters, but they are also expected to be younger, more attractive, and more deferential than their male counterparts (Craft,

1988; M. Sanders & Rock, 1988). Furthermore, women correspondents are given more fringe assignments and paid less than male correspondents. Whether having more women both behind and in front of the camera would actually affect what news is transmitted is debatable. Right now, only about 10% of news stories focus on women ("Study Reports Sex Bias," 1989). However, the predominance of males in authoritative positions conveys its own message to viewers—that is, that men are important and knowledgeable and that women are not.

Commercials The gender stereotypes are even more explicit in TV commercials than in regular programming, although women and men appear equally often as central characters (Bretl & Cantor, 1988; Ferrante, Haynes, & Kingsley, 1988; Lovdal, 1989; Osborn, 1989). Since the early 1970s, gender stereotyping has decreased somewhat, but women still are most often presented in the home in the role of wife and/or mother. When they are depicted as employed, their range of occupations is broader than it once was but is still traditionally feminine. Men, whose depiction as husband and/or father has increased, still are more frequently presented in other roles, especially ones in the business world. Women are most often seen in ads for food, and they are more likely than men to be shown using the products they advertise. Men are most often seen in ads for automotive products and alcohol. Women in commercials are much younger than the men, who can range between young and middle-aged. Relations between the sexes typically are portrayed in traditional ways. For example, detergent commercials still primarily depict a woman worrying about getting the dirt off her husband's clothes rather than vice versa. And women are presented as sex objects more frequently than men. On the other hand, men are increasingly likely to be the butt of jokes, especially when they show ignorance about nutrition and child care (Horovitz, 1989).

The most striking difference between women and men in commercials is the fact that men predominate (83%–90%) as the authoritative, dominant voice-overs, even when the products are aimed at women. Thus, again, the voice of authority is male, although research suggests that female voice-overs are just as effective (*Ms.*, February 1987, p. 30).

On children's shows, sexist stereotypes in commercials are rampant (Feldstein & Feldstein, 1982; O'Connor, 1989). Boys dominate both quantitatively and qualitatively. Boys are more likely to be portrayed in active roles, girls in passive ones. Indeed, commercials aimed at boys have a different format than commercials aimed at girls. Commercials aimed at boys have rapid action, frequent cuts, loud music, sound effects, and frequent scene changes. In contrast, commercials aimed at girls contain many fades and dissolves, background music, and female narration (R. L. Welch, Huston-Stein, Wright, & Plehal, 1979). Children as young as age 6 recognize these distinctions, which means that even if the content of a commercial doesn't sex type a product, the style in which it is produced might (A. C. Huston, Greer, Wright, Welch, & Ross, 1984). But most often the content is sex-typed as well. As discussed earlier, toys are markedly gender-labeled, with action toys tagged for boys, and domestic and cosmetic toys tagged for girls. Racism too is prevalent in children's commercials, with Black children almost always in supporting roles and other minority children completely invisible (O'Connor, 1989).

Thus, of all the television programming discussed so far, commercials are the most sexist. But they are rivaled by the sexism in an increasingly popular type of TV program, music television.

Music television Music television, shown on a number of cable stations, is viewed predominantly by teenagers, especially by females and Black males (J. D. Brown, Campbell, & Fisher, 1986). What they mostly see is male teenage fantasies (J. D. Brown & Campbell, 1986; B. L. Sherman & Dominick, 1986; Texier, 1990). White males predominate overall (more than two-to-one male-to-female ratio), and Black males predominate on Black entertainment video programs. Females are more likely to be shown dancing than singing or playing a musical instrument, trying to gain the attention of a man who ignores them, or engaging in passive and solitary activities. Females are less likely than males to be portrayed in professional work. Antisocial behavior (physical or verbal aggression, deception, disrespect for authority) is common for both White females and males (in fact, females are as likely as males to be aggressors) but not for Blacks. Some videos—for example, those by Billy Idol and David Lee Roth—are profoundly misogynistic and violent. Overall, most "concept videos," which dramatize the music, contain violence, graphic sexual content, and females as sex objects.

Rap music videos, a recent addition to the music scene, are mainly populated by Black men who promote themselves as dominant and sexually successful, such as 2 Live Crew (Pareles, 1990; Texier, 1990; Wallace, 1990). Women in these videos are presented almost exclusively as objects of male lust. Many male rappers have been criticized for their sexist and homophobic lyrics. However, there are female rappers who challenge the stereotypes by appearing to be dominant, level-headed, and in control. Queen Latifah, for example, presents a strong, regal female image and strikingly feminist lyrics. Unfortunately, these women get very little air time.

Less objectified images of women are presented in rock videos as well, but they are few in number and usually performed by women (E. A. Kaplan, 1987; L. A. Lewis, 1990; R. Roberts, 1990; Texier, 1990). For example, Janet Jackson tends to present a positive image of an active and sexually assertive female. Madonna, too, presents an image of a woman in control of her own sexuality, but she seems to revel in objectifying herself rather than breaking with that imagery. Interestingly, Black and White teenagers interpret Madonna's videos very differently, as do males and females, and fans and nonfans (J. D. Brown & Schulze, 1990).

As these last findings suggest, the meaning viewers take from music television cannot always be predicted or controlled. For example, White and Black female and Black male teenagers are more likely than White males to say they watch music videos to learn the latest fashions and dances (J. D. Brown et al., 1986). Females appear to use MTV to gain information about dominant male culture, whereas Blacks more often than Whites say they watch because they want to be like the people in the videos. This race and gender difference in viewer orientation makes the interpretation of such videos and their effects very difficult.

We do have evidence of some effects, however (C. H. Hansen & Hansen, 1988). For example, female viewers of MTV show a strong relationship between amount of exposure and acceptance of sexual violence (Dieter, 1989). That is, the more females watch MTV, the more likely they are to believe that men are violent toward women, that violence is part of love and sex, and that women cannot or should not defend themselves from male sexual aggression. Male viewers show less of a correlation, perhaps because males tend to accept sexual violence more than females, regardless of amount of MTV viewing. For both sexes, however, amount of MTV viewing is positively correlated with the view that both sexes tease and manipulate each other. Although the correlations exist, we do not know for

sure whether watching MTV causes attitudes to change, or whether people with certain attitudes are more likely to watch MTV. This issue will be discussed further in the next section.

Overall, sexism abounds in rock videos. The adolescent viewers of rock videos are confronted with images of male dominance and female subordination, and the sexualization of both.

Effects of TV viewing   As the results of research on music television suggest, what we see on television can affect us in sometimes powerful ways. Modeling is an important process in sex role development, as social learning theory predicts, and the models presented on TV are typically stereotyped to the extreme. As we have discussed, television viewers see a world in which men dominate. Men are more visible than women and are depicted as more important, competent, dominant, authoritative, and aggressive. These elements can help shape a child's developing gender schema.

Indeed, TV is a powerful source of influence on viewers' attitudes and behaviors. This influence appears to be particularly strong for children, who, as a group, are not as skilled as adults in distinguishing fantasy from reality (Eysenck & Nias, 1978). Working-class children in particular are likely to believe that television characters are real (Nikken & Peeters, 1988). The amount of time children spend watching TV has been found to be directly and positively related to their degree of acceptance of traditional sex roles as early as kindergarten age (McGhee & Frueh, 1980; Sprafkin & Liebert, 1978; D. M. Zuckerman, Singer, & Singer, 1980). Furthermore, whereas among light viewers of TV, the perception of male stereotypes declines with increasing age, among heavy viewers no such decline occurs. In a study comparing children who lived in a Canadian community without television to children in comparable communities with television, Kimball (1986) found that children in the communities without television were less stereotyped in their sex role attitudes. However, after television was introduced, the attitudes of these children became more stereotyped.

A number of factors may mediate the effects of television viewing. Parents' sex role attitudes may be important, and parents' presence during TV viewing may modify the TV message. Although children mostly watch TV alone, TV viewing is the single major recreational pursuit families do together (Timmer et al., 1985). A child's intelligence and level of cognitive development also may mediate the TV message. And not all TV shows are alike. Children who watch more educational TV programs tend to demonstrate less sex-stereotyped attitudes than children who watch little educational TV (Repetti, 1984). The same was found for young children who viewed such nontraditional shows as "The Cosby Show," "Who's the Boss?" and "Growing Pains" (Rosenwasser, Lingenfelter, & Harrington, 1989). Viewers of these shows tended to have nontraditional gender role perceptions.

The effect of TV is likely to be strongest among those who otherwise are least likely to hold traditional sex role views. Michael Morgan (1982), in a two-year study of the relationship between TV viewing and gender stereotypes in sixth through tenth graders, found support for this hypothesis. For males, high TV viewing did not predict sexism scores one year later, but for girls, amount of TV viewing was associated significantly with sexism scores one year later. This finding suggests that for girls, greater sexism was a result of watching a great deal of TV. Because girls, especially middle-class girls, are less sexist than boys to begin with, watching TV may affect them the most. These results parallel those found with respect to the effects of MTV. Thus, TV may "mainstream" children, creating in all viewers a homogeneous commonality of outlooks. Curiously, early sexism on the part of boys was a strong predictor of TV watching one year later, suggesting that those with strong stereotypes may enjoy the reinforcement of those attitudes that occurs on TV. Later research by Morgan (1987) demonstrated that television viewing makes an independent contribution to adolescents' sex role attitudes over time, although it is not clearly related to specific behaviors.

Race also may be an important variable mediating the effects of television. As we have seen, Black children watch TV much more than Whites and they seem to react to it quite differently, as research on rock videos has highlighted. Whereas heavy viewing seems to be normative for Black youths, it may be a sign of social deviancy for Whites (Tangney & Feshbach, 1988). Furthermore, although White children see people like themselves on the screen, Black children are viewing predominantly other-race individuals. We need to be cautious in generalizing from research on predominantly White subject populations to all others.

A number of studies have gone beyond the correlational to examine how specific television contact affects children's sex role attitudes. Pingree (1978) found that by showing third- and eighth-grade children commercials of either traditional women (housewives and mothers) or nontraditional women (professional business people), she could affect children's attitudes about women. All children, except eighth-grade boys, who saw the nontraditional commercials and who were told that the women were real people, became less traditional in their attitudes about women. And this was after only 5 minutes of viewing! Other research supports the idea that the portrayal of nonstereotyped characters can expand gender consciousness among children, although "masculine" boys appear to be the hardest to reach (Eisenstock, 1984).

Not only children and adolescents may be affected by the gender messages on television. Among college students and older adults as well, the amount of TV viewing of stereotyped programs has been found to be significantly and positively correlated with the amount of gender stereotyping in self-descriptions (L. Ross, Anderson, & Wisocki, 1982). Of course, especially in adult groups, the positive correlation may mean that sex-typed people prefer watching sex-typed shows. Still, frequent viewing is likely to be a powerful reinforcer of gender stereotypes. Viewing women and men in nontraditional as opposed to traditional roles in TV commercials has been found to improve women college students' self-confidence, independence of judgment, and achievement aspirations (Geis, Brown, Jennings, & Porter, 1984; Jennings, Geis, & Brown, 1980). Since children see about 20,000 traditional commercials a year, it is clear how TV can contribute to important gender differences.

In sum, television depicts marked gender stereotypes: men are presented as more important and dominant than women; women are presented as more subordinate and sexualized than men. These portrayals affect child viewers both by modeling different behaviors for females and males and by encouraging the development of a strong and stereotypic gender schema.

Films

Although television is the most pervasive visual medium, films also are enormously popular, especially with the advent of videocassette recorders, which allow viewers to rent a film to be shown at home on their television screen. About half of all U.S. households now own such a recorder (Edmondson, 1987).

Like television, films present stereotyped images of the sexes. Two images of women have been classically presented, their origins in the Bible: as virgin or saint and as whore. These images were clearly exemplified in the 1950s and 1960s by the brainless sexpot (for example, Marilyn Monroe) and the feminine homebody (for example, Doris Day). In 1990, we have Breathless Mahoney (Madonna) and Tess Trueheart (Glenne Headly) in *Dick Tracy*. It was only during the late 1930s and early 1940s, with the increased number of women in the labor force spurred by the women's movement of the 1920s and by World War II, that successful, achieving images of women emerged (as in roles portrayed by Katharine Hepburn). This ended when the war ended. When men reclaimed their jobs, women were pushed back into the home in films as well as in reality. The New Woman of the late 1960s and 1970s, although sexually active and more independent than her predecessors, usually was depicted in a negative way or was punished for her sexuality (Mellen, 1973). For example, in *Looking for Mr. Goodbar*, the main character gets killed by someone she meets in a singles' bar.

The women's movement of the 1960s finally had some effect on film images of women in the mid- to late 1970s, with credible and strong female characters in such films as *Alice Doesn't Live Here Anymore, An Unmarried Woman*, and *Julia* (James, 1989). But the 1980s saw considerable backlash, with such retrogressive film images as the brainless young woman (*The Woman in Red*) and the prostitute (*Pretty Woman*) (Haskell, 1988; Maslin, 1990). Motherhood and family came back, even (or especially) for working women (*Terms of Endearment, Fatal Attraction, Baby Boom*). Films about women's friendships have been particularly hard to find recently, especially ones where men don't become the focus of the film, unlike the popular male buddy films, where women are merely backdrops, if they appear at all (S. Isaacs, 1990). The backlash against strong women, and the conflict about how to depict them in a time of changing gender norms, led to a surprising absence of women in films during the mid- to late 1980s (Rickey, 1991). For example, most major box office stars have been male, and many films, especially the most popular ones, have glorified males and stereotypic masculinity (*Robocop, Die Hard, 48 Hours*). The roles for women have been smaller and more submissive. The intense reaction to the 1991 film *Thelma and Louise*, which depicted two strong women friends who used guns to protect themselves against male violence, clearly revealed how unacceptable strong women can be. The film was attacked by some male critics as a display of male bashing, despite the fact that most violent films depict gratuitous violence against women without being criticized for female bashing. Black women have been completely neglected in films, and this has been true throughout the history of filmmaking.

As some of the recent films suggest, cinematic images of masculinity also have held strongly to the gender stereotype. Whereas the realms of domesticity and sexual allure have been reserved for women, those of aggression, as in Westerns, war, and gangster movies, moral superiority, and intelligence, as in detective and mystery movies, have been reserved for men (S. Weitz, 1977). Because the male stereotype has more positive characteristics than the female one and because male characters usually are developed to a far greater degree than female characters because of their central role, men have not fared too badly in film. However, the overemphasis on violence and the depiction of superficial sexual encounters as the norm have tended to distort men's human characteristics. The brief attempt to make sensitive and emotionally competent men into film heroes during the 1970s (for example, Jon Voight in *Coming Home*, Kris Kristofferson in *Alice Doesn't Live Here Anymore*) (Starr, 1978) was slowly phased out during the 1980s. First we saw a return to male dominance by men taking over what were once considered female issues—for example, single parenting (*Kramer vs. Kramer*) and problems of divorce (*Starting Over*). Even *Tootsie*, a film praised for its perceptive insights into sex roles, can be analyzed as conveying another message as well—that men make better women than women do. Then we saw a return to the traditional definitions of maleness—adventure (*Indiana Jones and the Last Crusade*), sports (*Field of Dreams*), and violence (*Another 48 Hours*). The changes in the images of men and women in film can be attributed not only to changes in the social context but also to changing demographics. During the mid-1980s, the average moviegoer was a male between ages 14 and 24, and it was his fantasies that were being catered to. However, the youth audience is aging. In 1989, teenagers composed only 30% of the audience (Harmetz, 1990). Adults over 40 comprised a striking 23%. These changes are starting to be reflected in film fare, as evidenced by the surprising popularity of *Driving Miss Daisy*, a sensitive film about an elderly Jewish widow and her only slightly less elderly Black chauffeur. Sensitive males made a return in such 1991 films as *City Slickers* and *Regarding Henry* (Maslin, 1991).

Hopefully, the changing demographics will lead to more substantive and sensitive films, about real women and men, not just male fantasies of women and men. For example, acquaintance rape is rarely depicted on the screen as the sexual crime it really is (Warshaw, 1991). Hollywood still has a long way to go before there is true equality on, and behind, the silver screen. The same can be said for Broadway, although more progress has been made there, perhaps due to the rise of female playwrights ("Women Playwrights," 1989).

On a more sober note, the rise in home video viewing has led to increased concern about R- and X-rated films. Although the effects of pornography will be discussed in Chapter 12, it is worth noting in this section that most such films are aimed at a male audience and depict male dominance and/or exploitation of women (G. Cowan, Lee, Levy, & Snyder, 1988; Cowan & O'Brien, 1990). Most disturbing of all is the trend toward pairing sex with violence against women. As we will see in the later chapter, films that do this negatively shape men's attitudes toward women and toward sexual violence (Linz, Donnerstein, & Penrod, 1987b).

In sum, films portray traditional gender stereotypes, although their predominance has varied with the social context. We currently seem to be experiencing a backlash against feminism, which we can only hope will end soon. As with other forms of complex visual media, we cannot always predict what viewers will take away from viewing a film (see, for example, Pribram, 1988).

Print Media

Gender stereotypes are as present in print media as they are in visual media. We will examine fiction books, magazines, and newspapers.

Fiction   As we saw in the discussion of textbooks earlier in this chapter, children's books markedly portray boys and girls in stereotypic roles, and male characters tend to predominate. In books aimed at an adult audience, a wider variety of roles and behaviors is portrayed. Whereas earlier books written by men tended to present women as either pure or evil, madonna or whore/bitch (K. Snow, 1975), newer books have complex and strong female characters. Also new is racial, ethnic, and sexual diversity, as minority women writers have moved into the mainstream (for example, Alice Walker with *The Color Purple*). Feminist literary criticism has become increasingly popular and accepted, and many neglected women authors have been rediscovered and their works reprinted. *The Norton Anthology of Literature by Women* (Gilbert & Gubar) was released in 1985, marking a turning point in the acceptance of female writers and their works. The long history of systematic exclusion of women writers (see Spender, 1989) seems to be ending.

Along with this trend toward more inclusivity and gender equality, though, is another trend—the increasing popularity of the romantic historical novel, written and read primarily by women (for example, gothic novels). In these stories, the heroine is usually helpless or dependent upon a man to bring meaning to her life, although recent heroines have been more nontraditional in attitudes and behavior than in the past, and relationships are more often between equals (Modleski, 1982; Toth, 1984; Weston & Ruggiero, 1978). Despite their seeming confirmation of traditional female roles in a patriarchal society, modern romances also convey another message, according to Radway (1984)—that it is all right for women to be assertive, and for men to be nurturing and gentle. Indeed, it is this message that may account for the novel's appeal among women made anxious about changing gender definitions. These texts in many ways reveal the contradictions in women's lives under patriarchy (Modleski, 1982).

Popular books and fiction aimed at men, on the other hand (for example, James Bond thrillers), tend to present the male going off on some adventure, unencumbered by family ties. Themes of aggression predominate, and if females are presented, they are usually cast in a stereotyped sexual role (S. Weitz, 1977). Much male fiction is pornographic, with interconnected themes of sexuality, dominance, and violence against women (Dworkin, 1981; Griffin, 1981).

Magazines   Gender stereotypes abound in magazines as well, especially because the market for magazines is so segmented. That is, although visual media may have a predominant audience, they are available for all viewers. In contrast, advertisers aim magazines at a very narrow audience—for example, employed young mothers with joint annual incomes over $40,000. Magazines aimed at men focus on themes of sexuality (*Playboy*), sports (*Field and Stream*), and daring (*Road and Track*). Magazines aimed at women emphasize women's appearance and pleasing or helping others, especially men (M. Ferguson, 1983; Peirce, 1990). One thing that has changed in magazines aimed at women since the 1970s is the portrayal of women working outside the home (Geise, 1979; Ruggiero &

Weston, 1985), which has become positive. Specialized magazines even exist for these women, such as *Working Mother, Working Woman,* and *Savvy.* However, the circulation of men's sex magazines far surpasses the circulation of all women's magazines (Seager & Olson, 1986).

Advertisers, however, appear to be the last to acknowledge that women are multidimensional. For example, although women account for 39% of new car purchases and participate in buying another 42% of all new cars and trucks, automobile companies spend less than 3% of their advertising money in women's magazines ("Study: Women's Role," 1985). Advertisements in magazines aimed at one sex tend to use models predominantly of that sex (Masse & Rosenblum, 1988). As we saw with commercials, print advertisements frequently are more stereotypic than the contexts in which they are found. For example, one ad for suntan lotion that appeared in *Ms.* magazine depicted a man and woman devoted to being their "best": the man was Greg Louganis, a four-time Olympic gold medalist who clearly had to work hard to develop his abilities, and the woman was Christy Fichtner, a former Miss USA, whose "best" evidently was her looks. Women in print ads tend to be White, extremely young, and extremely thin, setting a standard of attractiveness that few women can attain (Silverstein, Perdue, Peterson, & Kelly, 1986). In fact, female models have become thinner each decade since 1950. The effects of such models on women's feelings about their body will be discussed in Chapter 8.

A well-kept secret is that advertising determines the content of women's magazines in ways unheard of in other magazines (Steinem, 1990). Advertisers in women's magazines require a certain number of pages of "complementary copy" for each of their ads, such as an article about hairstyling to accompany advertising for hair products. The result is that the vast majority of pages (from 75% to 90%) in such magazines as *Glamour* and *Family Circle* contain ads and ad-related copy. Advertisers also can refuse to advertise if they feel articles are unsympathetic to their products. For example, Clairol withdrew its advertising from *Ms.* magazine after *Ms.* reported on a congressional hearing into the carcinogenic potential of hair dyes, and Estee Lauder refused to advertise there because no articles on make-up appeared in the magazine. Thus, advertising virtually controls women's magazines, with the exception of the new *Ms.*—and that's only because *Ms.* takes no ads.

Equality between the images of men and women in ads has increased over the last 20 years (Sullivan & O'Connor, 1988). Ads now are equally as likely to show women in working roles as in nonworking roles. When people are depicted in the home, however, more women than men appear (Courtney & Whipple, 1983). Despite this greater diversity of settings and roles for females now than in the past, the most prominent thing about current advertisements is their emphasis on sexuality and "decoration." In this regard, indications that men's image in advertising has become more like women's is hardly comforting (Skelly & Lundstrom, 1981). It means that men have become more "decorative" as well. Sex sells, and it has become the prime advertising technique for a host of products (Muro, 1989). The fact that it dehumanizes both women and men and commodifies an intimate aspect of life seems to matter little.

Even the way an advertisement is composed visually conveys gender messages. Erving Goffman (1979) found numerous examples of genderisms that illustrate the position of men and women in our society: function ranking (male taller, in front, and in authoritative position), ritualization of subordination (for example, a woman at a man's feet), snuggling, mock assault games, and an overabundance of images of women on beds and floors. Females are also more likely to smile than males. Other research has confirmed Goffman's findings (for example, Masse & Rosenblum, 1988). Figure 7.4 is an example of function ranking—the man is pictured seated above, and leaning over, the woman. Men also are more likely than women to be depicted with their faces prominent, as opposed to their bodies (D. Archer, Iritani, Kimes, & Barrios, 1983; Nigro, Hill, Gelbein, & Clark, 1988). Such "face-ism" has been documented in periodicals both in the United States and in 11 other cultures, in artwork over six centuries, and in TV interview shows. This difference in facial prominence affects the viewers' perception of the person; for example, a person is perceived more favorably and is rated as more intelligent when the face is prominent than when it is not.

Thus, from both the content and the layout of advertisements, viewers receive the message that women are decorative, men more instrumental.

Newspapers   As with the other media, newspapers show a sexist bias in the treatment of women and men on the staff, in the news, and in the comic strips that are serialized. Women reporters generally have

Figure 7.4 Example of function ranking in magazine advertising. Note how the man is seated above, and leaning over, the woman. (Photo courtesy of Kenyon & Eckhardt Advertising, Inc., New York.)

a difficult time making the front page with their stories because women generally do not cover foreign, White House, or important news beats. In a survey of the front pages of ten leading newspapers in 1989, only one out of four of the signed articles were by women, from a low of 16% at the *New York Times* to a high of 41% at *USA Today* (Lipsyte, 1989; "Study Reports Sex Bias," 1989). Despite the fact that two out of three journalism graduates are women, they account for less than 2% of newspaper corporate management, 5% of publishers and general managers, and 13% of directing editors ("Women in Media," 1988).

Most newspaper articles are about men. Women are only 11% of the people quoted in newspapers ("Study Reports Sex Bias," 1989). When women are portrayed in the newspaper, their coverage is more likely to include mention of personal appearance, marital status, and spouse than is the coverage of men (Foreit et al., 1980). Such comments are not solely due to the fact that women are more likely than men to be written about in the "family" or "lifestyle" (that is, "women's") section. Wherever women appear in newspapers, their appearance and marital status is likely to be noted. Similarly, men's photographs outnumber women's three to one, and men are more likely to be depicted in their professional or athletic roles, whereas women are more likely to be depicted with their husbands or families (Luebke, 1989; "Study Reports Sex Bias," 1989). Some people argue that if more women were in the newsroom, coverage would deepen as well as broaden (K. Mills, 1988). Such a prediction remains to be tested.

Newspaper comic strips also perpetuate gender stereotypes. Men, especially White men, are represented far more than their proportion in the population warrants (Brabant & Mooney, 1986; Chavez, 1985). Furthermore, men are given preferential treatment in terms of number of appearances and number of careers depicted. Although many male and female characters are described in equally favorable or unfavorable terms, sex-typed characteristics often are emphasized for females (Potkay & Potkay, 1984). For example, women often are depicted either as a housewife or a sexpot (Blondie Bumstead, until her 1991 foray into the work force; Miss Buxley). Although a few comic strips portray employed mothers (for example, "For Better or For Worse" and "Sally Forth"), these women are depicted as superwomen—that is, doing everything (Mooney & Brabant, 1987). Furthermore, the home life of employed mothers is portrayed as less happy than that of traditional mothers. Thus, in the world of comic strips, as elsewhere in the media, traditional gender roles are portrayed most positively.

Other Media

By now, the picture is strikingly consistent: the media world presents a picture of traditional gender roles, despite some improvement in the last 20 years. We will note only briefly, two other forms of media: radio broadcasts and art.

Adolescents typically listen to about five hours of radio a day, with Black girls listening the most and White males the least (J. Brown et al., 1990). What they hear primarily is men and men's views of women. For example, Top 40 radio stations predominantly have male disc jockeys, newscasters, voice-overs, sportscasters, and weathercasters (Lont, 1990). Male artists outnumber female artists, especially in rock music and rap (J. D. Brown & Campbell, 1986; Endres, 1984). In popular songs, themes of love and sex are most common, followed by songs of social protest. Since most songs are written in the first person, and since most lyrics are written and sung by men, the male point of view predominates. Lyrics tend to be gender-stereotypic, although less so than the music videos that are made of them. For example, women are more likely to play passive rather than active roles, whereas for men, the reverse is true. Many lyrics in rock and rap depict women in a negative light, at least when men are the singers. Songs written and sung by female artists tend to be less stereotypic (Groce & Cooper, 1990). What effect does such music have? Research is scant on this topic but suggestive (see, for example, St. Lawrence & Joyner, 1991). It is likely that hearing sex-stereotypic lyrics contributes to the listener's stereotypic views of the sexes.

The art world also is male dominated, and works of art considered great have typically been done by men because of restrictions on women with respect to training, encouragement, and economic support (Broude & Garrard, 1982). Until this century, women were socially prohibited from seeing nude men. Drawing them was unheard of. Many of the paintings signed "Anonymous" have actually been done by women. But there also is the issue of bias. Much artwork done by women has been devalued due to the artist's sex and to the use of male-normed criteria. For example, the classification of painting and sculpture, which women traditionally had little access to, as "high" art, and pottery, needlework, and quilting, which primarily women did, as "low" art, shows a distinct male bias regarding aesthetic standards. Although discrimination against women artists has become less overt in recent years, a group of women artists known as the Guerrilla Girls still finds much to attack with respect to the art world's sexism and racism (R. Smith, 1990).

Feminist art criticism has become an important field (Broude & Garrard, 1982; Nochlin, 1989; H. Robinson, 1987; Saunders, 1990). From this perspective, traditional artwork can be viewed as reflecting women's lack of power and societal assumptions about women's "nature" and "place." Depiction of a nude woman amid a gathering of clothed men (Manet), the emphasis on female eroticism in modern art, the double images of either virgin or whore for women depicted in art versus use of images of men to represent all of humanity—these are only some of the ways women's status has been reflected in art.

In sum, in all forms of media, gender stereotypes are conveyed often in the most exaggerated way. Television commercials, print advertisements, and music videos tend to be particularly stereotypic. Since children are trying to understand gender-appropriate behavior and the world around them, they are especially vulnerable to influence by these distorted images. What children see is male power and female subordination. They see the home and child care as women's special province. They also see women frequently reduced to being sexual objects. They seldom see either women or men portrayed in their diversity and complexity. To the extent that children are exposed to the mass media, and we already have noted how extensive that exposure typically is, children appear to develop an increasingly marked and stereotypic gender schema.

▲ Summary

What is most striking from this review of socializing forces is the consistency of the gender stereotypes conveyed. Through the structure of the English language itself, through play activities, the school environment, religious messages, and media depictions, the two sexes are portrayed as differing widely in behavior and status. Females typically are characterized as unimportant, incompetent, passive, and nurturant homebodies and homemakers; males, as important, competent, active, and aggressive wage earners and athletes. Throughout a child's developing years, these images are emphasized through continuous repetition. Even if parents are nonstereotypic and try to inculcate similar values and behaviors in their children, the gender stereotypes conveyed by other socializing forces mitigate or overpower their influence. Parents need to strongly limit their children's television viewing, as well as find an atypical school environment, to successfully raise gender-aschematic children. For most children, gender schematization comes with normal socialization. Thus, we can understand why there is such a high degree of concordance regarding the gender stereotypes. A child cannot help but learn them if she or he grows up in such a stereotypic culture. What is surprising is that anyone can escape being gender-stereotypic. Given the pervasiveness of the gender stereotypes in our culture, we can better understand why changing them is so difficult, regardless of individual experience.

▲ Recommended Reading

Messner, M. A., & Sabo, D. F. (Eds.). (1990). *Sport, men, and the gender order: Critical feminist perspectives.* Champaign, IL: Human Kinetics. A fascinating collection of articles analyzing the role sports play in maintaining male dominance over women and a competitive dominance hierarchy with other men.

Miller, C., & Swift, K. (1988). *The handbook of nonsexist writing* (2nd ed.). New York: Harper & Row. A useful guide to understanding the need for nonsexist writing and learning how to do it.

Pearson, C. S., Shavlik, D. L., & Touchton, J. G. (Eds.). (1989). *Educating the majority: Women challenge tradition in higher education.* New York: American Council on Education/Macmillan. A comprehensive collection of articles on the importance of recognizing diversity among women college students, with suggestions regarding reconceptualizing and transforming the educational process.

Plaskow, J., & Christ, C. P. (Eds.). (1989). *Weaving the visions: New patterns in feminist spirituality.* San Francisco: Harper & Row. A heterogeneous collection of articles, representing the diversity of feminist thought with respect to religious experience.

Steinem, G. (1990, July/August). Sex, lies & advertising. *Ms.*, pp. 18–28. An eye-opening article on the role advertisers play in shaping the content and direction of women's magazines.

▲▲▲▲▲▲▲▲▲▲▲▲▲▲▲▲▲▲▲▲▲▲

Part 3 Summary

In Part 3, an answer to the question of how gender roles and stereotypes are acquired has been explored on two levels—historical derivations and current socialization practices. Initially, the roles and stereotypes arose from the division of labor by sex in previous societies as a function of the subsistence base of the society, the supply of labor, and the functional requirements of childbearing. Even though a division of labor is no longer functional or even practical, the roles and stereotypes remain.

In each generation, a child experiences, from the moment of birth, socialization pressures based on her or his sex that, in most cases, incorporate gender roles and stereotypes. From parents, teachers, and peers, and from the social forces of language, play, media, school, religion, and work, the child develops a gender schema and acquires a gender identity. This socialization process occurs through direct reinforcement, modeling, and imitation, as a function of the cognitive development of the child, and as a function of the gender distinctions the child's society makes. Boys, especially, receive intense socialization pressures and are particularly strongly sex-typed.

The consequences of such rigid sex role images are numerous and, as will be shown in Part 4, almost overwhelmingly negative. This does not mean that children should not form a separate and distinct gender identity. Clearly, they need to do so as part of their developing self-identity and for future reproductive functioning, if they so choose. But, as Money and Ehrhardt (1972) note, nature supplies the basic, irreducible elements of sex differences (women can menstruate, gestate, and lactate; men, impregnate). Sharply differing behaviors for the two sexes are simply unnecessary to accomplish the goal.

> Provided that a child grows up to know that sex differences are primarily defined by the reproductive capacity of the sex organ, and to have a positive feeling of pride in his or her own genitalia and their ultimate reproductive use, then it does not much matter whether various childcare, domestic, and vocational activities are or are not interchangeable between mother and father. (Money & Ehrhardt, 1972, p. 14)

What is being argued here is that rigid sex typing is neither necessary nor functional to the individual, to her or his relationships, or to society as a whole. Part 4 will discuss these consequences in detail.

Part 4
Consequences of Gender Stereotypes and Roles

In the preceding chapters, the development of gender stereotypes and roles and their transmittal to successive generations were shown to occur despite little demonstrable support for the existence of the traits depicted by the stereotypes. Except for aggressive behavior and for mathematical and verbal abilities, the sexes differ very little during childhood: indeed, there appear to be more differences *among* members of a sex than *between* the sexes. Yet, once the stereotypes and gender identity are acquired by age 5 or 6, certain gender differences sometimes do emerge. Because the acquisition of gender stereotypes and roles by a child occurs through individual instruction, interpersonal observation, and more generalized social forces, it is important to examine the consequences of gender stereotypes and roles on these three levels—that is, on the personal, interpersonal, and societal levels.

Even if the existence and knowledge of the stereotypes—what females and males are "supposed" to be like—do not change behavior, they can have many consequences. As will be shown in the next five chapters, the effects of the stereotypes are far-reaching and, for the most part, negative for both females and males. Some of these negative consequences are a result of trying to live out the stereotyped gender roles to some degree. Other negative consequences are a result of the inconsistencies between actual behavior and characteristics, on the one hand, and expected sex role behaviors and characteristics on the other. Thus, both gender stereotypes and stereotyped gender roles frequently result in unpleasant consequences.

Chapter 8

Consequences for the Individual

The effects of gender stereotypes and roles can be seen most clearly on the individual level. Gender affects an individual's self-concept, mental health, and physical health. In fact, there is almost no aspect of human functioning that gender does not, in some way, affect.

▲ Self-Concept

A great golf course is like a good woman. Beautiful . . . and a little bit Bitchy.
—advertisement in a golf magazine

This quotation reveals one concept of womanhood. Such conceptions of the gender roles influence an individual's self-concept—the way in which an individual views herself or himself. This concept

incorporates several others: (1) how one thinks of oneself, known by the term *self-esteem*, which itself incorporates self-acceptance and self-regard; (2) an estimate of one's abilities, referred to as *self-confidence;* (3) a sense of control over one's life, including the attributions that one makes, called *locus of control;* and (4) how one sees and evaluates one's bodily self, called *body image.* These four aspects of self-concept—self-esteem, self-confidence, locus of control, and body image—will be examined in some detail in the following pages, with the concept of the ideal self considered as incorporated within self-esteem. Overall, we will find that females have a somewhat more negative self-concept than males.

Because the gender stereotypes suggest a greater number of negative characteristics for females than for males, as seen in this chapter's opening quote, such a finding of lower female self-concept should not be surprising. Yet it would not be correct to assume that all females have a more negative self-concept than all males in all situations. These findings depend on whether individuals are being compared to members of the same sex or the other sex, on methodological variations in measuring the self-concept, and on the task involved. A major variable in the findings concerns which aspect of the self-concept is being tapped—self-esteem, self-confidence, locus of control, or body image.

Self-Esteem

Males tend to score slightly higher than females on measures of global self-esteem (the general degree of negative or positive regard one has for oneself), although the differences tend to be small and do not always appear (R. M. Lerner, Sorell, & Brackney, 1981; Robison-Awana, Kehle, & Jenson, 1986; P. J. Watson, Taylor, & Morris, 1987). Gender differences are more likely to appear among Whites than Blacks, with White females demonstrating the lowest self-esteem (A. H. Jenkins, 1982; J. R. Porter & Washington, 1979; Richman, Clark, & Brown, 1985).

Three factors seem important in understanding the relationship between gender and self-esteem: a person's age, degree of sex typing, and the underlying bases for self-esteem.

Developmental differences A national study of more than 3000 fourth- through tenth-grade students found that gender differences in self-esteem increase once students leave elementary school (American Association of University Women, 1991). Figure 8.1 depicts this trend using a composite measure of

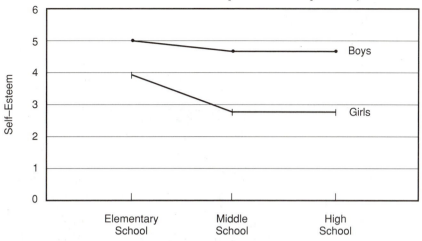

Figure 8.1 The gender gap in self-esteem widens during adolescence (From *Shortchanging Girls, Shortchanging America,* by American Association of University Women. Copyright © 1991 by The Greenberg-Lake Analysis Group. Reprinted by permission.)

self-esteem consisting of such items as "I'm happy the way I am," "I like most things about myself," and "I like the way I look." For boys, self-esteem decreases only slightly after elementary school; for girls, the drop is more dramatic and more sudden. Responses to the single item "I'm happy the way I am" showed the largest gender gap. For girls, the percentage agreeing went from 60% during elementary school to only 37% during middle school and 29% during high school. This decrease in self-esteem was largest for White and Hispanic girls, smallest for Black girls. In contrast, the percentage of boys agreeing went from 67% during elementary school to 56% during middle school to 46% during high school. Longitudinal research confirms this trend of decreasing self-esteem for girls between sixth and seventh grade (Schmich, 1984).

What happens to girls around age 12? Around puberty, girls are confronted with expectations to conform to a more restricted female role (AAUW, 1991; Gilligan, Lyons, & Hanmer, 1990; Gilligan, Ward, & Taylor, 1988). They receive conflicting messages about achievement, assertion, and popularity, wherein attaining the latter may mean sacrificing the former. The fundamental conflict is between staying in touch with their own feelings and beliefs and adjusting to the expectations of others. For many White and Hispanic girls, the solution to this conflict is to discredit their own feelings and thus to experience increased self-doubt. These conflicts are reflected in the decreased relationship between self-image and school achievement for girls

between sixth and seventh grade (L. R. Roberts et al., 1990). In contrast, achievement becomes more congruent with the male gender role during adolescence, which is reflected in the increased positive correlation between self-image and school achievement for boys between sixth and seventh grade. Many Black girls adopt a different solution because of strong family and community support—standing up for their own feelings, at the cost of disagreeing with authorities. The result is less of a decrease in general self-esteem but more distance from teachers and the educational system in general (AAUW, 1991).

The educational system itself may help to enhance the self-esteem of White males while decreasing the self-esteem of females during adolescence. As discussed in the last chapter, much of the typical school environment, including classroom dynamics, seems designed to meet White men's but not women's needs. This may be especially true at coeducational colleges. A study of 80 high school honors graduates found that upon graduation, 21% of the females and 23% of the males believed they were far above average in intelligence (Epperson, 1988). During college, the men's beliefs stayed relatively constant, but the women's changed: only 4% of the women believed that were far above average in their sophomore year, and none believed it in their senior year. In a similar vein, Black women at predominantly White institutions may feel outside the norm by virtue of both their sex and their race. Perhaps this is why the self-esteem of

Black females tends to be higher in predominantly Black or racially integrated schools than it is in predominantly White high schools and colleges (Chester, 1983; Pascarella, Smart, Ethington, & Nettles, 1987).

In general, it appears that life experiences after puberty may serve to lower the self-esteem of many females.

Sex typing   Sex-typing differences overshadow gender differences in predicting self-esteem. In general, the more instrumental ("masculine") characteristics that are present, the higher the individual's self-esteem. Starting as early as the third grade, self-esteem appears correlated mainly with instrumental-agentic traits, especially for females (Alpert-Gillis & Connell, 1989; Cate & Sugawara, 1986; Marsh, Antill, & Cunningham, 1987; Spence & Helmreich, 1978; Whitley, 1983, 1988a). This means that androgynous individuals—those who score high on both instrumental and expressive traits—along with masculine-sex-typed individuals (both male and female) have the highest self-esteem. Feminine-sex-typed individuals, especially females, have significantly lower self-esteem than androgynous and masculine groups. The undifferentiated individual (low on instrumental and expressive traits) appears to have the lowest level of self-esteem. This pattern has been found in other cultures as well (Basow, 1986; H. M. Carlson & Baxter, 1984; Lau, 1989).

Although a number of methodological and situational factors affect the relationship between sex typing and self-esteem (Flaherty & Dusek, 1980; Whitley, 1983), the beneficial effect of agentic-instrumental traits is clear, especially for females and especially as an individual matures. This relationship between agentic-instrumental traits and self-esteem may reflect societal valuing of agentic, as opposed to communal or expressive, qualities. Indeed, most self-esteem measures in fact may be measuring instrumental traits (Whitley, 1988a). That is, what most researchers mean by self-esteem is assertiveness and instrumentality. Stake (1979; Stake & Orlofsky, 1981) found at least two independent types of self-esteem: performance and social self-esteem. Whereas instrumental traits ("masculinity" scores) are significantly correlated with performance self-esteem (what most tests measure), expressive traits ("femininity" scores) are significantly correlated with social self-esteem. As this research suggests, the bases of self-esteem may differ for males and females.

Bases of self-esteem   Global self-esteem is generally measured by standardized paper-and-pencil questionnaires, such as the Coopersmith Self-Esteem Inventory. Generally, two distinct classes of items are included: those tapping *self-acceptance*, the degree to which one accepts oneself as one is, and *self-regard*, the degree to which one actively affirms one's worth and abilities (Deaux, 1976). If females score higher on the former items and males score higher on the latter items, then their total scores will be equal, even though they are responding positively to different items. There is some indirect support for this interpretation.

Females generally make more realistic estimates of their abilities and have lower aspirations than males (Erkut, 1983; Gitelson, Petersen, & Tobin-Richards, 1982; Ilardi & Bridges, 1988; Stake, 1983). Females, from first graders through college students, when given control of how much to pay themselves for some task, consistently pay themselves less than do their male counterparts, at least when no social comparison information is available (Callahan-Levy & Messe, 1979; Major, McFarlin, & Gagnon, 1984). These findings together suggest that females may have higher self-acceptance and lower self-regard than males, at least as related to the abilities measured. Males, in contrast to females, have higher expectations of their abilities and tend to overestimate them. Males also score higher than females on self-rated measures tapping feelings of superiority and narcissism (P. J. Watson et al., 1987). These findings suggest that males have higher self-regard and lower self-acceptance than females. One possible conclusion from these studies is that although the sexes do not seem to differ much in overall level of self-esteem as measured by questionnaires, the bases for self-esteem may be different and may be related to sex roles.

Not only are the components of self-esteem different for males and females, but the sexes also may use different standards against which to evaluate themselves. That is, females may compare themselves to the typical or ideal female, and males may compare themselves to the typical or ideal male, rather than both sexes' comparing themselves to some absolute standard. Research, mainly with college students, generally finds that women's self-descriptions match their ideal descriptions (both are somewhat androgynous) but not their view of a "typical woman," who is pictured as feminine-sex-typed (Deseran & Falk, 1982; D. Scher, 1984; Silvern & Ryan, 1983). In contrast, men's self-descriptions, which also are fairly androgynous, are lower on instrumental traits than considered both typical and ideal. These discrepancies between self and typical or ideal others may lead to lower self-esteem, as seems to happen with some women, or to more defensive self-esteem, as seems to happen with some men.

In general, there is evidence that adolescents who feel successful in the realm they consider appropriate (sociability for many girls; achievement, leadership, and strength for many boys) have high levels of self-esteem (Hodgson & Fischer, 1981; Tucker, 1983). What the person views as central to her or his self-concept is important, and these aspects may vary with gender and with the social context. Recent research with college students shows no gender differences in ratings of the importance of traditionally masculine domains, such as education, physical activities, and work (Blais, Vallerand, Briere, Gagnon, & Pelletier, 1990). However, the traditionally feminine domains, such as friends and relationships, still were rated as more important to women than men.

In summary, males and females may differ in the bases of their self-esteem, with males' self-esteem being more tied to their abilities and performance, and females' self-esteem tied to both performance and social relationships. Males tend to value themselves more than do females, although males also tend to be less self-acceptant. Overall, although males tend to score slightly higher than females on self-esteem questionnaires, the best predictor of self-esteem is instrumental ("masculine") personality traits.

Self-Confidence and Expectations
The research on self-regard, at least as related to task expectancy, is part of a considerable body of research on self-confidence. It is in this area that striking gender differences are observed. Males, on the average, consistently predict, over a wide range of ages and tasks, that they will do better than females predict for themselves (Erkut, 1983; Gitelson et al., 1982; A. R. Gold, Brush, & Sprotzer, 1980; Ryujin & Herrold, 1989; Vollmer, 1986). This gender difference becomes evident after the third grade, and increases during middle school and high school (AAUW, 1991). For example, during elementary school, 55% of the males compared to 45% of the females say that they are "good at a lot of things." During high school, however, the gender gap is wider: whereas 42% of high school males say that they are "good at a lot of things," only 23% of high school females do. The one exception to this

pattern of lower female self-confidence is once again Black females, whose self-confidence appears as high as that of males of both races (E. J. Smith, 1982).

Males' general self-confidence may lead many males to overestimate their abilities. However, it is also likely that it leads them to attempt more tasks. Such attempts give them more opportunities to increase their skill and to be rewarded. Females, who tend to underestimate their ability, may take themselves out of the running, refraining from attempting or continuing with new activities, thereby limiting their world and potential. Women's lower self-confidence also may make them particularly vulnerable to external assessments (Basow, Smither, Rupert, & Collins, 1989; T. Roberts, 1991). It is important to note, however, that although the sexes predict different levels of performance, there is little difference in actual performance. For example, despite predicting that they will receive lower grades than their male classmates, female college students perform similarly or even get better grades (Ryujin & Herrold, 1989). Indeed, in many ways, the aspirational level of boys seems much less tied to situational factors, such as past performance and performance feedback, than does the aspirational level of girls (Monahan, 1983). This may result in very real differences in the way the sexes evaluate current behavior and in the way they derive their expectancies of future performance. For example, males may be unaffected by failure experiences, whereas females may be unaffected by success experiences. This seems to be the case, as will be discussed in the next section.

The sex typing of the task or academic area under consideration is critical in research on self-confidence and expectancies. To the extent that an individual has a strong gender schema, it is likely that that individual will be hesitant to engage in gender-inappropriate behavior. Indeed, low female self-confidence is mainly found on tasks or in academic areas that are labeled masculine or that appear to be male-appropriate, such as math and science (Carr, Thomas, & Mednick, 1985; A. M. Lee, Nelson, & Nelson, 1988; Lenney, 1981; Linn & Hyde, 1989; McMahan, 1982). This pattern appears to be true for Blacks as well as for Whites. Even when grades are the same for females and males in such fields as math and science, females think they are less competent than males think themselves to be. Thus, females take fewer courses in those areas, and we have fewer women in those fields. Even when females continue in those areas, their self-doubt may remain. Many successful women report feeling like "imposters" (Clance, 1985). Even tasks or domains neutral on sex typing show a gender difference in level of aspiration, perhaps because achievement in general is viewed as masculine. However, when a task is labeled feminine or is female-linked, women frequently expect to do as well as men expect to. The fact that they don't expect to do better than males may reflect the "masculine" nature of competency and achievement themselves.

Thus, although females appear to have a set of lowered generalized expectancies about their achievement potential, it would be inaccurate to conclude that females always have less self-confidence than males in all achievement situations. Situational variables, such as specific ability area, availability of performance feedback, and the emphasis on social comparison, all affect females' self-confidence (Kimball & Gray, 1982; Lenney, Gold, & Browning, 1983; Stake, 1983). When the ability tapped relates to "feminine" behaviors (such as social skills) or is simply labeled as feminine, no gender difference in self-confidence in achievement settings generally is found. Similarly, gender differences generally disappear when clear performance feedback is available or when social comparison is not made salient.

Why do women generally have lower self-confidence than men? One reason may be their differential reinforcement history: males may be rewarded for being confident, while females may be rewarded for being modest. Related to this possibility is another one: that expressing low confidence is more acceptable from females than males. There is some evidence to support these hypotheses (J.H. Berg, Stephan, & Dodson, 1981; J.E. Parsons, Ruble, Hodges, & Small, 1976). Furthermore, the male gender role carries with it an aura of superiority and competence; the female gender role does not. The male gender role also emphasizes instrumental qualities, and these qualities are correlated with perceived ability and thereby with self-confidence (Vollmer, 1986). For change to occur, then, we must change the nature of the gender stereotypes and the behavior of socializing agents and forces. Both girls and boys need to develop instrumental traits and learn that they are expected to be competent. No one should learn that boys are "naturally" superior. As we have seen in Part 3, changing these messages is a tall order.

In general, females have lower self-confidence than males, especially in male-oriented situations and activities. This pattern could contribute to a negative self-image in some females.

Locus of Control and Attributions

If you were given a choice between playing a game of luck, such as the slot machine, or a game of skill, such as darts, which would you choose? Deaux, White, and Farris (1975) found that nearly 75% of the men studied chose a game described as requiring skill, whereas only 35% of the women did so. Women preferred games of chance, suggesting that they see themselves as less skilled than men and as having less control over the outcomes of their behavior.

Females, compared to males, seem to have a more external locus of control (that is, females tend not to believe that their own behavior will lead to desirable goals and reinforcements) (S. J. Johnson & Black, 1981; Lefcourt, 1976). Especially during the mid-1970s, when women became aware of the many external constraints (for example, discrimination) on their ability to achieve their goals in the labor force and elsewhere, women of all ages became strikingly more external than men in their locus of control (Doherty & Baldwin, 1985). The generally external locus-of-control orientation of females is associated with feelings of helplessness, with an avoidance of task-oriented behaviors, with fear of success, and with a preference for situations where luck, rather than skill, determines the outcome (Savage, Stearns, & Friedman, 1979).

Ethnicity and socioeconomic status also are related to locus of control, but in complex ways. For example, the higher one's income, the stronger one's internal locus of control, for all groups but Black and Native-American females (Guagnano, Acredolo, Hawkes, Ellyson, & White, 1986). Although Blacks and Hispanics frequently are found to have a more external locus of control than Whites, such differences may be due to differential socioeconomic status. Perhaps because of the double burden of racism and sexism, Black females, in particular, are most likely to construe control as a mixture of both internal and external factors, rather than as one or the other (D. Brown, Fulkerson, Furr, Ware, & Voight, 1984; B. Lykes, Stewart, & LaFrance, 1981).

Internal and external factors are just one way to attribute causality for an event or situation. Research on attribution patterns (the reasons given to explain why something happened) reveal three types of classifications: the cause is seen as due to (1) internal or external factors, (2) controllable or uncontrollable factors, and (3) stable or unstable factors. This classification system is presented in Table 8.1. Many individual and situational variables affect attributional patterns, along with a person's gender. The two most consistent findings with

Table 8.1 Three-way classification of causal attributions

	Internal	*External*
Controllable		
Stable	Effort (stable)	Others help or interfere consistently
Unstable	Effort (temporary state)	Others help or interfere in this situation only
Uncontrollable		
Stable	Ability	Task ease or difficulty
Unstable	Fatigue	Luck

Adapted from Wittig, 1985.

respect to gender differences in causal attributions is that women make stronger luck attributions than men and men make stronger ability attributions than women, regardless of task outcome (Whitley, McHugh, & Frieze, 1986).

There is some suggestion that the sexes may respond differently to success and failure. In general, females, especially Black females, are more likely than males to attribute their successes to external causes, like luck, or to unstable internal causes, like effort. In contrast, females are more likely than males to attribute failures to lack of ability or to another stable cause (D. Brown et al., 1984; Crombie, 1983; Erkut, 1983; Licht, Stader, & Swenson, 1989; Stipek, 1984). For example, when students are asked why they received a 90 on a test, females are more likely than males to say they were lucky, that the test was easy, that the teacher liked them, or that they studied very hard. Males are more likely to say they received such a high grade because they knew the material or because they were smart. In contrast, when a low grade is received, females are more likely to say it was

because they didn't know the material or were "dumb," whereas males are more likely to say it was because the test was unfair, the teacher didn't like them, or they didn't try. These tendencies are evident throughout the school years and become particularly striking in adolescence. Figure 8.2 illustrates gender differences in attribution patterns.

With the type of attribution process just described (attributing success to unstable or external factors and failure to lack of ability), it is very difficult for some females to feel good about themselves, as we have seen in the previous sections. Without taking credit for their successes, females cannot increase their self-confidence. With continued personal blame for their failures, females can only decrease their self-confidence further. Dweck (1986) and colleagues (Dweck, Goetz, & Strauss, 1980) found that girls showed greater discouragement than boys after failure both in a laboratory and in a classroom setting. This discouragement continued despite changes in the task and the teacher. Such a generalized low expectancy may lead to withdrawal from achievement situations, when possible, for many

Figure 8.2 Gender differences in attributional patterns. (CATHY Copyright 1990 Cathy Guisewite. Reprinted with permission of Universal Press Syndicate.)

females. This seems to be the case, especially in math and science. Females attribute their difficulties in such courses to lack of ability, whereas males attribute their difficulties to lack of effort or external factors (see also AAUW, 1991).

Thus, in contrast to the characteristic attribution pattern of many females, the attribution pattern of many males (attributing success to ability and failure to external causes) is very self-protective. In the face of failure, this attribution pattern protects a person's self-confidence and self-image; in response to success, this pattern increases a person's self-confidence and self-image. For example, college competitive swimmers who tended to blame failures on unstable external causes were more likely to do well after a failure experience than swimmers who tended to blame themselves for what went wrong ("Pessimistic Losers," 1988). This was true for both male and female swimmers. However, an ego-protective attribution pattern may have negative consequences, too, by making it difficult to learn from one's mistakes or to admit failure. For example, some researchers have found males, in general, to be more defensive than females following failure in sports events (Croxton & Klonsky, 1982). Another negative consequence of this pattern for many males is their increasing frustration when they discover that they have less ability than they had assumed. A male may unrealistically expect to receive a 90 on a test and be extremely disturbed and frustrated when he receives a 70 instead. This frustration itself may have serious negative consequences, such as increased aggressive behavior.

Yet such an attribution pattern does serve to increase males' continued striving. This, in turn, increases the probability of future success. Given the pressure on males to achieve, their self-protective attitude is facilitative. Furthermore, if males do have an internality bias, attributing most consequences both positive and negative to themselves, as some research suggests (Whitley et al., 1986), then their feeling of control and power is enhanced. Girls deliberately need to be taught to attribute their success to internal and stable causes, such as their ability, rather than to be "modest." Girls likewise need to be taught to attribute their failures to unstable yet controllable causes, like lack of effort. Such attributions can be taught (Dweck, 1975).

Although gender-related attribution patterns frequently are found, especially males' preference for ability attributions and general reluctance to use luck attributions, the size of the gender difference is small in magnitude, and varies with a host of situational, methodological, and personal factors (Travis, Burnett-Doering, & Reid, 1982; Whitley et al., 1986; Wittig, 1985). For example, some research suggests that apparent gender differences in attribution patterns really are gender differences in self-presentational goals, or in gender norms, or occur only among low-expectancy or low-ability students. Gender differences in attributions seem more likely to occur in laboratory settings than when men and women are in the same job (Heimovics & Herman, 1988). Sex typing also affects attributional patterns, but in complex ways (Basow & Medcalf, 1988). High "masculinity" scores seem related to internal locus of control and ability attributions, especially for females and especially under success conditions (Crombie, 1983; S. J. Johnson & Black, 1981; Kapalka & Lachenmeyer, 1988; Welch, Gerrard, & Huston, 1986). Thus, a variety of factors other than gender affect attributional patterns.

In sum, although the findings are complex, males more than females see themselves and their abilities as influential in what happens to them. Females see themselves as less in control of their destinies and more affected by luck. No wonder women prefer games of chance and men prefer games of skill! Such ways of thinking may have negative consequences for individual self-esteem and self-confidence, as we have seen, as well as for achievement behavior and mental and physical health. We will examine these latter two aspects of individual functioning after reviewing another important aspect of the self-concept—body image.

Body Image

Part of our self-concept is our body image, how we perceive and feel about our bodies. This aspect of the self-concept shows marked and consistent gender differences in one area—satisfaction with one's weight. Let's take a closer look at the findings.

On global measures of body satisfaction, females sometimes appear less satisfied than males, although the results are inconsistent (Cash & Brown, 1989; Koff, Rierdan, & Stubbs, 1990; Silberstein, Striegel-Moore, Timko, & Rodin, 1988). More consistent are the findings that females, compared to males, have a more differentiated body image (that is, they distinguish among parts of their body more frequently than males when making judgments). Furthermore, females of all ages are more dissatisfied with their weight than males, leading to lower appearance self-esteem (McCaulay, Mintz, & Glenn, 1988; Mintz & Betz, 1986; Pliner, Chaiken, & Flett, 1990; Silberstein et al., 1988). In particular, females tend to perceive themselves as overweight or slightly overweight, regardless of their actual weight. About 75% of college women report that at least some of the time they are preoccupied with the desire to be thinner (Basow & Schneck, 1983) and nearly half of all high school girls are trying to lose weight ("Nearly half," 1991).

Many males are dissatisfied with their weight, too, but they are equally, or more, likely to want to gain weight rather than to lose it. The discrepancy between a female's perception of her weight and her actual weight also tends to be larger than a male's (McCaulay et al., 1988). Furthermore, a male's dissatisfaction with his weight appears to be less related to his global level of self-esteem than is a female's (Mintz & Betz, 1986). That is, a female's feeling about her weight and her appearance seems more closely tied to her general feeling about herself than is a male's, perhaps because physical attractiveness is more important for a female than for a male (AAUW, 1991; R. Freedman, 1986). Feelings of dissatisfaction with one's weight start during childhood for females and dramatically increase during adolescence (Duncan, Ritter, Dornbusch, Gross, & Carlsmith, 1985; Richards, Boxer, Petersen, & Albrecht, 1990; Striegel-Moore, Silberstein, & Rodin, 1986). Weight dissatisfaction is directly related to sex typing, with feminine-sex-typed females the most dissatisfied and androgynous females the least (Franzoi, 1991).

Given these findings, plus the fact that women are more likely than men to be overweight (Zegman, 1983), it is not surprising that most women want to lose weight. Nor, given the close relationship between dieting and the eating disorders of anorexia nervosa and bulimia, is it surprising that 85 to 95% of such sufferers are women (Polivy & Herman, 1985). Negative body image also is associated with depression, which is two to three times more common in women than men (Mintz & Betz, 1986; Rierdan, Koff, & Stubbs, 1988). Furthermore, women's concern (bordering on obsession) with their weight is not unwarranted. People do seem to judge women by how much they eat. Women who eat lightly are perceived more positively than women who eat a larger meal (Basow & Kobrynowicz, 1990; Chaiken & Pliner, 1987). People also are more likely to judge a woman on the basis of her weight than they are a man, and are more likely to be critical of an overweight woman than an overweight man (Tiggemann & Rothblum, 1988). The media's promotion of an excessively thin standard of female attractiveness may play a role in women's widespread dissatisfaction with their weight (Silverstein et al., 1986).

Most of the research on body image has focused on White subjects. There is evidence, however, that Black females also tend to think they are too heavy, although to a lesser extent than do White females (R. Levinson, Powell, & Steelman, 1986; V. G. Thomas, 1989). Black females also are prone to body image distortion (that is, seeing themselves as heavier than others see them), but again, to a lesser extent than is found among White females. Although eating disorders do occur among Black women (Root, 1990), the incidence of such disorders is lower than it is among White women, perhaps because being overweight appears to be less a negative for Black women than it is for White women (V. G. Thomas & James, 1988).

Although more females than males are dissatisfied with their weight, it's important to remember that many men are dissatisfied with their bodies, too, especially if their physique does not match the male muscular ideal (Mishkind, Rodin, Silberstein, & Striegel-Moore, 1987; Tucker, 1982, 1983). Indeed, there are signs that our culture is increasingly emphasizing both women's and men's bodies, as we saw in our discussion of advertisements in the last chapter. More and more men appear to be exercising, lifting weights, and/or dieting in order to fit the cultural norm. As with women, such behaviors may lead to eating disorders or compulsive exercising. One group at high risk for developing such disorders is gay men. As is the case for heterosexual women, pleasing and attracting men seems to lead to an emphasis on physical attractiveness and thinness (Siever, 1988).

In sum, women are more dissatisfied with their weight than men, and this dissatisfaction negatively affects their body image and overall self-concept.

Discussion

The picture drawn with respect to the consequences of the gender stereotypes for males' and females' self-concepts suggests that females, in general, tend to have a more negative image of themselves than males; they have less self-regard, less self-confidence, less feeling of responsibility for their successes, and more dissatisfaction with their weight. This negative self-concept is offset by their being more self-acceptant than males. Males, on the other hand, tend to have a positive, although somewhat unrealistic, self-image. They have a high regard for themselves, are (over)confident of their abilities, feel responsible for their successes, and attribute their failures to external causes. They are, however, notably less self-acceptant. These varying self-concepts on the part of the sexes have direct consequences for their mental and physical health.

▲ Mental Health

Mental health is a difficult concept to define. We will examine three aspects of mental health—behavioral flexibility, psychological well-being, and mental illness. In all areas, it is again striking how strongly and how deeply the gender stereotypes and roles affect individuals. In general, both those individuals who feel they are not living up to their gender-appropriate stereotypes and those who hold to them most rigidly suffer from the greatest number of psychological problems.

Gender stereotypes, even if we do not conform to them, affect us directly as standards of behavior. They also affect us indirectly through effects on our self-concept. One consequence of the stereotypes can be seen in the flexibility of our behavior—that is, how comfortable and effective we are in engaging in a wide variety of behaviors.

Behavioral Flexibility

How comfortable and effective do you feel in situations requiring assertiveness? Empathy? Mechanical skills? Nurturance? Physical aggression? Social skills? Leadership? Intuition? The wider the range of behaviors one feels comfortable performing, the more flexible one is in one's behavior. To the extent that an individual is traditionally sex-typed, her or his behavioral repertoire will be considerably restricted. In addition, given the nature of the gender roles and gender socialization, males tend to be more behaviorally restricted than females.

As we have seen, boys receive more intense socialization pressures than girls starting in early childhood. Males are both punished and rewarded more than females, particularly with regard to gender-appropriate behaviors. As a result, males from age 3 through adulthood generally are more sex-typed and more reluctant than females to express a preference for, or engage in, other-sex activities. In contrast, females appear less rigidly sex-typed and have greater role flexibility than males, especially during childhood. Even during college, females rate a wider variety of activities as important to them than do males, and these activities cut across traditionally feminine, traditionally masculine, and neutral domains (Blais et al., 1990).

Males' intense socialization causes them a great deal of anxiety over anything vaguely feminine and leads them to deny certain aspects of themselves that have been associated with femininity, particularly feelings of dependence and vulnerability. As Fasteau (1974) notes, this denial sets up a classic scapegoating process whereby what is feared becomes disliked and those who display the feared behavior become hated and ridiculed. That boys often express dislike and contempt for girls is a common observation ("Yech, girls!"), but Fasteau remarks that this early misogyny never really disappears but only becomes more subtle and disguised. This scapegoating obviously will affect relationships between the sexes.

James O'Neil (1981a, 1981b, 1982) has described how men's gender role socialization and the masculine stereotype combine to create a fear of femininity in many males. As illustrated in Figure 8.3, this fear may manifest itself in six major ways: restrictive emotionality, homophobia, socialized power issues, restrictive sexual and affectionate behavior, obsession with achievement and success, and health care problems. The major consequence on the personal level is gender role conflict and strain. O'Neil and colleagues (O'Neil, Helms, Gable, David, & Wrightsman, 1986) have found that masculine-sex-typed men, in particular, experience conflict over success, power, and competition, score high in homophobia, and restrict their affectionate behavior toward men. These findings that intense gender socialization may be related to fear of femininity and gender role strain for some males are supported by other research as well (Babl, 1979; Hartley, 1959; Pleck, 1981b).

Females also are pressured to conform to traditional gender roles, but these pressures don't become intense until early adolescence, as previously noted. The consequences of such pressures are increased behavioral restrictiveness, especially in terms of females' personal environment, and increased gender role conflict. Still, modern gender role norms for women are more flexible than those for men. Indeed, women now may be expected to be and do everything (the Superwoman: career and marriage, nurturant and assertive behaviors). In contrast, the male role still is fairly narrowly defined.

More important than gender in its implications for behavioral flexibility is sex typing. It is mainly sex-typed individuals who are most inflexible behaviorally. In contrast, non-sex-typed individuals, especially androgynous ones, appear to be the most adaptive, flexible, and effective.

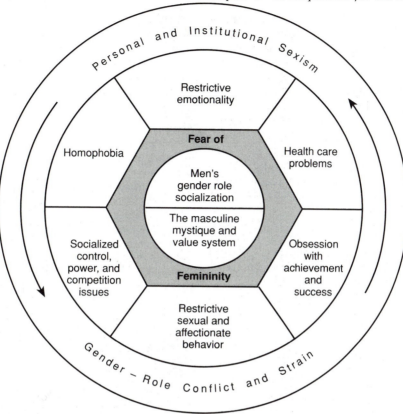

Figure 8.3 Six patterns of gender role conflict and strain in men. From "Patterns of Gender Role Conflict and Strain: The Fear of Femininity in Men's Lives" by J. M. O'Neil, 1981, *Personnel and Guidance Journal, 60,* p. 206. Copyright © 1981 American Association for Counseling and Development. Reprinted with permission.

Most of the research on sex typing is based on Sandra Bem's early work (1974, 1975a, 1975b, 1976, 1977; Bem & Lenney, 1976). In a sequence of studies, Bem and her associates found that masculine-sex-typed males were highly capable of effective performance when it came to instrumental behaviors, such as independence in a conformity situation and assertiveness in a request situation. But when it came to expressive behaviors, they performed poorly. For example, they were less nurturant to a human baby, less playful with a kitten, and less empathic to a lonely student. Feminine-sex-typed females, on the other hand, were the reverse—high in the expressive domain, except with the kitten, and low in the instrumental domain. Cross-sex-typed individuals showed the same pattern of behavioral restrictiveness as their other-sex partners; that is, "masculine" females and "feminine" males had the same behavioral patterns as "masculine" males and "feminine" females, respectively.

It was only the androgynous individuals who were able to perform well in both domains. Thus, both androgynous males and androgynous females could be nurturant and empathic as well as independent and assertive. In the study with the kitten, in fact, androgynous individuals were more nurturant than "feminine" individuals, because the situation required some initiative, which "feminine" individuals were unable to take. Thus, androgynous individuals are the most flexible behaviorally, and strongly sex-typed individuals are the most restricted.

The reason for this restriction in strongly sex-typed individuals seems to be that for them, engaging in cross-sex behavior is very uncomfortable and anxiety-producing. Sex-typed individuals are more likely than cross-sex-typed or androgynous individuals to prefer activities that are gender-appropriate and to resist those that are gender-inappropriate, even when those preferences incur a cost to the individual in terms of loss of offered payment for engaging in gender-inappropriate tasks (Bem & Lenney, 1976). For example, when sex-typed males were asked to choose between being photographed preparing a baby bottle for 4 cents and oiling a hinge for 2 cents, they were more likely to choose the oiling task than were androgynous or feminine-sex-typed males. Additionally, when sex-typed individuals did engage in cross-sex activity, they experienced discomfort and negative feelings about themselves. If male participants in the previous example did perform the bottle task, they said they felt uncomfortable and negative doing so more than did either the androgynous or feminine-sex-typed males.

These results are similar to those found with respect to achievement behavior and fear of success (see Chapter 3). Individuals, females and males, refrain from engaging in cross-sex activities or functions because they fear negative consequences from so doing. And it is primarily sex-typed individuals who appear concerned about the negative consequences. Androgynous individuals either do not expect such negative consequences or are not concerned about them. They seem the most balanced of all groups, with the most freedom and flexibility of behavior.

Androgyny is not a guarantee of behavioral flexibility, however. First, the effect of androgyny may differ for males and females (Flaherty & Dusek, 1980; Heilbrun, 1984; Wiggins & Holzmuller, 1978, 1981). For example, androgynous females may be more flexible and well adjusted than androgynous males. Second, people with high instrumental-agentic scores (masculine-sex-typed and androgynous individuals) may appear the most comfortable in a variety of situations or the most adaptive, perhaps because they are highest in self-esteem (Helmreich, Spence, & Holahan, 1979; W. H. Jones, Chernovetz, & Hansson, 1978). Overall, although androgyny may not be the only adaptive response mode, it does contribute to behavioral flexibility across both instrumental and expressive domains (Jose & McCarthy, 1988; Motowidlo, 1982; M. S. White, 1979). In terms of gender schema theory (S. L. Bem, 1985), androgynous individuals use gender less often than do sex-typed persons in processing information about the world around them. Therefore, the behavior of androgynous persons is less a function of the sex typing of a behavior or a situation than is the behavior of sex-typed persons.

In general, sex-typed individuals are more behaviorally restricted than androgynous individuals, and males tend to hold to the gender stereotypes even more rigidly than females. Behavioral restriction,

whatever the cause, hinders one in developing the skills needed to lead a full life—that is, both expressive and instrumental skills. Such restriction for many sex-typed males and females affects their emotional and physical well-being as well.

Psychological Well-Being
Mental health is often viewed as proper adjustment. A strongly prevailing assumption holds that individuals will be better off if they conform to their gender role (S. L. Bem, 1976). Thus, men who are doctors are considered, a priori, better adjusted than men who are nurses. The latter group, even if not considered disturbed, will certainly have their sexual identity questioned ("Is he gay?"). This view can be classified as the *traditional congruence model* of mental health. Two other models of mental health have been proposed as well: the *masculinity model*, which postulates that mental health is maximized when an individual possesses a high number of instrumental traits; and the *androgyny model*, which postulates that mental health is maximized when an individual incorporates a high number of both instrumental and expressive traits.

Research to date is fairly consistent in finding that gender conformity is not positively related to mental health, especially for females (Orlofsky & O'Heron, 1987; Roos & Cohen, 1987; Taylor & Hall, 1982; Whitley, 1984). Not only is the traditional congruence model of mental health not supported, but findings also suggest that gender conformity may be negatively related to good adjustment, especially for females. Support for the other two hypotheses is stronger, with more research supporting the masculinity model than the androgyny model, especially for males. Let's look more closely at these findings, since the most applicable model seems to vary as a function of an individual's gender.

The traditional congruence model Expressive (traditionally feminine) personality traits either are not associated with most measures of adjustment (DeGregorio & Carver, 1980; B. C. Long, 1989; Whitley, 1984) or the association is negative; that is, the higher the "femininity" score, the higher the anxiety, the lower the self-esteem, and the lower the social acceptance. Particular aspects of the feminine stereotype (verbal passive-aggressiveness and excessive conformity) have been found to be related negatively to self-esteem (Spence, Helmreich, & Holahan, 1979). However, strong expressive characteristics are associated with fewer adjustment problems involving interpersonal functioning for both women and men (Lubinski et al., 1983; F. D. Payne, 1987). In general, being traditionally sex-typed is not associated with the highest levels of overall adjustment for women.

Behaviorally as well, role conformity for women is either irrelevant or disadvantageous to women's well-being. For example, although women's traditional role has been home-oriented (wife and mother), women who work outside the home frequently are psychologically healthier and happier than noncareer women (Baruch, et al., 1983; Warr & Parry, 1982). Even if not better adjusted, employed women clearly are not more poorly adjusted than home-oriented women (Helson & Picano, 1990; Repetti, Matthews, & Waldron, 1989). Research since 1974 consistently shows a strong relationship between job satisfaction and life satisfaction for both men and women, both Black and White (Crohan, Antonucci, Adelmann, & Coleman, 1989; Tait, Padgett, & Baldwin, 1989).

These results do not mean that feminine-sex-typed or nonemployed women necessarily are poorly adjusted. The qualitative aspects of a woman's roles (wife, mother, and/or worker) are more predictive of her psychological well-being than the number of roles she holds (Baruch & Barnett, 1986b; Helson, Elliott, & Leigh, 1990; Kibria, Barnett, Baruch, & Pleck, 1990). (Multiple roles will also be discussed in Chapters 9 and 10.) Much has to do with an individual woman's expectations for herself with respect to gender conformity. Those women for whom gender roles are salient may feel less stress and strain when they conform than when they don't (Garnets & Pleck, 1979). What is crucial for adjustment may be consistency between attitude and behavior, not attitude or sex typing per se. For example, women who are career-oriented appear happier with themselves and their lives when they are employed full-time than when they are not employed or are employed part-time (Pietromonaco, Manis, & Markus, 1987; Repetti et al., 1989). In contrast, employment is not associated with the well-being of women who are not career-oriented.

The importance of living up to social expectations and social roles may partially explain the finding that women report slightly greater happiness than men (Gove & Zeiss, 1987). Based on a meta-analysis of 93 studies since 1963, Wood, Rhodes, and Whelan (1989) found that although men gave slightly higher ratings on general measures of well-being, women gave slightly higher ratings on measures of life satisfaction and happiness. The differences, however, are very small ($d = .03–.09$), and must be viewed in the context of findings that women, especially married women, also report greater negative feelings than men, as we will see in the next section. Thus, women simply may be more emotionally sensitive and expressive than men, as prescribed by the female gender role. Furthermore, some studies do find less satisfaction with life among women than men (Borges, Levine, & Dutton, 1984; C. S. Morgan, 1980).

The components of psychological well-being and life satisfaction are very similar for women and men, especially since the mid-1970s (Bryant & Veroff, 1982; C. S. Morgan, 1980). For both sexes, work satisfaction, marital/family satisfaction, and personal competence are very important. Whereas traditional male gender socialization is geared toward satisfying all three of the major components of life satisfaction, traditional female gender socialization is geared toward satisfying only one—the marital/family component. Thus, although marriage is positively related to psychological well-being for both men and women, Blacks and Whites (Broman, 1991; Crohan et al., 1989; Glenn & Weaver, 1988; Gove & Zeiss, 1987; Haring-Hidore, Stock, Okun, & Witter, 1985), marriage alone may not be sufficient. Women may experience dissatisfaction if they don't attain all three goals, and role strain if they do. Interestingly, the positive relationship between marriage and subjective well-being or happiness has decreased since 1972, especially for married females. We may be at a point in time when marriage is less beneficial for women than for men. Data on mental illness, discussed in the next section, support this hypothesis.

The masculinity model   The relationship between masculine sex typing and adjustment is more consistent and more positive for both sexes than is the relationship between feminine sex typing and adjustment. Possessing instrumental (traditionally masculine) traits is strongly associated with effective psychological functioning. We already have seen that instrumental qualities are strongly associated with high self-esteem. Now we see that high "masculinity" is strongly and positively correlated with high social competence, personal efficacy, and emotional well-being, as well as more problem-focused and preventive coping strategies. High "masculinity" is negatively correlated with feelings of anxiety, strain, depression, neuroticism, work impairment, achievement conflicts, stress symptoms, and dissatisfaction with current life circumstances (Della Selva & Dusek, 1984; Frank, McLaughlin, & Crusco, 1984; B. C. Long, 1989; Lubinski et al., 1983; Taylor & Hall, 1982; Whitley, 1984; Zeldow, Clark, & Daugherty, 1985). Strong instrumental traits, especially when combined with social support, seem to function as a buffer against stress (Roos & Cohen, 1987). Not all aspects of the masculine stereotype are related to healthy adjustment, however. Such negative "masculine" characteristics as arrogance, cynicism, and egocentrism are strongly and positively correlated with the occurrence of acting-out, sociopathic behaviors (Spence et al., 1979).

The androgyny model   Thus, instrumental personality traits are an important factor in psychological well-being. Combining instrumental traits with expressive ones (as occurs in androgynous individuals) may be particularly advantageous, but research results are less consistent. Although androgynous and masculine-sex-typed individuals generally appear to be better adjusted (have higher self-esteem, make fewer negative self-statements, show higher levels of psychosocial development, and exhibit more stable, nonneurotic personalities) than feminine-sex-typed and undifferentiated individuals, it is not always the case that androgynous individuals are better adjusted than masculine-sex-typed ones (Burchardt & Serbin, 1982; Della Selva & Dusek, 1984; Markstrom-Adams, 1989; Tzuriel, 1984). When androgynous individuals score highly on measures of adjustment, the results seem primarily due to strong instrumental traits, rather than to anything unique about combining instrumental and expressive characteristics (A. C. Baldwin et al., 1986; J. A. Hall & Taylor, 1985; Lubinski et al., 1983; Zeldow et al., 1985).

The relationship between androgyny and measures of adjustment may differ for males and females. Androgynous females have been found to be more likely than androgynous males to be competent socially, to have strong cognitive defenses, to have little tolerance for ambiguity, to blend expressive and instrumental behaviors, and to rate themselves as adjusted and happy (Burchardt & Serbin, 1982; Heilbrun, 1981, 1984; Shaw, 1982). Perhaps the combination of instrumental and expressive characteristics is more beneficial for females than males because instrumental traits are more socially valued than expressive traits. Males, whose gender is socially valued, may have less to gain from the addition of expressive traits, at least using traditional measures of adjustment, which may be heavily weighted toward instrumental functioning (C. J. Mills & Bohannon, 1983).

Measurement issues are particularly important in this area, since most measures of psychological well-being rely on self-reports. Furthermore, definitions of psychological well-being or adjustment vary tremendously. In the research just cited, well-being has been defined in terms of the presence of self-esteem, satisfaction, and happiness, and the absence of depression, anxiety, conflicts, stress, and so on. Not all these measures are intercorrelated. As Bryant and Veroff (1982) have demonstrated, three related but separate factors appear to be involved in psychological well-being: happiness or unhappiness (positive evaluation), strain or lack of anxiety (negative evaluation), and personal adequacy or inadequacy (competence). The types of thoughts or activities that contribute to such feelings may differ as a function of an individual's sex as well as social or historical circumstances. Thus, in a time period when attitudes toward sex roles are in flux, the relationships among sex typing, sex role conformity, and psychological well-being also are likely to be unstable.

In conclusion, instrumental traits, whether by themselves or in conjunction with expressive traits, appear to be associated most strongly with good adjustment; undifferentiated sex typing, with poor adjustment; and feminine sex typing, somewhere between the first and second groups. Thus, the belief that a high level of gender-appropriate traits facilitates a person's general psychological or social adjustment is not supported, at least for females. This is even more strikingly evident when more serious emotional problems are examined.

Mental Illness

Since Phyllis Chesler's ground-breaking book *Women and Madness* was published in 1972, research has proliferated on the relationship between gender and psychopathology (see, for example, Franks & Rothblum, 1983; Widom, 1984). Although mental disorders usually are multidetermined, reflecting various combinations of biological, psychological, and social factors, gender-related factors do appear to contribute to a number of disorders. One way they contribute is in the popular belief that women generally are more mentally disturbed than men. Certainly when statistics are examined, that's the picture that appears, at least until recently.

Numerous studies using data from community surveys, first admissions to psychiatric hospitals, psychiatric care in general hospitals, psychiatric outpatient care, private outpatient psychiatric care, and psychiatric illnesses in the practice of general physicians have shown that from 1950 to 1980, more women than men were likely to be mental patients, to experience nervous breakdowns, to suffer from depression, nervousness, insomnia, and nightmares, and to be in psychotherapy (Gove, 1979, 1980; Russo, 1990; Russo & Sobel, 1981). Although minority women are less likely than White women to suffer from depressive disorders, the finding of more female than male users of mental health services occurs across all ethnic groups.

However, a blanket statement that females are more mentally disturbed than males would be incorrect. It is only with regard to certain disorders and certain populations that the female incidence rate is higher than that of males. Table 8.2 summarizes the disorders in which gender differences in incidence have been found, based on the latest diagnostic

Table 8.2 Mental disorders that occur more frequently in one sex, by age of onset

Male	Female
Childhood	
1. Mental retardation (1.5 times more frequent)	1. Avoidant disorder
2. Autism (3 to 4 times more)	2. Elective mutism
3. Other pervasive developmental disorder	3. Dream anxiety disorder
4. Specific developmental disorder (reading, language) (2 to 4 times more)	
5. Attention deficit hyperactivity disorder (3 to 9 times more)	
6. Conduct disorder (4 times more)	
7. Gender identity disorder	
8. Tourette's disorder (3 times more)	
9. Transient tic disorder (3 times more)	
10. Functional encopresis	
11. Functional enuresis	
12. Stuttering (3 times more)	
13. Sleep terror disorder	
14. Sleepwalking	
15. Pyromania	
Adolescence	
16. Transsexualism	4. Anorexia nervosa (more than 9 times more)
17. Gender identity disorder, nontranssexual	5. Bulimia (9 times more)
	6. Multiple personality (3 to 9 times more)
Adulthood	
18. Multi-infarct dementia	7. Delusional (paranoid) disorder
19. Alcohol hallucinosis (4 times more)	8. Induced psychotic disorder
20. Substance abuse disorder	9. Depressive disorders (2 times more)
21. Social phobia	10. Dysthymia
22. Paraphilias	11. Panic disorder with agoraphobia (2 times more)
23. Factitious disorder with physical symptoms	12. Agoraphobia
24. Factitious disorder with psychological symptoms	13. Simple phobia
25. Intermittent explosive disorder	14. Somatization disorder
26. Pathological gambling	15. Somatoform pain disorder (3 times more)
27. Paranoid personality disorder	16. Hypoactive sexual desire
28. Antisocial personality disorder	17. Inhibited orgasm
29. Obsessive compulsive personality disorder	18. Borderline personality disorder
	19. Histrionic personality disorder
	20. Dependent personality disorder

Information derived from the DSM-III-R (American Psychiatric Association, 1987).

system, the *Diagnostic and Statistical Manual*, 3rd edition—revised (DSM-III-R), issued by the American Psychiatric Association in 1987. As can be seen in this table, when the entire spectrum of psychiatric disorders is examined across the life span, males actually suffer from more disorders than females. The greatest differential occurs during childhood, but even among adults, a number of disorders are more commonly found among men than among women—for example, certain personality disorders, alcoholism, and substance abuse disorders. These disorders often are considered developmental disorders or forms of social deviance rather than mental illness per se. Thus, even though males suffer from more disorders than females, they are less likely to be viewed as mentally ill.

Utilization of services also differs for females and males, possibly as a result of differential diagnoses. For example, although women predominate as inpatients in private mental hospitals and nonfederal general hospitals, men predominate as inpatients in state and county mental hospitals and Veterans Administration hospitals (Rosenstein, Steadman, Milazzo-Sayre, 1985; Rosenstein, Steadman, Milazzo-Sayre, MacAskill, & Manderscheid, 1986; Rosenstein, Steadman, MacAskill, & Manderscheid, 1987; Russo, 1990). Because private mental hospitals are outnumbered by other types of inpatient facilities, there actually were more male than female inpatients in 1980, when the last national survey was taken. Compared to female inpatients, male inpatients tend to be younger and are more likely to receive diagnoses of alcohol- or drug-related disorders; women are more likely than men to receive diagnoses of affective disorders. Thus, the finding of greater mental disturbance in women than men is not generally true when only inpatient statistics are examined.

Another factor that affects statistics on mental health is marital status (Gove, 1972; Rosenstein & Milazzo-Sayre, 1981; E. Walker, Bettes, Kain, & Harvey, 1985). The finding of greater mental disturbance in women than men is limited to married women compared to married men. When single (never married, divorced, widowed) individuals are compared, it is the single male who is more likely to be disturbed. For example, Table 8.3 shows the percentage of inpatients of each sex as a function of their marital status. Although males outnumber females as inpatients, a greater percentage of female than male inpatients are married, whereas a greater pecentage of male than female inpatients have never been married. (A greater percentage of

Table 8.3 The marital status of mental hospital (state and county, private and veterans administration) inpatients, 1980 (in percentages)

	Male	*Female*
Married	24.9	32.1
Never married	43.6	32.1
Divorced/separated	28.8	25.3
Widowed	2.7	10.4

Adapted from Rosenstein et al., 1985, 1986, 1987.

women inpatients also are widowed compared to men, but this is a function of women inpatients' older age and the higher incidence of widows than widowers in the general population.) The pattern for suicide attempts and completions is similar. When single individuals are compared to married ones, it is single men who are most suicidal (D. Lester, 1984). In general, however, married people of both sexes tend to have lower rates of mental illness than unmarried people (E. Walker et al., 1985).

A number of explanations are possible for why the sexes differ in the types of disorders they develop and for why married women appear to have higher rates of mental illness than married men. The differences may be due to sex bias, biological factors, gender roles, or role strain. Each explanation will be examined in turn.

Sex bias A closer look at our mental health system reveals sex biases in our definitions of mental health, our diagnostic categories, and our treatment approaches.

A double standard of mental health exists with respect to women and men, although it is not as prominent now as it was 20 years ago. In 1970, Inge Broverman and associates (Broverman, Broverman, Clarkson, Rosenkrantz, & Vogel, 1970) found that the 79 male and female psychologists, psychiatrists, and social workers they questioned made clear-cut distinctions between a healthy man and a healthy woman. The healthy woman, according to the participants in the study, is more emotional, more submissive, more concerned with her appearance, less independent, less aggressive, and less competitive than the healthy man. Even more disturbing than this negative assessment of females, however, is the finding that the behavior and characteristics judged healthy for an adult, sex unspecified, were similar to those judged healthy for an adult male but not for an adult female. Thus, mental health workers saw women as having more negative and less healthy characteristics than a typical adult—that is, a man—a clear example of a male-centered bias.

More recent research suggests that much of this apparent sex bias in expressed attitudes of clinicians has disappeared, especially in the case of female therapists (C. V. Davidson & Abramowitz, 1980; R. D. Phillips & Gilroy, 1985; Poole & Tapley, 1988). Therapists today no longer say that the characteristics of a healthy female and a healthy male are very different from each other. This reduction in overt stereotyping may be a result of greater awareness of this issue, or of improved methodology in the research (see, for example, Widiger & Settle, 1987). Yet some stereotyping still goes on, to the disparagement of females (Abramowitz & Herrera, 1981; Brodsky & Hare-Mustin, 1980; Hansen & Reekie, 1990; Teri, 1982).

This double standard of mental health, paralleling as it does societal gender stereotypes, is probably a reflection of an adjustment standard of mental health. In other words, a woman is seen as healthy if she is more emotional and submissive because that is what society has termed acceptable for females. Using this approach, an independent, assertive woman might be labeled deviant. Similarly, a man who stays home to care for his children may be seen as more disturbed than a man employed as an engineer (J. Robertson & Fitzgerald, 1990). Not only do clinicians holding an adjustment standard of mental health foster conformity and restrict the choices open to women and men, but they also may foster emotional problems. For example, sex-typed women are low in instrumental-active traits, which are important for high self-esteem and psychological well-being.

A double standard with respect to referrals may work against either females or males, depending upon whose problems go unrecognized and therefore untreated, or whose problems are seen as internal and personal or emotional as opposed to external and situational. For example, a recent epidemiological study of reading disability in second- and third-grade children found no gender difference in the prevalence of this disability when children were assessed by the researchers (Shaywitz, Shaywitz, Fletcher, & Escobar, 1990). However, school referral reports underestimated the prevalence of reading disability in girls, leading to a referral rate two to four times greater for boys than for girls. The cause of this referral bias may be teachers' expectations that boys have more reading problems than girls, or the possibility that teachers simply pay more attention to boys than

girls, or the fact that girls with reading problems tend to be less problematic behaviorally than boys with reading problems. Whatever the cause, the result is that girls with reading disability are not receiving needed corrective treatment. Conversely, females are more likely than males to be diagnosed as depressed, perhaps because depression in females is more expected and more likely to be recognized.

Because women are viewed as more emotional than men, and therefore as more vulnerable to emotional disorders, women may be encouraged and men discouraged from seeking psychological treatment for problems. For example, when people break the law, women (and Whites) are more likely to be referred to mental health services than men (and members of minority groups) (Steadman, Rosenstein, MacAskill, & Manderscheid, 1988). Male and minority group offenders may be viewed as more responsible for their deviant behavior than women and Whites. Thus, a woman and a man with the same type of behavioral problem may wind up in two different systems: the mental health system for women, the criminal justice system for men.

The categories used for diagnosing emotional problems have been strongly criticized for reflecting gender bias (Hare-Mustin, 1983; M. Kaplan, 1983; Landrine, 1989; Wakefield, 1987). The most widely used diagnostic system in the United States, the DSM-III-R, describes as personality disorders certain behavioral syndromes that are part of the female gender stereotype. For example, a woman who displays exaggerated emotions, irrational outbursts, overreactions to minor events, and vain, demanding, dependent, and helpless characteristics is likely to be classified as suffering from a histrionic personality disorder (formerly called hysterical personality). A constellation of other "feminine" traits may lead to a diagnosis of a dependent personality disorder. Thus, conforming to the female gender stereotype may lead to a psychiatric label, whereas there is no label for those who conform to the male gender stereotype. It should be noted that exaggerated "masculine" characteristics might lead to a label, such as antisocial or paranoid personality disorder. But in the case of females, the stereotypic traits or behaviors need not be exaggerated to lead to a psychiatric label.

The issue of gender bias in labeling has become very salient as the American Psychiatric Association develops DSM-IV. New categories of personality disorders have been proposed that are even more gender-linked than current ones. For example, "self-defeating personality disorder" might be the diagnosis for women who stay in abusive relationships. Such labeling focuses on pathology in the individual woman and ignores evidence that abusive situations can give rise to certain traits and behaviors in victims of chronic abuse (see Chapter 12). Thus, the diagnostic system may fail to distinguish between social deviance and true mental disorders, and therefore may lead to distorted patterns of incidence of mental disorders, such as found in Table 8.2. Although clinical diagnoses can still be useful when a problem has its roots in social factors (J. B. W. Williams & Spitzer, 1983), there is something wrong if socializing girls to conform to the female gender stereotype means they are being socialized into psychiatric categories (see also Caplan & Gans, 1991; Gelfond, 1991).

The way in which stereotypic female qualities tend to be pathologized is nowhere as clear as in the recent trend to label supportive empathic behavior as a sign of *codependency*, an addictive "disease" (Kaminer, 1990; H. G. Lerner, 1990; Tallen, 1990). Originally referring to the problems of people married to alcoholics, it now applies to any "overfocus" on another person, especially if such focusing leads to neglecting one's own needs. Given female socialization to focus on others more than the self, it is hardly surprising that most "codependents" are women, nor that most women could be labeled as codependent. The problem with the concept of codependency is that it is too broad and focuses on a "problem" within the individual, rather than on cultural and social norms. The result is that once again women are viewed as less mentally healthy than men.

Indeed, the mental health system seems set up for women. As Chesler (1972) and others (Hare-Mustin, 1983; Tennov, 1975) have noted, psychology and psychotherapy have traditionally served to keep women in their (second) place. According to Chesler, more women than men are in psychotherapy because psychotherapy is one of the two institutions socially approved for middle-class women; the other socially approved institution is marriage. Both institutions allow a woman to express and diffuse her feelings by experiencing them as a form of emotional illness. If a woman is married and her husband treats her well and provides for her (and for the children), then any feelings of dissatisfaction may be taken as a sign of some emotional problem on her part ("Why aren't you happy when you have everything a woman should want? There must be something wrong with you"). Both institutions also isolate women from each other and

emphasize individual, rather than social, solutions to problems (the problem is in you, rather than in society or your husband or marriage itself). Even family therapy traditionally has put the blame on the wife/mother for any problems in the family (see Luepnitz, 1988). Thus, more married women than married men may receive psychological treatment because marriage and psychotherapy fit so well together for women.

Thus, some groups of women may be drawn or referred to mental health treatment, which may serve to perpetuate their problems. Indeed, women are admitted to mental hospitals for less severe problems than men (Mowbray & Chamberlain, 1986). In contrast, the mental health needs of other groups of women appear to be severely neglected. The recent reports of the National Coalition for Women's Mental Health and the National Institute of Mental Health (A. Eichler & Parron, 1987; Russo, 1990) have targeted diagnosis and treatment of mental disorders, and mental health issues related to aging, violence, multiple roles, and poverty as priority areas for research with respect to women's mental health. Women are affected much more than men by all these mental health issues (aging, violence, multiple roles, and poverty), which may contribute to women's appearing more frequently than men in mental health statistics. The effect of ethnicity on mental health statistics and services also needs to be more closely researched (see, for example, Amaro & Russo, 1987).

When women enter the mental health system, they are more likely than their male counterparts to receive medication. Two-thirds of the prescriptions for psychotropic drugs are written for women, and there is concern that these drugs are overprescribed, perhaps because women are seen as more "dependent" or because acting-out behavior in women is less acceptable than is such behavior in men (McGrath, Keita, Strickland, & Russo, 1990). It therefore is not surprising that women are the major abusers of prescription drugs, such as Valium, although men predominate as abusers of other substances (Fidell, 1981; Verbrugge, 1982).

In sum, sex bias may account for the fact that females have higher rates of some emotional disturbances than males: a number of diagnostic categories may be biased against women, women may be diagnosed as disturbed even if they show "healthy adult" behaviors, and women are referred to the mental health system more than men. Yet although sex bias may account for some gender differences in incidence of disorders, it does not fully account for all the differences. Other explanations also must be examined.

Biology   As with any gender difference, people often suspect some biological factor involved. Yet there is no support for the hypothesis that women may be biologically more susceptible to mental problems than men, since single men have more mental health problems than single women. Perhaps the explanation is that the more biologically susceptible female and the less biologically susceptible male get married, while their "healthier" sisters and "sicker" brothers remain single either out of choice or because of inability to find a mate. Divorced and widowed individuals, then, having once been married, would be expected to have rates of mental illness similar to their married counterparts. This again is not the case. Divorced and widowed women have lower rates of mental illness than divorced and widowed men. Thus, a biological explanation cannot account for the data on mental illness and marital status.

Biological explanations are only slightly more useful in explaining the gender difference in incidence of mental disorders. In examining Table 8.2, we can infer that a number of problems more commonly found in males may have a biological component: mental retardation, attention deficit disorders, autism, various developmental disorders, multiple infarct dementia, alcohol hallucinosis, and antisocial personality disorders. As discussed in Chapter 2, males appear more biologically susceptible than females from birth, and this factor may be involved in some of the childhood disorders just mentioned. Gove (1985) suggests that sex differences in physical strength, energy, and drive during adolescence and young adulthood may lead to differential rates of social deviancy.

Biological factors may play a role in major depressive episodes, more commonly found in females after puberty. In particular, low levels of estrogen and/or progesterone, characteristic of the premenstrual, postpartum, and menopausal periods of a woman's life, have been suggested as causal agents of depression. Yet careful research on women during these time periods has not supported a purely biological hypothesis (McGrath et al., 1990; Nolen-Hoeksema, 1987, 1990). Although some women do seem to be extremely sensitive to hormonal fluctuations, most women are not. A review of the research on the premenstrual syndrome in Chapter 2 revealed widespread methodological problems and large individual differences. With

respect to postpartum depression, the best predictor is antepartum depression (that is, women who are depressed before and during pregnancy are most likely to be depressed after birth). The next best predictors are lack of employment plans and low levels of expressive-nurturant traits (Pfost, Lum, & Stevens, 1989). Most women do not develop a major depressive disorder after giving birth, although from 30 to 60% may have some depressive symptoms during the first day, better called "the blues" than depression (Nolen-Hoeksema, 1987, 1990; O'Hara, Zekoski, Philipps, & Wright, 1990). With respect to menopause, the biological evidence is even weaker. A major epidemiological study of 2500 randomly selected women between the ages of 45 and 55 revealed no relationship between natural menopause and depression (McKinlay, McKinlay, & Avis, 1989; see also Lennon, 1987). Three-quarters of the women say they are either relieved or have no feelings at all about menopause. Although 15% of the women were depressed at least occasionally, the best predictor was lack of social support. Further weakening a biological explanation of depression is the finding that among the Amish, an isolated group living an Old World lifestyle, no gender difference in affective disorders occurs (Egeland & Hosteller, 1983).

Whatever role biological factors play in the incidence of various mental disorders, they are unlikely to be sufficient to account for the differential pattern by sex. Those disorders that have the strongest biological bases, schizophrenia and bipolar depression, are just those disorders in which a gender difference in incidence is not found, at least among adults.

Gender roles   Another explanation for the mental health statistics centers on the definitions of male- and female-appropriate behavior—that is, the gender roles. Perhaps gender roles make certain types of disorders more likely in one sex than the other. Perhaps more females than males act emotionally disturbed or seek treatment because it is more acceptable that they do so. Perhaps females are more likely to be diagnosed as emotionally disturbed because that is part of our stereotype of femininity. All these interpretations have received some support. Although they, too, fail to account for the data on marital status, they do shed light on the gender difference in patterns of mental disorders.

The nature of the two gender roles may contribute directly to the different patterns of disorders found in the two sexes, as shown in Table 8.2. Since the *female gender role* emphasizes relationships and physical appearance and such traits as expressiveness and emotional sensitivity, it is not surprising that females are more prone than males to develop dependent and histrionic personality disorders, eating disorders, certain anxiety disorders, and depression. The most common mental disorders found in women are phobias and depressive disorders (Taube & Barrett, 1985). Earlier in this chapter, we saw how women are more likely than men to want to be thinner, a condition that makes them vulnerable to the development of eating disorders. In Chapter 3, we saw that females are more willing than males to admit fears, and such admissions are more acceptable in females than males. Women also are socialized to be fearful, especially of strange situations and men. Such differences in social acceptability of fearfulness may contribute to the higher incidence of phobias and anxiety disorders in women (Fodor, 1983; Gelfond, 1991; Wolfe, 1984).

Depression is particularly linked to the female gender role, and one out of every four women experiences clinical depression during her life (McGrath et al., 1990). In fact, descriptions of a depressed person are viewed by college students as identical to their stereotypes of a married woman (Landrine, 1988). Factors that have been linked to depression—learned helplessness (Cox & Radloff, 1984); making external and unstable attributions in success situations and internal, stable, and global attributions in failure situations (Abramson, Seligman, & Teasdale, 1978; Nolen-Hoeksema, Girgus, & Seligman, 1986); negative attitudes toward one's body (Mintz & Betz, 1986); attachment bonding (Weissman & Klerman, 1977); self-criticism and turning anger inward (Frank, McLaughlin, & Crusco, 1984)—all have been found to be more common in women than in men. In fact, as we have seen, these qualities are actually encouraged in women. For example, women are encouraged to be modest about their successes and abilities, to refrain from overt expressions of anger (it's not "ladylike"), to become strongly attached to another person, to dislike their bodies, and to act or be helpless (since active-instrumental traits are seen as masculine).

Women's lives add to their risk of being depressed. Certain demographic factors (being unemployed, being poor, holding a low-status job, having less education, being unmarried) and certain life factors (being a victim of sexual abuse, sex discrimination, and sexual harassment, being unhappily married) all are major predictors of depression and all occur more in women than men (Golding, 1988; McGrath et al., 1990). Ethnic minority women are particularly affected by these factors. Depression is greatest among young low-income women with young children, particularly those who are divorced or separated, or unemployed. These women may be the most prone to feelings of helplessness and disruptions of attachment. Given all the links between the female gender role and depression, it is no wonder that women are twice as likely as men to suffer from this disorder.

Since the *male gender role* emphasizes autonomy and such traits as dominance, aggressiveness, and activity, it is not surprising that men are more prone than women to acting-out disorders, such as substance abuse, pathological gambling, pyromania (fire setting), and intermittent explosive disorders. Men also are more likely to have an antisocial personality disorder, characterized by aggressive and impulsive behaviors. The most common mental disorders found in men are alcohol and drug abuse or dependence (Taube & Barrett, 1985).

Men cope with their feelings differently from women, and are more likely to externalize their feelings, such as by becoming physically aggressive (Frank et al., 1984; Stapley & Haviland, 1989), or by distracting themselves from their feelings, such as by engaging in a variety of activities (Nolen-Hoeksema, 1987, 1990). This is particularly the case with depressed feelings. When depressed, college women are more likely than men to cry, eat, smoke cigarettes, become irritable, lack confidence, and confront their feelings, whereas college men are more likely than women to become aggressive, express somatic concerns, engage in sexual behaviors, and withdraw socially (Chino & Funabiki, 1984; Oliver & Toner, 1990; Padesky & Hammen, 1981). Even among patients hospitalized for depression, men are more likely to show such gender-appropriate symptoms as somatic concerns and work-related problems (Vredenburg, Krames, & Flett, 1986). There also is evidence that men are more likely than women to use drugs and alcohol to cope with or mask depression, thus leading to higher rates of substance abuse in men and higher rates of depression in women (Weissman & Klerman, 1977; J. B. W. Williams & Spitzer, 1983). The traditional male role actually incorporates expectations regarding drinking beer and getting drunk (Landrine, Bardwell, & Dean, 1988). Given that substance abuse is the nation's number one mental health problem, it is not at all encouraging that the incidence of female alcoholics and substance abusers has increased steadily since the mid-1940s, with some leveling off in the 1970s (Colten & Marsh, 1984; Gomberg, 1986).

Suicide patterns also reveal the working of gender roles. Women are three times more likely than men to attempt suicide, but men are three times more likely than women to actually die from such attempts (D. Lester, 1984; Taube & Barrett, 1985). The difference between suicide attempts and suicide completions is due almost entirely to the different methods used in suicide attempts by males and females. In the United States, males are more likely than females to use firearms, whereas females are more likely than males to use pills. Unfortunately, women are starting to use increasingly lethal methods (J. R. Rogers, 1990).

Thus, the effect of gender roles is to make certain types of disorders more likely in one sex or the other. The female gender role encourages females to focus on their feelings, and therefore amplify them, whereas the male gender role encourages males to distract themselves from their feelings, and therefore damp them down (Ingram, Cruet, Johnson, & Wisnicki, 1988; Nolen-Hoeksema, 1987, 1990). Although there may be negative effects of the male pattern with respect to physical health and relationships, as will be discussed in later sections, the male pattern may be adaptive with respect to avoiding depression and anxiety. Furthermore, the disorders that men are more susceptible to—substance abuse, impulsive disorders, antisocial patterns—typically are viewed and treated as behavioral or social problems, not as emotional ones. This is true among children as well. Boys are most often referred to child guidance centers for aggressive, antisocial, and competitive behaviors; girls, for emotional problems, such as excessive fears, shyness, and feelings of inferiority (Anastas & Reinharz, 1984; Locksley & Douvan, 1979).

If gender roles affect the development of emotional or behavioral problems, we would expect that those individuals who are most sex-typed would show the most differences. This is precisely what is found. As discussed in the previous section, high "masculinity" scores are significantly related to high self-esteem and well-being, and low depression and anxiety. High "masculinity" scores seem particularly important in resisting the negative effects of helplessness and stressful life experiences and in avoiding depression, especially when such scores are accompanied by high "femininity" scores (Feather, 1985; Golding & Singer, 1983; Roos & Cohen, 1987; Stoppard & Paisley, 1987). Individuals

with high "masculinity" scores also appear to engage in more problem-focused and/or less emotion-focused coping styles in response to stressful situations (Conway, Giannopoulos, & Stiefenhofer, 1990; Ingram et al.,1988; Nezu & Nezu, 1987). Since both undifferentiated and feminine-sex-typed individuals are low in "masculine" traits, they are most prone to helplessness, depression, and anxiety (Baucom & Danker-Brown, 1984; Ingram et al., 1988; LaTorre, Yu, Fortin, & Marrache, 1983; Whitley, 1984). Feminine-sex-typed individuals may be particularly prone to such disorders since they tend to ruminate more than any other sex-typing group on their negative emotions.

High "masculinity" scores may not be completely positive with respect to mental health, however. For example, among children, masculine sex typing in boys appears related to conduct-disorder symptoms (Silvern & Katz, 1986). Among adults, high "masculinity" scores, especially hypermasculinity (macho) scores, appear related to alcohol abuse, especially when the individual is under stress (Snell, Belk, & Hawkins, 1987; Spence et al., 1979). Masculine sex typing in college students also is associated with anger-proneness and overt anger expression (Kopper & Epperson, 1991). Overall, sex typing may be more predictive than biological sex with respect to patterns of psychological problems.

Women may have higher rates of some emotional disorders than men not only because their gender role encourages the development of these disorders but also because their gender role encourages them to seek help for these problems. D. Phillips and Segal (1969) found that when the number of physical and psychiatric illnesses was held constant, women were more likely than men to seek medical and psychiatric care. They argued that in community studies, more women may appear mentally ill because it is more socially acceptable for them to talk about their psychological symptoms and to do something about them than it is for men. Other research supports the assertion that women may seek out health care services more frequently than men do (Padesky & Hammen, 1981; Scarf, 1979). This pattern develops sometime around puberty, a time when female-to-male ratios of mental health problems start changing (Gove, 1979). Since high "femininity" scores appear to be related to feeling that one is not responsible for solving one's problems, feminine individuals may be particularly prone to seek help when problems arise (C. L. Mitchell, 1987). Conversely, since part of the male sex role is autonomy and independence, it may be harder for men to ask for or receive help than for women. G. E. Good and colleagues (Good, Dell, & Mintz, 1989) found that male college students with traditional attitudes about the male role and concern about expressing emotions were significantly less likely to seek professional psychological assistance than were other men. Furthermore, men who had the strongest feelings about the importance of appearing "masculine" were the quickest to drop out of therapy (Riley, as cited in Goleman, 1990a).

In sum, the very nature of the gender roles makes it likely that women and men will develop different types of emotional problems and ways of expressing them. Simply being female may be a risk factor for certain mental disorders, as we further uncover the links between childhood sexual abuse (to which girls are more vulnerable) and emotional disorders such as multiple personality and depression (Bryer, Nelson, Miller, & Krol, 1987; Coons, Bowman, Pellow, & Schneider, 1989; Kluft, 1985). Gender roles also make it more likely that women will seek help for their problems, leading to the greater likelihood that women will receive psychiatric diagnoses. When we look further into the types of strains and conflicts that are likely within each gender role, we get a more complete explanation of the mental health statistics, including the marital and age patterns.

Role conflict   Another explanation for the mental health statistics centers on the concept of role conflict. It is not just that gender roles per se make males and females more susceptible to certain mental problems but also that some conflict or strain in the roles males and females hold promotes certain mental disorders. For example, the pressures of not fitting into culturally prescribed roles may account for the higher rates of alcohol addiction among women sex-typed as masculine, especially if they are in nontraditional roles (S. C. Wilsnack & Beckman, 1984).

Although marriage in general is beneficial to both men's and women's mental health, perhaps because of the emotional support provided by an intimate relationship, the marriage benefit is much greater for men than for women. This is somewhat ironic, given the fact the women are more likely than men to view marriage as their major goal in life, whereas men are more likely to view marriage as a trap to be avoided as long as possible. Yet women seem not to benefit as much from marriage as men with respect to emotional disorders. Why?

The major explanation for the differential rates of mental disorders among married women and men is

the greater role strain marriage produces in women compared to men, at least in contemporary society. The first source of role strain for married women may be with respect to multiple roles. Women's traditional role emphasizes homemaking and child-care activities, yet most married women, even those with young children, are in the labor force, mainly out of economic necessity. It is not that multiple roles are necessarily bad for women's psychological health, as we have seen in the section on psychological well-being, but that some women may have conflicts over multiple roles, either because of their traditional upbringing or because of their spouse's attitudes. It is this conflict or role strain that might produce stress. Furthermore, employed married women, especially those with children, tend to have more stress than their mates, because they are more likely to retain responsibility for the home and children, thus leading to two jobs (one inside and one outside the home). Women's jobs also tend to be less satisfying and more stressful than men's jobs since they involve less money, less prestige, fewer job openings, more career roadblocks, and so forth. (Work will be discussed in more detail in Chapter 11.)

Although multiple roles can lead to work overload and interrole conflict (Cooke & Rousseau, 1984; McBride, 1990), the critical variables are choice, social support, commitment to the work role, and quality of employment (Amatea & Fong, 1991; Baruch & Barnett, 1987; C. K. Holahan & Gilbert, 1979; Kibria et al., 1990). Workplace supports, such as personal days, flexible work hours, and leaves of absence, also reduce employed mothers' psychological strain (Moen & Forest, 1990). Married women with children who choose to work at a rewarding job, who have found satisfactory child care, and who have support from their husbands are in an extremely strong mental health position. Women with children who take jobs reluctantly and who receive few rewards from their work and little support from others are in an extremely vulnerable mental health position. Black women, who generally expect to combine family life with employment, report relatively little role conflict (Malson, 1983). These women tend to have support networks and role models that may alleviate some of the stresses of multiple roles. (This is not to say that other stresses, such as low-status jobs, poverty, and discrimination, don't affect Black women's mental health.)

A second source of strain for married women may be inequality in the marriage itself. In general, equality in the marital relationship is associated with lower depressive and somatic symptomatology in wives, at least when couples believe in an egalitarian ideal. In a study of 815 dual-career couples across the United States, Steil and Turetsky (1987a) found that when employed mothers were primarily responsible for the home and the children or had less decision-making responsibility, the women had higher levels of depressive symptomatology than did their peers whose husbands shared these responsibilities. Unfortunately, among dual-career couples with children, women tend to have greater responsibility than men for the home and children, and men tend to have greater responsibility than women for decision making (see also Chapters 9 and 10). Thus, regardless of employment status, women tend to be primarily responsible for domestic concerns. Such heavy responsibility may lead to household strain, which is a good predictor of depressive symptoms (Golding, 1990). Thus, Mexican-American women, who tend to hold more traditional roles than non-Hispanic White women, tend to have the highest levels of household strain and, consequently, of depression.

Related to inequality in the marital relationship is the issue of power itself. Research has shown that people who are relatively powerless have more symptoms of distress than people who are in powerful roles (Horwitz, 1982). For example, the less authority and influence married professional women with children have on the job, the more they suffer from depressive and physical symptoms (Reifman, Biernat, & Lang, 1991). In general, women have less power than men and, as we have seen, women tend to have higher levels of distress than men. The exceptions are married women who are the chief breadwinners of their family and married employed women without children. These two groups of women have some degree of power. The most distressed group of women are those who are unemployed and childless, perhaps because they are both powerless and deviant from sex role expectations.

A third source of role strain for married women may be exclusive parenting responsibilities, even if married women are not employed outside the home. In general, the transition to parenthood is more stressful for women than for men (McBride, 1990). For example, a young married mother may find that her major instrumental activities, such as raising children and keeping house, are frustrating and confusing, being often in conflict with her educational and intellectual attainments, having little prestige attached to them, and being virtually invisible. Wells (1988) found that mothers' sense of self-esteem was lower when they were with their children than when they were with adults. For nonemployed wives, children are associated with increased depression levels (C. E. Ross & Mirowsky, 1988). Yet such women are supposed to be happy, since they have attained what females are socialized to believe is their major life goal. Supporting this role-conflict explanation is the finding that housewives with liberal views toward sex roles, or who are dissatisfied with housework, or who have conflicts with their spouse over sex role expectations, are more depressed than housewives with traditional views or fewer conflicts (Kingery, 1985; Krause, 1983). Overall, depression is greatest among single and/or unemployed low-income women with young children, perhaps because the pressures (role, economic, social) on such women are extremely high. This pattern is true for both White and Black populations, although among younger Black women, marital status tends not to make a significant difference with respect to depressive symptomatology, perhaps because younger Black females are more independent than older ones (D. R. Brown, Milburn, Ahmed, Gary, & Booth, 1989–90; V. G. Thomas, Milburn, Brown, & Gary, 1988). Married men, who experience the least role strain, are least likely to suffer from depression.

Other sources of role strain for married women may be few social supports and unclear expectations. As we have seen, women are trained to give emotional support to others, while men tend not to receive such training. Thus, whereas married men may benefit from their spouse's emotional support and caretaking, married women frequently do not receive such support from their mate (due to his socialization) or female friends (because unemployed married women, especially those living in suburbia, tend to be isolated). Even among Black urban residents, women tend to have less reciprocal support networks than men (V. G. Thomas et al., 1988). Yet simply having a support network may be important. In a study of 238 White women between the ages of 35 and 55, Baruch and colleagues (1983) found that social supports were very important to a woman's overall well-being, especially if she was a homemaker.

For all these reasons—role overload, marital inequality, exclusive parenting responsibilities, unclear expectations, lack of support—marriage may be more stressful for women than men. If women's roles were clearer, were more highly valued, and demanded more time and skill, such strain would not occur. This was true for women before World War II. Indeed, mental health statistics bear this out—more men than women were hospitalized for mental illness at that time (Gove & Tudor, 1973, 1977). It should be noted, however, that the nature of psychiatric diagnosis has changed since that time (Dohrenwend & Dohrenwend, 1976). Since World War II, diagnoses have become broader and more inclusive, particularly regarding anxiety and depressive symptomatology. Hence, increasing rates of mental illness for women since World War II may reflect such methodological changes.

If mental health statistics are a product of the social system, it also can be predicted that those men who experience role conflict or strain or who are in relatively powerless positions should also have higher rates of emotional problems. There are numerous strains inherent in the male sex role, as described by Pleck (1976b, 1981b) and O'Neil (1981b, 1982; O'Neil et al, 1986). (See Figure 8.3.) It is these areas of strain that seem most associated with mental health problems. For example, male college students who scored high on O'Neil's scale measuring gender role conflict had higher depression scores than males who scored low (G. E. Good & Mintz, 1990). Unfortunately, these conflicted men are least likely to use psychological services.

As we have seen, marriage for men is of great psychological benefit. Because males are expected to devote themselves single-mindedly to achieving, single males are under more strain than single women and married males because they do not have anyone to take care of their other needs, both physical and emotional. Because of social inhibitions that keep males from expressing their emotions, especially to other men, wives are often the only source of emotional relief for men. Thus, we find that single men have higher rates of mental disorders than any other sex–marital status group. Single women tend to have more social supports and better caretaking skills than single men. Furthermore, treatment outcomes may be better for married than single men, as has been found in the case of male alcoholics (Cronkite & Moos, 1984). In contrast, marital status is unrelated to treatment outcome for alcoholic women.

In recent years, however, marriage may be getting more stressful for men (discussed further in the next chapter). Traditional marriages, in which the man is the sole breadwinner and the woman the sole domestic caretaker, are in the minority. Men's traditional position of dominance in the home and in decision making no longer is secure, as more wives join the labor force and demand more sharing of child-care and homemaking responsibilities.

Such pressures may be responsible for the fact that more men are seeking help for psychological distress than in the past (Bales, 1984; Goleman, 1984). Men with traditional attitudes toward gender roles may experience more stress and anxiety when their wives are employed than when they are not, either because they're not fulfilling their role as a "good provider" or because more is expected of them in the home (Kessler & McRae, 1982; Staines, Pottick, & Fudge, 1986). Yet men who believe in egalitarian relationships seem to benefit (in terms of decreased depressive symptomatology) from sharing responsibilities with their employed wives (Pleck, 1985; Steil & Turetsky, 1987a). Thus, a match between one's gender role expectations and one's life activities seems to be key for adequate mental health. Fortunately, both one's expectations and one's activities are open to change.

Because the major role for males centers on their working ability, in times of economic depression and high unemployment more men than women should experience problems. Statistics reported in Gove and Tudor (1973) bear this out, as do reports of increases in male depression, suicide, sexual impotence, child abuse, and so on accompanying the high unemployment rates of the 1970s (Drummond, 1977). Unemployed men show significantly more signs of both psychological and physiological distress than their employed male counterparts (Horwitz, 1982). One study (M. H. Brenner, 1979) found that, after looking at data from 750,000 New York State mental patients during a 127-year period, the only significant factor accounting for the rise and fall in admission to mental hospitals was employment. This negative effect of unemployment, supported by other studies, is true for women as well as men (P. B. Johnson, 1982; Kasl, 1979; Liem & Rayman, 1982; Warr & Parry, 1982). Retirement also may be stressful for women as well as for men (Herman, 1981). This may be because women's retirement often is involuntary, due to spouse's retirement or his failing health. These findings again point to the difficulty in dichotomizing the activities of the sexes and the consequences of these activities.

Role conflict and strain is a frequent occurrence among Black males in the United States. Most African-American men have internalized the cultural norms regarding masculinity (Cazenave, 1984), yet racism and economic exploitation have made it difficult, if not impossible, for most to attain the cultural norm of achievement, success, power, and so on. Nearly half of all Black children in the United States grow up in a home with an income below the federally defined poverty line.

Unemployment rates are much higher for Black males than for White males, and the gap in incomes between Black and White males has increased since the early 1970s (Cordes, 1985). In 1982, nearly 30% of all Black men between the ages of 20 and 64 were not employed, and about half of the 30% weren't even in the labor force, having given up looking for a job. Meanwhile, programs that support low- and moderate-income families were cut drastically during the Reagan administration and have yet to be restored. Some consequences of these stresses are the strikingly high number of mental and physical health problems among Black males, as well as the disproportionately high incidence of social deviancy among them (Cordes, 1985; Gary, 1981; J. T. Gibbs, 1988). Black male children appear to be more vulnerable to the detrimental effects of poverty than Black girls, and these boys show the highest rates of behavioral, learning, and emotional disorders (Patterson, Kupersmidt, & Vaden, 1990; M. B. Spencer, Dobbs, & Phillips, 1988). As adults, Black males have the highest admission rates as inpatients of any sex–race group to state and community mental hospitals, and they are admitted at younger ages (Rosenstein et al., 1986). The age period from 18 to 24 shows the greatest differential in admission rates as a function of sex–race grouping, suggesting that this age period, during which identity resolution occurs, may be particularly stressful for Black males. Depression is highest among young, poor, unemployed Black males, especially when they have conflictual relationships with women (Gary & Berry, 1985).

Like Blacks, lesbians and gay men are another stigmatized minority. However, just as being Black is not inherently pathological, so is same-gender sexual orientation not inherently pathological. Despite the fact that the American Psychiatric Association removed homosexuality from its classification system of disorders in 1973, and despite research indicating that homosexuals as a group are as emotionally stable as heterosexuals (A. Bell & Weinberg, 1978; Herek, 1990; Kurdek, 1987; Riess & Safer, 1979), many people, including many psychotherapists, believe that homosexuality is a type of mental disorder (Garfinkle & Morin, 1978). Given the stresses involved in being a heavily stigmatized group, some lesbians and gay men do develop problems with anxiety, depression, anger, and/or alienation, yet others develop stronger ego controls and better coping mechanisms than heterosexuals (Crocker & Major, 1989; M. Freedman, 1975; N. L. Thompson, McCandless, & Strickland, 1971). Thus, it is not same-gender sexual orientation itself that is related to emotional problems, but the strains involved in having an identity heavily stigmatized by the majority culture. Such strains may contribute to the finding that gay men and lesbians have three times the incidence of alcoholism and drug abuse as heterosexuals ("Report: Gays," 1990).

Using role conflict and role strain to explain emotional problems also helps explain certain age patterns as shown in Table 8.2. Adjustment pressures appear to be different for males and females at different ages. As was discussed previously, males experience the most intense socialization pressures during childhood, and it is then that males have higher rates of emotional, learning, and behavior problems than females (Anastas & Reinharz, 1984; Eme, 1984). Girls experience their most intense socialization pressures during and after adolescence, and it is then that the statistical trends just mentioned start reversing themselves. This is most apparent with respect to depression. Whereas boys show more depression than girls during childhood, the pattern is reversed during adolescence. Furthermore, those boys who have problems during adolescence are likely to have had problems in childhood, but girls are more likely to first show signs of psychological difficulty during adolescence (Petersen, 1988). By high school, girls attain greater anxiety, depression, and alienation scores than their male peers, report more stressful life events, and show signs of more negative body image and self-esteem (Allgood-Merten, Lewinsohn, & Hops, 1990; LaTorre et al., 1983; Petersen, 1988). The combination of negative self-appraisals and stressful life events may make adolescent girls particularly vulnerable to both depression and eating disorders. The latter disorders, which include both anorexia nervosa (self-starvation) and bulimia (the gorging-and-purging syndrome), affect adolescent females about nine times more frequently than males. Research on these disorders, which have increased in incidence since the mid-1970s, suggests that the following factors are predictive: low self-esteem; conflicts regarding sexuality, independence, assertiveness, competitiveness, and peer acceptance; and an obsession with thinness (Garfinkel & Garner, 1982; Steiner-Adair, 1990; Striegel-Moore et al., 1986; Striegel-Moore, Silberstein, Grunberg, & Rodin, 1990). All are more common in adolescent females than males.

There are other age patterns as well. Although community surveys taken in the mid-1950s and the 1960s found that impairment rates rose regularly among successive age groups, being higher for women than for men at all ages, follow-ups done in the 1970s showed women in their 40s and 50s were less impaired than in the past (Bird, 1979). In fact, their rates of impairment were comparable to those of their male peers (around 8% to 9%) and were the lowest among all age groups. The 50s may be the "prime of life" for women, despite the cultural stigma on aging women in the United States (see M. M. Gergen, 1990). Women in this age group tend to have better health, higher incomes, and more "empty nests" than other women, conditions related to confidence, involvement, security, and general well-being (Baruch et al., 1983; S. M. Black & Hill, 1984; V. Mitchell & Helson, 1990). Cross-cultural research supports the view that postmenopausal women are in their prime with regard to mental health and social influence (J. K. Brown & Kerns, 1985). The age group with the highest impairment rates (30%) in the most recent community surveys are women in their 30s. These are the women under the most stress in terms of role demands and often-conflicting work and family expectations.

In summary, role conflict and strain are important factors in the development of emotional and behavioral disorders. To the extent that individuals and society can reduce the conflicts and strains inherent in gender roles, the healthier individuals will be.

In this section we have seen how powerfully gender-related factors affect the incidence and patterns of mental disorders. Males and females tend to develop different disorders at different times in their lives. Different standards appear to be used to define mental problems in males and females, leading to some sex bias in diagnosis and treatment. Although female hormonal variability may make some women more susceptible to depression than men, biological factors appear to play a minor role in the disorders most differentiated by gender. Gender roles themselves play a larger role, making certain disorders more common in males (in particular, behavioral problems) and certain disorders more common in females (in particular, emotional problems). Certain instrumental traits, stereotyped as masculine, seem important in helping individuals avoid developing emotional disorders. These traits are more common among males than females. Gender roles also make it more likely for females than males to seek psychological help. All these aspects of gender roles contribute to females' overrepresentation in the mental health system. Role strain and conflict also are important

in the development of mental disorders. Analysis of the conflicts inherent in both the female and male gender roles today can account for many of the findings regarding marital status, ethnicity, and age patterns.

Discussion

The findings regarding the effect of gender stereotypic traits on mental health point in one direction—the more instrumental qualities an individual has, the better. Compared to other sex-typing groups, masculine- and androgynous-sex-typed persons tend to score higher on measures of psychological well-being and lower on measures of emotional disorders. Androgynous individuals tend to be the most behaviorally flexible. Thus, traditional feminine sex typing does not appear to be the most advantageous with respect to one's mental health. Indeed, the female gender role, combined with the stresses inherent within it, may predispose many females to the development of certain mental disorders starting during adolescence. The male gender role predisposes males to develop more behavioral disorders, especially during childhood.

Although marriage appears beneficial to one's mental well-being, the benefit of marriage is greater for men than women due to the role overload and stress involved in being a married woman in today's society. In contrast, more single men than single women experience role strain and conflict, and these stresses lead to more mental problems for them.

In sum, gender roles and stereotypes contribute greatly to an individual's mental health. They also contribute to an individual's physical health.

▲   Physical Health

As if their effect on self-concept and mental health were not enough, gender roles and stereotypes also affect one's physical health. As discussed in Chapter 2, males have a shorter life expectancy, contract more serious and fatal illnesses (such as cancer and heart attacks), and have more accidents than females. Men also are more likely than women to report ulcers, asthma, stomach symptoms, eye complaints, cardiovascular problems, and hypertension before age 60. Yet women have poorer health overall. Women compared to men have higher rates of acute and chronic health problems, use health services and medications more often, undergo more surgical procedures, and are more likely to have diabetes, anemia, rheumatoid arthritis, lupus, respiratory and gastrointestinal problems, weight difficulties, Alzheimer's disease, and hypertension after age 60 (Rodin & Ickovics, 1990; Seiden, 1979; Strickland, 1988; Verbrugge, 1987). Although some of these findings may be due to gender differences in reporting of problems, differential longevity, and biology, most researchers connect these findings to gender roles themselves—in particular, gender-related lifestyle patterns and stress, coping strategies, and personality characteristics. Of considerable note is the decreasing advantage for women in terms of mortality over the past decade, a time of decreasing gender differences in lifestyles and social roles (Rodin & Ickovics, 1990).

Lifestyle
The importance of lifestyle in affecting physical health is evident from research that shows that when environment and lifestyle are held relatively constant, there is a trend toward equalization of health-related statistics for both sexes. For example, the incidence of death from heart disease is similar for male and female long-term psychiatric patients, whereas in the general population, this cause of death affects men nearly four times more frequently than it does women (T. J. Craig & Lin, 1984). Similarly, among members of a kibbutz (where women participate fully in public life, where men are not expected to be "breadwinners," and where health and child care are communal responsibilities), there are no significant gender differences in health status or illness behavior (Anson, Levenson, & Bonneh, 1990). Furthermore, when lifestyle factors such as age, employment status, and job status are controlled statistically, gender differences in health status narrow greatly (Verbrugge, 1987). These findings support the hypothesis that lifestyle differences between the sexes, rather than differences in biological vulnerability, account for many of the gender differences in physical health.

Male gender role   What is it about the lifestyles of males and females that contributes to their differential health status? Examining the typical male role first, we've already noted how restrictive it is. As Brannon (1976) notes, the stereotyped male role has four major themes:

1. No Sissy Stuff: the need to be different from females.
2. The Big Wheel: the need to be superior to others.
3. The Sturdy Oak: the need to be self-reliant and independent.

4. Give 'em Hell: the need to be more powerful than others.

All four themes involve self-evaluation in terms of an external standard, and all four limit the expression of feelings. As discussed in the previous section and illustrated in Figure 8.3, many aspects of the male gender role cause conflict and strain. One consequence of this strain is poor physical health.

In looking more closely at the major causes of death listed in Table 2.1 that affect men more than women, we note that a number of them are directly attributable to certain behaviors, such as cigarette smoking, drinking, reckless driving, violence, and aggressive-competitive Type A or "coronary-prone" behavior. All these behaviors occur more in men than in women and all can be viewed as extreme forms of certain components of masculinity—risk taking, competition, striving for status and power, and violence. James Harrison (1978) suggests that such behaviors may develop as compensation for the anxiety derived from sex role expectations. Certain aspects of stereotypical masculinity—the need to be in charge, restricted emotionality, inhibited affection, and fear of femininity—have been linked to greater vulnerability to stress, more risk-taking practices, and avoidance of medical help (J. Alper, 1988; Harrell, 1986; Snell, Belk, & Hawkins, 1986). Thus, aspects of the male sex role may indirectly lead to men's higher rates of accidents and death.

Because many men's sole identity rests on their role as breadwinner, the stress is sometimes overwhelming when this role is threatened. A number of studies have found increased numbers of peptic ulcers, heart attacks, and strokes related to unemployment in middle-aged men (see Liem & Rayman, 1982). One study (Kasl & Cobb, 1979) found that 100 male blue-collar workers who were about to have their jobs terminated had significant increases in their cholesterol and norepinephrine levels and in their blood pressure in anticipation of their job loss. These changes continued for 24 months afterward. All of these changes adversely affect the cardiovascular system, and many of these men showed signs of coronary disease, dyspepsia, and hypertension. Women also experience adverse physiological effects from being unemployed, although the highest rates of illness appear to be for married men, perhaps because the stress of their unemployment is exacerbated by sex role expectations (Horwitz, 1982; Liem & Rayman, 1982).

The stress involved in being a minority male along with unhealthy lifestyle factors may contribute to the much poorer health status of Black males compared to White males. Black men are the most likely of any group to die from injuries on the job, and they die at higher rates than White men from heart disease, hypertension, cancer, strokes, cirrhosis of the liver, tuberculosis, diabetes, and lung diseases (Gary, 1981; J. T. Gibbs, 1988). Black males also have a greater likelihood than others of being homicide and accident victims. For example, one out of ten Black males aged 15 to 24 was a homicide victim in 1988, up 67% from the 1984 rate ("Dangers Rise," 1990). The life expectancy of Black males is about six and a half years shorter than the life expectancy of White males, whereas the life expectancy gap between Black and White females is only four years (Bovee, 1991a). These striking mortality and morbidity (illness) statistics reflect the greater number of risk factors in the Black male's environment: high rates of unemployment, poverty or low socioeconomic status, deteriorating housing and neighborhoods, substance abuse, tobacco use, unstable families, crime and delinquency, racism, and poor access to health care. Most of these factors affect Black females as well, but when combined with the expectations of the male gender role to be strong, dominant, and successful, they affect Black males particularly strongly. Thus, Black males have higher mortality and morbidity rates than Black females, although the health status of all minority groups is poorer than that of Whites (Coughlin, 1988; Ozer, 1986).

Female gender role   The female gender role also has implications for women's physical health. A number of aspects of the traditional female role may lead to healthier outcomes than the traditional male role—in particular, females' lower likelihood of engaging in risk-taking and violent activities, and their greater likelihood of seeking help for both physical and emotional problems. These factors may contribute to the findings of fewer accidents, homicides, and suicides among females than males, as well as fewer serious diseases (since women may seek treatment at an earlier stage than men). A nationwide survey of 1250 adults in 1989 found that women tend to have a healthier lifestyle than men, especially with respect to safe driving habits and proper nutrition (Wlazelek, 1989). Women also have had lower rates of tobacco and alcohol use than men, which have contributed to their lower rates of lung cancer and cirrhosis of the liver. Unfortunately, women's use of these substances has increased, as have their rates of lung cancer, heart attacks, and alcoholism, as cited in Chapter 2. One

of the most frequently suggested reasons for the increasing percentage of women who smoke is that cigarette smoking may have become a symbol of equality with men—"You've come a long way, baby." In fact, more young women than young men now are smoking (Reinhard, 1991). Between 1982 and 1986, the death rates from heart disease and cerebrovascular disease fell more for men than for women. For cancer, the male death rate decreased while the female death rate increased. The increased cancer death rate for women was due to a dramatic increase in deaths from lung cancer, almost entirely due to smoking ("Lung Cancer," 1990; Schmid, 1990). This is a sad testimonial for equality indeed.

Although some people have attributed the increase in certain health problems in women and their decreasing advantage with respect to mortality to women's increased likelihood of holding multiple roles (spouse, parent, and worker), a careful analysis of the data supports a very different conclusion. Just as multiple roles may contribute to women's mental health, so may multiple roles contribute to women's physical health. Again, the critical factors are the quality of the roles themselves and the degree of social support available (Barnett, Biener, & Baruch, 1987; Crosby, 1987; Repetti et al., 1989). For example, a number of studies have found that employed women actually have fewer physical ailments and fewer days in bed than housewives, especially if housewives have favorable attitudes toward employment (Horwitz, 1982; Verbrugge & Madans, 1985; Waldron & Herold, 1984). A longitudinal study of a national sample of middle-aged women found that labor force participation had the most beneficial effects on the health of unmarried women and married Black women (Waldron & Jacobs, 1989).

Yet there are aspects of the female role that are negatively related to physical health—in particular, women's lower status and lesser power. In general, feelings of control, appropriate power, and predictability are positively associated with health (Horwitz, 1982; Reifman et al., 1991; Strickland, 1988). Unfortunately, women compared to men tend to have less power in society and less control over their lives, and are more likely to live in an unpredictable environment. They also tend to have higher rates of illness. The least healthy women are those who are unemployed with neither spouse nor children (Verbrugge & Madans, 1985). For employed women, physical and emotional problems are associated with achievement conflicts and traditionally female jobs, such as clerical and sales work, especially for Blacks (Ehrenreich, 1979). Although many people assume that jobs with a great deal of responsibility (such as high-level managers) are more stressful than jobs with little responsibility (such as secretaries), the truth is exactly the reverse: the most stressful jobs are those that are demanding but low in status, and wherein the employee has little control and autonomy (Rodin & Ickovics, 1990). These types of jobs are disproportionately held by women. In fact, clerical/secretarial work is the second most hazardous occupation in regard to general health in the United States (U.S. Department of Labor, 1985b). Job stress is compounded when a worker also has sole or primary responsibility for the household and the children. Thus, the lifestyle of many women is extremely stressful due to the quality of their roles. The high stress involved in many of women's roles may account for the greater incidence of health problems found in women than in men. Black women, in particular, have poorer health than White women, and receive poorer health care (E. C. White, 1990). For example, Black women are three times as likely as White women to die of cervical cancer. The major stresses on Black women are poverty, racism, and role overload. However, research is clear that it is the quality and not the quantity of women's roles that contributes to women's higher morbidity level. Multiple roles in and of themselves are not the problem (Biener, 1990; Repetti et al., 1989; Rodin & Ickovics, 1990; Verbrugge, 1987; R. W. Wilsnack, Wilsnack, & Klassen, 1984).

Marriage   As is the case with mental health, marriage also is positively related to physical health for both men and women, but the benefit for men is greater. Married individuals of both sexes live longer than single people, lose fewer days from work, and see the doctor less often (Gove, 1973; "Study: Married," 1988; Trovato & Lauris, 1989). An example of the greater size of the marriage benefit for men than women can be found in the following statistics: Among women and men aged 45–54, 23% of the men who live without a spouse die within 10 years, compared to 11% of married men ("Bachelors," 1990). In contrast, only 7.7% of women who live without a spouse die within 10 years, compared to 4% of married women. Although these results can mean that sicker people are less likely to get or stay married than physically healthy people, other evidence suggests that marriage itself (or, more likely, a close intimate relationship) is beneficial, especially to men (Zick & Smith, 1991). Marriage is associated with increased income, and part of the protective effect of marriage is

economic. Married people, especially men, also tend to have healthier lifestyles than single people. Furthermore, close interpersonal ties are important for a sense of well-being, and married people tend to have larger social networks than nonmarried people. All these beneficial effects increase the marriage benefit for men more than women, since unmarried women still tend to have a healthy lifestyle and still tend to have close, intimate friendships.

For both men and women, involvement in marital and work roles is associated with the best physical health, followed by involvement in marital, work, and parental roles (L. M. Coleman, Antonucci, & Adelmann, 1987). These multiple roles may allow each spouse some degree of power and social support. Among women, unemployed single mothers tend to have the poorest physical health as they do mental health. This group of women tends to have the least power and control, as well as the least social support, compared to other women. For men, the worst physical health occurs among those who are married, have children, and are unemployed, perhaps due to the stress associated with not living up to the breadwinner role.

Equality in marriage is as important for women's physical health as it is for their mental health. Among married couples with children, more equal decision making is associated with fewer somatic complaints for women than in the more typical male-dominated pattern (Steil & Turetsky, 1987b). Of note is the finding that such equality does not negatively affect married men's health. For women at midlife, those who have followed a traditional life plan (exclusively homemakers) tend to have more chronic physical conditions and less energy than their peers who have followed a less traditional life plan (women without children and divorced mothers) (Helson & Picano, 1990).

In general, certain aspects of the male lifestyle are hazardous to men's physical health, and men benefit greatly by marriage. Women's lifestyle, though healthier in some ways than men's, is associated with less power and status and more stress. These factors negatively affect women's health.

Coping Styles
Lifestyle patterns may combine with gender differences in coping styles to contribute to gender differences in mortality and morbidity. Women tend to have larger support networks than men, and such networks are positively associated with health, perhaps because they serve to buffer the negative

effects of stress (N. Nelson, 1988; Rodin & Ickovics, 1990). This may be why unmarried men who live alone have the highest mortality rate of any group, almost double that of their married counterparts (Kobrin & Hendershot, 1977). Yet not all social support networks are mutually supportive. Women tend to provide most of the caring and support of others, whether that caring and support be physical or emotional, and regardless of a woman's employment status (Wethington, McLeod, & Kessler, 1987). This unequal caregiving may be a health burden on women. Family support is particularly important for women's ability to cope with stress (C. J. Holahan & Moos, 1985), and women's health is more severely affected than men's when stress is high and support is low (N. Nelson, 1988).

As with emotional problems, women are more likely than men to seek help for physical problems. It is not surprising, then, that 60% of all medical appointments are made for females (Scarf, 1979). The fact that women go to physicians regularly regarding reproductive functions may inflate these statistics, however. Furthermore, in controlled populations, gender differences in medically related behaviors do not always occur. For example, among college students, there are negligible gender differences in total symptom frequency, in delay in seeking medical consultation, and in the frequency with which medical treatment is obtained (S. Fisher & Greenberg, 1979). Still, if men really are less likely than women to go to doctors with physical problems, minor illnesses may develop into major ones, accounting somewhat for the higher rates of serious physical problems in men than in women.

As suggested previously, men and women may cope with stress differently. Women are more likely than men to turn toward other people in times of stress, whereas men are more likely to withdraw socially. Women are more likely than men to experience stress emotionally, and sometimes to dwell on those feelings. Men are more likely than women to distract themselves from stress through activities and depersonalization. Unfortunately, depersonalization is associated with greater consumption of alcohol, caffeine, and nicotine, all of which can have serious negative health effects (Ogus, Greenglass, & Burke, 1990). Avoidance coping responses, such as denying feelings or expressing them indirectly in hostile interpersonal encounters, are associated with greater physical and emotional strain (C. J. Holahan & Moos, 1985). Since the male gender role discourages men from directly expressing their feelings, men's gender role

conformity may lead to their higher rate of cardiovascular disorders and death.

Personality Traits

Related to both coping styles and lifestyles are personality traits. Certain traits and attitudes have been found critical in both women and men for avoiding the negative health consequences of stress: high self-esteem, low self-denigration, internal locus of control, a Type B (rather than a Type A) personality (low on competitiveness, time pressure, hostility, and achievement-orientation), and hardiness (a sense of commitment, control, and challenge) (Kobasa, 1987). As previously reviewed, gender roles encourage men to develop the first three qualities (high self-esteem, low self-denigration, and internal locus of control). However, men are actively discouraged from developing a Type B personality. We know little about whether males and females differ with respect to the last trait, hardiness. Thus, we can conclude that gender roles are not conducive to the health of either males or females.

The research on the Type A or B personality is instructive in revealing how unhealthy certain "masculine" personality traits can be. The Type A personality—competitive, achievement-oriented, time-pressured, aggressive, easily hostile—has been strongly linked to coronary heart disease (Matthews & Haynes, 1986). This constellation of traits also is strongly linked to stereotypic masculine traits and unrelated to stereotypic feminine traits (Blascovich, Major, & Katkin, 1981; DeGregorio & Carver, 1980; Grimm & Yarnold, 1985). Thus, Type A personalities are most likely to be masculine-sex-typed. In general, White males have the highest Type A scores, followed by White females, Black males, and Black females, in that order (Hunter, Johnson, Vizelberg, Webber, & Berenson, 1991). These gender and race differences appear as early as age 8. White males may be most Type A because they are most likely to be masculine-sex-typed or because people find a Type A White male to be more socially attractive than other Type A groups (Faulkner, Holandsworth, & Thomas, 1983). More likely, more White males than females tend to be in jobs or positions where Type A behavior is required or encouraged. For example, when employment or college status is similar, Type A personality traits do not occur more in men than in women. Traditionally male jobs, such as business executive, almost may demand Type A employees. Indeed, women in high-status occupations appear more likely to show the Type A behavior pattern than the more relaxed Type B pattern (Greenglass,

1984; K. E. Kelly & Houston, 1985; Waldron, 1978). Type A traits for women may be associated with even greater psychological distress than Type A traits for men, perhaps because such traits are gender-inappropriate as well as unhealthy (Musante, MacDougall, Dembroski, & Van Horn, 1983). Type A women also may experience more stress than Type A men because they may try to be "super-women"—expecting extremely high performance from themselves in multiple (worker, parent, and spouse) roles.

Thus, the relationship between sex typing and physical health is somewhat complex. Stereotypically masculine traits are associated with coronary-prone behaviors, lower levels of health, poor health practices, and impaired social networks (Downey, 1984; Helgeson, 1990). Furthermore, certain aspects of the male role, such as hyperaggressiveness, restrictive emotionality, and fear of femininity, may be lethal. Yet, it may be only extreme or "unmitigated agency" that's the problem. We may need to separate positive agentic traits from negative ones. As we have seen in the previous section, certain instrumental-active traits appear to be important in avoiding the negative effects of stressful life experiences, at least in terms of developing certain emotional disorders like depression. Many of these traits, especially when integrated with expressive-nurturant traits (as in some androgynous individuals) may be important in avoiding some physical effects of stress as well (Heilbrun & Mulqueen, 1987). Certainly, more research needs to be done on this topic.

Sex Bias in Health Care and Research

Another similarity with the data on emotional problems is the suggestion that doctors and other medical personnel may manifest a sex bias in treating their patients' physical complaints (Fidell, 1984; Wallston, DeVellis, & Wallston, 1983). In general, women's medical complaints are treated less seriously than men's, and women's symptoms are more often attributed to psychogenic rather than organic causes; the reverse is true for symptoms presented by men. Thus, women are twice as likely as men to have mood-modifying drugs prescribed (Gomberg, 1986), and one study found women patients recovering from coronary surgery were more likely to receive sedatives, which decrease anxiety, than a comparable group of men patients (Calderone, 1990). In fact, the men were administered pain medication, which decreases physical pain, significantly more frequently than the women, suggesting that women are less likely to be believed than men when they say they are in pain. Other signs of bias in health treatment exist as well. Women with symptoms of heart disease are considered for coronary bypass surgery or balloon angioplasty far less often than men with the same symptoms, even when patients' age and suspected severity of disease are taken into account (G. Kolata, 1991; Tobin et al., 1987). Women as well as minority men also tend to be recommended for and to receive transplants less frequently than White men ("White Men," 1989). Women with AIDS, who are most likely to be poor and either Black or Hispanic, have especially been neglected by the health care system ("Women with AIDS," 1991). Evidence of widespread sexism and racism in the U.S. health care industry is compelling (Ehrenreich & English, 1978; J. L. Weaver & Garrett, 1983).

Bias also occurs in medical research. Most studies examining the effect of a particular treatment on a particular medical condition, such as the effect of aspirin in preventing heart attacks, have used only White male subjects (Purvis, 1990; Roan, 1990). Consequently, we do not know if the findings generalize to minority group members or to White women. In a number of cases, generalizations based on White men's responses have not been warranted (see, for example, E. Rosenthal, 1991). Thus, we know less about effective treatments and preventive measures for women and minority men than we do for White men. This issue has become especially critical in research on AIDS, since minority men and women are the fastest growing population affected. Not only do we know less about women's responses to drugs than men's, we also know less about women's biology than we do about men's (E. Klein, 1990; "Too Little," 1990). As a result of this historical neglect, the National Institutes of Health in 1990 issued more stringent guidelines for research funding to ensure that women and minorities are adequately represented in federally funded research.

Discussion

Gender roles and stereotypes contribute to gender differences in physical health and longevity through their effect on lifestyle patterns, coping styles, and personality types. In particular, aspects of the male gender role appear related to men's earlier death, whereas aspects of the female gender role, along with possible gender bias in medical treatment, appear related to women's poorer health status.

▲ Summary

The evidence shows that gender roles and stereotypes have a variety of negative consequences on the individual level, affecting one's self-concept, mental health, and physical health. In regard to self-concept, it has been demonstrated that for females, strong feminine sex typing is associated with low self-confidence and low expectations. For males, sex typing is associated with high expectations and low self-acceptance. For both sexes, instrumental traits are positively associated with self-esteem. These differences in self-concept, combined with other aspects of the stereotypes, have direct consequences for behavior: feminine-sex-typed females perform poorly in "masculine" situations and activities requiring competition, independence, or assertiveness, all of which are abilities needed to function effectively in an industrial, competitive society; masculine-sex-typed males perform poorly in "feminine" situations and activities requiring empathy, nurturance, or expressiveness, which are needed in relating effectively to other individuals. Thus, to the extent that an individual is strongly sex typed, she or he is restricted from living a full and rewarding life.

Of even greater importance is the effect of the stereotypes on one's mental and physical health. For both sexes, instrumental traits are positively associated with psychological adjustment. Feminine-sex-typed and undifferentiated individuals tend to be more psychologically and socially maladjusted than masculine-sex-typed and androgynous individuals. Each sex also is more likely to develop certain disorders, partly as a function of gender socialization pressures. For example, women, particularly feminine-sex-typed women, are prone to depression. Men, particularly masculine-sex-typed men, are prone to behavior problems and coronary heart disease. Marriage is related to better physical and mental health than being single, but the marriage benefit is greater for men than for women, possibly because of the strains involved in being a married woman in today's society. Single males and unemployed males also show high rates of emotional disturbance and health problems, resulting from the strains of their roles. In general, males have higher mortality rates than females, whereas females have higher illness rates than males. Both results may be due to components of the gender roles and attendant lifestyle patterns.

This picture of the consequences of gender stereotypes and roles would be gloomy indeed if there also did not exist a model of a viable alternative. By examining those individuals who are not strongly sex-typed—that is, the nearly one-third of Americans who are androgynous—a picture emerges of individuals who can function effectively in a variety of situations and who tend to be emotionally well adjusted. Thus, these people serve as a reminder of the alternatives to the sex-typing trap. Increasing the variety of behaviors and traits allowed in male and female roles is also likely to decrease emotional tension and enhance personal growth for members of both sexes. And although there may be problems involved in such a changeover, the results certainly make a changeover seem worthwhile.

▲ Recommended Reading

Barnett, R. C., Biener, L., & Baruch, G. K. (Eds.). (1987). *Gender and stress.* New York: Free Press. An excellent collection of articles delineating the complex ways stress affects both women and men, with sufficient attention paid to ways in which the sexes differ. Both physical and mental health issues are examined.

Gibbs, J. T. (Ed.). (1988). *Young, black, and male in America: An endangered species.* Dover, MA: Auburn House. An important collection of articles delineating the high-risk aspects of life for minority males. Although an explicit gender analysis is not provided, the information speaks for itself.

McGrath, E., Keita, G. P., Strickland, B. R., & Russo, N. F. (Eds.). (1990). *Women and depression: Risk factors and treatment issues.* Hyattsville, MD: American Psychological Association. A comprehensive review of the research on depression by APA's Task Force on Women and Depression that emphasizes the importance of societal factors.

Sanford, L. T., & Donovan, M. E. (1984). *Women and self-esteem.* New York: Penguin. A self-help book with useful information about the causes of and remedies for low self-esteem in women.

Scher, M., Stevens, M., Good, G., & Eichenfield, G. A. (Eds.). (1987). *Handbook of counseling and psychotherapy with men.* Newbury Park, CA: Sage. A useful and comprehensive book describing different men's psychological needs and how counselors can best deal with them.

Chapter 9

Consequences for Friendships and Love Relationships

A couple with their 5-year-old daughter visits some friends who have a 5-year-old son. As the parents become involved in conversation, the boy tells his parents that he and the girl will go upstairs to his bedroom and play. Although the girl's parents do not consider this statement noteworthy, the boy's father remarks with a sly smile, "It won't be long before we'd think twice about letting them do that!"

This anecdote, modeled on a true story told by Sandra Bem, demonstrates that we have clear expectations regarding male-female relationships. Young children can have same- and other-sex friends. As children mature, however, we assume mixed-sex friendships will lead to sexual and/or romantic involvements. Such expectations are very much shaped by the gender roles and stereotypes of our society. And, of course, such expectations shape children's behaviors toward others.

In the previous chapter, the consequences for the individual of gender roles were examined. In many ways, the most negative consequences (lower self-confidence, higher incidence of some emotional disturbances, poorer health) occur predominantly in females, although males, as a group, certainly have their share of problems (for example, shorter life expectancy). In this chapter and the one to follow, the consequences of gender roles for relationships will be reviewed. It will become apparent that somewhat more negative consequences occur for males as a group than for females as a group, although, again, females also may suffer significantly.

This difference in area of most impairment (individual level for females, relationship level for males) parallels the differential emphasis on the appropriate sphere of activity for the sexes. Females generally are expected to operate on a relationship, or communal, level and are encouraged to develop related skills—interpersonal sensitivity, empathy, emotional expressiveness, nurturance. These skills facilitate females' expected major role, that of mother. Indeed, the self-identity formed by many females is one of a self-in-relation. Females generally are not expected to be independent or assertive, and many females, in fact, have difficulty demonstrating these qualities. For males, the picture is reversed; they are expected to be agentic, independent, achievement-oriented, and aggressive. These qualities facilitate the assumption of their expected major role, that of breadwinner. The self-identity formed by many males is one of an autonomous self. Males generally are not expected to be relationship-oriented, except as it may further their individual goals, such as sexual achievement and professional advancement. Most males are not encouraged to develop relationship skills and are taught, instead, to hide their emotions. Masking of emotion may facilitate competitive strivings, but it also may hinder the development of intimate relationships. Consequently, many men experience great difficulty in the area of relationships, which may be manifested in feelings of emptiness, isolation, and frustration.

Because of the mixed messages men receive about relationships (for example, "get close but not too close"), many men appear to perceive affiliative situations negatively and have lower affiliation motivation than women (Helgeson & Sharpsteen, 1987; Mark & Alper, 1985; Mazur, 1989; Pollak & Gilligan, 1982). As discussed in Chapter 3, more men than women perceive danger in affiliative situations, whereas more women than men perceive danger in achievement situations. Furthermore, from national surveys conducted in 1957 and 1976, men appear to be decreasing in their affiliative motive, whereas this motive for women has remained the same (Veroff et al., 1980). These same surveys found an increase among men in two power motives: motivation centered around fear of losing power and motivation to have power over others. Taken together, these findings suggest that some men may perceive the changing roles of women as threatening their traditional power. To compensate, these men increase their need to control others and decrease their need for relationships, wherein they might see themselves as weak. Such a trend has disturbing implications since relationships are so vital to emotional and physical well-being. For example, adults with an interest in and capacity for close relationships with others are generally happier and show fewer signs of strain than adults low in intimacy motivation (McAdams & Bryant, 1987).

For both sexes, the negative effects on relationships of believing in the gender stereotypes are far-reaching. In this chapter, the effects on friendships and love relationships will be examined. In the next chapter, the effects of gender on parental relationships and family functioning will be explored.

▲   Friendships

The term *friendship* has been used to describe a variety of relationships, from those with casual acquaintances to those with colleagues to those with intimates. In this discussion, *friendship* refers to an intimate, personal, caring relationship with attributes such as reciprocity, mutual choice, trust, loyalty, and openness. As discussed in Chapter 3, males and females generally have different types of friendships: males tend to have more numerous but less intimate same-sex friendships, while females tend to have same-sex friendships that are more intimate, disclosing, and emotional (Aukett, Ritchie, & Mill, 1988; Blyth & Foster-Clark, 1987; Reisman, 1990; Sapadin, 1988; Sharabany, Gershoni, & Hofman, 1981). This pattern is by no means universal, and a few studies find same-sex friendships for males and females to be more similar than different, especially among college students (Caldwell & Peplau, 1982; S. M. Rose, 1985b). Furthermore, individuals of both sexes choose friends who are similar to themselves demographically and behaviorally (D. B. Kandel, 1978). Similarity on personality

characteristics is relatively unimportant during adolescence, although value similarity increases in importance during the college years, especially for women (L. R. Davidson & Duberman, 1982; C. T. Hill & Stull, 1981; Rywick, 1984).

The general pattern of greater intimacy and disclosure in female than in male same-sex friendships exists throughout the life span, although it may be somewhat attenuated among older men and women (Antonucci & Akiyama, 1987; M. Fox, Gibbs, & Auerback, 1985; Roberto & Scott, 1986). Cultural influences certainly affect friendship patterns. For example, although gender differences in same-sex friendships exist among both White and African Americans, they are more extreme among Whites (D. L. Coates, 1987; D. L. DuBois & Hirsch, 1990; Stewart & Vaux, 1986). These ethnic differences may be due to Black males' greater intimacy than White males' with same-sex friends, and/or to Black females' relatively greater attachment to their family and consequent relatively less intimacy than White females with same-sex friends.

Expressive-nurturant traits appear to be strongly related to intimacy levels in both sexes. That is, "feminine" and androgynous individuals, when compared with "masculine" and undifferentiated individuals, tend to have more intimate relationships, more support from other people, and greater friendship satisfaction, and to be less lonely (Burda, Vaux, & Schill, 1984; D. C. Jones, Bloys, & Wood, 1990; L. Wheeler, Reis, & Nezlek, 1983; D. G. Williams, 1985). Thus, in contrast to research in the previous chapter that suggested that instrumental traits are most facilitative of mental health and achievement, research on relationships suggests that expressive traits are most facilitative. Again, being strong in both sets of traits may be optimal for the widest variety of situations and behaviors.

As we saw in Chapter 6, girls and boys start forming same-sex friendship networks very early, by age 3. Girls apparently find play with boys somewhat aversive due to boys' tendencies to engage in rough-and-tumble play and to resist girls' influence attempts (E. E. Maccoby, 1990; E. E. Maccoby & Jacklin, 1987). For girls, other girls are much more reinforcing. Sex-segregated play leads to greater gender distinctions with respect to social skills and interaction styles. Girls' greater use of language and enabling influence strategies (for example, use of polite suggestions) facilitates the development of close relationships. Boys' greater use of physical contact and restrictive influence strategies (for example, boasting) facilitates the development of dominance hierarchies but interferes with the development of intimacy. Yet the capacity for intimacy with friends in childhood appears important for overall social responsiveness and the later development of love relationships (Foot, Chapman, & Smith, 1977; Strommen, 1977). If some males are uncomfortable with intimacy and form less-intimate friendships, this situation suggests negative consequences for their future love and marital relationships.

A closer look at the nature of female-female, male-male, and male-female friendships of all ages seems warranted.

Female-Female Friendships

As has been noted, females as a group are more likely than males as a group to have close, intimate same-sex friendships. Female same-sex friendships have many positive qualities that are evident throughout the life span—trust, loyalty, enjoyment, nurturance, and attachment. Females converse with each other frequently and in great depth about such intimate topics as personal and family matters. Females tend to rate other females highly in terms of social support. Among feminist women and those who may be considered nonconventional (desirous of change and control over their lives, willing to take risks), same-sex friendships appear to be particularly important, close, and egalitarian, although the empirical data here are mixed (R. R. Bell, 1981; S. Rose & Roades, 1987). Overall, most women find their female friendships to be supportive and valuable. Indeed, some research suggests that the end of a friendship is more painful for a woman than the end of a romantic relationship, unlike the situation for men (Pierce, Smith, & Akert, 1984).

The establishment of close female friendships is facilitated by the socialization of females to value intimacy and connection. As discussed previously, girls grow up with a sense of self as embedded in relationships. A close relationship with one's mother correlates positively with intimacy in female friendships (M. Gold & Yanof, 1985). Furthermore, the personality traits encouraged in females—sensitivity, empathy, nurturance, caring, expressiveness—facilitate the development of intimate relationships.

Still, although many aspects of the female role and stereotype facilitate female same-sex friendships, a number of obstacles to such relationships also exist, including the taboo against females' displaying anger, competition for males, homophobia, the nuclear family, and society's deprecatory view of women. The general *taboo against displays of anger* in females makes it difficult for

many girls to learn how to express and resolve angry feelings that inevitably arise in intimate relationships. Thus, girls may use covert rather than overt forms of aggression in their friendships. For example, the friendship patterns of young girls frequently alternate between inclusion and exclusion, intimacy and repudiation (Bardwick, 1979; Gilligan et al., 1990). Most girls either experience or observe a close relationship between "best friends" that is broken by a third girl, only to have the triad reassemble in a different configuration shortly thereafter. White girls' friendships appear to be particularly exclusive (Hallinan & Kubitschek, 1990). It is difficult for girls, who tend to be raised in an atmosphere of connection, to establish a female identity in a culture that values separation (Eichenbaum & Orbach, 1987). Thus, females must struggle to find a comfortable balance between attachment and autonomy in their friendships, made all the more difficult by the threat of negative emotions, such as anger, envy, and competition. These experiences may lay the groundwork for girls to develop a core sense of mistrust of other females. Yet same-sex friendships are very important to female adolescents, ranking third in importance, after identity and sexuality, as an area of concern (Strommen, 1977). For males, autonomy ranks third in importance, the first two concerns being identical to those noted for girls. Despite the conflicts female friendships may involve, they are an important source of emotional support in times of personal crisis.

A second barrier to female same-sex friendships is *competition for males*. Since a female's identity traditionally has been determined by the status of the male to whom she is attached—for example, the high school football captain—girls may come to view other girls as competitors for the high-status males, thereby limiting friendships. Or they may view friendships with girls as unimportant, because no status accrues from such relationships. It is not uncommon for girls to break plans with their girlfriends if a date comes along. The girlfriend even is supposed to understand "the way it is." Candy and colleagues (Candy, Troll, & Levy, 1981) investigated female friendships in women aged 14 through 80. Although friendships providing intimacy and support remained important throughout the life span, friendships that enhanced status and power were greatest during teenage years and the 20s. After those years and through the 50s, these friendship functions decreased in importance. Thus, for young heterosexual women, relationships with men may get in the way of female friendships. For example, the most common reason for the breakup of female friendships in college is dating or marriage (S. M. Rose, 1983). For young men, the most common reason is physical separation.

A third barrier to female same-sex friendships is *homophobia*. In the 19th century in the United States, friendships between women were particularly emotionally intense, with love expressed verbally and in writing (Smith-Rosenberg, 1975). However, Freudian ideas about sexuality and unconscious motivation became generally accepted in Western cultures in the early part of the 20th century. After this shift in cultural beliefs, emotionally intense same-sex relationships frequently were viewed as an expression of latent homosexual feelings. Consequently, passionate avowals and physical expressions of love between same-sex friends became less acceptable, although the taboo has been stronger for men than for women, as will be discussed later. But the effect of homophobia on female friendships has been considerable (Pharr, 1988). To the extent that a heterosexual woman is afraid of being viewed as a lesbian, she may restrict her relationships with women and/or keep them clearly subordinated to her relationships with men. Similarly, a heterosexual woman may be afraid of forming friendships with known or suspected lesbians, further dividing women from each other. Women with a stereotypically feminine behavior pattern and traditional attitudes toward women have the most negative attitudes toward lesbians, and the most negative personal responses to homosexual advances and feelings (Newman, 1989; Whitley, 1987). Furthermore, nonfeminist heterosexual women have a greater preference than do feminist heterosexual women and feminist lesbians to be with other people when with their friend (S. Rose & Roades, 1987). These results again suggest that nonfeminist women may be more homophobic than feminist ones. Nonetheless, all three groups of women are equally satisfied with their friendships.

A fourth barrier to female same-sex friendships is *the heterosexual nuclear family*. Women's tendency to seek same-sex friendships is restricted by such factors as responsibility for small children and not being in the paid labor force (K. E. Davis & Todd, 1982). A married homemaker may have few opportunities to meet other women to form friendships. She therefore is likely to remain somewhat isolated, although there may be ethnic group and class differences in this regard. Furthermore, for married women, family needs come first (Oliker,

1989). However, with the friends they have, married women tend to be particularly self-disclosing, especially working-class women (Hacker, 1981). Furthermore, a married woman's friendships are more closely related to her psychological well-being than are the friendships of unmarried women (Goodenow & Gaier, 1986). Thus, female friendships are important for married women but may be hard to establish and maintain.

A further inhibiting factor in forming adult friendships is *the generally deprecatory view that society has of women* and that many women have accepted of each other. Many women believe that other women are gossipy, untrustworthy, and uninteresting. This view affects their interest in forming friendships with other women (Strommen, 1977). This deprecatory view of women may be held particularly by those women who have achieved some measure of success in male-dominated fields. Although such women might be expected to help other women after succeeding in their own struggles against sexist practices and expectations, in the past the reverse was more likely to be true. Women who achieved in male-dominated fields tended to identify with their male co-workers and superiors. Consequently, they tended to adopt the view that they had made it because they were different from most other women. This attitude and the resulting behaviors have been termed the Queen Bee syndrome (Staines, Tavris, & Jayaratne, 1974). In more recent years, however, empirical evidence of Queen Bee-ism has been hard to find, perhaps because more women have moved into male-dominated fields and because feminist attitudes have become more widespread (O'Leary, 1988). In fact, most professional organizations now have a women's caucus or networking group to provide support for women in their careers, and most professional women value same-sex friendships more than cross-sex ones (Sapadin, 1988).

If women manage to overcome these obstacles, the resulting friendships tend to be deep and rewarding. Fortunately, since the rise of the feminist movement in the 1960s, the value of female friendships has been increasingly recognized (see J. G. Raymond, 1986; L. B. Rubin, 1985). Even portrayals of women's friendships on television have become more positive, such as those shown in "The Golden Girls" (Spangler, 1989). In general, same-sex friendships play an important role in many women's lives. Many of these friendships serve as a model of a reciprocally supportive and egalitarian intimate relationship.

Male-Male Friendships

Despite the popular image of the closeness of male "buddies," in the past 15 years many male writers have acknowledged the poor quality of many male-male relationships (David & Brannon, 1976; Garfinkel, 1985; R. A. Lewis, 1978; McGill, 1985; S. Miller, 1983; Stoltenberg, 1989). Although boys as a group do have some intimate friendships during adolescence, these friendships generally are concerned less with interpersonal intimacy and sensitivity than are those of girls (Reis, Senchak, & Solomon, 1985; Strommen, 1977; D. G. Williams, 1985). The "gang" serves as a source of support in case of conflict with adults, rather than as a source of emotional support in personal crises. For adolescent and young adult men, male bonding frequently occurs at the expense of other groups—whether those groups be other male gangs, gay men, or females. For example, the sexist joke telling and sexual harassment and assault against women that sometimes occur when males are together serve as ways for some males to feel close to each other and separate from females (Hirsch, 1990; Lyman, 1987; Sanday, 1990).

These gender differences in same-sex friendships appear to be due in part to gender differences in affiliation motivation and in part to different expectations regarding same-sex friendships. Females seem to expect more intimacy in their friendships than males, which continues throughout the life span. Furthermore, the meaning of intimacy appears to be different for males and females (Caldwell & Peplau, 1982; Mark & Alper, 1985). For males, intimacy more often means doing things together or discussing work, sports, or politics. For females, intimacy more often means sharing feelings and concerns. Males tend to develop friendships with a wider network of other males to meet different needs, whereas females tend to develop a smaller network of other females to whom they can relate in a variety of areas (Barth & Kinder, 1988; McGill, 1985). In other words, males tend to have separate "sports friends," "work friends," "drinking buddies," and so on, whereas females tend to have a single set of friends with whom they do everything.

The lack of emotional sharing in many male same-sex friendships means that many males do not receive maximum benefits from friendships—the relief of being able to release feelings with someone else and receive support, and the opportunity to broaden interests and perspective. In fact, many adult males never have had a close male friend or known what it means to share affection and concern

with a male without fear of ridicule (Garfinkel, 1985; H. Goldberg, 1976; Komarovsky, 1974; Letich, 1991). As a result, men tend to report more feelings of loneliness than women, and the roots of their loneliness compared to that of women are more likely to lie in the lack of a cohesive set of friends (Borys & Perlman, 1985; Stokes & Levin, 1986).

As discussed earlier, being strong in expressive traits is most conducive to intimate relationships. Such traits generally are not encouraged in males. However, most males do appear capable of intimacy. For example, certain situational cues (like being asked to have an intimate conversation with their best friend) will elicit conversations similar to those that take place between female best friends (Reis et al., 1985). Thus, the lower level of intimacy in many male-male friendships seems to be due to a reluctance rather than an inability to be intimate. This reluctance to be intimate with another male probably stems from the male gender stereotype as inculcated through socialization practices—the emphasis on independence and competition, suppression of feelings and self-disclosure, an instilled fear of homosexuality, and the lack of appropriate role models. Let's take a closer look at these obstacles to close male same-sex friendships.

Competitiveness is a major obstacle to male same-sex friendships. Most males are socialized early into believing that actions are more important than feelings and that they must compete in everything they do to "win" or come out on top. This intense male competition may pervade nearly every area of encounter among men, including sports, work, sex, and conversation. It makes intimate relationships among men most unlikely (Fasteau, 1974; Garfinkel, 1985; Townsend, 1977). Using a questionnaire to measure gender role conflict in men, O'Neil and colleagues (1986) found that more than half of their sample of college males found these issues of competition and success to be conflictual for them. Because some males always are comparing themselves to other males, some relationships among men tend to be awkward and uncomfortable, sometimes marked by distrust and by an undercurrent of violence. It is difficult to be supportive toward people with whom one is competing.

It is not only socialization pressures that emphasize male-male competition but also the structural aspects of the roles that men are likely to inhabit (M. P. Farrell, 1986). From organized sports to hierarchical business organizations, competitiveness is emphasized. Not surprisingly, then, the values attached to competition and dominance for males also pervade the friendships that are formed. Male friendship groups are characterized by "dominance bonding," a form of connection in which members affirm and reaffirm their superiority (Farr, 1988). This time of jockeying for position within a group and assuming superiority over those outside the group (for example, females and gays) starts in the preschool years and can last a lifetime (Franklin, 1984; E. E. Maccoby, 1990; Sanday, 1990). Such friendship groups may take different forms, depending upon age, class, and ethnic background of the participants, but they all share the pattern of exaggerating "masculine" traits, whether they be toughness, financial success, heterosexuality, or dominance. In this way, ghetto males, fraternity men, "good ole boys," and upper-class men in private clubs all have similar types of friendship groups. Exclusivity and "one-upmanship" reign.

An even more important factor than competitiveness in inhibiting male friendships is the strong message most boys receive regarding *the need to suppress feelings*. Thus, maxims such as "Big boys don't cry," "Keep a stiff upper lip," and "Take it like a man" all pressure boys to keep their feelings hidden. If boys do not hide their emotions, they are likely to suffer marked loss in prestige, to be liked less, and to have difficulty assuming the competitive role society has set out for them. By sharing feelings, people become vulnerable. In a competitive atmosphere, this means that someone might take advantage of such vulnerability. According to male sex role prescriptions, showing feelings is weak and must be avoided at all costs. As we saw in Chapter 3, males self-disclose less than females, especially feelings of love, sadness, and happiness, and especially to other males. This is true even among identified friends (Mazur, 1989). Masculine-sex-typed males especially tend to be very low in self-disclosure to other males, although "masculinity" is not linked to males' self-disclosures to females (Winstead, Derlega, & Wong, 1984). Men from working-class backgrounds are particularly low in self-disclosure to other men, perhaps because they tend to be the most traditionally gender-stereotyped (Hacker, 1981).

Males begin to cover up their feelings as early as age 4. Yet the quality that most facilitates friendship formation is openness to others (Jourard, 1971; Strommen, 1977). Ironically, it is only in close relationships that men get emotional support, unlike the situation for women, who receive support from many different types of relationships, such as those among colleagues (D. G. Wilson & Stokes, 1983).

Low self-disclosure in men explains why many male conversations tend to be monologues rather than give-and-take communications, since responding to another may reveal feelings (see Chapter 3). Another reason male conversations tend to be monologues may be that both of the men involved may try to dominate and interrupt the conversation.

In general, male socialization and gender norms make it difficult for many men to self-disclose to other men. Instead, as we will discuss in the next section, men prefer to self-disclose to women, if they self-disclose at all.

Related to this fear of expressing feelings is an even more specific fear of expressing positive feelings toward other males—the fear of being thought a homosexual (*homophobia*). Imagine one man asking another to come over to his place just to talk, not to watch TV, go to a bar, or get together with other men or women. If the first time this happened, the man who was asked did not feel a little uncomfortable about possible implications, he would be unusual (Fasteau, 1974). In fact, males are more likely than females to engage in group friendship situations, perhaps because unstructured same-sex relationships are perceived as dangerous (Mazur, 1989; Mazur & Olver, 1987). In contrast, women seem to prefer unstructured dyadic interactions, which allow more intimacy.

Homophobia occurs in both men and women, but is stronger and more common among men than women (Kite, 1984; Kurdek, 1988a; Lieblich & Friedman, 1985). For example, in a 1989 nationwide survey of 3583 Americans, 51% of the men but only 28% of the women disapproved of homosexual rights (Barron, 1989). Similar percentages have been found in national surveys of American college freshmen (A. W. Astin, 1991). Heterosexual women also are more likely than heterosexual men to know a same-sex homosexual (Whitley, 1990). This male homophobia is so pervasive that intimacy between males often is deliberately suppressed. Fathers stop kissing and hugging sons; boys stop touching each other except in ritualized ways (handshakes, shoulder slaps, and fanny patting in sports). A stigma is attached to anything vaguely feminine. O'Neil and colleagues (1986) found that about three-fourths of their sample of college men were uncomfortable in situations where affectionate behavior between men was evident.

Male homophobia is not rational, since most beliefs about male homosexuals are false (Lehne, 1976; Morin & Garfinkle, 1978). For example, the majority of male homosexuals are not afraid of women, do not appear effeminate, are not limited to a few occupations, do not molest children, and are not psychologically abnormal or even unusual. Homophobia, then, is not a specifically sexual fear but rather a political one. It is related to a range of personality characteristics typical of prejudiced individuals: authoritarianism, conservative support of the status quo, and rigidity of sex roles. The best single predictor of homophobia is a belief in the traditional family ideology—a dominant father and a subservient mother. Individuals (male and female) with nontraditional sex role behaviors, attitudes, and personality characteristics are least likely to hold negative attitudes toward homosexuals (Krulewitz & Nash, 1980; Kurdek, 1988a; Lieblich & Friedman, 1985; Whitley, 1987). The real issue is the general maintenance by men of a society in which men control power through the regulation of sex roles. Homophobia serves this purpose by defining and reinforcing gender distinctions and the associated distribution of power. It keeps men within the boundaries of traditionally defined roles.

Homophobia and the stigmatization of gay men thus functions to maintain a traditional definition of masculinity by forcing men to deny their own homoerotic feelings and any qualities culturally viewed as feminine, such as sensitivity and nurturance (Herek, 1987). An experimental study by Karr (1978) exemplifies this social control factor. A group of college men were led to believe that one member of their group was homosexual. The labeled male was perceived by others in the group as being significantly less masculine and less preferred as a fellow participant in a future experiment than when the same individual had not been so labeled in a different group. Similar results have been found by others (Kite & Deaux, 1986; Krulewitz & Nash, 1980). Furthermore, the man in the group responsible for labeling the targeted individual (both men actually were experimental confederates) was perceived as more masculine and more sociable when he did the labeling than when, in another group, he did not. These results suggest that men are reinforced for publicly identifying homosexual men and that men have good reason to fear being labeled homosexual. The negative reactions to the labeled male and positive reactions to the labeler were even stronger when the subjects were homophobic men (that is, scored high on a scale measuring homophobic beliefs). The power of a male who labels another male as homosexual was supported by another study that found that this label was the worst thing a man could call another

man, at least in the eyes of college students (Preston & Stanley, 1987).

The price paid by men for conforming to male role expectations is great, since conforming to the male stereotype seriously impairs both same-sex and heterosexual relationships, causes severe anxiety, and narrows the range of legitimate male emotions, interests, and activities. In conjunction with this interpretation, Fasteau (1974) and others (Hirsch, 1990; Sanday, 1990) hypothesize that the real function of all-male groups is to provide mutual assurance of masculinity, to make personal communication difficult, and to defuse any assumption of intensity of same-sex feelings. Homophobia must be eliminated before a change in gender roles can be brought about. Dispelling homophobia clearly is necessary before close male relationships can occur, since men high on homophobia have been found to like a male stranger less and be less intimate with their male friends than are less homophobic men (Devlin & Cowan, 1985; Kite & Deaux, 1986).

Robert Lewis (1978) suggests that a fourth barrier to the expression of emotional intimacy between men is *the lack of role models* for such behaviors. We do not see many examples of affection giving between males, even between fathers and sons. This lack of warmth and affection by their fathers is a major complaint of men (Garfinkel, 1985; Komarovsky, 1976; Salk, 1982), yet their sons are likely to repeat the process. We know that children's emotional expressiveness is closely related to their parents' perceived expressiveness (Balswick, 1988). If a young boy grows up without seeing intimate emotions expressed by men, he most likely will inhibit his emotional expressiveness when he becomes an adult. Consequently, he will not be able to serve as a role model for such expressive behaviors for other young men. The pattern thus is likely to continue. Given all the other influences upon male expressive behavior, it is not surprising that Balswick (1988) found that only when a father is very expressive of love, is a son's emotional expressiveness likely to equal a daughter's.

Despite the barriers to intimate male-male friendships, men do appear to value the friendships they have. In most studies, males and females are equally satisfied with their same-sex friendships (Mazur, 1989). Furthermore, although gender differences in friendship quality are consistent, the magnitude of the differences is not very large. In particular, most of the differences in friendship patterns have been found between sex-typed males and females. Few differences have been found in the same-sex friendships of androgynous females and males (see, for example, Barth & Kinder, 1988). Again, we must remember to be cautious about making extreme distinctions between the behavior of males and females in this and in other areas.

Male-Female Friendships

If male-male friendships are difficult to establish, male-female ones are even more so. Most people have fewer other-sex friends than same-sex ones, although mixed-sex friendships have become more common among the younger generations. For example, in the mid-1980s, about one out of four college students named a member of the other sex as a best friend, whereas in the late 1970s, only 18% of a representative sample of middle-class Americans reported a close friendship with a member of the other sex (Block, 1980; K. E. Davis, 1985).

Barriers   Many barriers impede the establishment of cross-sex friendships, starting in preschool: gender segregation of activities, sexualization of male-female relationships, social pressures, ambiguity and lack of role models, sex-typed traits and behaviors, and gender inequality. (See O'Meara, 1989, for a structural analysis of these barriers.) All of these barriers are connected to gender stereotypes and gender roles.

Since to form friendships, people must first have an opportunity to get to know each other, the frequent *gender segregation of activities* inhibits the development of mixed-sex friendships. As we have seen, gender segregation begins during the preschool years, is widespread, and continues to a large extent into adulthood (E. E. Maccoby, 1990; E. E. Maccoby & Jacklin, 1987). Such segregation allows the sexes to develop distinctive interaction styles, which exaggerate both perceived and actual gender differences. Both males and females tend to believe that members of the other sex are significantly different from themselves in attitudes, interests, and personal styles, even though actual gender differences in these areas are small and certainly are not found consistently (Borges, Levine, & Naylor, 1982; H. R. Freeman, 1979). During college, both women and men think the other sex demands conformity to the gender stereotypes, even though such demands tend to be minimal (L. R. Davidson, 1981). Both sexes also perceive other-sex peers as less trustworthy than same-sex peers, and these differences in perceptions of trust are apparent by the second grade (Rotenberg, 1984, 1986). Since trust is critical in the formation of intimate relationships,

cross-sex friendships are difficult to establish under these circumstances. Furthermore, in some cases, boys' early socialization to reject anything vaguely feminine may lead to fear and hatred of females (Fasteau, 1974; O'Neil, 1982). Such feelings are unlikely to facilitate friendship formation between the sexes.

Compulsory heterosexuality and the *sexualization of male-female relationships* create additional barriers to male-female friendships. As the opening anecdote of this chapter indicates, many people have difficulty believing that heterosexual males and females can have purely platonic relationships. Not only does this view add social pressure and external scrutiny to mixed-sex friendships that do not exist for same-sex friendships, this sexualized expectation affects participants in cross-sex friendships as well. That is, sexual feelings nearly always must be dealt with in mixed-sex friendships between heterosexual individuals, whereas their same-sex friendships typically don't bear this burden (McGill, 1985; O'Meara, 1989). Indeed, sexualized expectations make forming mixed-sex friendships extremely difficult. Many existing mixed-sex friendships are formed only after a sexual-romantic relationship has not worked out or when one party has clearly rejected the possibility of a sexual-romantic relationship. For these reasons, male-female relationships wherein one or both parties is homosexual are much less problematical than those wherein both parties are heterosexual. Because of the sexualization of male-female relationships, mixed-sex friendships are particularly difficult when one or both parties are married.

Because of their socialization, males have a harder time than females leaving sex out of their mixed-sex encounters. Beginning in adolescence, many males start viewing females as sex objects (Townsend, 1977). Furthermore, many males learn that intimacy means sex, one reason why same-sex male friendships tend to be less intimate than same-sex female friendships (McGill, 1985). Thus, the idea of a male establishing a purely platonic relationship with a female is inconceivable to many. Indeed, research examining people's motives for establishing a mixed-sex friendship typically finds that men are motivated primarily by sexual attraction, whereas women are not (S. M. Rose, 1985b).

Considerable research evidence supports the observation that men tend to see women and their behaviors in a more sexualized way than women see men. For example, in a variety of laboratory studies, male observers of a male-female interaction tend to perceive more "sexiness" (for example, flirtatiousness, promiscuity) and less friendliness in the woman's behaviors than do female observers (Abbey, 1982; Abbey & Melby, 1986; C. B. Johnson, Stockdale, & Saal, 1991; Saal, Johnson, & Weber, 1989). Furthermore, college women actually report having had their friendliness misperceived as sexual interest by a member of the other sex more often than do college men (Abbey, 1987). These different perceptions of female behavior make the formation of male-female platonic relationships difficult.

Another barrier to the formation of male-female friendships is *stereotypic personality traits, behaviors, and ideology.* Generally speaking, the more stereotyped the individual, the less likely he or she is to form a friendship with a member of the other sex. In one study with college students, men and women were paired up on the basis of their sex-role orientation (as measured by the BSRI) and left on their own for five minutes (Ickes & Barnes, 1978). The ensuing interaction differed as a function of the sex typing combination. Dyads composed of a sex-typed man and a sex-typed woman showed significantly greater interpersonal incompatibility and stress than dyads in which one or both members were androgynous. For example, sex-typed couples verbalized to each other less and had fewer positive feelings about the interaction than other dyads. The researchers ruled out the possibility that the sex-typed individuals were more socially distant or less physically attractive than the non-sex-typed members of the other dyads. The lack of compatibility between sex-typed men and women may reflect their tendency to adopt highly stereotyped and socially opposed sex roles in such unstructured situations. Such roles would make establishing a friendship extremely difficult, although in a naturalistic setting, where expectations for male and female behavior tend to be clearer, such role-bound behavior might lead to more positive feelings. Nonetheless, sex-typed individuals of the other sex do appear to be regarded as less desirable as friends than androgynous individuals (L. A. Jackson, 1983; L. A. Jackson & Cash, 1985; Kulik & Harackiewicz, 1979; Major, Carnevale, & Deaux, 1981). This is so regardless of the rater's own sex type. In fact, sex-typed college women are less likely than androgynous college women to have a close male friend (Lavine & Lombardo, 1984). Thus, the evidence is fairly consistent in indicating that strict sex typing inhibits mixed-sex friendships.

Gendered patterns of communication, as discussed in Chapter 3, also make friendship formation between women and men difficult, as illustrated in Figure 9.1.

Figure 9.1 How adherence to gender stereotypes can affect relationships between the sexes. (Copyright 1973 by Bülbül. Reprinted by permission.)

In particular, since emotional sharing is the hallmark of an intimate relationship, males appear to be at a disadvantage in participating in such relationships, as we discussed in the section on male-male friendships. Indeed, some evidence exists that in mixed-sex relationships, females may provide a listening and support service ("ego boosting") for males without receiving any reciprocal service. It appears that both males and females prefer to self-disclose to another female, who may have had more experience and investment in being a good listener and in providing empathic support (Buhrke & Fuqua, 1987; Burda et al., 1984; Hacker, 1981; Sapadin, 1988; L. Wheeler et al., 1983). Thus, females may be less motivated than males by the prospect of obtaining needed emotional support in establishing a mixed-sex friendship. We need to examine the benefits of such relationships more closely.

Benefits Although the barriers just listed make the establishment of male-female friendships difficult, people who participate in such relationships generally find them to be rewarding. Mixed-sex friendships increase in frequency and intimacy during adolescence, with the transition occurring earlier for girls (seventh grade) than for boys (ninth grade) (Sharabany et al., 1981).

We have noted that for males, females may be the only people to whom they can, or are willing to, self-disclose (Fitzpatrick & Bochner, 1981). Even (or especially) among married men, female friends remain important recipients of self-disclosures (McGill, 1985). It appears that females contribute emotional closeness and meaningfulness to an interaction, whether that interaction be with another female or male. In short, females make good friends. Not surprisingly, men are more likely than women to nominate a member of the other sex as a close friend and to look to other-sex rather than same-sex friendships for emotional intimacy and support (Aukett et al., 1988; K. E. Davis, 1985; Reisman, 1990; F. W. Schneider & Coutts, 1985). Furthermore, men tend to describe their cross-sex relationships as closer than do women (Buhrke & Fuqua, 1987). However, we must be careful about generalizing from research using mainly White participants to all males and females. Different sex-race groups appear to have different patterns of friendship (D. L. Coates, 1987; Hallinan & Kubitschek, 1990).

In contrast to males, females rate their cross-sex friendships as less intimate and accepting than their same-sex friendships. Women see themselves as initiating more in cross-sex friendships and as wanting to give more than men (Buhrke & Fuqua, 1987). Women see more room for improvement in their cross-sex friendships than in their same-sex ones. If cross-sex friendships appear less rewarding than same-sex friendships for women, what motivates women to enter or maintain such mixed-sex relationships? Females receive a number of benefits from such friendships. In some situations, females feel more comfortable disclosing certain feelings (like love) to other-sex than to same-sex friends (Balswick, 1988). Second, females often enjoy the companionship and the lesser intensity offered by male friends. Third, male friends, by virtue of their societal and gender status, also can offer status to their female friends. Furthermore, both sexes may enjoy the different perspectives offered by friends of the other sex (Sapadin, 1988). In particular, mixed-sex friendships allow each member to get an "insider's" view of how the other sex thinks.

In general, cross-sex friendships appear to involve more role playing and less spontaneity than same-sex friendships (K. E. Davis, 1985; Fitzpatrick & Bochner, 1981; Hacker, 1981; S. M. Rose, 1985b). Females are perceived as being dependent on the male friend, and males are perceived as being nurturant toward the female friend. Men tend to reveal mainly their strengths, and women their weaknesses, in cross-sex friendships. Despite these differences, mixed-sex friendships tend to be valued by those who have them. Such friendships may be a necessary step in breaking down the gender stereotypes, since, as social psychological research has established firmly, personal contact on an equal footing between members of disparate groups is necessary for the elimination of prejudice.

Discussion

Gender roles clearly affect friendship relationships. Because of the emphasis on nurturant-expressive traits for females, female same-sex friendships tend to be particularly close and satisfying. Nonetheless, there are cultural barriers, such as the devaluation of females and competition for male approval, that must be overcome in order to establish and maintain such relationships. Close same-sex friendships are even harder to establish for males than for females. Males' relatively low levels of nurturant-expressive traits, high levels of competitive and dominant traits, and strong homophobia all make male same-sex friendships less intimate and more activity-based than female same-sex friendships. The most difficult friendships to establish are male-female ones, due to divergent gender roles, traits, and behaviors, as well as the sexualization of male-female encounters. Such friendships do occur, although the rewards of such relationships may be greater for males than females. Yet society conspires against such friendships and systematically steers members of the two sexes into romantic relationships.

▲ Heterosexual Dating

If friendship formation is affected by gender roles and stereotypes, the establishment of romantic relationships is affected by them even more. Heterosexual dating, marriage, and cohabitation, as well as homosexual relationships, all reflect society's messages about appropriate male-female behavior. We will examine each type of relationship in turn. Because sexual behavior was discussed in Chapter 4, it will be mentioned only briefly here.

Gender roles and stereotypes convey clear messages regarding how males and females are supposed to get along: both sexes are supposed to be attracted to sex-typed others (that is, women are supposed to prefer "masculine" men, men to prefer "feminine" women); men are supposed to initiate heterosexual encounters, although women can signal their interest in indirect, flirtatious ways; men are supposed to be dominant within the relationship; women and men are supposed to naturally be sexually attracted to each other, although sexual feelings are supposed to be more important for males than for females; and women are supposed to be more interested than men in love and in relationships. These messages all are part of a cultural heterosexual "script." In fact, the heterosexual dating script is so well known that when college students were asked to list the content and sequence of actions that would occur on a first date, agreement was strikingly high and strikingly gender-stereotyped (S. Rose & Frieze, 1989). Women's dating script focuses upon enhancing their appearance, making conversation, and controlling sexual behavior, whereas men's dating script focuses on planning and paying for the date as well as initiating sexual behavior. Although the heterosexual dating script, like the sexual one discussed in Chapter 4, constructs and exaggerates differences between women and men (women control the private sphere while men control the public one), its constructed nature is rarely questioned. The effects of gender roles and stereotypes on heterosexual dating relationships can be discerned in three areas: initiation, relationship development, and power differences.

Initiation

On the average, dating begins shortly after puberty, although game-playing precursors may begin much earlier. The beginning of dating signals the start of many anxieties about gender role and sexual competence. For both sexes, many dating and romantic involvements serve instrumental purposes—peer acceptance and conformity to sex role expectations—and not necessarily emotional ones. In fact, true intimacy often actually is discouraged between the sexes by the stereotypic emphasis on sexual achievement for males and on attracting a high-status mate for females. Being viewed as a status symbol by females may make some males feel superior, but it also may make them unduly attached to status-attaining activities, such as any that make money. Similarly, being viewed as a sex object by males may make some females feel attractive, but it also may cause some females to be overconcerned with their physical appearance. Analyses of personal advertisements in newspapers reflect these stereotypic patterns: men more than women emphasize that they are looking for physical characteristics, whereas women more than men emphasize that they are looking for status characteristics (S. Davis, 1990; Deaux & Hanna, 1984; J. E. Smith, Waldorf, & Trembath, 1990). When one's appeal is based on superficial qualities, trusting the other sex is difficult.

Intimacy also is discouraged by the highly ritualized nature of most dating situations and by the inequality in the dating relationship itself (Laws & Schwartz, 1977; S. Rose & Frieze, 1989). Traditionally, males do the asking and initiating; females can only refuse or accept. Despite changing sex role norms, men still initiate dates in the vast majority of instances, leading to the finding that more than one-third of college men experience dating anxiety, in contrast to one-quarter of college women (Himadi, Arkowitz, Hinton, & Perl, 1980). Furthermore, women who do initiate dates are viewed less positively than men who initiate dates (S. K. Green & Sandos, 1983). Yet women can and do signal their interest in specific males indirectly through a variety of nonverbal behaviors. One researcher catalogued 52 different flirtatious behaviors that effectively solicited male attention (M. M. Moore, 1985). Perhaps this is the reason women are stereotyped as indirect and manipulative. These qualities, rather than being intrinsic to females, seem like a function of the negative consequences women receive for being more direct.

The importance attached to sex for men and the double standard attached to sex for women are additional obstacles to be overcome in developing intimate heterosexual relationships. As discussed earlier, men frequently perceive sexual interest in a woman's behavior when she perceives only friendliness. This misunderstanding can lead to social discomfort and, in some cases, rape. As we will see in Chapter 12, men are more likely to hold rape myths than women; in particular, men are likely to believe that a woman doesn't really mean "no" when she says "no." Perhaps men's tendency to sexualize women's behavior should be expected given the cultural tendency to do the same, as seen in the media. Furthermore, since about one-third of college women sometimes do say "no" when they mean "yes," the resultant confusion and mistrust each sex has toward the other impedes relationship development (Muehlenhard & Hollabaugh, 1988; Muehlenhard & McCoy, 1991).

The gender stereotypes themselves cause much strain in male-female romantic relationships. Both sexes believe that the other sex expects them to live up to the gender stereotypes (Braito, Dean, Powers, & Bruton, 1981; Crovitz & Steinmann, 1980; L. R. Davidson, 1981; D. Scher, 1984). Despite the fact that the belief generally is wrong, especially on the part of males, the belief itself causes great strain as each person feels the pressure to conform to the impossible-to-attain standard. These mistaken beliefs are hard to eliminate since open communication between the sexes deviates from "playing the dating game." The training of many males to avoid expressing emotions and to avoid empathy works as another impediment to open communication. For all these reasons, Lillian Rubin (1983) refers to men and women together as "intimate strangers." In the Black community, especially, social life tends to be sex-segregated rather than couple-centered. This lack of companionship is a major source of disagreement between Black men and their partners (Gary, 1987).

Thus, despite the reality that most people, women and men, value both intimacy and egalitarian autonomy in relationships (Cochran & Peplau, 1985), both women and men must first break out of traditional gender roles and behaviors in order to attain these qualities. Research has found that strong masculine sex typing is associated with a strong game-playing attitude toward love and a weak possessive-dependent attitude, whereas strong feminine sex typing is associated with a weak game-playing and a strong possessive-dependent attitude (W. C. Bailey et al., 1987). Consequently, sex-typed partners may be quite opposite in their orientation toward love. Getting free of the conventional dating script appears to be easier for androgynous individuals than for others, probably because they are most likely to hold similar love attitudes and because they are the most behaviorally flexible and the least gender schematic (DeLucia, 1987).

Relationship Development

What happens when the sexes do get romantically involved with each other? How do the gender roles and stereotypes affect behaviors in heterosexual romantic relationships?

Although women generally are thought of as emotional and likely to fall in love easily, research suggests that men tend to fall harder, at least initially. Compared to women, men rate the desire to fall in love as a stronger motive in starting a relationship, they tend to fall in love more readily, they are less likely to end a relationship that appears ill-fated, and they are more upset when their relationship breaks up (Hatfield & Sprecher, 1986; C. T. Hill, Rubin, & Peplau, 1976; T. L. Huston & Ashmore, 1986; Pierce et al., 1984; Z. Rubin, Peplau, & Hill, 1981). Although women tend to be more cautious than men about falling in love, once past the early stages of dating, women and men tend to love with equal passion.

But what do men and women mean by love? Apparently, love means something different for the two sexes. Men tend to have a more game-playing attitude toward love than women, while women tend to be more pragmatic, possessive-dependent, and friendship-oriented in their love attitudes (W. C. Bailey et al., 1987; C. Hendrick & Hendrick, 1986). Cancian (1986, 1987) argues that in the United States, the current definition of love actually is feminine, with a heavy emphasis on emotional expressiveness. Since this aspect of love is one with which women feel more comfortable and at which they are more skilled, women tend to be viewed as the more loving sex. Such a definition works against recognizing as legitimate other manifestations of love, such as instrumental activities (like helping) or physical expressiveness (like sex). It is these other definitions of love that many men appear to use. Perhaps a more androgynous definition of love, one that combines both instrumental and expressive styles, is needed, together with more understanding of the value of such differences.

Gender differences with respect to the meaning and value of love are affected by the social and historical context. As a result of gender socialization, women may be more adept at cognitively managing their feelings. Alternatively, because women traditionally have been so dependent on their mate for their own status and economic situation, they may need to be more practical and utilitarian than men in choosing a mate. In contrast, men traditionally have been freer to follow their fancy. Research with college students in the mid-1960s found that romantic love was a precondition for marriage for two-thirds of the men but only one-fourth of the women (Kephart, 1967). Perhaps with the economic liberation of women, women too will become freer to marry for love or become less likely to marry at all. Both trends appear to be occurring. Among college students in the mid-1980s, four-fifths of both the men and the women view romantic love as a precondition for marriage (J. A. Simpson, Campbell, & Berscheid, 1986). The increased age of both sexes upon entering first marriages may indicate that women no longer have to get married to survive in this culture. In 1990, the median age of first-time newlyweds was 23.9 for the bride and 26.1 for the groom, the highest since the government started keeping these statistics in 1890 (Barringer, 1991). It is also possible that the later age at which first marriages occur reflects the changing norms regarding premarital sex. People no longer have to get married just to get sex. The fact that most people eventually do get married may mean that at least some marriages currently are being based on more than practical necessity. If so, these marriages may be stronger and last longer than those already in existence.

What factors facilitate good dating relationships? Some sharing of attitudes and values, and each partner's subjective judgment of intimacy appear important for relationship satisfaction and longevity (C. T. Hill, Peplau, & Rubin, 1981). Compatibility of gender ideology also appears important. Grush and Yehl (1979) found that both female college students with nontraditional attitudes toward gender roles in marriage and male college students with traditional attitudes toward gender roles in marriage had distinct preferences for partners who shared their ideology. Both groups rated similar other-sex individuals as more likable and as more desirable as dating and marital partners than they did other-sex individuals who had dissimilar views. For traditional women and nontraditional men, on the other hand, partner similarity was not important for ratings of likability and desirability. The researchers suggest that this interaction between gender and traditionality is due to the possibility that nontraditional women and traditional men have irreconcilable differences that would make

constant conflicts likely. In contrast, traditional women and nontraditional men are more likely to be adaptable to their partner's preferences.

More behaviorally, attachment and empathic behaviors appear strongly related to relationship satisfaction for women and men (Cochran & Peplau, 1985; N. L. Collins & Read, 1990; M. H. Davis & Oathout, 1987). However, the precise behaviors that predict dating relationship satisfaction differ somewhat for the sexes. For women, relationship satisfaction depends upon their partner's willingness to be emotionally close and to communicate. Perhaps because men tend to be less empathic, less self-disclosing, and less willing to become close than females, these behaviors when present carry great weight. Men too value empathic behaviors in their partner but are more sensitive than women to their partner's anxiety about being unloved or abandoned. Men's relationship satisfaction is higher when their partner's anxiety is low, perhaps because when such anxiety is present, men may feel restricted.

When problems arise in dating relationships, women are more likely than men to attempt to improve conditions (Rusbult, Johnson, & Morrow, 1986). Sex typing actually is more important than gender in predicting how an individual reacts to relationship problems, with those people high in nurturant-expressive traits and low in active-instrumental ones (that is, feminine-sex-typed individuals) being the most constructive in their attempts to resolve relationship problems (Rusbult, Zembrodt, & Iwaniszek, 1986). Women, of course, are more likely to be feminine-sex-typed than men. Perhaps because women have tried harder than men to overcome relationship problems in the past, when such problems persist, women may find it easier to conclude that the relationship cannot be saved.

Power Differences
Another factor affecting dating relationships is the traditional emphasis on male dominance. This "ideal" has been modified in recent years and the norm has increasingly become one of equality and intellectual companionship (Bachman, 1987; Herzog, Bachman, & Johnson, 1983). Yet a gap still remains between the ideal and the real, especially for males.

Peplau and colleagues (Peplau, Rubin, & Hill, 1976, 1977), in their two-year study of 231 dating couples in Boston, found that dating couples overwhelmingly favored equality as the norm in their relationships in intellectual and other areas. However, less than half the couples actually felt there was equality in their particular relationship. When individuals perceived an imbalance of power, it was usually in the direction of male dominance. Similarly, Komarovsky (1973, 1976), in her study of male seniors at an eastern Ivy League college, found that 30% of the men experienced some anxiety about not being intellectually superior to their dating partners. Of the 70% who expressed a desire for intellectual equality with their dating partners, most still felt their future wife should spend at least some of her life being a full-time homemaker, a role they held in low esteem. Virtually every study that examines attitudes toward gender roles finds that females have more egalitarian attitudes than males (see, for example, K. S. Larsen & Long, 1988).

With such male ambivalence about equality, it is not surprising that nearly one-half of one sample of college women reported having feigned intellectual inferiority on dates at least sometimes (Braito et al., 1981). (For college men, the percentage who "played dumb" at least sometimes was one-third.) Females are more likely than males to try to make their date feel superior in some way by making ego-boosting statements or by letting the date win in a game. Because more than half of all college students are female, the likelihood of female intellectual equality and even superiority occurring between dating partners is high. Ambivalence regarding the elimination of male dominance in a relationship may put tremendous strains on the individuals involved, especially with respect to willingness to self-disclose. Males may be reluctant to reveal their vulnerabilities, whereas females may be reluctant to reveal their strengths.

Other research confirms the findings that more men than women are looking for a traditional marriage. (Traditional refers to the preference for the pattern of employed husband and nonemployed wife.) For example, in Peplau and colleagues' study (1976, 1977) of dating couples, college men were consistently more traditional than women regarding their preferred marriage option 15 years later. Although dual-career marriage plans were popular among a sizable number of students of both sexes (65% of women, 48% of men), 20% of the men but only 5% of the women preferred the traditional marriage option. More recent research with high school and college students finds a similar gender gap in preference for and attitudes regarding the traditional marriage pattern. For example, a nationwide survey of high school students in 1986 found that 46% of the males but only 21% of the females agreed that "it is usually better for everyone involved if the man is the achiever outside the home

and the woman takes care of the home and the family" (Bachman, 1987). Similar results have been found among entering college students, although the gender gap is not as large. In 1990, 31% of the men agreed that married women's activities are best confined to home and family, in contrast to only 20% of the women (A. W. Astin, 1991). Thus, although norms regarding desired marriage patterns have been changing, they are changing more for females than for males. Such differences in preferences can cause problems in dating and marital relationships.

Still, there is no question that attitudes have changed dramatically in the last 50 years toward greater acceptance of employment for married women. A nationwide survey conducted in 1978 found that three-quarters of Americans approved of employed wives, a direct turnaround in the results of a similar survey conducted in 1938 (Yankelovich, 1981). At that time, three-quarters of the population disapproved of a married woman's earning money if she had a husband capable of supporting her. Other research confirms the increasingly liberated view of the female role since the 1960s in terms of employment, independence, and assertiveness, although some retrenchment was apparent in the 1980s (see, for example, Weeks & Botkin, 1987). Yet, although most high school and college students, as well as the general public, appear to accept an employed wife, there are many qualifiers. Approval of an employed wife goes down if she has children, especially young children. Approval also goes down if she is viewed as primarily career-oriented or highly ambitious (Bachman, 1987; Herzog et al., 1983; Michelini, Eisen, & Snodgrass, 1981; National Opinion Research Center, 1986). Careers may be OK, indeed attractive for women, but only when these careers take second place to family needs. Not coincidentally, such attitudes are the ones most commonly found among college women (Greenglass & Devins, 1982).

Differences appear to exist between Blacks and Whites with respect to appropriate gender roles within male-female relationships. Perhaps because the traditional pattern of a male breadwinner and female homemaker is mainly pertinent for middle-class Whites, negative attitudes toward maternal employment and a wife's career orientation appear less commonly among Blacks than among members of other ethnic groups (Crovitz & Steinmann, 1980; Herzog et al., 1983). Furthermore, there is little discrepancy between women's and men's views of the ideal female role among Black college students, unlike among White college students. However, relationship equality between Black men and women still has been hard to achieve, but for different reasons. Because Black women are more likely than Black men to be college graduates and to hold professional positions, and because both Black men and women continue to be victims of racism in employment settings, it often is not even possible for Black men to aspire to be the family breadwinner and protector (D. Bell, 1989; Cazenave, 1983). Many Black men resent what they perceive as Black women's (only relatively) greater advantages. This resentment of Black women causes its own problems in Black heterosexual relationships (Franklin, 1986).

Another indication that more men than women have traditional expectations of their romantic partners is the finding that for mates, women prefer relatively androgynous men, but men, especially traditional ones, prefer relatively sex-typed women (Alperson & Friedman, 1983; Keen & Zur, 1989; Kulik & Harackiewicz, 1979; Orlofsky, 1982; D. Scher, 1984). Interestingly, androgynous individuals have been found to be more loving (more aware of loving feelings, more willing to express feelings, more tolerant of faults) than either sex-typed or undifferentiated individuals (M. Coleman & Ganong, 1985). Non-sex-typed individuals also seem to be more satisfied with their relationships and less jealous than sex-typed individuals (G. L. Hansen, 1985; Stephen & Harrison, 1985).

Equality in a relationship is hard to achieve. A number of factors affect it: (1) belief in gender stereotypes (the more traditional, the more male power), (2) the degree of involvement of each member of the couple (the lesser the involvement, the greater the power), (3) the woman's educational career goals (the lower the goals, the greater the male power), (4) the man's self-esteem (the lower the self-esteem, the greater the preference for traditional roles), and (5) the sex typing of each member of the couple (the more androgynous the member, the greater the preference for an egalitarian relationship) (Grube, Kleinhesselink, & Kearney, 1982; Herzog et al., 1983; Hollender & Shafer, 1981; Peplau et al., 1976; Pursell, Banikiotes, & Sebastian, 1981; Sprecher, 1985). College students are more likely to rate their dating relationship as egalitarian when trust, commitment, and dependency are high (Grauerholz, 1987). Either these relationship qualities motivate people to behave in more egalitarian ways, or egalitarian relationships tend to be high in these qualities. A third possibility is that such qualities may disguise inequality between partners. That is, people may be more willing to overlook inequalities when other relationship qualities counteract them.

Another factor that may work against equality in a relationship is biology. According to a number of writers and researchers, each sex has a different role to play in sexual selection, based on evolutionary theory (for example, D. M. Buss, 1988, 1989b; W. Farrell, 1987). As discussed in Chapter 4, sociobiologists argue that males "naturally" want to spread their genes around (such as by copulating with many females who have a good chance of bearing their children), whereas females want to attract and retain the "best" male they can find (and thus obtain the "best" genes) to support them and their offspring during and after pregnancy. The best reproductive strategy for females then would be to emphasize their physical attractiveness, youthfulness, and general sexual appeal. The best reproductive strategy for males would be to emphasize their superiority through winning competitive encounters with other males, whether these be on the playing fields or in the workplace.

In general, male status and power attract females, whereas female physical appearance attracts males. What works for men may not work for women, and vice versa. (See Figure 9.2 for a humorous depiction of the effectiveness of different reproductive strategies.) Indeed, research has found that dominance behavior seems to increase the heterosexual attractiveness of males, whereas it has no effect on the attractiveness of females (Sadalla, Kenrick, & Vershure, 1987). Conversely, a judgment of sexiness appears important in males' interest in a female, whereas it has no influence on females' interest in a male (M. R. Cunningham, 1989). Similarly, a recent survey of young adults aged 18 to 24 by *Time* magazine (N. Gibbs, 1990) found that a well-paying job was viewed as an essential requirement for a spouse by 77% of the females and only 25% of the males. In contrast, physical attractiveness was viewed as essential by 41% of the males and only 19% of the females. According to an evolutionary argument, then, gender inequality within heterosexual relationships may be inevitable or at least necessary for the reproductive health of the species.

Although the roles women and men generally play in trying to attract each other frequently fit the overall theory, determining the cause of such different roles is difficult and politically charged. Even cross-cultural similarities in sex-linked reproductive strategies do not reveal their origin

Figure 9.2 Each sex appears to need a different strategy to attract the other sex. (CATHY Copyright 1989 Cathy Guisewite. Reprinted with permission of Universal Press Syndicate.)

(D. M. Buss, 1989b). It is just as possible for such roles to be socially constructed and transmitted as it is for them to be biologically determined. In fact, the evidence for social constructionism is stronger, although an interactive theory is possible. Furthermore, the things that men and women actually do to attract a mate are remarkably similar in kind and in effectiveness (D. M. Buss, 1988). In addition, when asked to rank a number of qualities desired in a romantic partner, men and women respond similarly, with kindness and considerateness being most important (Goodwin, 1990). This is also true of women's personal ads: the qualities most desired are understanding and a sense of humor (J. E. Smith et al., 1990). Even in the *Time* survey, more than 80% of both females and males indicated they want a spouse who is ambitious and hardworking (Gibbs, 1990).

Discussion

Overall, heterosexual dating relationships are heavily structured by gender role norms and stereotypes. Although equality between men and women in dating relationships is the prevailing ideal, it is hard to achieve in practice. Furthermore, although male dominance is less generally acceptable than it once was, role reversal is generally frowned upon. Most people still expect the male to be older, taller, more educated, and more sexually experienced, and to have a greater earning potential than the female. There is a great deal of ambivalence about eliminating male initiation of relationships (who asks whom out) and male dominance in controlling the relationship (who determines how often the couple will see each other, what they will do on dates, with whose friends they will associate, who will make a marriage proposal). Such ambivalence makes for

a great deal of confusion in dating relationships. Furthermore, males tend to hold more traditional views and expectations than females, especially about marital roles. This gender gap in expectations means that some males and females may have difficulty finding compatible marital partners. As a result, some members of each sex may be forced to compromise their views in ways that may strain the relationship and lead to unhappiness; others may resign themselves to doing without a heterosexual romantic relationship. Given the greater cultural importance attached to a relationship for women than for men, more women than men may end up compromising. Indeed, in a Roper Organization national poll of 3000 randomly selected women in 1989, the majority rated men negatively on their egos, sexual aggressiveness, and failure to help with household chores. Nonetheless, more than nine in ten women said it is better to be married than to live alone ("Male Bashing," 1990).

▲   **Marital Relationships**

From a heterosexual dating situation, men and women often move into marriage. Such a progression is no longer inevitable, especially in recent years. More and more couples are deciding to live together without a marriage ceremony. By the Census Bureau's conservative estimates, 2.9 million mixed-sex couples were living together in 1990, an 80% increase over 1980 (Barringer, 1991). This number constitutes over 4% of all couples, in contrast to 1% in 1970 ("Unmarried," 1986). Those under age 25 account for most of the increase. More women also are deciding to remain unattached.

Still, about 90% of the U.S. population will marry at some point in their lives, and some writers think that marriage is "back in style" ("Marriage," 1983). Such figures attest to the continued popularity of marriage or at least to the acceptance of the stereotype that a normal adult is a married one.

Traditionally, marriage has been viewed as one of two major goals of a woman's life, the other being the bearing of children. Once the marriage goal is attained, a woman has been expected to give up all other interests and devote herself to satisfying her husband's needs and those of her future children. See Figure 9.3 for a tongue-in-cheek look at what a marriage proposal might really mean. Reinforced by marriage laws, customs, and beliefs, this sexist view of a happy marriage has remained the ideal until challenged by the women's liberation movement. In this section we will look at the legal basis of marriage, marital division-of-labor patterns, and marital satisfaction. Throughout, the relevance of gender roles and stereotypes will be stressed.

The Meaning of Marriage

Marriage as a legal contract is based on a legal doctrine known as coverture. Although this doctrine has been modified in most states since 1960, before that time this doctrine meant that upon marriage, the wife lost her legal existence and was considered an extension of her husband's will and identity (Women in Transition, 1975). A wife took on her husband's name and place of residence, gave up her right to accuse her husband of rape (he was legally entitled to her sexual services), and agreed to provide domestic services without financial compensation. The husband agreed to provide shelter, food, and clothing for his wife and children according to his ability. A wife had no legal right to any part of her husband's cash income or any say in how it was spent. Although each state has its own marriage laws and there has been an increasing trend to define marriage partners as equals, in many states these legal elements still hold. For example, in nearly half the states, a wife cannot accuse her

Figure 9.3 What marriage might really mean. (Copyright © 1979 by Nicole Hollander. From the book *I'm in Training to Be Tall and Blonde*. Reprinted with special permission from St. Martin's Press, Inc., New York, NY.)

husband of rape, even if they are legally separated. Louisiana has a head-and-master law that allows a husband to sell the family home without his wife's consent and to cut off her credit even if she has her own salary. Few women or men, in contemplating marriage, consider these legal implications. If the relationship does not work out satisfactorily, however, these legalities may become extremely important.

In one type of analysis, marriage can be viewed as a bargaining situation—women trade domestic work and sex for financial support; men get their basic needs satisfied for a price (DeBeauvoir, 1953; Friedan, 1963). Few Americans think of marriage in these terms, however. Although it has not always been true and certainly is not true in many other cultures, in our culture romantic love is idealized as the basis for marriage. Some writers suggest that the current extremely high divorce rate (nearly one out of every two marriages ends in divorce) is due to the assumption that romantic love is necessary for a satisfactory marriage. Prince Charming will meet the Princess and they will live happily ever after. However, romantic love, with its strong sexual attraction and idealization of the partner, tends to fade over time. In contrast, companionate love, which involves deep attachment, caring, concern, and commitment, tends to endure (J. C. Coleman, 1984). These qualities often characterize intimate friendships. As was noted earlier, the likelihood of such friendships forming between the sexes is small, and males, in particular, prefer a different type of woman for romance than for friendship. Yet tradition and the media have led people, especially women, to believe and expect that finding true love means happiness ever after. A wife's general life happiness and overall well-being are more dependent upon marital happiness than are her husband's, and women consequently experience more dissatisfaction with their marriages than men. When the disillusionment comes, many marriages do not survive.

When the very unromantic legal meaning of marriage is made clear, it becomes easier to see the assumptions of male dominance and female subordination that are built into the institution of marriage. Both traditional gender roles and traditional marriages are based on men's higher status and greater power. The hidden power dynamic in marriage is maintained by gender ideology and by differential access to material resources (Komter, 1989). A power analysis helps one to understand better why so many people, especially men, feel threatened by changes in the traditional family structure. Such an analysis also helps one to understand better the shockingly high rates of wife abuse that occur in the United States and, undoubtedly, elsewhere. It has been estimated that one out of every three wives has been battered by her husband, yet most battered wives remain in their marriages due to their emotional and economic dependence and to the conspiracy of silence that surrounds abusive behavior by males. So powerful is the myth of the romantic marriage that other family members and friends tend to discount both verbal and nonverbal evidence of abuse. (See Chapter 12 for further discussion of wife abuse.)

Marital Division of Labor

Although the traditional type of marriage in which the husband is the breadwinner and the wife is the homemaker is still prominent as a cultural ideal (about half of the adults sampled in 1985 agreed that "it is much better for everyone if the man is the achiever and the woman takes care of the home and family"; National Opinion Research Center, 1986), in practice this type of marital arrangement is relatively uncommon and never was universal. For example, only certain families (mainly White middle- and upper-class) conformed to this model during the first half of this century. Among Blacks and working-class Whites, both spouses nearly always worked outside their home for wages. Furthermore, men began deserting the role of the good provider in the 1950s, long before the majority of wives were in the labor force in the late 1970s (Bernard, 1981; Ehrenreich, 1983). Still, until recently, the role of the good provider was a clear expectation for most married men. Now there is a new emphasis on an egalitarian relationship that provides love, companionship, and self-fulfillment. Marital role expectations are in transition, resulting in some role strain for both men and women (Goleman, 1984).

Four different types of marriages can be identified with respect to work and homemaking roles, excluding couples in which both spouses are unemployed (usually due to retirement) (C. E. Ross, Mirowsky, & Huber, 1983). In the Type I or traditional marriage, the wife is not employed by choice and she does all the housework and child care. In the Type II marriage, the wife is employed by necessity rather than by choice and she still does all the housework and child care. In the Type III marriage, the wife is employed by choice but she still does most of the home duties. This is the single most common type of marital arrangement. In the

Type IV or fully egalitarian marriage, both spouses are employed by choice and both share home duties.

Two out of three marriages (64%) in 1988 were dual-earner marriages, 17% had a sole male earner, 13% had no earners, and 6% had a sole female earner (Wilkie, 1991). Thus, marriages in which men are the sole breadwinner are a distinct minority of marriages now, in contrast to 1960 when they constituted nearly half of all marriages. Although most marriages now are dual-earner ones, they still tend to be conventional (Type II or III), because the wife's career usually is secondary to that of her husband and her primary interest is the family. It has been estimated that conventional dual-earner marriages outnumber dual-career marriages (in which both spouses are equally committed to their jobs and their families) by 10 to 1 (Parker, Peltier, & Wolleat, 1981). Employed wives are accepted mainly because two-income families have become an economic necessity for middle-class as well as blue-collar families. Society still shows some discomfort with the idea of female employment, as depicted in Figure 9.4. Yet national surveys show increasing support for a dual-career orientation. A 1985 survey found that only 36% of the 1500 people questioned thought that it was more important for a wife to help her husband's career than to have one herself, compared to 56% of a similar sample who thought so in 1977 (National Opinion Research Center, 1986).

Although most couples now share the income-earning role, wives still do most of the housework and, if children are present, most of the child care (this latter issue will be discussed in the next chapter). Across all couple types, wives perform about 80% of all housework (Berardo, Shehan, & Leslie, 1987). Husbands with traditional attitudes as well as those with "masculine" personality traits and less than a college education tend to spend less time doing housework than less traditional men (Atkinson & Huston, 1984; Gunter & Gunter, 1990; Nyquist, Slivken, Spence, & Helmreich, 1985). But even those husbands who express support for the sharing of household responsibilities tend not to share those responsibilities themselves. Every study of dual-career couples finds that wives have more responsibility than husbands for housework and child care (Hertz, 1986; Hochschild, 1989; Huber & Spitze, 1983; Steil & Turetsky, 1987a). The best predictor of marital equality in dual-career couples is perceived job importance: the more equal the two jobs are viewed as being, the more equality there is in the marriage. Since most employed wives still earn less than their husbands, it's no wonder that the marital division of labor is uneven. However, even when the wife has a high-powered career and earns more than her husband, her job still tends to be viewed as less important than his and she still spends as much time doing housework as her non-professionally employed counterpart, which is three times as many hours as the husband spends (Berardo et al., 1987; Steil & Weltman, 1991). Even when husbands do housework, they tend to concentrate on household repairs and outdoor chores, whereas women still dominate cooking and cleaning activities. Thus, women are constantly on duty while men can choose when to do "their" chores.

Change is occurring, albeit slowly. Married men now do about 30% of the housework and child care, up from 20% in the 1960s (Pleck, 1985). In 1985, women spent twice as long as men doing household chores (19.5 hours compared to 9.8 hours, respectively); in 1965, women spent 27 hours compared

Figure 9.4 The "dangers" that come from female employment. (SALLY FORTH Copyright 1984 by Greg Howard. Reprinted with special permission of North America Syndicate, Inc.)

to men's 4.6 hours ("Men Doing," 1988). Thus, not only is men's contribution to housework slowly increasing, but the total numbers of hours spent by a couple doing housework is decreasing as well. The picture is still one of inequality, however. The consequence of unequal sharing of household tasks is that most employed wives work at least two jobs (one in, one outside the home), whereas most employed husbands work only one.

Marital Satisfaction

Many factors affect marital satisfaction. Marital division of labor is only one factor and doesn't appear to be the strongest. More important is the matching of expectations between wives and husbands. Also important are couple sex typing, compatible communication styles, and social support. All these factors are affected by gender roles and stereotypes. In general, husbands are more satisfied by marriage than wives.

Division of labor   Which of the four types of marital division of labor is best? Much depends on how "best" is defined. In the traditional marriage, because both spouses' expectations are being met, the psychological benefits are high for both spouses, but more so for the husband (Fitzpatrick, 1988; C. E. Ross et al., 1983). His job generally lasts 8 hours a day, five days a week, whereas her "job" last 24 hours a day, seven days a week. Furthermore, his role is to provide for her physically whereas her role is to provide for him emotionally. Thus, his emotional needs are more likely to be met than hers. Yet a woman financially and emotionally dependent upon her husband can be an enormous burden. In addition, the less similar two people's daily activities are, the more difficult is any form of communication between them. A person who spends the entire day doing housework and child care usually is not a very stimulating or interesting partner for someone who spends the entire day working outside the home, as some househusbands have learned (see, for example, Roache, 1972).

Furthermore, if the wife in a traditional marriage actually prefers to be in the labor force but is not "permitted" to do so by her husband, resentment is likely to build. As was true with young women before marriage, most married women want to combine employment with a family life. Yet gender stereotypes, and particularly the attitudes of their mates, may hinder them from doing so. Fewer men than women want a marriage in which the wife combines family and paid work, although if these activities are done sequentially (for example, work for a while, take time off for raising a family, return to work), men tend to express positive attitudes. Whether the wife is able to focus on her career seems to be partly a function of the husband's power orientation. A longitudinal study of 51 male college graduates (Winter, Stewart, & McClelland, 1977) found that the greater the male's power motivation, the lower the likelihood of his wife's working and/or the lower the level of his wife's career. The power-motivated man may choose a non-career-oriented wife, or he may use his power to suppress her career goals once married. In the latter case, the marriage itself may be adversely affected (Seidenberg, 1973). When such differences are ignored, a wife may feel unfulfilled and try to get some compensation from her husband via money, material things, or vicarious achievements. In turn, a husband may feel increasingly resentful that his expectations have not been fulfilled, and he may withdraw defensively from his wife. From this sequence of events comes the nagging-wife/withdrawn-husband pattern of marital interaction that is the butt of so many jokes and appears so often in the offices of marriage counselors.

In Type II marriages, where the wife is employed by necessity rather than by choice but still does all the housework and child care, distress is the highest for both spouses (Rosen, 1987; C. E. Ross et al., 1983). Neither the wife's nor the husband's expectations have been fulfilled, and he may feel like a failure for not being able to be a "good provider." Indeed, it is mainly husbands with traditional attitudes toward gender roles who experience more stress and anxiety when their wives are employed than when they are not (Kessler & McRae, 1982; Staines et al., 1986). This sense of failing to live up to the male gender role "ideal" may lead to alcohol abuse as well as wife abuse. For the wife, the stresses of working essentially two jobs may lead to resentment, role conflict, and role overload, especially since her paid employment is likely to be low-level and unsatisfying. The strains on the marriage itself are enormous. Additionally, if husbands are not happy with child-care arrangements or if they must reduce their own time commitment to work in order to accommodate their wife's schedule, husbands of employed women tend to show slightly lower marital adjustment than if these things weren't true (Parasuraman, Greenhaus, Rabinowitz, Bedeian, & Mossholder, 1989). All these aspects of a Type II marriage may account for the finding that among lower-class families, marital happiness may be negatively related to the wife's employment, and more blue-collar than white collar women would stay home if they could (Dowd, 1983; Yogev, 1982).

In Type III marriages, the wife is employed by choice but she still does most of the home duties. This type of marital arrangement is the most common (J. C. Coleman, 1984; Hochschild, 1989; Huber & Spitze, 1983). In such cases, distress for the wife is high, although lower than for Type II wives (C. E. Ross et al., 1983). Many women in these marriages try to be "Superwoman," doing everything both traditional and modern wives are expected to do. For example, in most dual-career marriages, wives do 70% of the housework (Berardo et al., 1987). For the husband, psychological benefits are as high as in the Type I marriage. After all, the family's domestic needs still are being met without much behavior change on his part, and he has help financially supporting the family.

In the Type IV or fully egalitarian marriage, both spouses are employed by choice and both share home duties. Distress ratings for both spouses are the lowest among all four groups (C. E. Ross et al., 1983; Steil & Turetsky, 1987a). Although presently only a minority of marriages (estimates range from 10 to 20%), such marriages are on the rise (Hochschild, 1989). More and more young couples aspire to this type of marriage, although making it work takes a great deal of effort. One type of egalitarian marriage involves dual careers (in contrast to dual jobs, which involve less career commitment) for both partners. The practical problems of dual-career marriages are many (involving decisions about which spouse will be home to entertain clients, see to the laundry, take care of the children). Furthermore, with few role models to follow, many couples must overcome their own feelings of deviancy. Dual-career status does increase both personal and work stress, but it also increases relationship satisfaction. Many couples seem to be making such arrangements work, usually to the benefit of all involved (Steil & Turetsky, 1987a; Yogev & Brett, 1985). A relatively new pattern for dual-career couples is the commuter marriage, which offers both spouses equal career opportunities at a somewhat high price (Gerstel & Gross, 1984). (For more information on dual-career couples, see L. A. Gilbert, 1988, and Hertz, 1986).

Thus, the most satisfied couples are those whose expectations are being met and who share the work in either a similar (egalitarian marriage) or complementary (traditional marriage) fashion. Between these two types, however, the egalitarian marriage seems most beneficial, especially for women. The most difficulties beset the couples whose marriage takes a transitional form, either because it doesn't live up to both spouses' expectations (Type II) or because of the imbalance of the work load (Type III). In a recent national survey of 3000 women randomly sampled across the country, 60% of the employed women said juggling jobs and families put them under a great deal of stress and 52% cited their husbands' failure to help with household chores as a major cause of resentment ("Male Bashing," 1990). Only money caused more resentment. Wives are happiest when the division of labor is equal and when husbands share women's traditional chores (Aida & Falbo, 1991; Benin & Agostinelli, 1988). It should be noted that whereas only the Type II marriage is distressful for the husband, women have higher distress ratings than men for all types but the Type IV (egalitarian) marriage (C. E. Ross et al., 1983). The fact that most marriages are not Type IV explains why marriage benefits men so much more than it does women, as demonstrated in the last chapter. It is not surprising then that men, at least White men, express higher marital satisfaction than women (Antonucci & Akiyama, 1987; Staines & Libby, 1986; Suitor, 1991).

Thus, who does the housework is more closely tied to marital satisfaction, especially for women, than who earns the paycheck (Hochschild, 1989; Madden, 1987; Suitor, 1991). One way of allaying such dissatisfaction short of divorce is revising one's expectations. Hochschild (1989) found in her study of dual-career couples that elaborate rationalizations sometimes were spun to create a sense of equity. For example, one wife took care of the child and the house; her husband took care of the dog and the garage. Both felt the division of labor was equitable. Reframing thus is a major coping strategy used effectively by dual-career women (E. A. Anderson & Leslie, 1991). Other dual-career couples retain their belief in traditional gender roles by continuing to see the husband as more competent, intelligent, and of higher professional status than his wife, even when objective indexes of status are equal or indicate female superiority (Steil & Weltman, 1991; Yogev, 1987).

Although a couple's economic division of labor is less related to their marital satisfaction than their household division of labor, a wife's labor force participation is related to divorce rates. The higher a wife's economic status, the greater the probability of divorce (Trent & South, 1989). The most common explanation of this correlation is that as a woman gains economic independence, she is freer to leave an unhappy marriage. Alternatively, the higher a wife's economic status, the more threatened her husband may become, and the more unstable the marriage. A more recent explanation is that wives in unhappy marriages increase their participation in the labor force in anticipation of divorce (W. R. Johnson & Skinner, 1986). Thus, the cause-and-effect sequence between wives' income and marital instability is far from clear. Certainly it cannot simply be concluded that a wife's participation in the labor force will *cause* divorce. The key variables undoubtedly are the strength of the marital relationship to start with and the ability of the couple to structure time together for meals and recreation (Kingston & Nock, 1987).

Expectations   It follows from all this research that matched expectations between husband and wife regarding proper gender role behavior are critical for marital satisfaction. Indeed, spouses who have similar attitudes toward sex roles tend to be more satisfied with their marriage than spouses with dissimilar attitudes (K. Cooper, Chassin, & Zeiss, 1985). In point of fact, mismatched marriages with respect to marital expectations are unlikely to occur or survive. Peplau and colleagues (1976, 1977) found in their longitudinal study of dating couples that couples mismatched regarding attitudes about dual-career marriages were nearly twice as likely as other couples (41% compared to 26%) to break up in the year following the initial testing. Such couples also were less satisfied with their relationships while they were together. Once married, couples who disagree over the division of labor and the woman's career interests also tend to be more unstable and more troubled (Blumstein & Schwartz, 1983; Fowers, 1991; Hochschild, 1989; Nettles & Loevinger, 1983). In general, husbands tend to be more traditional than wives, and husbands in problem marriages tend to be the most traditional. Divorced women and divorced men tend to be even further apart in gender ideology than married people, suggesting that these differences may have contributed to their divorces (Finlay, Starnes, & Alvarez, 1985).

There may be differences among Black and White Americans regarding marital expectations. First, Blacks are less likely to marry than Whites, which makes marriage less likely to be a normative experience. Second, the importance of the husband's being the main economic provider is emphasized more by Black college students, especially males, than it is by White college students, especially females (Cazenave & Leon, 1987). Since dual-worker marriages are more common among Blacks than Whites and since economic and social discrimination reduces Black men's income, living up to this role expectation may prove especially difficult for Black men. One out of three Black married men do not earn enough to raise their family out of poverty (Wilkie, 1991). Perhaps that is why Black married men are significantly less satisfied with their lives than divorced, widowed, or single men (Ball & Robbins, 1986).

As we have seen, men who believe in traditional marital roles may experience role strain and negative mental health consequences when their wives are employed. Similarly, men whose wives earn more than they do (about one in every five dual job couples) also may experience role stress and strain if they have an emotional investment in being financially dominant (R. Lewis, 1990; C. E. Ross et al., 1983; Z. Rubin, 1983). Yet for dual-worker husbands who believe in egalitarian relationships, greater equality in domestic, child-care, and decision-making responsibilities is associated with greater mental health (decreased depressive symptomatology, more positive family adjustment) (Pleck, 1985; Steil & Turetsky, 1987a). Not being the sole or primary provider can be liberating for men whose egos aren't attached to being dominant.

Because of men's more traditional views regarding marital roles, women with a strong career interest may be less likely to marry than other women. For example, female scientists, who may be viewed as having a strong professional commitment, have a much lower marriage rate than male scientists or female nonscientists (Cuca, 1976). Furthermore, married men appear to be more career-oriented than married women and than cohabiting men and women (J. D. Cunningham, Braiker, & Kelley, 1982; Kotkin, 1983). Marriage, then, may be an asset for career-oriented men but not for career-oriented women. Male career success does seem to be related to male career precedence, marriage, and the conventional allocation of household tasks. Perhaps that is one reason that mail-order Asian brides have become increasingly popular (Belkin, 1986; Gavzer, 1988). Such women are stereotyped as being more traditional, compliant, and subservient than American women. Another trend that has developed in response to the incompatibility between some career-oriented men and women is the growing number of older women who marry younger, less traditional men (Gavzer, 1987).

Sex typing   Other factors besides the actual division of labor in the marriage and matched expectations affect the marital relationship. Sex typing in particular appears to be very influential. High nurturant-expressive scale scores for both partners are critically important in determining the happiness of the couple as well as each of its members (Antill, 1983; Bradbury & Fincham, 1988; C. D. Peterson, Baucom, Elliott, & Farr, 1989). When both partners are either androgynous or "feminine," they rate themselves as happier than couples in which at least one partner is low on nurturant-expressive traits. Couples with at least one undifferentiated spouse are the least happy. In general, as was found for male and female friendships, expressive-nurturant traits combined with instrumental-active traits facilitate relationships. Couples who are strongly sex-typed, although not perhaps the unhappiest of couples, also are not the happiest, despite their conformity to gender norms.

Sex typing may affect marital satisfaction indirectly in two different ways: the domestic division of labor and communication patterns. Spouses high in nurturant-expressive traits perform more domestic tasks than spouses low in such traits, which may be why having both spouses high in such traits is associated with marital satisfaction (Gunter & Gunter, 1990). Spouses high in such traits also may attend to the relationship itself more than spouses low in such traits. It certainly makes sense that for a relationship to work, at least one partner must attend to the relationship, whether primarily or in addition to outside employment. Traditionally, that one partner has been the wife, although a comprehensive nationwide study of couples in the early 1980s in the United States found that that pattern no longer was the norm (Blumstein & Schwartz, 1983). In only 36% of the couples was the wife the sole emotional caretaker; in 39% the husband was, and in the remaining 25%, both partners were relationship-centered. The key variable may be the sex typing of the spouses.

A second way sex typing affects marital satisfaction is through its effect on communication patterns. As discussed in Chapter 3, strong nurturant-expressive traits are related to emotional self-disclosure and perceptive decoding of verbal and nonverbal messages. Much research has found that marital satisfaction is closely related to a husband's ability to be tender and expressive, to send clear messages, and to decode his wife's messages accurately (Balswick, 1988; Blumstein & Schwartz, 1983; Noller, 1980, 1981; L. B. Rubin, 1983). Yet husbands tend to talk less and to view communication as less important than do wives, although this difference is mainly found among Whites (T. Adler, 1989b; McGill, 1985). A strongly stereotyped man usually is unable to satisfy his wife's emotional needs and may, in fact, find them threatening. Although improving a husband's ability to discuss feelings with his wife may help to increase her marital satisfaction, Cancian (1987) argues that women need to recognize that men may communicate their feelings through such instrumental behaviors as offering help or having sexual intercourse. Perhaps a greater appreciation of gender differences in communication styles is needed (see Tannen, 1990). Also needed is a recognition that individuals and couples differ not only in their communication skills but also in their communication needs (T. Adler, 1989b; Fitzpatrick, 1988). Thus, although most couples value self-disclosure in marriage, some prefer a more distant emotional style.

Social support   Although marital satisfaction depends primarily on factors involving the couple, external factors also play a role. Prominent among these external factors is social support, at least for women. Close female friendships and close ties with members of their extended families seem to bolster the marital relationship for women (Antonucci & Akiyama, 1987; Oliker, 1989). This bolstering effect may be due to the greater satisfaction of emotional needs women get from other women than they get from men. For Blacks, kin networks provide the major source of social support for both married and unmarried women (D. R. Brown & Gary, 1985). Without close relationships with other women, wives may find that their needs for intimacy remain unfulfilled. In contrast, men's emotional needs appear to be met fairly satisfactorily within their marriage. Close friendships and kin support also help wives work out problems they may be having in their marriage.

Given the different gender roles assigned women and men, it is not surprising that somewhat different factors affect their marital expectations and satisfactions. These gender differences can sometimes be so extreme that it may seem that each couple is part of two marriages: his, which is going fairly well, and hers, which can use improvement (Goleman, 1986).

Discussion

As we have seen, marriages traditionally have been based on male dominance. But the traditional pattern of employed husband, homemaker wife no longer is either the norm or the ideal. Contemporary marriages run along a continuum from the traditional to the egalitarian role-sharing ideal. Marital satisfaction is determined in large part by the match between the expectations of husbands and wives regarding the division of labor inside and outside the home. Although most wives are employed, they still bear primary responsibility for home and children. This weighs heavily on them. Since more men than women want a traditional marriage and many men are ego-invested in being dominant, many husbands feel stressed when their wife is in the labor force or when she earns as much as or more than he does. Most women, however, earn less than their husbands. Sex typing also affects marital satisfaction, with the happiest marriages reported by couples where both spouses possess strong nurturant-expressive traits. Expressivity is important in marriage, especially to wives. A traditionally sex-typed husband tends not to meet his wife's emotional needs, although his needs tend to be met.

What all this research suggests is that, in general, benefits from marriage are much greater for men than for women. As was discussed in Chapter 8 and earlier in this chapter, marriage appears to benefit men more than women physically, emotionally, and occupationally. The paradox here is that many men stereotypically view marriage as a trap, yet, statistically speaking, it does them a world of good, and they tend to remarry quickly if divorced or widowed. For many women, who stereotypically view marriage as their ultimate goal in life, marriage is less beneficial than it is for men, and women are less satisfied with their marriages than are men. A wife may experience more stress and strain in marriage than her husband, partly because she typically is the one expected to adapt to her husband's life and not vice versa, and partly because she typically receives little emotional support from him. Employed wives, in particular, are under great strain because they tend to work "double shifts" and they tend to earn less in the labor force than men. The most satisfied wives are those who enjoy their jobs and whose husbands share domestic responsibilities. Despite all these problems, being married does seem to be associated with greater subjective well-being than being single, although the differences are small and decreasing (Glenn & Weaver, 1988; Haring-Hidore et al., 1985).

In conclusion, adherence to the gender stereotypes may have negative consequences for marital satisfaction and stability, especially for women. A man's stereotypical lack of expressivity and interpersonal sensitivity may put great strain on his marriage. His stereotypical need to be dominant in the marriage may put great strain on his wife but also on himself. If men were not socialized to believe that males are, and should be, superior to women, men would not be so threatened by women's equality or, when it occurs, their economic superiority. Men have a great deal to gain from sharing the burden of financial support, although they also have much to lose by giving up their privileged status. Yet a truly open, rewarding relationship is possible only between equals. Breaking away from the gender stereotypes thus is imperative. In this regard, it is encouraging that the younger generation of men tends to have less traditional gender expectations regarding marriage than did their fathers. Eventually, then, marriage may prove as satisfying to women as it now is to men.

Lesbian and gay male relationships offer a good counterpoint to heterosexual relationships regarding the issue of equality. Let us briefly examine this type of intimate relationship.

▲   Lesbian and Gay Male Relationships

Despite general societal disapproval of lesbian and gay male relationships, especially by males, about 10% of both men and women are involved in such relationships, at least for part of their lives (see Chapter 4 for a discussion of the development of sexual orientation). Interestingly, research on the nature of homosexual relationships has found a great deal more equality and a great deal less role playing in such relationships than in heterosexual relationships. In this section we will look at the dynamics of gay male and lesbian relationships, as well as at factors affecting relationship satisfaction.

Despite the stereotype that in a homosexual couple, one plays the male ("butch") and one the female ("femme"), this pattern actually characterizes only a minority of such couples. Role playing is commonest among those who are older, at lower socioeconomic levels, and among men—groups least influenced by gay liberation and lesbian feminism (Cardell, Finn, & Maracek, 1981; Peplau, 1981). Gay male and lesbian relationships more closely resemble relationships between best friends, with an added sexual and romantic component, than they resemble heterosexual marriages.

The dynamics of gay male and lesbian relationships thus differ somewhat from heterosexual relationships and from each other due to the influence of gender roles and stereotypes. That is, men in same-gender and cross-gender sexual relationships are more similar to each other than gay men are to lesbians. Similarly, women in same-gender and cross-gender sexual relationships are more similar to each other than lesbians are to gay men. As we have seen, men's socialization trains them to separate sex from love and to be dominant, sexually active, and emotionally reticent. Relationships between two men should be especially marked by these characteristics. Indeed, gay male relationships have been characterized as the most sexually active and the least monogamous when compared with heterosexual marital and cohabiting relationships and with lesbian relationships (Blumstein & Schwartz, 1983, 1990). Compared with these other couples, gay male couples also are least likely to have at least one partner high in nurturant-expressive traits (Kurdek & Schmitt, 1986b). Compared to women, men in both gay and heterosexual relationships tend to be more interested in physical characteristics and less self-disclosing (Deaux & Hanna, 1984; Kurdek & Schmitt, 1986c; Schullo & Alperson, 1984). Gay men also engage in more role playing and power struggles than lesbians. Of all couple types, gay male partners are the most different with respect to age, income, and education (Kurdek & Schmitt, 1987a). Ironically, the powerful threat of AIDS and its decimation of a large segment of the gay community in the last five years have brought many gay men closer to each other. Not only have gay men become more involved in committed monogamous relationships but they have also learned how to physically and emotionally support each other in this time of crisis.

Compared to men, women tend to give greater importance to emotional expressiveness and personal compatibility. Women also are more self-disclosing, supportive, and sexually monogamous. These qualities are especially prominent in lesbian relationships. Sexual activity in such relationships is less frequent than it is in any other type of relationship, probably because of socialization (women have not been socialized to take the lead or to be interested in sex) and social norms (emotional rather than physical intimacy is emphasized in lesbian relationships) (Blumstein & Schwartz, 1990). Lesbian couples also tend to be less sex-typed and engage in less role playing than heterosexual couples or gay men (Cardell et al., 1981; Kurdek & Schmitt, 1986b, 1986c; Peplau, 1981). The latter finding may be due to the fact that gay men are less

influenced by feminism than are lesbians. Equality appears to be particularly strongly valued among lesbians, and most lesbian couples appear to be in an equal power relationship (Caldwell & Peplau 1984; Eldridge & Gilbert, 1990; Kurdek & Schmitt, 1986c; Peplau, 1981). In general, partner similarity is greatest for lesbian couples compared to gay male couples and to heterosexual married and cohabiting couples (Kurdek & Schmitt, 1987a).

The stresses on lesbian and gay male couples are greater than those on heterosexual couples, even those that are just cohabiting. The social stigma against homosexuality means that many lesbian and gay male couples cannot be public about their relationship. Lesbian and gay male partners frequently must go alone to couple functions, such as office parties, or else risk social ostracism or outright abuse. An additional stressor on gay male and lesbian couples is the lesser social support they receive for their relationship than do heterosexual couples, especially from family members (Kurdek, 1988b; Kurdek & Schmitt, 1987b). Furthermore, no legal ties bind gay male and lesbian partners to each other. Such ties have been found to increase the barriers to leaving a relationship (Kurdek & Schmitt, 1986c).

Despite these differences, gay male and lesbian couples share many similarities with heterosexual couples. For example, in their relationships, lesbians, gay males, and heterosexuals want both attachment and autonomy, are generally satisfied, and use similar power strategies (Falbo & Peplau, 1980; Howard et al., 1986; Kurdek & Schmitt, 1986c; Peplau, 1981). In long-term relationships, both heterosexual and homosexual, partners tend to be matched in terms of expressive characteristics, although lesbian and gay male partners are more similar to each other than are heterosexual partners, with lesbian partners being the most similar (Kurdek & Schmitt, 1987a; Schullo & Alperson, 1984). Both heterosexual and homosexual couples go through similar stages in their relationships, from early infatuation and high sexual activity through settling down and conflicting feelings to longer term maintenance activities (Kurdek & Schmitt, 1986a). As is true with heterosexual couples, lesbian and gay male couples with at least one androgynous or feminine-sex-typed partner report the highest relationship quality (Kurdek & Schmitt, 1986b).

The factors that determine relationship quality are similar for lesbian, gay male, and heterosexual couples (Eldridge & Gilbert, 1990; Kurdek &

Schmitt, 1986c; Lange & Worell, 1990). Relationship satisfaction is a function of strong attachment to and perceived attractiveness of the partner, a constructive attitude toward disagreements, few appealing alternatives to being in the relationship, receiving communal nurturance from one's partner, and shared decision making. Since partners in lesbian relationships have the greatest equality in decision making, the greatest similarity in terms of strength of attachment to the relationship, and high partner nurturance, it is not surprising that lesbian relationships are characterized by particularly high relationship satisfaction (Kurdek, 1989; Kurdek & Schmitt, 1987a). Indeed, the association between power equality and relationship satisfaction is stronger among lesbians than it is among heterosexuals, perhaps because heterosexuals assume more traditional (that is, unequal) gender roles (Peplau, 1979).

Not only are predictors of relationship quality similar between homosexual and heterosexual couples, but typical relationship conflicts are similar as well (Blumstein & Schwartz, 1983). For all couples, conflicts over the way work intrudes into the relationship are often associated with the couple's breaking up. For lesbians, differences between partners' levels of career commitment are related to relatively low relationship satisfaction (Eldridge & Gilbert, 1990). Money conflicts occur in all relationships, and the more equal the partners are in controlling how the money is spent, the more peaceful the relationship is. Economic self-sufficiency in a partner is generally a good thing, but lesbians are more tolerant of it than heterosexual males. Sexual conflicts also occur in all relationships, especially regarding monogamy. However, gay males tolerate outside sexual relations the best of all couples, perhaps because such activities are most likely to occur in those relationships.

Gay male and lesbian couples also have some unique problems. If not part of a homosexual community, gay and lesbian couples may feel isolated and overly dependent on each other. Lesbian couples in particular may have problems retaining separate identities due to a variety of reasons: the cultural pressure on women to put relationships before autonomy, the tendency for lesbian couples to be highly similar, and the high relationship satisfaction in such couples (Burch, 1987; G. D. Green & Clunis, 1988; Vargo, 1987). Such "merging" or "fusion" may account for lesbians' low sexual activity and may cause conflicts when interests and needs of the partners do diverge. Gay male relationships have

tended to be less stable than both heterosexual and lesbian relationships, partly because of more opportunities for outside sexual encounters and partly because of the relatively lower level of nurturant-expressive traits in the partners. Both gay male and lesbian relationships are more likely than heterosexual relationships to be interracial, with consequently greater potential for cultural conflicts (Garcia, Kennedy, Pearlman, & Perez, 1987). There is, however, very little research on this topic, just as there is very little research on violence within same-gender couples (one exception: Lobel, 1986).

In summary, lesbian and gay male couples share many similarities with heterosexual couples regarding qualities that affect relationship satisfaction. However, since gender roles and stereotypes are such powerful influences on interpersonal behavior, it is not surprising that some differences exist both between homosexual and heterosexual couples, and between gay male and lesbian couples. In general, lesbian and gay male couples compared to heterosexual couples are more characterized by equality and less by role playing. Of all couples, lesbians appear most equal and most satisfied.

▲ Summary

In this chapter, the effects of the gender stereotypes on friendship and love relationships have been examined. In general, females make good relationship partners due to their socialization to be relationship-oriented and to the facilitatory effect of strong nurturant-expressive traits (that is, those that are stereotypically feminine). Females are valuable friends and female-female friendships tend to be highly intimate and rewarding, although gender roles and stereotypes create obstacles that must be overcome. Males, on the other hand, are socialized for competition and dominance, not intimacy. Consequently, male-male friendships tend to be casual and activity-oriented. (These and all differences noted for males and females are group differences and are not necessarily true of all individuals in the group.) Male-male friendships also reflect males' stereotypical suppression of emotions and fear of homosexuality. Male-female friendships are difficult to form because of compulsory heterosexuality and the difficulty males have in sustaining any intimate relationship.

Romantic relationships also show the effects of the gender roles and stereotypes. Dating relationships often are characterized by much game playing and manipulation. Although equality in relationships has become more the norm among college students, there is still ambivalence on the part of many males and thus, in actual practice, male dominance still reigns. Despite prevailing opinion, both males and females have similar intimacy needs. However, due to traditional gender socialization practices, females are more able than males to satisfy such needs. Consequently, males tend to be more emotionally satisfied than females by their heterosexual relationships, and this is particularly true of married couples. Compared to women, men tend to fall in love faster and harder, and they tend to be more satisfied in their marriages. Since most marriages still reflect male dominance, this is not surprising. Although most wives are employed, they still do a disproportionate share of the domestic work. As egalitarian marriages become more common, men and women should become more similar in their marital satisfaction. In this transitional period, however, much stress exists in marriages as men struggle with the threat of equality and women struggle with resentment due to overwork. Changes in gender role expectations should help ease some of the stress. In contrast to heterosexual relationships, lesbian and gay male relationships tend to be more egalitarian and, for women, more emotionally satisfying.

Thus, nearly all relationships, particularly men's, suffer from adherence to the gender stereotypes. Men and women both would benefit if they could develop the expressive and agentic parts of their personalities. Androgynous individuals not only are rated as the most desirable friends, but they also tend to be in the most satisfying relationships, whether heterosexual or homosexual. Thus, strict sex typing is not most facilitative of good relationships with friends and lovers.

▲ Recommended Reading

Blumstein, P., & Schwartz, P. (1983). *American couples.* New York: Morrow. A thorough and fascinating sociological examination of a broad sample of American couples: married, heterosexual cohabiting, lesbian, and gay male.

Cancian, F. M. (1987). *Love in America: Gender and self-development.* Cambridge, England: Cambridge University Press. Changing gender roles require a changed definition of love—one combining both instrumental and expressive values—and a new relationship ideal—that of interdependence.

McGill, M. E. (1985). *The McGill report on male intimacy.* New York: Harper & Row. Based on research with over 5000 men and women and using many personal stories, this book provides a poignant glimpse of the difficulties men have being intimate in their closest relationships.

Rubin, L. B. (1985). *Just friends: The role of friendship in our lives.* New York: Harper & Row. Written for a general audience, this book examines the value of friendships for both women and men.

Chapter 10

Consequences for Family Relationships

In the last chapter, we examined the effects of gender roles and stereotypes on a variety of relationships—friendship, heterosexual dating, marital and homosexual relationships. All of these relationships are voluntary; that is, they usually are entered into intentionally and freely. But another powerful relationship that people have is not so intentional—that between parents and their children. Even if a child is planned, parents cannot predict exactly what characteristics their child will have, yet the relationship between a parent and a child may be the most profound relationship that either will ever have. And these relationships are strongly affected by gender roles and stereotypes.

For both parents, the birth of a child involves great changes—changes much greater than those involved in marriage. Both parents must adopt new roles, that of mother and father; both must adjust to a new member of the household who is very demanding of their time and energy; and both must learn new skills—for example, changing and soothing a baby. The marital relationship also undergoes change as each spouse must adjust to the new role and interests of the other. One of the changes that typically occurs is a reversion to, or renewed emphasis on, traditional gender norms (Belsky, Lang, & Huston, 1986; D. N. Ruble, Fleming, Hackel, & Stangor, 1988; Schaninger & Buss, 1986). Even egalitarian couples tend to fall into the pattern of the woman's being the primary caretaker. All these factors combine to make the birth of a child extremely stressful.

Families have been undergoing marked changes in recent years, spurred by the women's liberation movement and changing economic conditions. Only one out of four families in 1990 was composed of a married couple with one or more children under age 18, compared to 40% in 1970 ("Only One," 1991). The traditional family, with father as breadwinner and mother as homemaker and child-caretaker, represents even a smaller percentage of families today (less than 10% in 1988; National Commission on Working Women, 1989b). Along with these demographic changes have come changes in the mother and father roles. Although most mothers still are the major caretakers of children regardless of their labor force participation, many fathers are taking a more active role in child care. Yet traditional gender role expectations have been slower to change than have family roles. In this chapter, the effect of gender roles and stereotypes on mother-child and father-child relationships will be examined. First, however, let's look more closely at the American family today.

▲ The Changing American Family

The American family is changing: more mothers are in the labor force than ever before, women are having fewer children and at later ages, more births are occurring outside of marriage, female-headed and reconstituted families are on the rise, and the number of grown sons and elderly parents living with middle-aged family members has increased. Despite the profound changes, family ideology has remained stuck in the early 20th century.

The traditional White American family in the 20th century is a patriarchal one, with the father (the patriarch) as head and master. Since the mid-19th century, men have been expected to be the primary providers for their families, and typical male socialization has been aimed at enabling men to fulfill this role. By being competitive, dominant, active, and achievement-oriented, men will be motivated to get the "best" job. Since being a "good provider" for their family is a source of status and esteem for males, men will be motivated to become one. Thus, the traditional expectation of men as fathers is mainly economic. In contrast, typical female socialization has been aimed at enabling women to fulfill their major assigned role, that of mother. By being nurturant, expressive, selfless, and sensitive, women should be better equipped for raising children. Since being a "good mother" is a source of status and esteem for females, women will be motivated to become one. Thus, the traditional expectation of women as mothers is mainly relational.

These traditional expectations of mothers and fathers remain today, although they are accompanied by new ones as well. More is being expected of fathers in terms of relating to their children, and more is being expected of mothers in terms of providing for the children. Yet these mixed expectations can cause strain for individuals and families, especially since societal institutions remain attuned to the traditional roles. Most workplace settings assume a homemaker spouse who will take care of child care and domestic needs. Employers may expect employees to work overtime, entertain clients, or take business trips, all without thought to home needs. Similarly, few employers offer parental leave, flexible hours, or on-site day care. Most community services also assume a stay-at-home parent. Schools still count on mothers during the day for school parties, bake sales, parent-teacher conferences, delayed openings, and early dismissals. Delivery and repair persons assume someone with flexible time will be at home during the day. And day care facilities for preschoolers and sick children are inadequate for the need.

Yet American families have changed, and they are unlikely to assume the traditional form again. Our expectations and our institutions also must change if we want parents to function well and children to grow up healthy and strong. As we will see, children need many things, but the traditional American family is not the only or even the best way to meet these needs.

One of the most noticeable changes in the American family is the number of mothers who are in the labor force at least part-time. Figure 10.1 shows the percentage of mothers from 1950 to 1988 holding outside employment. In 1988, 73% of all mothers with school-aged children were employed, which was nearly two and a half times the percentage in 1950 (National Commission on Working Women, 1989b). The number of mothers in the labor force with children under 6 years old has nearly quintupled in the same period of time (from 12% in 1950 to 57% in 1988). Most dramatic of all is the increase in labor force participation of mothers with children under age 1, from less than 10% in 1950 to 51% in 1988. Much of this employment, however, is part-time or part-year. For example, although two-thirds (65%) of all mothers with children under 18 are now employed, only two-fifths (41%) are employed full-time (S. Rich, 1986). And of married mothers living with their husbands, only 29% worked full-time all year in 1985.

There are some ethnic group differences in maternal employment patterns, with Black mothers most likely and Hispanic mothers least likely to be in the labor force (National Commission on Working Women, 1989b). For example, when children are under age 3, 56% of Black mothers are in the labor force compared to 52% of White mothers and 39% of Hispanic mothers. But when children are school age, even most Hispanic mothers (59%) are in the labor force.

Child-bearing patterns also are changing (Bianchi & Spain, 1983). Women are having fewer children than ever before and are having them later in life. In 1959, the average American family had 3.7 children; by 1979, they had 1.8 children, lower than the level reached during the Depression of the 1930s. Since that time, the number of children per family has remained fairly steady, although there is some indication that birthrates are starting to increase (C. H. Schmitt, 1991). First births to women over 30 have increased dramatically, from 4% in 1970 to 16% in 1987 ("More Women," 1989). Most of these women who delay childbearing are employed and tend to be better educated and in higher income brackets than those who give birth earlier. The percentage of women who do not have children has increased slightly in the last 15 years, especially for women in high-status nontraditional jobs. For example, in a 1984 Gallup poll of a nationwide representative group of female executives with the title of vice-president or higher, 52% were childless compared to fewer than 10% of their male counterparts (Rogan, 1984). Yet despite changes in childbearing, 91% of all women do have at least one child by the time they are 44 (Dreyfous, 1991a).

Some of the decline in the birthrate in the 1970s may have been due to a forced-choice situation for

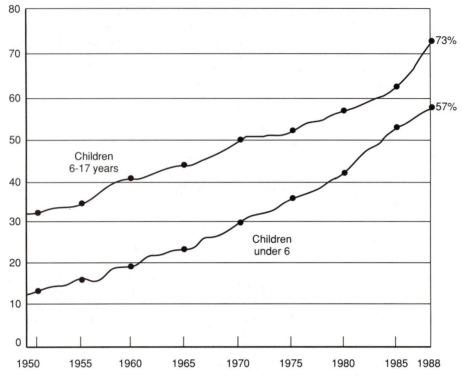

Figure 10.1 Percentage of mothers in the labor force, 1950–1988. (From National Commission on Working Women, 1989; S. Rich, 1985; R. E. Smith, 1979; U.S. Department of Labor, 1980.)

some women. Because most career patterns traditionally have ignored childbearing and child-care activities, women who have wanted both a career and a family may have felt forced to choose between the two. To some extent, the women's movement in the 1970s may have contributed to this conflict by emphasizing the importance of paid work, almost to the exclusion of family life. At the start of the 1980s, the movement began to focus on women's desire to have children, as well as on some ways in which family life and work could be integrated better (Friedan, 1981, 1983). As we have seen, recent polls of students and adults indicate that the vast majority of women today want and expect to combine jobs and family life. This changing attitude may be responsible for recent increases in births among both younger and older women (C. H. Schmitt, 1991; Vobejda, 1991).

Along with the overall decline in the birthrate and an increase in the age of first-time mothers is a high rate of teenage pregnancy, especially among Black females (Furstenberg, Brooks-Gunn, & Chase-Lansdale, 1989; Greenhouse, 1989; T. Lewin, 1988a). As discussed in Chapter 4, half of all teenage

females between ages 15 and 19 are sexually active (about the same as in other industrialized Western countries, with little difference by ethnic background), but less than half of these young women use contraception regularly. Consequently, pregnancy rates among teenagers in the United States are much higher than in other industrialized Western countries. In 1984, 19% of White females and 41% of Black females became pregnant by age 18. Although teenage pregnancy rates are high, the birthrate for female teenagers actually has declined since 1970. Only 48% of teenage pregnancies resulted in a live birth in 1984, mainly due to the availability of legal abortion. (More than a quarter of all abortions performed in the United States are performed on teenage girls, yet their access to legal abortion is increasingly being restricted by state laws.) Whether due to the increasing difficulty of obtaining an abortion or other reasons, more and more teenage girls, especially those under age 15, are keeping their babies ("More Teen Girls," 1991). Unfortunately, the young women who give birth are the least able to provide for their offspring. Most of the teenagers giving birth have below-average academic skills, tend not to complete high school, and come from poor families. Most also keep their babies and do not marry. Thus, these young women are most likely to raise their children in poverty, and their children suffer for it (low birth weight; physical, cognitive, and psychosocial problems; low school achievement). Teenage mothers also suffer compared to women who delay childbearing: they are less likely to complete high school and college, have fewer job skills, and are more likely to receive public assistance.

A related change with regard to families is the increasing number of single-parent households. Six out of ten Black children, one out of three Hispanic children, and one out of five White children under the age of 18 lived with one parent in 1989 (T. Lewin, 1990c). Overall, single parents head one-fourth of all families today, double the 1970 rate; 90% of these families are headed by the mother. The dramatic increase in single-parent households is due to two factors: a high divorce rate (about 40% of all children born in the late 1970s and early 1980s will experience their parents' divorce; Hetherington et al., 1989) and a large increase in the percentage of children born out of wedlock. In 1988, 26% of all newborns were born to an unmarried woman, compared to 18% of all newborns in 1980 ("Illegitimate," 1991). These percentages varied dramatically by ethnicity, with 18% of White babies, 34% of Hispanic babies, and 64% of Black babies born to unmarried women. Out-of-wedlock birth is more accepted now than in the past, especially in the Black community (T. Lewin, 1988a). A small but increasing number of out-of-wedlock births are occurring by choice among single women in their 30s (Smolowe, 1990). Between 1980 and 1988, the birthrate among unmarried White women in their 30s increased by two-thirds. Among this group are lesbians, who appear to be experiencing a baby boom, generally through the use of artificial insemination (S. Harris, 1991; G. Kolata, 1989).

Given the large number of divorces occurring among parents with young children and the relatively high rate of remarriage (80% for men, 75% for women), more and more children are growing up in reconstituted families (Hetherington et al., 1989). Despite the frequency of occurrence of this kind of family, norms and expectations regarding stepparents, stepchildren, stepgrandparents, half-siblings, noncustodial parents, and so on are vague and ill-defined for all concerned. (See Crosbie-Burnett, Skyles, and Becker-Haven, 1988, and Pasley and Ihinger-Tallman, 1987, for more information.)

In addition to changes in the size and composition of families with young children, families with adult children also have undergone change. One out of three single men aged 25 to 34 were living with their parents in 1990, a 50% increase over 1970 rates (J. Gross, 1991). For single women in that age group, living with parents is less appealing and only one out of five do so. For parents, especially mothers on whom caregiving responsibilities fall most heavily, this trend means that such responsibilities may never end. The increasing life expectancy of the elderly adds to the burden on middle-aged women. Just as women are the major caretakers of young children, they also are the major caretakers of the elderly. In fact, a 1989 report by the Older Women's League found that women are spending more time (an average of 18 years) caring for aged parents than they are caring for children (an average of 17 years) ("Mothers Bearing," 1989; M. B. Robinson, 1989). Women, whether they are daughters or daughters-in-law, employed or homemakers, outnumber men as caregivers more than three to one. The major reason men do not care for the elderly appears to be the prevailing view that "emotional work" is women's work (Finley, 1989). As we will see, such a view of the sexes' fields of "expertise" contributes to the differential expectations placed on mothers and fathers as well.

Thus, the traditional American (White) nuclear family model no longer is the norm. Most children live in families with a mother who is in the labor force at least part-time, and many live just with their mother, or with their mother and her partner. These new patterns are, in fact, becoming more similar to the historic pattern among Black families (P. H. Collins, 1990; Dill, 1979; Ladner, 1971; Stack, 1974; Willie, 1985). African Americans, brought over as slaves, developed family structures adapted to their unique and oppressive economic and political situation. Both Black men and women were forced to work, first in the fields, then elsewhere, to survive. Black women not only were expected to continue to work after giving birth, but frequently were expected to nurse White infants as well ("Mammy"). Among Blacks, communal child care in extended kin networks developed. Black children were the responsibility of the Black community, not just of their biological parents. Motherhood was never seen as a full-time occupation for Black women. Since both Black men and women worked and marriages frequently were discouraged, male-female relationships tended to be more egalitarian than was the case among Whites. Although slavery no longer exists, Blacks still are marginalized economically, politically, and structurally. Their family structures continue to reflect these conditions. Extended kin networks still are more common among Blacks than Whites. Many Black women still are socialized into a strong maternal role embedded in the Black community (Binion, 1990). As we have noted, Black mothers are more likely to be unmarried and in the labor force than White mothers. Black men, who still rarely can expect to earn enough to support a family, have a more difficult time establishing a family role for themselves. Perhaps that is why, as we saw in the last chapter, Black men tend to derive less benefit from marriage than White men. Unfortunately, the economic status of Black men is declining, and their unemployment rate is strongly linked to rates of single parenthood among Black women (R. M. Brewer, 1988; W. E. Schmidt, 1989; Wilkie, 1991). Given the dominance of White patriarchal cultural norms and of racism, it is not surprising that non-patriarchal Black families were described in the 1960s as "matriarchies" (see, for example, Moynihan, 1965). Rather than being viewed as the key to Black survival, Black mothers were blamed for all the problems Blacks suffered, especially poverty (see P. H. Collins, 1989, and Zinn, 1989, for critiques). Here was "mother blaming" of a high order.

Despite changes in family structures, the traditional family model still influences people's lives. Traditional assumptions about the "proper" parental roles for women and men significantly affect parent-child relations but in different ways for mothers and for fathers. In fact, father-child relationships until recently have been relatively ignored by most researchers—parental behavior has been assumed synonymous with maternal behavior. Therefore, both maternal and paternal relationships will be looked at separately in the following sections.

▲ Mother-Child Relationships

Phyllis Schlafly (1977) has written, "Why should a man marry a woman who refuses to be a mother to his children? He can get everything else he wants from women at a price much cheaper than marriage" (p. 51). As her quote illustrates, having children is usually viewed as a requirement for marriage and, for many, is a justification of female existence. Motherhood is chief among the requirements of the female role and has been considered a woman's major goal in life. Some writers (for example, Russo, 1976) go further and assert that even more than a goal that one theoretically chooses, motherhood is a mandate that women are required to fulfill. According to this mandate, every woman should have at least two children and "raise them well"—that is, spend most of her time with them. In this section, we will look at the myths of motherhood as well as the reality of motherhood for homemaking mothers, employed mothers, and single mothers.

The Myths of Motherhood

Numerous myths surround motherhood and are extremely resistant to refutation (see Oakley, 1974; A. Rich, 1986). One myth is the Motherhood Mandate: that all women need to be mothers or else they will be failures as human beings, a disgrace to their sex, or, at least, extremely unhappy. A second myth is that motherhood comes naturally to women and is women's most fulfilling and transcendant relationship. A third myth is that all children need their mother's (and only their mother's) exclusive and continuous attention. These myths all serve to support traditional gender roles, especially women's status as subordinate to men. Let us examine these myths more closely.

The motherhood mandate The belief that all women need to be mothers is a strong one and is part of many secular and religious ideologies. For example, Freudian psychoanalytic theory posits that the healthy resolution of the Electra complex for girls is a wish to have a child, particularly a male child. The Catholic church, too, posits that women's primary role in life is to bear children. Women who cannot bear children tend to be pitied, and women who are voluntarily child-free are viewed by others as misguided, maladjusted, or selfish (Dreyfous, 1991a; R. A. Peterson, 1983; J. Ross & Kahan, 1983). Due to these views, many women who have difficulty conceiving feel like failures and go to extraordinary lengths to try to conceive (Lasker & Borg, 1987). Many have turned to such new reproductive technologies as test-tube fertilization and ovum transfer, both of which are extremely expensive, enormously intrusive (women practically have to live at the clinic), and generally unsuccessful (success rates approximate 10%). Although many women who can afford to use these technologies appreciate their availability, many feminists have criticized these approaches as elitist, dehumanizing, and supportive of the view that the only "real" (valuable) woman is a mother (see Corea et al., 1987, and Spallone, 1989, for interesting critiques).

The Motherhood Mandate is transmitted in numerous ways. We have seen that the socialization girls receive emphasizes their future maternal role. From the emphasis on developing nurturant qualities, to the encouragement of "playing mommy" and baby-sitting activities, to the lack of attention to other options, most girls grow up trained to become mothers and, in many cases, only mothers. Girls' achievement aspirations sometimes become channeled into family production rather than career success through the message that the latter is less desirable than the former. For example, White women with high fear of success have been found to produce larger families than those with low fear of success (Russo, 1976). Societal norms that encourage females to be sexual but that restrict their ability to control reproduction by limiting contraceptive information and abortion availability also support the Motherhood Mandate. Indeed, the fight over abortion is part of the larger fight over women's reproductive freedom, which means freedom from the Motherhood Mandate (see S. E. Davis, 1988). The disturbingly high rate of teenage pregnancies in the United States is partly a reflection of this mandate. Teenage mothers are the ones with the least access to contraception and the fewest alternative life options.

The reality is that women can find life happiness in many ways. Not all women make good mothers, and not all women find motherhood rewarding. Much depends upon women's socialization experiences, personality, and expectations, as well as the social supports they receive. Women who are traditionally sex-typed or who have traditional sex role orientations tend to desire and have larger families than do non-sex-typed and nontraditional women (M. J. Gerson, 1980; W. J. Scott & Morgan, 1983). Traditional women also appear more personally interested in child rearing than more nontraditional women (Biaggio, Mohan, & Baldwin, 1985; M. J. Gerson, 1985). In one study of sexually active teenagers, those who got pregnant were found to be more traditional in sex role orientation than other young women (Ireson, 1984). Women who choose to remain child-free are even less traditional than other women with regard to their behavior, their attitudes, and their self-image (for example, they tend to have higher occupational status and more egalitarian marriages) (Baber & Dreyer, 1986; Bram, 1984; Yogev & Vierra, 1983). It is important to note that research on women late in life who

never had children find them no less happy or satisfied with their lives than women with at least one child (Houser, Berkman, & Beckman 1984). So much for the myth that all women need to be mothers.

The maternal instinct   Along with the belief that all women need to become mothers is the belief that all mothers need their children and know how to nurture them. Yet as we saw in Chapter 3, there is no such thing as a maternal instinct. Nurturance is learned, partly during childhood, and mostly as a function of interacting with infants and young children. Thus, boys who grow up caring for children are just as nurturant as girls who do so. Furthermore, taking care of an infant, even breast-feeding, is something that must be learned. Fathers who interact with their newborns become equally as proficient at caring for their baby and as nurturing as mothers who interact with their newborns. And many mothers are not nurturant and/or have no interest in their children.

Because of belief in the maternal instinct, many women who always expected to be mothers are startled to discover upon giving birth that they have no idea what to do or even what they feel. Many mothers undergo a difficult period of postpartum adjustment that is made more difficult by a mother's inability to share her feelings about motherhood and the marked inequality in caregiving and domestic responsibilities (Bram, 1983; Croghan, 1991; S. S. Feldman & Nash, 1984). Support for the mother is very important in facilitating her transition to motherhood (Power & Parke, 1984). Unfortunately, in a typical nuclear family, a mother may receive little support. Her husband may be unable or unwilling to give it, her own mother and other relatives may live at a distance, friends may not be that close, and societal supports, like day care, may be unavailable. Single mothers may receive even less social support than married mothers, although this typically is not the case in the Black community (P. H. Collins, 1990; Stack, 1974).

To say that there is no maternal instinct does not mean that women who give birth may not have special feelings for their newborn. Gestating a fetus for nine months 24 hours a day does give the new mother a head start on developing feelings of attachment and empathy, although in this age of ultrasound fetal pictures, some soon-to-be fathers also may develop such feelings. By the time many women give birth, they have already developed a very strong relationship with their newborn. Close bodily contact and interaction with a newborn immediately postpartum enhances the mother-infant bond (Klaus & Kennell, 1982). The experience of breast-feeding further enhances feelings of attachment since it is so mutually reinforcing. Hormonal changes in the new mother also may facilitate bonding. Thus, the mother-child bond indeed may be stronger than the father-child bond during the first few months of a baby's life, but this is not due to inevitable "instinct." Rather, this bond is a product of an interaction among biology, expectations, and experience (Ainsworth, 1989). We only need to read the accounts in the daily papers of mothers killing, maiming, or abandoning their babies to recognize that a loving attachment to a baby does not come automatically to biological mothers.

The controversy surrounding "surrogate" mothering (whereby a woman agrees to conceive and bear a child using her egg and another man's sperm, and then to give the child after birth to the biological father and his wife) reveals society's contradictory support of the motherhood myth that all women need their children. Although the public tends to sympathize with the woman who wants a baby using any means possible due to the Motherhood Mandate, the public also tends to be very hostile toward the woman who agrees to bear a child for another woman and later changes her mind, as happened in the case of Mary Beth Whitehead (Chesler, 1988). But since the "surrogate" mother actually is the biological mother, isn't she just conforming to the second motherhood myth, that there's a "sacred bond" or maternal instinct that binds mother to child? What the Whitehead case and others like it reveal is the purpose behind the myths of motherhood. These myths, although they primarily function to keep women subordinate to men, can be manipulated to maintain class privilege as well. After all, it is mainly privileged women and men who can pay less privileged women to have babies for them. Perhaps by agreeing to give up the baby in the first place, the surrogate mother has proven herself a "bad" mother and therefore undeserving of public sympathy. Thus, the motherhood myths can be invoked to support the privileged woman at the same time as they can be manipulated to vilify the less privileged one.

Throughout history, the institution of motherhood has responded to society's needs, and ideologies have developed to support societal values (A. Rich, 1986). Sometimes mothers have been expected to kill or abandon their newborns for reasons ranging from lack of financial resources to preference for a particular gender to euthanasia (as in ancient Rome). Sometimes mothers have been expected to hand over their newborns to another woman to suckle and raise, either temporarily (as many upper-class 19th-century women did) or permanently (as many unwed mothers did in the mid-20th century). As the birth rate of White upper-middle-class American women has dropped and their participation in the labor force risen, new myths of motherhood have sprung up in the late 20th century to encourage these women of the ruling class to stay home and reproduce. Not coincidentally, the fight over reproductive freedom has heated up. Such are the sexual politics of motherhood.

All children need their mothers   The third myth of motherhood is that all children need their biological mothers' exclusive and continuous attention. Thus, children are assumed to suffer if their mothers are employed and if they are cared for by a mother substitute, even if that substitute is the biological father. A direct corollary of this myth is that a "good" mother is a selfless one, ever subordinating her needs to those of her children. This myth is the basis of all the dire warnings about the effects of maternal employment and of day care.

Despite the strong belief that mothers should be home with their children, studies of other cultures have found that nowhere do mothers spend as much exclusive time with their children as did mid-20th century White American mothers (Dally, 1983; Greenfield, 1981). In less complex societies, the job of mothering is shared by other members of an extended family, including husbands, or by institutional supports, such as day-care facilities and children's houses. More important, research has shown that it is not in the interest of either the mother or her children for the mother to be kept dependent and housebound. Bronfenbrenner (1974), after reviewing the literature on child development, concludes that "to function effectively as a parent, a mother must also have the opportunity of being a total person" (p. 4). The best arrangement for the development of a young child may be one in which the mother is free to work outside the home part-time and in which the child is exposed to other caretakers, especially to the father (Dally, 1983; L. W. Hoffman, 1989).

The factors important for healthy infant and child development include consistent and sensitive care in a stable environment with physical and intellectual stimulation, love, and affection (Ainsworth, 1979; Scarr, 1984, 1990). While children need love and attention, they do not need it constantly from their biological mothers. Children respond as well (or better) to multiple mothering, to paternal attachment, or to any other regular caretaker (Beit-Hallahmi & Rabin, 1977; Goossens & van Ijzendoorn, 1990; Scarr, 1984, 1990).

Although it is important for parents to attend to the needs of their children in sensitive and supportive ways, it is not "selfish" for a mother also to want to meet some of her own needs, whether those needs involve employment, continuing education, friends, exercise, or just time of one's own. Mothers must have a self if they are to encourage their children to have one as well. Children need to have models of people who balance their own needs with those of others. Having one parent who attends to the needs of others at the expense of her own needs and another parent who attends to his own needs at the expense of others is not the best way to encourage children to develop a balanced sense of self. Maternal selflessness also may put an undue burden on children to live up to their mothers' expectations of them. One consequence of this norm of selflessness is that it is extremely easy for women to be viewed as "bad" mothers. All they have to do is express their own needs, whether these be sexual, work-related, or personal.

After surveying a broad range of studies (Clarke-Stewart, 1989; Gottfried & Gottfried, 1988; L. W. Hoffman, 1989; Rodman, Pratto, & Nelson, 1985; Scarr, 1984, 1990; Scarr, Phillips, & McCartney, 1990; Selkow, 1984; Tolman, Diekmann, & McCartney, 1989; Van Horn, 1989), one must conclude that there is absolutely no evidence that children of employed mothers are neglected or affected adversely on the whole. Most studies find little difference between children of employed mothers and children of nonemployed mothers. For example, both sets of children form similar interpersonal attachments. When differences are found, they tend to favor children of employed mothers. These children, compared to children of full-time housewives, tend to receive more independence training, have generally higher career goals and somewhat higher achievement motivation, and tend to have less traditional conceptions of the sex roles and a more positive evaluation of female competence. These results are particularly true for daughters, perhaps because employed mothers present a positive model of female achievement and because girls, under traditional child rearing, usually do not receive independence training. Sons of middle-class employed mothers do not fare quite as well as daughters in a few studies involving academic performance, although this finding has not been a consistent one. A more consistent finding is that middle-class sons of employed mothers tend to be less stereotyped in their conceptions of sex roles and to be better adjusted socially than middle-class sons of nonemployed mothers. Sons of working-class employed mothers appear to do as well as their sisters in terms of cognitive ability and social adjustment, although the sons tend to be somewhat stereotyped regarding sex roles. Thus, the guilt many employed mothers feel is unwarranted and may even be counterproductive. Mothers with positive attitudes toward their multiple roles are likely to have better-adjusted children than mothers with less positive attitudes (Etaugh, 1980). In conclusion, maternal employment in and of itself is not harmful. Its effects are mediated by the quality of alternative care, the mother's attitudes, the family environment (for example, economic status, single parenthood), and specific child-related qualities (age, gender, behavior).

The fear that children will be harmed if mothers do not stay home or sacrifice their needs to those of their family is a fear that some argue is perpetuated by men because it serves men's needs (someone takes care of all domestic responsibilities for them), because it eliminates women from competing with them in the labor force, and because it maintains their superior power in relation to women (Lowe & Hubbard, 1979; Polatnick, 1973–74). The norm of selflessness in women and not men means men's needs have primacy over women's. Furthermore, by promoting the myth that all children need their mothers (and only their mothers), the United States has dreadfully neglected its responsibilities toward children. Alone among industrialized countries, the United States has no consistent child-care policy and no parental leave policy. The government contributes no funds toward high quality child care. Consequently, there is a dearth of good alternative child care for families in need of such services (Scarr, 1990). And as we have seen, most families are in need of such services. The myths of motherhood, not mothers themselves, are putting the nation's children at risk.

These three myths—that all women must be mothers, that all mothers need their children, and that all children need their mothers—are pervasive. The effects of these myths are quite serious for women. The responsibility for a child limits a mother's access to life options, such as higher education or work. These myths support job discrimination against women because they maintain that women are likely to get pregnant and quit their jobs or at least quit focusing on them. These myths produce role conflict in those women who also want careers, since society provides little support for employed mothers—few part-time jobs, few day-care centers. Overall, these myths set women up for failure and guilt since no woman can live up to these myths in their entirety.

Not only do women blame themselves for failing to live up to these impossible myths, but society blames women as well. No one seems to blame the myths themselves. Psychology, medicine, and the law have a long history of blaming mothers for their children's behavior and problems (Caplan, 1989). For example, psychodynamic theory attributes nearly all psychological problems to some failure in the mother-child relationship (see H. G. Lerner, 1988, for a critique). The father-child relationship rarely is blamed, despite the important role fathers play in child development (see Chapter 6). One result of this maternal mythology and the resultant pattern of mother blame is that when fathers fight mothers for custody of children, mothers frequently lose. Chesler (1986) found that 70% of her sample of "good enough" mothers lost custody when challenged by the fathers for reasons ranging from the mother's being employed to having a sexual relationship. Such behavior on the part of the father did not prevent his being awarded custody.

It should be noted that it is not motherhood itself that is under attack here but rather the mandate that all women should experience motherhood and should devote their entire life to that purpose. When motherhood becomes a choice, not a requirement, the quality of the mother-child relationship should improve, as should the happiness of individual women and children. Some changes already are occurring, as noted earlier—the birthrate is decreasing, more women are having fewer children and at a later age, more women are deciding to remain child-free or have just one child, and more mothers are employed. These changes seem to be related to changing gender role expectations. The "best" mothers are women who are happy with their lives, whether they stay at home or are employed full-time. Thus, if as a society we really care about children, we should do everything possible to ensure that women have adequate opportunities to fulfill themselves and that when they become mothers, they have adequate support in their lives (personal, financial, and institutional). We are a long way from meeting this standard, as we shall see when we turn to women's experience of motherhood.

The Experience of Motherhood

Nine out of ten women become mothers. What do we know about their experience of motherhood? Until recently, we knew very little, relying instead upon the myths to tell us what mothers "must" feel. It is only in the last 20 years that a body of literature has accumulated about the experience of motherhood written by mothers themselves (for example, Lazarre, 1976; A. Rich, 1986). Unfortunately, most research studies only focus upon White middle-class mothers, which limits our ability to generalize about the experience of motherhood. As we will see, although there may be some universal experiences, by and large the experience of being a mother is very much shaped by such social factors as ethnicity, economic status, marital status, and employment status. Overlaying all these factors are, of course, the expectations based on gender. Nearly all women live in a patriarchal society that shapes the experience of motherhood for women and children. As we saw in Chapter 5, historically most children have been viewed as men's possessions (most take on the father's name and lineage). Women traditionally have been viewed as giving birth to and taking care of men's children. Although a mother's *connection* to her children is viewed today as important, indeed primary (as seen in the motherhood myths), fathers' *rights* still take precedence, as revealed in recent court decisions surrounding surrogacy, abortion, and custody (see Rothman, 1989, for an interesting discussion of these issues.)

Most women find the birth of their first child to be a major life event, for which no preparation is completely adequate (Mercer, 1986). Mothers must adapt to the birth experience biologically, psychologically, and socially. All mothers must acquire both a maternal "identity" and child-care skills. As we have noted, both aspects of motherhood are learned. This learning is affected by the mother's background, personality, and health; the birth and postpartum experience; the infant's temperament and health status; and the degree of social stress and social support present in the mother's life.

New mothers typically find themselves not only more involved in child-care activities than they had expected, but also doing more of the housework, regardless of the previous division of labor between couples and regardless of their employment status (Belsky et al., 1986; Croghan, 1991; D. N. Ruble et al., 1988). On the average, when a child under 5 years old is present, married women spend approximately 47 hours a week in home production activities (child care, chores, meal preparation, and so on) when they are not employed and 33 hours when they are employed (Douthitt, 1989). Approximately 40% of these hours are spent in direct child care—17 hours per week for nonemployed mothers compared to 14 hours per week for employed mothers. When the youngest child is over 5 years old, the amount of time mothers spend in direct child care decreases by about five hours a week for both employed and nonemployed mothers. Thus, taking care of preschool children is particularly time-consuming and mainly done by mothers. Fathers of such young children spend only 6 to 7 hours per week in child-care activities, mainly on weekends, regardless of their wife's employment status.

One major result of this traditional division of labor when a young child is present in the home is that marital satisfaction tends to decline, especially for the wife, as we saw in the last chapter. In general, the mother of a young child is under great stress, much greater than that of her husband, regardless of her labor force participation (E. A. Anderson & Leslie, 1991). The emotional and physical work involved in caring for and being responsible for a young, dependent child is tremendous, yet the myths of motherhood imply that such work should be assumed easily and eagerly by "good mothers." For single mothers without a supportive family network or sufficient income, the strains are even greater.

The developmental stage of a child significantly affects a mother's personal and social development. Women appear to undergo psychosocial transitions as a function of the phases of the family cycle, in contrast to men, whose psychosocial transitions are more associated with their own chronological age (such as a "midlife crisis" at age 40) (L. R. Fischer, 1981; R. L. Harris, Ellicott, & Holmes, 1986; Reinke, Holmes, & Harris, 1985; Silverberg & Steinberg, 1990). Important phases for women appear to be the birth of a child (preschool phase), when a daughter reaches puberty (pubertal phase), when the oldest child leaves home (launching phase), and when the last child leaves home (postparental phase). Marital and personal dissatisfactions tend to increase during the preschool, pubertal, and launching phases, but both satisfactions increase during the postparental phase. Thus, most women do not grieve over an "empty nest" when their last child leaves home but instead feel increased life satisfaction. Those women who do experience the "empty nest syndrome" tend to be women who incorporated the motherhood myths most strongly into their adult identity (Adelmann, Antonucci, Crohan, & Coleman, 1989).

A nationally representative sample of 1100 mothers between the ages of 18 and 80 was surveyed about their experience of motherhood (Genevie & Margolies, 1987). The majority of women (55%) expressed a great deal of ambivalence about motherhood. Although most felt that the good (the love, the enrichment, the fulfillment of expectations) outweighed the bad (the exhaustion, the limitations, the responsibility), most also felt disillusioned. The experience of motherhood was quite different from their expectations, and many mothers resented their husband's lack of involvement. About one out of five mothers found motherhood to be mostly negative. These women tended to feel pressured into motherhood and found the tasks of mothering to be burdensome and boring. These women also lacked the personal qualities of nurturance and patience, resented their husband's lack of support, and were disappointed in their children. In contrast, about one out of four mothers felt motherhood to be unambivalently satisfying. These mothers tended to have realistic expectations of what motherhood would be like, a strong desire for a close family, an involved husband who shared responsibilities, a great deal of both patience and luck, and a satisfying choice regarding employment (if they wanted to stay home full-time, they could; if they wanted to work outside the home, they did). Thus, motherhood is both rewarding and painful, and most mothers have contradictory feelings about it.

Unquestionably, motherhood is difficult, yet myths and stereotypes often make motherhood more difficult than it need be. Let's take a closer look at the experiences of different types of mothers.

Homemaker mothers   What do we call women with children under 18 who are not in the labor force? Most people just call them mothers, since they are fulfilling traditional expectations. We generally label the exceptions—the "employed mother," the "single mother." Yet full-time homemaker mothers are themselves the exception. Only one out of three women with children under 18 are not in the labor force. Most of these mothers have preschool children and view motherhood as a full-time job, at least until the children are in school. And, indeed, child care and homemaking are full-time jobs, since the average nonemployed mother spends over 45 hours a week in child-care and homemaking activities, plus being constantly on call for sick care, entertaining, and so on. She also gets little to no vacation or sick leave.

Most mothers who care for their children full-time today do so by choice. Genevie and Margolies's

(1987) national survey found that 70% of the full-time homemakers they interviewed experienced little or no conflict about staying home. Most of these women were happy and satisfied with their role, feeling a sense of fulfillment and pleasure in being there for their children. As we saw in Chapter 8, women who are feminine-sex-typed and/or who are primarily interested in being a wife and mother may be quite satisfied when they are able to fulfill these two roles, at least for part of their lives (Baruch et al., 1983; W. R. Gove & Zeiss, 1987; D. M. Hoffman & Fidell, 1979). Yet even women who feel little conflict about staying home may still have some dissatisfactions. Another survey of mothers found that 56% of full-time homemakers said they would choose to have a career if they had it to do all over again (DeChick, 1988). Full-time homemaking also may take its toll on a woman's mental and physical health. A longitudinal study found that at midlife, traditional homemakers appear to have somewhat inflexible personalities (Helson & Picano, 1990). Such women, when compared to nonmothers and mothers who had joined the labor force at some point, had more physical complaints and were less assertive and independent.

A significant minority of full-time homemakers (30%) do not even say they are content (Genevie & Margolies, 1987). They often experience conflict about their activities—feeling that they "should" stay home but not really enjoying it. Rather than fulfilled, they feel limited and trapped, with a lowered sense of self-worth. As discussed in Chapter 8, nonemployed mothers of young children tend to feel more depressed than other mothers (C. E. Ross & Mirowsky, 1988). Many feel taken for granted and unappreciated. As Figure 10.2 shows, homemakers

typically are not even thought of as working. Furthermore, given the motherhood myth of the necessity for selfless devotion to others, a stay-at-home mother may lose touch with her own identity and needs as well as with the world outside her domestic circle. She thus may experience little intellectual stimulation and personal growth. Wells (1988) found that mothers' sense of self-esteem was lower when they were with their children than when they were with adults.

Full-time homemaking may be a burden on the nonemployed woman and her family. Such mothers are more likely than others to interfere with their children's struggle for autonomy and privacy, to dominate their husbands and children, and to try to make their family feel guilty continually because they (the mothers) do "so much" (L. R. Ferguson, 1977; L. W. Hoffman, 1979; Wilborn, 1978). As noted previously, a certain amount of realistically timed pressure on the child toward independence and moderate levels of maternal warmth and protectiveness facilitate achievement behaviors in children. Thus, overprotective, overnurturing mothers may interfere with the development of achievement behaviors in their children.

What is critical is *choice*. Throughout the last 150 years, only middle- and upper-class women could "choose" to stay home with their children. Indeed, many of these women were prohibited by social norms and their husbands from doing otherwise, and many were extremely frustrated at home. Today, the economic situation of many families has placed some women in the opposite position: they would prefer to stay home but cannot afford to do so. Mothers who are forced to stay home as well as those forced to join the labor force tend to be more

Figure 10.2 When is work not thought of as work? When women do it in their home. (FOR BETTER OR FOR WORSE Copyright 1984 Lynn Johnston. Reprinted with permission of Universal Press Syndicate.)

conflicted and troubled than mothers who choose to stay home. The happiest homemaker mothers are those who prefer and can afford to do so. Thus, choice of lifestyle is critical. Even in terms of the division of labor within the family, if a woman is satisfied with her husband's contribution, regardless of how much it is, both she and her family tend to be happy (Pleck, 1981a; Suitor, 1991).

If a mother stays home for a number of years while her children are young, it often is difficult for her to enter the labor force in her late 30s (or later) and still achieve a significant degree of success. She may never have acquired job-related skills and therefore must settle for very low-level jobs. Her training may be outdated. She may be without the crucial informal contacts for professional success. She may have lost self-confidence through years of subverting her needs in favor of those of her family. She may have lost her ambition. The plight of displaced homemakers (women who lose their principal job of homemaking when their main source of income, their husband, is gone) is particularly tragic, since 57% end up in or near poverty (T. Lewin, 1990a). As Gloria Steinem once said, most women are one man away from poverty.

Increasing numbers of full-time homemakers are recognizing their economic vulnerability as well as the rewards of outside employment. Many middle-aged women are returning to school; more than one-fourth of all women attending college today are over age 35 (Liu, 1991). Labor force participation rates of women aged 35 to 44 also are extremely high, 75% in 1990 compared to 50% in 1970 (Uchitelle, 1990). Thus, full-time homemaking is mainly a temporary career today, engaged in primarily by women who want to stay home with a preschool child and who either have a husband who earns enough to support the family or who cannot afford the child-care expenses employment would entail.

Attitudes toward stay-at-home mothers appear to be changing slowly. Among high school seniors, three-fourths of the women and one half of the men in 1986 thought that "a working mother can establish just as warm and secure a relationship with her children as a mother who does not work" (Bachman, 1987). Nonemployed mothers tend to be viewed as more family-oriented but less instrumental and less professionally competent than employed mothers (Etaugh & Nekolny, 1990; Etaugh & Study, 1989). More positive attitudes toward maternal employment is a good sign, since most mothers will be in the labor force, even when their children are young.

Employed mothers   The primary experience of employed mothers is guilt. Most women have internalized the motherhood myths, and thus feel they are inadequate mothers if they are not with their children 24 hours a day. Especially if women are employed by choice, they experience conflict over what they feel they "should" do and what they want to do. Their conflict is understandable since a significant minority of the American public thinks that an employed woman makes a worse mother than a nonemployed woman.

A nationwide poll taken in November 1983 by the *New York Times* (Dowd, 1983) indicates that more than one-third of those interviewed (40% of the men, 31% of the women) believed employed women were worse mothers than those who devote all their time to the home. As Figure 10.3 shows, many (one out of four) employed women felt the same way. No wonder mothers who are engaged in outside employment often feel concerned about whether they are doing the right thing—one out of three Americans feels they are poor mothers! If a woman has a preschool child, attitudes toward her employment become even more negative. Three out of five men, from high school through adulthood, think that a preschool child is likely to suffer if the mother works (Bachman, 1987; "Changing Attitudes," 1986). Women tend to be a little more flexible than men in this regard, since less than half of them (35 to 46%) agree that a preschool child will suffer. Encouragingly, public opinion is moving in a more supportive direction, especially among women. In the *New York Times* survey, about 50% fewer women in 1983 than in 1970 thought employed mothers made poorer mothers. Similarly, about 15% more men and women in the mid-1970s than in the mid-1980s thought preschool children will suffer if the mother works.

Despite the slowly changing attitudes regarding maternal employment, many employed mothers still struggle with guilt feelings (B. J. Berg, 1986; Genevie & Margolies, 1987). Employed mothers often compensate for their absence by increasing the time they spend in direct interaction with the child when they are at home. Many also feel anxious about their child-care arrangements, sometimes due to the myth that only mothers can care well for children, but sometimes also due to uncertainties about the adequacy of alternative care (Clarke-Stewart, 1989; Scarr, 1990; Scarr et al., 1990). High-quality day care is scarce and extremely expensive. Most children of employed mothers are cared for in either their own (31%) or in another woman's

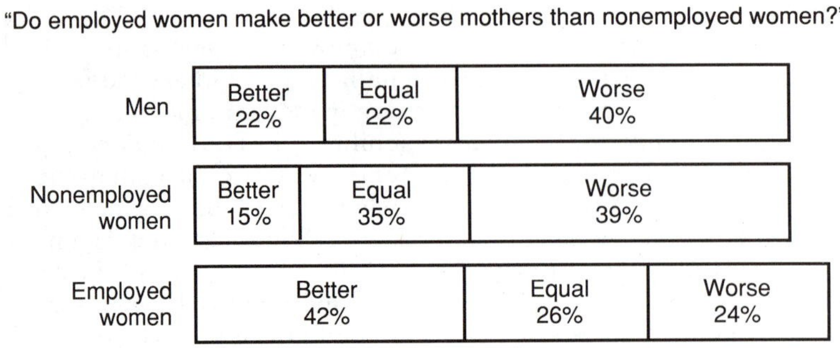

"Do employed women make better or worse mothers than nonemployed women?"

Men	Better 22%	Equal 22%	Worse 40%
Nonemployed women	Better 15%	Equal 35%	Worse 39%
Employed women	Better 42%	Equal 26%	Worse 24%

Figure 10.3 Opinions on mothers and wives who hold outside employment. (Adapted from Dowd, 1983. Poll taken by *New York Times*, November 1983.)

home (37%) (T. Lewin, 1988b). Only 25% are in organized child-care facilities, and some of these are of poor quality. Furthermore, since men hold more negative attitudes than women regarding maternal employment, a woman may receive little support from her spouse (and from her employer) if she chooses not to stay home. Not surprisingly, then, many employed mothers experience a great deal of stress and role conflict.

Mothers' guilt and anxiety about harming their children are particularly unfortunate since, as we have just seen, there is no evidence that maternal employment is harmful for children. Most child-care experts now agree that as long as the children get good alternative care and plenty of attention from their parents when they are home, the children will be fine. The mother's employment status is not the key variable; the kind of care the child receives is. Also important are personal and demographic factors. Many mothers do not provide adequate care; many day-care centers and baby-sitters provide excellent care. Thus, once we stop idealizing mothers as all-nurturant angels and perceive them as complex human beings with a variety of skills and interests, we will be further along in the development of a variety of enriching child-care options.

The effects of maternal employment on the mother also are important. As discussed in Chapter 8, most studies find little difference between the mental health status of employed women and homemakers. The *quality* of one's roles rather than the quantity of them appears to be key with respect to mental health (Crosby, 1987; Helson et al., 1990; Kibria et al., 1990). In a number of circumstances, paid employment is positively associated with a mother's psychological well-being—for example, among mothers with social support, positive occupational attitudes, and/or high-prestige jobs. Many women

appear to thrive on the challenges involved in juggling career and family lives. For example, Baruch et al. (1983) conducted interviews with 238 White women between the ages of 35 and 55, who were single, single with children, married, or married with children. Half of the married women were homemakers. These researchers found that the employed women had higher levels of mastery (self-esteem and a sense of control) than the nonemployed women and that a sense of mastery was vital for a woman's overall well-being. Interestingly, having children had no impact on well-being. Overall, for most women and men, combining work and family life leads to greater general satisfaction than either work or family alone.

Noting that employment may be beneficial or at least not unhealthy for mothers does not mean that multiple roles may not be stressful. The critical variables in determining work overload and inter-role conflict are choice, social support, commitment to the work role, quality of employment, and workplace supports (such as flexible work hours) (Baruch & Barnett, 1987; Holahan & Gilbert, 1979; Kibria et al., 1990; Moen & Forest, 1990). Mothers who are forced into the work force but who do not find their jobs rewarding and who still must do all or most of the housework and child care when they get home are likely to be the most stressed.

Nearly all employed mothers must deal with the stress of role overload since, as we have seen, employed mothers still remain primarily responsible for housework and child care. These responsibilities amount to a second full-time job for employed women, a "second shift." For example, in Arlie Hochschild's (1989) study of 50 dual-job couples with at least one child under age 6 at home, 80% were characterized by the fathers doing one-third or less of the domestic work (including child care). In only 20% of the families was domestic work shared somewhat equally. Still, the 30% of the housework and child care that most fathers with employed wives now seem to do is definitely an improvement (Pleck, 1985). In the 1960s, such men did only 20% of the domestic work. Some of the change in percentage is due, however, to the decreasing amount of time employed mothers are spending on household tasks like meal preparation (Douthitt, 1989).

How do employed mothers handle such a load of responsibilities? Some try to "do it all." The myth of "Supermom" abounds, encouraged by media reports of the exceptional woman who appears to have (and do) everything: a rewarding professional career, a close relationship with her children and participation in child-related activities such as the PTA and Girl Scouts, a sexy and romantic relationship with her husband, time for physical fitness activities, and a spotless home. Since this ideal is impossible to live up to, many women become exhausted trying, and many marriages may collapse under the weight. Other mothers are creating new options: job sharing (one job is split between two people), alternating shift work with their husbands, and working at home (Arkin & Dobrofsky, 1978a; Dullea, 1983; K. Rubin, 1987).

Most women, however, try to cope with existing options, using a variety of strategies (Basler, 1986; Dunlop, 1981; J. D. Gray, 1983; A. O. Harrison & Minor, 1983; Ogintz, 1983; K. Rubin, 1987). Employed mothers may (1) look primarily at the benefits of combining career and family, (2) decide in advance which role to emphasize (almost always the family) in case of conflicting demands, (3) compartmentalize the two roles as much as possible, (4) reduce standards within certain roles (like housekeeping), (5) get help from within and/or outside the family, (6) carefully schedule their time, (7) cut back on sleep and personal time, or (8) compromise their career to fit into family commitments. The last two options are the most common. The compromised career is a frequent solution and accounts for the fact that many women are underemployed and underpaid. The majority of traditionally female jobs, such as teaching and clerical work, are least in conflict with a primary commitment to home and family. Furthermore, about 25% of all employed mothers are employed part-time. Unfortunately, such compromising also reinforces the stereotype that women are not really serious about their work.

In conclusion, the lives of employed mothers are complex. For most, the benefits (financial and/or psychological) outweigh the costs. In 1988, only one out of five employed mothers said they would leave their jobs to stay home with their children if they had that option (DeChick, 1988). Many of the costs could be lessened, however, if employed mothers received more support. Fathers could share more equitably the responsibilities of child care and domestic work. Employers could offer more flexible hours, parental leaves, on-site day care, and professional part-time options. The government also could help. As noted, the United States is the only country among advanced industrial nations having no provisions assuring a parent of infant care leave of any kind. In fact, more than 100 countries guarantee workers some form of job-protected, partially paid, maternity-related benefits. In France, for example, all new mothers are guaranteed 10 weeks of paid leave after birth and 6 weeks of paid leave before, plus job security. Unpaid leave is possible for up to two years after birth and the government heavily subsidizes preschool care. In contrast, in 1990 a child-care bill that would have required employers of more than 50 people to offer at least 10 weeks *unpaid* job-protected leave to new mothers was vetoed by President Bush. Consequently, today about 60% of all working women have no paid parental leave (National Commission on Working Women, 1989b).

Single mothers Although mothers who are not married are included in the two preceding categories—that is, employed or nonemployed—their experience of motherhood differs in important ways from that of mothers who are married. In the first place, they are more likely to be poor. Second, they are viewed as nonnormative, at least among non-Black populations, despite their growing number. In March 1989, female-headed families comprised 13% of all families among Whites, 23% among Hispanics, and 44% among Blacks (U.S. Department of Commerce, 1989a). Third, the stresses upon them frequently are greater, partly due to the first two characteristics but also due to the lack of a co-parent.

What may be most difficult about single motherhood is the lack of economic resources. Half of all female-headed families live below the poverty level (Furstenberg, 1990). This is especially true of Black female-headed families and those headed by never-married mothers. (About 30% of all single mothers have never been married; Kamerman & Kahn, 1988.) Such dire economic circumstances means that most such families must cope with inadequate housing, food, health care, and education. The stress of such an existence is enormous. Poverty generates despair, substance abuse, and crime. As we will see in Chapter 12, the vast majority of the poor are single women and their children. Although most of the adult poor are mothers who never married, divorce also disadvantages mothers who have been married. Upon divorce, the standard of living of the custodial mother generally decreases 70% while the standard of living of the typical noncustodial father increases 40% (L. J. Weitzman, 1985). Most married women, especially those who devote themselves to full-time homemaking, are heavily dependent upon their husband's income. In a 1991 Census Bureau study, 43% of all mothers whose marriage broke up were not employed at the time ("When Dad," 1991). One-third were still out of work four months later. As we have seen, full-time homemakers generally are not prepared for full-time careers. Yet only 15% of divorced women are awarded alimony, and most of them are over age 40 (L. J. Weitzman, 1988). Child-support payments usually are not enough to cover even half the cost of raising a child, and fewer than half of the fathers comply fully with such awards. In general, fewer than one out of four single mothers receives regular and full child support (Furstenberg, 1990). Because of the dearth of affordable child care and/or lack of job skills, about one-third of single mothers cannot afford to join the labor force and are forced onto welfare (Aid to Families with Dependent Children), which offers below-poverty income (Dornbusch & Gray, 1988). Single mothers who do find jobs often find themselves in similarly poor economic straits since most women earn so little and child care generally consumes one-quarter of their income (National Commission on Working Women, 1989b). A second job may help, but it adds to the strain on single mothers. Between 1970 and 1990, the percentage of employed women with two or more jobs (nearly all single mothers) tripled, from 2% to 6% (Kilborn, 1990a). Overall, low income is a major source of stress for most single mothers and their children.

A second source of stress for many single mothers is their deviant social role. In the traditional (White) American family, mothers are expected to be married, and the institution of motherhood is based on this assumption. Divorced mothers tend to be viewed as less well adjusted and less nurturant than married mothers (Etaugh & Nekolny, 1990; Etaugh & Study, 1989). Thus, mothers who are not married, at least those in non-Black communities, often feel deviant and concerned that their children will suffer without a father. This concern is especially strong among divorced and separated mothers, who constitute about 60% of all single mothers (Kamerman & Kahn, 1988), especially if they feel responsible for the divorce. In fact, concern for the children is one of the main reasons unhappy couples stay together, at least until the children are grown. Yet research suggests that single-parent families are not necessarily less adequate families than two-parent ones. Children need love and acceptance; getting these from one parent is definitely better than not getting these from two.

Divorce may have both short-term and long-term negative effects on children, but such effects are not inevitable. When divorce produces long-term negative outcomes in a child, such as depression, social withdrawal, behavior problems, and poor academic performance, the cause is likely to be a poor relationship with the custodial parent, lack of sufficient quality contact with the noncustodial parent, inconsistency of discipline, interparental conflict, emotional distress in the mother, and lack of supportive relationships with nonparental adults (Allison & Furstenberg, 1989; Furstenberg, 1990; Hetherington et al., 1989; J. B. Kelly, 1988; Kline, Tschann, Johnston, & Wallerstein, 1989; Wallerstein & Blakeslee, 1989; Zaslow, 1988, 1989). The negative consequences are not necessarily the result of divorce or single parenthood per se. When pre-existing problems are taken into account, the effect of separation or divorce on a child's behavior problems and achievement is greatly reduced (Cherlin et al., 1991). The effects of divorce also appear to vary with the age and gender of the children. Younger children (ages 3 to 11) appear more negatively affected by divorce than older children. On the other hand, most infants adapt well in the long term if no new stressors are added. Sons appear more negatively affected than daughters by sole maternal custody, due, at least in part, to lack of contact with their father.

Many children in female-headed families appear well-adjusted. This is most likely to be true for girls when positive contact with the father continues, when parental conflict is absent or minimal, when the mother's emotional state is good, when there is an extended kin network, and when the mother receives sufficient emotional and financial support (Weinraub & Wolf, 1987). Type of custody arrangement, such as joint versus sole custody, appears to be less important to a child's emotional well-being than the quality of the child's relationships with each parent and the absence of parental conflict

(Kline et al., 1989; Luepnitz, 1986; Wolchik, Braver, & Sandler, 1985). In cases where the marriage had been extremely stressful and tension-filled, children may actually benefit from parental divorce (Hetherington et al., 1989).

A third major source of stress for single mothers is the lack of a co-parent. Although fathers tend not to do as much as mothers in terms of child care and housework, they still tend to do some. Thus, single mothers are faced with sole responsibility for domestic chores as well for their child's welfare. Such a heavy burden can take its toll (Genevie & Margolies, 1987). Fathers may have served not only to reduce maternal stress, but also to buffer the effects of maternal stress on the child (Weinraub & Wolf, 1987). Without his presence, stress may be high.

All these factors—being poorer, being nonnormative, being overburdened—make single motherhood particularly stressful. As we saw in Chapter 8, depression runs high among single mothers of young children. Single mothers who feel conflicted about being unmarried appear to experience motherhood most negatively (Genevie & Margolies, 1987). Many of these women try to compensate for their single status by being too permissive with their children. On the other hand, the majority of single mothers report that their relationships with their children improved after divorce or widowhood, due to mutual interdependency, less conflict in the household (especially over child-rearing decisions), and more time and energy for the children that previously had gone to the husband (Genevie & Margolies, 1987).

Lesbian mothers appear to be avoiding some of the stresses of single parenthood. Although unmarried in the conventional way, many lesbian mothers live in committed relationships with another woman who serves as co-parent to the children. In some cases, both partners are mothers, and both serve as co-parents. Yet living a socially stigmatized existence carries its own stresses (S. Crawford, 1987). Because of the social stigma against homosexuals and consequent social concern that children of homosexuals will be harmed by their parent's sexual orientation, lesbian mothers frequently must bear the social burden of proving that they are adequate parents. In custody battles, lesbian mothers lose custody more often than not (Falk, 1989). Yet lesbian mothers are not less nurturing than other mothers; in some studies, they appear more child-oriented than their heterosexual counterparts. Furthermore, studies of children of lesbian mothers find them to be similar to children of other single mothers with respect to psychological health, gender identity, sex role

behavior, and sexual orientation (Golombok, Spencer, & Rutter, 1983; Hoeffer, 1981; M. Kirkpatrick, Smith, & Roy, 1981). Most lesbian mothers have children from a previous heterosexual relationship, frequently a marriage, but increasing numbers of lesbians are choosing motherhood by alternative means, such as artificial insemination (Freiberg, 1990; S. Harris, 1991; G. Kolata, 1989). Although children of lesbian mothers have as much contact with their father as do children of other single mothers (Golombok et al., 1983; M. Hill, 1987), it is not clear what effect not having a known father will have on children whose mother was artificially inseminated. So far, the main issue artificial insemination has generated is one of custody if a lesbian couple splits up (Dreyfous, 1991b; Hendrix, 1990). Just as lesbians must deal with homophobic remarks from others, so may the children of lesbians. Yet this experience of "difference" may be empowering if the lesbian parent is "out" to the community, since such children have a role model of an adult standing up for her personal choices and convictions (Rohrbaugh, in Freiberg, 1990).

In sum, single mothers are a diverse group, consisting of employed mothers, nonemployed mothers, welfare mothers, teenage mothers, never-married mothers, widowed mothers, divorced mothers, lesbian mothers, and so on. Although the lives of many single mothers are extremely stressful, most of their problems are socially correctable. A sufficient income, adequate child care, social support, and societal acceptance would go a long way toward making the experience of motherhood less stressful for this group (Kamerman & Kahn, 1988).

Discussion

The experience of motherhood is intense and complex and belies the myths of motherhood: that all women must be mothers in order to be happy, that all mothers have a "natural" propensity (instinct) for caring for their children, and that all children must be cared for by their mothers or else they will be harmed. Motherhood can have many joys, but it does not make all women happy. Women must learn how to care for their children, and children's developmental and emotional needs can be met by a variety of people, not just their biological mother.

Although some commonalities can be found among women who experience motherhood, many differences also exist, due to both individual factors (personality traits, attitudes, health) and social factors (race, class, employment, marriage). Nearly all women find the experience of motherhood to be a major one in their lives, and nearly all must deal with the myths of motherhood. For most women, motherhood is characterized by ambivalence. Nonemployed married mothers best fit societal expectations, but they represent both a historical and cultural anomaly. Although most women who choose this role for part of their lives tend to be satisfied, many nonemployed married mothers are not satisfied. The trend is for mothers to combine child care activities with labor force activities, at least part-time. Although potentially stressful, multiple roles (parent, spouse, and worker) seem satisfying to most women. Such multiple roles would be even more satisfying if stress could be reduced. We need to eliminate the motherhood myths that employed mothers are bad for their children; we need to ensure that fathers share the burden of domestic and child-care activities; and we need to require society to offer more institutional supports, such as affordable high-quality child care and decent-paying jobs. Many of these changes would also help single mothers, who frequently must deal with the additional burdens of social stigma and poverty.

The problem with motherhood is not that it is a worthless activity. It can be argued quite convincingly that such activity is the most important thing anyone can do, if it is done well, because society's future depends on it. Rather, the problem is that the myths of motherhood are held in high esteem while mothers themselves are held in low esteem. The strains involved in being a mother are magnified by the lack of alternatives and supports for women in that role. As the motherhood myths recede, as institutional supports increase, and as people speak of parental, not specifically maternal, behavior, we can expect to find happier and better adjusted parents and children.

▲ Father-Child Relationships

Although there is no mandate for fatherhood comparable to the Motherhood Mandate, gender roles and stereotypes still strongly affect father-child relationships. One effect is the paucity of research on paternal relationships, at least until recently, especially in comparison with research on maternal relationships. The research that has been done on fathers typically has been guided by a particular theoretical perspective (Fein, 1978). The traditional research perspective (pre-1960) emphasized the aloof and distant father. The "modern" research perspective of the 1960s concentrated on certain child-outcome variables, such as gender development,

but ignored the positive effects of parenting on fathers and ignored men's capabilities in this area. The current emergent research perspective is based on the premise that men have the capacity to be effective nurturers of their children and that such behaviors would be beneficial to both children and parents.

These different research perspectives of fatherhood correspond, in part, to the changing role expectations of fathers (M. E. Lamb, 1986; Pleck, 1987; Rotundo, 1985). In the 18th and early 19th century in the United States, fathers were viewed as important moral teachers and educators. In a rural economy, father's workplace was also his home place. Children thus interacted with their father frequently and sons typically were trained to follow in their father's footsteps. As the country industrialized and the public and private spheres became more separate, the father role changed to that of the breadwinner. Home and child care were now exclusively "women's work." Freud's influence at the turn of the 20th century only further emphasized the critical role of the mother in parenting. Fathers were viewed as peripheral figures—important for income, unimportant for child development. After World War II, fathers again became important, but mainly as a sex role model for their children. The "devastating" effects of father absence were stressed by writers and researchers. This emphasis on the critical importance of father presence for their children's healthy sex role development served to buttress the heterosexual nuclear family model. Since the mid-1970s, a fourth image of fatherhood has emerged, that of an active, nurturant parent (for example, Pruett, 1987). The new "androgynous father," a product of the changes in women's roles, is expected to be involved with his children starting with his partner's pregnancy. He takes an active role in caring for both his sons and daughters. He is critically important in his children's development. These four different views of the father role all coexist today with some degree of tension. Although the nurturant father model is gaining strength, the breadwinning father model continues to be dominant, and the moral overseer model has experienced a resurgence, especially among religious fundamentalists. Furthermore, the culture of fatherhood (the ideology surrounding it) has changed more than the conduct of fatherhood (that is, what fathers actually do) (LaRossa, 1989).

Fatherhood is important to most men and is becoming increasingly so. Although most people believe women desire children more than do men, survey results paint a different picture. The same high proportion (over two-thirds) of both men and women say that raising a family is either "essential" or "highly important" to them (A. W. Astin, 1991; Bryant & Veroff, 1982; Gormly, Gormly, & Weiss, 1987). Some gender differences do arise, however, with respect to why people want children. Among college students, both men and women want children to expand themselves and to promote love and family ties (Gormly et al., 1987). But women are much more likely than men to view parenthood as a way to achieve adult status or social identity, not surprising given the Motherhood Mandate. Men are more likely than women to see marital, parental, and work roles as conflicting and to see children as lowering a person's life satisfaction (M. S. Richardson & Alpert, 1980; J. Ross & Kahan, 1983). Many men also experience doubts about their ability to be closely involved with their children (Goleman, 1984). As a result of these different factors, many men experience ambivalence about making a decision to have, or not have, a child (Baber & Dreyer, 1986).

Despite the professed importance of children to men, most men do not feel they should take an active caretaking role in their children's lives. For example, in surveys of high school seniors, no males expect to be a full-time homemaker, and only one-third think mothers and fathers should share child care responsibility equally (Bachman, 1987; Werrbach, Grotevant, & Cooper, 1990). Thus, although men may want children, most males do not see themselves as primary or even equal caretakers of them. And indeed, most men are not. In less than 2% of married couples is the father a full-time homemaker, and in less than 15% are child-care chores and responsibilities equally shared (B. Goldberg, 1991; Hochswender, 1990).

First we will take a look at the barriers to establishing rewarding father-child relationships. Then we will look at the actual experience of fatherhood.

Barriers

A number of factors serve as barriers to adequate father-child relationships. Among them are belief in the motherhood myths, the existence of strong sex typing, the power differences between the sexes, and the traditional pattern of divorce and custody arrangements.

Motherhood myths   Belief in the myths that only mothers can establish an intimate relationship with their children and that children need only their mothers unavoidably makes men feel that their role

as father is secondary and inadequate. Yet, as we have seen, there is no such thing as a maternal instinct. Nurturing behavior is learned, and fathers are equally capable of acquiring such behaviors, especially if they have early contact with the child. In addition, although mothers are biologically equipped to bear and nurse children, there is no biologically decreed responsibility to rear and care for them (just as there is no biological prerequisite for doing housework, often seen as part of a mother's "natural" work). In fact, Harlow (1958) found with his studies of monkeys that the critical aspect of mothering is not the provision of food but the provision of warm, comforting physical contact. Fathers are equally as capable as mothers of providing this.

Yet the father role for males usually is consistently ignored during a boy's socialization or is specifically deemphasized. As we have seen in Chapters 6 and 7, boys generally do not have any early experience with parental behaviors, such as playing with dolls and doing baby-sitting. They often see in their own homes and in the media that fatherhood is either irrelevant or only a minor part of the masculine role; achieving comes first. Because of the lack of role models for involved fatherhood, many men who want to be more involved with their own children feel insecure. In addition, there is no clear role for fathers. They used to be the benevolent disciplinarians and mentors ("Father knows best"), but such a role is no longer viable in our current egalitarian family ideal. As a result, fathers often feel like outsiders, not knowing what role to play, often opting simply to avoid the situation completely. Some research suggests that a father's adaptation to the birth of a child is improved if the father makes a decision to assume either the traditional or the involved father role, rather than vacillating between them (Pedersen, 1980; Zaslow & Pedersen, 1981).

In many families, women actually may discourage their husbands from becoming involved in child care, probably because child care has been the one area in which women have been allowed to feel competent (Cordes, 1983). Consequently, one strong predictor of a father's interaction time with his children is his wife's attitude toward paternal involvement (Barnett & Baruch, 1987; Palkovitz, 1984). As more women challenge the Motherhood Mandate for themselves, more women are welcoming men's participation in child care.

Sex typing   A major obstacle in father-child relationships is the masculine personality itself. Men who are uncomfortable with expressing their emotions may be inhibited from establishing closeness and intimacy with their children. As illustrated in Figure 10.4, some men may feel uncomfortable being seen in a silly or less-than-authoritative role. Typically, fathers are perceived as much less expressive than mothers, except for the physical expression of anger, regardless of race or social class (Balswick, 1988). A study of first-time fathers in single-earner families found that the best predictor of father involvement was the degree to which the father had high self-esteem and was sensitive to the feelings of others (Volling & Belsky, 1991). Small children cannot be dealt with using reason alone, and they need more direct expressions of affection than roughhousing, slaps on the back, or material rewards. In addition, the pressure of the male gender role to achieve concrete things (money, status, top grades, and so on) makes it difficult for many men to appreciate the much subtler rewards of feelings and relationships. Consequently, if fathers do spend any time with their children, which is often difficult if they are the primary breadwinner, they may displace their achievement strivings onto their children and engage in competition with them. Some fathers also may make their children feel they must earn their father's love in mechanical ways (Garfinkel, 1985; McGill, 1985).

Men who have a nontraditional sex role ideology and who are androgynous in terms of personality characteristics (strong nurturant-expressive as well as active-instrumental traits) tend to participate more in child care than other men (Baruch & Barnett, 1981; Nyquist et al., 1985; Palkovitz, 1984). Such results need to be interpreted cautiously,

however. It may be that nurturance in men leads them to participate in child care more, but it also may be that greater participation in child care leads to increased nurturance. There is evidence for both sequences.

Power differences   Another reason that men, as a group, do not rear children may be that it is to their advantage, in a power sense, not to be the caretakers. Polatnick (1973–74) analyzes the advantages of avoiding child-rearing responsibilities and taking on breadwinning responsibilities. Full-time child rearing limits the opportunities one has to engage in other activities, whereas the breadwinning role earns money, status, and power in society as well as in the family. Consequently, many men have an interest in defining child rearing as exclusively a woman's role—it limits women's occupational activities and thus their competition, and it enables men to have children without limiting their own occupational activities. As Wetzsteon (1977) has noted, "The real difficulty men have in becoming feminists . . . lies in the fact that American capitalism . . . still gives a strong competitive edge to men with traditional masculine values" (p. 59). Having a wife who cares for home and children is a strong advantage to men in the professional and business worlds. Although it is true that breadwinners must shoulder the financial burden involved in raising children, many men at least have the possibility of selecting work suited to their interests, and they can take time off from such work. In contrast, many women are arbitrarily assigned to child rearing on a 24-hour-a-day, 365-day-a-year basis.

Figure 10.4 Can "masculine" men be effective fathers? (FOR BETTER OR FOR WORSE Copyright 1980 Lynn Johnston. Reprinted with permission of Universal Press Syndicate.)

Cross-cultural studies of the time mothers and fathers spend in child care indicate that nowhere do fathers spend more time with children than do mothers (M. C. Lamb & Sagi, 1983; Mackey, 1985). American fathers may not be the worst in this regard, but neither are they the best. For example, fathers from Eastern European countries seem to spend more time with their children than Western fathers, probably because workaholic personalities are less rewarded there. The degree of male dominance in a society is strongly related to the degree to which fathers are involved in child-care activities: the more male societal dominance, the less involvement (Coltrane, 1988). So men may indeed lose some power in the public sphere if they participate more equally in child-care activities. As we will see in Chapter 12, this might be a very good thing.

With respect to career development as well, men actively engaged in parenting activities may have something to lose (L. A. Gilbert, 1985; C. Lawson, 1991; Skrzycki, 1990b). In most cases, the limitations on careers are chosen voluntarily. That is, some men consciously choose to forgo some career advancement for the sake of more time with their family. In other cases, however, employers may view involved fathers as less serious about their work, exactly what mothers have been hearing for years. Involved fathers face the additional problem of being viewed as "wimps." More encouragingly, however, negative career consequences do not occur for the majority of men as a result of involvement in child care and appear negligible in the long run. Using a life-span perspective, no difference is found in the career success of involved fathers when compared to a control group of less involved fathers (Snarey, Pleck, & Maier, as cited in M. Roberts, 1989).

Our society has a major structural flaw: the workplace is not set up to accommodate parenting activities. The same factors that make it stressful for women to juggle career and family responsibilities (for example, lack of affordable day care and flex-time schedules) are present for men as well. In fact, structural barriers are even stronger for men since paternal involvement in child care is viewed as deviant and traditionally male jobs (like business executive) are least flexible and most time-consuming (Bohen & Viveros-Long, 1981). We have noted that maternity leave policies are unavailable or inadequate for most female employees. The situation for fathers is even more restrictive: most companies have no parental leave policy at all, and those that do, have an extremely limited one (C. Lawson, 1991). For example, the average maximum length of the leave for mothers is 56 days; for fathers it is 18 days. Even when companies have such leaves for fathers, men are discouraged from using them since "it would make them appear soft in their commitment to work and prevent advancement" (C. Lawson, 1991). No one seriously has suggested a "Daddy track" comparable to a "Mommy track" in terms of career development—that is, a path that would allow greater integration of work and home responsibilities at the price of less rapid career development. Men are assumed to be single-mindedly devoted to their career or, at least, to earning money. Therefore, for many men, being involved in child care means reduced earnings and status, two qualities men are socialized to value highly. Furthermore, given the wage gap between women and men (discussed in Chapter 11), many families cannot afford to lose the father's salary in whole or in part.

Socially as well, men may lose prestige if they do not put their career first. In Herzog and colleagues' (1983) national survey of high school seniors, the researchers found marked rigidity regarding expectations of men. Although there was a preference for sharing child-care responsibilities between wife and husband, anything less than full-time employment for a husband was frowned upon. In contrast, anything more than part-time employment for a mother was frowned upon. Thus, father's involvement with children could hardly be fully equal. Even students who have liberal or neutral attitudes toward the mother role tend to have traditional attitudes toward the father role (Rao & Rao, 1985). And male full-time homemakers are viewed more negatively than female homemakers, unless they bring in some money through free-lance work (Rosenwasser, Gonzales, & Adams, 1985). Thus, although more young men than ever before are expressing interest in an active parenting role, the barriers (psychological, social, economic, and structural) to their assuming such a role are enormous. The gender script requires men to be dominant. That cannot occur if men participate actively in child care.

Divorce   Still another factor has contributed to the difficulties of the father-child relationship: the typical pattern of child custody has been to award custody of children to the mother if a couple divorces. This custom is, of course, both a result and a cause of distance in father-child relationships. The awarding of children to the mother has been a result of the 20th century's emphasis on maternal care of children and the diminution of the father's role in child rearing. Before the 20th century, children were considered property, and as such "belonged" to the male head of household. Although fathers' "rights" with respect to their children have been receiving renewed support (see Chesler, 1986; Smart & Sevenhuijzen, 1989), the fact is that most children (90%) live with their mother when their parents divorce. And when ex-wives have custody, paternal involvement with the children drops off dramatically, especially as time since the divorce increases (Furstenberg, 1990). Nearly half of all noncustodial White fathers and 60% of noncustodial Black fathers had not seen their children in the previous year (Furstenberg & Harris, in T. Lewin, 1990b). (See later section on single fathers.)

The main reason custody usually is awarded to the mother is the simple fact that, until recently, very few fathers requested custody. Since fathers typically spent very little time caring for their children when they were married, it is not surprising that most did not request custody of the children when they divorced. Many divorce lawyers and judges also were reluctant to recommend and grant custody to fathers for two reasons: (1) the stereotyped belief that mothers are "naturally" the better parent, and (2) the more than a century of mother-oriented custodial rules and traditions. Yet that pattern is changing. Increasing numbers of divorced fathers are requesting and, in many cases, obtaining custody of their children after divorce. Part of the pressure has come from men's rights organizations, which have active memberships in more than 30 states, and from the National Congress for Men, organized in 1981 by men who wanted to reform divorce settlements (Astrachan, 1984; Silver & Silver, 1981). Unfortunately, in some cases, a father's petition for custody is just part of a power struggle with the mother and does not arise out of a true desire to nurture the child. As we have seen, it is relatively easy to argue that a mother is "unfit" if the motherhood ideal is used as a standard. Since fathers compared to mothers are more likely to be economically stable and remarried, and since their very request for custody suggests unusual paternal involvement to judges, more fathers are gaining custody than ever before. Of the 5% of custody cases that go to court, approximately half (between 30% and 70%, depending upon jurisdiction) are won by fathers (Chesler, 1986; Loewen, 1988).

Yet most fathers who petition for custody are men who have come to terms with their own nurturing capabilities and with what they view as the best interest of their children. Many mothers, indeed, may not be the best caretakers of their children. Joint custody arrangements also recognize the contributions of both parents to the welfare of the children. In 1980, California was the first state to enact a joint-custody law in which preference was given to such arrangements. By 1989, 29 other states had followed (Hetherington et al., 1989). Today, about 10% of divorces involve some form of joint custody (Streitfeld, 1986). However, experience has proved that joint custody is not necessarily best for children, especially if the parents cannot get along with each other (Kline et al., 1989). Furthermore, even with joint custody, most women continue to maintain principal responsibility for child care and fathers tend to diminish their contact over time (Furstenberg, 1990).

Thus, divorce, or the prospect of it, may serve as a barrier to close father-child relationships.

Overall, many barriers to close father-child relationships exist. The motherhood myths set the stage for a father role that is peripheral to children's lives. This barrier is augmented by men's traditional gender socialization and their higher status in the work force and the community. Finally, high divorce rates and the tradition of maternal custody of children further distance many fathers.

The Experience of Fatherhood

Despite all the barriers to fatherhood, the transition to parenthood is a powerful experience for fathers as well as mothers (Berman & Pedersen, 1987). Changes occur in men's psychological state, family relations, and work lives. Let's look more closely at men's experience of fatherhood. We will first examine developmental changes in the fatherhood experience, and then the lives of fathers who are employed, unemployed, and single. One pattern is important: class differences among fathers are stronger than differences based on race or ethnicity (McAdoo, 1988; Mirande, 1988; G. D. Weaver, 1986).

The development of the father   Men vary with respect to when, if ever, they feel closely connected to their child. Since the 1970s, such a connection is likely to occur at the birth of the child (Daniels & Weingarten, 1988). Pregnancy increasingly is becoming a two-parent event (see, for example, Worth, 1988). With the popularity of ultrasound imagery, some expectant fathers begin feeling some attachment to their soon-to-be child even before birth. A newly patented device called the "Empathy

Belly" allows soon-to-be fathers to experience something of what it feels like to be pregnant (Duckett, 1990). At least among the middle class, fathers frequently attend birthing classes with their partners. About 80% of all fathers now attend the birth of their child, in contrast to only 25% in 1975 (Buie, 1989). The father's presence during the first few minutes of the baby's life helps to encourage father-infant bonding. As we have seen, it is experience with a newborn that leads to the development of such bonds, not biology alone (Ainsworth, 1989). Immediately after their child is born, fathers often become completely engrossed in their child, showing immediate, strong affective responses (M. Greenberg & Morris, 1974; Parke & Sawin, 1977). The traditional pattern of keeping fathers from the delivery room and from immediate contact with the newborn discourages the development of such bonds. Father's interaction with his child soon wanes, and both are deprived of continuing, meaningful intimacy.

As previously described, many factors combine to make fathers the less involved parent. For all these reasons, fathers are less active in feeding and caretaking activities, spend less time with, and feel less responsible for the infant than mothers (Berman & Pedersen, 1987). Consequently, fathers become less experienced in caretaking activities and less sensitive than mothers in discerning the baby's needs. Indeed, at two or three months after the birth of a first child, both fathers and mothers rate the husband's effectiveness as a father as poorer than expected (Entwisle & Doering, 1988). As we have seen, traditional gender roles reassert themselves soon after birth (LaRossa & LaRossa, 1981). However, fathers still play an important role in their infant's life. Fathers tend to stimulate and be more physically playful with their infant than mothers, which helps the child's physical and cognitive development (Berman & Pedersen, 1987; Bronstein, 1984; M. E. Lamb, 1981a; Parke, 1981). Furthermore, when fathers do undertake the traditionally female tasks of child care, they do very well.

A number of factors predict a father's involvement with his infant child. Father involvement with infants is best predicted by the wife's encouragement of such involvement. Without such encouragement and considerable social support, it is unlikely that a father will spend much time in infant care (Berman & Pedersen, 1987). Whereas women appear to separate their relationship with their children from their relationship with their husband, men seem less able to do so. Men tend to view marriage

and children as a package. Thus, if the marital relationship isn't strong, fathers are less likely to get involved in child care (Berman & Pedersen, 1987). In an 18-month longitudinal study, C. P. Cowan and Cowan (1987) found that fathers who were most involved in caring for their 18-month-old infant tended to take more responsibility for household tasks in general, to be satisfied with marital decision making, to be employed fewer hours while their wife was employed more hours, to have child-centered parenting attitudes, and to have expected to be involved in child care. Father involvement in traditionally female child-care tasks (feeding and diapering) is most likely to occur if fathers are specifically instructed in these aspects of child care and if the child is a boy (Dickie, 1987; Parke, 1981; Parke & Tinsley, 1981). In fact, regardless of instruction, fathers are more likely to touch and vocalize to first-born sons than first-born daughters or later-born children (G. Collins, 1979). A number of studies have found that parental behaviors in fathers are more easily influenced and more easily disrupted than parental behaviors in mothers, probably because men's socialization for parenthood has been less extensive and their role as a parent is less well defined (Berman & Pedersen, 1987).

Being involved in child care and being satisfied with such involvement are two different things. In Cowan and Cowan's (1987) longitudinal study, fathers' satisfaction with their involvement at 18 months was best predicted by the men's satisfaction with the couple's decision making, level of self-esteem, and participation in household tasks before the birth. Fathers who held more child-centered parenting attitudes also tended to be more satisfied with their own involvement in child care. Fathers who experienced the most stress with parenting tended to have less positive relationships in their family of origin, lower self-esteem, lower satisfaction with the marriage and with couple decision making, and less predicted involvement in caring for the child.

As children get older, expectations regarding father involvement change as well. Whereas infants typically are viewed as needing their mothers almost exclusively, older children, especially sons, are viewed as needing a father's "guidance" and his model of male functioning. Many factors affect the degree of involvement fathers have with their children: motivation; skills and self-confidence; gender ideology; support, especially from the mother; and institutional practices, such as employment flexibility or rigidity (M. E. Lamb, 1986;

G. Russell, 1986). The best predictors of paternal involvement continue to be a flexible view of the male role and maternal employment (Radin & Harold-Goldsmith, 1989).

Fathers today, although spending more time with their children than they did previously, still typically are less involved than mothers. A review of the literature suggests that fathers typically spend from one-fifth to one-third as much time as mothers engaged with their children on a one-to-one basis (M. E. Lamb, 1987; Pleck, 1985). Fathers also tend to be less accessible (that is, available if needed) than mothers to their children. Perhaps most important, fathers assume less than 10% of the responsibility for caring for their children (for example, remembering doctors' appointments, time last fed, and so on). Maternal employment does not affect these figures very much. Although the proportion of child care men do increases when wives are employed (from one-fifth to one-third), the actual time men spend in direct child care increases by less than a half hour per week, from 6.2 to 6.6 hours, when a child under 5 years of age is present (Douthitt, 1989). The reason for this confusing picture is that as employed mothers decrease the number of hours they are engaged in child-care activities, the *relative* amount of time their husbands spend increases.

The time fathers do spend with their children takes place mainly on weekends (Douthitt, 1989) and can be characterized as "semi-involved" (M. E. Lamb, 1987; LaRossa & LaRossa, 1981). When fathers are with their children, they are more likely to play with them, share an activity (such as watching television), or simply be present. Fathers are much less likely than mothers to attend to children's physical and affective needs (Jump & Haas, 1987). LaRossa (1989) describes this pattern as being "technically present but functionally absent" (p. 6). Yet such involvement still is important to children. As we saw in Chapter 6, fathers influence their children's gender role development, and, in part, their cognitive development. The lack of a warm father-child relationship may contribute to rigid and polarized gender roles, especially for sons. Fathers also enhance child development by helping to both reduce stress on the mother as well as to buffer the effects of maternal stress on the child (Weinraub & Wolf, 1987). In general, there are very few differences in paternal behavior between Black and White fathers when social class is held constant (McAdoo, 1988; G. D. Weaver, 1986).

When fathers are heavily involved in child care by choice, both sons and daughters benefit. In general, children with highly involved fathers evidence accelerated intellectual development, increased cognitive competence and empathy, less sex-stereotyped beliefs, and a more internal locus of control (L. W. Hoffman, 1989; M. E. Lamb, 1986; Pruett, 1987; Radin, 1988; G. Russell, 1986). The differences are slight, but they certainly suggest that families have nothing to fear from increased father involvement. In particular, gender identification in children is normal, even when fathers are the primary caretaker. A longitudinal study of more than 200 fathers over four decades revealed that fathers' family participation generally improved their children's lives as young adults: sons tended to be more confident and skillful and daughters tended to be more mature and autonomous (Snarey et al., in M. Roberts, 1989).

Given the small amount of time fathers generally spend engaged with their children, it is not surprising that most children and teenagers report a closer and better relationship with their mother than with their father (Balswick, 1988; McGill, 1985). The father-son relationship appears to be particularly problem-filled (Garfinkel, 1985; Stoltenberg, 1989). Men express a clear preference for sons and they are more involved with and attached to their sons than their daughters from infancy on. Indeed, fathers with sons are less likely to divorce than fathers with daughters (S. P. Morgan et al., 1988). Yet fathers also are stricter and less permissive with their sons than their daughters, which causes frequent friction between the two. Competition and dominance issues frequently arise, and expressions of affection and love frequently remain hidden. As a result, a major regret of grown men is that they were not closer to their father (T. Gabriel, 1990; Garfinkel, 1985).

The rewards of father involvement for the father are only beginning to be calculated. The joys of nurturance and the pleasures of exchanging love with children are allowing some fathers to get in touch with the emotional aspects of themselves that they previously had shut off. Involved fathers appear to develop closer relationships with their children, increased sensitivity toward others, enhanced self-esteem and satisfaction with their parental role, and improved marital satisfaction, at least when the involvement is by choice (L. W. Hoffman, 1989; G. Russell, 1986). In Snarey and colleagues' longitudinal study (in M. Roberts, 1989), the more fathers nurtured their children, the more caring and giving these men were when they reached middle age. Involved fathers tended to assume responsibilities outside of their families later in life, a continuation of their nurturing, generative focus.

Because men on the whole are more involved in child care than their fathers were, many feel quite pleased with their performance. As depicted in Figure 10.5, the standards against which we judge ourselves affect the way we feel about our behavior. Thus, whereas mothers tend to feel guilty when they are not full-time homemakers, fathers tend to feel proud of their less-than-one-third contribution to child care. Many fathers, in fact, overestimate their involvement (Jump & Haas, 1987). Mothers are complicit in excusing fathers from equal involvement with their children (Croghan, 1991; Hochschild, 1989; LaRossa, 1989). For example, a mother may agree that the father needs a "night out with the boys" even though she gets no relief from full-time child care. Children, too, tend to hold fathers less responsible than they hold mothers (Pogrebin, 1990). For example, when a father forgets a child's birthday or gets the child an inappropriate gift, he may be excused, or the mother may be blamed for not reminding him. However, were a mother to do these things, she would be seen as a bad mother. Unless our expectations of mothers and fathers become more similar, we cannot expect their behaviors to be.

Participation in child care can be stressful for some fathers. Employment responsibilities frequently conflict with child-care responsibilities, as noted previously. Social support for paternal involvement in child care tends to be minimal. Involved fathers frequently are viewed as odd, although this is becoming less common. Caring for children also may elicit men's vulnerable side, which may be experienced as threatening by some men. In addition, there are few role models of involved fatherhood for men to follow. Men are encountering 1990s expectations with only a 1960s preparation.

In general, the experience of fatherhood is quite variable, changing with the age and sex of the child and as a function of father's personality, gender ideology, social support, and contextual factors (for example, social class). Let's take a closer look at two specific contexts: employment and marital status.

Employment issues Employment is not a major factor in men's experience of parenthood, especially when contrasted with the effect of employment on women's experience of parenthood. This is because gender role expectations are different. Men are expected to devote most of their energies to their work, regardless of their parental status. Indeed, all working-age men are expected to be employed, and about 75% are (Uchitelle, 1990). Statistics are not even kept on what proportion of fathers are employed compared to nonfathers, nor the average number of hours fathers are employed compared to nonfathers. Research exploring the effects of a father's employment on his family role suggests that for men, hours of paid work and job schedule (for example, night or day shifts) have very little effect on hours of child care (Pleck, 1985, 1986). In fact, hours of paid work and job schedule affect the amount of housework fathers do more than they

Figure 10.5 Why fathers don't feel guilty. (DOONESBURY Copyright 1987 G. B. Trudeau. Reprinted with permission of Universal Press Syndicate. All rights reserved.)

affect the amount of child care fathers do. Caring for children, especially young ones, is simply not men's work.

In the traditional division of labor, mothers fulfill their parental responsibility through nurturing the children and fathers fulfill their parental responsibility by providing economically for them. Many fathers, especially those with traditional values and a homemaker wife, expect to relax once they get home. Working-class fathers are particularly likely to feel this way, and such fathers appear not to evaluate themselves as fathers based on their infant's adjustment (Entwisle & Doering, 1988). In contrast, middle-class fathers tend to evaluate their competence as fathers in terms of how well their baby is doing, suggesting different self-expectations. Indeed, we have seen that expectations of fathers have been changing more among the middle than among the upper and working classes.

In traditional families, fathers assume a secondary role in caretaking activities. Not only does a traditional father spend minimal time with his children, but a greater proportion of that time is devoted to play activities, or semi-involved ones, like watching television together (LaRossa, 1989; M. E. Lamb, 1987). Significant predictors of paternal involvement in child care when the wife is not employed are the father's personality traits and his attitude toward the quality of fathering he received as a child. Fathers who are more interpersonally-oriented and who have a positive marital relationship spend more time with their infants than do other traditional fathers (Volling & Belsky, 1991). Fathers who have negative attitudes toward the type of fathering they received also tend to spend more time with their own children than do fathers who were satisfied (Barnett & Baruch, 1988). In general, husbands of nonemployed wives tend to decrease their interaction time with their child as the child gets older, and father-child relationships in traditional families tend to be distant and formal, not typically characterized as intimate or close.

What affects a man's experience of fatherhood more than his own employment is his wife's employment. Because an employed wife must reduce some of the hours she spends in child-care activities, there is more pressure on her husband to increase his involvement. As we have seen, husbands with employed wives do slightly increase their contribution to child care, but not dramatically so. Other child-care providers, usually paid, typically fill in the gap created by the mother's labor force participation. If men have participated in domestic responsibilities before the birth of their child, they are more likely to be involved in basic child care once the infant is born (Volling & Belsky, 1991). A father's participation is greatest when an employed mother works long hours, earns more than the father, and supports the father's involvement in child care (Barnett & Baruch, 1988; Steil & Weltman, 1991). These fathers are most likely to be middle- to upper-class professional men who espouse an egalitarian philosophy and who are married to professional women (Jump & Haas, 1987). Even they, however, still generally fall short of egalitarian parenting. In only 20% of dual-career relationships do fathers share child-care responsibilities equitably with mothers (Hochschild, 1989).

Married fathers are the primary caretakers in a very small percentage of families (2%) and this pattern tends to be short-lived (Radin, 1988). Factors that determine whether a father will be a primary caretaker are early childhood experiences of both the mother and the father, current employment involvement (she's more involved than he, or his hours are more flexible), negative attitudes toward alternative child-care arrangements, and only a brief episode (if any at all) of the mother's being the primary caretaker. Factors that contribute to the continuation of paternal primary caregiving for at least four years are satisfaction with the arrangement, sufficient income from the mother's salary, continued flexibility of the father's hours, absence of pressure on the mother to stay home, and small family size. All of these conditions are unlikely to be met, and primary care by the father rarely lasts more than two years.

Although fathers may feel pressured to participate in child care when their wife is employed, forced participation in child care can be stressful for fathers, as it is for mothers. As we've seen, fathers frequently are not prepared psychologically, behaviorally, or socially for such a role. Job demands and friends may not be supportive. Indeed, as fathers become more involved in child care, their concern about how such activities might interfere with their careers increases, at least among middle-class families (Baruch & Barnett, 1986a). Pressure by the wife to assume more child care responsibilities than the father desires may be a major cause of marital disagreement and stress (Cowan & Cowan, 1987; Volling & Belsky, 1991). Even when a father increases his participation, marital friction may continue, since increased father participation is strongly associated with increased criticism of the wife's parenting (Baruch

& Barnett, 1986a). And one-to-one interactions with children are not always rewarding, as mothers have known for years. Tension, fatigue, and boredom are common among caregivers.

Thus, a number of studies have found that men tend to be less satisfied with their life, especially with their marriage, when their wife is employed and they are assuming some domestic responsibilities than when the traditional division of labor is present in the home (Baruch & Barnett, 1986a; L. W. Hoffman, 1989; Parasuraman et al., 1989). This is especially true for blue-collar men and for fathers who hold traditional sex role ideologies. There are many possible reasons for this result. Men with a traditional gender ideology may feel that child care is women's work and therefore their masculinity and position of dominance in the family may be threatened when their involvement increases. Second, the type of paternal participation may change. In single-wage families, paternal involvement may mean playing with the child when the father feels like it; in dual-wage families, paternal involvement may mean carrying out less pleasurable child-care tasks, such as feeding and diapering. Indeed, even among dual-career fathers, assuming traditionally feminine physical caretaking tasks is bothersome (Jump & Haas, 1987). Third, increased involvement in domestic responsibilities means less personal and relaxation time, and less time for job demands. Thus, the dissatisfaction of some involved fathers may reflect the stresses of combining paid work with family work, something employed mothers have had to deal with for years. It should be emphasized, however, that the benefits from paternal involvement in child care remain despite the costs.

Thus, as we found for mothers, caring for children creates highly ambivalent feelings in fathers, with multiple rewards and multiple disadvantages. As with mothers, the best results occur when child care is a chosen activity. Among such fathers, satisfaction with paternal roles runs high (see, for example, Jump & Haas, 1987).

Unemployed fathers tend to spend more time in child-care activities than employed men (McLoyd, 1989; Radin & Harold-Goldsmith, 1989). However, the quality of that involvement may not be very high, especially if the men feel unhappy about it. For nearly all men (and women, for that matter), unemployment is extremely stressful. Many men respond with increased anxiety, depression, and hostility, which may cause them to be less nurturant and more punitive and arbitrary in interactions with their children (McLoyd, 1989). Thus, even though unemployed men have more time, their emotional state, cognitive beliefs, and behavioral training may preclude either their greater involvement in child care or the beneficial effects of such involvement. As for women, choice is the critical variable mediating the effects of parental involvement. The best predictor of father involvement for unemployed men is sex role ideology (Radin & Harold-Goldsmith, 1989). As we have seen, part of most men's gender identity is being the dominant breadwinner. When they cannot fulfill that role, they may feel like failures. Since child care is viewed as a traditionally female activity, involvement in child care may appear as one more blow to their masculine identity.

Overall, paternal unemployment has negative effects on children, mediated by loss of income, greater parental stress, changes in the father's moods and behaviors, and changes in the marital relationship (McLoyd, 1989). Unfortunately, unemployment and job loss for fathers has been increasing since 1980. Hardest hit have been African-American men and their families. Not only do single Black fathers have high rates of unemployment, around 50% in some communities, but even married Black fathers have twice the unemployment rates of White fathers (Noble, 1986). Not being able to provide for their family may make some Black fathers withdraw (McAdoo, 1988). As noted earlier, unemployment rates among Black males are directly related to the incidence of Black female-headed households.

The single father   Single fathers, at least those who do not have custody of their children, tend to be relatively absent from their children's lives. Upon divorce, many noncustodial fathers go through a very difficult mourning period, grieving not only over the breakup of the marriage but also over the loss of regular contact with their children (Hetherington & Hagan, 1986; Loewen, 1988). Traditional custody arrangements typically permit the noncustodial father to see his children only one weekend every two weeks. This is hardly enough time to sustain a relationship, especially with very young children.

Most noncustodial fathers tend to drop out of their children's lives. Others frequently wind up playing "Disneyland Daddy" (Loewen, 1988); that is, taking their children to recreational activities and buying them things to compensate for the father's usual absence. In the first two years after marital disruption, 30% of children go a month or more without seeing their father and 60% never sleep over at their father's residence (Furstenberg, 1990). Only half speak to their fathers on the telephone at least once a week. As length of separation increases, amount of father-child contact decreases. For children who have not lived with their father for ten or more years, three-fourths never see or speak to their fathers in a typical month. Noncustodial fathers appear more likely to maintain contact with sons than daughters, but the differences are small (Hetherington & Hagan, 1986). Age of the child when the separation occurred, and race do not seem to affect estrangement patterns (Furstenberg, 1990). Furthermore, divorced fathers tend to withdraw economic support of their children as well as emotional support. Less than half of all noncustodial fathers required to pay child support actually do so regularly and in full. The result, as we have seen, is that many children of divorce live in poverty.

The reasons for paternal withdrawal after divorce when mothers have custody of the children are complex (Furstenberg, 1990; Loewen, 1988; D. Meredith, 1985). Many fathers appear to view wife and children as part of one package; divorcing one means divorcing the other. Other factors also are involved: geographical distance, increased economic demands, remarriage, conflict with ex-wife, fathers' own discomfort or pain in relating to their children, lack of sufficient court-ordered visitation rights, and/or the nature of the predivorce father-child relationship. If fathers had little contact with their children before the divorce, they are less likely to have contact with them afterward than are fathers who had much contact with them prior to the divorce. Such limited contact is especially true in working-class families. Yet many fathers spend more time or have qualitatively more meaningful interactions with their children after the divorce than previously. Often such parent-child experiences lead to personal change for the father. Many fathers report increased personal growth, more expressiveness, greater sensitivity to others, and less concern about work as a consequence of their parenting involvement (Greif, 1985; Hetherington & Hagan, 1986). Such changes suggest some of the rewards men are likely to obtain from increased parenting.

One result of paternal withdrawal is that both boys and girls from divorced families perceive their relationship with their father more negatively than children in intact families (M. A. Fine, Moreland, & Schweibel, 1983). Children's adjustment to the divorce itself also suffers. As noted earlier, one of the key factors in children's adjustment to divorce is the frequency of the child's contact with the noncustodial parent, usually the father, as well as the relationship between the ex-spouses. Sons, in particular, appear to suffer from lack of contact with their father, and may do better living with him than with their mother (Hetherington et al., 1989; Zaslow, 1988, 1989). In general, children living in the custody of a same-sex parent seem somewhat better adjusted than children living with an other-sex parent (J. B. Kelly, 1988). Thus, despite the motherhood myths and judicial custom, fathers are important to their children too. However, contact alone is not the critical variable, as recent studies of families practicing joint custody have discovered. It is the quality of the contact that matters.

The number of single-parent families headed by fathers has more than doubled since 1970, but the proportion has remained relatively unchanged at 11% (Hanson, 1988). More White single-parent families are headed by fathers (13%) than is the case among Hispanics (8%) and Blacks (5%). The percentage of custodial fathers may increase slowly as women's and men's lives become more similar and as courts begin reflecting society's changing attitudes toward gender roles. Research to date suggests that parent-child relationships and children's emotional adjustment are similar in families headed by custodial fathers compared with families headed by custodial mothers (Greif, 1985; J. B. Kelly, 1988; Santrock & Warshak, 1986). Personal qualities, not gender itself, matter with respect to good parenting. As we have seen, qualities such as nurturance, sensitivity, and communication skills are not gender-specific. It also helps that children in father-custody families still tend to maintain contact with their noncustodial mother on a regular basis (Furstenberg, 1990).

A key factor in determining whether a father will seek custody of his children is his own experiences with his family when he was a child (Hanson, 1988). Male custody-seekers tend to have had close relationships with their mothers and somewhat distant relationships with their fathers. Typically, custodial fathers were making a conscientious effort to be closer to their children than their own father had been to them and they tended to have been involved in child care since their children's early infancy. In some cases, they felt themselves to be the better parent. Overall, single custodial fathers appear to be doing very well in terms of social, emotional, and familial well-being; that is, their well-being is similar to that of custodial mothers and better than that of noncustodial fathers (Buehler, 1988; Greif, 1985; Hanson, 1988). Of course, fathers who seek child custody may be quite different, as a group, from fathers who do not seek custody.

Many single fathers were never married. This is most often the case among teenagers and among Blacks. Unfortunately, males typically are socialized to be sexually active rather than sexually responsible. Sex can be disconnected from parenthood for males in ways not usually possible for females. No statistics even are kept on the number of unmarried fathers. Indeed, some males don't even know when they have fathered a child. Because of this, many unmarried fathers play no role in their child's life (Furstenberg et al., 1989). Since many unmarried fathers are poor because of unemployment or low salaries, they also contribute nothing to their child's financial support. Indeed, male unemployment is likely to discourage men from marrying the mother of their child (W. E. Schmidt, 1989; Wilkie, 1991). Nonetheless, many of these fathers develop and maintain some connection to their children, especially in Black communities, where kin networks tend to be strong (Stack, 1974). Teenage fathers, although less adversely affected by early parenthood than young mothers, tend to have higher dropout rates from high school than teenage males who are not fathers (Furstenberg et al., 1989). Since some males intentionally try to get their partner pregnant to prove the male's "virility," any prevention program aimed at reducing rates of teenage pregnancy must be aimed at males as well as females.

Single fatherhood may be particularly difficult for gay fathers (Bozett, 1988). Many gay men marry, often before recognizing the depth of their attraction to men. Typically, as their awareness of their own sexual orientation increases or becomes harder to deny, the marriage ends. However, the feelings gay fathers have for their children remain, as is the case with other divorced men. A gay father's adjustment to his role as single father is complicated by his adjustment to his new sexual identity and to the seeming contradiction between the two roles. Custody arrangements tend to be typical (that is, about 10% of gay fathers have custody of their children), and noncustodial gay fathers struggle with the same barriers to maintaining their relationship with their children as do other noncustodial fathers. In fact, they must overcome even more barriers: the lack of role models and lack of social support from the gay community. Coming out to one's children is another difficulty gay parents must face. Nonetheless, the few studies of gay fathers that have been done (see Bozett, 1988), suggest that such fathers try harder to be good parents and they appear to be successful at it, especially when they are comfortable with their own sexuality. As is true with lesbian mothers, gay fathers appear to have no influence on their children's later sexual orientation.

In general, single fathers, like married fathers, are a diverse group. Children generally are important to fathers and fathers who do not have custody of their children generally miss them. Fathers who do have custody appear to be doing a fine job. What is clear is that a person who takes on the role of primary caretaker typically develops the skills and traits necessary for fulfilling that role. Men are as capable as women of being good, nurturing parents, at least when the proper motivation is present.

Discussion

The "new father" is a nurturing one. More men are sharing child-care responsibilities with their wives than ever before, in a variety of patterns—househusband, two part-time jobs, morning-evening shifts, weekly shifts, dual careers, and more. More companies are offering family leave time, available to mothers and fathers, and more men are making use of such leaves. Nonetheless, the number of men actively involved in child care still is small, and these men are predominantly middle class. And the number of men participating in the truly critical aspect of parenting—the sense of emotional responsibility—is smaller still. The dominant pattern of fathering is still the traditional breadwinner one. Our ideology has changed faster than our behavior. Thus, most fathers play a minor role in their children's daily lives, and they, their children, and their wives all suffer for it. The benefits of involved fathering are numerous for all concerned, although not without costs.

Societal structures (for example, workplace expectations and lack of child-care facilities) combined with traditional ideology and traditional practices make an active paternal role and shared child care difficult. These barriers can be overcome by a combination of structural and social changes. Such changes already have begun. Many fathers are beginning to realize how much they are missing by not sharing child-care responsibilities. Many mothers are insisting that fathers get involved. The lessons learned in parenting—relating to someone weaker and dependent in a socially responsive way—may carry over into men's relations with the rest of the world and may lead to a more caring, humane society. At the very least, greater involvement in child care would permit men to both work and love, to touch the parts of their emotional lives they have kept hidden. And because men would be sharing child-care responsibilities, women would be freer to develop their competencies in other areas. The end result might be the development of more fully functioning individuals—mothers, fathers, and children.

▲   Summary

Parental relationships suffer from adherence to gender stereotypes and roles. Indeed, the core part of the female role is motherhood. Sex role expectations force women to believe they should be mothers and stay home with their children. The same expectations neglect the important role fathers play with their children. If women live up to the Motherhood Mandate, they may feel frustrated and take out their feelings on their families. If they are employed, they are generally happy but tend to feel guilty, despite there being no evidence of any negative effect of maternal employment on children.

Paternal relationships have been viewed as less important than maternal relationships due to gender role stereotypes. Effective father-child relationships are difficult to establish because of the motherhood myths, men's lack of training, the characteristics of the stereotyped masculine personality, and the career disadvantages of parenting. However, fathers are important to children and children are important to fathers. Fortunately, cultural ideology is changing toward the ideal of the nurturant father. More men than ever before are becoming involved in child-care activities, although the numbers still are small.

More than consciousness raising is needed, however, to ameliorate some of the negative effects of the Motherhood Mandate. Many of the social and structural barriers to shared child care must be overcome. This means that the Motherhood Mandate needs to be eliminated and we must start expecting mothers and fathers to be equally responsible for rearing their children. We must socialize our children with these new models of parenting in mind. But most important, structural barriers to equality must be eliminated. Affordable high-quality day care, family leave options, good part-time jobs, flexible-hour jobs, and so on must be made available to ease the child-care burden that falls disproportionately on women. These suggested changes would go a long way toward making parenthood predominantly rewarding—a choice, not an obligation; an opportunity for growth, not a burden.

We can go further. Perhaps we need to rethink the entire structure of work and family life. Rather than the current "masculine" model of separation, where employment involves single-minded continuous devotion to a job without any "intrusion" from one's personal and domestic domains, we need a more balanced ideal. With the current model, nearly all employees (both men and women) would benefit from a traditional wife and mother—someone whose job it is to take care of domestic responsibilities. Thus, employed mothers, fathers with employed wives, and those who wish to be involved in their children's lives are at a distinct disadvantage in the workplace. The option of having a traditional wife is not available for women and is becoming increasingly less available for men. Thus, we need to find a way to integrate better our work, family, and personal lives. We need to reduce the emphasis on having a high-powered, fast-track career and increase our support of parenting activities. The benefits from such changes would be enormous for mothers, fathers, and children.

The next chapter will examine the workplace in more detail.

▲   Recommended Reading

Bronstein, P., & Cowan, C. P. (Eds.). (1988). *Fatherhood today: Men's changing role in the family.* New York: Wiley. A comprehensive collection of articles on the experience of fatherhood in a wide variety of personal and family contexts.

Crosby, F. J. (Ed.). (1987). *Spouse, parent, worker: On gender and multiple roles.* New Haven: Yale University Press. An excellent collection of articles on how multiple roles affect both men and women.

Dornbusch, S. M., & Strober, M. H. (Eds.). (1988). *Feminism, children, and the new families.* New York: Guilford. An excellent collection of articles describing the current diversity of family forms and the relationship between feminist ideology and family functioning.

Hoffman, L. W. (1989). Effects of maternal employment in the two-parent family. *American Psychologist, 44,* 283–292. A comprehensive summary of the research literature on a highly charged topic.

Rich, A. (1986). *Of woman born: Motherhood as experience and institution* (10th anniversary ed.). New York: Norton. A new edition of the 1976 classic, which examines both the myths and the experiences of mothering.

Rothman, B. K. (1989). *Recreating motherhood: Ideology and technology in a patriarchal society.* New York: Norton. A thought-provoking book, arguing for the need to reconceptualize mothering in terms of a certain kind of relationship rather than in terms of biology or law.

Chapter 11

Consequences for the Labor Force

As discussed in the last three chapters, gender roles and stereotypes seriously affect nearly all aspects of personal and interpersonal functioning. Gender roles and stereotypes also affect societal functioning. Indeed, gender roles are an instrinsic component of social and occupational roles. As social-role theory (discussed in Chapter 1) suggests, one way of viewing gender-stereotypic characteristics is to see them as a product of the social roles women and men are expected to enact. Women are expected to be mothers, hence they are encouraged to develop nurturant-expressive characteristics; men are expected to be wage earners, hence they are encouraged to develop active-instrumental characteristics. These differential expectations carry over to everything men and women do. Thus, even when women are in the labor force, as the majority are, they are seen as most

suitable for human service jobs—nursing, teaching, social work, domestic work. Conversely, men are seen as most suitable for jobs involving leadership and strength—management, politics, manual labor.

Overlapping with social role expectations are status expectations. As we have seen, men by virtue of their gender have a higher status than women. This too carries over into societal functioning. Not only are higher status positions seen as most suitable for men, but whatever men do is viewed as superior. This dynamic is reflected in salary differentials: women employed full-time earn only two-thirds of the salary earned by men employed full-time. The status dynamic can also be seen in the changing status of a profession when its gender composition changes. As more women enter a profession, the status of the profession declines and men start exiting. This happened in the past with respect to jobs like elementary-school teaching and bank telling. This is happening today in such fields as medicine, psychology, and religious service (C. Raymond, 1989).

Because societal effects are so pervasive, this book can, of necessity, only examine a few areas. This chapter will focus on the labor force and barriers to equality within it; the next, on structural power and abuses of power.

▲ Labor Force Patterns

Volumes of data have been accumulated regarding women and men in the labor force. Because of the wealth of data, only a cursory survey will be attempted here. The interested reader is encouraged to read Blau and Ferber (1986), Statham, Miller, and Mauksch (1988), and the additional sources cited within this chapter for more detail.

In general, women in the labor force have been underemployed, underpaid, and discriminated against. Figure 11.1 gives a simplified view of how the gender stereotypes influence our work lives. Occupational tracking and salary inequities are just two of the major consequences. We will discuss both in this section after reviewing the data on participation rates.

Participation Rates

As Figure 11.2 indicates, participation by women in the labor force has been steadily increasing since 1950, whereas participation by men has been slowly declining. Nearly three-fifths of all women (58%) are currently in the labor force, compared to about

Figure 11.1 For this you went to college? One example of how the gender stereotypes influence our work lives. (Copyright 1973 by Bülbül. Reprinted with permission.)

three-quarters (77%) of all men (U.S. Department of Labor, 1991a). Among women, the rates are highest for African Americans (59%) and lowest for Hispanics (54%) (National Commission on Working Women, 1990).

The greatest increase in labor force participation has been by women aged 25 to 34. Between 1970 and 1990, their participation rate advanced nearly 30 percentage points, from 45% to 73%. These are the women who historically remained at home to rear children. Some ceiling may have been reached in this group's labor force participation, however, since their rate of increase has slowed dramatically in the last few years. The problems of combining child care and paid employment, noted in the previous chapter, probably create a barrier to this group's increased labor force participation. Then, too, the slowdown in service economy jobs (where women are overrepresented) in the last few years also has slowed the pace of entry into the labor force of women of all ages. Still, by the year 2000, 61% of women and 80% of men aged 25 to 54 are expected to be in the work force (J. Bailey, 1988; National Commission on Working Women, 1989a).

Who are these women in the labor force? Contrary to American family mythology, more than half (56%) of all women workers are married (National Commission on Working Women, 1990). The remaining 44% are single women, either never married or presently separated, divorced, or widowed. Most support not only themselves but also their families. As discussed in the last chapter, the traditional image of the American family as consisting of a breadwinning husband, a homemaking wife, and at least one child is actually atypical and when such a pattern occurs, usually temporary. Most married women are in the labor force, at least part-time, even when there is a preschool child in the household (participation rates are about 55% for married women with a child under age 6). As children get older, married women's labor force participation increases to about 75%. For women who maintain families, two out of three are in the labor force.

Despite the stereotypes that men are workers and women are homemakers, the actual labor force is nearly half female (46% in 1991, 47% expected in 2000) (Randle, 1990; U.S. Department of Labor, 1991a). By the year 2000, White males will constitute only

Percent of Population in Labor Force

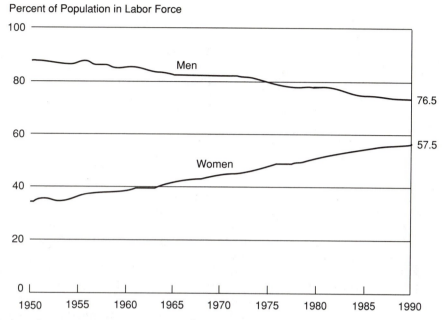

Figure 11.2 Labor force participation rates of women and men, annual averages, 1950–1990. (From U.S. Department of Labor, 1977, 1991a.)

39% of the labor force: 35% will be White women, 14% will be minority men, and 12% will be minority women. More than nine out of every ten women work for pay at some point during their lives. Given the current large participation of women in the labor force and projections for an increase, it is high time to revise our image of the world of paid employment from one exemplified by White males to one reflective of racial and gender diversity.

The reasons for the increasing participation of women in the labor force are numerous. Among them are economic necessity, rising educational attainments, changing demographic trends, and changing employer needs.

Economic necessity   Like men, most women are employed out of economic necessity. In addition to the 44% of female workers who are single, nearly another 20% have husbands earning equal to or less than a poverty-level salary (U.S. Department of Labor, 1985c). The economic situation since 1980 has increased the pressure on both spouses in working-class and middle-income families to be in the labor force (Hewlett, 1990). Wages for men have gone down while taxes have risen. In addition, living costs, such as housing prices and college tuitions, have soared. Thus, two wages are needed simply to maintain a family's former standard of living. In

fact, family income dropped 3% from 1973 to 1984 despite the increased presence of two wage earners. However, the drop would have been greater (10%) without the extra income earned by wives (Lawrence, 1986).

As we saw in the last chapter, the plight of single mothers who head households is particularly alarming. Not only have their numbers been increasing dramatically, but so has their poverty level. Half of all single mothers live at or below the poverty level today. Their dire economic situation is due to a number of factors: starting off poor, inadequate vocational preparation, low educational attainment, lack of equitable financial division upon divorce, lack of adequate child-care payments, lack of affordable child care, and low salaries in traditionally female jobs. Thus, even though the majority of female heads of families are in the labor force (70% of White female heads of families, 62% of African-American female heads, and 48% of Hispanic female heads), many of these employed women still have incomes below poverty level (53% of African Americans, 52% of Hispanics, 28% of Whites) (National Commission on Working Women, 1990).

Rising educational attainments   Another reason more women are in the labor force is that more women are obtaining college and advanced degrees, giving them access to jobs for which they were previously unqualified. Table 11.1 illustrates this trend. More than half of all bachelor's and master's degrees now are awarded to women. On the highest educational levels, the increase in percentage of women has been dramatic. Women received only 2.7% of first-professional degrees in 1961 but received 36.3% of them in 1990. Doctoral degrees to women have nearly quadrupled since 1961, with nearly two out of five such degrees now going to women. Attaining a postsecondary degree increases an individual's employability. It is predicted that by the year 2000, 86% of all jobs will require post-secondary education or training (National Commission on Working Women, 1990).

Postsecondary education also increases the likelihood that women will want to be in the labor force. In all income brackets, wives who have completed college are more likely to be employed and have positive attitudes toward employment than wives with less education (Houser & Beckman, 1980; U.S. Department of Labor, 1980). Also, because college-educated women are more likely to have been employed for a longer period of time before both marriage and childbearing, they are accustomed to employment outside the home and therefore less likely to drop out of the paid labor force (Van Dusen & Sheldon, 1976).

Changing demographic trends   Women's marital and family status is changing and these changes affect their participation in the labor force. As discussed in the previous chapter, young persons in the 1980s remained single longer than in previous decades, and the trend seems likely to continue in the 1990s. The percentage of women in their early 20s who have not married rose from 36% in 1970 to 61% in 1988 (Women's Research and Education Institute, 1990). Too, families are decreasing in size and are being started later in the parents' lives than in previous decades. Consequently, more women are experiencing longer periods of time during

which they may advance their careers. The average American woman can expect to spend around 30 years of her life in the work force, compared with 37 years for men (U.S. Department of Labor, 1983).

Changing employer needs   Another factor contributing to women's entry into the paid labor force has been the growth of industries that have primarily employed women. The post–World War II baby boom created the need for more services—educational, medical, governmental, and recreational. These services, especially the professional ones, have been traditional employers of women. Consequently, the demand for female workers has increased significantly since the 1940s. For example, in 1950, 62% of all clerical workers and 45% of all service workers (other than household workers) were women. In February 1991, the numbers were 79% and 59%, respectively (U.S. Department of Labor, 1991a). Between 1972 and 1985, the number of women working in clerical and professional occupations (mainly teaching and nursing) rose by more than 50%. A substantial increase also occurred in the service occupations, which were 64% female in 1991. These three job categories currently account for more than three-fifths of all female workers (U. S. Department of Labor, 1991a).

The demand for female workers is increasing. In the year 2000, nearly 90% of all new jobs will be in the service sector (National Commission on Working Women, 1990). Increasing demand also results from the facts that women outnumber men in the population, population expansion has been halted, and the participation rate of males in the labor force has been declining due to earlier retirement and the slowdown in industries that have traditionally employed men.

Other factors   Another factor that may contribute to the increasing participation of women in the labor force is diminishing social prejudice against the idea of women working outside of the home. As discussed in the previous chapter, the majority of adult Americans, and the vast majority of college students, support the idea of married women being in the labor force. Legislation promoting equality in employment and education, and advances in household technologies, also have aided women's entry into the world of paid work.

It should be noted that the reasons women are employed are virtually identical to the reasons men are employed: economic necessity, work as part of their identity, a desire for achievement, and the

Table 11.1 Percentage of degrees awarded to women, 1961–1990

	1961	1970	1980	1990
B.A.	38.2	43.0	49.0	52.1
M.A.	32.3	39.7	49.4	51.0
Doctoral	10.5	13.3	29.6	38.9
First-professional	2.7	13.3	29.6	36.3

From U.S. Department of Commerce, 1990.

satisfaction of meaningful, rewarded activity (Renwick & Lawler, 1978; Thom, 1984).

Occupational Segregation

The increasing gender parity in labor force participation rates obscures the fact that most workers are employed in gender-segregated occupations. Nine out of ten workers have co-workers of the same sex (Kassell, 1984). Thus, there are really two labor markets—one male, one female—and the two groups rarely compete for the same jobs. Segregation of jobs by gender is even more severe than segregation of jobs by race (Blau & Ferber, 1986). (See Jacobs, 1989, for a thorough analysis of this problem.)

In 1991, nearly three out of four female employees worked in one of three job categories—clerical/administrative support (28%), managerial/professional (27%; mainly teaching and administrative), and service (18%) (U.S. Department of Labor, 1991a). In contrast, male employees are spread more evenly among a number of job categories—managerial/professional (26%), operatives (20%), precision production/craft (19%), sales (11%), and service (10%). Figure 11.3 illustrates the gender segregation of the labor force. Women are particularly underrepresented as precision workers, transportation workers, farmers, and nonretail sales workers, and are overrepresented as service workers, retail sales workers, noncollege teachers, administrative support workers, and private household workers. In 1989, only 9% of all employed women were employed in jobs in which 75% or more of those employed were men (National Commission on Working Women, 1990). Black women are the most segregated, with more than 70% employed in the nonprofit sector, such as hospitals (Kassell, 1984; Woody, 1989).

Not only are women concentrated in a few female-dominated occupations, but these occupations also tend to have the lowest status and be the

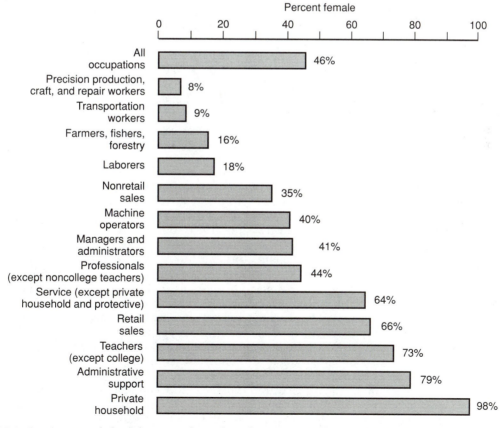

Figure 11.3 Occupational distribution of employed women, February 1991. (From U.S. Department of Labor, 1991a.)

lowest paying. Of the 500 occupations listed by the U.S. Census Bureau, women primarily are concentrated in the 22 lowest paid job classifications (" 'That's Women's,' " 1985). Even within the same occupations, women usually are assigned the lowest paying tasks. For example, most female sales workers are employed as retail sales clerks, whereas most male sales workers are employed as manufacturing sales representatives. Even in retail sales, women are likely to be selling less expensive products (like clothes), men the more expensive ones (like automobiles). Thus, men make more money in commissions and, as a result, earn more than twice what female sales workers earn (Blau & Ferber, 1986). Even in high-status fields such as medicine, men are more likely than women to be administrators and surgeons, powerful positions, whereas women tend to be overrepresented in the relatively low-status positions of teacher, general practitioner, and pediatrician (Recer, 1991; S. R. Sherman & Rosenblatt, 1984). In 1988, women doctors earned only 63% of what their male counterparts earned, a disparity not due to differences in amount of experience (Hilts, 1991).

Thus, the pattern of occupational segregation by gender is one of social stratification. As previously discussed (see also Chapter 5), males hold the highest paid and highest status jobs in this as well as in other societies. The more an occupation is dominated by women, the less it pays (Hartmann & Treiman, 1981). As the salary and status of an occupation increase, the proportion of women in that occupation decreases (Feldberg, 1984; Jacobs & Powell, 1985).

Underlying the gender labeling of jobs are factors that have traditionally influenced female participation in the labor force but that no longer are valid for many female workers. Most traditional "women's jobs" do not require long-term commitment. The hours are flexible, the jobs exist all over the country, and the jobs do not necessitate employer investment in training. Hence, women can drop in and out of these jobs according to family needs and personal desires. Most temporary and part-time employees are women (62% and 67%, respectively, in 1989), another reflection of women's domestic responsibilities and consequently weaker "commitment" to the labor force (National Commission on Working Women, 1990). Female-dominated jobs also are viewed as an extension of "natural female functions"—nurturing, servicing others, housework, and so on (Van Dusen & Sheldon, 1976). The fact that women are limited to a few jobs and may have

limited mobility (they traditionally have lived where their husbands are employed) means that many constitute a reserve pool of qualified women outside the paid labor market (Blau & Ferber, 1986). This, in turn, allows salaries to be kept low.

Since the 1960s, occupational segregation has shown a slight decrease and social acceptance of nontraditional career choices a slight increase, especially among younger cohorts (C. Raymond, 1989; Reskin & Roos, 1990). Top management remains mostly male, but women have made strong inroads in other professional jobs. In 1989, women constituted nearly 18% of doctors, 22% of lawyers, 32% of computer systems analysts, and nearly half of accountants and auditors (Castro, 1990). Still, most people choose traditional careers, and the small decrease in job segregation from 1960 to 1990 was due mainly to the increase in less gender-segregated occupations, such as computer specialties, and to an increase in the number of women in a few managerial jobs (C. Raymond, 1989; Rytina & Bianchi, 1984). Few women are moving into (and staying in) traditionally male craft and operative jobs and fewer men are moving into traditionally female-dominated jobs. When such changes do occur, salary and status changes follow. That is, women in traditionally male jobs earn less than men do, and men in traditionally female jobs earn more than women do. Because the majority of emerging jobs are in the female-dominated service sector, only small declines in occupational segregation are predicted through 2000 (National Commission on Working Women, 1990).

Management jobs represent a good example of what has been transpiring in the labor force as a whole. The number of management and professional positions has been increasing since the mid-1980s, but the number of traditional position-holders, White males, has been decreasing. Thus, organizations have been forced to diversify their employees. Yet although women have nearly doubled their representation in management between 1972 and 1990 to about a third of all managers, they remain concentrated in positions of least authority and lowest pay (Blum & Smith, 1988; Morrison & Von Glinow, 1990). Women confront a "glass ceiling" when trying to reach the top-ranked jobs. In 1990, fewer than 3% of the 6502 top jobs at Fortune 500 companies were held by women, although this is up from 1% a decade before (K. Ball, 1991b; Castro, 1990). At the current rate of increase, gender equality will be reached in the executive suite in the year 2466. The situation of minority males is similar. Female managers also are paid less than their male counterparts (Morrison & Von Glinow, 1990). One result of this pattern is that women and Black men appear to be leaving such jobs to start their own businesses at a much higher rate than White men.

High technology, rather than helping women to break free of their traditional low-salary jobs, actually has worked to enmesh women there. Women perform most of the low-skilled high-tech labor and receive even lower salaries than men in the same positions (A. D. Stanley, 1983). Indeed, many high-tech companies locate assembly plants in areas where the pool of women workers is large—for example, along Mexico's border (J. Nash & Fernandez-Kelly, 1983; Rytina & Bianchi, 1984). Technology also may reinforce "pink-collar ghettos," such as clerical jobs. By automating and fragmenting clerical tasks, technology is increasingly isolating clerical workers from other workers and decreasing the level of skill needed. Thus, such jobs are becoming even more dead-end than they were before (J. Bailey, 1988).

The underutilization of women in such traditionally male fields as science and technology impacts both women and society negatively. Women lose out by losing access to high-paying and high-prestige jobs, but society also loses out because it wastes a substantial portion of its talent. Society also suffers from the fact that crucial decisions made in the areas of science and technology will be made with little input from women with technical expertise (Ehrhart & Sandler, 1987).

In sum, the labor force is both gender-segregated and gender-stratified. A closer look at salary inequities by gender will complete the picture of the labor force.

Salary

What is a woman worth? In terms of employment compensation, only about two-thirds of the worth of a man (see Table 11.2). When part-time workers are included, the average earned income of women relative to men is even less, about one half. Even though women's labor force participation has increased over the last 35 years, the salary differential between men's median income and that of women has shown only slight fluctuations around the 60% mark. Women belonging to minority groups are especially at a disadvantage. In 1988, Black women employed full-time earned only 61% of the salary earned by White men, and 81% of that earned by Black men (National Commission on

Table 11.2 The wage gap, 1955–1989: Women's median full-time earnings as compared to men's

Year	For Every Dollar a Man Earns, A Woman Earns
1955	63.9¢
1960	60.8¢
1965	60.0¢
1970	59.4¢
1975	58.8¢
1980	60.2¢
1985	64.8¢
1989	68.0¢

From Kane, 1991; U.S. Department of Labor, 1975, 1983, 1985a.

Working Women, 1990). For Hispanic women, the situation is even worse: employed full-time Hispanic women earned only 54% of the salary earned by White men, and 83% of the salary earned by Hispanic men. One hopeful sign is that the salary gap between women and men is narrowest (about 90%) for younger workers—those under age 25 (Women's Research and Education Institute, 1990). By the year 2000, it is expected that the wage gap should narrow to about 75% (J. P. Smith & Ward, 1989).

In general, women are overrepresented in the lowest paying jobs and underrepresented in the highest paying ones. In 1988, nearly half (46%) of all female employees earned less than $10,000 per year, compared to 26% of all male workers (National Commission on Working Women, 1990). Two-thirds (65%) of all minimum wage earners are women. In contrast, 41% of male employees earned more than $25,000 per year in 1988 compared to only 15% of women workers.

One factor that contributes to this salary differential is occupational segregation. As noted previously, most women and men are not employed in the same jobs. Women are concentrated in a small number of the lowest paying jobs. About 25% of the earnings gap between women and men has been attributed to gender segregation (Jacobs, 1989). Related to occupational segregation is the fact that until recently, men went further in school and received more vocational training than women, which prepared them for higher paying positions. Indeed, salaries for both women and men tend to increase with increasing education (Women's Research and Education Institute, 1990). Differential qualifications may account for up to one-half of the wage differential (Blau & Ferber, 1986). Yet educational differences do not fully account for wage inequality since female college graduates employed full-time earned roughly the same as male high school graduates employed full-time (Bovee, 1991c). A comparison of annual salaries of those with college degrees in 1989 showed that Black women earned 65%, White women 67%, and Black men 76% of what their White male counterparts earned (Bovee, 1991b). When level of degree, field of study, and prior work experience is controlled, men still earn more than women (U.S. Department of Education, 1988b).

Even when women and men are employed in the same occupations, men earn more. This is true for male-dominated occupations as well as female-dominated occupations (National Commission on Working Women, 1990). For example, in 1989, female motor vehicle operators (6% of all such workers) earned 75% of what their male counterparts earned, while female bookkeepers (91% of all such workers) earned 84% of what their male counterparts earned. Table 11.3 shows the salary differential for several occupational groups in 1990. The salary differential is greatest for sales workers and least for farmers/fishers/forestry workers and nonfarm laborers. The salaries of these latter two occupational groups are notably low, however (U.S. Department of Labor, 1991b).

A contributing factor to the salary differential in similar positions is the increasing number of women in entry-level positions. Another factor may be the greater likelihood of women's taking time out for child-care activities and therefore not accumulating seniority as rapidly as men. Domestic responsibilities also make it more difficult for women than men to work overtime or in second jobs, although this difference between women and men is decreasing and accounts for only 8% of the gender gap in wages (Kilborn, 1990a; Shelton & Firestone, 1989). Overall, research examining labor market attachment (absenteeism, limitations on job location or hours, work interruptions) indicates that this factor explains very little of the wage differential between women and men—maybe 15% (Blau & Ferber, 1986).

Given the pervasiveness of occupational segregation, ensuring equal pay for the same work will do little to redress the overall salary inequity between women and men. One proposed solution to wage inequality between women and men is the principle of *comparable worth*, requiring equal pay for comparable work (Acker, 1989; Remick, 1984). Jobs that require similar amounts of education, similar skill levels, similar experience, similar supervisory responsibilities, and so on, should be similarly compensated. This standard would get at what many think is the most critical factor involved in salary inequality—differential valuation of what women and men do. For example, dog pound attendants, who are mostly male, earn more than child-care attendants, who are mostly female, even though the latter job requires more education than the former. Correcting for differences in the valuation of measurable traits would reduce gender-based salary inequities by about 50% (Jacobs, 1989).

Since 1983, different states, communities, and businesses have tried to implement a comparable worth approach, based on a broad interpretation of the Title VII provision of the 1964 Civil Rights Act, which prohibits sex discrimination in employment. By 1987, 28 states had begun job-evaluation

Table 11.3 Median weekly earnings of full-time employees by occupation and sex, 1990

Occupation and Earnings Industry Group	Median Weekly Earnings		Women's as % of Men's
	Women	Men	
Farm, forestry, fishing	216	263	82
Nonfarm laborers	250	308	81
Transportation operators	314	418	75
Clerical/admin. support	332	440	75
Professional	534	720	74
Technical	417	570	73
Service	230	320	72
Machine operators	260	391	66
Managerial	485	742	65
Precision production/craft	316	488	65
Sales	292	505	58

From U.S. Department of Labor, 1991b.

studies and 20 states had begun to make some kind of pay equity adjustments. At least 166 localities in 20 states had enacted comparable worth, either through legislation or collective bargaining. The state of Minnesota, and its more than 1600 local jurisdictions, has been among the more thorough and progressive sites of implementation of pay equity for public employees (see S. M. Evans & Nelson, 1989, for details). The results of such implementation between 1983 and 1987 were paradoxical, however: although female employees at the lowest ranks received more money, a smaller salary gap still existed and managers (mostly male) emerged with more power by virtue of their ability to reclassify jobs in line with technocratic rather than wage justice concerns. Furthermore, although work done by women and men now is judged by a uniform set of standards (for example, amount of technical skill required), the standard still is primarily male-based (for example, valuing product over process). Other problems with implementation that some jurisdictions have encountered are continued gender segregation in the labor force and the loss of workers in male-dominated jobs to private industry, which now pays more than the public sector (Kilborn, 1990b).

Comparable worth touches a fundamental issue with respect to wages, an issue that is very gender-bound: whether wages should reflect traditional supply-and-demand factors (for example, the number of women in the reserve labor pool, women's willingness to work for lower wages) or whether wages should reflect the principle of equal pay for comparable work. There is some evidence that traditionally female jobs are less sensitive to supply-and-demand forces than traditionally male jobs (Buttner & Rosen, 1987). Even salaries for traditionally male jobs are based on more than supply and demand; for example, men's salaries traditionally have been based on men's social role (that of breadwinner) (Kessler-Harris, 1990). Women were supposed to earn less than men in order to ensure women's economic dependence. If the comparable worth position is established, it will lead to questioning the market basis of all wages. This questioning might lead to a reevaluation of all the work women do, both inside and outside the home, which in turn might challenge the gender hierarchy in society (Feldberg, 1984). In this context, comparable worth is a radical concept indeed.

For every dollar earned by men, women currently earn 68 cents. Many factors contribute to wage inequality—occupational segregation, years in the labor force, gender differences in training, and domestic responsibilities. An overriding factor is differential valuation of male and female activities and traits. This factor itself can be subsumed under a larger one—discrimination. A major longitudinal study of a nationally representative sample of American families found that two-thirds of the wage gap between White men and White women, and three-quarters of the gap between White men and Black women, cannot be accounted for by gender differences in skills, work participation, or labor force attachment (M. Corcoran, Duncan, & Hill, 1984). The major factor explaining the salary differential appears to be direct and indirect discrimination.

In sum, women comprise nearly half of the labor force, and their representation is increasing. Most women, even married ones with children, are employed. Women's position in the labor force belies their numbers, however. Women are over-represented in the lowest paying, lowest status jobs, and they earn only two-thirds what their male counterparts earn. Although occupational segregation accounts for some of these differences, the barriers to women's equality in the labor force are complex. We will examine these barriers more closely in most of the remainder of the chapter.

▲ Barriers to Equality

As noted previously, women's position in the labor force is lower than men's in terms of status, opportunities, and salaries. The reasons for women's lower status are complex and involve both women's socialization and societal factors—work/family arrangements, direct and indirect discrimination, and the nature of the work environment. We will examine each of these factors in this section. The societal barriers are more important and more serious than the personal barriers, yet people often deliberately ignore external problems to focus on internal ones. It is easier to "blame the victim" than to institute social change, and psychologists have been as responsible as anyone else for this misdirected emphasis (see Kahn & Yoder, 1989). Therefore, after noting some of the internal barriers developed through socialization, we will focus on some of the external ones.

Before addressing the barriers themselves, a review of three main theoretical models will be useful to provide a framework for the ensuing discussion.

Theoretical Perspectives

Economists and sociologists have viewed women's participation in the labor force in terms of three major theoretical frameworks: gender role socialization theory, human capital theory, and social-structural theories.

Socialization theory is perhaps the most intuitive. Girls and boys are socialized into different roles, with different traits and skills. As we saw in Part 2, there is considerable evidence that this occurs. With respect to the labor force, males are socialized to take an active role in it and to compete for positions of power and status. Females primarily are socialized to be mothers, and to care for and nurture others. Therefore, females tend not to be as career- or achievement-oriented as males, and they gravitate toward human service and low-level jobs that require little commitment. Males, in contrast, are concerned about achievement, competition, status, and power in the work force, as elsewhere.

Human capital theory rests on the neoclassical economic assumption that people make rational choices to maximize their own utility. Since women are viewed as investing their "capital" in bearing and raising children, they don't invest themselves in extensive preparation for careers and they don't choose occupations that require considerable training, uninterrupted employment, or considerable advancement or salary potential. Women only choose jobs that fit with their maternal role. Women's "investment" goes into attracting a dependable mate and into developing their own nurturant qualities. In contrast, because men invest their "capital" in the labor force, they build up skills that will be to their advantage—vocational training and education, membership in "old boy" networks, competitiveness, aggressiveness, leadership, and so on. A considerable amount of evidence casts doubt on this model. For example, rational choice in vocational decisions seems less prominent than social constraints; and many male-dominated jobs fit the model of requiring little skill, training, or commitment, but women still don't enter them (England & McCreary, 1987; Epstein, 1988). Yet some decrease in labor force segregation during the 1970s and 1980s may be due to women's recognition that they would be spending a considerable portion of their life in the labor force, possibly without a mate.

The *social structural models* posit that women are restricted from entering occupations traditionally dominated by men. The degree of globality of these barriers depends upon the breadth of the specific structural model employed. Some models narrowly focus on the labor force; others focus on society at large. Barriers to equal access to jobs are multiple: entrance requirements, discrimination, lack of solutions to work/family conflicts, inadequate mentors, and so on. From a radical feminist perspective, however, the very nature of patriarchy requires that positions of power and status remain in men's hands, lest men's dominance be threatened. Therefore, women are systematically excluded from positions of power and status in the labor force and elsewhere (Chapter 12 will explore other power bases). Indeed, intrinsic to patriarchy is the devaluation of whatever women do, thus explaining why when women enter a job category, its salary and status decline. Such a model also suggests why comparable worth strategies won't ever completely eliminate occupational segregation or wage inequality, since standards employed still will be male-based. A Marxist perspective would add that private property requires men to control women's sexuality (to assure paternity) and therefore leads to the subordination of women throughout society.

A related way of looking at gender patterns in the labor force is through a power analysis (Ragins & Sundstrom, 1989). Power (the ability of one person to influence others) rests disproportionately in men's hands. Since power stems from organizational, interpersonal, or personal factors, all three factors must be examined in order to understand the relationship between gender and power. As we will see, women are disadvantaged personally due to socialized differences in career aspirations, personality traits, skills and education, and nonwork responsibilities. Women are disadvantaged interpersonally due to gender stereotypes and interpersonal perceptions, and lack of mentors, networks, and subordinate support. Organizationally, women are disadvantaged by recruitment and selection practices, performance appraisal, training, and tracking. Thus, gender differences in power that we see in the labor force reflect gender differences in access to a variety of resources for power.

All three theories have something to offer, although the last type has the greatest explanatory value. As Ragins and Sundstrom (1989) note, gender makes the path to power for women an obstacle course whereas gender is either immaterial or an asset for men. We will examine barriers to gender equality in the labor force in more detail in the following pages.

Socialization

As just described, the socialization girls and boys receive contributes to gendered labor force patterns, especially women's lower labor force participation and overrepresentation in low-status, low-paying jobs. Female socialization steers girls into a maternal role, whereas male socialization steers boys into an employment role. Related to this differential role socialization is the encouragement of different attitudes, values, personality traits, and styles in males and females.

Future roles   The most critical personal factor barring women from equal achievement in the labor force is the different life plans for the sexes into which children are socialized. Despite the facts that nine out of ten women will work in the paid labor force at some point in their lives, many women are employed their entire adult lives, and more than three out of five mothers are employed, most girls grow up unprepared psychologically and professionally to assume a career. Traditionally, girls grow up expecting to be mothers; boys grow up expecting to have jobs. Today, most young women plan on motherhood *and* employment, but the importance of the former still typically supersedes that of the latter.

Because of these different life plans, boys are encouraged through all the socializing forces of our culture (toys, education, media, role models) to prepare for their future role by pursuing vocational training, continued education, mentors, and so on, more so than girls. They invest in their employment-related "human capital." Salary considerations are important because males are socialized into assuming a breadwinner role. In contrast, employment is of secondary concern in traditional female socialization. For middle- and upper-class White females, jobs traditionally have been optional. Certainly, salary considerations traditionally have been deemphasized due to the expectation that a woman would be married to an employed man who would economically provide for her. This has been less true among Black and working-class White females, who traditionally have expected to combine employment and motherhood (Murrell, Frieze, & Frost, 1991; E. J. Smith, 1982; V. G. Thomas & Shields, 1987). Black female adolescents also emphasize financial reward with respect to employment. Yet most Black female adolescents still aspire to traditionally female-dominated social service jobs (V. G. Thomas, 1986). This is not true of Black female college students, who tend to aspire to traditionally male occupations even more than do White female college students, and more for economic reasons (Murrell et al., 1991).

Given traditional socialization toward different future roles, it is not surprising that, until recently, more males than females received a college education. If women were primarily mothers, money invested in a college education might be viewed as wasted. Men still are more likely than women to attain advanced professional degrees, which can lead to some of the most lucrative and prestigious jobs. Even with respect to blue-collar jobs, males are more likely to pursue vocational training that will qualify them for well-paying positions, such as mechanics, whereas females are more likely to pursue vocational training for such poorly paid jobs as hairdresser. As noted earlier, gender differences in job qualifications partially account for wage inequality and occupational segregation.

Since girls are supposed to invest their "capital" in preparing for motherhood, vocational and salary concerns are secondary. Jobs that are easiest to combine with motherhood—that is, that require little work commitment and training—are preferred. Certainly, most of the traditionally female jobs in the clerical and service sectors fall into this category. Even professional jobs that are female-dominated —teaching and nursing—fit well with motherhood due to their flexible hours and availability in every community. Furthermore, since motherhood and marriage are linked, young women are encouraged to focus on finding a mate. Doing so may require them to keep their career aspirations and salary achievements below that of their partners so as not to threaten men's position of dominance. A study of young women in the 1970s found that those who had traditional marriages frequently gave up their own career goals to focus on their husbands' career advancement and on having children (K. Gerson, 1985). This was especially likely when husbands had a strong need to control (Winter et al., 1977). Indeed, research has found that among adolescent girls, those who have a high commitment to marriage and family and who begin dating early tend to have lower educational and occupational aspirations than other girls (Danziger, 1983; Holms & Esses, 1988; Marini, 1978). Among college women as well, the greater the number of children desired, the lower the career aspirations in female-dominated careers (Murrell et al., 1991).

For those women aspiring to a career, men's attitudes may play an important role. Adolescent girls' aspirations for nontraditional careers in particular are inversely related to their desire to marry, especially in the near future (Sandberg, Ehrhardt, Mellins, Ince, & Meyer-Bahlburg, 1987). Men appear to prefer as a romantic partner women who aspire to a traditionally female as opposed to a traditionally male job (Pfost & Fiore, 1990). Furthermore, college women who perceive traditional sex role expectations in their male friends expect more negative outcomes from success and have lower career aspirations than women who do not perceive such expectations in their male friends (Canter, 1979; Lemkau, 1983).

Since gender roles emphasize men's labor force potential and not women's, it is not surprising that more factors predict males' career and educational aspirations than females'. For example, number of siblings, socioeconomic background, and academic ability and performance are stronger predictors of a boy's educational and occupational aspirations than they are of a girl's (Danziger, 1983; Harmon, 1981; Marini, 1978; Tittle, 1981). Girls' aspirations are more affected than boys' by family factors (support, cohesiveness), female role models, and their own marital plans (Basow & Howe, 1980; King, 1989; Sandberg et al., 1987; V. G. Thomas, 1986). For example, a longitudinal study of 81 high school valedictorians found that whereas White males continued to achieve at the top of their classes in college and then moved quickly into prestigious jobs, the women divided into two groups: those who lowered their career and eductional aspirations due to plans to start a family soon, and those who retained high aspirations due to plans to delay family life (Denny & Arnold, in Moses, 1991b). The high-achieving women also received more social support from professionals and mentors than did those who had lowered their aspirations.

Much is changing with respect to future role expectations. As noted in previous chapters, the vast majority of high school and college women now expect to combine employment and motherhood. (Fewer than 5% of high school girls in the late 1980s expected to be full-time homemakers.) College women today typically report equal interest in and support for domestic and occupational activities (see, for example, Stake & Rogers, 1989). In fact, the goals and aspirations of male and female college students are becoming increasingly similar, especially with regard to vocational achievement and financial rewards (H. S. Astin, 1990; Fiorentine, 1988). In addition, an increasing minority of young women are putting careers ahead of motherhood in their aspirations. What effect these new life plans will have on women's future occupational status and achievement remains to be seen. Much will

depend upon how much other barriers to equality have been eliminated or reduced.

Attitudes and values   Related to future roles is the differential encouragement of certain values and attitudes in males and females. Since males are supposed to be primary wage earners, they are encouraged to value competition, achievement, and status. Since females are supposed to be primary child rearers, they are encouraged to value helping and nurturing others. As we saw in Chapter 3, girls typically do tend to develop a stronger interpersonal orientation than boys, and boys typically do tend to develop a stronger power orientation than girls. These different attitudes and values affect women's and men's roles in the labor force.

National surveys of college and high school students consistently show that females are more concerned than males with helping others, and are less concerned than males with prestige or status factors in their career decisions (see, for example, Bridges, 1989). Thus, women may be more motivated than men to pursue jobs in the service sector, which typically are low-status and low-paying jobs, whereas men may be more motivated than women to pursue jobs with clear advancement potential. Of all first-year college students in the United States in 1990, 71% of the females compared with 51% of the males considered it essential or very important to help others who are in difficulty (A. W. Astin, 1991). Helping others is a major factor in both Black and White college women's career choice, although it is less important for White women aspiring to traditionally male jobs (Murrell et al., 1991). This value may contribute to the greater likelihood of college women's versus college men's majoring in the humanities and social sciences. Unfortunately, such college majors do not prepare women for high-paying jobs, such as in technology and the sciences.

College women's interest in being very well-off financially has been increasing over the last 20 years (as has men's) and may signal a shift in women's bases for career decisions (H. S. Astin, 1990). But just as men's interest in raising a family doesn't necessarily mean they personally are interested in staying home to do so, so it may be that women's interest in being very well-off doesn't necessarily mean they personally are interested in earning that income. Finding ways to meet one's most important objectives may be difficult for today's college students since the labor force is not designed to accommodate career and domestic interests simultaneously. If forced to choose, many will likely let socialized role expectations take precedence.

The relatively greater relationship orientation of women as a group and women's greater interest in helping others has many labor force implications. Women are more likely than men to be interested in teaching, nursing, waitressing, child care, and other human service jobs, but because masculine cultural values dominate, these jobs have low status and relatively low remuneration. Even men and women in the same job may gravitate toward different aspects of their profession. For example, female physicians are more likely to choose primary care than men, who are more likely to choose surgery (S. C. Martin et al., 1988). Not coincidentally, surgery pays much more than primary care. Female professionals—doctors, lawyers, and executives—also appear to have a more caring and humanistic style than male professionals (Gilligan & Pollak, 1988; Jack & Jack, 1988; S. C. Martin et al., 1988; Rosener, 1990). Although a relational style may lead to greater client satisfaction, it has not traditionally led to job advancement or high salary. It is unlikely to do so in the future, given dominant cultural values, although more is being written about "the female advantage" in leadership style (see, for example, Helgesen, 1990). Most college students today still see professional jobs as requiring an exclusively "masculine" (that is, competitive) value orientation (Sacks, 1989). This belief may keep many women from aspiring to professional careers, despite these careers' high status and salary.

Gender differences in other work-related attitudes, besides those in interpersonal and power concerns, occur as well. Perhaps most salient is the importance of one's job to one's sense of self. Since men are trained to view employment as part of their male identity, they may be more emotionally invested in their work status than women. Since women are trained to view motherhood and not employment as part of their female identity, they may be less emotionally invested in their work status than males. Thus, not only may men be more motivated than women to achieve in the labor force, but they may be more invested than women in seeing their work in gendered terms. This dynamic may account for men's greater reluctance to work in nontraditional (that is, other-sex-dominated) jobs and men's greater resistance to having members of the other sex enter their work environment than is true for women. In fact, males are more likely than females to see jobs in gender terms in the first place.

For example, girls are more likely than boys to rate most jobs as suitable for both males and females (C. J. Archer, 1984; Franken, 1983). In one major Rand Corporation study of more than 13,000 adolescents, three out of four males chose traditionally male jobs, whereas only 47% of the females picked traditionally female jobs (Parachini, 1985).

Men's greater resistance to diversifying their work environment can be seen in studies of how men in the Marine Corps and in police teams actively resisted women's entry into their profession and attempted to limit their job opportunities. In contrast, female nurses welcomed men into their profession and even steered them into the highest status and paying specialties (Ott, 1989; C. L. Williams, 1989). Status seems a part of each sex's gender identity and carries over into labor force dynamics. Perhaps that is part of the reason that both men and women in male-dominated jobs are more satisfied than both men and women in female-dominated jobs (T. Adler, 1989c; Cassidy & Warren, 1991). Despite women's satisfaction in male-dominated jobs, however, they frequently move into more female-dominated ones over time, perhaps due to men's resistance and outright hostility. In a six-year longitudinal study of women, Harmon (1981) found that the occupations considered became more traditional in sex type and lower in socioeconomic status over time.

A strong career focus itself is nontraditional for women. Whereas 55% of full-time male workers think of their work as a career rather than a job, only 46% of full-time female workers feel similarly (Belkin, 1989). This lesser career focus in women than men is related to the types of jobs each typically holds. Women in clerical, sales, and service occupations (all traditionally female and low-status jobs) tend to have less of a career orientation than women in professional jobs (Spenner & Rosenfeld, 1990). A traditional attitude toward women's roles is associated with low career salience and with more female-dominated college majors and occupations, among Blacks as well as Whites (Burlew, 1982; Murrell et al., 1991). Such an attitude also is negatively related to the number of hours employed mothers work each week (Krogh, 1985). Although it is logical to assume that nontraditional attitudes may lead to nontraditional career behavior, it also is possible that engaging in nontraditional career behavior (for example, working as a business executive) may liberalize a woman's attitudes. Perhaps encouragingly, younger women (those aged 18 to 29) are as likely as their male peers to call their work a career.

Overall, while gendered attitudes and values may provide some explanation for gendered labor force patterns, such a personal explanation ignores strong individual differences that cut across gender as well as the numerous external barriers that steer males and females into certain jobs.

Personality traits and styles   In addition to gender differences in some attitudes and values, we have noted that men and women also tend to differ with respect to some personality traits and styles that may have labor force implications.

Although people in low-status, low-paying jobs (mainly women) may be suspected of being less achievement-motivated than people in other jobs (mainly men), no gender difference in need for achievement exists, as discussed in Chapter 3. How these needs get expressed, however, may differ for females and males due to societal messages and barriers. For example, in a study of more than 100 young women tested in their senior year in college and 14 years later, women high in need for achievement tended to pursue teaching careers, a traditionally female career congenial to women's achievement and affiliative interests (S. R. Jenkins, 1987). Entrepreneurial business careers, although competitive and therefore potentially appealing to people high in achievement motivation, are not viewed as congenial to women's interests. Perhaps most provocative is the finding that need for achievement actually increases in women who are employed in highly competitive achievement-oriented positions, such as college teaching and entrepreneurial business careers. To the extent that men are more likely than women to be in such occupations, men may appear to be more achievement-oriented. However, the cause of such a gender difference then would be situational, not personality-related.

Similarly, explanations that rely on a presumed personality defect in women, such as high fear of success, also have not been supported by research, as reviewed in Chapter 3. Both men and women may fear success if such success is viewed as gender-inappropriate and leads to negative social consequences. For example, women who strive to achieve in traditionally masculine careers are viewed as less desirable as romantic partners and friends by their peers than women who strive to achieve in traditionally feminine careers (Pfost & Fiore, 1990). Again, the problem is less personal than social.

With respect to self-confidence, we saw in Chapter 8 that men tend to have higher self-regard than women. This means that men frequently overestimate their abilities while women frequently underestimate theirs, at least in situations viewed as gender-inappropriate. Although overestimation can lead to frequent disappointments, such a style is likely to lead to more attempts to achieve at higher levels. In the labor force, this might lead men to aspire to a greater variety of jobs, more advanced positions, and higher salaries. In contrast, underestimation can lead to lowered aspirations and settling for jobs and salaries beneath one's abilities. Higher expectations in gender-appropriate occupations and lower expectations in gender-inappropriate occupations also would steer women into traditionally feminine jobs (Bridges, 1988). This description of implications certainly parallels the labor force patterns we have seen.

Although gender differences in attribution patterns are complex and not always found (see Chapter 8), in some cases they may contribute to women's lower status in the labor force. In particular, men may use more internal attributions than women, especially for success (see, for example, Deaux, 1979). This pattern would lead to continued strivings. Indeed, an internal locus of control is strongly related to career aspirations for both females and males (King, 1989). Women are somewhat more likely than men to use "luck" explanations, especially for success, even when they are on national boards of directors of major U.S. corporations (Klemesrud, 1979). However, rather than viewing attribution patterns as purely personal, it's important to recognize that they may be realistic. That is, women's careers may indeed be more determined by luck than men's, whereas men's careers may indeed appear to be more under their own control. Larwood and Gattiker (1987) found that top positions in 17 major corporations were predictable for men on the basis of their earlier positions or successes. In contrast, for older women, no important paths predicted their attainment of top positions, suggesting the operation of chance.

Related to occasional gender differences in self-confidence and attributions are occasional gender differences in feelings of entitlement in the work domain—that is, what people feel they are due for their work. Research on distributive justice patterns reveals two consistent patterns: when objective accomplishments are similar, women tend to allocate fewer rewards to themselves than do men;

despite lower rewards, women generally are as satisfied as men with their jobs and their salary (see Major, 1987, for a summary of this research). Why do women take less for themselves than men? Why don't they feel deprived when they receive less? It's not because women pay everyone less; men and women don't differ when it comes to allocating rewards to others. It's also not because women don't realize that men earn more. They do. The important variables seem to be what reference group women use when considering their rewards and the perceived justifiability of the reward procedures. Women appear to compare themselves to other women more than to men. With a same-sex comparison group, the low rewards an individual woman receives may appear fair. Second, to the extent women believe that life is fair and that they have some control over their lives, they may be reluctant to acknowledge the degree to which they personally are discriminated against, although they may recognize injustice in the work situation of other women (Crosby, 1982; Unger & Sussman, 1986). Thus, increased awareness of personal discrimination plus increased use of men as referents should elevate women's expectations for themselves. This does seem to occur, although both changes probably are needed simultaneously. For example, just disclosing actual starting salaries alone does not eliminate gender differences in salary expectations among college seniors applying for similar jobs (B. A. Martin, 1989). It's important to remember that women and men are not usually applying for similar jobs because most occupations are dominated by one gender. In such cases, same-sex comparison groups would be hard to avoid and discrimination would be less visible.

Sex typing also affects labor force patterns. Among adolescents and college students, feminine sex typing is associated with choice of female-dominated majors and occupations, whereas masculine sex typing is associated with choice of male-dominated majors and occupations (Harren, Kass, Tinsley, & Moreland, 1979; Sztaba & Colwill, 1988; Young, 1984). Agentic traits also are associated with strong commitment to a career among adolescent girls (Holms & Esses, 1988). Among adults, agentic traits are associated with a higher level of occupational attainment than are expressive-nurturant traits (Chow, 1987). This may be due to the linkage between sex-typed personality traits and sex-typed occupations. That is, in male-dominated jobs like law, most employees (female

and male) have strong active-instrumental characteristics (androgynous and masculine-sex-typed); in female-dominated jobs like nursing, most employees (female and male) have strong nurturant-expressive characteristics (androgynous and feminine-sex-typed) (Doerfler & Kammer, 1986; Lemkau, 1983; S. W. Williams & McCullers, 1983). Especially in male-dominated fields, instrumental traits appear positively associated with greater levels of responsibility and achievement than expressive traits (Dimitrovsky, Singer, & Yinon, 1989; Jagacinski, 1987; Wong, Kettlewell, & Sproule, 1985). For example, people who hold upper-level management jobs have significantly stronger instrumental-active traits than individuals holding low-level management jobs (Fagenson, 1990). The causal sequence here is not clear, however. Experienced woman managers may have even more autonomous traits than experienced men managers (Hatcher, 1991). Sex typing may lead some individuals to choose certain career paths, whereas for others, being in a particular occupation may lead to the development of certain sex-typed personality traits. There is evidence of both patterns (Canter, 1979; Eagly, 1987b). Thus, again we see that what at first appears to be solely an internal personal variable—sex typing—actually may interact with situational factors to yield differential labor force patterns for males and females.

In sum, girls and boys clearly have different socialization experiences that impact on their future labor force participation. Boys are trained to assume an active achievement-oriented occupational role and are encouraged to develop traits and attitudes that will enhance that role. Girls are trained to assume a maternal role, with traits and attitudes that will enhance their role performance. Since the labor force is dominated by masculine values and patterns, women in the labor force are at a distinct disadvantage. To the extent they have developed according to the traditional female norm, they may be best suited for subordinate jobs, typically in human services.

But socialization cannot fully account for women's status in the labor force. In the first place, as we have seen repeatedly throughout the book, not all (or even most) women conform to the traditional female stereotype. Second, differences between women as a group and men as a group on most traits and behaviors are minimal. Those that exist are more likely to *result from* different social roles than *lead to* different social roles. Third, young women's career aspirations typically are less traditional than the occupations they later hold (Jacobs, 1989). We need to examine those social forces that shape and control our occupational experiences in order to truly understand women's subordinate status in the labor force. One of the most important barriers is the structural conflict between work and family activities.

Work-Family Conflicts

As discussed in the previous chapter, more than 100 countries provide some form of job-protected leave for new mothers. The United States stands alone among advanced industrialized countries in having no statutory provisions to guarantee infant care leave. In France, for example, all new mothers, including adoptive ones, can take a ten-week paid leave from their jobs. Pregnant women also are entitled to paid leave during the last six weeks of pregnancy. Furthermore, women can take up to two years unpaid leave after birth or they can work part-time. Nationally subsidized quality day care also is available. In contrast, in the United States, only 60% of all employed women are entitled to *unpaid* leave for childbirth, and this leave is limited to the time period the woman is physically "disabled," usually six weeks. Fathers, parents who adopt a child, and parents of a sick child generally are not entitled to any leave, because such leaves typically are part of disability coverage. Fewer than half of all employed women are entitled to a maternity leave that includes even partial pay and a job guarantee (National Commission on Working Women, 1989b).

Even these tend to be limited to six to eight weeks. Figure 11.4 depicts the reasoning behind these policies. Yet research in states where unpaid leave time for family care is mandated in certain firms (17 states in 1991) has found that businesses have had little difficulty complying with the law (K. Ball, 1991a; Trzcinski & Finn-Stevenson, 1991). What these policies, or lack thereof, mean is that many employed women are forced to choose between their jobs and their child. Such a choice is not a happy one, especially for the majority of women whose jobs are economically necessary. For this and other reasons, nearly three out of four new mothers are remaining in the labor force (Trost, 1990). Of those who take time off, about two-thirds return before the end of the year. Even when women are allowed unpaid leave for childbirth, few low-income women can afford to take it. One out of five low-income women take less than the medically recommended six weeks off (K. Ball, 1991a).

Four out of five female employees are of child-bearing age and 90% eventually will have children. Thus, many female workers are women with children, frequently very young children. Yet the workplace is set up for employees without domestic responsibilities. Indeed, most professional jobs are designed for two people: one employed (and paid) and one who provides the backup (entertaining clients, taking care of home and family). Such a career pattern is most suitable for traditional men with a traditional wife. Women with children have less time available than men and women without children for overtime and extraprofessional activities, like entertaining and golfing. It is not

Figure 11.4 The comfort of illusions, or why the United States lags behind the rest of the industrialized world with respect to parental leave policies. (CATHY Copyright 1987 Cathy Guisewite. Reprinted with permission of Universal Press Syndicate.)

surprising, then, that greater numbers of professional women are childless than is true of professional men. For example, 90% of male executives 40 years of age and younger have children, compared to only 35% of their female counterparts (F. N. Schwartz, 1989). Professional women also are less likely to be married than professional men and than nonprofessional women (Olson, Frieze, & Detlefsen, 1990).

Employees with domestic responsibilities, especially child-care concerns, are at a marked disadvantage in professional careers. These employees are predominantly women. Besides having limitations on their time for extraprofessional activities, such women also bear the burden of having to arrange their work life around the availability of child care. When things go wrong with such arrangements (for example, when the child or child-care worker becomes ill), it is they who must leave work, take a day off, or quit. A 1987 survey of 600 workers found that 30% of employed parents with children under 12 said they gave up jobs or promotions because of a lack of child-care options ("Lack of Child Care," 1987). Professional women with families also may be less mobile than men with families or than women without families, since women are more likely to move for their husband's job than vice versa. This problem of geographic constraint or reluctant relocation may contribute to the status and salary differences between professional men and women, at least in academia (Gutek & Burley, 1988; Marwell, Rosenfeld, & Spilerman, 1979). The problems caused by such moves have made many dual-career couples very reluctant to accept transfers, and this resistance is increasing (Kraft, 1991). About 60% of corporate transfers involve dual-career families, and when such transfers fail, the main reason is lack of family adjustment. Only one out of four companies offer spouse career assistance, but more will need to do so to make job transfers attractive to dual-career spouses.

Even when all goes well, employed mothers bear the extra stress of worrying about domestic factors. Work-home conflicts are associated with high stress in employed women, and such stress takes its toll on a woman's physical and mental health. Yet women by and large are unprepared for the degree of conflict that arises between domestic and career responsibilities (Tangri & Jenkins, 1986). Interestingly, work-home conflicts do not appear to be related to women's career progress, job satisfaction, or productivity (J. R. Cole & Zuckerman, 1987; D. L. Nelson, Quick, Hitt, & Moesel, 1990). These findings may be due to the fact that work appears to interfere more with family life than family life interferes with work activities (Bolger, DeLongis, Kessler, & Wethington, 1989; Gutek, Repetti, & Silver, 1988). It is important to recognize that work-home conflicts are not inevitable. When families are supportive of a mother's labor force participation and when workplace supports such as flexible scheduling exist, stress tends to be low and job satisfaction high (Moen & Forest, 1990; Rudd & McKenry, 1986; also see Chapter 8). Another point to note is that work-family conflicts affect men as well as women, although research typically has focused mainly on the latter. In fact, when both sexes are studied, men appear more likely than their employed wives to bring home stress into the workplace (Bolger et al., 1989). However, to the extent that less is expected of fathers than mothers with respect to domestic responsibilities, men experience less work-family conflict than women. For example, in a national survey of men and women employed full-time, 83% of the women with children under 18 said they feel torn between the demands of their job and wanting to spend more time with their family at least sometimes, compared to 72% of comparable men (Belkin, 1989). For the first time in 1990, a slight majority of employed women (56%) in a national survey said they would stop working if they had enough money (Balter, 1991). The stress of carrying two full-time jobs (in the labor force and at home) is wearing many women out. Of course, increased sharing of domestic responsibilities is an alternative solution to reducing labor force involvement.

Jobs that are most compatible with domestic responsibilities are the traditionally female ones, as noted earlier. Jobs such as waitress, hairdresser, nurse, and clerk can be done part-time, frequently on shifts. Such jobs also can be entered and departed without much problem since they tend to be plentiful and no career ladder is involved. Unfortunately, such jobs are among the lowest paying ones. Part-time work, which most mothers of young children would prefer, also tends to be low paying and frequently without any health benefits or possibilities for advancement (McHenry & Small, 1989). The highest paying jobs, especially in the white-collar category, tend to be male-dominated and are least compatible with domestic responsibilities. For example, job interruptions and part-time work have a more negative effect on the salaries of women with master's degrees in business (a male-dominated career) than on the salaries of women with master's degrees in library science (a female-dominated career) (Olson et al., 1990). This appears true for other career-ladder jobs as well. Once someone steps off the ladder, it's hard to get back on. The strongest negative effect is on salaries, with work interruptions alone accounting for approximately 15% of the gender salary differential (Schneer & Reitman, 1990; "Women Making," 1987). Although no full-time career is completely compatible with family responsibilities, male-dominated ones seem least so. Perhaps that is why turnover rates in management are higher for women than men (F. N. Schwartz, 1989).

As the data on job relocations suggest, men too are affected by work and family conflicts. Nearly half of all corporate transfers involve a husband "trailing" his wife (Kraft, 1991). Men who want to take time off to raise children or even just to adjust to the birth of a child frequently are met with corporate disapproval and/or loss of employment (C. Lawson, 1991; Saltzman, 1991). In fact, discontinuous employment histories affect men more negatively than women with respect to future income and career satisfaction, at least in managerial careers (Schneer & Reitman, 1990). Only 1% of men take paternity leave, even when their workplace allows it. Yet men are becoming more interested in combining their work and family lives. A 1991 survey by Du Pont found that 56% of male employees were interested in more flexible work schedules so that they could have more time with their families, up from 37% just five years earlier (Saltzman, 1991). Another survey of young Americans found that nearly half of the men said they would be interested in staying at home and raising children if they had the opportunity (N. Gibbs, 1990). Such opportunities are unlikely given the structure of the workplace and economic realities. Only by changing the structure of the workplace to enable both fathers and mothers to take parental leave and/or create alternative work schedules without penalties will companies begin to reduce work-family conflicts for their employees (Pleck, 1986).

Thus, work-family conflicts are not the sole province of women and cannot be solved by recommendations directed at women alone—for example, to get out of the labor force when their children are young (Mason, 1988) or to develop greater acceptance of the dominant and nurturant parts in themselves, what Patricia McBroom (1986) refers to as the creation of a "third sex." As we have seen, most employed mothers work out of economic necessity, and the problems they encounter in the workplace are due to familial and workplace structures, not

personality variables. Even solutions to work and family conflicts that center only upon facilitating women's ability to manage dual roles are insufficient. For example, Felice Schwartz (1989) suggested that corporations recognize two types of female employees: career-primary women (those who put their careers first); and career-and-family women (those with dual concerns), the latter being more numerous. Corporations must adjust the work environment to support the different needs of each group in order to reap maximum gains in terms of job commitment and productivity. Although meant to be helpful to professional women, the creation of a "Mommy track," as the media came to call it, is likely to stigmatize career-and-family women, especially because such women are seen as costing the corporation more than career-primary women and than men. The creation of a "Mommy track" also ignores men's role in family life. Men too have children, but no one has suggested a "Daddy track." The real problem is not that women have children, but the unwillingness of most fathers to share domestic responsibilities, the unwillingness of most employers to change the structure of the workplace to accommodate such responsibilities on the part of all workers, and the unwillingness of the state to support modern family life.

Without more plentiful and affordable child care, without more sharing of domestic responsibilities, and without structural changes in the workplace to allow for parental leaves, flexible hours, and more career-track part-time jobs, women's subordinate status in the work force is unlikely to change. We may in fact have reached the maximum amount of labor force participation of women aged 25 to 34—73% during the late 1980s—due to these barriers. Although some companies are making an effort to accommodate workers' family needs by developing generous leave policies and part-time and flex-time positions that do not remove women from the career track (C. H. Deutsch, 1990a; Trost, 1987), much more change is needed. Fewer than 1 company in 100 provides some form of child-care assistance to their employees (National Commission on Working Women, 1989b). Direct federal outlays for child-care programs, which benefit mainly low-income families, declined between 1977 and 1986. In 1990, President Bush vetoed a modest family leave bill and threatens to do the same with any future bills passed by Congress. As Victor Fuchs (1988) notes, as long as responsibility for children is borne primarily by women, women's economic status will suffer. Child-centered national policies (such as child allowances for all mothers and high-quality, affordable day care) and workplace flexibility are needed.

As we have seen, solutions to work-family conflicts require major societal changes, but such changes will benefit everyone, especially women and children. Without such changes, a major barrier to women's equality in the workplace will remain.

Discrimination

Work-family conflicts exist because work and family lives have been conceptualized by society and by employers as two separate and nonoverlapping spheres. Women are supposed to be responsible for family life, men for work life. As we have seen, such a picture has little correspondence to today's realities. Nonetheless, this picture contributes to two related barriers to women's equality—prejudicial attitudes and discriminatory behavior. Negative attitudes about women frequently interact with a variety of myths about women employees to create a discriminatory work environment for women. What women do is generally devalued, even when women and men do the exact same thing. Stereotypic expectations also affect the types of jobs offered women and men, and the types of recommendations made regarding job changes and advancement. Because such discrimination frequently is quite subtle and done unconsciously, it is hard to see. Therefore, in this section we will examine research studies depicting how gender prejudice works, myths regarding women workers, and evidence of discrimination in the workplace.

Gender prejudice   What evidence is there that men and women are prejudiced against women solely on the basis of their gender? In Philip Goldberg's (1968) classic study, female college students were asked to evaluate journal articles for their value, persuasiveness, and profundity. They also evaluated the authors for their writing style, professional competence, status, and ability to persuade the reader. The articles were from predominantly "masculine" fields (such as law and city planning), predominantly "feminine" fields (elementary school teaching and dietetics), and "neutral" ones (linguistics and art history). They differed only in that the author was presented as male in half of the articles and as female in the other half. The results showed that college women consistently found an article more valuable and its author more competent when the article bore a male rather than a female name. These differences in evaluation as a function

of author sex were significant only in the traditionally masculine fields and the "neutral" field of linguistics. The importance of the sex typing of the field has been overlooked frequently by later researchers.

From the vast amount of research in this area since 1968, it now is clear that Goldberg's findings were too simple and overstated. For example, Swim, Borgida, Maruyama, and Myers (1989), in a meta-analysis of over 100 studies based on Goldberg's paradigm, found only very small differences ($d = -.07$) in overall ratings of women and men, although the difference was in the predicted direction. The size of the difference is on the same order as gender differences in problem-solving abilities (see Chapter 3) and can be considered negligible. This finding does not mean that prejudice against women does not exist, only that evidence of such prejudice is subtle and probably only becomes manifest under certain conditions and in interaction with other variables. Let's look more closely at what some of the important variables might be.

1. *Amount of information available.* The less information provided, the more likely stereotypic expectations will be used and women will be evaluated less favorably (Locksley et al., 1980; Powell, 1987; Swim et al., 1989). Qualifications carry much greater weight than does gender in determining evaluations and recommendations (Olian, Schwab, & Haberfeld, 1988). When a great deal of specific information is provided (for example, when you have had a chance to interact with someone at length), ratings are likely to be less influenced by gender variables.

2. *Violation of stereotypes.* Although the findings are complex, prejudice against women is most likely to occur toward those women who are seen as violating gender stereotypes (Etaugh & Riley, 1983; Lenney, Mitchell, & Browning, 1983; Paludi & Bauer, 1983; Ward, 1981). For example, women writing about "masculine" topics (à la Goldberg) or engaging in "masculine" behavior (such as dominance) or applying for "masculine" jobs (such as college teacher or construction worker) are likely to receive more negative ratings than identically described men. Even gender-neutral situations sometimes may elicit bias against women, although such bias appears to be abating (Etaugh & Foresman, 1983). Only ratings of women with respect to "feminine" topics, behaviors, or jobs show no bias against women and may even occasionally show bias in the opposite direction. For

example, men in nontraditional settings or engaging in nontraditional behavior sometimes receive somewhat more negative ratings than identically described women (Etaugh & Riley, 1983; M. M. Gross & Geffner, 1980; M. B. Isaacs, 1981). Women also may be evaluated more positively than identically described men when their behavior is described as supercompetent, perhaps because exceptional performance on the part of a woman is particularly surprising and thus viewed as more noteworthy (P. P. Abramson, Goldberg, Greenberg, & Abramson, 1977; Basow & Howe, 1987; Taynor & Deaux, 1975).

3. *Sex-typed traits.* Depending on the situational context, women and men may be judged differently for exhibiting the same sex-typed traits (Basow, 1990; Major, Carnevale, & Deaux, 1981; Stoppard & Kalin, 1983; Wiley & Eskilson, 1985). Whereas men may be evaluated positively when exhibiting agentic traits alone, women may need to combine agentic and expressive traits (that is, be androgynous) in order to receive positive ratings, especially in "masculine" situations.

4. *Attitudes toward women.* Prejudice against women is most likely to be shown by people with traditional attitudes about women's roles (Brabeck & Weisgerber, 1989; C. K. Holahan & Stephan, 1981; A. Kahn, 1981; Spence & Helmreich, 1972). Education also may affect attitudes toward women, with college-educated persons showing somewhat less traditional attitudes than non-college-educated persons (M. M. Gross & Geffner, 1980).

5. *Rater gender.* Since men hold more traditional attitudes than women, more prejudice tends to be shown by men, especially in conjunction with nontraditional target persons (Basow & Silberg, 1987; M. B. Isaacs, 1981; Kaschak, 1978; Paludi & Strayer, 1985; Ward, 1981). In a number of situations and with respect to specific questions, same-sex preference appears, with women rating female target persons and men rating male target persons most positively (Basow & Howe, 1979).

6. *Status/success of target.* Prejudice against women is most common when women are viewed as aspiring to recognition or a high-status job. When women are described as award winners or as successful, however, they tend to be evaluated as favorably as identically described men (Heilman, Block, Martell, & Simon, 1989; M. B. Isaacs, 1981; Kaschak, 1981a; Starer & Denmark, 1974; Taynor & Deaux, 1973). Thus, external "legitimization" equalizes perceptions of women and men; without such legitimization, however, women may be devalued.

7. *Race.* Race also may interact with gender to affect ratings, but the findings are inconsistent and complex. Although Blacks tend to be rated lower than Whites, especially when Whites are doing the rating (Greenhaus, Parasuraman, & Wormley, 1990; Kraiger & Ford, 1985), Black women are not always rated the lowest (which might be expected due to both racism and sexism) (Gerdes, Miner, Maynard, Dominguez, & Joshl, 1988; Nkomo & Cox, 1989; Pulakos, White, Oppler, & Borman, 1989; D. E. Thompson & Thompson, 1985). Class too may interact with race in complex ways, at least for men (Jussim, Coleman, & Lerch, 1987).

8. *Rating context.* Rating context also affects findings of prejudice, with most bias found when ratings are made of job resumes and job applications rather than articles (the Goldberg paradigm) (Swim et al., 1989). This finding obviously has workplace implications, although even here the effects frequently are subtle. When raters have more than one person to rate, more bias against women appears than when raters judge only one candidate (Olian et al., 1988). This too has implications for the workplace, since most job evaluators rate more than one employee or potential employee.

Other factors also may interact with gender and related variables to affect evaluations: for example, the marital status of the target person (Etaugh & Stern, 1984) and whether the ratings are done in same-sex or mixed-sex groups (Etaugh, Houtler, & Ptasnik, 1988; L. A. Gilbert, Holt, & Long, 1988; Toder, 1980). (See also Top, 1991).

All these factors, though individually of perhaps minor importance, can work together to either maximize or minimize bias. From the research literature, we can conclude that bias against women is minimized when people with nontraditional attitudes toward women's roles evaluate a well-qualified woman, about whom a great deal is known, with respect to her neutral or gender-appropriate behavior or interests. Conversely, bias against women is maximized when people with traditional attitudes toward women's roles evaluate an aspiring unknown woman candidate or job applicant for a nontraditional job or promotion. These latter conditions are met most frequently in the labor force with respect to male-dominated jobs. Such settings will be discussed in more detail later in this chapter.

Although prejudice in evaluations may be minimized for successful individuals, differential sexist attributions regarding the reasons for success may remain. For example, men generally are viewed as succeeding because of their own abilities, whereas women's success may be viewed more in terms of external factors (such as luck or ease of the task) or in terms of effort, which, although an internal factor, is a variable one (Deaux & Emswiller, 1974; L'Heureux-Barrett & Barnes-Farrell, 1991; O'Leary & Hansen, 1985) (see Chapter 8 for a discussion of attributions). For example, a man who obtains a highly valued sales account might be viewed as exceptionally capable, whereas a women with the same success might be viewed as lucky or benefiting from her looks. Conversely, when success does not occur, attributions are more likely to be made involving women's lack of ability and men's lack of effort or unfortunate circumstances. For example, when a highly valued sales account is lost, a man may be criticized for not trying hard enough, but a woman may be suspected of not having the ability to do the job. Given the current social climate where overt prejudice no longer is socially acceptable, prejudice is more likely to be seen indirectly in terms of attributions made rather than directly in terms of differential evaluations.

One specific personal quality that affects women more than men, especially in the labor force, is physical attractiveness. Because this quality is seen as more appropriate for females than males, women who don't conform to the level of physical attractiveness expected of them may be described more negatively than similarly unattractive males (Bar-Tal & Saxe, 1976; Cash, Gillen, & Burns, 1977; Wallston & O'Leary, 1981). Many traditionally female jobs, such as receptionist, may "unofficially" require female attractiveness. However, being very physically attractive may be a negative for women who aspire to nontraditional jobs, such as in management, perhaps because attractive women are taken less seriously than attractive men (Cash & Trimer, 1984; Dullea, 1985; Heilman & Stopeck, 1985). This negative effect of attractiveness for nontraditional women is strongest when raters are men (Holahan & Stephan, 1981). Even when attractive women are rated positively, their successful performance is more likely to be attributed to external factors (such as favoritism by others) than to their own abilities (B. A. Spencer & Taylor, 1988). Thus, women aspiring to executive positions may be well advised to wear tailored clothes, little makeup and jewelry, and a conservative hairstyle. The popular film *Working Girl* demonstrated how important it is for a secretary who aspires to an executive job to tone down her traditionally feminine appearance.

With respect to facial expressiveness, too, women are judged more critically, at least by White college students (F. M. Deutsch, LeBaron, & Fryer, 1987). If women do not smile and act warmly, they are evaluated more negatively than similarly behaving men. Women in professional positions may be in a bind: if they act too "feminine" by using too much makeup and jewelry and by smiling too much, they may be taken less seriously than male colleagues; however, if professional women do not use makeup or smile, they may be judged as too "masculine." A very narrow spectrum of behavior is considered appropriate for professional women, unlike for professional men. (See also Wolf, 1991.)

In summary, much of the sex bias demonstrated in laboratory research appears to operate unconsciously (V. Brown & Geis, 1984) and in increasingly subtle ways. Evaluations of individuals on the basis of their gender are affected by a variety of situational and personal factors, some of which may favor women. Still, to the extent that an irrelevant variable such as gender enters into any evaluation of an individual, it is unfair. Furthermore, many workplace settings where personal evaluations are important (such as for promotions) are traditionally male-dominated. In such settings, prejudice tends to operate against women. We will examine evidence of gender discrimination in the workplace after first evaluating some of the myths people hold regarding women workers.

Myths about women employees   Many myths exist regarding women employees. These myths contribute to workplace discrimination either directly (when a women isn't hired because of a myth) or indirectly (by virtue of the general attitude toward women employees as different from "regular"— read "male"—employees). Let's examine some of the most common myths more closely.

Myth 1: Women work just for "pin money." *Fact:* As discussed earlier, most women work out of economic necessity, as do men.

Myth 2: Women don't really want to work or to have a career. *Fact:* Although it is true that men are more likely than women to think of their work as a career, this is true only among workers over age 29 (Belkin, 1989). Furthermore, most employed women still would work even if they did not have to, although employed mothers are increasingly feeling squeezed by the double burden (labor force and domestic responsibilities) they carry (Balter, 1991). The reason some women employees appear less committed to the work force than men employees is due to women's greater likelihood of being in low-status, low-paying jobs. When organizational job level is held constant, female and male workers view job dimensions and work outcomes in similar ways (Rosenbach, Dailey, & Morgan, 1979). Women and men are equally concerned about getting ahead when they have a realistic chance of being promoted, and are equally concerned that work be self-actualizing (Kanter, 1977; Renwick & Lawler, 1978; Yankelovich, 1981). Furthermore, men and women require similar job characteristics to be satisfied in their jobs (Pines & Kafry, 1981; Voydanoff, 1980). The one exception to the overall pattern of women's general attachment to the work force is blue-collar women, half of whom would choose to stay home if they could. Interestingly, we don't know how many men employees would do the same.

Myth 3: Women are less reliable employees than men. *Fact:* Although it is true that women are more likely than men to be absent from work—5.5 days a year for women, 4.3 days a year for men ("Study Finds," 1989)—the reasons for these absences appear different for the two sexes. Women are out more often for shorter periods of time because of acute illnesses; men are out for longer periods of time because of chronic illnesses. But employee illness probably does not account fully for employee absences, especially for women. Rather, women are more likely than men to be absent due to child-care-related activities. Since such absences are not officially excused, women tend to report these absences as personal illnesses (Englander-Golden & Barton, 1983). Therefore, if women had more support for child care from partners, companies, or communities, women's work absences probably would decrease. Supporting evidence for this hypothesis comes from statistics on women and men without children, who do not differ significantly in sick-leave hours. Thus, women are not by virtue of their gender less reliable employees; rather, some women are disproportionately burdened with the responsibility of young children, which, in turn, occasionally affects work attendance.

Myth 4: Women have a higher job turnover rate than men and thus their training and education often are wasted. *Fact:* Among young people (under age 25), there is no difference in turnover rates between women and men in the labor force in general, or in traditionally male-dominated jobs in particular (U.S. Department of Labor, 1985c; Waite & Berryman, 1985). Between ages 35 and 44, however, men average 7.7 years in their job compared with 4.6 years for women. This difference is due to

the greater likelihood of women's than men's interrupting their work history to care for children. However, women today are increasingly likely to stay in the labor force even when they have young children. Most employed women are out of the labor force less than one year after childbirth. The main factor that determines whether a pregnant woman will quit the labor force upon childbirth is her earnings: the lower, the more likely she is to quit (Glass, 1988). When low earnings are combined with structural constraints (such as inconvenient work hours and lack of adequate child care), job quitting becomes even more likely.

Factors other than childbirth and child rearing also affect job turnover rates. Job dissatisfaction and low earnings are strong predictors of job change for women (Glass, 1988). As we have seen, women tend to have less education and be in lower-paying, lower-status jobs than men. When skill level, education level, age of worker, and length of service are controlled for, there is no significant difference between the sexes in job turnover (U.S. Department of Labor, 1975). Among professionals, women may have somewhat higher turnover rates than men, but they do not appear to be leaving jobs to stay home. (Fewer than 10% quit to stay home; C. H. Deutsch, 1990b.) Rather, women are more likely than men to leave because they are unhappy with gender-related aspects of the job, such as work-family conflicts, sexual harassment, and a general "old boys" atmosphere (these last two aspects of jobs will be discussed later) (Graddick & Farr, 1983; Saltzman, 1991; F. N. Schwartz, 1989).

As the amount of time women interrupt their employment continues to decrease, differences between the length of women's and men's work lives will continue to shrink. As it is, women average 11 fewer years in the labor force than men, but they still put in between 24 and 35 years (U.S. Department of Labor, 1983). Thus, job training for women is not wasted. If the workplace became more congenial to women in general and ways were found to reduce the conflict between work and family life in particular, women's job interruptions and turnover rates would be reduced even further.

Myth 5: Women have different aptitudes than men and therefore should stick to "women's jobs." *Fact:* As reviewed in Part 2, there are very few group differences between males and females in aptitudes, intelligence, or behavior, and what differences exist are not all-or-none (for example, some females are better at mathematics than some males). In addition, most jobs are genderless—tradition and status, not aptitudes, have labeled jobs as more appropriate for one sex than another. For example, it is commonly believed that women have greater manual dexterity than men, a belief used to justify employing women in low-paying jobs like typing and making electronics components (Messing, 1982). Great manual dexterity is also required in surgery and mechanics, yet these jobs are nearly exclusively male ones.

Myth 6: Women take jobs away from men. *Fact:* Women and men traditionally have not competed for the same jobs. As we have seen, the labor force is markedly segregated by gender. Because women make up about 45% of the work force, if they all quit, the economy would collapse. The reason that nearly two-thirds of the displaced workers in the United States in the 1980s were men was that the manufacturing field, which predominantly employed men, has been shrinking, not because more women entered the labor force (Serrin, 1984). Most women entering the labor force go into the service sector, which has been expanding. Yet men are reluctant to move into "women's jobs." As more women enter the work force and apply for nontraditional jobs, however, they will be competing with men. Thus, some women may get jobs that otherwise would have gone to men. However, those jobs don't belong to men exclusively, nor do men necessarily need a job more than women. In a society that prides itself on equal opportunity and the hiring of the best worker, this situation simply will have to be accepted.

Myth 7: Mixing the sexes in the work environment disrupts concentration. *Fact:* Laboratory research has found that mixed-sex groups perform as well as or better than single-sex groups (Wood, 1987). This may be due to combining men's typically more task-oriented style with women's typically more interpersonally oriented style. Although mixed-sex groups initially may be more self-conscious than single-sex groups, they tend to adjust with time (Aries, 1977; Kanter, 1977). Group members of both sexes may be better motivated in mixed-sex groups than in same-sex groups or individually (N. L. Kerr & Sullaway, 1983).

If there are problems in mixed-sex groups, they do not revolve around productivity but rather group dynamics. In general, women in mixed-sex groups tend to be less assertive, less competitive, less influential, and perceived as less competent than men, at least in laboratory settings (Wood & Karten, 1986). In the workplace, women may be at a disadvantage in mixed-sex groups mainly when they are in the minority or hold only "token" status. In such circumstances, gender becomes more salient, and

the token tends to feel isolated and powerless (Cota & Dion, 1986; Hans & Eisenberg, 1985; Hennig & Jardim, 1977; Kanter, 1977; Kanter & Stein, 1980). When men are tokens, however, they still tend to be influential, another indication of how gender is related to social status (J. M. Craig & Sherif, 1986; Yoder, 1991). Thus, women in mixed-sex groups may need extra support, and men in such groups may need to become more sensitive to gender dynamics. Given training and time, increased numbers of women in mixed-sex groups, and institutional supports, such problems should be reduced.

Myth 8: Women cannot handle positions of power and men would not want to work under them. *Fact:* Much field research has demonstrated that sex does not strongly affect leadership style or ability, although it may affect co-workers' expectations and perceptions of the leader (Dobbins & Platz, 1986; Powell, 1988). Eagly and Johnson (1990) conducted a meta-analysis of 269 studies done in organizational settings and concluded that there was no overall gender difference in leadership. Furthermore, subordinates usually are equally satisfied with male and female supervisors (see O'Leary, 1988, for a review of the literature). However, people who have not had a woman supervisor generally say they prefer men as bosses, possibly due to gender stereotypes of men as leaders and men's greater access to power.

Agentic traits appear important in a manager, but such traits can be possessed by women as well as men (Arkkelin & Simmons, 1985; Brenner, Tomkiewicz, & Schein, 1989; Powell & Butterfield, 1989). Thus, masculine-sex-typed and androgynous managers tend to be preferred over feminine-sex-typed and undifferentiated managers, regardless of gender. Current thinking suggests that optimal leadership may require androgynous behaviors—that is, a blend of communal and agentic behaviors—and not solely agentic behaviors as is sometimes thought, especially by men (Cann & Siegfried, 1990). Interestingly, most of the individuals in supervisory leadership positions appear to be androgynous, although this is truer for women than men (Kapalka & Lachenmeyer, 1988).

Recently, there has been some discussion of women managers' greater tendency to use a more democratic or participative style of managing as opposed to a more autocratic style, at least when given the opportunity to do so ($d = .21$ in Eagly and Johnson's 1990 meta-analysis; see also Helgesen, 1990; Rosener, 1990). A democratic leadership style has certain advantages with respect to worker morale and for tasks involving discussion and negotiation (Kushell & Newton, 1986; Wood, 1987). Such a leadership style, then, may be beneficial in terms of worker retention and therefore long-term productivity. (See Figure 11.5 for a "humorous" glimpse of how a democratic style may be perceived by others.) Yet it would be incorrect to conclude that a democratic style is always better than an autocratic style or that all women use one leadership style and all men another. Much depends on the specific task and the specific situation. When short-term productivity is the objective, an autocratic style may be most efficient. Furthermore, when women are in extremely male-dominated roles, they tend to use stereotypically masculine styles of leadership (S. Gordon, 1991). Companies can either encourage or discourage one style or a variety of styles in their managers. Interestingly, as Japanese businesses have become ascendant in the world, American companies are starting to adopt aspects of Japan's more cooperative management style (see, for example, Kanter, 1983). This has meant sending many male managers to training workshops to learn management styles that already are in the repertoire of many female managers.

Although women and men perform equally well in leadership positions, it is true that subordinates bring gender-related expectations to a job setting that may disadvantage women leaders. Each sex appears to prefer a leadership style congruent with their own gender (Statham, 1987). Men may find it difficult to work with a democratic-style leader and women may find it difficult to work with an autocratic-style leader. Even when men and women leaders engage in similar behaviors, they may be perceived and reacted to differently. For example,

in a laboratory study of group members' nonverbal reactions to different leaders, women leaders were responded to more negatively than men leaders, even though their behavior was scripted and therefore exactly the same (Butler & Geis, 1990). Women thus may be perceived as less effective leaders than men, although they don't actually behave any differently (V. Brown & Geis, 1984). Such gender-related expectations can account for why men are more likely than women to assume leadership and/or be perceived as leaders in unstructured situations (as discussed in Chapter 3), as well as be given leadership roles in job situations.

People in leadership positions in the workplace must be given the necessary power and authority to carry out their jobs effectively; otherwise, they may become petty and punitive. Unfortunately, women supervisors and managers sometimes are given less power than men supervisors and managers (Kanter, 1976; Liden, 1985; Riger & Galligan, 1980), which has given rise to the image of the "bitchy boss." The bad news, then, is that women and men leaders may not have equal access to power. The good news, however, is that when men and women have similar types of power, they are rated similarly by white-collar subordinates (Ragins, 1989b). Women leaders in strongly male-dominated fields, however, still may have their authority challenged more than their male peers (Sterling & Owen, 1982). So too may minority managers, especially Black women (G. W. Domhoff & Dye, 1987). As more women and minority men move into positions of leadership and power and as more attention is paid to the value of a variety of leadership styles, more adjustment will occur.

Figure 11.5 Female managers generally receive positive evaluations from their employees. (SALLY FORTH Copyright 1984 by Greg Howard. Reprinted with special permission of North America Syndicate, Inc.)

Myth 9: Women have come a long way already. *Fact:* Women's status in the labor force still has a long way to go before equity is reached, whether the criterion is salaries, occupational segregation, or presence in high-status jobs. The 1950s were a particularly bad period for women vis-à-vis the labor force, and progress since then has been slow, as demonstrated by salaries (Table 11.3), labor force participation rates (Figure 11.2), and attainment of advanced educational degrees (Table 11.1). Only in 1985 did the wage gap start decreasing from its previous record in 1955 (Table 11.2). The percentage of doctorates in science awarded to women has just begun to surpass the rate during the 1920s (nearly 30%) (J. W. Brown, Aldrich, & Hall, 1978). Finally, occupational segregation shows little sign of decreasing much further, because the fastest growing jobs are in the female-dominated service sector.

These nine myths all serve to perpetuate job discrimination against women. Let's look more closely at how such discrimination becomes manifest in the labor force.

Workplace discrimination As discussed earlier, although differential education, experience, and work interruptions can partially account for the salary and status differential between women and men in the labor force, much of the differential remains unexplained. This unexplained difference can be attributed either directly or indirectly to discrimination. From our review of circumstances likely to elicit gender prejudice and the myths commonly held about female workers, we can begin to see how and where workplace discrimination can occur.

The first opportunity for discrimination comes about in the hiring process and is most apparent with respect to sex-typed jobs. Generally speaking, when hypothetical job candidates (identical except for applicant sex) apply for traditionally male jobs (such as college professor or business manager), male applicants are more likely to be considered, and recommended for higher positions, than similarly qualified female applicants (Bronstein, Black, Pfennig, & White, 1986; Firth, 1982; Glick, Zion, & Nelson, 1988; Landy & Farr, 1980; Powell, 1988). Conversely, female applicants are more likely to be hired for traditionally female jobs (such as receptionist/secretary). For gender-neutral jobs (such as administrative assistant in a bank), gender alone does not appear to be a major factor in evaluations. Employers tend to match applicant gender with the gender of those already in the job, although such gender bias is subtle and not always found

(Powell, 1987; Swim et al., 1989). Thus, gender segregation of the labor force contributes to occupational stereotyping, which contributes to differential hiring, which contributes to continued segregation. A vicious cycle thus is perpetuated.

Branscombe and Smith (1990) outline a model of how stereotypes affect decision making. First, the target's gender and/or race activates the relevant group stereotype. For example, a woman job candidate will automatically activate stereotypes about women. Second, this stereotype filters or enhances other information about the target. For example, a rater learning that a particular female candidate is independent might remember this quality more than she or he would if a male job candidate were described similarly. Third, in order to make a decision about a minority target in contrast to a White male target, additional information may be needed for the rater to feel confident. For example, since an independent woman may be viewed as unusual, more information is needed to determine what this woman really is like. Finally, a decision is made based not only on the preceding processes but also on the rater's own identity as a prejudiced or unprejudiced person. For example, gender stereotypes may negatively affect the way a female job candidate is perceived, but she still may be recommended for the job if the rater considers it socially desirable to do so or wants to appear unprejudiced. Thus, discerning bias in decision making is a complex undertaking, especially in a social climate that discourages overt expressions of prejudice.

From these and other research studies, we can list a number of factors that can reduce hiring discrimination. When job candidates are individuated, such as happens in real-life interviews, less outright discrimination occurs for entry-level positions (Graves & Powell, 1988; Swim et al., 1989). When specific counterstereotypic information is available (for example, when the female job applicant for a traditionally male job is described as possessing strong agentic traits or as calling herself "Ms."), gender discrimination also is reduced (Dion & Schuller, 1990; Glick et al., 1988). Furthermore, when employers signal that gender discriminatory behavior is unacceptable or undesirable, gender discrimination also is minimized (D. Katz, 1987; Larwood, Szwajkowski, & Rose, 1988).

Perhaps more common today than entry-level discrimination is discrimination in the related areas of tracking and job advancement. These areas are difficult to research because subjective factors (such as "fitting in") play such a large role here.

Young women with college or advanced degrees applying for white-collar jobs now stand as much chance of being hired as their male peers, although they may be hired for or tracked into slightly different jobs. Blue-collar and pink-collar applicants, older applicants, and applicants with less than a college education may face more gender discrimination in hiring than white-collar applicants. Women compared to men tend to be employed in smaller organizations, which may have more variable salary and promotion practices (Dreher, Dougherty, & Whitely, 1989). Even women and men in the same organization with the same education and experience may be given different employment opportunities, which in turn constrain future employment options. For example, in legal departments, male lawyers are more likely than female lawyers to be assigned professionally advantageous big business cases, often because the men have greater outside contacts and greater geographic mobility (Roach, 1990). Similarly, the U.S. State Department has been found guilty of discriminating against women in the assignment and promotion of foreign service officers (Rowley, 1987). Men were more likely to be assigned jobs above their rank and in the more prestigious political and economic areas; women were more likely to be assigned jobs below their rank and in the less prestigious consular areas.

The reasoning for differential job assignments may not appear gender-specific, but the results are: White men soon surpass women and minority men in salary and status. As we have seen, as job status increases in every field, the percentage of women decreases. Minority women, in particular, are over-represented in the lowest status, lowest paying jobs and earn less than their minority male peers (P. H. Collins, 1990; Woody & Malson, 1984). In general, White men tend to experience unlimited career opportunities; women and minority men tend to experience blocked mobility, the "glass ceiling" effect (Blum & Smith, 1988; Greenhaus et al., 1990; Morrison & Von Glinow, 1990; O'Leary & Ickovics, 1991). Contrary to a prevailing stereotype, Black women in management do not appear to be "doubly advantaged" (Fulbright, 1987; Nkomo & Cox, 1989). Other groups frequently facing workplace discrimination are lesbians and gay men (M. P. Levine & Leonard, 1984; Melton, 1989).

Why do (White) male employees receive more and bigger promotions than female employees (J. R. Cole, 1979; Gupta, Jenkins, & Beehr, 1983; "You've Come," 1984)? Why, when female and male workers are matched for skill, education, tenure on the job, and so on, does the salary gap still remain (Crosby,

1982; Linscott, 1984)? The answer typically is not conscious gender discrimination, in the sense that most supervisors do not think they are making decisions based exclusively on their employee's gender. Nevertheless, gender factors are involved. For example, a survey of male and female business school graduates similar in work experience and socioeconomic backgrounds found that by five years after graduation, the men earned significantly more money than the women (Dreher et al., 1989). Part of this salary difference may have been due to women's greater likelihood of working for small organizations (because they were more likely to be hired for such jobs in the first place). However, part of the salary difference appeared due to men's greater success in negotiating higher salaries. Men who bargain with their employers (for example, who offer superiors an exchange or who remind them of past favors) are more likely to receive higher salaries than those who don't, whereas women who bargain with their employers are likely to receive smaller salaries than those who don't. Thus, the same behaviors on the part of men and women may be perceived and reacted to differently, a finding we have encountered in other contexts. For example, a woman speaking to a man in an assertive style is less influential than a man speaking in such a style (Carli, 1989a). Men seem to be more influenced by women who speak in a tentative style, although women listeners are not. Thus, women may have a narrower range of acceptable behavior than men, and they may need to adapt their behavior to the gender of their evaluator in ways unnecessary for men.

A classic case of a different standard's being applied to a woman than to a man aspiring to a high-status position is the case of Ann Hopkins, who successfully sued the accounting firm of Price Waterhouse for sex discrimination after she was denied partnership in the firm (Fiske, Bersoff, Borgida, Deaux, & Heilman, 1991). Ms. Hopkins joined Price Waterhouse in 1978 and successfully brought in $40 million in new business, more than any of the 87 other candidates (all male) nominated for partnership in 1982. Whereas 47 of the candidates were invited to become partners, Ms. Hopkins's nomination was placed on hold. To become a partner, a candidate is evaluated by the existing partners. Of the 32 partners who evaluated Ms. Hopkins, 8 recommended against her and 3 recommended postponing the decision. Most of the opposition came from partners who had had limited contact with her. The opposition centered on her "interpersonal skills," which many felt were "unfeminine."

For example, she was described as authoritative, tough, and prone to using profanity. It was recommended that she wear makeup and jewelry and learn how to walk, talk, and dress "more femininely." When she was not renominated for partnership the following year, Ms. Hopkins left the company and filed suit, finally settled in federal district court in 1990, which found that such gender stereotyping qualifies as sex discrimination. This case indicates how subjective the criteria are in many promotion decisions, and how the same behavior that may be viewed as laudable in a man may be viewed as a problem in a woman. Many of the significant factors that promote gender bias and discrimination were present in Hopkins's case: she violated gender stereotypes, she aspired to a high-status, male-dominated position, her critics did not know her well, and the criteria for promotion were ambiguous. As numerous studies have shown, the more ambiguous the job or evaluation criteria, the more likely it is that stereotypical evaluations will occur (Lenney et al., 1983; Martinko & Gardner, 1983; Siegfried, 1982).

Awareness of sex discrimination has increased since the early 1970s, and today, a majority of the adult public believes that women are discriminated against in the labor force (Thom, 1984). Of employed women, nearly half say they personally have been discriminated against in the workplace (Dowd, 1983). However, many women still are not aware of sex discrimination; if aware of it, they downplay its effects in their own job situation. People seem reluctant to acknowledge being personally disadvantaged (Crosby, Pufall, Snyder, O'Connell, & Whalen, 1989). Some women just accept sex discrimination as a condition of employment, especially if they have a male supervisor or work on a male-sex-typed task (Calder & Ross, 1977). Because women generally compare themselves to other women in deciding how good their own job is, they may not notice or feel affected by the fact that their male colleagues earn much more than they do or advance further and faster (Crosby, 1982). Therefore, just asking women employees if they personally feel discriminated against is not a good index of workplace discrimination.

Overall, gender discrimination in the workplace typically operates in indirect ways through occupational and personal stereotyping, through different job assignments and advancement opportunities, and through ambiguous evaluative criteria. A survey of more than 200 chief executive officers found that almost three-fourths were aware of barriers to women's advancement in corporations (Skrzycki, 1990a). The major stumblings blocks identified were stereotyping and preconceptions (81%), a reluctance to take risks with women in line positions (49%), and a lack of careful career planning and planned job assignments (47%). To counteract such subtle processes, employers need to set up clear evaluation criteria, train supervisors in the use of such criteria and in awareness of gender and racial stereotypes, support employees who have both cultural and job-related minority status, and send clear messages that gender and race discrimination are undesirable and will not be tolerated.

Overt discrimination can be reduced, if not completely eliminated. More difficult to change are the subtle aspects of a workplace environment that may serve as barriers to equal opportunity on the job. To these we now turn.

The Workplace Environment

The barriers to equality that women and minorities face in the labor force go beyond direct discrimination. Intangible aspects of the workplace environment may be much more salient on an everyday basis. The general atmosphere in the work setting, including the values that are promoted, affects workers' feelings of comfort and belonging. The behavior of one's colleagues—whether supportive, as in the presence of mentors, or nonsupportive, as in the presence of sexual harassment—also affects one's ability to fit in and advance.

Atmosphere and values   Men and women perceive the workplace environment very differently. Whereas most men tend to perceive the workplace as one where women have equal opportunity, most women perceive the workplace as inhospitable. For example, in a survey of middle managers and executives at Fortune 500 companies, 56% of the men but only 23% of the women believed a woman could become a CEO based on performance alone (Hymowitz, 1989). Similarly, half the men but only one-third the women believed men and women work well together and that men accept women as peers. In a national sample of over 800 employees, 55% of the women but only 33% of the men reported that most men don't take women seriously at work (Belkin, 1989). Among astronomers as well, 40% of the women felt they had been discriminated against in terms of general social treatment but only 12% of their male colleagues shared their perception (Flam, 1991).

Why do men and women perceive the work environment for women in different ways? Part of the reason may stem from the difficulty any privileged group has in acknowledging how they benefit from unearned privilege, whether that privilege be due to gender, race, religion, sexual orientation, or other factors (McIntosh, 1988). When institutions in general, and workplace settings in particular, are designed for (White) men's lives, experiences, interests, and styles, such environments seem "normal" for men. That is, (White) men define the norm, and others who want "in" have to fit in. Thus, most male-dominated fields, and professional careers in general, are based on a full-time, uninterrupted work career and characterized by competitive and hierarchical work arrangements. To the extent that women's lives, experiences, interests, and styles differ from those of men (for example, because of work interruptions due to child bearing or a preference for cooperative, democratic work arrangements), women are disadvantaged in traditionally male environments. Minority men may be disadvantaged as well.

Given the "masculine" work atmosphere and values of most male-dominated jobs, it is not surprising that many women perceive themselves and are perceived by others as not fitting in. Most college women view such traditionally male characteristics as competitiveness, assertiveness, aggressiveness, and a loud voice as being necessary for women's success in professional jobs (Sacks, 1989). Such traditionally female characteristics as vulnerability, emotionality, or soft-spokenness are seen as handicaps for professional women. To the extent that women do not see themselves as masculine-sex-typed, they may decide against professional careers. To the extent that such careers do indeed demand exclusively masculine-sex-typed characteristics, only a small group of women would qualify. Even these women may not fit in, however, since they may be seen as "unfeminine," as was the case with Ann Hopkins. More to the point, however, may be the cost to people, corporations, and society of rejecting so completely the presence of expressive-nurturant traits in corporate leaders (see Gordon, 1991; P. A. McBroom, 1986). As noted earlier, the best managers and leaders actually may be androgynous.

Beyond desirable personality characteristics, however, is the management style that is promoted and rewarded. To the extent that women prefer to use and to work for people who use a democratic management style, women will feel less comfortable in traditionally male work environments, which tend to be characterized by an autocratic management style (see "Myth 8" earlier). Since the higher one goes in terms of salary and status in the work force, the greater is the male dominance, such

dynamics serve to keep the majority of women out of the top positions. It's not that women cannot use autocratic styles; they can, and indeed may have to in order to advance in the corporate world. It's more that such styles may be less comfortable for more women than men. This dynamic may explain why women managers have a higher turnover rate than men managers. Women leave not to stay home (only 7% do) but because of an "inhospitable corporate climate" (Loden, 1986). Many wind up starting their own businesses, where they can create their own work atmosphere (Parrish, 1986; Saltzman, 1991). By 1995, women will start half of all new businesses, up from 10% in 1960. The irony is that corporations are losing talented women and minority men as managers at a time when the number of White males in the labor force is decreasing and research is revealing the benefits of different management styles and traits (Castro, 1990; Helgesen, 1990). To get the best people, corporations will have to cultivate and appreciate diversity. Such change is just beginning.

Traditionally male-dominated blue-collar jobs present an even more formidable barrier for many women. Not only are masculine traits and values dominant, but co-worker hostility may also be more overt than in white-collar jobs. Perhaps because white-collar males are closer to the top of the status pyramid than blue-collar males, the latter feel more threatened by competition from women. If blue-collar men are not dominant in society, as men "should be," at least they can be dominant over women. When women enter such workplaces, they typically are met with a great deal of male co-worker resistance and direct hostility (G. A. Fine, 1987a; Palmer & Lee, 1990; Schroedel, 1990; Swerdlow, 1989). For example, women may be singled out for the worst assignments or publicly belittled. The workplace itself may become sexualized, with sexual jokes and sexual images abounding. Men may relate to female co-workers in a sexualized manner, propositioning and/or harassing them. Such behaviors help men accommodate women in traditionally male settings because such behaviors reestablish the traditional male-female role of dominance/submission, whether in terms of competence or sexuality. If a man is older and a woman younger, a "father-daughter" relationship may occur. Over time, if women stay in such jobs, the men may begin to treat them individually as equals. Typically, however, men retain their views of women as inferior workers and sexual objects. Such an atmosphere still may be hard for many women to take. They may become "one of the boys," or at least accept "boys' rules," but many find this adaptation to be a strain. Thus, despite the better pay, many women leave traditionally male blue-collar jobs for lower paying but more "compatible" female-dominated ones. This is one more way gender segregation of the workplace is maintained.

Women workers who belong to unions have an advantage over nonunion women, especially with respect to harassment on the job. Unions offer workers a structured grievance process for filing complaints, and union grievances carry more weight than those individually filed. Union women also earn 30% more than nonunion women and have greater access to job mobility and educational opportunities (Grenier, 1988; National Commission on Working Women, 1990). For all these reasons, plus the growing recognition among women that only by organizing can they make gains, women are more likely than men to vote for a union in their workplace. The fastest growing unionization efforts are taking place in occupations dominated by women (for example, household workers, nurses, secretaries). Although only 16% of women workers were unionized in 1985, one out of three new union members was a woman. Because of this trend, although most unions still are run by men, "women's issues" (such as pay equity, child care, and parental leave) have become union issues and thus have garnered more attention.

Co-worker behavior   As we have seen with respect to blue-collar workers, co-worker behavior can have direct and indirect effects on one's comfort in one's job and one's prospects for advancement. In traditionally male jobs, co-worker behavior generally operates to support men and to deter women. Such deterrence can take direct forms, such as sexual harassment. But it can also take indirect forms, such as the lack of mentors and role models for women and minority men. Let's look more closely at these behaviors.

Women are particularly vulnerable to *sexual harassment* in the workplace, which the Equal Employment Opportunity Commission defines as follows: "Unwelcome sexual advances, requests for sexual favors, and other verbal or physical conduct of a sexual nature constitute sexual harassment when (1) submission to such conduct is made explicitly or implicitly a term or condition of an individual's employment, (2) submission to or rejection of such conduct by an individual is used as the basis for employment decisions affecting such

individual, or (3) such conduct has the purpose or effect of unreasonably interfering with an individual's work performance or creating an intimidating, hostile, or offensive working environment" ("Equal Employment," 1980, p. 25025). Sexual harassment can range from demands for sexual intercourse to brushes against one's body to suggestive jokes or ogling. The key aspect of sexual harassment is the undesired highlighting of one's sexual identity that interferes with one's ability to do one's job. Such behavior is not only undesirable and unpleasant, but it is also illegal since it is a form of sex discrimination. Not only is the harasser legally liable, but employers are as well if they do nothing about such situations when they are brought to the employers' (or supervisors') attention.

Numerous studies since the late 1970s have documented that about half of all women employees have experienced some form of sexual harassment (L. Fitzgerald, Shullman, et al., 1988; Gutek, 1985; U.S. Merit Systems Protection Board, 1988). Although men sometimes are sexually harassed as well (about 10 to 15% of men report harassment), nearly all harassers are male and the most common pattern is a man harassing a woman. Such harassment can result in stress, lowered self-esteem, poor performance, and damaged careers. About 10% of women have quit a job because of sexual harassment. Unfortunately, few victims of sexual harassment recognize their victimization (M. B. Brewer & Berk, 1982; MacKinnon, 1979). Some women think such behaviors are "normal" from men, or are "just part of the job," or that they may be "oversensitive" or even, somehow, to blame. Many people are unaware that sexual harassment is a crime (it was only recognized as such in 1976). These factors, together with a belief that organizations will do nothing to correct the situation, result in the fact that only a small minority of women file a formal complaint. The perception that organizations will be unresponsive unfortunately is true. In one study of 160 big corporations, 90% had received complaints from female employees concerning sexual harassment, but most had done nothing about them ("Ninety Percent," 1988). Yet the situation is changing slowly, as more and more court cases demonstrate that employers are legally liable for maintaining a workplace free of sexual harassment (Coles, 1986; Pollack, 1990).

Sexual harassment in the workplace primarily is due to patriarchal norms and sex role spillover, the process by which one's gender role "spills over" into one's work role (Gutek, 1985). Because the male gender role involves power and sexual aggressiveness, and because the female gender role involves submissiveness, nurturance, and sexual objectification, workplace settings in which men and women come in contact with each other may elicit such spillover. Those work settings that are most likely to elicit sex role spillover are those in which one sex predominates. In such settings, gender and sexual issues become most salient. In female-dominated settings, token males are more likely to be "mothered" than harassed, due to the nature of the female sex role (Ott, 1989). But in male-dominated settings, token females are likely to be treated in a sexual fashion, partly so men can act out their role expectations, but also partly to keep women in their place. Surveys of women in male-dominated occupations find that over 75% have experienced at least one form of sexual harassment (Ellis, 1990; Lafontaine & Tredeau, 1986; Schroedel, 1990). The intent of sexual harassment often is to demonstrate power and/or privilege rather than sexual interest or desire, although sexual contact may occur. Such behavior is very effective: the more sexualized a woman's work environment, the lower her job satisfaction and the greater the likelihood of her quitting (Gutek, 1985). In contrast, men's reactions to a sexualized work environment are rarely negative. If men do receive sexual overtures from women, they are more likely to be flattered than threatened. But women's overtures are much less frequent than men's and carry less threat since women, both physically and in their work role, typically are less powerful than men. (See Chapter 12 for further discussion of the dynamics of sexual harassment.)

Companies will need to do more than they're currently doing to eliminate sexual harassment in the workplace. Not only is such behavior a barrier to equal employment opportunity for women, but such behavior is also costing companies nearly $7 million a year in expenses for such related costs as low productivity, absenteeism, and employee turnover ("Ninety Percent," 1988). A long-term solution would be to eliminate gender segregation of occupations, since sexual harassment is least likely to occur when men and women are represented in equal numbers in the work setting. A more short-term solution involves sending a clear signal from the top that sexual harassment will not be tolerated and that those who work to eliminate it will be rewarded (Gutek, 1985).

Another aspect of work environments, especially male-dominated ones, that disadvantages women is the *old boy network.* In many professional fields,

career advancement takes place through informal social contacts. Someone knows someone who has a job. Someone plays golf with or belongs to the same country club as a senior executive. Someone has a top student who is just right for that postdoctoral opening heard about over drinks at a professional conference. What all these scenarios have in common is the importance of personal contacts. Jobs and promotions frequently go to people who are known, either directly or indirectly, to employers. Given that (1) most of the people with power in organizations are White men, and (2) most social networks are gender- and race-segregated, it should not be surprising that White male employees fit more easily into such networks than women and minority men. For example, an examination of over 4000 businesses found that word-of-mouth recruiting tended to reproduce existent racial patterns for mixed-sex jobs (Braddock, 1990).

Women tend not to become as involved as men in colleague systems, especially where they are numerically a minority (Kanter, 1977; O'Leary & Ickovics, 1991; Riger & Galligan, 1980). In such settings, as we have seen, women frequently feel like and are perceived as outsiders. Women belong to fewer professional organizations, limit their own professional interactions, and generally put in fewer hours (often because they have family responsibilities). In addition, women usually are excluded (and exclude themselves) from informal channels of communication, like lunches, in which they may stand out and feel uncomfortable. A number of private clubs, such as the Bohemian Club in California, actually exclude women. Yet these are places where major career contacts are made and strengthened (W. Domhoff, 1981; McQuade, 1985). Such "outsider" status carries professional costs. For example, women tend to be cited in professional publications less frequently than men, which may contribute to their work's being underrecognized and undersupported (Helmreich, Spence, Beane, Lucker, & Matthews, 1980; J. S. Long, 1990; Persell, 1983).

To counteract the "old boy network," scores of professional women's groups have begun in the last 20 years—for example, the Women's Forum, Women in Business, and the Association for Women in Psychology. Most of these groups were formed deliberately to create an "old girl network." Indeed, women have been instructed in how to make networking work for them (see, for example, B. B. Stern, 1981). How effective such networks are remains to be seen. Certainly they provide women with needed support. They may not, however, be as effective as men's networks in helping to build a professional reputation (S. M. Rose, 1985a).

Not only do White men fit most easily into an "old boy network," but White men also are more likely than other groups to have a *mentor*, someone who takes you under his or her wing and guides your career (Fulbright, 1987; S. E. K. Hill, Bahniuk, Dobos, & Rouner, 1989; Noe, 1988; Ragins, 1989a). Having a mentor is critically important for socialization into a profession and for professional advancement (Bahniuk, Dobos, & Hill, 1990; R. M. Hall & Sandler, 1983; O'Leary & Ickovics, 1991). For example, collaboration with a mentor is the most important factor affecting productivity for scientists (J. S. Long, 1990). Yet women and minority men in male-dominated fields are unlikely to find mentors, due both to the lack of enough women and minority men in high enough positions to serve as mentors and to the fact that White men often are reluctant to assume that role with women for gender-based reasons. Black women may have the most difficulty obtaining mentor relationships (Morrison & Von Glinow, 1990). Potential female and minority mentors, even when present, typically have less time available than men to be a mentor because of their own continued struggle for advancement. Potential male mentors for women may be concerned about possible sexual attraction or office gossip, or they may be less certain about women's career commitment or stamina than men's. The presence of young children appears to decrease women but not men scientists' opportunities for collaboration during their years of graduate study. The result of this lack of collaboration disadvantages women at the start of their career. Since later success builds upon early advantages, early disadvantages are likely to have long-term effects.

Even men who don't have a personal mentor relationship are likely to have male *role models*, people whom they admire and aspire to be like. Given the prevalence of White men in positions of achievement, White men have little difficulty finding such models. Because women and minority men in positions of achievement are harder to find, aspiring women and minority men are at a disadvantage. Yet having a successful female role model has been found to be particularly important for women, especially with regard to integrating work and family lives, and especially for nontraditional careers (Burlew, 1982; Erkut & Mokros, 1983; Gilbert, Gallessich, & Evans, 1983; Lemkau, 1983; G. Simpson, 1984; D. M. Zuckerman, 1981).

Overall, the atmosphere of most work environments serves to maintain the status quo: White men move up the career ladder while women and minority males stay at the bottom.

Overcoming the Barriers

Although barriers to equality in the workplace are numerous and powerful, ways to reduce them do exist. Major transformations are needed in society in general and workplace practices in particular. Socialization practices need to be changed so that girls are better prepared for a lifetime of employment, and boys are better prepared for accepting females as colleagues and for sharing domestic responsibilities. Conflicts between work and family life need to be addressed by the government, businesses, and men, and not just dumped in women's laps to resolve. Prejudice and discrimination against women must be eliminated, and women must assume their rightful place beside men in setting standards for *human* behavior and humane work practices. Both men and women deserve work environments that will support them and the development of their skills and aptitudes. Sexual harassment and gender favoritism should not be tolerated.

Some specific factors can help women and minority men. Training managers and supervisors in how to promote a nondiscriminatory work environment is important, as is punishing those who discriminate. Structuring the work situation also aids women and minority men. The less ambiguous the job-related requirements and expectations are, the greater the likelihood is of underrepresented groups' being fairly evaluated. Women must be placed in positions central to the operation of their organization, not just in marginal, invisible positions (O'Leary & Ickovics, 1991). Support systems and mentor programs for women and minority men also help such employees maximize their employment potential, as do programs that help underrepresented groups learn the corporate culture.

Laws can help underrepresented groups in the workplace as well, if they are used and enforced. The 1972 amendments (Title VII) to the Civil Rights Act of 1964 and the Equal Pay Act of 1963 make job and salary discrimination illegal. Sexual harassment also is illegal through a 1976 interpretation of Title VII. Laws banning sex discrimination exist; enforcing such laws is a problem. Complaints often take years to be resolved, and many employees simply do not bother. Since 1980 when the Reagan administration took office, enforcement of these laws has been markedly curtailed. For example, the number of cases filed by the Equal Employment Opportunity Commission (EEOC) involving sex discrimination in employment dropped more than 70% between 1981 and 1983 (Kennelly, 1984). EEOC's emphasis shifted away from the more far-reaching class-action lawsuits and toward more individual cases of bias (G. Evans & Fields, 1985). This change in emphasis may have made large employers less concerned about discriminating on the basis of sex. As we noted with respect to sexual harassment, most big businesses do nothing to address complaints, and most employees do not pursue their complaints through the courts. A 1989 decision by the Supreme Court restricted a 1866 civil rights law prohibiting racial discrimination to hiring situations only. Since that decision, federal judges have dismissed over 100 discrimination claims regarding racial harassment on the job ("Civil Rights," 1989).

Affirmative action legislation, meant to increase the hiring of underrepresented groups, is a good example of the limited help legislation can provide unless it is backed up by monitoring and sanctions. Affirmative action for women and minorities was mandated in the 1960s by executive orders, but did not have effective regulations for enforcement until after enactment of the Equal Employment Act of 1972. This act specified that all federal contractors with 50 or more employees must ensure the fair treatment of all employees without regard to their race, color, religion, sex, or national origin, and must establish goals and timetables for correcting deficiencies based on past discriminatory employment practices. Affirmative action involves actively recruiting underrepresented job applicants and giving preference to qualified women and minorities over equally qualified White men until such time as numerical equity is reached. During the 1970s, when monitoring and sanctions occurred, underrepresented groups were helped by affirmative action policies, Black women more than White women (J. P. Smith & Ward, 1989). Since 1980, however, when sanctions were eliminated by the Reagan administration, progress has been limited (Leonard, 1989). Although the productivity of work sites where affirmative action policies are in effect is similar to that of non–affirmative action worksites, many people still believe that affirmative action requires the hiring of unqualified workers. These beliefs lead to different attributions for performance by members of targeted groups. Their successes are more likely to be attributed to luck, and failures to race or sex, than is the case for the

performance of White males. Thus, affirmative action policies may reinforce stereotypes, which, in turn, may lead to self-fulfilling prophecies (Crosby & Clayton, 1990). For affirmative action to have the desired effect, it must have the appearance of fairness and be accompanied by accurate information regarding what it involves. It also must include monitoring and sanctions. Given President Bush's philosophy and the current composition of the Supreme Court, affirmative action programs look dead.

Changes in the law in the last 30 years have certainly helped, although more change still is needed. Furthermore, when employers are warned about illegal discrimination, more bias in favor of male applicants sometimes occurs (Siegfried, 1982). The federal minimum wage law still does not apply to household workers, 97% of whom are women. Part-time workers, most of whom are women, also are denied major benefits from employers. We already have noted the absence of any national family and medical leave plan, which is a major barrier for women in the workplace. Most important, there still is no federal Equal Rights Amendment.

Until now, we have mainly been examining women's role in the labor force. As has been shown, the gender roles and stereotypes markedly affect what kinds of jobs a woman might have as well as the salary she might earn. But the roles and stereotypes also affect men's role in the labor force. And, contrary to prevailing opinion, not all effects are beneficial. We will briefly examine some of these effects.

▲ Men and the Labor Force

Whereas many women have had to struggle to enter the labor force, such participation usually is required of men by virtue of the male sex role. A woman's identity traditionally has been defined by her relationships; a man's, primarily by his job. Just as women appear always to retain responsibility for the emotional and physical well-being of their family, so men appear always to retain responsibility for the financial well-being of their family (Farrell, 1991). Although work can provide a sense of satisfaction and self-worth and is usually necessary for satisfying one's material needs, the overexaggeration of the work role for men has consequences for them that are as serious as the consequences of the overexaggeration of the home-maker role for women.

In the first place, as discussed in previous chapters, the pressure on most males to participate in the work force encourages males to develop a high achievement and competitiveness orientation. Success and status become the bedrock of the male sex role, and "masculinity" is often measured by the amount of money a man earns or by his material possessions (David & Brannon, 1976; Doyle, 1983; O'Neil, 1981b). As Warren Farrell (1991) notes, men have become "success objects," evaluated for what they produce and earn, not for who they are as people. This goal orientation and competition often obliterate other rewards of working, such as mastery of a skill. They also may lead to finding substitute ways of gaining status—one-upmanship, athletic prowess, emphasis on sexual performance— especially if one's job is not intrinsically rewarding (Fasteau, 1974; Tolson, 1977). Such intense competition and stress to achieve also may make many men more vulnerable to certain stress-related diseases.

As a result of such an achievement and competitiveness focus, some men's relationships may suffer. As discussed in Chapters 9 and 10, because they are usually trained to develop these qualities and neglect their emotional side, it is difficult for many men to trust other men and form close relationships with them, with women, and especially with their children. When work becomes a primary focus in one's life, other things and people are excluded. Many jobs actually require such exclusion. Men often are expected to work overtime, to put in many hours in work-related activities (for example, cocktail parties, golf), to travel, and so forth. Research has shown the business executive and the blue-collar worker to be particularly caught in the masculine stereotype, the former because he believes he can "make it" (Bartolome, 1972; M. Maccoby, 1976); the latter, because he realizes he cannot (Astrachan, 1986; Cazenave, 1984; Tolson, 1977). In any case, many families rarely see their "breadwinner," causing serious damage to the marital and the parent-child relationships.

In addition, when an individual's identity is defined solely by one thing, when that one thing ends, emotional problems may result. Thus, women who are identified solely as mothers may experience marked depression and loss of self-esteem when their children leave home. Similarly, many men who are unemployed or retired may experience marked depression and loss of self-esteem, often leading to alcoholism, suicide, heart attacks, and other ailments (see Chapter 8). Black men, who have the highest unemployment rates, may suffer the most severe consequences. Unemployment among men is increasing due to a decrease in jobs traditionally held by men, such as in manufacturing. Young men's earnings plunged by almost one-third between 1973 and 1984 ("Report Notes Decline," 1987). Ironically, most new jobs are in the service or clerical sector and are regarded as "women's work." Most men, given their socialization experiences plus the low salaries attached to such jobs, won't apply for such positions. Even among men who are employed, most (85%) no longer are the sole family breadwinner. The decline in the breadwinner role is most pronounced for minority men, older men, and those with little education (Wilkie, 1991). This loss of social and economic dominance may be experienced as ego-threatening. Thus, more and more men may be feeling like failures, which may be associated with disturbed interpersonal relationships and acting-out behaviors, such as drug abuse and violence.

Another negative consequence of men's viewing work as part of their masculine identity comes when women start entering traditionally male jobs. As we have seen, such women typically are met with a great deal of resistance and hostility. Many men feel threatened by equality with women, as if men's worth resides exclusively in their difference from and superiority over women. Such insecurity on the part of some men not only makes life difficult for co-workers, but is also stressful for the men who feel that way. If men's sense of self were less invested in asserting dominance over women, much job-related stress would be reduced.

Gender role factors affect men's career choices perhaps even more than women's (O'Neil & Fishman, 1986). As we have seen, men's socialization is stricter than women's with respect to avoiding gender-inappropriate activities. Thus, women are more likely than men to be interested in nontraditional jobs, and such interests on the part of women are more accepted than such interests on the part of men. For example, undergraduates consider men in nontraditional jobs to be significantly less likable, less well adjusted, and less physically attractive than women in nontraditional occupations (Shinar, 1978). Thus, although more jobs are viewed as appropriate for men than for women, gender stereotyping of occupations does limit men's career choices.

Some men do go into female-dominated jobs, despite the stigma. These men appear to be comfortable with themselves and their masculine sexuality, contrary to stereotypes (Chusmir, 1990). Men in nontraditional jobs score somewhat lower on agentic-instrumental traits than men in traditional jobs, probably because traditionally female jobs require fewer of those traits. Interestingly, men who go into nontraditional jobs generally have advantages over women who do so. As we have noted, men in predominantly female jobs tend to be supported by their co-workers, whereas women in predominantly male jobs tend to be harassed by theirs. In fact, men in predominantly female fields tend to earn more and advance faster than women in those fields. In a study of 50 such employees, Schreiber (1979) found that the nontraditional women wanted to be regarded as like the men with whom they worked, but the nontraditional men wanted to be viewed as different from and superior to their female co-workers. Thus, as we've repeatedly noted throughout the book, gender conveys status irrespective of behavior.

As many women have rejected their sex typing, many men, especially the younger ones, also are doing so. As a result of both the questioning of sex roles prompted by the women's movement and the fact that most paid work no longer provides the sense of self-worth that it is supposed to, many men are also beginning to question the responsibility and expectations placed on them (Doyle, 1983; Friedan, 1981; O'Neil & Fishman, 1986; Voydanoff, 1984). Like women, many men want more options and more satisfaction. Some retire early. Others drop out of the work force because of health problems, lack of education, or because they are economically able to do so. Still others are becoming less willing to transfer from one location to another. Many men now show a preference for shorter or more flexible work hours, and some are increasing their participation in household maintenance and child-care functions. Some even interrupt their careers to care for their children. Many men also are rejecting the whole notion of a career as being the sole means of male identity. They want a richer, fuller life, one that makes use of their full range of human potentialities. Instead of adjusting to the "Establishment," many are expecting the Establishment to become more androgynous and to adjust to them (Bernard, 1971).

▲ Summary

In this chapter we have reviewed how gender roles and stereotypes affect labor force patterns. Regardless of the measure used (status, salaries, promotional opportunities, and so on), White men are at the top of the employment hierarchy; women, especially minority women, are at the bottom.

Although women constitute almost half of all workers, they are overrepresented in the lowest paying, lowest status jobs. The labor market is gender-segregated not only vertically (men at the top, women at the bottom), but also horizontally (most employees work in same-sex workplaces).

The barriers to full equality for women in the labor force are numerous and interact in complex ways. Not only are girls and boys socialized to assume different adult roles (employment for males, motherhood for females), but also the attitudes and traits associated with these roles disadvantage females when they enter the labor force, as nearly all of them do. More important, structural barriers disadvantage women. Resolution of work and family conflicts is left entirely to women, who often must work part-time or in low-paying jobs in order to retain needed time flexibility. Stereotypic attitudes toward women's and men's capacities and traits frequently lead to discrimination against women and unearned privilege for White men in the labor force. Each sex tends to be steered into different types of jobs and given different responsibilities, which later result in differences in advancement potential. Cultural attitudes regarding women's worth have led to the devaluation of women's activities both in the home and in the labor force. Thus, traditionally female jobs have low status and low salaries. In traditionally male occupations, White men tend to experience a supportive work environment, one with compatible norms and expectations, where mentors and role models are likely to be available. In contrast, women and minority men in traditionally male occupations tend to experience a nonsupportive work environment, one whose norms and expectations may be unfamiliar and incompatible. The outsider status of women and minority men makes it more difficult for them to be part of collegial networks ("the old boy system") and to find mentors and role models. Not only is the work environment less supportive of women and minority men than it is for White men, but it is more openly hostile as well. Women and minority men frequently must deal with hostility and harassment based on their sex and/or race. Thus, the workplace operates to maintain the gender status quo.

Gender roles and stereotypes, although frequently an advantage for White males in the labor force, may have negative consequences for men as well. The compulsory nature of work and status expectations for males may restrict the development of men's full human potential and may affect their relationship with others and their own health. Many men suffer from the pressure to achieve at all costs, to define success in only material ways. The pressure to dominate and be "number one" takes its toll, especially in a declining economy where most men no longer can expect to support a family on their wages alone. Decreased occupational sex typing and decreased identification of masculinity with dominance may reduce the pressures on some men. Both women and men need to be free to develop their achievement potential in the world of work, but they can only do so in a society where domestic responsibilities are shared and where balance in and integration of home and work concerns are supported.

The workplace is changing. White males soon will be a minority of workers. If we are to make maximum use of our human resources, we must learn to deal with diversity. Change is needed in five major areas to allow women full entry into the labor force:

1. Gender stereotyping and sexist assumptions about appropriate activities for women and men must be eliminated. We must do away with the steering of males and females into different roles and occupations based solely on their gender. A revaluation of "women's work" also is needed.
2. A comprehensive family support system is needed with adequate day care and after-school care arrangements for all who need them. Parental and family leave must be available for whoever desires it, and women must receive paid maternity leave when they give birth. Men must share responsibility for domestic activities.
3. Greater job flexibility must be developed, such as with flex-time opportunities (whereby individuals work 40 hours a week but not necessarily from 9 to 5), job sharing, and part-time jobs with advancement potential. Greater flexibility in the traditional life-cycle patterns is needed, allowing males and females to alternate periods of study, employment, and work in the home without penalty.
4. Workplaces need to train managers and supervisors to encourage and support nontraditional workers and a diversity of management and interpersonal styles. Vigorous recruitment and training efforts must be made. New programs, such as assigned mentors, may be needed.
5. Strict enforcement of existing laws prohibiting sex and race discrimination, including sexual harassment, must take place. Not only employers but also the government must take active measures to ensure compliance with laws that prohibit discrimination.

All these changes entail a reordering of American priorities with greater choice for the individual and improved quality of life in contrast to the traditional concern for productivity. Whether or not we, as a society, will embrace this new goal remains to be seen. Some organizations are, in fact, changing toward a more androgynous ideal (Kanter, 1983; Peters & Waterman, 1982). Many jobs now require more emphasis on human relations and less on simple hierarchical relationships. In some cases, competition is becoming less important and, in fact, dysfunctional. Many modern businesses are requiring nonstereotyped, multifaceted functioning from workers for maximum effectiveness.

More than business practices will have to change, however, before equality is realized in the labor force. The whole basis of our society is patriarchal and therefore requires male dominance. As we will see in the next chapter, societal power resides in (White) men's hands. Thus, to eliminate inequality in the labor force means to eliminate inequality everywhere. This is a tall order, indeed.

▲ Recommended Reading

Fuchs, V. R. (1988). *Women's quest for economic equality.* Cambridge, MA: Harvard University Press. A well-developed argument that women's near-exclusive responsibility for children is at the root of women's subordinate status in the labor force.

Gutek, B. A. (1985). *Sex and the workplace: The impact of sexual behavior and harassment on women, men, and organizations.* San Francisco: Jossey-Bass. A scholarly examination of the role sex plays in work environments, based on interviewing over 1200 people and interpreted in terms of sex role spillover.

Jacobs, J. A. (1989). *Revolving doors: Sex segregation and women's careers.* Stanford, CA: Stanford University Press. A careful analysis of sex segregation in the workplace, emphasizing a social control explanation.

O'Neil, J. M., & Fishman, D. M. (1986). Adult men's career transitions and gender-role themes. In Z. Leibowitz & D. Lea (Eds.), *Adult career development: Concepts, issues, and practices* (pp. 132–162). Alexandria, VA: American Association for Counseling and Development Press. A review of research on men's career development and transitions and the importance of gender-related issues.

Schwartz, F. N. (1989). Management women and the new facts of life. *Harvard Business Review, 89,* 65–76. A controversial article describing two types of female managers—those primarily focused on their careers and those trying to balance careers and family life. Different treatment is recommended for each.

Chapter 12

Structural Power and Abuses of Power

Gender roles and stereotypes portray not only differences between the sexes and between "feminine" and "masculine" characteristics, but also power relationships. In terms of power in American society (the ability to influence others, to get done what you want to get done), women are generally at a marked disadvantage. Males, and all things viewed as masculine, have more power and higher status than females and all things viewed as feminine. In Chapter 3, we saw that males are more interested in developing power over others than are females and that males as a group do tend to exert more power over others through dominant and aggressive behaviors than do females. These gender differences in personal power are magnified at the institutional level. As Catherine MacKinnon notes,

Men's physiology defines most sports, their needs define auto and health insurance coverage, their socially designed biographies define workplace expectations and successful career patterns, their perspectives and concerns define quality in scholarship, their experiences and obsessions define merit, their objectification of life defines art, their military service defines citizenship, their presence defines family, their inability to get along with each other—their wars and ruler-ships—defines history, their image defines god, and their genitals define sex. (1987b, p. 36)

In the previous chapter, we saw how gender roles and stereotypes operate in the labor force. One clear conclusion is that women, especially those of color, are at the bottom of the labor force hierarchy in terms of job prestige, salaries, and advancement potential. This differential status is built into the very structure and fabric of society, as reflected in other societal institution, such as the economy, politics, law, and the military. In this chapter, we will examine how gender roles and stereotypes are involved in the operation of structural power as well as in the abuse of power. (For further examination of the relationship between gender and power, see Connell, 1987; Lips, 1991).

▲ Structural Power

Power in America is predominantly in the hands of the "White male club," from which women and minority males traditionally and deliberately have been excluded. Table 12.1 shows evidence of this club. In every public office, particularly the most powerful, men predominate. This is true around the world (United Nations, 1991). Patriarchy prevails, as does women's relative powerlessness. For example, fewer than 10% of the world's parliamentarians were women in 1987.

Power is important because, as a number of writers have noted (for example, Blumberg, 1979; A. Kahn, 1984), it is differential power that underlies all inequality. Western society is characterized by an ideology of domination based on gender, race, class, and sexual orientation. We need to understand how such a matrix of domination shapes both individual experience and social structures (P. H. Collins, 1990). Therefore, it will be instructive to examine four forms of structural power (economic,

Table 12.1 How men run America, 1979 and 1989

	Percentage Male	
	1979	*1989*
U.S. population	48.7	48.7
U.S. Congress	97	94
U.S. Supreme Court	100	89
Federal judgeships	95	96
Governorships	96	94
State legislatures	90	83
Statewide elective offices	89	86
County governing boards	97	91
Mayorships and councilorships	92	87

Data compiled by the Center for the American Woman and Politics.

political, legal, and military) and the sexes' relationship to them in more detail.

Economic Power

Women have less economic power than men since women are overrepresented among those in the lowest income brackets. Poverty is a women's issue and a racial one. One out of 3 Black women lived in poverty in 1980, compared to 1 out of 5 Black men, 1 out of 10 White women, and 1 out of 15 White men (McLanahan, Sorensen, & Watson, 1989). Overall, more than 3 out of 5 of the people over 17 years of age who are living below the poverty line are women. The reasons for the high rate of female poverty are complex, but three factors are important: low salaries, single parenthood, and increased longevity.

Low salaries As discussed in the previous chapter, women earn about two-thirds of what men earn. Minority women earn even less. Three out of five employed Black women earn incomes below the poverty level (Woody & Malson, 1984). Most available new jobs offer workers little chance to climb out of poverty because such jobs are in the low-paying service sector. Two-thirds of all minimum wage earners are women (National Commission on Working Women, 1990). In contrast, 41% of male employees earned more than $25,000 per year in 1988, compared to only 15% of all women workers. As income increases, the percentage of women and minority men represented at a given income level decreases. For example, 14% of White men earned $50,000 or more in 1990, compared to 4% of Black men, 2% of White women, and 1% of Black women

(Bovee, 1991b). Among those earning the highest incomes are virtually only a handful of women. Women's progress up the career ladder is slow and tends to stop in middle management. Fewer than 3% of top corporate jobs were held by women in 1990 (K. Ball, 1991b). The slight progress that has occurred for some women in professional fields over the last ten years camouflages the fact that the percentage of women in poverty has remained fairly constant during that time.

Part of what has happened economically to women since 1980 has happened to men too. During the Reagan and Bush administrations, the gap between the rich and the poor exceeded all previous records (Meisler, 1990). The income of the wealthiest 20% of Americans rose by one-third, that of the middle 60% rose only slightly, while that of the poorest 20% dropped 5%. Many working-class and middle-class families have been hard-hit by recessionary forces (high unemployment, inflation, little real salary growth) and increased taxes. The increased participation of wives in the labor force has offset slightly the effect of these factors on White family income. Among Blacks, who earn less than three-fifths the income of Whites, economic progress has been virtually stalled (Bovee, 1991b; Moses, 1989). Black men have been particularly hard-hit by the recession, and their declining economic status is a major factor in Black family poverty and female-headed households (R. M. Brewer, 1988; Wilkie, 1991).

Unemployment rates have been increasing for both women and men (U.S. Department of Labor, 1991a). Women's unemployment rate tends to be slightly higher than men's, but women are underrepresented among recipients of unemployment benefits and services (Pearce, 1985). This underrepresentation is due to the greater likelihood that female employees work part-time, at temporary jobs, and at jobs not covered by unemployment insurance (such as waitressing). Women also have been hurt by the presumption that married women are not committed to working and therefore are not entitled to unemployment benefits.

Single parenthood A major factor in the high poverty rates among women, especially Black women, is the increased number of female-headed households. Single parents head one-fourth of all families today, double the 1970 rate (Lewin, 1990c). Ninety percent of these families are headed by the mother. More than half of all Black and Hispanic female-headed families and more than one out of four White female-headed families live below the poverty level (U.S. Department of Commerce, 1988). Female-headed families represented 55% of all poor families in the United States in 1985 (Arendell, 1987). The National Advisory Council on Economic Opportunity predicts that by the year 2000, nearly the entire poverty population will be women and children living in female-headed households.

Female-headed families are in such dire economic straits for many reasons already discussed: women bear the responsibility of child care, which limits their labor force participation, child-care costs are high and usually offset employment income among the poor, displaced homemakers have few job-related skills, predominantly female jobs offer low wages, most fathers do not contribute adequately toward the economic support of their children, and government financial support is insufficient to raise families out of poverty. In essence, divorce spells poverty or near-poverty for about half of all women, and the economic plight of never-married mothers is even more severe ("Child Support Lags," 1990; Lewin, 1990a).

Increased longevity   Age also is a factor in women's poverty. Women live longer than men and 20% of all women over 60 years of age have incomes below the poverty level, with another 20% with incomes only slightly higher (K. Collins, 1988; "Social Security," 1985). Minority women have the highest poverty rate: 42% of all elderly Black women and 31% of all elderly Hispanic women live in poverty. Women over age 65 are nearly twice as likely to be poor as men over age 65, at least among Whites (McLanahan et al., 1989). The poverty of elderly women is a result of their spending most of their lives as homemakers or in low-paying jobs with few benefits. As a result, they rarely have pensions of their own, and only 10% receive pension benefits from their husband's plan if they outlive him, as 85% of married women do. Only 20% of elderly women, in contrast with 43% of elderly men, receive pension income in addition to Social Security (B. Kandel, 1986). Although older women rely more heavily on Social Security income than do men, women actually receive 20% less in such income than men (K. Collins, 1988). Thus, women who've followed traditional gender role expectations by not investing heavily in the labor force are the most penalized in their old age, especially if their spouse divorces or predeceases them.

Consequences   One consequence of men's economic dominance can be seen within the family. Economic power generally translates into family power, and traditional marriages have been based on female financial dependence. As we saw in Chapter 9, the more money a woman brings in, the more power in the family she tends to have and the more egalitarian the marriage arrangement tends to become. Interestingly, the more money a woman brings in, the more likely it is that the couple will divorce. Because a woman generally does not earn as much as her husband, the husband's dominance still is somewhat assured. This fact may work directly or indirectly to keep the salary differential wide. Women's economic status also is linked to their societal status. It should be recalled from Chapter 5 that throughout history and across cultures, the more women work in the main productive activity of a society, the more money they earn and the greater their ability to control their personal destiny—marriage, divorce, sex, children, free movement, education, and household power. Thus, women's economic power is the strongest predictor of their relative equality and freedom.

Because of patriarchal ideology, the male-dominated upper-class nuclear family is idealized, and the needs of women, especially women not living in such families, are ignored. Figure 12.1 gives one example of this deliberate blindness. Because of this insensitivity, public policies generally affect women adversely. For example, when President Reagan took office in 1981, he systematically cut federal social welfare expenditures—food stamps, Medicaid, Aid to Families with Dependent Children (AFDC)—with a consequent increase in the number of people living in poverty, most of whom were women. These cuts also decreased even further the poor's already inadequate quality of life (Rix, 1988). In 1987, the total federal share of AFDC was less than 1% of the federal budget while national defense consumed 27% (Funiciello, 1990). The massive transfer of government funds from the civilian economic sector, where 99% of employed women work, to military production also affected women negatively. It is clear that women and children are low priorities for our government: in 1990, the total federal share of AFDC was just over 1% of the cost of bailing out savings and loan institutions. Overall, the United States spends a smaller proportion of its gross national product on social programs than any other advanced industrial nation except Japan (Rix, 1988).

Figure 12.1 How to maintain the image of America as the land of good and plenty: Ignore the lives of women and other people without power. (Copyright © 1982 by Field Enterprises, Inc. From the book, *My Weight Is Always Perfect For My Height—Which Varies*, by Nicole Hollander. Reprinted with permission from St. Martin's Press, Inc., New York, NY.)

The consequences of male dominance of the economy are manifest not only in the power men exert in the family and in society, but also in the way the economy, especially business, is run. The way business is run, in turn, affects all members of the society, workers and nonworkers alike. Because business executives succeed based on their ability to make decisions that maximize corporate profit, and because such executives usually epitomize the rational, nonemotional, insensitive, competitive male, these decisions often are contrary to human needs. Thus, we live in a country of enormous wealth, natural resources, and productivity, yet many children suffer from malnutrition and inadequate health care, the number of homeless people is soaring, our air and water have become increasingly polluted, and our safety standards for motor vehicles and consumer products are low. The hierarchical structure of the business world (as well as the political and military worlds) implies control of the many by a few. This hierarchical structure then becomes the primary mode in which many men operate—being dominated and oppressed at work and going home to dominate their wives and children.

Valuing only work that earns cash income means that most of the work done by women simply doesn't count. Domestic work done in one's own home, reproduction and child care, subsistence farming (the bulk of the farming done around the world, almost exclusively by women), voluntary community work—none of these are computed in determining the gross national product of a country or in determining public policy. Yet, as Marilyn Waring (1989) argues,

such activities are essential to society and enable all other work to get done. We have an economic system in which women's work is invisible and devalued, a fact that both reflects and supports the devaluation of women themselves. A 1991 study by the United Nations' International Fund for Agricultural Development revealed that the number of rural women living in poverty in developing countries has increased 50% since 1970, primarily due to the fact that development projects ignore women's roles (J. Dixon, 1991).

Institutions may use and perpetuate the masculine stereotype because it serves their purpose. Through the emphasis on getting ahead and "staying cool," many men fit right into institutions "whose function is not to increase general human welfare but to enhance the profit, power and prestige of the few who control them" (Pleck & Sawyer, 1974, pp. 126–127). The fact that many women are now entering these bastions of male power may mean that they will need to adopt similar ways of dealing with situations—competitively, hierarchically, and unfeelingly. Whether this is a desirable state of affairs is, of course, a value judgment. It is the opinion of the author that the integration of instrumental and expressive qualities should be an ideal of institutional as well as individual functioning, that the traditionally masculine aim of achievement should be tempered by the traditionally feminine concern for people. As we saw in the last chapter, some women managers do appear to use a more democratic management style than has been traditional, and some companies are encouraging this shift among all their managers.

Society will certainly benefit as a result, but such a shift is not inevitable, nor innately gender-linked. Humanization of institutions is as much a goal of the women's liberation movement as is human liberation (see also S. Gordon, 1991).

Political Power

Salaries, a small part of economic power, are an even smaller part of political power. But political power can and does influence salaries and the work situation in general. And politically, women have consistently had negligible power. Women won the right to vote in the United States in 1920 and currently make up 53% of the nation's registered voters. Since 1980, women have been voting with the same (low) frequency as men. In fact, starting in 1986, a slightly higher percentage of women have been voting than men, a pattern visible across all ethnic groups (National Commission on Working Women, 1988). Although voting is an important political activity, its impact on public policy pales compared to other activities. Women still are underrepresented in the party hierarchies and in elected and appointed offices (see Table 12.1). Laws and policies are made and enforced primarily by men, from a male perspective.

On the political party level, women have served as indispensable volunteers, but rarely in positions of responsibility or decision making. Few of the top jobs of the major presidential campaigns have been held by women. The presence of women as party delegates at national conventions, however, has been more equitable, at least in the Democratic Party. For the 1980 convention, Democrats required that half their delegates be women and thus Democrats have had an equal number of female and male delegates at the last three national conventions. Republicans have aimed for similar representation without setting quotas, but reached only 29% female representation in 1980, 44% in 1984, and 38% in 1988. Although delegates are visible and women's increasing representation in such positions certainly is an improvement, these are not the most powerful party positions. For these reasons and others, such as that neither party adequately addresses women's issues, the National Organization for Women in 1989 set up a commission to consider establishing a new political party dedicated to equality.

Women still occupy fewer than 20% of all elected offices in the United States, with Black and Hispanic women underrepresented even more than White women ("Hispanic Elected," 1990). As with labor force patterns, women's representation is highest at the lowest levels and lowest at the highest levels. But the increased representation of women at the state and local levels has been impressive. By 1990, the number of women who had been elected to state legislatures had increased more than four times from what it had been in 1969 (from 4% to 17.1%). Even greater gains have been made in local government, but primarily in positions traditionally reserved for women, such as on library boards or in part-time, poorly paid elective offices. However, 13% of all mayors were women in 1990, compared to 1% in 1971. Minorities, both women and men, are underrepresented in government, but Black women have been faring slightly better than White women on the state and local levels ("Eyes on the Prize," 1989). For example, in 1987 women comprised 25% of Black state legislators but only 15% of White state legislators. Few women are state governors (3 in 1991), mainly because women are more readily accepted as representatives than leaders.

On a federal level, the number of women in Congress is still minimal, as shown in Table 12.2. Since 1947, the proportion of women in Congress has fluctuated between 2% and its all-time high in 1991 of 5.8%. Representation in the Senate, however, has been strikingly low and has never surpassed more than two women—2%. Since Jeannette Rankin was first elected to the House of Representatives in 1917, women's representation there has increased, although with fluctuations. Shirley Chisholm in 1968 was the first Black woman to serve in Congress. Since that time, only seven other Black women, one Asian-American woman, and one Hispanic woman have served in the House, none in the Senate. In the 1991–92 Congress, there were 29 women in the House, 6 of whom were women of color—a record. Women in Congress serve an average of four years less than men (6.6 years compared to 10.8). Consequently, few women who have served in Congress have been able to build up enough seniority to be powerful. At the current pace of change, women will achieve equal representation in Congress in the year 2582 (Whicker, 1990).

In other positions on the federal level, women also have little power. When Ronald Reagan took office in 1981, the number of women and minorities in top jobs plummeted (Pear, 1987). Reagan was the first president in over a decade who failed to appoint more women to top-level positions than his immediate predecessor. In the Ford administration, women's representation was 14%; in Carter's, women's representation was 18%; in Reagan's, women's representation was 15%. In Bush's first two years in

Table 12.2 Number of women in Congress, 1947–1992

Congress	Year	Senate	House	Total
80th	1947–1948	0	8	8
81st	1949–1950	1	9	10
82nd	1951–1952	1	10	11
83rd	1953–1954	2	11	13
84th	1955–1956	1	16	17
85th	1957–1958	1	15	16
86th	1959–1960	1	16	17
87th	1961–1962	2	17	19
88th	1963–1964	2	11	13
89th	1965–1966	2	10	12
90th	1967–1968	1	11	12
91st	1969–1970	1	10	11
92nd	1971–1972	1	12	13
93rd	1973–1974	0	16	16
94th	1975–1976	0	19	19
95th	1977–1978	2	18	20
96th	1979–1980	1	16	17
97th	1981–1982	2	19	21
98th	1983–1984	2	22	24
99th	1985–1986	2	23	25
100th	1987–1988	2	23	25
101st	1989–1990	2	28	30
102nd	1991–1992	2	29	31

office, 19% of his appointments have been women, but these are mainly at lower levels (Dowd, 1991). Only 1 out of 14 members of Bush's cabinet and 1 out of 15 officials on the White House senior staff are women. Certain appointive posts have rarely been held by a woman, most noticeably in the State, Justice, and Defense departments.

On the international scene, women are underrepresented as well. Among the 159 member states of the United Nations, only 6 were led by women in 1989—3.7%. About the same percentage of women were represented at the cabinet level in these countries, with 10% female representation in the 130 countries with national parliaments (United Nations, 1989). The United States has one of the worst records for the holding by women of national public office. For example, in mid-1989, women made up more than a third of the parliaments in Norway, Sweden, and Cuba, compared to our 5%, and nearly half of Norway's cabinet was composed of women, compared to our 16%.

Why has women's progress on the political scene been so slow and what are its implications? After reviewing the barriers to women in poiitics, we will look at the growing gender gap present in voting and political attitudes. We will conclude this section with an examination of the consequences of men's dominance of the political scene.

Barriers to women in politics   The barriers to women's participation in politics are numerous and are similar to those present for women in the work force. One set of barriers arises from gender socialization. Many women and men still think politics is "masculine" and are concerned that political participation would somehow "coarsen" women (Bernard, 1979). Consequently, women have a difficult time developing the self-confidence needed to run for public office. They also tend to believe that family responsibilities should come first. Women in politics do not appear to be less politically ambitious than men holding comparable elective offices (S. J. Carroll, 1985a; Merritt, 1982). However, politically ambitious women do appear to have a special approach to office, one that emphasizes public service rather than power brokerage or personal career advantages.

The major barriers to women's participation in politics are situational, such as motherhood, and educational and occupational background; societal, such as public attitudes and stereotypes; and institutional, such as political procedures (Randall, 1987). Among situational factors, the constraints of motherhood may be the most immediate. The fact that women traditionally are responsible for domestic and child-care activities means that their available time and resources for pursuing political office are limited. This is especially the case for national political positions, which often require extensive campaigning and travel. Not surprisingly, then, women entering Congress tend to have grown children and be older than men. Most women who have been elected to office also have been widowed or divorced (N. Lynn, 1975; Whicker, 1990). Jobs and educational background also have limited women. Most politicians have had at least a college education, a factor that favored men until recently. Most politicians also tend to have backgrounds in law or business, two careers in which women have been a minority. For example, in 1988, over half the U.S. representatives and nearly two out of three U.S. senators were lawyers (C. G. Bell & Price, 1989). Not only are there fewer women lawyers than men lawyers, but women lawyers also appear less interested than men lawyers in political careers (Briscoe, 1989).

Societal attitudes also have been important. Most people associate politics with men and masculine-stereotyped traits and therefore may have difficulty perceiving women as appropriate for political office, especially when power and prestige are involved (Rosenwasser & Dean, 1989). This may explain why women are more readily accepted for office on a local than on a national level, and as a representative rather than as a governor or president. In a 1987 national survey of 1500 registered voters, 31% thought that a woman would do a worse job than a man as president, but this percentage decreased steadily when the political position in question went from governor to U.S. senator to state legislator to school board member (C. Green, 1987). In fact, for school board member, women were rated 15 points better than men. Those most reluctant to support female candidates tend to be voters over age 60, rural and small-town residents, voters in the South, those with less than a college education, and those who are homemakers or working in blue-collar or low-paying white-collar jobs.

Women are perceived to have an advantage over men with respect to a wide range of social issues and in holding down government spending, possibly because women are seen as being more compassionate, honest, and moral than men. In contrast, men are perceived to have an advantage over women with respect to dealing with taxes, arms control, military spending, and foreign trade, possibly because men are seen as being tougher, more decisive, and more emotionally stable than women. Since those issues in which men are perceived to have an advantage also are evaluated as being more important for presidential candidates than those issues in which women are perceived to have an advantage, it is not surprising that men are perceived as more suitable for and more likely to win a presidential election (Rosenwasser & Dean, 1989). For other positions, however, being a female may be advantageous. A survey taken after the 1988 elections found that women candidates had distinct advantages among voters with respect to favoring women's rights, standing up for what they believe, fighting for voters' interests, and having new ideas ("Post-election Survey," 1989).

Thus, gender stereotypes affect attitudes about political candidates and such opinions turn into votes. In a 1984 study of five congressional races between a man and a woman, 40% of those surveyed said the men could handle the emotional demands of public life while 27% said the women were prepared to do so ("Poll," 1985). Four out of five of the men won in the actual elections. In another study using hypothetical gubernatorial candidates, people tended to vote for men despite their stating that the sex of the candidate would not affect their vote (Basler, 1984). Only when women clearly were more qualified than men did people vote for women. Again, the stereotypes were strongest among men, older voters, the less educated, and those in lower income groups.

In practice, women candidates are subject to closer scrutiny than the familiar White male candidate. In particular, women's age, height, weight, clothing, and physical attractiveness play a big role in how seriously she is taken as a candidate (Mandel, 1981). For example, during the 1984 campaign, Democratic vice-presidential candidate Geraldine Ferraro was scrutinized endlessly with regard to how she wore her hair, where she got her clothes, and so on. Such topics were ignored in discussions of her male rival, George Bush. Ironically, of course, there is never a "right" way for a woman candidate to be since she will never be male. She is either too young or too old, too shrill or too quiet, too fat or too thin, and so on. In one study wherein women and men read the same political speech at identical decibel levels, observers rated the women as more shrill and aggressive than the men (M. Carlson, 1990).

Even when a woman has some political power, she may not be able to wield it as effectively as a man in the same situation because of gender stereotypes. Female politicians may be reproached for assuming male prerogatives (Abzug, 1984; Mandel, 1981). Outspoken women, in particular, may be negatively evaluated, especially by women. An interesting example of the difficulties facing women in politics occurred in February 1979 when Queen Elizabeth II of England visited the Persian Gulf countries. In order to be received by her Moslem male hosts and be accorded the honors generally bestowed upon a visiting chief of state, Queen Elizabeth had to become an "honorary man" and cover herself with veils and wrist-to-ankle clothes. Women in most of these countries generally are not even allowed to speak in front of men.

The institutional structure of politics also works to women's disadvantage. In the United States, political campaigns require large budgets. Not only are women less likely than men to have access to personal wealth, but women traditionally have had more trouble than men raising funds as well. This pattern appears to be changing, but women still bear the burden of being outsiders in a political system that tends to reelect incumbents (S. J. Carroll, 1985b; Whicker, 1990). In fact, the single greatest barrier to more women in politics, especially in Congress, is the fact that men tend to stay in office until they retire and incumbents nearly always get reelected. In addition, political clubs and social activities (the "smoke-filled back rooms") usually exclude women formally and informally. Party leaders may force women into a no-win position by encouraging them when a nomination seems worthless and ignoring them when it looks valuable.

The outlook is improving, however, and the traditional attitudes and barriers to women's involvement in politics can be broken down. The 1990 election set a record for women: women ran for, were nominated to, and won office at higher levels than ever before (Cohan & Altman, 1990). There now are unprecedented numbers of women as state legislators, lieutenant governors, governors, and national representatives. Even those who didn't win elections may have benefited women in the long run by gaining political experience, serving as role models for other women, and educating the public about women's viability as political candidates.

Attitudes also are changing and becoming more acceptant of women politicians. More people than ever before report that they are willing to vote for a woman, even for president. For example, a 1987 Gallup poll found that 82% said they would vote for a woman if she were their party's presidential nominee, up from 52% found in 1958 (Houston, 1987). Although 31% of the voters sampled in 1987 thought a woman would do a worse job than a man as president, more thought so in 1984. Political analysts attribute the decreasing resistance to women in high office to Geraldine Ferraro's candidacy and voters' increasing experience with women as political leaders. Also, as older, more traditional voters leave the electorate, attitudes toward women politicians become more acceptant. Seven out of 10 voters in 1986 said the gender of the candidate makes no difference (Grenier, 1986). Unfortunately, for those for whom it is a factor, it is more likely to be a negative than a positive one.

The gender gap   The term *gender gap* was coined in 1980 to explain gender differences in voting patterns in that year's presidential election. For the first time, women and men were found to vote differently. Since that time, the term has been used to refer not only to gender differences in voting patterns but also to gender differences in political attitudes.

In the 1980 presidential election, men were found to back Ronald Reagan against Jimmy Carter by a 54% to 37% edge, whereas women split their votes 46% to 45% (Abzug, 1984). Among Blacks, only 23% of the men supported Reagan, still greater than the 16% of Black women who supported him. In the 1984 presidential election, although the majority of both sexes voted for Reagan, a gender gap still was evident. Men favored Reagan over Mondale by 62% to 36%, whereas women went for Reagan by 54% to 44% (Stetson, 1991). The gender gap appeared in the 1988 presidential election as well, although it was not as large on election day as it had been earlier in the campaign. Whereas men voted for Bush over Dukakis 57% to 41%, women were more evenly split, with just 50% voting for Bush (Madigan, 1989).

The gender gap in voting is apparent in other elections as well. Since 1980, exit poll data from state and national elections has shown that women vote significantly differently from men in more than half the races. Since women now represent a higher percentage of registered voters than men, and since women also are beginning to vote in greater proportion than men, more and more races are being won by virtue of women's votes. For example, in 1986, nine U.S. senators and three governors, all but one of whom were Democrats, won with the votes of women ("Agenda '88," 1988). As these results suggest, women in recent elections are more likely than

White men to vote Democratic, although party and ideological identification (conservative, moderate, liberal) traditionally have shown little gender difference. That is starting to change. Since 1980, the gender gap in political affiliation has widened due to White men's increasing affinity with the Republican party (Clymer, 1991). Women remain more affiliated with the Democratic party, 38% to 29%. (One-third of all voters do not identify with either party.)

What accounts for this consistent gender gap in voting patterns? A number of factors are important: gender differences in economic status, in political attitudes, and in political values. Perceptions about the health of the economy are critical factors in shaping voters' choices (E. Klein & Farah, 1988). Not only do women occupy a more disadvantaged economic position than men, but women also worry more than men about the economy and related concerns (such as health care). As we have seen, Reagan's and Bush's policies have had a disparate negative impact on the poorer segments of our society. A 1988 nationwide survey found that only 40% of women voters said they had benefited from the Reagan administration's economic policies, compared to 55% of the men (McQueen, 1988). Thus, although Republican campaign rhetoric, especially in the 1988 presidential campaign, successfully cast doubt on the Democratic candidate's ability to manage the economy, women remained more skeptical than men regarding the Republican's economic agenda. Bush's support was least among poor women, elderly women, single women, and Black women. But women at higher income levels also were less likely to vote for Reagan and Bush than were men at higher incomes, making explanations based solely on economic self-interest and economic vulnerability inadequate (S. J. Carroll, 1984b).

Attitudes toward the economy are of more importance in voting than voter economic status itself.

Gender differences in economic attitudes are part of a pattern of gender differences in political attitudes and values. Women have been socialized to be more compassionate than men; men have been socialized to be more concerned with dominance and toughness (see Chapter 3). Such training results in different priorities. Nationwide polls taken since 1987 indicate that women tend to be more concerned than men about environmental and social welfare issues, such as unemployment, health care, child care, and care for the elderly and the poor. In contrast, men tend to be more concerned than women about foreign policy, national defense, and crime ("Agenda '88," 1988; McQueen, 1988). See Table 12.3 for an example of the size of the gender gap in attitudes. Thus, the Republican campaign rhetoric in recent years, which has emphasized a tough foreign policy posture, war imagery (war on crime, war on drugs), and cuts in social programs aimed at the disadvantaged, appeals more to men than to women. Although there is some support for this argument, one must remember that the gender differences noted are matters of degree, not of kind. Not all men are concerned with toughness nor all women with social programs. The actual size of the gender gap varies across demographic groups, which suggests that the gap is not a purely gender-related phenomenon. For example, in the 1988 presidential election, there was a larger gender gap among single voters than married voters, among college graduates than those with less education, among voters in the West than those in the South, and among voters between ages 18 and 44 than among voters over age 45 (E. Klein & Farah, 1988). Feminism may be a better explanatory factor than gender (Abzug, 1984). Since women tend to hold

Table 12.3 The gender gap in attitudes, 1987 (in percentages)

	Women	*Men*
Think the economy is in good shape	47	60
Favor raising taxes to improve health care for the elderly	55	39
Favor raising taxes to build a stronger national defense	16	23
Approve U.S. policy in the Persian Gulf	50	67
Oppose military aid to Nicaragua	61	49
Favor more strict handgun control	66	53
Favor cutting back nuclear power plant operation until more strictly regulated	76	55

From National Commission on Working Women, 1988.

more feminist attitudes than men, this may account for gender differences in voting patterns. Among those who agree with the basic tenets of feminist ideology, the gender gap generally is minimal.

Since the gender gap first was noted in 1980, women appear to be gaining power during election campaigns as an important interest group. Many view the selection of a female vice-president by the Democratic party in 1984 as a response to this gender gap. Despite all hopes to the contrary, however (for example, Abzug, 1984; Smeal, 1984), women still do not vote as a self-conscious interest group, although they are more likely to vote for women and women's issues than ever before (Grenier, 1987; K. E. Lewis & Bierly, 1990). For example, in the 1990 elections, the gender gap helped defeat antiabortion initiatives and helped elect more pro-choice legislators, male and female (Smeal, Raphael, & Mulvihill, 1990). The strongest supporters of women candidates are young, college-educated working women, whose numbers are increasing; the strongest opponents are older men and women who are most likely to believe that female candidates are less capable than male candidates (Hepp, 1989).

Consequences   The consequences of male dominance of the political system are long-standing and far-reaching. As Wendy Brown (1988) argues, Western political thought is based on men's lives and values. The stereotypic male preoccupations with dominance and mastery and the need to prove masculinity by being tough and unemotional have had tremendous impact on both domestic and foreign policy since Aristotle's time. Any sign of "weakness"—which can be revealed by tears, psychotherapy, or even too much compassion—can destroy political careers, especially in the United States.

A number of writers (Farrell, 1974; Fasteau, 1974; Steinem, 1972) have argued persuasively that the United States' reactions to the Cuban missile crisis and, particularly, the Vietnam War, were significantly colored by the needs of Presidents Kennedy, Johnson, and Nixon to prove their toughness. The same came to be said of Presidents Reagan and Bush with respect to more recent U.S. involvements in Grenada, Panama, and the Persian Gulf. As I. F. Stone (1974) notes, "The first rule of this small boy statecraft is that the leader of a gang, like the leader of a tribe, horde, or nation, dare not appear 'chicken'" (p. 131). Not only must a leader prove his toughness to other leaders, but he also must be at least as tough as his predecessors. Thus, President Johnson was concerned that he would be thought

less of a man than Kennedy if he did not follow through with Vietnam. Nixon was particularly obsessed with winning, saving face, and being tough, as the Pentagon papers and the White House tapes all too clearly show. The cult of toughness reappeared with Reagan and Bush, after the Carter administration's emphasis on human rights, which many thought of as too soft.

All this is not to say that standing firm, threatening, or using force is never valid. Clearly, certain situations require such responses, as President Carter learned during the Iran and Afghanistan crises of 1979 and 1980. What is being questioned is the use of such responses to satisfy a psychological or political need, rather than as a clearly thought-out and appropriately humanitarian foreign policy. A study of State Department staff and policy disagreements between U.S. presidents and secretaries of state between 1898 and 1975 revealed a connection between aggressive "masculine" traits and hard-line foreign policy (Etheredge, 1978). A specific example of how the masculine sex role may influence foreign policy can be found in the Pentagon papers. They revealed that in March 1965, the U.S. aims in South Vietnam were only 20% to keep South Vietnam out of Chinese hands, only 10% to allow the South Vietnamese a freer, better way of life, but 70% to avoid a "humiliating defeat" (in Fasteau, 1974). More recently, Bush's foreign policy ventures during his first two years in office, which involved sending U.S. troops into Panama and the Persian Gulf region, can be viewed as an attempt to prove that he is not "a wimp," a characterization made of him when he was vice president, which in itself reveals the gender politics of politics. (See Figure 12.2.)

Bush had the difficult task of succeeding Reagan, known for his "macho" image. This image was a major factor in Reagan's appeal to White men, who flocked to him in droves even though most were registered Democrats. As Reagan's 1984 campaign director said, "Ronald Reagan is a man's man. He is a leader. He is providing direction, whether you agree with the direction or not. He's not afraid of taking action, decisive action. And that appeals to men" (S. Friedman, 1983). In a 1983 poll, half of the women surveyed feared Reagan's policies would get us into war; only 36% of the men felt that way. Black and Jewish women overwhelmingly opposed the president because they felt that Reagan lacked compassion and would too easily use military force (Perlez, 1984). Much of the 1984 presidential campaign rhetoric hinged on who would be the

Figure 12.2 The "wimp factor" in U.S. politics. (DOONESBURY Copyright 1990 G. B. Trudeau. Reprinted with permission of Universal Press Syndicate. All rights reserved.)

strongest and toughest leader—Reagan or Mondale. Reagan, with his strong and tough but sincere cowboy image, prevailed, especially for White males. Bush worked hard during the 1988 campaign to use the same rhetoric, characterizing Dukakis as weak and soft.

As is true with business institutions, if women want to achieve positions of political power, they often must prove themselves even tougher than men. Yet women, for the most part, are not obsessed with proving their strength, saving face, or gaining prestige. Polls consistently show women generally to be against specific wars and against military solutions to international problems. For example, about 5% more women than men thought U.S. entry into World War I was a mistake. In December 1990, just before the United States entered the war in the Persian Gulf, 73% of the women polled opposed attacking Iraqi forces occupying Kuwait, compared to 48% of the men (E. Goodman, 1990). More than half of the women (56%) preferred giving sanctions more time to work, compared to only 37% of the men (Quindlen, 1991). Indeed, women have been less likely than men to support all issues having to do with the military or violence, such as defense spending and capital punishment (J. M. Silverman & Kumka, 1987; Steinem, 1984). In contrast, women tend to show greater support than men for issues having to do with peace, equality, and social welfare (such as health and education).

Women politicians apparently reflect these views when they vote. Studies of the voting patterns of women in Congress since 1917 show them to be more humanistic and altruistic than men (M. Carlson, 1990; S. J. Carroll, 1984a; E. Klein, 1984). One of the few people in Congress to vote against

the United States' entering World War I and the only person to vote against the United States' entering World War II was the first woman to serve in Congress, Jeannette Rankin. Women, regardless of whether they describe themselves as conservative, moderate, or liberal, have been more likely than men to take feminist positions on women's issues, such as ratification of the Equal Rights Amendment, opposition to curbs on abortion, government support for child care, and Social Security for homemakers. Women politicians also typically differ from men politicians on attitudes toward military strength, nuclear power plants, and capital punishment, with women less likely to favor these issues than men. The gender gap on all issues tends to be greater among those elected to higher levels of office. Women in Congress have been the sponsors of legislation frequently overlooked by men: family and medical leave, help for middle-income families in financing homes, reformed pension laws, education for the disabled, and the network of veterans' hospitals. At all levels, Black women holding elective office have been the most liberal. Thus, women politicians as a group do seem to be different from men politicians as a group, more humanitarian and public-service oriented.

If more women were in positions of political power, would domestic and foreign policy be different? Some feminists think so, citing gender differences in political attitudes and values for support (French, 1985; R. Morgan, 1991). With more women in power, we might expect more humane policies, more concern with social and environmental issues, and less concern with displays of toughness and bravado. Yet political institutions, by their very structure, tend to operate on "masculine" aggressive, nonhumanitarian, competitive principles, and women who make it to the top often have adopted those values. To expect more humane politics just because women are in power is a sexist as well as a false notion, as Indira Gandhi in India and Margaret Thatcher in England have demonstrated. Most women leaders around the world have owed their positions to male dynasties rather than to feminist politics (Chua-Eoan, 1990). The system itself must change and become more concerned with human values and connections between people. These are feminist values, not solely the province of women. We need a "post-masculinist politics," one wherein power is defined less as hierarchical dominance and more as empowering others and getting things done (W. Brown, 1988). Such a system would work to break down not only gender oppression but race and class oppression as well, as all oppressions are interconnected. What we are describing is eliminating patriarchy, rule by "the fathers." Given the scope of this vision, it is not surprising that resistance is high and change is slow.

Legal Power

Not only is public policy made mainly by White men generally from a White male perspective, but laws are as well. In addition, mainly White men are responsible for enforcing and interpreting the law. Not surprisingly then, laws encode a patriarchal world view, where White Christian middle-class heterosexual men are the norm and women are defined mainly by their sexual and reproductive role (see Eisenstein, 1989; MacKinnon, 1987b, for well-developed arguments of this point). As we have seen throughout this book, gender is about power and inequality, not just about difference.

Few women serve in the judiciary of the United States, especially in the higher courts, and few serve in the political offices responsible for making and enforcing laws. Only one woman has served on the U.S. Supreme Court, and she was appointed only in 1981. Judicial appointments are particularly important because judges can strike down laws as unconstitutional and can order the executive branch to perform specified actions. Unlike President Carter, who was committed to increasing female representation in the judiciary, President Reagan was committed to appointing young conservative men (S. V. Roberts, 1988). Whereas women represented 16% of Carter's appointments to lifetime federal judgeships, women represented only 8% of Reagan's. Black appointments were strikingly low—only 2% of all federal judgeships went to Blacks, well below the rate of Carter (14%), Ford (6%), and even Nixon (3%). Since Reagan appointed about half the federal judiciary during his eight years and Bush continues to appoint conservative White men to the bench, we now have a predominantly conservative judiciary. Since many of these new appointments have been to relatively young individuals (under age 45), the effects of such appointments will last for the next 20 to 30 years. We have been seeing the consequences of these appointments in recent judicial decisions.

Women are, however, becoming lawyers in increasing numbers. In 1986, 18% of all lawyers were women, up from 9% in 1976 (Mullins, 1987). And more are on their way, because more than 40% of those entering law school now are women. These numbers represent a tremendous change since 1873, when U.S. Supreme Court Justice Bradley allowed Illinois to bar Myra Bradwell from practicing law because women "naturally" belonged in the domestic sphere (Rhode, 1990). Unfortunately, minority representation still is low, with Blacks constituting only 5% of first-year law students and Hispanics 4%. Because law is the route to legal as well as political power, we may expect to see some changes in male dominance of this area in the future.

Would having more women as lawyers and judges make a difference? Some feminists would argue yes. The history of women lawyers in American shows that they have been the leaders in the fight for women's rights (the vote, protection from abuse), humane reforms (such as child welfare, work safety, and worker's compensation), and the practice of public interest law (as opposed to business and corporate law) (Morello, 1986). Black women lawyers were in the forefront early in the fight for civil rights. As noted in the previous section, women tend to have more humanitarian attitudes than men and therefore may practice law differently (see, for example, Jack & Jack, 1988). However, some of these attitudinal differences may come from being relatively powerless rather than being socialized as female. As women gain more power in a system that rewards "masculine" behaviors and attitudes (aggressiveness, competitiveness, unemotionality), it is debatable how much of a difference more women would make. One study of women judges in the late 1970s found that the sentences they imposed were similar to those imposed by male judges (Epstein, 1988). To effect real change, we need more than an increase in the numbers of women judges and lawyers. We need to change the legal system itself so that it becomes more reflective of and responsive to the lives of all citizens, not just White males.

Because male dominance and belief in sexual difference are part of the law and its enforcement, women are generally at a marked disadvantage under the law. Unfair treatment still exists despite significant changes in the laws and their enforcement over the past 20 years toward the reduction of discrimination against women in employment, salaries, education, family planning, and credit (for example, the Equal Employment Opportunity Act of 1972; the Equal Pay Act of 1963 as amended by the Education Amendments of 1972; Title IX of the Education Amendments of 1972 as amended by the Bayh Amendment of 1974 and the Education Amendments of 1976; the Equal Credit Opportunity Act of 1975; and the Pregnancy Discrimination Act of 1978). These are statutory laws, however; judicial decisions (common law) are made by legislators and judges, who are usually men, some of whom may not be able to transcend their own socialized belief that women and men are meant to have distinct and different roles in life.

To prove sex discrimination, a plaintiff must show that she (or he) was denied some benefit (a job, promotion, salary increase, or such) solely on account of being female (or male). The assumption is that women and men who are similar should be treated similarly. But women and men are almost never "similarly situated" because of differential power and differential life options (MacKinnon, 1987b; Rhode, 1990). For example, women and men have different experiences with sexual violence, reproductive autonomy, occupational segregation, poverty, and divorce. Therefore, sex discrimination laws help primarily upper middle-class White women; they do not help the majority of women who do not and cannot have "vitae" that are identical to those of men. In fact, seemingly gender-neutral standards may penalize women, such as when custody arrangements are based solely on financial resources. Such a criterion typically gives preference to men, especially if women have concentrated on domestic and child-care activities. This is one reason why, as we saw in Chapter 10, men who contest custody more often than not have been awarded it in the last few years.

Gender roles and stereotypes affect in many other ways the types of laws made and enforced (for a good history of women's changing legal status, see Hoff-Wilson, 1988). Until 1971 and the *Reed v. Reed* case, sex was always held to be a difference that warranted different legal treatment. In that case,

a woman was prevented from administering an estate due to a state law giving automatic preference to men. The Supreme Court, for the first time, held a state statute to be unconstitutional because it discriminated against women on "arbitrary" grounds. However, in 1974, the Supreme Court upheld a Florida law (*Kahn v. Shevin*) that granted widows a property tax exemption but did not extend the benefit to widowers. Since that time, the law has been inconsistent with respect to how it treats gender—although no longer a category requiring differential treatment, gender still has not been given the status of a suspect classification as has race. This means that laws still can make distinctions on the basis of gender in some cases. For example, women are excluded from registering for the draft nationwide; women are allowed to marry younger than men in most states; in some states, statutory rape laws only apply to males; and property laws in some states may differentiate between the responsibilities of husbands and wives. As can be seen from this sampling, unequal treatment by the law affects men as well as women, sometimes negatively.

The reason gender still can be used for making legal distinctions is that the United States Constitution does not guarantee women equality. The Equal Rights Amendment (ERA), designed to redress this neglect, was introduced into every Congress between 1923 and 1972 until it passed. It then fell three states short of being ratified despite having its deadline extended to June 30, 1982. Although reintroduced into every Congress since then, it has yet to get out of committee. The ERA states that "equality of rights under the law shall not be denied or abridged by the United States or by any State on account of sex." It would provide clear constitutional recognition of equal rights and responsibilities for men and women. It would eliminate legislative inertia that keeps discriminatory laws on the books. And it would serve as a clear statement of the nation's moral and legal commitment to full gender equality.

The defeat of the ERA was not due to lack of popular support. Every poll at the time found that it was favored by a majority of the populace. It still is, even more so. For example, a 1987 Harris poll found that 78% of all Americans favored an equal rights amendment to the U.S. Constitution, compared to 51% in 1975 (Creager, 1989). But popular support doesn't matter when it is state legislatures that must do the ratifying and the vast majority of state legislators are White men. The successful fight against the ERA shows clearly that the country's politicians and other power holders find equality threatening. A campaign of misinformation and scare tactics characterized the national fight. For example, opponents of the ERA deliberately publicized falsely that separate bathrooms for the sexes would no longer be legal and that husbands no longer would support families. In the 1986 Vermont campaign for a state equal rights amendment, opponents used the scare tactic of suggesting that passage of such an amendment would lead to a greater incidence of AIDS, since it would eliminate "natural" sex roles and thus lead to an increase in homosexuality. Although these tactics were successful, their falsity is clear since none of the predicted horrors has occurred in the 14 states that now have their own equal rights amendments (Smeal, 1987). Although some strategic mistakes may have been made by supporters of the national ERA battle, opponents prevailed mostly because they had the money and institutionalized power to do so (M. F. Berry, 1986; Mansbridge, 1986).

What underlies much of the opposition to the ERA and much of current discriminatory law is a fear of eliminating patriarchy, often described as "traditional family values." Traditional families, of course, are ones in which there is a husband who is the main financial provider, a wife who is the main caretaker of home and family, and at least two children. As we saw in Chapter 10, such a "tradition" was always limited to a particular race, class, and historical period that is long past. The fantasy lingers, however, especially for White males, whose power is threatened both at home and at work by previously marginalized and subordinated groups—women and minority males. Since 1980 and the conservative swing of the country and especially the judiciary, the concern about women's becoming too autonomous has become the basis of an increasing number of judicial decisions. Thus, laws limiting access to abortion, contraception, and even abortion-related information have increased. Affirmative action has been cut back. Comparable worth claims have been dismissed. Employed parents have no legal protection against losing their jobs if they must take time off to care for young children or sick family members. Many employed women have no protection against losing their jobs if they take time off to give birth. Pension and Social Security benefits discriminate against women, especially against homemakers. Lesbians and gay men still can be discriminated against.

Even when nondiscriminatory laws are on the books, enforcement can be curtailed by restricting necessary funding. For example, Reagan's cuts in funds for the Equal Employment Opportunity Commission hampered their prosecution of discrimination cases. The number of cases filed by the commission involving sex discrimination in employment dropped more than 70% between 1981 and 1983 (Kennelly, 1984).

Judicial practices also frequently discriminate against women. State task forces studying the situation of women and the courts in Maryland, Massachusetts, Nevada, New Jersey, New York, and Rhode Island found a consistent pattern of judges' giving less credibility to lawyers, witnesses, experts, and probation officers who were women than to their male counterparts (A. R. Gold, 1989). For example, women lawyers are more likely than men lawyers to be addressed by their first name or by a term of endearment (such as "honey"). Female plaintiffs and defendants also receive discriminatory, frequently paternalistic, treatment. For example, women tend to be put on probation longer than men convicted of similar crimes. Whereas women sometimes may be treated more leniently by the courts than are their male counterparts, women are likely to be treated more punitively when they violate gender role norms in addition to the law (Chesney-Lind, 1986; K. Daly, 1989; Mann, 1984). For example, female prostitutes typically are dealt with more severely than their customers. Female adolescents accused of a noncriminal "status offense," such as promiscuity, running away from home, or "bad behavior," tend to be detained and held longer than male adolescents accused of criminal offenses.

MacKinnon (1987b) argues that the legal debate about whether women should be treated just like men or should get special treatment perpetuates the use of men as the legal norm and the view of women as different. Women aren't just different in the eyes of the law; they are inferior. To effect change, we must first recognize that law is about power relationships and that current law encodes male dominance over women. From such a perspective, "sex discrimination stops being a question of morality and starts being a question of politics" (MacKinnon, 1987b, p. 44).

Military Power

Women traditionally have been excluded from gaining military power. They have not been subject to the draft in the United States, and it has only been since the draft ended in 1972 that women have entered the services in significant numbers. They now constitute about 11% of all military personnel, more than five times the 2% cap previously mandated by law (Schafer, 1990a). With the recession in the late 1980s and early 1990s, the military has been a particularly attractive employer, especially to minorities. About one-third of all enlisted women are African American and 4% are Latina (Flanders, 1990). Despite the increased presence of women in the military over the last 20 years, discriminatory regulations and practices abound.

By federal statute, women are prohibited from combat duty and from jobs that are labeled combat-related in the U.S. Navy, Marines, and Air Force. The U.S. Army has followed suit on its own initiative. The proportion of jobs open to military women varies with branch of service. In 1991, 20% of Marine Corps jobs were open to women, 51% of Army jobs, 59% of Navy jobs, 97% of Air Force jobs, and 100% of Coast Guard jobs (McNeil, 1991). Not all the jobs from which women are excluded are designated as combat or combat-support positions. Additional positions are reserved for men to facilitate rotation of positions and to provide men with career opportunities. Lack of acceptable housing also disqualifies women from many overseas positions. The fact that women are barred from serving in combat makes them exempt from the 1980 law requiring registration for the draft, at least according to a 1981 Supreme Court decision—this despite the fact that in the last draft, fewer than 1% of the men eligible were inducted and subsequently assigned to a combat unit. A prohibition against women's serving in combat does not mean that women are protected from combat, as the 1991 Gulf War clearly demonstrated. Women are not prohibited from combat zones where they, along with everyone else, are vulnerable to missile and ground attacks. In modern warfare, there is no well-defined "front line." The prohibition against women in combat is really a prohibition against giving women weapons. In practice, it also prohibits women from promotions and top-paying jobs.

The result of these restrictions, coupled with sexism and traditional gender socialization, is that women are overrepresented in the less prestigious, lower paying jobs in the military, as they are in civilian life. Approximately 83% of enlisted women are in the four lowest pay grades, as compared to 68% of men ("The Registration," 1980). The four highest pay grades hold 23% of enlisted men and only 3% of enlisted women. Fewer than 1% of the top 15,000 senior enlisted positions are held by women ("Resolutions," 1990). As in civilian life,

women seem to prefer traditional specialties, such as those in offices and hospitals and in communications. However, men appear to prefer these jobs as well; similarly, both women and men leave traditionally male jobs at comparable rates (Stiehm, 1989). These patterns suggest more about the jobs themselves than about gender.

During the 1970s, the military gradually began opening up to women. Not only did more women join the military in the 1970s, but the pattern of job specialties also began to change. Between 1973 and 1978, the percentage of army women in traditional jobs declined by more than 30%, while the percentage in nontraditional jobs increased by 20% (Savell, Woelfel, Collins, & Bentler, 1979; Woelfel, 1981). In 1978, 57% of army women were in traditional jobs, 20% in nontraditional ones. The Army's Reserve Officers Training Program (ROTC) first admitted women in the 1973–74 academic year. In the 1978–79 academic year, women made up 25% of the total enrollment (Card & Farrell, 1983). The service academies opened their doors to women in 1976 after being ordered to do so by federal legislation. By 1989, about 12% of cadets at the Air Force Academy and 9% at the Naval Academy were women (Wittman, 1989).

In 1977, the armed forces adopted a recommendation by the Brookings Institute to move toward less restrictive personnel policies so that more women could enter the services. The Brookings report recommended that women constitute 22% of the forces; the Pentagon's final goal was 12.5%. The Pentagon's goal could be met even if women still were excluded from front-line combat jobs. However, that five-year plan was scrapped after the Reagan administration took over and after a slumping economy made it possible to enlist enough men (Stiehm, 1989). New strength standards were set for specialty positions that eliminated more than 90% of the eligible women, despite the fact that women were serving in those specialties at the time with no evidence of deficiency.

Branches of the armed forces differ in their openness to women. The Air Force, with the greatest percentage of women (13.6% in 1990), is the most receptive (Schafer, 1990a). After the 1991 Gulf War, the House of Representatives passed a provision repealing restrictions on women's flying combat aircraft (Nordheimer, 1991). In contrast, the Marine Corps is least receptive, with only 4.8% female representation. Because the Marine Corps is infantry-oriented and such positions are the most physically demanding, it is not surprising that female representation is lowest there. Also not surprising is the intense masculine mystique that surrounds this branch of the service.

Women in the military have to face an environment oftentimes overtly hostile to them. Clothes and equipment generally are not designed for most women and short-statured men; standards of performance do not take women's different strengths into account (for example, leg as opposed to upper-body strength); and family and social services are poor (Cheatham, 1984; J. Johnson, 1989; Rustad, 1982). For example, there are not enough day-care slots for children of military personnel, and many day-care centers are overcrowded and hazardous. As the 1991 Gulf War revealed, single parents (more often mothers) and military couples often face an insurmountable burden with respect to finding adequate child care, especially when they are mobilized on short notice (J. Gross, 1990b). Another factor for women in the military is the high degree of sexual harassment present. A 1988 Pentagon survey of 38,000 military women and men found that two out of three women had experienced some form of sexual harassment, compared to only 17% of the men (Schafer, 1990b). Most of the harassment took the form of sexual jokes or remarks, suggestive looks or gestures, and physical contact such as touching or pinching, but 15% of the females said they had been pressured for sexual favors and 5% reported actual or attempted rape or sexual assault. Although these percentages are similar to those found in traditionally male civilian work settings, the consequences still are severe. For example, the frequency of vulgar and obscene language directed at women is significantly correlated with women's ratings of their own job dissatisfaction (Woelfel & Savell, 1981). On many bases overseas, military leaders foster and condone an atmosphere of sexual harassment by ignoring complaints, by allowing on-base sexually-oriented entertainment, and in some cases by setting an example (Katzenstein, 1990).

Homophobia also is high in the military and officially sanctioned. The armed forces prohibit lesbians and gay men from serving in the military, despite lack of evidence demonstrating harm from their presence (J. Gross, 1990a; Melton, 1989). In fact, two studies commissioned by the Pentagon in 1989 found no evidence that gay men and lesbians disrupted the military. The reports went further, praising the performance of gay men and lesbians and urging their retention. Even a Navy commander who was urging his officers to vigorously root out lesbian sailors noted that these sailors were "hard-working, career-oriented, willing to put in long hours on the job and among the command's top performers" (reported in J. Gross, 1990a). The military policy against homosexuals affects both gay men and lesbians, but lesbians are more systematically rooted out and dismissed. For example, three times as many lesbians as gay men are dismissed from the armed forces each year. Mainly because women who are engaged in nontraditional occupations and activities are frequently accused of being lesbian, lesbian-baiting has been one more way women, both gay and straight, have been harassed (Katzenstein, 1990).

No rational basis exists for denying women an equal role in the military. Studies (reported in Stiehm, 1989) have shown that women in the military learn fast, perform well, stay in service longer and have a lower rate of lost time for illnesses and absenteeism (including time lost for pregnancy) than men (because men lose more time than women for disciplinary reasons). Studies of women army recruits given regular male basic training and extended field exercises have found little difference in relative performance when these women were compared to an equal number of men, using scientifically based standards ("Registration," 1980). Although men may be stronger on the average than women and therefore more suitable for infantry positions, a criterion-based rather than a gender-based standard seems most reasonable. Most women at the service academies are doing well, although attrition rates are higher for females than males, and males still are more likely than females to be perceived as leaders (J. Adams, 1984; R. W. Rice, Yoder, Adams, Priest, & Prince, 1984).

Military men's attitudes toward women in the military have become more acceptant over the years, especially since the Gulf War (Nordheimer, 1991; Stevens & Gardner, 1987). Within the military, the majority of men and women now favor the concept of assigning women to traditionally male jobs, including assignments to combat units or aboard naval vessels. However, about half of military respondents think women would be poorer front-line soldiers than men (Woelfel, 1981). Among the American public, close to two-thirds in 1990 approved of women volunteering to serve in combat roles but not being assigned to such roles (Sciolino, 1990).

The hypocritical nature of regulations regarding women in the military was pointed up quite clearly in the 1991 war against Iraq. Thirty-five thousand U.S. women were called up along with 505,000 men and sent to a region where women have few, if any, legal rights. American women fought, were injured, taken prisoner, and died alongside men, yet the image of women somehow being "protected" by men was still part of official policy. Uncomfortable with the realities of women and men working together relatively equally, the media played up women's maternal role by focusing on the poignancy of children seeing their mothers go off to war (see Flanders, 1990). Little was said about the pain children experienced watching their fathers go off to war. The truth was that both women and men adjusted relatively well to the sudden mobilization of the armed forces, especially the reserves (J. Gross, 1990b).

Many people, especially older military officers, are highly resistant to the idea of women in combat. They argue that men's greater aggressiveness, strength, and daring make men better combatants than women (see, for example, Gilder, 1979; B. Mitchell, 1989). Putting women into such positions thus would make a combat unit less effective. Furthermore, the presence of women would lower men's morale, since women have lower status than men. Brian Mitchell (1989) argues that the presence of women in the military "feminizes" it, making it less attractive to "manly" men and therefore weaker as a fighting force. This puts our nation in peril. George Gilder (1979) suggests that women in combat threaten society in another way. Unless men have sole responsibility for protecting women's welfare, social barriers to male aggression against women will break down and the result may be "nothing more nor less than a move toward barbarism" (p. 46). (This is an odd statement given the tremendous amount of male violence against women that exists now, as will be discussed later.) As retired Marine Corps commandant General Robert Barrow testified before the Senate Armed Services Committee's manpower and personnel subcommittee in 1991, "Women give life, sustain life, nurture life, they can't take it. If you want to make a combat unit ineffective, assign women to it" (in Mower, 1991). Thus, in this line of thinking, women must be excluded from combat.

It is important to note that only 10 to 15% of our defensive force consists of front-line troops. Technology has displaced brute strength in conventional combat situations. And if women were eligible for combat service, it is most likely that only women with the same minimum skills as men would be allowed in a combat situation. The "brute strength" argument against women is further diminished by recognizing the fact that most Asian men are smaller than American women, yet size was no apparent disadvantage for Asian fighters in the Korean and Vietnam wars. In addition, women have

fought in national struggles of resistance around the world, from Greece to Palestine to Nicaragua.

The main argument for allowing women in combat situations is that it is sex discrimination not to. For women officers, the prohibition also limits their career advancement since top positions in the armed forces require combat experience (Nordheimer, 1991). An additional argument is that by enlarging the pool of potential officers to include women, the military would be ensured of getting the smartest, most capable people available. The critical issue seems to be whether to allow women to be killed in wartime. To some extent, the issue is more abstract than real since women have participated and died in every war that has ever been fought. To date, neither Congress nor the Supreme Court is ready to put women into military combat. It is indeed a terrible thing to have to decide whose life to risk, but if defending one's country is a duty of citizenship and women and men are supposedly equal citizens, it is difficult for many people to justify sparing one sex over the other as a general rule.

Those in favor of opening combat roles to women argue that women already live in a war zone in their own country, vulnerable to rape, intimidation, and brainwashing. Therefore, "real" combat should pose little additional threat. Exempting women from combat perpetuates the stereotype that women need protection and are not as capable as men. Furthermore, as the 1991 Gulf War showed, the protection women receive is more illusory than real. Why not then give women the benefits of equality, since they already are absorbing the costs?

Feminists themselves are split over this issue (Elshtain & Tobias, 1990; A. Harris & King, 1989; Ruddick, 1989; Stiehm, 1989). Those against the presence of women in combat argue that feminism should mean nonviolence and that war is a masculine "game" in which women should play no role, especially because women have little to no policymaking power. Until women and men have equal rights as civilians and equal opportunity to make and shape policy decisions, it is unreasonable to give women an equal opportunity to die. Some feminists add that women, because they are life-bearers, are more oriented toward peace than war and therefore shouldn't be forced into killing.

One consequence of current military policy is that more men do risk their lives as combat troops during war. The military has been viewed by some writers as the last bastion of masculinity, where men can prove their toughness physically through aggressiveness, risk taking, and violence (Arkin &

Dobrofsky, 1978b; Pleck & Sawyer, 1974; Raphael, 1988). And the military has fostered this image of masculinity in order to train men to kill and to risk their lives. "Be a real man," the ads say. The U.S. Marines want "men at their best." As we saw in Chapter 5, warriors hold high status within society, partly as a reward for risking their lives. Thus, keeping warrior roles for men preserves their higher status. This masculine image of the military may account for some of the marked resistance to allowing women's equal participation.

Another outgrowth of "macho" military training is that military men often engage in unnecessary violence and wanton acts of killing and destruction. Seymour Hersh (1970) analyzed the My Lai massacre in Vietnam as a predictable outcome of military exaggerations of the male gender stereotypes. Such atrocities occur in every war by every army, and gender roles may have much to do with it.

The consequences of men and not women being the warriors extend far beyond military life. Socialization trains boys and not girls to be soldiers. Dominance, aggressiveness, competitiveness—all valued in military life—are characteristics of the male gender role. As a result of this socialization, even nonmilitary men are more militaristic than women and, as we will discuss shortly, more likely to use violence to solve interpersonal problems. Furthermore, the military model of dominating an opponent through the use of force becomes the model of (male) societal thinking as well. Thus, all forms of domination—on the basis of race, gender, class, species, national origin, sexual orientation—become more possible (see Stoltenberg, 1989).

The effect of women on the military remains to be seen. Because so much training goes into the making of a soldier, it seems clear that women recruits can be trained to be equally as cold, aggressive, and deadly as male recruits. A study of West Point cadets during the first three years of coeducation found few personality differences between the men and women (J. Adams, 1984). Both groups were strong in agentic characteristics (for example, competitiveness, independence), potential for leadership, and motivation to achieve. Nearly half of the women did not see themselves as having children in the future, compared to fewer than 20% of the men. Another study found senior cadets to be more agentic than freshmen, suggesting that military training may have a "masculinizing" effect (Apao, 1982). Indeed, agentic personality characteristics are linked to suitedness of military recruits for military functions (Dimitrovsky et al., 1989).

Given the tendency, because of socialization, for more women than men to be against war in general and to be humanistic, it is possible that not many women will desire a military role. But it only seems fair to let those who do desire that role to have access to it. An important point is the fact that in peacetime, service in the military is a job with excellent educational and training opportunities, excellent fringe benefits, and good chance for advancement. It is the kind of job from which women have traditionally been barred. In addition, all individuals who have served in the military—in the past, predominantly men—receive five points' preference on federal civil service exams. In some states (for example, Massachusetts), veterans receive an absolute preference, a procedure upheld by the Supreme Court in 1979. Historically, veterans' preference points have hurt women's job chances. Consequently, although women make up 41% of those who pass the Civil Service Professional and Administrative Career Exam, they are only 27% of those who are hired ("Veterans," 1978). Allowing women full equality in the military will go a long way toward allowing them an equal role in society. It will also alleviate the burden now placed on men.

▲ Abuses of Power

Inherent in the preceding discussion regarding different forms of power is the observation that not only are men more likely than women to have structural power, but they are also more likely to abuse such power—as seen in economic greed, political corruption, self-serving legal maneuvering, and military massacres. Perhaps power leads to abuse, especially absolute power ("Power tends to corrupt and absolute power corrupts absolutely"—Lord Acton, 1887). Thus, men's greater abuse of power simply may be a function of their greater likelihood of being in positions of power. Yet gender is not incidental to men's having greater structural power than women, nor is it incidental to the use of violence, the major form of abuse. As we saw in Chapter 3, males are expected and encouraged to act aggressively. Although males, in general, do seem to have a greater predisposition toward aggression than females, aggressive behavior is definitely learned and is responsive to a wide range of situational conditions. In our culture, far more than in most others, male aggressiveness appears to be viewed ambivalently. While violence and its social effects (crime, rapes, wars) are overtly condemned, aggression and violence are covertly glorified in the media (films, books, and especially TV) and in daily interactions. Action films like the "Rambo" series are box-office hits mainly because the "action" is violent.

Because of the link between masculinity and violence, one way of "proving" one's masculinity is by some form of aggression or violence. We have seen how male political leaders may try to prove their masculinity through macho talk and military intervention. In this sense, war may be viewed as the ultimate proof of manhood. This may explain, in part, the strong resistance to allowing women in combat. Terrorism, too, whether by the Right or the Left, whether officially sanctioned or officially punished, can be viewed as a consequence of the cultural linkage of masculinity and violence since it is an act overwhelmingly committed by men (R. Morgan, 1989). Indeed, the terrorist—aggressive, dedicated, passionate, risk-taking—may be a male cultural idol.

In sports as well, masculinity is tied to aggression and violence. The greater the danger of injury and the more combative the activities, the more likely it is that the sport and its players will be viewed as masculine (Fasteau, 1974; Raphael, 1988). Thus, contact sports (such as football, hockey, boxing, wrestling, basketball, and soccer) are viewed as more masculine than sports such as golf or swimming, which are neither combative nor extremely competitive. Perhaps not coincidentally, athletes in the contact "masculine" sports tend to be more violent in their attitudes and behaviors than comparable groups of nonathletes or than athletes in noncontact sports, at least on college campuses (J. M. Brown, 1982; J. M. Brown & Davies, 1978). In particular, male high school and college athletes in contact sports have been implicated in a disproportionate number of rapes and other sexual assaults (Eskinazi, 1990; Neimark, 1991). (See Miedzian, 1991, for further discussion of the link between masculinity and violence.)

As this last finding suggests, criminal activities too reflect gender roles; in particular, men's crimes are more likely than women's to involve violence. Men constitute more than 80% of those who commit crimes and more than 90% of those who commit violent crimes ("Status Report," 1988). This pattern holds true around the world (Seager & Olson, 1986). Most crimes are committed by men between the ages of 13 and 24, mostly poor. Criminal behavior is often a way for a young man to prove his masculinity at a time when such proof is important—that is, during adolescence and young adulthood. Violence in particular may be a way for young men to display their "toughness" and gain peer approval when more acceptable paths of attaining status (such as via money, a prestigious job, athletic success) are unavailable due to poverty, racism, lack of education, and lack of hope (Freiberg, 1991a; Messerschmidt, 1986). The use of violence by powerless men to prove their masculinity may explain why nearly one in four young Black men is in jail, on probation, or on parole.

Violent street crime tends to be committed by powerless men, but powerful men also commit crimes, although they are less likely to be charged or convicted of them (Messerschmidt, 1986). Corporate crime, which may involve deliberate corporate neglect of workplace and product safety (for example, the defective Ford Pinto and the unsterilized Dalkon shield), may result in injury and death far exceeding that which results from street crime. Although appearing to be far removed from violent street crime, corporate crime reflects masculine stereotypes too, especially those relating to ambition, competition, and lack of concern for others.

Females predominate only with respect to crimes of prostitution and juvenile running away, both of which are considered "victimless crimes" and both of which may result from female sexual victimization (U.S. Department of Commerce, 1989b). Female criminals usually are interested more in improving their financial circumstances than in violence or dominance, and women's motives are more "need-based than greed-based" (Daly, as cited in "Women's Booty," 1987). The crimes that have increased the most for females have been embezzlement, larceny, forgery, and fraud—all nonviolent crimes—although violent crime committed by young urban girls may be on the rise as well (F. Adler, 1981; F. R. Lee, 1991; Mann, 1984). As women's work experiences become more similar to men's, their temptations may be similar as well. For example, with more women working in banks, embezzlement by women becomes more possible. However, most of women's crimes are unrelated to their paid work. As with men, powerlessness in the form of poverty and racism is strongly associated with crime and especially with criminal convictions (Redmond, 1990).

Men not only are more likely than women to use violence, but they are more likely to be victims of violence as well, at least in terms of police statistics. Race also is a factor, mediated by the greater likelihood of Blacks and Hispanics than Whites to be poor and live in crime-infested neighborhoods.

One out of ten Black males between ages 15 and 24 were homicide victims in 1988, the highest rate of any group ("Dangers," 1990). In their lifetime, non-White males have a 1 in 38 chance of becoming a murder victim, non-White females a 1 in 138 chance, White males a 1 in 204 chance, and White females a 1 in 437 chance ("Non-white," 1989). The homicide rate in the United States is higher than in 21 other industrialized countries, largely due to the easy availability of firearms, the violence of the crack trade, and the glorification of violence (by men) in the media ("Report: Homicide Rate," 1990).

Although men, at least minority men, are more likely to be murder victims than women, violence against women has escalated since the early 1960s (Caputi & Russell, 1990). The magnitude of the violence committed against women is enormous—murder, rape, sexual abuse, assault, robbery, sexual slavery (forced prostitution), sexual harassment—yet much of it never gets officially reported or classified. A probability sampling of 930 San Francisco-area women aged 18 or older revealed that nearly one out of three women had been a victim of rape or attempted rape, more than one out of three had been a victim of childhood sexual abuse, and one out of five had been a victim of marital violence (D. E. H. Russell, 1984). Fewer than 10% had reported these crimes to the police. Even more chilling than the magnitude of the violence committed by men against women is the fact that most of it is committed by men known to the victim. For example, more than half of all female homicide victims are killed by current or former partners, compared to a minority of male homicide victims (L. E. A. Walker, 1989b).

The gender politics involved in violence against women frequently goes unrecognized. Most women are victims of violent crimes because they are female, not just because they are a specific human being. For example, Marc Lepine murdered 14 female engineering students at the University of Montreal in 1989 because they were women ("You're all fucking feminists," Lepine shouted as he opened fire in a classroom after ordering all the men out; reported in Caputi & Russell, 1990). Serial killings, a crime on the increase, are nearly always committed against women by White men. As Jane Caputi (1989) notes, "Sexual murder is the ultimate expression of sexuality as a form of power" (p. 439). The most frequent victims of rape, sexual abuse, sexual slavery, sexual harassment, and domestic abuse are women. This pattern is true worldwide, as a 1989 report by the Worldwatch Institute documented ("Violence Against Women," 1989). All these acts terrify not only the actual victims but all women, who become afraid to talk back, to go out alone, to be alone. Carole Sheffield (1989) describes male sexual violence as "'sexual terrorism," "a system by which males frighten and, by frightening, control and dominate females" (p. 3). Underlying the dynamics of such crimes is the socialized belief that men are entitled to women's obedience and women's bodies, and men's socialized need for power and status.

Violence against women is often accepted as "normal," so much so that until recently, it wasn't even named as such. For example, only in the last 20 years have we had names for sexual harassment, acquaintance rape, sexual abuse of young girls, and battering. Much of male behavior toward women that now is viewed as unacceptable had been rationalized in the past as "just the way men are." Since the second wave of the women's movement in the early 1970s, such behaviors increasingly have been identified, analyzed, and criminalized. Gender roles and stereotypes are integrally connected to such behaviors, as will become clearer as we review the research in three areas: sexual harassment, rape, and domestic abuse. The controversial issue regarding whether pornography can be considered a form of violence against women also will be examined as it relates to rape.

Sexual Harassment

It already has been noted that women in college (Chapter 7), in the workplace (Chapter 11), and in the military are subject to unwanted sexual attention that interferes with their ability to work or that creates an "intimidating, hostile, or offensive working environment." Sexual harassment affects one out of two or three female college students, one out of two employed women, and two out of three military women.

Sexual harassment is an abuse of power. It is engaged in by those with more power against those with less power. It functions as a social control mechanism to keep a minority group in its place. Yet sexual harassment is not gender neutral. Women in positions of power are much less likely than men in power to engage in sexually harassing behaviors (Gutek, 1985; U.S. Merit Systems Protection Board, 1988). And male targets of unwanted sexual behaviors from women are less likely to experience such behaviors as unpleasant. Given the status inequality encoded in gender roles and the socialization of men to view sexual dominance as a way of proving masculinity, it is not surprising that sexual harassment is fairly gender-specific. Sexist remarks, seductive behaviors, sexual bribery, and sexual coercion all serve to remind women that they are primarily sexual objects, not equal human beings.

The operation of this social control aspect of sexual harassment can be discerned when the dynamics of sexual harassment are examined. The main victims of sexual harassment are non-White women, young women, single women, women who work in nonsupervisory jobs, and women who work in a primarily male workplace (Fain & Anderton, 1987; Lafontaine & Tredeau, 1986). Thus, women who are vulnerable because of age, marital status, job status, and ethnic minority status, as well as those who threaten men's dominance by "invading their territory," are most likely to be sexually harassed.

Not all men engage in sexually harassing behaviors, but those who do tend to do so repeatedly. Sexual harassers appear to adhere very strongly to the stereotypic male role in terms of traits and attitudes. Research has found that men who are most likely to engage in sexually exploitative behavior (such as using their position to coerce sexual favors from a woman) hold adversarial sexual beliefs (such as, that all sexual relationships are fundamentally exploitative), believe women enjoy male sexual dominance and coercive sex, have difficulty taking another person's perspective, and describe themselves as possessing stereotypically masculine characteristics, especially those that are socially undesirable and those that contrast most strongly with stereotypic femininity (Pryor, 1987). From reports of victims, most sexual harassers appear to be older than and of the same race as their victims, married, and in co-worker positions (Gutek, 1985; U.S. Merit Systems Protection Board, 1988).

Given the way sexual harassment is embedded in gender and power dynamics, it is not surprising that many women view sexually harassing behaviors as "normal," meaning "to be expected." For example, in one study, fewer than a third of the female graduate students who had received unwelcome sexual attention from a professor (27%) believed they had been sexually harassed (L. F. Fitzgerald, Shullman, et al., 1988). Women victims may be blamed for sexual harassment ("What did I/she do to bring this on?"), especially by those who hold traditional attitudes toward women (Malovich & Stake, 1990). Laws that define sexual harassment as a form of sex discrimination and therefore illegal have been in place only since 1976. Consciousness has been rising steadily since then, although many employment and academic settings still have inadequate procedures for filing and processing complaints (Gutek, 1985; C. Robertson, Dyer, & Campbell, 1988). Labeling an experience as sexual harassment appears to be a function of gender (women are more likely than men to label behaviors as sexually harassing), age (graduate students and employed women are more likely to label experiences as sexual harassment than are college students), attitudes toward women (those with less traditional attitudes are less tolerant of harassment behavior), and the severity of the behavior (sexually coercive experiences are more likely to be defined as harassment than are unwanted sexual attention, leering, and deliberate touching) (D. D. Baker, Terpstra, & Larntz, 1990; L. F. Fitzgerald & Ormerod, 1991; C. B. Johnson et al., 1991; Malovich & Stake, 1990). Labeling is important, since only those who label experiences as sexual harassment will report it. However, reporting does not always correct the problem, since women who bring complaints may be viewed as troublemakers ("Why are you trying to hurt his career?") or their complaint may be trivialized ("You should be flattered" or "Can't you take a joke?").

Of course, if women don't report sexual harassment, their credibility is also questioned, as the nation all too vividly witnessed in the 1991 Senate confirmation hearings of Supreme Court Justice Clarence Thomas. Former employee Anita Hill's experience of and reaction to his alleged sexual harassment was typical (for example, the harassment was verbal and occurred in private, she told only her closest friends, and tried to cope with the situation herself). Unfortunately, public reaction also was typical. Professor Hill was characterized as lying, vengeful, hysterical, and, as a Black women testifying against a Black man, a traitor to her race. In the end, her testimony was viewed as either false or trivial by a nearly all-male and all-White Senate.

Sexual harassment is not trivial. As we have seen, such behaviors serve as barriers to women's achievement in academia, the labor force, and the military. Such behaviors also have enormous psychological effects, causing women to feel violated, depressed, inferior, and inadequate. There are physical effects as well, especially if the harassment is ongoing, since chronic stress takes its toll. As we saw in Chapter 8, the higher rates of depression and anxiety-related disorders (both physical and emotional) in women than men can be linked to women's greater likelihood of experiencing sexual victimization.

Eliminating sexual harassment will be difficult, especially if only specific behaviors are targeted. Although learning that certain behaviors are illegal and will be punished is an important first step, both the power structure and societal attitudes must change as well. When men are given more status than women simply by virtue of their gender, and when male gender socialization encourages men to view women as their sexual property and to define themselves in terms of dominance over others, sexual violence against women is to be expected. This is strikingly evident with respect to rape.

Rape

About one woman in four will be a rape victim during the course of her lifetime, and an additional 20% will experience an attempted rape (Allgeier, 1987; D. E. H. Russell, 1984). Only a minority of these rapes get reported to authorities (fewer than 10%), although the rate of reported rape has been increasing since 1977 ("Rape," 1991). Yet the current high rate of forcible rape is not a recent phenomenon. In fact, the rate of rape among women and teenage girls appears to have remained unchanged since 1973, when community surveys first were done. Gender roles and men's power over women are integrally connected to this all-too-common crime.

In this section, we will examine myths about rape, cultural and psychological factors contributing to rape, and enforcement/prevention issues. (See Allgeier, 1987, for an excellent summary of the psychological research on coercive sexual interactions.)

Rape myths   The myths that have been perpetuated about rape illustrate masculine prejudice and are most likely to be believed by males, older and less educated people, and those high in gender stereotyping, sexist attitudes, adversarial sexual beliefs, and acceptance of interpersonal violence as a legitimate way to gain compliance (Burt, 1980; Feild, 1978; E. R. Hall, Howard, & Boezio, 1986).

Myth 1: Women provoke rape by their appearance or actions. *Fact:* Men rape women; therefore men are responsible for rape. As many as 90% of rapes are premeditated—for example, a decision is made to rape the next unaccompanied female who enters an elevator. Thus, what a victim does or wears cannot be considered relevant (M. Lester, 1976; Scully, 1990). The only characteristic that distinguishes rape victims from non–rape victims is being female. Three out of four college rape victims

cannot be predicted by any suggested risk factor (for example, amount of drinking) (Koss & Dinero, 1989). Furthermore, nothing a woman could do (drink, wear revealing clothes, go to a bar alone, kiss a man) merits a response of rape.

Myth 2: Rape is a sex crime committed by sexually abnormal males. *Fact:* One out of 12 college men admit to having engaged in behaviors that meet the legal definition of rape or attempted rape (Koss, Gidycz, & Wisniewski, 1987). One out of three college men admit they would rape a woman if no one were likely to find out (Allgeier, 1987). If all rapists were sexually abnormal, this would implicate a very large number of men. In fact, numerous studies reveal that men who commit rape are psychologically indistinguishable from other men in terms of psychiatric problems, heterosocial skills, and adequacy of their sex life (Briere & Malamuth, 1983; Koss & Dinero, 1988; Muehlenhard & Falcon, 1990; Scully, 1990). Rape is a crime of violence, a form of assault, not a crime of passion.

Myth 3: Most rapes are committed by strangers in dark alleys. *Fact:* The vast majority of rapes (80 to 90%) are committed by someone known to the victim, and half of all rapes occur in the victim's residence (Allgeier, 1987; D. E. H. Russell, 1984). However, acquaintance rapes are least likely to be reported to the police (only 5% of college women who have been raped report their assault) (Koss et al., 1987). Thus, reported rapes are most likely to be stranger rapes. Women don't report rapes for a number of reasons: they don't label what has been done to them "rape" (most common in cases of acquaintance rape), they think they're at fault (Myth #1), they fear others will disbelieve or blame them (this is likely to be true), and they think they'll be able to "forget about it" more quickly if they don't tell (this is not true).

Myth 4: Most women want to be raped. *Fact:* Virtually no women report a wish to be raped, even if no one were to know what had happened (Malamuth, Haber, & Feshbach, 1980). Rape is an act of violence and experienced as such. Nearly all victims suffer severe aftereffects, both emotionally and in their relationships with others. Studies have found that even one year after a rape, victims are more anxious, fearful, suspicious, and confused than matched nonvictims (Kilpatrick, Resick, & Veronen, 1981; Scheppele & Bart, 1983). One out of three rape victims consider suicide after being raped, and 80% become more distrustful of men in general (Koss, Dinero, Seibel, & Cox, 1988). Victims of acquaintance rape are just as severely affected as victims of stranger rape.

Myth 5: Many reports of rape are unfounded. *Fact:* Fewer than 10% of rape complaints are unfounded, about the same as for other violent crimes. In some areas, the percentage of false reports may be as low as 2% (M. Lester, 1976). As noted previously, the opposite is more likely to be true: the vast majority of rapes never get reported.

Myth 6: Most rapes are performed by Black men on White women. *Fact:* Over 75% of reported rapes are intraracial, with White male offenders and White female victims the most common pairing (Amir, 1971; South & Felson, 1990). This myth reflects both sexism and racism—the White woman viewed as valuable property of the White man, and the Black man viewed as especially lusting after White men's property. Research on the racial patterning of rape indicates that rape is more a matter of opportunity than of racial animosity.

The preposterousness of such myths is illustrated in the following story using a robbery as an analogy for rape.

A man was testifying regarding his having been robbed while walking down a street.
Prosecutor: Can you tell the jury what time the alleged crime occurred?
Victim: About 11:30 P.M.
Prosecutor: And what exactly were you doing?
Victim: Just walking down the street.
Prosecutor: Alone?
Victim: Yes.
Prosecutor: And what were you wearing?
Victim: Oh, a three-piece suit.
Prosecutor: An expensive suit?
Victim: Well, I do like to dress well.
Prosecutor: Let me ask you this. Have you ever given money away?
Victim: Why, of course . . .
Prosecutor: In fact, Mr. D., you have quite a reputation for philanthropy. So here you are, a well-dressed man, with a history of giving money away, walking alone late at night, practically advertising yourself as a mark. Why, if we didn't know better, Mr. D., we might even say that you were asking for it!

Cultural factors   The cultural aspect of rape is revealed through a number of different lines of evidence: cross-cultural research, the linkage of sex and domination/submission, the role of pornography, sexual scripts, and gender roles. The research is conclusive that cultural factors are major contributors to the incidence of rape.

Cross-cultural research reveals that the occurrence of rape varies among cultures. Rape-prone societies, like the United States, are characterized by male dominance, an ideology of male toughness and interpersonal violence, and a view of nature as something to be dominated and exploited (Sanday, 1981b, 1986). In cultures where women are respected and influential, where "feminine" qualities such as nurturance are valued and nature is revered, rape rarely occurs. In a sample of 95 band and tribal societies, approximately one-half were relatively rape-free (for example, West Sumatra) and 20% clearly rape-prone. These findings demonstrate that rape is an expression of male dominance, not innate male sexuality. When a culture devalues "the feminine" (nurturance, vulnerability, tenderness), males devalue females and demonstrate their devaluation by means of rape and other forms of domination (see also Griffin, 1981).

Rape and other forms of sexual assault can be viewed as the inevitable outcome of *the linkage of sex and domination/submission*—equating masculinity with power, dominance, and sexual aggressiveness, and femininity with pleasing men, sexual passivity, and lack of assertiveness. In the United States and many other cultures, domination and subordination are eroticized and sex and violence linked (see Brownmiller, 1975; MacKinnon, 1987b, for excellent discussions of this subject). The words we use for sex demonstrate this connection with violence: sexual "conquest," "screw," "bang," and so forth. Such an equation makes rape the "perfect" combination to prove masculinity: it is aggressive, it is sexual, and it involves dominance over and denigration of a woman (Griffin, 1975).

Given the way sexual behavior fits into a culture that encourages male dominance, male sexual abuse of children perhaps should not be surprising. It has been estimated that between one-third to two-thirds of all women have been victims of sexual abuse before age 18, at least half of it by family members or acquaintances (Clutter, 1990; Koss, 1990; D. E. H. Russell, 1984). Only 2 to 6% of cases ever get reported to police. Although boys too are sexually abused (about 10%), three out of four victims are female and nearly all perpetrators are male. Father-daughter incest in particular is much more common than previously thought, although apparently not new (Armstrong, 1987; Rush, 1980). Freud, for example, in the late 19th century, was aware of many reports of female children abused by their fathers or other family members, but chose to disbelieve his women patients. Father-daughter incest is most likely to occur in highly patriarchal families, and the effects on the daughter are devastating and long-lasting. Women who have been sexually abused as children are likely to suffer from a host of psychological problems, including multiple personality disorders, borderline disorders, eating disorders, generalized anxiety, and depression. Thus, the higher rates of these disorders for women than men (as seen in Chapter 8) may be due to the greater likelihood of women's having been sexually victimized.

Laboratory and survey research confirms the linkage of sex and violence for many American men. For example, most college men have fantasies of forced sex and domination (Greendlinger & Byrne, 1987), about 70% experience some sexual arousal to the thought of "forcing a female to do something she didn't want to," and about 40% find rape scenes sexually arousing (Malamuth, Check, & Briere, 1986). Those men who are most aroused or most likely to fantasize about forced sex are most likely to use or to have used force in a sexual interaction with a woman, and these men also are most likely to use force in nonsexual aggressive ways as well. Thus, there appears to be a reciprocal relationship between sexual arousal and aggression for at least some men: the more aggressive the stimuli, the greater the sexual arousal.

The linkage of sex and violence, sex and domination is the main theme of *pornography*, an $8-billion-a-year industry (Douglas, 1987). Although any definition of pornography is likely to be controversial, the term will be used here to refer to materials that graphically depict the sexual subordination and degradation of a human being, such as dehumanized portrayals of women, presenting pain or bondage as pleasurable, and sex between unequals (such as between adult and child) (MacKinnon, 1987b; Steinem, 1983). In contrast, *erotica* refers to materials that portray consensual and mutually pleasurable sexual interactions between adults. Most "adult"-oriented and X-rated materials fit the category of violent pornography. Content analysis of 45 widely available X-rated videocassettes found that most (four out of five) contained sexually explicit scenes depicting male domination or exploitation of women (Cowan et al., 1988). In three out of four of these videos, male physical aggression against women was depicted; in half, rape was specifically shown.

There is enormous debate, fueled by political and religious objections to sexual material and

feminists' concern over degrading portrayals of women, about whether pornography has negative effects on the viewer and on society. The research evidence is clear, however, that it is not sexually explicit material per se that has negative effects on the viewer, but sexually violent material, the most frequent kind (Donnerstein, Linz, & Penrod, 1987). In most such material, women are portrayed as willing victims, even when pain cues are presented. For example, women rape victims typically are depicted as sexually aroused by the rape, despite (because of?) being brutalized.

What effect does viewing violent pornography have on the viewer? Numerous studies conducted by Neil Malamuth and Edward Donnerstein and colleagues using mainly college students in controlled laboratory settings have found that viewing violent sexual material can lead to men's increased acceptance of rape myths, increased sexual arousal to rape scenes, and increased self-reported likelihood to commit rape (Donnerstein et al., 1987; Malamuth & Briere, 1986). Men whose sexual arousal increases in response to exposure to pornography also are more likely to aggress against women in nonsexual ways, at least in laboratory settings. Repeated exposure to violent pornography results in reduced negative reactions (such as anxiety and depression) to the material and reduced sensitivity to female victims of violence in other contexts (Linz, Donnerstein, & Penrod, 1984). Survey research with men finds a significant correlation between amount of exposure to pornography and such attitudinal variables as acceptance of rape myths, general sexual callousness, and acceptance of violence against women (Malamuth & Briere, 1986). Although we cannot say that all men who view violent pornography actually will go out and rape a woman, we can say that exposure to such materials desensitizes men to rape and therefore may make such crimes more likely (Demare, Briere, & Lips, 1988). Thus, the effect of pornography may be indirect, affecting violence against women by affecting thought patterns supportive of such violence.

Research with convicted rapists and serial killers supports a link between exposure to violent pornography and violence against women (Caputi, 1989). Such men admit to a much higher incidence of viewing violent pornography than do other men. An analysis of state to state variations in reported rapes found that the best predictor of rape reports is the circulation level of sexually explicit magazines, followed by the level of gender inequality (for example, the percentage of women holding political office and women's median income relative to men's), and the level of social disorganization (for example, divorce rates and the number of female-headed families) (Baron & Straus, 1989). Although all this research is correlational and therefore cannot tell us what caused what (does pornography predispose or disinhibit a tendency to rape women in some men or do rapists seek out more pornography than non-rapists?), the pattern is as predicted.

These results and others have fueled an intense debate about whether pornography should be made illegal. Public opinion is divided along gender lines, with 72% of the women sampled in 1986 agreeing that laws against pornography were not strict enough, compared to only 41% of the men (B. Sussman, 1986). Half of the men thought the laws were about right, compared to only 23% of the women. There also is disagreement among feminists. On one side are feminists like Catharine MacKinnon and Andrea Dworkin and groups like Women Against Pornography who argue that pornography infringes on the civil rights of women and thus is a form of sex discrimination (Dworkin, 1981; Leidholdt & Raymond, 1990; MacKinnon, 1987b; Stoltenberg, 1989). Ordinances supporting this view were passed in Minneapolis in 1983 and in Indianapolis in 1984, but both were later defeated—the former by the mayor's veto, and the latter by the Supreme Court, which found it unconstitutional. The argument that such material harmed women as a class was not considered as important as the pornographers' right of free speech. On the other side are feminists and groups such as the Feminist Anti-Censorship Taskforce who argue that any form of censorship is dangerous and likely to be ineffective (Vance, 1984). They recommend educational measures instead. The 1986 Meese Commission report, which concluded that sexually explicit material causes sexual violence, did not help resolve the difficult issue of distinguishing among different types of such material, nor did it help determine what should be done about the different types. The debate continues (see Gubar & Hoff, 1989).

Not all men are rapists, of course, and not all men have callous attitudes toward coercive sex. Yet male *gender role expectations and sexual scripts* do contribute to the incidence of rape in this country. Male sexual scripts encourage men to view sex as a proving ground of their masculinity (see Chapter 4). "Getting sex" is important for men; less important is how sex is obtained. Although finding a willing female partner is one way of obtaining sex, the use of some persuasion or coercion to obtain sex may be even more satisfying to some males since such

sexual circumstances demonstrate dominance and achievement. The lines between persuasion, manipulation, and force are thin and somewhat subjective. In a national survey of college students, although 8 to 9% of the men admitted to behaviors that met the legal definition of rape or attempted rape, 84% of these men believed that their behavior definitely was not rape (Koss et al., 1987). Perhaps this denial is due to the belief that rape refers only to coerced sex with a stranger. But even men who rape strangers tend to deny the criminality of their behavior. One study of incarcerated men convicted of rape found that few felt that what they had done was inappropriate or wrong, and even those who admitted they had committed a wrong felt that external circumstances (such as alcohol or drug use) were responsible (Scully, 1990). What women view as coercive, some men may view as persuasive; what women view as rape, some men may view as "rough sex." There is considerable evidence that males and females perceive heterosexual interactions in different ways, with males seeing sex where females perceive friendliness or force (Abbey, 1987; Goodchilds, Zellman, Johnson, & Giarrusso, 1988; C. B. Johnson et al., 1991).

The female gender role and sexual script may work against women's recognizing certain behaviors as rape, as well. One study found that only 27% of college women who had been the victim of behaviors that met the legal definition of rape actually believed they were rape victims (Koss et al., 1987). Since 84% of the victims knew their attacker, it is likely that the myth of stranger rape worked against these victims' acknowledging that they had indeed been raped. Other research confirms that adolescents are unlikely to label as rape nonconsensual sex that occurs between dating partners, even when physical force is involved (Goodchilds et al., 1988). The cultural norm for men to dominate and women to submit, combined with sexual scripts that require men to be sexually aggressive and women to appear sexually disinterested, may make both women and men genuinely confused as to what constitutes "normal" consensual sex. The majority (from 55 to 75%) of college women report having been coerced or manipulated into some type of sexual encounter at least once (Koss et al., 1987; Poppen & Segal, 1988). In addition, more than one out of three college women admit to having said no to sex at least once when they didn't mean it (Muehlenhard & Hollabaugh, 1988; Muehlenhard & McCoy, 1991). Such "token resistance" may confirm men's belief that "no" does not mean "no," and thus may increase the probability of rape. In fact, in half the cases where a woman gave token resistance, the man persisted in engaging in sexual intercourse despite never getting the woman's consent. Such findings suggest that truly consensual sex may not even be the norm (see Dworkin, 1987, for an even more extreme view).

There appears to be a continuum of sexual aggression against women, ranging from no aggression to manipulative sexual behavior (such as making false promises, exerting verbal pressure, threatening to end a relationship, getting a woman intoxicated) to coercive sexual behavior (persisting in having sexual intercourse when the woman doesn't want to) to sexual assault and rape (using or threatening to use physical force to engage in sexual behaviors, including intercourse) (Lisak & Roth, 1988). Although a minority of sexually active men actually commit rape, more engage in coercive and manipulative sex: about 50% of college men (Lisak & Roth, 1988; Poppen & Segal, 1988; Rapoport & Burkhart, 1984). In fact, only a minority of college men (between 20 and 40%) would be classified as completely nonaggressive in their attitudes and behaviors toward sex. This estimate excludes men who admit to having felt like using force in order to have intercourse (about 12% of college men) and those who indicate some likelihood of using force if no one were to find out (from 35 to 60% of college men; Briere & Malamuth, 1983; Malamuth, 1981). Again, sex and aggression appear linked for most men.

What do we know about men who rape women or who admit that they might under some circumstances? Numerous research studies indicate that such men tend to be hypermasculine (that is, they possess exaggeratedly "macho" attitudes regarding sex and dominance) and to believe strongly in rape myths and traditional gender roles and stereotypes (Allgeier, 1987; Koss & Dinero, 1988; Lisak & Roth, 1988; Muehlenhard & Falcon, 1990). Compared to non–sexually aggressive men, such men also tend to have greater feelings of hostility toward women, greater feelings of inadequacy with women, and less control over their impulses. When all these attitudes and feelings are present in one man, the probability of his committing sexual aggression is very high (Malamuth, 1986). Exposure to family violence including sexual abuse, exposure to pornography, and early sexual experiences also seem to serve as preconditions to rape.

What factors appear to precipitate rape? Two are most important: the use of drugs and/or alcohol and membership in a group that holds rape-supportive attitudes. At least three out of four college men who

commit rape are intoxicated at the time of the rape (Koss & Dinero, 1988). Drugs and alcohol may serve to reduce inhibitions against sexual aggression. The peer social environment also plays a big role in males' sexually aggressive behaviors. All-male groups that emphasize stereotypical conceptions of masculinity—dominance, competition, heterosexual activity, group loyalty—also tend to hold attitudes that encourage rape. Fraternities, male athletic teams, and male juvenile delinquent groups tend to support the view that women are sexual objects, sex is a matter of dominance/submission, and coercion (especially through using alcohol) is an appropriate way to obtain sex (Ageton, 1983; Eskinazi, 1990; P. Y. Martin & Hummer, 1989). Men from such groups are overrepresented among those who rape. Gang rapes in particular appear to be a way for men to bond with each other, to forge ties of "brotherhood" on women's bodies (Neimark, 1991; Sanday, 1990).

Thus, a variety of cultural factors contribute to the extremely high rates of rape in the United States: the male-dominant cultural ethos, the erotization of aggression toward women, the prevalence of violent pornography, and stereotypical gender role norms and divergent sexual scripts for women and men. Before focusing on preventive strategies, we will look at the role played by the legal system in the incidence of rape.

Rape and the law   Laws against rape originated to protect the rights of men, not the rights of women (Brownmiller, 1975; Estrich, 1987). Women traditionally have been viewed as the property of men, first the father, then the husband. Consequently, rape has been viewed as an affront to the man, a violation of his "property rights," rather than as a violation of women's bodily and psychological integrity. Under traditional law, women had no rights. Hence, wife rape was not considered rape, since the wife "belonged" to her husband and he was entitled to unlimited sexual access. Only stranger rape was considered "real" rape in the eyes of the law, and only under certain circumstances. Because virginity in an unmarried woman ensured exclusive "ownership" for the prospective husband, the rape of a virgin was considered more serious than the rape of a nonvirgin. Similarly, it was considered impossible for a female prostitute to be raped. Because she "sold sex" under some circumstances, she was the property of any man who wanted her and therefore not entitled to legal protection. The determination of rape was based on the victim's behavior (for example, her clothing and degree of resistance), not the man's. And when it was just the woman's word against the man's, she frequently was disbelieved.

The laws against rape and their enforcement have improved during the last 20 years, mainly as a function of the women's movement (Heilbrun & Heilbrun, 1986; Largen, 1988). For example, it no longer is legal to ask about the victim's previous sexual history. Nor is it necessary that there be a witness to the crime. Husbands can be accused of wife rape in 27 states, although 23 still permit it, at least while the couple is living together (Seager & Olson, 1986). However, people's attitudes change slowly and there still are misconceptions. Acquaintance rape still is the most difficult to accept. Not surprisingly, such cases are least likely to be reported to police. As noted earlier, fewer than 10% of all acquaintance rapes are reported to police. The percentage may be as low as 3 to 5%. Once reported, only 25% of rape complaints result in an arrest and only 2% of initial complaints end with a conviction, although these percentages are higher when the rape is committed by a stranger using physical force (Estrich, 1987; "New Report," 1978). Still, more women are reporting rape, especially acquaintance rape, than ever before (Largen, 1988; Mansnerus, 1989).

Because of rape myths and misconceptions, rape victims often are treated insensitively and antagonistically by the police, medical personnel, and the courts. Field research and personal reports have indicated that police officers often believe rape myths and consequently treat the victim as if she were the guilty party (Feild, 1978; Holmstrom & Burgess, 1981). Judges too may hold such attitudes. For example, in a June 1977 rape trial in Wisconsin, a judge released a 15-year-old boy who had been convicted of rape, remarking that he had reacted only "normally" in a community known to be "permissive." In that situation, the community mobilized and successfully sought to recall the judge. Such consequences are not frequent. In the same state in 1981, another judge called a 5-year-old female victim of sexual assault by a 24-year-old man "an unusually sexually permissive young lady" ("Judge," 1982). Minority women are especially unlikely to be believed, due to racist assumptions about the value and sexual nature of such women (Feldman-Summers & Ashworth, 1981). Not surprisingly, minority women are least likely to report rape.

Most police, doctors, and judges are men, and research studies consistently find that men compared to women respond less favorably toward the female rape victim and more leniently toward the male perpetrator (Gerdes, Dammann, & Heilig, 1988; J. D. Johnson & Jackson, 1988; Kleinke & Meyer, 1990). Males, especially Black and Hispanic males, are less likely than females to view acquaintance rape as rape (Bourque, 1989; G. J. Fischer, 1987; Goodchilds et al., 1988). Situational and attitudinal factors also affect people's perceptions of the victim and the case. For example, victim age, attractiveness, and sexual history, defendant age and attractiveness, degree of victim resistance, sex of defense attorney, and sex role attitudes of the observer all appear to affect the degree to which people believe the victim and attribute responsibility for the crime to either her or to her assailant (Acock & Ireland, 1983; Check & Malamuth, 1983; Howard, 1984; Villemur & Hyde, 1983).

Certainly the law and its enforcement officers need to become more sensitive to women's experience of rape. Such change is occurring slowly, especially on college campuses (Collison, 1991). But something more than better enforcement is needed: prevention.

Prevention   Because nearly half of all women will be victims of attempted or actual rape at some point in their lives, the fear of rape serves as an important form of social control (M. T. Gordon & Riger, 1989; Griffin, 1979). This fear keeps women passive and dependent, especially on men. Fear of rape develops early, generally by age 10, and affects the personal and work lives of a majority of women (Rozee, 1988). Brownmiller (1975) argues that rape thus serves as "a conscious process of intimidation by which all men keep all women in a state of fear" (p. 15). Most rape prevention programs reinforce this type of social control by recommending that females not go out at night, not go out alone, not anger their assailant. In fact, if a woman is confronted with someone wanting to rape her, the best thing for her to do (unless he is armed) is to fight back actively using multiple strategies, such as yelling and kicking (Bart & O'Brien, 1985; Levine-MacCombie & Koss, 1986).

Most campus rape prevention programs inadvertently reinforce the societal view that women are to blame for rape (Corcoran, 1991). Programs aimed at instructing women in ways to avoid rape (don't drink, don't go to his apartment/room, know self-defense) imply that women can avoid rape. Therefore if a woman gets raped, it must have been her fault. Of course it is important for women to be aware of high-risk situations and behaviors and to learn how to protect themselves, but the reality is that men rape and only men can stop rape. Men must learn not to force a woman into having sex and they must learn that "no" means "no." Men also must stop reinforcing coercive sexual behaviors and attitudes in other men. Innovative campus programs aimed at men are just beginning, especially for those most at risk, such as fraternity men (Mahlstedt, 1991; Moses, 1991a).

In sum, rape can be viewed as an inevitable outgrowth of a culture that glorifies sex and violence. We need to change the aspects of our culture that support rape, rather than try to dismiss rape as due to pathology on the part of a small group of men or to "poor judgment" on the part of a somewhat larger group of women. We all are part of the problem.

The increased publicity over acquaintance rape and childhood sexual abuse has begun to bring a change in some people's attitudes, especially those of women. But another crime, also an extension of the glorification of aggression, violence, and dominance in the male sex role, still is misunderstood and devalued—the battering of women by their domestic partners.

Battering

From 10 to 20% of all women suffer physical abuse by their husbands or male domestic partners (D. E. H. Russell, 1984; Straus & Gelles, 1986). This battering often occurs in conjunction with rape and other forms of sexual abuse. It is difficult to get precise estimates of the number of women affected because most cases are not reported to the police. Although women sometimes engage in violence against husbands, this is rare and usually a response to aggression by the man. More than 90% of all violent crime between spouses appears due to men aggressing against women; less than 5% is due to women aggressing against men (Kurz, 1989).

Until relatively recently, wife beating was considered a husband's right, rather than a crime. The expression "rule of thumb" is derived from English common law, which allowed a husband to beat his wife with a stick no bigger than the diameter of his thumb. This view still is prevalent today, and most cases of wife abuse are considered "family matters," rather than crimes (Kurz, 1989). As we saw with rape, we are only just starting to recognize that the occurrence of a crime should be based on the behavior in question, not the degree of relationship between the perpetrator and the victim.

Most husbands obtain power in marriage not because of individual resources or personal competence but simply because they are male. Indeed, men often define themselves in terms of the power they exert over others, particularly over women. This dynamic is a major factor in men's physical abuse of their wives and lovers. Studies of batterers reveal that they use violence as a way to control their female partners, often in conjunction with other forms of intimidation and isolation (Yllo & Bograd, 1988). When men are socialized to view women, especially wives, as their property and dominance over them as their right, wife abuse is not surprising, especially in a culture where violence is accepted as a means of social control. Cross-cultural research on family violence confirms that sexual inequality, male domestic authority, and acceptance of violence as a form of conflict resolution are major factors in its occurrence (D. Levinson, 1989).

A cycle of violence typically occurs in battering relationships (L. E. Walker, 1984). First is the phase of tension building, wherein the man becomes increasingly abusive in his behaviors short of physical violence and wherein the woman might be able to fend off blows by being extremely compliant. However, an explosion inevitably occurs when acute battering takes place. This phase generally is followed by a marked reduction in tension and, often, loving contrition. This last phase frequently convinces both partners that such abuse never will happen again. Nevertheless, it usually does, with the cycle repeating itself until one of the partners leaves or dies. Over half of all women homicide victims are killed by current or former partners.

Why do women stay in such relationships? This question is asked far more frequently than why men batter. Research has revealed that women in battering relationships frequently suffer from the *battered women's syndrome*, a psychological state wherein a woman becomes so demoralized and defeated by repeated uncontrollable beatings that she feels fearful, acquiescent, and helpless to leave. She may deny the seriousness of the abuse or feel that she deserves it (L. E. Walker, 1984; L. E. A. Walker & Browne, 1985). Female socialization to be compliant and "stand by your man," combined with previous experiences of victimization as children, also contribute to women's vulnerability to and acceptance of violence. In addition, all too frequently there is nowhere for her to go, especially if she has children and is economically dependent upon her partner. Most cases of female homicide are committed by battered women against their batterer when escape appears impossible and the women believe their batterer is likly to kill them (Browne, 1987; L. E. A. Walker, 1989b).

Whether the incidence of such assaults against women is increasing or whether just the reporting of them is, the numbers are startling and serious. The criminal justice system slowly is becoming more responsive to women who have been abused (for example, restraining orders are relatively easy to obtain although they are not always effective). Yet more needs to be done. Many "domestic complaints" still get dismissed too easily, and female victims frequently are treated insensitively. In many communities, women's groups have succeeded in setting up shelters for battered women, but funds are low and the need often is greater than the available resources. But even more than treating the problem, we need to find ways to prevent it. Male physical abuse of women is not limited to a marital relationship; recent evidence suggests that violence occurs in dating relationships as well (Mahlstedt, 1992; Pirog-Good & Stets, 1989). Both women and men must be educated about the unacceptability of physical abuse and women must be encouraged to become economically independent. As with other forms of violence against women, eliminating wife beating means changing social norms, such as that men should dominate women, that a man's home is his castle, and that interpersonal violence is acceptable.

Discussion

The evidence is overwhelming that violence is primarily a male phenomenon, linked closely to stereotypic gender roles and traits. Violence against women, in particular, reveals the gender dynamics of power and the cultural support of its maintenance, however many pronouncements are made to the contrary. Until societal power becomes more equally redistributed, until the male gender role becomes disassociated from dominance over women, until norms develop that truly support equality and nonviolence, it is unlikely that we will see much change in the statistics of sexual harassment, rape, and battering. If anything, the numbers appear to be increasing as more women start reporting such crimes. In the meantime, more steps can be taken to help the victims of male violence and to punish the offenders.

▲   Summary

This chapter has examined how gender roles and stereotypes affect societal functioning in two major

areas: structural power and abuses of power. Overwhelmingly, societal power remains in the hands of White men—economically, politically, legally, and militarily. At the bottom of the power structure are women of color. Although women are making gains in all areas, their progress is extraordinarily slow and difficult. Women's lack of power means White men virtually run our society. Consequently, society generally functions using the standards of the White male gender stereotype: competition, achievement, aggression, hierarchical relationships, and insensitivity to feelings. Thus, our society, in general, has been run for profit and the good of a few, those at the top of the status hierarchy, rather than for the benefit of the many. Whether having more women in positions of power would change the way society is run is an open question. Until we have eliminated male dominance, we cannot know how to reconstruct the state and its institutions because our very thinking is limited by gender politics. Only when women can define themselves rather than be defined by men will a new way of thinking be possible (MacKinnon, 1989).

Men's overrepresentation in positions of power carries over to men's overrepresentation as abusers of power. Masculinity, aggression, and sexuality are strongly interrelated, and nowhere is this linkage more overt than with respect to crimes of violence, especially violence against women. Violent crime may be one way otherwise powerless males can "prove" their masculinity. Sexual harassment, rape, and wife beating are inextricably linked to gender role norms, male dominance, sexual scripts, and general societal support of violence. These crimes affect between half to three-fourths of all women directly, and all women indirectly. They serve as a form of sexual terrorism that keeps women subordinate to men.

Thus, not only do gender roles and stereotypes affect societal functioning, but societal functioning also maintains gender inequality. Clearly, for any change in gender roles to occur, it must occur on a variety of levels—individual, interpersonal, and societal. The next chapter will examine the process of change in more detail.

▲   Recommended Reading

Brown, W. (1988). *Manhood and politics: A feminist reading in political theory.* Totowa, NJ: Rowman & Littlefield. A fascinating analysis of how the "ethos of manhood" marks Western political thought, as seen in the theories of Aristotle, Machiavelli, and Max Weber.

Donnerstein, E., Linz, D., & Penrod, S. (1987). *The question of pornography: Research findings and policy implications.* New York: Free Press. An excellent summary of the research on the effects of pornography on the viewer and on society.

Harris, A., & King, Y. (Eds.). (1989). *Rocking the ship of state: Toward a feminist peace politics.* Boulder, CO: Westview Press. An excellent collection of articles exploring how patriarchal politics leads to wars and how a feminist politics can lead to peace.

MacKinnon, C. A. (1987). *Feminism unmodified: Discourses on life and law.* Cambridge, MA: Harvard University Press. An insightful and provocative collection of speeches delivered by one of the most exciting feminist legal scholars of the day.

Sidel, R. (1986). *Women and children last: The plight of poor women in affluent America.* New York: Viking. A disturbing examination of the social factors that have led to the high rate of poverty among women and children, ending with a call for a new and far-reaching national family policy.

Warshaw, R. (1988). *I never called it rape.* New York: Harper & Row. An accessible summary of Mary Koss's national survey of rape among college students, with helpful suggestions for preventing and surviving rape.

▲▲▲▲▲▲▲▲▲▲▲▲▲▲▲▲▲▲▲

Part 4 Summary

In the preceding five chapters, the effects of gender stereotypes and roles on individuals, their relationships, and society in general have been examined. The evidence is persuasive that the stereotypes and roles negatively affect nearly all aspects of human and societal functioning, for men as well as for women.

On a personal level, many women, especially feminine-sex-typed ones, experience a negative self-concept, particularly low self-confidence and self-blame for failures; constricted behavior in masculine-defined activities; and problems in adjustment and mental health, particularly depression. Many men, especially masculine-sex-typed ones, suffer from physical health problems as well as from overconfidence and behavioral rigidity, especially in feminine-defined activities. All these consequences can be traced to the gender stereotypes.

On a relationship level, males experience difficulty with intimacy, which may account for the sometimes superficial quality of their relationships with friends, lovers, spouses, and children. Close male same-gender friendships may be particularly difficult to establish. Women, who more often are trained for and steered into interpersonal relationships, frequently experience marked disappointment in the relationship with men. This disappointment, combined with inequality in the marital division of labor, tends to make marriage more stressful for women than for men. Because of the Motherhood Mandate, many women become trapped in that role. Negative effects then may occur for the woman, her husband, and the children. Fathers may become trapped in the breadwinner role, resulting in minimal interactions with their children and negative effects on the entire family.

On a societal level, the gender stereotypes and roles have led to marked prejudice against women by both men and women; underutilization of and discrimination against women in the world of work in terms of hiring, status, and salary; a dramatic lack of power by women vis-à-vis men in the areas of economics, politics, law, and military affairs; and high rates of male aggression and violence, as revealed in crimes, especially against women, of sexual harassment, rape, and battering.

The effects of male dominance may be seen in the priorities of American society—profit, concrete rewards, competitiveness, dominance, unemotional functioning, aggression—that is, the masculine stereotype. This is in contrast to a society in which human life and human qualities are valued above profits, a less hierarchical and authoritarian mode of operation, greater concern with the quality of life, cooperative efforts—that is, the feminine stereotype. Evidence was presented to argue that androgynous functioning, the incorporation of positive masculine and feminine stereotyped characteristics—the agentic with the expressive, as in an action-oriented concern about the environment—would improve not only individual functioning and adjustment but societal functioning as well.

The next part will explore the implication of such changes and ways to achieve them. Problems that might arise also will be discussed.

Part 5
Toward the Future

In the preceding chapters, the traditional gender stereotypes and roles, their underpinnings, origins, and consequences have been examined in some detail. A study of the material leads to the conclusion that such stereotypes and roles have little basis in fact and, in today's world, are dysfunctional for individuals, their relationships, and society in general. This part will address itself to some alternatives to rigid gender roles and sex typing, ways to achieve such changes, and the implications of such changes for our society.

Chapter 13

Beyond Gender Stereotypes and Roles

Instead of a society where females attempt to be "feminine" (nurturant, emotional, intuitive) and fear being called "mannish," and males attempt to be "masculine" (aggressive, logical, strong) and fear being called "effeminate," imagine a society where each individual can develop in her or his own unique way. Neither sex automatically is steered toward adopting certain social roles (worker or homemaker; leader or subordinate). Both sexes are considered equal and the interests and experiences of both sexes are at the center of all public policies. This chapter will examine how we can transcend traditional gender stereotypes and roles. Models and modes of change, problems, and some of the implications for individuals, society, and institutions will be considered.

▲ Goals

Moving beyond gender stereotypes and roles is an enormous and difficult endeavor. The first difficulty is having some idea of what we are changing to, or toward. Since gender is embedded within our social system, we need to look at goals on three levels—personal, social, and institutional. Agreement on any single goal is unlikely, but in this section we will sketch some possibilities.

Personal Goals

On the personal level, change would involve the elimination of strict sex typing. Two useful and related concepts have been proposed: androgyny and sex role transcendence or gender aschematicity. The current emphasis is on the latter idea, but it will be helpful to review the former as well.

As discussed in Chapter 1, *androgyny* refers to the combination of strong agentic ("masculine") and expressive ("feminine") traits (S. L. Bem, 1976). As a proposed goal for individuals, however, androgyny refers to more than a linear combination of such traits. Rather, flexibility and integration of such traits in unique ways is emphasized (A. Kaplan, 1979; A. Kaplan & Bean, 1976). Thus, a woman who is always very competitive and aggressive at work but very passive and dependent at home (or vice versa) and who is unable to adjust her behavior to what the situation requires is neither integrated nor flexible and therefore is not androgynous. Uniqueness refers to the fact that because androgynous individuals are no longer restricted by stereotyped behavior, it is impossible to predict their behavior across situations. For example, an individual may be nurturant in one situation, assertive in another, sensitive in a third, and rational in a fourth. Thus, each androgynous individual has the opportunity to develop his or her potential to its fullest, without the restriction that only gender-appropriate behaviors are allowed.

Although the concept of androgyny has appeal, it also has problems. As discussed in previous chapters, concerns are both methodological and definitional. For example, different androgyny scales apparently measure different things, yet all use the same terminology. For our current purposes, a bigger problem is definitional. If androgyny is defined as a combination of "feminine" and "masculine" traits, the sex linking of such traits is maintained. In this sense, androgyny as a concept has obsolescence built in (S. L. Bem, 1979; Locksley & Colten, 1979). If people stop adhering to such characteristics and if the two gender roles become modified and less distinct from each other, the current definition of androgyny no longer will be meaningful. This problem can be circumvented by speaking of agentic and expressive attributes, instead of sex role attributes, as Spence and Helmreich (1980) suggest. Thus, androgyny can mean a flexible integration of agentic and expressive qualities; sex typing of these qualities can be ignored.

Another problem involves using androgyny as a new standard of mental health. Requiring each person to develop an even larger set of traits may be as restrictive as traditional sex roles. Just as the "superwoman" model of the female gender role urges women to enact all the traditionally female behaviors as well as some traditionally male ones, such a model just adds to the expectations placed on individuals without subtracting anything. We also do not have enough evidence that androgyny always is better than agentic traits alone. As discussed in Chapter 8, although androgynous people have the most behavioral flexibility, it is people high on the active-instrumental scale (which includes masculine-sex-typed as well as androgynous individuals) who have the highest self-esteem and lowest depression. What we need is to define healthy human functioning independent of gender-related characteristics. That is, we need to construct an ideal of adult behavior without reliance on traditional concepts of femininity and masculinity. We also need to pay more attention to situational factors, because different traits are used in different situations. We need to determine those situations in which androgyny is more functional than sex typing, those in which sex typing is more functional than androgyny, and those in which sex typing per se is irrelevant (Locksley & Colten, 1979).

Alexandra Kaplan (1979) proposes that androgyny really has two stages. The first is the dualistic stage where "masculine" and "feminine" characteristics coexist but are not necessarily integrated. The second, more advanced level, is the hybrid stage where each group of characteristics truly becomes integrated and tempered by the other. Indeed, in this advanced stage, speaking of androgyny at all is misleading since such a term implies two differing sets of gender-related characteristics. As Garnets and Pleck (1979) suggest, we need to go beyond merely broadening the sex role norms. Rather, we

need to transcend the norms themselves and help make sex roles less salient.

In the *transcendence* model, personality traits would be divorced from biological sex. People would stop developing and using a strong gender schema in processing the world (S. L. Bem, 1983, 1985). Gender-aschematic people use gender distinctions less frequently than sex-typed persons in perceiving and structuring their environment. Whereas a sex-typed person might describe a social situation by first noting the number or proportion of males and females present, a non-sex-typed individual might describe the same situation without making any note of gender facts. When such gender transcendence occurs, people can be just people—individuals in their own right, accepted and evaluated on their own terms.

Some writers have suggested that without strict sex typing and gender roles, a society of neuters would develop, with males and females indistinguishable from each other in behavior and appearance (for example, Winick, 1968). In this view, a likely consequence of such a development might be a lack of sexual attraction between the sexes and the eventual extinction of the species. This conjecture, besides being obviously alarmist (sexual attraction is learned and is not contingent on hairstyles or behavior), is not realistic. Without gender stereotypes, society would not be neuter or regulated in its conformity at all. Gender would be restricted to biological sex differences and future reproductive roles rather than broadly generalized to encompass nearly everything one does, from the colors one wears to the foods one eats. Individual differences abound and are much greater than gender differences for nearly all measurable behaviors and attributes. Such differences would remain, but the negative consequences now experienced by individuals who do not conform to current gender norms would be eliminated.

Becoming gender aschematic means being raised that way, since a gender schema develops at a very early age (see S. L. Bem, 1983, for suggestions on how to raise gender-aschematic children). Since the world makes such strong distinctions between the sexes, raising gender-aschematic children is very hard to do. Perhaps more feasible is learning to transcend strict sex typing, something that may not be possible until late adolescence.

Five stages appear to be involved in reaching sex role transcendence, part of a dialectical process

(Eccles, 1987a; Rebecca, Hefner, & Olenshansky, 1976). First is the stage of the thesis or initial proposition. Stage 1 represents an undifferentiated conception of gender, such as exists in very young children who have not yet learned the sex dichotomy. From this stage stems the antithesis, the opposite of the initial proposition. Stage 2 is a polarized either/or conception of gender roles. Here, males and females are seen as opposite and distinct from each other in nearly all behaviors. This stage is cognitively necessary in order for a young child to organize her or his world and occurs between ages 3 and 7 (see Chapter 6). Everything is classified absolutely into black or white, good or bad, masculine or feminine, and so on. In stage 3 (ages 7 to 11), some of the polarization present in the previous stage subsides as gender is recognized as a stable aspect of individuals. Sex role differentiation still occurs, however, and gender stereotypes still have a somewhat prescriptive quality. During adolescence (stage 4), gender concepts are in transition. Early adolescence (ages 12 to 14) brings with it sharp concerns about fitting in, and gender stereotypes may return to being extremely rigid. By middle adolescence (ages 15 to 18), however, females and males are capable of transcending strict gender roles if androgynous role models are present and the social environment is relatively egalitarian.

Stage 5, gender role transcendence, requires a strong personal identity not linked to strict gender differentiation. This stage combines or synthesizes previously held gender polarities into a new and more balanced whole. Here, an individual is able to move and behave freely and adaptively as a function of the situation. For example, a person might act tenderly with a child, forcefully with subordinates, and sympathetically with a friend, all without concern for whether the behavior was gender-appropriate. Few individuals reach stage 5 functioning. It evolves over a long period of time, is facilitated by societal supports, and is a dynamic process, not a final destination. As we saw in Chapters 3 and 6, many individuals move toward gender role transcendence as they leave behind the tasks and expectations of raising children and establishing themselves in the labor force. Thus, middle age may be a time of maximal gender role transcendence.

Androgyny, gender aschematicity, and gender role transcendence provide alternatives to strict sex typing. Androgyny may, in fact, be one step on the path to transcending gender roles. It certainly is not the only nor necessarily the best way for personal change to occur.

Social Goals

More than individual change in terms of personality traits is needed. An important goal of any change process is changing social roles. As discussed in Chapter 1 and throughout the book, Eagly's (1987b) social-role theory suggests that females and males develop different traits and behaviors because of the different roles they are forced to play. If we want to change the gender stereotypes, we must change the gender roles. No more can men be solely linked with employment and power and women solely linked with child care and submission. Indeed, as we have seen, the labor force is not the sole province of men. Most women, including most mothers of young children, are employed. Thus, we need to start changing our expectations of the two sexes.

Although a division of labor by sex is present in nearly all human societies (see Chapter 5), it is amenable to change. Women and men, although they do not have to do exactly the same things, should both be involved in productive and reproductive work, and the former should not be viewed as superior to the latter (Gailey, 1987). Women and men need to achieve equality in terms of income, culturally powerful positions, and household responsibilities (Chafetz, 1989). Change in only one area will block changes in others. For example, women's increased participation in the labor force without commensurate decreased participation in household responsibilities or increased social power to support such changes has not translated into gender equality.

As this example suggests, women's roles have changed more than men's. Women now are expected to have and take care of children as well as others (the traditional female role), but they also are expected to earn a living (in whole or in part). Thus, the expectations placed on women have multiplied with nothing subtracted. As discussed in Chapter 8, playing multiple roles can be life-enhancing, but only when such roles are freely chosen and adequate personal, social, and institutional support is in place. The support system is what is so often lacking. Husbands may feel threatened by their wife's earnings, parents may criticize their daughter or son for putting grandchildren in day care, the workplace may have inflexible hours and job expectations, and society may provide few affordable resources (parental leave, adequate day care) to help manage the load. The outcome, frequently, is a stressed and exhausted woman who feels guilty for not spending enough time with her children.

Men's roles are only beginning to change (Allis, 1990; Clatterbaugh, 1990; Kimbrell, 1991). Men still are expected to be a good breadwinner and to be dominant in employment and social situations. But more and more, men are being expected, often by wives who are themselves employed, to be sensitive and involve themselves in child-care activities. Although the increase in such activities for men has been slight, it is on the rise. One consequence is that many men feel the same stress as their wives from multiple roles since employment expectations haven't been reduced and many men find engaging in "feminine" activities to be humiliating. Men also receive less social support for engaging in nontraditional activities than do women. For example, even fewer men than women are entitled to parental leave, and such leaves are shorter for men than they are for women. In addition, traditional parents and friends may see a father who is involved in domestic activities as less of a man for doing "women's work."

This is a difficult transitional time for many women and men today. Gender role expectations are unclear. Traditional role expectations are still strong but new expectations have been added. Since it is difficult to do everything, especially in a world that only supports traditional roles, many women and men are stressed and confused. One way of resolving such stress and confusion is to return to traditional roles. That seems to be a trend in the 1990s. But another way is to work to change society to be more supportive of nontraditional roles. This means not only changing expectations placed on individuals but also changing the way societal institutions work. Indeed, real change in gender roles means changing the whole basis of society.

Institutional Goals

Gender involves more than different personality traits and social roles. Gender also is about differential power. As we have seen throughout the book, men (and all things masculine) are associated with power and high status, while women (and all things feminine) are associated with powerlessness and low status. Societal institutions encode such distinctions. We live in a patriarchy where men and "masculine" values rule. Nearly all societal institutions reflect this gender dynamic, as we saw in the last chapter. Thus, business, law, politics, and the military are run not only primarily by men but also primarily from a male point of view using a value system compatible with the male role (dominance, competition, aggression, and personal insensitivity). To truly change gender stereotypes and roles, we must

change the patriarchal system in which we live and make societal institutions more reflective of and responsive to the entire citizenry.

Feminism refers to the belief that women and men are equal and should be equally valued as well as have equal rights (see Offen, 1988, for a detailed historical definition). Thus, all feminists seek to end women's subordination. All generally believe that both equality and liberation are needed: equality means differential valuing of each sex must end, and liberation means that the gender roles themselves must be changed since they are restrictive. As suggested in Figure 13.1, however, men and women may define equality in different terms. Feminists also differ among themselves with respect to their analyses of the causes of women's subordination as well as the solutions proposed to end it. There are three main types of feminism: liberal feminism, socialist feminism, and radical feminism. We will discuss each in turn, starting with the most traditional and conservative (see Donovan, 1985; Jaggar & Struhl, 1978; Tong, 1989 for more details).

Liberal feminism   In liberal feminism, the stress is on equality of opportunity between the sexes. Indeed, liberal feminism is sometimes referred to as "equal opportunity feminism." There is no critique of societal inequalities, such as between social classes or races. The goal is to obtain for women economic, political, and social rights equal to those of men within the existing system. Gender roles are seen as inhibiting both women and men, although possible "innate" differences between the sexes are acknowledged to exist. Because the roots of women's oppression are seen in terms of sexist discrimination, actions that stem from this model are aimed at changing the institutional and organizational levels of society where inequities occur.

This model dates back to the 1792 publication of Mary Wollstonecraft's book *A Vindication of the Rights of Woman*. Current feminists such as Betty Friedan and Eleanor Smeal, and organizations like the National Organization for Women, work within this model of social change. Their actions are directed at changing laws (for example, passing the Equal Rights Amendment) and equalizing educational and employment opportunities. Because a central emphasis of this model is that a person's abilities are learned through socialization, liberal feminists believe that a relearning of traditional sex role attitudes and behaviors must occur before egalitarian gender relations are possible. This model is the mainstream feminist perspective, and

WHAT'S YOUR OPINION/ How do you feel about equality for women?

I feel that women should get equal pay for equal work.

I think it's only simple justice that women get equal pay for equal work.

Equality for women means that our potential for physical, intellectual and emotional growth be supported and nurtured. It means women recognized as full and valuable members of this society. It means being given a chance to risk, to grow, to make a contribution to a better world side by side with men.

I think if a woman's doing the same job as a man is doing, she should get the same pay.

Figure 13.1   Gender difference in the meaning of equality? (Copyright © 1982 by Field Enterprises, Inc. From the book, *My Weight Is Always Perfect For My Height—Which Varies*, by Nicole Hollander. Reprinted with permission from St. Martin's Press, Inc., New York, NY.)

its adherents tend to be middle-class and upper-middle-class professional and career women. Some men also are involved. This model has the most widespread appeal of the three, since it reflects Western cultural values of individualism and personal achievement.

This model is sometimes referred to as an assimilation model, in which women are encouraged to assume the lifestyle and characteristics of the mainstream male culture. The assumption underlying this model creates problems. Institutions run by "masculine" values (that is, most institutions) are goal- (that is, profit-) oriented, competitive, aggressive, and insensitive to human values. Furthermore, women are unlikely to be assimilated into high-paying jobs where competition with men would be the strongest. Because many higher positions require an unpaid wife to fulfill social obligations and take care of domestic functioning, women would still be at a disadvantage even if they obtained such positions. Adjusting women's lives to the standards of the Establishment (Bernard, 1971) would do little to alleviate the negative consequences of

such institutional practices. Women would just learn to be as competitive, aggressive, and insensitive as many men. Because the uninterrupted work pattern would continue to be the norm, women and men interested in child rearing would continue to be at a disadvantage.

Furthermore, class and race distinctions are ignored in this model. Only a small group of women, mainly White middle-class ones, can hope to compete with men on male terms (for example, go to the same colleges and professional schools, have uninterrupted careers). Doing so generally requires middle-class women to use working-class women (often women of color) to care for their children, clean their houses, and sometimes even have their babies (as in "surrogate" motherhood). Thus, liberal feminism serves the interest of a minority of women while it perpetuates the class and race oppression that is a component of patriarchal societies.

Such problems have caused a backlash against liberal feminism in the last few years. Many women writers (S. Gordon, 1991; Hewlett, 1986; Mason, 1988) have blamed women's increasing poverty and increasingly stressful lives on liberal feminists. By emphasizing equality issues, liberal feminists have tried to use gender-neutral standards with respect to employment, divorce, laws, and so on. But women's lives are not gender-neutral. Women's childbearing capacity and vulnerability to sexual assault make women's life and experience different from that of men. Gender-neutral standards thus are really men's standards (MacKinnon, 1987b). For example, no-fault divorce penalizes most women (those who have devoted themselves to caregiving and thus have less earning potential) while advantaging most men. Although such criticisms of liberal feminism may be valid, it is important to recognize that it is not liberal feminists who are holding women back but the male-dominated power structure. Besides, liberal feminists have recognized that women are the predominant caretakers of children and have fought for increased child-care options and parental leave programs, for example. They've simply been less successful at obtaining such changes than others. Rather than engage in "horizontal hostility," women need to assign blame where it is due—that is, to the patriarchal system that maintains women's oppression.

Socialist feminism   Socialist feminism is based on, but goes beyond, the traditional Marxist view of society. It arose in the 1970s as a result of feminists' dissatisfaction with the traditional Marxist perspective on women and the family (see Chapter 5; also Eisenstein, 1979; A. Ferguson, 1989; Hartmann, 1976; MacKinnon, 1989). In contrast to liberal feminism, this model emphasizes the necessity of changing our economic system as a precondition for the establishment of gender equality. Economic oppression and sexist oppression both are seen as fundamental and as reinforcing each other. A few wealthy White men exploit the working class and all men exploit women, because women earn less than men in the marketplace and their labor at home receives no pay at all.

Because of their emphasis on cultural institutions, like the family, within a class society, socialist feminists emphasize the distinct problems faced by women in different classes and from different racial groups. For example, the issue of birth control for working-class and Third World women is different from the issue of birth control for White upper-middle-class women. Liberal feminists ignore these distinctions and have concentrated on obtaining the right to safe and legal abortions for all women. But Third World and working-class women also must

face the problems of compulsory sterilization and the right to conceive and bear children free from poverty and discrimination (A. Y. Davis, 1986). Most of those involved in socialist feminism are students and workers from the working class and middle class, and women from such traditional New Left groups as the civil rights movement. Current democracy movements in Latin America are the best examples of the growing convergence between feminism and Marxism (Chinchilla, 1991).

Most of the activities of socialist feminists are aimed at educating people about the relationship between women's oppression and economic class oppression. Women are organized around these economic issues as well as around health-care and child-care issues. Men's sexist attitudes are seen as stemming from the capitalist economic system. Therefore, socialist feminists believe, the system itself must be changed.

An examination of women's lives in countries around the world partially supports the view that socialism is associated with more gender equality than capitalism. For example, a 1988 study of women's status in 99 countries conducted by the Population Crisis Committee found that women came closest to equality in Sweden, followed by Finland, the United States, East Germany, Norway, Canada, and Denmark, in that order ("The Status of Women," 1988). (Five out of the seven are socialist or social welfare states.) Women's status was poorest in Bangladesh, Mali, Afghanistan, North Yemen, and Pakistan. Similarly, a study of gender stereotypes across six cultures (Norway, Sweden, Denmark, Finland, England, and the United States) revealed that the countries with the longest and most well-established commitment to social welfare (Sweden and Denmark) were also the countries with fewest gender differences (J. H. Block, 1973). Still, even Sweden does not have complete gender equality (discussed further later on), and different models of socialism do not seem as supportive of gender equality as does the Scandinavian model. In particular, women do not fare as well in the communist systems of Eastern Europe, the Soviet Union, and the People's Republic of China. Although employment and salary figures show relative gender equality, domestic responsibilities fall entirely on women, the work force still is gender-segregated, and positions of power are still solidly in men's hands (Kruks et al., 1989; Mamonova, 1989; Stacey, 1983). Thus, Marxist models do not lead inevitably to gender equality, although socialism may be more compatible with such equality than capitalism. As illustration, the rise of market economies from former communist states in Eastern Europe in the early 1990s has led to increased restrictiveness on reproductive rights, loss of maternity policies and jobs for women, loss of political representation, and a general resurgence of traditional roles (Bohlen, 1990; "Women Parliamentarians," 1990).

Radical feminism   Whereas socialist feminists emphasize the importance of both economic and sexist oppression, radical feminists argue that men's oppression of women is primary and serves as the model for all other oppression (for example, economic and racial oppression). There are a number of variants of radical feminism: for example, lesbian feminism and cultural feminism. All agree, however, that women's oppression was the first oppression historically, that it exists in virtually all societies, and that it will not be eliminated solely by social changes, such as by the abolition of a class society (see Echols, 1989, for a history of radical feminism).

Disagreement exists among radical feminists as to the root causes of women's oppression. Some argue it rests in women's child bearing capacities and women's resultant physical dependence on men (see, for example, Firestone, 1970). Thus, the full liberation of women may depend upon extrauterine production of children, a possibility that is becoming increasingly feasible. Other radical feminists (for example, G. Rubin, 1975) emphasize the importance of kinship systems that were set up to control women's sexuality and reproductive processes. As a result, offspring became products, and women were bartered and exchanged. (See Chapter 5 for further hypotheses on the origins of patriarchy.)

The goal of radical feminism is to abolish class and gender inequality and create a new culture based on a more balanced synthesis of male and female modes of power. To end women's oppression by men, woman-centered systems and beliefs must be established. Thus, change is sought on all levels, both personal and institutional. In this context, the personal is seen as political. The goals of radical feminism can be accomplished through grassroots organizations, confrontational politics, and by building an alternative culture. Some radical feminists argue that only lesbians, whose primary attachments are to other women, can fight sexism fully, since heterosexual women's attachments to men keep them from breaking free of male opinion and power (Bunch, 1975; M. Daly, 1978). Proponents of radical feminism tend to be middle-class women

from the New Left and those never before involved in politics.

A nonpolitical variant of radical feminism is *cultural feminism,* where gender differences between women and men are emphasized but where "women's" qualities of nurturance, caring, cooperativeness, and nonviolence are viewed as superior to "men's" qualities. Emphasis is on creating a separate female counterculture based on a "feminine" value system. Attention is focused on individual change and the creation of alternatives rather than on reforming current institutions. As Sonia Johnson (1987, 1989) recommends, women must "take our eyes off the guys" and develop their own woman culture. In this view, paying attention to men and male institutions, even by struggling against them, only serves to perpetuate the status quo and uses up women's energies in the process. Women should use their energies to benefit each other.

Integration?   Integrating all three major forms of feminism is not completely possible given the different analyses that underlie each view. The starkest contrast is between liberal feminism and radical feminism. Socialist feminism is more compatible with the latter than the former. In the views of both socialist and radical feminism, society must change. It is not sufficient to encourage women to adapt their lives to the Establishment, as some feel liberal feminists have done. Rather, the Establishment itself must be changed and adapted to the lives of women. Whereas liberal feminists emphasize women's getting their fair share of the pie, radical and socialist feminists emphasize baking a new pie altogether, one composed of healthier ingredients. Although these objectives are different, some feminists suggest that we can embrace both sets: working to gain equal rights in the short term (liberal feminism) while trying to transform society in the long term (radical and socialist feminism) (Jaggar, 1990).

Socialist and radical feminism differ as to how to achieve this new society. Socialist feminists view the overthrow of capitalism as primary, but stipulate that it should be done with the active involvement of committed socialist feminists. This will ensure the demise of sexism. Radical feminists, on the other hand, believe that overthrowing patriarchy is primary in order to destroy sexism. For them, overthrowing patriarchy will result in the institution of socialism. As we have seen, there is some empirical support for this linkage of socialism with a reduction in sexism.

If we integrate radical and socialist feminism, we come to view sexism as a result of a number of factors: the division of labor according to gender, the emergence of class systems, the formation of patriarchal relations, and the social organization of the family. We are forced to look not only at gender oppression, but at race and class oppression as well. Integrating the two models and examining sexism as it interacts with race and class factors appears to be the current trend in the development of feminist theory. Influenced by postmodernism, feminism today is struggling to recognize the diversity among women as well as to maintain some sense of unity (Fox-Genovese, 1991; Nicholson, 1990; Spelman, 1988). Writings by women of color have been particularly important in this regard (for example, Hooks, 1984, 1989).

Both socialist and radical feminism partly grew out of the dissatisfaction of many New Left women in the late 1960s, who became fed up with the sexist and patronizing behavior of their male colleagues in what they had thought was a joint struggle against the Vietnam War and for civil rights for Blacks. A historical look at what is loosely called "the women's liberation movement" will help throw light on the development of these three models of change. Although the cry for women's liberation has been at the heart of the movement, it is important to recognize that men too would be liberated from the restrictiveness of their gender roles. The men's liberation movement, begun in the early 1970s, reflects this perspective.

▲ Liberation Movements

A social movement, to be considered as such, must meet several criteria (Sherif, 1970). People (both those directly affected and those who sympathize) must first come together around a specific problem (for example, equal rights for women). They must develop a specific ideology with a focus on social change via specific means (for example, developing a feminist ideology and pressure tactics to get Congress to pass a constitutional amendment). The movement also must be socially identifiable with the issues in the public's mind (for example, through newspaper articles describing the movement's progress). Clearly, the women's movement meets these criteria. It has a strong feminist ideology that attributes a number of problems specific to women to a structured system of gender inequality. It also involves a network of organizations capable of

attracting mass support and of using a variety of tactics. Chafetz and Dworkin (1986) suggest that there are two types of social movements, based on comprehensiveness: ameliorative movements, which focus on specific problems; and totalistic movements, which seek to alter the entire social system. "First wave" movements tend to be ameliorative, while "second wave" movements tend to be more totalistic. The women's movement in the United States has gone through both waves, while the men's movement currently still is in the first wave.

The Women's Movement

In the United States, the movement to grant women legal rights began in the early 1820s, and, for a time, was tied to the abolitionist movement (see Cott, 1987; Deckard, 1983, for excellent histories). Much of the focus was on including women in the Constitution, as can be seen in the Declaration of Sentiments and Resolutions from the Seneca Falls Convention of 1848, which was modeled directly on the Declaration of Independence. After the Fourteenth and Fifteenth amendments were introduced in Congress in 1866, women felt betrayed. They had expected equality for both Black males and all women, but these amendments only granted all male citizens the right to vote. In fact, these amendments introduced the word *male* into the Constitution for the first time. In response, feminists like Susan B. Anthony and Elizabeth Cady Stanton formed organizations to guarantee women equal rights. At the beginning, the goals of the movement were broad, including equality with respect to education, property rights, employment, social status, and societal responsibilities, as well as freedom from men's violence. By the end of the 19th century, the focus had narrowed to the issue of suffrage, for strategic reasons. It was an issue that united all women, although it always was more important to middle-class White women than to Black and working-class women. From the beginning of the 20th century to 1920, the women's rights movement gained momentum and culminated in the passage of the Nineteenth Amendment, guaranteeing women's right to vote. However, after this goal was achieved, most of the women's rights groups disappeared, having fulfilled their mission. Many women experienced an increased number of social options during the 1920s, especially with respect to paid employment and reproductive control, which worked against their identification as women with common concerns. Still, some women continued the fight against women's oppression. The Equal Rights

Amendment, drafted by Alice Paul and her National Women's Party, was successfully introduced into Congress in 1923 but was not passed. Women were active in labor movements, in temperance and social welfare movements, and in a variety of women's clubs. Thus, although the women's liberation movement as a visible and broad-based social movement appeared to have become dormant, it did not really die. It reemerged in the 1960s with renewed vigor.

After World War II, many women who had been urged to join the labor force during the war were urged to leave to make room for the returning male soldiers. Of course, many others willingly quit to have families. During the 1950s, the "feminine mystique" was promoted (Friedan, 1963): women should be mothers, housewives, and consumers, roles very profitable to an industrialized capitalistic society changing over from peak wartime production to peacetime production. During the early 1960s, society itself began to change: the "baby-boom" children rediscovered a social conscience and became active in civil rights, the New Left, and the antiwar movement. Some males began rejecting the masculine mystique and the goals of blind patriotism and productivity. Some also began rediscovering sensuality and emotionality. Hence, the occurrence of "hippies," draft resistance, and concern about ecology. On another level, career women also were becoming mobilized. In 1961, the federal Commission on the Status of Women was formed and documented women's second-class status. State commissions followed, and the federal Equal Employment Opportunity Commission (EEOC) was established on the basis of, among other things, complaints of sex discrimination.

Two forces—younger New Left women and older career women—became welded together into a movement in the late 1960s as a result of a series of crises (J. Freeman, 1989). Their orientations and values, however, remained different. The older group became dissatisfied with the refusal of EEOC to take sex discrimination complaints seriously and they formed their own political and professional organizations. The National Organization for Women (NOW) was founded in 1966 by Betty Friedan, followed by the Women's Equity Action League, Federally Employed Women, and many professional women's caucuses.

At the same time, women from New Left and civil rights organizations became dissatisfied with the traditional roles they were being forced to take in the movements (making coffee, typing, and so forth).

They spontaneously formed their own groups in 1967 and 1968, focusing on personal revolution through grassroots organizing and consciousness-raising groups.

These two groups remained separate. The older branch functioned as a pressure group, focusing on political, legal, and economic changes, and developed into what we have termed liberal feminism. The younger branch focused on consciousness raising and individual changes and, later, societal changes. This younger branch was divided into two groups, socialist feminists and radical feminists. Despite their differences, all groups agreed on two theoretical concerns: criticism of the gender-stereotyped division in our society, and the view that sexism exists as institutionalized discrimination, sometimes beyond conscious awareness. The goal of the women's movement, then, is to eradicate sexism and replace it with concepts of equality and liberation.

During the 1980s, the women's movement became fragmented (see Ferree & Hess, 1985). Rather than a single movement, there now are a variety of groups operating to eliminate sexism in different ways. As we have seen, there are at least three different models of feminism—liberal feminism, socialist feminism, and radical feminism. Each model attacks sexism from a different perspective. And there are subgroups as well—cultural feminists, lesbian feminists, Third World feminists, and so on. In the 1990s, the two most dominant forms are liberal feminists (who emphasize gender equality) and cultural feminists (who emphasize gender difference). These groups are increasingly at odds with each other.

Postmodernism also has influenced the women's movement by emphasizing the impossibility of a single totalizing point of view (Nicholson, 1990). When the women's movement has presented one point of view in the past, it typically has been that of White middle-class heterosexual women (Spelman, 1988). The pendulum has swung so far the other way, however, that it is hard to speak of women as a unified group. This has led to difficulty organizing women around common objectives, but it has been necessary in order to recognize the diversity among women, something previously ignored. The solution may be increased emphasis on "coalition politics," wherein groups with separate goals can come together to work on specific issues, such as reproductive rights (Reagon, 1983).

In 1985, a nonpartisan coalition group composed of leaders of the largest national women's organizations formed to press for common goals (Harder,

1990). This Council of Presidents, composed of more than 40 organizations (such as the Mexican American Women's National Association, the Older Women's League, and the YWCA), represents 10 million grassroots citizen-activists. Their 1988 "Women's Agenda" included policies aimed at supporting families (such as access to housing, child and elder care, family and medical leave), economic opportunity (such as pay equity and welfare reform), comprehensive health care and safety, a federal budget that balanced issues of national defense with those of human development, and equality under the law (such as ERA and reproductive choice).

Another trend in the women's movement is toward making it international (Bernard, 1987; Iglitzin & Ross, 1986; R. Morgan, 1984). 1975 began the United Nations Decade for Women, culminating in a 1985 conference in Nairobi. Links between women in different countries have been solidified since then, as women lend their experience and energies to each other to fight local battles against female genital mutilation, dowry deaths, illiteracy, and so on.

Thus, the women's movement is alive and well despite repeated claims that the movement is dead and that we are in a "postfeminist" period (see, for example, N. Davidson, 1988; M. Dixon, 1983). The movement may be invisible to some because much of feminist ideology has been absorbed into mainstream thought. For example, most women and men now agree that women should have an equal role with men in running business, industry, and government, whereas 20 years ago, this was a minority view (Deckard, 1983; N. Gibbs, 1990; Harder, 1990). Women, in particular, have become more feminist in their attitudes if not in their identification. The gap between attitudes and identification is interesting and may explain why some people think feminism is dead. Although between 82% and 94% of American women in 1989 thought the women's movement was helping to improve the lives of women and had given women more control over their lives and helped women to become more independent, a similar percentage also said they paid little attention or no attention to the movement and only one-third identified themselves as feminists (Wallis, 1989). Other surveys find a similar gap between feminist attitudes and feminist identification. For example, a survey of more than 500 college women found that almost all supported the goals of the women's movement but only 16% identified strongly as feminists (Buhl, 1989). Some of the problem with identifying as a feminist may be a

misunderstanding of the term. Many people incorrectly believe feminists hate men, want to dominate men, and/or are lesbians. As we have seen, feminists believe in equality and though they are profemale, they are not antimale. Nevertheless, seven out of ten college women believe men dislike feminists (Buhl, 1989). Not surprisingly then, young women are less likely than older women to call themselves feminists.

Still, despite reluctance to claim a feminist identity, most women and most men support the goals of the women's movement and think such a movement is necessary. For example, three out of five Americans believe that the United States continues to need a strong women's movement to push for changes that benefit women (Belkin, 1989). This is not to say that the women's movement is seen as unproblematic. Along with the belief that the women's movement has made it easier for women to lead satisfying lives, is the belief that the women's movement has made it harder for women to combine jobs and family responsibilities, for marriages to be successful, and for parents to raise children (DeStefano & Colasanto, 1990).

The women's movement today may be less visible than it once was since much of the change now taking place in society is occurring from within organizations rather than from the outside (Katzenstein, 1990). Despite its relatively successful impact on ideology, the women's movement still has a long way to go before sexism is eradicated. Behaviors are harder to change than beliefs, and institutions are the hardest of all to change. As we have seen, the women's movement is a dynamic, ever-changing social movement, with a long history (more than 100 years) and undoubtedly an extended future.

The Men's Movement
As a result of the changes women were making and the questions they were asking, and also as a result of the inherent strain of the male role, many men began reevaluating their roles and raising their own consciousness. To this end, the men's liberation movement arose in the early 1970s and has been slowly growing, especially in urban areas (Astrachan, 1986; Clatterbaugh, 1990; Doyle, 1989; Fiebert, 1987; Kimbrell, 1991; Shiffman, 1987). The focus is on the changes men want in their lives and how best to achieve them. The men's movement generally has not been driven by a passion to change the system, because most men derive ample benefit from the existing social, political, and economic systems. Instead, the men's movement has tried to give men a forum in which to air and discuss their

confusions and distress, as well as to gain other men's support in personal and social areas.

Initially, the main concern of the fledgling men's movement was the stress caused by changes in women's roles and expectations. Men began to examine what it meant to be a man, primarily through consciousness-raising (CR) groups and books (such as Farrell, 1974; Fasteau, 1974; Pleck & Sawyer, 1974). Although many of the men in such groups did not consider themselves part of a movement, others began to organize. The first National Conference on Men and Masculinity was held in 1975 and this conference has been held nearly every year since then.

Two separate men's movements developed during the 1980s: the "profeminist" camp (who support a feminist analysis of patriarchy) and the "pro-masculinist" camp (who emphasize men as victims) (Astrachan, 1986; Clatterbaugh, 1990; Fiebert, 1987). *Profeminists,* who organized the first men's CR groups in 1970, analyze men's problems as stemming from a patriarchal social system that privileges men, especially White middle-class heterosexual ones. As with feminists, some profeminists are more liberal (for example, W. Farrell, 1974) and some are more radical (for example, Stoltenberg, 1989). The former emphasize gender roles, the latter patriarchal oppression. But both groups view men as forced into oppressive behaviors that distort men's character and limit their functioning. Liberating men thus requires eliminating patriarchy and restrictive gender roles. Profeminist men are fully aligned with feminist women in working for social and political change, and many such men supported the 19th-century women's movement as well (Kimmel, 1989). Current profeminists also work to overcome homophobia within both themselves and the culture, since such attitudes maintain the gender hierarchy and alienate men from each other (see also Chapter 9).

In 1983, profeminist men formed the National Organization for Changing Men (changed in 1990 to the National Organization for Men Against Sexism), whose goals are to transcend the traditional male sex role, to support women's struggle for equality, and to support gay rights and fight homophobia (Doyle, 1989). This organization, with around 500 to 600 dues-paying members in 1989, has national and regional meetings and regularly publishes a newsletter, *Brother.* It also has a variety of task forces on topics such as ending men's violence, fathering, gay rights, male-female relationships, and men's studies. Most profeminist men appear to be White, middle-class, and college-educated, and a large number identify as gay or bisexual (A. Gross, Smith, & Wallston, 1983; Shiffman, 1987). Academic men constitute a large percentage of profeminist men, especially those involved in the field of men's studies (for example, Brod, 1987).

The second branch of the men's movement is composed of the *promasculinist* groups. Although far from unitary, promasculinists tend to focus on supporting men's rights and "masculinity" (for example, Bly, 1990; W. Farrell, 1987; H. Goldberg, 1976). These groups tend to see men as victims of oppressive gender roles as well as feminist anger. The forerunners of current promasculinists can be found in the movement against "Momism" of the early 20th century. In response to increasing compartmentalization of gender roles with increasing industrialization (the public/private split), many middle-class men became concerned about the effects of too much female influence on growing boys (Filene, 1986; Kimmel, 1989). One outcome was the development of boys' clubs—for example, the YMCA and the Boy Scouts—to combat "feminization." Another outcome was increased militarization and sports consciousness. (President Theodore Roosevelt was a symbolic hero of this movement.) In the early 1970s, the main emphasis of promasculinists was on divorce reform and defending against feminist attacks (Astrachan, 1986; Clatterbaugh, 1990). At that time, divorce and child custody awards were two of the few areas in which women sometimes had a real advantage over men, although the men tended either to ignore statistics that showed how few men actually pay alimony or child support, or to oppose legislation to enforce payment. At first, these men formed local organizations, like Fathers United for Equal Rights. In 1981, they formed their own national organization, the National Congress for Men, later joined by men who felt they had no reason to feel guilty in their relationships with women. This "no-guilt" group had initially been part of an organization called Coalition for Free Men. In general, the National Congress for Men emphasizes legal issues related to "men's rights," especially "fathers' rights." It also is interested in protecting and promoting the common interests of males (see Doyle, 1989). Like the profeminist National Organization for Men Against Sexism, the promasculinist National Congress for Men had about 500 to 600 dues-paying members in 1989, holds national and regional meetings, and regularly publishes a newsletter, *NetWORK.* Men in this group tend to be well-educated White professionals who know how to lobby and use the legal system for their benefit.

In the early 1990s, another branch of the promasculinist group has been gaining momentum—men who recognize they have been stunted in their personal development by the rigidity of male gender socialization and role expectations and who are searching for spiritual healing and growth (Clatterbaugh, 1990). The path to such healing frequently is through therapy, CR groups, and rituals all focused on releasing the "wild man" inside the civilized man. Myths (such as Iron John) are heavily used to provide men with a positive image of masculinity, one that combines strength with tenderness. Based on the works of poet Robert Bly (1990), therapist John Rowan (1987), and others (Keen, 1991; R. Moore & Gillette, 1990; K. Thompson, 1991), this "wildman" movement is based on the belief that only men can initiate males into manhood. Through the use of rituals, men get in touch with their inner feelings and heal the emptiness and alienation caused by the absence of fathers, the oppressive nature of corporate culture, and feminist attacks on men. Around the country, retreats (called wildman gatherings) encourage men to overcome the barriers separating them from developing intimate friendships with each other (Gabriel, 1990). Similar to the views of the early 20th-century promasculinists, modern men are depicted as endangered by too much of "the feminine." Either they become "soft" as a result, or they rebel and become "macho" ("savage man"). What's needed is a healthier balance. Similar to cultural feminists, then, wildmen emphasize gender differences and the importance of valuing one's own "side."

In general, the men's movement, though still small, appears to be growing, especially the academic and personal growth components (discussed further in the next section). Since the mid-1970s, the number of books, newsletters (for example, *Changing Men: Issues in Gender, Sex, and Politics*), magazine articles, and research articles has increased dramatically (see Doyle, 1989, for more information). Certainly, men need to change if society is going to change. However, the relative lack of emphasis on political and social change is disconcerting, since, as we have seen, gender is created from and embedded in a specific social context. Unless the social context changes, individual change will be hard to maintain.

Discussion

Both men's and women's liberation movements appear to be expanding slowly and infiltrating our cultural consciousness. As noted previously, the goals of the women's movement have been accepted by the majority of men and women, even if they don't identify as feminists. Since the early and mid-1970s, there also has been a decrease in traditional attitudes toward women (Helmreich, Spence, & Gibson, 1982; W. H. McBroom, 1987). In general, women have changed more than men, younger people are changing more than older people, and increased education is associated with less traditional attitudes. Still, attitude change has occurred across both class and race lines (Dionne, 1989; Ferree, 1983). Whereas 20 years ago women who wanted both to work outside the home and to have a family might have had their mothering abilities questioned, this is much less true today. Indeed, the goal of combining employment and family life has become the norm for most young women. Similarly, 20 years ago, few men could talk about cooking, doing the laundry, or child care without having their masculinity questioned; this too is much less true today.

Betty Friedan (1981, 1985) argues that the second stage of feminism must include men. Men must be helped to overcome the "masculine mystique" created by the polarization of the sexes. Only when this barrier is overcome will men be able to unite with women. She sees the needs of both sexes converging as they try to live together and raise children in dual-career marriages. Men and women need to work out the trade-offs at work and at home. Friedan's message is strongly within the liberal feminist tradition and, as such, it neglects structural changes in society. Still, it is a message that appeals to a large number of people today. After all, feminism does not mean dominance by women, but the equality of women and men. As argued throughout this book, such equality and liberation will be beneficial to all members of society.

Perhaps because of the changes in personal attitudes, many women and men today are confused and frustrated at the slower pace of social and institutional change. Traditional roles no longer are the norm either in actuality or in fantasy, but nontraditional roles are not fully accepted either. Cultural beliefs and institutional practices still are geared to the old roles, which makes living the new ones difficult. There also is a strong backlash against the changes that have been made, which will be discussed later. The result has been a retreat to the personal level (which is more under one's control), as can be seen in the rise of cultural feminism and the wildman movement. Maintaining an assault on systems of power can be wearying as well as dangerous.

We need to take a closer look at the process of change. How can we help individuals and society move beyond gender stereotypes and roles? How can we equalize the power structure? The following section suggests some alternatives.

▲   Modes of Change

Change needs to occur on individual, social, and institutional levels. No one tactic or orientation will accomplish the entire task. People choose their tactics based on personal preferences and their diagnoses of the problem. Their approach will be influenced by whether they view women's oppression as due, for example, to gender socialization, value differences between masculine and feminine culture, the power inequality between women and men, or capitalism itself, with its view that women are property and cheap labor (Polk, 1976).

Personal Change
Regardless of perspective, changing the self is an important part of any alteration in the social order. Ways to achieve such change are numerous and include consciousness-raising groups, psychotherapy, experiential groups, general education, explicit training, and experimenting with new behaviors.

Consciousness-raising groups   Perhaps the most prevalent and valuable contribution of the women's movement has been the consciousness-raising (CR) group as a way to achieve personal and social change. CR groups generally consist of 7 to 15 same-sex individuals who meet together, usually weekly, to focus on members' common values, attitudes, and experiences. Many personal problems are seen as having a social cause and a political solution. Through sharing of experiences, members increase their awareness of gender stereotypes and their consequences, receive support, explore new ways of behaving and relating, and learn to trust and respect other members of their sex (J. Freeman, 1989; Nassi & Abramowitz, 1978; N. B. Rosenthal, 1984).

A key aspect of CR groups is the alteration of traditional (that is, masculine) hierarchical leadership norms. Most groups are run democratically with no fixed leader, and each member is regarded as an expert. This new norm applies to the women's liberation movement itself and partially explains why many observers view the movement as disorganized and fragmented. When an organization has no recognizable leader or spokesperson, the media have a difficult time focusing on it—the male norm expectation here is evident.

Research has documented many changes that appear to occur as a result of CR groups: an altered world view and greater understanding of social, political, and economic factors; a clearer sense of identity and job-career orientation; a greater sense of self-acceptance and higher self-esteem and self-confidence; more egalitarian relationships with members of the other sex and increased trust and respect for members of the same sex; and a feeling of group solidarity (Astrachan, 1986; Kravetz, 1978; Lieberman, Solow, Bond, & Reibstein, 1979; R. Weitz, 1982). The strongest findings have been with regard to the development of profeminist attitudes. The most equivocal data have been with regard to the promotion of self-esteem and personal growth. Although self-reports verify such psychological changes, results from various psychometric measures have been conflicting and few in number (Nassi & Abramowitz, 1978). Furthermore, people who join such groups may be different from people who don't join. Still, all researchers agree that CR groups are potent vehicles for resocialization. For men, especially, CR groups appear to be extremely powerful. By their egalitarian structure and their concern with talking about feelings and doubts, these groups challenge male gender stereotypes. For this reason, men's CR groups are more difficult to start and to continue than women's CR groups, but the experience itself often is profound (W. Farrell, 1974; A. Gross et al., 1983; Shiffman, 1987; Tolson, 1977).

During the 1960s and early 1970s, most people joining CR groups were trying to develop a political awareness of how seemingly personal issues (for example, who does the housework) are in fact political. As noted previously, for many women, such groups were a gateway into the women's movement. CR groups during the late 1970s and 1980s were more oriented toward personal change and support, and most women who joined the more recent groups were already members of the women's movement (Kravetz, Marecek, & Finn, 1983; Lieberman et al., 1979; N. B. Rosenthal, 1984). Modern men's CR groups also emphasize personal change and support more than politics, and many of the men involved have no interest in becoming part of the men's movement (Astrachan, 1986; Shiffman, 1987). Thus, although CR groups appear to produce real personal change and intensify the individual's ideological commitment, they do not inevitably propel group members into political action. This is true with all individual change strategies. Still, such groups are important, and some feminists have called for a new round of consciousness raising for the women brought up to believe that they could "have it all" (Friedan, 1985). Such women need to see that their failure to have it all is not a personal failure, but rather a societal one.

Psychotherapy   A second and more traditional way of achieving personal change has been through psychotherapy. Despite popular misconception, psychotherapy is not reserved for individuals who are severely emotionally disturbed. Rather, it is a way to increase self-awareness and effect behavioral and emotional changes. This method is likely to be beneficial to most people since most of us can benefit from learning more about ourselves and our behaviors. But, as was discussed in Chapter 8, traditional psychotherapy may discriminate against women in a number of ways. It may incorporate a double standard of mental health. It may "blame the victim" by looking for personal solutions to social problems. And it may reinforce powerlessness by the hierarchical nature of the therapist-client relationship itself. Awareness of these problems has brought changes in therapeutic techniques and has given rise to a new approach, feminist therapy (Brodsky, 1980; Brodsky et al., 1978; D. Howard, 1986; Robbins & Siegel, 1983; Rosewater & Walker, 1985).

Feminist therapy emphasizes awareness of gender roles and stereotypes, as well as of sexism. Clients are helped to appreciate the social-political context of their behavior, and self-nurturance is encouraged. Issues of equality, anger, and dependence are dealt with, and the ultimate goal is self-empowerment. The therapist-client relationship is nonauthoritarian and the therapist serves as a role model of gender-role transcendence. Although there are many variations of feminist therapy, they all have in common the recognition that the social context is an important determinant of human behavior, and that the gender roles and statuses prescribed by society are disadvantageous to both sexes, but especially to women. Feminist therapy can be applied to couple and family counseling (Hare-Mustin, 1978; Luepnitz, 1988), group counseling (C. M. Brody, 1987; Fedele & Harrington, 1990), and to counseling with nontraditional clients, including ethnic minorities (L. S. Brown & Root, 1990). It is especially effective with women who have been victimized by sexual assault and family violence.

Because feminism refers to equality between the sexes, men as well as women can be feminist therapists or clients of feminist therapists. That is,

feminist therapy is not for women only, although women have been its primary practitioners and clients. Still, there is some support for the argument that each sex might do better with same-sex therapists since the therapist's role as a model can be one of the most powerful aspects of therapy, and this would be enhanced in a same-sex dyad. There are power issues as well. For example, some people (such as Chesler, 1972) argue that only women should be therapists for other women because the male therapist–female client dyad replicates the gender power structure that disempowers women. Research tends to support this conclusion, especially when the female client is young, single, and/or uncertain in her relationships with men (Brodsky, 1980; H. G. Lerner, 1988; Orlinsky & Howard, 1976). Clients of feminist therapists generally feel empowered and supported, not forced into adopting particular behaviors. In contrast, some clients of traditional therapists report feeling forced into a traditional mode (Chambers & Wenk, 1982; Marecek, Kravetz, & Finn, 1979). The female therapist–female client dyad also tends to be the most emotionally intense (Mintz & O'Neil, 1990). Yet a woman is not a better therapist simply by virtue of her sex. The key seems to be sensitivity to and awareness of issues particularly relevant to women. Certainly men can become aware and sensitive. It may be, however, at this point in time, that feminist female therapists have more to offer other women than feminist male therapists, who perhaps would be more effective working with men.

The question of using psychotherapy for males who are trying to adopt nontraditional gender roles has received increased attention from a number of writers since the early 1980s (L. E. Good, Gilbert, & Scher, 1990; O'Neil, 1981a, 1982; M. Scher et al., 1987; Solomon & Levy, 1982). These writers have argued that counseling practitioners need to assess, conceptualize, and intervene in gender role conflicts of clients. In particular, counselors can help men examine the degree to which gender role conflicts limit their interpersonal, physical, and emotional lives. Problems with psychotherapy could arise from the fact that many therapists may not be sensitive to the negative effects of gender stereotypes on males, some therapists may have difficulty accepting non-sex-typed behavior in men, and different psychotherapeutic techniques may be needed with men than are needed with women. For example, men-only groups and programs may be particularly important for men to break down the barriers to self-disclosure built up by traditional male socialization (Buie, 1990; Croteau & Burda, 1983).

Men as well as women can benefit from feminist therapy, although men may view such therapy as unsuitable for themselves. To get around the word barrier, some therapists recently have coined the term "gender aware therapy," which synthesizes feminist therapy and knowledge about gender (L. E. Good et al., 1990). The five principles of such an approach are (1) regard conceptions of gender as integral aspects of counseling and mental health; (2) consider problems within their societal context; (3) actively seek to change gender injustices experienced by women and men; (4) emphasize development of collaborative therapeutic relationships; and (5) respect clients' freedom to choose.

Having begun as a grassroots movement during the 1970s, feminist therapy is now a legitimate school of thought (Kaschak, 1981b). As such, it continues to evolve and to influence more traditional forms of therapy in such a way that even if a therapy is not explicitly feminist, it still may be nonsexist.

Experiential groups   A third vehicle for personal change is experiential groups or training groups ("T-groups"). These groups have been particularly helpful in opening men up to their feelings and in improving their listening skills and interpersonal sensitivity. For this reason, some businesses have instituted such programs to improve the effectiveness of their staff (Saltzman, 1991). Interestingly, it is in precisely these areas that most women already are competent due to gender socialization. Putting more women who are otherwise qualified in influential positions also might achieve the business objectives, although anything that helps men increase their interpersonal sensitivity should be encouraged.

As noted earlier, "wildman gatherings" have become increasingly popular around the country (Gabriel, 1990). So have intimacy workshops conducted at men's conferences (R. A. Lewis, 1978). These workshops focus on developing self-disclosure communication skills and the ability to extend affection. Other groups, especially those on college campuses, are more structured, aimed at helping men become more aware of their sex role conditioning and its effects on their lives. These groups also help men learn how to live free of traditional masculine roles (Croteau & Burda, 1983).

Workshops and groups to help individuals break down internalized racism, anti-Semitism, and homophobia also have been successful (see, for example, Pheterson, 1986). Overcoming internalized oppression and domination is crucial in order for people to form alliances across subgroup boundaries.

Education   Education, both general and specific, is a fourth way to promote individual change. Women's studies, men's studies, courses on gender and the psychology of women, and so on have proliferated in the last 20 years on the college and, in a few cases, the high school level. The American Psychological Association (APA) officially accepted the psychology of women as a legitimate field of study by establishing a separate division for it in 1973. By 1979, this division had nearly 2000 female and male members and published its own journal. Work in the field is growing, as indicated by the increasing number of papers presented at meetings and in books, journal articles, and dissertations. The National Women's Studies Association was founded in 1976, and in 1990 there were more than 600 women's studies programs (see M. Johnson, 1982, for more information on the psychology of women; see Bowles and Duelli-Klein, 1983, and Stimpson, 1986, for more information on women's studies). Black women's studies (Guy-Sheftall & Bell-Scott, 1989a; Hull, Scott, & Smith, 1982) and lesbian studies (Cruikshank, 1982) are two offshoots of these developments.

Men's studies also has developed as a field (Brod, 1987). A men's studies newsletter, *Men's Studies Review,* began in 1972 and is now published quarterly by the Men's Studies Association of the National Organization for Men Against Sexism. In 1975, the University of Southern California established a Division for the Study of Women and Men in Society, followed by the first professorship in men's studies in 1984. There also are specific courses within disciplines, such as "The Sociology of Masculinity" or "The Male Experience" (Carrigan, Connell, & Lee, 1987; Kimmel, 1987b) As does women's studies, men's studies examines the effects of gender stereotypes and roles within a sociopolitical context. Thus, men's studies explores masculinities and the male experience using a feminist framework. Although it is true that men traditionally have been the center of nearly all knowledge, they haven't previously been studied as male humans, but rather as generic humans. The effects of gender on males thus have been hidden.

Parallel to increased interest in men's studies is increased interest in gender studies and the transformation of all traditional curricula so that gender issues (as well as those of race, class, and ethnicity) are made more salient and the existing White male bias corrected (E. C. DuBois et al., 1985; Minnich, 1990; Schmitz, 1985). For example, a course called "Modern Literature" might more accurately be called "White Male European Literature since 1920," if such is truly its content. Better still might be the inclusion of previously underrepresented groups (such as women, ethnic minorities, and non-Western cultures) in the course content. Peggy McIntosh (1989) has outlined five phases of curricular transformation: (1) women and minority men are completely left out and no notice is made of their absence; (2) some women and minority men are included but only to the extent that they have succeeded on traditional White male terms; (3) there is recognition of systems of oppression and how they have worked to exclude women and minority men from the curriculum; (4) a dramatic shift in consciousness takes place so that the focus is on "How was/is it for people?"; and (5) consciousness, perception, and behavior are entirely reconstructed. There are over 100 curriculum integration projects in progress, most of which are at phase 3. McIntosh believes it will take 100 years before phase 5 is achieved.

The general focus of all these educational endeavors is to encourage people to challenge traditional gender stereotypes and assumptions and to consider seriously the consequences of such sexism. This challenge threatens the status quo, which may account for the recent outbreak of hostility by conservatives toward a more inclusive curriculum. Research on the effects of women's studies and psychology of women courses suggests that the effects duplicate some of the results of CR groups; that is, after such courses women tend to gain in self-esteem, assertiveness, and instrumental-active traits; they become more feminist and less traditional in their sex role attitudes; and they may even become more certain and motivated with respect to future jobs (Bargad & Hyde, 1991; Howe, 1985; G. P. Jones & Jacklin, 1988; O'Connell, 1989; Stake & Gerner, 1987; D. M. Zuckerman, 1983). Men, too, appear to make similar gains from such courses, but less research has been done on them since they are a small percentage of students in those classes.

Explicit training   A fifth method of achieving personal change is through explicit training. For example, some women might benefit from explicit training in problem solving, mathematics, career planning, management and leadership skills, and self-defense. Some men could benefit from training in sensitivity

to women's concerns and effective listening techniques. For instance, workshops designed to retrain men's perceptions of pornography have met with some success (Astrachan, 1986). Both sexes may need training in assertiveness (Alberti & Emmons, 1978). In assertiveness training, individuals are taught to discriminate among passive responses (letting others violate your rights, particularly common among women), aggressive responses (infringing upon the rights of others, particularly common among men), and assertive responses (respecting your own rights and those of others). Through role playing and homework assignments, stereotypic sex role behaviors can be changed. A six-week group treatment program incorporating principles of both assertiveness training and consciousness raising was found to increase the assertiveness and instrumental-active trait scores of participating feminine-sex-typed college women when these women were compared one year after participation with a matched control group who had been placed on a waiting list (Gulanick, Howard, & Moreland, 1979). Another study (Lewittes & Bem, 1983) found that undergraduate women who received three sessions of behavioral training in assertiveness later increased their participation in mixed-sex discussion groups when compared with control groups of women. It would be interesting to assess the consequences of similar programs on males.

Changing behavior   A sixth way of achieving individual attitude change is through focusing on changing behaviors. As was discussed in Chapter 10, increasing numbers of men are trying out the role of househusband and are learning much about themselves in the process. In Chapter 11 we saw that women executives are learning how to deal with situations they have never before encountered, and many wind up reevaluating previously held beliefs. Other changes are occurring on a smaller, more personal scale—a wife going out to work, a husband doing the laundry, a woman asking a man for a date, a man refusing a sexual overture, and so on. Because behaviors and attitudes interact, such behavioral changes often increase the individual's level of awareness.

All these changes, by their very nature, occur on the individual level and thus touch only one part of the problem. They often are slow and limited to a few highly motivated people. In addition, individual change itself is not always linear. As Alexandra Kaplan and Bean (1976) suggest, we seem to follow the pendulum principle: at the beginning, there may be a move from one extreme to another, as in a move from passive to aggressive behavior. With time, however, modifications are made and a middle ground is gradually attained, as in the development of assertive behavior. Such a middle position is never static, however; an external force is able to start the swing again at any time. The point to remember is that in order to reject an old, extreme behavior or attitude, a new, equally extreme behavior or attitude may temporarily be needed. It's the dialectical process again: first the thesis, then the antithesis, and finally the synthesis. Although this process may be difficult for those dealing with someone at the time of antithesis, knowledge of its necessity and temporary nature might help.

Downing and Roush (1984) propose a five-stage model of feminist identity development in women, based on models of African-American identity development (Cross, 1978). Stage 1 is passive acceptance, in which women not only deny or are unaware of sexism but also believe traditional roles are beneficial. Stage 2 is revelation, in which a woman becomes aware of sexism, frequently accompanied by anger and bipolar thinking (for example, men are bad, women are good). In stage 3, embeddedness-emanation, women become immersed in women's culture and feel connected to other women. With stage 4, synthesis, women begin to transcend gender roles and recognize individual differences among men and women. Stage 5 is the active commitment stage, wherein the individual commits herself to working for social change. This model has received some empirical support (Bargad & Hyde, 1991; Rickard, 1989), although its relevance for men is unclear. It's important to note that part of a feminist identity is a commitment to social change. It is to such change that we now turn.

Social Change

Changes in individual consciousness only go so far. To be effective, individuals must join together to urge changes at social and institutional levels. The importance of group work cannot be overestimated: not only do groups carry more social and political clout because they amplify what might otherwise be dismissed as a lone individual voice, but groups also provide needed support for their members since working for change can be a frustrating and sometimes isolating process.

Since gender is socially constructed, it first needs to be socially deconstructed and then reconstructed, with equality rather than domination/subordination

as the model (see Connell, 1990, for an example of the process). Change on the social level must incorporate changes in our basic ideology, socialization practices, and relationships with others.

Ideology   The liberation movements have gone a long way toward changing the ideology of our culture. As noted previously, most people agree with the goals of the women's movement. Equality and freedom of choice are becoming more the norm in personal relationships and individual functioning, although they are not always practiced (see Chapters 9 and 10). Standards of mental health, intelligence, creativity, achievement, and child rearing are all changing in a non-sex-typed direction although progress is slow and by no means continuous. Since ideology is the backdrop against which all constructions of roles and behaviors occur, the fact that gender ideology has become more egalitarian bodes well for future changes.

More is needed than egalitarian beliefs, however. An egalitarian ideology may even be a hindrance to social change if there also is an ideology of individualism. That is, just believing that women and men should have equal rights is unlikely to lead to social change if people also believe that individuals generally get what they deserve based on their own merits. This belief in individualism and a meritocracy is a basic one in the United States and leads people to believe that change will inevitably occur without a strong and coherent social movement. This belief also leads people, especially women, to believe they can make it on their own, without institutions, or even other people, changing (see Sidel, 1990). So we have a situation where most people don't themselves identify with the women's movement or with feminism, although they believe the movement is important. Yet an egalitarian ideology is not sufficient to create systemic change, especially in the face of organized resistance. Systems need to be pushed in order to change, as we will discuss in the next section, and the best "pushers" are people organized around specific issues.

In this sense, it is important that more people than ever before are recognizing sexism in everyday life. About half of all adults in 1989 (49%) believed that men have a better life in this country than women, in contrast to only one-third who believed this in 1975 (DeStefano & Colasanto, 1990). Younger women (aged 18 to 40) are even more likely to see men as better off (63%). This recognition may lead to increased demands for change.

Interestingly, even though women tend to have more egalitarian values than men and an increasing awareness of the disparities in status between men and women, women generally do not have a group consciousness—that is, a sense of identification with other women (E. Klein, 1984). Without such a sense of identification, which other minority groups such as Blacks and the elderly have, organizing and acting together to bring about change can be very difficult. Some indication of this was the 1984 presidential election, where the majority of women voted for President Reagan even though they recognized his policies were damaging to the status of women. As discussed in Chapter 12, women are just starting to recognize that the discrepancies between what should exist and what does is the result of the inadequacy of social institutions rather than of individual failures. In the last ten years, women have been more likely to vote as a bloc for issues and candidates of importance to them.

Socialization Because we learn our sex roles through socialization, radical changes need to be made in this area. Parents need to be made aware of the potentially maladaptive consequences of rigid sex typing. Child-rearing practices deliberately need to foster non-sex-typed functioning, such as by encouraging independence in girls and emotional sensitivity and expressiveness in boys (see Pogrebin, 1981, for some suggestions). Parents also need to try to raise their children without a schema for gender, as advocated by Sandra Bem (1983) and discussed in Chapter 6. This means deemphasizing the importance of gender in children's lives, including in matters of choosing toys, games, clothes, and colors. Because males very likely will continue to display higher levels of aggression due to hormonal differences, they may need greater reinforcement of gentleness than girls (Gullahorn, 1977).

Socializing forces too need to change (see Chapter 7). For example, language needs to become less discriminatory (for example, *Ms.* and *Mr.*, not *Miss, Mrs.,* and *Mr.*) and more egalitarian (for example, chair*person*, not chair*man*). The media need to give a more accurate and liberated picture of the roles available to women and men. To these ends, many pressure groups have formed that are having some effect. For example, Women on Words and Images, an outgrowth of the Princeton NOW chapter, studied sex typing in children's books. Many of their recommendations have been incorporated by publishers and adopted by school systems. Women Against Violence Against Women, an activist organization

based in Los Angeles, successfully instituted boycotts against socially irresponsible companies who use images of violence against women as an advertising gimmick. Men Organized Against Sexism and Institutionalized Stereotypes (OASIS), based in Boston, have developed an educational slide show regarding the images of men in advertising. There also are groups against pornography (for example, Women Against Pornography) and groups concerned about television images (for example, Action for Children's Television).

Changing sex typing in schools also is imperative. As discussed in Chapter 7, present school practices and organization, textbooks, curricula, and counseling all perpetuate sex typing. Laws banning any form of sex discrimination in any educational institution receiving public funds could help remedy the situation, but the laws have been narrowly interpreted, and enforcement is weak. Additionally, the changing of regulations does not necessarily change attitudes or behavior. As Guttentag and Bray (1977) found when they tried to institute curriculum changes to counteract sexism in kindergarten, fifth, and ninth grades, the teachers' own attitudes and the age and sex of the children were the most important factors: teachers who cared about the issue of sexism could change the attitudes of their students, and kindergarteners and females were especially affected by the six-week program. Thus, change can be effected in the schools, but it also can be thwarted by teachers' attitudes and practices. Perhaps specific training for our nation's teachers in avoiding sexism is needed (as well as training in avoiding racism, which many schools already have instituted). As a result of the Women's Equity Act of 1974, many resource materials for teachers of all grades have been developed (see S. S. Klein, 1985). However, many of these federally funded programs have been targeted for extinction by the Reagan/Bush administrations, saved mainly by congressional insistence. Parents' groups might be particularly effective in monitoring teacher behavior and school compliance with federal regulations. On the college and university level, the Project on the Status and Education of Women of the Association of American Colleges has a number of resource materials to help monitor and decrease sexism in higher education.

Just as socializing agents and forces currently construct traditional roles and attitudes in children, these same agents and forces can construct nontraditional roles and attitudes. The process generally is the same; the content is radically different.

Relationships Changing relationships is a key aspect of social change and is where many people get bogged down. This is particularly true with respect to female-male relationships, particularly within families.

In general, although most people have become less traditional in their attitudes toward gender roles over the last 20 years, women have changed more than men, especially White men (Belkin, 1989; Cherlin & Walters, 1981; Thom, 1984). Life experience, especially entry into marriage, seems to increase women's nontraditional gender attitudes (W. H. McBroom, 1987). Women's life experience in general tends to radicalize women as they move from relatively equal educational experiences to sexist environments in the workplace and at home. The reverse is true for men. Their life experience (of gender privilege in the workplace and in the home) tends to reinforce traditional gender ideology. Thus, women and men have different stakes in maintaining the status quo: men may perceive less traditionalism as eroding their power, while women may perceive such a change as increasing theirs. This differential stake in the status quo may lead to conflict between women and men.

Although both sexes believe that men's attitudes toward women have changed for the better in the past 20 years, men think they've changed more than women think men have changed (Belkin, 1989). For example, 57% of women aged 18 to 44 but only 35% of comparably aged men believe men are only willing to let women get ahead if women still do all the housework at home. The result of this gender gap in social perception has been increased criticism of men by women and increased strain in male-female relationships. For example, more than half of all women now believe "most men think only their own opinions about the world are important" (58%) and "most men find it necessary for their egos to keep women down" (55%) ("Male Bashing," 1990).

Greater balance in the division of labor between the sexes, especially in the home, is integral to transcending gender roles and achieving gender equality. As we have noted, male participation in child rearing enhances the public status of women (Coltrane, 1988). Without a more equal division of labor, women wind up with low status in the public sphere (including the workplace) and a "second shift" at home (Hochschild, 1989; L. Segal, 1990). This is the area of most conflict between women and men, as discussed in Chapters 9 and 10. Although many men are increasing their participation in household chores and child care, the burden of such activities still falls disproportionately on the shoulders of women.

Couples need to work out new patterns of responsibilities that correspond to current realities and gender equality. Women need to expect men to participate more in the home, and they must hold them to it by refusing to "overfunction" in that area (H. G. Lerner, 1989). Similarly, women must stop doing all the emotional work in a relationship. Unless women hold men responsible for expressing their own feelings and meeting their own emotional needs, many men will continue to underfunction in that area. Conversely, men must stop reinforcing their female partners for helpless, dependent behaviors. When conflicts arise, they must be worked through rather than buried. Conflict confrontations may be needed in order to prevent the substitution of subtle, informal discrimination for structural, institutional discrimination (Safilios-Rothschild, 1979). It is in relationships that have a strong degree of affective and esteem feelings (such as friendships, love and marital relationships) that such confrontations can lead to personal change and eventually to a gradual diminution of interpersonal conflict.

To change the division of labor in the home, more than good will is needed, however. As discussed in previous chapters, the workplace and traditional gender socialization steer women and men into their different roles in society. Thus, women may in fact find more pleasure in child-care activities than employment activities because they are trained for the former role and their role in the workplace frequently is unrewarding (see Chapter 11). This pattern is starting to change, as young women increase their commitment to the labor force and young men increase their interest in family life (N. Gibbs, 1990). Still, until socialization and institutional practices change, it will be hard to attain gender equality within relationships. This issue will be discussed further in the next section.

Even in less personal relationships, confrontation can restructure roles. For example, exposure to overt sexist statements and actions has been found to raise the consciousness, and lead to less traditional sex role attitudes, of other group members (R. J. Dworkin & Dworkin, 1983). Even without direct confrontation, it is important not to become complicit in gender oppression, such as by laughing at sexist jokes and engaging in homophobic or sexist behaviors toward others.

Alternative lifestyles A fourth way to effect change on the social level might be to provide for living situations other than the nuclear family. In a nuclear family, father dominance tends to prevail, a strict division of labor by sex often is encouraged, and family members often feel isolated. Popularization of communes, spread of living complexes with communal cooking and child-care arrangements, and increased acceptance of single women living alone, unmarried couples living together, gay and lesbian families, and single-parent families, all represent ways of providing more alternatives for more people and facilitate breaking away from traditional sex-typed behaviors and patterns. (See Macklin, 1980; Pogrebin, 1983, for general discussions of alternatives.) However, research on communes in America suggests that such a lifestyle, although resulting in less competitive, hostile, and independent behaviors among its members than among noncommune peers, nevertheless frequently maintains traditional roles and statuses for women and men (Minturn, 1984; Wagner, 1982). In order for nontraditional gender roles to be accepted, they must be explicitly targeted and supported by the environment (for example, Latkin, 1989).

Institutional Change

Even though change has been progressing on the individual level and some change is beginning on the social level, the institutional level has been markedly resistant to change—although many confrontations have occurred. This level represents "the incorporation of ideology into legally required or generally expected actions" (A. Kaplan & Bean, 1976, p. 386). Laws, politics, the division of work and family, direct action, and alternative institutions come under this heading and will be examined in succeeding paragraphs. The master variable on the institutional level is *power*. As discussed in the last chapter, power in our society rests predominantly in White male hands; significant change is impossible without a reallocation of society's resources, including power. This is difficult because those in control of societal power administer it in ways that work to their continuing advantage and privilege (see Boneparth & Stoper, 1988; Lipman-Blumen & Bernard, 1979, for an excellent collection of articles on the interface between sex roles and social policy). Many feminists view electoral politics as the key to changing the power structure (for example, Katzenstein, 1984); others emphasize more radical changes from outside the system (for example, S. Johnson, 1987). Even when laws change, however, socialized beliefs take time to follow.

Laws As discussed in the last chapter, there has been some movement toward enacting legislation prohibiting discrimination on the basis of sex. Yet, despite affirmative action guidelines, Title IX of the Higher Education Act of 1972, and other legislation, enforcement still is a problem. Since 1980 the Equal Employment Opportunity Commission has had its funds and staff cut, is behind in hearing sex discrimination cases, and has done only a minimum amount of actual prosecution. Much existing legislation is neither comprehensive nor mandatory, and some regulatory agencies still do not enforce the legal statutes already on the books.

Perhaps most discouraging have been the failure to ratify the Equal Rights Amendment (ERA) and the assault on reproductive choice. The ERA, proposed yearly since 1923, finally was passed by Congress in 1972. It fell 3 states short of ratification by the required 38 states by its 1982 deadline despite support by the majority of the population. Although reintroduced in Congress yearly, the ERA has yet to be passed again. It was defeated by a combination of forces: organized opposition by politically conservative organizations such as the Conservative Caucus, the John Birch Society, the American Conservative Union, and fundamentalist and Mormon churches; a virulent and effective misinformation campaign; the lack of a unified pro-ERA organization; and the inability of pro-ERA forces to face head-on the implications of full equality (such as that women could no longer be exempt from the draft, although they still could be exempt from combat) (M. F. Berry, 1986; Mansbridge, 1986). The states that did not ratify (mostly Deep South and Sun Belt states) have a politically conservative tradition. Despite findings from opinion polls that a majority of voters in those states favored passage of the ERA, the legislators (mainly White males) voted it down.

The ERA would go a long way toward affirming women's equality under the law. Fourteen states already have a state equal rights amendment, but a national policy is needed so that all citizens are covered. Such an event seems unlikely in the current conservative political climate, despite popular support for such an amendment. In 1980, the Republican party reversed its 40-year support for the ERA and has maintained its opposition since then. Judging by the history of other constitutional amendments (for example, the right to vote for women took 72 years to obtain), it is likely that it will take another 10 to 20 years to get an ERA into the Constitution.

It should be noted, however, that not all feminists think the ERA is the way to achieve gender equality. As discussed previously, the emphasis on equal *rights* ignores the fact that women's lives are fundamentally different from men's by virtue of women's reproductive capacity. Women can (and do) have babies and they can be (and are) victimized by sexual violence in disproportionate numbers. Thus, a standard of equal rights generally means a male standard (see the discussion in the last chapter and in the section on institutional goals). As we have seen, women are increasingly disadvantaged in child custody decisions because of a "gender-neutral" standard, such as earnings capacity. The old argument about whether women need some form of "protective" legislation because of their (potential) role as mothers (which can and has worked against them in the labor force) or whether women should be treated exactly the way men are treated (which has worked against them in the domestic sphere) has resurfaced. Catherine MacKinnon (1987b) and others (for example, Eisenstein, 1989) argue that we must stop focusing on gender *differences* and start focusing on gender *inequality*, which takes into account the effect that difference produces. Of course men and women are different; but such difference does not mean that they should be unequal under the law unless only a male standard of rights is utilized. Such is the present situation: men are the norm; women are viewed as different and hence inferior. Women's views and needs are not the basis of law. Hence pornographers are protected by the Bill of Rights ("freedom of speech") while women who are victimized by such materials (for example, by being degraded and dehumanized in the eyes of many viewers of pornography, or by being sexually assaulted because such materials increased men's likelihood of committing rape; see Chapter 12) have no rights at all.

Nowhere is this issue of women's inequality under the law more pressing today than in the current fight to maintain reproductive choice. The 1973 U.S. Supreme Court ruling that restrictions on abortions are unconstitutional (*Roe v. Wade*) has increasingly been eroded. In 1976, Congress passed the Hyde amendment, which prevented Medicaid funds from being used for abortions, a law upheld by the Supreme Court in 1980. This, in effect, denied low-income women the right to a legal and safe abortion. Since then, further restrictions have occurred, as the Republicans gained the White House on an anti-choice platform and began appointing anti-choice justices. "Right to life" groups have continuously pressured Congress to ban legal abortions through a constitutional amendment. Such groups also have pressured abortion clinics, through picketing, sit-ins, and even bombings, to stop providing services. President Reagan actively supported restrictive anti-choice family planning measures, including a "gag rule" that prohibits any clinic that receives federal funds (such as Planned Parenthood) from counseling clients about abortion or even telling clients that abortion is a legal option. This policy was upheld by the Supreme Court in 1991 (*Rust v. Sullivan*). Although Congress passed a new law barring such restrictions, President Bush vetoed it. Other restrictions on abortion access have occurred on the state level. For example, a number of states now require parents (one or both) to be notified if a minor has an abortion, and/or husbands to give their consent for their wife's abortion, even if the child is not theirs. Some states also bar abortions at public clinics or hospitals and impose criminal sentences on physicians who provide abortions.

All restrictions increase the likelihood of women's delaying abortions (with increased risk since later abortions are more complicated than early ones) or seeking illegal abortions, with their much higher health risk. For example, an Indiana teenager (Becky Bell) died in 1990 from an illegal abortion due to the parental notification requirement in that state. She hadn't wanted to tell her parents for fear of disappointing them. Such restrictions also mean that some women who do not want a child are forced to have one. For example, the birth rate for 15- to 17-year-olds increased by nearly 40% in Minneapolis after passage of a parental consent law (Freiberg, 1991c). Unfortunately, unwanted children are twice as likely as wanted children to end up abused, delinquent, on welfare, or with serious emotional problems (H. P. David & Baldwin, 1979). At the time of this writing, it is very likely that the now strongly conservative Supreme Court will increase restrictions on abortion or overturn *Roe v. Wade* entirely. This assault on reproductive choice is occurring despite the fact that national surveys consistently show that a majority of both sexes (62%) oppose a constitutional ban on abortion ("Most," 1989). Although most Americans (61% in 1989) consider abortion to be morally wrong, 74% also agree that whether or not to have an abortion should be a decision made by the woman for herself.

The right of women to control their own bodies is an integral part of the women's movement. The issue is a complex one, involving religious, philosophical, political, economic, and other factors. Being against abortion does not necessarily mean being against women. However, a distinction needs to be made between a personal decision and a legal option. Although someone may be personally against abortions, he or she still can support a woman's legal right to choose. Without such a legal right, some women would be forced to find "home remedies" or have unsafe illegal abortions. Others would be forced to bear unwanted children, which might force them to abandon their jobs or education and/or enter pregnancy-related marriages that might have little chance of success. Thus, without reproductive freedom and reproductive choice, women's control over their lives would be reduced dramatically. It is not coincidental that the fight against reproductive choice is waged most strongly by those who wish to maintain traditional gender roles. Many of the same people who are against legal abortion also are against birth control as well as sex education. Since the courts are firmly in the hands of conservatives, the main hope for those who wish to retain reproductive choice is to elect pro-choice legislators.

Although women increasingly are being forced to bear children, the government has no interest in helping them or their families. As discussed previously, the United States is one of only two industrialized countries (South Africa is the other) not offering any guaranteed maternity leave for women. Even many developing countries offer such leave. The Parental and Medical Leave Act, passed by Congress and vetoed by President Bush in 1990, is desperately needed to guarantee for parents the right to take time off from their job to care for a child or other family member without job loss or punishment. Even this bill is too modest, only providing unpaid leave for a short period of time (about 10 weeks) and only to employees working in businesses with more than 50 employees. Other desirable options include paid leave, longer leave, a family allowance, and subsidized child care. Families also need comprehensive health care coverage as well as adequate food, clothing, and shelter. Thus, we need to overhaul the welfare system and provide national health insurance to all.

Legal action is needed in the following other areas as well:

1. Equal opportunity in employment and salaries must be supported. This involves the effective enforcement of all laws, including affirmative action programs. It also involves the passage of displaced homemakers legislation and legislation increasing part-time and flex-time work opportunities. Legislation is needed to reduce the veteran's preference and to expand the opportunities and benefits of women in the military.

2. Full sex equity in education must be achieved. The scope of Title IX needs to be broadened and the amendment needs to be enforced. Math and science equity legislation also needs to be passed.

3. Legislation is needed to assure economic equity, especially for married couples. This involves the reform of Social Security regulations and federal and military pensions to give both spouses equity and benefits. Tax reform is needed to ensure that families with two wage earners are not penalized. Appropriation of adequate funds is needed to enforce the Equal Credit Opportunity Act. Legislation barring sex discrimination in insurance and pension coverage must be passed. Divorce settlements must take account of a woman's nonmonetary investments in her husband's career potential.

4. Women need legislation to protect them against violence, such as the Violence Against Women Act, sponsored by Senator Joseph Biden and Representative Barabara Boxer in the 101st Congress (1990). This bill authorized money to be used for training, education, prevention, and victim services, such as rape crisis centers and battered women's shelters. The bill explicitly recognized sexual assault against women as an act of sex discrimination, thus entitling victims to sue assailants for damages and other forms of civil relief.

5. Legislation is also needed to guarantee equal rights for lesbians and gay men. Denying such groups equal rights feeds homophobia, which supports sexism and gender inequality.

In sum, with equal treatment under the law, protection from discrimination based on sex, and the right to physical self-determination, political and economic power for women as a class should increase.

Politics As discussed in the last chapter and suggested earlier in this chapter, political life is dominated by White males. Women are slowly increasing their representation as officeholders, but their representation decreases as the status of the office increases. Even more difficult than getting women elected is getting feminists elected. Since to be acceptable to either of the two dominant political parties means supporting their traditional policies to some extent, many women who get elected are indistinguishable from their male counterparts. To really make a change in politics-as-usual, we may need a third political party, one with a feminist agenda (see Boneparth & Stoper, 1988). In 1990, NOW organized a task force to study the issue. Although starting a feminist party seems radical, it's been done before in this country and is occurring in other countries. For example, Alice Paul headed the National Women's Party in the 1920s, which existed through the 1950s. Unfortunately, it appeared to be oriented toward a single issue (the ERA) and did not have support from most progressive women leaders of that time. In contrast, feminist parties in Norway and Iceland have significantly increased women's influence in these governments and helped move social policies in more feminist directions, including the election of a feminist woman prime minister in Norway (Edgar, 1987; Steinem, 1988).

To be successful, a women's (or feminist) party would have to cut across party lines and appeal to a wide range of women and men. It would need to have strong leaders who could appeal to disparate groups. It's not clear such an approach could work in the United States, but such a party might bring certain issues (such as the feminization of poverty and violence against women) into the forefront of political debate. This might put pressure on both Republicans and Democrats to do something about these issues. At the very least, feminists must organize to support candidates sympathetic to their issues and to work against antifeminists.

Reorganization of work and family In contrast to changing laws and electing sympathetic representatives, another way to effect institutional change is by changing our way of compartmentalizing work and family functions. As we have seen, for an egalitarian society, women need to be truly integrated into the occupational world and men need to be truly integrated into the domestic sphere. Although a number of nations have attempted the former, very few have attempted the latter. The result has been that everywhere in industrialized societies, many women must bear the burden of two jobs—one in the work force and one at home. This lack of inclusion of men in domestic and child-care responsibilities, and the work overload for employed women partially account for the redifferentiation of sex roles that has occurred on most Israeli kibbutzim, contrary to the initial inhabitants' professed ideology (Agassi, 1989; Palgi, Blasi, Rosner, & Safir, 1983; Snarey, Friedman, & Blasi, 1985). Even in socialist countries, such as the Soviet Union and the People's Republic of China, whose founding ideals included gender equality, women must work a double day—first outside, then inside the home. This double-day pattern is one reason those countries have failed to achieve true gender equality, even though in both countries 90% of the women are employed (see earlier section on socialist feminism).

When both men and women share domestic as well as subsistence activities, sex roles tend to be relatively egalitarian, since men develop a more communal orientation and no longer can be paternalistic and distant. This can be seen in primitive hunting and gathering and horticultural societies (see Chapter 5) and currently in Sweden, the country that has gone the farthest over the longest time (since the 1970s) to encourage women's and men's active participation in both parenthood and the labor force.

While Swedish society in practice is not completely egalitarian, Sweden has come farther than any other country in egalitarian ideology and national policy (Baude, 1979; Moen & Forest, 1990; Pogrebin, 1982; Safilios-Rothschild, 1979). Perhaps the most important aspect of the Swedish model is that the government has strongly emphasized men's role changes. To accomplish this, the Swedes have reformed textbooks, changed school curricula, and developed nonsexist parent education. Nearly all boys learn homemaking and child-care skills, and preference usually is given to male applicants for preschool teacher training. The government has offered a system of incentives to employers to combat traditional sex typing of occupations; provided occupational counseling, grants-in-aid for education, and training for women; and taken care of child-care costs. Either mother or father can take child-care leave (nine months at 90% salary plus three additional months at a fixed rate) or child-sickness leave (10 days per child per year) or work reduced hours (six hours per day, with no loss of benefits until their child is 8 years old) and receive the child-care allowance paid to parents of children under 16. Child care is publicly supported and available. Each adult is considered economically independent and pays individual income taxes. The percentage of mothers with young children who participate in the labor force was 86% in 1986, much higher than our 57% that same year (Moen & Forest, 1990). Not surprisingly, Sweden ranks number one in the world in terms of the status of women ("The Status of Women," 1988).

Yet true equality has lagged behind national policy. For example, in 1981, 25% of employed mothers with a preschool child took a leave of absence from the workplace, compared to 3% of fathers. More than half of all mothers (55%) worked part-time, compared to 5% of fathers (Moen & Forest, 1990). Thus, although Swedish fathers are more likely to take on domestic responsibilities than American fathers, women still bear most of the responsibility, but with less psychological distress than before such workplace supports were in place. Perhaps because Swedish women, like their American counterparts, earn somewhat less (about 10%) than men and work mainly in sex-segregated low-status jobs, Swedish women are more willing than men to reduce their labor force role to care for young children. Still, work and family roles are better balanced in Sweden than in the United States, and many of the stresses on employed mothers of young children have been reduced.

Some elements of the Swedish model can be incorporated here. Our country needs a national policy, not just piecemeal efforts toward equality. Important changes would be increasing child-care options, such as leaves of absence for either parent (preferably paid), job protection and benefits to accompany part-time and flex-time options, and federally subsidized and community-controlled day-care centers. (See Figure 13.2 for one way to get more day-care centers.) Companies that have instituted parental leave policies have not found them to be problematic or costly. But the bigger problem is encouraging men to make use of such policies. This requires a major overhaul of gender role expectations. As long as a man's worth is defined in terms of his income and job status, most men will never risk reducing their investment in the labor force. As long as women and all things associated with them have low status, most men will never risk increasing their involvement in "women's work." Thus, change must occur on all levels simultaneously—the individual, the social, and the institutional—before men's roles will change. A key part of such change will be the collapsing of the artificial division between work and family roles for men as well as for women. Recognition and support by employers of most workers' (men's and women's) dual roles will help break down this division.

Direct action   While legal and political actions are powerful tactics to employ in trying to change male domination of institutions, other tactics also can be effective, such as direct action and conflict confrontations (Polk, 1976; Safilios-Rothschild, 1979). Through a variety of actions, women increasingly are being not only heard but also heeded. Some organizations, like Women Against Violence Against Women and NOW, are engaging in sit-ins and economic boycotts against products, companies, and states that disparage or discriminate against women. Other women have applied moral pressure by publicizing reports of sex discrimination, sexual harassment, and rape. Still others are organizing and unionizing groups of secretaries, nurses, and household workers. Women often need help in learning such tactics, and skill building is an important part of many feminist projects (Polk, 1976).

Some feminists (for example, Friedan, 1985; Safilios-Rothschild, 1979) urge women to become actively involved in crucial issues and protest

Figure 13.2 How to accomplish change in the structure of work and family relationships: get men to bear children. (Copyright © 1982 by Field Enterprises, Inc. From the book, *My Weight Is Always Perfect For My Height—Which Varies*, by Nicole Hollander. Reprinted with permission from St. Martin's Press, Inc., New York, NY.)

movements other than those specifically related to women in order to achieve maximum sex role change. Because some changes are occurring on the personal and social levels, confrontations on an institutional level are currently being eroded. By joining with other groups and issues, confrontations can continue. This may speed up the acceptance of nonsexist legislation and social policies as well.

Whereas the 1960s and 1970s were the heyday of street politics and pressure group activity, the 1980s were characterized by "unobtrusive mobilization" —working for change from within institutions (Katzenstein, 1990). Although the danger of co-optation always exists when women enter male-dominated settings (that is, they might adopt "masculine" values once they get inside), many women seem to be pushing to make such institutions more responsive to the needs of women. This can be seen particulary clearly in the case of the military (where attention has been focused on gender discrimination and sexual harassment) and the Catholic church (where issues of social justice have been interwoven with women's concerns about inclusion and representation). Thus, we need to take direct action from within as well as from outside of societal institutions.

Alternative institutions   A fifth approach to accomplishing institutional change is by building alternative institutions (Polk, 1976). The women's movement itself represents an alternative to masculine hierarchical authoritarian organizations, and many groups have begun to use the nonhierarchical model—feminist therapy, the Association for Women in Psychology, women's studies courses, and so forth. Numerous self-help organizations have challenged the traditional male monopoly on medical, legal, and psychotherapeutic information and have helped large numbers of people whom the professional institutions had turned off, put down, and overcharged. Collective living situations, as discussed earlier under "Alternative Lifestyles," also provide couples and single individuals with an alternative to the nuclear family. Such an alternative may facilitate sex role change if the group makes that a conscious goal.

As noted earlier, cultural feminists in particular emphasize the development of a "women's culture." In the 1980s and 1990s many women-only or women-dominated activities developed: music festivals, spirituality groups, conferences, weekend retreats, and so on. Although most women, even most feminists, want to live and work with men,

many feel that male-dominated institutions have proven themselves to be inadequate: destructive of people and the environment. Thus, many feel women must take the lead in developing alternatives based on "women's values" of concern for others and cooperative interactive styles.

▲   Problems

Change must occur on all three levels: personal, social, and institutional. We are talking about a complete overhaul of societal structure and practice. The difficulties of instituting such a massive change in society are enormous. Among the problems are those of integrating changes occurring on three levels, dealing with diversity, and overcoming resistance.

Integrating Changes
Unless changes occur on all levels—personal (attitudes), social (ideology), and institutional (power)— the likelihood of achieving a truly egalitarian society where each individual can develop according to his or her potential and society itself can be run in an effective and humanistic way is small. Legislation without comparable changes in people's attitudes will raise unrealistic hopes and increase resentments. Changes in attitudes without changes in socialization forces and institutions will lead to frustration and hostility. As social psychologists and sociologists have learned, the relationship between attitudes and behavior change is complex (see Bernard, 1976; Branscombe & Deaux, 1991). Changes in behavior sometimes can lead to changes in attitudes and of the social norm. For example, female premarital virginity no longer is the norm it once was. It is also possible that the norm may change and behavior will follow. For example, equality in relationships now is the norm and behavior is slowly changing. On the other hand, the norm may change and behavior may not follow. For example, the Civil Rights Bill of 1964 legislated racial and sexual equality but equality has yet to be achieved. Or behavior may change but the norm may not. For example, most mothers work outside the home, but the norm is that they do not. Clearly, the relation is a complex one and difficult to predict. Time and persistence are undoubtedly crucial variables.

Further evidence of problems that occur when the three levels of change are not integrated currently can be seen in communist countries, especially those of Eastern Europe (Kruks et al.,

1989; H. Scott, 1979). In their initial stages of development, communist societies generally facilitate progress toward sexual equality, especially when such countries first are moving toward industrialization. Labor is scarce at that time, and women are needed in the labor force. Their participation thus is encouraged through emphasis on equality. But once such advances begin to pose a threat to the male political hierarchy or to lead to greatly reduced fertility, sexist policies reappear. Change never really has taken place on the individual or relationship level. Incorporating women into the work force has meant only that women have been called on to perform two roles while men still performed one. When other policy matters become more important, the interest in "equality" abates. Thus, when communism collapses, there is no ideology or social support to sustain gender equality, and traditional roles reassert themselves.

Integration of changes also is important to avoid the "superwoman effect." With changing sex role ideologies, many women now feel they can, and should, do everything—have a stimulating career, establish intimate relationships, rear children, engage in recreational activities, and so on. Without social support from family and friends—and institutional support, such as child-care assistance and flexible work schedules—"doing it all" can be overwhelming. Given the American emphasis on individualism, people have had a hard time acknowledging that individual change alone is insufficient, and they blame themselves for "failure." But people make choices based not only on personal preference but also on social expectations and restrictions. If we want women and men to have equal choices of life options, we must support those choices socially and institutionally.

Dealing with Diversity
Not only is it difficult to work for change on all levels, it also is difficult to integrate diverse perspectives and goals. If you can't work on everything all at once, where do you start? Whose perspective guides the way?

As discussed under "Institutional Goals," different feminists have emphasized different objectives: male profeminists and cultural feminists often focus on personal and social (relationship) change and tend not to be politically active. Liberal feminists emphasize working within the system to attain change, especially within the legal and political systems. Socialist feminists focus on social (ideological) and institutional (political) change.

Radical feminists focus on change on all three levels and are the most committed to developing new institutions. Unfortunately, these groups often are at odds with each other and too much feminist energy is expended in defining who is a true feminist. The truth is we need change in all areas. If different groups and individuals chip away at different pieces of the system, the system itself gradually may be eroded. Furthermore, extremists make moderates look more reasonable. If no one were pushing a radical agenda, liberal feminists might not have attained the changes they already have. For example, 20 years ago parental and family leave programs were viewed as radical; today they are supported by the majority of people in Congress. Conflicts within feminism can be productive and enhancing, as divergent views on critical issues provoke deeper and more comprehensive responses (M. Hirsch & Keller, 1990).

Problems also arise in trying to integrate the perspectives of people with very different life experiences, especially when those differences are not acknowledged. As discussed in Chapter 1, the experience of gender intersects with the experience of class, race, ethnicity, sexual orientation, age, religion, and so on. This is true for all of us, although we tend to see only women as having a gender, only people of color as having a race, only working-class people as having a class, and only homosexuals as having a sexual orientation. The tendency to define White heterosexual middle-class experience as the norm has pervaded the women's movement as it has pervaded our entire society (Spelman, 1988). This tendency caused the women's movement in the 1960s and 1970s to focus on primarily White middle-class concerns (such as entry into professional jobs) rather than on concerns that affect a larger group of women (such as poverty and adequate health care). This tendency also has led to the perception that the women's movement is for White middle-class women only. This, of course, is not the case.

There are both similarities and differences among women that must be recognized and reconciled. Difference does not have to be divisive. To work together, we need to understand different women's experiences. Whereas White heterosexual middle-class women suffer primarily from sexism, Third World women suffer from racism and sexism and often from poverty as well. Lesbians suffer additionally from homophobia. Because of dual, sometimes triple, oppression, minority women tend to be on the bottom of the status hierarchy. For example, although women as a group earn less than men as a group, White men earn the most and Hispanic women earn the least. As a result, many minority women have had difficulty identifying with the women's movement, although many have supported the movement's objectives (Hemmons, 1980; D. K. Lewis, 1977; Lorde, 1984; B. Smith, 1982).

Blacks, Asians, Hispanics, and Native Americans each have a unique cultural background and a unique position vis-à-vis the dominant White male culture (Anzaldua, 1987, 1990; J. B. Cole, 1986; Hooks, 1989; Hull et al., 1982; Moraga & Anzaldua, 1981; A. Smith & Stewart, 1983; B. Smith, 1983). Yet despite ethnic group differences, certain similarities emerge among Third World women. As a group, they are a minority in a White culture. They tend to hold the lowest status, lowest paying jobs. They generally have been made to feel inadequate as women regarding their physical appearance and behavior. They may have difficulty establishing their own identity. And they often disagree with the (White) women's movement on a number of issues. They are likely to define racial oppression rather than sexual oppression as the top priority. They are also likely to favor the traditional structure of the family and to be against birth control and abortion, which may be viewed by them as genocidal and racist and are particular problems for Catholic Chicanas.

The life experience of Black women generally has made them more rejecting of culturally dominant gender roles and attitudes than any other group. For example, in a national Harris poll taken in 1984 (see Table 13.1), Black women appeared more aware of sex discrimination and more supportive of women's rights than White women (Thom, 1984). In contrast, Black men appeared similar to or more conservative than White men, except on questions of equal rights. Black women also are more likely than any other race-gender group to support the women's movement. For example, a 1989 poll by the *New York Times* found that 85% of Black women agreed that the United States continues to need a strong women's movement to push for changes that benefit women, compared to 76% of Hispanic women, 64% of White women, 63% of Black men, 49% of White men, and 47% of Hispanic men (Dionne, 1989). Black women also feel they've benefited more from the women's movement than any other race-gender group. Because Black women traditionally have combined work and family responsibilities, they feel less tension than White women between their work and family roles. Black women are strong supporters of equality in the labor force and politics, although not necessarily in domestic life (Dugger, 1988). Whereas White women experience families as oppressive, Black women tend to experience families

Table 13.1 Views of discrimination: Black women in the lead (results of a Louis Harris and Associates poll in March 1984).

	Black Women	White Women	Black Men	White Men
Women often do not receive the same pay as men for doing exactly the same job	79%	74%	59%	64%
Women often have much more trouble than men in getting credit, bank loans, and mortgages	74	63	56	57
Women are often discriminated against in being promoted for supervisory and executive jobs	75	62	55	55
Women often receive lower pensions or pay more on annuities than men doing the same work	62	44	40	40
Women often do not receive the same pay as men for doing comparable jobs with similar skill and training	82	71	56	64
Women are discriminated against in being able to earn enough to support themselves independently	74	56	45	50
Favor the Equal Rights Amendment	71	63	58	55
Believe ERA will pass	68	62	78	54
It is very important that women's rights be strengthened	76	55	57	44
Would vote for woman for Congress if man and woman equally qualified	46	42	22	17
Favor woman for vice-president in 1984	68	69	66	72

From "The All-Time Definitive Map of the Gender Gap" by M. Thom, July 1984, *Ms.*, p. 59. Used with permission.

as a refuge from an oppressive White culture (J. B. Cole, 1986; Hooks, 1984). Being a single mother tends to be radicalizing, and since more Black than White women are single mothers, Black women are most challenging of traditional gender roles.

Despite differences, women do share certain similarities with each other, and minority group membership and feminism need not be antithetical. Women of all cultures are exposed to sexism, violence against women, and issues surrounding reproduction and childbearing. All women work (whether inside the home or out) and all are primarily responsible for domestic and child-care activities. Groups can work with and learn from each other on issues they have in common. Blacks, for example, already have role integration to a certain degree since circumstances have required Black women to work and be strong. As a result of their heritage, Black women have found ways of coping and surviving that could be helpful to other women (Lykes, 1983; Reid, 1984). We can hope that the current trend in the women's movement to acknowledge and learn from the differences that exist among women will continue and coalesce into a stronger and more united front. True liberation means respect for all individuals and an acceptance of diversity. To achieve that goal, we each have to work on our internalized oppression and domination (see Pheterson, 1986).

Overcoming Resistance

A third major problem in instituting change is the resistance of people and of institutions. Some resistance may stem from a general fear of the unknown and some from confusion about the sexual and nonsexual aspects of gender roles. But much resistance stems directly from feminism's threat to male dominance. (See Faludi, 1991, for a cogent analysis of the current backlash against feminism.)

Male resistance   Because men typically have been the dominant sex with most of the power, it is much more difficult for them to give some up than it is for those without power to acquire some. This especially is true as long as power remains the criterion by which status is determined. Second, as children, most males define themselves by avoiding anything even vaguely feminine. To now alter their self-definition to include "feminine" behavior may mean a perceived loss of status and self-esteem for some men. Third, the unemotional nature of the male sex role mitigates against some men's recognizing problems they may have as a result of their

sex role, and certainly mitigates against their expressing such problems.

Arnold Kahn (1984) hypothesizes that because power is such an integral part of masculine self-esteem, all men have difficulty handing power over to women. Men with the least diversified power base experience power loss most keenly and attempt to regain power with the only power base they have left—coercive power. Thus, the increased reports of rape, battering, sexual harassment, and sexual abuse of children by men in recent years may be one indication of this type of male resistance. For men with more diversified bases of power, such as expert, reward, informational, or legitimate power, the reaction may be more subtle. Their resistance may appear in hiring and promotion decisions, in decisions concerning how women are portrayed in the media, and so on. For those men who intellectually believe in equal rights, behavioral change is more possible, but probably only after they learn how to act differently.

Given the strength and the broad-based nature of the women's movement since the late 1960s, it is not surprising that men's concern about retaining their power has been increasing. In two representative national surveys of adults done in 1957 and 1976, Veroff and colleagues (1980) found that men's power motives (fear of weakness and desire for influence over others) had increased since the 1950s. This quest for power over others seems to make it difficult to establish affiliative concerns as well. Thus, as women have been gaining more rights in American society, men have become more concerned with power. Certainly the 1980s and 1990s have seen increased male resistance to women's fight for equality: the ERA has been defeated, the right of women to control their own bodies is threatened, women's advances up the career ladder in politics and business have reached a "glass ceiling"; and "profamily" campaigns are trying to put women back in the homemaker role.

The Reagan/Bush era, with its emphasis on "traditional" (read "patriarchal") values, has made antifeminism popular again. The new/old rhetoric blames feminists/women for all of society's social problems (N. Davidson, 1988; Gilder, 1986). Women are too tired from working double shifts? It's feminists' fault for urging them into the workplace. Increased problems of youth (drugs, violence, pregnancy)? It's feminists' fault for encouraging women to "neglect" their maternal role. Increased divorces and single mothers? It's feminists' fault for not focusing on keeping their mate happy. Men increasingly violent? It's feminists'/women's fault for not doing their job of civilizing them. Blaming women directs attention away from men (and questions like why fathers aren't helping with children and housework and why men aren't responsible for their own behavior) and from society (and issues like the economic circumstances that force women into the labor force and the lack of adequate child-care facilities). Even some members of the promasculinist men's movement have a strong antifeminist, sometimes antiwoman, tone (see Clatterbaugh, 1990).

The strength of the backlash suggests how strong the momentum toward change already is. Anthony Astrachan (1986) believes that the backlash is real but that the underlying revolution is irreversible. Increasing numbers of men are welcoming at least some of the changes in gender relations. For example, 56% of young men in one survey said they would be willing to give up as much as a quarter of their salary to have more family or personal time; 45% said they'd refuse a promotion if it meant sacrificing family time (Wallis, 1989). Economic conditions guarantee that employers will continue to need women workers, and few families can afford to live on just one income. In addition, the pendulum swing of history suggests that a backlash will be replaced by a new synthesis in which power is redistributed in a more balanced fashion.

We have seen repeatedly throughout this book that men tend to hold more traditional attitudes toward women and gender roles than do women. Robert Sigel's (1991) interviews with more than 200 men revealed that most men are not disturbed by evidence of gender inequality, and even those who are disturbed by it don't think it requires remedial action on their part. Astrachan (1986), from his interviews with more than 400 men, estimates that only about one-third of men support women's demands for independence and equality and most of these are for pragmatic reasons (for example, men who don't want to have all the financial responsibility). Still, surveys show that about half of all men believe a strong women's movement is necessary for women and 15% of all men believe the women's movement has made their life better (Dionne, 1989). Black men are the most supportive.

Although men stand to lose some degree of power and status from women's liberation, they also stand to gain from it. Warren Farrell (1974) describes 21 benefits for men from the women's movement. These benefits mainly focus on the fact that if a man were no longer the primary breadwinner, he probably would experience less fear about losing his job and greater freedom to choose an interesting, low-paying one over an unfulfilling, high-paying one. He might feel less need to compete and less pressure to be the sole source of his partner's happiness. He might be able to devote more time to his children, to the pursuit of nonvocational goals, and to alternative household arrangements. His relationships might be based more on feelings than on security or dominance. Sexual interest might increase, and his relationships probably would be more rewarding. Men most likely would experience a reduction of anxiety about their sex role and about homosexuality, an increase in autonomy and intellectual achievement, and might develop a new set of values that accompany true listening and a more balanced ego. Men also would become free of many legal burdens that currently fall on them.

Despite the backlash and men's resistance to change, most people do think men's attitudes toward women have changed for the better in the past 20 years (Belkin, 1989). There have been signs that American men as a group are becoming more sensitive and less macho (Ehrenreich, 1984; Franklin, 1984), especially when compared to the 1950s. The 90s man has been called a "New Romantic" (J. Warren, 1991), but many feminists are concerned that in becoming more sensitive, men also are becoming more narcissistic, more class-conscious, and more self-indulgent. Truly feminist goals would include equality among men and women as well as between them, and the ability to make and keep relationships. Those goals are still to be realized.

Female resistance   Of course, men are not the only group resistant to sex role change; many women are resistant as well. Some of the backlash can be seen in books like Marabel Morgan's (1975) *Total Woman* and Toni Grant's (1988) *Being a Woman: Fulfilling Your Femininity and Finding Love*, where women are encouraged to use their "feminine wiles" to get what they want out of "their man." Women's resistance may stem partly from misunderstanding the goals of the liberation movements. This misunderstanding is perpetuated by myths, such as those about the ERA and about the word *feminist*. Women's resistance also may stem from a resistance to any change and from women's own internalized sexism. Many women have accepted male standards as the norm and as the way it "should" be. Some women may have religious or philosophical reasons for preferring present gender role norms. For example, many women (and men) feel it is God's law for women to be inferior to and dependent upon men. Most antifeminists are associated with the New Right (Dworkin, 1983; Rowland, 1986).

A strong undercurrent in much antifeminist rhetoric is the belief that men basically are animalistic and selfish and must be forced (through legal and social restrictions) to be sexually monogamous, support their children economically, and refrain from violence and sexual assault (Ehrenreich, 1983; Grant, 1988; Paglia, 1990; Rowland, 1986; Schlafly, 1977). If women were to be considered independent persons and equal to men, men would abandon their families and basically go wild. It is only through strict laws (for example, those requiring men to support their family), strict social customs ("good" women know not to trust men sexually and therefore don't go out alone or drink or go to men's apartments), and traditionally feminine behaviors (for example, making men feel superior and needed) that men are made to behave in a halfway civilized fashion. Feminism, with its emphasis on gender equality, appears to get men off the hook. The fear that men will abandon their families was played upon in the anti-ERA campaign.

The 1980s saw a slew of self-help books aimed at women (for example, *Women Who Love Too Much* and *Too Smart for Her Own Good*), all of which implied that women's main problems are finding and keeping a man. Their solution? Women must change. No mention is made of women's real problems (as determined by national surveys)— equality on the job, balancing work and family, child care (Dionne, 1989). Nor is mention made that perhaps men should change and be more accepting of independent women. Nor is there any critique of the assumption that finding and keeping a man should be a woman's highest priority. Such books, even when well intentioned, wind up blaming the victim. As such, they contain an antifeminist message.

Nonemployed working-class women without a college education, who may be most economically dependent upon a husband, tend to hold the most traditional attitudes toward women (Houser & Beckman, 1980). Still, even most of them support the women's movement and only a minority (about 4%) are overtly hostile toward it (Dionne, 1989; Ehrenreich, 1987; Ferree, 1983). Those who are hostile tend to confuse the movement with uninhibited sexuality, or to be committed to the idea of separate-but-equal spheres of activity and association.

Greater publicity about the social, political, and economic factors involved in the current role of women and more accurate portrayals of the women's movement and its goals by the media may change the views of some of these women. A direct effort may be needed to reach women feeling alienated from the women's movement because they cannot identify with some of the extreme positions taken. The women's movement appears to have entered a new stage with its current emphasis on family, health, and employment issues. Such concerns may appeal to many of the men and women who previously have felt alienated from the women's movement.

Institutional resistance   Institutional resistance has been more difficult to overcome. Part of the problem involves the inertia of institutions in general that keeps them from responding to any type of change. Another part of the problem involves the paternalistic nature of institutional discrimination against women. This form of discrimination encourages women to maintain their dependence on men and fragments the position of women as a group while strengthening the position of men as a group (Safilios-Rothschild, 1979). For example, by allowing a few women into high-ranking positions, the illusion is created that all women can now "make it." Thus, class interests often overshadow gender ones. A third part of the problem involves the lack of a clear image of what a more sex-egalitarian future society would look like (Boulding, 1979). This unknown is frightening since it may involve undesirable as well as desirable changes and certainly would involve a redistribution of power. It is this redistribution of power that undoubtedly accounts for most institutional resistance. As we have seen, institutions were developed and are run primarily by White upper-and middle-class men, based on their values and perspectives. Letting other people (women, men of color) in will mean major institutional change and loss of power for those now holding it. It is easier (and cheaper) to try to destroy the social movement attempting change than it is to actually change the system (Toch, 1966).

Thus, resistance stems mainly from fear of change and fear of loss of power, however perceived. What will the future bring? Let's turn to some speculations.

▲   Toward the Future

Despite the current politically conservative climate and the backlash against feminism, it is unlikely that the movement toward gender equality will be halted. It has infiltrated too far into our cultural ideology to be easily rooted out. Women are getting less tolerant of male resistance, as we have seen. In fact, the backlash may even serve as an organizing tool for the women's movement. In the face of institutional resistance, more people are beginning to realize the importance of group efforts for social change. For example, membership in NOW increased by over 100,000 (from 160,000) after the 1988 *Webster* decision, which restricted abortions (Wallis, 1989). (NOW's previous peak membership was 220,000 in 1982).

Given the fact that each of us is a product of our society, it is hard to break out of trained ways of seeing the world to imagine a truly gender-equal society. Figure 13.3 gives a satiric view of one possible future. Inequality distorts the character and vision of both the oppressors and the oppressed. Nevertheless, we will try to describe what the future would be like if all the goals described in the beginning of the chapter were achieved.

Figure 13.3 Where old roles might go. (Copyright 1978 by National Lampoon, Inc. Reprinted with permission.)

Personal and Social Possibilities

Although non-sex-typed males and females probably would not be differentiable by activities, interests, or personality patterns, they still would maintain their separate gender identities. Gender identity is basically one's sense of maleness or femaleness (see Chapter 2). It involves appreciating and valuing one's genitals and, later, one's secondary sex characteristics and their potentialities. It has little intrinsic connection to gender roles. Sexual attraction between women and men still would occur, although since heterosexuality no longer would be compulsory and homophobia would be eliminated, we might see some increase in same-sex experiences and relationships. More likely would be an increase in bisexuality since a forced choice between same-sex and other-sex partners would be unnecessary. It is likely that sexual experiences would be more gratifying than they are presently since good sex requires openness, trust, vulnerability, assertiveness, and activity—all part of an androgynous individual but only partially represented in sex-typed individuals (see Chapter 4). The sexual double standard should no longer exist.

Because both women and men would develop expressive and nurturant traits, all relationships should be enriched. Male same-sex friendships would become more intimate and male-female relationships would provide emotional support for both partners. Since women no longer would need to look for economic security in a mate, both men and women could choose mates on the basis of companionability, understanding, tenderness, physical attractiveness, or sexual ability. Because a woman would no longer have to marry to fulfill herself, there might be fewer marriages and they probably would occur at a later age—a trend that has already begun. The resulting marriages, however, might be stronger and more emotionally satisfying because they would be based on free choice, not social expectations and economic survival. Because marriage would be an equal partnership, wives would be less dependent and husbands would be less tyrannical (see Chapter 9). Women would no longer have to tolerate abusive relationships out of economic dependence.

Because marriages might come later and divorces no longer would be viewed as a sign of failure, there would be more single people in the population at a given time than currently exist. Thus, there should be an increase in single-person households, a trend already begun, and in alternative living situations such as single parents and communal arrangements.

Same-sex relationships would be legally acknowledged. These alternatives probably no longer would be considered deviant.

In an egalitarian society, parents probably would serve as non-sex-typed models for their children, sharing responsibility for work and family. Through their behavior and their own example, such parents should produce non-sex-typed children who believe in gender equality (see Chapter 7). In a world of equality, stress on both females and males would be reduced tremendously. Consequently, females should have better mental and physical health—less anxiety and depression, higher self-esteem. Males too should have better health as they abandon risk-taking and self-destructive behaviors (such as drugs, violence). Other negative consequences of gender roles and stereotypes discussed in Chapters 8 through 10 also should be eliminated, leading to better feelings about oneself and better relationships with same- and other-sex individuals and with children.

The division between work and family roles would collapse. Both women and men would participate in labor force and domestic activities. The labor force would reflect these changes. Relatively equal numbers of women and men would be in the labor force and gender segregation of positions would be greatly reduced. Thus, most occupations would show a mix of races and genders, and women's income should be the same as men's, since salaries would be based on comparable worth. Job competition would mean that the best person would be in any specified position. Greater job flexibility would mean that both women and men would be freer to quit, take leaves, work part-time, and make career changes. There would be more flex-time and part-time opportunities, and both sexes would avail themselves of them.

Because women still would bear children, they might take more leave time than men, but their jobs would be secure and their leave time would be compensated. Either parent would be entitled to paid parental leave for child-care activities. If a parent decided to stay home longer than the leave (about one year), she or he might receive a percentage of the spouse's pay and be entitled to pension fund and/or Social Security benefits and a job training allowance if divorced. An adequate program of government income support would exist for people who could not enter the labor market, either because they had to care for young children or because they could not find jobs. Child care itself would be restructured. More day and after-school care would be available, sponsored by government, business, or the community. Housework might become professionalized and greater status (pay and benefits) might be accorded to child care. Major alterations in life-cycle stages, such as alternate periods of study, employment, and work in the home, probably also would occur.

Given that people's life spans are increasing, if more people entered the labor force they probably could not all work 40-hour weeks until age 70. This means that there might be more leisure time for all. More activities and hobbies could be pursued by women and men. Women and men with more leisure time could fill the gap left by women who used to be available for traditional community voluntary activities. Since a man's identity would no longer be based solely on his role as worker and breadwinner, much of the emotional and physical stress now experienced by men who retire or who are laid off would be reduced or eliminated.

It might be argued that many of the possible changes depend on society's being affluent. However, even in economically depressed times, non-sex-stereotyped functioning still should lead to change. Although employment might be difficult to obtain, layoffs and limited hiring practices should affect both sexes equally. Child care still could be shared by parents and helped by institutional support. Housework too could be shared, since one sex would not be more likely than the other to be employed outside the home.

Greater equality, then, would enhance personal and relationship functioning. It would improve institutional functioning as well.

Institutional Possibilities

In an egalitarian society, industry as well as politics might become more humane and socially oriented. There should be a move away from power, competition, and dominance, and toward democracy and group decision making. More women would be in managerial and top political posts and in other positions of power. Such restructuring of society might lead to more humane domestic and foreign politics. For example, our support of corrupt, inhumane foreign dictatorships for economic reasons might be reduced. International development projects would include women and would take into consideration the long-term implications of development for human and natural resources (Shiva, 1988; Tinker, 1990). Health care would improve, malnutrition and poverty-related illnesses should decrease, ecological implications of policies would be weighed more strongly, and inhumane work practices would be reduced. When women are valued, nature should

be more valued as well since the male need to dominate and control would be eliminated. Thus, environmental abuses should decrease (I. Diamond & Orenstein, 1990; Hynes, 1989). Traditional science and technology would be infused with a feminist perspective so that their products would be respectful of human life and human dignity rather than exploitative (see, for example, Bleier, 1988; Keller, 1985; Rothschild, 1983).

If violence became less tied to the masculine sex role and women became equally respected, we would expect less violent behavior by men. Women always have been in the forefront of peace movements, and a society that incorporates egalitarian values would be more inclined to nonviolence than violence and to settling conflicts peaceably rather than forcefully (L. Gordon, 1990; A. Harris & King, 1989; Ruddick, 1989). A society structured around egalitarian values also would be one in which the incidence of crimes against women, especially sexual abuse, would be greatly reduced. Indeed, all crimes based on dominance and power, such as rape, incest, and child abuse, should be lessened. Violent pornography should find no market and therefore would disappear. Sexist advertising and other forms of media sexism also no longer would be tolerated. We might also expect to find more interest in nonviolent sports.

In an egalitarian society, ethnic and racial diversity would be acknowledged and embraced, rather than stigmatized and punished. Without patriarchy as a model, the need for one group to dominate another group would be diminished. Moving "beyond power" means moving beyond all hierarchical systems that require someone to lose in order that someone else may win (French, 1985). Thus, equality is the basis of true democracy.

In sum, an egalitarian society is nothing to fear. Although men no longer would have power and status by virtue of their sex, they have much to gain personally and interpersonally from equality. Women too have much to gain. Most of all, the world would be a better, safer, cleaner place to live.

▲   Summary

In this chapter, the process of moving toward new conceptions of gender stereotypes and roles has been examined. Change must occur on the personal, social, and institutional levels. Desirable goals on an individual level involve transcending rigid sex typing in terms of behavior, traits, and attitudes.

On the social level, the meaning of gender would be reconstructed in terms of equality rather than domination/subordination. Social roles would become more flexible and less gender-specific, except for those relating to reproductive roles. On the institutional level, society itself would have to change to become more equal and inclusive not only of the two sexes but also of different racial and ethnic groups. Different models of feminism have somewhat different analyses regarding the causes and solutions of gender inequality, but all emphasize the need for equality and liberation from current gender role conceptions. Socialist feminist and radical feminist models are the clearest with respect to the need to completely restructure society.

Many avenues for change exist. An egalitarian society will not come about automatically, even if people become less sex-typed individually. Institutions run on a different dynamic than individuals, and a concerted, deliberate, and persistent effort will be needed before social change becomes a reality. On the personal level, change can be made through consciousness-raising groups, psychotherapy, experiential groups, education, and alterations in behavior. On the social level, change can occur through changes in ideology, socialization practices, relationships, and the development of alternate lifestyles. On the institutional level, change can occur via the law, politics, reorganization of work and family, direct action, and alternative institutions. Such changes will not come easily. First, there needs to be an integration of the changes occurring on the three levels, institutional change being the most difficult to achieve. Second, issues of diversity must be addressed continuously and substantively. Any vision of the future must be inclusive of all groups in society, not just the White heterosexual middle class. Third, resistance by both women and men as well as social institutions needs to be expected and handled constructively. Working for change is a long-term process, not a short-term project. Support and organization of efforts are crucial.

If such changes occur, and our society and the individuals it contains become less sex-typed and more egalitarian, the ramifications will be widespread, occurring on personal, social, and institutional levels. Some changes already have begun; others will be more difficult to implement. The future, however, is open. What is at stake is no less than the happiness and effectiveness of our entire country. Eliminating gender stereotypes and redefining gender in terms of equality does not mean simply liberating women, but liberating men and our society as well. What we have been talking about is allowing people to be more fully human and creating a society that will reflect that humanity. Surely that is a goal worth striving for.

▲   Recommended Reading

Anzaldua, G. (Ed.). (1990). *Making face, making soul/Haciendo caras: Creative and critical perspectives by women of color.* San Francisco: Aunt Lute. An exciting interdisciplinary blend of stories, poems, and articles illustrating the perspective of minority women.

Brod, H. (Ed.). (1987). *The making of masculinities: The new men's studies.* Boston: Allen & Unwin. A diverse collection of articles analyzing how gender has affected men's lives, using a feminist framework.

Brown, L. S., & Root, M.P.P. (Eds.). (1990). *Diversity and complexity in feminist therapy.* New York: Harrington Park. Timely collection of articles urging therapists to consider multicultural, multiracial, as well as individual perspectives in their approach to helping women.

Clatterbaugh, K. (1990). *Contemporary perspectives on masculinity: Men, women, and politics in modern society.* Boulder, CO: Westview Press. A clear description of six different contemporary views of men and masculinity, including men's responses to feminism.

Donovan, J. (1985). *Feminist theory: The intellectual traditions of American feminism.* New York: Frederick Ungar. An excellent and accessible summary of the different forms of American feminism and their implications for a wide variety of issues.

Faludi, S. (1991). *Backlash: The undeclared war against American women.* New York: Crown. A provocative analysis of how the media and popular culture have tried to halt women's progress toward equality.

References

Abbey, A. (1982). Sex differences in attributions for friendly behavior: Do males misperceive females' friendliness? *Journal of Personality and Social Psychology, 42,* 830–838.

Abbey, A. (1987). Misperceptions of friendly behavior as sexual interest: A survey of naturally occurring incidents. *Psychology of Women Quarterly, 11,* 173–194.

Abbey, A., & Melby, C. (1986). The effects of nonverbal cues on gender differences in perceptions of sexual intent. *Sex Roles, 15,* 283–298.

Abramowitz, S. J., & Herrera, H. R. (1981). On controlling for patient psychopathology in naturalistic studies of sex bias: A methodological demonstration. *Journal of Consulting and Clinical Psychology, 49,* 597–603.

Abramson, L. Y., Seligman, M. E. P., & Teasdale, J. D. (1978). Learned helplessness in humans: Critique and reformulation. *Journal of Abnormal Psychology, 87,* 49–74.

Abramson, P. P., Goldberg, P. A., Greenberg, J. H., & Abramson, L. M. (1977). The talking platypus phenomenon: Competency ratings as a function of sex and professional status. *Psychology of Women Quarterly, 2,* 114–124.

Abramson, P. R., & Mosher, D. L. (1979). An empirical investigation of experimentally induced masturbatory fantasies. *Archives of Sexual Behavior, 8,* 27–39.

Abzug, B., with Keller, M. (1984). *Gender gap: Bella Abzug's guide to political power for American women.* Boston: Houghton Mifflin.

Academe. (1990, March–April). Some dynamic aspects of academic careers: The urgent need to match aspirations with compensation. Pp. 3–20.

Acker, J. (1989). *Doing comparable worth: Gender, class, and pay equity.* Philadelphia: Temple University Press.

Acock, A. C., & Ireland, N. K. (1983). Attribution of blame in rape cases: The impact of norm violation, gender, and sex-role attitude. *Sex Roles, 9,* 179–193.

Adams, D. B., Gold, A. R., & Burt, A. D. (1978). Rise in female-initiated sexual activity at ovulation and its suppression by oral contraceptives. *New England Journal of Medicine, 299* 1145–1150.

Adams, J. (1984). Women at West Point: A three-year perspective. *Sex Roles, 11,* 525–541.

Adams, K. A. (1980). Who has the final word? Sex, race, and dominance behavior. *Journal of Personality and Social Psychology, 38,* 1–8.

Adams, K. A. (1983). Aspects of social context as determinants of black women's resistance to challenges. *Journal of Social Issues, 39,* 69–78.

Adamsky, C. (1981). Changes in pronominal usage in a classroom situation. *Psychology of Women Quarterly, 5,* 773–779.

Adelmann, P. K., Antonucci, T. C., Crohan, S. E., & Coleman, L. M. (1989). Empty nest, cohort, and employment in the well-being of midlife women. *Sex Roles, 20,* 173–189.

Adler, F. (Ed.). (1981). *The incidence of female criminality in the contemporary world.* New York: New York University Press.

Adler, T. (1989a, June). Early sex hormone exposure studied. *APA Monitor,* p. 9.

Adler, T. (1989b, August). For couples, value of talk is all relative. *APA Monitor,* pp. 10–11.

Adler, T. (1989c, August). Happiest workers are in fields dominated by their own gender. *APA Monitor,* pp. 12–13.

Adler, T. (1990a, January). Causes, cure of PMS still elude researchers. *APA Monitor,* p. 10.

Adler, T. (1990b, January). Differences explored in gays and straights. *APA Monitor,* p. 27.

Adler, T. (1990c, January). Roots of PMS seen as biological. *APA Monitor,* p. 11.

Adler, T. (1990d, March). Restraint is in style, new sex surveys find. *APA Monitor,* p. 24.

African women seek larger role. (1985, January 6). *Morning Call,* p. 5.

Agassi, J. B. (1989). Theories of gender equality: Lessons from the Israeli kibbutz. *Gender and Society, 3,* 160–186.

Agenda '88: Women and the presidency. (1988, April). *Ms.,* pp. 75–79.

Ageton, S. S. (1983). *Sexual assault among adolescents.* Lexington, MA: D. C. Heath.

Aida, Y., & Falbo, T. (1991). Relationships between marital satisfaction, resources, and power strategies. *Sex Roles, 24,* 43–56.

Aiken, S. H., Anderson, K., Dinnerstein, M., Lensink, J. N., & MacCorquodale, P. (Eds.). (1988). *Changing our minds: Feminist transformations of knowledge.* Albany: State University of New York Press.

Ainsworth, M.D.S. (1979). Infant-mother attachment. *American Psychologist, 34,* 932–937.

Ainsworth, M.D.S. (1989). Attachments beyond infancy. *American Psychologist, 44,* 709–716.

Alagna, S. W. (1982). Sex role identity, peer evaluation of competition, and the responses of women and men in a competitive situation. *Journal of Personality and Social Psychology, 43,* 546–554.

Alagna, S. W., & Hamilton, J. A. (1986). Social stimulus perception and self-evaluation: Effects of menstrual cycle phase. *Psychology of Women Quarterly, 10,* 327–338.

Alberti, R., & Emmons, M. D. (1978). *Your perfect right.* San Luis Obispo, CA: Impact.

Allen, I. L. (1984). Male sex roles and epithets for ethnic women in American slang. *Sex Roles, 11,* 43–50.

Allen, M. J., & Hogeland, R. (1978). Spatial problem-solving strategies as a function of sex. *Perceptual and Motor Skills, 47,* 348–350.

Allen, R. C. (1985). *Speaking of soap operas.* Chapel Hill: University of North Carolina Press.

Allgeier, E. R. (1981). The influence of androgynous identification on heterosexual relations. *Sex Roles, 7,* 321–330.

Allgeier, E. R. (1987). Coercive versus consensual sexual interactions. In V. P. Makosky (Ed.), *The G. Stanley Hall Lecture Series,* Vol. 7 (pp. 7–63). Washington, DC: American Psychological Association.

Allgood-Merten, B., Lewinsohn, P. M., & Hops, H. (1990). Sex differences and adolescent depression. *Journal of Abnormal Psychology, 99,* 55–63.

Allis, S. (1990, Fall). What do men really want? *Women: The road ahead* [Special issue of *Time* magazine], pp. 80–82.

Allison, P. D., & Furstenberg, F. F., Jr. (1989). How marital dissolution affects children: Variations by age and sex. *Developmental Psychology, 25,* 540–549.

Alper, J. (1988, June). Fear of femininity. *Psychology Today,* pp. 64–65.

Alper, J. S. (1985). Sex differences in brain asymmetry: A critical analysis. *Feminist Studies, 11,* 7–37.

Alper, T. G. (1974). Achievement motivation in college women: A now-you-see-it-now-you-don't phenomenon. *American Psychologist, 29,* 194–203.

Alperson, B. L., & Friedman, W. J. (1983). Some aspects of the interpersonal phenomenology of heterosexual dyads with respect to sex-role stereotypes. *Sex Roles, 9,* 453–474.

Alpert-Gillis, L. J., & Connell, J. P. (1989). Gender and sex-role influences on children's self-esteem. *Journal of Personality, 57,* 97–114.

Amaro, H., & Russo, N. F. (Eds.) (1987). Hispanic women and mental health: Contemporary issues in research and practice [Special issue]. *Psychology of Women Quarterly, 11*(4).

Amatea, E. S., & Fong, M. L. (1991). The impact of role stressors and personal resources on the stress experience of professional women. *Psychology of Women Quarterly, 15,* 419–430.

American Association of University Women. (1991). *Shortchanging girls, shortchanging America.* Washington, DC: The Greenberg-Lake Analysis Group.

American Psychiatric Association. (1987). *Diagnostic and statistical manual of mental disorders* (3rd ed.—revised). Washington, DC: Author.

Ames, N. R. (1984, Winter). The socialization of women into and out of sports. *Journal of the National Association for Women, Deans, Administrators, and Counselors, 47,* 3–8.

Amir, M. (1971, November). Forcible rape. *Sexual Behavior,* pp. 26–36.

Anastas, J. W., & Reinhartz, H. (1984). Gender differences in learning and adjustment problems in school: Results of a longitudinal study. *American Journal of Orthopsychiatry, 54,* 110–122.

Anderson, E. A., & Leslie, L. A. (1991). Coping with employment and family stress: Employment arrangement and gender differences. *Sex Roles, 24,* 223–237.

Anderson, N. S. (1987). Cognition, learning, and memory. In M. A. Baker (Ed.), *Sex differences in human performance* (pp. 37–54). Chichester: Wiley.

Angier, N. (1990, July 19). Scientists say gene on Y chromosome makes a man a man. *New York Times,* pp. A1, A19.

Anson, O., Levenson, A., & Bonneh, D. Y. (1990). Gender and health on the kibbutz. *Sex Roles, 22,* 213–231.

Antill, J. K. (1983). Sex role complementarity vs. similarity in married couples. *Journal of Personality and Social Psychology, 45,* 145–155.

Antill, J. K. (1987). Parents' beliefs and values about sex roles, sex differences, and sexuality: Their sources and implications. In P. Shaver & C. Hendrick (Eds.), *Sex and gender* (pp. 294–328). Newbury Park, CA: Sage.

Antill, J. K., & Cunningham, J. D. (1982). Sex differences in performance on ability tests as a function of masculinity, femininity, and androgyny. *Journal of Personality and Social Psychology, 42,* 718–728.

Antonucci, T. C., & Akiyama, H. (1987). An examination of sex differences in social support among older men and women. *Sex Roles, 17,* 737–749.

Anzaldua, G. (1987). *Borderlands/La Frontera: The new mestiza.* San Francisco: Spinsters/Aunt Lute.

Anzaldua, G. (Ed.) (1990). *Making face, making soul/Haciendo caras: Creative and critical perspectives by women of color.* San Francisco: Aunt Lute.

Apao, W. K. (1982, April). *Women among men: Androgyny and sex-role attitudes of women in a military college.* Paper presented at the meeting of the Eastern Psychological Association, Baltimore.

Arch, E. C., & Cummins, D. E. (1989). Structured and unstructured exposure to computers: Sex differences in attitude and use among college students. *Sex Roles, 20,* 245–254.

Archer, C. J. (1984). Children's attitudes toward sex-role division in adult occupational roles. *Sex Roles, 10,* 1–10.

Archer, D., Iritani, B., Kimes, D. D., & Barrios, M. (1983). Face-isms: Five studies of sex differences in facial prominence. *Journal of Personality and Social Psychology, 45,* 725–735.

Archer, J. (1989). The relationship between gender-role measures: A review. *British Journal of Social Psychology, 28,* 173–184.

Arendell, T. J. (1987). Women and the economics of divorce in the contemporary United States. *Signs: Journal of Women in Culture and Society, 13,* 121–135.

Aries, E. (1977). Male-female interpersonal styles in all male, all female, and mixed groups. In A. Sargent (Ed.), *Beyond sex roles* (pp. 292–299). St. Paul: West.

Aries, E. (1987). Gender and communication. In P. Shaver & C. Hendrick (Eds.), *Sex and gender* (pp. 149–176). Newbury Park, CA: Sage.

Aries, E. J., & Olver, R. R. (1985). Sex differences in the development of a separate sense of self during infancy: Directions for future research. *Psychology of Women Quarterly, 9,* 515–531.

Arkin, W., & Dobrofsky, L. R. (1978a). Job sharing. In R. Rapoport & R. Rapoport (Eds.), *Working couples* (pp. 122–137). New York: Harper & Row.

Arkin, W., & Dobrofsky, L. (1978b). Military socialization and masculinity. *Journal of Social Issues, 34* (1), 131–168.

Arkkelin, D., & Simmons, R. (1985). The "good manager": Sex-typed, androgynous, or likable? *Sex Roles, 12,* 1187–1198.

Arms and the woman: Equal opportunity in the military. (1977, Spring). *WEAL Washington Report,* pp. 1–6.

Armstrong, L. (1987). *Kiss daddy goodnight: Ten years later.* New York: Pocket Books.

Ashmore, R. D., & Del Boca, F. K. (1979). Sex stereotypes and implicit personality theory: Toward a cognitive-social psychological conceptualization. *Sex Roles, 5,* 219–248.

Ashmore, R. D., Del Boca, F. K., & Wohlers, A. J. (1986). Gender stereotypes. In R. D. Ashmore and F. K. Del Boca (Eds.), *The social psychology of female-male relations: A critical analysis of central concepts* (pp. 69–119). New York: Academic Press.

Ashton, E. (1983). Measures of play behavior: The influence of sex-role stereotyped children's books. *Sex Roles, 9,* 43–47.

Asso, D. (1987). Cyclical variations. In M. A. Baker (Ed.), *Sex differences in human performance* (pp. 55–80). Chichester: Wiley.

Astin, A. W. (1977). *Four critical years: Effects of college on beliefs, attitudes, and knowledge.* San Francisco: Jossey-Bass.

Astin, A. W. (1991, January 30). The American freshman: National norms for fall 1990. *Chronicle of Higher Education,* p. A31.

Astin, H. S. (1990). Educating women: A promise and a vision for the future. *American Journal of Education, 98,* 479–493.

Astrachan, A. (1984, August). Men: A movement of their own. *Ms.,* pp. 91–94.

Astrachan, A. (1986). *How men feel: Their response to women's demands for equality and power.* Garden City, NY: Anchor Press.

Atkinson, J., & Huston, T. L. (1984). Sex role orientation and division of labor early in marriage. *Journal of Personality and Social Psychology, 46,* 330–345.

Atkinson, J. W., & Feather, N. T. (1966). *A theory of achievement motivation.* New York: Wiley.

Aukett, R., Ritchie, J., & Mill, K. (1988). Gender differences in friendship patterns. *Sex Roles, 19,* 57–66.

Austin, A.M.B., Salehi, M., & Leffler, A. (1987). Gender and developmental differences in children's conversations. *Sex Roles, 16,* 497–510.

Baber, K. M., & Dreyer, A. S. (1986). Gender-role orientations in older child-free and expectant couples. *Sex Roles, 14,* 501–512.

Babl, J. D. (1979). Compensatory masculine responding as a function of sex role. *Journal of Consulting and Clinical Psychology, 47,* 252–257.

Bachelors told marriage is a real lifesaver. (1990, October 6). *Morning Call,* p. A26.

Bachman, J. G. (1987, July). An eye on the future. *Psychology Today,* pp. 6–7.

Baenninger, M., & Newcombe, N. (1989). The role of experience in spatial test performance: A meta-analysis. *Sex Roles, 20,* 327–344.

Bahniuk, M. H., Dobos, J., & Hill, S.E.K. (1990). The impact of mentoring, collegial support, and information adequacy on career success: A replication. In J. W. Neuliep (Ed.), Handbook of replication research in the behavioral and social sciences [Special issue]. *Journal of Social Behavior and Personality, 5,* 431–452.

Bailey, J. (1988, July). Jobs for women in the nineties. *Ms.,* pp. 74–79.

Bailey, W. C., Hendrick, C., & Hendrick, S. S. (1987). Relation of sex and gender role to love, sexual attitudes, and self-esteem. *Sex Roles, 16,* 637–648.

Bakan, D. (1966). *The duality of human existence.* Chicago: Rand McNally.

Baker, D. D., Terpstra, D. E., & Larntz, K. (1990). The influence of individual characteristics and severity of harassing behavior on reactions to sexual harassment. *Sex Roles, 22,* 305–325.

Baker, M. A. (1987). Sensory functioning. In M. A. Baker (Ed.), *Sex differences in human performance* (pp. 5–36). Chichester: Wiley.

Baldwin, A. C., Critelli, J. W., Stevens, L. C., & Russell, S. (1986). Androgyny and sex role measurement: A personal construct approach. *Journal of Personality and Social Psychology, 51,* 1081–1088.

Baldwin, R. O. (1984). Stability of masculinity-femininity scores over an 11-year period. *Sex Roles, 10,* 257–260.

Baldwin, R. O. (1987). Femininity-masculinity of blacks and whites over a 14-year period. *Psychological Reports, 60,* 455–458.

Bales, J. (1984, November). Men troubled by societal changes. *APA Monitor,* p. 22.

Ball, K. (1991a, May 23). Family leave poses few problems, survey finds. *Morning Call,* p. B23.

Ball, K. (1991b, August 26). Many staffs lack distaff. *Morning Call,* p. A3.

Ball, R. E., & Robbins, L. (1986). Marital status and life satisfaction among Black Americans. *Journal of Marriage and the Family, 48,* 389–394.

Balswick, J. (1988). *The inexpressive male.* Lexington, MA: Lexington Books.

Balter, T. (1991, September 1). Survey finds fast-track mothers running out of gas. *Morning Call,* pp. E1, E2.

Bancroft, J. (1987). A physiological approach. In J. H. Geer & W. T. O'Donohue (Eds.), *Theories of human sexuality* (pp. 411–421). New York: Plenum.

Bandura, A. (1965). Influence of the model's reinforcement contingencies on the acquisition of imitative responses. *Journal of Personality and Social Psychology, 1,* 589–595.

Bandura, A. (1969). *Principles of behavior modification.* Stanford. CA: Stanford University Press.

Bandura, A. (1973). *Aggression: A social learning analysis.* Englewood Cliffs, NJ: Prentice-Hall.

Bandura, A., & Walters, R. H. (1963). *Social learning and personality development.* New York: Holt, Rinehart & Winston.

Banner, L. (1977). *Women in the college curriculum.* Princeton, NJ: Princeton Project on Women in the College Curriculum.

Bardwell, J. R., Cochran, S. W., & Walker, S. (1986). Relationship of parental education, race, and gender to sex role stereotyping in 5-year-old kindergartners. *Sex Roles, 15,* 275–281.

Bardwick, J. M. (1979). *In transition.* New York: Holt, Rinehart & Winston.

Barfield, A. (1976). Biological influences on sex differences in behavior. In M. S. Teitelbaum (Ed.), *Sex differences: Social and biological perspectives* (pp. 62–121). New York: Anchor Press.

Bargad, A., & Hyde, J. S. (1991). Women's studies: A study of feminist identity development in women. *Psychology of Women Quarterly, 15,* 181–201.

Barnett, R. C., & Baruch, G. K. (1987). Determinants of fathers' participation in family work. *Journal of Marriage and the Family, 49,* 29–40.

Barnett, R. C., & Baruch, G. K. (1988). Correlates of fathers' participation in family work. In P. Bronstein & C. P. Cowan (Eds.), *Fatherhood today: Men's changing role in the family* (pp. 66–79). New York: Wiley.

Barnett, R. C., Biener, L., & Baruch, G. K. (Eds.). (1987). *Gender and stress.* New York: Free Press.

Baron, L., & Straus, M. A. (1989). *Four theories of rape in American society.* New Haven: Yale University Press.

Barringer, F. (1991, June 7). Changes in U.S. households: Single parents amid solitude. *New York Times,* pp. A1, A18.

Barron, J. (1989, June 25). Homosexuals see two decades of gains but fear setbacks. *New York Times,* pp. 1, 25.

Barry, R. J. (1980). Stereotyping of sex role in preschoolers in relation to age, family structure, and parental sexism. *Sex Roles, 6,* 795–806.

Bar-Tal, D., & Saxe, L. (1976). Physical attractiveness and its relationship to sex-role stereotyping. *Sex Roles, 2,* 123–133.

Bart, P. B., & O'Brien, P. H. (1985). *Stopping rape: Effective survival strategies.* New York: Pergamon.

Barth, R. J., & Kinder, B. N. (1988). A theoretical analysis of sex differences in same-sex friendships. *Sex Roles, 19,* 349–363.

Bartol, K. M., & Martin, D. C. (1986). Women and men in task groups. In R. D. Ashmore and F. K. Del Boca (Eds.), *The social psychology of female-male relations: A critical analysis of central concepts* (pp. 259–310). New York: Academic Press.

Bartolome, F. (1972, November–December). Executives as human beings. *Harvard Business Review,* pp. 62–69ff.

Baruch, G., & Barnett, R. (1981). Fathers' participation in the care of their preschool children. *Sex Roles, 7,* 1043–1055.

Baruch, G. K., & Barnett, R. (1986a). Consequences of fathers' participation in family work: Parents' role strain and well-being. *Journal of Personality and Social Psychology, 51,* 983–992.

Baruch, G. K., & Barnett, R. (1986b). Role quality, multiple role involvement, and psychological well-being in midlife women. *Journal of Personality and Social Psychology, 51,* 578–585.

Baruch, G. K., & Barnett, R. C. (1987). Role quality and psychological well-being. In F. J. Crosby (Ed.), *Spouse, parent, worker: On gender and multiple roles* (pp. 63–73). New Haven: Yale University Press.

Baruch, G. K., Barnett, R., & Rivers, C. (1983). *Lifeprints: New patterns of love and work for today's women.* New York: McGraw-Hill.

Basler, B. (1984, Feb. 12). Study finds sex stereotypes affect voters at polls. *New York Times,* p. 4.

Basler, B. (1986, December 7). Putting a career on hold. *New York Times Magazine,* pp. 152, 153, 158, 160.

Basow, S. A. (1984a). Cultural variations in sex-typing. *Sex Roles, 10,* 577–585.

Basow, S. A., (1984b). Ethnic group differences in educational achievement in Fiji. *Journal of Cross-Cultural Psychology, 15,* 435–451.

Basow, S. A. (1986). Correlates of sex-typing in Fiji. *Psychology of Women Quarterly, 10,* 429–442.

Basow, S. A. (1990). Effects of teacher expressiveness: Mediated by teacher sex-typing? *Journal of Educational Psychology, 82,* 599–602.

Basow, S. A., & Howe, K. G. (1979). Sex bias and career evaluations. *Perceptual and Motor Skills, 49,* 705–706.

Basow, S. A., & Howe, K. G. (1980). Role model influence: Effects of sex and sex-role attitudes in college students. *Psychology of Women Quarterly, 4,* 558–572.

Basow, S. A. & Howe, K. G. (1987). Evaluations of college professors: Effects of professors' sex-type and sex, and students' sex. *Psychological Reports, 60,* 671–678.

Basow, S. A., & Kobrynowicz, D. (1990, August). *How much is she eating? Impressions of a female eater.* Paper presented at the meeting of the American Psychological Association, Boston. (ERIC Document Reproduction Service No. ED 326 827)

Basow, S. A., & Medcalf, K. L. (1988). Academic achievement and attributions among college students: Effects of gender and sex typing. *Sex Roles, 19,* 555–567.

Basow, S. A., & Schneck, R. (1983, April). *Eating disorders among college women.* Paper presented at the meeting of the Eastern Psychological Association, Philadelphia. (ERIC Document Reproduction Service No. ED 243 049)

Basow, S. A., & Silberg, N. T. (1987). Student evaluations of college professors: Are males prejudiced against women professors? *Journal of Educational Psychology, 79,* 308–314.

Basow, S. A., Smither, J. W., Rupert, L., & Collins, H. (1989). The effect of satisfaction and gender on self-evaluations of task performance. *Sex Roles, 20,* 413–427.

Basow, S. A., & Spinner, J. (1984). Social acceptability of college athletes: Effects of sport sex-typing, athlete sex, and rater sex. *International Journal of Sport Psychology, 15,* 79–87.

Baucom, D. H., Besch, P. K., & Callahan, S. (1985). Relation between testosterone concentration, sex role identity, and personality among females. *Journal of Personality and Social Psychology, 48,* 1218–1226.

Baucom, D. H., & Danker-Brown, P. (1984). Sex role identity and sex stereotyped tasks in the development of learned helplessness in women. *Journal of Personality and Social Psychology, 46,* 422–430.

Baude, A. (1979). Public policy and changing family patterns in Sweden 1930–1977. In J. Lipman-Blumen & J. Bernard (Eds.), *Sex roles and social policy: A complex social science equation* (pp. 145–175). Beverly Hills, CA: Sage.

Baumeister, R. F. (1988). Should we stop studying sex differences altogether? [Letter to the editor]. *American Psychologist, 43,* 1092–1095.

Beauvais, C., & Spence, J. T. (1987). Gender, prejudice, and categorization. *Sex Roles, 16,* 89–100.

Becker, B. J. (1986). Influence again: Another look at studies of gender differences in social influence. In J. S. Hyde & M. C. Linn (Eds.), *The psychology of gender: Advances through meta-analysis* (pp. 178–209). Baltimore: Johns Hopkins University Press.

Becker, B. J., & Hedges, L. N. (1984). Meta-analysis of cognitive gender differences: A comment on an analysis by Rosenthal and Rubin. *Journal of Educational Psychology, 76,* 583–587.

Bee, H. L., Mitchell, S. K., Barnard, K. E., Eyres, S. J., & Hammond, M. A. (1984). Predicting intellectual outcomes: Sex differences in response to early environmental stimulation. *Sex Roles, 10,* 783–803.

Beit-Hallahmi, B., & Rabin, A. I. (1977). The kibbutz as a social experiment and as a child-rearing laboratory. *American Psychologist, 32,* 534–551.

Belenky, M. F., Clinchy, B. M., Goldberger, N. R., & Tarule, J. M. (1986). *Women's ways of knowing: The development of self, voice, and mind.* New York: Basic Books.

Belkin, L. (1986, May 11). The mail-order marriage business. *New York Times Magazine,* pp. 28, 51–53, 73, 76, 78.

Belkin, L. (1989, August 20). Bars to equality of sexes seen as eroding, slowly. *New York Times*, pp. 1, 26.

Bell, A., & Weinberg, M. (1978). *Homosexualities*. New York: Simon & Schuster.

Bell, A. P., Weinberg, M. S., & Hammersmith, S. K. (1981). *Sexual preference: Its development in men and women*. Bloomington: Indiana University Press.

Bell, C. G., & Price, C. M. (1989). Lawyer-legislators: The capitol's endangered species. *California Journal, 20*, 181–183.

Bell, D. (1989). The effects of affirmative action on male-female relationships among African Americans. *Sex Roles, 21*, 13–24.

Bell, R. R. (1981). Friendships of women and of men. *Psychology of Women Quarterly, 5*, 402–417.

Bellinger, D. C., & Gleason, J. B. (1982). Sex differences in parental directives to young children. *Sex Roles, 8*, 1123–1139.

Belsky, J., Lang, M., & Huston, T. L. (1986). Sex typing and division of labor as determinants of marital change across the transition to parenthood. *Journal of Personality and Social Psychology, 50*, 517–522.

Belzer, E. (1981). Orgasmic expulsions of women: A review and heuristic inquiry. *Journal of Sex Research, 17*, 1–12.

Bem, D., & Allen, A. (1974). On predicting some of the people some of the time: The search for cross-situational consistencies in behavior. *Psychological Review, 81*, 506–520.

Bem, S. L. (1974). The measurement of psychological androgyny. *Journal of Consulting and Clinical Psychology, 42*, 155–162.

Bem, S. L. (1975a). Androgyny versus the tight little lives of fluffy women and chesty men. *Psychology Today, 9*, pp. 58–59ff.

Bem, S. L. (1975b). Sex role adaptability: One consequence of psychological androgyny. *Journal of Personality and Social Psychology, 31*, 634–643.

Bem, S. L. (1976). Probing the promise of androgyny. In A. Kaplan & J. Bean (Eds.), *Beyond sex role stereotypes: Readings toward a psychology of androgyny* (pp. 47–62). Boston: Little, Brown.

Bem, S. L. (1977). On the utility of alternative procedures for assessing psychological androgyny. *Journal of Consulting and Clinical Psychology, 45*, 196–205.

Bem, S. L. (1979). Theory and measurement of androgyny: A reply to the Pedhazur-Tetenbaum and Locksley-Colton critiques. *Journal of Personality and Social Psychology, 37*, 1047–1054.

Bem, S. L. (1981a). *Bem Sex-Role Inventory, professional manual*. Palo Alto, CA: Consulting Psychologists Press.

Bem, S. L. (1981b). Gender schema theory: A cognitive account of sex typing. *Psychological Review, 88*, 354–364.

Bem, S. L. (1983). Gender schema theory and its implications for child development: Raising gender-aschematic children in a gender-schematic society. *Signs: Journal of Women in Culture and Society, 8*, 598–616.

Bem, S. L. (1985). Androgyny and gender schema theory: A conceptual and empirical integration. In T. B. Sonderegger (Ed.), *Nebraska Symposium on Motivation, 1984: Psychology and gender*, Vol. 32 (pp. 179–226). Lincoln, NE: University of Nebraska Press.

Bem, S. L. (1987). Gender schema theory and the romantic tradition. In P. Shaver & C. Hendrick (Eds.), *Sex and gender* (pp. 251–271). Newbury Park, CA: Sage.

Bem, S. L. (1989). Genital knowledge and gender constancy in preschool children. *Child Development, 60*, 649–662.

Bem, S. L., & Bem, D. J. (1970). Case study of a nonconscious ideology: Teaching the woman to know her place. In D. J. Bem (Ed.), *Beliefs, attitudes, and human affairs*. Monterey, CA: Brooks/Cole.

Bem, S. L., & Lenney, E. (1976). Sex-typing and the avoidance of cross-sex behavior. *Journal of Personality and Social Psychology, 33*, 48–54.

Bem, S., Martyna, W., & Watson, C. (1976). Sex-typing and androgyny: Further exploration of the expressive domain. *Journal of Personality and Social Psychology, 34*, 1016–1023.

Benbow, C. P. (1988). Sex differences in mathematical reasoning ability in intellectually talented preadolescents: Their nature, effects, and possible causes. *Behavioral and Brain Sciences, 119*, 169–232.

Benbow, C. P., & Arjmand, O. (1990). Predictors of high academic achievement in mathematics and science by mathematically talented students: A longitudinal study. *Journal of Educational Psychology, 82*, 430–441.

Benbow, C. P., & Stanley, J. C. (1980). Sex differences in mathematical ability: Fact or artifact? *Science, 210*, 1262–1264.

Benbow, C. P., & Stanley, J. C. (1983). Sex differences in mathematical reasoning ability: More facts. *Science, 222*, 1029–1031.

Benderly, B. L. (1987). *The myth of two minds: What gender means and doesn't mean*. New York: Doubleday.

Benderly, B. L. (1989, November). Don't believe everything you read . . . *Psychology Today*, pp. 67–69.

Bengtson, V. L., & Robertson, J. F. (Eds.). (1985). *Grandparenthood*. Beverly Hills, CA: Sage.

Benin, M. H., & Agostinelli, J. (1988). Husbands' and wives' satisfaction with the division of labor. *Journal of Marriage and the Family, 50*, 349–361.

Benjamin, J. (1988). *The bonds of love: Psychoanalysis, feminism, and the problem of knowledge*. New York: Pantheon.

Bennett, R. S., Whitaker, K. G., Smith, N.J.W., & Sablove, A. (1987). Changing the rules of the game: Reflections toward a feminist analysis of sport. *Women's Studies International Forum, 10*, 369–379.

Berardo, D. H., Shehan, C. L., & Leslie, G. R. (1987). A residue of tradition: Jobs, careers, and spouses' time in housework. *Journal of Marriage and the Family, 49*, 381–390.

Berg, B. J. (1986). *The crisis of the working mother: Resolving the conflict between family and work*. New York: Summit Books.

Berg, J. H., Stephan, W. G., & Dodson, M. (1981). Attributional modesty in women. *Psychology of Women Quarterly, 5*, 711–727.

Berger, C., & Gold, D. (1979). Do sex differences in problem solving still exist? *Personality and Social Psychology Bulletin, 5*, 109–113.

Berman, P. W. (1980). Are women more responsive than men to the young? A review of developmental and situational variables. *Psychological Bulletin, 88*, 668–695.

Berman, P. W., & Pedersen, F. A. (Eds.). (1987). *Men's transitions to parenthood: Longitudinal studies of early family experience*. Hillsdale, NJ: Erlbaum.

Berman, P. W., & Smith, V. L. (1984). Gender and situational differences in children's smiles, touch, and proxemics. *Sex Roles, 10*, 347–356.

Bernard, J. (1971). *Women and the public interest*. Chicago: Aldine.

Bernard, J. (1976). Change and stability in sex-role and behavior. *Journal of Social Issues, 32*(3), 207–223.

Bernard, J. (1979). Women as voters: From redemptive to futurist role. In J. Lipman-Blumen & J. Bernard (Eds.), *Sex roles and social science equation* (pp. 279–286). Beverly Hills, CA: Sage.

Bernard, J. (1981). The good-provider role. *American Psychologist, 36*, 1–12.

Bernard, J. (1987). *The female world from a global perspective*. Bloomington: Indiana University Press.

Bernard, J. (1989). Educating the majority: The feminist enlightenment. In C. S. Pearson, D. L. Shavlik, & J. G. Touchton (Eds.), *Educating the majority: Women challenge tradition in higher education* (pp. 413–440). New York: American Council on Education/Macmillan.

Berndt, T. J., & Heller, K. A. (1986). Gender stereotypes and social inferences: A developmental study. *Journal of Personality and Social Psychology, 50,* 889–898.

Berry, J. W. (1966). Temne and Eskimo perceptual skills. *International Journal of Psychology, 1,* 207–229.

Berry, M. F. (1986). *Why the ERA failed: Politics, women's rights and the amending process.* Bloomington: Indiana University Press.

Berryman-Fink, C. L., & Wilcox, J. R. (1983). A multivariate investigation of perceptual attributions concerning gender appropriateness in language. *Sex Roles, 9,* 663–681.

Best, R. (1983). *We've all got scars: What boys and girls learn in elementary school.* Bloomington: Indiana University Press.

Bettelheim, B. (1962). *Symbolic wounds.* New York: Collier.

Biaggio, M. K., Mohan, P. J., & Baldwin, C. (1985). Relationships among attitudes toward children, women's liberation, and personality characteristics. *Sex Roles, 12,* 47–62.

Bianchi, S., & Spain, D. (1983). *American women: Three decades of change.* Washington, DC: U.S. Government Printing Office.

Biener, L. (1990, Spring). Substance abuse in women: A consequence of emancipation or the lack of it? *Psychology of Women Newsletter,* pp. 8–9.

Bigler, R. S., & Liben, L. S. (1990). The role of attitudes and interventions in gender-schematic processing. *Child Development, 61,* 1440–1452.

Biller, H. B. (1981a). Father absence, divorce, and personality development. In M. Lamb (Ed.), *The role of the father in child development* (2nd ed.) (pp. 489–552). New York: Praeger.

Biller, H. B. (1981b). The father and sex role development. In M. Lamb (Ed.), *The role of the father in child development* (2nd ed.) (pp. 319–358). New York: Wiley.

Bilsker, D., Schiedel, D., & Marcia, J. (1988). Sex differences in identity status. *Sex Roles, 18,* 231–236.

Binion, V. J. (1990). Psychological androgyny: A Black female perspective. *Sex Roles, 22,* 487–507.

Bird, C. (1979, June). The best years of a woman's life. *Psychology Today,* pp. 20–66.

Birnbaum, D. W., & Croll, W. L. (1984). The etiology of children's stereotypes about sex differences in emotionality. *Sex Roles, 10,* 677–691.

Birnbaum, D. W., Nosanchuk, T. A., & Croll, W. L. (1980). Children's stereotypes about sex differences in emotionality. *Sex Roles, 6,* 435–443.

Birrell, S., & Richter, C. M. (1987). Is a diamond forever? Feminist transformations of sport. *Women's Studies International Forum, 10,* 395–409.

Bishops publish new Catholic Bible. (1987, April 5). *Easton Express,* p. A1.

Black, S. M., & Hill, C. E. (1984). The psychological well-being of women in their middle years. *Psychology of Women Quarterly, 8,* 282–292.

Blais, M. R., Vallerand, R. J., Briere, N. M., Gagnon, A., & Pelletier, L. G. (1990). Significance, structure, and gender differences in life domains of college students. *Sex Roles, 22,* 199–212.

Blakemore, J.E.O. (1990). Children's nurturant interactions with their infant siblings: An exploration of gender differences and maternal socialization. *Sex Roles, 22,* 43–57.

Blanck, P. D., Rosenthal, R., Snodgrass, S. E., DePaulo, B. M., & Zuckerman, M. (1981). Sex differences in eavesdropping on nonverbal cues: Developmental changes. *Journal of Personality and Social Psychology, 41,* 391–396.

Blascovich, J., Major, B., & Katkin, E. S. (1981). Sex-role orientation and Type A behavior. *Personality and Social Psychology Bulletin, 7,* 600–604.

Blau, F. D., & Ferber, M. A. (1986). *The economics of women, men, and work.* Englewood Cliffs, NJ: Prentice-Hall.

Blaubergs, M. S. (1978). Changing the sexist language: The theory behind the practice. *Psychology of Women Quarterly, 2,* 244–261.

Bleier, R. (1979). Social and political bias in science: An examination of animal studies and their generalizations to human behaviors and evolution. In E. Tobach & B. Rosoff (Eds.), *Genes and gender II* (pp. 49–69). Staten Island: Gordian Press.

Bleier, R. (1984). *Science and gender: A critique of biology and its theories on women.* New York: Pergamon Press.

Bleier, R. (1986). Sex differences research: Science or belief? In R. Bleier (Ed.), *Feminist approaches to science* (pp. 147–164). New York: Pergamon Press.

Bleier, R. (1988). A decade of feminist critiques in the natural sciences. *Signs: Journal of Women in Culture and Society, 14,* 186–195.

Block, J. D. (1980). *Friendship.* New York: Macmillan.

Block, J. H. (1973). Conceptions of sex-roles: Some cross-cultural and longitudinal perspectives. *American Psychologist, 28,* 512–526.

Block, J. H. (1984). *Sex-role identity and ego development.* San Francisco: Jossey-Bass.

Blum, L., & Smith, V. (1988). Women's mobility in the corporation: A critique of

the politics of optimism. *Signs: Journal of Women in Culture and Society, 13,* 528–545.

Blumberg, R. L. (1977). Women and work around the world: A cross-cultural examination of sex division of labor and sex status. In A. Sargent (Ed.), *Beyond sex roles* (pp. 412–433). St. Paul: West.

Blumberg, R. L. (1979). A paradigm for predicting the position of women: Policy implications and problems. In J. Lipman-Blumen & J. Bernard (Eds.), *Sex roles and social policy: A complex social science equation* (pp. 113–142). Beverly Hills, CA: Sage.

Blumberg, R. L. (1984). A general theory of gender stratification. In R. Collins (Ed.), *Sociological theory* (pp. 23–101). San Francisco: Jossey-Bass.

Blumberg, R. L. (1989). Toward a feminist theory of development. In R. A. Wallace (Ed.), *Feminism and sociological theory* (pp. 161–199). Newbury Park, CA: Sage.

Blumberg, R. L. (in press). *Women and the wealth of nations: Theory and research on gender and global development.* New York: Praeger.

Blumstein, P., & Schwartz, P. (1983). *American couples.* New York: Morrow.

Blumstein, P., & Schwartz, P. (1990). Intimate relationships and the creation of sexuality. In D. P. McWhirter, S. A. Sanders, & J. M. Reinisch (Eds.), *Homosexuality/heterosexuality: Concepts of sexual orientation.* New York: Oxford University Press.

Bly, R. (1990). *Iron John: A book about men.* Reading, MA: Addison-Wesley.

Blyth, D. A., & Foster-Clark, F. S. (1987). Gender differences in perceived intimacy with different members of adolescents' social networks. *Sex Roles, 17,* 689–718.

Bodenhausen, G. V. (1988). Stereotypic biases in social decision making and memory: Testing process models of stereotype use. *Journal of Personality and Social Psychology, 55,* 726–737.

Bohen, H. H., & Viveros-Long, A. (1981). *Balancing jobs and family life.* Philadelphia: Temple University Press.

Bohlen, C. (1990, November 25). East Europe's women struggle with new rules, and old ones. *New York Times,* pp. E1, E2.

Boldizar, J. P., Perry, D. G., & Perry, L. C. (1989). Outcome values and aggression. *Child Development, 60,* 571–579.

Bolger, N., DeLongis, A., Kessler, R. C., & Wethington, E. (1989). The contagion of stress across multiple roles. *Journal of Marriage and the Family, 51,* 175–183.

Boneparth, E. & Stoper, E. (Eds.). (1988). *Women, power, and policy: Toward the year 2000* (2nd ed.). New York: Pergamon Press.

Booth, A., Shelley, G., Mazur, A., Tharp, G., & Kittok, R. (1989). Testosterone and winning and losing in human competition. *Hormones and Behavior, 23,* 556–571.

Borges, M. A., Levine, J. R., & Dutton, L. J. (1984). Men's and women's ratings of life satisfaction by age of respondent and age interval judged. *Sex Roles, 11,* 345–350.

Borges, M. A., Levine, J. R., & Naylor, P. A. (1982). Self-ratings and projected rating of sex-role attitudes. *Psychology of Women Quarterly, 6,* 406–414.

Borges, M. A., & Vaughn, L. S. (1977). Cognitive differences between the sexes in memory for names and faces. *Perceptual and Motor Skills, 45,* 317–318.

Borys, S., & Perlman, D. (1985). Gender differences in loneliness. *Personality and Social Psychology Bulletin, 11,* 63–74.

Boserup, E. (1970). *Women's role in economic development.* London: Allen & Unwin.

Boulding, E. (1979). Introduction. In J. Lipman-Blumen & J. Bernard (Eds.), *Sex roles and social policy: A complex social science equation* (pp. 7–14). Beverly Hills, CA: Sage.

Bourque, L. B. (1989). *Defining rape.* Durham, NC: Duke University Press.

Bovee, T. (1991a, August 29). Black life expectancy greater, but still years less than whites. *Morning Call,* p. A18.

Bovee, T. (1991b, September 20). Blacks continue to trail whites at the pay window. *Philadelphia Inquirer,* p. 14C.

Bovee, T. (1991c, November 14). Women suffer pay gap bias. *Morning Call,* p. A3.

Bowles, G., & Duelli-Klein, R. (Eds.). (1983). *Theories of women's studies.* London: Routledge & Kegan Paul.

Boyer, P. J. (1986, February 16). TV turns to the hard-boiled male. *New York Times,* pp. H1, H29.

Bozett, F. W. (1988). Gay fatherhood. In P. Bronstein & C. P. Cowan (Eds.), *Fatherhood today: Men's changing role in the family* (pp. 214–235). New York: Wiley.

Brabant, S., & Mooney, L. (1986). Sex role stereotyping in the Sunday comics: Ten years later. *Sex Roles, 14,* 141–148.

Brabeck, M. M., & Weisgerber, K. (1988). Responses to the *Challenger* tragedy: Subtle and significant gender differences. *Sex Roles, 19,* 639–650.

Brabeck, M. M., & Weisgerber, K. (1989). College students' perceptions of men and women choosing teaching and management: The effects of gender and sex role egalitarianism. *Sex Roles, 21,* 841–857.

Bradbard, M. R., & Endsley, R. C. (1983). The effects of sex-typed labeling on preschool children's information-seeking and retention. *Sex Roles, 9,* 247–260.

Bradbury, T. N., & Fincham, F. D. (1988). Individual difference variables in close relationships: A contextual model of marriage as an integrative framework. *Journal of Personality and Social Psychology, 54,* 713–721.

Braddock, J. H. (1990, August). Race and sex difference in the role of education for occupational success. Abstracted in the *Spencer Foundation Newsletter,* pp. 1–2.

Braito, R., Dean, D., Powers, E., & Bruton, B. (1981). The inferiority games: Perceptions and behavior. *Sex Roles, 7,* 65–72.

Bram, S. (1983). The effects of childbearing on woman's mental health: A critical review of the literature. In E. Tobach & B. Rosoff (Eds.), *Genes and gender IV* (pp. 143–160). Staten Island: Gordian Press.

Bram, S. (1984). Voluntarily childless women: Traditional or nontraditional? *Sex Roles, 10,* 195–206.

Brannon, R. (1976). The male sex role: Our culture's blueprint of manhood and what it's done for us lately. In D. David & R. Brannon (Eds.), *The 49-percent majority.* Reading, MA: Addison-Wesley.

Brannon, R. (1978). Measuring attitudes toward women (and otherwise): A methodological critique. In J. Sherman & F. Denmark (Eds.), *The future of women: Issues in psychology* (pp. 647–709). New York: Psychological Dimensions.

Branscombe, N. R., & Deaux, K. (1991). Feminist attitude accessibility and behavioral intentions. *Psychology of Women Quarterly, 15,* 411–418.

Branscombe, N. R., & Smith, E. R. (1990). Gender and racial stereotypes in impression formation and social decision-making processes. *Sex Roles, 22,* 627–647.

Brehm, S. S., Powell, L., & Coke, J. S. (1984). The effects of empathic instructions upon donating behavior: Sex differences in young children. *Sex Roles, 10,* 405–416.

Brehony, K. A., & Geller, E. S. (1981). Relationship between psychological androgyny, social conformity, and perceived locus of control. *Psychology of Women Quarterly, 6,* 204–217.

Bremer, T. H., & Wittig, M. A. (1980). Fear of success: A personality trait or a response to occupational deviance and role overload? *Sex Roles, 6,* 27–46.

Brenner, M. H. (1979). Influence of the social environment on psychopathology: The historic perspective. In J. S. Barrett (Ed.), *Stress and mental disorder* (pp. 161–177) New York: Raven Press.

Brenner, O. C., Tomkiewicz, J., & Schein, V. E. (1989). The relationship between sex role stereotypes and requisite management characteristics revisited. *Academy of Management Journal, 32,* 662–669.

Bressler, L. C., & Lavender, A. D. (1986). Sexual fulfillment of heterosexual, bisexual, and homosexual women. *Journal of Homosexuality, 12,* 109–122.

Bretl, D. J., & Cantor, J. (1988). The portrayal of men and women in U. S. television commercials: A recent content analysis and trends over 15 years. *Sex Roles, 18,* 595–609.

Brewer, M. B., & Berk, R. A. (Eds.). (1982). Beyond nine to five: Sexual harassment on the job [Special issue]. *Journal of Social Issues, 38*(4).

Brewer, R. M. (1988). Black women in poverty: Some comments on female-headed families. *Signs: Journal of Women in Culture and Society, 13,* 331–339.

Bridges, J. S. (1988). Sex differences in occupational performance expectations. *Psychology of Women Quarterly, 12,* 75–90.

Bridges, J. S. (1989). Sex differences in occupational values. *Sex Roles, 20,* 205–211.

Briere, J., & Malamuth, N. M. (1983). Self-reported likelihood of sexually aggressive behavior: Attitudinal versus sexual explanations. *Journal of Research in Personality, 17,* 315–323.

Briscoe, J. B. (1989). Perceptions that discourage women attorneys from seeking public office. *Sex Roles, 21,* 557–567.

Brod, H. (Ed.). (1987). *The making of masculinities: The new men's studies.* Boston: Allen & Unwin.

Brodsky, A. M. (1980). A decade of feminist influence on psychotherapy. *Psychology of Women Quarterly, 4,* 331–344.

Brodsky, A. M., & Hare-Mustin, R. T. (Eds.). (1980). *Women and psychotherapy: An assessment of research and practice.* New York: Guilford.

Brodsky, A. M., Holroyd, J., Payton, C. R., Rubenstein, E. A., Rosenkrantz, P., Sherman, J., Zell, F., Cummings, T., & Suber, C. J. (1978). Source materials for non-sexist therapy. JSAS: *Catalog of Selected Documents in Psychology, 8*(2), 40. (Ms. No. 1685)

Brody, C. M. (Ed.). (1987). *Women's therapy groups: Paradigms of feminist treatment.* New York: Springer.

Brody, L. R. (1984). Sex and age variations in the quality and intensity of children's emotional attributions to hypothetical situations. *Sex Roles, 11,* 51–59.

Brody, L. R. (1985). Gender differences in emotional development: A review of theories and research. *Journal of Personality, 53,* 102–149.

Brody, L. R., Hay, D. H., & Vandewater, E. (1990). Gender, gender role identity, and children's reported feelings toward the same and opposite sex. *Sex Roles, 23,* 363–387.

Broman, C. L. (1991). Gender, work-family roles, and psychological well-being of Blacks. *Journal of Marriage and the Family, 53,* 509–520.

Bronfenbrenner, U. (1974). Developmental research, public policy and the ecology of childhood. *Child Development, 45*, 1–5.

Bronfenbrenner, U. (1977). Toward an experimental ecology of human development. *American Psychologist, 32*, 513–531.

Bronstein, P. (1984). Differences in mothers' and fathers' behaviors to children: A cross-cultural comparison. *Developmental Psychology 20*, 995–1003.

Bronstein, P., Black, L., Pfennig, J., & White, A. (1986). Getting academic jobs: Are women equally qualified—and equally successful? *American Psychologist, 41*, 318–321.

Bronstein, P., & Cowan, C. P. (Eds.). (1988). *Fatherhood today: Men's changing role in the family.* New York: Wiley.

Brooks-Gunn, J. (1986). The relationship of maternal beliefs about sex typing to maternal and young children's behavior. *Sex Roles, 14*, 21–35.

Brooks-Gunn, J., & Furstenberg, F. F., Jr. (1989). Adolescent sexual behavior. *American Psychologist, 44*, 249–257.

Brophy, J. (1985). Interactions of male and female students with male and female teachers. In L. C. Wilkinson & C. B. Marrett (Eds.), *Gender influences in classroom interaction* (pp. 115–142). Orlando, FL: Academic Press.

Broude, N., & Garrard, M. (1982). *Feminism and art history.* New York: Harper & Row.

Broverman, D. M., Klaiber, E. L., Kobayaski, Y., & Vogel, W. (1968). Roles of activation and inhibition in sex differences in cognitive abilities. *Psychological Review, 75*(11), 5–7, 23–50, 167.

Broverman, I., Broverman, D. M., Clarkson, F. E., Rosenkrantz, P. S., & Vogel, S. R. (1970). Sex-role stereotypes and clinical judgments of mental health. *Journal of Consulting and Clinical Psychology, 34*, 1–7.

Broverman, I., Vogel, S. R., Broverman, D. M., Clarkson, F. E., & Rosenkrantz, P. S. (1972). Sex role stereotypes: A current appraisal. *Journal of Social Issues, 28*(2), 59–78.

Brown, A., Larsen, M. B., Rankin, S. A., & Ballard, R. A. (1980). Sex differences in information processing. *Sex Roles, 6*, 663–673.

Brown, B. A., Frankel, B. G., & Fennell, M. P. (1989). Hugs or shrugs: Parental and peer influence on continuity of involvement in sport by female adolescents. *Sex Roles, 20*, 397–412.

Brown, C. E., Dovidio, J. F., & Ellyson, S. L. (1990). Reducing sex differences in visual displays of dominance: Knowledge is power. *Personality and Social Psychology Bulletin, 16*, 358–368.

Brown, D., Fulkerson, K. F., Furr, S., Ware, W. B., & Voight, N. L. (1984). Locus of control, sex role orientation, and self-concept in black and white third- and sixth-grade male and female leaders in a rural community. *Developmental Psychology, 20*, 717–721.

Brown, D. R., & Gary, L. E. (1985). Social support network differentials among married and nonmarried Black females. *Psychology of Women Quarterly, 9*, 229–241.

Brown, D. R., Milburn, N. G., Ahmed, F., Gary, L. E., & Booth, J. (1989–90). Depression and marital status among Black females. *Urban Research Review, 12*(2), 11, 12, 14, 16.

Brown, J., Childers, K. W., Bauman, K. E., & Koch, G. G. (1990). The influence of new media and family structure on young adolescents' television and radio use. *Communication Research, 17*, 65–82.

Brown, J. D., & Campbell, K. (1986). Race and gender in music videos: The same beat but a different drummer. *Journal of Communication, 36*, 94–106.

Brown, J. D., Campbell, K., & Fisher, L. (1986). American adolescents and music videos: Why do they watch? *Gazette, 37*, pp. 19–32.

Brown, J. D., & Schulze, L. (1990). The effects of race, gender, and fandom on audience interpretations of Madonna's music videos. *Journal of Communication, 40*(2), 88–102.

Brown, J. K. (1970). Economic organization and position of women among the Iroquois. *Ethnohistory, 17*, 151–167.

Brown, J. K. (1976). An anthropological perspective on sex roles and subsistence. In M. Teitelbaum (Ed.), *Sex differences: Social and biological perspectives* (pp. 122–137). New York: Anchor Press.

Brown, J. K., & Kerns, V. (Eds.). (1985). *In her prime: A new view of middle-aged women.* South Hadley, MA: Bergin & Garvey.

Brown, J. M. (1982, April). *Attitude towards violence and self-reports of participation in contact sports.* Paper presented at the meeting of the Eastern Psychological Association, Baltimore.

Brown, J. M., & Davies, N. (1978, May). Attitude towards violence among college athletes. *Journal of Sport Behavior, 1*, pp. 67–70.

Brown, J. W., Aldrich, M. L., & Hall, P. Q. (1978). *The participation of women in scientific research.* Washington, DC: National Science Foundation.

Brown, L. S., & Root, M.P.P. (Eds.). (1990). *Diversity and complexity in feminist therapy.* New York: Harrington Park.

Brown, V., & Geis, F. L. (1984). Turning lead into gold: Evaluations of men and women

leaders and the alchemy of social consensus. *Journal of Personality and Social Psychology, 46*, 811–824.

Brown, W. (1988). *Manhood and politics: A feminist reading in political theory.* Totowa, NJ: Rowman & Littlefield.

Browne, A. (1987). *When battered women kill.* New York: Free Press.

Brownmiller, S. (1975). *Against our will: Men, women, and rape.* New York: Simon & Schuster.

Bryant, F. B., & Veroff, J. (1982). The structure of psychological well-being: A sociohistorical analysis. *Journal of Personality and Social Psychology, 43*, 653–673.

Bryden, M. P. (1979). Evidence for sex-related differences in cerebral organization. In M. A. Wittig & A. C. Petersen (Eds.), *Sex-related differences in cognitive functioning: Developmental issues* (pp. 121–143). New York: Academic Press.

Bryden, M. P. (1983). *Sex-related differences in perceptual asymmetry.* Paper presented at the meeting of the American Psychological Association, Anaheim.

Bryden, M. P. (1986). Dichotic listening performance, cognitive ability, and cerebral organization. *Canadian Journal of Psychology, 40*, 445–456.

Bryden, M. P., & Vrbancic, M. I. (1988). Dichotic lateralization, cognitive ability, and age at puberty. *Developmental Neuropsychology, 4*, 169–180.

Bryer, J. B., Nelson, B. A., Miller, J. B., & Krol, A. A. (1987). Childhood physical and sexual abuse as factors in adult psychiatric illness. *American Journal of Psychiatry, 144*, 1426–1430.

Bryson, L. (1987). Sport and the maintenance of masculine hegemony. *Women's Studies International Forum, 10*, 349–360.

Buck, R. (1977). Nonverbal communication of affect in preschool children. Relationships with personality and skin conductance. *Journal of Personality and Social Psychology, 35*, 225–236.

Budd, B. E., Clance, P. R., & Simerly, D. E. (1985). Spatial configurations: Erikson reexamined. *Sex Roles, 12*, 571–577.

Buehler, C. (1988). The social and emotional well-being of divorced residential parents. *Sex Roles, 18*, 247–257.

Buhl, M. (1989, September–October). The feminist mystique. *In View*, p. 16.

Buhrke, R. A., & Fuqua, D. R. (1987). Sex differences in same- and cross-sex supportive relationships. *Sex Roles, 17*, 339–352.

Buie, J. (1989, August). Course helps fathers know best. *APA Monitor*, p. 28.

Buie, J. (1990, March). "Men-only" therapy programs emerge. *APA Monitor*, pp. 16–17.

Bunch, C. (1975). Lesbians in revolt. In M. Myron & C. Bunch (Eds.), *Lesbianism and the women's movement* (pp. 29–38). Oakland, CA: Diana Press.

Bunker, B. B., Forcey, B., Wilderom, C.P.M., & Elgie, D. M. (1984, August). *The competitive behaviors of men and women: Is there a difference?* Paper presented at the meeting of the American Psychological Association, Toronto, Canada.

Burch, B. (1987). Barriers to intimacy: Conflicts over power, dependency, and nurturing in lesbian relationships. In Boston Lesbian Psychologies Collective (Ed.), *Lesbian psychologies: Explorations and challenges* (pp. 126–141). Urbana: University of Illinois Press.

Burchardt, C. J., & Serbin, L. A. (1982). Psychological androgyny and personality adjustment in college and psychiatric populations. *Sex Roles, 8*, 835–851.

Burda, P. C., Jr., Vaux, A., & Schill, T. (1984). Social support resources: Variation across sex and sex role. *Personality and Social Psychology Bulletin, 10*, 119–126.

Burke, P. J. (1989). Gender identity, sex, and school performance. *Social Psychology Quarterly, 52*, 159–169.

Burlew, A. K. (1982). The experience of black females in traditional and nontraditional professions. *Psychology of Women Quarterly, 6*, 312–326.

Burns, A., & Homel, R. (1989). Gender division of tasks by parents and their children. *Psychology of Women Quarterly, 13*, 113–125.

Burt, M. R. (1980). Cultural myths and supports for rape. *Journal of Personality and Social Psychology, 38*, 217–230.

Buss, A. H., & Finn, S. E. (1987). Classification of personality traits. *Journal of Personality and Social Psychology, 52*, 432–444.

Buss, D. M. (1981). Sex differences in the evaluation and performance of dominant acts. *Journal of Personality and Social Psychology, 40*, 147–154.

Buss, D. M. (1988). The evolution of human intrasexual competition: Tactics of mate attraction. *Journal of Personality and Social Psychology, 54*, 616–628.

Buss, D. M. (1989a). Conflict between the sexes: Strategic interference and the evocation of anger and upset. *Journal of Personality and Social Psychology, 56*, 735–737.

Buss, D. M. (1989b). Sex differences in human mate preferences: Evolutionary hypotheses tested in 37 cultures. *Behavioral and Brain Sciences, 12*, 1–49.

Bussey, K., & Bandura, A. (1984). Influence of gender constancy and social power on sex-linked modeling. *Journal of Personality and Social Psychology, 47*, 1292–1302.

Bussey, K., & Maughan, B. (1982). Gender differences in moral reasoning. *Journal of Personality and Social Psychology, 42*, 701–706.

Bussey, K., & Perry, D. G. (1982). Same-sex imitation: The avoidance of cross-sex models or the acceptance of same-sex models? *Sex Roles, 8*, 773–784.

Butcher, J. E. (1989). Adolescent girls' sex role development: Relationship with sports participation, self-esteem, and age at menarche. *Sex Roles, 20*, 575–593.

Butler, D., & Geis, F. L. (1990). Nonverbal affect responses to male and female leaders: Implications for leadership evaluations. *Journal of Personality and Social Psychology, 58*, 48–59.

Buttner, E. H., & Rosen, B. (1987). The effects of labor shortages on starting salaries for sex-typed jobs. *Sex Roles, 17*, 59–71.

Byrne, D. (1977). Social psychology and the study of sexual behavior. *Personality and Social Psychology Bulletin, 3*, 3–30.

Cahill, S. E. (1983). Reexamining the acquisition of sex roles: A social interactionist approach. *Sex Roles, 9*, 1–15.

Calder, B. G., & Ross, M. (1977). Sexual discrimination and work performance. *Personality and Social Psychology Bulletin, 13*, 429–433.

Caldera, Y. M., Huston, A. C., & O'Brien, M. (1989). Social interactions and play patterns of parents and toddlers with feminine, masculine, and neutral toys. *Child Development, 60*, 70–76.

Calderone, K. L. (1990). The influence of gender on the frequency of pain and sedative medication administered to postoperative patients. *Sex Roles, 23*, 713–725.

Caldwell, M. A., & Peplau, L. A. (1982). Sex differences in same-sex friendship. *Sex Roles, 8*, 721–732.

Caldwell, M.R., & Peplau, L.A. (1984). The balance of power in lesbian relationships. *Sex Roles, 10*, 587–599

Callahan-Levy, C. M., & Messe, L. A. (1979). Sex differences in the allocation of pay. *Journal of Personality and Social Psychology, 37*, 433–446.

Cameron, E., Eisenberg, N., & Tryon, K. (1985). The relations between sex-typed play and preschoolers' social behavior. *Sex Roles, 12*, 601–615.

Cancian, F. M. (1986). The feminization of love. *Signs: Journal of Women in Culture and Society, 11*, 692–709.

Cancian, F. M. (1987). *Love in America: Gender and self-development.* Cambridge, England: Cambridge University Press.

Candy, S. G., Troll, L. E., & Levy, S. G. (1981). A developmental exploration of friendship functions in women. *Psychology of Women Quarterly, 5*, 456–472.

Cann, A., & Siegfried, W. D. (1990). Gender stereotypes and dimensions of effective leader behavior. *Sex Roles, 23*, 413–419.

Cannon, L. W., Higginbotham, E., & Leung, M.L.A. (1988). Race and class bias in qualitative research on women. *Gender and Society, 2*, 449–462.

Cano, L., Solomon, S., & Holmes, D. S. (1984). Fear of success: The influence of sex, sex-role identity, and components of masculinity. *Sex Roles, 10*, 341–346.

Canter, R. J. (1979). Achievement-related expectations and aspirations in college women. *Sex Roles, 5*, 453–470.

Canter, R. J., & Ageton, S. S. (1984). The epidemiology of adolescent sex-role attitudes. *Sex Roles, 11*, 657–676.

Canter, R. J., & Meyerowitz, B. C. (1984). Sex-role stereotypes: Self-reports of behavior. *Sex Roles, 10*, 293–306.

Cantor, A. (1983). The Lilith question. In S. Heschel (Ed.), *On being a Jewish feminist: A reader* (pp. 40–50). New York: Schocken.

Cantor, M. G., & Pingree, S. (1983). *The soap opera.* Beverly Hills, CA: Sage.

Caplan, P. J. (1989). *Don't blame mother: Mending the mother-daughter relationship.* New York: Harper & Row.

Caplan, P. J., & Gans, M. (1991). Is there empirical justification for the category of "self-defeating personality disorder"? *Feminism and Psychology, 1*, 263–278.

Caplan, P. J., MacPherson, G. M., & Tobin, P. (1985). Do sex-related differences in spatial abilities exist? A multilevel critique with new data. *American Psychologist, 40*, 786–799.

Caplan, P. J., MacPherson, G. M., & Tobin, P. (1986). The magnified molehill and the misplaced focus: Sex-related differences in spatial ability revisited [Letter to the editor]. *American Psychologist, 41*, 1016–1018.

Caputi, J. (1989). The sexual politics of murder. *Gender and Society, 3*, 437–456.

Caputi, J., & Russell, D.E.H. (1990, September–October). "Femicide": Speaking the unspeakable. *Ms.*, pp. 34–37.

Card, J. J., & Farrell, W. S., Jr. (1983). Nontraditional careers for women: A prototypical example. *Sex Roles, 9*, 1005–1022.

Cardell, M., Finn, S., & Marecek, J. (1981). Sex-role identity, sex-role behavior, and satisfaction in heterosexual, lesbian, and gay male couples. *Sex Roles, 5*, 488–494.

Carli, L. L. (1989a). Gender differences in interaction style and influence. *Journal of Personality and Social Psychology, 56*, 565–576.

Carli, L. L. (1989b, August). *Social influence as a function of gender and language.* Paper presented at the meeting of the American Psychological Association, New Orleans.

Carlson, B. E. (1984). The father's contribution to child care: Effects on children's perceptions of parental roles. *American Journal of Orthopsychiatry, 54,* 123–136.

Carlson, H. M., & Baxter, L. A. (1984). Androgyny, depression, and self-esteem in Irish homosexual and heterosexual males and females. *Sex Roles, 10,* 457–467.

Carlson, J. E. (1976). The sexual role. In F. I. Nye (Ed.), *Role structure and analysis of the family.* Beverly Hills, CA: Sage.

Carlson, M. (1990, Fall). It's our turn. *Women: The road ahead* [Special issue of *Time* magazine], pp. 16–18.

Carr, P. G., & Mednick, M. T. (1988). Sex role socialization and the development of achievement motivation in Black preschool children. *Sex Roles, 18,* 169–180.

Carr, P. G., Thomas, V. G., & Mednick, M. T. (1985). Evaluation of sex-typed tasks by Black men and women. *Sex Roles, 13,* 311–316.

Carrigan, T., Connell, B., & Lee, J. (1987). Toward a new sociology of masculinity. In H. Brod (Ed.), *The making of masculinities: The new men's studies* (pp. 63–100). Boston: Allen & Unwin.

Carroll, J. L., Volk, K. D., & Hyde, J. S. (1985). Differences between males and females in motives for engaging in sexual intercourse. *Archives of Sexual Behavior, 14,* 131–139.

Carroll, S. J. (1984a). Women candidates and support for feminist concerns: The closet feminist syndrome. *Western Political Quarterly, 37,* 307–323.

Carroll, S. J. (1984b, August). *Women's autonomy and the gender gap.* Paper presented at the meeting of the American Psychological Association, Toronto, Ontario.

Carroll, S. J. (1985a). Political elites and sex differences in political ambition: A reconsideration. *Journal of Politics, 47,* 1231–1243.

Carroll, S. J. (1985b). *Women as candidates in American politics.* Bloomington: Indiana University Press.

Carter, B. (1991, May 1). Children's TV, where boys are king. *New York Times,* pp. A1, C18.

Carter, D. B. (1987). The roles of peers in sex role socialization. In B. Carter (Ed.), *Current conceptions of sex roles and sex typing: Theory and research* (pp. 101–121). New York: Praeger.

Cash, T. F., & Brown, T. A. (1989). Gender and body images: Stereotypes and realities. *Sex Roles, 21,* 361–373.

Cash, T. F., Gillen, B., & Burns, D. S. (1977). Sexism and "beautyism" in personnel consultant decision making. *Journal of Applied Psychology, 62,* 301–310.

Cash, T. F., & Trimer, C. A. (1984). Sexism and beautyism in women's evaluations of peer performance. *Sex Roles, 10,* 87–98.

Cassidy, M. L., & Warren, B. O. (1991). Status inconsistency and work satisfaction among professional and managerial women and men. *Gender and Society, 5,* 193–206.

Castro, J. (1990, Fall). Get set: Here they come! *Women: The road ahead* [Special issue of *Time* magazine], pp. 50–52.

Cate, R., & Sugawara, A. I. (1986). Sex role orientation and dimensions of self-esteem among middle adolescents. *Sex Roles, 15,* 145–158.

Catholics for a Free Choice. (1988, November–December). *Conscience* [Whole issue].

Cazenave, N. A. (1983, July). Black male-black female relationships: The perceptions of 155 middle-class black men. *Family Relations,* pp. 341–350.

Cazenave, N. A. (1984). Race, socioeconomic status, and age: The social context of American masculinity. *Sex Roles, 11,* 639–656.

Cazenave, N. A., & Leon, G. H. (1987). Men's work and family roles and characteristics: Race, gender, and class perceptions of college students. In M. S. Kimmel (Ed.), *Changing men: New directions in research on men and masculinity* (pp. 244–262). Newbury Park, CA: Sage.

Chafetz, J. (1984). *Sex and advantage: A comparative macrostructural theory of sex stratification.* Totowa, NJ: Rowan & Allanheld.

Chafetz, J. S. (1978). *Masculine/feminine or human?* (2nd ed.). Itasca, IL: F. E. Peacock.

Chafetz, J. S. (1989). Gender equality: Toward a theory of change. In R. A. Wallace (Ed.), *Feminism and sociological theory* (pp. 135–160). Newbury Park, CA: Sage.

Chafetz, J. S., & Dworkin, A. G. (1986). *Female revolt: Women's movements in world and historical perspective.* Totowa, NJ: Rowan & Allanheld.

Chaiken, S., & Pliner, P. (1987). Women, but not men, are what they eat: The effect of meal size and gender on perceived femininity and masculinity. *Personality and Social Psychology Bulletin, 13,* 166–176.

Chambers, D. L., & Wenk, N. M. (1982). Feminist versus nonfeminist therapy: The client's perspective. *Women and Therapy, 1,* 57–65.

Changing attitudes. (1986, November 23). *New York Times,* p. E26.

Chaplin, W. F., & Goldberg, L. R. (1985). A failure to replicate the Bem and Allen study of individual differences in cross-situational consistency. *Journal of Personality and Social Psychology, 47,* 1074–1090.

Chassler, S. (1988, December 18). What teen boys think about sex. *Parade Magazine,* pp. 16–17.

Chavez, D. (1985) Perpetuation of gender inequality: A content analysis of comic strips. *Sex Roles, 13,* 93–102.

Cheatham, H. E. (1984). Integration of women into the U.S. military. *Sex Roles, 11,* 141–153.

Check, J.V.P., & Malamuth, N. M. (1983). Sex role stereotyping and reactions to depictions of stranger versus acquaintance rape. *Journal of Personality and Social Psychology, 45,* 344–356.

Cherlin, A., & Walters, P. (1981). Trends in United States men's and women's sex-role attitudes: 1972–1978. *American Sociological Review, 46,* 453–460.

Cherlin, A. J., Furstenberg, F. F., Jr., Chase-Lansdale, P. L., Kiernan, K. E., Robins, P. K., Morrison, D. R., & Teitler, J. O. (1991). Longitudinal studies of effects of divorce on children in Great Britain and the United States. *Science, 252,* 1386–1389.

Cherry, F., & Deaux, K. (1978). Fear of success versus fear of gender-inappropriate behavior. *Sex Roles, 4,* 97–101.

Cherry, L., & Lewis, M. (1976). Mothers and two-year-olds: A study of sex-differentiated aspects of verbal interaction. *Developmental Psychology, 12,* 278–282.

Chesler, P. (1972). *Women and madness.* New York: Doubleday.

Chesler, P. (1978). *About men.* New York: Simon & Schuster.

Chesler, P. (1986). *Mothers on trial: The battle for children and custody.* New York: McGraw-Hill.

Chesler, P. (1988). *Sacred bond: The legacy of Baby M.* New York: Times Books.

Chesney-Lind, M. (1986). Women and crime: The female offender. *Signs: Journal of Women in Culture and Society, 12,* 78–96.

Chester, N. L. (1983). Sex differentiation in two high school environments: Implications for career development among black adolescent females. *Journal of Social Issues, 39*(3), 29–40.

Child support lags for mothers never married. (1990, August 2). *Morning Call,* p. A17.

Chinchilla, N. S. (1991). Marxism, feminism, and the struggle for democracy in Latin America. *Gender and Society, 5,* 291–310.

Chino, A. F., & Funabiki, D. (1984). A cross-validation of sex differences in the expression of depression. *Sex Roles, 11,* 175–187.

Chipman, S. F., Brush, L. R., & Wilson, D. M. (Eds.). (1985). *Women and mathematics: Balancing the equation.* Hillsdale, NJ: Erlbaum.

Chodorow, N. (1978). *The reproduction of mothering: Psychoanalysis and the sociology of gender.* Berkeley: University of California Press.

Chodorow, N. J. (1990). *Feminism and psychoanalytic theory*. New Haven: Yale University Press.

Chow, E. N. (1985). The acculturation experience of Asian American women. In A. Sargent (Ed.), *Beyond sex roles* (2nd ed.) (pp. 238–251). St. Paul, MN: West.

Chow, E. N. (1987). The influence of sex-role identity and occupational attainment on the psychological well-being of Asian American women. *Psychology of Women Quarterly, 11,* 69–81.

Christy, C. A. (1987). *Sex differences in political participation: Processes of change in 14 nations*. New York: Praeger.

Chua-Eoan, H. G. (1990, Fall). All in the family. *Women: The road ahead* [Special issue of *Time* magazine], pp. 33–34.

Chusmir, L. H. (1990). Men who make nontraditional career choices. *Journal of Counseling and Development, 69,* 11–16.

Cicirelli, V. G. (1982). Sibling influence throughout the lifespan. In M. Lamb & B. Sutton-Smith (Eds.), *Sibling relationships: Their nature and significance across the lifespan* (pp. 267–284). Hillsdale, NJ: Erlbaum.

Cicone, M. N., & Ruble, D. N. (1978). Beliefs about males. *Journal of Social Issues, 34*(1), 5–16.

Civil rights decision hurting fight against discrimination, group says. (1989, November 20). *Morning Call*, p. D5.

Clance, P. R. (1985). *The imposter phenomenon: Overcoming the fear that haunts your success*. Atlanta: Peachtree.

Clarke, A. E., & Ruble, D. N. (1978). Young adolescents' beliefs concerning menstruation. *Child Development, 49,* 231–234.

Clarke-Stewart, A. (1989). Infant day care: Malignant or maligned? *American Psychologist, 44,* 266–273.

Clatterbaugh, K. (1990). *Contemporary perspectives on masculinity: Men, women, and politics in modern society*. Boulder, CO: Westview Press.

Clutter, S. (1990, May 3). Gender may affect response and outrage to sex abuse. *Morning Call*, p. D14.

Clymer, A. (1991, July 14). Poll finds GOP growth erodes dominant role of the Democrats. *New York Times*, pp. 1, 16.

Coates, D. L. (1987). Gender differences in the structure and support characteristics of Black adolescents' social networks. *Sex Roles, 17,* 719–736.

Cobb, N. J., Stevens-Long, J., & Goldstein, S. (1982). The influence of televised models on toy preference in children. *Sex Roles, 8,* 1075–1080.

Cochran, S. D., & Peplau, L. A. (1985). Value orientations in heterosexual relationships. *Psychology of Women Quarterly, 9,* 477–488.

Cohan, A., & Altman, E. (1990, November–December). 1990 elections reveal women to be a growing force. *National NOW Times*, pp. 1, 2.

Cohn, L. D. (1991). Sex differences in the course of personality development. *Psychological Bulletin, 109,* 252–266.

Coker, D. R. (1984). The relationship among concepts and cognitive maturity in preschool children. *Sex Roles, 10,* 19–31.

Cole, E., & Rothblum, E. (1991). Lesbian sex at menopause: As good or better than ever. In B. Sang, A. Smith, & J. Warshow (Eds), *Lesbians at midlife*. San Francisco: Spinsters/Aunt Lute.

Cole, J. B. (Ed.). (1986). *All American women: Lines that divide, ties that bind*. New York: Free Press.

Cole, J. R. (1979). *Fair science*. New York: Free Press.

Cole, J. R., & Zuckerman, H. (1987). Marriage, motherhood, and research performance in science. *Scientific American, 256,* 119–125.

Coleman, J. C. (with S. Basow & P. Railey). (1984). *Intimate relationships, marriage, and family*. Indianapolis, IN: Bobbs-Merrill.

Coleman, L. M., Antonucci, T. C., & Adelmann, P. K. (1987). Role involvement, gender, and well-being. In F. J. Crosby (Ed.), *Spouse, parent, worker: On gender and multiple roles* (pp. 138–153). New Haven: Yale University Press.

Coleman, M., & Ganong, L. H. (1985). Love and sex-role stereotypes: Do "macho" men and "feminine" women make better lovers? *Journal of Personality and Social Psychology, 49,* 170–176.

Coles, F. S. (1986). Forced to quit: Sexual harassment complaints and agency response. *Sex Roles, 14,* 81–95.

Collier, J. F., & Rosaldo, M. Z. (1981). Politics and gender in simple societies. In S. Ortner & H. Whitehead (Eds.), *Sexual meanings: The cultural construction of gender and sexuality* (pp. 275–329). Cambridge, England: Cambridge University Press.

Collins, G. (1979, June 1). A new look at life with father. *New York Times Magazine*, pp. 30–31 ff.

Collins, K. (1988, December 15). Many older women denied fair share of the gold. *Easton Express*, p. C5.

Collins, N. L., & Read, S. J. (1990). Adult attachment, working models, and relationship quality in dating couples. *Journal of Personality and Social Psychology, 58,* 644–663.

Collins, P. H. (1989). The social construction of Black feminist thought. *Signs: Journal of Women in Culture and Society, 14,* 745–773.

Collins, P. H. (1990). *Black feminist thought: Knowledge, consciousness, and the politics of empowerment*. New York: HarperCollins Academic.

Collison, M. N. (1987, December 9). More young Black men choosing not to go to college. *Chronicle of Higher Education*, pp. Al, A26, A27.

Collison, M. N. (1990, December 12). 20 years later, women on formerly all-male campuses fight to change their institutions' "old boy" images. *Chronicle of Higher Education*, pp. A23, A24.

Collison, M. N. (1991, May 15). Increase in reports of sexual assaults strains campus disciplinary systems. *Chronicle of Higher Education*, pp. A29–30.

Colten, M. A., & Marsh, J. C. (1984). A sex-roles perspective on drug and alcohol use by women. In C. Widom (Ed.), *Sex roles and psychopathology* (pp. 219–248). New York: Plenum.

Coltrane, S. (1988). Father-child relationships and the status of women: A cross-cultural study. *American Journal of Sociology, 93,* 1060–1095.

Comes the revolution. (1978, July 26). *Time*, pp. 54–59.

Condry, J., & Dyer, S. (1976). Fear of success: Attribution of cause to the victim. *Journal of Social Issues, 32*(3), 63–83.

Condry, S. M., Condry, J. C., Jr., & Pogatshnik, L. W. (1983). Sex differences: A study of the ear of the beholder. *Sex Roles, 9,* 697–704.

Connell, R. W. (1987). *Gender and power: Society, the person, and sexual politics*. Stanford, CA: Stanford University Press.

Connell, R. W. (1990). A whole new world: Remaking masculinity in the context of the environmental movement. *Gender and Society, 4,* 452–478.

Connor, J. M., & Serbin, L. A. (1978). Children's responses to stories with male and female characters. *Sex Roles, 4,* 637–645.

Connor, J. M., & Serbin, L. A. (1985). Visual-spatial skill: Is it important for mathematics? Can it be taught? In S. Chipman, L. Brush, & D. Wilson (Eds.), *Women and mathematics: Balancing the equation* (pp. 151–174). Hillsdale, NJ: Erlbaum.

Connor, J. M., Serbin, L. A., & Ender, R. A. (1978). Responses of boys and girls to aggressive, assertive, and passive behaviors of male and female characters. *Journal of Genetic Psychology, 133,* 59–69.

Constantinople, A. (1979). Sex-role acquisition: In search of the elephant. *Sex Roles, 5,* 121–133.

Conway, M., Giannopoulos, C., & Stiefenhofer, K. (1990). Response styles to sadness are related to sex and sex-role orientation. *Sex Roles, 22,* 579–587.

Cook, A. S., Fritz, J. J., McCornack, B. L., & Visperas, C. (1985). Early gender differences in the functional usage of language. *Sex Roles, 12*, 909–915.

Cooke, R. A., & Rousseau, D. M. (1984). Stress and strain from family roles and work-role expectations. *Journal of Applied Psychology, 69*, 252–260.

Coons, P. M., Bowman, E. S., Pellow, T. A., & Schneider, P. (1989). Post-traumatic aspects of the treatment of victims of sexual abuse and incest. *Psychiatric Clinics of North America, 12*, 325–335.

Cooper, H. M. (1979). Statistically combining independent studies: A meta-analysis of sex differences in conformity research. *Journal of Personality and Social Psychology, 37*, 131–146.

Cooper, J., Hall, J., & Huff, C. (1990). Situational stress as a consequence of sex-stereotyped software. *Personality and Social Psychology Bulletin, 16*, 419–429.

Cooper, K., Chassin, L., & Zeiss, A. (1985). The relation of sex-role attitudes to the marital satisfaction and personal adjustment of dual-worker couples with preschool children. *Sex Roles, 12*, 227–241.

Cooper, K. J. (1989, April 28). SATs sex-biased, a think tank says. *Philadelphia Inquirer*, p. 12A.

Corcoran, C. B. (1991, August). *Sexual assault programs: From victim control to feminist social change.* Paper presented at the meeting of the American Psychological Association, San Francisco.

Corcoran, M., Duncan, G. J., & Hill, M. S. (1984). The economic fortunes of women and children: Lessons from the panel study of income dynamics. *Signs: Journal of Women in Culture and Society, 10*, 232–248.

Cordes, C. (1983, December). Researchers make room for father. *APA Monitor*, pp. 1, 9, 10.

Cordes, C. (1985, January). At risk in America. *APA Monitor*, pp. 9–11, 27.

Corea, G., Klein, R. D., Hanmer, J., Holmes, H. B., Hoskins, B., Kishwar, M., Raymond, R., Rowland, R., & Steinbacher, R. (1987). *Man-made women: How new reproductive technologies affect women.* Bloomington: Indiana University Press.

Costos, D. (1990). Gender role identity from an ego developmental perspective. *Sex Roles, 22*, 723–741.

Cota, A. A., & Dion, K. L. (1986). Salience of gender and sex composition of ad hoc groups: An experimental test of distinctiveness theory. *Journal of Personality and Social Psychology, 50*, 770–776.

Cott, N. F. (1987). *The grounding of modern feminism.* New Haven: Yale University Press.

Coughlin, E. K. (1988, September 1). Condition of black men in American society presents challenge for behavioral sciences. *Chronicle of Higher Education*, pp. A4–5.

Courtney, A. E., & Whipple, T. W. (1983). *Sex stereotyping in advertising.* Lexington, MA: D. C. Heath.

Coutts, J. S. (1987). Masculinity-femininity of self-concept: Its effect on the achievement behavior of women. *Sex Roles, 16*, 9–17.

Cowan, C. P., & Cowan, P. A. (1987). Men's involvement in parenthood: Identifying the antecedents and understanding the barriers. In P. W. Berman & F. A. Pedersen (Eds.), *Men's transitions to parenthood: Longitudinal studies of early family experience* (pp. 145–174). Hillsdale, NJ: Erlbaum.

Cowan, G., Drinkard, J., & MacGavin, L. (1984). The effects of target age and gender on the use of power strategies. *Journal of Personality and Social Psychology, 47*, 1391–1398.

Cowan, G., Lee, C., Levy, D., & Snyder, D. (1988). Dominance and inequality in X-rated videocassettes. *Psychology of Women Quarterly, 12*, 299–311.

Cowan, G., & O'Brien, M. (1990). Gender and survival vs. death in slasher films: A content analysis. *Sex Roles, 23*, 187–196.

Cox, S., & Radloff, L. S. (1984). Depression in relation to sex roles: Differences in learned susceptibility and precipitating factors. In C. Widom (Ed.), *Sex roles and psychopathology* (pp. 123–144). New York: Plenum.

Craft, C. (1988). *Too old, too ugly, and not deferential to men: An anchorwoman's courageous battle against sex discrimination.* Rockland, CA: Prima.

Craig, J. M., & Sherif, C. W. (1986). The effectiveness of men and women in problem-solving groups as a function of group gender composition. *Sex Roles, 14*, 453–466.

Craig, T. J., & Lin, S. P. (1984). Sex differences in mortality rate among long-stay psychiatric inpatients. *Sex Roles, 10*, 725–732.

Crane, M., & Markus, H. (1982). Gender identity: The benefits of a self-schema approach. *Journal of Personality and Social Psychology, 43*, 1195–1197.

Crawford, M. (1988). Agreeing to differ: Feminist epistemologies and women's ways of knowing. In M. Crawford & M. Gentry (Eds.), *Gender and thought: Psychological perspectives* (pp. 128–145). New York: Springer-Verlag.

Crawford, M., & MacLeod, M. (1990). Gender in the college classroom: An assessment of the "chilly climate" for women. *Sex Roles, 23*, 101–122.

Crawford, M., & Marecek, J. (1989). Psychology reconstructs the female: 1968–1988. *Psychology of Women Quarterly, 13*, 147–165.

Crawford, S. (1987). Lesbian families: Psychosocial stress and the family-building process. In the Boston Lesbian Psychologies Collective (Ed.), *Lesbian psychologies: Explorations and challenges* (pp. 195–214). Urbana: University of Illinois Press.

Creager, E. (1989, January 23). Ignored for years, drive for ERA is on again. *Easton Express*, p. A6.

Crocker, J., & Major, B. (1989). Social stigma and self-esteem: The self-protective properties of stigma. *Psychological Review, 96*, 608–630.

Croghan, R. (1991). First-time mothers' accounts of inequality in the division of labour. *Feminism and Psychology, 1*, 221–246.

Crohan, S. E., Antonucci, T. C., Adelmann, P. K., & Coleman, L. M. (1989). Job characteristics and well-being at midlife: Ethnic and gender comparisons. *Psychology of Women Quarterly, 13*, 223–235.

Crombie, G. (1983). Women's attribution patterns and their relation to achievement: An examination of within-sex differences. *Sex Roles, 9*, 1171–1182.

Cronkite, R. C., & Moos, R. H. (1984). Sex and marital status in relation to treatment and outcome of alcoholic patients. *Sex Roles, 11*, 93–112.

Crosbie-Burnett, M., Skyles, A., & Becker-Haven, J. (1988). Exploring stepfamilies from a feminist perspective. In S. M. Dornbusch & M. H. Strober (Eds.), *Feminism, children, and the new families* (pp. 297–326). New York: Guilford.

Crosby, F. J. (1982). *Relative deprivation and working women.* New York: Oxford University Press.

Crosby, F. J. (Ed.) (1987). *Spouse, parent, worker: On gender and multiple roles.* New Haven: Yale University Press.

Crosby, F. J., & Clayton, S. (1990). Affirmative action and the issue of expectancies. *Journal of Social Issues, 46*(2), 61–79.

Crosby, F. J., Pufall, A., Snyder, R. C., O'Connell, M., & Whalen, P. (1989). The denial of personal disadvantage among you, me, and all the other ostriches. In M. Crawford & M. Gentry (Eds.), *Gender and thought: Psychological perspectives* (pp. 79–99). New York: Springer-Verlag.

Cross, W. E. (1978). The Thomas and Cross models of psychological nigrescence: A review. *Journal of Black Psychology, 5*, 13–31.

Croteau, J. M., & Burda, P. C., Jr. (1983). Structured group programming on men's roles: A creative approach to change. *Personnel and Guidance Journal, 62* 243–245.

Crovitz, E., & Steinmann, A. (1980). A decade later: Black-White attitudes toward women's familial role. *Psychology of Women Quarterly, 5,* 170–176.

Croxton, J. S., Chiacchia, D., & Wagner, C. (1984, April). *Gender differences in attitudes toward sports and reactions to competitive situations.* Paper presented at the meeting of the Eastern Psychological Association, Baltimore.

Croxton, J. S., & Klonsky, B. G. (1982). Sex differences in causal attributions for success and failure in real and hypothetical sport settings. *Sex Roles, 8,* 399–409.

Cruikshank, M. (1982). *Lesbian studies: Present and future.* Old Westbury, NY: Feminist Press.

Cuca, J. (1976, March). Women psychologists and marriage: A bad match? *American Psychologist,* p. 3.

Culp, R. E., Cook, A. S., & Housley, P. C. (1983). A comparison of observed and reported adult-infant interactions: Effects of perceived sex. *Sex Roles, 9,* 475–479.

Cunningham, J. D., & Antill, J. K. (1984). Changes in masculinity and femininity across the family life cycle: A reexamination. *Developmental Psychology, 20,* 1135–1141.

Cunningham, J. D., Braiker, H., & Kelley, H. H. (1982). Marital-status and sex differences in problems reported by married and cohabitating couples. *Psychology of Women Quarterly, 6,* 415–427.

Cunningham, M. R. (1989). Reactions to heterosexual opening gambits: Female selectivity and male responsiveness. *Personality and Social Psychology Bulletin, 15,* 27–41.

Dabbs, J. M., Jr., & Morris, R. (1990). Testosterone, social class, and antisocial behavior in a sample of 4462 men. *Psychological Science, 1,* 209–211.

Dahlberg, F. (Ed.). (1981). *Woman the gatherer.* New Haven: Yale University Press.

Dally, A. (1983). *Inventing motherhood: The consequences of an ideal.* New York: Schocken.

Dalton, K. *The menstrual cycle.* New York: Pantheon.

Daly, K. (1989). Rethinking judicial paternalism: Gender, work-family relations, and sentencing. *Gender and Society, 3,* 9–36.

Daly, M. (1974). *Beyond God the father.* Boston: Beacon Press.

Daly, M. (1978). *Gyn/ecology.* Boston: Beacon Press.

Dan, A. J. (1976). Patterns of behavioral and mood variation in men and women: Variability and the menstrual cycle. *Dissertation Abstracts International, 37,* 3145B–3146B.

Dan, A. J. (1979). The menstrual cycle and sex-related differences in cognitive variability. In M. A. Wittig & A. C. Petersen (Eds.), *Sex-related differences in cognitive functioning: Developmental issues* (pp. 241–260). New York: Academic Press.

Dangers rise for young black males. (1990, December 7). *Morning Call,* p. A3.

Daniels, P., & Weingarten, K. (1988). The fatherhood click: The timing of parenthood in men's lives. In P. Bronstein & C. P. Cowan (Eds.), *Fatherhood today: Men's changing role in the family* (pp. 36–52). New York: Wiley.

Danziger, N. (1983). Sex-related differences in the aspirations of high school students. *Sex Roles, 9,* 683–695.

Darden, B. J. (1983). Sex, sex-role identity, and self-control: Correlates of negative and positive assertion. *Dissertation Abstracts International, 43,* 2693B–2694B.

David, D. S., & Brannon, R. (Eds.). (1976). *The 49-percent majority: The male sex role.* Reading MA: Addison-Wesley.

David, H. P., & Baldwin, W. P. (1979). Childbearing and child development. *American Psychologist, 34,* 866–871.

Davidson, C. V., & Abramowitz, S. I. (1980). Sex bias in clinical judgment: Later empirical returns. *Psychology of Women Quarterly, 4,* 377–395.

Davidson, L. R. (1981). Pressures and pretense: Living with gender stereotypes. *Sex Roles, 7,* 331–347.

Davidson, L. R., & Duberman, L. (1982). Friendship: Communication and interactional patterns in same-sex dyads. *Sex Roles, 8,* 809–822.

Davidson, N. (1988). *The failure of feminism.* Buffalo: Prometheus.

Davis, A. J. (1984). Sex-differentiated behavior in nonsexist picture books. *Sex Roles, 11,* 1–16.

Davis, A. Y. (1986). Racism, birth control, and reproductive rights. In J. B. Cole (Ed.), *All American women: Lines that divide, ties that bind* (pp. 239–255). New York: Free Press.

Davis, D. M. (1990). Portrayals of women in prime-time network television: Some demographic characteristics. *Sex Roles, 23,* 325–332.

Davis, K. E. (1985, February). Near and dear: Friendship and love compared. *Psychology Today,* pp. 22, 24–28, 30.

Davis, K. E., & Todd, M. J. (1982). Friendship and love relationships. *Advances in Descriptive Psychology, 2,* 79–122.

Davis, M., & Weitz, S. (1982). Sex differences in body movements and positions. In C. Mayo & N. Henley (Eds.), *Gender and nonverbal behavior* (pp. 81–92). New York: Springer-Verlag.

Davis, M. H., & Oathout, H. A. (1987). Maintenance of satisfaction in romantic relationships: Empathy and relational competence. *Journal of Personality and Social Psychology, 53,* 397–410.

Davis, S. (1990). Men as success objects and women as sex objects: A study of personal advertisements. *Sex Roles, 23,* 43–50.

Davis, S. E. (Ed.) (1988). *Women under attack: Victories, backlash and the fight for reproductive freedom.* Boston: South End Press.

Davis, S. W., Williams, J. E., & Best, D. L. (1982). Sex trait stereotypes in the self- and peer descriptions of third grade children. *Sex Roles, 8,* 315–331.

Deaux, K. (1976). *The behavior of women and men.* Monterey, CA: Brooks/Cole.

Deaux, K. (1979). Self-evaluations of male and female managers. *Sex Roles, 5,* 571–580.

Deaux, K., & Emswiller, T. (1974). Explanations of successful performance on sex-linked tasks: What's skill for the male is luck for the female. *Journal of Personality and Social Psychology, 29,* 80–85.

Deaux, K., & Hanna, R. (1984). Courtship in the personals column: The influence of gender and sexual orientation. *Sex Roles, 11,* 363–375.

Deaux, K., & Kite, M. E. (1987). Thinking about gender. In B. B. Hess & M. M. Ferree (Eds.), *Analyzing gender: A handbook of social science research* (pp. 92–117). Newbury Park, CA: Sage.

Deaux, K., Kite, M. E., & Lewis, L. (1985). Clustering and gender schemata: An uncertain link. *Personality and Social Psychology Bulletin, 11,* 387–397.

Deaux, K., & Lewis, L. (1984). Structure of gender stereotypes: Interrelationships among components and gender label. *Journal of Personality and Social Psychology, 46,* 991–1004.

Deaux, K., & Major, B. (1987). Putting gender into context: An interactive model of gender-related behavior. *Psychological Bulletin, 94,* 369–389.

Deaux, K., White, L. J., & Farris, E. (1975). Skill or luck: Field and lab studies of male and female preferences. *Journal of Personality and Social Psychology, 32,* 629–636.

Deaux, K., Winton, W., Crowley, M., & Lewis, L. L. (1985). Level of categorization and content of gender stereotypes. *Social Cognition, 3,* 145–167.

DeBeauvoir, S. (1953). *The second sex.* (H. M. Parshey, Trans.). New York: Knopf.

DeBold, J. F., & Luria, Z. (1983). Gender identity, interactionism, and politics: A reply to Rogers & Walsh. *Sex Roles, 9,* 1101–1108.

DeChick, J. (1988, July 19). Most mothers want a job, too. *USA Today,* p. Dl.

Deckard, B. S. (1983). *The women's movement: Political, socioeconomic, and* psychological issues. New York: Harper & Row.

DeGregorio, E., & Carver, C. S. (1980). Type A behavior pattern, sex role orientation, and psychological adjustment. *Journal of Personality and Social Psychology, 39,* 286–293.

De Lacoste-Utamsing, C., & Holloway, R. L. (1982). Sexual dimorphism in the human corpus callosum. *Science, 216,* 1431–1432.

DeLamater, J. (1987). Gender differences in sexual scenarios. In K. Kelley (Ed.), *Females, males, and sexuality: Theories and research* (pp. 127–139). Albany: State University of New York Press.

Del Boca, F. K., & Ashmore, R. D. (1980). Sex stereotypes through the life cycle. In L. Wheeler (Ed.), *Review of Personal and Social Psychology,* Vol. 1. (pp. 163–192). Beverly Hills, CA: Sage.

Del Boca, F. K., Ashmore, R. D., & McManus, M. A. (1986). Gender-related attitudes. In R. D. Ashmore & F. K. Del Boca (Eds.), *The social psychology of female-male relations: A critical analysis of central concepts* (pp. 121–163). New York: Academic Press.

De Lisi, R., & Gallagher, A. M. (1991). Understanding of gender stability and constancy in Argentinean children. *Merrill-Palmer Quarterly, 37,* 483–502.

De Lisi, R., & McGillicuddy-De Lisi, A. V. (1988). Individual differences in adolescents' horizontality representation: Associations with vocational major and gender. *Merrill-Palmer Quarterly, 34,* 437–449.

De Lisi, R., & Soundranayagam, L. (1990). The conceptual structure of sex stereotypes in college students. *Sex Roles, 23,* 593–611.

Delk, J. L., Madden, R. B., Livingston, M., & Ryan, T. T. (1986). Adult perceptions of the infant as a function of gender labeling and observer gender. *Sex Roles, 15,* 57–534.

Della Selva, P., & Dusek, J. B. (1984). Sex role orientation and resolution of Eriksonian crises during the late adolescent years. *Journal of Personality and Social Psychology, 47,* 204–212.

DeLucia, J. L. (1987). Gender role identity and dating behavior: What is the relationship? *Sex Roles, 17,* 153–161.

Demare, D., Briere, J., & Lips, H. M. (1988). Violent pornography and self-reported likelihood of sexual aggression. *Journal of Research in Personality, 22,* 140–153.

D'Emilio, J., & Freedman, E. B. (1988). *Intimate matters: A history of sexuality in America.* New York: Harper & Row.

Denmark, F., Russo, N. F., Frieze, I. H., & Sechzer, J. A. (1988). Guidelines for avoiding sexism in psychological research: A report of the Ad Hoc Committee on Nonsexist Research. *American Psychologist, 43,* 582–585.

Denny, N. W., Field, J. K., & Quadagno, D. (1984). Sex differences in sexual needs and desires. *Archives of Sexual Behavior, 13,* 233–245.

Derlega, V. J., & Chaikin, A. L. (1976). Norms affecting self-disclosure in men and women. *Journal of Consulting and Clinical Psychology, 44,* 376–380.

Derlega, V. J., Durham, B., Gockel, B., & Sholis, D. (1981). Sex differences in self-disclosure: Effects of topic content, friendship, and partner's sex. *Sex Roles, 7,* 433–447.

Deseran, F. A., & Falk, W. W. (1982). Women as generalized other and self theory: A strategy for empirical research. *Sex Roles, 8,* 283–297.

Desertrain, G. S., & Weiss, M. R. (1988). Being female and athletic: A cause for conflict? *Sex Roles, 18,* 567–582.

DeStefano, L., & Colasanto, D. (1990, February 25). Men have it better, poll says. *Philadelphia Inquirer,* pp. K1, K7.

Deutsch, C. H. (1990a, January 28). Saying no to the "Mommy track." *New York Times,* p. F29.

Deutsch, C. H. (1990b, April 29). Why women walk out on jobs. *New York Times,* p. F27.

Deutsch, F. M., LeBaron, D., & Fryer, M. M. (1987). What is in a smile? *Psychology of Women Quarterly, 11,* 341–351.

Devereux, G. (1937). Institutionalized homosexuality of the Mohave Indians. *Human Biology, 9,* 498–527.

Devlin, P. K., & Cowan, G. A. (1985). Homophobia, perceived fathering, and male intimate relationships. *Journal of Personality Assessment, 49,* 467–473.

Diamond, I., & Orenstein, G. F. (Eds.) (1990). *Reweaving the world: The emergence of ecofeminism.* San Francisco: Sierra Club Books.

Diamond, M. (1982). Sexual identity, monozygotic twins reared in discordant sex roles. A BBC follow-up. *Archives of Sexual Behavior, 11,* 181–186.

Dickie, J. R. (1987). Interrelationships within the mother-father-infant triad. In P. W. Berman & F. A. Pedersen (Eds.), *Men's transitions to parenthood: Longitudinal studies of early family experience* (pp. 113–143). Hillsdale, NJ: Erlbaum.

Dieter, P. (1989, March). *Shooting her with video, drugs, bullets, and promises.* Paper presented at the meeting of the Association of Women in Psychology, Newport, RI.

Dill, B. T. (1979). The dialectics of black womanhood. *Signs: Journal of Women in Culture and Society, 4,* 535–555.

Dimitrovsky, L., Singer, J., & Yinon, Y. (1989). Masculine and feminine traits: Their relation to suitedness for and success in training for traditionally masculine and feminine army functions. *Journal of Personality and Social Psychology, 57,* 839–847.

Dion, K. L., & Cota, A. A. (1991). The Ms. stereotype: Its domain and the role of explicitness in title preference. *Psychology of Women Quarterly, 15,* 403–410.

Dion, K. L., & Schuller, R. A. (1990). Ms. and the manager: A tale of two stereotypes. *Sex Roles, 22,* 569–577.

Dionne, E. J., Jr. (1988, June 19). Why Bush faces a problem winning women's support. *New York Times,* pp. 1, 20.

Dionne, E. J., Jr. (1989, August 22). Struggle for work and family fueling women's movement. *New York Times,* pp. 1, A18.

Dixon, J. (1991, July 29). Number of women in rural poverty growing, U.N. says. *Morning Call,* p. A3.

Dixon, M. (1983). *The future of women.* San Francisco: Synthesis.

Dixson, A. F. (1980). Androgens and aggressive behavior in primates: A review. *Aggressive Behavior, 6,* 37–67.

Dobbins, G. H., & Platz, S. J. (1986). Sex differences in leadership: How real are they? *Academy of Management Review, 11,* 118–127.

Dodge, S. (1990, September 5). Average score on verbal section of '89–90 SAT drops. *Chronicle of Higher Education,* pp. A33–34.

Doerfler, M. C., & Kammer, P. P. (1986). Workaholism, sex, and sex-role stereotyping among female professionals. *Sex Roles, 14,* 551–560.

Doering, C. H., Brodie, H.K.H., Kramer, H. C., Becker, H. B., & Hamburg, D. A. (1974). Plasma testosterone levels and psychological measurements in men over a two-month period. In R. C. Friedman, R. M. Richart, & R. L. Vande Wiele (Eds.), *Sex differences in behavior* (pp. 413–421). New York: Wiley.

Doherty, W. J., & Baldwin, C. (1985). Shift and stability in locus of control during the 1970's: Divergence of the sexes. *Journal of Personality and Social Psychology, 48,* 1048–1053.

Dohrenwend, B. P., & Dohrenwend, B. S. (1976). Sex differences and psychiatric disorders. *American Journal of Sociology, 18,* 1447–1454.

Domhoff, G. W., & Dye, R. R. (1987). *Power elites and organizations.* Newbury Park, CA: Sage.

Domhoff, W. (1981). *Bohemian Grove and other retreats.* New York: Harper & Row.

Donelson, E. (1977). Development of sex-typed behavior and self concept. In E. Donelson & J. Gullahorn (Eds.), *Women: A psychological perspective* (pp. 119–139). New York: Wiley.

Donenberg, G. R., & Hoffman, L. W. (1988). Gender differences in moral development. *Sex Roles, 18,* 701–717.

Donnerstein, E., Linz, D., & Penrod, S. (1987). *The question of pornography: Research findings and policy implications.* New York: Free Press.

Donovan, J. (1985). Feminist theory: *The intellectual traditions of American feminism.* New York: Frederick Ungar.

Dorans, N. J., & Livingston, S. A. (1987). Male-female differences in SAT-Verbal ability among students of high SAT-Mathematical ability. *Journal of Educational Measurement, 24,* 65–71.

Dornbusch, S. M., & Gray, K. D. (1988). Single-parent families. In S. M. Dornbusch & M. H. Strober (Eds.), *Feminism, children, and the new families* (pp. 274–296). New York: Guilford.

Dornbusch, S. M., & Strober, M. H. (Eds.) (1988). *Feminism, children, and the new families.* New York: Guilford.

Doty, R. L., Applebaum, S., Zusho, H., & Settle, R. G. (1985). Sex differences in odor identification ability: A cross-cultural analysis. *Neuropsychologia, 23,* 667–672.

Douglas, C. A. (1987, June). Review of *Feminism unmodified. off our backs,* pp. 12–13.

Douthitt, R. A. (1989). The division of labor within the home: Have gender roles changed? *Sex Roles, 20,* 693–704.

Dovidio, J. F., Ellyson, S. L., Keating, C. F., Heltman, K., & Brown, C. E. (1988). The relationship of social power to visual displays of dominance between men and women. *Journal of Personality and Social Psychology, 54,* 233–242.

Dowd, M. (1983, December 4). Many women in poll equate values of job and family life. *New York Times,* pp. 1, 66.

Dowd, M. (1991, May 20). Bush giving more jobs to women. *Morning Call,* pp. Al, A2.

Dowling, C. (1981). *The Cinderella complex.* New York: Summit Books.

Downey, A. (1984). The relationship of sex-role orientation to self-perceived health status in middle-aged males. *Sex Roles, 11,* 211–225.

Downing, N., & Roush, K. (1984). From passive acceptance to active commitment: A model of feminist identity development for women. *Counseling Psychologist, 13,* 695–709.

Downs, A. C. (1983). Letters to Santa Claus: Elementary school-age children's sex-typed toy preferences in a natural setting. *Sex Roles, 9,* 159–163.

Downs, A. C., & Langlois, J. H. (1988). Sex typing: Construct and measurement issues. *Sex Roles, 18,* 87–100.

Doyle, J. A. (1983). *The male experience.* Dubuque, IA: William C. Brown.

Doyle, J. (1989). *The male experience* (2nd ed.). Dubuque, IA: William C. Brown.

Dreher, G. F., Dougherty, T. W., & Whitely, W. (1989). Influence tactics and salary attainment: A gender-specific analysis. *Sex Roles, 20,* 535–550.

Dreyfous, L. (1991a, March 17). Childless couples confront family norms of society. *Morning Call,* pp. A6, A7.

Dreyfous, L. (1991b, April 21). Gay couples are redefining parenthood. *Morning Call,* pp. A24, A25.

Drummond, H. (1977, September–October). The epidemics nobody tries to treat. *Mother Jones,* pp. 11–12.

Dubbert, J. L. (1979). *A man's place: Masculinity in transition.* Englewood Cliffs, NJ: Prentice-Hall.

DuBois, D. L., & Hirsch, B. J. (1990). School and neighborhood friendship patterns of blacks and whites in early adolescence. *Child Development, 61,* 524–536.

DuBois, E. C., Kelly, G. P., Kennedy, E. L., Korsmeyer, C. W., & Robinson, L. S. (1985). *Feminist scholarship: Kindling in the groves of academe.* Urbana: University of Illinois Press.

Duckett, J. (1990, May 3). A bellyful of empathy. *Morning Call,* pp. Dl, Dll.

Dugger, K. (1988). Social location and gender-role attitudes: A comparison of Black and White women. *Gender and Society, 2,* 425–448.

Dullea, G. (1983, October 31). When parents work on different shifts. *New York Times,* p. B12.

Dullea, G. (1985, June 3). On corporate ladder, beauty can hurt. *New York Times,* p. C13.

Duncan, P. D., Ritter, P. L., Dornbusch, S. M., Gross, R. T., & Carlsmith, J. M. (1985). The effects of pubertal timing on body image, school behavior, and deviance. *Journal of Youth and Adolescence, 14,* 227–235.

Dunlop, K. H. (1981). Maternal employment and childcare. *Professional Psychology, 12,* 67–75.

Dweck, C. S. (1975). The role of expectations and attributions in the alleviation of learned helplessness. *Journal of Personality and Social Psychology, 31,* 674–685.

Dweck, C. S. (1986). Motivational processes affecting learning. *American Psychologist, 41,* 1040–1048.

Dweck, C. S., Davidson, W., Nelson, S., & Enna, B. (1978). Sex differences in learned helplessness. II. The contingencies of evaluative feedback in the classroom. III. An experimental analysis. *Developmental Psychology, 14,* 268–276.

Dweck, C. S., Goetz, T. E., & Strauss, N. L. (1980). Sex differences in learned helplessness: IV. An experimental and naturalistic study of failure generalization and its mediators. *Journal of Personality and Social Psychology, 38,* 441–452.

Dworkin, A. (1981). *Pornography: Men possessing women.* New York: Perigee/Putnam.

Dworkin, A. (1983). *Right-wing women: The politics of domesticated females.* London: Women's Press.

Dworkin, A. (1987). *Intercourse.* New York: Free Press.

Dworkin, R. J., & Dworkin, A. G. (1983). The effect of intergender conflict on sex-role attitudes. *Sex Roles, 9,* 49–57.

Dwyer, D., & Bruce, J. (Eds.). (1988). *A home divided: Women and income in the Third World.* Stanford, CA: Stanford University Press.

Dziech, B. W., & Weiner, L. (1984). *The lecherous professor: Sexual harassment on campus.* Boston: Beacon Press.

Eagly, A. H. (1987a). Reporting sex differences [Letter to the editor]. *American Psychologist, 42,* 756–757.

Eagly, A. H. (1987b). *Sex differences in social behavior: A social-role interpretation.* Hillsdale, NJ: Erlbaum.

Eagly, A. H. (1990). On the advantages of reporting sex comparisons [Letter to the editor]. *American Psychologist, 45,* 560–562.

Eagly, A. H., & Carli, L. L. (1981). Sex of researchers and sex-typed communications as determinants of sex differences in influenceability: A meta-analysis of social influence studies. *Psychological Bulletin, 90,* 1–20.

Eagly, A. H., & Chrvala, C. (1986). Sex differences in conformity: Status and gender-role interpretations. *Psychology of Women Quarterly, 10,* 203–220.

Eagly, A. H., & Crowley, M. (1986). Gender and helping behavior: A meta-analytic review of the social psychological literature. *Psychological Bulletin, 100,* 283–308.

Eagly, A. H., & Johnson, B. T. (1990). Gender and leadership style: A meta-analysis. *Psychological Bulletin, 108,* 233–256.

Eagly, A. H., & Karau, S. J. (1991). Gender and the emergence of leaders: A meta-analysis. *Journal of Personality and Social Psychology, 60,* 687–710.

Eagly, A. H., & Kite, M. E. (1987). Are stereotypes of nationalities applied to both women and men? *Journal of Personality and Social Psychology, 53,* 451–462.

Eagly, A. H., & Mladinic, A. (1989). Gender stereotypes and attitudes toward women and men. *Personality and Social Psychology Bulletin, 15,* 543–558.

Eagly, A. H., & Steffen, V. J. (1984). Gender stereotypes stem from the distribution of women and men into social roles. *Journal of Personality and Social Psychology, 46,* 735–754.

Eagly, A. H., & Steffen, V. J. (1986a). Gender and aggressive behavior: A meta-analytic review of the social psychological literature. *Psychological Bulletin, 100,* 309–330.

Eagly, A. H., & Steffen, V. J. (1986b). Gender stereotypes, occupational roles, and beliefs about part-time employees. *Psychology of Women Quarterly, 10,* 252–262.

Eagly, A. H., & Wood, W. (1982). Inferred sex differences in status as a determinant of gender stereotypes about social influence. *Journal of Personality and Social Psychology, 43,* 915–928.

Eagly, A. H., & Wood, W. (1985). Gender and influenceability: Stereotype versus behavior. In V. O'Leary, R. Unger, & B. Wallston (Eds.), *Women, gender, and social psychology* (pp. 225–256). Hillsdale, NJ: Erlbaum.

Eagly, A. H., Wood, W., & Fishbaugh, L. (1981). Sex differences in conformity: Surveillance by the group as a determinant of male nonconformity. *Journal of Personality and Social Psychology, 40,* 384–394.

Eaton, W. O., & Enns, L. R. (1986). Sex differences in human motor activity level. *Psychological Bulletin, 100,* 19–28.

Eaton, W. O., & Yu, A. P. (1989). Are sex differences in child motor activity level a function of sex differences in maturational status? *Child Development, 60,* 1005–1011.

Eccles, J. (1985). Sex differences in achievement patterns. In T. B. Sonderegger (Ed.), *Nebraska Symposium on Motivation: Psychology and gender,* Vol. 32 (pp. 97–132). Lincoln, NE: University of Nebraska Press.

Eccles, J. S. (1987a). Adolescence: Gateway to gender-role transcendence. In B. Carter (Ed.), *Current conceptions of sex roles and sex typing: Theory and research* (pp. 225–241). New York: Praeger.

Eccles, J. S. (1987b). Gender roles and women's achievement-related decisions. *Psychology of Women Quarterly, 11,* 135–172.

Eccles, J. S. (1989). Bringing young women to math and science. In M. Crawford & M. Gentry (Eds.), *Gender and thought: Psychological perspectives* (pp. 36–58). New York: Springer-Verlag.

Eccles, J. S., & Jacobs, J. E. (1986). Social forces shape math attitudes and performance. *Signs: Journal of Women in Culture and Society, 11,* 367–380.

Echols, A. (1989). *Daring to be bad: Radical feminism in America 1967–1975.* Minneapolis: University of Minnesota Press.

Edgar, J. (1987, December). Iceland's feminists: Power at the top of the world. *Ms.,* pp. 30–33.

Edmondson, B. (1987, August). Reality on screen. *American Demographics, 9,* p. 21.

Edwards, H. (1988, August). The single-minded pursuit of sports. *Ebony,* pp. 138, 140.

Edwards, V. J., & Spence, J. T. (1987). Gender-related traits, stereotypes, and schemata. *Journal of Personality and Social Psychology, 53,* 146–154.

Egeland, J. A., & Hostetler, A. M. (1983). Amish study, 1: Affective disorders among the Amish. *American Journal of Psychiatry, 140,* 56–62.

Ehrenreich, B. (1979, May). Is success dangerous to your health? *Ms.,* pp. 4, 97–101.

Ehrenreich, B. (1983). *The hearts of men: American dreams and the flight from commitment.* Garden City, NY: Anchor Press.

Ehrenreich, B. (1984, May 20). A feminist's view of the new man. *New York Times Magazine,* pp. 36–41, 44, 46, 48.

Ehrenreich, B. (1987, July–August). The next wave. *Ms.,* pp. 166–168, 216–217.

Ehrenreich, B., & English, D. (1978). *For her own good: 150 years of the experts' advice to women.* Garden City, NY: Anchor Press.

Ehrhardt, A. A. (1985). Psychobiology of gender. In A. Rossi (Ed.), *Gender and the life course* (pp. 81–96). Hawthorne, NY: Aldine.

Ehrhardt, A. A., Meyer-Bahlburg, H.F.L., Rosen, L. R., Feldman, J. F., Veridiano, N. P., Zimmerman, I., & McEwen, B. S. (1985). Sexual orientation after prenatal exposure to exogenous estrogen. *Archives of Sexual Behavior, 14,* 57–77.

Ehrhart, J. K., & Sandler, B. R. (1987). *Looking for more than a few good women in traditionally male fields.* Washington, DC: Association of American Colleges, Project on the Status and Education of Women.

Eichenbaum, L., & Orbach, S. (1987). *Between women: Love, envy, and competition in women's friendships.* New York: Viking.

Eichler, A., & Parron, D. L. (Eds.). (1987). *Women's mental health: Agenda for research.* Rockville, MD: National Institute of Mental Health.

Eichler, M. (1988). *Nonsexist research methods: A practical guide.* Boston: Allen & Unwin.

Eisenberg, A. R. (1988). Grandchildren's perspectives on relationships with grandparents: The influence of gender across generations. *Sex Roles, 19,* 205–217.

Eisenberg, N., & Lennon, R. (1983). Sex differences in empathy and related capacities. *Psychological Bulletin, 94,* 100–131.

Eisenberg, N., Schaller, M., Miller, P. A., Fultz, J., Fabes, R. A., & Shell, R. (1988). Gender-related traits and helping in a nonemergency situation. *Sex Roles, 19,* 605–618.

Eisenstein, Z. (Ed.). (1979). *Capitalist patriarchy and the case for socialist feminism.* New York: Monthly Review Press.

Eisenstein, Z. R. (1989). *The female body and the law.* Berkeley: University of California Press.

Eisenstock. B. (1984). Sex-role differences in children's identification with counter-stereotypical televised portrayals. *Sex Roles, 10,* 417–430.

Eisler, R. (1987). *The chalice and the blade: Our history, our future.* San Francisco: Harper & Row.

Eldridge, N. S., & Gilbert, L. A. (1990). Correlates of relationship satisfaction in lesbian couples. *Psychology of Women Quarterly, 14,* 43–62.

Ellis, L. (1990, April 1). Women stake their claim in macho field. *Philadelphia Inquirer,* pp. D1, D2.

Ellis, L., & Ames, M. A. (1987). Neurohormonal functioning and sexual orientation: A theory of homosexuality-heterosexuality. *Psychological Bulletin, 101,* 233–258.

Elshtain, J. B., & Tobias, S. (Eds.). (1990). *Women, militarism, and war: Essays in history, politics, and social theory.* Savage, MD: Rowan & Littlefield.

Ember, C. R. (1981). A cross-cultural perspective on sex differences. In R. H. Munroe, R. L. Munroe, & B. B. Whiting (Eds.), *Handbook of cross-cultural human development.* New York: Garland STPM Press.

Eme, R. F. (1984). Sex-related differences in the epidemiology of child psychopathology. In C. Widom (Ed.), *Sex roles and psychopathology* (pp. 279–316). New York: Plenum.

Emihovich, C. A., Gaier, E. L., & Cronin, N. C. (1984). Sex-role expectations changes by fathers for their sons. *Sex Roles, 11,* 861–868.

Emmerich, W., Goldman, K. L., Kirsh, B., & Sharabany, R. (1977). Evidence for a transitional phase in the development of gender constancy. *Child Development, 48,* 930–936.

Endres, K. L. (1984). Sex role standards in popular music. *Journal of Popular Culture, 18,* 9–18.

Engeler, A. (1989, October 1). For women golfers, life in the rough. *New York Times Magazine,* pp. 42, 46, 52, 54, 55.

Engels, F. (1972). *The origins of the family, private property, and the state.* (E. Leacock; Ed.) New York: International Publishers. (Original work published 1884)

England, P., & McCreary, L. (1987). Gender inequality in paid employment. In

B. B. Hess & M. M. Ferree (Eds.), *Analyzing gender: A handbook of social science research* (pp. 286–320). Newbury Park, CA: Sage.

Englander-Golden, P., & Barton, G. (1983). Sex differences in absence from work: A reinterpretation. *Psychology of Women Quarterly, 8,* 185–188.

Entwisle, D. R., & Doering, S. (1988). The emergent father role. *Sex Roles, 18,* 119–141.

Epperson, S. E. (1988, September 16). Studies link subtle sex bias in schools with women's behavior in the workplace. *Wall Street Journal,* p. 27.

Epstein, C. F. (1988). *Deceptive distinctions: Sex, gender and the social order.* New Haven, CT: Yale University Press.

Equal employment opportunity guidelines on sexual harassment. (1980). *Federal Register, 45,* 25025.

Erikson, E. (1963). *Childhood and society* (2nd ed.). New York: Norton.

Erikson, E. (1964). Inner and outer space: Reflections on womanhood. *Daedalus, 93,* 582–606.

Erikson, E. (1970). *Identity through the life cycle* (2nd ed.). New York: Norton.

Erkut, S. (1983). Exploring sex differences in expectancy, attribution, and academic achievement. *Sex Roles, 9,* 217–231.

Erkut, S., & Mokros, J. R. (1983). *Professors as models and mentors for college students* (Working Paper No. 65). Wellesley, MA: Wellesley College Center for Research on Women.

Eskinazi, G. (1990, June 3). Athletic aggression and sexual assault. *New York Times,* pp. H1, H4.

Estrich, S. (1987). *Real rape.* Cambridge, MA: Harvard University Press.

Etaugh, C. (1980). Effects of nonmaternal care on children. *American Psychologist, 35,* 309–319.

Etaugh, C., & Duits, T. (1990). Development of gender discrimination: Role of stereotypic and counterstereotypic gender cues. *Sex Roles, 23,* 215–222.

Etaugh, C., & Foresman, E. (1983). Evaluations of competence as a function of sex and marital status. *Sex Roles, 9,* 759–765.

Etaugh, C., Grinnell, K., & Etaugh, A. (1989). Development of gender labeling: Effect of age of pictured children. *Sex Roles, 21,* 769–773.

Etaugh, C., Houtler, B. D., & Ptasnik, P. (1988). Evaluating competence of women and men: Effects of experimenter gender and group gender composition. *Psychology of Women Quarterly, 12,* 191–200.

Etaugh, C., & Nekolny, K. (1990). Effects of employment status and marital status on perceptions of mothers. *Sex Roles, 23,* 273–280.

Etaugh, C., & Riley, S. (1983). Evaluating competence of women and men: Effects of marital and parental status and occupational sex-typing. *Sex Roles, 9,* 943–952.

Etaugh, C., & Stern, J. (1984). Person-perception: Effects of sex, marital status, and sex-typing occupation. *Sex Roles, 11,* 413–424.

Etaugh, C., & Study, G. G. (1989). Perceptions of mothers: Effects of employment status, marital status, and age of child. *Sex Roles, 20,* 59–70.

Etaugh, C., & Whittler, T. E. (1982). Social memory of preschool girls and boys. *Psychology of Women Quarterly, 7,* 170–174.

Etheredge, L. (1978). *A world of men: Private sources of American foreign policy.* Cambridge, MA: MIT Press.

Ethier, K., & Deaux, K. (1990). Hispanic in Ivy: Assessing identity and perceived threat. *Sex Roles, 22,* 427–440.

Etienne, M., & Leacock, E. (1980). *Women and colonization.* New York: Praeger.

Evans, G., & Fields, C. M. (1985, February 20). Equal-employment agency to focus its probes on individual victims of bias. *Chronicle of Higher Education,* p. 25.

Evans, R. G. (1984). Hostility and sex guilt: Perceptions of self and others as a function of gender and sex-role orientation. *Sex Roles, 10,* 207–215.

Evans, S. M., & Nelson, B. J. (1989). *Wage justice: Comparable worth and the paradox of technocratic reform.* Chicago: University of Chicago Press.

Eyes on the prize: Black women in politics. (1989, April). *Psychology Today,* p. 10.

Eysenck, H. J., & Nias, D.K.B. (1978). *Sex, violence and the media.* New York: Harper Colophon.

Fagenson, E. A. (1990). Perceived masculine and feminine attributes examined as a function of individuals' sex and level in the organizational power hierarchy: A test of four theoretical perspectives. *Journal of Applied Psychology, 75,* 204–211.

Fagley, N. S., & Miller, P. M. (1990). The effect of framing on choice: Interactions with risk-taking propensity, cognitive style, and sex. *Personality and Social Psychology Bulletin, 16,* 496–510.

Fagot, B. I. (1977). Consequences of moderate cross-gender behavior in preschool children. *Child Development, 48,* 902–907.

Fagot, B. I. (1978). The influence of sex of child on parental reaction to toddler behaviors. *Child Development, 49,* 459–465.

Fagot, B. I. (1981a). Male and female teachers: Do they treat boys and girls differently? *Sex Roles, 7,* 263–271.

Fagot, B. I. (1981b). Stereotypes versus behavioral judgements of sex differences in young children. *Sex Roles, 7,* 1093–1096.

Fagot, B. I. (1984). Teacher and peer reactions to boys' and girls' play styles. *Sex Roles, 11,* 691–702.

Fagot, B. I. (1985). A cautionary note: Parents' socialization of boys and girls. *Sex Roles, 12,* 471–476.

Fagot, B. I., & Hagan, R. (1985). Aggression in toddlers: Responses to the assertive acts of boys and girls. *Sex Roles, 12,* 341–351.

Fagot, B. I., Hagan, R., Leinbach, M. D., & Kronsberg, S. (1985). Differential reactions to assertive and communicative acts of toddler boys and girls. *Child Development, 56,* 1499–1505.

Fagot, B. I., & Leinbach, M. D. (1987). Socialization of sex roles within the family. In B. Carter (Ed.), *Current conceptions of sex roles and sex typing: Theory and research* (pp. 89–100). New York: Praeger.

Fagot, B. I., & Leinbach, M. D. (1989). The young child's gender schema: Environmental input, internal organization. *Child Development, 60,* 663–672.

Fain, T. C., & Anderton, D. L. (1987). Sexual harassment: Organizational context and diffuse status. *Sex Roles, 17,* 291–311.

Falbo, T. (1982). PAQ types and power strategies used in intimate relationships. *Psychology of Women Quarterly, 6,* 399–405.

Falbo, T., & Peplau, L. A. (1980). Power strategies in intimate relationships. *Journal of Personality and Social Psychology, 38,* 618–628.

Falk, P. J. (1989). Lesbian mothers: Psychosocial assumptions in family law. *American Psychologist, 44,* 941–947.

Faludi, S. (1991). *Backlash: The undeclared war against American women.* New York: Crown Publ.

Farkas, G., Grobe, R. P., Sheehan, D., & Shuan, Y. (1990). Cultural resources and school success: Gender, ethnicity, and poverty groups within an urban school district. *American Sociological Review, 55,* 127–142.

Farmer, H., & Sidney, J. S. (1985). Sex equity in career and vocational education. In S. Klein (Ed.), *Handbook for achieving sex equity through education.* Baltimore: Johns Hopkins University Press.

Farr, K. A. (1988). Dominance bonding through the Good Old Boys Sociability Group. *Sex Roles, 18,* 259–278.

Farrell, M. P. (1986). Friendship between men. *Marriage and Family Review, 9,* 163–197.

Farrell, W. (1974). *The liberated man.* New York: Random House.

Farrell, W. (1982, April). Risking sexual rejection: Women's last frontier? *Ms.,* p. 100.

Farrell, W. (1987). *Why men are the way they are*. New York: McGraw-Hill.

Farrell, W. (1991, May–June). Men as success objects. *Utne Reader*, pp. 81–84.

Fasteau, M. F. (1974). *The male machine*. New York: McGraw-Hill.

Faulkner, E. E., Holandsworth, J. G., Jr., & Thomas, L. M. (1983, November). *Social perceptions of Type A vs. Type B behavior: A replication and extension.* Paper presented at the meeting of the Association for the Advancement of Behavior Therapy.

Fausto-Sterling, A. (1985). *Myths of gender: Biological theories about women and men.* New York: Basic Books.

Fay, R. E., Turner, C. F., Klassen, A. D., & Gagnon, J. H. (1989). Prevalence and patterns of same-gender sexual contact among men. *Science, 243*, 338–348.

Feather, N. T. (1984). Masculinity, femininity, psychological androgyny, and the structure of values. *Journal of Personality and Social Psychology, 47*, 604–620.

Feather, N. T. (1985). Masculinity, femininity, self-esteem, and subclinical depression. *Sex Roles, 12*, 491–500.

Feather, N. T., & Simon, J. C. (1975). Reactions to male and female success and failure in sex-linked occupations: Impressions of personality, causal attributions and perceived likelihood of different consequences. *Journal of Personality and Social Psychology, 31*, 20–31.

Fedele, N. M., & Harrington, E. A. (1990). *Women's groups: How connections heal* (Working Paper No. 47). Wellesley, MA: The Stone Center, Wellesley College.

Feild, H. S. (1978). Attitudes toward rape: A comparative analysis of police, rapists, crisis counselors, and citizens. *Journal of Personality and Social Psychology, 36*, 156–178.

Fein, R. (1978). Research on fathering: Social policy, and an emergent perspective. *Journal of Social Issues, 34*(1), 122–135.

Feingold, A. (1988). Cognitive gender differences are disappearing. *American Psychologist, 43*, 95–103.

Feinman, S. (1981). Why is cross-sex-role behavior more approved for girls than for boys? A status characteristic approach. *Sex Roles, 7*, 289–300.

Feinman, S. (1984). A status theory of the evaluation of sex-role and age-role behavior. *Sex Roles, 10*, 445–456.

Feiring, C., & Lewis, M. (1987). The child's social network: Sex differences from three to six years. *Sex Roles, 17*, 621–636.

Feldberg, R. L. (1984). Comparable worth: Toward theory and practice in the United States. *Signs: Journal of Women in Culture and Society, 10*, 311–328.

Feldman, N. S., & Brown, E. (1984, April). *Male vs. female differences in control strategies: What children learn from Saturday morning television.* Paper presented at the meeting of the Eastern Psychological Association, Baltimore.

Feldman, S. S., & Nash, S. C. (1984). The transition from expectancy to parenthood: Impact of the firstborn child on men and women. *Sex Roles, 11*, 61–78.

Feldman-Summers, S., & Ashworth, C. D. (1981). Factors related to intentions to report a rape. *Journal of Social Issues, 37*, 53–70.

Feldman-Summers, S., Montano, D. E., Kasprzyk, D., & Wagner, B. (1980). Influence attempts when competing views are gender-related: Sex as credibility. *Psychology of Women Quarterly, 5*, 311–320.

Feldstein, J. H., & Feldstein, S. (1982). Sex differences on televised toy commercials. *Sex Roles, 8*, 581–587.

Ferguson, A. (1989). *Blood at the root: Motherhood, sexuality, and male dominance.* London: Pandora.

Ferguson, L. R. (1977). The woman in the family. In E. Donelson & J. Gullahorn (Eds.), *Women: A psychological perspective* (pp. 214–227). New York: Wiley.

Ferguson, M. (1983). *Forever feminine: Women's magazines and the cult of femininity.* Exeter, NH: Heinemann Educational Books.

Ferrante, C. L., Haynes, A. M., & Kingsley, S. M. (1988). Image of women in television advertising. *Journal of Broadcasting & Electronic Media, 32*, 231–237.

Ferree, M. M. (1983). The women's movement in the working class. *Sex Roles, 9*, 493–505.

Ferree, M. M., & Hall, E. J. (1990). Visual images of American society: Gender and race in introductory sociology textbooks. *Gender and Society, 4*, 500–533.

Ferree, M. M., & Hess, B. B. (1985). *Controversy and coalition: The new feminist movement.* Boston: G. K. Hall/Twayne.

Fewer black men going to college. (1989, January 14). *Easton Express*, p. A16.

Fidell, L. S. (1981). Sex differences in psychotropic drug use. *Professional Psychology, 12*, 156–162.

Fidell, L. S. (1984). Sex roles in medicine. In C. Widom (Ed.), *Sex roles and psychopathology* (pp. 375–389). New York: Plenum.

Fiebert, M. (1987). Some perspectives on the men's movement. *Men's Studies Review, 4*(4), 8–10.

Filene, P. G. (1986). *Him/her/self: Sex roles in modern America* (2nd ed.). Baltimore: Johns Hopkins University Press.

Fine, G. A. (1987a). One of the boys: Women in male-dominated settings. In M. S. Kimmel (Ed.), *Changing men: New directions in research on men and masculinity* (pp. 131–147). Newbury Park, CA: Sage.

Fine, G. A. (1987b). *With the boys: Little League baseball and preadolescent culture.* Chicago: University of Chicago Press.

Fine, M. (1987). Why urban adolescents drop into and out of high school. In G. Natriello (Ed.), *School dropouts: Patterns and policies* (pp. 89–105). New York: Teachers College Press.

Fine, M. (1988). Sexuality, schooling, and adolescent females: The missing discourse of desire. *Harvard Educational Review, 58*, 29–53.

Fine, M., & Gordon, S. M. (1989). Feminist transformations of/despite psychology. In M. Crawford & M. Gentry (Eds.), *Gender and thought: Psychological perspectives* (pp. 146–174). New York: Springer-Verlag.

Fine, M. A., Moreland, J. R., & Schweibel, A. I. (1983). Long-term effects of divorce on parent-child relationships. *Developmental Psychology, 19*, 703–713.

Fink, D. (1983, April 19). The sexes agree more about sex. *USA Today*, pp. 1D–2D.

Finkelhor, D. (1984). *Child sexual abuse: Theory and research.* New York: Free Press.

Finlay, B., Starnes, C. E., & Alvarez, F. B. (1985). Recent changes in sex-role ideology among divorced men and women: Some possible causes and implications. *Sex Roles, 12*, 637–653.

Finley, N. J. (1989). Theories of family labor as applied to gender differences in caregiving for elderly parents. *Journal of Marriage and the Family, 51*, 79–86.

Finn, J. D. (1980). Sex differences in educational outcomes. A cross-national study. *Sex Roles, 6*, 9–26.

Finney, J. C., Brandsma, J. M., Tondoro, M., & Lemaistre, G. (1975). A study of transsexuals seeking gender reassignment. *American Journal of Psychology, 132*, 962–967.

Fiorentine, R. (1988). Increasing similarity in the values and life plans of male and female college students? Evidence and implications. *Sex Roles, 18*, 143–158.

Fiorenza, E. S. (1985). *Bread not stone: The challenge of feminist biblical interpretation.* Boston: Beacon Press.

Firestone, S. (1970). *The dialectic of sex.* New York: Morrow.

Firth, M. (1982). Sex discrimination in job opportunities for women. *Sex Roles, 8*, 891–901.

Fischer, G. J. (1987). Hispanic and majority student attitudes toward forcible date rape as a function of differences in attitudes toward women. *Sex Roles, 17*, 93–101.

Fischer, L. R. (1981). Transitions in the mother-daughter relationship. *Journal of Marriage and the Family, 43*, 613–622.

Fisher, S., & Greenberg, R. P. (1979). Masculinity-femininity and response to somatic discomfort. *Sex Roles, 5*, 453–485.

Fisher, W. R., & Byrne, D. (1978). Sex differences in response to erotica? Love versus lust. *Journal of Personality and Social Psychology, 36*, 117–125.

Fisk, W. R. (1985). Responses to "neutral" pronoun presentations and the development of sex-biased responding. *Developmental Psychology, 21*, 481–485.

Fiske, S. T., Bersoff, D. N., Borgida, E., Deaux, K., & Heilman, M. E. (1991). Social science on trial: Use of sex stereotyping research in *Price Waterhouse v. Hopkins. American Psychologist, 46*, 1049–1060.

Fitzgerald, H. E. (1977). Infants and caregivers: Sex differences as determinants of socialization. In E. Donelson & J. Gullahorn (Eds.), *Women: A psychological perspective* (pp. 101–118). New York: Wiley.

Fitzgerald, L. F., & Ormerod, A. J. (1991). Perceptions of sexual harassment: The influence of gender and academic context. *Psychology of Women Quarterly, 15*, 281–294.

Fitzgerald, L. F., Shullman, S. L., Bailey, N., Richards, M., Swecker, J., Gold, Y., Ormerod, M., & Weitzman, L. (1988). The incidence and dimensions of sexual harassment in academia and the workplace. *Journal of Vocational Behavior, 32*, 152–175.

Fitzgerald, L. F., Weitzman, L. M., Gold, Y., & Ormerod, M. (1988). Academic harassment: Sex and denial in scholarly garb. *Psychology of Women Quarterly, 12*, 329–340.

Fitzpatrick, M. A. (1988). *Between husbands and wives: Communication in marriage.* Newbury Park, CA: Sage.

Fitzpatrick, M. A., & Bochner, A. (1981). Perspectives on self and other: Male-female differences in perceptions of communication behavior. *Sex Roles, 7*, 523–535.

Fivush, R. (1989). Exploring sex differences in the emotional content of mother-child conversations about the past. *Sex Roles, 20*, 675–691.

Flaherty, J. F., & Dusek, J. B. (1980). An investigation of the relationship between psychological androgyny and components of self-concept. *Journal of Personality and Social Psychology, 38*, 984–992.

Flam, F. (1991). Still a "chilly climate" for women? *Science, 252*, 1604–1606.

Flanders, L. (1990, November–December). Military women and the media. *New Directions for Women*, pp. 1, 9.

Flax, J. (1981). A materialist theory of women's status. *Psychology of Women Quarterly, 6*, 123–136.

Flax, J. (1987). Postmodernism and gender relations in feminist theory. *Signs: Journal of Women in Culture and Society, 12*, 621–643.

Fleischer, R. A., & Chertkoff, J. M. (1986). Effects of dominance and sex on leader selection in dyadic work groups. *Journal of Personality and Social Psychology, 50*, 94–99.

Fleming, J. (1978). Fear of success, achievement-related motives and behavior in black college women. *Journal of Personality, 46*, 694–716.

Fleming, J. (1982). Fear of success in black male and female graduate students: A pilot study. *Psychology of Women Quarterly, 6*, 327–341.

Fleming, J. (1983). Black women in black and white college environments: The making of a matriarch. *Journal of Social Issues, 39*(3), 41–54.

Fleming, J. (1984). *Blacks in college.* San Francisco: Jossey-Bass.

Foa, U. G., Anderson, B., Converse, J., Jr., Urbansky, W. A., Cawley, M. J., III, Mulhausen, S. M., & Tornblom, K. Y. (1987). Gender-related sexual attitudes: Some crosscultural similarities and differences. *Sex Roles, 16*, 511–519.

Fodor, I. G. (1983). Toward an understanding of male/female differences in phobic anxiety disorders. In I. Al-Issa (Ed.), *Gender and psychopathology* (pp. 179–197). New York: Academic Press.

Fogel, R., & Paludi, M. A. (1984). Fear of success and failure, or norms for achievement? *Sex Roles, 10*, 431–443.

Foot, H. C., Chapman, A. J., & Smith, J. R. (1977). Friendship and social responsiveness in boys and girls. *Journal of Personality and Social Psychology, 35*, 401–411.

Ford, M. R., & Lowery, C. R. (1986). Gender differences in moral reasoning: A comparison of the use of justice and care orientations. *Journal of Personality and Social Psychology. 50*, 777–783.

Foreit, K. G., Agor, T., Byers, J., Larue, J., Lokey, H., Palazzini, M., Patterson, M., & Smith, L. (1980). Sex bias in the newspaper treatment of male-centered and female-centered news stories. *Sex Roles, 6*, 475–480.

Foucault, M. (1978). *The history of sexuality*, Vol. 1 (Robert Hurley, Trans.). New York: Pantheon.

Foushee, H. C., Helmreich, R. L., & Spence, J. T. (1979). Implicit theories of masculinity and feminity: Dualistic or bipolar? *Psychology of Women Quarterly, 3*, 259–269.

Fowers, B. J. (1991). His and her marriage: A multivariate study of gender and marital satisfaction. *Sex Roles, 24*, 209–221.

Fox, L. H. (1981). *The problem of women and mathematics.* New York: Ford Foundation.

Fox, L. H., & Cohn, J. J. (1980). Sex differences in the development of precocious mathematical talent. In L. H. Fox, L. Brody, & D. Tobin (Eds.), *Women and the mathematical mystique* (pp. 94–112). Baltimore: Johns Hopkins University Press.

Fox, M., Gibbs, M., & Auerback, D. (1985). Age and gender dimensions of friendship. *Psychology of Women Quarterly, 9*, 489–502.

Fox-Genovese, E. (1991). *Feminism without illusions: A critique of individualism.* Chapel Hill, NC: University of North Carolina Press.

Frable, D.E.S. (1987). Sex-typed execution and perception of expressive movement. *Journal of Personality and Social Psychology, 53*, 391–396.

Frable, D.E.S. (1989). Sex typing and gender ideology: Two facets of the individual's gender psychology that go together. *Journal of Personality and Social Psychology, 56*, 95–108.

Frable, D. E. S., & Bem, S. L. (1985). If you're gender-schematic, all members of the opposite sex look alike. *Journal of Personality and Social Psychology, 49*, 459–468.

Frank, S. J., McLaughlin, A. M, & Crusco, A. (1984). Sex role attributes, symptom distress, and defensive style among college men and women. *Journal of Personality and Social Psychology, 47*, 182–192.

Franken, M. W. (1983). Sex role expectations in children's vocational aspirations and perceptions of occupations. *Psychology of Women Quarterly, 8*, 59–68.

Franklin, C. W., II. (1984). *The changing definition of masculinity.* New York: Plenum.

Franklin, C. W. (1986). Black male-black female conflict: Individually caused and culturally nurtured. *The Black Family, 6*, 106–112.

Franks, V., & Rothblum, E. D. (Eds.). (1983). *The stereotyping of women: Its effects on mental health.* New York: Springer.

Franzoi, S. L. (1991, August). *Gender role orientation and female body perception.* Paper presented at the meeting of the American Psychological Association, San Francisco.

Freedman, M. (1975, March). Homosexuals may be healthier than straights. *Psychology Today*, pp. 28–32.

Freedman, R. (1986). *Beauty bound.* Lexington, MA: D. C. Heath.

Freeman, H. R. (1979). Sex-role stereotypes, self-concepts, and measured personality characteristics in college women and men. *Sex Roles, 5*, 99–103.

Freeman, H. R. (1987). Structure and content of gender stereotypes: Effects of somatic appearance and trait information. *Psychology of Women Quarterly, 11*, 59–67.

Freeman, J. (1989). Feminist organization and activities from suffrage to women's liberation. In J. Freeman (Ed.), *Women: A feminist perspective* (4th ed.) (pp. 541–555). Mountain View, CA: Mayfield.

Freiberg, P. (1990, December). Lesbian moms can give kids empowering models. *APA Monitor*, p. 33.

Freiberg, P. (1991a, March). Black men may act cool to advertise masculinity. *APA Monitor*, p. 30.

Freiberg, P. (1991b, May). Separate classes for black males? *APA Monitor*, pp. 1, 47.

Freiberg, P. (1991c, July). Parental-notification laws termed harmful. *APA Monitor*, p. 28.

Freimuth, M., & Hornstein, G. A. (1982). A critical examination of the concept of gender. *Sex Roles, 8*, 515–532.

French, M. (1985). *Beyond power: On women, men and morals.* New York: Summit Books.

Freud, S. (1964a). The dissolution of the Oedipus complex. In J. Strachey (Ed. and Trans.), *The standard edition of the complete psychological works of Sigmund Freud,* Vol. 19 (pp. 173–179). London: Hogarth Press. (Original work published 1924)

Freud, S. (1964b). Some psychical consequences of the anatomical distinction between the sexes. In J. Strachey (Ed. and Trans.), *The standard edition of the complete psychological works of Sigmund Freud,* Vol. 19 (pp. 243–258). London: Hogarth Press. (Original work published 1925)

Freud, S. (1964c). Three essays on the theory of sexuality. In J. Strachey (Ed. and Trans.), *The standard edition of the complete psychological works of Sigmund Freud,* Vol. 7 (pp. 125–245). London: Hogarth Press. (Original work published 1905)

Friedan, B. (1963). *The feminine mystique.* New York: Dell.

Friedan, B. (1981). *The second stage.* New York: Summit Books.

Friedan, B. (1983, February 27). Twenty years after the feminine mystique. *New York Times Magazine,* pp. 38, 39, 42, 54–57.

Friedan, B. (1985, November 3). How to get the women's movement moving again. *New York Times Magazine,* pp. 27, 28, 66, 67, 84, 85, 89, 98, 106, 108.

Friedl, E. (1975). *Women and men: An anthropologist's view.* New York: Holt, Rinehart & Winston.

Friedman, S. (1983, December 24). Polls: White males Reagan's biggest supporters. *Easton Express,* p. A10.

Friedman, W. J., Robinson, A. B., & Friedman, B. L. (1987). Sex differences in moral judgments? A test of Gilligan's theory. *Psychology of Women Quarterly, 11*, 37–46.

Frieze, I. H., & Ramsey, S. J. (1976). Nonverbal maintenance of traditional sex roles. *Journal of Social Issues, 32*(3), 133–141.

Frisch, H. L. (1977). Sex stereotypes in adult-infant play. *Child Development, 48,* 1671–1675.

Frodi, A., Macaulay, J., & Thome, P. R. (1977). Are women always less aggressive than men? A review of the experimental literature. *Psychological Bulletin, 84,* 634–660.

Fuchs, V. R. (1988). *Women's quest for economic equality.* Cambridge, MA: Harvard University Press.

Fuentes, A., & Ehrenreich, B. (1983). *Women in the global factory.* Boston: South End Press.

Fulbright, K. (1987). The myth of the double-advantage: Black female managers. In M. C. Simms & J. M. Malveaux (Eds.), *Slipping through the cracks: The status of Black women.* New Brunswick, NJ: Transaction.

Funiciello, T. (1990, November–December). The poverty industry: Do government and charities create the poor? *Ms.,* pp. 33–40.

Furstenberg, F. F., Jr. (1990). Divorce and the American family. *Annual Review of Sociology, 16,* 379–403.

Furstenberg, F. F., Jr., Brooks-Gunn, J., & Chase-Lansdale, L. (1989). Teenaged pregnancy and childbearing. *American Psychologist, 44,* 313–320.

Gabriel, S. L., & Smithson, I. (Eds.). (1990). *Gender in the classroom: Power and pedagogy.* Urbana: University of Illinois Press.

Gabriel, T. (1990, October 14). Call of the wildmen. *New York Times Magazine,* pp. 36–39, 42, 47.

Gaeddert, W. P. (1985). Sex and sex role effects on achievement strivings: Dimensions of similarity and difference. *Journal of Personality, 53,* 286–305.

Gailey, C. W. (1987). Evolutionary perspectives on gender hierarchy. In B. B. Hess & M. M. Ferree (Eds.), *Analyzing gender: A handbook of social science research* (pp. 32–67). Newbury Park, CA: Sage.

Galambos, N. L., Almeida, D. M., & Petersen, A. C. (1990). Masculinity, femininity, and sex role attitudes in early adolescence: Exploring gender intensification. *Child Development, 61,* 1905–1914.

Gallagher, S. A. (1989). Predictors of SAT mathematics scores of gifted male and gifted female adolescents. *Psychology of Women Quarterly, 13,* 191–204.

Garcia, N., Kennedy, C., Pearlman, S. F., & Perez, J. (1987). The impact of race and culture differences: Challenges to intimacy in lesbian relationships. In Boston Lesbian Psychologies Collective (Ed.), *Lesbian psychologies: Explorations and challenges* (pp. 142–160). Urbana: University of Illinois Press.

Garfinkel, P. (1985). *In a man's world: Father, son, brother, friend, and other roles men play.* New York: New American Library.

Garfinkel, P. E., & Garner, D. M. (1982). *Anorexia nervosa: A multidimensional perspective.* New York: Brunner/Mazel.

Garfinkle, E., & Morin, S. (1978). Psychologists' attitudes toward homosexual psychotherapeutic clients. *Journal of Social Issues, 34*(3), 101–112.

Garnets, L., & Pleck, J. H. (1979). Sex role identity, androgyny, and sex role transcendence: A sex role strain analysis. *Psychology of Women Quarterly, 3,* 270–283.

Garrett, C. D., Ein, P. L., & Tremaine, L. (1977). The development of gender stereotyping of adult occupations in elementary school children. *Child Development, 48,* 507–517.

Garrison, S., & Jenkins, J. O. (1986, October). Differing perceptions of Black assertiveness as a function of race. *Journal of Multicultural Counseling and Development,* pp. 157–166.

Garrod, A., Beal, C., & Shin, P. (1990). The development of moral orientation in elementary school children. *Sex Roles, 22,* 13–27.

Gartrell, N., & Mosbacher, D. (1984). Sex differences in the naming of children's genitalia. *Sex Roles, 10,* 869–876.

Gary, L. E. (1981). *Black men.* Beverly Hills, CA: Sage.

Gary, L. E. (1987). Predicting interpersonal conflict between men and women: The case of black men. In M. S. Kimmel (Ed.), *Changing men: New directions in research on men and masculinity* (pp. 232–243). Newbury Park, CA: Sage.

Gary, L. E., & Berry, G. L. (1985). Depressive symptomatology among Black men. *Journal of Multicultural Counseling and Development, 13,* 121–129.

Gastil, J. (1990). Generic pronouns and sexist language: The oxymoronic character of masculine generics. *Sex Roles, 23,* 629–643.

Gavzer, B. (1987, May 24). Why more older women are marrying younger men. *Parade Magazine,* pp. 12–13.

Gavzer, B. (1988, August 7). Would you order a mate through the mail? *Parade Magazine,* pp. 14–15.

Geer, J. H., & Broussard, D. B. (1990). Scaling sexual behavior and arousal: Consistency and sex differences. *Journal of Personality and Social Psychology, 58,* 664–671.

Geis, F. L., Boston, M. B., & Hoffman, N. (1985). Sex of authority role models and achievement by men and women: Leadership performance and recognition.

Journal of Personality and Social Psychology, 49, 636–653.

Geis, F. L., Brown, V., Jennings, J., & Porter, N. (1984). TV commercials as achievement scripts for women. *Sex Roles, 10,* 513–525.

Geise, L. A. (1979). The female role in middle class women's magazines from 1955 to 1976: A content analysis of nonfiction selections. *Sex Roles, 5,* 51–62.

Gelfond, M. (1991). Reconceptualizing agoraphobia: A case study of epistemological bias in clinical research. *Feminism and Psychology, 1,* 247–262.

The gender factor in math. (1980, December 15). *Time,* p. 57.

Genevie, L., & Margolies, E. (1987). *The motherhood report: How women feel about being mothers.* New York: Macmillan.

George, V. D. (1986). Talented adolescent women and the motive to avoid success. *Journal of Multicultural Counseling and Development, 14,* 132–139.

Gerbner, G., & Gross, L. (1976, April). The scary world of TV's heavy viewer. *Psychology Today,* pp. 41–45ff.

Gerdes, E. P., Dammann, E. J., & Heilig, K. E. (1988). Perceptions of rape victims and assailants: Effects of physical attractiveness, acquaintance, and subject gender. *Sex Roles, 19,* 141–153.

Gerdes, E. P., Miner, R. S., Maynard, M. A., Dominguez, M. C., & Joshl, R. (1988, March). *White males' bias against Black female job applicants.* Paper presented at the meeting of the Association for Women in Psychology, Bethesda, MD.

Gergen, K. J. (1985). The social constructionist movement in modern psychology. *American Psychologist, 40,* 266–275.

Gergen, M. M. (1988). Building a feminist methodology. *Contemporary Social Psychology, 13*(2), 47–53.

Gergen, M. M. (1990). Finished at 40: Women's development within the patriarchy. *Psychology of Women Quarterly, 14,* 471–493.

Gerrard, M. (1982). Sex, sex guilt, and contraceptive use. *Journal of Personality and Social Psychology, 42,* 153–158.

Gerrard, M. (1987). Sex, sex guilt, and contraceptive use revisited: The 1980s. *Journal of Personality and Social Psychology, 52,* 975–980.

Gerson, K. (1985). *Hard choices: How women decide about work, career, and motherhood.* Berkeley: University of California Press.

Gerson, M. J. (1980). The lure of motherhood. *Psychology of Women Quarterly, 5,* 207–218.

Gerson, M. J. (1985). Feminism and the wish for a child. *Sex Roles, 11,* 389–399.

Gerstel, N., & Gross, H. (1984). *Commuter marriage: A study of work and family.* New York: Guilford.

Gervasio, A. H., & Crawford, M. (1989). Social evaluations of assertiveness: A critique and speech act reformulation. *Psychology of Women Quarterly, 13,* 1–25.

Geschwind, N., & Behan, P. (1982). Left-handedness: Association with immune disease, migraine, and developmental learning disorder. *Proceedings of the National Academy of Sciences, 79,* 5097–5100.

Geschwind, N., & Galaburda, A. M. (1985). Cerebral lateralization: Biological mechanisms, associations, and pathology: I and II. A hypothesis and a program for research. *Archives of Neurology, 42,* 428–459; 521–552.

Gibbs, J. T. (Ed.). (1988). *Young, black, and male in America: An endangered species.* Dover, MA: Auburn House.

Gibbs, N. (1990, Fall). The dreams of youth. *Women: The road ahead* [Special issue, *Time* magazine], pp. 11–14.

Gilbert, L. A. (1985). *Men in dual-career families: Current realities and future prospects.* Hillsdale, NJ: Erlbaum.

Gilbert, L. A. (1988). *Sharing it all. The rewards and struggles of two-career families.* New York: Plenum.

Gilbert, L. A. & Evans, S. L. (1985). Dimensions of same-gender student-faculty role-model relationships. *Sex Roles, 12,* 111–123.

Gilbert, L. A., Gallessich, J. M., & Evans, S. L. (1983). Sex of faculty role model and students' self-perceptions of competency. *Sex Roles, 9,* 597–607.

Gilbert, L. A., Holt, R., & Long, K. M. (1988). Teaching gender-related material: The effect of group sex composition on perceptions of a female instructor. *Sex Roles, 19,* 241–254.

Gilbert, S. M., & Gubar, S. (1985). *The Norton anthology of literature by women: The tradition in English.* New York: Norton.

Gilder, G. (1979, January 28). The case against women in combat. *New York Times Magazine,* pp. 29–30ff.

Gilder, G. (1986). *Men and marriage.* London: Pelican.

Gill, D. L. (1986, August). *Gender differences in competitiveness.* Paper presented at the meeting of the American Psychological Association, Washington, DC.

Gill, S., Stockard, J., Johnson, M., & Williams, S. (1987). Measuring gender differences: The expressive dimension and critique of androgyny scales. *Sex Roles, 17,* 375–400.

Gilligan, C. (1982). *In a different voice: Psychological theory and women's development.* Cambridge, MA: Harvard University Press.

Gilligan, C., & Attanucci, J. (1988). Two moral orientations. In C. Gilligan, J. V. Ward, & J. M. Taylor (Eds.), *Mapping the moral domain* (pp. 73–86). Cambridge, MA: Harvard University Press.

Gilligan, C., Lyons, N. P., & Hanmer, T. J. (Eds.). (1990). *Making connections: The relational worlds of adolescent girls at Emma Willard School.* Cambridge, MA: Harvard University Press.

Gilligan, C., & Pollak, S. (1988). The vulnerable and invulnerable physician. In C. Gilligan, J. V. Ward, & J. M. Taylor (Eds.), *Mapping the moral domain* (pp. 245–262). Cambridge, MA: Harvard University Press.

Gilligan, C., Ward, J. V., & Taylor, J. M. (Eds.). (1988). *Mapping the moral domain.* Cambridge, MA: Harvard University Press.

Gilmore, D. D. (1990). *Manhood in the making: Cultural concepts of masculinity.* New Haven: Yale University Press.

Gimbutas, M. (1990). *The language of the goddess.* New York: Harper & Row.

Gitelson, I. B., Petersen, A. C., & Tobin-Richards, M. H. (1982). Adolescents' expectancies of success, self-evaluations, and attributions about performance on spatial and verbal tasks. *Sex Roles, 8,* 411–419.

Glass, J. (1988). Job quits and job changes: The effects of young women's work conditions and family factors. *Gender and Society, 2,* 228–240.

Glenn, N. D., & Weaver, C. N. (1988). The changing relationship of marital status to reported happiness. *Journal of Marriage and the Family, 50,* 317–324.

Glick, P., Zion, C., & Nelson, C. (1988). What mediates sex discrimination in hiring decisions? *Journal of Personality and Social Psychology, 55,* 178–186.

Goffman, E. (1979). *Gender advertisements.* New York: Harper & Row.

Goktepe, J. R., & Schneier, C. E. (1989). Role of sex, gender roles, and attraction in predicting emergent leaders. *Journal of Applied Psychology, 74,* 165–167.

Gold, A. R. (1989, July 2). Sex bias is found pervading courts. *New York Times,* p. 14.

Gold, A. R., & Adams, D. B. (1981). Motivational factors affecting fluctuations of female sexual activity at menstruation. *Psychology of Women Quarterly, 5,* 670–680.

Gold, A. R., Brush, L. R., & Sprotzer, E. R. (1980). Developmental changes in self-perceptions of intelligence and self-confidence. *Psychology of Women Quarterly, 5,* 231–239.

Gold, D., Crombie, G., & Noble, S. (1987). Relations between teachers' judgments of girls' and boys' compliance and intellectual competence. *Sex Roles, 16,* 351–358.

Gold, M., & Yanof, D. S. (1985). Mothers, daughters, and girlfriends. *Journal of Personality and Social Psychology, 49,* 654–659.

Goldberg, A. S., & Shiflett, S. (1981). Goals of male and female college students: Do traditional sex differences still exist? *Sex Roles, 7,* 1213–1222.

Goldberg, B. (1991, June 16). More dads choose kids over career. *Morning Call,* pp. D1, D11.

Goldberg, H. (1976). *The hazards of being male: Surviving the myth of masculine privilege.* New York: Nash.

Goldberg, P. (1968). Are women prejudiced against women? *Trans-Action, 5*(5), 28–30.

Goldberg, S. (1974). *The inevitability of patriarchy.* New York: Morrow.

Golden, G. A., & Cherry, F. (1982). Test performance and social comparison choices of high school men and women. *Sex Roles, 8,* 761–772.

Golding, J. M. (1988). Gender differences in depressive symptoms: Statistical considerations. *Psychology of Women Quarterly, 12,* 61–74.

Golding, J. M. (1990). Division of household labor, strain, and depressive symptoms among Mexican Americans and non-Hispanic whites. *Psychology of Women Quarterly, 14,* 103–117.

Golding, J. M., & Singer, J. L. (1983). Patterns of inner experience: Daydreaming styles, depressive moods and sex roles. *Journal of Personality and Social Psychology, 45,* 663–675.

Goldman, A. L. (1990, July 29). Black women's bumpy path to church leadership. *New York Times,* pp. 1, 24.

Goldman, J.D.G., & Goldman, R. J. (1983). Children's perceptions of parents and their roles: A cross-national study in Australia, England, North America, and Sweden. *Sex Roles, 9,* 791–812.

Goldstein, E. (1979). Effect of same-sex and cross-sex role models on the subsequent academic prosperity of scholars. *American Psychologist, 34,* 407–410.

Goleman, D. (1984, August 21). As sex roles change, men turn to therapy to cope with stress. *New York Times,* pp. C1, 5.

Goleman, D. (1986, April 1). Two views of marriage explored: His and hers. *New York Times,* pp. C1, C11.

Goleman, D. (1989, April 11). Subtle but intriguing differences found in the brain anatomy of men and women. *New York Times,* pp. C1, C6.

Goleman, D. (1990a, April 10). Stereotypes of the sexes persisting in therapy. *New York Times,* pp. C1, C8.

Goleman, D. (1990b, July 17). Aggression in men: Hormone levels are a key. *New York Times,* pp. C1, C6.

Golombok, S., Spencer, A., & Rutter, M. (1983). Children in lesbian and single-parent households: Psychosexual and psychiatric appraisal. *Journal of Child Psychology and Psychiatry, 24,* 551–572.

Golub, S., & Harrington, D. M. (1981). Premenstrual and menstrual mood changes in adolescent women. *Journal of Personality and Social Psychology, 41,* 961–965.

Gomberg, E. S. (1982). Historical and political perspective: Women and drug use. *Journal of Social Issues, 38*(2), 9–23.

Gomberg, E.S.L. (1986). Women: Alcohol and other drugs. *Drugs and Society, 1,* 75–109.

Good, G. E., Dell, D. M., & Mintz, L. B. (1989). Male role and gender role conflict: Relations to help seeking in men. *Journal of Counseling Psychology, 36,* 295–300.

Good, G. E., & Mintz, L. B. (1990). Gender role conflict and depression in college men: Evidence for compounded risk. *Journal of Counseling and Development, 69,* 17–21.

Good, L. E., Gilbert, L. A., & Scher, M. (1990). Gender aware therapy: A synthesis of feminist therapy and knowledge about gender. *Journal of Counseling and Development, 68,* 376–380.

Good, P. R., & Smith, B. D. (1990). Menstrual distress and sex-role attributes. *Psychology of Women Quarterly, 4,* 482–491.

Goodchilds, J. D., Zellman, G. L., Johnson, P. B., & Giarrusso, R. (1988). Adolescents and their perceptions of sexual interactions. In A. W. Burgess (Ed.), *Rape and sexual assault II* (pp. 245–270). New York: Garland.

Goodenow, C., & Gaier, E. L. (1986, August). *Best friends: Close reciprocal friendships of married and unmarried women.* Paper presented at the meeting of the American Psychological Association, Washington, DC.

Goodman, E. (1990, December 4). Will gender gap calm winds of war? *Morning Call,* p. 10.

Goodman, M. J., Griffin, P. B., Estioko-Griffin, A. A., & Grove, J. S. (1985). The compatibility of hunting and mothering among the Agte hunter-gatherers of the Philippines. *Sex Roles, 12,* 1199–1209.

Goodnow, J. J. (1988). Children's household work: Its nature and functions. *Psychological Bulletin, 103,* 5–26.

Goodwin, R. (1990). Sex differences among partner preferences: Are the sexes really very similar? *Sex Roles, 23,* 501–513.

Goossens, F. A., & van Ijzendoorn, M. H. (1990). Quality of infants' attachments to professional caregivers: Relation to infant-parent attachment and day-care characteristics. *Child Development, 61,* 832–838.

Gordon, L. (1990). The peaceful sex? On feminism and the peace movement. *NWSA Journal, 2,* 624–634.

Gordon, M. T., & Riger, S. (1989). *The female fear.* New York: Free Press.

Gordon, S. (1983). What's new in endocrinology? Target: Sex hormones. In M. Fooden, S. Gordon, & B. Hughley (Eds.), *Genes and gender IV* (pp. 39–48). Staten Island, NY: Gordian Press.

Gordon, S. (1991). *Prisoners of men's dreams: Striking out for a new feminine future.* Boston: Little, Brown.

Gormly, A. V., Gormly, J. B., & Weiss, H. (1987). Motivations for parenthood among young adult college students. *Sex Roles, 16,* 31–39.

Gottfried, A. E., & Gottfried, A. W. (Eds.). (1988). *Maternal employment and children's development: Longitudinal research.* New York: Plenum.

Gough, K. (1975). The origin of the family. In J. Freeman (Ed.), *Women: A feminist perspective.* Palo Alto, CA: Mayfield.

Gove, W. (1972). The relationship between sex roles, marital status, and mental illness. *Social Forces, 51,* 34–44.

Gove, W. (1973). Sex, marital status, and mortality. *American Journal of Sociology, 79,* 45–67.

Gove, W. (1979). Sex differences in the epidemiology of mental disorder: Evidence and explanations. In E. S. Gomberg & V. Franks (Eds.), *Gender and disordered behavior: Sex differences in psychopathology* (pp. 23–68). New York: Brunner/Mazel.

Gove, W., & Tudor, J. F. (1973). Adult sex roles and mental illness. In J. Huber (Ed.), *Changing women in a changing society.* Chicago: University of Chicago Press.

Gove, W. & Tudor, J. F. (1977). Sex differences in mental illness: A comment on Dohrenwend and Dohrenwend. *American Journal of Sociology, 82,* 1327–1336.

Gove, W. R. (1980). Mental illness and psychiatric treatment among women. *Psychology of Women Quarterly, 4,* 345–362.

Gove, W. R. (1985). The effect of age and gender on deviant behavior: A biopsychosocial perspective. In A. Rossi (Ed.), *Gender and the life course* (pp. 115–144). New York: Aldine.

Gove, W. R., & Zeiss, C. (1987). Multiple roles and happiness. In F. J. Crosby (Ed.), *Spouse, parent, worker: On gender and multiple roles* (pp. 125–137). New Haven: Yale University Press.

Graddick, M. M., & Farr, J. S. (1983). Professionals in scientific discipline: Sex-related differences in working life commitments. *Journal of Applied Psychology, 68,* 641–645.

Grady, K. E. (1981). Sex bias in research design. *Psychology of Women Quarterly, 5,* 628–636.

Gralewski, C., & Rodgon, M. M. (1980). Effect of social and intellectual instruction on achievement motivation as a function of role orientation. *Sex Roles, 6,* 301–309.

Grant, L. (1985). Race-gender status, classroom interaction, and children's socialization in elementary school. In L. C. Wilkinson & C. B. Marrett (Eds.), *Gender influences in classroom interaction* (pp. 57–77). Orlando, FL: Academic Press.

Grant, T. (1988). *Being a woman: Fulfilling your femininity and finding love.* New York: Random House.

Grauerholz, E. (1987). Balancing the power in dating relationships. *Sex Roles, 17,* 563–571.

Grauerholz, E., & Serpe, R. T. (1985). Initiation and response: The dynamics of sexual interaction. *Sex Roles, 12,* 1041–1059.

Graves, L. M., & Powell, G. N. (1988). An investigation of sex discrimination in recruiters' evaluations of actual applicants. *Journal of Applied Psychology, 73,* 20–29.

Gray, H. (1986). Television and the new Black man: Black male images in prime-time situation comedy. *Media, Culture, and Society, 8,* 223–242.

Gray, J. D. (1983). The married professional woman: An examination of her role conflicts and coping strategies. *Psychology of Women Quarterly, 7,* 235–243.

Gray, L. S. (1983, November 11). Schools that overcome girls' computer shyness. *New York Times,* Sect. 12, p. 9.

Green, C. (1987, August 13). Poll finds women still face voter bias. *Philadelphia Inquirer,* p. 21A.

Green, G. D., & Clunis, G. M. (1988). *Lesbian couples.* Seattle, WA: Seal Press.

Green, S. K., & Sandos, P. (1983). Perceptions of male and female initiators of relationships. *Sex Roles, 9,* 849–852.

Greenberg, D. F. (1988). *The construction of homosexuality.* Chicago: University of Chicago Press.

Greenberg, M., & Morris, N. (1974). Engrossment: The newborn's impact upon the father. *American Journal of Orthopsychiatry, 44,* 520–531.

Greendlinger, V., & Byrne, D. (1987). Coercive sexual fantasies of college males as predictors of self-reported likelihood to rape and overt sexual aggression. *Journal of Sex Research, 23,* 1–11.

Greenfield, P. M. (1981). Childcare in cross-cultural perspective: Implications for the future organization of childcare in the U.S. *Psychology of Women Quarterly, 6,* 41–45.

Greenglass, E. R. (1984, May-June). *Psychological implications of Type A behavior in employed women.* Paper presented at the meeting of the Canadian Psychological Association, Ottawa.

Greenglass, E. R., & Devins, R. (1982). Factors related to marriage and career plans in unmarried women. *Sex Roles, 8,* 57–71.

Greenhaus, J. H., Parasuraman, S., & Wormley, W. M. (1990). Effects of race on organizational experiences, job performance evaluations, and career outcomes. *Academy of Management Journal, 33,* 64–86.

Greenhouse, L. (1989, July 16). Abortion law fight turns to rights of teen-agers. *New York Times,* pp. 1, 23.

Greif, G. (1985). *Single fathers.* Lexington, MA: Lexington Books.

Grenier, J. E. (1986, November). Election briefing: The woman-versus-woman races. *Ms.,* p. 27.

Grenier, J. E. (1987, Spring). Gender gap exists for women. *Women's Political Times,* pp. 1, 8.

Grenier, J. E. (1988, Summer). Women and the unions. *Women's Political Times,* p. 8.

Griffin, S. (1975). Rape: The All-American crime. In J. Freeman (Ed.), *Women: A feminist perspective* (pp. 25–40). Palo Alto, CA: Mayfield.

Griffin, S. (1979). *Rape: The power of consciousness.* San Francisco: Harper & Row.

Griffin, S. (1981). *Pornography and silence: Culture's revenge against nature.* New York: Harper & Row.

Griffiths, M. (1988). Strong feelings about computers. *Women's Studies International Forum, 11,* 145–154.

Griffitt, W. (1987). Females, males, and sexual responses. In K. Kelley (Ed.), *Females, males, and sexuality: Theories and research* (pp. 141–173). Albany: State University of New York.

Griffitt, W., & Hatfield, E. (1985). *Human sexual behavior.* Glenview, IL: Scott, Foresman.

Grimm, L., & Yarnold, P. R. (1985). Sex typing and the coronary-prone behavior pattern. *Sex Roles, 12,* 171–178.

Groce, S. B., & Cooper, M. (1990). Just me and the boys? Women in local-level rock and roll. *Gender and Society, 4,* 220–229.

Gross, A., Smith, R., & Wallston, B. (1983). The men's movement: Personal vs. political. In J. Freeman (Ed.), *The politics of social movements.* New York: Longmans.

Gross, A. E. (1978). The male role and heterosexual behavior. *Journal of Social Issues, 34*(1), 87–107.

Gross, J. (1990a, September 2). Navy is urged to root out lesbians despite abilities. *New York Times,* p. A24.

Gross, J. (1990b, December 9). Needs of family and country: Missions on a collision course. *New York Times,* pp. 1, 16.

Gross, J. (1991, June 16). More young single men hang onto apron strings. *New York Times,* pp. 1, 18.

Gross, M. M., & Geffner, R. A. (1980). Are the times changing? An analysis of sex-role prejudice. *Sex Roles, 6,* 713–722.

Grube, J. W., Kleinhesselink, R. R., & Kearney, K. A. (1982). Male self-acceptance and attraction toward women. *Personality and Social Psychology Bulletin, 8,* 107–112.

Grush, J. E., & Yehl, J. G. (1979). Marital roles, sex differences, and interpersonal attraction. *Journal of Personality and Social Psychology, 37,* 116–123.

Guagnano, G., Acredolo, C., Hawkes, G. R., Ellyson, S., & White, N. (1986). Locus of control: Demographic factors and their interactions. *Journal of Social Behavior and Personality, 1,* 365–380.

Gubar, S. & Hoff, J. (Eds.). (1989). *Adult users only: The dilemma of violent pornography.* Bloomington: Indiana University Press.

Gulanick, N. A., Howard, G. S., & Moreland, J. (1979). Evaluation of a group program designed to increase androgyny in feminine women. *Sex Roles, 5,* 811–827.

Gullahorn, J. E. (1977). Sex roles and sexuality. In E. Donelson & J. Gullahorn (Eds.), *Women: A psychological perspective* (pp. 226–281). New York: Wiley.

Gunter, N. C., & Gunter, B. G. (1990). Domestic division of labor among working couples: Does androgyny make a difference? *Sex Roles, 14,* 355–370.

Gupta, N., Jenkins, D., Jr., & Beehr, T. A. (1983). Employee gender, gender similarity, and supervisor-subordinate cross-evaluations. *Psychology of Women Quarterly, 8,* 174–184.

Gurwitz, S. B., & Dodge, K. A. (1975). Adults' evaluation of a child as a function of sex of adult and sex of child. *Journal of Personality and Social Psychology, 33,* 822–828.

Gutek, B. A. (1985). *Sex and the workplace: The impact of sexual behavior and harassment on women, men, and organizations.* San Francisco: Jossey-Bass.

Gutek, B. A., & Burley, K. (1988, August). *Relocation, family, and the bottom line: Results from the Division 35 survey.* Paper presented at the meeting of the American Psychological Association, Atlanta.

Gutek, B. A., Repetti, R. L., & Silver, D. L. (1988). Nonwork roles and stress at work. In C. L. Cooper & R. Payne (Eds.), *Causes, coping, and consequences of stress at work* (pp. 141–174). New York: Wiley.

Gutmann, D. L. (1987). *Reclaimed powers: Toward a new psychology of men and women in later life.* New York: Basic Books.

Guttentag, M., & Bray, H. (1975, December). Tough to nip sexism in the bud. *Psychology Today,* p. 58.

Guttentag, M., & Bray, H. (1977). Teachers as mediators of sex-role standards. In A. Sargent (Ed.), *Beyond sex roles* (pp. 395–411). St. Paul, MN: West.

Guttentag, M., & Secord, P. F. (1983). *Too many women? The sex ratio question.* Beverly Hills, CA: Sage.

Guy-Sheftall, B., & Bell-Scott, P. (1989a). Black women's studies: A view from the margin. In C. S. Pearson, D. L. Shavlik, & J. G. Touchton (Eds.), *Educating the majority: Women challenge tradition in higher education* (pp. 205–218). New York: American Council on Education/Macmillan.

Guy-Sheftall, B., & Bell-Scott, P. (1989b). Finding a way: Black women students and the academy. In C. S. Pearson, D. L., Shavlik, & J. G. Touchton (Eds.), *Educating the majority: Women challenge tradition in higher education* (pp. 47–56). NY: American Council on Education/Macmillan.

Haaken, J. (1988). Field dependence research: A historical analysis of a psychological construct. *Signs: Journal of Women in Culture and Society, 13,* 311–330.

Haas, A. (1981). Partner influences on sex-associated spoken language of children. *Sex Roles, 7,* 925–935.

Hacker, H. M. (1951). Women as a minority group. *Social Forces, 30,* 60–69.

Hacker, H. M. (1981). Blabbermouths and clams: Sex differences in self-disclosure in same-sex and cross-sex friendship dyads. *Psychology of Women Quarterly, 5,* 385–401.

Hahn, W. K. (1987). Cerebral lateralization of function: From infancy through childhood. *Psychological Bulletin, 101,* 376–392.

Halberstadt, A. G., & Saitta, M. B. (1987). Gender, nonverbal behavior, and perceived dominance: A test of the theory. *Journal of Personality and Social Psychology, 53,* 257–272.

Hale-Benson, J. E. (1986). *Black children: Their roots, culture, and learning styles* (rev. ed.). Provo, UT: Brigham Young University Press.

Hall, E. G., & Lee, A. M. (1984). Sex differences in motor performance of young children: Fact or fiction? *Sex Roles, 10,* 217–230.

Hall, E. R., Howard, J. A., & Boezio, S. L. (1986). Tolerance of rape: A sexist or antisocial attitude? *Psychology of Women Quarterly, 10,* 101–117.

Hall, J. A (1984). *Nonverbal sex differences: Communication accuracy and expressive style.* Baltimore: Johns Hopkins University Press.

Hall, J. A. (1987). On explaining gender differences: The case of nonverbal communication. In P. Shaver & C. Hendrick (Eds.), *Sex and gender* (pp. 177–200). Newbury Park, CA: Sage.

Hall, J. A., & Braunwald, K. G. (1981). Gender cues in conversations. *Journal of Personality and Social Psychology, 40,* 99–110.

Hall, J. A., & Halberstadt, A. G. (1986). Smiling and gazing. In J. S. Hyde & M. C. Linn (Eds.), *The psychology of gender: Advances through meta-analysis.* (pp. 136–158). Baltimore: Johns Hopkins University Press.

Hall, J. A., & Taylor, M. C. (1985). Psychological androgyny and the masculinity × femininity interaction. *Journal of Personality and Social Psychology, 49,* 429–435.

Hall, R. M., with Sandler, B. R. (1982). *The classroom climate: A chilly one for women?* Washington, DC: Association of American Colleges, Project on the Status and Education of Women.

Hall, R. M., & Sandler, B. R. (1983). *Academic mentoring for women students and faculty: A new look at an old way to get ahead.* Washington, DC: Association of American Colleges, Project on the Status and Education of Women.

Hall, R. M., & Sandler, B. R. (1984). *Out of the classroom: A chilly campus climate for women.* Washington, DC: Association of American Colleges, Project on the Status and Education of Women.

Hall, T. (1984, October 10). Many women decide they want their careers rather than children. *Wall Street Journal,* p. 35.

Hallinan, M. T., & Kubitschek, W. N. (1990). Sex and race effects of the response to intransitive sentiment relations. *Social Psychology Quarterly, 53,* 252–263.

Hallinan, M. T., & Sorensen, A. B. (1987). Ability grouping and sex differences in mathematics achievement. *Sociology of Education, 60,* 63–72.

Halpern, D. F. (1985). The influence of sex-role stereotypes on prose recall. *Sex Roles, 12,* 363–375.

Halpern, D. F. (1989). The disappearance of cognitive gender differences: What you see depends on where you look [Letter to the editor]. *American Psychologist, 44,* 1156–1158.

Hamburg, D. A., & Lunde, D. T. (1966). Sex hormones in the development of sex differences in human behavior. In E. E. Maccoby (Ed.), *The development of sex differences* (pp. 1–24). Stanford, CA: Stanford University Press.

Hamilton, M. (1983, April). *Sex differences in memory for social stimuli.* Paper presented at the meeting of the Eastern Psychological Association, Philadelphia.

Hamilton, M. C. (1988). Using masculine generics: Does generic *he* increase male bias in the user's imagery? *Sex Roles, 19,* 785–799.

Hamilton, M. C. (1991). Masculine bias in the attribution of personhood: People = male, male = people. *Psychology of Women Quarterly, 15,* 393–402.

Hampson, E., & Kimura, D. (1988). Reciprocal effects of hormonal fluctuations on human motor and perceptual-spatial skills. *Behavioral Neuroscience, 102,* 456–459.

Handal, P. J., & Salit, E. D. (1985). Gender-role classification and demographic relationships: A function of type of scoring procedures. *Sex Roles, 12,* 411–419.

Hans, V. P., & Eisenberg, N. (1985). The effects of sex-role attitudes and group composition on men and women in groups. *Sex Roles, 12,* 477–490.

Hansen, C. H., & Hansen, R. D. (1988). How rock music videos can change what is seen when boy meets girl: Priming stereotypic appraisal of social interactions. *Sex Roles, 19,* 287–316.

Hansen, F. J., & Reekie, L. (1990). Sex differences in clinical judgments of male and female therapists. *Sex Roles, 233,* 51–64.

Hansen, G. L. (1985). Dating jealousy among college students. *Sex Roles, 12,* 713–721.

Hanson, S.M.H. (1988). Divorced fathers with custody. In P. Bronstein & C. P. Cowan (Eds.), *Fatherhood today: Men's changing role in the family* (pp. 166–194). New York: Wiley.

Haraway, D. (1989). *Primate visions: Gender, race, and nature in the world of modern science.* New York: Routledge.

Harder, S. (1990). Flourishing the mainstream: The U.S. women's movement today. In Women's Research & Education Institute (Eds.), *The American woman 1990-1991: A status report* (pp. 273–286). New York: Norton.

Harding, S. (Ed.). (1987). *Feminism and methodology: Social science issues.* Bloomington: Indiana University Press.

Hare-Mustin, R. T. (1978, June). A feminist approach to family therapy. *Family Process, 17,* 181–194.

Hare-Mustin, R. T. (1983). An appraisal of the relationship between women and psychotherapy: 80 years after the case of Dora. *American Psychologist, 38,* 593–601.

Hare-Mustin, R. T., & Marecek, J. (1988). The meaning of difference: Gender theory, postmodernism, and psychology. *American Psychologist, 43,* 455–464.

Hare-Mustin, R. T., & Marecek, J. (1990). *Making a difference: Psychology and the construction of gender.* New Haven: Yale University Press.

Haring-Hidore, M., Stock, W. A., Okun, M. A., & Witter, R. A. (1985). Marital status and subjective well-being: A research synthesis. *Journal of Marriage and the Family, 47,* 947–953.

Harlow, H. F. (1958). The nature of love. *American Psychologist, 13,* 673–685.

Harlow, H. F. (1962). The heterosexual affectional system in monkeys. *American Psychologist, 17,* 1–9.

Harlow, H. F. (1965). Sexual behavior in the rhesus monkeys. In F. A. Beach (Ed.), *Sex and behavior.* New York: Wiley.

Harmetz, A. (1990, May 13). Hollywood pays court to the young adult. *New York Times,* pp. H17, H18.

Harmon, L. W. (1981). The life and career plans of young adult college women: A follow-up study. *Journal of Counseling Psychology, 28,* 416–427.

Harrell, A. W. (1986). Masculinity and farming-related accidents. *Sex Roles, 15,* 467–478.

Harren, V. A., Kass, R. A., Tinsley, H.E.A., & Moreland, J. R. (1979). Influences of gender, sex-role attitudes, and cognitive complexity on gender-dominant career choices. *Journal of Counseling Psychology, 26,* 227–234.

Harrington, D. M., & Andersen, S. M. (1981). Creativity, masculinity, femininity, and three models of psychological androgyny. *Journal of Personality and Social Psychology, 41,* 744–757.

Harris, A., & King, Y. (Eds.) (1989). *Rocking the ship of state: Toward a feminist peace politics.* Boulder, CO: Westview Press.

Harris, M. (1977a). *Cannibals and kings.* New York: Random House.

Harris, M. (1977b, November 13). Why men dominate women. *New York Times Magazine,* pp. 46ff.

Harris, M. (1981). *Why America changed: Our cultural crisis.* New York: Simon & Schuster.

Harris, R. L., Ellicott, A. M., & Holmes, D. S. (1986). The timing of psychosocial transitions and changes in women's lives: An examination of women aged 45 to 60. *Journal of Personality and Social Psychology, 51,* 409–416.

Harris, S. (1991, October 27). "Gayby boom" is bundle of hope for homosexuals. *Morning Call,* p. A24.

Harrison, A. O., & Minor, J. H. (1983). Inter-role conflict, coping strategies, and role satisfaction among single and married employed mothers. *Psychology of Women Quarterly, 6,* 354–360.

Harrison, J. (1978). Male sex role and health. *Journal of Social Issues, 34*(1), 65–86.

Hartley, R. E. (1959). Sex role pressures and the socialization of the male child. *Psychological Reports, 5,* 457–468.

Hartmann, H. (1976). Capitalism, patriarchy, and job segregation by sex. *Signs: Journal of Women in Culture and Society, 1,* 137–169.

Hartmann, H. I., & Treiman, D. J. (Eds.). (1981). *Women, work, and wages.* Washington, DC: National Academy Press.

Hartup, W. W. (1983). The peer system. In P. Mussen & E. Heatherington (Ed.), *Handbook of child psychology,* Vol. 4 (4th ed.) (pp. 104–196), New York: Wiley.

Harway, M. (1980). Sex bias in educational-vocational counseling. *Psychology of Women Quarterly, 4,* 412–423.

Harway, M., & Astin, H. S. (1977). *Sex discrimination in career counseling and education.* New York: Praeger Press.

Haskell, M. (1984, February). Good girls, earth mothers, and sluts in film. *Ms.,* pp. 35, 37.

Haskell, M. (1988, May). Hollywood Madonnas. *Ms.,* pp. 84, 86, 88.

Hatcher, M. A. (1991). The corporate woman of the 1990s: Maverick or innovator. *Psychology of Women Quarterly, 15,* 251–259.

Hatfield, E., & Sprecher, S. (1986). Measuring passionate love in intimate relationships. *Journal of Adolescence, 9,* 383–410.

Hatfield, E., Sprecher, S., Pillemer, J. T., Greenberger, D., & Wexler, P. (1988). Gender differences in what is desired in the sexual relationship. *Journal of Psychology and Human Sexuality, 1,* 39–52.

Hatton, G. J. (1977). Biology and gender: Structure, sex and cycles. In E. Donelson & J. E. Gullahorn (Eds.), *Women: A psychological perspective* (pp. 49–64). New York; Wiley.

Haviland, J. J., & Malatesta, C. Z. (1982). The development of sex differences in nonverbal signals. In C. Mayo & N. Henley (Eds.), *Gender and nonverbal behavior* (pp. 183–208). New York: Springer-Verlag.

Hayduk, L. A. (1983). Personal space: Where we now stand. *Psychological Bulletin, 94,* 293–335.

Hearn, J. (1987). *The gender of oppression: Men, masculinity, and the critique of Marxism.* New York: St. Martin's.

Heilbrun, A. B., Jr. (1981). Gender differences in the functional linkage between androgyny, social cognition, and competence. *Journal of Personality and Social Psychology, 41,* 1106–1118.

Heilbrun, A. B., Jr. (1984). Sex-based models of androgyny: A further cognitive elaboration of competence differences. *Journal of Personality and Social Psychology, 46,* 216–229.

Heilbrun, A. B., Jr., & Heilbrun, M. R. (1986). The treatment of women within the criminal justice system: An inquiry into the social impact of the Women's Rights Movement. *Psychology of Women Quarterly, 10,* 240–251.

Heilbrun, A. B., Jr., & Mulqueen, C. M. (1987). The second androgyny: A proposed revision in adaptive priorities for college women. *Sex Roles, 17,* 187–207.

Heilbrun, A. B., Jr., & Schwartz, H. L. (1982). Sex-gender differences in level of androgyny. *Sex Roles, 8,* 201–214.

Heilman, M. E., Block, C. J., Martell, R. F., & Simon, M. C. (1989). Has anything changed? Current characterizations of men, women, and managers. *Journal of Applied Psychology, 74,* 935–942.

Heilman, M. E., & Stopeck, M. H. (1985). Attractiveness and corporate success: Different causal attributions for males and females. *Journal of Applied Psychology, 70,* 379–388.

Heiman, J. R. (1975, April). The physiology of erotica: Women's sexual arousal. *Psychology Today,* pp. 90–94.

Heimovics, R. D., & Herman, R. D. (1988). Gender and the attribution of chief executive responsibility for successful or unsuccessful organizational outcomes. *Sex Roles, 18,* 623–635.

Helgesen, S. (1990). *The female advantage: Women's ways of leadership.* New York: Doubleday Currency.

Helgeson, V. S. (1990). The role of masculinity in a prognostic predictor of heart attack severity. *Sex Roles, 22,* 755–774.

Helgeson, V. S., & Sharpsteen, D. J. (1987). Perception of danger in achievement and affiliation situations: An extension of the Pollak and Gilligan versus Benton et al. debate. *Journal of Personality and Social Psychology, 53,* 727–733.

Heller, S. (1986, September 10). Fewer blacks are entering the academic pipeline. *Chronicle of Higher Education,* pp. 1, 24.

Helmreich, R., Spence, J. T., Beane, W. E., Lucker, G. W., & Mathews, K. A. (1980). Making it in academic psychology: Demographic and personality correlates of attainments. *Journal of Personality and Social Psychology, 39,* 896–908.

Helmreich, R. L., Spence, J. T., & Gibson, R. H. (1982). Sex-role attitudes: 1972–1980. *Personality and Social Psychology, 37,* 1631–1644.

Helmreich, R. L., Spence, J. T., & Holahan, C. K. (1979). Psychological androgyny and sex role flexibility: A test of two hypotheses. *Journal of Personality and Social Psychology, 37,* 1631–1644.

Helson, R., Elliott, T., & Leigh, J. (1990). Number and quality of roles: A longitudinal personality view. *Psychology of Women Quarterly, 14,* 83–101.

Helson, R., & Moane, G. (1987). Personality change in women from college to midlife. *Journal of Personality and Social Psychology, 53,* 176–186.

Helson, R., & Picano, J. (1990). Is the traditional role bad for women? *Journal of Personality and Social Psychology, 59,* 311–320.

Hemmer, J. D., & Kleiber, D. A. (1981). Tomboys and sissies: Androgynous children? *Sex Roles, 7,* 1205–1212.

Hemmons, W. M. (1980). The women's liberation movement: Understanding black women's attitudes. In L. F. Rodgers-Rose (Ed.), *The black woman* (pp. 285–299). Beverly Hills, CA: Sage.

Hendrick, C., & Hendrick, S. (1986). A theory and method of love. *Journal of Personality and Social Psychology, 50,* 392–402.

Hendrick, S. S., Hendrick, C., Slapion-Foote, M. J., & Foote, F. F. (1985). Gender differences in sexual attitudes. *Journal of Personality and Social Psychology, 48,* 1630–1642.

Hendrix, K. (1990, August 19). Lesbians clash over child custody. *Morning Call,* p. A22.

Hengkietisak, S., & Cleary, T. A. (1989, August). *Gender differences in mathematics ability: A meta-analysis of mathematics aptitude and achievement test scores.* Paper presented at the meeting of the American Psychological Association, New Orleans.

Henley, N., & Thorne, B. (1977). Womanspeak and manspeak: Sex differences and sexism in communication, verbal and nonverbal. In A. Sargent (Ed.), *Beyond sex roles* (pp. 201–218). St. Paul, MN: West.

Henley, N. M. (1977). *Body politics: Power, sex, and nonverbal communication.* Englewood Cliffs, NJ: Prentice-Hall.

Henley, N. M. (1989). Molehill or mountain? What we know and don't know about sex bias in language. In M. Crawford & M. Gentry (Eds.), *Gender and thought: Psychological perspectives* (pp. 59–78). New York: Springer-Verlag.

Hennig, M., & Jardim, A. (1977). *The managerial woman.* New York: Doubleday.

Hensley, K. K., & Borges, M. A. (1981). Sex role stereotyping and sex role norms: A comparison of elementary and college age students. *Psychology of Women Quarterly, 5,* 543–554.

Hepburn, C. (1985). Memory for the frequency of sex-typed versus neutral behaviors: Implications for the maintenance of sex stereotypes. *Sex Roles, 12,* 771–776.

Hepp, C. (1989, June 7). A political edge: The female factor. *Philadelphia Inquirer,* pp. 1A, 12A.

Herek, G. M. (1987). On heterosexual masculinity: Some psychical consequences of the social construction of gender and sexuality. In M. S. Kimmel (Ed.), *Changing men: New directions in research on men and masculinity* (pp. 68–82). Newbury Park, CA: Sage.

Herek, G. M. (1990). Gay people and government security clearances: A social science perspective. *American Psychologist, 45,* 1035–1042.

Herman, R. (1981, May 3). Men and women also grow old in different ways. *New York Times,* p. E7.

Hersh, S. (1970). *My Lai 4.* New York: Random House.

Hertz, R. (1986). *More equal than others: Women and men in dual-career marriages.* Berkeley, CA: University of California Press.

Herzog, A. R., & Bachman, J. G. (1982). *Sex-role attitudes among high school seniors.* Ann Arbor: University of Michigan, Institute of Social Research.

Herzog, A. R., Bachman, J. G., & Johnson, L. D. (1983). Paid work, child care, and housework: A national survey of high school seniors' preferences for sharing responsibilities between husband and wife. *Sex Roles, 9,* 109–135.

Heschel, S. (Ed.). (1983). *On being a Jewish feminist: A reader.* New York: Schocken.

Hetherington, E. M., & Hagan, M. S. (1986). Divorced fathers: Stress, coping, and adjustment. In M. E. Lamb (Ed.), *The father's role: Applied perspectives* (pp. 103–134). New York: Wiley.

Hetherington, E. M., Stanley-Hagan, M., & Anderson, E. R. (1989). Marital transitions: A child's perspective. *American Psychologist, 44,* 303–312.

Hewlett, S. A. (1986). *A lesser life: The myth of women's liberation in America.* New York: Morrow.

Hewlett, S. A. (1990, Fall). Running hard just to keep up. *Women: The road ahead* [Special issue of *Time* magazine], p. 54.

Hier, D. B., & Crowley, W. F. (1982). Spatial ability in androgen-deficient men. *New England Journal of Medicine, 306,* 1202–1205.

Hill, C. E., Hobbs, M. A., & Verble, C. (1974). A developmental analysis of the sex-role identification of school-related objects. *Journal of Educational Research, 67,* 205–206.

Hill, C. T., Peplau, S. A., & Rubin, Z. (1981). Differing perceptions in dating couples: Sex roles vs. alternative explanations. *Psychology of Women Quarterly, 5,* 418–434.

Hill, C. T., Rubin, Z., & Peplau, A. (1976). Breakups before marriage: The end of 103 affairs. *Journal of Social Issues, 32,* 147–168.

Hill, C. T., & Stull, D. E. (1981). Sex differences in effects of social and value similarity in same-sex friendship. *Journal of Personality and Social Psychology, 41,* 488–502.

Hill, C. T., & Stull, D. E. (1987). Gender and self-disclosure: Strategies for exploring the issues. In V. J. Derlega & J. H. Berg (Eds.), *Self-disclosure: Theory, research, and therapy.* New York: Plenum.

Hill, M. (1987). Child-rearing attitudes of Black lesbian mothers. In the Boston Lesbian Psychologies Collective (Ed.), *Lesbian psychologies: Explorations and challenges* (pp. 215–226). Urbana: University of Illinois Press.

Hill, S.E.K., Bahniuk, M. H., Dobos, J., & Rouner, D. (1989). Mentoring and other communication support systems in the academic setting. *Group and Organization Studies, 14,* 355–368.

Hilts, P. J. (1991, September 10). Women still lag behind in medicine. *New York Times,* p. C7.

Himadi, W. G., Arkowitz, H., Hinton, R., & Perl, J. (1980). Minimal dating and its relationship to other social problems and general adjustment. *Behavior Therapy, 11,* 345–352.

Hines, M. (1982). Prenatal gonadal hormones and sex differences in human behavior. *Psychological Bulletin, 92,* 56–80.

Hines, M., & Shipley, C. (1984). Prenatal exposure to diethylstilbestrol (DES) and the development of sexually dimorphic cognitive abilities and cerebral lateralization. *Developmental Psychology, 20,* 81–94.

Hirsch, K. (1990, September-October). Fraternities of fear. *Ms.,* pp. 52–56.

Hirsch, M., & Keller, E. F. (Eds.). (1990). *Conflicts in feminism.* New York: Routledge.

Hispanic elected officials members jumps by 12.6 percent to record. (1990, Fall). *Women's Political Times,* pp. 4, 8.

Hirt, J., Hoffman, M. A., & Sedlacek, W. E. (1983, January). Attitudes toward changing sex-roles of male varsity athletes versus nonathletes: Developmental perspectives. *Journal of College Student Personnel,* pp. 33–38.

Hite, S. (1976). *The Hite report: A nationwide study of female sexuality.* New York: Macmillan.

Hite, S. (1981). *The Hite report on male sexuality.* New York: Macmillan.

Hochschild, A. (1989). *The second shift: Working parents and the revolution at home.* New York: Viking.

Hochswender, W. (1990, June 17). For today's fathers, their holiday seems a bit set in its ways. *New York Times*, pp. 1, 22.

Hodges, K. K., Brandt, D. A., & Kline, J. (1981). Competence, guilt, and victimization: Sex differences in attribution of causality in television dramas. *Sex Roles, 7,* 537–546.

Hodgson, J. W., & Fischer, J. L. (1981). Pathways of identity development in college women. *Sex Roles, 7,* 681–690.

Hoeffer, B. (1981). Children's acquisition of sex-role behavior in lesbian-mother families. *American Journal of Orthopsychiatry, 51,* 536–544.

Hoferek, M. J., & Hanick, P. L. (1985). Woman and athlete: Toward role consistency. *Sex Roles, 12,* 687–695.

Hoff-Wilson, J. (1988). *Balancing the scales: The changing legal status of U.S. women from the colonial period to the present.* Bloomington: Indiana University Press.

Hoffman, C., & Hurst, N. (1990). Gender stereotypes: Perception or rationalization? *Journal of Personality and Social Psychology, 58,* 197–208.

Hoffman, D. M., & Fidell, L. A. (1979). Characteristics of androgynous, undifferentiated, masculine, and feminine middle-class women. *Sex Roles, 5,* 765–781.

Hoffman, L. W. (1977). Changes in family roles, socialization, and sex differences. *American Psychologist, 32,* 644–657.

Hoffman, L. W. (1979). Maternal employment: 1979. *American Psychologist, 34,* 859–865.

Hoffman, L. W. (1989). Effects of maternal employment in the two-parent family. *American Psychologist, 44,* 283–292.

Holahan, C. J., & Moos, R. H. (1985). Life stress and health: Personality, coping, and family support in stress resistance. *Journal of Personality and Social Psychology, 49,* 739–747.

Holahan, C. K., & Gilbert, L. A. (1979). Interrole conflict for working women: Careers versus jobs. *Journal of Applied Psychology, 64,* 86–90.

Holahan, C. K., & Stephan, C. W. (1981). When beauty isn't talent: The influence of physical attractiveness, attitudes toward women, and competence on impression formation. *Sex Roles, 7,* 867–876.

Hollender, J., & Shafer, L. (1981). Male acceptance of female career roles. *Sex Roles, 7,* 1199–1203.

Hollway, W. (1989). *Subjectivity and method in psychology: Gender, meaning, and science.* London: Sage.

Holms, V. L., & Esses, L. M. (1988). Factors influencing Canadian high school girls' career motivation. *Psychology of Women Quarterly, 12,* 313–328.

Holmstrom, L. L., & Burgess, A. W. (1981). *The victim of rape: Institutional reaction.* New York: Wiley.

Hood, K. E., Draper, P., Crockett, L. J., & Petersen, A. C. (1987). The ontogeny and phylogeny of sex differences in development: A biopsychosocial synthesis. In B. Carter (Ed.), *Current conceptions of sex roles and sex typing: Theory and research* (pp. 49–77). New York: Praeger.

Hooks, B. (1984). *Feminist theory: From margin to center.* Boston: South End Press.

Hooks, B. (1989). *Talking back: Thinking feminist, thinking black.* Boston: South End Press.

Hopkins, J. R. (1977). Sexual behavior in adolescence. *Journal of Social Issues, 33*(2), 67–85.

Hopson, J., & Rosenfeld, A. (1984, August). PMS: Puzzling monthly symptoms. *Psychology Today,* pp. 30–35.

Hopson, J. L. (1987, August). Boys will be boys, girls will be . . . *Psychology Today,* pp. 61–66.

Horner, M. J. (1968). *Sex differences in achievement motivation and performance in competitive-noncompetitive situations.* Unpublished doctoral dissertation, University of Michigan.

Horner, M. J. (1972). Toward an understanding of achievement-related conflicts in women. *Journal of Social Issues, 28,* 157–176.

Horney, K. (1973). On the genesis of the castration complex in women. In J. B. Miller (Ed.), *Psychoanalysis and women.* New York: Brunner/Mazel. (Original work published 1922)

Horovitz, B. (1989, August 10). In TV commercials, men are more often the butt of the jokes. *Philadelphia Inquirer,* pp. 5B, 6B.

Hort, B. E., Fagot, B. I., & Leinbach, M. D. (1990). Are people's notions of maleness more stereotypically framed than their notions of femaleness? *Sex Roles, 23,* 197–212.

Horwitz, A. V. (1982). Sex-role expectations, power, and psychological distress. *Sex Roles, 8,* 607–623.

Houser, B. B., & Beckman, L. J. (1980). Background characteristics and women's dual-role attitudes. *Sex Roles, 6,* 355–366.

Houser, B. B., Berkman, S. L., & Beckman, L. J. (1984). The relative rewards and costs of childlessness for older women. *Psychology of Women Quarterly, 8,* 395–398.

Houseworth, S., Peplow, K., & Thirer, J. (1989). Influence of sport participation upon sex role orientation of Caucasian males and their attitudes toward women. *Sex Roles, 20,* 317–325.

Houston, P. (1987, Fall). Three out of 5 back woman president. *Los Angeles Times,* as cited in *Women's Political Times,* p. 16.

How college women and men feel today about sex, AIDS, condoms, marriage, kids. (1987, August). *Glamour,* pp. 261–263.

How Title IX has helped. (1984, March-April). *Women's Political Times,* p. 3.

Howard, D. (Ed.). (1986). *The dynamics of feminist therapy.* New York: Haworth.

Howard, J. A. (1984). Societal influences on attribution: Blaming some victims more than others. *Journal of Personality and Social Psychology, 47,* 494–505.

Howard, J. A., Blumstein, P., & Schwartz, P. (1986). Sex, power, and influence tactics in intimate relationships. *Journal of Personality and Social Psychology, 51,* 102–109.

Howe, K. G. (1985). The psychological impact of a women's studies course. *Women's Studies Quarterly, 13,* 23–24.

Hrdy, S. B. (1981). *The woman that never evolved.* Cambridge, MA: Harvard University Press.

Hrdy, S. B. (1986). Empathy, polyandry, and the myth of the coy female. In R. Bleier (Ed.), *Feminist approaches to science* (pp. 119–146). New York: Pergamon Press.

Hubbard, R. (1990). *The politics of women's biology.* New Brunswick, NJ: Rutgers University Press.

Huber, J., & Spitze, G. (1983). *Sex stratification: Children, housework, and jobs.* New York: Academic Press.

Hughes, J. O., & Sandler, B. R. (1988). *Peer harassment: Hassles for women on campus.* Washington, D.C: Association of American Colleges, Project on the Status and Education of Women.

Hull, G. T., Scott, P. B., & Smith, B. (Eds.). (1982). *But some of us are brave: Black women's studies.* Old Westbury, NY: Feminist Press.

Hunt, M. (1974). *Sexual behavior in the 1970s.* Chicago: Playboy Press.

Hunter, S. M., Johnson, C. C., Vizelberg, I. A., Webber, L. S., & Berenson, G. S. (1991). Tracking of Type A behavior in children and young adults: The Bogalusa Heart Study. *Journal of Social Behavior and Personality, 6,* 71–84.

Huston, A. C. (1983). Sex-typing. In P. H. Mussen & E. M. Hetherington (Eds.), *Handbook of child psychology, Vol. IV: Socialization, personality, and social development* (4th ed.) (pp. 387–468). New York: Wiley.

Huston, A. C. (1985). The development of sex typing: Themes from recent research. *Developmental Review, 5,* 1–17.

Huston, A. C., Greer, D., Wright, J. C., Welch, R., & Ross, R. (1984). Children's comprehension of televised formal features with masculine and feminine connotations. *Developmental Psychology, 20,* 707–716.

Huston, T. L., & Ashmore, R. D. (1986). Women and men in personal relationships. In R. D. Ashmore & R. K. Del Boca

(Eds.), *The social psychology of female-male relations* (pp. 167–209). New York: Academic Press.

Hyde, J. S. (1981). How large are cognitive gender differences? A meta-analysis using *v* and *d. American Psychologist, 36*, 892–901.

Hyde, J. S. (1984). Children's understanding of sexist language. *Developmental Psychology, 20*, 697–706.

Hyde, J. S. (1986). Gender differences in aggression. In J. S. Hyde & M. C. Linn (Eds.), *The psychology of gender: Advances through meta-analysis* (pp. 51–66). Baltimore: Johns Hopkins University Press.

Hyde, J. S. (1990). Meta-analysis and the psychology of gender differences. *Signs: Journal of Women in Culture and Society, 16*, 55–73.

Hyde, J. S., Fennema, E., & Lamon, S. J. (1990). Gender differences in mathematics performance: A meta-analysis. *Psychological Bulletin, 107*, 139–155.

Hyde, J. S., Fennema, E., Ryan, M., Frost, L. A., & Hopp, C. (1990). Gender comparisons of mathematics attitudes and affect: A meta-analysis. *Psychology of Women Quarterly, 14*, 299–324.

Hyde, J. S., & Linn, M. C. (1988). Gender differences in verbal ability: A meta-analysis. *Psychological Bulletin, 104*, 53–69.

Hyde, J. S., Rosenberg, B.G., & Behrman, J. (1977). Tomboyism. *Psychology of Women Quarterly, 2*, 73–75.

Hyland, D. A. (1978, January 26). Participation in athletics: Is it worth all the suffering? *New York Times*, p. S2.

Hymowitz, C. (1989, February 16). Gender gap is how you perceive it. *Wall Street Journal*, p. B1.

Hynes, H. P. (1989). *The recurring silent spring.* New York: Pergamon Press.

Ickes, W., & Barnes, R. D. (1978). Boys and girls together—and alienated: On enacting stereotyped sex roles in mixed-sex dyads. *Journal of Personality and Social Psychology, 36*, 669–683.

Iglitzin, L. B., & Ross, R. (Eds.). (1986). *Women in the world, 1975–1985: The women's decade* (2nd. rev. ed.). Santa Barbara, CA: ABC-Clio.

Ilardi, B. C., & Bridges, L. J. (1988). Gender differences in self-esteem processes as rated by teachers and students. *Sex Roles, 18*, 333–342.

Illegitimate births top million mark. (1991, June 14). *Morning Call*, p. A2.

Ingram, R. E., Cruet, D., Johnson, B. R., & Wisnicki, K. S. (1988). Self-focused attention, gender, gender role, and vulnerability to negative affect. *Journal of Personality and Social Psychology, 55*, 967–978.

Inoff-Germain, G., Arnold, G. S., Nottelmann, E. D., Susman, E. J., Cutler, G. B. Jr., & Chrousos, G. P. (1988). Relations between hormone levels and observational measures of aggressive behavior of young adolescents in family interactions. *Developmental Psychology, 24*, 129–139.

Ireson, C. J. (1984). Adolescent pregnancy and sex roles. *Sex Roles, 11*, 189–201.

Irvine, J. J. (1986). Teacher-student interactions: Effects of student race, sex, and grade level. *Journal of Educational Psychology, 78*, 14–21.

Isaacs, M. B. (1981). Sex role stereotyping and the evaluation of the performance of women: Changing trends. *Psychology of Women Quarterly, 6*, 187–195.

Isaacs, S. (1990, January 14). Sisterhood isn't so powerful in the movies. *New York Times*, pp. H1, H37.

Israel, J., & Eliasson, R. (1971). Consumption society, sex-role, and sexual behavior. *Acta Sociologica, 14*, 68–82.

Israeli women insulted at return to stereotype. (1982, June 21). *Easton Express*, p. A9.

Jack, D., & Jack, R. (1988). Women lawyers: Archetype and alternatives. In C. Gilligan, J. V. Ward, & J. M. Taylor (Eds.), *Mapping the moral domain* (pp. 263–288). Cambridge, MA: Harvard University Press.

Jacklin, C. N. (1989). Female and male: Issues of gender. *American Psychologist, 44*, 127–133.

Jacklin, C. N., Maccoby, E. E., & Doering, C. H. (1983). Neonatal sex steroid hormones and timidity in 6-to-18-month-old boys and girls. *Developmental Psychobiology, 16*, 163–168.

Jackson, A. D. (1982). Militancy and black women's competitive behavior in competitive versus noncompetitive conditions. *Psychology of Women Quarterly, 6*, 342–353.

Jackson, L. A. (1983). The perception of androgyny and physical attractiveness: Two is better than one. *Personality and Social Psychology Bulletin, 9*, 405–413.

Jackson, L. A. (1987). Gender and distributive justice: The influence of gender-related characteristics on allocations. *Sex Roles, 17*, 73–91.

Jackson, L. A., & Cash, T. F. (1985). Components of gender stereotypes: Their implications for inferences on stereotypic and nonstereotypic dimensions. *Personality and Social Psychology Bulletin, 11*, 326–344.

Jackson, L. A., Ialongo, N., & Stollak, G. E. (1986). Parental correlates of gender role: The relations between parents' masculinity, femininity, and child-rearing behaviors and their children's gender roles. *Journal of Social and Clinical Psychology, 4*, 204–224.

Jackson, L. A., & Sullivan, L. A. (1990). Perceptions of multiple role participants. *Social Psychology Quarterly, 53*, 274–282.

Jacobs, J. A. (1989). *Revolving doors: Sex segregation and women's careers.* Stanford, CA: Stanford University Press.

Jacobs, J. A., & Powell, B. (1985). Occupational prestige: A sex-neutral concept. *Sex Roles, 12*, 1061–1071.

Jagacinski, C. M. (1987). Androgyny in a male-dominated field: The relationship of sex-typed traits to performance and satisfaction in engineering. *Sex Roles, 17*, 529–547.

Jaggar, A. (1990). Sexual difference and sexual equality. In D. Rhode (Ed.), *Theoretical perspectives on sexual difference* (pp. 239–254). New Haven: Yale University Press.

Jaggar, A. M., & Struhl, P. R. (1978). *Feminist frameworks: Alternative theoretical accounts of the relations between women and men.* New York: McGraw-Hill.

James, C. (1989, July 16). Are feminist heroines an endangered species? *New York Times*, pp. H15, H20.

Janda, L. H., O'Grady, K. E., & Capps, C. F. (1978). Fear of success in males and females in sex-linked occupations. *Sex Roles, 4*, 43–50.

Janman, K. (1989). One step behind: Current stereotypes of women, achievement, and work. *Sex Roles, 21*, 209–230.

Jeffreys, S. (1986). *The spinster and her enemies: Feminism and sexuality, 1880–1930.* London/Boston: Routledge & Kegan Paul/Pandora.

Jeffreys, S. (1990). Eroticizing women's subordination. In D. Leidholdt & J. G. Raymond (Eds.), *The sexual liberals and the attack on feminism* (pp. 132–135). New York: Pergamon Press.

Jenkins, A. H. (1982). *The psychology of the Afro-American: A humanistic approach.* New York: Pergamon Press.

Jenkins, S. R. (1987). Need for achievement and women's careers over 14 years: Evidence for occupational structure effects. *Journal of Personality and Social Psychology, 53*, 922–932.

Jennings, J. W., Geis, F. L., & Brown, V. (1980). The influence of television commercials on women's self-confidence and independent judgment. *Journal of Personality and Social Psychology, 38*, 203–210.

Johnson, C. B., Stockdale, M. S., & Saal, F. E. (1991). Persistence of men's misperceptions of friendly cues across a variety of interpersonal encounters. *Psychology of Women Quarterly, 15*, 463–475.

Johnson, D. D. (1973–1974). Sex differences in reading across cultures. *Reading Research Quarterly, 9*, 67–86.

Johnson, J. (1989, June 25). A child care crisis confronts parents who are in uniform. *New York Times*, pp. 1, 22A.

Johnson, J. D., & Jackson, L. A., Jr. (1988). Assessing the effects of factors that might underlie the differential perception of acquaintance and stranger rape. *Sex Roles, 19*, 37–45.

Johnson, M. (Ed.) (1982). Teaching psychology of women [Special issue]. *Psychology of Women Quarterly, 7.*

Johnson, P. B. (1982). Sex differences, women's role and alcohol use: Preliminary national data. *Journal of Social Issues, 38*(2), 95–116.

Johnson, S. (1987). *Going out of our minds: The metaphysics of liberation.* Freedom, CA: Crossing Press.

Johnson, S. (1989). *Wildfire: Igniting the she/volution.* Albuquerque: Wildfire.

Johnson, S. J., & Black, K. N. (1981). The relationship between sex-role identity and beliefs in personal control. *Sex Roles, 7*, 425–431.

Johnson, W. R., & Skinner, J. (1986). Labor supply and marital separation. *American Economic Review, 76*, 455–469.

Jolly, E. J., & O'Kelly, C. G. (1980). Sex-role stereotyping in the language of the deaf. *Sex Roles, 6*, 85–292.

Jones, D. C., Bloys, N., & Wood, M. (1990). Sex roles and friendship patterns. *Sex Roles, 223*, 133–145.

Jones, G. P., & Jacklin, C. N. (1988). Changes in sexist attitudes towards women during introductory women's and men's studies courses. *Sex Roles, 18*, 611–622.

Jones, W. H., Chernovetz, M. E., & Hansson, R. O. (1978). The enigma of androgyny: Differential implications for males and females? *Journal of Consulting and Clinical Psychology, 46*, 298–313.

Jordan, J. V. (1987). *Clarity in connection: Empathic knowing, desire, and sexuality* (Work in Progress, No. 29). Wellesley, MA: Wellesley College, The Stone Center.

Jorgenson, C., Davis, J., Opella, J., & Angerstein, G. (1979, September). *Hemispheric asymmetry in the processing of Stroop stimuli: An examination of gender, hand-preference, and language differences.* Paper presented at the meeting of the American Psychological Association, New York.

Jose, P. E. (1989). The role of gender and gender role similarity in readers' identification with story characters. *Sex Roles, 21*, 697–713.

Jose, P. E., & McCarthy, W. J. (1988). Perceived agentic and communal behavior in mixed-sex group interactions. *Personality and Social Psychology Bulletin, 14*, 57–67.

Jourard, S. (1971). *The transparent self.* New York: Van Nostrand.

Judge blames sex assault on 5-year-old victim. (1982, January-February). *National NOW Times*, p. 6.

Jump, T. L., & Haas, L. (1987). Fathers in transition: Dual-career fathers participating in child care. In M. S. Kimmel (Ed.), *Changing men: New directions in research on men and masculinity* (pp. 98–114). Newbury Park, CA: Sage.

Jung, C. G. (1956). *Two essays on analytical psychology.* New York: Meridian.

Jussim, L., Coleman, L. M., & Lerch, L. (1987). The nature of stereotypes: A comparison and integration of three theories. *Journal of Personality and Social Psychology, 52*, 536–546.

Kahn, A. (1981). Reactions of profeminist and antifeminist men to an expert woman. *Sex Roles, 7*, 857–866.

Kahn, A. (1984). The power war: Male response to power loss under equality. *Psychology of Women Quarterly, 8*, 234–247.

Kahn, A., & Gaeddert, W. P. (1985). From theories of equity to theories of justice: The liberating consequences of studying women. In V. O'Leary, R. Unger, & B. Wallston (Eds.), *Women, gender, and social psychology* (pp. 129–148). Hillsdale, NJ: Erlbaum.

Kahn, A. S., & Yoder, J. D. (1989). The psychology of women and conservatism: Rediscovering social change. *Psychology of Women Quarterly, 13*, 417–432.

Kahn, S., Zimmerman, G., Csikszentmihalyi, M., & Getzels, J. W. (1985). Relations between identity in young adulthood and intimacy at midlife. *Journal of Personality and Social Psychology, 49*, 1316–1322.

Kalichman, S. C. (1988). Individual differences in water-level task performance: A component-skills analysis. *Developmental Review, 8*, 273–295.

Kamerman, S. B., & Kahn, A. J. (1988). *Mothers alone: Strategies for a time of change.* Dover, MA: Auburn House.

Kaminer, W. (1990, February 11). Chances are you're codependent too. *New York Times Book Review*, pp. 1, 26, 27.

Kandel, B. (1986, May 11). Many elderly women are poor and alone. *Easton Express*, p. A5.

Kandel, D. B. (1978). Similarity in real-life adolescent friendship pairs. *Journal of Personality and Social Psychology, 36*, 306–312.

Kane, M. (1991, September 26). Women's wage gap narrows. *Morning Call*, p. B16.

Kanter, R. M. (1976, May). Why bosses turn bitchy. *Psychology Today*, pp. 56–59ff.

Kanter, R. M. (1977). *Men and women in the corporation.* New York: Basic Books.

Kanter, R. M. (1983). *The change masters: Innovations for productivity in the*

American corporation. New York: Simon & Schuster.

Kanter, R. M., & Stein, B. (1980). *A tale of "O": On being different in an organization.* New York: Harper & Row.

Kapalka, G. M., & Lachenmeyer, J. R. (1988). Sex role flexibility, locus of control, and occupational status. *Sex Roles, 19*, 417–427.

Kaplan, A. (1979). Clarifying the concept of androgyny: Implications for therapy. *Psychology of Women Quarterly, 3*, 223–230.

Kaplan, A., & Bean, J. P. (1976). From sex stereotypes to androgyny: Considerations of societal and individual change. In A. Kaplan & J. Bean (Eds.), *Beyond sex-role stereotypes* (pp. 383–392). Boston: Little, Brown.

Kaplan, E. A. (1987). *Rocking around the clock: Music television, postmodernism, and consumer culture.* New York: Methuen.

Kaplan, H. S. (1979). *Disorders of desire.* New York: Simon & Schuster.

Kaplan, M. (1983). A woman's view of DSM-III. *American Psychologist, 38*, 786–792.

Karabenick, S. A. (1983). Sex-relevance of content and influenceability: Sistrunk & McDavid revisited. *Personality and Social Psychology Bllletin, 9*, 243–252.

Karpoe, K. P., & Olney, R. L. (1983). The effect of boys' or girls' toys on sex-typed play in preadolescents. *Sex Roles, 9*, 507–518.

Karr, R. G. (1978). Homosexual labeling and the male role. *Journal of Social Issues, 34*(3), 73–83.

Kaschak, E. (1978). Sex bias in student evaluation of college professors. *Psychology of Women Quarterly, 3*, 235–243.

Kaschak, E. (1981a). Another look at sex bias in students' evaluation of professors: Do winners get the recognition that they have been given? *Psychology of Women Quarterly, 5*, 767–772.

Kaschak, E. (1981b). Feminist psychotherapy: The first decade. In S. Cox (Ed.), *Female psychology: The emerging self* (2nd ed.) (pp. 387–401). New York: St. Martin's.

Kasl, S. (1979). Changes in mental health status associated with job loss and retirement. In J. Barrett (Ed.), *Stress and mental disorder.* New York: Raven Press.

Kasl, S., & Cobb, S. (1979). Some mental health consequences of plant closing and job loss. In L. Ferman & J. Gordus (Eds.), *Mental health and the economy.* Kalamazoo, MI: Upjohn Institute.

Kassell, P. (1984, July-August). Equal pay. *New Directions for Women*, p. 7.

Katz, D. (1987). Sex discrimination in hiring: The influence of organizational climate and need for approval on decision–making behavior. *Psychology of Women Quarterly, 11*, 11–20.

Katz, P. (1979). The development of female identity. *Sex Roles, 5*, 115–178.

Katz, P. A. (1986). Gender identity: Development and consequences. In R. D. Ashmore and F. K. Del Boca (Eds.), *The social psychology of female-male relations: A critical analysis of central concepts* (pp. 21–67). New York: Academic Press.

Katz, S. (1988). Sexualization and the lateralized brain: From craniometry to pornography. *Women's Studies International Forum, 11*, 29–41.

Katzenstein, M. F. (1984). Feminism and the meaning of the vote. *Signs: Journal of Women in Culture and Society, 10*, 4–26.

Katzenstein, M. F. (1990). Feminism within American institutions: Unobtrusive mobilization in the 1980s. *Signs: Journal of Women in Culture and Society, 16*, 27–54.

Kearins, J. M. (1981). Visual-spatial memory in Australian aboriginal children of desert regions. *Cognitive Psychology, 13*, 434–460.

Keen, S. (1991). *Fire in the belly: On being a man.* New York: Bantam.

Keen, S., & Zur, O. (1989, November). Who is the new ideal man? *Psychology Today*, pp. 54–60.

Keller, E. F. (1985). *Reflections on gender and science.* New Haven: Yale University Press.

Kelly, J. A., O'Brian, G. G., & Hosford, R. (1981). Sex roles and social skills considerations for interpersonal adjustment. *Psychology of Women Quarterly, 5*, 758–766.

Kelly, J. A., & Worell, J. (1976). Parent behaviors related to masculine, feminine, and androgynous sex role orientations. *Journal of Consulting and Clinical Psychology, 44*, 843–851.

Kelly, J. B. (1988). Longer-term adjustment in children of divorce: Converging findings and implications for practice. *Journal of Family Psychology, 2*, 119–140.

Kelly, K. E., & Houston, B. K. (1985). Type A behavior in employed women: Relation to work, marital, and leisure variables, social support, stress, tension, and health. *Journal of Personality and Social Psychology, 48*, 1067–1079.

Kelly-Gadol, J. (1977). Did women have a renaissance? In R. Bridenthal & C. Koonz (Eds.), *Becoming visible: Women in European history* (pp. 137–164). Boston: Houghton Mifflin.

Kemper, S. (1984). When to speak like a lady. *Sex Roles, 10*, 435–443.

Kennelly, E. (1984, September-October). Republicans in fear of gender gap, feature women at convention. *National NOW Times*, p. 3.

Kenrick, D. T. (1987). Gender, genes, and the social environment: A biosocial interactionist perspective. In P. Shaver & C. Hendrick (Eds.), *Sex and gender* (pp. 14–43). Newbury Park, CA: Sage.

Kenrick, D. T., Gutierres, S. E., & Goldberg, L. L. (1989). Influence of popular erotica on judgments of strangers and mates. *Journal of Experimental Social Psychology, 25*, 159–167.

Kenrick, D. T., & Trost, M. R. (1987). A biosocial theory of heterosexual relationships. In K. Kelley (Ed.), *Females, males, and sexuality: Theories and research* (pp. 59–100). Albany: State University of New York Press.

Kephart, W. M. (1967). Some correlates of romantic love. *Journal of Marriage and the Family, 29*, 470–474.

Kerr, N. L., & Sullaway, M. E. (1983). Group sex composition and member task motivation. *Sex Roles, 9*, 403–417.

Kerr, P. (1984, September 16). Women in take-charge roles stride into TV's limelight. *New York Times*, pp. H29–30.

Kershner, J. R., & Ledger, G. (1985). Effect of sex, intelligence, and style of thinking on creativity: A comparison of gifted and average IQ children. *Journal of Personality and Social Psychology, 48*, 1033–1040.

Kessler, R. C., & McRae, J. A., Jr. (1982). The effect of wives' employment on the mental health of married men and women. *American Sociological Review, 47*, 216–227.

Kessler, S. J., & McKenna, W. (1978). *Gender: An ethnomethodological approach.* New York: Wiley.

Kessler, S. J. (1990). The medical construction of gender: Case management of intersexed infants. *Signs: Journal of Women in Culture and Society, 16*, 3–26.

Kessler-Harris, A. (1990). *A woman's wage: Symbolic meanings and social consequences.* Lexington, KY: University of Kentucky Press.

Kibria, N., Barnett, R. C., Baruch, G. K., & Pleck, J. H. (1990). Homemaking-role quality and the psychological well-being and distress of employed women. *Sex Roles, 22*, 327–347.

Kiesler, S., Sproull, L., & Eccles, J. (1985). Poolhalls, chips, and war games: Women in the culture of computing. *Psychology of Women Quarterly, 9*, 451–462.

Kilborn, P. T. (1990a, February 15). For many women, one job just isn't enough. *New York Times*, pp. A1, A22.

Kilborn, P. T. (1990b, May 31). Wage gap between sexes is cut in test, but at a price. *New York Times*, pp. A1, D22.

Kilpatrick, D. G., Resick, P. A., & Veronen, L. J. (1981). Effects of a rape experience: A longitudinal study. *Journal of Social Issues, 37*(4), 105–122.

Kimball, M. M. (1986). Television and sex-role attitudes. In T. M. Williams (Ed.), *The impact of television: A natural experiment in three communities* (pp. 265–301). Orlando, FL: Academic Press.

Kimball, M. M. (1989). A new perspective on women's math achievement. *Psychological Bulletin, 105*, 198–214.

Kimball, M. M., & Gray, V. A. (1982). Feedback and performance expectancies in an academic setting. *Sex Roles, 8*, 999–1007.

Kimble, C. E., Yoshikawa, J. C., & Zehr, H. D. (1981). Vocal and verbal assertiveness in same-sex and mixed-sex groups. *Journal of Personality and Social Psychology, 40*, 1047–1054.

Kimbrell, A. (1991, May-June). A time for men to pull together. *Utne Reader*, pp. 66–74.

Kimmel, M. S. (Ed.). (1987a). *Changing men: New directions in research on men and masculinity.* Newbury Park, CA: Sage.

Kimmel, M. S. (1987b). Teaching a course on men. In M. S. Kimmel (Ed.), *Changing men: New directions in research on men and masculinity* (pp. 278–294). Newbury Park, CA: Sage.

Kimmel, M. S. (1989). From pedestals to partners: Men's responses to feminism. In J. Freeman (Ed.), *Women: A feminist perspective* (4th ed.) (pp. 581–594). Mountain View, CA: Mayfield.

Kimura, D. (1985, November). Male brain, female brain: The hidden difference. *Psychology Today*, pp. 50–58.

Kimura, D. (1987). Are men's and women's brains really different? *Canadian Psychology, 28*, 133–147.

Kimura, D. (1989a, June). *The effect of exogenous estrogen on motor programming skills in post-menopausal women.* Research Bulletin #684. University of Western Ontario, London, Canada: Department of Psychology.

Kimura, D. (1989b, November). How sex hormones boost or cut intellectual ability. *Psychology Today*, pp. 62–66.

King, S. (1989). Sex differences in a causal model of career maturity. *Journal of Counseling and Development, 68*, 208–215.

Kingery, D. W. (1985). Are sex-role attitudes useful in explaining male/female differences in rates of depression? *Sex Roles, 12*, 627–636.

Kingston, P. W., & Nock, S. L. (1987). Time together among dual-earner couples. *American Sociological Review, 52*, 391–400.

Kinsey, A. E., Pomeroy, W. B., & Martin, C. E. (1948). *Sexual behavior in the human male.* Philadelphia: Saunders.

Kinsey, A. E., Pomeroy, W. B., Martin, C. E., & Gebhard, P. H. (1953). *Sexual behavior in the human female.* Philadelphia: Saunders.

Kirkpatrick, C. S. (1980). Sex roles and sexual satisfaction in women. *Psychology of Women Quarterly, 4,* 444–459.

Kirkpatrick, M., Smith, C., & Roy, R. (1981). Lesbian mothers and their children: A comparative study. *American Journal of Orthopsychiatry, 51,* 545–551.

Kirshner, L., & Johnston, L. (1983). Effects of gender on inpatient psychiatric hospitalization. *Journal of Nervous and Mental Disease, 171,* 651–657.

Kishwar, M. (1987). The continuing deficit of women in India and the impact of amniocentesis. In G. Corea et al. (Eds.), *Man-made women: How new reproductive technologies affect women* (pp. 30–37). Bloomington: Indiana University Press.

Kite, M. E. (1984). Sex differences in attitudes toward homosexuals: A meta-analytic review. *Journal of Homosexuality, 10,* 69–81.

Kite, M. E., & Deaux, K. (1986). Attitudes toward homosexuality: Assessment and behavioral consequences. *Basic and Applied Social Psychology, 7,* 137–162.

Kite, M. E., & Deaux, K. (1987). Gender belief systems: Homosexuality and the implicit inversion theory. *Psychology of Women Quarterly, 11,* 83–96.

Kitzinger, C. (1987). *The social construction of lesbianism.* London: Sage.

Klass, P. (1988, April 10). Are women better doctors? *New York Times Magazine,* pp. 32–35, 46, 48, 96, 97.

Klaus, M. H., & Kennell, J. H. (1982). *Maternal-infant bonding* (2nd ed.). St. Louis: Mosby.

Klein, E. (1984). *Gender politics: From consciousness to mass politics.* Cambridge, MA: Harvard University Press.

Klein, E. (1990, November-December). Specialty urged in women's health. *New Directions for Women,* pp. 1, 5.

Klein, E., & Farah, B. G. (1988, November 17). *What happened to the gender gap?* Paper presented at the meeting of the Mid-Atlantic Seminar on Women and Culture, Philadelphia.

Klein, S. S. (Ed.). (1985). *Handbook for achieving sex equity through education.* Baltimore, Md.: Johns Hopkins University Press.

Kleinke, C. L., & Meyer, C. (1990). Evaluation of rape victim by men and women with high and low belief in a just world. *Psychology of Women Quarterly, 14,* 343–353.

Klemesrud, J. (1979, March 11). Women executives: View from the top. *New York Times,* p. 50.

Kline, M., Tschann, J. M., Johnston, J. R., & Wallerstein, J. S. (1989). Children's adjustment in joint and sole physical custody families. *Developmental Psychology, 25,* 430–438.

Kluft, R. P. (Ed.). (1985). *Childhood antecedents of multiple personality disorder.* Washington, DC: American Psychiatric Association.

Knafo, D., & Jaffe, Y. (1984). Sexual fantasizing in males and females. *Journal of Research in Personality, 18,* 451–462.

Kobasa, S.C.O. (1987). Stress responses and personality. In R. C. Barnett, L. Biener & G. K. Baruch (Eds.), *Gender and stress* (pp. 308–329). New York: Free Press.

Koblinsky, S. A., & Sugawara, A. I. (1984). Nonsexist curricula, sex of teacher, and children's sex role learning. *Sex Roles, 10,* 357–367.

Kobrin, F. E., & Hendershot, G. E. (1977). Do family ties reduce mortality? Evidence from the United States, 1966-1968. *Journal of Marriage, 39,* 737–745.

Koenenn, C. (1987, November-December). Women, gays lambast Pope. *New Directions for Women,* p. 3.

Koeske, R. K., & Koeske, G. F. (1975). An attributional approach to moods and the menstrual cycle. *Journal of Personality and Social Psychology, 31,* 473–478.

Koff, E., Rierdan, J., & Stubbs, M. L. (1990). Gender, body image, and self-concept in early adolescence. *Journal of Early Adolescence, 10,* 56–68.

Kohlberg, L. A. (1966). A cognitive-developmental analysis of children's sex-role concepts and attitudes. In E. E. Maccoby (Ed.), *The development of sex differences* (pp. 82–173). Stanford, CA: Stanford University Press.

Kohlberg, L. (1969). Stage and sequence: The cognitive-developmental approach to socialization. In D. A. Goslin (Ed.), *Handbook of socialization and research* (pp. 347–480). Chicago: Rand McNally.

Kohlberg, L., & Ullian, D. Z. (1974). Stages in the development of psychosexual concepts and attitudes. In R. C. Friedman, R. M. Richart, & R. L. Vande Wiele (Eds.), *Sex differences in behavior.* (pp. 209–222). New York: Wiley.

Kolata, G. (1983). Math genius may have hormonal basis. *Science, 222,* 1312.

Kolata, G. (1989, January 30). Lesbian partners find the means to be parents. *New York Times,* p. A13.

Kolata, G. (1991, July 25). Women's cardiac care may be lacking heart. *Morning Call,* pp. A1, A14.

Kolata, G. B. (1974). !Kung hunter-gatherers: Feminism, diet and birth control. *Science, 185,* 932–934.

Komarovsky, M. (1973). Cultural contradictions and sex roles: The masculine case. *American Journal of Sociology, 78,* 873–874.

Komarovsky, M. (1974). Patterns of self-disclosure in male undergraduates. *Journal of Marriage and the Family, 36,* 677–687.

Komarovsky, M. (1976). *Dilemmas of masculinity: A study of college youth.* New York: Norton.

Komter, A. (1989). Hidden power in marriage. *Gender and Society, 3,* 187–216.

Kopper, B. A., & Epperson, D. L. (1991). Women and anger: Sex and sex-role comparisons in the expression of anger. *Psychology of Women Quarterly, 15,* 7–14.

Koss, M. P. (1990). The women's mental health research agenda: Violence against women. *American Psychologist, 45,* 374–380.

Koss, M. P., & Dinero, T. E. (1988). Predictors of sexual aggression among a national sample of male college students. In V. I. Quinsey & R. Prentky (Eds.), *Human sexual aggression: Current perspectives* (pp. 133–147). New York Academy of Sciences.

Koss, M. P., & Dinero, T. E. (1989). A discriminant analysis of risk factors for rape among a national sample of college women. *Journal of Consulting and Clinical Psychology, 57,* 242–250.

Koss, M. P., Dinero, T. E., Seibel, C. A., & Cox, S. L. (1988). Stranger and acquaintance rape: Are there differences in the victim's experience? *Psychology of Women Quarterly, 12,* 1–24.

Koss, M. P., Gidycz, C. J., & Wisniewski, N. (1987). The scope of rape: Incidence and prevalence of sexual aggression and victimization in a national sample of higher education students. *Journal of Consulting and Clinical Psychology, 55,* 162–170.

Koss, M. P., & Oros, C. J. (1982). Sexual experiences survey: A research instrument investigating sexual aggression and victimization. *Journal of Consulting and Clinical Psychology, 50,* 455–457.

Kotkin, M. (1983). Sex roles among married and unmarried couples. *Sex Roles, 9,* 975–985.

Kraft, I. (1991, February 24). Dual-career families face "trailing spouse syndrome." *Morning Call,* p. B21.

Kraiger, K., & Ford, J. K. (1985). A meta-analysis of ratee race effects in performance ratings. *Journal of Applied Psychology, 70,* 56–65.

Krasnoff, A. G. (1981). The sex difference in self-assessed fears. *Sex Roles, 7,* 19–23.

Krause, N. (1983). Conflicting sex-role expectations, housework dissatisfaction, and depressive symptoms among full-time housewives. *Sex Roles, 9,* 1115–1125.

Kravetz, D. (1978). Consciousness-raising groups in the 1970s. *Psychology of Women Quarterly, 3,* 168–186.

Kravetz, D., Marecek, J., & Finn, S. E. (1983). Factors influencing women's participation in consciousness-raising groups. *Psychology of Women Quarterly, 7,* 257–271.

Krogh, K. M. (1985). Women's motives to achieve and to nurture in different life stages. *Sex Roles, 12,* 75–90.

Kruks, S., Rapp, R., & Young, M. B. (Eds.). (1989). *Promissory notes: Women in the transition to socialism.* New York: Monthly Review Press.

Krulewitz, J. E., & Nash, J. E. (1980). Effects of sex role attitudes and similarity on men's rejection of male homosexuals. *Journal of Personality and Social Psychology, 38,* 67–74.

Krupnick, C. G. (1985, May). Women and men in the classroom: Inequality and its remedies. *On Teaching and Learning: The Journal of the Harvard-Danforth Center for Teaching and Learning,* pp. 18–25.

Kulik, J. A., & Harackiewicz, J. (1979). Opposite-sex interpersonal attraction as a function of the sex roles of the perceiver and the perceived. *Sex Roles, 5,* 443–452.

Kurdek, L. A. (1987). Sex role self schema and psychological adjustment in coupled homosexual men and women. *Sex Roles, 17,* 549–562.

Kurdek, L. A. (1988a). Correlates of negative attitudes toward homosexuals in heterosexual college students. *Sex Roles, 18,* 727–738.

Kurdek, L. A. (1988b). Perceived social support in gays and lesbians in cohabitating relationships. *Journal of Personality and Social Psychology, 54,* 504–509.

Kurdek, L. A. (1989). Relationship quality in gay and lesbian cohabiting couples: A 1-year follow-up study. *Journal of Social and Personal Relationships, 6,* 39–59.

Kurdek, L. A., & Schmitt, J. P. (1986a). Early development of relationship quality in heterosexual married, heterosexual cohabiting, gay, and lesbian couples. *Developmental Psychology, 22,* 305–309.

Kurdek, L. A., & Schmitt, J. P. (1986b). Interaction of sex role self-concept with relationship quality and relationship beliefs in married, heterosexual cohabiting, gay, and lesbian couples. *Journal of Personality and Social Psychology, 51,* 365–370.

Kurdek, L. A., & Schmitt, J. P. (1986c). Relationship quality of partners in heterosexual married, heterosexual cohabiting, and gay and lesbian relationships. *Journal of Personality and Social Psychology, 51,* 711–720.

Kurdek, L. A., & Schmitt, J. P. (1987a). Partner homogamy in married, heterosexual, cohabiting, gay, and lesbian couples. *Journal of Sex Research, 23,* 212–232.

Kurdek, L. A., & Schmitt, J. P. (1987b). Perceived emotional support from family and friends in members of homosexual, married, and heterosexual cohabiting couples. *Journal of Homosexuality, 14,* 57–68.

Kurtz, D. (1989). Social science perspectives on wife abuse: Current debates and future directions. *Gender and Society 3,* 489–505.

Kushell, E., & Newton, R. (1986). Gender, leadership style, and subordinate satisfaction: An experiment. *Sex Roles, 14,* 203–209.

Lacher, M.R.B. (1978). On advising undergraduate women: A psychologist's advice to academic advisors. *Journal of College Student Personnel, 19,* 488–493.

Lack of child care limits career. (1987, June 14). *Easton Express,* p. E6.

Ladner, J. (1971). *Tomorrow's tomorrow: The black woman.* New York: Doubleday.

Lafontaine, E., & Tredeau, L. (1986). The frequency, sources, and correlates of sexual harassment among women in traditional male occupations. *Sex Roles, 15,* 433–442.

LaFrance, M. (1982). Gender gestures: Sex, sex-role, and nonverbal communication. In C. Mayo & N. Henley (Eds.), *Gender and nonverbal behavior* (pp. 129–150). New York: Springer-Verlag.

LaFrance, M., & Carmen, B. (1980). The nonverbal display of psychological androgyny. *Journal of Personality and Social Psychology, 38,* 36–49.

Lakoff, R. (1975). *Language and woman's place.* New York: Harper & Row.

Lakoff, R. T. (1990). *Talking power: The politics of language in our lives.* New York: Basic Books.

Lamb, M. C., & Sagi, A. (Eds.). (1983). *Fatherhood and family policy.* Hillsdale, NJ: Erlbaum.

Lamb, M. E. (1981a). The development of father-infant relationship. In M. E. Lamb (Ed.), *The role of the father in child development* (2nd ed.) (pp. 459–488). New York: Praeger.

Lamb, M. E. (Ed.). (1981b). *The role of the father in child development* (2nd ed.). NY: Wiley.

Lamb, M. E. (1986). The changing roles of fathers. In M. E. Lamb (Ed.), *The father's role: Applied perspectives* (pp. 3–27). New York: Wiley.

Lamb, M. E. (1987). Introduction: The emergent American father. In M. E. Lamb (Ed.), *The father's role: Cross-cultural perspectives* (pp. 3–25). Hillsdale, NJ: Erlbaum.

Landers, S. (1989, April). NY: Scholarship awards are ruled discriminatory. *APA Monitor,* p. 14.

Landers, S. (1990, April). Sex, condom use up among teenage boys. *APA Monitor,* p. 25.

Landrine, H. (1985). Race × class stereotypes of women. *Sex Roles, 13,* 65–75.

Landrine, H. (1988). Depression and stereotypes of women: Preliminary empirical analyses of the gender-role hypothesis. *Sex Roles, 19,* 527–541.

Landrine, H. (1989). The politics of personality disorder. *Psychology of Women Quarterly, 13,* 325–339.

Landrine, H., Bardwell, S., & Dean, T. (1988). Gender expectations for alcohol use: A study of the significance of the masculine role. *Sex Roles, 19,* 703–712.

Landy, F. J., & Farr, J. L. (1980). Performance rating. *Psychological Bulletin, 87,* 72–107.

Lange, S. J., & Worell, J. (1990, August). *Satisfaction and commitment in lesbian and heterosexual relationships.* Paper presented at the meeting of the American Psychological Association, Boston.

Largen, M. A. (1988). Rape-law reform: An analysis. In A. W. Burgess (Ed.), *Rape and sexual assault II* (pp. 271–292). New York: Garland.

LaRossa, R. (1989, Spring). Fatherhood and social change. *Men's Studies Review, 6,* 1–9.

LaRossa, R., & LaRossa, M. M. (1981). *Transition to parenthood: How infants change families.* Beverly Hills, CA: Sage.

Larsen, K. S., & Long, E. (1988). Attitudes toward sex roles: Traditional or egalitarian? *Sex Roles, 19,* 1–12.

Larsen, R. J., & Seidman, E. (1986). Gender schema theory and sex role inventories: Some conceptual and psychometric considerations. *Journal of Personality and Social Psychology, 50,* 205–211.

Larwood, L., & Gattiker, U. E. (1987). A comparison of the career paths used by successful women and men. In B. A. Gutek & L. Larwood (Eds.), *Women's career development* (pp. 129–156). Beverly Hills, CA: Sage.

Larwood, L., Szwajkowski, E., & Rose, S. (1988). Sex and race discrimination resulting from manager-client relationships: Applying the rational bias theory of managerial discrimination. *Sex Roles, 18,* 9–29.

Lasker, J. N., & Borg, S. (1987). *In search of parenthood: Coping with infertility and high-tech conception.* Boston: Beacon Press.

Latkin, C. A. (1989). Gender roles in the experimental community: Rajneeshpuram. *Sex Roles, 21,* 629–652.

LaTorre, R. A., Yu, L., Fortin, L., & Marrache, M. (1983). Gender-role adoption and sex as academic and psychological risk factors. *Sex Roles, 9,* 1127–1136.

Lau, S. (1989). Sex role orientation and domains of self-esteem. *Sex Roles, 21*, 415–422.

Lavelle, M., & Ramunni, R. (1986, June 14). Methodists in throes of revising hymnals. *Easton Express*, p. C1, C3.

Lavine, L. O., & Lombardo, J. P. (1984). Self-disclosure: Intimate and nonintimate disclosures to parents and best friends as a function of Bem Sex-Role category. *Sex Roles, 11*, 735–744.

Lawrence, J. (1986, May 11). Working moms' pay essential to families. *Easton Express*, p. A5.

Laws, J. L., & Schwartz, P. (1977). *Sexual scripts: The social construction of female sexuality*. Hinsdale, IL: Dryden.

Lawson, A. (1988). *Adultery: An analysis of love and betrayal*. New York: Basic Books.

Lawson, C. (1989, June 15). Toys: Girls still apply makeup, boys fight wars. *New York Times*, pp. C1, C10.

Lawson, C. (1991, May 26). Time off the job for new fathers still elusive. *Morning Call*, p. A13.

Lazarre, J. (1976). *The mother knot*. New York: McGraw-Hill.

Leahy, R. L., & Shirk, S. R. (1984). The development of classificatory skills and sex-trait stereotypes in children. *Sex Roles, 10*, 281–292.

Leary, M. R., & Snell, W. E., Jr. (1988). The relationship of instrumentality and expressiveness to sexual behavior in males and females. *Sex Roles, 18*, 509–522.

Lee, A. M., Nelson, K., & Nelson, J. K. (1988). Success estimations and performance in children as influenced by age, gender, and task. *Sex Roles, 18*, 719–726.

Lee, F. R. (1991, December 1). More girls joining gangs to get things they want. *Morning Call*, p. A30.

Lee, R. B. (1972). The !Kung Bushmen of Botswana. In M. G. Bicchieri (Ed.), *Hunters and gatherers today*. New York: Holt, Rinehart & Winston.

Lee, V. E., & Bryk, A. S. (1986). Effects of single-sex secondary schools on student achievement and attitudes. *Journal of Educational Psychology, 7*, 381–395.

Lee, V. E., & Ekstrom, R. B. (1987). Student access to guidance counseling in high school. *American Educational Research Journal, 24*, 287–310.

Lee, V. E., & Marks, H. M. (1990). Sustained effects of the single-sex secondary school experience on attitudes, behaviors, and values in college. *Journal of Educational Psychology, 82*, 578–592.

Lefcourt, H. (1976). *Locus of control: Current trends in theory and research*. Hillsdale, NJ: Erlbaum.

Lehne, G. K. (1976). Homophobia among men. In D. David & R. Brannon (Eds.), *The 49-percent majority* (pp. 66–88). Reading, MA: Addison-Wesley.

Leiblum, S. R. (1990). Sexuality and the midlife woman. *Psychology of Women Quarterly, 14*, 495–508.

Leibowitz, L. (1979). Universals and male dominance among primates: A critical examination. In E. Tobach & B. Rosoff (Eds.), *Genes and gender II* (pp. 35–46). Staten Island, NY: Gordian Press.

Leibowitz, L. (1983). Origins of the sexual division of labor. In M. Lowe & R. Hubbard (Eds.), *Women's nature: Rationalizations of inequality* (pp. 123–147). New York: Pergamon Press.

Leidholdt, D., & Raymond, J. G. (Eds.). (1990). *The sexual liberals and the attack on feminism*. New York: Pergamon Press.

Leinbach, M. D., & Fagot, B. I. (1986). Acquisition of gender labels: A test for toddlers. *Sex Roles, 15*, 655–666.

Lemkau, J. P. (1983). Women in male-dominated professions: Distinguishing personality and background characteristics. *Psychology of Women Quarterly, 8*, 144–165.

Lenney, E. (1981). What's fine for the gander isn't always good for the goose: Sex differences in self-confidence as a function of ability area and comparison with others. *Sex Roles, 7*, 905–924.

Lenney, E., Gold, J., & Browning, C. (1983). Sex differences in self-confidence: The influence of comparison to others' ability level. *Sex Roles, 9*, 925–942.

Lenney, E., Mitchell, L., & Browning, C. (1983). The effect of clear evaluation criteria on sex bias in judgments of performance. *Psychology of Women Quarterly, 7*, 313–328.

Lennon, M. C. (1987). Is menopause depressing? An investigation of three perspectives. *Sex Roles, 17*, 1–16.

Leonard, J. S. (1989). Women and affirmative action. *Journal of Economic Perspectives, 3*, 61–75.

Lerner, G. (1986). *The creation of patriarchy*. New York: Oxford University Press.

Lerner, H. G. (1988). *Women in therapy*. Northvale, NJ: Jason Aronson.

Lerner, H. G. (1989). *The dance of intimacy*. New York: Harper & Row.

Lerner, H. G. (1990, April). Problems for profit. *Women's Review of Books*, pp. 15–16.

Lerner, R. M., Sorell, G. T., & Brackney, B. E. (1981). Sex differences in self-concept and self-esteem of late adolescents: A time-lag analysis. *Sex Roles, 7*, 709–722.

Lester, D. (1984). Suicide. In C. Widom (Ed.), *Sex roles and psychopathology* (pp. 145–156). New York: Plenum.

Lester, M. (1976, January 26). Rape: A report. *New York Times Magazine*, pp. 4–16.

Letich, L. (1991, May-June). Do you know who your friends are? *Utne Reader*, pp. 85–87.

Levay, S. (1991). A difference in hypothalmic structure between heterosexual and homosexual men. *Science, 253*, 1034–1037.

Levin, J., & Arluke, A. (1985). An exploratory analysis of sex differences in gossip. *Sex Roles, 12*, 281–286.

Levine, L., & Barbach, L. (1984). *The intimate male*. New York: Doubleday.

Levine, M. P., & Leonard, R. (1984). Discrimination against lesbians in the work force. *Signs: Journal of Women in Culture and Society, 9*, 700–710.

Levine-MacCombie, J., & Koss, M. P. (1986). Acquaintance rape: Effective avoidance strategies. *Psychology of Women Quarterly, 10*, 311–320.

Levinson, D. (1978). *The seasons of a man's life*. New York: Knopf.

Levinson, D. (1989). *Family violence in cross-cultural perspective*. Newbury Park, CA: Sage.

Levinson, R., Powell, B., & Steelman, L. C. (1986). Social location, significant others, and body image among adolescents. *Social Psychology Quarterly, 49*, 330–337.

Lévi-Strauss, C. (1956). The family. In H. Shapiro (Ed.), *Man, culture, and society*. New York: Oxford University Press.

Levy, G. D. (1989a). Developmental and individual differences in preschoolers' recognition memories: The influences of gender schematization and verbal labeling of information. *Sex Roles, 21*, 305–324.

Levy, G. D. (1989b). Relations among aspects of children's social environments, gender schematization, gender role knowledge, and flexibility. *Sex Roles, 21*, 803–823.

Levy, G. D., & Carter, D. B. (1989). Gender schema, gender constancy, and gender-role knowledge: The roles of cognitive factors in preschoolers' gender-role stereotype attributions. *Developmental Psychology, 25*, 444–449.

Levy, J., & Reid, M. (1978). Variations in cerebral organization as a function of handedness, hand posture in writing, and sex. *Journal of Experimental Psychology: General, 107*, 119–144.

Lewin, M., & Tragos, L. M. (1987). Has the feminist movement influenced adolescent sex role attitudes? A reassessment after a quarter century. *Sex Roles, 16*, 125–135.

Lewin, T. (1988a, March 20). Fewer teen mothers, but more are unmarried. *New York Times*, p. E4.

Lewin, T. (1988b, June 5). Day care becomes a growing burden. *New York Times*, p. 22.

Lewin, T. (1990a, June 2). Data show rising plight of displaced homemakers. *New York Times*, p. 13.

Lewin, T. (1990b, June 16). Fathers desert children at alarming rate, study says. *New York Times*, p. 22.

Lewin, T. (1990c, July 15). Rise in single-parent families found continuing. *New York Times*, p. 24.

Lewis, D. K. (1977). A response to inequality: Black women, racism, and sexism. *Signs: Journal of Women in Culture and Society*, 3, 339–361.

Lewis, E. T., & McCarthy, P. R. (1988). Perceptions of self-disclosure as a function of gender-linked variables. *Sex Roles*, 19, 47–56.

Lewis, K. E., & Bierly, M. (1990). Toward a profile of the female voter: Sex differences in perceived physical attractiveness and competence of political candidates. *Sex Roles*, 22, 1–12.

Lewis, L. A. (1990). *Gender politics and MTV: Voicing the difference*. Philadelphia: Temple University Press.

Lewis, M. (1987). Early sex role behavior and school age adjustment. In J. M. Reinisch, L. A. Rosenblum, & S. A. Sanders (Eds.), *Masculinity/femininity* (pp. 202–226). New York: Oxford University Press.

Lewis, M., & Weinraub, M. (1979). Origins of early sex-role development. *Sex Roles*, 5, 135–153.

Lewis, R. (1990, January 25). Wife's higher earnings can tax a marriage. *Morning Call*, pp. D1, 2.

Lewis, R. A. (1978). Emotional intimacy among men. *Journal of Social Issues*, 34(1), 108–121.

Lewittes, H. J., & Bem, S. L. (1983). Training women to be more assertive in mixed-sex task-oriented discussions. *Sex Roles*, 9, 581–596.

Lewontin, R. C., Rose, S., & Kamin, L. J. (1984). *Not in our genes: Biology, ideology, and human nature*. New York: Pantheon.

L'Heureux-Barrett, T., & Barnes-Farrell, J. L. (1991). Overcoming gender bias in reward allocation: The role of expectations of future performance. *Psychology of Women Quarterly*, 15, 127–139.

Liben, L. S., & Golbeck, S. L. (1986). Adults' demonstration of underlying euclidean concepts in relation to task context. *Developmental Psychology*, 22, 487–490.

Liben, L. S., & Signorella, M. L. (1980). Gender-related schemata and constructive memory in children. *Child Development*, 51, 11–18.

Liben, L. S., & Signorella, M. L. (Eds.). (1987). *Children's gender schemata*. San Francisco: Jossey-Bass.

Licht, B. G., Stader, S. R., & Swenson, C. C. (1989). Children's achievement-related beliefs: Effects of academic area, sex, and achievement level. *Journal of Education Research*, 82, 253–260.

Lichter, S. R., Lichter, L. S., & Rothman, S. (1986, September-October). From Lucy to Lacey: TV's dream girls. *Public Opinion*, pp. 16–19.

Lichter, S. R., Lichter, L. S., Rothman, S., & Amundson, D. (1987, July-August). Prime-time prejudice: TV's images of Blacks and Hispanics. *Public Opinion*, pp. 13–16.

Liden, R. C. (1985). Female perceptions of female and male managerial behavior. *Sex Roles*, 12, 421–432.

Lieberman, M. A., Solow, N., Bond, G. R., & Reibstein, J. (1979). The psychotherapeutic impact of women's consciousness-raising groups. *Archives of General Psychiatry*, 36, 161–168.

Lieblich, A., & Friedman, G. (1985). Attitudes toward male and female homosexuality and sex-role stereotypes in Israeli and American students. *Sex Roles*, 12, 561–570.

Liem, R., & Rayman, P. (1982). Health and social costs of unemployment: Research and policy considerations. *American Psychologist*, 37, 1116–1123.

Lii, S., & Wong, S. (1982). A cross-cultural study on sex-role stereotypes and social desirability. *Sex Roles*, 8, 481–491.

Lim, L.Y.C. (1990). Women's work in export factories: The politics of a cause. In I. Tinker (Ed.), *Persistent inequalities: Women and world development* (pp. 101–119). New York: Oxford University Press.

Linehan, M. M., & Seifert, R. F. (1983). Sex and contextual differences in the appropriateness of assertive behavior. *Psychology of Women Quarterly*, 8, 79–88.

Linn, M. C., & Hyde, J. S. (1989, November). Gender, mathematics, and science. *Educational Researcher*, pp. 17–27.

Linn, M. C., & Petersen, A. C. (1985). Emergence and characterization of sex differences in spatial ability: A meta-analysis. *Child Development*, 56, 1479–1498.

Linn, M. C., & Petersen, A. C. (1986). A meta-analysis of gender differences in spatial ability: Implications for mathematics and science achievement. In J. S. Hyde & M. C. Linn (Eds.), *The psychology of gender: Advances through meta-analysis* (pp. 67–101). Baltimore: Johns Hopkins University Press.

Linscott, J. (1984, March 15). Road still rougher for career women. *Easton Express*, p. C2.

Linz, D., Donnerstein, E., & Penrod, S. (1984). The effects of multiple exposure to filmed violence against women. *Journal of Communications*, 34(3), 130–147.

Linz, D., Donnerstein, E., & Penrod, S. (1987a). The findings and recommendations of the Attorney General's Commission on Pornography: Do the psychological "facts" fit the political fury? *American Psychologist*, 42, 946–953.

Linz, D., Donnerstein, E., & Penrod, S. (1987b). Sexual violence in the mass media: Social psychological implications. In P. Shaver & C. Hendrick (Eds.), *Sex and gender* (pp. 95–123). Newbury Park, CA: Sage.

Lipman-Blumen, J., & Bernard, J. (Eds.). (1979). *Sex roles and social policy: A complex social science equation*. Beverly Hills, CA: Sage.

Lips, H. M. (1991). *Women, men, and power*. Mountain View, CA: Mayfield.

Lips, H. M., & Temple, L. (1988, August). *Majoring in computer science: Causal models for women and men*. Paper presented at the meeting of the American Psychological Association, Atlanta.

Lipsyte, M. (1989, May-June). She blasts racist media. *New Directions for Women*, p. 8.

Lisak, D., & Roth, S. (1988). Motivational factors in nonincarcerated sexually aggressive men. *Journal of Personality and Social Psychology*, 55, 795–802.

Liu, A. E. (1991, February). Going back and moving forward. *Lear's*, pp. 28-29.

Lobel, K. (Ed.). (1986). *Naming the violence: Speaking out about lesbian battering*. Seattle, WA: Seal Press.

Lockheed, M. E. (1985). Some determinants and consequences of sex segregation in the classroom. In L. C. Wilkinson & C. B. Marrett (Eds.), *Gender influences in classroom interaction* (pp. 167–184). Orlando, FL: Academic Press.

Lockheed, M. E., & Hall, K. P. (1976). Conceptualizing sex as a status characteristic and applications to leadership training strategies. *Journal of Social Issues*, 32(3), 111–124.

Locksley, A., Borgida, E., Brekke, N., & Hepburn, C. (1980). Sex stereotypes and social judgement. *Journal of Personality and Social Psychology*, 39, 821–831.

Locksley, A., & Colten, M. E. (1979). Psychological androgyny: A case of mistaken identity? *Journal of Personality and Social Psychology*, 37, 1017–1031.

Locksley, A., & Douvan, E. (1979). Problem behavior in adolescents. In E. S. Gomberg & V. Franks (Eds.), *Gender and disordered behavior: Sex differences in psychopathology* (pp. 71–100). New York: Brunner/Mazel.

Loden, M. (1986, February 9). A machismo that drives women out. *New York Times*, p. D2.

Loevinger, J. (1976). *Ego development: Conceptions and theories*. San Francisco: Jossey-Bass.

Loewen, J. W. (1988). Visitation fatherhood. In P. Bronstein & C. P. Cowan (Eds.), *Fatherhood today: Men's changing role in the family* (pp. 195–213). New York: Wiley.

Lohman, D. F. (1988). Spatial abilities as traits, processes, and knowledge. In R. J. Sternberg (Ed.), *Advances in the psychology of human intelligence*, Vol. 4 (pp. 181–248). Hillsdale, NJ: Erlbaum.

Lombardo, W. K., Cretser, G. A., Lombardo, B., & Mathis, S. L. (1983). For cryin' out loud—There is a sex difference. *Sex Roles, 9*, 987–995.

Long, B. C. (1989). Sex-role orientation, coping strategies, and self-efficacy of women in traditional and nontraditional occupations. *Psychology of Women Quarterly, 13*, 307–324.

Long, J. S. (1990). The origins of sex differences in science. *Social Forces, 68*, 1297–1315.

Lont, C. M. (1990). The roles assigned to females and males in non-music radio programming. *Sex Roles, 22*, 661–668.

Lorde, A. (1984). *Sister outsider.* Trumansburg, NY: Crossing Press.

Lott, B. (1978). Behavioral concordance with sex role ideology related to play areas, creativity and parental sex typing of children. *Journal of Personality and Social Psychology, 36*, 1087–1100.

Lott, B. (1985). The potential enrichment of social/personality psychology through feminist research, and vice versa. *American Psychologist, 40*, 155–164.

Lott, B. (1989). Sexist discrimination as distancing behavior: II. Prime-time television. *Psychology of Women Quarterly, 13*, 341–355.

Lovdal, L. T. (1989). Sex role messages in television commercials: An update. *Sex Roles, 21*, 715–724.

Lowe, M., & Hubbard, R. (1979). Sociobiology and biosociology: Can science prove the biological basis of sex differences in behavior? In E. Tobach & B. Rosoff (Eds.), *Genes and gender II* (pp. 91–112). Staten Island, NY: Gordian Press.

Lubinski, D., Tellegen, A., & Butcher, J. N. (1983). Masculinity, femininity, and androgyny viewed and assessed as distinct concepts. *Journal of Personality and Social Psychology, 44*, 428–439.

Luebke, B. F. (1989). Out of focus: Images of women and men in newspaper photographs. *Sex Roles, 20*, 121–133.

Luepnitz, D. A. (1986). A comparison of maternal, paternal, and joint custody: Understanding the varieties of post-divorce family life. *Journal of Divorce, 9*, 1–12.

Luepnitz, D. A. (1988). *The family interpreted: Feminist theory in clinical practice.* New York: Basic Books.

Lummis, M., & Stevenson, H. W. (1990). Gender differences in beliefs and achievement: A cross-cultural study. *Developmental Psychology, 26*, 254–263.

Lung cancer increasing faster among women. (1990, December 7). *Morning Call*, p. A12.

Lykes, B., Stewart, A., & LaFrance, M. (1981, April). *Control and aspirations in adolescents: A comparison by race, sex, and social class.* Paper presented at the meeting of the Eastern Psychological Association, New York.

Lykes, M. B. (1983). Discrimination and coping in the lives of black women: Analyses of oral history data. *Journal of Social Issues, 39*(3), 79–100.

Lykes, M. B. (1985). Gender and individualistic vs. collectivist bases for notions about the self. *Journal of Personality, 53*, 356–383.

Lykes, M. B., & Stewart, A. J. (1986). Evaluating the feminist challenge to research in personality and social psychology: 1963–1983. *Psychology of Women Quarterly, 10*, 393–412.

Lyman, P. (1987). The fraternal bond as a joking relationship. In M. S. Kimmel (Ed.), *Changing men: New directions in research on men and masculinity* (pp. 148–163). Newbury Park, CA: Sage.

Lynn, D. B. (1959). A note on sex differences in the development of masculine and feminine identification. *Psychological Review, 66*, 126–135.

Lynn, D. B. (1969). *Parental and sex role identification: A theoretical formulation.* Berkeley: McCutchan.

Lynn, D. B. (1979). *Daughters and parents: Past, present, and future.* Monterey, CA: Brooks/Cole.

Lynn, N. (1975). Women in American politics: An overview. In J. Freeman (Ed.), *Women: A feminist perspective* (pp. 364–385). Palo Alto, CA: Mayfield.

Lytton, H., & Romney, D. M. (1991). Parents' differential socialization of boys and girls: A meta-analysis. *Psychological Bulletin, 109*, 267–296.

MacArthur, R. S. (1967). Sex differences in field dependence for the Eskimo. *International Journal of Psychology, 2*, 139–140.

Maccoby, E. E. (1966). Sex differences in intellectual functioning. In E. E. Maccoby (Ed.), *The development of sex differences* (pp. 25–55). Stanford, CA: Stanford University Press.

Maccoby, E. E. (1990). Gender and relationships: A developmental account. *American Psychologist, 45*, 513–520.

Maccoby, E. E., & Jacklin, C. N. (1974). *The psychology of sex differences.* Stanford, CA: Stanford University Press.

Maccoby, E. E., & Jacklin, C. N. (1987). Gender segregation in childhood. *Advances in Child Development and Behavior, 20*, 239–287.

Maccoby, M. (1976, December). The corporate climber. *Fortune*, pp. 98–101, 104–108.

MacCormack, C., & Strathern, M. (1981). *Nature, culture, and gender.* Cambridge, England: Cambridge University Press.

MacDonald, K. B., & Parke, R. D. (1986). Parent-child physical play: The effects of sex and age of children and parents. *Sex Roles, 15*, 367–378.

MacKay, D. G. (1980). Psychology, prescriptive grammar, and the pronoun problem. *American Psychologist, 35*, 444–449.

Mackey, W. C. (1985). A cross-cultural perspective on perceptions of paternalistic deficiencies in the United States: The myth of the derelict Daddy. *Sex Roles, 12*, 509–534.

MacKinnon, C. A. (1979). *Sexual harassment of working women: A case of sex discrimination.* New Haven: Yale University Press.

MacKinnon, C. A. (1987a). A feminist/political approach: "Pleasure under patriarchy." In J. H. Geer & W. T. O'Donohue (Eds.), *Theories of human sexuality* (pp. 65–90). New York: Plenum.

MacKinnon, C. A. (1987b). *Feminism unmodified: Discourses on life and law.* Cambridge, MA: Harvard University Press.

MacKinnon, C. A. (1989). *Toward a feminist theory of the state.* Cambridge, MA: Harvard University Press.

Macklin, E. D. (1980). Nontraditional family forms: A decade of research. *Journal of Marriage and the Family, 42*, 905–922.

Madden, M. E. (1987). Perceived control and power in marriage: A study of marital decision making and task performance. *Personality and Social Psychology Bulletin, 13*, 73–82.

Madigan, C. M. (1989, January 12). Women focus on politics. *Easton Express*, p. C10.

Mahlstedt, D. (1991, August). *Fraternity violence education project: When men take action.* Paper presented at the meeting of the American Psychological Association, San Francisco.

Mahlstedt, D. (1992). *Female survivors of dating violence and their social networks.* Manuscript submitted for publication.

Major, B. (1987). Gender, justice, and entitlement. In P. Shaver & C. Hendrick (Eds.), *Sex and gender* (pp. 124–148). Newbury Park, CA: Sage.

Major, B., & Adams, J. B. (1984). Situational moderators of gender differences in reward allocations. *Sex Roles, 11*, 869–880.

Major, B., Bylsma, W. H., & Cozzarelli, C. (1989). Gender differences in distributive justice preferences: The impact of domain. *Sex Roles, 21*, 487–498.

Major, B., Carnevale, P.J.D., & Deaux, K. (1981). A different perspective on androgyny: Evaluation of masculine and feminine personality characteristics. *Journal of Personality and Social Psychology, 41*, 988–1001.

Major, B., McFarlin, D., & Gagnon, D. (1984). Overworked and underpaid: On the nature of gender differences in personal entitlement. *Journal of Personality and Social Psychology, 47,* 1399–1412.

Major, B., Schmidlin, A. M., & Williams, L. (1990). Gender patterns in social touch: The impact of setting and age. *Journal of Personality and Social Psychology, 58,* 634–643.

Malamuth, N. M. (1981). Rape proclivity among males. *Journal of Social Issues, 37*(4), 138–157.

Malamuth, N. M. (1986). Predictors of naturalistic sexual aggression. *Journal of Personality and Social Psychology, 50,* 953–962.

Malamuth, N. M., & Briere, J. (1986). Sexual violence in the media: Indirect effects on aggression against women. *Journal of Social Issues, 42,* 75–92.

Malamuth, N. M., Check, J.V.P., & Briere, J. (1986). Sexual arousal in response to aggression: Ideological, aggressive, and sexual correlates. *Journal of Personality and Social Psychology, 50,* 330–340.

Malamuth, N. M., & Donnerstein, E. (Eds.). (1984). *Pornography and sexual aggression.* New York: Academic Press.

Malamuth, N. M., Haber, S., & Feshbach, S. (1980). Testing hypotheses regarding rape: Exposure and sexual violence, sex differences and the "normality" of rapists. *Journal of Research in Personality, 14*(1), 121–137.

Male bashing: Women less enamored with men, survey finds. (1990, April 26). *Morning Call,* p. A13.

Malinowski, B. (1932). *The sexual life of savages.* London: Routledge.

Malovich, N. J., & Stake, J. E. (1990). Sexual harassment on campus: Individual differences in attitudes and beliefs. *Psychology of Women Quarterly, 14,* 63–81.

Malson, M. R. (1983). Black women's sex roles: The social context for a new ideology. *Journal of Social Issues, 39*(3), 101–113.

Mamonova, T. (Ed.). (1984). *Women and Russia: Feminist writings.* (R. Park & C. A. Fitzpatrick, Trans.). Boston: Beacon Press.

Mamonova, T. (1989). *Russian women's studies: Essays on sexism in Soviet culture.* New York: Pergamon Press.

Mancini, J. A., & Orthner, D. K. (1978). Recreational sexuality preferences among middle-class husbands and wives. *Journal of Sex Research, 14*(2), 96–106.

Mandel, R. (1981). *In the running: The new woman candidate.* New York: Ticknor & Fields.

Mann, C. R. (1984). *Female crime and delinquency.* Tuscaloosa, AL: University of Alabama Press.

Mansbridge, J. J. (1986). *Why we lost the ERA.* Chicago: University of Chicago Press.

Mansnerus, L. (1989, February 19). The rape laws change faster than perceptions. *New York Times,* p. E20.

Marcus, S., & Overton, W. F. (1978). The development of cognitive gender constancy and sex role preferences. *Child Development, 49,* 434–444.

Marecek, J., Kravetz, D., & Finn, S. (1979). Comparison of women who enter feminist therapy and women who enter traditional therapy. *Journal of Consulting and Clinical Psychology, 47,* 734–742.

Marini, M. M. (1978). Sex differences in the determination of adolescent aspirations: A review of research. *Sex Roles, 4,* 723–753.

Mark, E. W., & Alper, T. G. (1985). Women, men, and intimacy motivation. *Psychology of Women Quarterly, 9,* 81–88.

Markowitz, J. (1984). The impact of the sexist-language controversy and regulation on language in university documents. *Psychology of Women Quarterly, 8,* 337–347.

Markstrom-Adams, C. (1989). Androgyny and its relation to adolescent psychosocial well-being: A review of the literature. *Sex Roles, 21,* 325–340.

Markus, H., Crane, N., Bernstein, S., & Siladi, M. (1982). Self-schemas and gender. *Journal of Personality and Social Psychology, 42,* 38–50.

Marriage: It's back in style. (1983, June 20). *U.S. News and World Report,* pp. 44–50.

Marsh, H. W., Antill, J. K., & Cunningham, J. D. (1987). Masculinity, femininity and androgyny: Relations of self-esteem and social desirabiity. *Journal of Personality, 55,* 661–685.

Marsh, H. W., Antill, J. K., & Cunningham, J. D. (1989). Masculinity and femininity: A bipolar construct and independent constructs. *Journal of Personality, 57,* 625–663.

Marsh, H. W., & Jackson, S. A. (1986). Multidimensional self-concepts, masculinity, and femininity as a function of women's involvement in athletics. *Sex Roles, 15,* 391–415.

Marshall, D. S. (1971, February). Too much in Mangaia. *Psychology Today,* pp. 43–44.

Martin, B. A. (1989). Gender differences in salary expectations when current salary information is provided. *Psychology of Women Quarterly, 13,* 87–96.

Martin, C. L. (1987). A ratio measure of sex stereotyping. *Journal of Personality and Social Psychology, 52,* 489–499.

Martin, C. L. (1989). Children's use of gender-related information in making social judgments. *Developmental Psychology, 25,* 80–88.

Martin, C. L. (1990). Attitudes and expectations about children with nontraditional and traditional gender roles. *Sex Roles, 22,* 151–165.

Martin, C. L., & Halverson, C. F., Jr. (1983). Gender constancy: A methodological and theoretical analysis. *Sex Roles, 9,* 775–790.

Martin, C. L., & Halverson, C. F., Jr. (1987). The roles of cognition in sex role acquisition. In B. Carter (Ed.), *Current conceptions of sex roles and sex typing: Theory and research* (pp. 123–137). New York: Praeger.

Martin, C. L., & Little, J. K. (1990). The relation of gender understanding to children's sex-typed preferences and gender stereotypes. *Child Development, 61,* 1427–1439.

Martin, C. L., Wood, C. H., & Little, J. K. (1990). The development of gender stereotype components. *Child Development, 61,* 1891–1904.

Martin, E. (1991). The egg and the sperm: How science has constructed a romance based on stereotypical male-female roles. *Signs: Journal of Women in Culture and Society, 16,* 485–501.

Martin, P. Y., & Hummer, R. A. (1989). Fraternities and rape on campus. *Gender and Society, 3,* 457–473.

Martin, S. C., Arnold, R. M., & Parker, R. M. (1988). Gender and medical socialization. *Journal of Health and Social Behavior, 29,* 333–343.

Martinko, M. J., & Gardner, W. L. (1983). A methodological review of sex-related access discrimination problems. *Sex Roles, 9,* 825–839.

Marwell, G., Rosenfeld, R., & Spilerman, S. (1979). Geographic constraints on women's careers in academia. *Science, 205,* 1225–1231.

Maslach, C., Santee, R. T., & Wade, C. (1987). Individuation, gender role, and dissent: Personality mediators of situational forces. *Journal of Personality and Social Psychology, 53,* 1088–1093.

Maslin, J. (1990, June 17). Bimbos embody retro rage. *New York Times,* pp. H13, H14.

Maslin, J. (1991, July 2). Give him a puppy and get the lady a gun. *New York Times,* pp. H1, H19.

Mason, M. A. (1988). *The equality trap.* New York: Simon & Schuster.

Masse, M. A., & Rosenblum, K. (1988). Male and female created they them: The depiction of gender in the advertising of traditional women's and men's magazines. *Women's Studies International Forum, 11,* 127–144.

Masters, W. H., & Johnson, V. (1966). *Human sexual response.* Boston: Little, Brown.

Masters, W. H., & Johnson, V. (1970). *Human sexual inadequacy.* Boston: Little, Brown.

Masters, W. H., & Johnson, V. (1974). *The pleasure bond: A new look at sexuality and commitment.* Boston: Little, Brown.

Masters, W. H., & Johnson, V. (1979). *Homosexuality in perspective*. Boston: Little, Brown.

Matteo, S. (1986). The effect of sex and gender-schematic processing on sport participation. *Sex Roles, 15*, 417–432.

Matteo, S. (1988). The effect of gender-schematic processing on decisions about sex-inappropriate sport behavior. *Sex Roles, 18*, 41–58.

Matthews, K. A., & Haynes, S. G. (1986). Type A behavior pattern and coronary disease risk. *American Journal of Epidemiology, 123*, 923–960.

Maugh, T. H., II. (1991, May 30). Gene tied to common retardation. *Morning Call*, p. A3.

Mayo, C., & Henley, N. (1981). *Gender and nonverbal behavior*. New York: Springer-Verlag.

Mazur, E. (1989). Predicting gender differences in same-sex friendships from affiliation motive and value. *Psychology of Women Quarterly 13*, 277–292.

Mazur, E., & Olver, R. R. (1987). Intimacy and structure: Sex differences in imagery of same-sex relationships. *Sex Roles, 16*, 539–558.

McAdams, D. P., & Bryant, F. B. (1987). Intimacy motivation and subjective mental health in a nationwide sample. *Journal of Personality, 55*, 395–413.

McAdoo, J. L. (1988). Changing perspectives on the role of the Black father. In P. Bronstein & C. P. Cowan (Eds.), *Fatherhood today: Men's changing role in the family* (pp. 79–92). New York: Wiley.

McArthur, L. Z., & Eisen, S. V. (1976). Achievements of male and female storybook characters as determinants of achieving behavior by boys and girls. *Journal of Personality and Social Psychology, 33*, 467–473.

McBride, A. B. (1990). Mental health effects of women's multiple roles. *American Psychologist, 45*, 381–384.

McBroom, P. A. (1986). *The third sex: The new professional woman*. New York: Morrow.

McBroom, W. H. (1981). Parental relationships, socioeconomic status, and sex role expectations. *Sex Roles, 7*, 1027–1033.

McBroom, W. H. (1987). Longitudinal change in sex role orientations: Differences between men and women. *Sex Roles, 16*, 439–452.

McCaulay, M., Mintz, L., & Glenn, A. A. (1988). Body image, self-esteem, and depression-proneness: Closing the gap. *Sex Roles, 18*, 381–391.

McClelland, D. C., Atkinson, J. W., Clark, R. A., & Lowell, E. G. (1953). *The achievement motive*. New York: Appleton-Century-Crofts.

McCoy, N., Cutler, W., & Davidson, J. M. (1985). Relationships among sexual behavior, hot flashes, and hormone levels in perimenopausal women. *Archives of Sexual Behavior, 14*, 385–394.

McCoy, N. L. (1977). Innate factors in sex differences. In A. Sargent (Ed.), *Beyond sex roles*. St. Paul, MN: West.

McDonald, K. (1984, March 21). Female athletes are competing at levels close to those of men in some sports. *Chronicle of Higher Education*, p. 23.

McFarland, C., Ross, M., & DeCourville, N. (1989). Women's theories of menstruation and biases in recall of menstrual symptoms. *Journal of Personality and Social Psychology, 57*, 522–531.

McFarlane, J., Martin, C. L., & Williams, T. M. (1988). Mood fluctuations: Women versus men and menstrual versus other cycles. *Psychology of Women Quarterly, 12*, 201–223.

McGhee, P. E., & Frueh, T. (1980). Television viewing and the learning of sex-role stereotypes. *Sex Roles, 6*, 179–188.

McGill, M. E. (1985). *The McGill report on male intimacy*. New York: Harper & Row.

McGillicuddy-De Lisi, A. V. (1985). The relationship between parental beliefs and children's cognitive level. In I. E. Sigel (Ed.), *Parental belief systems: The psychological consequences for children* (pp. 7–24). Hillsdale, NJ: Erlbaum.

McGillicuddy-De Lisi, A. V. (1988). Sex differences in parental teaching behaviors. *Merrill-Palmer Quarterly, 34*, 147–162.

McGlone, J. (1980). Sex differences in human brain asymmetry: A critical survey. *Behavioral and Brain Sciences, 3*, 215–263.

McGrath, E., Keita, G. P., Strickland, B. R., & Russo, N. F. (Eds.). (1990). *Women and depression: Risk factors and treatment issues*. Hyattsville, MD: American Psychological Association.

McGuinness, D., & Pribram, K. (1978). The origins of sensory bias in the development of gender differences in perception and cognition. In M. Bortner (Ed.), *Cognitive growth and development—Essays in honor of Herbert G. Birch*. New York: Brunner/Mazel.

McHale, S. M., Bartko, W. T., Crouter, A. C., & Perry-Jenkins, M. (1990). Children's housework and psychosocial functioning: The mediating effects of parents' sex-role behaviors and attitudes. *Child Development, 61*, 1413–1426.

McHenry, S., & Small, L. L. (1989, March). Does part-time pay off? *Ms.*, pp. 88–93.

McHugh, M. C., Koeske, R. D., & Frieze, I. H. (1986). Issues to consider in conducting non-sexist psychological research: A guide for researchers. *American Psychologist, 41*, 879–890.

McIntosh, P. (1988). *White privilege and male privilege: A personal account of coming to see correspondences through work in Women's Studies* (Working Paper No. 189). Wellesley, MA: Wellesley College Center for Research on Women.

McIntosh, P. M. (1989). Curricular re-vision: The new knowledge for a new age. In C. S. Pearson, D. L. Shavlik, & J. G. Touchton (Eds.), *Educating the majority: Women challenge tradition in higher education* (pp. 400–412). New York: American Council on Education/Macmillan.

McIntyre, L. D., & Pernell, E. (1985). The impact of race on teacher recommendations for special education placement. *Journal of Multicultural Counseling and Development, 13*, 112–120.

McKenna, W., & Kessler, S. (1977). Experimental design as a source of sex bias in social psychology. *Sex Roles, 3*, 117–128.

McKinlay, S. M., McKinlay, J. B., & Avis, N. E. (1989, Spring). The Massachusetts Women's Health Study: A longitudinal study of the health of mid-aged women and the epidemiology of the menopause. *Psychology of Women, Newsletter of Division 35, American Psychological Association*, pp. 1, 3, 4.

McLanahan, S. S., Sorensen, A., & Watson, D. (1989). Sex differences in poverty, 1950–1980. *Signs: Journal of Women in Culture and Society, 15*, 102–122.

McLoyd, V. C. (1989). Socialization and development in a changing economy: The effects of paternal job and income loss on children. *American Psychologist, 44*, 293–302.

McMahan, I. (1982). Expectancy of success on sex-linked tasks. *Sex Roles, 8*, 949–958.

McMillen, L. (1986, September 10). Women flock to graduate school in record numbers. *Chronicle of Higher Education*, pp. 1, 25.

McMillen, L. (1989, April 26). Foundations are being drawn into colleges' debate over cultural diversity in the curriculum. *Chronicle of Higher Education*, pp. 25–27.

McNeil, D. G., Jr. (1991, July 21). Should women be sent into combat? *New York Times*, p. E3.

McNeill, S., & Petersen, A. C. (1985, Winter). Gender role and identity in early adolescence: Reconsideration of theory. *Academic Psychology Bulletin, 7*, 299–315.

McQuade, W. (1985, August 5). The male manager's last refuge. *Fortune*, pp. 37–42.

McQueen, M. (1988, September 23). Economic issues split sexes in their choice of Bush or Dukakis. *Wall Street Journal*, pp. 1–6.

Mead, M. (1935). *Sex and temperament*. New York: Morrow.

Mednick, M.T.S., & Puryear, G. R. (1975). Motivational and personality factors related to career goals of Black college women. *Journal of Social and Behavioral Sciences, 12*, 1–30.

Megargee, E. (1969). Influence of sex roles on the manifestation of leadership. *Journal of Applied Psychology, 53,* 377–382.

Meillassoux, C. (1981). *Maidens, meal, and money: Capitalism and the domestic community.* Cambridge, England: Cambridge University Press.

Meisler, S. (1990, July 24). Incomes of the richest jumped 87% in the '80s. *Morning Call,* p. A5.

Mellen, J. (1973). *Women and their sexuality in the new film.* New York: Dell.

Melson, G. F., & Fogel, A. (1988, January). Learning to care. *Psychology Today,* pp. 39–45.

Melton, G. B. (1989). Public policy and private prejudice: Psychology and law on gay rights. *American Psychologist, 44,* 933–940.

Men doing more housework but still less than women. (1988, November 30). *Easton Express,* p. A2.

Mendonsa, E. L. (1981). The status of women in Sisala society. *Sex Roles, 7,* 607–625.

Mercer, R. T. (1986). *First-time motherhood: Experiences from teens to forties.* New York: Springer.

Meredith, D. (1985, June). Dad and the kids. *Psychology Today,* pp. 63–67.

Meredith, N. (1984, January). The gay dilemma. *Psychology Today,* pp. 56–62.

Merritt, S. (1982). Sex roles and political ambition. *Sex Roles, 8,* 1025–1036.

Messerschmidt, J. W. (1986). *Capitalism, patriarchy, and crime: Toward a socialist feminist criminology.* Totowa, NJ: Rowman & Littlefield.

Messing, K. (1982). Women have different jobs because of their biological differences. In E. Fee (Ed.), *Women and health: The politics of sex in medicine* (pp. 139–148). Farmingdale, NY: Baywood.

Messing, S. (1987, May-June). Co-ed gym: Boost or bust for average school girls? *New Directions for Women,* p. 7.

Messner, M. (1987). The life of a man's seasons: Male identity in the life course of the jock. In M. S. Kimmel (Ed.), *Changing men: New directions in research on men and masculinity* (pp. 53–67). Newbury Park, CA: Sage.

Messner, M. (1989). Masculinities and athletic careers. *Gender and Society, 3,* 71–88.

Messner, M. A., & Sabo, D. F. (Eds.). (1990). *Sport, men, and the gender order: Critical feminist perspectives.* Champaign, IL: Human Kinetics.

Metha, A. A. (1983). Decade since Title IX: Some implications for teacher education. *Action in Teacher Education, 5,* 21–27.

Meyer-Bahlburg, H.F.L. (1984). Psychoendocrine research on sexual orientation: Current status and future options. *Progress in Brain Research, 61,* 375–398.

Meyer-Bahlburg, H.F.L., Feldman, J. F., Cohen, P., & Ehrhardt, A. A. (1988). Perinatal factors in the development of gender-related play behavior: Sex hormones versus pregnancy complications. *Psychiatry, 51,* 260–271.

Michelini, R. L., Eisen, D., & Snodgrass, S. R. (1981). Success orientation and the attractiveness of competent males and females. *Sex Roles, 7,* 391–401.

Miedzian, M. (1991). *Boys will be boys: Breaking the link between masculinity and violence.* New York: Doubleday.

Mies, M. (1988). Social origins of the sexual divisions of labour. In M. Mies, V. Bennholdt-Thomsen, & C. von Werlhof (Eds.), *Women: The last colony.* (pp. 67–95). London: Zed.

Mies, M., Bennholdt-Thomsen, V., & von Werlhof, C. (Eds.). (1988). *Women: The last colony.* London: Zed.

Miles, R. (1988). *The women's history of the world.* New York: Harper & Row.

Milgram, S. (1965). Some conditions of obedience and disobedience to authority. *Human Relations, 18,* 57–76.

Miller, C., & Swift, K. (1988). *The handbook of nonsexist writing* (2nd ed.) New York: Harper & Row.

Miller, C. L. (1987). Qualitative differences among gender- stereotyped toys: Implications for cognitive and social development in girls and boys. *Sex Roles, 16,* 473–487.

Miller, C. T. (1984). Self-schemas, gender, and social comparison: A clarification of the related attributes hypothesis. *Journal of Personality and Social Psychology, 46,* 1222–1229.

Miller, J. B. (1976). *Toward a new psychology of women.* Boston: Beacon Press.

Miller, J. B. (1984). *The development of women's sense of self* (Work in Progress, No. 12). Wellesley, MA: Wellesley College, The Stone Center.

Miller, J. Y. (1989, July 6). A girl who can dish out Little League hardball. *Morning Call,* p. D2.

Miller, S. (1983). *Men and friendship.* New York: Houghton Mifflin.

Millet, K. (1970). *Sexual politics.* New York: Doubleday.

Millham, J., & Smith, L. E. (1981). Sex-role differentiation among Black and White Americans: A comparative study. *Journal of Black Psychology, 7,* 77–90.

Mills, C. J. (1983). Sex-typing and self-schemata effects on memory and response latency. *Journal of Personality and Social Psychology, 45,* 163–172.

Mills, C. J., & Bohannon, W. E. (1983). Personality, sex-role orientation, and psychological health in stereotypically masculine groups of males. *Sex Roles, 9,* 1161–1169.

Mills, C. J., & Tyrrell, D. J. (1983). Sex-stereotypic encoding and release from proactive interference. *Journal of Personality and Social Psychology, 45,* 772–781.

Mills, K. (1988). *A place in the news: From the women's pages to the front page.* New York: Dodd, Mead.

Mills, R.S.L., Pedersen, J., & Grusec, J. E. (1989). Sex differences in reasoning and emotion about altruism. *Sex Roles, 20,* 603–622.

Minnich, E. K. (1990). *Transforming knowledge.* Philadelphia: Temple University Press.

Minor, C. W. (1989). Toward a new concept of career development. In C. S. Pearson, D. L. Shavlik, & J. G. Touchton (Eds.), *Educating the majority: Women challenge tradition in higher education* (pp. 346–361). New York: American Council on Education/Macmillan.

Minturn, L. (1984). Sex-role differentiation in contemporary communes. *Sex Roles, 10,* 73–85.

Mintz, L. B., & Betz, N. E. (1986). Sex differences in the nature, realism, and correlates of body image. *Sex Roles, 15,* 185–195.

Mintz, L. B. & O'Neil, J. M. (1990). Gender roles, sex, and the process of psychotherapy: Many questions and few answers. *Journal of Counseling and Development, 68,* 381–387.

Mirande, A., (1988). Chicano fathers: Traditional perceptions and current realities. In P. Bronstein & C. P. Cowan (Eds.), *Fatherhood today: Men's changing role in the family* (pp. 93–106). New York: Wiley.

Mischel, W. (1966). A social learning view of sex differences in behavior. In E. E. Maccoby (Ed.), *The development of sex differences* (pp. 56–81). Stanford, CA: Stanford University Press.

Mischel, W. (1968). *Personality and assessment.* New York: Wiley.

Mishkind, M. E., Rodin, J., Silberstein, L. R., & Striegel-Moore, R. H. (1987). The embodiment of masculinity: Cultural, psychological, and behavioral dimensions. In M. S. Kimmel (Ed.), *Changing men: New directions in research on men and masculinity* (pp. 37–52). Newbury Park, CA: Sage.

Mitchell, B. (1989). *Weak link: The feminization of the American military.* Washington, DC: Regnery Gateway.

Mitchell, C. L. (1987). Relationship of femininity, masculinity, and gender to attribution of responsibility. *Sex Roles, 16,* 151–163.

Mitchell, J. (1971). *Women's estate.* New York: Pantheon.

Mitchell, J. E., Baker, L. A., & Jacklin, C. N. (1989). Masculinity and femininity in twin children: Genetic and environmental factors. *Child Development, 60,* 1475–1485.

Mitchell, V., & Helson, R. (1990). Women's prime of life: Is it the 50s? *Psychology of Women Quarterly, 14,* 451–470.

Mitgang, L. (1988, September 20). Flat SAT scores only fuel debate. *Easton Express,* pp. 1, 2.

Miura, I. T. (1987). The relationship of computer self-efficacy expectations to computer interest and course enrollment in college. *Sex Roles, 16,* 303–311.

Modleski, T. (1982). *Loving with a vengeance: Mass-produced fantasies for women.* New York: Methuen.

Moely, B. E., Skarin, K., & Weil, S. (1979). Sex differences in competition-cooperation behavior of children at two age levels. *Sex Roles, 5,* 329–342.

Moen, P., & Forest, K. B. (1990). Working parents, workplace supports, and well-being: The Swedish experience. *Social Psychology Quarterly, 53,* 117–131.

Monagan, D. (1983, March). The failure of coed sports. *Psychology Today,* 58–63.

Monahan, L. (1983). The effects of sex differences and evaluation on task performance and aspiration. *Sex Roles, 9,* 205–215.

Monahan, L., Kuhn, D., & Shaver, P. (1974). Intrapsychic versus cultural explanations of the fear of success motive. *Journal of Personality and Social Psychology, 29,* 60–64.

Money, J. (1986). *Venuses penuses: Sexology, sexosophy, and exigency theory.* Buffalo, NY: Prometheus.

Money, J. (1987). Sin, sickness, or status? Homosexual gender identity and psychoneuroendocrinology. *American Psychologist, 42,* 384–399.

Money, J. (1988). *Gay, straight, and in-between: The sexology of erotic orientation.* New York: Oxford University Press.

Money, J., & Ehrhardt, A. A. (1972). *Man and woman, boy and girl.* Baltimore: Johns Hopkins University Press.

Mooney, L., & Brabant, S. (1987). Two martinis and a rested woman: "Liberation" in the Sunday comics. *Sex Roles, 17,* 409–420.

Moore, H. A., & Porter, N. K. (1988). Leadership and nonverbal behaviors of Hispanic females across school equity environments. *Psychology of Women Quarterly, 12,* 147–163.

Moore, M. M. (1985). Nonverbal courtship patterns in women: Context and consequences. *Ethology and Sociobiology, 6,* 237–247.

Moore, R., & Gillette, D. (1990). *King, warrior, magician, lover: Rediscovering the archetype of the mature masculine.* San Francisco: HarperCollins.

Moos, R., Kopell, B., Melges, F., Yalum, I., Lunde, D., Clayton, R., & Hamburg, D. (1969). Variations in symptoms and mood during the menstrual cycle. *Journal of Psychosomatic Research, 13,* 37–44.

Moraga, C., & Anazaldua, G. (Eds.) (1981). *This bridge called my back: Writings by radical women of color.* Watertown, MA: Persephone Press.

Morawski, J. G. (1987). The troubled quest for masculinity, femininity, and androgyny. In P. Shaver & C. Hendrick (Eds.), *Sex and gender* (pp. 44–69). Newbury Park, CA: Sage.

More teen girls keeping their babies, report says. (1991, August 31). *Morning Call,* p. A24.

More women postponing first child. (1989, December 1). *Morning Call,* p. A6.

Morello, K. B. (1986). *The invisible bar: The woman lawyer in America 1638 to the present.* New York: Random House.

Morelock, J. C. (1980). Sex differences in susceptibility to social influence. *Sex Roles, 6,* 537–548.

Morgan, C. S. (1980). Female and male attitudes toward life: Implications for theories of mental health. *Sex Roles, 6,* 367–380.

Morgan, M. (1975). *The total woman.* New York: Pocket Books.

Morgan, M. (1982). Television and adolescents' sex role stereotypes: A longitudinal study. *Journal of Personality and Social Psychology, 43,* 947–955.

Morgan, M. (1987). Television, sex-role attitudes, and sex-role behavior. *Journal of Early Adolescence, 7,* 269–282.

Morgan, M. Y. (1987). The impact of religion on gender-role attitudes. *Psychology of Women Quarterly, 11,* 301–310.

Morgan, R. (Ed.). (1984). *Sisterhood is global: The international women's movement anthology.* Garden City, NY: Anchor Press.

Morgan, R. (1989). *The demon lover: On the sexuality of terrorism.* New York: Norton.

Morgan, R. (1991, January-February). Complicit trust. *Ms.,* p. 1.

Morgan, S. P., Lyle, D. N., & Condran, G. A. (1988). Sons, daughters, and the risk of marital disruption. *American Journal of Sociology, 94,* 110–129.

Morin, S. F., & Garfinkle, E. M. (1978). Male homophobia. *Journal of Social Issues, 34*(1), 29–47.

Morokoff, P. J. (1985). Effects of sex, guilt, repression, sexual arousability, and sex experience on female sexual arousal during erotica and fantasy. *Journal of Personality and Social Psychology, 49,* 177–187.

Morris, N. M., Udry, J. R., Khan-Dawood, F., & Dawood, M. Y. (1987). Marital sex frequency and midcycle female testosterone. *Archives of Sexual Behavior, 16,* 27–37.

Morrison, A. M., & Von Glinow, M. A. (1990). Women and minorities in management. *American Psychologist, 45,* 200–208.

Moses, S. (1989, October). Economic progress of blacks has stalled. *APA Monitor,* p. 18.

Moses, S. (1991a, March). Rape prevention "must involve men." *APA Monitor,* pp. 35–36.

Moses, S. (1991b, July). Ties that bind can limit minority valedictorians. *APA Monitor,* p. 47.

Mosher, D. L., & Abramson, P. R. (1977). Subjective sexual arousal to films of masturbation. *Journal of Consulting and Clinical Psychology, 45,* 796–807.

Moss, H. (1967). Sex, age, and state as determinants of mother-infant interaction. *Merrill-Palmer Quarterly, 13,* 19–36.

Most consider abortion immoral but a right. (1989, March 19). *Morning Call,* p. A11.

Mothers bearing a second burden. (1989, May 14). *CA Times,* p. 26.

Motowidlo, S. J. (1982). Sex role orientation and behavior in a work setting. *Journal of Personality and Social Psychology, 42,* 935–945.

Mowbray, C. T., & Chamberlain, P. (1986). Sex differences among the long-term mentally disabled. *Psychology of Women Quarterly, 10,* 383–391.

Mower, J. (1991, June 19). Military brass uneasy about women in combat. *Morning Call,* p. A3.

Moynihan, D. P. (1965). *The negro family: The case for national action.* Washington, DC: Department of Labor, Office of Policy Planning and Research.

Muehlenhard, C. L., & Falcon, P. L. (1990). Men's heterosocial skill and attitudes toward women as predictors of verbal sexual coercion and forceful rape. *Sex Roles, 23,* 241–259.

Muehlenhard, C. L., & Hollabaugh, L. C. (1988). Do women sometimes say no when they mean yes? The prevalence and correlates of women's token resistance to sex. *Journal of Personality and Social Psychology, 54,* 872–879.

Muehlenhard, C. L., & McCoy, M. L. (1991). Double standard/double bind: The sexual double standard and women's communication about sex. *Psychology of Women Quarterly, 15,* 447–461.

Mulac, A., Incontro, C. R., & James, M. R. (1985). A comparison of the gender-linked language effect and sex-role stereotypes. *Journal of Personality and Social Psychology, 49,* 1098–1109.

Mullins, H. P. (1987, June). Women and the law. *Ms.,* pp. 64–65.

Munroe, R. L., & Munroe, R. H. (1969). A cross-cultural study of sex, gender, and social structure. *Ethnology, 8*(2), 206–211.

Munroe, R. L., & Munroe, R. H. (1980). Perspectives suggested by anthropological data. In H. C. Triandis & W. W. Lambert (Eds.), *Handbook of cross-cultural psychology*, Vol. 1. Boston: Allyn & Bacon.

Munroe, R. H., Shimmin, H. S., & Munroe, R. L. (1984). Gender understanding and sex role preference in four cultures. *Developmental Psychology, 20*, 673–682.

Muro, M. (1989, April 23). Comment: New era of eros in advertising. *Morning Call*, pp. D1, D16.

Murphy, L. O., & Ross, S. M. (1987). Gender differences in the social problem-solving performance of adolescents. *Sex Roles, 16*, 251–264.

Murrell, A. J., Frieze, I. H., & Frost, J. L. (1991). Aspiring to careers in male- and female-dominated professions: A study of Black and White college women. *Psychology of Women Quarterly, 15*, 103–126.

Musante, L., MacDougall, J. M., Dembroski, T. M., & Van Horn, A. E. (1983). Component analysis of the Type A coronary-prone behavior pattern in male and female college students. *Journal of Personality and Social Psychology, 45*, 1104–1117.

Myers, A. M., & Gonda, G. (1982). Empirical validation of the Bem Sex-Role Inventory. *Journal of Personality and Social Psychology, 43*, 304–318.

Myers, A. M., & Lips, H. M. (1978). Participation in competitive amateur sports as a function of psychological androgyny. *Sex Roles, 4*, 571–588.

Nadler, A., Maler, S., & Friedman, A. (1984). Effects of helper's sex, subjects' androgyny, and self-evaluation on males' and females' willingness to seek and receive help. *Sex Roles, 10*, 327–339.

Nadler, R. D. (1987). Behavioral dimorphisms in the sexual initiative of great apes. In J. M. Reinisch, L. A. Rosenblum, & S. A. Sanders (Eds.), *Masculinity/femininity* (pp. 129–149). New York: Oxford University Press.

Narus, L. R., Jr., & Fischer, J. L. (1982). Strong but not silent: A reexamination of expressivity in the relationships of men. *Sex Roles, 8*, 159–168.

Nash, J., & Fernandez-Kelly, M. P. (Eds.). (1983). *Women, men, and the international division of labor*. Albany: State University of New York Press.

Nash, S. C. (1979). Sex role as a mediator of intellectual functioning. In M. A. Wittig & A. C. Petersen (Eds.), *Sex-related differences in cognitive functioning: Developmental issues* (pp. 263–302). New York: Academic Press.

Nash, S. C., & Feldman, S. S. (1981). Sex-related differences in the relationship between sibling status and responsibility to babies. *Sex Roles, 7*, 1035–1042.

Nassi, A. J., & Abramowitz, S. I. (1978). Raising consciousness about women's groups: Process and outcome research. *Psychology of Women Quarterly, 3*, 139–156.

Nathan, S. (1981). Cross-cultural perspectives on penis envy. *Psychiatry, 44*(1), 39–44.

National Association of Scholars. (1989, November 8). Is the curriculum biased? Advertisement in *Chronicle of Higher Education*, p. 23.

National Center for Education Statistics. (1983). *Faculty salaries, tenure, and benefits survey*. Washington, DC: Author.

National Center for Education Statistics. (1984). *High school seniors: A comparative study of the classes of 1972 and 1980*. Washington, DC: U. S. Government Printing Office.

National Commission on Working Women of Wider Opportunities for Women. (1988). *Women and the vote—1988*. Washington, DC: Author.

National Commission on Working Women of Wider Opportunities for Women. (1989a, January). *Women, work, and the future*. Washington, DC: Author.

National Commission on Working Women of Wider Opportunities for Women. (1989b, May). *Women, work, and child care*. Washington, DC: Author.

National Commission on Working Women of Wider Opportunities for Women. (1990, March). *Women and work*. Washington, DC: Author.

National Opinion Research Center. (1986, November 23). Changing attitudes. *New York Times*, p. E26.

National Research Council. (1989, March 15). Survey of earned doctorates, 1987. *Chronicle of Higher Education*, p. A13.

National Science Foundation. (1986). *Women and minorities in science and engineering* (NSF 86-301). Washington, DC: Author.

Nearly half of teen girls trying to diet, survey says. (1991, November 11). *Morning Call*, p. A7.

Neimark, J. (1991, May). Out of bounds: The truth about athletes and rape. *Mademoiselle*, pp. 196–199, 244–246.

Nelson, D. L., Quick, J. C., Hitt, M. A., & Moesel, D. (1990). Politics, lack of career progress, and work/home conflict: Stress and strain for working women. *Sex Roles, 23*, 169–185.

Nelson, L. J., & Cooper, J. (1990). *Children's reactions to success and failure with computers*. Manuscript submitted for publication.

Nelson, M. B. (1991). *Are we winning yet? How women are changing sports and sports are changing women*. NY: Random House.

Nelson, N. (1988, April). *Gender differences in response to life stress and social support: A meta-analysis*. Paper presented at the meeting of the Eastern Psychological Association, Buffalo, NY.

Nettles, E. J., & Loevinger, J. (1983). Sex role expectations and ego level in relation to problem marriages. *Journal of Personality and Social Psychology, 45*, 676–687.

New Edition of the Bible to eliminate many masculine references. (1977, June 5). *New York Times*, p. B6.

New report on rape shows underreporting. (1978, August 26). *New York Times*.

Newcomb, M. D., Huba, G. J., & Bentler, P. M. (1986). Determinants of sexual and dating behaviors among adolescents. *Journal of Personality and Social Psychology, 50*, 428–438.

Newcombe, N., & Bandura, M. M. (1983). Effect of age at puberty on spatial ability: A question of mechanism. *Developmental Psychology, 19*, 215–224.

Newcombe, N., & Dubas, J. S. (1987). Individual differences in cognitive ability: Are they related to timing of puberty? In R. M. Lerner & T. T. Foch (Eds.), *Biological-psychosocial interactions in early adolescence* (pp. 249–302). Hillsdale, NJ: Erlbaum.

Newcombe, N., Dubas, J. S., & Baenninger, M. (1989). Associations of timing of puberty, spatial ability, and lateralization in adult women. *Child Development, 60*, 246–254.

Newcomer, S., & Udry, J. R. (1985). Oral sex in an adolescent population. *Archives of Sexual Behavior, 14*, 41–46.

Newcomer, S., & Udry, J. R. (1988). Adolescents' honesty in a survey of sexual behavior. *Journal of Adolescent Research, 3*, 419–423.

Newman, B. S. (1989). The relative importance of gender role attitudes to male and female attitudes toward lesbians. *Sex Roles, 21*, 451–465.

Nezu, A. M., & Nezu, C. M. (1987). Psychological distress, problem solving, and coping reactions: Sex role differences. *Sex Roles, 16*, 205–214.

Nicholson, L. J. (Ed.) (1990). *Feminism/postmodernism*. New York: Routledge.

Nielsen Media Research. (1989). *'89 Nielsen report on television*. Northbrook, IL: Author.

Nielsen, J. M. (1990). *Sex and gender in society: Perspective on stratification* (2nd ed.). Prospect Heights, IL: Waveland.

Nieves-Squires, S. (1991). *Hispanic women: Making their presence on campus less tenuous*. Washington, DC: Association of American Colleges, Project on the Status and Education of Women.

Nigro, G. N., Hill, D. E., Gelbein, M. E., & Clark, C. L. (1988). Changes in the facial prominence of women and men over the last decade. *Psychology of Women Quarterly, 12,* 225–235.

Nikken, P., & Peeters, A. L. (1988). Children's perceptions of television reality. *Journal of Broadcasting & Electronic Media, 32,* 441–452.

Ninety percent of big firms get sex complaints. (1988, November 23). *Easton Express,* p. D9.

Nkomo, S. M., & Cox, T., Jr. (1989). Gender differences in the upward mobility of black managers: Double whammy or double advantage? *Sex Roles, 21,* 825–839.

Noble, K. B. (1986, March 16). More U.S. mothers are holding jobs. *New York Times,* p. 35.

Nochlin, L. (1989). *Women, art, and power, and other essays.* New York: Harper & Row.

Noe, R. A. (1988). Women and mentoring: A review and research agenda. *Academy of Management Review, 13,* 65–78.

Nolen-Hoeksema, S . (1987). Sex differences in unipolar depression: Evidence and theory. *Psychological Bulletin, 101,* 259–282.

Nolen-Hoeksema, S. (1990). *Sex differences in depression.* Stanford: Stanford University Press.

Nolen-Hoeksema, S., Girgus, J. S., & Seligman, M.E.P. (1986). Learned helplessness in children: A longitudinal study of depression, achievement, and explanatory style. *Journal of Personality and Social Psychology, 51,* 435–442.

Noller, P. (1980). Misunderstandings in marital communication: A study of couples' nonverbal communication. *Journal of Personality and Social Psychology, 39,* 1135–1148.

Noller, P. (1981). Gender and marital adjustment level differences in decoding messages from spouses and strangers. *Journal of Personality and Social Psychology, 41,* 272–278.

Non-white males most apt to be murdered. (1989, January 13). *Easton Express,* p. A7.

Nordheimer, J. (1991, May 26). Women's role in combat: The war resumes. *New York Times,* pp. 1, 28.

Nyquist, L., Slivken, K., Spence, J. T., & Helmreich, R. L. (1985). Household responsibilities in middle-class couples: The contribution of demographic and personality variables. *Sex Roles, 12,* 15–34.

Nyquist, L. V., & Spence, J. T. (1986). Effects of dispositional dominance and sex-role expectations on leadership behaviors. *Journal of Personality and Social Psychology, 50,* 87–93.

Oakley, A. (1972). *Sex, gender, and society.* New York: Harper & Row.

Oakley, A. (1974). *Woman's work: The housewife past and present.* New York: Pantheon.

Oberlander, S. (1989, June 21). Advocates for women's sports say 1988 Civil Rights Act has not brought hoped-for equity with men. *Chronicle of Higher Education,* p. A23.

O'Brien, M. (1981). *The politics of reproduction.* Boston: Routledge & Kegan Paul.

O'Connell, A. N. (1989). Psychology of women students' self-concepts, attitudes, and assertiveness: A decade of research. *Teaching of Psychology, 16,* 178–181.

O'Connor, J. J. (1989, June 6). What are commercials selling to children? *New York Times,* p. 28.

Offen, K. (1988). Defining feminism: A comparative historical approach. *Signs: Journal of Women in Culture and Society, 14,* 119–157.

Ogilvie, B. C., & Tutko, T. (1971, October). Sport: If you want to build character, try something else. *Psychology Today,* p. 61ff.

Ogintz, E. (1983, December 8). 19 million mothers juggling jobs, homelife. *Easton Express,* pp. C1–C2.

Ogletree, S. M., & Williams, S. W. (1990). Sex and sex-typing efects on computer attitudes and aptitude. *Sex Roles, 23,* 703–712.

Ogus, E. D., Greenglass, E. R., & Burke, R. J. (1990). Gender-role differences, work stress, and depersonalization. *Journal of Social Behavior and Personality, 5,* 387–398.

O'Hara, M. W., Zekoski, E. M., Philipps, L. H., & Wright, E. J. (1990). Controlled prospective study of postpartum mood disorders: Comparison of childbearing and non-childbearing women. *Journal of Abnormal Psychology, 99,* 3–15.

O'Keefe, E.S.C., & Hyde, J. S. (1983). The development of occupational sex-role stereotypes: The effects of gender stability and age. *Sex Roles, 39,* 481–492.

O'Leary, V. E. (1988). Women's relationships with women in the workplace. In B. A. Gutek, L. Larwood, & A. Stromberg (Eds.), *Women and work: An annual review,* Vol. 3 (pp. 189–214). Beverly Hills, CA: Sage.

O'Leary, V. E., & Hansen, R. D. (1985). Sex as an attributional fact. In T. B. Sonderegger (Ed.), *Nebraska Symposium on Motivation, 1984. Psychology and gender,* Vol. 32 (pp. 133–177). Lincoln, NE: University of Nebraska Press.

O'Leary, V. E., & Ickovics, J. R. (1991). Cracking the glass ceiling: Overcoming isolation and alienation. In U. Sekeran & F. Leong (Eds.), *Pathways to excellence: New patterns for human utilization.* Beverly Hills. CA: Sage.

Olian, J. D., Schwab, D. P., & Haberfeld, Y. (1988). The impact of applicant gender compared to qualifications on hiring recommendations: A meta-analysis of experimental studies. *Organizational Behavior and Human Decision Processes, 41,* 180–195.

Oliker, S. (1989). *Best friends and marriage: Exchange among women.* Berkeley, CA: University of California Press.

Oliver, S. J., & Toner, B. B. (1990). The influence of gender role typing on the expression of depressive symptoms. *Sex Roles, 22,* 775–790.

Olson, J. E., Frieze, I. H., & Detlefsen, E. G. (1990). Having it all? Combining work and family in a male and a female profession. *Sex Roles, 23,* 515–533.

Olweus, D. (1986). Aggression and hormones: Behavioral relationships with testosterone and adrenaline. In D. Olweus, J. Block, & M. Radke-Yarrow (Eds.), *Development of antisocial and prosocial behavior: Research, theories, and issues* (pp. 51–71). Orlando, FL: Academic Press.

O'Meara, J. D. (1989). Cross-sex friendship: Four basic challenges of an ignored relationship. *Sex Roles, 21,* 525–543.

O'Neil, J. M. (1981a). Male sex-role conflicts, sexism, and masculinity: Psychological implications for men, women, and the counseling psychologist. *Counseling Psychologist, 9,* 61–80.

O'Neil, J. M. (1981b). Patterns of gender role conflict and strain: The fear of femininity in men's lives. *Personnel and Guidance Journal, 60,* 203–210.

O'Neil, J. M. (1982). Gender role conflict and strain in men's lives: Implications for psychiatrists, psychologists, and other human service providers. In K. Solomon & N. B. Levy (Eds.), *Men in transition: Changing male roles, theory, and therapy* (pp. 5–44). New York: Plenum.

O'Neil, J. M., & Fishman, D. M. (1986). Adult men's career transitions and gender-role themes. In Z. Leibowitz & D. Lea (Eds.), *Adult career development: Concepts, issues, and practices* (pp. 132–162). Alexandria, VA: American Association for Counseling and Development.

O'Neil, J. M., Helms, B. J., Gable. R. K., David, L., & Wrightsman, L. S. (1986). Gender-role conflict scale: College men's fear of femininity. *Sex Roles, 14,* 335–350.

Only one U.S. family in four is "traditional." (1991, January 30). *New York Times,* p. 24.

Orlinsky, D., & Howard, K. (1976). The effects of sex of therapist on the therapeutic experience of women. *Psychotherapy: Theory, Research, and Practice, 13,* 82–88.

Orlofsky, J. L. (1979). Parental antecedents of sex-role orientation in college men and women. *Sex Roles, 5,* 495–512.

Orlofsky, J. L. (1982). Psychological andro-gyny, sex typing, and sex-role ideology as predictors of male-female interpersonal attraction. *Sex Roles, 8,* 1057–1073.

Orlofsky, J. L., & Stake, J. E. (1981). Psycho-logical masculinity and femininity: Rela-tionship to striving and self-concept in the achievement and interpersonal domains. *Psychology of Women Quarterly, 6,* 218–233.

Orlofsky, J. L., & O'Heron, C. A. (1987). Stereotypic and nonstereotypic sex role trait and behavior orientations: Implica-tions for personal adjustment. *Journal of Personality and Social Psychology, 52,* 1034–1042.

Ortner, S. B. (1974). Is female to male as nature is to culture? In M. Z. Rosaldo & L. Lamphere (Eds.), *Women, culture, and society.* Stanford, CA: Stanford University Press.

Ortner, S. B. (1981). Gender and sexuality in hierarchical societies. In S. B. Ortner & H. Whitehead (Eds.), *Sexual meanings: The cultural construction of gender and sexuality* (pp. 359–409). Cambridge, England: Cambridge University Press.

Ortner, S. B., & Whitehead, H. (Eds.) (1981). *Sexual meanings: The cultural construc-tion of gender and sexuality.* Cambridge, England: Cambridge University Press.

Osborn, S. (1989, May). *Gender depictions in television advertisements: 1988.* Paper presented at the meeting of the Inter-national Communications Association, San Francisco.

Ott, E. M. (1989). Effects of the male-female ratio at work: Policewomen and male nurses. *Psychology of Women Quarterly, 13,* 41–57.

Ozer, E. (1986). *Health status of minority women.* Washington, DC: American Psychological Association, Office of Ethnic Minority Affairs.

Padesky, C. A., & Hammen, C. L. (1981). Sex differences in depressive symptom expression and help-seelcing among college students. *Sex Roles, 7,* 309–320.

Paglia, C. (1990). *Sexual personae: Art and decadence from Nefertiti to Emily Dickinson.* New Haven: Yale University Press.

Paige, K. E. (1971). The effects of oral contra-ceptives on affective fluctuations associated with the menstrual cycle. *Psychosomatic Medicine, 33,* 515–537.

Paige, K. E., & Paige, J. M. (1973). The politics of birth practices: A strategic analysis. *American Sociological Review, 38,* 663–676.

Paikoff, R. L., & Savin-Williams, R. C. (1983). An exploratory study of dominance inter-actions among adolescent females at a summer camp. *Journal of Youth and Adolescence, 12,* 419–433.

Palgi, M., Blasi, J., Rosner, M., & Safir, M. (Eds.). (1983). *Sexual equality: The Israeli kibbutz tests the theories.* Norwood, PA: Norwood Editions.

Palkovitz, R. (1984). Parental attitudes and fathers' interactions with their 5-month-old infants. *Developmental Psychology, 20,* 1054–1060.

Palmer, H. T., & Lee, J. A. (1990). Female workers' acceptance in traditionally male-dominated blue-collar jobs. *Sex Roles, 22,* 607–625.

Paludi, M. A. (1984). Psychometric proper-ties and underlying assumptions of four objective measures of fear of success. *Sex Roles, 10,* 765–781.

Paludi, M. A. (Ed.). (1990). *Ivory power: Sexual harassment on campus.* Albany: State University of New York Press.

Paludi, M. A., & Bauer, W. D. (1983). Goldberg revisited: What's in an author's name. *Sex Roles, 9,* 387–390.

Paludi, M., & Fankell-Hauser, J. (1986). An idiographic approach to the study of women's achievement striving. *Psychology of Women Quarterly, 10,* 89–100.

Paludi, M. A., & Strayer, L. A. (1985). What's in an author's name? Differential evalua-tions of performance as a function of author's name. *Sex Roles, 12,* 353–361.

Palmer, H. T., & Lee, J. A. (1990). Female workers' acceptance in traditionally male-dominated blue-collar jobs. *Sex Roles, 22,* 607–625.

Parachini, A. (1985, May 9). Study: Turnover of women in "men's" jobs isn't high. *Easton Express,* p. C10.

Parasuraman, S., Greenhaus, J. H., Rabinowitz, S., Bedeian, A G., & Mossholder, K. W. (1989). Work and fam-ily variables as mediators of the relation-ship between wives' employment and husbands' well-being. *Academy of Management Journal, 32,* 185–201.

Pareles, J. (1990, October 21). The women who talk back in rap. *New York Times,* pp. H33, H36.

Parke, R. (1981). *Fathers.* Cambridge, MA: Harvard University Press.

Parke, R. D., & Sawin, D. B. (1977, June). Fathering: Its major role. *Psychology Today,* pp. 108–112.

Parke, R. D., & Tinsley, B. R. (1981). The father's role in infancy: Determinants of involvement in caregiving and play. In M. Lamb (Ed.), *The role of the father in child development* (2nd ed.) (pp. 429–457). New York: Wiley.

Parker, M., Peltier, S., & Wolleat, P. (1981, September). Understanding dual career couples. *Personnel and Guidance Journal,* 14–18.

Parlee, M. B. (1973). The premenstrual syndrome. *Psychological Bulletin, 80,* 454–465.

Parlee, M. B. (1982a). Changes in moods and activation levels during the menstrual cycle in experimentally naive subjects. *Psychology of Women Quarterly,* 7,119-131.

Parlee, M. B. (1982b, September). New find-ings: Menstrual cycles and behavior. *Ms.,* pp. 126–128.

Parrish. J. B. (1986, February 9). Why many women opt to go it alone. *New York Times,* p.D2.

Parsons, J.K., Ruble, D.N., Hodges, K.L. & Small, A.W.(1976). Cognitive developmen-tal factors in sex differences in achievement-related expectancies. *Journal of Social Issues,* 32(3), 47-61.

Parsons, T., & Bales, R. F. (1955). *Family, socialization, and interaction process.* Glencoe, IL: Free Press.

Pascarella, E. T., Smart, J. C., Ethington, C. A., & Nettles, M. T. (1987). The influence of college on self-concept: A considera-tion of race and gender differences. *American Educational Research Journal, 24,* 49–77.

Pasley, N. K., & Ihinger-Tallman, M. (Eds.). (1987). *Remarriage and stepparenting: Current research and theory.* New York: Guilford.

Patterson, C. J., Kupersmidt, J. B., & Vaden, N. A. (1990). Income level, gender, eth-nicity, and household composition as predictors of children's school-based competence. *Child Development, 61,* 485–494.

Payne, F. D. (1987). "Masculinity," "femi-ninity," and the complex construct of adjustment. *Sex Roles, 17,* 359–374.

Payne, T. J., Connor, J. M., & Colletti, G. (1987). Gender-based schematic process-ing: An empirical investigation and reevaluation. *Journal of Personality and Social Psychology, 52,* 937–945.

Pear, R. (1987, March 22). Number of blacks in top jobs in administration off sharply. *New York Times,* pp. 1, 30.

Pearce, D. M. (1985). Toil and trouble: Women workers and unemployment compensation. *Signs: Journal of Women in Culture and Society, 10,* 439–459.

Pearson, C. S., Shavlik, D. L., & Touchton, J. G. (Eds.). (1989). *Educating the majority: Women challenge tradition in higher edu-cation.* New York: American Council on Education/Macmillan.

Pearson, J. L., & Ferguson, L. R. (1989). Gender differences in patterns of spatial ability, environmental cognition, and math and English achievement in late adolescence. *Adolescence, 24,* 421–431.

Pearson, J. L., & Ialongo, N. S. (1986). The relationship between spatial ability and environmental knowledge. *Journal of Environmental Psychology, 6,* 299–304.

Pedersen, F. A. (Ed.). (1980). *The father-infant relationship: Observational studies in the family setting.* New York: Praeger.

Pedhazur, E. J., & Tetenbaum, T. J. (1979). Bem Sex Role Inventory: A theoretical and methodological critique. *Journal of*

Personality and Social Psychology, 37, 996–1016.

Peirce, K. (1990). A feminist theoretical perspective on the socialization of teenage girls through *Seventeen* magazine. *Sex Roles, 23*, 491–500.

Peplau, L. A. (1979). Power in dating relationships. In J. Freeman (Ed.), *Women: A feminist perspective* (2nd ed.). Palo Alto, CA: Mayfield.

Peplau, L. A. (1981, March). What do homosexuals want. *Psychology Today*, pp. 28–38.

Peplau, L. A., Rubin, Z., & Hill, C. T. (1976, November). The sexual balance of power. *Psychology Today*, p. 142ff.

Peplau, L. A., Rubin, Z., & Hill, C. T. (1977). Sexual intimacy in dating relationships. *Journal of Social Issues, 33*(2), 86–109.

Percival, L., & Quinkert, K. (1987). Anthropometric factors. In M. A. Baker (Ed.), *Sex differences in human performance* (pp. 121–139). Chichester: Wiley.

Perlez, J. (1984, June 24). Women, power, and politics. *New York Times Magazine*, pp. 22–27, 29, 31, 72, 76.

Perry, D. G., & Bussey, K. (1979). The social learning theory of sex differences: Imitation is alive and well. *Journal of Personality and Social Psychology, 37*, 1699–1712.

Perry D. G., Perry, L. C., & Weiss, R. J. (1989). Sex differences in the consequences that children anticipate for aggression. *Developmental Psychology, 25*, 312–319.

Perry, J., & Whipple, B. (1981). Pelvic muscle strength of female ejaculators: Evidence in support of a new theory of orgasm. *Journal of Sex Research, 17*, 22–39.

Perry, M. (1982, April 21). Being "macho" can be a short-lived experience. *Easton Express*. A-14.

Perry, R., & Greber, L. (1990). Women and computers: An introduction. *Signs: Journal of Women in Culture and Society, 16*, 74–101.

Persell, C. H. (1983). Gender rewards and research in education. *Psychology of Women Quarterly, 8*, 33–47.

Pessimistic losers. (1988, November). *Psychology Today*, p. 18.

Peters, T. J., & Waterman, R. H., Jr. (1982). *In search of excellence: Lessons from America's best-run companies.* New York: Warner Books.

Petersen, A. C. (1979). Hormones and cognitive functioning in normal development. In M. A. Wittig & A. C. Petersen (Eds.), *Sex-related differences in cognitive functioning: Developmental issues* (pp. 189–214). New York: Academic Press.

Petersen, A. C. (1982). A biopsychosocial perspective on sex differences in the human brain. *Behavioral and Brain Sciences, 2*, 312.

Petersen, A. C. (1983). *The development of sex-related differences in achievement.*

Invited address at the meeting of the American Psychological Association, Anaheim.

Petersen, A. C. (1988). Adolescent development. *Annual Review of Psychology, 39*, 583–607.

Petersen, A. C., & Wittig, M. A. (1979). Sex-related differences in cognitive functioning: An overview. In M. A. Wittig & A. C. Petersen (Eds.), *Sex-related differences in cognitive functioning: Developmental issues* (pp. 1–17). New York: Academic Press.

Peterson, C. D., Baucom, D. H., Elliott, M. J., & Farr, P. A. (1989). The relationship between sex role identity and marital adjustment. *Sex Roles, 21*, 775–787.

Peterson, R. A. (1983). Attitudes toward the childless spouse. *Sex Roles, 9*, 321–331.

Pfost, K. S., & Fiore, M. (1990). Pursuit of nontraditional occupations: Fear of success or fear of not being chosen? *Sex Roles, 23*, 15–24.

Pfost, K. S., Lum, C. U., & Stevens, M. J. (1989). Femininity and work plans protect women against postpartum dysphoria. *Sex Roles, 21*, 423–431.

Pharr, S. (1988). *Homophobia: A weapon of sexism.* Little Rock, AR: Chardon.

Phelps, S., & Austin, N. (1975). *The assertive woman.* San Luis Obispo, CA: Impact.

Pheterson, G. (1986). Alliances between women: Overcoming internalized oppression and internalized domination. *Signs: Journal of Women in Cultlure and Society, 12*, 146–160.

Philips, S. U., Steele, S., & Tanz, C. (Eds.). (1987). *Language, gender, and sex in comparative perspective.* Cambridge, England: Cambridge University Press.

Phillips, D., & Segal, B. (1969). Sexual status and psychiatric symptoms. *American Sociology Review, 34*, 58–72.

Phillips, R. D., & Gilroy, F. D. (1985). Sex-role stereotypes and clinical judgments of mental health: The Broverman's findings reexamined. *Sex Roles, 12*, 179–193.

Phillips, S., King, S., & DuBois, L. (1978). Spontaneous activities of female versus male newborns. *Child Development, 49*, 590–597.

Piedmont, R. L. (1988). An interactional model of achievement motivation and fear of success. *Sex Roles, 19*, 467–490.

Pierce, K., Smith, H., & Akert, R. M. (1984, April). *Terminating adult same-sex friendships: The role of gender and decision to terminate in the break-up process.* Paper presented at the meeting of the Eastern Psychological Association, Baltimore.

Pietromonaco, P. R., Manis, J., & Markus, H. (1987). The relationship of employment to self-perception and well-being in women: A cognitive analysis. *Sex Roles, 17*, 467–477.

Pietropinto, A., & Simenauer, J. (1977). *Beyond the male myth: What women want to know about men's sexuality.* New York: Times Books.

Piliavin, J. A., & Unger, R. K. (1985). The helpful but helpless female: Myth or reality? In V. O'Leary, R. Unger, B. Wallston (Eds.), *Women, gender, and social psychology* (pp. 149–189). Hillsdale, NJ: Erlbaum.

Pines, A., & Kafry, D. (1981). Tedium in the life and work of professional women as compared with men. *Sex Roles, 7*, 963–977.

Pingree, S. (1978). The effects of nonsexist TV commercials and perceptions of reality on children's attitudes about women. *Psychology of Women Quarterly, 2*, 262–277.

Pirog-Good, M. A., & Stets, J. E. (Eds.). (1989). *Violence in dating relationships: Emerging social issues.* New York: Praeger.

Plaskow, J., & Christ, C. P. (Eds.). (1989). *Weaving the visions: New patterns in feminist spirituality.* San Francisco: Harper & Row.

Pleck, J. H. (1976a). My male sex role and ours. In D. David & R. Brannon (Eds.), *The 49-percent majority* (pp. 253–264). Reading, MA: Addison-Wesley.

Pleck, J. H. (1976b). The male sex role: Definitions, problems, and sources of change. *Journal of Social Issues, 32*(3), 155–164.

Pleck, J. H. (1981a). *Changing patterns of work and family roles* (Working Paper No. 81). Wellesley, MA: Wellesley College Center for Research on Women.

Pleck, J. H. (1981b). *The myth of masculinity.* Cambridge, MA: MIT Press.

Pleck, J. H. (1983). Husbands' paid work and family roles: Current research issues. In H. Z. Lopata & J. H. Pleck (Eds.), *Research on the interweave of social roles, Vol. 3: Families and jobs.* Greenwich, CT: JAI Press.

Pleck, J. H. (1985). *Working wives, working husbands.* Beverly Hills, CA: Sage.

Pleck, J. H. (1986). Employment and fatherhood: Issues and innovative policies. In M. E. Lamb (Ed.), *The father's role: Applied perspectives* (pp. 385–412). New York: Wiley.

Pleck, J. H. (1987). American fathering in historical perspective. In M. S. Kimmel (Ed.), *Changing men: New directions in research on men and masculinity* (pp. 83–97). Newbury Park, CA: Sage.

Pleck, J. H., & Sawyer, J. (Eds.). (1974). *Men and masculinity.* Englewood Cliffs, NJ: Prentice-Hall.

Pliner, P., Chaiken, S., & Flett, G. L. (1990). Gender differences in concern with body weight and physical appearance over the life span. *Personality and Social Psychology Bulletin, 16*, 263–273.

Plumb, P., & Cowan, G. (1984). A developmental study of stereotyping and androgynous activity preferences of tomboys, nontomboys, and males. *Sex Roles, 10,* 703–712.

Pogrebin, L. C. (1981). *Growing up free: Raising your child in the 80's.* New York: Bantam.

Pogrebin, L. C. (1982, April). A feminist in Sweden. *Ms.,* pp. 66–70, 82–88.

Pogrebin, L. C. (1983). *Family politics: Love and power on an intimate frontier.* New York: McGraw-Hill.

Pogrebin, L. C. (1990, September-October). The Teflon father. *Ms.,* pp. 95–96.

Polatnick, M. (1973–74). Why men can't rear children: A power analysis. *Berkeley Journal of Sociology, 18,* 45–86.

Polivy, J., & Herman, C. P. (1985). Dieting and bingeing: A causal analysis. *American Psychologist, 40,* 193–201.

Polk, B. B. (1976). Male power and the women's movement. In S. Cox (Ed.), *Female psychology: The emerging self* (pp. 400–413). Chicago: SRA.

Poll rates candidates by gender. (1985, January 20). *New York Times,* p. 45.

Pollack, W. (1990). Sexual harassment: Women's experience vs. legal definitions. *Harvard Women's Law Journal, 13,* 35–85.

Pollak, S., & Gilligan, C. (1982). Images of violence in Thematic Apperception Test stories. *Journal of Personality and Social Psychology, 42,* 159–167.

Pollak, S., & Gilligan, C. (1983). Differing about differences: The incidence and interpretation of violent fantasies in women and men. *Journal of Personality and Social Psychology, 45,* 1172–1175.

Polyson, J. (1978). Sexism and sexual problems: Societal censure of the sexually troubled male. *Psychological Reports, 42,* 843–850.

Pomerleau, A., Bolduc, D., Malcuit, G., & Cossette, L. (1990). Pink or blue: Environmental stereotypes in the first two years of life. *Sex Roles, 22,* 359–367.

Poole, D. A., & Tapley, A. E. (1988). Sex roles, social roles, and clinical judgments of mental health. *Sex Roles, 19,* 265–272.

Poppen, P. J., & Segal, N. J. (1988). The influence of sex and sex role orientation on sexual coercion. *Sex Roles, 19,* 689–701.

Porter, J. R., & Washington, R. E. (1979). Black identity and self-esteem: A review of studies of Black self-concept 1968–1978. *Annual Review of Sociology, 5,* 53–74.

Porter, N., & Geis, F. (1982). Women and nonverbal leadership cues: When seeing is not believing. In C. Mayo & N. Henley (Eds.), *Gender and nonverbal behavior* (pp. 39–61). New York: Springer-Verlag.

Porter, N., Geis, F. L., Cooper, E., & Newman, E. (1985). Androgyny and leadership in mixed-sex groups. *Journal of Personality and Social Psychology, 49,* 808–823.

Porter, N., Geis, F., & Jennings (Walstedt), J. (1983). Are women invisible as leaders? *Sex Roles, 9,* 1035–1049.

Post-election survey '88. (1989, Winter). *Women's Political Times,* p. 10.

Potera, C., & Kort, M. (1986, September). Are women coaches an endangered species? *Women's Sports and Fitness,* pp. 34–36.

Potkay, C. R., & Potkay, C. E. (1984). Perceptions of female and male comic strip characters. II: Favorability and identification are different dimensions. *Sex Roles, 10,* 119–128.

Powell, G. N. (1987). The effects of sex and gender on recruitment. *Academy of Management Review, 12,* 731–743.

Powell, G. N. (1988). *Women and men in management.* Newbury Park, CA: Sage.

Powell, G. N., & Butterfield, D. A. (1989). The "good manager": Did androgyny fare better in the 1980s? *Group and Organization Studies, 14,* 216–233.

Power, T. G., & Parke, R. D. (1984). Social network factors and the transition to parenthood. *Sex Roles, 10,* 949–972.

Powlishta, K. K., & Maccoby, E. E. (1990). Resource utilization in mixed-sex dyads: The influence of adult presence and task type. *Sex Roles, 23,* 223–240.

Preston, K., & Stanley, K. (1987). "What's the worst thing . . . ?" Gender-directed insults. *Sex Roles, 17,* 209–219.

Pribram, E. D. (Ed.). (1988). *Female spectators: Looking at film and television.* London: Verso.

Proctor, E. B., Wagner, N. M., & Butler, J. C. (1974). The differentiation of male and female orgasms: An experimental study. In N. M. Wagner (Ed.), *Perspectives in human sexuality.* New York: Human Sciences.

Progress slow for women in network news. (1985, January 1). *TV Guide,* p. A-1.

Project on the Status and Education of Women. (1984, Spring). Women get less financial aid than men. *On Campus with Women,* p. 6.

Pruett, K. D. (1987). *The nurturing father: Journey toward the complete man.* New York: Warner Books.

Pryor, J. B. (1987). Sexual harassment proclivities in men. *Sex Roles, 17,* 269–290.

Pulakos, E. D., White, L. A., Oppler, S. H., & Borman, W. C. (1989). Examination of race and sex effects on performance ratings. *Journal of Applied Psychology, 74,* 770–780.

Purcell, P., & Stewart, L. (1990). Dick and Jane in 1989. *Sex Roles, 22,* 177–185.

Pursell, S., Banikiotes, P. G., & Sebastian, R. J. (1981). Androgyny and the perception of marital roles. *Sex Roles, 7,* 201–215.

Purvis, A. (1990, Fall). A perilous gap. *Women: The road ahead* [Special issue of *Time* magazine], pp. 66–67.

Quante, A. L. (1981, April). *Attitudes toward sexually assertive women.* Paper presented at the meeting of the Eastern Psychological Association, New York.

Quina, K., Wingard, J. A., & Bates, H. G. (1987). Language style and gender stereotypes in person perception. *Psychology of Women Quarterly, 11,* 111–122.

Quindlen, A. (1991, January 13). In the shadow of war. *New York Times,* p. E19.

Radin, N. (1981). The role of the father in cognitive, academic, and intellectual development. In M. Lamb (Ed.), *The role of the father in child development* (2nd ed.) (pp. 379–427). New York: Wiley.

Radin, N. (1988). Primary caregiving fathers of long duration. In P. Bronstein & C. P. Cowan (Eds.), *Fatherhood today: Men's changing role in the family* (pp. 127–143). New York: Wiley.

Radin, N., & Harold-Goldsmith, R. (1989). The involvement of selected unemployed and employed men with their children. *Child Development, 60,* 454–459.

Radway, J. R. (1984). *Reading the romance: Women, patriarchy, and popular literature.* Chapel Hill, NC: University of North Carolina Press.

Ragins, B. R. (1989a). Barriers to mentoring: The female manager's dilemma. *Human Relations, 42,* 1–22.

Ragins, B. R. (1989b). Power and gender congruency effects in evaluations of male and female managers. *Journal of Management, 15,* 65–76.

Ragins, B. R., & Sundstrom, E. (1989). Gender and power in organizations: A longitudinal perspective. *Psychological Bulletin, 105,* 51–88.

Randall, V. (1987). *Women and politics: An international perspective* (2nd ed.). Chicago: University of Chicago Press.

Randle, W. (1990, January 14). Influx of women, minorities changing face of work force. *Morning Call,* p. D1.

Rao, V.V.P., & Overman, S. J. (1984). Sex-role perceptions among black female athletes and nonathletes. *Sex Roles, 11,* 601–614.

Rao, V.V.P., & Rao, V. N. (1985). Sex-role attitudes: A comparison of sex-race groups. *Sex Roles, 12,* 939–953.

Rape now an "epidemic," Biden says. (1991, March 22). *Morning Call,* p. A2.

Raphael, R. (1988). *The men from the boys: Rites of passage in male America.* Lincoln, NE: University of Nebraska Press.

Rapoport, K. & Burkhart, B. R. (1984). Personality and attitudinal correlates of sexually coercive college males. *Journal of Abnormal Personality, 93,* 216–221.

Rapping, E. (1989, May-June). Talk shows pervert feminism. *New Directions for Women,* p. 8.

Rashid, H. M. (1989). Divergent paths in the development of African-American males: A qualitative perspective. *Urban Research Review, 12*(1), 1–2, 12–13.

Raskin, P. A., & Israel, A. C. (1981). Sex-role imitation in children: Effects of sex of child, sex of model, and sex-role appropriateness of modeled behavior. *Sex Roles, 7,* 1067–1077.

Rasmussen, J. L., & Moely, B. E. (1986). Impression formation as a function of the sex role appropriateness of linguistic behavior. *Sex Roles, 14,* 149–161.

Raymond, C. (1989, October 11). Shift of many traditionally male jobs to women. *Chronicle of Higher Education,* pp. A4, A6.

Raymond, J. G. (1979). Transsexualism: An issue of sex-role stereotyping. In E. Tobach & B. Rosoff (Eds.), *Genes and gender II* (pp. 131–141). Staten Island, NY: Gordian Press.

Raymond, J. G. (1986). *A passion for friends: Towards a philosophy of female affection.* Boston: Beacon Press.

Reagon, B. J. (1983). Coalition politics: Turning the century. In B. Smith (Ed.), *Home girls: A Black feminist anthology* (pp. 356–368). New York: Kitchen Table/Women of Color Press.

Rebecca, M., Hefner, R., & Olenshansky, B. (1976). A model of sex role transcendence. *Journal of Social Issues, 32*(3), 197–206.

Recer, P. (1991, September 8). Feminist report shows gender gap in medicine. *Morning Call,* p. A3.

Redmond, P. (1990, March-April). Record numbers of women in prison. *New Directions for Women,* pp. 1, 11.

The registration and drafting of women in 1980. (1980, March). *National NOW Times,* pp. 1, 4–9.

Reid, P. T. (1984). Feminism versus minority group identity: Not for Black women only. *Sex Roles, 10,* 247–255.

Reifman, A., Biernat, M., & Lang, E. L. (1991). Stress, social support, and health in married professional women with small children. *Psychology of Women Quarterly, 15,* 431–445.

Reinhard, K. (1991, January 14). Following the pack. *Morning Call,* pp. D1, D2.

Reinisch, J. M., Gandelman, R., & Spiegel, F. S. (1979). Prenatal influences on cognitive abilities: Data from experimental animals and syndromes. In M. A. Wittig & A. C. Petersen (Eds.), *Sex-related differences in cognitive functioning: Developmental issues* (pp. 215–239). New York: Academic Press.

Reinisch, J. M., Rosenblum, L. A., & Sanders, S. A. (Eds.). (1987). *Masculinity/femininity: Basic perspectives.* New York: Oxford University Press.

Reinke, B. J., Holmes, D. S., & Harris, R. L. (1985). The timing of psychological changes in women's lives: The years 25 to 45. *Journal of Personality and Social Psychology, 48,* 1353–1364.

Reis, H. T., & Jackson, L. A. (1981). Sex differences in reward allocation: Subjects, partners, and tasks. *Journal of Personality and Social Psychology, 40,* 465–478.

Reis, H. T., & Jelsma, B. (1978). A social psychology of sex differences in sport. In W. Straub (Ed.), *Sport psychology: An analysis of athlete behavior* (pp. 178–188). Ithaca, NY: Mouvement.

Reis, H. T., Senchak, M., & Solomon, B. (1985). Sex differences in the intimacy of social interaction: Further examination of potential explanations. *Journal of Personality and Social Psychology, 48,* 1204–1217.

Reisman, J. M. (1990). Intimacy in same-sex friendships. *Sex Roles, 23,* 65–82.

Remick, H. (Ed.). (1984). *Comparable worth and wage discrimination.* Philadelphia: Temple University Press.

Renwick, P. A., & Lawler, E. E. (1978, December). What you really want from a job. *Psychology Today,* pp. 53–65ff.

Repetti, R. L. (1984). Determinants of children's sex-stereotyping: Parental sex-role trait and television viewing. *Personality and Social Psychology Bulletin, 10,* 457–468.

Repetti, R. L., Matthews, K. A., & Waldron, I. (1989). Employment and women's health: Effects of paid employment on women's mental and physical health. *American Psychologist, 44,* 1394–1401.

Report: Gays abuse more alcohol, drugs. (1990, October 9). *Morning Call,* p. A7.

Report: Homicide rate high for U.S. men. (1990, June 27). *Morning Call,* p. A12.

Report notes decline in earnings of young men, especially blacks. (1987, June 12). *Easton Express,* p. C7.

Reskin, B. F., & Roos, P. A. (1990). *Job queues, gender queues: Explaining women's inroads into male occupations.* Philadelphia: Temple University Press.

Resolutions passed on women in the military. (1990, Fall). *National NOW Times,* p. 5.

The Revolution is over. (1984, April 9). *Time,* pp. 74–83.

Rhode, D. L. (1990). Definitions of difference. In D. L. Rhode (Ed.), *Theoretical perspectives on sexual difference* (pp. 197–212). New Haven: Yale University Press.

Rhodes, A. L. (1983). Effects of religious denominations on sex differences in occupational expectations. *Sex Roles, 9,* 93–108.

Rice, J. K. & Hemmings, A. (1988). Women's colleges and women achievers: An update. *Signs: Journal of Women in Culture and Society, 13,* 546–559.

Rice, R. W., Yoder, J. D., Adams, J., Priest, R. F., & Prince, H. T., II. (1984). Leadership ratings for male and female military cadets. *Sex Roles, 10,* 885–901.

Rich, A. (1980). Compulsory heterosexuality and lesbian existence. *Signs: Journal of Women in Culture and Society, 5,* 631–660.

Rich, A. (1986). *Of woman born: Motherhood as experience and institution* (10th anniversary ed.). New York: Norton.

Rich, S. (1986, November 3). Most moms stay home until children are 18, study says. *Morning Call,* p. A12.

Richards, M. H., Boxer, A. M., Petersen, A. C., & Albrecht, R. (1990). Relation of weight to body image in pubertal girls and boys from two communities. *Developmental Psychology, 26,* 313–321.

Richardson, D., Vinsel, A., & Taylor, S. P. (1980). Female aggression as a function of attitudes toward women. *Sex Roles, 6,* 265–271.

Richardson, M. S., & Alpert, J. L. (1980). Role perceptions: Variations by sex and roles. *Sex Roles, 6,* 783–793.

Richman, C. L., Clark, M. L., & Brown, K. P. (1985). General and specific self-esteem in late adolescent students: Race × gender × SES effects. *Adolescence, 20,* 555–566.

Rickard, K. M. (1989). The relationship of self-monitored dating behaviors to level of feminist identity on the feminist identity scale. *Sex Roles, 20,* 213–226.

Rickey, C. (1991, March 24). Too male and too pale. *Philadelphia Inquirer Magazine,* pp. 14, 15, 32–35.

Riddle, D. I., & Morin, S. F. (1977, November). Removing the stigma: Data from individuals. *APA Monitor,* pp. 16, 28.

Rierdan, J., Koff, E., & Stubbs, M. L. (1988). Gender, depression, and body image in early adolescents. *Journal of Early Adolescence, 8,* 109–117.

Riess, B. F., & Safer, J. M. (1979). Homosexuality in females and males. In E. S. Gomberg & V. Franks (Eds.), *Gender and disordered behavior: Sex differences in psychopathology* (pp. 257–286). New York: Brunner/Mazel.

Riger, S. & Galligan, P. (1980). Women in management. *American Psychologist, 35,* 902–910.

Riger, S., & Gordon, M. T. (1981). The fear of rape: A study in social control. *Journal of Social Issues, 37*(4) 71–92.

Rix, S. E. (1988). The Reagan years: Budgetary backlash. In E. Boneparth & E. Stoper (Eds.), *Women, power and policy: Toward the year 2000* (2nd ed.) (pp. 66–85). New York: Pergamon Press.

Roach, S. L. (1990). Men and women lawyers in in-house legal departments: Recruitment and career patterns. *Gender and Society, 4,* 207–219.

Roache, J. P. (1972, November). Confessions of a house husband. *Ms.,* pp.1, 25–27.

Roan, S. (1990, August 4). Sexual, racial bias seen in drug studies. *Morning Call,* p. A40.

Robbins, J. H., & Siegel, R. J. (Eds.). (1983). *Women changing therapy: New assessments, values and strategies in feminist therapy.* New York: Haworth.

Roberto, K. A., & Scott, J. P. (1986). Friendships of older men and women: Exchange patterns and satisfaction. *Psychology and Aging, 1,* 103–109.

Roberts, L. R., Sarigiani, P. A., Petersen, A. C., & Newman, J. L. (1990). Gender differences in the relationship between achievement and self-image during early adolescence. *Journal of Early Adolescence, 10,* 159–176.

Roberts, M. (1989, March). The benefits of fatherhood. *Psychology Today,* p. 76.

Roberts, R. (1990). "Sex as a weapon": Feminist rock music videos. *NWSA Journal, 2,* 1–15.

Roberts, S. V. (1988, October 9). Reagan's legions of nominees put his own stamp on the judiciary. *New York Times,* p. E6.

Roberts, T. (1991). Gender and the influence of evaluations on self-assessments in achievement settings. *Psychological Bulletin, 109,* 297–308.

Robertson, C., Dyer, C. E., & Campbell, D. (1988). Campus harassment: Sexual harassment policies and procedures at institutions of higher learning. *Signs: Journal of Women in Culture and Society, 13,* 792–812.

Robertson, J., & Fitzgerald, L. F. (1990). The (mis)treatment of men: Effects of client gender role and life-style on diagnosis and attribution of pathology. *Journal of Counseling Psychology, 37,* 3–9.

Robinson, C. C., & Morris, J. T. (1986). The gender-stereotyped nature of Christmas toys received by 36-, 48-, and 60-month-old children: A comparison between non-requested vs requested toys. *Sex Roles, 15,* 21–32.

Robinson, H. (Ed.). (1987). *Visibly female: Feminism and art today.* New York: Universe.

Robinson, M. B. (1989, May 11). Women bear the burden of caregiving, study finds. *Morning Call,* p. A8.

Robison-Awana, P., Kehle, T. J., & Jenson, W. R. (1986). But what about smart girls? Adolescent self-esteem and sex role perceptions as a function of academic achievement. *Journal of Educational Psychology, 78,* 179–183.

Rodin, J., & Ickovics, J. R. (1990). Women's health: Review and research agenda as we approach the 21st century. *American Psychologist, 45,* 1018–1034.

Rodman, H., Pratto, D. J., & Nelson, R. S. (1985). Child care arrangements and children's functioning: A comparison of self-care and adult-care children. *Developmental Psychology, 21,* 413–418.

Rogan, H. (1984, October 30). Executive women find it difficult to balance demands of job, home. *Wall Street Journal,* pp. 35, 55.

Rogers, J. R. (1990). Female suicide: The trend toward increased lethality in method of choice and its implications. *Journal of Counseling and Development, 69,* 37–38.

Rogers, L., & Walsh, J. (1982). Shortcomings of the psychomedical research of John Money and co-workers in sex differences in behavior: Social and political implications. *Sex Roles, 8,* 269–281.

Rohrbaugh, J. B. (1979, August). Femininity on the line. *Psychology Today,* p. 30ff.

Romer, N., & Cherry, D. (1980). Ethnic and social class differences in children's sex-role concepts. *Sex Roles, 6,* 245–263.

Roos, P. E., & Cohen, L. H. (1987). Sex roles and social support as moderators of life stress adjustment. *Journal of Personality and Social Psychology, 52,* 576–585.

Root, M.P.P. (1990). Disordered eating in women of color. *Sex Roles, 22,* 525–536.

Rose, R. M., Gordon, T. P., & Bernstein, I. (1972). Plasma testosterone levels in the male rhesus: Influence of sexual and social stimuli. *Science, 178,* 643–645.

Rose, R. M., Holaday, J. W., & Bernstein, I. (1971). Plasma testosterone, dominant rank, and aggression behavior in male rhesus monkeys. *Nature, 231,* 366–368.

Rose, S., & Frieze, I. H. (1989). Young singles' scripts for a first date. *Gender and Society, 3,* 258–268.

Rose, S., & Roades, L. (1987). Feminism and women's friendships. *Psychology of Women Quarterly, 11,* 243–254.

Rose, S. M. (1983, August). *Friendship termination patterns of college women and men.* Paper presented at the meeting of the American Psychological Association, Anaheim.

Rose, S. M. (1985a). Professional networks of junior faculty in psychology. *Psychology of Women Quarterly, 9,* 533–547.

Rose, S. M. (1985b). Same-sex and cross-sex friendships and the psychology of homosociality. *Sex Roles, 12,* 63-74.

Rosen, E. I. (1987). *Bitter choices.* Chicago: University of Chicago Press.

Rosenbach, W. E., Dailey, R. C., & Morgan, C. B. (1979). Perceptions of job characteristics and affective work outcomes for women and men. *Sex Roles, 5,* 267–277.

Rosenberg, M. (1973). The biological basis for sex role stereotypes. *Contemporary Psychoanalysis, 9,* 374–391.

Rosener, J. (1990, November-December). Ways women lead. *Harvard Business Review,* pp. 119–125.

Rosenkrantz, P., Vogel, S. R., Bee, H., Broverman, I. K., & Broverman, D. M. (1968). Sex role stereotypes and self-concepts in college students. *Journal of Consulting and Clinical Psychology, 32,* 287–295.

Rosenstein, M., & Milazzo-Sayre, L. J. (1981). *Characteristics of admissions to selected mental health facilities, 1975: An annotated book of charts and tables.* Washington, DC: U.S. Government Printing Office.

Rosenstein, M. J., Steadman, H. J., & Milazzo-Sayre, L. J. (1985, November). *Characteristics of admissions to private psychiatric hospital inpatient services, United States, 1980* (Mental Health Statistical Note No. 174). Rockville, MD: Department of Health and Human Services.

Rosenstein, M. J., Steadman, H. J., Milazzo-Sayre, L. J., MacAskill, R. L., & Manderscheid, R. W. (1986, September). *Characteristics of admissions to the inpatient services of state and county mental hospitals, United States, 1980* (Mental Health Statistical Note No. 177). Rockville, MD: Department of Health and Human Services.

Rosenstein, M. J., Steadman, H. J., MacAskill, R. L., & Manderscheid, R. W. (1987, October). *Characteristics of admissions to Veterans Administration medical center psychiatric inpatient services, United States, 1980* (Mental Health Statistical Note No. 184). Rockville, MD: Department of Health and Human Services.

Rosenthal, E. (1991, September 4). High blood pressure may pose less of a danger for women. *New York Times,* p. C11.

Rosenthal, N. B. (1984). Consciousness raising: From revolution to re-evaluation. *Psychology of Women Quarterly, 8,* 309–326.

Rosenthal, R. (1966). *Experimenter effects in behavioral research.* New York: Appleton-Century-Crofts.

Rosenthal, R., & DePaulo, B. M. (1979). Sex differences in eavesdropping on nonverbal cues. *Journal of Personality and Social Psychology, 37,* 273–285.

Rosenthal, R., Hall, J. A., DiMatteo, M. R., Rogers, P. L., & Archer, D. (1979). *Sensitivity to nonverbal communication: The PONS test.* Baltimore: Johns Hopkins University Press.

Rosenthal, R., & Jacobson, L. (1968). *Pygmalion in the classroom: Teacher expectations and pupils' intellectual development.* New York: Holt, Rinehart & Winston.

Rosenthal, R., & Rubin, D. B. (1982). Further meta-analytic procedures for assessing cognitive gender differences. *Journal of Educational Psychology, 74,* 708–712.

Rosenwasser, S. M., & Dean, N. G. (1989). Gender role and political office: Effects of perceived masculinity/femininity of candidate and political office. *Psychology of Women Quarterly, 13,* 77–85.

Rosenwasser, S. M., Gonzales, M. H., & Adams, V. (1985). Perceptions of a housespouse: The effects of sex, economic productivity, and subject background variables. *Psychology of Women Quarterly, 9,* 258–264.

Rosenwasser, S. M., Lingenfelter, M., & Harrington, A. F. (1989). Nontraditional gender role portrayals on television and children's gender role perceptions. *Journal of Applied Developmental Psychology, 10,* 97–105.

Rosewater, L. B., & Walker, L.E.A. (Eds.). (1985). *Handbook of feminist therapy: Women's issues in psychotherapy.* New York: Springer.

Ross, C. E., & Mirowsky, J. (1988). Child care and emotional adjustment to wives' employment. *Journal of Health and Social Behavior, 29,* 127–138.

Ross, C. E., Mirowsky, J., & Huber, J. (1983). Dividing work, sharing work, and inbetween: Marriage patterns and depression. *American Sociological Review, 48,* 809–823.

Ross, H., & Taylor, H. (1989). Do boys prefer Daddy or his physical style of play? *Sex Roles, 20,* 23–33.

Ross, J., & Kahan, J. P. (1983). Children by choice or by chance: The perceived effects of parity. *Sex Roles, 9,* 69–77.

Ross, L., Anderson, D. R., & Wisocki, P. A. (1982). Television viewing and adult sex-role attitudes. *Sex Roles, 8,* 589–592.

Ross, S. I., & Jackson, J. M. (1991). Teachers' expectations for Black males' and Black females' academic achievement. *Personality and Social Psychology Bulletin, 17,* 78–82.

Rosser, P. (1989, May-June). SATs no gauge of students' abilities. *New Directions for Women,* pp. 1, 7.

Rosser, S. V. (1988). Good science: Can it ever be gender-free? *Women's Studies International Forum, 11,* 13–19.

Rossi, A. S. (1985). Gender and parenthood. In A. Rossi (Ed.), *Gender and the life course* (pp. 161–191). Hawthorne, NY: Aldine.

Rossi, J. D. (1983). Ratios exaggerate gender differences in mathematical ability [Comment]. *American Psychologist, 38,* 348.

Rotenberg, K. J. (1984). Sex differences in children's trust in peers. *Sex Roles, 11,* 953–957.

Rotenberg, K. J. (1986). Same-sex patterns and sex differences in the trust-value

basis of children's friendship. *Sex Roles, 15,* 613–626.

Rothman, B. K. (1989). *Recreating motherhood: Ideology and technology in a patriarchal society.* New York: Norton.

Rothschild, J. (Ed.). (1983). *Machina ex dea: Feminist perspectives on technology.* New York: Pergamon Press.

Rotkin, K. F. (1976). The phallacy of our sexual norm. In A. G. Kaplan & J. P. Bean (Eds.), *Beyond sex-role stereotypes: Readings toward a psychology of androgyny* (pp. 154–162). Boston: Little, Brown.

Rotundo, E. A. (1985). American fatherhood: A historical perspective. *American Behavioral Scientist, 29,* 7–23.

Rowan, J. (1987). *The horned god: Feminism and men as wounding and healing.* New York: Routledge & Kegan Paul.

Rowland, R. (1986). Women who do and women who don't, join the women's movement: Issues for conflict and collaboration. *Sex Roles, 14,* 679–692.

Rowley, J. (1987, March 26). Court: State Department has discriminated against women. *Easton Express,* p. A3.

Rozee, P. (1988, August). *The effects of fear of rape on working women.* Paper presented at the meeting of the American Psychological Association, Atlanta.

Rubber sales expanding. (1988, October). *Psychology Today,* p. 11.

Rubin, G. (1975). The traffic in women. In R. Reiter (Ed.), *Toward an anthropology of women* (pp. 157–211). New York: Monthly Review Press.

Rubin, J. Z., Provenzano, F. J., & Luria, Z. (1974). The eye of the beholder: Parents' views on sex of newborns. *American Journal of Orthopsychiatry, 44,* 512–519.

Rubin, K. (1987, March). Whose job is child care? *Ms.,* pp. 32–44.

Rubin, L. B. (1983). *Intimate strangers: Men and women together.* New York: Harper & Row.

Rubin, L. B. (1985). *Just friends: The role of friendship in our lives.* New York: Harper & Row.

Rubin, L. B. (1990). *Erotic wars: What happened to the sexual revolution?* New York: HarperCollins.

Rubin, Z. (1983). Are working wives hazardous to their husbands' mental health? *Psychology Today,* pp. 70–72.

Rubin, Z., Peplau, L. A., & Hill, C. T. (1981). Loving and leaving: Sex differences in romantic attachments. *Sex Roles, 7,* 821–835.

Ruble, D. N. (1977). Premenstrual symptoms: A reinterpretation. *Science, 197,* 291–292.

Ruble, D. N., Fleming, A. S., Hackel, L. S., & Stangor, C. (1988). Changes in the marital relationship during the transition to first-time motherhood: Effects of

violated expectations concerning division of household labor. *Journal of Personality and Social Psychology, 55,* 78–87.

Ruble, T. L. (1983). Sex stereotypes: Issues of change in the 1970s. *Sex Roles, 9,* 397–402.

Rudd, N. M., & McKenry, P. C. (1986). Family influences on the job satisfaction of employed mothers. *Psychology of Women Quarterly, 10,* 363–371.

Ruddick, S. (1989). *Maternal thinking: Toward a politics of peace.* Boston: Beacon Press.

Ruether, R. R. (1987). *Women-Church: Theology and practice of feminist liturgical communities.* San Francisco: Harper & Row.

Ruggiero, J. A., & Weston, L. C. (1985). Work options for women in women's magazines: The medium and the message. *Sex Roles, 12,* 535–547.

Rumenik, D. K., Capasso, D. R., & Hendrick, C. (1977). Experimenter sex effects in behavioral research. *Psychological Bulletin, 84,* 852–877.

Rusbult, C. E., Johnson, D. J., & Morrow, G. D. (1986). Impact of couple patterns of problem solving on distress and nondistress in dating relationships. *Journal of Personality and Social Psychology, 50,* 744–753.

Rusbult, C. E., Zembrodt, I. M., & Iwaniszek, J. (1986). The impact of gender and sex role orientation on responses to dissatisfaction in close relationships. *Sex Roles, 15,* 1–20.

Rush, F. (1980). *The best kept secret: Sexual abuse of children.* Englewood Cliffs, NJ: Prentice-Hall.

Russell, D.E.H. (1984). *Sexual exploitation: Rape, child sexual abuse, and workplace harassment.* Beverly Hills, CA: Sage.

Russell, D.E.H. (1986). *The secret trauma: Incest in the lives of girls and women.* New York: Basic Books.

Russell, G. (1978). The father role and its relation to masculinity, femininity, and androgyny. *Child Development, 49,* 1174–1181.

Russell, G. (1986). Primary caretaking and role-sharing fathers. In M. E. Lamb (Ed.), *The father's role: Applied perspectives* (pp. 29–57). New York: Wiley.

Russett, C. E. (1989). *Sexual science: The Victorian construction of womanhood.* Cambridge, MA: Harvard University Press.

Russo, N. F. (1976). The Motherhood Mandate. *Journal of Social Issues, 32*(3), 143–153.

Russo, N. F. (1990). Overview: Forging research priorities for women's mental health. *American Psychologist, 45,* 368–373.

Russo, N. F., & Sobel, S. B. (1981). Sex differences in the utilization of mental health facilities. *Professional Psychology, 12,* 7–19.

Rustad, M. (1982). *Women in khaki: The American enlisted women.* New York: Praeger.

Ryan, S. (1975, January). Gynecological considerations. *Journal of Health, Physical Education, and Recreation,* pp. 40–44.

Rytina, N. F., & Bianchi, S. M. (1984, March). Occupational reclassification and changes in distribution by gender. *Monthly Labor Review, 107*(3), 11–17.

Ryujin, D. H., & Herrold, A. J. (1989). Cross-sex comparisons: A word of caution. *Sex Roles, 20,* 713–719.

Rywick, T. (1984, April). *A SYMLOG analysis of friendship.* Paper presented at the meeting of the Eastern Psychological Association, Baltimore.

Saal, F. E., Johnson, C. B., & Weber, N. (1989). Friendly or sexy? It may depend on whom you ask. *Psychology of Women Quarterly, 13,* 263–276.

Saario, T. N., Jacklin, C. N., & Tittle, C. K. (1973). Sex role stereotypes in the public schools. *Harvard Educational Review, 43*(3), 386–416.

Sacks, R. (1989, November-December). Women at work. *In View,* p. 16.

Sacks, R. (1990, March-April). Sex on campus. *In View,* p. 16.

Sadalla, E. K., Kenrick, D. T., & Vershure, B. (1987). Dominance and heterosexual attraction. *Journal of Personality and Social Psychology, 52,* 730–738.

Sadd, S., Miller, F. D., & Zeitz, B. (1979). Sex roles and achievement conflicts. *Personality and Social Psychology Bulletin, 5,* 352–355.

Sadker, M., & Sadker, D. (1985, March). Sexism in the schoolroom of the '80s. *Psychology Today,* pp. 54, 56, 57.

Sadker, M., & Sadker, D. (1986, March). Sexism in the classroom: From grade school to graduate school. *Phi Delta Kappan,* pp. 512–515.

Sadker, M., Sadker, D., & Steindam, S. (1989, March). Gender equity and educational reform. *Educational Leadership,* pp. 44–47.

Safilios-Rothschild, C. (1977). *Love, sex, and sex roles.* Englewood Cliffs, NJ: Prentice-Hall.

Safilios-Rothschild, C. (1979). Women as change agents: Toward a conflict theoretical model of sex role change. In J. Lipman-Blumen & J. Bernard (Eds.), *Sex roles and social policy: A complex social science equation* (pp. 287–301). Beverly Hills, CA: Sage.

St. Lawrence, J. S., & Joyner, D. J. (1991). The effects of sexually violent rock music on males' acceptance of violence against women. *Psychology of Women Quarterly, 15,* 49–63.

Salk, L. (1982). *My father, my son: Intimate relationships.* New York: Putnam.

Saltzman, A. (1991, June 17). Trouble at the top. *U.S. News and World Report,* pp. 40–48.

Sanday, P. R. (1973). Toward a theory of the status of women. *American Anthropologist, 75,* 1682–1700.

Sanday, P. R. (1974). Female status in the public domain. In M. Z. Rosaldo & L. Lamphere (Eds.), *Women, culture, and society* (pp. 189–207). Stanford, CA: Stanford University Press.

Sanday, P. R. (1981a). *Female power and male dominance: On the origins of sexual inequality.* Cambridge, England: Cambridge University Press.

Sanday, P. R. (1981b). The socio-cultural context of rape: A cross-cultural study. *Journal of Social Issues, 37*(4), 5–27.

Sanday, P. R. (1986). Rape and the silencing of the feminine. In S. Tomaselli & R. Porter (Eds.), *Rape* (pp. 84–101). Oxford: Basil Blackwell.

Sanday, P. R. (1990). *Fraternity gang rape: Sex, brotherhood, and privilege on campus.* New York: New York University Press.

Sandberg, D. E., Ehrhardt, A. E., Mellins, C. A., Ince, S. E., & Meyer-Bahlburg, H.F.L. (1987). The influence of individual and family characteristics upon career aspirations of girls during childhood and adolescence. *Sex Roles, 16,* 649–668.

Sanders, G., & Ross-Field, L. (1987). Neuropsychological development of cognitive abilities: A new research strategy and some preliminary evidence for a sexual orientation model. *International Journal of Neuroscience, 36,* 1–16.

Sanders, M., & Rock, M. (1988). *Waiting for prime time: The women of television news.* Urbana, IL: University of Illinois Press.

Sanford, L. T., & Donovan, M. E. (1984). *Women and self-esteem.* New York: Penguin.

Santrock, J. W., & Warshak, R. A. (1986). Development of father custody, relationships, and legal/clinical considerations in father-custody families. In M. E. Lamb (Ed.), *The father's role: Applied perspectives* (pp. 135–163). New York: Wiley.

Sapadin, L. A. (1988). Friendship and gender: Perspectives of professional men and women. *Journal of Social and Personal Relationships, 5,* 387–403.

Saunders, G. (1990). *The nude: A new perspective.* New York: Harper & Row.

Saurer, M. K., & Eisler, R. M. (1990). The role of masculine gender role stress in expressivity and social support network factors. *Sex Roles, 23,* 261–271.

Savage, J. E., Jr., Stearns, A. D., & Friedman, P. (1979). Relationship of internal-external locus of control, self-concept, and masculinity-femininity to fear of success in Black freshmen and senior college women. *Sex Roles, 5,* 373–383.

Savell, J. M., Woelfel, J. C., Collins, B. E., & Bentler, P. M. (1979). A study of male and female soldiers' beliefs about the "appropriateness" of various jobs for women in the Army. *Sex Roles, 5,* 41–62.

Saxby, L., & Bryden, M. P. (1985). Left visual-field advantage in children for processing visual emotional stimuli. *Developmental Psychology, 21,* 253–261.

Sayers, J. (1987). Science, sexual difference, and feminism. In B. B. Hess & M. M. Ferree (Eds.), *Analyzing gender: A handbook of social science research* (pp. 68–91). Newbury Park, CA: Sage.

Scarf, M. (1979, November). The more sorrowful sex. *Psychology Today,* pp. 44–52, 89–90.

Scarr, S. (1984). *Mother care/Other care.* New York: Basic Books.

Scarr, S. (1988). Race and gender as psychological variables: Social and ethical issues. *American Psychologist, 43,* 56–59.

Scarr, S. (1990). Mother's proper place: Children's needs and women's rights. *Journal of Social Behavior and Personality, 5,* 507–515.

Scarr, S., Phillips, D., & McCartney, K. (1990). Facts, fantasies, and the future of child care in the United States. *Psychological Science, 1,* 26–35.

Schacter, S., & Singer, J. E. (1962). Cognitive, social, and physiological determinants of emotional state. *Psychological Review, 63,* 379–399.

Schafer, S. M. (1990a, April 15). Debate still rages over role of women in military. *Morning Call,* p. E8.

Schafer, S. M. (1990b, September 13). Pentagon survey: Harassment exists. *Philadelphia Inquirer,* p. 2.

Schaninger, C. M., & Buss, W. C. (1986). The relationship of sex role norms to couple and parental demographics. *Sex Roles, 15,* 77–94.

Schau, C. G., & Scott, K. P. (1984). Impact of gender characteristics of instructional materials: An integration of the research literature. *Journal of Educational Psychology, 76,* 183–193.

Scheppele, K. L., & Bart, P. B. (1983). Through women's eyes: Defining danger in the wake of sexual assault. *Journal of Social Issues, 39*(2), 63–81.

Scher, D. (1984). Sex-role contradictions: Self-perceptions and ideal perceptions. *Sex Roles, 10,* 651–656.

Scher, M., Stevens, M., Good, G., & Eichenfield, G. A. (Eds.) (1987). *Handbook of counseling and psychotherapy with men.* Newbury Park, CA: Sage.

Schlafly, P. (1977). *The power of the positive woman.* New Rochelle, NY: Arlington House.

Schmich, M. T. (1984, November 12). Young teen-age girls find that stereotypes die hard. *Easton Express*, p. 3.

Schmid, R. E. (1990, April 11). Closing the gap: Men catching up in population tally. *Morning Call*, p. 3.

Schmidt, G. (1975). Male-female differences in sexual arousal and behavior during and after exposure to sexually explicit stimuli. *Archives of Sexual Behavior, 4,* 353–364.

Schmidt, G., & Sigusch, V. (1973). Women's sexual arousal. In J. Zubein & J. Money (Eds.), *Contemporary sexual behavior: Critical issues in the 1970s* (pp. 117–143). Baltimore: Johns Hopkins University Press.

Schmidt, W. E. (1989, January 15). Study links male unemployment and single mothers in Chicago. *New York Times*, p. 16.

Schmitt, B. H., & Millard, R. T. (1988). Construct validity of the Bem Sex Role Inventory (BSRI): Does the BSRI distinguish between gender-schematic and gender-aschematic individuals? *Sex Roles, 19,* 581–588.

Schmitt, C. H. (1991, June 10). Signs point to a turnaround in the long decline of the American family. *Morning Call*, pp. D1, D2.

Schmitz, B. (1985). *Integrating women's studies into the curriculum: A guide and bibliography.* Old Westbury, NY: Feminist Press.

Schneer, J. A., & Reitman, F. (1990). Effects of employment gaps on the careers of M.B.A.'s: More damaging for men than for women? *Academy of Management Journal, 33,* 391–406.

Schneider, F. W., & Coutts. L. M. (1985). Person orientation of male and female high school students: To the educational disadvantage of males? *Sex Roles, 13,* 47–63.

Schneider, S. W. (1986). Jewish women in the nuclear family and beyond. In J. Cole (Ed.), *All-American women: Lines that divide, ties that bind* (pp. 198–215). New York: Free Press.

Schreiber, C. T. (1979). *Changing places.* Boston: MIT Press.

Schroedel, J. R. (1990). Blue-collar women: Paying the price at home and on the job. In H. Y. Grossman & N. L. Chester (Eds.), *The experience and meaning of work in women's lives* (pp. 241–260). Hillsdale, NJ: Erlbaum.

Schullo, S. A., & Alperson, B. L. (1984). Interpersonal phenomenology as a function of sexual orientation, sex, sentiment, and trait categories in long-term dyadic relationships. *Journal of Personality and Social Psychology, 47,* 983–1002.

Schwartz, F. N. (1989). Management women and the new facts of life. *Harvard Business Review, 89,* 65–76.

Schwartz, L. A., & Marham, W. T. (1985). Sex stereotyping in children's toy advertisements. *Sex Roles, 12,* 157–170.

Sciolino, E. (1985, June 23). U.N. finds widespread inequality for women. *New York Times*, p. 10.

Sciolino, E. (1990, January 25). Battle lines are shifting on women in war. *New York Times*, pp. 1, D23.

Scott, H. (1979). Women in Eastern Europe. In J. Lipman-Blumen & J. Bernard (Eds.), *Sex roles and social policy: A complex social science equation* (pp. 177–197). Beverly Hills, CA: Sage.

Scott, W. J., & Morgan, C. S. (1983). An analysis of factors affecting traditional family expectations and perceptions of ideal fertility. *Sex Roles, 9,* 901–914.

Scully, D. (1990). *Understanding sexual violence: A study of convicted rapists.* Boston: Unwin Hyman.

Seager, J., & Olson, A. (1986). *Women in the world: An international atlas.* New York: Simon & Schuster.

Seaman, B. (1972). *Free and female.* Greenwich, CT: Fawcett Crest.

Sears, D. O. (1986). College sophomores in the laboratory: Influences of a narrow data base on social psychology's view of human nature. *Journal of Personality and Social Psychology, 51,* 515–530.

Secord, P. F. (1983). Imbalanced sex ratios: The social consequences. *Personality and Social Psychology Bulletin, 9,* 525–543.

Sedney, M. A. (1987). Development of androgyny: Parental influences. *Psychology of Women Quarterly, 11,* 311–326.

Sedney, M. A. (1989). Conceptual and methodological sources of controversies about androgyny. In R. Unger (Ed.), *Representations: Social constructions of gender* (pp. 126–144). Amityville, NY: Baywood.

Segal, J., & Yahraes, H. (1978, June). Bringing up mother. *Psychology Today*, pp. 90–96.

Segal, L. (1990). *Slow motion: Changing masculinities, changing men.* New Brunswick, NJ: Rutgers University Press.

Seiden, A. M. (1979). Gender differences in psycho-physiological illness. In E. S. Gomberg & V. Franks (Eds.), *Gender and disordered behavior: Sex differences in psychopathology* (pp. 426–449). New York: Brunner/Mazel.

Seidenberg, R. (1973). *Marriage between equals.* Garden City, NY: Anchor Press.

Seidman, C. (1979, December 30). Women athletes gained recognition and also respect. *New York Times*, p. 57.

Selkow, P. (1984). Effects of maternal employment on kindergarten and first-grade children's vocational aspirations. *Sex Roles, 11,* 677–690.

Sells, L. W. (1980). The mathematics filter and the education of women and minorities. In L. H. Fox, L. Brody & D. Tobin (Eds.), *Women and the mathematical mystique.* Baltimore: Johns Hopkins University Press.

Selnow, G. W. (1985). Sex differences in uses and perceptions of profanity. *Sex Roles, 12,* 303–312.

Senneker, P., & Hendrick, C. (1983). Androgyny and helping behavior. *Journal of Personality and Social Psychology, 45,* 916–925.

Serbin, L. A., & Connor, J. M. (1979). Sex-typing of children's play preference and patterns of cognitive performance. *Journal of Genetic Psychology, 134,* 315–316.

Serbin, L. A., Connor, J. M., & Citron, C. C. (1981). Sex differentiated free play behavior: Effects of teacher modeling, location, and gender. *Developmental Psychology, 17,* 640–646.

Serbin, L. A., O'Leary, K. D., Kent, R. N., & Tonick, I. J. (1973). A comparison of teacher response to the pre-academic and problem behavior of boys and girls. *Child Development, 44,* 796–804.

Serbin, L. A., Zelkowitz, P., Doyle, A., Gold, D., & Wheaton, B. (1990). The socialization of sex-differentiated skills and academic performance: A mediational model. *Sex Roles, 23,* 613–628.

Serrin, W. (1984, December 9). White men discover it's a shrinking job market. *New York Times*, p. E2.

Sex on campus. (1982, October). *Playboy*, pp. 144–149ff.

Sharabany, R., Gershoni, R., & Hofman, J. E. (1981). Girl friend, boy friend: Age and sex differences in development of intimate friendships. *Developmental Psychology, 17,* 800–808.

Shaw, J. S. (1982). Psychological androgyny and stressful life events. *Journal of Personality and Social Psychology, 43,* 145–153.

Shaywitz, S. E., Shaywitz, B. A., Fletcher, J. M., & Escobar, M. D. (1990). Prevalence of reading disability in boys and girls. *Journal of the American Medical Association, 264,* 998–1002.

Sheffield, C. J. (1989). Sexual terrorism. In J. Freeman (Ed.), *Women: A feminist perspective* (pp. 3–19). Mountain View, CA: Mayfield.

Shelton, B. A., & Firestone, J. (1989). Household labor time and the gender gap in earnings. *Gender and Society, 3,* 105–112.

Shepelak, N. J., Ogden, D., & Tobin-Bennett, D. (1984). The influence of gender labels on the sex typing of imaginary occupations. *Sex Roles, 11,* 983–996.

Sherfey, M. J. (1974). *The nature and evolution of female sexuality.* New York: Aronson.

Sherif, M. (1970). On the relevance of social psychology. *American Psychologist, 25,* 144–156.

Sherman, B. L., & Dominick, J. R. (1986). Violence and sex in music videos, TV, and rock-n-roll. *Journal of Communication, 36,* 79–93.

Sherman, J. (1978). *Sex-related differences in cognition: An essay on theory and evidence.* Springfield, IL: Charles C Thomas.

Sherman, J. (1982a). Continuing in mathematics: A longitudinal study of the attitudes of high school girls. *Psychology of Women Quarterly, 7,* 132–140.

Sherman, J. (1982b). Mathematics, the critical filter: A look at some residues. *Psychology of Women Quarterly, 6,* 428–444.

Sherman, J. (1983). Factors predicting girls' and boys' preparatory mathematics. *Psychology of Women Quarterly, 7,* 272–281.

Sherman, J., & Fennema, E. (1978). Distribution of spatial visualization and mathematical problem-solving scores: A test of Stafford's X linked hypotheses. *Psychology of Women Quarterly, 3,* 157–167.

Sherman, S. R., & Rosenblatt, A. (1984). Women physicians as teachers, administrators, and researchers in medical and surgical specialties. *Sex Roles, 11,* 203–209.

Shields, S. (1975). Functionalism, Darwinism, and the psychology of women: A study in social myth. *American Psychologist, 30,* 739–754.

Shields, S. (1987). Women, men, and the dilemma of emotion. In P. Shaver & C. Hendrick (Eds.), *Sex and gender* (pp. 229–250). Newbury Park, CA: Sage.

Shiffman, M. (1987). The men's movement: An exploratory empirical investigation. In M. Kimmel (Ed.), *Changing men: New directions in research on men and masculinity* (pp. 295–314). Newbury Park, CA: Sage.

Shigetomi, C. C., Hartmann, D. P., & Gelfand, D. N. (1981). Sex differences in children's altruistic behavior and reputations for helpfulness. *Developmental Psychology, 19,* 434–437.

Shinar, E. H. (1978). Person perception as a function of occupation and sex. *Sex Roles, 4,* 679–693.

Shinedling, M., & Pedersen, D. M. (1970). Effects of sex of teacher versus student on children's gain in quantitative and verbal performance. *Journal of Psychology, 76,* 79–84.

Shiva, V. (1988). *Staying alive: Women, ecology, and development.* London: Zed.

Sidel, R. (1986). *Women and children last: The plight of poor women in affluent America.* New York: Viking.

Sidel, R. (1990). *On her own: Growing up in the shadow of the American dream.* New York: Viking.

Siegfried, W. D. (1982). The effects of specifying job requirements and using explicit warnings to decrease sex discrimination in employment interviews. *Sex Roles, 8,* 73–82.

Siem, F. M., & Spence, J. T. (1986). Gender-related traits and helping behaviors. *Journal of Personality and Social Psychology, 51,* 615–621.

Siever, M. D. (1988, August). *Sexual orientation, gender, and the perils of sexual objectification.* Paper presented at the meeting of the American Psychological Association, Atlanta.

Sigel, R. S. (1991). *How men and women cope when gender role orientations change.* Paper presented at the meeting of the International Society for Political Psychology, Helsinki, Finland.

Signorella, M. L., & Jamison, W. (1986). Masculinity, femininity, androgyny, and cognitive performance: A meta-analysis. *Psychological Bulletin, 100,* 207–229.

Signorella, M. L., Jamison, W., & Krupa, M. H. (1989). Predicting spatial performance from gender stereotyping in activity preferences and in self-concept. *Developmental Psychology, 25,* 89–95.

Signorella, M. L., & Vegega, M. E. (1984). A note on gender stereotyping of research topics. *Personality and Social Psychology Bulletin, 10,* 107–109.

Signorella, M. L., Vegega, M. E., & Mitchell, M. E. (1981). Subject selection and analyses for sex-related differences: 1968–1970 and 1975–1977. *American Psychologist, 36,* 988–990.

Signorielli, N. (1989). Television and conceptions about sex roles: Maintaining conventionality and the status quo. *Sex Roles, 21,* 341–360.

Silberstein, L. S., Striegel-Moore, R. H., Timko, C., & Rodin, J. (1988). Behavioral and psychological implications of body dissatisfaction: Do men and women differ? *Sex Roles, 19,* 219–232.

Silver, G. A., & Silver, M. (1981). *Weekend fathers.* Los Angeles: Stratford Press.

Silverberg, S. B., & Steinberg, L. (1990). Psychological well-being of parents with early adolescent children. *Developmental Psychology, 26,* 658–666.

Silverman, J. M., & Kumka, D. S. (1987). Gender differences in attitudes toward nuclear war and disarmament. *Sex Roles, 16,* 189–203.

Silverman, L. H., & Fisher, A. K. (1981). The Oedipus complex: Studies in adult male behavior. In L. Wheeler (Ed.), *Review of Personality and Social Psychology,* Vol. 2 (pp. 43–67). Beverly Hills, CA: Sage.

Silverman, W. K., & Nelles, W. B. (1987). The influence of gender on children's ratings of fear in self and same-aged peers. *Journal of Genetic Psychology, 148,* 17–21.

Silvern, L. E. (1977). Children's sex-role preferences: Stronger among girls than boys. *Sex Roles, 3,* 159–171.

Silvern, L. E., & Katz, P. A. (1986). Gender roles and adjustment in elementary-school children: A multidimensional approach. *Sex Roles, 14,* 181–202.

Silvern, L. E., & Ryan, V. L. (1983). A reexamination of masculine and feminine sex-role ideals and conflicts among ideals for the man, woman, and person. *Sex Roles, 9,* 1223–1248.

Silverstein, B., Perdue, L., Peterson, B., & Kelly, E. (1986). The role of the mass media in promoting a thin standard of bodily attractiveness for women. *Sex Roles, 14,* 519–532.

Simon, W., & Gagnon, J. H. (1987). A sexual scripts approach. In K. Kelley (Ed.), *Females, males, and sexuality: Theories and research* (pp. 363–383). Albany: State University of New York Press.

Simpson, G. (1984). The daughters of Charlotte Ray: The career development process during the exploratory and establishment stages of black women attorneys. *Sex Roles, 11,* 113–139.

Simpson, J. A., Campbell, B., & Berscheid, E. (1986). The association between romantic love and marriage: Kephart (1967) twice revisited. *Personality and Social Psychology Bulletin, 12,* 363–372.

Sinnott, J. D. (1986). *Sex roles and aging: Theory and research from a systems perspective.* New York: S. Karger.

Sinnott, J. D. (1987). Sex roles in adulthood and old age. In B. Carter (Ed.), *Current conceptions of sex roles and sex typing: Theory and research* (pp. 155–177). New York: Praeger.

Six, B., & Eckes, T. (1991). A closer look at the complex structure of gender stereotypes. *Sex Roles, 24,* 57–71.

Skelly, G., & Lundstrom, W. (1981). Male sex roles in magazine advertising, 1959–1979. *Journal of Communication, 31,* 52–57.

Skrypnek, B. J., & Snyder, M. (1982). On the self-perpetuating nature of stereotypes about women and men. *Journal of Experimental Social Psychology, 18,* 277–291.

Skrzycki, C. (1990a, February 25). The ladder for women still hits "glass ceiling." *Morning Call,* pp. D1, D11.

Skrzycki, C. (1990b, December 30). Dual-career families are putting more men on the daddy track. *Morning Call,* p. E2.

Slaby, R. G., & Frey, K. S. (1975). Development of gender constancy and selective attention to same-sex models. *Child Development, 46,* 849–856.

Slife, B. D., & Rychlak, J. F. (1982). Role of affects assessment in modeling aggressive behavior. *Journal of Personality and Social Psychology, 43,* 861–868.

Slusher, M. P., & Anderson, C. A. (1987). When reality monitoring fails: The role of imagination in stereotype maintenance. *Journal of Personality and Social Psychology, 52,* 653–662.

Smart, C., & Sevenhuijzen, S. (Eds.). (1989). *Child custody and the politics of gender.* New York: Routledge.

Smeal, E. (1984). *Why and how women will elect the next president.* New York: Harper & Row.

Smeal, E. (1987, July–August). The ERA: Should we eat our words? *Ms.,* pp. 170, 218.

Smeal, E., Raphael, T., & Mulvihill, S. (1990, November–December). 1990 elections: Breakthrough year for women. *National NOW Times,* p. 4.

Smith, A. (1983). Nonverbal communication among black female dyads: An assessment of intimacy, gender, and race. *Journal of Social Issues, 39*(3), 55–67.

Smith, A., & Stewart, A. J. (Eds.). (1983). Racism and sexism in black women's lives [Special issue]. *Journal of Social Issues, 39*(3).

Smith, B. (1982). Racism and women's studies. In G. Hull, P. Scott, & B. Smith (Eds.), *But some of us are brave* (pp. 48–51). Old Westbury, NY: Feminist Press.

Smith, B. (Ed.). (1983). *Home girls: A black feminist anthology.* New York: Kitchen Table/Women of Color Press.

Smith, E. A., Udry, J. R., & Morris, N. M. (1985). Pubertal development and friends: A biosocial explanation of adolescent sexual behavior. *Journal of Health and Social Behavior, 26,* 183–192.

Smith, E. J. (1982). The Black female adolescent: A review of the educational, career, and psychological literature. *Psychology of Women Quarterly, 6,* 261–288.

Smith, J. E., Waldorf, V. A., & Trembath, D. L. (1990). "Single white male looking for thin, very attractive . . ." *Sex Roles, 23,* 675–685.

Smith, J. P., & Ward, M. (1989). Women in the labor market and in the family. *Journal of Economic Perspectives, 3,* 9–23.

Smith, P. A., & Midlarsky, E. (1985). Empirically derived conceptions of femaleness and maleness: A current view. *Sex Roles, 12,* 313–328.

Smith, R. (1990, June 17). Waging guerrilla warfare against the art world. *New York Times,* pp. H1, H31.

Smith, R. E. (Ed.). (1979). *The subtle revolution: Women at work.* Washington, DC: The Urban Institute.

Smith-Rosenberg, C. (1975). The female world of love and ritual: Relations between women in nineteenth-century America. *Signs: Journal of Women in Culture and Society, 1,* 1–29.

Smolowe, J. (1990, Fall). Last call for motherhood. *Women: The road ahead* [Special issue of *Time* magazine], p. 76.

Smye, M. D., & Wine, J. D. (1980). A comparison of female and male adolescents' social behaviors and cognitions: A challenge to the assertiveness literature. *Sex Roles, 6,* 213–230.

Snarey, J., Friedman, K., & Blasi, J. (1985). *Sex role strain among Kibbutz women: a developmental perspective* (Working Paper No. 151). Wellesley, MA: Center for Research on Women.

Snell, W. E., Jr. (1989). Development and validation of the Masculine Behavior Scale: A measure of behaviors stereotypically attributed to males vs. females. *Sex Roles, 21,* 749.

Snell, W. E., Jr., Belk, S. S., & Hawkins, R. C. (1986). The masculine role as a moderator of stress-distress relationships. *Sex Roles, 15,* 359–366.

Snell, W. E., Jr., Belk, S. S., & Hawkins, R. C. (1987). Alcohol and drug use in stressful times: The influence of the masculine role and sex-related personality attributes. *Sex Roles, 16,* 359–373.

Snell, W. E., Jr., Miller, R. S., Belk, S. S., Garcia-Falconi, R., & Hernandez-Sanchez, J. E. (1989). Men's and women's emotional disclosures: The impact of disclosure recipient, culture and the masculine role. *Sex Roles, 21,* 467–486.

Snitow, A., Stansell, C., & Thompson, S. (Eds.). (1983). *Powers of desire: The politics of sexuality.* New York: Monthly Review Press.

Snodgrass, S. E. (1985). Women's intuition: The effect of subordinate role upon interpersonal sensitivity. *Journal of Personality and Social Psychology, 49,* 146–155.

Snow, K. (1975). Women in the American novel. In J. Freeman (Ed.), *Women: A feminist perspective* (pp. 279–292). Palo Alto, CA: Mayfield.

Snow, L. J., & Parsons, J. L. (1983). Sex role orientation and female sexual functioning. *Psychology of Women Quarterly, 8,* 133–143.

Snyder, M., Tanke, E. D., & Berscheid, E. (1977). Social perception and interpersonal behavior: On the self-fulfilling nature of social stereotypes. *Journal of Personality and Social Psychology, 35,* 656–666.

Snyder, T. D. (1987). *Digest of education statistics.* Washington, DC: Department of Education.

Social Security is a women's issue. (1985, May). *National NOW Times,* p. 10.

Sollie, D. L., & Fischer, J. L. (1985). Sex-role orientation, intimacy of topic, and target person differences in self-disclosure among women. *Sex Roles, 12,* 917–929.

Solomon, K., & Levy, N. (Eds.). (1982). *Men in transition: Changing male roles, theory, and therapy.* New York: Plenum.

Sommer, B. (1984, August). PMS in the courts: Are all women on trial? *Psychology Today,* pp. 36–38.

South, S. J., & Felson, R. B. (1990). The racial patterning of rape. *Social Forces, 69,* 71–93.

Spallone, P. (1989). *Beyond conception: The new politics of reproduction.* Granby, MA: Bergin & Garvey.

Spangler, L. C. (1989). A historical overview of female friendships on prime-time television. *Journal of Popular Culture, 22,* 13–23.

Spelman, E. V. (1988). *Inessential woman: Problems of exclusion in feminist thought.* Boston: Beacon Press.

Spence, J. T. (1983). Commenting on Lubinski, Tellegen, and Butcher's "Masculinity, femininity, and androgyny viewed and assessed as distinct concepts." *Journal of Personality and Social Psychology, 44,* 440–446.

Spence, J. T. (1985). Gender identity and its implications for concepts of masculinity and femininity. In T. B. Sonderegger (Ed.), *Nebraska Symposium on Motivation, 1984. Psychology and gender,* Vol. 32 (pp. 59–96). Lincoln, NE: University of Nebraska Press.

Spence, J. T. (1991). Do the BSRI and PAQ measure the same or different concepts? *Psychology of Women Quarterly, 15,* 141–165.

Spence, J. T., & Helmreich, R. (1972). Who likes competent women? Competence, sex-role congruence of interests, and subjects' attitude toward women as determinants of interpersonal attraction. *Journal of Applied Social Psychology, 2,* 197–213.

Spence, J. T., & Helmreich, R. (1978). *Masculinity and femininity: The psychological dimensions, correlates, and antecedents.* Austin: University of Texas Press.

Spence, J. T., & Helmreich, R. L. (1980). Masculine instrumentality and feminine expressiveness: Their relationships with sex role attitudes and behavior. *Psychology of Women Quarterly, 5,* 147–163.

Spence, J. T. & Helmreich, R. L. (1981). Androgyny versus gender schema: A comment on Bem's gender schema theory. *Psychological Review, 88,* 365–368.

Spence, J. T. & Helmreich, R. L. (1983). Achievement-related motives and behaviors. In J. T. Spence (Ed.), *Achievement and achievement motivation: Psychological and sociological approaches* (pp. 7–74). San Francisco: Freeman.

Spence, J. T., Helmreich, R. L., & Holahan, C. K. (1979). Negative and positive components of psychological masculinity and femininity and their relationship to self-reports of neurotic and acting out behaviors. *Journal of Personality and Social Psychology, 37,* 1673–1682.

Spence, J. T., Helmreich, R., & Stapp, J. (1974). The Personal Attributes Questionnaire: A measure of sex role stereotyping and masculinity and femininity. *JSAS selected documents in psychology* (Ms. No. 617).

Spence, J. T., & Sawin, L. L. (1985). Images of masculinity and femininity: A reconceptualization. In V. O'Leary, R. Unger, & B. Wallston (Eds.), *Women, gender and social psychology* (pp. 35–66). Hillsdale, NJ: Erlbaum.

Spencer, B. A., & Taylor, G. S. (1988). Effects of facial attractiveness and gender on causal attributions of managerial performance. *Sex Roles, 19,* 273–285.

Spencer, M. B., Dobbs, B., & Phillips, D. (1988). African American adolescents: Adaptational processes and socioeconomic diversity in behavioral outcomes. *Journal of Adolescence, 11,* 117–137.

Spender, D. (1989). *The writing or the sex? Or why you don't have to read women's writing to know it's no good.* New York: Pergamon Press.

Spenner, K. I., & Rosenfeld, R. A. (1990). Women, work, and identities. *Social Science Research, 19,* 266–299.

Sprafkin, J. N., & Liebert, R. M. (1978). Sex-typing and children's television preferences. In G. Tuchman, A. K. Daniels, & J. Benet (Eds.), *Hearth and home: Images of women in the mass media* (pp. 228–239). New York: Oxford University Press.

Sprague, J., & Quadagno, D. (1987). Gender and sexual motivation: An exploration of two assumptions. *Journal of Psychology and Human Sexuality, 2,* 57–76.

Sprecher, S. (1985). Sex differences in bases of power in dating relationships. *Sex Roles, 12,* 449–462.

Stacey, J. (1983). *Patriarchy and socialist revolution in China.* Berkeley, CA: University of California Press.

Stack, C. (1974). *All our kin: Strategies for survival in a Black community.* New York: Harper & Row.

Stack, C. (1986). The culture of gender: Women and men of color. Signs: *Journal of Women in Culture and Society, 11,* 321–324.

Staines, G. L., & Libby, P. L. (1986). Men and women in role relationships. In R. D. Ashmore & R. K. Del Boca (Eds.), *The social psychology of female-male relations* (pp. 211–258). New York: Academic Press.

Staines, G. L., Pottick, K. J., & Fudge, D. A. (1986). Wives' employment and husbands' attitudes toward work and life. *Journal of Applied Psychology, 71,* 118–128.

Staines, G. L., Tavris, C., & Jayaratne, T. E. (1974, January). The Queen Bee syndrome. *Psychology Today,* pp. 55–60.

Stake, J. E. (1979). The ability/performance dimension of self-esteem: Implications for women's achievement behavior. *Psychology of Women Quarterly, 3,* 365–377.

Stake, J. E. (1983). Ability level, evaluative feedback, and sex differences in performance expectancy. *Psychology of Women Quarterly, 8,* 48–58.

Stake, J. E. (1985). Exploring the basis of sex differences in third-party allocations. *Journal of Personality and Social Psychology, 48,* 1621–1629.

Stake, J. E., & Gerner, M. A. (1987). The women's studies experience: Personal and professional gains for women and men. *Psychology of Women Quarterly, 11,* 277–283.

Stake, J. E., & Orlofsky, J. L. (1981). On the use of global and specific measures in assessing the self-esteem of males and females. *Sex Roles, 7,* 653–662.

Stake, J. E., & Rogers, L. L. (1989). Job and home attitudes of undergraduate women and their mothers. *Sex Roles, 20,* 445–463.

Stangor, C. (1988). Stereotype accessibility and information processing. *Personality and Social Psychology Bulletin, 14,* 694–708.

Stangor, C., & Ruble, D. N. (1987). Development of gender role knowledge and gender constancy. In L. Liben & M. L. Signorella (Eds.), *Children's gender schemata* (pp. 5–22). San Francisco: Jossey-Bass.

Stanley, A. D. (1983, September 19). High tech will hurt women. *New York Times,* p. A19.

Stanley, J. P. (1977). Paradigmatic woman: The prostitute. In D. L. Shores & C. P. Hines (Eds.), *Papers in language variation* (pp. 303–321). Tuscaloosa: University of Alabama Press.

Stapley, J. C., & Haviland, J. M. (1989). Beyond depression: Gender differences in normal adolescents' emotional experiences. *Sex Roles, 20,* 295–308.

Star, S. L. (1979). Sex differences and the dichotimization of the brain: Methods, limits, and problems in research on consciousness. In E. Tobach & B. Rosoff (Eds.), *Genes and gender II* (pp. 113–130). Staten Island, NY: Gordian Press.

Starer, R., & Denmark, F. (1974). Discrimination against aspiring women. *International Journal of Group Tensions, 4,* 65–71.

Starhawk. (1982). *Dreaming the dark: Magic, sex, and politics.* Boston: Beacon Press.

Starr, P. (1978, July 16). Hollywood's new ideal of masculinity. *New York Times,* Sect. 2, p. 1ff.

Statham, A. (1987). The gender model revisited: Differences in the management styles of men and women. *Sex Roles, 16,* 409–429.

Statham, A., Miller, E. M., & Mauksch, H. O. (Eds.). (1988). *The worth of women's work: A qualitative synthesis.* Albany: State University of New York Press.

Statham, A., Richardson, L., & Cook, J. A. (1991). *Gender and university teaching: A negotiated difference.* Albany: State University of New York Press.

The status of women. (1988, September 18). *Parade Magazine,* p. 14.

Status report: Women and crime. (1988, February). *Ms.,* p. 26.

Steadman, H. J., Rosenstein, M. J., MacAskill, R. L., & Manderscheid, R. W. (1988). A profile of mentally disordered offenders admitted to inpatient psychiatric services in the United States. *Law and Human Behavior, 12,* 91–99.

Steenland, S. (1988). Ten years in prime time: An analysis of the image of women on entertainment television from 1979 to 1988. *Celebrate the changing image of working women.* Washington, DC: National Commission on Working Women of Wider Opportunities for Women.

Steenland, S., & Whittemore, L. (1987, November). *Women out of view: An analysis of female characters on 1987–88 TV programs.* Washington, DC: National Commission on Working Women of Wider Opportunities for Women.

Steil, J. M., & Turetsky, B. A. (1987a). Is equal better? The relationship between marital equality and psychological symptomatology. In S. Oskamp (Ed.), *Applied social psychology annual,* Vol. 7 (pp. 73–97). Newbury Park, CA: Sage.

Steil, J. M., & Turetsky, B. A. (1987b). Marital influence levels and symptomatology among wives. In F. J. Crosby (Ed.), *Spouse, parent, worker: On gender and multiple roles* (pp. 74–90). New Haven: Yale University Press.

Steil, J. M., & Weltman, K. (1991). Marital inequality: The importance of resources, personal attributes, and social norms on career valuing and the allocation of domestic responsibilities. *Sex Roles, 24,* 161–179.

Stein, J. S., & Yaworsky, K. B. (1983, August). *Menstrual cycle and memory for affective and neutral words.* Paper presented at the meeting of the American Psychological Association, Anaheim.

Stein, P. J., & Hoffman, S. (1978). Sports and male role strain. *Journal of Social Issues, 34*(1), 136–150.

Steinbacher, R., & Gilroy, F. (1990). Sex selection technology: A prediction of its use and effect. *Journal of Psychology, 124,* 283–288.

Steinbacher, R., & Holmes, H. B. (1987). Sex choice: Survival and sisterhood. In G. Corea et al. (Eds.), *Man-made women: How new reproductive technologies affect women* (pp. 52–63). Bloomington: Indiana University Press.

Steinem, G. (1972). The myth of the Masculine Mystique. *International Education, 1,* 30–35.

Steinem, G. (1983). *Outrageous acts and everyday rebellions.* New York: Holt, Rinehart & Winston.

Steinem, G. (1984, July). How women live, vote, think. . . . *Ms.,* pp. 51–54.

Steinem, G. (1988, January). Gro Harlem Brundtland. *Ms.,* pp. 74–75.

Steinem, G. (1990, July–August). Sex, lies, and advertising. *Ms.,* pp. 18–28.

Steiner-Adair, C. (1990). The body politic: Normal female adolescent development and the development of eating disorders. In C. Gilligan, N. P. Lyons, & T. J. Hanmer (Eds.), *Making connections: The relational worlds of adolescent girls at Emma Willard School* (pp. 162–182). Cambridge, MA: Harvard University Press.

Stephen, T. D., & Harrison, T. M. (1985). A longitudinal comparison of couples with sex-typical and non-sex-typical orientations to intimacy. *Sex Roles, 12,* 195–206.

Stericker, A. B., & Kurdek, L. A. (1982). Dimensions and correlates of third through eighth graders' sex-role self-concepts. *Sex Roles, 8,* 915–929.

Sterling, B. S., & Owen, J. W. (1982). Perceptions of demanding versus reasoning male and female police officers. *Personality and Social Psychology Bulletin, 8,* 336–340.

Stern, B. B. (1981). *Is networking for you? A working woman's alternative to the Old Boy System.* Englewood Cliffs, NJ: Prentice-Hall.

Stern, M., & Karraker, K. H. (1989). Sex stereotyping of infants: A review of gender labeling studies. *Sex Roles, 20,* 501–522.

Sternglanz, S. H., & Serbin, L. A. (1974). Sex role stereotyping in children's TV programs. *Developmental Psychology, 10,* 710–715.

Stetson, D. M. (1991). *Women's rights in the U.S.A.: Policy debates and gender roles.* Pacific Grove, CA: Brooks/Cole.

Stevens, G., & Gardner, S. (1987). But can she command a ship? Acceptance of women by peers at the Coast Guard Academy. *Sex Roles, 16,* 181–188.

Stevenson, M. B., Leavitt, L.A., Thompson, R. H., & Roach, M. A. (1988). A social relations model analysis of parent and child play. *Developmental Psychology, 24,* 101–108.

Stewart, D., & Vaux, A. (1986). Social support resources, behaviors, and perceptions among black and white college students. *Journal of Multicultural Counseling and Development, 14,* 65–72.

Stiehm, J. H. (1989). *Arms and the enlisted woman.* Philadelphia: Temple University Press.

Stier, D. S., & Hall, J. A. (1984). Gender differences in touch: An empirical and theoretical review. *Journal of Personality and Social Psychology, 47,* 440–459.

Stillion, J. M. (1985). *Death and the sexes.* Washington, DC: Hemisphere.

Stimpson, C. R, with Cobb, N. K. (1986). *Women's studies in the United States.* New York: Ford Foundation.

Stipek, D. J. (1984). Sex differences in children's attributions for success and failure on math and spelling tests. *Sex Roles, 11,* 969–981.

Stockard, J., & Dougherty, M. (1983). Variations in subjective culture: A comparison of females and males in three settings. *Sex Roles, 9,* 953–974.

Stockard, J., & Johnson, M. M. (1979). The social origins of male dominance. *Sex Roles, 5,* 199–218.

Stokes, J., & Levin, I. (1986). Gender differences in predicting loneliness from social network characteristics. *Journal of Personality and Social Psychology, 51,* 1069–1074.

Stoller, R. J. (1968). *Sex and gender: On the development of masculinity and femininity.* New York: Science House.

Stoltenberg, J. (1989). *Refusing to be a man: Essays on sex and justice.* Portland, OR: Breitenbush Books.

Stone, I. F. (1974). Machismo in Washington. In J. Pleck & L. Sawyer (Eds.), *Men and masculinity* (pp. 130–133). Englewood Cliffs, NJ: Prentice-Hall.

Stone, M. (1976). *When God was a woman.* San Diego: Harcourt Brace Jovanovich.

Stoneman, Z., Brody, G. H., & MacKinnon, C. E. (1986). Same-sex and cross-sex siblings: Activity choices, roles, behavior, and gender stereotypes. *Sex Roles, 15,* 495–511.

Stoppard, J. M., & Kalin, R. (1983). Gender typing and social desirability of personality in person evaluation. *Psychology of Women Quarterly, 7,* 209–218.

Stoppard, J. M., & Paisley, K. J. (1987). Masculinity, femininity, life stress, and depression. *Sex Roles, 16,* 489–496.

Storms, M. D. (1980). Theories of sexual orientation. *Journal of Personality and Social Psychology, 38,* 783–792.

Storms, M. D., Stivers, M. L., Lambers, S. M., & Hill, C. A. (1981). Sexual scripts for women. *Sex Roles, 7,* 699–707.

Straus, M. A., & Gelles, R. J. (1986). Societal change and change in family violence from 1975 to 1985 as revealed by two national surveys. *Journal of Marriage and the Family, 48,* 465–479.

Streitfeld, D. (1986, December 7). Experts exchange views on joint custody. *Morning Call,* p. E22.

Strickland, B. R. (1988). Sex-related differences in health and illness. *Psychology of Women Quarterly, 12,* 381–399.

Striegel-Moore, R. H., Silberstein, L. R., Grunberg, N. E., & Rodin, J. (1990). Competing on all fronts: Achievement orientation and disordered eating. *Sex Roles, 23,* 697–702.

Striegel-Moore, R. H., Silberstein, L. R., & Rodin, J. (1986). Toward an understanding of risk factors for bulimia. *American Psychologist, 41,* 246–263.

Stroman, C. A. (1989). To be young, male, and Black on prime-time television. *Urban Research Review, 12,* pp. 9–10.

Strommen, E. A. (1977). Friendship. In E. Doneleon & J. Gullahorn (Eds.), *Women: A psychological perspective* (pp. 154–167). New York: Wiley.

Study of Black females cites role of praise. (1985, June 25). *New York Times,* p. C5.

Study finds women take more sick days than men. (1989, May 9). *Morning Call,* p. A22.

Study: Girls encouraged to write better than boys. (1989, May 16). *Morning Call,* p. 2.

Study: Married people healthier than singles. (1988, November 16). *Easton Express,* p. A3.

Study reports sex bias in news organizations. (1989, April 11). *New York Times,* p. C22.

Study: Women's role in car buying ignored. (1985, March 13). *Easton Express,* p. C11.

Suchner, R. W. (1979). Sex Ratios and occupational prestige: Three failures to replicate a sexist bias. *Personality and Social Psychology Bulletin, 5,* 236–239.

Sugg, R. S. (1978). *Motherteacher: The feminization of American education.* Charlottesville: University Press of Virginia.

Suitor, J. J. (1991). Marital quality and satisfaction with the division of household labor across the family life cycle. *Journal of Marriage and the Family, 53,* 221–230.

Sullivan, G. L., & O'Connor, P. J. (1988). Women's role portrayals in magazine advertising: 1958–1983. *Sex Roles, 18,* 181–188.

Surrey, J. L. (1985). *Self-in-relation: A theory of women's development* (Work in Progress, No. 13). Wellesley, MA: Wellesley College, The Stone Center.

Susman, E. J., Inoff-Germain, G., Nottelmann, E. D., Loriaux, D. L., Cutler, G. B. Jr., & Chrousos, G. P. (1987). Hormones, emotional dispositions, and aggressive attributes in young adolescents. *Child Development, 58,* 1114–1134.

Susman, E. J., Nottelmann, E. D., Inoff-Germain, G., Dorn, L. D., & Chrousos, G. P. (1987). Hormonal influences on aspects of psychological development during adolescence. *Journal of Adolescent Health Care, 8,* 492–504.

Sussman, B. (1986, March 22). Pornography concerns women more than men. *Easton Express,* p. A4.

Sussman, N. M., & Rosenfeld, H. M. (1982). Influences of culture, language, and sex on conversational distance. *Journal of Personality and Social Psychology, 42,* 66–74.

Svare, B., & Kinsley, C. H. (1987). Hormones and sex-related behavior: A comparative analysis. In K. Kelley (Ed.), *Females, males, and sexuality: Theories and research* (pp. 13–58). Albany: State University of New York Press.

Swap, W. C., & Rubin, J. Z. (1983). Measurement of interpersonal orientation. *Journal of Personality and Social Psychology, 44,* 208–219.

Swerdlow, M. (1989). Men's accommodations to women entering a nontraditional occupation: A case of rapid transit operatives. *Gender and Society, 3,* 373–387.

Swim, J., Borgida, E., Maruyama, G., & Myers, D. G. (1989). Joan McKay versus John McKay: Do gender stereotypes bias evaluations? *Psychological Bulletin, 105,* 409–429.

Switzer, J. Y. (1990). The impact of generic word choices: An empirical investigation of age- and sex-related differences. *Sex Roles, 22,* 69–82.

Symons, D. (1979). *The evolution of human sexuality.* Oxford, England: Oxford University Press.

Symons, D. (1987). An evolutionary approach. In J. H. Geer & W. T. O'Donohue (Eds.), *Theories of human sexuality* (pp. 91–125). New York: Plenum.

Sztaba, T. I., & Colwill, N. L. (1988). Secretarial and management students: Attitudes, attributes, and career choice considerations. *Sex Roles, 19,* 651–665.

Tait, M., Padgett, M. Y., & Baldwin, T. T. (1989). Job and life satisfaction: A reevaluation of the strength of the relationship and gender effects as a function of the date of the study. *Journal of Applied Psychology, 74,* 502–507.

Talan, J. (1986, December 9). Tracking the chemistry of the motherhood instinct. *Morning Call,* p. D2.

Tallen, B. S. (1990). Twelve-step programs: A lesbian feminist critique. *NWSA Journal, 2,* 390–407.

Tanaka, J. S., Panter, A. T., & Winborne, W. C. (1988). Dimensions of the need for cognition: Subscales and gender differences. *Multivariate Behavioral Research, 23,* 35–50.

Tangney, J. P., & Feshbach, S. (1988). Children's television-viewing frequency: Individual differences and demographic correlates. *Personality and Social Psychology Bulletin, 14,* 145–158.

Tangri, S. S., & Jenkins, S. R. (1986). Stability and change in role innovation and life plans. *Sex Roles, 14,* 647–662.

Tannen, D. (1990). *You just don't understand: Women and men in conversation.* New York: Morrow.

Tannen, D. (1991, June 19). Teachers' classroom strategies should recognize that men and women use language differently. *Chronicle of Higher Education,* pp. B1, B3.

Taube, C. A., & Barrett, S. A. (Eds.). (1985). *Mental health, United States 1985* (DHHS Publication No. ADM 85–1378). Washington, DC: National Institute of Mental Health.

Tauber, M. A. (1979). Parental socialization techniques and sex differences in children's play. *Child Development, 50,* 225–234.

Tavris, C. (1973). Who likes women's liberation and why: The case of the unliberated liberals. *Journal of Social Issues, 29*(4), 175–194.

Tavris, C., & Offir, C. (1977). *The longest war: Sex differences in perspective.* New York: Harcourt Brace Jovanovich.

Taylor, M. C. (1979). Race, sex, and the expression of self-fulfilling prophecies in a laboratory teaching situation. *Journal of Personality and Social Psychology, 37,* 897–912.

Taylor, M. C., & Hall, J. A. (1982). Psychological androgyny: Theories, methods, and conclusions. *Psychological Bulletin, 92,* 347–366.

Taynor, J., & Deaux, K. (1973). When women are more deserving than men: Equity, attribution, and perceived sex differences. *Journal of Personality and Social Psychology, 28,* 360–367.

Taynor, J., & Deaux, K. (1975). Equity and perceived sex differences: Role behavior as defined by the task, the mode, and the action. *Journal of Personality and Social Psychology, 32,* 381–390.

Teen sex: Not for sale. (1989, May). *Psychology Today,* pp. 10, 12.

Tennov, D. (1975). *Psychotherapy: The hazardous cure.* New York: Abelard-Schuman.

Teri, L. (1982). Effects of sex and sex-role style on clinical judgement. *Sex Roles, 8,* 639–649.

Tetenbaum, T. J., & Pearson, J. (1989). The voices in children's literature: The impact of gender on the moral decisions of storybook characters. *Sex Roles, 20,* 381–395.

Texier, C. (1990, April 22). Have women surrendered in MTV's battle of the sexes? *New York Times,* pp. H29, H31.

"That's women's work." (1985, Winter). *On Campus with Women,* p. 8.

Theberge, N. (1987). Sport and women's empowerment. *Women's Studies International Forum, 10,* 387–393.

Thom, M. (1984, July). The all-time definitive map of the gender gap. *Ms.,* pp. 55–60.

Thoma, S. J. (1986). Estimating gender differences in the comprehension and preference of moral issues. *Developmental Review, 6,* 165–180.

Thomas, J. R., & French, K. E. (1985). Gender differences across age in motor performance: A meta-analysis. *Psychological Bulletin, 98,* 260–282.

Thomas, V. G. (1986). Career aspirations, parental support, and work values among Black female adolescents. *Journal of Multicultural Counseling and Development, 14,* 177–185.

Thomas, V. G. (1989). Body-image satisfaction among Black women. *Journal of Social Psychology, 129,* 107–112.

Thomas, V. G., & James, M. D. (1988). Body image, dieting tendencies, and sex role traits in urban Black women. *Sex Roles, 18,* 523–529.

Thomas, V. G., Milburn, N. G., Brown, D. R., & Gary, L. E. (1988). Social support and depressive symptoms among Blacks. *Journal of Black Psychology, 14,* 35–45.

Thomas, V. G., & Shields, L. C. (1987). Gender influences on work values of Black adolescents. *Adolescence, 22,* 37–43.

Thompson, D. E., & Thompson, T. A. (1985). Task-based performance appraisal for blue-collar jobs: Evaluation of race and sex effects. *Journal of Applied Psychology, 70,* 747–753.

Thompson, E. H., Jr., & Pleck, J. H. (1987). The structure of male role norms. In M. S. Kimmel (Ed.), *Changing men: New directions in research on men and masculinity* (pp. 25–36). Newbury Park, CA: Sage.

Thompson, H. L., & Richardson, D. R. (1983). The Rooster effect: Same-sex rivalry and inequity as factors in retaliative aggression. *Personality and Social Psychology Bulletin, 9,* 415–425.

Thompson, K. (Ed.). *To be a man: Developing conscious masculinity.* Los Angeles: Tarcher.

Thompson, N. L., McCandless, B. R., & Strickland, B. B. (1971). Personal adjustment of male and female homosexuality and heterosexuality. *Journal of Abnormal Psychology, 78,* 237–240.

Thorne, B., Kramarae, C., & Henley, N. (Eds.) (1983). *Language, gender, and society.* Rowley, MA: Newbury House.

Tiano, S. (1987). Gender, work, and world capitalism: Third World women's role in development. In B. B. Hess & M. M. Ferree (Eds.), *Analyzing gender: A handbook of social science research.* (pp. 216–243). Newbury Park, CA: Sage.

Tice, D. M., & Baumeister, R. F. (1985). Masculinity inhibits helping in emergencies: Personality does predict the bystander effect. *Journal of Personality and Social Psychology, 49,* 420–428.

Tidball, M. E. (1989). Women's colleges: Exceptional conditions, not exceptional talent, produce high achievers. In C. S. Pearson, D. L. Shavlik, & J. G. Touchton (Eds.), *Educating the majority: Women challenge tradition in higher education* (pp. 157–172). New York: American Council on Education/Macmillan.

Tiefer, L. (1987). In pursuit of the perfect penis: The medicalization of male sexuality. In M. S. Kimmel (Ed.), *Changing men: New directions in research on men and masculinity* (pp. 165–184). Newbury Park, CA: Sage.

Tiggemann, M., & Rothblum, E. D. (1988). Gender differences in social consequences of perceived overweight in the United States and Australia. *Sex Roles, 18,* 75–86.

Timmer, S. G., Eccles, J., & O'Brien, K. (1985). How children use time. In F. T. Juster & F. P. Stafford (Eds.), *Time, goods, and well-being.* Ann Arbor, MI: University of Michigan, Institute for Social Research.

Tinker, I. (Ed.). (1990). *Persistent inequalities: Women and world development.* New York: Oxford University Press.

Tittle, C. K. (1981). *Careers and family: Sex roles and adolescent life plans.* Beverly Hills, CA: Sage.

Tobias, S. (1982, January). Sexist equations. *Psychology Today,* pp. 14–17.

Tobin, J. N., et al. (1987). Sex bias in considering coronary bypass surgery. *Annals of Internal Medicine, 107,* 19–25.

Toch, H. (1966). *The social psychology of social movements.* London: Methuen.

Toder, N. L. (1980). The effect of the sexual composition of a group on discrimination against women and sex-role attitudes. *Psychology of Women Quarterly, 5,* 292–310.

Tolman, A. E., Diekmann, K. A., & McCartney, K. (1989). Social connectedness and mothering: Effects of maternal employment and maternal absence. *Journal of Personality and Social Psychology, 56,* 942–949.

Tolson, A. (1977). *The limits of masculinity: Male identity and women's liberation.* New York: Harper & Row.

Tong, R. (1989). *Feminist thought: A comprehensive introduction.* Boulder, CO: Westview Press.

Too little known about female biology, scientists say. (1990, December 7). *Morning Call,* p. A12.

Top, T. J. (1991). Sex bias in the evaluation of performance in the scientific, artistic, and literary professions: A review. *Sex Roles, 24,* 73–106.

Toth, E. (1984, February). Who'll take romance? *Women's Review of Books,* pp. 11–13.

Touhey, J. C. (1974). Effects of additional women professionals on ratings of occupational prestige and desirability. *Journal of Personality and Social Psychology, 29,* 86–89.

Townsend, R. C. (1977). The competitive male as loser. In A. Sargent (Ed.), *Beyond sex roles* (pp. 228–242). St. Paul, MN: West.

Towson, S.M.J., & Zanna, M. P. (1982). Toward a situational analysis of gender differences in aggression. *Sex Roles, 8,* 903–914.

Towson, S.M.J., Zanna, M. P., & MacDonald, G. (1989). Self-fulfilling prophecies: Sex role stereotypes as expectations for behavior. In R. Unger (Ed.), *Representations: Social constructions of gender* (pp. 97–107). Amityville, NY: Baywood.

Tracy, D. M. (1987). Toys, spatial ability, and science and mathematics achievement: Are they related? *Sex Roles, 17,* 115–138.

Travis, C. B. (1988). *Women and health psychology: Biomedical issues.* Hillsdale, NJ: Erlbaum.

Travis, C. B., Burnett-Doering, J., & Reid, P. T. (1982). The impact of sex, achievement domain, and conceptual orientation on causal attributions. *Sex Roles, 8,* 443–454.

Travis, C. B., McKenzie, B. J., Wiley, D. L., & Kahn, A. S. (1988). Sex and achievement domain: Cognitive patterns of success and failure. *Sex Roles, 19,* 509–525.

Treadwell, P. (1987). Biologic influences on masculinity. In H. Brod (Ed.), *The making of masculinities: The new men's studies* (pp. 259–285). Boston: Allen & Unwin.

Tremaine, L. S., Schau, C. G., & Busch, J. W. (1982). Children's occupational sex-typing. *Sex Roles, 8,* 691–710.

Trent, K., & South, S. J. (1989). Structural determinants of the divorce rate: A cross-societal analysis. *Journal of Marriage and the Family, 51,* 391–404.

Tresemer, D. W. (1977). *Fear of success.* New York: Plenum.

Trevarthen, C. (1974). Cerebral embryology and the split brain. In M. Kinsbourne & W. L. Smith (Eds.), *Hemispheric disconnection and cerebral function* (pp. 208–236). Springfield, IL: Charles C Thomas.

Tronto, J. C. (1987). Beyond gender difference to a theory of care. *Signs: Journal of Women in Culture and Society, 12,* 644–663.

Trost, C. (1987, November 30). Best employers for women and parents. *Wall Street Journal,* p. 23.

Trost, C. (1990, May 9). Childbirth isn't seen as career ending for women today. *Wall Street Journal,* p. B2.

Trotter, R. J. (1983, August). Baby face. *Psychology Today,* pp. 15–20.

Trovato, F., & Lauris, G. (1989). Marital status and mortality in Canada: 1951–1981. *Journal of Marriage and the Family, 51,* 907–922.

Trzcinski, E., & Finn-Stevenson, M. (1991). A response to arguments against mandated parental leave: Findings from the Connecticut Survey of Parental Leave Policies. *Journal of Marriage and the Family, 53,* 445–460.

Tucker, L. A. (1982). Relationship between perceived somatotype and body cathexis of college males. *Psychological Reports, 50,* 983–989.

Tucker, L. A. (1983). Muscular strength and mental health. *Journal of Personality and Social Psychology, 45,* 1355–1360.

Turkewitz, G., & Ross-Kossak, P. (1984). Multiple modes of right-hemisphere information processing: Age and sex differences in facial recognition. *Developmental Psychology, 20,* 95–103.

Turkle, S. (1984). *The second self: The computer and the human spirit.* New York: Simon & Schuster.

Turkle, S., & Papert, S. (1990). Epistemological pluralism: Styles and voices within the computer culture. *Signs: Journal of Women in Culture and Society, 16,* 128–157.

Twelve-year growth in number of female presidents has slowed since 1984. (1988, March 30). *Chronicle of Higher Education,* p. A15.

Tzuriel, D. (1984). Sex role typing and ego identity in Israeli, Oriental, and Western adolescents. *Journal of Personality and Social Psychology, 46,* 440–457.

Uchitelle, L. (1990, November 24). Women's push into work force seems to have reached plateau. *New York Times,* pp. 1, 28.

Udry, J. R., & Talbert, L. M. (1988). Sex hormone effects on personality at puberty. *Journal of Personality and Social Psychology, 54,* 291–295.

Udry, J. R., Talbert, L. M., & Morris, N. M. (1986). Biosocial foundations for adolescent female sexuality. *Demography, 23,* 217–230.

Ullian, D. (1976). The development of conceptions of masculinity and femininity. In B. Lloyd & J. Archer (Eds.), *Exploring sex differences* (pp. 24–48). New York: Academic Press.

Ullian, D. (1984). "Why girls are good": A constructivist view. *Sex Roles, 11,* 241–256.

Ungar, S. B. (1982). The sex-typing of adult and child behavior in toy sales. *Sex Roles, 8,* 251–260.

Unger, R. K. (1983). Through the looking glass: No wonderland yet! (The reciprocal relationship between methodology and models of reality.) *Psychology of Women Quarterly, 8,* 9–32.

Unger, R. K. (1989a). Sex, gender, and epistemology. In M. Crawford & M. Gentry (Eds.), *Gender and thought: Psychological perspectives* (pp. 17–35). New York: Springer-Verlag.

Unger, R. K. (1989b). Sex in psychological paradigms—From behavior to cognition. In R. K. Unger (Ed.), *Representations: Social constructions of gender* (pp. 15–20). Amityville, NY: Baywood.

Unger, R. K., & Siiter, R. (1975). Sex role stereotypes: The weight of a "grain of truth." In R. Unger (Ed.), *Sex-role stereotypes revisited: Psychological approaches to women's studies* (pp. 10–13). New York: Harper & Row.

Unger, R. K., & Sussman, L. E. (1986). "I and thou": Another barrier to societal change? *Sex Roles, 14,* 629–636.

United Nations Department of Public Information. (1989, November). *Women in politics: Still the exception?* (DPI/1012—41080). New York: United Nations Publications.

United Nations. (1991). *The world's women 1970–1990: Trends and statistics.* New York: United Nations Publications.

U.S. Commission on Civil Rights. (1977). *Window dressing on the set: Women and minorities on television.* Washington, DC: U.S. Government Printing Office.

U.S. Commission on Civil Rights. (1979). *Window dressing on the set: An update.* Washington, DC: U.S. Government Printing Office.

U.S. Commission on Civil Rights. (1980). *More hurdles to clear: Women and girls in competitive athletics* (Report No. 63). Washington, DC: U.S. Government Printing Office.

U.S. Department of Commerce, Bureau of the Census. (1988). *Money income and poverty status in the United States: 1987* (Current Population Reports, Series P-60, No. 159). Washington, DC: U. S. Government Printing Office.

U.S. Department of Commerce, Bureau of the Census. (1989a). *Households, families, marital status, and living arrangements: March 1989.* Washington, DC: U. S. Government Printing Office.

U.S. Department of Commerce, Bureau of the Census. (1989b). *Statistical abstracts of the United States, 1989.* Washington, DC: U. S. Government Printing Office.

U.S. Department of Commerce, Bureau of the Census. (1990). *Statistical abstracts of the U.S., 1990* (110th ed.). Washington, DC: U.S. Government Printing Office.

U.S. Department of Education, National Center for Education Statistics. (1988a, April). *Targeted forecast: Doctoral and first-professional degrees awarded to women projected to increase.* Washington, DC: U. S. Government Printing Office.

U.S. Department of Education, National Center for Education Statistics. (1988b, August). *Employment outcomes of recent master's and bachelor's degree recipients* (CS 88-251). Washington, DC: U. S. Government Printing Office.

U.S. Department of Health, Education, and Welfare, Bureau of Occupational and Adult Education. (1979). *Summary data, vocational education, project year 1978.* Washington, DC: U.S. Government Printing Office.

U.S. Department of Health and Human Services, National Center for Health Statistics. (1990a, August 30). Annual summary of births, marriages, divorces, and deaths: United States, 1989. *Monthly Vital Statistics Report. 38*(13).

U.S. Department of Health and Human Services, National Center for Health Statistics. (1990b, November 28). Advance report of final mortality statistics, 1988. *Monthly Vital Statistics Report, 39*(7, Supplement).

U.S. Department of Labor, Women's Bureau. (1975). *1975 handbook on women workers* (Bulletin 297). Washington, DC: U.S. Government Printing Office.

U.S. Department of Labor, Women's Bureau. (1977). *Women in the labor force, 1976–1977, April.* Washington, DC: U.S. Government Printing Office.

U.S. Department of Labor, Women's Bureau. (1980). *Twenty facts on women workers.* Washington, DC: U.S. Government Printing Office.

U.S. Department of Labor, Bureau of Labor Statistics. (1983). *Women at work: A chartbook.* Washington, DC: U.S. Government Printing Office.

U.S. Department of Labor, Bureau of Labor Statistics. (1985a). *Employment and earnings, April 1985.* Washington, DC: U.S. Government Printing Office.

U.S. Department of Labor. Bureau of Labor Statistics. (1985b). *Occupational injuries and illnesses in the United States by industry* (Bulletin No. 2236). Washington, DC: U.S Government Printing Office.

U.S. Department of Labor, Women's Bureau. (1985c). *Facts on U.S. working women* (Fact Sheet No. 85–7). Washington, DC: U.S. Government Printing Office.

U.S. Department of Labor, Bureau of Labor Statistics. (1991a). *Employment and earnings, February 1991.* Washington, DC: U.S. Government Printing Office.

U.S. Department of Labor, Bureau of Labor Statistics. (1991b, February 8). *Usual weekly earnings of wage and salary workers: Fourth quarter 1990.*

U.S. Merit Systems Protection Board. (1988). *Sexual harassment in the federal government: An update 2.* Washington, DC: Author.

Unmarried couples increase in number. (1986, December 17). *Morning Call,* p. A16.

Urberg, K. A. (1982). The development of the concepts of masculinity and femininity in young children. *Sex Roles, 8,* 659–668.

Vance, C. S. (Ed.). (1984). *Pleasure and danger: Exploring female sexuality.* Boston: Routledge & Kegan Paul.

Vandenberg, S. G. (1987). Differences in mental retardation and their implications for sex differences in ability. In J. M. Reinisch, L. A. Rosenblum, & S. A. Sanders (Eds.), *Masculinity/femininity: Basic perspectives* (pp. 157–171). New York: Oxford University Press.

Vandenberg, S. G., & Kuse, A. R. (1979). Spatial ability: A critical review of the sex-linked major gene hypothesis. In M. A. Wittig & A. C. Petersen (Eds.), *Sex-related differences in cognitive functioning: Developmental issues* (pp. 67–95). New York: Academic Press.

Van Dusen, R. R., & Sheldon, E. B. (1976). The changing status of American women: A life cycle perspective. *American Psychologist, 31,* 106–117.

Van Hecke, M. T., Van Keep, P. A., & Kellerhals, J. M. (1975). The aging women. *Acts Obstetrica et Gynecologia, 51,* Scandinavica Supplement, 17–27.

Van Horn, J. E. (1989, February 16). Studies find latchkey children are doing fine. *Morning Call,* p. B10.

Vargo, S. (1987). The effects of women's socialization on lesbian couples. In Boston Lesbian Psychologies Collective (Ed.), *Lesbian psychologies: Explorations and challenges* (pp. 161–173). Urbana: University of Illinois Press.

Vazquez-Nuttall, E., Romero-Garcia, I., & De Leon, B. (1987). Sex roles and perceptions of femininity and masculinity of Hispanic women: A review of the literature. *Psychology of Women Quarterly, 11*, 409–425.

Verbrugge, L. M. (1982). Sex differences in legal drug use. *Journal of Social Issues, 38*(2), 59–76.

Verbrugge, L. M. (1987). Role responsibilities, role burdens, and physical health. In F. J. Crosby (Ed.), *Spouse, parent, worker: On gender and multiple roles* (pp. 154–166). New Haven: Yale University Press.

Verbrugge, L. M., & Madans, J. H. (1985, March). Women's roles and health. *American Demographics, 7*(3), 36–39.

Verhovek, S. H. (1990, March 4). Girls win 51.3% in Regents series. *New York Times*, p. 28.

Vernon-Gerstenfeld, S. (1989). Serendipity? Are there gender differences in the adoption of computers? A case study. *Sex Roles, 21*, 161–173.

Veroff, J., Depner, C., Kula, R., & Douvan, E. (1980). Comparison of American motives: 1957 versus 1976. *Journal of Personality and Social Psychology, 39*, 1249–1262.

Veterans preference hurts women. (1978, August). *National NOW Times*, p. 15.

Villemur, N. K., & Hyde, J. S. (1983). Effects of sex of defense attorney, sex of juror, and age and attractiveness of the victim on mock juror decision making in a rape case. *Sex Roles, 9*, 879–889.

Violence against women rampant, report says. (1989, March 9). *Morning Call*, p. A23.

Vobejda, B. (1991, January 20). U.S. childbirths booming; experts wondering why. *Morning Call*, p. A22.

Vogel, L. (1984). *Marxism and the oppression of women: Toward a unitary theory.* New Brunswick, NJ: Rutgers University Press.

Volling, B. L., & Belsky, J. (1991). Multiple determinants of father involvement during infancy in dual-earner and single-earner families. *Journal of Marriage and the Family, 53*, 461–474.

Vollmer, F. (1986). Why do men have higher expectancy than women? *Sex Roles, 14*, 351–362.

Von Baeyer, C. L., Sherk, D. L., & Zanna, M. P. (1981). Impression management in the job interview: When the female applicant meets the male (chauvinist) interviewer. *Personality and Social Psychology Bulletin, 7*, 45–51.

Voydanoff, P. (1980). Perceived job characteristics and job satisfaction among men and women. *Psychology of Women Quarterly, 5*, 177–185.

Voydanoff, P. (Ed.) (1984). *Work and family: Changing roles of men and women.* Palo Alto, CA: Mayfield.

Vredenburg, K., Krames, L., & Flett, G. L. (1986). Sex differences in the clinical expression of depression. *Sex Roles, 14*, 37–49.

Waber, D. P. (1976). Sex differences in cognition: A function of maturation rate? *Science, 192*, 572–574.

Waber, D. P. (1977). Sex differences in mental abilities, hemispheric lateralization, and rate of physical growth at adolescence. *Developmental Psychology, 13*, 29–38.

Waber, D. P., Mann, M. B., Merola, J., & Moylan, P. M. (1985). Physical maturation rate and cognitive performance in early adolescence: A longitudinal examination. *Developmental Psychology, 21*, 666–681.

Wagner, J. (1982). *Sex roles in contemporary American communes.* Bloomington: Indiana University Press.

Waite, L. J., & Berryman, S. E. (1985). *Women in nontraditional occupations: Choice and turnover* (Report R-3106-FF). New York: Rand Corp.

Wakefield, J. C. (1987). Sex bias in the diagnosis of primary orgasmic dysfunction. *American Psychologist, 42*, 464–471.

Waldron, I. (1976). Why do women live longer than men? *Journal of Human Stress, 2*, 1–13.

Waldron, I. (1978). Type A behavior pattern and coronary heart disease in men and women. *Social Science and Medicine, 12*, 167–170.

Waldron, I., & Herold, J. (1984, May). *Employment, attitudes toward employment, and women's health.* Paper presented at the meeting of the Society of Behavioral Medicine, Philadelphia.

Waldron, I., & Jacobs, J. A. (1989). Effects of labor force participation on women's health—New evidence from a longitudinal study. *Journal of Occupational Medicine, 30*, 977–983.

Walker, E., Bettes, B. A., Kain, E. L., & Harvey, P. (1985). Relationship of gender and marital status with symptomatology in psychotic patients. *Journal of Abnormal Psychology, 94*, 42–50.

Walker, L. E. (1984). *The battered woman syndrome.* New York: Springer.

Walker, L.E.A. (1989a). Psychology and violence against women. *American Psychologist, 44*, 695–702.

Walker, L.E.A. (1989b). *Terrifying love: Why battered women kill.* New York: Harper & Row.

Walker, L.E.A., & Browne, A. (1985). Gender and victimization by intimates. *Journal of Personality, 53*, 179–195.

Walker, L. J. (1984). Sex differences in the development of moral reasoning: A critical review. *Child Development, 55*, 667–691.

Walker, L. J. (1989). A longitudinal study of moral reasoning. *Child Development, 60*, 157–166.

Walker, L. J., de Vries, B., & Trevethan, S. D. (1987). Moral stages and moral orientations in real-life and hypothetical dilemmas. *Child Development, 58*, 842–858.

Wallace, M. (1979). *Black macho and the myth of the superwoman.* New York: Dial Press.

Wallace, M. (1990, July 29). When Black feminism faces the music, and the music is rap. *New York Times*, p. H26.

Wallerstein, J. S., & Blakeslee, S. (1989). *Second chances: Men, women, and children a decade after divorce.* New York: Ticknor & Fields.

Wallis, C. (1989, December 4). Onward, women! *Time*, pp. 80–89.

Wallston, B. S., DeVellis, B. M., & Wallston, K. (1983). Licensed practical nurses' sex role stereotypes. *Psychology of Women Quarterly, 7*, 199–208.

Wallston, B. S., & Grady, K. E. (1985). Integrating the feminist critique and the crisis in social psychology: Another look at research methods. In V. O'Leary, R. Unger, & B. Wallston (Eds.), *Women, gender, and social psychology* (pp. 7–33). Hillsdale, NJ: Erlbaum.

Wallston, B. S., & O'Leary, V. (1981). Sex makes a difference: Differential perceptions of women and men. In L. Wheeler (Ed.), *Review of personality and social psychology*, Vol. 2 (pp. 9–41). Beverly Hills, CA: Sage.

Ward, C. (1981). Prejudice against women: Who, when, and why? *Sex Roles, 7*, 163–171.

Ward, C. (1985). Sex trait stereotypes in Malaysian children. *Sex Roles, 12*, 35–45.

Wardle, M. G., Gloss, M. R., & Gloss, D. S., III. (1987). Response differences in M. A. Baker (Ed.), *Sex differences in human performance* (pp. 107–120). Chichester: Wiley.

Waring, M. (1989). *If women counted: A new feminist economics.* New York: Harper & Row.

Warr, P., & Parry, G. (1982). Paid employment and women's psychological well-being. *Psychological Bulletin, 91*, 498–516.

Warren, C.A.B. (1988). *Gender issues in field research.* Newbury Park, CA: Sage.

Warren, J. (1991, February 18). Survey finds men are "reinventing themselves." *Morning Call*, pp. D1, D5.

Warshaw, R. (1988). *I never called it rape.* New York: Harper & Row.

Warshaw, R. (1991, May 5). Ugly truths of date rape elude the screen. *New York Times*, pp. H17, H22.

Wartik, N. (1986, October). Where the girls are: The state of women's colleges. *Ms.*, pp. 32, 34.

Wasserman, G. A., & Lewis, M. (1985). Infant sex differences: Ecological effects. *Sex Roles, 12,* 665–675.

Watson, P. J., Taylor, D., & Morris, R. J. (1987). Narcissism, sex roles, and self-functioning. *Sex Roles, 16,* 335–350.

Watson, V. M. (1990, March). APA TV task force criticizes programs. *APA Monitor,* p. 26.

Wattenawaha, N., & Clements, M. A. (1982). Qualitative aspects of sex-related differences in performances on pencil-and-paper spatial questions, grades 7–9. *Journal of Educational Psychology, 74,* 878–887.

Weaver, G. D. (1986). Black fathering. *Urban Research Review, 11*(1), 6–10.

Weaver, J. L., & Garrett, S. D. (1983). Sexism and racism in the American health care industry: A comparative analysis. In E. Fee (Ed.), *Women and health: The politics of sex and medicine* (pp. 79–116). Farmingdale, NY: Baywood.

Webb, N. M. (1984). Sex differences in interaction and achievement in cooperative small groups. *Journal of Educational Psychology, 76,* 33–44.

Weeks, M. O., & Botkin, D. R. (1987). A longitudinal study of the marriage role expectations of college women: 1961–1984. *Sex Roles, 17,* 49–58.

Wehren, A., & De Lisi, R. (1983). The development of gender understanding: Judgments and explanations. *Child Development, 54,* 1568–1578.

Weinraub, M., & Wolf, B. M. (1987). Stressful life events, social supports, and parent-child interaction: Similarities and differences in single parent and two parent families. In C.F.Z. Boukydis (Ed.), *Research on support for parents and infants in the postnatal period* (pp. 114–135). Norwood, NJ: Ablex.

Weisner, T. S., & Wilson-Mitchell, J. E. (1990). Nonconventional family life-styles and sex typing in 6-year-olds. *Child Development, 61,* 1915–1933.

Weissman, M. M., & Klerman, G. L. (1977). Sex differences and the epidemiology of depression. *Archives of General Psychiatry, 34,* 98–111.

Weisstein, N. (1969, October). Woman as nigger. *Psychology Today,* pp. 20–22, 58.

Weitz, R. (1982). Feminist consciousness raising, self-concept, and depression. *Sex Roles, 8,* 231–241.

Weitz, R. (1989). What price independence? Social reactions to lesbians, spinsters, widows, and nuns. In J. Freeman (Ed.), *Women: A feminist perspective,* 4th ed. (pp. 446–456). Palo Alto, CA: Mayfield.

Weitz, S. (1977). *Sex roles: Biological, psychological, and social foundations.* New York: Oxford University Press.

Weitzman, L. J. (1985). *The divorce revolution: The unexpected social and economic consequences for women and children in America.* New York: Free Press.

Weitzman, L. J. (1988). Women and children last: The social and economic consequences of divorce law reforms. In S. M. Dornbusch & M. H. Strober (Eds.), *Feminism, children, and the new families* (pp. 212–248). New York: Guilford.

Weitzman, L. J., & Rizzo, D. (1974). *Images of males and females in elementary school textbooks.* New York: NOW Legal Defense and Education Fund.

Weitzman, N., Birns, B., & Friend, R. (1985). Traditional and nontraditional mothers' communication with their daughters and sons. *Child Development, 56,* 894–898.

Welch, M. R., & Page, B. M. (1981). Sex differences in childhood socialization patterns in African societies. *Sex Roles, 7,* 1163–1173.

Welch, R., Gerrard, M., & Huston, A. (1986). Gender-related personality attributes and reaction to success/failure: An examination of mediating variables. *Psychology of Women Quarterly, 10,* 221–233.

Welch, R. L., Huston-Stein, A., Wright, J. C., & Plehal, R. (1979). Subtle sex-role cues in children's commercials. *Journal of Communication, 29,* 202–209.

Wells, A. J. (1988). Variations in mothers' self-esteem in daily life. *Journal of Personality and Social Psychology, 55,* 661–668.

Welter, B. (1966). The cult of true womanhood, 1820–1860. *American Quarterly, 18,* 244–256.

Wentworth, D. K., & Anderson, L. R. (1984). Emergent leadership as a function of sex and task type. *Sex Roles, 11,* 513–524.

Werner, D. (1984). Child care and influences among the Mekranoti of Central Brazil. *Sex Roles, 10,* 395–404.

Werner, P. D., & LaRussa, G. W. (1985). Persistence and change in sex-role stereotypes. *Sex Roles, 12,* 1089–1100.

Werrbach, G. B., Grotevant, H. D., & Cooper, C. R. (1990). Gender differences in adolescents' identity development in the domain of sex role concepts. *Sex Roles, 23,* 349–362.

Weston, L. C., & Ruggiero, J. A. (1978). Male-female relationships in best-selling "Modern Gothic" novels. *Sex Roles, 4,* 647–655.

Wethington, E., McLeod, J. D., & Kessler, R. C. (1987). The importance of life events for explaining sex differences in psychological distress. In R. C. Barnett, L. Biener & G. K. Baruch (Eds.), *Gender and stress* (pp. 144–156). New York: Free Press.

Wetzsteon, R. (1977, November). The feminist man? *Mother Jones,* pp. 52–59.

Wheeler, L., Reis, H., & Nezlek, J. (1983). Loneliness, social interactions, and sex roles. *Journal of Personality and Social Psychology, 45,* 943–953.

When dad leaves, poverty hits kids, Census study says. (1991, March 2). *Morning Call,* p. A34.

Where have all the smart girls gone? (1989, April). *Psychology Today,* p. 20.

Whicker, M. L. (1990, October-November). Women in Congress. Cited in *The National Voter,* pp. 12–14.

White, E. C. (Ed.). (1990). *The Black women's health book: Speaking for ourselves.* Seattle, WA: Seal Press.

White, J. W., & Roufail, M. (1989). Gender and influence strategies of first choice and last resort. *Psychology of Women Quarterly, 13,* 175–189.

White, M. S. (1979). Measuring androgyny in adulthood. *Psychology of Women Quarterly, 3,* 293–307.

White men give, get most transplant organs. (1989, May 30). *Morning Call,* p. A6.

Whiting, B., & Edwards, C. P. (1973). A cross-cultural analysis of sex differences in the behavior of children aged 3 through 11. *Journal of Social Psychology, 91,* 171–188.

Whiting, B. B., & Edwards, C. P. (1988). *Children of different worlds: The formation of social behavior.* Cambridge, MA: Harvard University Press.

Whitley, B. E., Jr. (1983). Sex role orientation and self-esteem: A critical meta-analytic review. *Journal of Personality and Social Psychology, 44,* 765–778.

Whitley, B. E., Jr. (1984). Sex-role orientation and psychological well-being: Two meta-analyses. *Sex Roles, 12,* 207–225.

Whitley, B. E., Jr. (1987). The relationship of sex role orientation to heterosexuals' attitudes toward homosexuals. *Sex Roles, 17,* 103–113.

Whitley, B. E., Jr. (1988a). Masculinity, femininity, and self-esteem: A multitrait-multimethod analysis. *Sex Roles, 18,* 419–432.

Whitley, B. E., Jr. (1988b). The relation of gender role orientation to sexual experience among college students. *Sex Roles, 19,* 619–638.

Whitley, B. E., Jr. (1990). The relationship of heterosexuals' attributions for the causes of homosexuality to attitudes toward lesbians and gay men. *Personality and Social Psychology Bulletin, 16,* 369–377.

Whitley, B. E., Jr., McHugh, M. C., & Frieze, I. H. (1986). Assessing the theoretical models for sex differences in causal attributions of success and failure. In J. S. Hyde & M. C. Linn (Eds.), *The psychology of gender: Advances through meta-analysis.*

(pp. 102–135). Baltimore: Johns Hopkins University Press.

Widiger, T. A., & Settle, S. A. (1987). Broverman et al. revisited: An artifactual sex bias. *Journal of Personality and Social Psychology, 53,* 463–469.

Widom, C. S. (Ed.). (1984). *Sex roles and psychopathology.* New York: Plenum.

Wiggins, J. S., & Holzmuller, A. (1978). Psychological androgyny and interpersonal behavior. *Journal of Consulting and Clinical Psychology, 46,* 40–52.

Wiggins, J. S., & Holzmuller, A. (1981). Further evidence on androgyny and interpersonal flexibility. *Journal of Research in Personality, 15,* 67–80.

Wilborn, B. L. (1978). The myth of the perfect mother. In L. Harmon, J. Bert, L. Fitzgerald, & M. F. Tanney (Eds.), *Counseling women* (pp. 241–249). Monterey, CA: Brooks/Cole.

Wilcox, S., & Udry, J. R. (1986). Autism and accuracy in adolescent perceptions of friends' sexual attitudes and behavior. *Journal of Applied Social Psychology, 16,* 361–374.

Wiley, M. G., & Eskilson, A. (1985). Speech style, gender stereotypes, and corporate success: What if women talk more like men? *Sex Roles, 12,* 993–1007.

Wilkie, J. R. (1991). The decline in men's labor force participation and income and the changing structure of family economic support. *Journal of Marriage and the Family, 53,* 111–122.

Wilkinson, L. C., & Marrett, C. B. (Eds.). (1985). *Gender influences in classroom interaction.* Orlando, FL: Academic Press.

Williams, C. L. (1989). *Gender differences at work: Women and men in nontraditional occupations.* Berkeley: University of California Press.

Williams, D. G. (1985). Gender, masculinity-femininity, and emotional intimacy in same-sex friendship. *Sex Roles, 12,* 587–600.

Williams, J.B.W., & Spitzer, R. L. (1983). The issue of sex bias in DSM-III. *American Psychologist, 38,* 793–798.

Williams, J. E., & Best, D. L. (1990). *Measuring sex stereotypes: A multination study* (rev. ed.). Newbury Park, CA: Sage.

Williams, J. H. (1973). Sexual role identification and personality functioning in girls: A theory revisited. *Journal of Personality, 41*(1), 1–8.

Williams, S. W., & McCullers, J. C. (1983). Personal factors related to typicalness of career and success in active professional women. *Psychology of Women Quarterly, 7,* 343–357.

Williamson, N. E. (1976). *Sons and daughters: a cross-cultural survey of parental preferences.* Beverly Hills, CA: Sage.

Willie, C. (1985). *Black and white families: A study in complementarity.* Bayside, NY: General Hall.

Willis, S. L., & Schaie, K. W. (1988). Gender differences in spatial ability in old age: Longitudinal and intervention findings. *Sex Roles, 18,* 189–203.

Wilsnack, R. W., Wilsnack, S. C., & Klassen, A. D. (1984). Women's drinking and drinking problems: Patterns from a 1981 national survey. *American Journal of Mental Health, 74,* 1231–1238.

Wilsnack, S. C., & Beckman, L. J. (Eds.). (1984). *Alcohol problems in women.* New York: Guilford.

Wilson, D. G., & Stokes, J. P. (1983, August). *Gender differences in social support.* Paper presented at the meeting of the American Psychological Association, Anaheim.

Wilson, F. R., & Cook, E. P. (1984). Concurrent validity of four androgyny instruments. *Sex Roles, 11,* 813–837.

Wilson, J. (1978). *Religion in American society.* Englewood Cliffs, NJ: Prentice-Hall.

Wilson, L. K., & Gallois, C. (1985). Perceptions of assertive behavior: Sex combination, role appropriateness, and message type. *Sex Roles, 12,* 125–141.

Winick, C. (1968). *The new people and desexualization in American life.* New York: Pegasus.

Winstead, B. A., Derlega, V. J., & Wong, P.T.P. (1984). Effects of sex-role orientation on behavioral self-disclosure. *Journal of Research in Personality, 18,* 541–553.

Winter, D., Stewart, A., & McClelland, D. (1977). Husband's motive and wife's career level. *Journal of Personality and Social Psychology, 35,* 159–166.

Winter, D. G. (1988). The power motive in women—and men. *Journal of Personality and Social Psychology, 54,* 510–519.

Wise, E., & Rafferty, J. (1982). Sex bias and language. *Sex Roles, 8,* 1189–1196.

Witelson, S. F. (1976). Sex and the single hemisphere: Specialization of the right hemisphere for spatial processing. *Science, 193,* 425–427.

Witkin, H. A., Dyk, R. B., Faterson, H. F., Goodenough, D. R., & Karp, S. A. (1962). *Psychological differentiation.* New York: Wiley.

Witkin, H. A., & Goodenough, D. R. (1981). *Cognitive styles: Essence and origins.* New York: International Universities Press.

Witt, S. H. (1981). The two worlds of native women. In S. Cox (Ed.), *Female psychology* (2nd ed.) (pp. 149–155). New York: St. Martin's.

Wittig, M. A. (1979). Genetic influences on sex-related differences in intellectual performance: Theoretical and methodological issues. In M. A. Wittig and A. C. Petersen (Eds.), *Sex-related differences in cognitive functioning: Developmental issues* (pp. 21–66). New York: Academic Press.

Wittig, M. A. (1985). Sex-role norms and gender-related attainment values: Their role in attributions of success and failure. *Sex Roles, 12,* 1–13.

Wittig, M. A. (1989, August). *Frameworks for a feminist psychology of gender: Reconciling scientific and feminist values.* Paper presented at the meeting of the American Psychological Association, New Orleans.

Wittman, B. (1989, November 5). Women veterans reflect on changes in military. *Morning Call,* p. B25.

Wlazelek, A. (1989, February 16). Women drive safer, eat better, and live longer, study says. *Morning Call,* p. B8.

Woelfel, J. C. (1981). Women in the United States Army. *Sex Roles, 7,* 785–800.

Woelfel, J. C., & Savell, J. M. (1981). Marital satisfaction, job satisfaction, and retention in the army. In E. Hunter & D. Nice (Eds.), *Military families: Adaptation to change.* New York: Praeger.

Wojcicka-Sharff, J. (1981, March). Free enterprise and the ghetto family. *Psychology Today,* p. 41, 43, 44, 46–48.

Wolchik, S. A., Braver, S. L., & Sandler, I. N. (1985). Maternal versus joint custody: Children's post-separation experiences and adjustment. *Journal of Clinical Child Psychology, 14,* 5–10.

Wolf, N. (1991). *The beauty myth: How images of beauty are used against women.* New York: Morrow.

Wolfe, B. E. (1984). Gender ideology and phobias in women. In C. Widom (Ed.), *Sex roles and psychopathology* (pp. 51–72). New York: Plenum.

Women account for half of college enrollment in U.S., three other nations. (1986, September 17). *Chronicle of Higher Education,* p. 1.

Women gaining in senior administrative posts. (1985, Spring). *On Campus with Women,* p. 5.

Women in media say careers hit "glass ceiling." (1988, March 2). *Easton Express,* p. A9.

Women in Transition, Inc. (1975). *Women in transition.* New York: Scribner's.

Women making some gains at work. (1987, September 4). *Easton Express,* p. A6.

Women on Words and Images. (1972). *Dick and Jane as victims.* Princeton, NJ: Author.

Women parliamentarians. (1990, November-December). *Ms.,* p. 10.

Women playwrights: Themes and variations. (1989, May 7). *New York Times,* pp. H1, H42.

Women taking charge. (1987, August 14). *Easton Express,* p. A2.

Women with AIDS feel overlooked by doctors, society. (1991, April 20). *Morning Call*, p. A23.

Women's booty from crimes is less than men's. (1987, July 26). *Easton Express*, p. A13.

Women's Research and Education Institute. (1990). *The American woman, 1990–91: A status report*. New York: Norton.

Women's Sports Foundation. (1988). *The Wilson report: Moms, Dads, daughters, and sports*. New York: Women's Sports Foundation.

Women's Sports Foundation. (1989). *Minorities in sports*. New York: Women's Sports Foundation.

Wong, P.T.P., Kettlewell, G., & Sproule, C. F. (1985). On the importance of being masculine: Sex role, attribution, and women's career achievement. *Sex Roles, 12*, 757–769.

Wood, W. (1987). Meta-analytic review of sex differences in group performance. *Psychological Bulletin, 102*, 53–71.

Wood, W., & Karten, S. J. (1986). Sex differences in interaction style as a product of perceived sex differences in competence. *Journal of Personality and Social Psychology, 50*, 341–347.

Wood, W., Rhodes, N., & Whelan, M. (1989). Sex differences in positive well-being: A consideration of emotional style and marital status. *Psychological Bulletin, 106*, 249–264.

Woody, B. (1989). Black women in the emerging services economy. *Sex Roles, 21*, 45–67.

Woody, B., & Malson, M. (1984). *In crisis: Low income Black employed women in the U.S. workplace* (Working Paper No. 131). Wellesley, MA: Wellesley College Center for Research on Women.

Worth, C. (1988). *The birth of a father*. New York: McGraw-Hill.

Wrisberg, C. A., Draper, M. V., & Everett, J. J. (1988). Sex role orientations of male and female collegiate athletes from selected individual and team sports. *Sex Roles, 19*, 81–90.

Yankelovich, D. (1981, April). New rules in American life: Searching for self-fulfillment in a world turned upside down. *Psychology Today*, pp. 35–39ff.

Yarczower, M., & Daruns, L. (1982). Social inhibition of spontaneous facial expressions in children. *Journal of Personality and Social Psychology, 43*, 831–837.

Yee, D. K., & Eccles, J. S. (1988). Parent perceptions and attributions for children's math achievement. *Sex Roles, 19*, 317–333.

Yllo, K., & Bograd, M. (Eds.). (1988). *Feminist perspectives on wife abuse*. Newbury Park, CA: Sage.

Yoder, J. D. (1991). Rethinking tokenism: Looking beyond numbers. *Gender and Society, 5*, 178–192.

Yogev, S. (1982). Happiness in dual-career couples: Changing research, changing values. *Sex Roles, 8*, 593–605.

Yogev, S. (1987). Marital satisfaction and sex role perceptions among dual-earner couples. *Journal of Social and Personal Relationships, 4*, 35–46.

Yogev, S., & Brett, J. M. (1985). Patterns of work and family involvement among single and dual-earner couples. *Journal of Applied Psychology, 70*, 754–768.

Yogev, S., & Vierra, A. (1983). The state of motherhood among professional women. *Sex Roles, 9*, 391–396.

Young, R. A. (1984). Vocational choice and values in adolescent women. *Sex Roles, 7/8*, 485–492.

Yount, K. (1986). A theory of productive activity: The relationships among self-concept, gender, sex-role stereotypes, and work-emergent traits. *Psychology of Women Quarterly, 10*, 63–88.

Youssef, N. H., & Hartley, S. F. (1979). Demographic indicators of the status of women in various societies. In J. Lipman-Blumen & J. Bernard (Eds.), *Sex roles and social policy: A complex social science equation* (pp. 83–112). Beverly Hills, CA: Sage.

You've come a long way, baby—But not as far as you thought. (1984, October 1). *Business Week*, pp. 126–128.

Zammuner, V. L. (1987). Children's sex-role stereotypes: A cross-cultural analysis. In P. Shaver & C. Hendrick (Eds.), *Sex and gender* (pp. 272–293). Newbury Park, CA: Sage.

Zanna, J. J., & Pack, S. J. (1975). On the self-fulfilling nature of apparent sex differences in behavior. *Journal of Experimental Social Psychology, 11*, 583–591.

Zarbatany, L., Hartmann, D. P., Gelfand, D. M., & Vinciguerra, P. (1985). Gender differences in altruistic reputation: Are they artifactual? *Developmental Psychology, 21*, 97–101.

Zaslow, M. J. (1988). Sex differences in children's response to parental divorce: 1. Research methodology and postdivorce family forms. *American Journal of Orthopsychiatry, 58*, 355–378.

Zaslow, M. J. (1989). Sex differences in children's response to parental divorce: 2. Samples, variables, ages, and sources. *American Journal of Orthopsychiatry, 59*, 118–141.

Zaslow, M. J., & Pedersen, F. A. (1981). Sex role conflicts and the experience of childbearing. *Professional Psychology, 12*, 47–55.

Zegman, M. A. (1983). Women, weight, and health. In V. Franks & E. D. Rothblum (Eds.), *The stereotyping of women*. New York: Springer.

Zeldow, P. B., Clark, D., & Daugherty, S. R. (1985). Masculinity, femininity, Type A behavior, and psychosocial adjustment in medical students. *Journal of Personality and Social Psychology, 48*, 481–492.

Zick, C. D., & Smith, K. R. (1991). Marital transitions, poverty, and gender differences in mortality. *Journal of Marriage and the Family, 53*, 327–336.

Zilbergeld, B. (1978). *Male sexuality: A guide to sexual fulfillment*. Boston: Little, Brown.

Zinn, M. B. (1989). Family, race, and poverty in the eighties. *Signs: Journal of Women in Culture and Society, 14*, 856–874.

Zuckerman, D. M. (1981). Family background, sex-role attitudes, and life goals of technical college and university students. *Sex Roles, 7*, 1109–1126.

Zuckerman, D. M. (1983). Women's studies, self-esteem, and college women's plans for the future. *Sex Roles, 9*, 633–642.

Zuckerman, D. M., Singer, D. S., & Singer, J. L. (1980). Children's television viewing, racial and sex-role attitudes. *Journal of Applied Social Psychology, 10*, 281–294.

Zuckerman, M., DeFrank, R. S., Spiegel, N. H., & Larrance, D. T. (1982). Masculinity-femininity and encoding of nonverbal cues. *Journal of Personality and Social Psychology, 42*, 548–556.

Subject Index

Author Index